WORLD ENCYCLOPEDIA OF PEACE

(SECOND EDITION)

WORLD ENCYCLOPEDIA OF PEACE

(SECOND EDITION)

VOLUME III

Honorary Editor-in-Chief

Javier Perez De Cuellar

Editor-in-Chief

Young Seek Choue

OCEANA PUBLICATIONS, INC.®
NEW YORK

•

SEOUL PRESS

World Encyclopedia of Peace (Second Edition)

Published in the United States of America in 1999 and distributed exclusively throughout the world, except in Korea, by
Oceana Publications Inc.
75 Main Street
Dobbs Ferry, New York 10522
Phone: (914) 693-8100
Fax: (914) 693-0402

ISBN: 0-379-21401-6 (Volume III)
ISBN: 0-379-21398-2 (Set)

Library of Congress Cataloging-in-Publication Data

World encyclopedia of peace / honorary editor-in-chief, Javier Perez de Cuellar, editor-in-chief, Young Seek Choue. -- 2nd ed.
  p. cm.
  Includes bibliographical references and indexes.
  ISBN 0-379-21398-2 (clothbound set : alk. paper)
  1. Peace Encyclopedias. I. Perez de Cuellar, Javier, 1920-
  II. Young Seek Choue, 1921-
  JZ5533 .W67 1999
  327.1'03--dc21   99-34811
                                                                 CIP

Published simultaneously in the Republic of Korea in 1999 by
Seoul Press
Jin Wang Kim, Publisher
Room 303, Jeodong Bldg., 7-2, Jeodong, Chung-ku
Seoul 100-032, Korea
Phone: (02) 2275-6566
Fax: (02) 2278-2551

ISBN: 89-7225-099-6   94330 (Volume III)
ISBN: 89-7225-096-1 (Set)

Printed in the Republic of Korea by Seoul Press

I

Idea of a Liberal Democratic Peace

An impressive literature has developed in recent years dealing with the topic of a liberal democratic peace. A debate has been conducted in North American and British political science journals such as *International Security, American Political Science Review, Comparative Political Studies* and *Review of International Studies* about the validity of the hypothesis that the growth in the number of states with liberal-democratic polities will lead to a more stable and harmonious international order. In the literature on democratic peace Kant (see *Kant, Immanuel*) has been much referred to: it is true to say that he has become an emblem of the thesis. This is so to such an extent that authors need only cite Kant in their title to show that they are engaging with the debate. Others make play with Kant's name to demonstrate their topicality such as Christopher Layne's title to his article 'Kant or Cant: The Myth of the Democratic Peace' in *International Security* 19 (1994). Accordingly I shall follow through the liberal-democratic peace thesis here in terms of the three main principles laid down in Kant's seminal essay *Perpetual Peace* (see *Perpetual Peace*). These are the requirements of his three definitive articles:

(a) that the constitution of states should be republican,

(b) that the basis of international law should be a federation of free states,

(c) that each individual is entitled to be treated with hospitality when meeting the inhabitants of other states.

In these three articles we have a measure of the contemporary peace theory and also its main source. In the final section I shall look at the thesis through the perspective of Kant's guarantee of lasting peace.

1. Michael Doyle

The debate on the democratic peace has its origins in a resurgence of interest in Kant's political philosophy and international relations which occurred in the early 1980s. One of the writers who most effectively caught on to this trend was Michael Doyle, who in two articles in *Philosophy and Public Affairs* in 1983 highlighted Kant's legacy to liberalism and internationalism which were then distilled into the one key article in the *American Political Science Review* 80 (1986) 'Liberalism and World Politics.' Although in the *APSR* article Kant is cited along with Machiavelli and Schumpeter it is clear that Kant forms the centrepiece of Doyle's argument. For Doyle Kant's views on politics not only have a valuable policy component in that they show how American foreign relations ought best to be framed but also have a significant empirical relevance in that Kant is 'a liberal republican whose theory of internationalism best accounts for what we are.' Doyle's object then is to put forward Kant's political theory as a model of good practice for liberal democratic states to follow.

Doyle's thesis has a moral and empirical side to it. The moral side is naturally that policy-makers should be informed by Kant's liberal internationalism and the empirical side is to show that where policy-makers have been informed by Kant's principles that in terms of peace it has turned out to be quite successful. In the liberal democratic thesis the behaviour of states that conform as near as possible to Kant's model of a republic comes under close scrutiny. The *APSR* article has a three-page appendix where all the liberal regimes which have existed from 1700-1982 are listed and all the international wars since 1817 onwards are given chronologically. Doyle rests some of his conclusions upon this evidence. As he states in the abstract of his article, 'liberal states are different. Liberal states have created a separate peace, as Kant argued they would.' The evidence therefore is mixed but in no sense refutes the position Doyle believes Kant and other liberals to hold. Living by the rules outlined by Kant in his Definitive Articles to *Perpetual Peace* can pay in terms of the avoidance of war. Indeed Doyle seems to believe that even closer attention to Kant's arguments might have paid off because he fears that in some respects the rulers of liberal democratic states may have been prone to be 'trigger happy' contrary to Kant's pacific recommendations. Where contrary to their liberal beliefs liberal democratic states have got involved in wars to defend liberal causes this has often turned out badly. In so far as western democratic states have found liberal grounds for aggression Doyle thinks they have strayed from Kant's conceptions.

2. Fukuyama

Further credence has been given to the democratic peace thesis by Francis Fukuyama's writing on the *End of History*. Fukuyama gets to democratic peace via a very different route from Doyle. Fukuyama is particularly struck by the notion of a struggle for recognition that occurs in human history. He borrows this notion of a struggle for recognition from Hegel's philosophy (see *Hegel, Georg Wilhelm Friedrich*). Fukuyama uses the notion of the struggle for recognition—a struggle which affects all human individuals—as a means of dismissing all but the democratic republic as a legitimate form of government. The difficulty with all non-democratic forms of government is that they prevent the struggle for recognition which always occurs between free human individuals from working itself out in a non-destructive form. Earlier, more authoritarian, forms of government stand in the way of such an equal form of recognition. They are based upon forms of recognition which elevate one individual or a group of individuals above the rest. Like Doyle, Fukuyama provides his own list of democratic states in his writings. Fukuyama sees the spread of democracies as part of the universal history of mankind which is leading to the worldwide recognition of all individuals as equals. Fukuyama is highly optimistic about this course of events. In liberal democratic states no adults are excluded from the political process. This widening of participation in the political process takes the edge off the natural competition for preference amongst individuals. States that allow such full democratic civil competition fall outside history and those who fail to allow it are regarded as still within history. Fukuyama believes that Kant foresaw such a condition of universal peace in his political philosophy. Kant provided the basis for the development of a convincing liberal internationalism. Although it is Hegel who inspires Fukuyama's vision of the universal homogenous state Fukuyama gains his vision of a democratic world peace from Kant. Fukuyama is aware that many of the liberal internationalist movements inspired by Kant, such as the League of Nations (see *League of Nations*), have ended in failure. But Fukuyama argues that 'what many people have not understood, however, is that the actual incarnation of the Kantian idea has been seriously flawed from the start by not following Kant's own precepts.'

Broadly speaking Fukuyama believes the movement towards peace and democracy represents an irreversible process. The leaders of states may make poor choices or fail properly to see the road ahead. Their desire for power and prestige may momentarily stand in the way of their seeking mutual recognition in the world. But Fukuyama believes that the growth of modern science and the technological improvement which follows from it mean that human desire and human reason point in the same direction. Economic efficiency flows from the adoption of liberal democratic practices and rules. No state can afford to go it alone in the modern world economy. To flourish states have to open their markets and encourage both trade and investment. In this respect Fukuyama envisages a kind of economic determinacy which forces people towards greater democracy and the opportunity of peace. This argument seems very similar to the 'guarantee' of eternal peace which nature provides which Kant puts forward in the first supplement to *Perpetual Peace*. With Fukuyama the democratic peace theory ceases to be a hypothesis and becomes instead a reality.

3. 'Liberalism and World Politics'

The empirical tone of the debate is most marked in both Fukuyama and Doyle. Their focus is upon the factual reality or otherwise of Kant's outline for perpetual peace. At the general philosophical level it should be borne in mind that Kant is more often regarded as a transcendental idealist rather than a straightforward defender of empiricism. Kant was very impressed by the empiricist philosophies of Locke and Hume but ultimately wished to differ with them about the importance of observation in the construction of human knowledge. Kant wanted to emphasize in his critical philosophy the active human part played in the production of knowledge as well as the passive part played by the absorption of data. This brings us to the most striking overall difference between Doyle/Fukuyama's approach to the growth of a peaceful world order and Kant's. In many respects Doyle and Fukuyama play the role of passive spectators in observing the role of liberal republican regimes in bringing about peace whereas Kant's main emphasis is on the role that the leaders of states and an enlightened public can play in realizing the goal. Kant's *Perpetual Peace* represents the most explicit kind of moral advocacy where facts are brought in to demonstrate that Kant's goals are not wholly unrealistic whereas Doyle and Fukuyama's work is directed more to showing the empirical feasibility of the goal of a democratic peace and its possible moral desirability. For Doyle and Fukuyama the lure of the democratic peace thesis lies mainly in its apparent present empirical validity whereas for Kant the allure of his thesis stands independently of particular present facts. For Kant we ought to aim at a world made up of free, republican states because this is the right thing to do even if present circumstances do not indicate with total clarity that this will bring lasting peace. Kant thinks that we have to work on the assumption that the thesis can be shown both morally *as well as* empirically to be correct.

Doyle's argument is therefore not at odds with Kant's arguments for peace. The criticism that might legitimately be levelled at Doyle and Fukuyama is that they tell only part of the story. As Doyle eloquently puts it, 'beginning in the eighteenth century and slowly growing since then, a zone of peace, which Kant called the 'pacific federation' or 'pacific union,' has begun to be established among liberal societies. More than 40 liberal states currently make up the union. It is interesting to note that Doyle draws his argument primarily from one section only of Kant's essay on *Perpetual Peace* in which Kant outlines the three definitive articles for a lasting peace. Doyle does have a strong justification in that the three definitive articles represent the main positive points that Kant wished to highlight with his essay. These stipulate the requirements for a republican form of government (a); for a federation of free states (b); and for cosmopolitan law to be limited to the right of universal hospitality (c). These three definitive laws provide the backbone for Doyle's argument and the first two are also highlighted by Fukuyama. Neither discuss in great detail the 'guarantee' for perpetual peace which Kant discusses in the first supplement and would seem, dealing as it does with the course of history upon the development of peace, to have an important bearing upon their arguments. Overlooked also are Kant's views on the role of the philosopher, his discussions of morality and politics and his reflections on the role of publicity in politics.

Doyle's account of Kant is therefore a highly selective one. But in those matters he chooses to discuss Doyle is accurate and persuasive. Indeed, in very many respects both Doyle and Fukuyama get

Kant right. Doyle in particular provides a highly accurate report of the kind of internal social and political structure it is important to have in order to ensure the most rapid progress towards peace, and his discussion of Kant's cosmopolitanism is illuminating and valuable. Although Doyle's Kantian argument has been called the democratic peace theory Doyle himself sensibly stresses that Kant's main emphasis is upon the republican nature of the ideal form of government. This is in line with Kant's views. In fact we can add that in his original account of the kind of rule most suitable for bringing international harmony in *Perpetual Peace,* Kant is quite hostile to the democratic form. Kant's republican ideal is intended to prevent all kinds of despotism, not only the despotism of one individual who rules arbitrarily from the top but also the despotism of a group of the people who might seek to rule arbitrarily from the bottom. In a republic, as Kant understands it, there has to be a proper separation of powers between the executive, legislature, and judiciary. Not only are the rulers not allowed to make the law; they are also not allowed to interfere in the adjudication of infringements to the law.

4. The First Definitive Article

This very strict separation of powers rules out direct democracy as an ideal of government for Kant. Just as it would not be right if one individual sought to control each branch of the government order so also it has to be wrong if the people as a body seeks to control the executive, legislature and judiciary. As Kant puts it, 'any form of government which is not representative is essentially an anomaly.' Doyle stresses this point. But there is a large gap in Doyle's presentation of Kant's thesis in relation to democracy. Although Doyle makes no attempt to suggest that Kant is an enthusiast about democracy Doyle does not bring out the objections Kant has. We can not, for instance, glean from Doyle's discussion that Kant rules out democracy as a possible form of government. Kant thinks there are essentially only two forms of government: the despotic or the republican. It might be argued here that Kant has in mind with his critique a more radical kind of direct democracy than is now usual in Western states. Yet still, I would argue, there are elements of Kant's objections to democracy which have a bearing on the current practices of Western democracies and on the application of Kant's peace theory. Although Kant's advocacy of the republican form of government can be read as very much favouring the kind of representative democracy to be found in countries such as the United States, Germany and France, it can also be read as a warning against tendencies towards a majoritarian style of democracy which from time to time influence the government of these countries. Like Mill and Tocqueville, Kant fears the tyranny of the majority and believes a genuinely rational form of government has to be properly structured to prevent it from occurring. For example, it is difficult to see how Kant's republicanism might wholly embrace the kind of party politics now prevalent in Western States. It is conceivable that Kant's guidelines are compatible with parties competing for representation within legislatures and so with their success putting forward a certain legislative programme. However, it is difficult to see how Kant's principles might be used to endorse parties competing for sole executive authority, particularly if that dominance were matched by an equal dominance in the legislature. Where a party uses executive authority to press through its own programme, and this programme is willed by a certain section of the population and not all, then the government must, according to Kant, tend towards despotism. It is true that most parties in Western states are not monolithic structures and have their own internal representative features which mitigates the problem. But where such parties tend towards unity or uniformity the danger of straying towards despotism (as Kant understands it) must exist. Thus, peculiarly, from Kant's standpoint the more diverse, open, representative and pluralist a party the more it will conform to his ideal of government should it gain executive power.

That Kant's prescription for the ideal polity requires that majoritarian tendencies be kept in check has important implications for his peace thesis. Kant would regard states whose representative systems were liable to factional control as possibly more inclined to belligerence that other states where the republican model he outlines is more rigidly adhered to. Democratic states which allowed one party to control both its legislature and executive might be more prone to war than others; just as democratic states which allowed one set of opinions to predominate at the expense of others through inadequate public debate might be seen as less peaceable. Doyle and Fukuyama's optimistic approach to Kant's thinking seems to overlook these possibilities which surely would have exercised Kant. It is very important for Kant that all citizens should regard the rulers as acting on their behalf, and with their authority, even if in many respects they disagree with the policies being pursued. Should political structures within a state systematically exclude one section of the population (which might be seen as occurring where some discriminatory political principles are taken to their extreme) then they can not be fully regarded as co-citizens.

5. The Second Definitive Article

What Doyle also perhaps glosses over in his writings and the liberal treatment of Kant in general has to deal with carefully is Kant's attitude to the role of women as citizens. Essentially Kant excludes all women from active citizenship, as he does all dependents including wageworkers, servants and those without jobs. Kant thinks that such independent individuals who form a republic will be unlikely to seek war with other states, first, because they would through their representatives be making the decision on their own behalf and, secondly, if there were any costs to be borne they themselves would have to bear them.

In this respect Doyle believes that 'the apparent absence of war between liberal states, whether adjacent or not, for almost 200 years thus may have significance.' In states where the Kantian features of a separation of powers, representative government and some form of adult suffrage have been absent there seems not to have been the same restraint shown in relation to other states. What Doyle finds particularly striking is the behaviour of liberal states (which best approximate to the Kantian model) when major wars actually occur. As Doyle puts it, 'when states are forced to decide on which side of an impending world war they will fight, liberal states all wind up on the same side despite the complexity of the paths that take them there.'

Doyle is correct to emphasize how the behaviour of non-despotic states tends to point in the same direction. But it is doubtful that Kant would see this as proof of his contention. Because even if the leaders of a republican state were to take the 'wrong' side in a world war (which Finland is alleged to have done at the time of the Second World War in some of the literature calling the democratic theory into doubt) this would not absolve the leaders of all states from the duty of trying to hold to the project of perpetual peace in all their future actions. It is interesting that in *Perpetual Peace* Kant does not cite the behaviour of republican states to demonstrate the truth of his plan but rather he refers to such states from the standpoint of the example they might set to other states. He makes this clear in his comments upon the second definitive article where he states: ' If by good fortune one powerful and enlightened nation can form a republic (which by its nature is inclined to seek perpetual peace) this will provide a focal point for federal association among other states.'

A great deal of the discussion in the democratic peace debate has focussed on the extent to which states with Kantian style constitutions form a pacific union. Enthusiasts for the proposition have discovered that states with liberal constitutions tend to keep the peace in relation to each other and those who question the peace theory suggest that there is a great deal of evidence that states with such constitutions are still liable to war. Doyle's thesis is that 'liberal republics will progressively establish peace amongst themselves by means of the pacific federation (foedus pacificium) described in Kant's Second Definitive Article.' In Doyle's view, 'most liberal theorists have offered inadequate guidance in understanding the exceptional nature of liberal pacification.' Where many fall down, in Doyle's view, is in their inability to explain the way in which some liberal states tend also to get embroiled in war. In this respect Doyle thinks, 'Immanuel Kant offers the best guidance.' Kant is able to understand the tendency of liberal states to form with each other islands of peace and their tendency to be less at home with non-liberal states.

Doyle understands Kant to be recommending in his Second Definitive Article neither a formal federation nor any institutionalized form of co-operation. Mainly Kant is emphasizing a disposition of states with republican constitutions not to attack each other militarily. But Doyle does go a bit further to suggest that Kant 'appears to have in mind a mutual nonaggression pact, perhaps a collective security agreement.' This seems very close to what Kant suggests where he states in his Second Definitive Article that the 'law of nations should be based on a federalism of free states.' Particularly important in the way in which Kant formulates the Second Definitive Article is its markedly counterfactual nature. Kant is not speaking directly of any empirical state of affairs, present or future, in the article itself. He has in mind much more the intellectual presuppositions which form the basis for an effective international law.

Indeed, I think that the main thrust of Kant's Second Definitive Article for perpetual peace is a criticism of prevailing conceptions of international law which ground international law in the unrestricted sovereignty of states. The recommendation that a pacific federation of free states be formed is one that flows from this initial objection. Kant holds that very little progress can be attained in international politics

if the leaders of states behave as rulers of entirely self-contained and wilfully independent territories who can declare war whenever they see fit upon any other such sovereign entities. The very conception of an international politics based upon such wholly unrestricted sovereignty carries the seeds of its own destruction. As Kant sees it, the concept of a law of nations becomes meaningless if interpreted as the right to go to war. Doyle is highly conscious of the federative aspect of Kant's peace plan but does not bring out this indictment of the traditional notions of state sovereignty which underlie Kant's critique of international law. Doyle notes that Kant's 'pacific union is not a single peace treaty ending one war, a world state, nor a state of nations. Kant finds the first insufficient. National sovereignty precludes reliable subservience to a state of nations; a world state destroys the civic freedom on which the development of human capacities rests.' It is indeed true that Kant rules out for the foreseeable future a world state resting upon a world-wide civil society but this is not because the pursuit of such a condition is morally wrong. In Kant's view we ought to give up the total and arbitrary independence of our national state and seek to approximate to a world state. What prevents us from attaining the condition of world statehood which reason prescribes is the sheer physical difficulty of coordinating government over huge tracts of territory some of which are not developed (in Kant's day this was of course a much greater problem than it is now) and the entrenched habits of the leaders of sovereign states. In Kant's view the second poses the greatest difficulty. The attainment of state sovereignty is indeed a great step forward in the development of the human race, but it is not an absolutely valid arrangement. As Kant sees it, state sovereignty attains its proper validity when it merges over into a wider international sovereignty of free states. The splendid majesty of the absolutely unrestricted sovereign state is an obstacle to world peace.

We might thus expect that civilized peoples, each united with itself as a state, would hasten to abandon so degrading a condition as soon as possible. Fukuyama also does not realize the extent to which Kant's Second Definitive Article implies a critique of the traditional notion of state sovereignty and international law. Kant wants to rewrite the rules of international society in a rational form, whereas Fukuyama is more concerned to point out how international society has already taken on a rational form. In keeping with Kant Fukuyama argues that 'international law is merely domestic law writ large' yet there is no direct recognition of the kind of mutation of state sovereignty this might involve. In the kind of world Kant envisages no one state can prevail over another, each has always to accommodate itself to the next as though they were neighbouring citizens within a civil society and state. But Fukuyama and Doyle both realize that in a peaceful condition of the Kantian variety state sovereignty can not play the role it once did. Without clearly stating it both imply that the kind of unrestricted state sovereignty that once prevailed in international society has had its day.

6. The Third Definitive Article

One of the great virtues of democratic peace theory is its moral egalitarianism. Each human individual for the proponent of a democratic peace counts for as much as every other. With Fukuyama this moral egalitarianism is evident in his emphasis upon what he calls *isothymia*. Fukuyama defines the term in relation to its opposite *megalothymia*. This is the 'desire to be recognized as superior to other people' whereas 'its opposite is *isothymia*, the desire to be recognized as the equal of other people.' Francis Fukuyama's thesis is that the world must change, and is changing, to a situation where each person lives under a system of rule which fosters *isothymia* or equal recognition. He sees this happening, however, mainly within states. In drawing this picture of extending world-wide equality Fukuyama's inspiration is Hegel who in his conception of the state properly develops the idea of mutual democratic recognition.

By definition human individuals who are the only rational animals are equal. It is an offence against our dignity as human individuals to treat another human individual or group as inherently unequal to us. In this respect Doyle captures the spirit of Kant's philosophy well. Doyle sees that Kant's cosmopolitanism (see *Cosmopolitanism*) leads to a different style of international politics from that to which we are now accustomed. Kant's doctrine of right would provide no grounds for the western imperial project of the modern world nor for any missionary intention to civilize forcefully non-Western countries. Kant rules out a patriarchal approach to government both internally and externally. The development of societies outside Europe must possess a voluntary dimension. Natives have to play a part themselves in drawing towards civilization. This comes out in Doyle's interpretation of the Third Definitive Article to *Perpetual Peace*. 'Hospitality,' Doyle says, 'does not require extending to foreigners either the right to citizenship or the right to settlement, unless the foreign

visitors would perish if they were expelled. Foreign conquest and plunder also find no justification under this right.' Imperialism of any kind is ruled out (see *Imperialism*). 'Hospitality does appear to include the right of access and the obligation of maintaining the opportunity for citizens to exchange goods and ideas without imposing the obligation to trade (a voluntary act in all cases under liberal constitutions).

Doyle argues that liberal states, despite their internal liberal structures, have been prone to war with non-liberal societies. As he puts it: 'the historical liberal legacy is laden with popular wars fought to promote freedom, to protect private property, or to support liberal allies against nonliberal enemies.' As Doyle suggests, Kant's position would be at odds with this outcome. Partly these wars have occurred because the leaders of liberal states have demanded more than hospitality for their citizens and subjects in their relations with other states. In seeking to promote the freedom and advantage of visitors to foreign territories they often have asked not simply for safe passage but that a certain form of life be respected which is contrary to native traditions. Kant believes we ought not to venture beyond peaceful persuasion in trying to advance the condition of other nationals in their own states. Similarly liberal states are in no position to guarantee the property of their nationals abroad simply through the exertion of their own powers. The civil order of a foreign state is primarily its own responsibility.

7. The Guarantee of Perpetual Peace

In one of the most interesting supplements to *Perpetual Peace* Kant outlines what he describes as a guarantee provided by 'the great artist nature herself.' Kant argues here that the apparently unguided course of historical development tends in the direction of human improvement often against our will. Kant cites a number of mechanisms that help bring this about such as our competitiveness, our self-interested pursuit of trade, the rivalry amongst nations and even war itself. Both Doyle and Fukuyama cite this mechanism of nature with approval. They approve of Kant's guarantee because it highlights an empirical process which can help underpin the liberal democratic peace. For Doyle the guarantee works not because we are politically moral beings but through our less agreeable side. Whereas it might be argued that Kant is quite happy to see human short-sightedness and downright evil inadvertently playing a progressive role and this conflicting with the moral spirit within us, Doyle wants to unify the two forces. Those who are entirely focussed on their selfish interests are also playing a moral role. With Doyle the 'hidden plan' of nature complements our ethical duty. However with Kant the hidden plan steps in only where we fail in our ethical duty. For Kant the hidden plan is not right in itself, rather it provides us with an incentive to do what is right.

Kant argues that we can not depend on the guarantee from a theoretical standpoint. We can rightly suppose that there are natural mechanisms at work which promote the aim of lasting peace. Despite the expressed aims of less scrupulous political leaders and their subjects we can discern over the longer term underlying trends which appear to be taking the human race forward. Perversely war itself might further these trends by bringing home to people the doleful effects of war. Societies who engage in this aggressive behaviour are forced to modernise quickly in order to employ the most advanced means for engaging in war. But this modernisation takes place with a concomitant growth in the potential and demand for freedom within the state. Self-interest is, above all, what brings the progressive mechanism of nature into play. The hard-nosed pursuit of economic gain may have peaceful consequences. Although primarily motivated by the pursuit of profit those professionally engaged in trade and commerce come to dislike the disruption caused by wars. Over the long term Kant thinks that business prefers peace to war.

Kant realizes that such projections about the progressive mechanism of history are not subject to clear empirical proof. Kant's object is not to create sufficient certainty from a scientific standpoint but rather sufficient certainty from a moral standpoint. He thinks there is enough evidence to justify us from a moral standpoint pursuing progressive policies. Doyle and Fukuyama tend to overlook the voluntary side of human progress which forms the essential part of Kant's guarantee. Both Doyle and Fukuyama are enthusiastic about the natural mechanism, especially Fukuyama who devotes several passages in his writings to the economic, social and political forces that drive us willy-nilly towards cooperation. Successful material acquisition under a free market system requires long-term peace and security. According to Fukuyama, a preoccupation with acquiring more consumer goods diverts people away from aggressive foreign policies and war. In keeping with Doyle and Fukuyama's interest in the determinist side of Kant's 'hidden plan' the literature on democratic peace concentrates heavily on the empirical verifiability of the perpetual peace thesis. This may not take us entirely off the Kantian track, since the more

empirical evidence for the thesis which exists the fewer excuses there can be for refusing to seek progress in external policy. However, in the light of Kant's priorities the emphasis is still a little one-sided. Kant's main purpose is to bring morality and politics into accord, only then will perpetual peace be achieved.

8. Conclusion

What does our examination of the liberal democratic peace thesis advanced by Doyle and Fukuyama from the standpoint of Kant's original peace theory tell us? Our first conclusion might justifiably be that there is more to Kant's original view than the democratic peace theorists convey. There are elements in Kant's argument, such as his powerful objections to forcible intervention in the affairs of other states, which are not fully considered. Just as Doyle and Fukuyama's new interpretations of Kant's thinking have uncovered many valuable ideas we might legitimately claim that there is even more to be discovered which might not only add to the democratic peace thesis but also provide insights in other connected areas of politics. Classical political theory, such as Kant's essay on *Perpetual Peace*, provides a permanent source of new insight into current national and international issues.

Kant would have himself emphasized that we have to judge what constitutes knowledge and understanding ourselves. Kant's political writings should of course be treated with respect, but not slavishly followed. Doyle and Fukuyama are each in their own way critically receptive. Two particular issues stand out as problematic in Kant's account: (a) Kant's exclusion of women from politically relevant roles; (b) His apparently optimistic view of the role finance and trade (operating through self-interest) can play in the forging of international peace.

In terms of the first, it would be fair to say that empirically the facts run against Kant's exclusion of women. The seeds of wars seem often to lie in conflicts of economic interests. Although Doyle stresses once again the peaceful impetus brought about by overlapping economic interests the optimistic Kantian picture has to be weighed against the ambiguous, if not entirely contrary, empirical evidence. It is true to say that Kant was not depending on the world economic system automatically to bring about peace. Kant's point is that in the long term contract—upon which trade and commerce rest—can not function without trust and a sense of community. From an intelligible or logical standpoint war and trade are at odds.

There is an irony here in that contemporary democratic peace theory has strongly emphasized the empirical dimension of Kant's thinking. Above all, the literature has concentrated on analyzing the behaviour of states with constitutions approximating to the one recommended to Kant. Their conclusion is that in relation to each other such states behave well, but they do not tell us it is because of the convergence of economic interests of these states or the peaceful intentions of their rulers. From a Kantian perspective the main gap in the contemporary literature is its tendency to underemphasize the moral side of Kant's argument. Kant's allusion to empirical developments is intended primarily to strengthen his moral argument rather than to provide conclusive proof. Those who require absolutely convincing proof of the viability of the peace project before signing up to it are precisely those Kant was not aiming to attract to his argument. His case for perpetual peace is made to those who already have moral intentions in politics. The liberal democratic peace will work only for those who aim to live in a morally regulated peace with others.

See also: *Peace and Democracy; Peace with Freedom*

Bibliography —————————————

Bachteler T, Russett B (Comm.) 1997 Explaining the democratic peace: The evidence from Ancient Greece reviewed. *J. Peace Research* 34

di Zerega G 1995 Democracies and peace: The self-organizing foundation for the democratic peace. *Rev. Polit.* 57

Doyle M 1986 Liberalism and world politics. *Am. Polit. Sci. Rev.* 80

Doyle M 1983 Kant, liberal legacies and foreign affairs. *Philosophy and Public Affairs* 12

Fukuyama F 1992 *The End of History and the Last Man*. Penguin, London

Gartzke E 1998 Kant we all just get along? Opportunity, willingness, and the origins of the democratic peace. *Am. J. Political Science* 42

Kant 1991 *Political Writings*. (ed. H. Reiss), Cambridge University Press, Cambridge

Kegley C W Jr, Hermann M G 1997 Putting military intervention into the democratic peace: A research note. *Comparative Political Studies* 30

Krain M, Myers M E 1997 Democracy and civil war: A note on the democratic peace proposition. *International Interactions*

Layne C 1994 Kant or cant: The myth of the democratic peace. *International Security* 19

Lemke D, Reed W 1996 Regime type and status quo evaluations: Power transition theory and the democratic peace. *International Interactions* 22

Mansfield E D, Snyder J 1995 Democratization and the danger of war. *International Security* 20

Maoz Z 1998 Realist and cultural critique of the democratic peace: A theoretical and empirical reassessment. *International Interactions* 24

Oneal J R, Ray J L 1997 New tests of the democratic peace: Controlling for economic interdependence, 1950-85. *Polit. Res. Q.* 50

Raknerud A, Herge H 1997 The hazard of war: Reassessing the evidence for the democratic peace. *J. Peace Research* 34

Ray J L 1995 *Democracy and International Conflict: An Evaluation of the Democratic Peace Proposition*. University of South Carolina Press, Columbia, SC

Russet B, Layne C, Spiro D E, Doyle M 1995 The democratic peace. *International Security* 19

Russet B M 1993 *Grasping the Democratic Peace: Principles for a post-Cold War World*. Princeton University Press, Princeton, NJ

Russett B 1995 Correspondence: The democratic peace. *International Security* 19

Tanji M, Lawson S 1997 "Democratic peace" and "Asian democracy": A universalist-particularist tension. *Alternatives* 22

Thompson W R, Tucker R, Farber H (Comm.), Gowa J (Comm.), Mansfield E E (Comm.), Snyder J (Comm.) 1997 A tale of two democratic peace critiques. *J. Conflict Resolution* 41

Williams H 1983 *Kant's Political Philosophy*. Blackwell, Oxford

HOWARD WILLIAMS

Imperialism

In our century "imperialism" is one of the most frequently used phrases in the sphere of international political and ideological warfare. Its meaning is ambiguous and has repeatedly changed since the term first appeared. Its usage—precisely described by Koebner and Schmidt in 1964—seems to have started in the first half of the nineteenth century in France. "*Impérialisme*" there became a synonym for "*Bonapartisme*" expressing the desire to restore the glories connected with the name of Napoleon. During the reign of Louis Napoleon (1852-70) the word was employed occasionally by British authors, too, as a critique of this French system of government which to them looked like Caesarism or despotism.

In Great Britain afterwards the term developed, changing its meaning like a chameleon. So in the 1870s the Liberals used it as an anti-Israeli slogan, referring to military splendor, despotic rule, adventures abroad, and Empire expansion. In the 1880s the Liberals, now in government, gave imperialism a strictly new and positive sense. It expressed the growing Empire enthusiasm looking for a "Greater Britain," and a closer union of the white Anglo-Saxons living in different parts of the world.

There was a strong relationship between this enthusiasm and a feeling of racial and national superiority which, at a time when the "scramble for Africa" was turning more and more parts of Africa (and Asia) into British colonies, helped to widen the understanding of Empire and imperialism so as to incorporate tropical regions, not settled by Britons, too. Kipling and some of his contemporaries interpreted this process as "the White man's burden" to civilize the black races; other "imperialists," the most prominent among them being Joseph Chamberlain, regarded empire expansionism as necessary to secure markets and to solve the problem of Great Britain's growing population.

Not all of those interested in politics accepted such views. It was the Boer War (1899-1902) which finally changed the imperialist mood drastically. Reports on burning Boer farms and on the setting up of concentration camps shook the confidence of the British in the moral character of imperialism. Again it acquired a pejorative connotation. Simultaneously the Boer War strengthened the efforts being made to look behind the scenes, to understand the causes of this aggressive expansionism which was leading to dangerous conflicts between the rival colonial powers.

The British journalist and economist John A. Hobson, in publishing his famous "Imperialism," in 1902, became the founding father of imperialism as an (economic) theory explaining the imperialist race by structural defects of the capitalist system.

Numerous theories followed as imperialism came to be recognized as a world phenomenon. But before analyzing the different interpretations of imperialism, it is interesting to follow up the development of the term. Imperialism gradually became an international issue. Its discussion was even taken up in those countries which had become the objects and victims of imperialistic expansion. "So it came about that in the period following the First World War, imperialism rose to global eminence as the leading slogan of three world struggles, the struggle against capitalism, against Anglo-Saxon domination, and the struggle against white colonial power" (Koebner and Schmidt 1964 p. 279).

For the further understanding of imperialism, the communist doctrine developed by Lenin and Stalin is of great significance. For Lenin (1917), following on from the work of Hobson, imperialism was identical with the newest, that is, the "monopolist stage of capitalism." By drawing political and strategical consequences from this concept, Stalin (1919) simplified the meaning of imperialism even more. He saw the world dichotomously split into two camps, the camp of imperialism and that of socialism (see *Marxist-Leninist Concepts of Peace and Peaceful Coexistence*).

After the Second World War the process of diluting the meaning of the term imperialism continued. Globally imperialism was used as a discriminatory label with which almost every political group or nation attacked its ideological opponents in the international arena. There was the old but also a new capitalist imperialism, a Soviet (social) imperialism, a Chinese, Indian, Israelite or Vietnamese imperialism, and so on. This confusion of terminology always reached its climax when imperialists denounced other imperialists as imperialists. The end of the Cold War stopped this career of imperialism as a political slogan and hate word. It almost disappeared from the political scene. Now looking back at the entire history of the term imperialism one has to realize that in an academic sense it has gradually lost any precise meaning. Hancock (1950), for example, called it "a word for the illiterates of social science." Nevertheless it cannot be eliminated from the scientific analysis of phenomena which were called imperialism by some authors or political groups. Thus, if the term is used, its precise meaning has to be defined within its context, at least.

1. Classical Interpretations of Imperialism

Which concrete historical events did the famous theories of imperialism try to explain? Let us again start with Hobson, the progenitor of the classical approach. He explicitly looked at the phenomenon of rule expansion in the last three decades of the nineteenth century. "During that period a number of European nations, Great Britain being first and foremost, have annexed or otherwise asserted political sway over vast portions of Africa and Asia, and over numerous islands in the Pacific and elsewhere" (1902 p. 13; see also Table 1).

But such an expansion of European nations was not a new phenomenon in history. Why did it nevertheless suddenly evoke numerous theories of imperialism? One reason is that this new expansionism followed a period in which a number of signs indicated that colonialism and (formal) empire building were done with, because they seemed too costly on the one hand and unnecessary on the other. But from the 1870s onward, without any obvious reason, this phase was suddenly followed by a very hectic race of the old colonial powers and of some latecoming have-nots to bring all territories still "free" under their control. Apparently these competing powers were driven by strong interests. This seems clear from the fact that many colonial conflicts arose. If they could not be settled peacefully (as in the case of the Fashoda crisis in 1898) they even led to wars, for instance the Boer War, the Spanish-American War (1898), and the Russo-Japanese War (1904-05). And at the end of this period, the First World War broke out—in Lenin's eyes a pure imperialistic war.

Taking these aspects into consideration, those who tried to understand this new wave of aggressive international policy believed that there must also be some new motives, interests, or special causes at work. Hobson very thoroughly complied and analyzed most of the then discussed expansionist incentives, declared as potential motives. His conclusion was that imperialistic policy had been bad for the British nation as a whole but good for certain "economic parasites," especially for some Jewish investors who were driven to look for profitable capital outlets abroad because of the capitalist system's tendencies to underconsumption and maldistribution. Thus he located the "taproot of imperialism" in the sphere of economics by connecting the phenomenon of competitive empire building in the late nineteenth century with some supposed structural defects of modern capitalism.

Hobson provided the starting point for a broad theoretical discussion about the new imperialism in the following decades. Although his concept was opposed by other approaches, the idea that economic causes were primarily responsible for modern imperialism prevailed for a considerable time, thus exerting a strong influence upon many political-ideological movements in different countries and a distinct impact on the further development of international relations (see also sect. 2).

Within the broad outline of the economic interpretation of imperialism different groups of arguments were developed. Some authors, most of them Marxists like Hilferding (1910), Lenin (1917) or—later on—Sweezy (1942), regarded the main impulse behind imperialism to be the increasing efforts of capitalist entrepreneurs to abolish competition by creating cartels, syndicates, or trusts (that is, monopolizing the markets) to overcome the secular tendency to declining profits, this being an important element of Marxist theory. In this view imperialist actions were the

Table 1

The colonial empires in 1876 and 1914 (area in millions of square kilometers, population in millions)[a]

	Colonies				Metropoles		Total	
	1876		1914		1914		1914	
	km²	Pop.	km²	Pop.	km²	Pop.	km²	Pop.
Great Britain	22.5	251.9	33.5	393.5	0.3	46.5	33.8	440.0
Russia[b]	17.0	15.9	17.4	33.2	5.4	136.2	22.8	169.4
France	0.9	6.0	10.6	55.5	0.5	39.6	11.1	95.1
Germany	–	–	2.9	12.3	0.5	64.9	3.4	77.2
United States[b]	–	–	0.3	9.7	9.4	97.0	9.7	106.7
Japan	–	–	0.3	19.2	0.4	53.0	0.7	72.2
Italy	–	–	2.3	1.8	0.3		2.6	
Belgium	–	–	2.4		<0.1		2.4	
Netherlands	2.1	24.5	2.1		<0.1		2.1	
Portugal	1.8	6.8	2.1		0.1		2.2	
Spain	0.4	8.4	0.3		0.5		0.8	
Total	44.7	313.5	74.2		17.4		91.6	
Spheres of interest (China, Persia, Turkey)							14.5	361.2
The other countries							28.0	289.9

a Source: Hampe 1976, p. 22 b It is especially difficult to separate the metropole and its colonies in the cases of Russia and the United States since both—with a few exceptions—did not expand overseas but on their own continents, a process which began well before the later nineteenth century. In the table the continental possessions are only regarded in the case of Russia.

necessary instrument to secure the largest possible part of the world market for the national capitalists as compensation for the monopolistically restricted inner market. Goods and idle capital thus could be exported profitably.

Another approach explained imperialism in terms of defects in the dynamics of a capitalist economy. Rosa Luxemburg (1913) regarded continuous accumulation of capital (that is economic growth) as impossible unless an effective demand is found among noncapitalist groups and/or countries to "realize" the surplus of production. In this interpretation imperialism was a necessary means of lengthening the life of capitalism which would finally come to an end only when all countries and territories were included in the capitalist system.

An alternative interpretation, going back to Hobson and reaffirmed by some non-Marxist authors even after the Second World War (see, for example, Wehler 1969 and Hampe 1976 pp. 126-35) explained the imperialist expansion as an attempt to offset the periodic depressions which can be regarded as a characteristic part of the trade cycle in a capitalist economy.

An attempt was also made to explain imperialism in economic terms, but independent of a specific economic system. To a few authors the combination of a growing population and constraints upon agrarian production seemed to reduce the *Lebensraum* in some industrializing countries. In their eyes, imperialist policy was designed simply to secure or enlarge the national food basis (Hampe 1976 pp. 184-90).

1.1 Criticisms

Most of the arguments of these economic interpretations of classical imperialism have not remained unchallenged. They have provoked a criticism which has increased in recent decades on the basis of new empirical and theoretical knowledge (the literature on problems of imperialism in the decades following the Second World War has increased immensely (see for instance Halstead and Porcari's bibliography of 1974) so that in the remainder of this article very few titles or authors can be mentioned as paradigmatic references). Principally, doubts were raised from three sides: how valid is the economic theory underlying the above-mentioned interpretations of imperialism? Were the premises presupposed by the theories of imperialism empirically met by the imperialist countries? Can the imperialist actions in the decades before the First World War be better explained with the help of other lines of argument? The critique of the economic interpretation of imperialism can be summarized as follows:

Economic history and modern economic theory have shown that a tendency for growing monopolism does not necessarily occur in capitalism, nor does capitalism fundamentally need noncapitalist demand for "realizing" the national product. Even in periods of depression or slump a recovery can be achieved without the help of foreign trade surpluses. Many arguments of the *Lebensraum* theory are based on weak theoretical arguments, too.

Some authors, Schumpeter (1919) being the most prominent, have tried to show that capitalism per se does not initiate imperialism or war but is likely to foster peaceful international relations. These authors have argued that imperialism will slowly wither away with expanding capitalism. And indeed, to ascribe the new imperialism before the First World War primarily to capitalism was, to say the least, a superficial judgment. Not all countries that engaged in imperialist expansion were capitalist ones or surplus producing (Russia and Japan, for example). On the other hand, capitalist states existed which did not take part in imperialist actions, for example Switzerland and the countries of Scandinavia. Furthermore, it is relatively obvious why Marxist authors in particular insisted on a strong connection between capitalism and imperialism: this interpretation sustained some basic tenets of Marxist theory which would otherwise appear to be refuted by historical developments. For instance, contrary to Marxist expectations, capitalism was still alive at the beginning of the twentieth century. Thus the theory of capitalist imperialism was to show that imperialism brought with it a lengthening effect on the lifetime of capitalism which was sure to collapse later, nevertheless.

With regard to late nineteenth century imperialism, most of the new territories acquired or brought under indirect rule by the imperialist countries did not promise great economic advantages. It is not surprising therefore that the greater part of capital exports and foreign trade of the imperialist countries did not go to the newly won (dependent) territories but to the rival capitalist, that is industrial, countries. Even the share of raw material and/or food coming from their territories abroad was relatively small. The colonies on the other hand traded in some cases with foreign countries to a higher degree than with their metropoles.

In recent decades, new research by historians and social scientists has thrown more light on the process of the imperialist partition of the world beginning in the second half of the nineteenth century. By clarifying for example the decision-making processes in the imperialist headquarters, they argue that expansionism was caused by a very complex pattern of motives and events, partly in the sphere of domestic policy, partly of foreign policy, which differed from one imperialist country to another.

This new picture differs markedly from the relatively simple picture which the classical theories of economic imperialism have drawn. This does not mean that the process of expansion of European rule was at that time free from economic interests or speculations. But the economy apparently neither played the only nor always the main role and often worked in a way other than that which the classical theories claimed (for the criticisms see especially Fieldhouse 1973; Hampe 1976; Mommsen 1979; Platt 1968; Robinson and Gallagher 1962; Wehler 1969).

2. The Concept of Neoimperialism

A theory which links imperialism with capitalism in the sense that the former was necessary for the existence of the latter must meet additional difficulties in the period of decolonization which reached its climax after the Second World War. How could the capitalist states survive without colonies? Why did they experience a period of economic growth and prosperity never before seen in history? Above all, neo-Marxist authors in Europe and in North and South America as well as prominent leaders of developing nations tried to solve the mystery with the help of the idea of neocolonialism and neoimperialism respectively. This approach could trace its argument to the phenomenon that, even in the nineteenth century, imperialism was not truly identical with formal colonialism (see *Colonialism; Neocolonialism*). An extreme thesis along these lines was developed by the two British historians, Gallagher and Robinson, in their unconventional essay "The imperialism of free trade" (1953). They showed that to identify the British Empire with its constituent parts was only half the truth. In a number of cases, for instance in Latin America, in China, Persia, Turkey, or Morocco, and in the Balkans, Great Britain and other imperialist countries were—or had to be—satisfied with winning spheres of interest or influence, exercising alone or together with other imperialist nations some sort of—informal—hegemony (see *Hegemony*) over the above-mentioned regions by imposing treaties of "free trade and friendship," by winning concessions for capital investment, by controlling their financial systems, or—as a last resort—by military intervention (see *Intervention*). In Gallagher and Robinson's eyes the British imperialist policy followed the principle "trade with informal control if possible; trade with rule when necessary" throughout the nineteenth century (p. 13). According to this theory, the general strategy of the policy was to win areas as "complementary satellite economies which would provide raw materials and food for Great Britain, and also provide widening markets for its manufactures" (p. 9). Or more generally: "Both formal and informal imperialism appear as variable political functions of the extending pattern of overseas trade, investment, emigration and culture" (p. 6).

It is not difficult to see the similarity between this approach and the concept of neoimperialism which gradually won predominance in the discussions on the North-South conflict from the middle 1960s onward (see *North-South Conflict*). Contrary to the classic theories of imperialism which tried to explain the motives and causes of the imperialist policy of capitalistic-industrial states, the concept of neoimperialism was focused primarily upon the effects of imperialism on the countries concerned. Thus, in the first instance it intended to explain the widening economic gap between the developed countries and most of the developing countries, which occurred in spite of numerous national, bilateral, and international measures for developing the former colonial regions ("foreign aid"). And the main reason for this international economic rift was seen in different forms of economic *dependencia* (dependency) which were believed exploit the underdeveloped countries and to enrich the capitalist ones at the same time. According to this view, economic underdevelopment is not a sign of insufficient economic management but the necessary consequence of the further development of worldwide capitalism. Thus, the neoimperialism of invisible empires seemed to fulfill the same functions for the capitalist system as did previously the formal imperialism of colonial empires according to the mentioned classical interpretations of imperialism (see Sec. 1).

As for the concrete mechanisms of neoimperialist exploitation, different arguments were used by different authors. To classify and to comment on them here is only possible in outline:

Continuing to a certain extent Lenin's thesis of imperialism by capital export, Baran (1957), Frank (1967), Magdoff (1969), Nkrumah (1965), Dos Santos (1970), and others have accused the multinational companies (see *Multinational Corporations and Peace*) of exploiting the developing countries by means of their direct investments. They mostly illustrated this by activities of United States firms, particularly in Latin American and some oil-producing countries. These investments took place only in highly profitable fields, above all in the raw material sectors, and tended—so the argument runs—to harden the monocultural structures of the underdeveloped countries which they had inherited from colonial times; furthermore the multinational companies were said to decapitalize the underdeveloped countries by repatriating high profits to the imperialistic headquarters and to control the economies of the underdeveloped countries from outside in conformity with their interests (see *Maldevelopment*).

Another chain of arguments was derived from the assured structures and tendencies in the international trade area which can be summarized under the heading of "unequal exchange."A first and very well-known argument was the thesis that the terms of trade worsen in the long run for underdeveloped countries (partly as a result of highly monopolized international markets), which means that underdeveloped countries have to export more goods to pay for a constant import volume (see, for instance, Jalée 1969, Marini 1974, Prebisch 1968). On a more theoretical level it was maintained that even given the assumptions of the classical economic theory of foreign trade (that is, flexible prices, full competition, full employment, and free trade), international trade between more and less developed countries leads to a "nonequivalent exchange." The thesis was explained by differences in economic efficiency and/or applied technology (Amin 1973; Kohlmey 1962) or by different wage levels (Emmanuel 1969) all of which were said to lead to hidden transfers of resources or real incomes from the less to the more developed countries.

Quite another mechanism lies at the center of Johan Galtung's impressive "Structural theory of imperialism" (1971) in which, beyond the aspect of neoimperialism, he tried to integrate all historical and modern aspects and forms of imperialism (for a similar argument see Amin 1973). For Galtung "the world consists of Center and Periphery nations; and each nation, in turn, has its center and periphery" (p. 81). According to this view, imperialism is a relationship between a center and a periphery nation so that above all there is harmony of interest between the center in the center nation and the center in the periphery nation, based on a "bridgehead" which the former establishes in the latter for the joint benefit of both, whereas a disharmony of interests exists within both nations between the center and periphery of each and between the periphery in the center nation and the periphery in the periphery nation (pp. 81-83) (see *Global Economic Interdependence: Why Crisis?*).

The mechanisms of imperialistic exploitation are explained by two principles of interaction. The first one is that of "vertical trading": who benefits more by foreign trade between a center and a periphery nation in Galtung's view depends mostly on "the gap in processing level" between both nations (p. 87). The nation which, according to the international division of labor, specializes in most refined, finished products will gain high "spin-off effects" (that is, external economies) which stimulate economic growth and occur not only in the production sector but additionally bring with them benefits in skills, research, communication, and social structure, not to mention psychological, military, and political advantages. On the other hand, low processing patterns, which are typical for underdeveloped countries normally having only one or very few primary products to export, result in very low spin-offs. Thus vertical interaction is seen by Galtung as "the major source of the inequality of this world" (p. 89) (see *Equitable Equality: Gandhian Concept*). And this inequality is maintained and reinforced by a second mechanism, "the feudal interaction structure" (p. 89). This principle in its purest form assumes that the periphery nation only has interaction with one center nation, but not with other center or periphery nations, resulting in high concentration of trade partners. The overall consequence of Galtung's structural imperialism is that it tends to perpetuate worldwide inequalities. They can be reduced only by changing these structures (p. 107).

Even "foreign aid" was seen by some authors as a special form of neoimperialism. They argued that foreign aid is determined mostly by the economic interests of the donor countries in securing and promoting their exports and investments. The United States especially were reproached for using their aid as an instrument for the "Pax Americana," (see *Pax-Americana*) namely for their anticommunist "containment policy" (see *Containment*) to prevent underdeveloped countries from leaving the zone of capitalist influence or from becoming communist satellites (see *Containment*). In a similar way the economic and military aid of the former Soviet Union clearly seemed to be determined by its economic, strategic, and ideological interests.

If foreign aid is granted under such conditions it is not difficult to conclude that, far from responding to the developmental needs of developing countries, it primarily tends to strengthen their economic, political, and cultural dependence.

What was said about bilateral foreign aid was also maintained of multilateral aid. In this context several international organizations have been accused of merely playing the role of additional instruments for controlling the developing countries (see for instance Hayter 1971; Jalée 1969; Magdoff 1969; Nuscheler 1971; Steel 1968).

The most damning charge derived from all of the above-mentioned arguments of neoimperialism or neocolonialism culminated in the thesis that the so called policy of developing the developing countries was in truth a policy of "developing their underdevelopment" (Frank 1967), that is to say the wealth of the rich center nations originates from the exploitation of the periphery nations.

2.1 Criticisms

The various arguments in the debate on neoimperialism have not remained unchallenged. Some of them were criticized even by advocates of the idea of a persistent exploitation of the developing countries insofar as they centered the main root of the evil on another special aspect. Naturally the criticism raised by principal opponents of the neoimperialism approach, who see the underdevelopment of so many countries not, or not only, as caused by the above-mentioned factors, is much more biting. Deutsch (1974), for example, pointed out circularities in some of the arguments and called Galtung's contribution "a brilliant piece of simplification" which becomes highly dubious on closer examination (pp. 17-19). Waltz spoke of "selfverifying theories" which at best offered descriptions rather than explanations (1975 pp. 25-27). And for Mommsen they fascinate more because of their moral and ideological strength than their analytical efficiency (1987 p. 108, 121). To make this critique more substantial, some special arguments and questions should be enumerated:

By separating imperialism more and more from political respectively governmental activities, the idea of neoimperialism contributed considerably to enlarge and thus dilute the meaning of the term imperialism. Every sort of interaction between countries with differing levels of economic development now stood under suspicion of being imperialist. But how should one prove this, how should one separate imperialist from nonimperialist activities? Is the level of economic development a sufficient criterion for differentiation? And if one puts forward a specific structure of foreign trade, namely the exportation of raw materials when importing manufactured goods, as an indicator of imperialist dependence and exploitation, then one additionally obtains the strange result that, for instance, the former Soviet Union was impe-

rialistically exploited even by her own East European satellites (not to mention the fact that the world's major exporter of raw materials is the United States).

While Lenin and other Marxists had believed that imperialism would have the side-effect of developing the colonies by making them capitalist and thus ripe for revolution, quite contrary effects on development were now boldly stated, even by adherents of Marxist thought.

Most neoimperialist views are theoretically and/or empirically too superficial or too biased to prove their main theses. For example, there was and is no definite tendency for the terms of trade of underdeveloped countries to deteriorate in the long run (Boeckh 1982 p. 139, Osterkamp 1984): The drastic raising of oil prices by the members of the Organization of Petroleum Exporting Countries (OPEC) in 1973 and 1979 was the most spectacular example of breaking through the barrier of *dependencia*. And "feudal trading" was and is in most cases by no means as characteristic for the developing countries as Galtung's model pretends (see his own table, pp. 110-11).

As some authors have shown (for instance Samuelson 1976, Schmidt 1982) the theory of "unequal exchange" in the version of Emmanuel or Kohlmey does not explain why countries develop unequally because of their foreign trade.

Contrary to the neoimperialist approach, in developing countries a long and clear tendency of decreasing importance as a field of operation for Western private capital could be observed. Thus the desire of underdeveloped countries for foreign capital was and is in many cases greater than the willingness of capitalist countries to invest there. Only in the last decade a turnaround can be seen due to the dynamic economic development of some "threshold countries" which attract large amounts of private capital.

But also the fact that some originally underdeveloped countries have developed enormously in spite of, or because of, intensive economic contacts with more advanced countries (see the United States or Germany in the late nineteenth century, Japan after World War II and a lot of countries in Asia and South America in the last decades) generally stands in contradiction to the neoimperialist thinking. It better coincides with the classical theory of Adam Smith or David Ricardo, that economic transactions between developed countries in general are not only not harmful but very advantageous to their prosperity. And if this is true, the premise of the neoimperialist approach that the capitalist countries have a strong interest in maintaining the Third World in the status of underdevelopment is dubious.

What is the essence of this criticism? Surely, there was, and is, in fact a widening economic gap between the industrial countries (including some "Tigers" and some oil-producing states) and many poorer countries (especially in Africa) in spite of all efforts in the manifold fields of "foreign aid" (see for example Broad and Landi 1996). But neoimperialist thought does not tell us the whole story why this is happening.

At best it throws light on some aspects, raises important questions, and stimulates helpful hypotheses, whereas at worst it serves to obscure relevant causal relations. Nevertheless the neoimperialist explanations had their own political effects. By blaming the capitalist or highly developed countries for the underdevelopment of developing countries they distracted attention from these countries' own responsibilities and those of their governments and thus aggravated the North-South conflict. On the other hand, neoimperialist accusations may partly have contributed in western countries to create a climate hostile to imperialist activities as well as perhaps a stronger willingness to help the developing countries.

3. Imperialism as a Constant Historical Phenomenon

As demonstrated earlier the process of empire building in the decades before the First World War initiated numerous theories of imperialism. Attempts were made to explain it primarily as a result of characteristics which came into existence only in this period. But empire building is a much more general historical phenomenon. It predates the nineteenth century's "age of imperialism," it can equally be observed in the twentieth century, and perhaps it may be a pattern of international politics in the future, as well.

The question remains as to the reasons for imperialism in earlier times. Moreover, did these reasons not play any role in modern times, as the theories pretend, which put so much stress on the capitalistic system? Looking back in history it becomes obvious that imperialism in different times and different cases was connected with quite different types of economic, social, and/or political systems. Most well-known theorists of capitalist imperialism did not discuss it in a broader historical context. They made the mistake of interpreting a specific historical correlation—namely the simultaneous advent of the new wave of imperialism in the late nineteenth century and of the new economic system of capitalism or of its structural change—as a relationship of cause and effect.

A common root of all historical examples of imperialism as well as of similar tendencies in recent times is the existence of considerable power differentials. "Where gross imbalances of power exist, and where the means of transportation permit the export of goods and of the instruments of rule, the more capable people ordinarily exert a considerable influence and control over those less able to produce surpluses. Weakness invites control; strength tempts one to exercise it, even if only for the 'good' of other people" (Waltz 1975 pp. 22-23). Certainly, this common basis of imperialism does not tell us the whole truth about all imperialistic activities in history. As demonstrated above one can distinguish different methods of imperialistic control, some more direct ones such as (formal) colonialism, some more indirect ones such as (informal) preponderance or hegemony over satellites. Beyond this formal aspect one can usually distinguish different persons and groups within various countries who called for imperialism in different historical situations; and they did and do so with widely varying imperialistic motivations, aiming at very different goals, economic as well as political or ideological ones. By means of foreign expansion they tried, and still try, for example,

(a) to increase the dynasty's, or the nation's, or the system's security;

(b) to aggrandize the dynasty's, or the nation's prestige and/or power;

(c) to spread their own ideology and/or culture (for example, "the White man's burden" or "*am deutschen Wesen soll die Welt genesen*," or the "world revolution");

(d) to open up, to secure, and/or to exploit foreign markets;

(e) to make foreign regions accessible for their own settlement;

(f) to prevent their rival's expansionism;

(g) to integrate or to divert different groups or classes of their own society.

Logically these imperialistic incentives can best be attained by global hegemony, which in history was only reached—and here only approximately—by Rome in the second and by Great Britain in the nineteenth centuries (that is, Pax Romana, and Pax Britannica, respectively).

In the period after World War II a system of "bimultipolarity" (Rosecrance) developed which restricted the imperialistic options for the two Superpowers.

Pax Americana or Pax Sovietica could at most be half global, especially under the threat of mutual nuclear destruction. Thus, both Superpowers mainly took pains to avoid losing allies (see *Brezhnev Doctrine*). Moreover they supported tendencies of disintegration in the rival camp, they tried to prevent neutral countries from coming under the opponent's control, and they tried to recruit new allies from the neutral world. However, after the Soviet empire collapsed the international scene changed dramatically. On the one hand, a global Pax Americana now became possible, at least in the military sphere. On the other hand the structure of the international system has tended more toward multipolarity than toward US hegemony. In addition, the Americans themselves do not seem to strive for real global hegemony, though they energetically stand up for their own interests all over the world, which are expressed also in their striving for worldwide peace, freedom, free trade and for the respect of human rights.

Thus, the future of imperialism is unclear. In a decolonized, multipolar and more and more economically and technologically globalized world it seems less possible and less necessary to dominate other nations. But as history has demonstrated there always exists such a variety of incentives that new imperialistic actions including cultural and religious ones cannot be ruled out.

See also: *World Economy, Social Change and Peace; Peace Theory: An Introduction*

Bibliography

Amin S 1973 *Le développement inégal.* Minuit, Paris [1975 *Die ungleiche Entwicklung.* Hamburg]

Baran P A 1957 *The Political Economy of Growth.* Monthly Review Press, New York [1966 *Politische Ökonomie des Wirtschaftlichen Wachstums.* Luchterhand, Berlin]

Boeckh A 1982 Abhängigkeit, Unterentwicklung und Entwicklung: Zum Erklärungswert der Dependencia-Ansätze. In: Nohlen D, Nuscheler F (eds.) 1982 *Handbuch der Dritten Welt*, Vol.1, 2nd edn. Hoffmann und Campe, Hamburg

Broad R, Landi Ch M 1996 Whither the North-South Gap? *Third World Q.* 17(1)

Daalder H 1968 Imperialism. *International Encyclopedia of the Social Sciences*, Vol.7. Macmillan, New York

Deutsch K W 1974 Imperialism and neocolonialism. *The Papers of the Peace Science Society* (*International*) 23

Dos Santos T 1970 The structure of dependence. *Am. Econ. Rev.* 60

Emmanuel A 1969 *L'echange inégal.* Maspero, Paris [1972 *Unequal Exchange.* Monthly Review Press, New York]

Fieldhouse D K 1973 *Economics and Empire 1830-1914.* Weidenfeld and Nicolson, London

Frank A G 1967 *Capitalism and Underdevelopment in Latin America.* Monthly Review, New York [1968 *Capitalisme et sous-development en Amérique latine.* Maspero, Paris; 1969 *Kapitalismus und Unterentwicklung in Latein Amerika.* Europäische Verlagsanstalt, Frankfurt]

Gallagher J, Robinson R 1953 The imperialism of free trade. *Econ. History Rev.* 2nd series

Galtung J 1971 A structural theory of imperialism. *J. Peace Research* 8

Halstead J P, Porcari S 1974 *Modern European Imperialism: A Bibliography of Books and Articles, 1815-1972.* Boston, Massachusetts

Hampe P 1976 *Die "Ökonomische Imperialismustheorie."* Beck, Munich

Hancock W K 1950 *Wealth of Colonies.* Cambridge University Press, Cambridge

Hayter T 1971 *Aid as Imperialism.* Penguin, Harmondsworth

Hilferding R 1910 *Das Finanzkapital.* Brand, Vienna

Hobson J A 1902 *Imperialism.* Allen and Unwin, London. [1968 *Der Imperialismus.* Kiepenheuer and Witsch, Cologne]

Jalée P 1969 *L'imperialisme en 1970.* Maspero, Paris

Koebner R, Schmidt H D 1964 *Imperialism: The Story and Significance of a Political Word, 1840-1960.* Cambridge University Press, Cambridge.

Kohlmey G 1962 Karl Marx' theorie von den internationalen Werten mit einigen Schlussfolgerungen . . . *Jahrbuch des Instituts für Wirtschaftswissenschaft* 5

Lenin V I 1917 *Imperialism: The Highest State of Capitalism.* International Publishers, New York

Luxemburg R 1913 *Die Akkumulation des Kapitals.* Berlin [1951 *The Accumulation of Capital.* Routledge, London]

Magdoff H 1969 *The Age of Imperialism.* Monthly Review Press, New York [1970 *Das Zeitalter des Imperialismus.* Frankfurt]

Marini R M 1974 Die Dialektik der Abhängigkeit. In: Senghaas D (ed.) 1974 *Peripherer Kapitalismus.* Suhrkamp, Frankfurt

Mommsen W J 1979 *Der Europäische Imperialismus.* Vandenhoeck and Ruprecht, Göttingen

Mommsen W J 1987 *Imperialismustheorien*, 3rd. edn Vandenhoeck and Ruprecht, Göttingen

Nkrumah K 1965 *Neo-colonialism: The Last Stage of Imperialism.* Nelson, London

Nohlen D, Nuscheler F (eds.) 1982 *Handbuch der Dritten Welt*, Vol. 1, 2nd edn. Hoffmann and Campe, Hamburg

Nuscheler F 1971 Dritte Welt und Imperialismustheorie. *Civitas* 10

Osterkamp R 1984 Der Aussenhandel. In: Opitz P J (ed.) 1984 *Die Dritte Welt in der Krise.* Beck, Munich

Owen R, Sutcliffe B (eds.) 1972 *Studies in the Theory of Imperialism*. Longman, London

Platt D C M 1968 *Finance, Trade, and Politics in British Foreign Policy 1815-1914*. Clarendon, Oxford

Prebisch R 1968 *Für eine bessere Zukunft der Entwicklungsländer*. East Berlin

Robinson R, Gallagher J 1962 *Africa and the Victorians*. Macmillan, London

Samuelson P A 1976 Illogic of neo-Marxian doctrine of unequal exchange. In: Belsley D A et al., (eds.) 1976 *Inflation, Trade and Taxes*. Columbus

Schmidt A 1982 Ungleicher Tausch. In: Nohlen D, Nuscheler F (eds.) 1982 *Handbuch der Dritten Welt*, Vol.1, 2nd edn. Hoffmann and Campe, Hamburg

Schumpeter J A 1919 Zur Soziologie der Imperialismen. *Archiv für Sozialwissenschaft und Sozialpolitik* 46 [1951 *Imperialism and Social Classes*. Kelley, New York and Blackwell, Oxford]

Stalin J 1919 *Izvestia*, February 22 [1953 *Works*, Vol. 4. Moscow]

Steel R 1968 *Pax Americana*. Hamish Hamilton, London

Sweezy P M 1942 *The Theory of Capitalist Development*. Dennis Dobson, London [1970 *Theorie der Kapitalistischen Entwicklung*. Suhrkamp, Frankfurt]

Waltz K N 1975 Theory of international relations. In: Greenstein F I, Polsby N W (eds.) 1975 *Handbook of Political Science*, Vol. 8. Addison-Wesley, Reading, Massachusetts

Wehler H U 1969 *Bismarck und der Imperialismus*. Kiepenheuer Witsch, Cologne

PETER HAMPE

India: Historical Concepts and Institutions of Peace

Indian society has long been concerned with peace (*Shanti*). There is hardly any Hindu ritual which does not start or end with a *Shanti-Path* (recitation and call for peace). The fact is that *Shanti* has much deeper meanings and wider implications which could be fruitfully brought to bear on the peace movements of our times. One such historical dimension is that long before people started talking of peace in outer space, on the high seas, beneath the sea, and beneath the earth, Indian society was fully conscious of the cosmic view of peace, as is illustrated by one of the famous *Shanti-Path* talks concerning peace in the minds of people, peace on earth, in outer space, on the seas, and beneath the sea and earth. Compared with this broad vision of peace, even the concept of structural violence appears to be limited and shallow. A second dimension of *Shanti* was that it was as much concerned with groups and institutions as with individuals. In fact, in the Indian concept of peace, an individual being at peace with himself or herself was considered to be absolutely crucial to peace on all fronts and in all places. It was assumed that society, and in fact the entire cosmos, could not remain fully peaceful unless people were fully at peace with themselves. For instance, one of the greatest aspirations and achievements of a Hindu was to become *Jivan-Mukta* (free in life)—an individual of high spiritual achievement who has attained a rare equanimity of mind so as to remain unaffected by all vicissitudes of life. Viewed from this perspective, individuals who had come to terms with themselves were to be the foundation upon which the entire edifice of societal and cosmic peace and harmony was to be built.

A very elaborate and detailed design for life was conceived and a complete structure of intellectual and institutional society was erected to achieve and promote peace and harmony both at the individual and at the societal level.

The intellectual vision which supported this peaceful and harmonious living was based on a deeper philosophical vision of the universe in which all beings, both animate and inanimate, had a symbiotic relationship with one another, and with the whole. This was the *Adaitic* (nondualistic) view of the universe—a much deeper and wider concept than today's equivalent, the ecosystem. Another dimension was a person's relationship with the ultimate reality—God. There was no concept of "original sin" and people needed no mediation between themselves and their creator. Thus a person was a part of the same divinity—*Twa twam Asi* (that art thou). All that was needed was to remove the veil of *Avidya* (lack of knowledge) and this was achieved by an educational system based on the *Guru-Shishya Parampara* (teacher-disciple relationship). Thus the role of external agencies like the church and state was kept at a minimal level and every person was to find his or her own path to salvation. Such a view of human beings and the universe promoted peaceful and harmonious relationships between people and the environment on the one hand, and people and their fellow beings on the other.

The second intellectual pillar which contributed greatly to this peace and harmony in society was the concept of truth which was taken to be *Apaursheya* (not human-made). The underlying concept of this truth was the feeling that truth is of paramount importance but there are different roads leading to it and that it is not possible to say which road is the best road. It was left up to the individual to decide which of the three paths—*Karma* (action), *Bhakti* (devotion), and *Jhyan* (knowledge)—to follow in keeping with his or her own development, and the question of one path being superior to another did not arise. This created an atmosphere of tolerance and broadmindedness. It is remarkable that there was no concept of the renegade and even when people like Buddha and Mahabir and later on the saint poets challenged some of the basic tenets of Hinduism, they were neither prosecuted nor attacked. Buddha was integrated into one of the tenth *Avatars* of Hinduism. It was again the same quality of intellectual tolerance and broadmindedness which helped Indian society to absorb and integrate the vast numbers of invaders who came to India until the medieval period when Islam confronted Indian society. Such a view of truth gave Indian society a tremendous capacity for renewal and regeneration.

A third pillar of this harmonious and peaceful living was the concept of the four *Purushharth* (the ends of human life)—*Arth, Dharma, Kam*, and *Moksha*. It should be noted here that in these ends of human life there was a real balance between the demands of the body and those of the spirit. While the first two *Purushharth*, that is, *Arth* and *Kam*, dealt with the needs of the body, the other two— *Dharma* and *Moksha*—took care of the needs of the spirit. Thus at the individual level the desire of *Arth* and *Kam* is to be adjusted and controlled in the context of a person's higher aspirations of *Dharma* and *Moksha*. Thus an attempt was made to achieve rare balance between the needs of the body and those of spirit. Thus developed a philosophy of life which openly and unequivocally went against the ever-rising needs of a person—rather it developed the concept of limited needs.

Another intellectual element in this perception of life was that there was no concept of individual rights in the Western sense. Rather the concept of *Dharma* was emphasized. *Dharma* has been defined as:

> Sacred law and duty, justice, religious merit . . . . The commentators have explained it, as denoting an act which produces the quality of the soul called *apurva*, the cause of the heavenly bliss and of final liberation. In ordinary usage, however, it has a far wider meaning than this, and may denote established practice or custom of any caste and community. (*Encyclopaedia of Religion and Ethics*, Vol. IV p. 702)

Accordingly, there were specific duties for every segment of society including the king. The king was the authority to enforce *Des Dharma* (rules relating to a particular country), *Jati Dharma* (regarding caste), and *Kul Dharma* (customs related to a family). The concept of *Swadharma* (one's own duty) was developed according to which every person had to perform an assigned duty according to his or her ability and station in life and society. That also created a situation of harmonization of conflicts. However, the possibility of conflict arising between the weak and the strong was not totally ruled out. The protection of the weak did not arise from their rights, as in Western society, but it was the duty of the strong to protect the weak. Thus the concept of *Avadhya* (one that cannot be harmed or killed) was propounded as a major instrument for keeping conflict to manageable proportions and for protecting the weak from the onslaught of the strong. This category of the weak included women, children, widows, handicapped people, and pet animals. By failing to protect the weak, the strong and powerful stood condemned in their own eyes and also in those of society. This arrangement served two purposes. First, it kept conflict to a minimal level as the weak did not seek protection by asserting their rights, thus further accentuating the conflict situation, and second it reminded the strong of their duty to protect the weak. Such a system was morally and spiritually uplifting for both the parties and there was no concept of two adversaries being party to a dispute both asserting their rights. Another advantage of the system was the right of both community and individual to be protected but not at the cost of each other.

This intellectual and philosophical vision of life and the universe to a great extent contributed toward a peaceful and harmonious life in society by promoting an atmosphere of general tolerance and goodwill. What sustained, nurtured, and supported this view of life was the institutional structure which was created to keep society on an even keel by minimizing the arena of conflicts both at individual and societal level.

Foremost in the institutional structure was the concept of *Varna Ashram Dharma* (fourfold division of society with specific duty for each one of them). This kind of social arrangement may have many weaknesses, but there is no denying the fact that it developed an institutional framework in which everyone found a fixed role in life and was entrusted with a particular kind of task which suited him or her, and which prevented a situation in which everyone competed with everyone else. Viewed in an historical context, this might be the most stability-oriented superstructure which human beings have ever conceived, erected, and promoted. That it ultimately degenerated into the caste system is another issue and not very relevant to the point under discussion.

A second institution which supported this harmony and peace on society was the family structure. It created a concept of the extended family in which people of many generations lived under the same roof. In several ways this family structure contributed to the peace and harmony in society. In the first place, it was in the family that the man learnt his first lesson in performance of his *Dharma* (duty) and noninsistence on his rights. The pivotal role of the family head as the *Karta* (actor) of the family played a significant role in harmonizing the interests of the members, more often than not to his own cost. Thus it was at the level of the family that man learnt his first lesson in living for others, emphasizing duty instead of his individual rights, and harmonizing the conflicting interests of various members in an atmosphere of goodwill and understanding. Thus the *Grihastha* (householder) played a key role in society, and the harmonious family structure became society in miniature.

This social structure was further supported by the institution of the Indian system of education. It has several distinguishing features. In the first place, education was not a training for carrying out a profession, but for the total development of a person. Second, the *Guru-Shishya Parampara* (teacher-disciple relationship) took care of the problem of internalization of values, the process becoming easier because of the close personal relationship between the *Guru* and *Shishya*. Third, the oral tradition took care of those who were not fortunate enough to participate in the long process of education in the *Guru-Shishya Parampara*. This oral tradition had several roles to perform. It worked through the devotional songs of poets, and the *Kath Vachak* (reader) of the scriptures. It passed the whole gamut of cultural heritage from one generation to another and from the higher to the lower castes and thus raised the consciousness of the entire community.

A fourth institution which greatly contributed to conflict resolution was the village *Panchayats* and caste *Panchayat*. These associations played a mediatory role in the case of clashes of interest among various individuals or groups. These institutions proved to be better instruments of conflict resolution than institutions based on the legal juridical system of the Western model which is primarily based on the adjudication between two adversaries on the basis of elaborate but rigid rules which may not take care of certain situations. This indigenous system of justice and adjudication has several advantages over the Western model. First, administration of justice and adjudication did not take place between two adversaries fortified by written laws and extensive commentaries. Rather justice was done on the basis of firsthand knowledge. Second, justice was done in such a way that it was acceptable to the whole society.

The productive system also contributed in a significant way to peaceful living. The whole foundation was based on the concept of self-sufficient villages. Geographical mobility was discouraged and people worked and lived, from generation to generation, in the same area and thus their body-mind system was attuned to the immediate environment. Besides, the whole economic system was noncompetitive and based on the use and mobilization of local resources. The social order was not marked by great inequality, and conflict was kept at a minimal level.

At the individual level, there were a number of norms which individuals were to observe and any violation of these norms brought social sanction in its train. The three important instruments of conflict resolution at the individual level were the institution of *Sadhna* (practice), *Prayaschit* (expiation), and *Paschtap* (repentance). A person went through a process of individual *sadhana* which helped him or her to internalize the values of good social living by strengthening the process of inner discipline. In case there was deliberate or non-deliberate violation of *Swadharma*, a person was to undergo a process of *Prayaschit* and *Paschtap* which has a purifying impact on his or her body and mind and thus enables him or her to strengthen the resolve to live a peaceful and harmonious life.

That does not mean that there was no system of punishment (*Danda*). In fact, various types of *Danda* were provided for people who failed to observe their *Swadharma* (self-duty) (Tähtinen 1982).

Indian society underwent a change and the system of conflict management which it had assiduously built up collapsed in the course of time. The old structure collapsed partly under its own weight as distortion crept in, and partly as a result of a kind of social stratification or social atrophy. The colonial rule under which India remained for a long time was also a contributory factor in the process of historical decay and disintegration. Perhaps both processes worked simultaneously and reinforced each other.

The most significant change that took place in Indian society internally was the system of *chutur varna* being turned into a cast-iron and stratified caste system. This created a severe imbalance in the social order leading to great differences, and to tension and conflict situations.

Colonial rule also led to several fundamental changes in the socioeconomic structure of Indian society. In the first place, it destroyed the old economic order of the country which had been the bulwark of peaceful and harmonious social living by introducing a system of private ownership of land which led to conflict and confrontation in the villages. Second it destroyed the balanced growth of village industry and agriculture and thus created a new class of landless labor which became the greatest destabilizing force in the country. Third, it destroyed the indigenous industrial structure and thus turned India into a marketplace for its finished produce. Subsequently, the process of industrialization which was introduced on a limited scale led to the creation of a society with deep and irreconcilable class differences. The emergence of a class society brought about a change in the country creating a situation of class conflict and confrontation at several levels.

However, the worst victims of the colonial rule were the educational and cultural systems of the country. It destroyed the indigenous system of education which had stood the test of time and in fact had taken the Indian people to the highest peak of intellectual achievements. This was replaced by a British system of education which had several consequences. In the first place, it sought to destroy the true consciousness of the people by superimposing a false consciousness of alien symbols and images. Second, it destroyed the strong oral tradition of education which was the major vehicle of transmitting cultural heritage from one generation to the next and also for bringing it to the reach of the lower strata of society. Third, it led to the emergence of a new class of colonized elite which was totally cut off from its indigenous cultural roots and in fact had contempt for its own heritage.

Another consequence of the colonial rule was that conflict between different communities was accentuated. This was done by playing one community off against the other. The Hindu-Moslem animosity which arose from these developments finally led to the partition of the country.

Thus by the time India achieved independence in 1947, the traditional modes of conflict resolution had virtually collapsed.

Bibliography ——————————————————

Tähtinen U 1982 *Non-violent Theories of Punishment: Indian and Western.* Moti Lal Banarsi Das, Delhi

RAM C. PRADHAN

Indian Ocean:
The Duality of Zone of Peace Concept and Politics of Security Revisited

1. Introduction

On December 16, 1971 the United Nations General Assembly passed resolution 2832 (XXVI), the thrust of which was to declare the "Indian Ocean as a zone of peace." Proposed by two littoral states, Sri Lanka and Tanzania, the resolution acknowledged" . . . the right to free and unimpeded use of the zone by the vessels of all nations . . . ." But, more substantively, it calls

> . . . upon the great powers to enter into consultation with the littoral states of the Indian Ocean with a view to halting the further expansion of their military presence in the Indian Ocean from the area of all bases, military installations, nuclear weapons and weapons of mass destruction and any manifestation of great power presence conceived in the context of great power rivalry.

Sustained military presence by the great powers was deemed to be heightening tension in the Ocean zone. It was, therefore, inimical to the peace and security of the developing littoral states. But, fifteen years later, the ideals of that resolution have still not been realized. On the contrary, any chance of realizing them seems to have receded further with time. Nevertheless, verbal commitment to the ideals has endured, particularly among the littoral states. At the UN, the Non-aligned Conferences, and other international forums, these states still reiterate their demand and receive support from their peers. The great powers, whom the resolution address, appeared responsive in the 1970s with the superpowers actually embarking on Naval Arms Limitation Talks (NALT). This initiative cooled off toward the close of the decade and the powers became less forthcoming about the initiative both in attitude and behavior.

Thus a coordinated and allied pattern of military deployment started. Diego Garcia, the most significant Anglo-American base in the Indian Ocean was acquired against this background. In April 1965

Britain excised from its colonies, Mauritius and Seychelles, a series of islands to form the British Indian Ocean Territory (BIOT). Seychelles regained its possession when they were deemed to be unfit. But Mauritius was given £3 million and its territories, the Chagos Archipelago including Diego Garcia were retained.

Seemingly independent, but still allied with the West, is the French presence. Like Britain, France also followed the imperial tradition of consolidating bases in the former colonies. These include coastal Djibouti and island bases like Mayotte, Reunion, Juan de Nova, Bassas de India and so on which France acquired from its former colonies, Comoro and Malagasy. This network enables France to pursue its own policy through separate command deployment while at the same time lending weight and muscle toward western interests.

On the other side, the former Soviet Union made its first debut into the Indian Ocean in March 1968. The timing of the debut eroded the Anglo-American claims of "countering Soviet threat" in that activities a prepositioning took place on their side long before any effective Soviet presence was established there. However, given the competitive posture between the two blocs, once the West succeeded in establishing some enduring presence there, it just became a matter of time before a Soviet presence was established.

The UN Zone of Peace resolution of December 16, 1971 was passed against this background. It was preceded by a similar resolution at the Non-aligned summit conference in Lusaka, Zambia the previous year. Further, since the early 1970s, the former colonies have also moved to reclaim the island bases excised from them before independence. Thus Mauritius claims Diego Garcia; the Comoros claims Mayotte; while Malagasy claims Glorieuses, Juan De Nova and Basses de India.

But under the veneer of agreement, the littoral states harbor an intricate network of relationships among themselves on the one hand, and between them and the great powers whom they want to remove from the Indian Ocean on the other. Local conflicts, uneasy relations with respective neighbors, and domestic political behaviour force the littoral states to seek allies in order to supplement their own strength. Invariably the choice is one of the powers with a reach to the Indian Ocean. In this way, a pattern of bilateral and multilateral relationships was nurtured. The upshot is that the littoral states individually find themselves strengthening the same forces that they collectively seek to contain. Thus, parallel to their quest for demilitarization, the littoral states also pursue other policies based on different dictates which render the collective demand inoperative.

Hence the 1971 resolution is being gradually upset in the 1980s by the formula of "balanced presence advocated by among others Australia, Malaysia, Mauritius, Singapore, Somalia and some Gulf states. These being Western inclined nations, their advocacy is interpreted as favorable to the West. This has, consequently, invoked a counterview which contends that the choke points, that is, the entrances to the Indian Ocean at the Strait of Malacca, Suez Canal, West Australia and the Cape are controlled by countries that are strategically closer to the West. As such, this view accepts Soviet presence as less threatening. Hence, perhaps not surprisingly, by the turn of the decade the 45-member UN Committee on the Indian Ocean has not made any impact of consequence.

In terms of independent resolve, the policy positions of the powers over the decade are also pertinent. In September 1973, two years after the UN resolution, France established a separate Indian Ocean naval command. And in February 1978, France announced a 200-mile economic exclusion zone around its island bases. In October 1972, the United Kingdom and the United States reached another agreement over Diego Garcia to complement that of December 1966. Since then two other agreements have been reached, in February 1976 and June/July 1981 respectively. The terms of these exchanges would allow Diego Garcia to be transformed into a hard naval base capable of servicing B-52 strategic bombers, nuclear submarines, and aircraft carriers. The spate of construction on Diego Garcia demonstrates that Anglo-American behavior has been governed more by geo-strategic assessment than by anything else. And that is not lost on the former Soviet Union.

Ultimately, that strategic perception has an adverse effect on the naval arms strategic talks (NALT). In February 1978, the United States withdrew from NALT ostensibly in protest at Soviet-Cuban intervention on the Ethiopian side in the Ogden war. However, a more important reason would be the behavior of the superpowers based on subjective perception of strategic stakes.

The 1970s closed with Soviet intervention in Afghanistan in December 1979. The 1980s opened with an American response, the Carter Doctrine of February 1980 which pledged that:

> An attempt by any outside force to gain control of the Persian Gulf region will be regarded as an assault on the vital interests of the United States. And such an attempt will be repelled by any means necessary including military force.

The doctrine translated to a fresh commitment to Diego Garcia and the formation of the Rapid deployment Force (RDF) as a key element of United States defense policy in the 1980s.

This bout of militarization demonstrates that the pursuit of demilitarization is closely linked to the strategic perception and behavior of the non-Indian Ocean powers and their littoral allies. The point is pertinent since the inclination of the littoral states to cooperate (albeit for their own reasons) strengthens the strategic anchorage of the great powers.

Thus, the pursuit of zone of peace concept survives only verbally. In the practical sense, it has long been rendered less credible and less attainable by the twin disposition of great power search for primacy and the strategic calculation of the littoral states. The concept has been overwhelmed by the various dimensions of Indian Ocean politics.

The above synopsis is an abridgement of an article in two journals.[1] In this setting the review and re-evaluation of its conceptual thrust, analysis and conclusion forms the basis of this article. The aim is to determine the existing situation with regard to the duality of the zone of peace concept and the politics of security in the Indian Ocean in the context of the fundamental changes that have been taking place in the trend of international relations from the mid-1980s to date (1998).

In essence, this means evaluating the continuous pursuit of the implementation of the UN General Assembly resolution 2832 (XXVI) of December 16, 1971 declaring the Indian Ocean as a zone of peace by the various parties involved. And this is going to be done against the background of the conclusion that as of the mid-1980s the undertaking survived only verbally while,

> In the practical sense it has been long rendered less credible and less attainable by the twin disposition of great power search for primacy and the strategic calculation of the littoral states.[2]

Proceeding from this conclusion and within the context of the prevailing trends in international relations, the approach is to determine whether the subsequent run of pursuit has notched up any accomplishments in the process, or whether it continued to stagnate, or even more negatively whether it suffered debilitating reversals. And for this purpose the original framework revolving around the three themes would be retained. The themes include: One, the perceived militarization of the Indian Ocean. Two, the behavior of the littoral states as the sponsors of the zone of peace resolution. And three, the responses of the non-Indian Ocean powers as the target of the resolution.

2. *International Relations since the Mid-1980s: An Overview*

The trend of international relations since the mid-1980s, has been completely overshadowed, and inevitably so, by the collapse of the bipolar structure which emerged at the end of the Second World War in 1945. The decision by the contracting parties to dismantle the Warsaw Pact military alliance in March 1991[3] marked the beginning of the physical end of the network of communist bloc centered in Eastern Europe. Finally, in December 1991, the Soviet Union itself, the superpower that served as the anchor and nerve centre of the communist bloc disintegrated spawning fifteen new sovereign states. Thus the period from 1985 when the erstwhile Soviet Union embarked on fundamental reforms and re-structuring, and 1991 when the communist bloc and its superpower core finally unravelled, stand in good comparison with other landmark years that historically signify the end of one era and the beginning of another. In this regard the disintegration of the Soviet Union in 1991 marked the formal end of the pattern of ideological and military rivalry and proxy wars between the eastern and western blocs under the rubric of Cold War which started at the end of the Second World War and the beginning of a succeeding era known variedly as the post-Cold War era or the new world order (NWO).

As an outcome of a systematically pursued pattern of rivalries and contests including proxy wars, the NWO, at least up to this point (1998) could be likened more to a western bloc era on the basis of three considerations. First, western institutions (e.g., European Union), and values (e.g., system of economic management and notions of political democracy), in triumph became more popularized globally. In sum, western victory was unambiguous.[4] Thus it transpires that the erstwhile communist bloc opponents have since turned full circle by adopting the very western values and seeking the full membership of the very western institutions that they were confronting during the Cold War.[5] For those east European states that were once bound to the communist bloc, domestic political and economic reforms and full membership of the dominant Western institutions like the European Union and the North Atlantic Treaty Organization (NATO) (see *North Atlantic Treaty Organization (NATO)*) signify not just a break with a defeated system, but equally important, a move towards securing international guarantees for their new independence. For its part, the Russian Federation as the legatee of the erstwhile Soviet Union, signed a Charter with NATO in May 1997, under which the two sides affirmed that "they do not consider each other adversaries."[6]

Second, the West as a geo-political system of states has become more confident and coherent[7] aided both by its triumph in the Cold War and the long established process of institutional integration particularly that propelling the European Union (see *European Union (EU)*) and NATO (see *Integration, Regional*). Correspondingly, other broad international groupings such as the non-aligned movement, are undermined by their diversity and the international political atmosphere created by the advent of the NWO.[8] Those other organizations with narrow regional focus such as the Arab League (see *League of Arab States*), the OAU, OAS and ASEAN (see *Association of Southeast Asian Nations (ASEAN)*) are constrained by their power limitations in the realm of power politics. They cannot successfully contest the renewed preponderance of the western bloc.

And third, the United States, as the lone surviving superpower and as the leading power within the West, has become enhanced as a hegemon (see *Hegemony*) and a unit-bloc in its own right more capable of holding sway over other countries including its own Western allies under certain circumstances. Thus where before it used to be checked and counter balanced by the former Soviet Union whether at the United Nations, the outer space or in the waters of the Indian Ocean, it now confronts little opposition. And that comparatively little opposition comes essentially from China and the European Union.

With regard to the special focus on the Indian Ocean, the new preponderance of the West in the international framework cast by the NWO has two implications: First, that at present, the military presence in the Indian Ocean which the 1971 Zone of Peace resolution was contesting is, exclusively, Western. Thus, the full implementation of the resolution or the de-militarization of the Indian Ocean as envisaged under it, means in practice the complete withdrawal of Western military presence there.

The second aspect relates to the behavior of the littoral states both in terms of how much cohesion and unity of purpose they could maintain among themselves in pursuing the implementation of the resolution and in terms of how much success they could possibly have against any probable and contingent western resistance or even rejection of their aim. Clearly, this situation anticipates that the littoral

states would either persist and achieve their aims as set out in the resolution, or else they would compromise and find some working arrangement with the western military powers outside the terms of the resolution.

The trend of events around the rim of the Indian Ocean since the mid-1980s is going to be observed against this background. This is necessary because in the context of the zone of peace resolution, the advent of the NWO and its impact on international relations defines only one broad segment (albeit the major one) in the framework. The direct experiences or the defining trends in the littoral states around the rim of the Indian Ocean, which is the zone of activity, is posited as the other main segment. With specific regards to the politics of the Indian Ocean, it is certain that the trend of events within individual littoral states would have significant consequences even if the old order had continued.

At the Cape, South Africa moved from apartheid, white minority rule to multi-racial democracy in April 1994. Although this shift took place after the NWO has emerged, South Africa's transformation has a unique significance because it ended an established pattern of racially and culturally motivated (allowing that apartheid had no international dimensions) alliance with the West. At its broadest, the new South Africa would be more internationalist than Western. Otherwise, it would be simply African. Further up in Mozambique the civil war that grounded the country for some twenty years ended in October, 1994 with a multi-party elections under UN supervision. Notably, the new South Africa became one of the stabilizing agents in the peace process where before de-stabilizing Mozambique (and other neighboring states) was one of the strategic objectives actively pursued by the apartheid regime.

At the Horn of Africa, Somalia collapsed as a modern, functional state under the multiple weight of clan based internecine civil war and the attendant destruction aided and abetted by natural disasters like drought (see *Ethnic Conflict and International Relations*). In 1991, northern Somalia seceded and formed the Republic of Somaliland.[9] In the rest of Somalia, international efforts to restore peace to the country between 1992 and 1995 ended in bitter disappointment and failure with some $3 billion expended.[10] In Ethiopia, the long Civil War culminated in the secession of Eritrea. In May 1993, Eritrea declared itself formally independent following the outcome of a UN monitored referendum in April. By that, Ethiopia ceased being an Indian Ocean littoral state. That status has now fallen on Eritrea with ports in Assab and

Massawa.[11] For its part, Djibouti remains under the continuous threat of ethnic insurgency revolving around the Afars and the Issas.[12] Sudan is in a similar situation except that the configuration of its conflict is comparatively larger. Its long Civil War, renewed yet again since 1983, is pitched along a broad north-south and African-Arab divide.[13]

On the other bank of the Red Sea, the Gulf of Aden acquired a new strategic face following the unification of North and South Yemen in May 1990. With a population of some 14 million, the United Republic of Yemen is larger than all the other states in the Arabian peninsula combined. Further its coastline covers the entire south-western flank of the Arabian peninsula. And although it is still comparatively poorer in per capita income, united Yemen has proven oil reserves of its own in addition to possessing the most extensive areas of fertile land in the region. Significantly, united Yemen is also the only non-monarchical republican state in the peninsula and equally the only non-member of the Gulf Cooperation Council (GCC).[14]

The GCC, made up of Bahrain, Kuwait, Oman, Saudi Arabia and the United Arab Emigrates (UAE) was formally established in May 1981 to provide a security framework for its members against the background of the strategic situation created by the Iraq-Iran war which has been raging since September, 1980. In the war that eventually lasted for eight years, the GCC members supported Iraq thereby effectively designating Iran as the main source of threat in the region. That view altered on August 2, 1990 when Iraq invaded and subsequently annexed Kuwait. In 1991, Iraq itself was defeated and ejected from Kuwait by a US-led multinational force operating under the aegis of the United Nations. Since its defeat, Iraq has been under an assorted range of UN sanctions.

Further out, the littoral rim stretching from India through south-east Asia to Australia, New Zealand and the Antarctic,[15] the situation generally remained placid during the period under review with only what could be termed, the occasional high points or bursts in the diplomatic routine occurring. Against the backdrop of the stringent terms mandated by the 1987 constitution, American military bases in the Philippines were closed between 1991 and 1992.[16] For members of the Association of South East Asian Nations (ASEAN) that development translated into the type of significant regional de-militarization as envisaged by ASEAN's 1976 Declaration of Concord in pursuit of a Zone of Peace, Freedom and Neutrality (ZOFPAN).[17] But at the same time, it created a new strategic equation for Japan, the United States and others with shared concern about the security of the sea lanes crossing that region.

In June 1989, New Zealand's parliament enacted the Nuclear Free Zone (see *Nuclear-Weapons-Free Zones: A History and Assessment*) Disarmament and Arms Control bill which made into law the banning of nuclear-capable ships in its ports. Earlier on, the Labor government of prime minister David Lange applied the ban as a stated policy with countries like the United States primarily in focus. In response, the US suspended security guarantees to New Zealand in August 1986 claiming that the ban has made the Australia, New Zealand, United States alliance (ANZUS) inoperable. In that regard, the 1989 bill hardened New Zealand's position even further. The change of government in 1990 mellowed New Zealand's tone significantly but the national political attitude towards promoting nuclear free zones endured.[18]

The background to this national attitude is cast by the South Pacific Nuclear Free Zone Treaty or the Treaty of Rarotonga which came into effect in December 1986. The former Soviet Union ratified it in April 1988 while China did so in December, 1988. But the other three nuclear powers who in addition also have territories in the zone (i.e., Britain, France and US) refused to ratify it. In the context of the Cold War, they saw the treaty as hampering their options. Eventually, after the end of the Cold War, they accepted the treaty in 1996.[19]

The 1980s were dominated by the stand-off between New Zealand and United States. The early 1990s pitched all the members of the South Pacific Forum*, the progenitors of the SPNFZ treaty, against France over its nuclear tests in the Muroroa Atolls. Their campaigns did not stop the tests, but France allowed that they would be its last. With that, it can be said that more than the efforts of the regional states, the end of the Cold War and technological advancement in nuclear testing methods constituted the major forces that brought about the accomplishment of the SPNFZ treaty.[20]

In June 1995, African states adopted the African Nuclear-Weapon-Free Zone Treaty (ANWFZ) or the Pelindaba treaty.[21] Among the signatories, the treaty had the quickest and greatest impact on South Africa as the only internationally acknowledged nuclear weapons capable member state. In March 1993 while the transition process was under negotiations, Mr. F.W. de Klerk (see Nobel Peace Prize Laureates: *F.W. de Klerk*), the last white president under the apartheid regime confirmed in parliament that South Africa actually developed up to six atomic bombs in the 1980s. But he added that after he took office in

1989, the devices were destroyed, the nuclear plants were downgraded and the blue-prints were shredded.[22] Even with this level of assurance, the negotiators still sought maximum guarantees on the issue of "declaration, dismantling, destruction or conversion of nuclear explosive devices" in Africa.[23] Article 6 of the treaty was directly aimed at ensuring that compliance from member states based on South Africa's experience even though apartheid belonged to a separate diplomatic era.

With specific regard to the Indian Ocean, the ANWFZ treaty compliments similar treaties covering the South Pacific (Rarotonga 1986) the Antarctic (Treaty of Washington 1959) as well as the treaty governing the seabed and ocean floor.[24] Further it also compliments the ZOFPAN initiative of the ASEAN members. Relatedly, these treaties in combination with the UN zone of peace resolution, bring Diego Garcia, the hard Anglo-American military base in the Indian Ocean, into greater focus and scrutiny.

But unlike the nuclear free zones treaties which are issue specific, the zone of peace concept embraces the whole gamut of regional, multilateral, cooperation including de-militarization efforts. Thus, in the context of the NWO wherein civil issues bearing on political dialogue, economic cooperation, trade, environmental protection and military restraint are deemed to have come to the fore, the notion of zone of peace has acquired an even wider definition. In the prevailing international environment, the zone of peace concept envisages a form of "Indian Ocean community consciousness"[25] with institutionalized mechanisms for advancing shared interests including common security. While it may be linked to the advent of the NWO, this idea is not entirely new for as early as 1982, an Indian Ocean Commission has been set up to promote economic cooperation among the smaller island nations. And since the demise of apartheid in 1994, Australia, India, South Africa, Singapore and Mauritius have met and agreed to set up a regional framework to be known as the International Forum of the Indian Ocean.[26] Intended to operate on an informal basis, the forum would debate economic, trade, security and social issues.

If it were ever to progress beyond ideals and good intent, the pursuits of an Indian Ocean forum would have the pattern of political and economic cooperation; among the countries of the Pacific Basin. Further just as the Pacific Basin forum includes the United States and Canada, an equivalent covering the Indian Ocean rim could include Britain, France and the United States in some informal capacities on the basis of historic and existing involvement in the region. They are the non-Indian Ocean powers against whom the zone of peace resolution is primarily directed at.

Thus conceptually, the zone of peace resolution can be expected to fare better under the influence of the new world order with both the littoral states and the non-Indian Ocean powers initiating new approaches commensurate with the times.

3. The Militarization

The systematic collapse of the communist bloc beginning with the dismantling of the Warsaw Pact and ultimately the demise of the then Soviet Union in December, 1991 effectively eliminated the condition, the basis and the strategic-military logic upon which the militarization of the Indian Ocean first took place. Thus, in essence, the end of the Cold War and with it, the collapse of the world order which emerged after the Second World War, marked the end of the first phase of the militarization of the Indian Ocean. In this regard, the subsequent political and strategic rapprochement between the Western bloc and the Russian Federation as the legatee of the defunct Soviet Union as notable by Russia's participation in the Group of Seven (G-7) summit under the banner of political G-8, and its acceptance of the 1997 Charter with NATO that formally ended all historical adversary relationship, served only to confirm anew how decisive the formal end of the first phase was. Further, from the Russian perspective, the end of the historical phase also provided a safe distance from the political tumult and civil wars that have engulfed littoral states like Ethiopia (until the emergence of Eritrea), Somalia and Iraq where it used to have its military bases during the Cold War. South Yemen, another ally, united with its northern half creating a situation that could have undermined its military position in the country on the basis of the renewed sense of nationalism that tend to bloom under such circumstances and the traditional hostility of the defunct North Yemen.[27]

However, the end of the first phase of militarization and the advent of the new world order left the Western military-strategic position severally and collectively intact. The only discernible shifts in the Western position were the transformation of South Africa away from apartheid and the hard knocks which the ANZUS alliance took in the 1980s over New Zealand's attitude towards port calls by nuclear capable ships. Even at the height of the Cold War, these relatively minor shifts could not have altered the balance against the West. Besides under the new world order, the West has been amply compensated by the adoption of the ANWFZ treaty and the ratification of the SPNFZ. With the existing treaty status of the Antarctic and South-east Asia's ZOFPAN, the Indian Ocean is enclosed by nuclear-free zones with the exception of the area covering the Arabian peninsula, Persian Gulf and South Asia. In this zone, the nuclear policies of Iran, India, and Pakistan remain intact.[28] Iraq, the other participant in the nuclear field, has been subjected to systematic dismantling of its programme under United Nations sanctions since its defeat in 1991 which, coincidentally, became one of the landmark events heralding the advent of the new world order. However, as a strategic boon to the Western position, none of them poses as a rival in the Indian Ocean, while each one of them is a signatory to the zone of peace resolution.

Thus, in this setting, under the new world order, the Indian Ocean has, in effect, become one vast Western strategic lake without any credible threat of challenge from another source. The Anglo-American base in the island of Diego Garcia, remains intact although the dispute about its sovereignty is unresolved. Inevitably, the status of Diego Garcia has acquired a special position in Mauritius which claims it as part of the Chagos Archipelago. It is a regular issue in Mauritius' domestic politics and foreign policy with its tempo rising and falling according to electoral swings.[29] Similarly, the position of France in the islands of Mayotte and Reunion remains intact. Notably, they are also part of the network of French Overseas Territories, and as such, France is even more secure since it does not have to contend with external claims of sovereignty. Symbolically, the domestic crisis in the Comoros which led the island of Anjouan to secede in August, 1997 with the avowed aim of seeking a membership of the community of the French overseas territories[30] provides yet another boost to the strategic position of the West in general and that of France in particular. For France, the prestige lies in the historical fact that during the referendum for independence in 1975, Mayotte voted to remain under French administration while Anjouan and the other three islands voted for independence. Consequently, independent Comoros continued to claim sovereignty over Mayotte. Next, France also remains entrenched in Djibouti which continues to retain the status of being host to the largest French military base in Africa.[31]

Then, collectively and severally, all the three non-Indian Ocean powers (i.e., Britain, France and the US) are engaged with the GCC members in military cooperation.[32] And, separately on its own, the United States enjoys base facilities in Bahrain, Qatar, Kuwait and Oman.[33]

This new Western military-strategic position in the Indian Ocean can also be looked at in another way apart from the viewpoint of its being a carry-over from the Cold War period. And that is the perspective of the openly stated intentions of the powers involved. For Britain and the United States, their position on Diego Garcia is no less secured than that of France in Mayotte and Reunion which are an integral part of French overseas territories. Both Britain and the United States are openly committed to retaining their joint control over Diego Garcia regardless of the claims by Mauritius or any historic sense of injustice linked to notions about excision of territories from colonies before their national independence and the movement of native populations elsewhere.[34] Thus in November, 1989, in response to demonstrations in front of the American embassy organized by the Youth Wing of the Mauritius Socialist Movement, demanding the return of Diego Garcia, the US Assistant Secretary of State for African Affairs, Herman Cohen said:

> We do not accept the argument that our presence constitutes a destabilizing force. On the contrary, the Indian Ocean has been at peace for the whole of the period of our presence.[35]

Similarly, in response to demands such as made in front of the American embassy, the then British High Commissioner to Mauritius, Michael Howell, declared on November 20, 1991 that British sovereignty over the Chagos Archipelago (of which Diego Garcia is a part) was not negotiable. But at the same time, Britain is interested in dialogue with Mauritius so that the issue would not be internationalized.[36]

Relatedly, the recent military re-organisation under which France still kept its base in Djibouti as both the largest in Africa[37] and as the forward position for military involvements in the Persian Gulf region (e.g., joint exercises with UAE forces code-named 'Gulf '96'),[38] compliments the general Western oriented operations of US Central Command. The Central Command (cent com) formed in the 1980s to replace the Rapid Deployment Force (RDF) covers American military operations stretching,

> from Suez Canal to Pakistan and from the Gulf to the coast of Kenya across more than 19.5 million square kilometers (7.5 million square miles) of land and sea.[39]

Diego Garcia and a chain of other bases in the GCC states and Turkey support the operations or Centcom.[40]

Against this background the decision by these powers (Britain, France and the US) to vote against the UN General Assembly resolution 48/82 or December 16, 1993 only serves to demonstrate their independent and collective attitudes towards the militarization of the Indian Ocean even further. Remarkably, both China and Russia voted in favour. The resolution focused on the activities of the Ad Hoc Committee on Indian Ocean set up by the General Assembly with the aim of using the opportunities offered by the new world order to advance the implementation of the December 1971 Zone of Peace resolution. Hence it invited member states to submit "their views on new alternative approaches" to the Secretary-General after noting

> that great-power rivalry is being replaced by a new and welcome phase of confidence, trust and cooperation, and that the improved international political environment following the end of the Cold War has created favorable opportunities to renew comprehensive multilateral and regional efforts towards the realization of the goals of peace, security and stability in the Indian Ocean.[41]

It is evident from the foregoing that the advent of the new world order did not lead to the de-militarization of the Indian Ocean. In fact, there is as yet no tangible sign of even reduction in the near future. The non-Indian Ocean powers are, presently, openly committed to preserving their military-strategic positions individually and collectively. For them, the main pre-occupation is not compliance with the Zone of Peace resolution to roll back, but to maintain a steady phase or even expand on the basis of their respective strategic quests for primacy.

How much the littoral states could do to challenge that open commitment remains to be seen. Unlike the old order when competitive deployment along east-west lines obtained, there is, under the new order, only a pattern of engagement between the littoral states and the non-Indian Ocean powers.

4. The Littoral States

The open, unambiguous stand of the non-Indian Ocean powers with regards to preserving their individual and collective (e.g., Western alliance) primacy amounts to open challenge for the littoral states to compromise or abide by the militarization of the Indian ocean. A yet another alternative is for them to forge a clear strategic relationship with the powers whose inevitable meaning and consequence would be to re-cast the whole concept of de-militarization of

the Indian Ocean as intended under the terms of the UN General Assembly resolution 2832 (XXVI) of December 1971. Objectively either of these alternatives is feasible if the littoral states cannot (or are unwillingly to) summon the diplomatic and other means to "eject" the foreign military powers from the Indian Ocean.

Officially, the declared position of the littoral states is the continuous pursuit of the 1971 Zone of Peace resolution. This is underlined by their collective support for the activities of the UN General Assembly Ad Hoc Committee on the Indian Ocean. But thus far, the Ad Hoc Committee has not notched up any success because the primary non Indian Ocean powers (i.e., Britain, France and the United States) continue to oppose it. In effect, this stand-off appears to neutralise the UN framework as a vehicle for the littoral states and it forces on them the above mentioned choices of alternatives to compromise, abide by or enter into partnership with the military powers. But since the declared stand of the littoral states remains officially unchanged in favour of the Zone of Peace resolution, their true stand can only be determined, deductively, by reviewing and analysing the nature and substance of their strategic relations with the non-Indian Ocean powers.

Ultimately, the pattern of that relationship is deemed to be predicated on three factors: First, against the background of the apparent stalemate at the UN, it should be ascertained whether the littoral states possess other means or framework for collective pursuit and how they have been faring with it. Second, with regards to individual states, the dimensions of the domestic and sub-regional security and strategic issues that confront them should be determined as a means of measuring the pressures that could influence their priorities. And third, the existing patterns of direct ties between individual and groups of the littoral states and the non-Indian Ocean powers should be assessed as a means of understanding the extent of shared strategic objectives between the two sides in contrast and in opposition to the aims of the Zone of Peace resolution.

4.1 A Framework for Collective Action

The littoral states have no parallel or equivalent organisation that can support and compliment the UN. The plan by Australia, India, Mauritius, Singapore and South Africa to establish an International Forum for the Indian Ocean appears to have lapsed without a tangible break-through. At any rate, as the plan of a select group with a commercial focus, it would have considerable difficulty with making any significant impact on the Zone of Peace process.

Similar observations can be made of the other sub-regional groupings to which clutches of the littoral states belong. The Organisation of African Unity (OAU), the Arab league, the Gulf Cooperation Council (GCC), the Association of South East Asian Nations (ASEAN) and the South Pacific Forum (SPF), each has a fixed, localized focus even though the mention of the Indian Ocean comes up from their ranks occasionally in communiques designed to boost the diplomatic stand of a given member state- e.g. Mauritius over its claims on Diego Garcia. But then such resolutions cannot be extended to the whole of the littoral states.

The Non-Aligned Movement (NAM) draws its membership from each of these sub-regional groups and its resolutions dwell on the Indian Ocean often. But, it is still grossly inadequate as an alternative of sorts for the littoral states in comparison to the UN or as a medium of pressure against the non-Indian Ocean powers. It lacks the requisite diplomatic reach in terms of influence and bargaining power. This is particularly true of its situation under the new world order dominated by the West.

4.2 Littoral States: Domestic and Sub-Regional Strategic Priorities

Underneath the common, declared concern for the future of the Indian Ocean, the littoral states are weighed down by a range of strategic anxieties. Such anxieties pose a serious dilemma for the affected member states in that even as they worry for the militarization of the Indian Ocean, they find themselves amenable to cooperation with the same powers deploying military resources there. The examples are numerous enough to constitute a definitive sample.

In August 1997, the island of Anjuoan seceded from the rest of the Comoros and openly called upon France to admit it into its network of African overseas territories which is presently made up of Mayotte and Reunion, both in the Indian ocean. This dramatic turn of events in colonial history was preceded by the collapse of Somalia and secession of Eritrea from Ethiopia. In the course of its bitter civil war, Somalia experienced both the nominal secession of its northern province (the Republic of Somaliland) and the intervention of a US-led UN forces. Sudan is locked in a bitter civil war while Djibouti is under the pressure of domestic insurgent forces. In the Arabian peninsula, the GCC member states (Bahrain, Kuwait, Oman, Saudi Arabia, and the UAE) are locked in separate disputes with Iran and Iraq. On their own, Iran and Iraq, having fought each other throughout

the 1980s remain uneasy neighbours. The same can be said of South Asia where India and Pakistan are locked in a serious rivalry going back to their partition and independence in 1947.

Taken together, the impact of these strategic anxieties is discernible in the creation of a bloc within the littoral states. The bloc is not one of a united front with shared priorities that work against the Zone of Peace resolution directly. Instead, it is a bloc of disparate states and interests united only by their shared preoccupation with other strategic objectives that compels them to down-grade the Zone of Peace resolution as a matter of urgency. In the short to medium terms, at least, their respective national security interests clashes with any attempt at an ardent pursuit of the Zone of Peace resolution. This perspective has become systematically embedded into the broader pattern of relations between the littoral states and the non-Indian ocean powers. It has created a situation where the pattern of relations between the littoral states and the powers operate along separate strategic strands in direct competition with the pursuit of the Zone of Peace resolution and without according it any priority.

4.3 The Tiers of Ties Between the Littoral States and the Non-Indian Ocean Powers

If observed strictly from the point of view of the Zone of Peace resolution, the relations between the littoral states and the military powers is contentious. This is so because the powers (specifically Britain, France and US) reject any idea of de-militarizing the Indian Ocean and they show no inclination to accommodate the Zone of Peace resolution in any form. On their part, the littoral states offer no alternative to the resolution other than appealing to the military powers to cooperate with the UN General Assembly AD Hoc Committee on the Indian Ocean. But when the relation between the two sides is examined beyond the narrow purview of the Zone of Peace resolution, taking in the international politics of the Indian Ocean as a whole, the statement at the UN becomes less contentious and less serious. From the broader perspective, the statement becomes even logical as the product not just of a disagreement over a single resolution but as the outcome of a combination of several decisions from different sources each representing a strand or a tier of relations between the littoral states and the non-Indian Ocean powers. At present (1998) up to four such tiers of relations can be identified in the context of the international politics of the Indian Ocean.

The first bears on the relationship between Australia and New Zealand on one hand and the military powers on the other. While the Zone of Peace resolution may point to a disagreement, Australia and New Zealand are an integral part of the Western bloc in world politics. Beyond that the decision by France to halt all future nuclear tests in the South pacific and the decline of the issue of port calls by nuclear ships between New Zealand and the United States have removed the sources of scorging disagreements between these Western allies. This ensures that any disagreement over the Zone of Peace resolution would not be too upsetting for the alliance particularly if the military powers could be persuasive about the advantages of their presence to the interests of the West as a whole, or to the vital interests of their respective countries.

This perspective adjoins the second tier—i.e., the relationship between the military powers as a group and the GCC member states as a bloc. The military powers can (and indeed do) explain that relationship in terms of safeguarding the interests of the West as a whole by ensuring the security of oil supplies from the Persian Gulf. If a military presence is deemed to be necessary to underpin that relationship, it would be hard for Australia and New Zealand to argue against that.

Thus the GCC states and the military powers are engaged militarily, strategically and commercially. At the beginning, the threat to the mutual interests was determined as coming from the upheavals unleashed by the Islamic revolution in Iran. Then came the Iran-Iraq war which dominated the whole of the 1980s. The 1990s saw Iraq's invasion and attempted annexation of Kuwait. In each case, the GCC states were compelled to accept the conclusion that, on their own, they do not possess the military power to guarantee their security. They needed the West, particularly the United States, Britain and France, to do that. Thus, presently the GCC states have active military agreements with these powers; grant them base rights, allow them to pre-position military equipment in their territories, engage in joint exercises with them and pay the costs[42] of some of their operations such as the war to liberate Kuwait and the enforcement of UN sanctions against Iraq. In terms of acceding to the realities of sub-regional security, there is at present, complete strategic coordination between the GCC states and non-Indian Ocean powers regardless of the terms of the Zone of Peace resolution.

Separate, but complemental, the strategic relationship between France and Djibouti also falls into this category. In strategic terms, the French position in

Djibouti serves as a bridge between the Horn of Africa and the Arabian peninsula.

The third tier draws considerable inspiration, justification and logic from the others above. If there is a genuine balance of strategic interests between some members of the littoral states and the powers, then their presence becomes quite relevant and legitimate in certain ways. The succumbing of a section of the littoral states opens the avenue for the non-Indian Ocean powers to use their presence to pursue their own independent objectives with relative ease even if such pursuits were directed against some littoral states. There is a strategic gap to be exploited.

The American policy of dual containment against Iran and Iraq[43] and its policy of opposing the Islamist government in Sudan by supporting the insurgents in the Civil War,[44] fall into this category. Given the regional power position of Iran and Iraq and the ideological orientation of their governments revolving around Islamism (Iran) and radical nationalism (Iraq), it is conceivable that the United States would be drawn to act against them in the broader interest of maintaining a balance of power (see *Balance of Power*) in the Middle East even if the GCC states were not as apprehensive as they are at present. The declared American policy objectives of guaranteeing the security of Israel, ensuring unimpeded flow of oil from the Persian Gulf to the West and supporting "friendly" Arab states against those it deems too radical, Islamist or anti-West,[45] support this assertion.

The American opposition to Sudan falls under the categories of Islamism and perceived anti-Western posture. By extension, the situation is further aggravated by Sudan's close ties with Iran.[46]

The fourth tier draws from all the others above. It can be presented by its protagonists as supportive of Western interests, supportive of closer ties between "friendly" littoral states (e.g., the GCC states) and the military powers, and that it facilitates quicker response in times of crisis. In yet another consideration, it can be presented as a separate, sovereign affair exclusive to those directly involved. This tier relates to the status of the military bases over which the non-Indian Ocean powers claim sovereign control or some other equivalent under international law. Specifically, they refer to two cases: First, the military presence of France in Mayotte and Reunion, the island states that are part of the network of French overseas territories. And second, the British and American military presence in Diego Garcia.

In both cases the powers concerned could argue that the Zone of Peace resolution cannot apply to them because the military bases there are partial extensions of their sovereignty. And by this logic, they are themselves of the Indian Ocean. This line is particularly simple for France because Mayotte and Reunion are French in terms of sovereign jurisdiction. Thus at its widest, France is also a littoral state in the Indian Ocean.

But the Anglo-American presence in Diego Garcia is, comparatively, more complicated than that because any claims of sovereignty is subject to dispute from two sources. First, the on again, off again campaign by Mauritius to regain control of Diego Garcia which was excised from it before Britain granted it independence. The style of the campaign reflects both the weakness of Mauritius relative to Britain and the dispute between the two countries about the sequence of events from the excision of the Chagos Archipelago before the independence of Mauritius to the present. Did Mauritius consent to some agreement involving the sale of the island? Did Mauritius ever have genuine sovereignty over the islands historically, or was the linkage to it merely for British colonial administrative convenience? Is Diego Garcia under some extended lease or has Mauritius lost it for good? Any sense of ambiguity about the status of Diego Garcia seems to be expunged by Britain's avowals that its claims are "not negotiable."[47] That forecloses all options for Mauritius except a recourse to the International Court of Justice (see *International Court of Justice*).

The second source of dispute over Diego Garcia is the stand of the Ilois, the original inhabitants of the islands who were moved to Mauritius. The islands were de-populated before they were transformed into an Anglo-American base. There is a range of arguments about the status of the Ilois people beginning with the contention that the islands were virtually uninhabitated at the time of their discovery and ending in whether they were actually expelled in the 1960s or were paid out to leave. Presently, the British position is that they departed voluntarily, they were compensated and they have renounced any claims or rights of return following the compensation. But the Ilois insist they were deceived and coerced to leave and they still retain their right to return. They feel not bound by any agreements which Britain and Mauritius reached over their fate.[48]

However, the tangles over sovereignty claims and rights of return aside, Anglo-American presence in Diego Garcia and French presence in Mayotte and Reunion provide these powers the means to maintain independent military bases which they can use as a leverage against the littoral states. Where there is a merger of interests, the bases offer a deep and secure

reserve to draw from. In the alternative, if there is a disagreement, they enable the powers the means to act separately and independently by arguing exclusive rights and sovereign prerogatives.

In sum, such is the circumstantial reality of the littoral states whenever it comes to action or a critical review of their relations with the non-Indian ocean powers over the issue of implementing the Zone of Peace resolution. The military powers are clear and firm in refusing to abide by it. Confronted with that resolve, the littoral states find themselves weakened and debilitated by three critical factors—i.e., the lack of a complimentary organisation to boost their stand at the UN; the burden of individual national and sub-regional security and strategic preoccupations and the restrictions emanating from different tiers in the complex network of their relationship with the military powers.

5. Conclusion

From the passage of the Zone of Peace resolution to date (1998), the international politics of the Indian Ocean has followed a course marked by the pairing of crucial events that define the given moment. First, the period 1971-1998 can be noted for two defining events—i.e., the passage of time long enough to create an analytical impression and the shift of international relations from dominance of the Cold War to the new world order. Second, that in the old as in the new order, the international politics of the Indian Ocean has continued to be dominated by great power search for strategic primacy and the dilemma of the littoral states in trying to balance individual quests for security cooperation with the military powers and the desire to pursue the implementation of the Zone of Peace resolution. And third, that under the new world order, the military powers have been greatly uplifted by the overall preponderance of the West following the collapse of the communist bloc, while in the context of the Indian Ocean politics, the littoral states became clearly less powerful and cohesive. This pairing arose from the fact that with the absence of the competition from the Soviet bloc, Britain, France and United States have emerged as the powers in virtually the sole strategic control of the Indian Ocean, while the cohesion of the littoral states has been undermined by the collapse of the Comoros and Somalia, the emergence of Eritrea and the strategic alliance which the GCC states have forged with them. In addition, the military powers possess bases in Diego Garcia, Mayotte and Reunion that are, for the moment, under their own respective sovereign control. Given the importance of the Persian Gulf sub-region as the epicenter of foreign oil supplies to the Western bloc, the convergence of a strategic world view between the GCC states and the military powers permits the latter to re-cast both the content and the direction of the international politics of the Indian ocean.

Against this background, it can be concluded that under the prevailing circumstance, the Zone of Peace resolution has become inoperable. Equally, pursuing its implementation has steadily become impractical and unrealistic. The military powers, unimpressed by the resolution from the beginning, have become more powerful and significantly more on demand by "local friends" to ignore it altogether now while the littoral states have failed to evolve a functional sense of Indian Ocean community.

Notes

1. Bukar Bukarambe, "Zone of Peace or Strategic Primacy: Politics of Security in the Indian Ocean," *Bulletin of Peace Proposals* (IPRS, Oslo), Vol.16, No.1, 1985.

____, "Zone of Peace or Strategic Primacy: Politics of Security in the Indian Ocean," *The Journal of Peace Studies* (IIPS, Seoul), Vol.5, No.2, February 1986.

2. Ibid.

3. "Member States of the Warsaw Treaty, acting as sovereign states with equal rights, decided that by March 31, 1991, they will dismantle the military organs and structures of the treaty," *International Herald Tribune* (London), February 26, 1991.

4. Zbgniew Brzezinski, "The Cold War and its Aftermath," *Foreign Affairs*, Vol.17, No.4, Fall 1992.

5. In July 1997, The Czech Republic, Hungary and Poland were invited to join NATO by 1999. These and other former communist east European states are slated to join the EU. *International Herald Tribune*, October 23, 1997, p. 6.

6. *International Herald Tribune* (London), May 28, 1997, p. 1.

7. Lawrence Freedman, "Order and Disorder in the New World," *Foreign Affairs*, Vol.71, No.1, 1992, p. 26.

8. There is a current school of thought which argues that NAM is relevant even under the new order. See R.S. Yadar, "NAM in the New World Order," *India Quarterly* (New Delhi), Vol. XLIX, No.3, July-September 1993.

9. *International Herald Tribune* (London), October 1, 1993, p. 2. But the new republic has not won international recognition.

10. *The Observer* (London), March 5, 1995, p. 15. See also, Jeffrey Clark, "Debacle in Somalia," *Foreign Affairs*, Vol. 72, No. 1, 1993.

11. *Africa Research Bulletin*, May 1-31, 1993, pp. 10995-8.

12. *Africa Research Bulletin*, November 1-30, 1991, pp. 110349-50. See also: Thomas Marks, "Djibouti: A Strategic French Toehold in Africa," *African Affairs*, Vol.73, No. 290, January 1974.

13. In recent years that configuration has been slightly tampered by the emergence of groups like the National Democratic Alliance which has membership form both northern and southern Sudan. The NDA has among its members, Sadiq El-Mahdi, a former prime minister. But the actual war on the ground still follows a broad Arab-African; north-south divide; *Financial Times* (London), August 31, 1997, p. 4.

14. *The Middle East* (London), July 1990, pp. 5-8.

15. Madan Mohan Puri, "Geopolitics in the Indian Ocean: The Antarctic Dimension," *International Studies* (New Delhi), Vol.23, No.2, 1986.

16. Gregory P. Corning, "The Philippine Bases and US Pacific Strategy," *Pacific Affairs*, Vol.63, No.1 Spring 1990. Ian Brown, "Philippines: History," *The Far East and Australasia*, 1994 (London: Europa Publication Ltd. 1993), pp. 838-848.

17. "Association of South East Asian Nations," *Ibid.*, p. 1024.

18. Jeanine Graham, "New Zealand: History," *Ibid.*, pp. 636-640.

19. Keith Sutter, "Treaty of Raratonga: US Signs on at last," *The Bulletin of the Atomic Scientists*, March-April, 1996, pp. 12-13.

20. Gabriele Kittel, Manfred Makowitzki, Thomas Nielebock, and Ralf Ott, "Nuclear Weapon Free Zones: Re-evaluating a Political Concept of Peace-Making," *Bulletin of Peace Proposals* (IPRS, Oslo), Vol.22, No.2, June 1991.

21. Disarmament: (UN. New York), Vol.XIX, No.1,, 1996.

22. *International Herald Tribune* (London), March 25, 1993, pp. 1&6.

23. Olu Adeniji, "The Pelindaba Text and its Provisions," *Disarmament, op. cit.* p. 6.

24. Kittel, Makowitzki, Nielebock and Ott, "Nuclear Weapon Free Zone. . . ," *op. cit.* Wojciech Multan, "The Past and Future of Nuclear Weapon-Free Zones," *Bulletin of Peace Proposals* (IPRS, Oslo), Vol.16, No.4, 1985.

25. Madan Mohan Puri "Geopolitics in the Indian Ocean," *op. cit.* p. 165.

26. *The Financial Times* (London), June 14, 1995, p. 8.

27. There is a perspective that the demise of the Soviet Union actually proved useful for the process of Yemeni unification. Alan George and Eric Watkins, "This Time it is Really Happening," *The Middle East* (London), May, 1990, p. 8.

28. SIPRI Year Book 1995; *Armaments, Disarmament and International Security* (Oxford University Press 1995), pp. 656-661.

29. *Africa Research Bulletin* (London), December 15, 1989, p. 9503.

30. *International Herald Tribune* (London), September 9, 1997, p. 7.

31. *The Times* (London), July 25, 1997, p. 13.

32. *The Middle East* (London), October, 1992, p. 21; December, 1993, p. 10, December 1996, pp. 14-15.

33. *International Herald Tribune* (London), June 17, 1997, p. 7. *Financial Times* (London), June 28, 1995, p. 5.

34. Monoranjan Beeboruah, US Strategy in the Indian Ocean; The International Response (New York, Praeger Publishers, 1977); John Madeley, "Diego Garcia: An Indian Ocean Storm Centre," *The Round Table* (London), July 1981.

35. *Africa Research Bulletin* (London), December 15, 1989, p. 9503.

36. *Africa Research Bulletin* (London), November 1-30, 1991, p. 10361.

37. *The Times* (London), July 25, 1997, p. 13.

38. *The Middle East* (London), December 1996, pp. 14-15.

39. Eric Watkins, "The Unfolding US Policy in the Middle East," *International Affairs*, Vol.73, No.1, 1997, p. 11.

40. *The Middle East* (London), June 1991, p. 12; December 1991, pp. 15-16. *The Times* (London), February 6, 1998, p. 12.

41. *Year Book of the United Nations*, 1993, Vol.47 (Department of Public Information, UN, New York), p. 124.

42. *The Financial Times* (London), February 27, 1998, p. 6.

43. Anthony Lake, "Confronting Backlash States," *Foreign Affairs*, Vol. 73, No.2, March-April 1994, p. 45.

44. *The Financial Times* (London), August 31, 1997, p. 4. The Times (London), November 5, 1997, p. 18. *International Herald Tribune* (London), March 26, 1998, p. 6.

45. Shahram Chubin, Security in the Gulf: The Role of Outside Powers (Gower, Aldershot for IISS), No.4, 1982. Richard Falk, *Iran and American Geopolitics in the Gulf; Horn of Africa* (N.J.), Vol.2, April-June 1979. Walid Khadduri, "Oil and Politics in the Middle East," *Security Dialogue*, Vol.27 (2)

1996.

46. Amir Taheri, "Sudan: An Expanding Civil War with an Iranian Connection," *International Herald Tribune*, April 9, 1997, p. 8.

47. *Africa Research Bulletin*, December 15, 1989, p. 9503.

48. Carl Honore, "The Islanders who still hope to regain paradise," *The Sunday Observer* (London), January 31, 1993, p. 17. *The New Statesman*, September 27, 1996, p. 34.

BUKAR BUKARAMBE

Integration, Regional

Regional integration, regionalism (or regionalization), a term that has been used to describe very different institutionalized preferences and trends in international political, military, or economic relations within sets of countries has been promoted by many of its advocates as an interconnecting, unifying process that is a natural outgrowth of bilateral relations. In the early 1960s, Harlan Cleveland characterized regionalism as "a halfway house at a time when single nations are no longer viable and the world is not ready to become one."[1] According to this definition, regionalism could be seen as a bridge between bilateral and global cooperation. The pursuit of regional cooperation has a long, varied, and checkered history.[2] For centuries, attempts have been made in Europe to create regions of peace and cooperation, thereby eliminating the causes of tensions and conflicts between nations. In the 18th century, the establishment of the United States on the American continent inspired political thinkers and statesmen to construct similar federal arrangements in other parts of the world. Some of the Hungarian revolutionaries in the mid-19th century dreamt about a federation of nations in the valley of the Danube that would be established on the ruins of the Austrian empire (see *Peace and Regional Integration*). 19th century Latin American revolutionaries like Simon Bolivar sought to create a federal structure to maintain, protect, or increase the autonomy of the new countries of Latin America against external powers. In this century, many African revolutionaries have thought in terms of a united, federal Africa. The vision of a united Arab world has been promoted time and again, with pragmatic, albeit ultimately unsuccessful, steps taken toward its realization by such pan-Arabist politicians as Egyptian president Gamal Abdel Nasser (see *Pan-Arabism*). In the early stages of planning for the post World War II order, Winston Churchill (see *Churchill, Winston*) suggested the establishment of a number of regional councils through which the great powers could exercise leader-

ship in the world. These are examples of unfulfilled ambitions. In the post World War II era, however, a large number of regional organizations have been successfully established in a wide range of areas. These organizations include military alliances like NATO (see *North Atlantic Treaty Organization (NATO)*), essentially political groups like the OAS, the OAU, and the Arab League (see *Organization of African Unity (OAU); Organization of American States (OAS); League of Arab States*); and economic bodies like the European Economic Community, which on the basis of the Maastricht Treaty signed in February 1992, has been called officially European Union (see *European Union*). There are about 30 other regional integration or cooperation groups and free trade areas in different continents of the world.

Regional organizations have differed in their geographical breadth; in their specific mandates and political, economic, or military responsibilities; and in their relations to global cooperation structures.

Regional economic integration (see *Economic Integration*) presupposes that the states may have considerable common interests and, therefore, may be ready to renounce sovereignty in certain areas by internationalizing their national economic policy decisions. However, the process is contradictory. In the more developed part of the world, the process of integration is the result of internationalization (see *Internationalization*) achieved, while in the less developed regions, the objective to promote economic development in the age of internationalization in an efficient way could be the main motive force. On this level integration is also a potential regional pool of scarce human and material resources and an instrument to use the limited capacity of the regional market for the benefit of the producers from the region. The differences determine to a great extent the propensity for establishing supranational institutions and for renouncing the right of nation-states to decision making. These attitudes are not identical even in the individual member countries of the European Community (EC), which is considered to be the most advanced form of international integration in the West.

The EU has been by far the most successful and important regional organization, exercising considerable influence on both its member states and the international system as a whole. Most of the conceptual and theoretical foundations of the integration process are based on the historical experiences of the post World War II integration in Europe. First, integration is an institutionalized political and economic development process. It can be the result of the internationalization process, which may take place in a comprehensive way (i.e., simultaneously throughout all major fields of economic activity) or by sectors. Second, it can emerge at a given stage, when relations are already intensive and multiple, between countries. Alternatively, it may emerge as a target to promote deliberately economic cooperation among states in such a way as to internationalize the production, consumption, and infrastructure of several countries within a given region.

In interpreting the economic integration of states, the mainstream Western economics literature usually focuses on the removal of obstacles to different flows (goods, services, capital, personnel), and usually regards it as a sufficient condition (see *Regionalism, Economic Security and Peace: The Asia-Pacific*). The European integration process proved the limitations of this approach. The removal of barriers is a necessary condition of the progress in the integration of the national economies. With the progress of the liberalization, new needs emerge, for the harmonisation of policies and institutions and the process more or less automatically results in the conferring of more and more responsibilities on the collective institutions. The Maastricht treaty for example envisaged the following measures on the level of the Union: the coordination, supervision and appropriate enforcement of sound economic policies, particularly in competition and budgetary measures, the maintenance of equity and where necessary, the redistribution of wealth between the richer and poorer regions, the management of common external policy, the preservation of law and order, etc. Community of interests may also develop on the basis of different, often conflicting, economic and political factors resulting from specific problems which the member countries try to resolve, but their position may change (see *Problem Solving in Internationalized Conflicts*). Moreover, as economic development is not even across states, the benefits are not constant either, and the conditions of realization are subject to

alteration. Compromises and agreements based on them are bound to break up. If the economic and political ties established by the community of interests are not strong enough, and there is no conscious and constant pressure and determination to settle emerging problems, then the conflicts necessarily arising in the course of development may paralyze the integrational organizations and programs, while steadily reproducing the disintegrating forces. The question of when, if at all, any integration group arrives at the point of no return (i.e., at the point from which there is no way back to the earlier national markets, to national economic policies) cannot be answered definitely. It depends mainly on the effect of economic, political, and institutional development taking place within its framework, the transformation of the production and consumption patterns of the member countries, the mergers of the large corporations, and state organs. It is also an open question, to what extent the widening of an integration group, like the EU is slowing down or blocking its deepening. This, to a large extent depends on the flexibility of the institutions and on the capabilities for the harmonization of the changing interests of the countries.

The integration of the developing countries also has its specific problems. The scope of the national economies of the developing countries is usually rather narrow, and hence it is clear that for most developing countries regional integration is the only possibility for faster economic growth. The plans for and ideas of integration in the developing countries arise primarily from the fact that their productive forces are underdeveloped, their national markets are narrow both in absolute and relative terms, and they are short of capital and qualified personnel. It is well known that the creation of the most up-to-date industries, especially in the branches of heavy industry, is profitable only on an optimum scale. This would unambiguously require a number of developing countries today either to renounce industrial development or to trust the use of a considerable part of their existing productive capacities to unpredictable export opportunities. Further problems are caused by the fact that the development aims of most developing countries follow the same direction and lead to the establishment of the same industries. In addition, the strengthening of integration efforts in the developing countries is also connected with the high costs of infrastructural investment and the favorable utilization possibilities of common establishments. This applies, in the first place, to railways, hydroelectric plants, harbors, channels, and highways. It is plain that the integration of the developing countries is subject to several economic and political preconditions, and it is no easy task to satisfy them.

At the end of the 1990s, three main trends are apparent in regionalization: the consolidation of regional integration groups; progress toward the establishment of regional security arrangements and institutions (see *Security Regimes: Focusing on Asia-Pacific*); and the development of larger "economic spaces" within which countries make preferential agreements for free trade, create customs unions, and harmonize their policies. The European economic space is, first of all an extension of the EU to countries which may join it later. This extension is based on association agreements that focus on liberalizing trade relations with the community. The creation of an American economic space, known in the Western hemisphere as the "American Enterprise," was declared as a continental goal by President George Bush in June 1990, when he spoke of establishing a free trade zone "from Anchorage to Tierra del Fuego."[3] The realization of the North American Free Trade Agreement (NAFTA) has been widely regarded as the first major step toward achieving this goal (see *North American Free Trade Area (NAFTA)*). NAFTA, however, could represent a significant step toward splitting the American continent into blocs, each of which would establish preferential trade and investment conditions for its members. The idea of a third economic space centered on the Pacific has been raised by a number of Asian countries and pursued by the United States. A concrete step was taken in 1989 with the establishment of the Asia-Pacific Economic Community (APEC) (see *Asia Pacific Economic Cooperation (APEC)*). Proposals made in 1993 to strengthen APEC (an idea that did not receive universal support from within the region) were justified in part by the need to respond to the "escalation of inward-looking regionalism throughout the world," a thinly veiled reference to the EC.[4]

Post-Cold War regionalism in its different forms has many political and economic sources, the most important of which is probably the failure of global cooperation regimes to create a credible structure of global security and peace and to respond effectively to regional conflicts. In the post Cold War era, most international political disputes and military conflicts are widely expected to be confined to a given region. At least in principle, the management and resolution of these conflicts should prove easier to accomplish if undertaken by entities with a more limited geographic and political scope than that of the UN Security Council. Another reason why regionalism will become more important is the emergence of a multipolar

world. Russia is certain to be substantially less involved in remote regions of the world than was the Soviet Union. For Russia, the main sphere of interest and influence will be the territory of the former Soviet Union. The United States too seems likely to show less interest in many regions of the world than it did during the Cold War. In the absence of a globally pervasive bipolarity, many regional powers will have the opportunity to strengthen their international positions by forming regional structures within which they can enjoy great influence. Regionalism also offers many less powerful countries especially those in the developing world the chance to improve their bargaining positions in the global policy making arena. A growth in regionalism accords with the direction of several ongoing economic trends. Capital flows and technological cooperation have been increasing more rapidly within certain regions, Europe and Asia, most notably than between regions. In addition, certain currencies are playing a more prominent role within particular regions. In Europe, the leading currency is the German mark, which, is the main pillar of the EU. The EURO, which will be the de facto common currency may further strengthen the regional structures. Likewise in the Far East, economic currents are shaping a yen-based economic bloc. The progress of regionalization and globalization (and the fragmentation of existing structures) is tied to specific political and economic interests of countries and powerful groups such as the transnational corporations. Regional institutions like the EU are also playing a demonstrative and self-generating role, promoting integration as part of their institutional duty (see *Security and Cooperation in Europe*). However, regional cooperation is also facing significant obstacles and uncertainties. In Europe, for example, the question is often asked: Can the momentum that resulted in regionalism be sustained in view of the changing interests of the participating countries? Another fundamental question concerns the extent to which regional cooperation can more efficiently satisfy the political, security, and economic needs of countries than can traditional forms of bilateral cooperation or global multilateralism. A further, more delicate question is whether or not regionalism will be able to provide greater political and economic security for smaller nations against the actions of regional hegemons than global institutions have been able to achieve.

Where regional cooperation is most advanced, the impediments to its further progress tend to be more concrete. For example, Europe will have to grapple with several major problems. One such problem concerns the widening and deepening of the EC. To date, the EC has been able to maintain a delicate balance of collective and national interests. Any further increase in the membership or powers of the community might easily upset this balance, imperilling the interests of member countries and provoking domestic opposition to supranational policies (see *Supranationalism*). The experiences of other regions are even more discouraging. Although such continental organizations as the OAU and the OAS serve as forums for negotiations, they have achieved only limited success in building security structures and promoting qualitative improvements in economic cooperation. In many subregions of the developing world, the work of integration groups has hardly progressed beyond the declaration of intentions. Regional cooperation institutions are not always more effective than are global organizations and regimes. Indeed, both regional and global bodies suffer from similar problems: the heterogeneity of interests of their member states, an unreliable propensity for cooperation, inadequate financial resources and expertise, bureaucratization, and so forth. Joseph Nye has enumerated three arguments against the establishment of economic blocs in Europe, the Far East, and North America: one, they run counter to the thrust of global technological trends and the interests of transnational corporations; two, they are counter to interests of smaller states, which need a global system to protect them against domination by their larger neighbors; and three, they cannot diminish the fears of nonnuclear nations regarding their nuclear neighbors in the region.[5] Although these arguments are sound, we cannot afford to disregard the possibility that 21st century power politics may be characterized by increasing interregional conflicts and regionalism, with competing regions structured as security and economic networks centered around major regional powers. The regionalization of the global bargaining process and of security issues, the establishment of regional security complexes, and the compartmentalization of global cooperation and institutional structures could, very possibly obstruct global cooperation if different regions choose to structure themselves as regional fortresses (see *Global Integration*). The preferential trade liberalization features of such agreements could be a major source of trade diversion which may well offset their trade-creating effects. Moreover, regionalization could have adverse overspill effects since it may induce outsiders who bear the brunt of trade diversion to retaliate by seeking preferential trade agreements among themselves so as to offset their loss of markets and strengthen their bargaining power. This process of competitive regionalization

may undermine the multilateral system and, far from contributing to global liberalization, could turn the world into one of hostile economic blocs and discriminatory trade regimes similar to those that prevailed in the 1930s. In such a situation, interregional relations would become a zero-sum game played by competitive blocs. Alternatively, however, more intensive regional cooperation could complement and enhance global cooperation and networking. As Harlan Cleveland suggested, regionalism could serve as a bridge between countries and global processes by facilitating internationalization and greater liberalization within regional structures. Compared to their global counterparts, regional structures are more transparent and more familiar to their member states; they enjoy the cohering effects of common cultural and economic ties; and they allow the gains and losses that cooperation produces to be more easily balanced. Furthermore, regional structures could promote different forms of cooperation between countries in a wide variety of areas, ranging from the fight against poverty and the control of migration to the development of physical infrastructure and the establishment of regional information and telecommunications structures. Regional agreements may make negotiations more manageable: a relatively small number of like-minded countries are involved, it reduces the likelihood that liberalization will be held hostage by a recalcitrant power.[6]

In principle, bilateral or regional and global multilateral cooperation should not necessarily be considered as contradictory forms of relations (see *Multilateralism*). They can coexist, and may even be mutually supportive in open democratic institutional systems. In closed or constrained systems of cooperation, however, they may be conflictual. In this context, it may be noted that the transnational business sector could better harmonize the processes of globalization and regionalization within its corporate structure than could the small-business sector. The economic future of regionalism will depend to a large extent on the ability of regional structures to satisfy their members' needs for economic development (higher output and incomes, greater trade and capital flows, increased entrepreneurship, and so forth). Another factor shaping the future of regionalism is the institutional efficiency of regional governance: its cost effectiveness; its timely and flexible response to the needs of member countries; its management of relations within the region and with the rest of the world; and its ability to sustain development and cooperation on a global level, satisfying the new needs of the participants in the global system.

See also: *Interdependence, International; Globalization; Integration Theories*

Notes ———————————————

1. Harlan Cleveland, "Reflections on the Pacific Community," *Department of State Bulletin* 48, no. 1243 (April 22, 1963): 614.
2. A region can be defined in many ways. The geographical concept of a region is usually based on the physical characteristics of a given area. From an economic point of view, a region is a zone within which countries cooperate more intensively among themselves than with the rest of the world. Geostrategically, a region is a specific area of cooperative and/or conflictual political relationships. The cultural definition of a region may emphasize similarities in historical development in regard to such factors as ethnicity, religion, life-style, or language. Regions can, of course, be identified within countries or within a larger, international framework. The international character of a region is the one used in this book.
3. See R. E. Feinberg and Dalia M. Boylan, "Modular Multilateralism," *The Washington Quarterly* 15, no. 1 (Winter 1991) 195.
4. Quoted from an edited excerpt of a confidential report to the Asia-Pacific summit meeting. See "Now Let's Build an Asia-Pacific Economic Community, " *International Herald Tribune*, November 4, 1993, 8.
5. Joseph S. Nye, Jr. , "What New World Order?" *Foreign Affairs* 71, no. 2 (Spring 1992): 87.
6. OECD Forum for the Future, Long-Term Prospects for the World Economy: Outlook, Main Issues and Summary of Discussions (Paris: OECD, 1992), 17, 18.

Bibliography ———————————————

Asian Development Bank 1993 *Subregional Economic Cooperation*. Manila
Economic Integration, Worldwide, Regional, Sectoral. 1976 Papers and Proceedings of the 4th Congr. International Economic Association. Macmillan, London
Oman C 1994 *Globalisation and Regionalisation*. OECD, Paris
Robinson P 1993 *The Economics of International Integration*. Routledge, London
Simai M 1981 *Interdependence and Conflicts in the World Economy*. Akademia, Budapest
Simai M, Garam K (eds.) 1977 *Economic Integration: Concepts, Theories and Problems*. Akademia Kiado, Budapest
Simai M 1994 *The Future of Global Governance*. USIP Press, Washington, DC

MIHALY SIMAI

Integration Theories

Integration, of itself, is neither a good thing nor a bad thing. However, it has a certain inevitability. Any relationship other than one of total isolation implies some degree of social and political linkage. What, therefore, do we mean by integration? The first distinction must be between conceptions of integration which are largely based upon the free-will of actors, knowingly exercised without any substantial constraints of either overt violence or structural violence, and those conceptions which are based on some element of coercion. Enforced integration, whether overtly or structurally enforced, is a form of imperialism, and it is excluded from the rest of this analysis as being normatively unacceptable. The frameworks for cooperation identified here are freely and mutually acceptable ones by which the parties can come to terms with difficulties and manage them to their mutual satisfaction, or, more positively, take advantage together of opportunities to the benefit of all in a process which involves an element of integration.

In the literature, integration is sometimes defined as the property of a state of affairs, and sometimes as a process. Integration as a state of affairs simply means that authors define the characteristics of what they think constitutes integration, and then examine practical cases to see whether they have matched the standards laid down. Integration as a process is an analysis of those variables which are likely to induce movement along a spectrum between the opposite poles of complete separation and complete integration. Consideration of integration as either a state of affairs or a process is mutually compatible, and we intend, briefly, to consider both.

1. Integration as a State of Affairs

There is an abundant literature setting out criteria for what constitutes a state of integration. In describing a political community, Etzioni[1] suggests that it must have three properties, namely: "effective control over the use of the means of violence"; a decision-making centre "able to affect significantly the allocation of resources and rewards throughout the community"; and to be "the dominant focus of political identification of the large majority of politically aware citizens." What, however, these three criteria also require is some form of self-sufficiency, that is internal mechanisms to secure their maintenance under their own steam.

Karl Deutsch[2] elaborated a conception of a "security community" in which a group of people has become "integrated." For Deutsch this meant "the attainment, within a territory, of a 'sense of community' and of institutions and practices strong enough and widespread enough to assure, for a 'long' time, dependable expectations of 'peaceful change' among its population." This entailed, in his mind, the notion that the group was convinced that any difficulties that arose would be resolved through peaceful change, which implied the normal resolution of such problems by institutionalised procedures without any large-scale physical force being used.

The structural functionalists urge us to think of any organisation as being required to fulfil four basic functions. The structures through which these different organisations fulfil the four functions vary considerably, but one way of establishing the degree to which any organisation, no matter how disparate, is integrated, is by analysing the extent to which the organisation is able to fulfil these functions. If it is to survive, and no judgement is made about whether or not it should survive, any social organisation must be able to adapt to its social and ecological environment, and for that purpose it requires open lines of communication between both its external and internal environments. It needs, therefore, to be able to receive information and to impart information. An organisation needs also to be able to integrate its subunits into a whole. But administrative integration is not enough, there must also be a sense of identitive commitment. At some point, the actors in an organisation must have some conception that they form part of a whole. In short, there must be a 'we' feeling. If there is no level at which they can say 'we,' then there is no integration and no organisation. Finally, any organisation in order to survive, needs enough self-knowledge to be able to set goals. It is no good having excellent channels of communication, well integrated sub-units and a strong sense of commitment if there is no sense of direction. But a sense of direction can only come from the collective memory which is the repository of previous experiences from which desirable and undesirable goals can be identified. Organisational amnesia leads to collapse, for we can have no sense of direction.

Sociologists such as Tönnies pointed out long ago that such organisations could be identified on a spectrum between two ideal types which Tönnies called *Gemeinschaft* and *Gesellschaft*. A *Gemeinschaft* is a closely-knit and ascriptive community in which the propensity for change and adaptation is low. It is, however, an extremely secure community in which everything is in its place and there is a place for everything. At the same time that assurance and security can be suffocating because of its ultra-stable nature. A *Gesellschaft* on the other hand is extremely achievement-oriented, and is therefore much more

insecure. Its adaptability implies a high rate of change which can, in itself, make severe demands upon individuals. While a *Gemeinschaft* is holistic, a *Gesellschaft* is in constant motion.

If we reflect upon these different approaches, a composite set of properties suggest itself for defining integration as a state of affairs. There must be a high degree of shared values which engenders a will to collective action for the promotion of mutual interest. This collective action need not be embodied in a single decision-making centre, but can be part of a more diffused decision-making process. Nevertheless, it does require the ability to fulfil the four functions mentioned above to a very high level which involves the identification and pursuit of mutual interests. This process is based upon long-term expectations of acceptable behaviour on the part of the members of the community. In short, there will be peaceful change. Finally, the process must be able to maintain itself from within its own resources, and not be dependent upon outside influences, resources or pressures.

It is clear that few if any social organisations are unlikely to achieve these demanding requirements, but if complete integration is not necessarily the goal, some integration is inevitable and thus we must consider integration not only as a state of affairs, but also as a process.

2. Integration as a Process

By integration as a process is meant movement between the poles of complete integration and complete separation. There are no necessary normative implications in either more or less integration. Etzioni[3] is again helpful in pointing to three sets of variables which are important in the process of integration and disintegration. These variables are utilitarian, affective and coercive in nature. Utilitarian variables concern practical matters such as trade flows, the transport infrastructure, energy policy, agriculture and the like. In short, they are concerned with the practical integration of daily life. Affective variables, on the other hand, are psycho-social in their characteristics, that is, not only are we integrated in practical questions, but also in a sense of commitment to that process of integration—a commitment which is political, psychological and social. The relationship between the two forms of integration, both utilitarian and affective, is a matter of controversy. The previous assumption that the degree of integration would proceed in step, that is, that utilitarian integration would engender affective integration and *vice versa*, has been found wanting. Difficulties arise where there is a large gap between the two elements of the process which takes us into the third set of variables that Etzioni mentioned, namely coercive variables.

We have already defined integration based on coercion as being imperialism (see *Imperialism*) and beyond the ambit of this discussion. Nevertheless, Etzioni[4] points out that a successful integration process may require the use of coercion at a particular point, although it cannot in the long run be based largely on coercion. Of course, such forms of coercion do not necessarily have to be violent, but they may be. However, there is no guarantee that even such short-term, if intense, periods of violence or coercion can hold the integration process together, and there is a real danger that they will evolve into imperialism.

The literature suggests a number of factors likely to facilitate integration. It is, however, important to remember that these factors are in no sense a recipe. It is merely that if they are evident in abundance, the question of integration is likely to be on the agenda, and if it is pursued, the passage is likely to be relatively smooth.

A pre-existing degree of homogeneity between the integrating units is often a facilitating factor. While societies with differing religious values have been able to integrate, it is likely that homogeneity of religious values and normative frameworks is a permissive factor for integration. Also of significance is homogeneity of wealth which may obviate any difficulties about variations in size. But it is not only objective levels that need to be taken into consideration. The likelihood of integration is enhanced by shared levels of expectations in political, economic, social, cultural and, perhaps indeed, military affairs.

If homogeneity of wealth, values and expectations is a bedrock on which integration can be built, the idea of integration is not relevant without transactions. However, these transactions must be highly legitimised, that is, acceptable, freely and with full knowledge, by all parties. As Karl Deutsch has pointed out in his seminal work *Nationalism and Social Communication*,[5] increased transactions give rise to mutual knowledge, and the confidence engendered thereby provides a climate in which functional specialisation can emerge. Such factors are likely to be particularly important in societies characterised by a high degree of urbanisation, industrialisation and trade. All of these imply specialisation, and we are only likely to specialise if we are confident that others will be prepared to supply our remaining needs in a manner acceptable to us. Such a division of labour is the very stuff of integration. In short, integration is likely to be on the agenda where there is a strong functional imperative leading to task expansion and spillover.

The functional imperative does not work in a political void. It can be reined back sharply by political actors. This points to the relevance of the attitude of elites and also to the decision-making process. Where the decision-making process reflects political systems which are widely different, it is unlikely to engender a framework for integration at more than a minimal instrumental level. Nevertheless, effective leadership can overcome many barriers, but it usually requires that there be a broadening of the elite as well as elite socialisation into the policy and underlying goals and norms of the integration process. This must be based on effective means of communication not only between elites, but also, in the long run, among masses and between elites and masses. Moreover, government must be effective and equally so. Any gross disparities in effectiveness, despite an intention of creating homogeneity, may cause friction and lead to a process more of disintegration rather than integration if such friction is allowed to fester. In part, this is because actors joining an integration process are usually aware that they are making a commitment of considerable import. They are more likely to accept a process in which they know that their future behaviour is likely to be considerably constrained if they are able to predict, with some degree of assurance, the future behaviour patterns of their partners and the framework that they are creating. Thus, not only do gross disparities in shared values create a climate of unpredictability which acts as a brake upon the process of integration, but so also do gross disparities in governmental effectiveness.

Even utilitarian integration may have difficulty if it is based merely on a redistribution of existing resources, for that means the taking from one in order to give to the other. Integration processes, therefore, are much more relevant in a climate of growth when there need be no losers. But even in such a situation, a perceived equity of distribution of the benefits of growth is an important factor in engendering affective integration, and without a substantial degree of affective integration, the level of utilitarian integration is likely to be reined back. The gap between the two can only be so big before either a stalemate sets in or coercion rears its ugly head. A sense of relative deprivation, that is of inequity in distribution of benefits in this instance, is a powerful stimulus to revolt, or at least disaffection. Such a disaffection is envenomed if the group perceiving itself to be in an inequitable situation also finds itself to be in a permanent minority status. In such a situation, the relevant strategy is secession rather than integration.

Geographical neighbours may find that they have an interest in developing ties and a thriving transactional base leading to mutual knowledge, which puts the question of further integration high on the agenda, but it is also a fact that neighbours fight with each other more frequently than with other actors. Geography may engender relevance, but geographical distance does not prevent similarities. Moreover, geographical distance should not be confused with psychological or political distance. Albania is a long way from Britain in the psychological and political sense, whereas New Zealand is not. Psychological distance may in itself be a reflection of previous experiences. Positive experiences bring peoples closer, negative experiences drive them apart, if not literally, at least politically and psychologically. Indeed, until perceptions of psychological and political distance from and between each of the potential partners are reasonably consonant, there is a gross danger of misunderstanding which may inhibit or, indeed, wreck, the process of integration.

In some instances groups have integration thrust upon them, not so much by coercion, as by the expectations of others. Labelling theory suggests that if an actor is labelled in a particular way, then that actor may well fulfil the expectations placed upon it. If a unit aspires to be an integrated community and others treat it as such, then this may be a significant fillip towards integration. Of course, it is one of the oldest adages of political life that an external threat can, in some circumstances, lead to internal unity, although some political leaders have found out to their great cost, and that of their society, that wild foreign adventures do not always increase internal unity. Indeed, the reverse may be dramatically and catastrophically the case. In either instance, the attitude of third parties to an integration process, whether they are encouraging it, ignoring it, or trying to nullify it, is of significance.

This survey of factors deemed in the literature likely to facilitate integration implies no political conclusions of whether this is a good or a bad thing. It does, however, suggest that utilitarian integration may be easier to achieve than affective integration, but that unless there is a degree of affective integration, eventually the brakes will be put upon the process of utilitarian integration. What forms might such integration take? It is to that subject that we now turn, and again, there is a rich variety from which to choose.

3. General Categories for Cooperation[6]

It is convenient to divide the forms of cooperation most often found in the literature into three different categories. Actors may plumb for adjustment processes, constitutional changes or non state-centric frameworks. Adjustment processes are those in which actors seek to broach problems or to take advantage of opportunities within the existing system of states by adopting techniques which do not, in the last resort, undermine state sovereignty. Thus, while they may attenuate such sovereignty, in the final analysis state actors retain their autonomy to act independently. There are thus no fundamental structural implications in the processes of cooperation. The repertoire of techniques for adjustment is wide, and includes cooperation, coordination, harmonisation, regionalism, association and parallel national action. Such techniques are likely to prove opposite in relations where there is a relative weakness of the factors likely to facilitate integration.

Constitutional theories, on the other hand, do have significant implications for the existing state system. They do not question the appropriateness of acting through a state system, but they seek to refashion it in a manner more suitable for contemporary and future tasks and opportunities. Such constitutional theories include federalism, neo-functionalism, consociationalism and theories of disintegration, that is of building down to smaller units rather than building up to larger ones.

It may be that the nature of the tasks envisaged and the problems and opportunities which present themselves renders any state system an inappropriate structural framework through which to broach major issues. Such non state-centric theories therefore take us beyond the existing, or any, state system, not necessarily by abolishing it, but through bypassing it, overlaying it and perhaps marginalising it. Such theories are those of functionalism, networking, complex interdependence and regimes. This implies a further development towards notions of global governance.

4. Adjustment Processes

At its simplest level, adjustments within the existing state system between various parties may involve simple examples of cooperation. These are separate, discrete agreements which involve a limited engagement of the parties in a joint enterprise which is focused on a specific predetermined objective with no hint or intention that it should go beyond the scope and duration of the cooperation that has been agreed. In short, it seeks to deny any aspect of the functional imperative of spillover or task expansion into other areas. A dramatic if extreme form of the limitations of cooperation might be the exchange of prisoners of war in the course of hostilities between two states.

Coordination envisages a continuing programme in which there is a constant adjustment of government policies through a process of intensive consultation, often within the framework of an international institution, frequently in the context of striving to achieve goals which can only be obtained by working together, but to which each separately, and from its own point of view, attaches considerable significance. This process of intensive and continuing consultation is one from which governments can stand aside if they so wish, but they are unlikely to do so because they are enmeshed in a set of relationships which become increasingly interdependent. In such a framework a secretariat can also play a catalytic role.

Out of such processes of consultation, harmonisation may result. Harmonisation involves discussion and analysis in order to arrive at an agreed standard of conduct in a particular domain. Once such a standard has been set, states agree that they will try to implement it, even though they are not, strictly speaking, bound by the standard. It is a statement of intention, but it is nevertheless a very effective one, since any states that do not conform with the standard have, since they themselves have recognised its merit, the obligation to give good cause why they have not done so, at least in political and moral terms. In short, they have laid a rod across their own backs. There are many examples of this technique, such as the standards of the ILO and the Universal Declaration of Human Rights (see *Declaration of the Rights of Man*). Just as coordination brings a degree of policy alignment and helps to bring about the early recognition and elimination of unintended consequences of particular policies chosen by individual governments, so harmonisation brings a degree of integration through the setting of universal or regional standards, and their gradual implementation through national policies.

Regionalism, at least as it is conceived in the framework of the UN Charter (see *United Nations Charter*), has in some sense the notion of a geographical basis. It is an assertion that geography is a key variable as a guide to behaviour. It assumes that because a group lives in a particular geographic region, then there are likely to be similarities of interest, values, methods and institutions, and that geography may be an important factor in giving rise to common cultures and knowledge and understanding between groups. It is sometimes asserted that the region is a natural building block between individual states and world government. Yet, while not wishing to discount geographical factors, there seems to be virtually no evidence to suggest that geography is this sort of master variable. Indeed, Bruce Russett[7] has made the not surprising finding that although geographical regions may exist in particular functional dimensions, there are no multidimensional regions easily discernible on the globe. If that is so, we must ask whether such a region should be created as an act of policy or whether it may emerge as a response to the processes of globalisation.

A weaker form of regional and trans-regional linkage is the idea of association. In many ways the association is a device to allow actors to be in that enviable situation of having their cake and eating it at the same time. It allows groups to come together for particular purposes while remaining apart for other purposes. This means that there are activities in which a particular actor can join without belonging to the institution as a full member. Sometimes, however, association agreements between a group of states in an international organisation and a non-member constitute an interim arrangement before that state becomes a full member. Europe provides many examples of this. On other occasions, association agreements are used to link actors who have one vital area in common, but who are otherwise disparate. The Lomé agreements, linking together the EU countries with the ACP countries, are a case in point. Finally, we should not forget that a commonwealth is an association of states and peoples. The Commonwealth of Nations, which grew out of the British Empire, acknowledges both the severance of ties of Empire as well as the continuing myriad of relationships which gives rise to an impressive movement of goods, services, peoples and ideas within a framework that acknowledges a common bond.[8] However, such an association is one of sovereign states who are constrained neither to join nor to leave. La Francophonie and the Commonwealth of Independent States are like organisations, at least in aspiration.

The Scandinavian countries have long been adept at a pragmatic approach to integration which does not deny their sovereignty, but at the same time, allows a considerable degree of integration. This process can be described as parallel national action. The result has been a network of ties in which a conscious effort is made to coordinate legislation in particular areas in the five countries. This makes it easy to extend the benefits of such parallel legislation to citizens of all five countries, wherever they may be in Scandinavia, while paying due account to minor variations to meet local peculiarities, and local control through national parliaments to ensure that there is a degree of grassroots participation. Such a process commends itself as a method whereby countries which have significant differences in many domains may, nevertheless, in areas where they have common interests, promote a considerable degree of integration by acting in a parallel manner and then reciprocating the obligations and benefits of the legislation to those who are acting in parallel.

None of these techniques should be seen as a royal road to cooperation, nor are they formulae, since the approaches described are rarely, in practice, to be found in a pure form. Nevertheless they do provide a menu from which politicians can choose if their aim is to further cooperation, while at the same time keeping their distance through the preservation of the possibility of the exercise of sovereignty.

5. Constitutional Theories

The rationale of constitutional changes is that the existing state system is no longer capable of meeting the needs of actors in a number of important domains. It is, therefore, necessary to move beyond adjustment within the existing state system, towards rebuilding the state system on a different basis. The principal approaches to rebuilding the state system are federalism, neofunctionalism, consociation and theories of disintegration. A federation is based on a constitution which divides sovereign powers between the federal and the regional governments. Each government remains sovereign in its area, and relates directly to its citizens. While the balance between the federal and regional governments can change, as a minimum, federal governments usually have control of external affairs, defence and monetary matters. A federation recognises that there are advantages to centralisation, while at the same time other matters can best be dealt with separately. The division is specified in a constitution and normally takes place on the basis of territory. But a society is a living organism, and the nature of relationships can change as can the degree of their territoriality. The constitutional and territorial division decided upon at the time of the creation of a federation may not be relevant some years thereafter. Thus as time passes, federations may become less appropriate unless they are reformulated to meet new conditions. Neo-functionalism is, in reality, the proceeding to a federation by installments. It has nothing to do with functionalism

as a theory, except that it shares in common a belief of the efficacy of the functional imperative.[9]

The purpose of consociation is to bring together groups which desire unity, but which at the same time have deep cleavages in certain aspects of their relationships. The principle of consociation is to avoid majority rule, because in such circumstances it bids fair to be a tyranny of the majority which will only engender a desire for secession by the permanent minority. Governance therefore, has to be joint and consensual in which all the major groups are represented in a grand coalition, and in which the groups retain a good deal of autonomy in the management of their own affairs. These groups may exercise that autonomy on a territorial basis or on a non-territorial basis as is most appropriate.

Constitutional theories are not only about building bigger: they may also be about building smaller, that is, building down rather than building up. There is an evident need in the contemporary world to study movements away from unitary government and aspirations towards autonomy, devolution, secession or aterritorial units. However, theories of disintegration have a negative connotation which is unfortunate since the world needs more diverse forms in order to deal with its complexity. Much of the theorising in this area has been the by-product of other theorising, such as negative theories of integration or negative theories of cohesion, but building down is somewhat different from falling apart. More direct theories of building down are associated with internal colonialism and some form of ethnicity or communalism. Internal colonialism is based on the idea that the centre exploits the periphery, both globally and within states. The periphery, therefore, in order to protect itself, may seek either to change the power relations between the centre and periphery through revolution, or, and especially if it is ethnically different, to break away from the centre. Communalism arises when the expression of identity is an efficient means of enhancing the position of the group with a view to obtaining or safeguarding a share of scarce resources. However, both the above theories are essentially conflictual theories for building down. There are also more positive reasons for regionalisation on the model of the European Union (see *European Union*). To be sure, such movements are a response to greater demands for an acknowledgement of identity and a need for participation, but they are also a response to an awareness that systems of transactions have different boundaries. Some systems are growing in size, others are dividing into smaller or less territorially based groupings. Sovereignty was never complete and the process of building up and down from the existing state system is simply an acknowledgement of the diffuse nature of sovereignty in the late twentieth century. We are, in short, moving towards a more complex framework in which ambiguity and anomaly can find a useful place, and there is something to be learned from previous systems such as the Christian Commonwealth of Europe, the Ottoman Empire, or the governance of India in British times and before. Such systems turn our attention to those approaches which go beyond the state system, in the sense of bypassing it, overlying it, ignoring it or undermining it.

6. Beyond the State System: Non State-Centric Approaches

David Mitrany is considered by many to be one of the fathers of functionalism. *A Working Peace System*[10] is a seminal essay from which we can distill the essence of this approach. For Mitrany, the basic idea was that form should follow function, that is, where a system of transactions delineated itself, the institutional form for the governance of that system of transactions should grow out of the function being performed. He observed that too often the sequence of events was the reverse, namely, that a functional system was forced into a pre-existing institutional framework for its governance and that consequently the pre-existing framework was often ill-adapted to the functional needs which had expressed themselves in transactional patterns. Thus, the nineteenth century European state system was inappropriate, in his view, for the security, economic and welfare needs of the mid-twentieth century. He was not suggesting that states should be abolished, but where there was a clear functional need to go beyond the state system, on either a territorial or an aterritorial basis, then there should be no compunction in creating a new functional framework (see *Peace, Systems View of*). Within such a framework, Mitrany urged that decision-making should be by experts rather than negotiated by politicians. The experts, in his view, would be able to start from the problems of the function being performed, whereas politicians and diplomats would negotiate from the strength of the parties, often at the expense of felt functional needs. Mitrany's claim was that if such a network of functional institutions was able to develop, it would move us in the direction of three cherished goals which had been so wanting in the twentieth century, namely, peace, prosperity and participation.

A working peace system would evolve through the development of a sense of community whereby individuals from different countries worked together at the same functional task for their mutual benefit in response to their individually felt needs. Such cross-cutting loyalties that would evolve as a result of cooperating together for mutual benefit would point to the immediate costs of an inter-state conflict. To go to war would therefore be self-evidently a case of cutting off the nose to spite the face. Moreover, superordinate goals would develop which could only be arrived at through cooperation. Gradually, in Mitrany's view, a working peace system would emerge which would be characterised, not by the so-called security of the antagonist armed camps with the manipulation of threats, the arms race and the like, but rather by security through association, that is, security coming from the fact that an actor was providing services to others which were valued by both parties and *vice versa*, thereby creating a strong disincentive for conflicts of a dysfunctional nature.

It is not difficult to share Mitrany's goals of peace, prosperity and participation, nevertheless, we cannot treat his approach as a panacea. There are a number of objections to it, not least of which is his easy assumption that the learning process of cooperation would be characterised by a strong degree of automaticity. Moreover, decision-making by experts cannot take the politics out of functional issues. Decisions can only be made on the basis of expert knowledge once value choices have been made, at least in setting the parameters within which the experts can operate. There may be, of course, advantages in pushing back the parameters of political choice to give a wider field for experts, but such choices there must be. Moreover not everything is rosy in a functionalised world. Conflict, for example, is not abolished, although its incidence and its form may be lessened and changed. Finally, we should note that, as we saw above, identitive loyalties do not follow *pari passu* with the satisfaction of felt needs in a utilitarian sense. Yet we should not dismiss the functionalist's approach too hastily, not only because it has been espoused by practical men of the world, but also because of the startling success of a functionalist-style strategy in helping to resolve the Franco-German conflict which lay at the heart of three massive European civil wars which wreaked havoc in far-flung corners of the world.

What Mitrany had in mind was the development of a psycho-social community. Such a community is a characteristic of networks which are in fact sets of nodes which have flows between each node which evolve and change in response to new challenges and opportunities. A network reflects a need to gain strength and dynamism without going to a coordinating umbrella authority which can, over time, develop into a social dinosaur. In networks the emphasis is on special knowledge, but omniscience is not imputed to key organisations. Relationships are essentially lateral rather than being the product of vertical integration and communication. Indeed the network is utilised far more for the communication of information and advice than for issuing instructions and taking decisions. Such bodies are highly adaptable and can often form lookout agencies picking up items which are likely to be features on future agendas.

We have been describing a world of increasingly complex interdependence. Interdependence is a situation in which there is an element of reciprocity in relationships, although these relationships are likely to be asymmetrical. As Keohane and Nye[11] point out, such asymmetries give rise to the politics of interdependence, since even if everyone benefits from the relationship, nevertheless, the balance of benefits and of costs may reflect the asymmetries of power and resources. Unfortunately Keohane and Nye restrict themselves to the power politics of interdependence, and they do not explore, indeed they may well deny the existence of, a politics of interdependence based on legitimised relationships and a sense of equity (see *Interdependence, International*). In such a situation the balance of benefits and costs is not decided by the ability of some to thrust the burden of the costs on others by virtue of asymmetries in their favour, but rather on agreed views of what constitutes need and equity.

Stephen Krasner has coined a well-known definition of regimes as phenomena which have grown out of a situation of complex interdependence, giving use to "sets of implicit or explicit principles, norms, rules, and decision-making procedures around which actors' expectations converge in a given area of international relations."[12] This definition signifies phenomena which are more than temporary in duration, and which are not based solely on short term calculations of interest. Indeed, they frequently embody a carefully nurtured conception of the common interest, and a growing realisation that self-interest includes a strong element of the common interest. It is evident that we can all survive better in cooperation with others than without them, for as Aristotle noted, we are social animals. It is therefore in our interest that the common interest survives and flourishes. This implies that we must fulfil our obligations, otherwise the benefits of common endeavour will be withdrawn from us, if we are small, and that the system will collapse, if we are a major actor, for the want of fulfilment of our obligations.

The question of the formation of regimes is an interesting one which has aroused some controversy. Neo-realists and structural realists stress the importance of a hegemonic patron who goads, cajoles, and if needs be, coerces actors into recognising a system of governance for a particular area. Others acknowledge different motivations for the establishment of regimes. They can arise from the gradual realisation of mutual interests and the need for coordination of a group of equals, and the codification of established, if informal practices. However, once regimes have been formed, they may well outlive the circumstances of their formation and develop a life of their own, constraining their begetters, whether there are hegemonic patrons or not. The reason for this is that they bring an element of certainty and there may be no alternative easily available. They may also become the expression of community interest, but this is not to suggest that they cannot, in other circumstances, collapse in short order.

Much of the literature on regimes has assumed that state actors are the sole or predominant participants. Such need not, however, be the case, either at the formal or the informal level. Indeed, the range of effective actors in world politics, and more broadly in world society, goes far beyond state actors. Regimes are therefore one way of enfranchising actors which are excluded by the formalities of the inter-state system (see *Security Regimes: Focusing on Asia-Pacific*). Beyond formal inter-governmental ties, living systems develop and demand an institutional form which reflects their complex and diverse nature. The concept of a regime enables us to broach the essence of this nature although much North American literature on regimes does not reflect this adequately. Nevertheless, non-state-centric frameworks have with them the seeds better to understand the ties which can bond us together in a more equitable and more highly participatory manner.

7. Global Governance

Global governance is a phrase which is much bruited about, as is the term globalisation. Globalisation is a phenomenon frequently commented upon by international political economists who see the dominance of global markets over states as a new and remarkable situation (see *Globalization*). They are correct to remark upon this phenomenon, although the ensuing interaction is not so much markets *versus* states, as markets *and* states. However, the debate about globalisation from the economic point of view does not give much truck for global governance, since either the global market will decide, or states will decide, or there will be some interaction between the two (see *Global Integration*). Yet the process of globalisation is multifaceted and throws up a variety of global problems in many dimensions that provide the agenda for global governance.

Global problems are new phenomena in their extent and importance, and their nature can, perhaps, best be seized upon by comparison with the world problems with which we are familiar. World problems may touch upon each part of the globe, but do not necessarily do so, whereas global problems of necessity involve everyone and all parts of the globe. In short, they are problems from which there can be no escape.

The dreadful possibility of nuclear war, and the globalisation of the world economy, are but two examples. Our awareness of environmental questions and their ecological implications is now much greater than it was hitherto. Moreover, there are religious, political, social and cultural movements, the consequences of which are felt globally, which are transmitted to and diffused all over the world through the growing effectiveness of transmission belts, not only of ideas, but also of people. A growing concern for human rights is a case in point since this may involve demands for participation, separateness and even revolution. It often brings a heightened awareness of identity, particularly ethnic identity, and may involve violence, the movement of refugees, and acts of terrorism. In such a context the notion of global governance is difficult to contemplate. Yet global governance is necessary, for if we are not able to broach global problems by hanging together, then we shall surely hang separately. This is surely an indicator that there is no way to avoid some element of integration.

There is no such thing as global governance in the sense of a world government, or even a strengthened United Nations (see *United Nations Governance*). Rather, it is a process which has many component parts. It is multi-polar in nature and encompasses a wide range of differing actors, governmental and non-governmental, and a plethora of transnational actors which contribute to the essential multi-dimensionality of the notion. Their transactions give rise to a decentralised public process for the governance of global civil society. The outcome of this formal and informal process is a set of norms, rules and decisions for the management of global issues. Global governance, therefore, is the decision-making process in formal and informal institutions whereby issues, which by their very nature are global, are broached and to a certain extent managed. It is multi-polar, multi-dimensional and complex, and its procedures are decentralised. It represents that minimum degree of integration necessary if we are to survive when faced by global problems that necessarily affect us all.

There are many embryonic institutions of global governance. P5 and the Security Council is one. G8 and G15 are another in the economics sphere. The annual Davos meetings of world leaders, both governmental and non-governmental, are another case in point, as are the many global conferences of the UN system, bringing together, as they do, both governmental and non-governmental actors, including multinational corporations. None of these have yet cohered into a formal system of an holistic nature. Perhaps that is no bad thing since we need complexity, diversity, flexibility and a wide range of modes of participation to match the range of global problems which must be addressed. It is not likely, therefore, that any particular approach of adjustment, constitution building or moving beyond the state system will suffice to secure that degree of global cohesion and integration so that we hang together in the management of our problems, rather than hang separately in our failure to handle them. We have made some progress, albeit fitfully. A regional experience that has achieved a fair degree of success is the example of the European Union, which is surely an archetypical hybrid.

In Europe there is a fourfold process building up at one level to what the European Commission itself has called the joint management of pooled sovereignty. The process is not a federal one, but a form of consociation in which the governmental elites of the member states together manage a particular function, sometimes on the basis of a simple or qualified majority, and sometimes on the basis of a unit veto system or consensus. Associated with this process is the Commission, whose function varies from that of administrator to that of conscience and initiator. The Parliament and Court both have specific roles and a political and judicial overview role. There is no federal authority, nor is there a constitution, since the entire process is based principally upon the Treaty of Rome, The Single Act, and the Treaty of Maastricht.

The governance of Europe is not only a form of elite consociation in Brussels, it is also about building down to regions within Europe, including some transnational regions. The regions of the European Union are often regions which have an historical, or indeed, an ethnic basis. They are, in some instances, imagined communities of the past which have been brought to life again. The existence of regions is an important conflict prophylactic, since it may allow ethnic and other groups to have a substantial increase in local autonomy and to be able to act in a framework wider than the state, but one which is still a coherent unit to which all belong on an equal basis.

Again, there is the dimension of building across, that is the fostering and consolidation of ties between groups on a transnational basis, often with a very important functional connotation, although it has to be admitted that those who participate most are the elite social categories. The final dimension is that of building beyond, in the form of a wide set of association agreements in Europe and partnerships with other regions of the world. During the last half century Western Europe has been mainly concerned with its own internal affairs, but the new millennium will bring greater activity beyond the Union. Beyond the many close relations at the present time, such as the Lomé agreements, we can see already the development of new ties, such as in the relationships which are developing with East Asia. In some ways the development of integration within regions such as the EU and co-ordination between regions are the response to the globalisation of markets and a greater awareness of the imperatives of global problems.

The European experience in the form of the EU has brought about a metamorphosis from a balance of power system which, as David Mitrany put it, kept the people fearfully apart in rival alliance systems to a coalescing system of collective security and European governance, which at one and the same time has brought people fructuously together for some things, but has enabled them to exert a separate identity in other dimensions. Moreover, this has been achieved without a firm constitutional arrangement, and with a high degree of flexibility. The movement has been essentially in one direction, but with spurts in the degree and kind of cooperation, periods of consolidation, and periods of hesitation and even withdrawal.

There is no panacea that can be taken from the Western European experience in the European Union, but the characteristics of the associative cooperation there suggests that the complexity of society requires a flexible response to diversity. There is no one way, but several ways simultaneously, through which enough confidence can be generated that collective security can take root, and good governance grow. Perhaps integration in the end is a process to which there is no end.

See also: *Economic Integration; Integration, Regional; European Political Community*

Notes —————————————————

1. Amatai Etzioni: *Political Unification*, New York, Holt, Rinehart & Winston, 1965, p. 4.
2. Karl Deutsch *et al.* in (Amatai Etzioni, ed.) *International Political Communities*, New York, Doubleday, 1966, p. 2.
3. Etzioni, Political Unification, *op. cit.*
4. *Ibid.*
5. Karl Deutsch: *Nationalism and Social Communication*, London, MIT Press, 1966.
6. For a more detailed exposition of such frameworks, see A.J.R. Groom and Paul Taylor (eds) : *Frameworks for International Cooperation*, London, Pinter, 1990.
7. Bruce Russett: *International Regions and the International System*, Chicago, Rand McNally, 1967.
8. See A.J.R. Groom: 'The Commonwealth: A Bond that Held' in Paul Taylor and A.J.R. Groom (eds): *International Institutions at Work*, London, Pinter, 1988 and A.J.R. Groom: 'The Commonwealth of Nations Towards the Millennium' in Coral Bell (ed): *National Region and Context*, Canberra, Australian National University, 1995.
9. See A.J.R. Groom: 'Neofunctionalism: A Case of Mistaken Identity,' *Political Science*, July 1978.
10. David Mitrany: *A Working Peace System*, Chicago, Quadrangle Press, 1966.
11. Robert Keohane and Joseph Nye: *Power and Interdependence*, Boston, Little Brown, 1989, 2nd edition.
12. Stephen Krasner in Stephen Krasner (ed.): 'International Regimes,' *International Organization*, Special Issue, Spring 1982, p. 186.

A.J.R. GROOM

Intercultural Relations and Peace Studies

The field of intercultural relations investigates the dynamics of relationships between people from different cultural backgrounds. This new field is interdisciplinary, building on traditional disciplines such as anthropology, sociology, psychology, foreign language studies, and philosophy. It studies the inter-relationship of language and culture as well as international/global communication, and human relations. Along with the related fields of cross-cultural psychology and multicultural education it studies inter-group, interracial, and cultural diversity. The contemporary field of intercultural relations includes studies of international communication, leadership and collaboration.

Although intercultural communication has existed since the dawn of humanity, the field of intercultural relations/cross cultural studies is relatively new. The publication in 1959 of Edward T. Hall's seminal and widely read book, *Silent Language*, offered the first comprehensive analysis of the relationship between communication and culture. The researcher Geert Hofstede investigated the nature of work values in different cultures. In his influential 1980 book, *Cultures Consequences*, he pointed out the need for industrial/organizational psychology to expand its theories to include the effects of culture on work-related attitudes and behaviors.

Relations between countries, institutions and individuals have always been strongly influenced by cultural backgrounds. Countries have their own unique identity, esthetic standards, linguistic expressions, patterns of thinking, behavioral norms, systems of nonverbal communication, history, ways of doing things and symbols. Conflict results when people from different cultures challenge each other's ways of behaving as wrong or inferior (see *Chauvinism*). Information about cultural differences helps prepare people for intercultural encounters. By obtaining this knowledge, people can reduce culture shock.

The development of a sense of global citizenship is an essential condition for global peace (see *Education for Global Citizenship*). There has never been as much contact between the people and products of the nations of the world as now. There are increasing numbers of "global citizens" who are socially and psychologically a product of the inter-weaving of cultures. These people's identifications and loyalties transcend the boundaries of nationalism as they sense themselves to be members of global communities (see *Supranationalism*). Being a multicultural, international person is a recognition of our increasingly interconnected world. It does not preclude the positive effects of having a unique cultural background. The world will most likely remain culturally diverse and this diversity can contribute to expanding perspectives and problem solving.

Information about cultures and customs alone does not necessarily reduce misunderstanding. Bias and prejudice is formed over centuries and certainly through an individual's lifetime. If not viewed with sensitivity, divergent values and behaviors can fuel conflict. Intercultural peace efforts and the movement towards global citizenship involves learning on myriad levels. The values, behaviors and beliefs which have been formed by one's culture, family and formal education must be systematically reviewed and revised (see *Peace and Peace Education: A Holistic View*). This self assessment coupled with accurate information, provides a foundation for improved intercultural communication.

The field of intercultural relations has much to offer for developing international understanding and peace. The American Field Service is one non-profit student exchange organization which provides intercultural learning opportunities. They aim to "help people develop the knowledge, skills and understanding needed to create a more just and peaceful world and to act as responsible, global citizens working for peace and understanding in a diverse world." The AFS mission statement "acknowledges that peace is a dynamic concept threatened by injustice, inequity, and intolerance."

1. Applications

A search of the Internet sites associated with the topics "intercultural" and "peace" yields resources such as student exchange programs, international education programs, peace study programs, psychologists' efforts in war torn countries, conflict management, programs in business and education, and contributions in the field of art. Related topics include biculturalism, cross-cultural training, cross-cultural awareness, cultural exchange, cultural pluralism, ethnic relations, foreign culture, intercultural programs, international communication, multicultural education, and multilingualism. There are discussion groups on the Internet which involve people from different nations exploring the implications of cultural differences and bias toward cultural groups (see *Internet: A New Vehicle for Global Peace Efforts*).

The theories about intercultural communication and human relations intersect to form the foundation for the conceptual tools used in teaching and training in multicultural education (see *Communication: Key to World Peace*). The end product of such education is the increased ability of people to successfully resolve intercultural conflict and misunderstanding. This knowledge and skill about education and training in intercultural relations has many applications such as governmental agencies welcoming refugees, the increasing mobilization of business people, businesses looking for new markets, tourism, and foreign students exchanges. The study of intercultural relations is relevant as well to subgroups within countries. Multicultural studies help to resolve the misunderstandings and conflicts which result from contact between people with obvious differences such as language, skin color, length of hair, dress and sexual behavior. It provides ways to approach complex conflicts involving people with different lifestyles, values, and ways of perceiving the world. Because of heightening interaction between cultural groups both internationally and domestically, educational, psychological and organizational development experts have created curricula and methodologies for providing the information and skills that will reduce conflict and increase peace and productivity.

See also: *Cultural Roots of Peace; Language and Peace*

Bibliography ————————————————

Hall E T 1959 *Silent Language*. Doubleday and Co., New York

Hofstede G 1980 *Culture's Consequences*. Sage Publications, Beverly Hills, California

Hoopes D 1979 *Intercultural Sourcebook Cross-cultural Training Methodologies*. The Society for Intercultural Education Training and Research

Klopf D, Park M S 1982 *Cross-Cultural Communication: An Introduction to the Fundamentals*. Han Shin Publishing Co. Seoul, Korea

Milhouse V 1996 Intercultural communication education and training goals, content, and methods. *Int. J. Intercultural Relations* 20(1)

Pruegger V, Rogers T 1994 Cross-cultural sensitivity training: Methods and assessment. *Int. J. Intercultural Relations* 18(3)

Pusch M 1981 *Multicultural Education: A Cross Cultural Training Approach*. Intercultural Network, Inc. Chicago, Illinois

ROBERT C. SMITH; STEVI LISCHIN

Interdependence, International

In the theory of systems analysis, a system is conceived as a total sum of interdependent variables (elements and blocs). The structure of a system is the cumulative totality of the functional interdependent variables. Since the 1960s economics and political science have shown a great predilection for using the concept of "interdependence" to characterize partly the progress of internationalization and partly the increasing impact of one state on another through different channels. In political science, mostly the pluralist school of thoughts put the emphasis on interdependence. This school was focusing on international development between states in the Western world. In economics, the school of international political economy studied the issue of interdependence mainly from the perspective of the outcome of interstate distributive relations.

The concept of interdependence has been welcomed as a new discovery in economics. The category was extremely popular in the "golden age" of the 1960s, and appeared in the new framework of the 1970s amidst the problems and crises of the world economy. Interdependence, though, is not a new notion. More than a century ago, Marxist political economy (see *Socialism, "Scientific"*) had already understood and illuminated the causes which had led to the internationalization (see *Internationalization*) of economic development under the then prevailing conditions of capitalism. In the *Communist Manifesto*, first published in February 1848, Marx and Engels wrote that by exploiting the world market, the bourgeoisie had internationalized the production and consumption of all countries. They pointed out the role of modern industry in this process, using raw materials imported from the remotest areas to create products which were consumed all over the world, and that national seclusion and self-sufficiency were being replaced by a "universal interdependence of nations" (see *Imperialism*). They added that this process was taking place not only in material but also in intellectual production and that the intellectual products of individual nations were becoming the common treasure of humankind. Since the formulation of these ideas in the last century, the process has further advanced albeit with many distortions and disruptions.

Since the 1960s a voluminous literature has been published in economics, political science, and other related disciplines on the notion of international interdependence in the industrial western countries. The expression has also gained currency in the rhetoric of politicians and the press. While the literature about interdependence has contributed to a better understanding of the world system, it has also created great confusion and often reduced the concept to pseudoscientific platitudes. In order to understand the implications, several authors have tried to define the concept of international interdependence. A report prepared for the US legislature some years ago has provided one of the most comprehensive definitions: "Interdependence has great many meanings . . . . According to the interpretation given to it in the study, it is a dynamic condition system on which the forces of growth and change compel the states and peoples of the world to depend to a greater extent on one another for their security and welfare, while they also (and decisively) rely on themselves (see *World Economy, Social Change and Peace*). Thus interdependence also implies both self-reliance and bi- and multi-lateral cooperation." (*Science, Technology and Diplomacy in the Age of Interdependence* 1976)

This definition is correct in the sense that interdependence is a multidimensional notion but in concrete analysis it must be defined more precisely. This interpretation is also one-sided because it fails to take into account the stages, divergent intensity, importance, and consequences of relations. Thus it does not explain, for example, historical changes in interstate relations. In addition, the definition is problematic also because it identifies actual mutual dependence with one-sided dependence. Yoshikazu Sakamoto (1976) has offered an alternative definition:

First: interdependence may be classified as negative and positive interdependence. The former refers to those interactions which arise from mutual withdrawals and mutual denials, while the latter from expectations connected with mutual benefits. Secondly: interdependence may be symmetric and asymmetric. The former indicates that interdependence takes place on equal terms while the latter refers to disproportionate interdependence. The combination of these two criteria leads to the following possible sub-notions: (a) Negative symmetric interdependence, exemplified by nuclear deterrence existing then between the United States and the former Soviet Union, (b) Negative asymmetric interdependence represented by the colonial system, (c) Positive symmetric interdependence based on equitable partnership relations, e.g., horizontal division of labour among the developing countries, (d) Positive asymmetric interdependence. The definition of Sakamoto describes all forms of international relations or interstate effects as interdependence, irrespective of their character and intensity. It is important to note here that, while cases of negative symmetric, negative asymmetric, and positive symmetric interdependence are rather common in history, few successful examples of positive asymmetric interdependence relationships can be established between the North and the South without asymmetric dependence assuming a dominant role. Thus the question is this: is a positive asymmetric kind of cooperation possible, and is it a politically and economically realistic objective?

The pioneers of the notion of interdependence in the political science of the US, Keohane and Nye, (1977) give the following definition of interdependence: Interdependence, defined in the simplest way, means mutual dependence. Interdependence in world politics refers to a situation characterized by interactions among states of agents [of world politics] in the different countries . . . we do not confine interdependence to mutual utility. Such a definition would presuppose that a policy concept is useful only where. . . threat by military power is rare and the level of conflicts is low. The concept expressed by Henry Kissinger was not far from the views of Keohane and Nye: . . . the traditional themes of foreign affairs—power relations among the leading countries, the security of states—no longer define out dangers and possibilities. We are entering a new era. The traditional international structure is decaying. The world has become interdependent in the fields of economy, telecommunications and human endeavors (*A New National Partnership*, News Release, January 24, 1975, US Department of State, p. l). Kissinger in fact puts the emphasis also on the growing internationalization of national politics. Interdependence in fact has undermined—much more the effective sovereignty of states for economic transactions.

In the practical life of the world of the end of the 20th Century, and in the framework of the global political and economic system an immeasurable number of linkages exist and develop constantly between states, which extends to the production and utilization of material goods, acts many-sidedly on economic life and in the eco-system. It is also strengthened by the expanding information flows. They constantly create, change and restructure interdependent relations. National policies could often be nullified by new international transactions over which the decision makers have no control. The process exert a great influence on the interests of the countries, and on the way of thinking of persons who, as decision makers, play a role in the given area.

The scope of the problems relating to the management of "mutual dependence" or interdependence is extremely complex. Interdependence means mutual vulnerability. It has become an important new dimension of political, economic and environmental security of the countries. As the consequence of the fact, that the life, the existence, of states is complexly interwoven with the consequences of the life, the existence of other states (and those of the various social classes and groups within them), their objectives in a number of areas can be realized only if the impact of other countries is taken into account in political and economic fields, in environmental management, though not necessarily in a symmetrical way (see *World Peace Order, Dimensions of a*). Interdependent relations may strengthen the mutuality of interests, but can become the sources of tensions and conflicts. The ways, the different countries interact, may become the source of chaotic relations in international life and the loss of control over many areas of national life. Interdependence may become an incentive for being less dependent, in the case of many countries, but it can stimulate collective policies and actions. The international consequences of interdependence are particularly important in the global problems, which created not only new interactions between states, but made their cooperation indispensable. The environmental and social sustainability of global development depends to a great extent to the capabilities of nations to manage their interdependent relations (see *Human Right and Environmental Rights: Their Sustainable Development Compatibility*).

The management of interdependence requires appropriate national institutions and international, multilateral organizations in the framework of which mutually accepted rules, norms and forms of cooperation can be developed for the international harmonisation of the cost and benefits so that conflicts emerging in the different areas of political or economic relations may be resolved equitably. It presupposes the increasing coordination of economic policies. The evolving concept and practice of global governance is in fact a necessary condition for the management of interdependence.

See also: *Global Integration; Integration, Regional;*

Transnationalism; Maldevelopment; Global Economic Interdependence: Why Crisis?

Bibliography —————————————

Camps M 1981 *Collective Management.* Council of Foreign Relations, New York
Goldmann K, Sjostedt G 1979 *Power, Capabilities, Interdependence.* Sage, London
Interdependence and Structural Change, 7th World Congress of the International Economic Association, 1983 Ilustre Colegio de Economistas de Madrid, Madrid
Keohane R O, Nye J S 1977 *Power and Interdependence.* Little, Brown, Boston, Massachusetts
Marx K, Engels F 1952 *Manifesto of the Communist Party.* Progress Publishers, Moscow
Sakamoto Y 1976 The state of the globe. Mimeo of a lecture delivered at the Conference on War and Peace, University of Pennsylvania, Philadelphia, Pennsylvania
Science, Technology and Diplomacy in the Age of Interdependence. 1976 US Government Printing Office, Washington, DC
Simai M 1981 *Interdependence and Conflicts in the World Economy.* Sijthoff and Noordhoff, Rockville, Maryland
Simai M 1994 *The Future of Global Governance. Managing Risk and Change in the International System.* USIP Press, Washington, DC

MIHALY SIMAI

Internal War

Internal war is a concept that was popularized during the 1960s, initially by Harry Eckstein in a collection of essays on *Internal War: Problems and Approaches* (1964). It seems to have been used first by nineteenth century writers who sought to distinguish internal from external war. In modern usage two different meanings have been attributed to the concept, one broad and one narrow.

A broad definition is used by Eckstein: internal wars "are attempts to change by violence, or threat of violence, a government's policies, rulers, or organization" (1964 p. 1). In this conception internal war is a synonym of other general terms for violent internal conflict such as "civil strife" and "political violence." Included in internal wars, according to Eckstein, are revolutions, civil wars, guerrilla wars, localized rioting, terrorism, mutinies, and *coups d'état* (1964 p. 3). Internal war often combines different types of violence in space and time, for example guerrilla warfare in one region and terrorism in another. The main purpose

served by this conception of internal war was to direct scholars' attention to the comparative study of a diverse set of phenomena which had a single defining property: the concerted use of violence against authorities to bring about political change. Most previous research had concentrated on narrower categories of political conflicts such as revolution, coups, and racial rioting, with little or no attempt to develop more general explanations which encompassed all of them.

A narrower conception of internal war limits it to conflicts which are large in scale, organized, and reflect fundamental divisions within society. Modelski for example characterizes internal wars as violent conflicts in which "All the essential structures of the political system—the structures of authority, solidarity, culture, and resources-split in two . . ." (Rosenau 1964 p. 14). This usage was given impetus by the results of a series of empirical studies using factor analysis which sought to identify the underlying dimensions of conflict behavior, using data on the frequency with which different kinds of events occurred in a large number of countries. Most of these studies suggested that there were two substantially different forms or types of internal conflict: small-scale, disorganized, spontaneous conflict such as rioting, clashes, and demonstrations (labeled turmoil or protest): and large-scale, organized, and more deadly conflicts such as civil and guerrilla wars. The latter dimension was first labeled internal war by Tanter (1965), a usage which was followed by most other scholars doing quantitative work during the 1960s and 1970s (reviewed in Zimmermann 1983 pp. 44-45).

Although the term "internal war" is not used as often in the 1980s as it was in previous decades, there seems to be general agreement among conflict theorists that it should be used in the more restricted sense rather than in Eckstein's broad sense (see Zimmermann 1983 p. 14). It continues to serve a useful purpose, which is to remind scholars that large-scale, deadly political con-flicts such as revolutions, civil and guerrilla wars, and terrorist campaigns have some common characteristics, and that it is useful to seek general theories which explain those common characteristics.

Bibliography

Eckstein H (ed.) 1964 *Internal War: Problems and Approaches.* Free Press of Glencoe, New York

Rosenau J N (ed.) 1964 *International Aspects of Civil Strife.* Princeton University Press, Princeton, New Jersey

Tanter R 1965 Dimensions of conflict behavior within nations, 1955-1960: Turmoil and internal war. *Peace Research Society Papers* 3

Zimmermann E 1983 *Political Violence, Crises and Revolutions: Theory and Research.* Schenkman, Cambridge, Massachusetts

TED ROBERT GURR; JEFFREY IAN ROSS

International Association of University Presidents (IAUP)

1. Founding and Early Years

The first half of the 1960s appeared on the surface to be economically optimistic: futurologists predicted the imminent realization of a post-industrial society on a global scale in which spending would become a virtue. On the other hand, many undesirable byproducts of industrialization pervaded, at the same time, all parts of the world. More than anything else, world peace was at stake as seen by the construction of the Berlin wall, the Cuban missile crisis and the emergence of the third nuclear powers.

Against this complex historical backdrop, five university leaders met first in 1964 at Oxford, England and resolved to create an international organization to respond to the challenge creatively. Their objective, in the words of one founder, Dr. Young Seek Choue, was to create an organization "to make university education truly universal, international and transnational—all geared to planting peace in the minds of students and people."

The five founders were Dr. Young Seek Choue, president and subsequently chancellor of Kyung Hee University in Seoul, Korea; Dr. Peter Sammartino, president of Fairleigh Dickinson University in the United States of America; Dr. Jaime Benitez, president of the University of Puerto Rico; Dr. Carlos Romulo, president and chancellor of the University of the Philippines (and a major contributor to the establishment of the Philippine nation and of the United Nations); and Dr. Rocheforte Weeks, president of the University of Liberia. The founders agreed on a name for the organization, the International Association of University Presidents (IAUP), and the timing and arrangements for a founding conference.

1.1 Triennial I

The inaugural conference of IAUP was held at Wroxton College and Oxford University, England from June 29 to July 1, 1965. The theme of the conference as "What are the Common Elements of a University Education in all the Countries of the World." About 170 presidents, chancellors, vice chancellors and rectors attended from 21 nations. Among the prominent speakers were historian Arnold Toynbee and Ambassador Adlai Stevenson. Dr. Peter Sammartino was elected to be founding president of IAUP.

The original IAUP Charter drafted by the preparatory committee at the founding conference was in outline only and did not elaborate on peace education and cooperation in higher education among nations as its main emphasis. Finally, it was revised with a major role of Dr. Sammartino and Dr. Young Seek Choue in the subsequent years to become more specific, and came to reflect the spirit of the UN in the IAUP Charter. The essence of the Charter reads as follows:

The purpose of the IAUP shall be to promote peace,

welfare, and security for mankind through education, to generate friendship, understanding and confraternity among leaders of higher education, to arrange for joint research through the exchange of faculty members, students and academic materials, and to facilitate cultural and academic exchange as a means of helping in the maintenance of world peace as well as the advancement of the cultures of mankind.

In the inaugural conference of the IAUP, the resolutions were presented by Dr. Young Seek Choue and ratified by all members. The gist of the resolutions is as follows:

We, members of the International Association of University Presidents, reaffirm the basic aim of this organization as embodied in the articles of its Charter:

(a) Emphasis on cooperation among members for the purpose of creating a new civilized world through true advancement of science and technology under the control of human reason;

(b) Emphasis on realization of the lasting world peace by promoting the common prosperity of mankind and eliminating international discord based on mutual respect and understanding;

(c) Emphasis on proper guidance of younger generations in a direction where their vigour and strength will be used for the creation of a better world in harmony with established order and values;

(d) Emphasis on promotion of common research projects and exchange programs of scholarship students, professors, and other academic materials in cognizance of universities' mission to make cultural progress of mankind through the advancement of learning and technology.

These early years of IAUP were the formative ones of organization building. Dr. Sammartino continued as president for two triennial periods (1965-68) (see later section on organization). The members of IAUP agreed at the 1965 founding conference to meet again in 1968.

1.2 Triennial II

The Second IAUP Triennial Conference was convened in Seoul with the proposal of Dr. Young Seek Choue. At that time, there was a strong doubt about its capacity and competence because Korea still stood at the bottom of the developing world. However, the global meetings of the conference went on smoothly, much more so than initially expected, being impeccably organized and effectively managed with full preparations. Noteworthy is that the late President of Korea, Chung Hee Park, immediately grasped the importance

of the conference and rendered moral and financial support in the name of the Korean government.

The major theme of the conference was "The Harmony of Cultures of the East and the West and the Promotion of World Peace," which was a most proper subject for discussion among the participants coming from all corners of the world, particularly in view of the bleak reality of the times. This theme was a foretaste of a consistent line of interest and activity in the IAUP through today.

Some 280 university presidents and the like from 63 countries participated in the Triennial II Conference. Among the speakers were very famous personalities and intellectuals such as Dr. Lin Yu-tang, Dr. Carlos Romulo, Ex-President of the UN General Assembly, Dr. Thanat Khoman, the then Foreign Minister of Thailand, and the then President Chung-Hee Park of the Republic of Korea.

In view of the conviction that the university, as the cradle of future leaders, had to respond to the critical situation, the 1968 IAUP Conference in Seoul marked a new turning point not only for the growth of the young Association but also in the history of humankind. A spacious Commemoration Hall was opened on the fourth floor of Kyung Hee Library Building to preserve for generations to come all the materials and articles that were used for and at the Conference as historic relics in the hope of recalling the epochal success of the IAUP Conference hosted by the University.

1.3 Triennial III

The participants in at Seoul agreed upon the Triennial III Conference to be held in Monrovia, Liberia under the auspices of the University of Liberia. This conference encountered difficulties of various kinds, including governmental and financial ones. The conference was greeted by the President of Liberia, as one of his last official acts. Dr. Rocheforte Weeks, the President of the University of Liberia and an IAUP founder, was elected president of IAUP, and Dr. Young Seek Choue of Korea was elected vice-president. Because of the inconvenience of transportation and the weakness of world economy then, it was not easy to travel to Africa. The Conference was attended by no more than fifty members and observers. Just shortly after the conference, President Tubman of Liberia died. His successor chose Dr. Weeks to be Foreign Minister, and then Dr. Weeks necessarily resigned as President of IAUP. Dr. Choue, following the then by-laws, became Acting President.

Dr. Young Seek Choue became president of IAUP in 1971 and led the organization up to 1981. The focus for the organization during his years of leadership had two programmatic themes, peace and the role of universities, and the work of universities in developing nations.

These years also saw the beginning of a new phase of organization building; *Lux Mundi*, the bulletin of IAUP was distributed worldwide to recruit as many members as possible. The distribution in a large scale was the basis for the great success of the Triennial IV Conference. It had been published quarterly without a break during the presidency of Dr. Young Seek Choue. Membership grew significantly as the 1974 Triennial IV Conference approached, the number was 450.

1.4 Triennial IV

The Triennial IV Conference was originally planned in Tunisia. Unfortunately, not long before the projected time of the conference, the government of Tunisia withdrew its invitation to IAUP because of internal unrest in the country. Then an active IAUP Executive Committee member, Dr. Albert Whiting, the then president of North Carolina Central University in the USA, made a proposal leading to a joint conference with the American Association of State Colleges and Universities (AASCU) in Boston for November of 1975. Finally, the joint conference was held with a theme "Toward a New Direction in Higher Education for the Twenty-First Century," and two sub-themes: "Education for What?" and "Reconstruction of the World Community through Education." The Triennial IV Conference was a success, and it was at that conference that the concept of major structural changes was first discussed.

Attended by over six hundred leaders of higher education from forty-five nations representing both IAUP and AASCU, and with many intellectual giants delivering interesting messages, the conference made great contributions to bridging the gap between universities of different countries, charting a new course of higher education for the future, declaring a new goal for mankind to pursue. After discussing the proper role of universities in relation to the peace, welfare and security of humankind, the Boston Conference unanimously resolved to declare the following five principles to all the peoples of the world as a new goal for mankind to pursue: humancentrism, democratic pacifism, the development and control of scientific technology, cultivation of a sound human spirit, and mankind-consciousness.

Activities of IAUP between triennials were rather informal without systematic and administrative provisions, but through the 1975 Boston Conference,

they needed more efficient administrative system of its organization. With adoption of some amendments of the Charter in the Conference, the Executive Committee was formed and began to meet regularly each year. In addition, a sub-group of Regional Council Chairs was formed to build a world-wide structure of regional councils and regional leadership. Dr. Leland Miles, then president of the University of Bridgeport, emerged as an important figure in this structuring activity, and later in 1981 became President of IAUP. As the 1978 Triennial V approached, a further proposal to provide for stable succession in IAUP was formulated. This called for the election at each Triennial conference of a President-Elect and a Secretary General-Elect, thus assuring that, at the close of each Triennial, there would be strong and able leadership for a period of six years ahead.

1.5 Triennial V

All these changes were adopted at the Triennial V Conference in Teheran, Iran. The Triennial V Conference was held in late June 1978. Memorable was the scene of the opening session in the Parliamentary Hall. The royal couple—His Majesty Shah and Her Majesty Farah—were seated on the floor. Only one person seated at the podium was Dr. Young Seek Choue as the president of IAUP. After his opening remarks, the Shah was invited to the podium to give his welcome address to the participants. There was little or no comprehension, however, among the participants that very soon Teheran and all of Iran would be plunged into revolution.

In spite of the political tension seething under the surface, the conference, attended by 560 university presidents from 49 countries, was in many ways a spectacular success for its pageantry, papers, and the approval of important organizational changes.

The triennium of 1978-81 was a transitional one with the leadership of IAUP beginning to pass from one of the founders to a new generation of leaders. The informal and continuing activities of member presidents continued through the period. The initial regional councils, called for in the actions of 1975-78, were established. The leadership of IAUP expanded in numbers. Dr. Leland Miles, the president-elect, assumed responsibility for the 1981 Triennial VI conference and for planning activities from 1981-84.

1.6 Triennial VI

The Triennial VI Conference was held in San Jose, Costa Rica in late June and early July of 1981. More than 700 presidents and others from 49 countries participated in the conference. Concluded was a remarkable period of leadership by Dr. Choue and Dr. Won Sul Lee, then Dean of the Graduate School at Kyung Hee University and IAUP Secretary-General from 1971 to 1981. Dr. Lee was the first IAUP Secretary-General and, in many ways, shaped the role. The theme of the conference, "World Peace Education," was a continuation of a consistent thread which had run through IAUP activities almost from the beginning.

The decade of the 1980s opened with increasing tension, conflicts and complicated problems in the world. It seemed that Armageddon might break out at any place, at any time, on any issue. Many military specialists such as Dr. Henry Kissinger prognosticated that the middle of the 1980s would be some of the most dangerous times of human history.

Mindful of this dreadful global crisis, Dr.Young Seek Choue proposed the following resolution: "The members of IAUP request the United Nations to set up a Day of Peace and a Year of Peace." Armed with this Costa Rican Resolution, Dr. Choue, after the conclusion of the conference, travelled to a number of countries in Latin America urging them to support the IAUP recommendation at the UN General Assembly. His devotion and unceasing efforts had a good influence over minds of many UN people.

It seemed unbelievable, but the proposal for the Day of World Peace was unanimously adopted at the 36th session of the UN General Assembly on November 30, 1981. The UN designated the third Tuesday of every September as the UN International Day of Peace. In the meantime, the UN also designated the year of 1986 as the UN International Year of Peace at the session of its General Assembly on November 16, 1982 and declared it officially at the 40th Anniversary of the UN on October 24, 1985.

At the close of the 1981 Triennial, Dr. Leland Miles became President of IAUP, and his colleague, Dr. Raymond Allen, also then of the University of Bridgeport, became Secretary-General. At the 1981 Triennial, a major focus was the newly established University for Peace in Costa Rica. This was a creation of the United Nations in response to a proposal from the Costa Rican government. Support and encouragement of the University for Peace was to be a major theme for the 1981-84 period. This was a time which saw the creation of additional regional councils, obtaining membership from areas of the world not previously involved with IAUP.

1.6.1 The World Atmosphere after the Birth of the International Day and Year of Peace

In November, 1985, Secretary-General of the former Soviet Union, Mr. Gorbachev, took the initiative of suggesting to President Reagan of the USA to hold a meeting to share their thoughts on the critical world atmosphere and to find a way to avoid World War III. Encouraged by the UN International Year of Peace, Secretary-General Gorbachev took another initiative to suggest to President Reagan to have new year TV interviews in the morning of the first day of 1986, the UN International Year of Peace. They exchanged peace messages for the people of the opposite side. The two leaders of the superpowers pledged that they would do their best to save mankind from a nuclear war. The two leaders finally agreed in principle to abolish their strategic nuclear weapons. It was certainly a promising outcome for positive changes in the world atmosphere in years to come. The INF treaty signed by the two leaders in the following year was the beginning of the end of the Cold War era.

The then Secretary-General Gorbachev decided to adopt the policy of Perestroika and Glasnost for reconstruction of his own society. As ensuing events, the Soviet forces withdrew unilaterally from Afghanistan, end of military conflicts in many parts of the world occurred. Instead, socialist states were transformed into competitive state systems and moved toward a pluralistic representative political system.

Considering these positive and rapid changes in the world atmosphere, the 6th IAUP Triennial Conference in Costa Rica is a historical turning point in human history. The UN International Day and Year of Peace, which was a fruitful result of the Costa Rica Conference, was the sign and initial force to end the Cold War era and to begin a new era of detente.

1.7 Triennial VII

At the 1981 Triennial, the members elected Dr. Nibondh Sasidhorn of Thailand as President-Elect and Dr. Charoen Khantawongs as Secretary General-Elect. Dr. Sasidhorn was former Minister of Education in Thailand and university president.

"Higher Education for International and National Development," was the main theme of the meeting which was hosted by the Government of Thailand with full support from Prime Minister Prem Tinsulanonda and Deputy Prime Minister Thanat Khoman. With a massive participation by the Thai private and government institutes of higher learning, the event saw presidents and their representatives from more than 600 universities and colleges gather together.

This three-year period saw the consolidation of many past efforts and the creation of the High Commission for Peace (HCP).

1.7.1 Creation of the HCP and its Activities

The High Commission for Peace (HCP) was created in July, 1985 at the IAUP Executive Committee meeting in Bangkok as a major achievement during the presidency of Dr. Nibondh Sasidhorn to promote commemorative activities for the International Year of Peace in 1986 as a special commission, Dr. Young Seek Choue's efforts for realizing peace have been greatly activated to produce many a successful result.

The HCP has greatly contributed to promoting a peaceful world atmosphere by holding annual Commemoration Ceremonies, International Peace Seminars, and other celebration activities in commemoration of the UN International Day of Peace including publication of regular HCP *Activities Report* since 1982 without any intermission. Especially, grand celebration activities were held for the 1986 UN International Year of Peace. The United Nations has dispatched a special envoy of the Secretary-General of UN to the commemoration ceremony of the UN International Day of Peace seven times for 16 years since 1982.

In commemoration of the International Year of Peace in 1986, for the first time in human history, *World Encyclopaedia of Peace* (Pergamon Press, UK) was published. To meet the rapidly changed world atmosphere since then and to commemorate the 10th Anniversary of the UN International Year of Peace, 1996, the Institute of International Peace Studies of Kyung Hee University in cooperation with the HCP is now preparing the second edition of *World Encyclopaedia of Peace*. With the initiative of HCP and Kyung Hee University, *Textbook on World Citizenship* was also published for education of universal democracy.

In recognition of a significant contribution to the programme and objectives of the International Year of Peace, proclaimed by the United Nations General Assembly, the Secretary-General of the United Nations designated the International Association of University Presidents as a Peace Messenger on September 15, 1987.

Some noteworthy ambitious projects are now envisaged by HCP under the auspices of Kyung Hee University acting as Secretariat of HCP. The establishment of UN Peace Park and International Peace Museum in Korea are a good example. These two projects were committed to IAUP by the former Secretary-General, Boutros-Boutros Ghali and recommended by New York Metropolitan Peace Museum.

1.8 Triennial VIII

The leadership of IAUP moved once again in 1987.

Dr. Luis Garibay, the rector of the Autonomous University of Guadalajara was elected President-Elect and Dr. Alvaro Romo Secretary General-Elect at the Bangkok conference in 1984. The Triennial VIII was held in late June of 1987. Major presenters from all parts of the world participated, totalling as many as 600 individuals. The theme of the conference was "Important Missions of Universities in Developing Countries."

The years 1987-90 saw the first movement of IAUP in programmatic directions, beyond the consistent theme of peace-related activities. President Luis Garibay wrote "one of the priorities established as IAUP President was to promote continuous activities in the period between the VIII and IX Triennial Conference." The following three activities stand out.

The IAUP had long engaged in activities which related with other international organizations, especially those in the United Nations family. Dr. Garibay moved to establish delegations to the United Nations, a formal delegation to the UN in New York in 1988 and additional representation in Geneva and Vienna.

President Garibay and others recognized the need for creating an atmosphere of cooperation with other international organizations, most especially with the International Association of Universities, the only other world-wide university organization.

At the 1989 Executive Committee meeting in Tokyo, two members presented the concept of a project focussing on higher education and human resource development in the Pacific Basin. President Garibay enthusiastically supported this, and thus began a sustained series of action-oriented seminars.

1.9 Triennial IX

In 1990, Dr. Rafael Cartagena, the former Chancellor of the San Juan campus of the Interamerican University of Puerto Rico and Secretary of Education in Puerto Rico, became IAUP president. Dr. Alvaro Romo de la Rosa continued as Secretary-General. Even though Dr. Cartagena's homeland is Puerto Rico, the University of Valladolid in Spain offered to host the IX Triennial Conference with an extended visit to the Universities of Salamanca & Leon. Dr. Maria Jose Crespo Allue, Vice Rector of the University of Valladolid, was the chair of the organizing committee.

The Triennial was a spectacular success. The theme was "The Challenge of the University Facing a New Century." The leadership of Dr. Cartagena was most notable for the promotion of the further internationalization of IAUP. He travelled tirelessly and worked to establish regional offices. Again, the 1990's are a continuum in the development of IAUP.

1.10 Triennial X

The 1993-96 leadership group was led by Dr. Kanichi Miyaji, then President of the University of the Air in Japan, and included Dr. Yukiyasu Harano, the Secretary-General of the Association of Independent Colleges and Universities of Japan as Secretary-General, and Dr. Alvaro Romo, then of the University of Houston, as Treasurer. Dr. Miyaji appointed two very able countrymen as Assistant Secretaries-General: Dr. Ichiro Tanioka and Dr. Mitsuaka Sukigara.

The Triennial X Conference in Kobe, Japan, in July of 1993 attracted 628 participants from 49 countries of the world, accomplished by a joint concerned effort between the 1993-96 officers and the 1996-99 officers-elect and their executive officers in their efforts to build leadership. The conference was a most substantial success measured by the breadth of attendance internationally and the substance of the program. The theme of the conference was "The Contribution of the University to a Global Society."

1.11 Triennial XI

The 1996 XIth Triennial Conference was in San Francisco. The theme of the conference was "Strengthening the Quality of Higher Education Through Technology." The membership conference participation was the greatest in number in the history of IAUP, again the result of a continued recruitment effort to presidents, chancellor, and rectors world-wide, along with the conference's substantive program.

Donald R. Gerth, President of California State University, Sacramento, became President of IAUP. Maurice Harari, emeritus from both the American Association of State Colleges and Universities and California State University, Long Beach, became Secretary-General; Robert G. Jones, Vice-President for University Affairs at California State University, Sacramento, became Treasurer. Additionally, Mr. Sven Caspersen, Rector of the University of Aalborg in Denmark, Mr. Josef Van der Perre, Secretary-General of the Flemish Association of Universities, and Dr. Michael Daxner, President of the University of Oldenburg in Germany were elected respectively to the President-elect, the Secretary General-elect, and Treasurer-elect positions.

2. The Organization

IAUP is a presidentially based organization, including vice chancellors, rectors, chancellors, principals, and university level chief-executives by various titles. Only a few non-presidents (or former presidents who are eligible, one of IAUP's strengths) are members. They are typically major officers of IAUP and others who have played key roles in the organization. Provisions for presidents, vice chancellors, and rectors have been created to continue their membership in IAUP either at a reduced rate from institutional members or as lifetime members with a one-time payment.

IAUP is governed by a set of three world-wide officers (president, secretary-general, and treasurer) and six vice-presidents, all of whom are elected. There are presently nine Regional Councils with chairs (Africa, Europe, Latin America, North America, North Asia, South Asia, South East Asia, South Pacific, and South West Asia/North Africa). Some of these regions have encouraged national chapters. The Executive Committee is the operating representative group between IAUP Triennial Conferences. The Executive Committee included all of the above mentioned officers, vice-president, and chairs as well as a number of individuals appointed by the president for her/his Triennial period to give international opinions and involvement and to provide world-wide leadership for various IAUP projects and activities.

Continuity is deliberately provided for. At each Triennial, the world-wide officers-elect are also chosen. In other words, at the 1996 Triennial the president-elect, secretary general-elect, and treasurer-elect were chosen for leadership from 1999 to 2002. The officers-elect serve on the Executive Committee, as do the immediate past officers.

For years, IAUP has published annually and sometimes the periodical *Lux Mundi*, a report of IAUP activities, as a bulletin for members and other interested individuals. IAUP has also published complete proceedings of triennial conferences. More recently, *Lux Mundi* has become a quarterly bulletin and newsletter submitted for mailing to all IAUP registered members. Condensed proceedings of the 1996 Triennial were published. A new series of publications, a set of policy statements, is now being published and can be found on the World Wide Web site by searching www.csus.edu/iaup/IAUP.PDF. The first two were published in 1996 and 1997 and addressed the internationalization of universities and technology and telecommunication.

In the 1987-90 triennium, then President Luis Garibay established a Council of Senior Advisors (CSA). The Council was to be composed of major world leaders, from the public and private sectors, who would bring support of all kinds, including material support to IAUP. Initial appointments were made and these continue. Former presidents of IAUP are included among the members. CSA members are included in all IAUP functions and are invited to Executive Committee meetings.

3. The Culture of Peace

As noted in earlier sections of this article, IAUP has had a major and consistent interest virtually from the founding in relationships of the universities of the world to the age long quest for peace. This was a consistent theme in all of the early triennial conferences, beginning with Dr. Young Seek Choue's presidency.

After Dr. Young Seek Choue left the IAUP presidency, he devoted his major IAUP work to the issue of peace. In the early eighties, IAUP petitioned the United Nations successfully for the creation of an International Day of Peace and an International Year of Peace. IAUP also endorsed and became a parent to the High Commission for Peace a group and set of activities devoted to every effort to bring about a greater level of peace in the world. Dr. Choue's university, Kyung Hee University, created a Graduate Institute of Peace Studies in 1984. Dr. Choue's contributions to world peace were recognized by UNESCO which awarded the Graduate Institute of Peace Institute the 1993 UNESCO Peace Prize for Education.

Dr. Leland Miles, another IAUP former president, devoted many years to the same issue. In 1989 he proposed a joint IAUP-United Nations effort. Members at the Triennial IX in Valladolid, Spain in 1990 unanimously approved a joint commission; thereafter the United Nations also approved. The IAUP/United Nations Commission on Disarmament Education was born. The first meeting of the Commission, at the United Nations in New York, was on June 12, 1991.

The Commission mandate was to assess the state of academic arms control and to find ways of advancing teaching and research in that field.

The Commission was no small undertaking. The first group was 160 persons, one-third on a Steering Committee, two-thirds corresponding, drawn from academic, diplomatic, governmental, military, and other professional communities, including journalism and law. This was by no means an IAUP solo work, and many of the academics were not from IAUP institutions. The Commission sponsored projects that included fundamental research and the development of curriculum, seminars around the world, programs at various IAUP meetings, and the 1993 and 1996 Triennials, and the like. The work of the Commission was funded by foundations, public sector agencies, and others. The Commission became the vehicle for the IAUP Non-Governmental Organization status and in 1993 was largely responsible for the designation of IAUP-as a category II NGO.

Dr. Miles had invited to join him as co-chair of the Commission Dr. L. Eudora Pettigrew, president of the State University of New York at Old Westbury. In 1995, Miles indicated to then President-elect Gerth that he, Miles, wished to step aside at the close of the 1996 Triennial. Gerth then indicated that he would ask Dr. Pettigrew to become Chair of the Commission for the 1996-99 triennium, and Dr. Pettigrew undertook an assessment of the work of the Commission. Any reasonable judgement about the work of the Commission from 1991 to 1996 would be concluded that the Commission was pioneering and productive. The activity was renamed the Commission on Disarmament Education, Peace, and Conflict Resolution at the 1996 Triennial. The Commission deliberately set out to bring more IAUP universities into its activity.

IAUP Triennial Conferences

I	1965	June 28-July 1	Oxford & Wroston, England
II	1968	June 18-20	Seoul, Korea
III	1971	June	Monrovia, Liberia
IV	1975	November 11-14	Boston, USA
V	1978	June 25-27	Teheran, Iran
VI	1981	June 28-July 3	San Jose, Costa Rica
VII	1984	July 16	Bangkok, Thailand
VIII	1987	June 21-26	Guadalajara & Mexico City, Mexico
IX	1990	July 8-14	Valladolid, Salamanca & Leon
X	1993	July 11-14	Kobe, Japan
XI	1996	July 14-17	San Francisco, USA
XII	1999	July 11-14	Brussels, Belgium

IAUP Roster of Presidents and Secretaries-General

Period	President	Secretary-General	Treasurer
1964-68	Dr. Peter Sammartino	Not Designated	
1968-71	Dr. Peter Sammartino	Not Designated	
1971-75	Dr. Young Seek Choue	Dr. Won Sul Lee	
1975-78	Dr. Young Seek Choue	Dr. Won Sul Lee	
1978-81	Dr. Young Seek Choue	Dr. Won Sul Lee	
1981-84	Dr. Leland Miles	Dr. William Allen	
1984-87	Dr. Nibondh Sasidhorn	Dr. Charoen Khantawongs	
1987-90	Dr. Luis Garibay	Dr. Alvaro Romo de la Rosa	
1990-93	Dr. Rafael Cartagena	Dr. Alvaro Romo de la Rosa	
1993-96	Dr. Kan Ichi Miyaji	Dr. Yukiyasu Harano	Dr. Alvaro Romo
1996-99	Dr. Donald R. Gerth	Dr. Maurice Harari	Mr. Robert Jones
1999-2002	Mr. Sven Caspersen	Mr. Jef Van der Perre	Dr. Michael Daxner

4. A Diversifying Organization

IAUP was in its early years an organization which provided an arena for presidents to meet and work together. The emphasis was not on program, save for the peace related activities. The 1987-90 triennium marked the beginning of a change, to an organization with a programmatic thrust, albeit still an organization providing an arena sometimes the arena for presidents to meet and work together.

The first move was made at the 1989 Executive Committee meeting in Tokyo with the approval of the seminar series "Higher Education and Human Resource Development in the Pacific Basin." These conferences began in Sacramento, California in 1991 with the sixth conference to be in Australia in April of 1998. These seminar-conferences have been highly productive of practical steps and increasingly well attended. Earlier in this article these were more thoroughly described.

A small IAUP task force with the leadership of Secretary-General Maurice Harari put together a major paper on internationalizing universities and curricula. This has now been published as a first major policy statement.

In 1997 a second major policy statement on telecommunications and technology was published. The international group was headed by Dr. Edward Walsh of Limerick University in Ireland and the documents created by Dr. Spencer have worldwide impact as universities everywhere implement approaches to technology and linkages among universities made possible by technology. The 1996 Triennial XI program had as a consistent sub-theme the matter of university linkages through technology.

New initiatives launched at the 1996 Triennial further extended the process of diversification. The new IAUP leadership proposed a worldwide series of business and higher education forums modelled on successful such efforts in a number of countries. It is intended to bring together business and university leaders not only in the advanced industrialized nations but also in all nations to the end of establishing cooperation and support.

In South America, a major IAUP undertaking, with the leadership of Dr. Ricardo Popovsky, has been a collaborative effort among university leaders to address accreditation issues. A regional conference was held in Buenos Aires in May of 1997.

Working relationships with international organizations have received significant attention from IAUP in recent years. Reference has already been made to United Nations NGO status and the joint IAUP/United Nations Commission.

In 1994-95, a second IAUP/United Nations joint project was developed. This was a proposal for a joint commission to address socio-economic development capacity in universities in 22 selected countries, with 22 pairs of universities, each pair including one university in a developing nation where the university wanted to build a capacity to address socio-economic development and one university which already had such a capacity. The project was approved by the then Secretary General of the United Nations, but subsequently delayed in the transition to a new Secretary General.

IAUP leaders, as long as 1989, sought to establish a relationship with UNESCO. Complex discussions were initiated and finally a formal application was made for NGO status. With little progress of the matter, then President-elect Donald R. Gerth visited UNESCO headquarters in December of 1993 to solve issues in the way by meeting with senior staff in the higher education unit and it was effective. Since then, good relationship with UNESCO has remained.

In early 1996, the Director General asked to be the keynote speaker at the Triennial XI Conference, and he was warmly welcomed. Subsequently, Dr. Donald Gerth and the UNESCO leadership (with a small number of other world figures in higher education) are working together on the UNESCO 1998 World Conference on Higher Education. IAUP is working aggressively in two areas at this time. The first is program. The scope of IAUP activity has been widened greatly to cover issues and areas of university leadership responsibility worldwide, being extended to such topics as economic development, access, financing, and globalization. The second is an open door policy of its membership. The object of building membership in IAUP is to be inclusive of the university leaders of all countries and cultures. Universities are the backbone of a country's strength. The pattern of membership which IAUP seeks is to be a reflection of this developing strength.

5. IAUP Issues

In any organization, perhaps especially in any international organization, building membership needs attention. In past years, IAUP membership has been fluid. Many "members" did not pay dues. Some could not; others who could did not. In a very real sense, the IAUP membership base was not firm. In the mid-1990s, a determined effort was made to make firm the IAUP membership base. Members were defined as individuals who paid dues. Provision was made for a limited number of fellows, individual presidents who did not have access to hard currency or sometimes any funding for IAUP and others activity; this was achieved specifically to support fellowship members through private donors.

This approach has worked. Members pay dues. At the same time, a concerted effort has been made through membership campaigns and other means to bring in presidents of accredited and recognized university-level institutions. Dr. Fred Young, membership Chair for 1996-99, has announced his goal: "1000 by 2000."

This leads directly to the matter of stabilizing and institutionalizing IAUP. The organization is maturing. In the 1993-96 triennium, the secretary general-elect and the president-elect presented a paper in several drafts over a two-year period on the stabilization of IAUP. The paper called for the eventual establishment of an endowment fund and the creation of a small permanent office, possibly at the United Nations headquarters in New York.

The IAUP has been moving firmly in the recent years to an organization that has a program that is responsive to its members. In the 1960s, university presidents may have needed an arena in which to meet. In the 1990s and in the next century, university presidents need ways and mechanisms for collaboration and cooperation among themselves and with other sectors of society internationally. IAUP has been that place and provides those mechanisms.

Serious students and leaders of higher education are discovering that universities now work in a global marketplace. This marketplace can be either the arena for new and unheard of positive collaboration, or a level of competition and unhealthy behaviour that will eventually be self-destructive and certainly will not contribute to peace and progress.

In a very real sense, IAUP has the opportunity to bring about a measure of collaboration that will help lead to peace and to economic development and to decent and humane cultural and civic values. This is the opportunity of IAUP.

See also: *International Day of Peace and International Year of Peace; Year of Peace (1986): Initiation, Promulgation and Commemoration*

DONALD GERTH

International Bill of Human Rights

At the United Nations Conference on International Organization that convened in 1945 to draft the UN Charter, it was already proposed that the Charter should embody a Declaration on the Essential Rights of Man (see *Declaration of the Rights of Man*). When the first UN General Assembly opened in London in 1946 a draft for such a Declaration was transmitted to the new Commission on Human Rights which, in 1947, began to formulate an International Bill of Human Rights that would include, respectively, a Declaration, a Convention to be known as a Covenant, and measures for implementing the latter.

The Universal Declaration of Human Rights was duly completed, and finally proclaimed on December 10, 1948. Its worldwide influence, relying, like the Charter itself, on moral force as a statement to be subscribed to by every member state, has been enormous. Adopted by fifty-one states without a dissenting vote, its entry into force was a truly historic achievement. Its provisions have been incorporated or reflected in many of the newer national constitutions, and it has formed a basis for all subsequent work on human rights as well as a yardstick by which to appraise their observance throughout the world.

The Declaration (reproduced in full at the end of this article) comprises four groups of articles, of which the first group, 1 to 3, sets out those basic conditions on which human rights depend. Articles 4 to 21 embrace a wide range of civil and political rights, and Articles 22 to 27 concentrate on those economic, social, and cultural rights whose full enjoyment depends upon the state's available resources, as well as on national effort and a degree of international harmony. The remaining three articles recognize everyone's entitlement to a social and international order in which the forgoing rights can be realized. They also define an individual's duties to the community and state how far any rights enumerated may be limited by a need to secure recognition and respect for the rights of others.

In the ensuing years work continued on the next stage in erecting an International Bill of Human Rights. In place of the single binding Covenant that had been foreseen, the Human Rights Commission found it necessary to draft two such covenants, to cover respectively civil and political rights and economic, social and cultural rights. To a large extent this undertaking sought to transform the principles of the Universal Declaration into definite treaty provisions establishing legal obligations on any ratifying state. That task occupied the Commission and the General Assembly's Third Committee for the next eighteen years, so that the two Covenants, plus an Optional Protocol on Civil and Political Rights, were finally adopted by the General Assembly on December 18, 1966, although they did not enter into force until early 1976, nearly 10 years later.

While the Universal Declaration proclaimed those principles of humane conduct that follow from the essential nature and social situation of human beings, the covenants are designed to translate those same principles into a series of basic policy statements mandatory for the guidance of any ratifying state. The preamble is common to both covenants, as is part I of each, which contains certain new ideas not included in the Declaration. These are, first, that states party to the covenants, including those responsible for dependent or trust territories, shall promote respect for, and realization of, the right to self-determination which all peoples have, and by virtue of which they freely determine their political status and pursue economic, social, and cultural development. Secondly, that all peoples may freely dispose of their natural wealth and resources without prejudice to any obligations arising out of international cooperation and international law. In no case may a people be deprived of its own means of subsistence. These ideas have subsequently been developed further in a number of other international instruments adopted or under study by the UN, including a Charter of the Economic Rights and Duties of States (1974) and a Declaration on the Right to Development (1986).

Part II of each covenant includes four articles which state the principles underlying a ratifying state's undertakings and the extent to which any rights distinguished can be derogated in particular circumstances. The rights themselves are set out in Part III of each covenant.

With a few secondary modifications the substantive parts of each covenant are those of the Universal Declaration, but they are often considerably elaborated as well as being couched in a form appropriate to the requirements of states, since it is states that accede to the covenants. Thus Article 14 of the Covenant on Civil and Political Rights runs to more than a page, as compared to under four lines in the Declaration. The same is true of Article 13 in the Covenant on Economic, Social, and Cultural Rights, which deals with education.

Part IV of each covenant sets out the procedure under which states undertake to report on progress made and measures they have adopted to secure observance of the rights in question. For the Covenant on Economic, Social, and Cultural Rights reports on performance are submitted to, and evaluated periodically by, a Committee on that subject. For the Covenant on Civil and Political Rights, party states undertake to furnish reports as requested to a Human Rights Committee. In turn, both Committees prepare an annual statement for ECOSOC and the UN General Assembly. The remainder of each covenant deals with procedural matters, except in the case of the Covenant on Civil and Political Rights, which incorporates two further refinements. First, under optional provisions of that Covenant's Article 41, the Human Rights Committee may consider communications from any ratifying state alleging that another ratifying state is not fulfilling its obligations under the Covenant.

A second important instrument that completes the International Bill of Human Rights is an Optional Protocol which accompanies the Civil and Political Covenant. This allows the Human Rights Committee to consider communications from private individuals who have "exhausted all available domestic remedies" and who claim to suffer from a violation, by a state party to the Protocol, of any right defined in the Covenant. The Committee's findings are communicated to the state concerned. A further Optional Protocol deals with abolition of the death penalty.

There is little question that the two International Covenants and the Optional Protocols have had a fundamental effect in serving to spread the acceptance of a global frame of human rights and duties throughout the world community, and hence to create conditions for a peaceful world. This is because they serve as explicit guides to states on how to fulfil the letter and spirit of the Universal Declaration of Human Rights. So far their influence on the working of national legal systems is grossly insufficient, though it should increase as true development proceeds and also as the number of ratifications increases. By July 1992 the number of ratifications or accessions to the two Covenants was one hundred and thirteen for the Covenant on Civil and Political Rights and one hundred and fourteen for that on Economic, Social and Cultural Rights—over sixty per cent of the present number of member states. The Optional Protocol to the former had been ratified by sixty-seven states and a second Optional Protocol on the death penalty by thirteen states.

Further measures are still needed in practice to create conditions for proper human rights observance, as well as further binding international instruments. It is also true that a lack of strong standing machinery is still as much of a handicap in the human rights field as it is in the prevention of armed conflict (see *Global Ethics, Human Rights Laws and Democratic Governance*).

Universal Declaration of Human Rights
Adopted and proclaimed by General Assembly Resolution 217 A (III) of 10 December 1948

PREAMBLE

Whereas recognition of the inherent dignity and of the equal and inalienable rights of all members of the human family is the foundation of freedom, justice and peace in the world,

Whereas disregard and contempt for human rights have resulted in barbarous acts which have outraged the conscience of mankind, and the advent of a world in which human beings shall enjoy freedom of speech and belief and freedom from fear and want has been proclaimed as the highest aspiration of the common people,

Whereas it is essential, if man is not to be compelled to have recourse, as a last resort, to rebellion against tyranny and oppression, that human rights should be protected by the rule of law,

Whereas it is essential to promote the development of friendly relations between nations,

Whereas the peoples of the United Nations have in the Charter reaffirmed their faith in fundamental human rights, in the dignity and worth of the human person and in the equal rights of men and women and have determined to promote social progress and better standards of life in larger freedom,

Whereas Member States have pledged themselves to achieve, in co-operation with the United Nations, the promotion of universal respect for and observance of human rights and fundamental freedoms,

Whereas a common understanding of these rights and freedoms is of the greatest importance for the full realization of this pledge,

Now, therefore,

The General Assembly

Proclaims this Universal Declaration of Human Rights as a common standard of achievement for all peoples and all nations, to the end that every individual and every organ of society, keeping this Declaration constantly in mind, shall strive by teaching and education to promote respect for these rights and freedoms and by progressive measures, national and international, to secure their universal and effective recognition and observance, both among the peoples of Member States themselves and among the peoples of territories under this jurisdiction.

Article 1

All human beings are born free and equal in dignity and rights. They are endowed with reason and conscience and should act towards one another in a spirit of brotherhood.

Article 2

Everyone is entitled to all the rights and freedoms set forth in this Declaration, without distinction of any kind, such as race, colour, sex, language, religion, political or other opinion, national or social origin, property, birth or other status.

Furthermore, no distinction shall be made on the basis of the political, jurisdictional or international status of the country or territory to which a person belongs, whether it be independent, trust, non-self-governing or under any other limitation of sovereignty.

Article 3

Everyone has the right to life, liberty and security of person.

Article 4

No one shall be held in slavery or servitude; slavery and the slave trade shall be prohibited in all their forms.

Article 5

No one shall be subjected to torture or to cruel, inhuman or degrading treatment or punishment.

Article 6

Everyone has the right to recognition everywhere as a person before the law.

Article 7

All are equal before the law and are entitled without any discrimination to equal protection of the law. All are entitled to equal protection against any discrimination in violation of this Declaration and against any incitement to such discrimination.

Article 8

Everyone has the right to an effective remedy by the competent national tribunals for acts violating the fundamental rights granted him by the constitution or by law.

Article 9

No one shall be subjected to arbitrary arrest, detention or exile.

Article 10

Everyone is entitled in full equality to a fair and public hearing by an independent and impartial tribunal, in the determination of his rights and obligations and of any criminal charge against him.

Article 11

1. Everyone charged with a penal offence has the right to be presumed innocent until proved guilty according to law in a public trial at which he has had all the guarantees necessary for his defence.

2. No one shall be held guilty of any penal offence on account of any act or omission which did not constitute a penal offence, under national or international law, at the time when it was committed. Nor shall a heavier penalty be imposed than the one that was applicable at the time the penal offence was committed.

Article 12

No one shall be subjected to arbitrary interference with his privacy, family, home or correspondence, nor to attacks upon his honour and reputation. Everyone has the right to the protection of the law against such interference or attacks.

Article 13

1. Everyone has the right to freedom of movement and residence within the borders of each State.

2. Everyone has the right to leave any country, including his own, and to return to his country.

Article 14

1. Everyone has the right to seek and to enjoy in other countries asylum from persecution.

2. This right may not be invoked in the case of prosecutions genuinely arising from non-political crimes or from acts contrary to the purposes and principles of the United Nations.

Article 15

1. Everyone has the right to a nationality.

2. No one shall be arbitrarily deprived of his nationality nor denied the right to change his nationality.

Article 16

1. Men and women of full age, without any limitation due to race, nationality or religion, have the right to marry and to found a family. They are entitled to equal rights as to marriage, during marriage and at its dissolution.

2. Marriage shall be entered into only with the free and full consent of the intending spouses.

3. The family is the natural and fundamental group unit of society and is entitled to protection by society and the State.

Article 17

1. Everyone has the right to own property alone as well as in association with others.

2. No one shall be arbitrarily deprived of his property.

Article 18

Everyone has the right to freedom of thought, conscience and religion; this right includes freedom to change his religion or belief, and freedom, either alone or in community with others and in public or private, to manifest his religion or belief in teaching, practice, worship and observance.

Article 19

Everyone has the right to freedom of opinion and expression; this right includes freedom to hold opinions without interference and to seek, receive and impart information and ideas through any media and regardless of frontiers.

Article 20

1. Everyone has the right to freedom of peaceful assembly and association.

2. No one may be compelled to belong to an association.

Article 21

1. Everyone has the right to take part in the government of his country, directly or through freely chosen representatives.

2. Everyone has the right of equal access to public service in his country.

3. The will of the people shall be the basis of the authority of government; this will shall be expressed in periodic and genuine elections which shall be by universal and equal suffrage and shall be held by secret vote or by equivalent free voting procedures.

Article 22

Everyone, as a member of society, has the right to social security and is entitled to realization, through national effort and international co-operation and in accordance with the organization and resources of each State, of the economic, social and cultural rights indispensable for his dignity and the free development of his personality.

Article 23

1. Everyone has the right to work, to free choice of employment, to just and favourable conditions of work and to protection against unemployment.

2. Everyone, without any discrimination, has the right to equal pay for equal work.

3. Everyone who works has the right to just and favourable remuneration ensuring for himself and his family an existence worthy of human dignity, and supplemented, if necessary, by other means of social protection.

4. Everyone has the right to form and to join trade unions for the protection of his interests.

Article 24

Everyone has the right to rest and leisure, including reasonable limitation of working hours and periodic holidays with pay.

Article 25

1. Everyone has the right to a standard of living adequate for the health and well-being of himself and of his family, including food, clothing, housing and medical care and necessary social services, and the right to security in the event of unemployment, sickness, disability, widowhood, old age or other lack of livelihood in circumstances beyond his control.

2. Motherhood and childhood are entitled to special care and assistance. All children, whether born in or out of wedlock, shall enjoy the same social protection.

Article 26

1. Everyone has the right to education. Education shall be free, at least in the elementary and fundamen-
tal stages. Elementary education shall be compulsory. Technical and professional education shall be made generally available and higher education shall be equally accessible to all on the basis of merit.

2. Education shall be directed to the full development of the human personality and to the strengthening of respect for human rights and fundamental freedoms. It shall promote understanding, tolerance and friendship among all nations, racial or religious groups, and shall further the activities of the United Nations for the maintenance of peace.

3. Parents have a prior right to choose the kind of education that shall be given to their children.

Article 27

1. Everyone has the right freely to participate in the cultural life of the community, to enjoy the arts and to share in scientific advancement and its benefits.

2. Everyone has the right to the protection of the moral and material interests resulting from any scientific, literary or artistic production of which he is the author.

Article 28

Everyone is entitled to a social and international order in which the rights and freedoms set forth in this Declaration can be fully realized.

Article 29

1. Everyone has duties to the community in which alone the free and full development of his personality is possible.

2. In the exercise of his rights and freedoms, everyone shall be subject only to such limitations as are determined by law solely for the purpose of securing due recognition and respect for the rights and freedoms of others and of meeting the just requirements of morality, public order and the general welfare in a democratic society.

3. These rights and freedoms may in no case be exercised contrary to the purposes and principles of the United Nations.

Article 30

Nothing in this Declaration may be interpreted as implying for any State, group or person any right to engage in any activity or to perform any act aimed at the destruction of any of the rights and freedoms set forth herein.

See also: *Human Rights and Peace; Human Rights and Environmental Rights: Their Sustainable Development Compatibility*

Bibliography ————————————————————

Brownlie I 1981 *Basic Documents on Human Rights*, 2nd edn. Oxford University Press, Oxford

Cranston M 1973 *What are Human Rights?* Bodley Head, London

Dilloway A J 1983 *Human Rights and World Order*. H.G. Wells Society, London

Dilloway A J 1986 *Is World Order Evolving? An Adventure into Human Potential*. Pergamon, Oxford

Donnelly J 1985 *The Concept of Human Rights*. Croom Helm, London

United Nations 1994 *Human Rights: A Compilation of International Instruments*. United Nations, New York

United Nations 1988 *The United Nations and Human Rights*. United Nations, New York

JAMES DILLOWAY

International City

The term international city is generally used to describe a city, or port, which, alone with its environs, has been placed under the sovereignty, the effective control, or the protection of a group of states. In this sense it is but one form of what might otherwise be designated an "internationalized territory." Such entities have varied considerably in their nature and in their origins. They have been established both as a means of protecting the interests and privileges of minorities, and because the cities in question have had some peculiar cultural, economic, or strategic significance which has disallowed them from being possessed by any one power. International regimes have also been imposed on cities when sovereignty over them has been disputed, during periods of military occupation, and when it has been necessary to set up a temporary administration pending the settlement of a conflict.

One of the earliest example of an international city is that of Cracow. The free city, or republic, of Cracow was a product of the Vienna settlement of 1815, and its establishment along with that of the so called "Congress Kingdom" of Poland, which formed part of the dominions of the Russian emperor, gave some recognition to the continued existence of a Polish nation. It was endowed with a liberal constitution, and its three Great Power neighbors, Austria, Prussia, and Russia, each of which had shared in previous partitions of Poland, supervised its political development and guaranteed its independence and neutrality. This left the citizens of Cracow and its surrounding territory with the freedom to manage their own internal affairs. But insurrections in congress Poland during 1830 and 1831 led the Russians to send an army into Cracow in pursuit of Polish revolutionaries, and the danger of the city becoming a center for Polish irredentism caused the protecting powers to meddle in the administration of the republic. Then in 1846 troubles amongst the Polish population of Galicia provided the Austrians with an excuse to eliminate the troublesome free city, and with the consent of Prussia and Russia, Cracow was merged with the other lands of the Habsburg monarchy.

Cracow's fate was engineered by its guarantors, who had come to regard its independence as a menace to their security. But in the 1840s a very different form of international administration, whose purpose was to safeguard the interests of the United States and the imperial powers of Europe, was evolving in the Far East. The international settlement of Shanghai owed its existence to treaties imposed upon China, in the first instance by Britain, France and the United States, which granted to those powers "concessions" in various Chinese cities. These were originally conceived of as areas in which European traders could settle and enjoy extraterritorial privileges under the jurisdiction and protection of their consuls. Mutual jealousy amongst the powers prevented the important port of Shanghai from becoming the concession of any single state, and the amalgamation in 1866 of the US and British concessions there brought formally into existence the international settlement. Although it remained in theory under Chinese sovereignty, its municipal council, which was composed of representatives of the foreign residents, came in time to exercise a large degree of local autonomy. Indeed, so weak was the Chinese central government that in 1899 it was compelled to accept a trebling in the size of the settlement's territory, and the disorders which followed the revolution of 1911 allowed the authorities at Shanghai to arrogate further powers to themselves. The settlement also survived the demands made by Chinese nationalists in the aftermath of the First World War for the abolition of foreign concessions. The Sino-Japanese conflicts of the 1930s had, however, a destablizing effect upon the region, and the municipal council ceased to function when, following the bombardment of Pearl Harbor, Japan's forces extended their occupation of the settlement. One year later, in January 1943, the British and US governments negotiated an agreement with the nationalist government of Chiang K'ai-shek by which they gave up their extraterritorial rights. Their example was followed by other countries after the conclusion of the Second World War, and the international settlement came to an end as a political institution.

A parallel has been drawn between the situation at Shanghai and the international city, or zone, of Tangier. Both resulted from engagements which local rulers were forced to accept, and both were examples of the institutionalization of extraterritorial privileges. But the creation of the international city of Tangier was also intimately connected with the division of Morocco into French and Spanish protectorates. That partition was foreseen in 1904 when the British government, with a view to preventing the establishment of another major naval power on the coast opposite to Gibraltar, agreed to give its diplomatic support to France's ambitions in Morocco, only on condition that the Mediterranean littoral of the country should form part of a Spanish sphere of influence. But in subsequent negotiations between Paris and Madrid the French insisted that Tangier should retain the special character given to it by the presence of the diplomatic corps and its internationally controlled municipal and sanitary institutions. In London it was assumed that this would mean the internationalization of Tangier, and when after two major international crises over Morocco in 1905 and 1911, the French and Spaniards proceeded to establish their protectorates, the British required agreement on a constitution for the city which would not allow France, as the principal protector of the Sultan, to become predominant there. The issue generated a good deal of friction between Britain and France both before and after the First World War, and it was November 1923 before they reached agreement on the form of an international administration that would take over the running of the city. This provided for a legislative assembly composed of representatives of the native and foreign communities of Tangier, under the presidency of a delegate of the Sultan, and for an administration which would carry out the decisions of the assembly.

The constitution, which the Sultan promulgated in February 1924, was to remain in force throughout the interwar years. But the military defeat of France in the spring of 1940 allowed the Spaniards, who had long hoped that Tangier would eventually be included in their zone of Morocco, the opportunity to send their troops into Tangier on the pretext of defending its neutrality. Their occupation of the city lasted barely five years, and at the end of the Second World War a provisional international administration was established which enabled both the United States and the then Soviet Union to participate in the work of the city's committee of control. Finally, the French decision to grant full independence to Morocco in 1956 led to a dissolution of the two protectorates, and a dismantling of the international administration at Tangier.

The internationalization of Cracow, Shanghai, and Tangier was in each case effected by agreements and understandings amongst several states. No international organization as such was involved. But when at the Paris peace conference of 1919 the victorious Allies decided to remove the Baltic port of Danzig from German sovereignty, and to transform it into a free city, it was also agreed that it should have the protection of the newly founded League of Nations. The free city's constitution was to be drafted by its representatives in agreement with a high commissioner appointed by the League, and it was to be placed under the League's guarantee. Differences arising over the provisions of the Versailles Treaty were to be resolved by the high commissioner, and ultimately by the League itself. Danzig's status was, however, complicated by the requirements of the peace treaty that an agreement be negotiated between the free city and Poland which would include Danzig in a Polish customs union, ensure to the Poles the free use of the port, and provide Poland with the responsibility for conducting the foreign relations of the city.

The purpose of these arrangements was to reconcile the claim of the recently resurrected Polish republic that Danzig was vital to its economy, with the rights of the city's largely German population to national self-determination. The Danzigers were thus separated from Germany, but unlike the inhabitants of the rest of West Prussia they were not included in Poland. Unfortunately, the compromise worked out at Paris gave little satisfaction to either the citizens of the free city or the government in Warsaw, which did its best to restrict Danzig's autonomy. As a result there was a long series of legal wrangles between the Polish authorities and the Danzig senate, in which the League frequently had to arbitrate. The situation was not eased by the prevailing uncertainty about where sovereignty over Danzig was vested. And the natural reluctance of governments of Weimar Germany to accept as permanent the territorial requirements of the Versailles *Diktat* appeared only to strengthen

Poland's resolve to defend its rights. Matters were, however, to change after the accession of Hitler to power in Germany in January 1933. Although subsequent elections in Danzig gave the National Socialists a majority in the city's legislative assembly (*Volkstag*), Hitler, who wished to separate the Poles from their French allies, adopted a conciliatory approach towards Warsaw, and the Danzig senate was encouraged to pursue a similar line. In the meanwhile neither the League nor its high commissioner were capable of defending the constitutional liberties of those Danzigers who opposed the Nazis.

The free city finally disappeared in September 1939 when, following the refusal of Poles to accept Hitler's proposals for frontier rectifications and the restoration of Danzig to the German Reich, German forces invaded Poland. At the end of the Second World War most of the German population of the city fled to the West, and Danzig, like other parts of Germany lying to the east of the Oder-Neisse line was colonized by Poles. Since then it has been administered as part of Poland, and has become more generally known in the English-speaking world by its Polish name of Gdansk.

One other German city for which an international solution was envisaged was Memel, the most northerly port of East Prussia. In order to provide the new Lithuanian republic with secure access to the sea, Germany was required by the Versailles Treaty to cede the port to the Allied powers. They, in their turn, examined the possibility of setting up an international administration under the auspices of the League. But in January 1923, before any decision had been reached, the Lithuanians, who had themselves become victims of Polish aggression, dispatched troops to Memel, compelled the French garrison there to surrender, and established their own administration. The city was granted a degree of local autonomy, which afforded some protection to its German population, but Lithuania's sovereignty over Memel was recognized by the League, and plans for its internationalization were dropped. A similar fate awaited the former Hungarian port of Fiume. Its mixed population of Italians and Croats permitted both Italy and Yugoslavia to put forward claims to it at the end of the First World War, and internationalization was suggested as a solution to the dispute. However, after only a brief period during which Fiume functioned as an independent city-state, Mussolini cajoled the government in Belgrade into accepting a settlement which involved Italy's acquisition of the city itself, and the cession of its hinterland to Yugoslavia.

Italy's defeat in the Second World War enabled the Yugoslavs to secure from the Italians not only Fiume, but also the Istrian peninsula. This gave rise to a quarrel over the future of Trieste which bore a marked resemblance to the previous squabble over Fiume. Again the territory in question contained an urban population which was in large part Italian, and a rural and suburban population which was of Slavonic origin. Once more internationalization was proposed as a solution, and by the Italian peace settlement of 1947 it was agreed that Trieste should be a free city with its independence and integrity guaranteed by the security council of the United Nations. But the Yugoslavs continued to hope that they would eventually acquire the port, and differences within the United Nations, especially over the appointment of a governor, delayed the establishment of a free city. In the end, after seven years during which British and US forces occupied the center of the city and the harbor, and Yugoslav forces occupied the environs, the decision was taken to divide the administration between Italy and Yugoslavia.

Even after it had become apparent that there were many obstacles in the way of converting Trieste into a free city, the idea of internationalization continued to find favor in the United Nations. Thus in its endeavor to settle the problem of Palestine the United Nations resolved in November 1947 that Jerusalem should become an international city under the direct control of the organization's trusteeship council. A statute was drafted to serve this purpose. But the outbreak of the Arab-Israeli war in 1948 made impossible its application, and Jerusalem, like Trieste, was for the time being partitioned rather than internationalized.

The latest example of what could be termed as an international city had been the then West Berlin. At the end of the Second World War the German capital, along with its environs, was occupied by British, French, Soviet, and US forces, and it was placed under an inter-Allied governing authority. But the onset of the Cold War impeded further cooperation between the former allies, and by 1948 the collective operation of this body had ceased. Moreover, whilst the United Kingdom, France and the United States have continued to claim the right to exercise supreme authority over their sectors of the city within the framework of four-power responsibility, they have entrusted the normal diplomatic relations of West Berlin to the former Federal Republic of Germany. Moreover, the German Democratic Republic regards the Soviet sector of East Berlin as an integral part of its territory. The result of these developments has been the de facto partition of Berlin, with the Western sectors functioning as though they were extraterritorial to the Federal Republic, but under the sovereignty and protection of the occupying powers. Ironically, what were once conceived of as temporary arrangements designed to meet the requirements of a city under military administration have seemed to become a permanent feature of the political map of Europe. West Berlin might indeed prove to be one of the most durable of the international cities.

It should be evident from this brief survey that the term international city can be applied to a variety of political structures. The only common feature of the cities listed here is that each of them has been subject to some degree of international protection and control. Because of this it is difficult to generalize about the advantages and disadvantages of such regimes. Two of those which have endured the longest, the Shanghai settlement and Tangier, belonged to an age of imperialism during which Asian and African potentates were compelled to yield to the will of the United States and the European powers. West Berlin, in so far as it may be regarded as an international city, is a unique by-product of the Cold War and the division of Germany. The internationalization of cities has in any case been more often proposed than imposed in the twentieth century. It has been obstructed by an absence of consensus on the part of the guaranteeing and protecting powers, and prevent-

ed by the military intervention of neighboring states. Even when fully constituted an international city may, as in the case of Danzig, prove to be more of a source of conflict than a solution to a dispute. Internationalization can offer the prospect of a just compromise. It provides no certainty of prolonged peace.

Bibliography ——————————————————

Crawford J 1979 *The Creation of States in International Law.* Oxford University Press, Oxford

Kimmich C M 1968 *The Free City, Danzig and German Foreign Policy, 1919-1934.* Yale University Press, New Haven, Connecticut

Levine H S 1970 *Hitler's Free City: A History of the Nazi Party in Danzig, 1925-39.* University of Chicago Press, Chicago, Illinois

Novak B C 1970 *Trieste, 1951-1954: The Ethnic, Political, and Ideological Struggle.* University of Chicago Press, Chicago, Illinois

Rusinow D I 1969 *Italy's Austrian Heritage, 1919-1946.* Oxford University Press, Oxford

Stuart G H 1955 *The International City of Tangier.* Stanford University Press, Stanford, California

Ydit M 1961 *Internationalised Territories: From the "Free City of Cracow" to the "Free City of Berlin."* Sijthoff, Leyden

KEITH HAMILTON

International Conflicts and Equilibria

The notions of equilibrium and international conflict are at the center of many discussions in the social sciences today. A glance at each epistemological and scientific transition of contemporary culture (relative to the concept of systems, limits, predictions, games, etc.) can be useful in redefining the very concepts of equilibrium and conflict. A brief historical *excursus* can help us to place and better understand the nature of modern problems.

The ways in which a particular society tackles the problem of differences among its members—economic, material, and cultural, of status or prestige, racial or religious—are extremely revealing of the direction of its reproductive mechanisms. Most societies in the course of human history—most "primitive" and peasant societies—were characterized by the ratification of necessity and by the "naturality" of spatial, temporal, economic, material, and symbolic boundaries in which a particular form of life was achieved. In this logic, every good—whether materi-

al or nonmaterial—was thought to be available in a fixed or established quantity once and for all. The acquisition of a good by one member of a society was equal to the loss of this good by another member. The differences among the members were disciplined by a "grammatical" hierarchy, and hence the society can be represented in the form of a huge zero-sum game. This "grammar" generated innumerable structures and mechanisms for the maintenance of these societies. Such structures and mechanisms were, for example, the compulsory gifts, such as the potlatch, which tended to reestablish symbolically an order shattered by the sudden enrichment of a member; or the figure of the scapegoat which upheld the differences between members of a society by extolling the difference.

Modern tradition constitutes a context for the discussion of necessity and of the naturality of "limit." With the ideas of "progress" and "the future" came the concept of the open system. In such a system, society cannot be represented in terms of a zero-sum game: gain for one member of society does not necessarily correspond to a loss for another member of that society. From this perspective, the breakdown of spatial-temporal boundaries of the medieval cosmos, the great geographical discoveries, the growth of social mobility, the creation of the free market, and the invention of science based on observation and experimentation were all essential processes in the production of modern Western societies. If the existence of differences is a necessary condition to the operation—indeed to the existence itself—of every type of society, the nature of concrete differences becomes contingent, changeable, fickle. This has explosive effects. Having forever lost the "natural" allotted place from which to order his or her experience in the cosmos, the individual (every individual) continually seeks a new context for his or her experiences. The potential for conflicts between individuals and between humankind and nature are multiplied. For its own correct operation, the strategy of modernity necessarily assumes and requires the existence of open spaces (material *and* symbolic) and hence of an abundance of reserves in which to locate these quests. Nevertheless, situations of contraction and scarcity continue to occur, determined each time by the specific limits of the particular society. Modernity has recurrently undergone this conflict between the systemic necessity of expansion and the objective situation of contraction. In dealing with this conflict it has produced certain regulating ideals that have been presented repeatedly as nonhistorical and atemporal necessities, and as the keystone for control and dominion of history and society. Significant mechanisms in these attempts at dominion and control have included scientism, the idea of a *dernière science*, the demon of Laplace, the *Panopticon* of Bentham, the invisible hand of economists, and above all the image of the evolutive and historical course centralized around the ideas of Progress and Prediction.

Societies and cultural traditions of the modern age have formed themselves by long processes of decentralization, never really completed. Of these, the most evident is the one that has produced a progressive broadening of the notion of society, and a consequent retreat of the frontier of this society, so that what is considered external environment is constantly diminishing. From ethnic groups humankind has passed to a planetary society, via nationhood and the integration of relatively homogeneous continental areas. The passage from a zero-sum game to a game which tries to guarantee benefits to a greater number of players (or, optimally, to all players), that is, a

non-zero-sum game or a win-win solution, is an important decentralization. It is a decentralization that leads from a knowledge of well-balanced action on the level of the real to a well-balanced idea on the level of the possible. Many of the key notions of modern culture have in themselves the traces of these decentralizations, whether in the latest results that they contain or, obversely, in the persistence of ancient strategies, rooted in the dawn of humanity. One of these key notions is that of international equilibrium (regional, continental, or worldwide according to historical periods or circumstances).

The genesis and development of such a notion can certainly tell us much about these processes of decentralization. For the purpose of this article, however, it will be examined as an already adult notion in the features that it developed in the course of the nineteenth century (beginning with the Congress of Vienna, 1814-15). The international equilibrium, the balance of power (among "Great Powers") appeared then as a regulating ideal of politics and of the relations among nations, like necessity and the changeable independence by which all the concrete strategies of action are disciplined. As such, it was located at a very precise stage in the process of decentralization. In the notion of international equilibrium was recognized the idea of a system in which powers, with symmetrical and interacting partners were, in some way, part of a community larger than that which the laws were laid down for, and in which behaviors were disciplined. On the other hand, it also recognized the right of all partners not only to survive, but if possible, to expand and win. But at whose expense? Certainly not at the expense of the vital interests of another Great Power, or of another partner, symmetric and interacting. The fundamental "discovery" of this utilization of the notion of international equilibrium was that of identifying "areas" (geographical, but also technological and symbolic) through which the system and individual powers within it could achieve primary objectives (thus fulfilling the drive to expansion) without coming into conflict. In this way, the system recognized not only the equilibrium, of the partner, but also the equilibrium of the future developments of the partner. The territorial arrangements proposed by the Congress of Vienna were deeply imbued with this strategy. The equilibrium among the powers was guaranteed by buffer states, by partitions, by geographical areas in which local conflicts of interest were "permitted" and contained. These arrangements ensured that escalation to the level of global conflict did not occur precisely because of the rigorous delimitation of the acknowledged scenario (Italy, Germany, Poland, the Balkans, are all—in 1815—clear illustrations of the occurrence of this principal strategy).

The idea worked for about 100 years. It worked in a double sense. First of all it guaranteed global equilibrium from its starting point, Europe, notwithstanding serious moments of crisis (1848 and 1870) and notwithstanding the political, cultural, and technological changes taking place in the meanwhile. But above all, it became a model to organize that which retrospectively appears as one of the key processes of the nineteenth century, the first emergence of a network of interaction and connections. Wherever the problem of the enlargement of modern society occurred, the model could be reconstituted from the definition of a system able to expand unhindered into a surrounding indefinite environment. The conquest of the frontier and the race for gold were realizations of this strategy just as significant as local wars and colonial divisions.

The worldwide situation at the beginning of the twentieth century represented a kind of generalized equilibrium that in some manner appeared as necessary and guaranteed. Of course various crises arose but the general conviction was held that the strategies of control and isolation of the crisis would be able to continue indefinitely to be effective. Among these strategies the more widely used ones consisted in moving the development of, and solution to, a crisis to an area considered remote or marginal (at the beginning of the twentieth century such areas comprised at least three-quarters of the planet). Such areas were conceived of as a vast protective belt: open space and abundant "containers" which allowed the unloading of conflicts without touching the nucleus of that equilibrium which the nineteenth century appeared to have constructed.

The year 1914 was the sign that every "external" space, every "container" of abundance was progressively failing, and, even more, that the system was becoming progressively a single system (polysystem) closed in upon itself. The end-point of this development is that every local crisis becomes, potentially, a global crisis. The expansion and the increasing density of the planetary network of interactions produced a change not simply quantitative, but qualitative. The paradigm of control revealed itself to be impossible and often damaging and the problem of error gained increasing prominence. In 1914, this problem was realized in a specific event at Sarajevo. Since then, Sarajevo has recurrently haunted the twentieth century, and our century seems constantly to seek the pos-

sibility of its future in a new understanding of the "nature of Sarajevo."

The limit of this notion of international equilibrium is most evident in its acceptance of bonds imposed by the historical condition as a necessity that cannot be disregarded and as an independent variable, operating in such a manner as to narrow the possibility of choice and decision. This is no less true as far as the years following 1945 are concerned, even though they were dominated by the centrality of a worldwide structure of equilibrium. In the name of this equilibrium, vast potentialities have been neglected, not least in the cultural and technological realms. The situation of scarcity that characterized the planet following the Second World War led the parties concerned in the matter to resort again to this regulative figure, committing itself to a game which appeared to be bilateral and zero-sum. On the other hand, the idea that an enormous reserve of superabundance would soon be available was promoted. This would have had the effect of transforming the game into one in which all players would have been able to win (precisely at the expense of this reserve). But, in reality, this reserve has not become available, and in fact the same regulative figure of equilibrium—with the decisions that it has imposed—has been utilized, serving only to drain and render impossible one of its creative interventions. The energy crisis of the early 1970s can be considered the most evident symptom of this situation. But perhaps more important still is the dramatic failure of the ideas of "the future" and planning. In a closed system, there is a risk that the game will take a direction other than the one desired. There is a risk that all players will lose, a well-known game, described by Rene Girard in the following terms:

> The players are opposite but similar, and in fact, interchangeable since they make the exact same gesture . . . . The players are *partners*, which means that they understand each other, but only in disagreements. Nobody wants to lose, and yet, it's a strange thing, in that there are only losers:" . . . they all growled, they all grunted, and they all cursed each other." Each, we know, makes the *other one* responsible for the bad luck that oppresses him. (Girard 1961 pp. 107-8)

Even in this phase of historical development—which is the phase characterized by the constitution of a true planetary polysystem in which the various social, cultural, and human systems developed in the course of the modern age intertwine—the problem arises of locating new spaces in which to pursue the further development of the system. As always these spaces are contemporaneously geographical, technological, symbolic, and cosmic: they are the intensive and extensive conquest of new spaces for agricultural production, the revolution produced through the service of low-cost and rapid information, the identification of new energy sources, or the research for the utilization of already known energy sources in more comfortable conditions, the possibility of the creation, from outer space to earth of an *outer frontier*, energetic and industrial with significant retroaction on the economic situation of the planet. The temptation to repropose already known plans, to identify in these spaces protective belts able to locate and postpone conflicts and the chances of conflict, is strong. The ever-decreasing efficacy of these strategies of postponement is also evident in the moment in which the technological means available today render directly classifiable all the new elements, in the traditional games, that come to add themselves to the planetary system. The risk is that the potentialities available become a reserve in which to develop a game where everybody loses.

Can this risk be avoided? It is a fundamental question for the culture of contemporary peace. Above all, is it possible to create a process of reciprocal amplification among the implicit possibilities in the technological, symbolic, and cosmic developments of the planetary system? Is it possible to create a culture of possibility that would have as its goal the redefinition of games played in the planet, the redefinition of the players of these games, and also, as a final appeal, the redefinition of the notions themselves of the limits of the system, of its contraction and expansion?

One of the research directions that appears more promising, and fundamental in any case in order to give an answer to these question, is the reexamination of those concepts of control, dominion, and forecasting, that supported and still support the strategies of the players of planetary games, and to the representations that these same players make of their games. In this sense system science can assist in a reexamination of the necessities of certain regulative figures that are characteristic of the whole of science and the whole of modern culture. To rethink about nature and the status of ideas of control, of domination, of forecasting, implies a final attempt to place oneself at the root of the changes which characterize modern science. The science of the second half of the twentieth century is really produced in the awareness of a change in the definition of the relationship between *laws* and *history*, between *rules* and *games*. This passage takes us from a strategy that we can define as *applicative* to a strategy definable as *constructive* and it is marked by the failure of the regulative ideal of a fundamental place of explanation and observation. In classical science "laws" occupied this fundamental place. The ideal of a *dernière science* entrusted to science, as its specific task, the research of laws on which basis, in a necessary and predictable manner, the course of phenomena may be deduced. No deduction of such a kind defines the goals and the nature of contemporary sciences in which the passage from a science of necessity to a science of games is realized. Rather, laws are proposed as bonds, as preconditions that define a vast ensemble of possibilities. In this sense they are very similar to the rules of a game that define a range of possibilities in which some moves are made, in preference to others, on the basis of the ability or deficiency of the players. Which of these possibilities is actually verified is not presented in advance. The evolutive discourse depends upon a real—and for that same reason really constructive—interaction between causal and independent chains, interaction between bonds of different orders, and contingent and aleatory (chance-dependent) events.

The center of gravity of contemporary knowledge seems to be moving from a key notion of necessity to a key notion of possibility. It is on the inside of this epistemological transition that appears a reformulation of concepts and problems of boundaries, of expansion and contraction of systems, of equilibrium of cooperation, of conflicts of parts in a game and, in the final analysis, of history and evolution. The compelling practical problems of the management of equilibrium and of international conflicts can also be planned in this framework, and in this framework they can find more adequate formulations. The problem of peace is also a theoretical question, a question that depends mostly on the overviews that are being used in the ways of thinking of contemporary humankind.

See also: *Game Theory; Peace, Systems View of*

Bibliography

Bocchi G, Ceruti M (eds.) 1985 *La sfida della complessità*. Feltrinelli, Milan
Ceruti M 1986 *Il vincolo e la possibilità*. Feltrinelli, Milan
Dumouchel P, Duputy J P (eds.) 1983 *L'Auto-organisation: De la physique au politique*. Seuil, Paris
Girard R 1961 *Mensonge romantique et vérité romanesque*. Grasset, Paris
Girard R 1978 *Des Choses cachées depuis la fondation du monde*. Grasset, Paris

Jantsch E 1980 *The Self-Organizing Universe*. Pergamon, Oxford

Laszlo E 1986 *Evolution*. New Science Library, Boston, Massachusetts

Morin E 1981 *Pour sortie du Vingtième Siècle*. Nathan, Paris

Prigogine I, Stengers T 1979 *La Nouvelle Alliance: Métamorphose de la science*. Gallimard, Paris [1984 *Order Out of Chaos*. New Science Library, Boston, Massachusetts]

MAURO CERUTI

International Conflicts, De-escalation of

Every international conflict de-escalates eventually. However intractable and destructive the conflict appears, at some time it decreases in the severity of the means used in waging the struggle and/or in the number of parties engaged in it. De-escalation is usually a preliminary phase in the ending of a conflict, although many de-escalations are short-lived. In the 1990s, a series of remarkable de-escalating transformations occurred in many parts of world. The Cold War between the United States of America and the then Union of Soviet Socialist Republics, which had dominated the world system and threatened a nuclear catastrophe, was transformed and then ended. Remarkable shifts toward de-escalation also occurred in the relations between the Palestine Liberation Organization (PLO) and the Israeli government, and within and among the countries of Southern Africa and Central America.

De-escalation is not generally understood to refer to reductions in the level of conflict behavior that are unilaterally imposed. Rather, it refers to varying degrees of mutual movement toward reducing the level of an ongoing conflict (see *Conflict Resolution, Process of*). It is important to recognize that many partisans and even outside observers are likely to regard de-escalation as wrong when it results in the acceptance of injustice. Therefore, they may argue for intensifying a struggle in order to gain a more just settlement. In this contribution, we do not assume that every de-escalation is necessarily desirable. We recognize that escalation may be needed to achieve worthwhile goals, but it is also assumed that escalation can be relatively constructive, and is not necessarily destructive.

De-escalations vary in several regards. Thus, they vary in duration, some for a brief interlude, others for decades, and others are preludes to a conflict's resolution. They also vary in the level of antagonism expressed in the relationship; for example, Indian-Pakistani relations, although de-escalated from the intensity of the occasional outbreaks of war, have been generally highly antagonistic. They also vary in the cumulativeness of the de-escalation movement; for example, the de-escalation phases in American-Soviet relations, including the Thaw of 1963, the détente of the early 1970s, and the accommodation of the late 1980s were cumulative in many ways. Transformative de-escalations are long cumulative processes, not brief clearly delineated events. Neither is the transition from escalation to de-escalation a single event; rather it is a shift produced by pressures building over time. Even if astounding moments of change occur, they usually follow from many less visible trends.

In this contribution, we examine the processes contributing to de-escalation, the changing conditions fostering it, and the policies that partisans and intermediaries pursue that help de-escalate conflicts. Consideration is given not only to international conflicts, but also to large-scale internal conflicts with international implications.

1. Processes of De-escalation

The processes that contribute to de-escalation occur within each adversary, in the relations between the adversaries, and also among other parties in the social environment.

In the case of large-scale struggles, the effects of these various processes must generally converge and re-enforce each other for de-escalation to proceed.

1.1 Internal Processes

Within each adversary country, both social psychological and organizational developments contribute to conflict de-escalation. We examine those processes as they occur under varying conditions, particularly those which are modifiable by policy choices. Certain processes can contribute to escalation or to de-escalation, depending on the circumstances.

1.2 Social-Psychological Processes

Cognitive dissonance, entrapment, and certain other cognitive and affective processes can contribute to conflict de-escalation, affecting individual leaders, group members, or the public at large (see *Psychology of Peace*). Cognitive dissonance theory suggests that if people make conciliatory moves toward an adversary, they will tend to justify their actions and value what they have done. Evidence for this can be found in survey data about approval of the country's president. This assumes that people regard actions taken in the name of an entity with which they identify, such as their country, as their own. For example, Americans tend to "rally-round-the flag;" that is, they support a military action or other forceful foreign policy initiative of their government or president, and even increase their approval of the president after such actions (Mueller 1973). Leaders anticipating this, may more readily undertake escalating moves. There is also survey evidence, however, that approval of the president will rise if he undertakes a conciliatory action (Borker, Kriesberg, and Abdul-Quader, 1985). That is less widely assumed and therefore less likely to affect conduct.

Once actions toward de-escalation have been taken, the contentious goal previously sought may become de-valued. That is a way to bring consistency between the values desired and the actual conduct. This mechanism helps explain how at least some people handle thinking their past actions had been wrong.

Entrapment, another process usually fostering escalation, can be controlled to help avoid escalation (Brockner and Rubin, 1985). Experimental evidence indicates, for example, that if individuals set limits on how far they will go prior to embarking on a possibly entrapping course, they tend to avoid entrapment. Thus, people may learn to avoid entering a struggle in which creeping escalation and entrapment seem likely; thus, a concern to avoid repeating the 1960s Vietnam war experience inhibited early US military intervention in the 1990s fighting within the former Yugoslavia.

Certain aspects of entrapment contribute directly to de-escalation. Once adversaries have initiated actions to de-escalate their conflict with each other, the process of entrapment may contribute to keeping them on that course. Taking de-escalating action in a conflict usually has incurred some costs and each adversary therefore has made investment in this course. The dynamics of entrapment is that one or both sides may find itself making greater and greater concessions in order to proceed consistently and not abandon the previous investments. Consequently, an antagonistic party may yield more than it had anticipated in order not to lose the investments already made. After all, the party abandoning the movement toward settlement would appear inconsistent and be admitting that its previous actions had been mistaken.

Additional cognitive and affective processes significantly contribute to conflict de-escalation. Sym-

pathizing and empathizing with others are such processes, and certain policies and experiences can trigger and sustain these processes, even between enemies. The construct of empathy stresses taking the role of the other, without losing one's identity (Goldstein and Michaels 1985).

1.3 Organizational Processes

Several organizational and social structural processes within one or more antagonistic countries may contribute to de-escalation. Under certain conditions, leadership competition fosters de-escalation rather than escalation. The development of a constituency for accommodation is an important condition for the emergence of a viable alternative leadership; the emergence of alternative leadership in turn tends to give legitimacy to further dissent from the hard-line policies sustaining conflict escalation.

Constituencies for de-escalation arise from many sources. Thus, the costs of continuing a struggle grow as the struggle goes on, raising doubts about the benefit of the goals sought. Moreover, the burdens of a long, escalating struggle often become increasingly unequal. The unfairness of that inequality arouses dissent and withdrawal of support; in a war, this may take the form of draft riots, desertion, and flight. This is illustrated by the Russian Imperial army's 1917 resistance to the war against Germany and its allies, resulting in Russia's withdrawal from World War I.

Leaders sometimes seek to stifle dissent among their constituencies in order to sustain a struggle. But trying to suppress dissent often drives people into further opposition, as their views are silenced. Branding people as disloyal can itself provoke acts of disloyalty.

Dissent and opposition to official hard-line policies can be mobilized readily insofar as groups of people favoring accommodation with the adversary have leaders with broad legitimacy and are linked by networks of communication. Thus, in the United States during the 1960s, opponents to the US intervention in Vietnam were able to mobilize demonstrations and other acts of resistance by their ties to previous peace movement organizations, to traditional peace churches, to student organizations, and to civil rights organizations (DeBenedetti 1995).

As a struggle escalates, a small group of persons affiliated with a cause may commit what most affiliated persons regard as outrageous acts; consequently, the cause may lose constituent support and legitimacy. For example, this contributed to the loss of support in France for the "dirty war" waged by the

French military forces against the National Liberation Front in Algeria, 1954-1962 (see *Nonintervention and Noninterference*).

Since the processes which limit consideration of alternatives in times of crises tend to engender further escalation, adopting special policies to avoid those destructive effects would be desirable. One such method is to have decisions made by a broad and diverse group of persons, following procedures that foster free discussion ensure consideration of alternatives. President John F. Kennedy's handling of the Cuban Missile Crisis is often regarded as exemplary of this method (Schlesinger 1965). When President Kennedy was presented evidence of Soviet missiles in Cuba, on October 16,1962, he called together a small but diverse group to consider possible responses. The group met secretly for six days and considered several possible responses, gathered information about the alternatives, and discussed each. In order to encourage open discussion and to avoid early closure on a decision, the President did not participate in the discussions.

Finally, once de-escalation has gotten underway, several organizational processes can come into play that make turning back difficult. The road to peace sometimes becomes a slippery slope. Thus, leaders who have initiated de-escalating steps are reluctant to appear to have made a mistake by changing the course they have undertaken.

Furthermore, their actions sometimes have actually altered the relations within their party and with other organizations, creating vested interests for continuing de-escalation. Particularly if large, public steps have been taken, the new course may seem irreversible.

1.4 Interaction Processes

Three general processes pertaining to the interaction between adversaries often contribute to de-escalation. These include reciprocity in interaction, issue containment, and linking between adversaries.

1.4.1 Reciprocity in Interaction

Three related processes of reciprocity in adversary interaction are conducive to de-escalation: reacting equivalently, learning about the struggle and the adversary, and developing shared norms. The first process entails each side reacting in a measured and equivalent level to the other. In this scenario, one or both sides avoid acting in ways that may be provocative or may invite an aggrandizing move by the other side. For example, the response selected by President Kennedy and his advisors to the Soviet emplacement of missiles in Cuba in 1962 was a "quarantine;" he

did treat the emplacement as of little consequence and did not simply lodge a protest at the United Nations, neither did he order a provocative air strike or an invasion of Cuba. President Kennedy was determined to allow time and space for discovering acceptable ways out of the crisis; avoiding a runaway escalation of words and actions, he took what he regarded as a measured response which would not provoke an escalating interaction. He also communicated directly with Soviet Chairman Nikita S. Khrushchev, inviting interaction and he closely monitored the operations of the US quarantine (Kennedy 1971). The actions by each side during the crisis were roughly equivalent (Holsti, Brody and North 1964).

The second interaction process which is often de-escalating is learning from experience with the adversary. Learning about conflicts in general or about a particular struggle encompasses a wide variety of phenomena (Breslauer and Tetlock 1991). Here, it refers to adversaries understanding more about each other and their conflict as they contentiously interact in recurrent disputes. As each side learns more about the other, each tends to make better estimates of how the other side will react to its actions. That reduces the likelihood of unintentional and ineffective escalation.

Finally, adversaries sometimes develop shared norms guiding some arenas in which they are in contention. The rules themselves may be matters of dispute for a time, but once agreed upon, they provide guidance for waging a conflict which constrains the antagonists from escalating very far. In international affairs, normative regimes sometimes develop to stabilize and manage particular areas of recurrent disputes.

1.4.2 Issue Containment

Although issues in a struggle often expand and spillover, incorporating other divisive matters, such expansion is not inevitable. An adversary may purposefully remain focused on a specific goal in order to isolate the opponent and concentrate its own energies.

As a struggle persists, contentious issues often begin to contract. One of the adversaries, failing to attain its grand goals, finds that settling for what it can get to be its best alternative. A conflict party that believes it is unable to impose its preferences will come to recognize that it must deal with its adversary. The great matters in contention between them tend to be broken down into more manageable sub-issues. When adversaries fractionate the conflict into specific issues, some may appear easily settled and trade offs among several issues seem possible (Fisher 1964).

Finally, inflammatory issues may be contained by

the development of superordinate goals; these are shared goals which are given primacy over the contentious ones. One kind of superordinate goal that sometimes emerges when a conflict persists is a mutual avoidance of destruction. Adversaries who think that continued escalation risks giving both sides their worst outcome may decide to coordinate their conduct to avoid such a result.

1.4.3 Developing Ties between Adversaries

As a struggle becomes protracted, some members of the opposing sides may undertake to communicate with each other in order to facilitate a de-escalation of the conflict. They serve as quasi-mediators, conveying information and suggestions between the antagonistic parties (Kriesberg 1995). They also may develop bonds with each other and thus form an interest group within their own camps to de-escalate the conflict.

Furthermore, if the conflict persists with recurrent confrontations, the representatives of the opposing sides themselves often develop shared expectations about how the next confrontation will be handled. If previous confrontations were contained and settled in a mutually acceptable fashion, the next one is likely to be guided by the previous experience. This is particularly likely in a setting in which the adversaries have an ongoing relationship.

1.5 Processes of Involvement with Other Parties

International adversaries contend with each other within a social context of many other parties, and some of the ways those other parties relate to the adversaries can foster de-escalation. First, they sometimes provide models of the way de-escalation could occur, or at least provide the vision that de-escalation is feasible. Second, other parties often set limits to the escalation of a conflict, and intervene to enforce those limits. Such outside intervention may try to use particular means or to ensure that one of the adversaries is not too badly damaged. Increasingly, international governmental organizations and other governments have begun to intervene within countries when the government has itself exercised extreme violence on its own people (see *Intervention*). Justifications in terms of humanitarian assistance or the upholding of human rights are occasionally given greater standing than those made in the name of sovereignty.

Finally, other parties frequently serve as intermediaries to assist the contending parties to find a way to de-escalate their conflict. They may facilitate the antagonists' accepting a move toward de-escalating their struggle, for example, by providing a face-sav-

ing way out of the fight. This includes offering a proposal which an adversary would not accept from its enemy, but which is accepted when offered by a mediator. The intermediaries may also forcefully intervene and help impose a settlement of the conflict, but such intervention often only freezes the conflict at its current status (see *Arbitration, International*).

2. Changing Conditions

De-escalation, in large measure, occurs as a result of changes in the conditions which underlay the emergence of a conflict in the first place, or which generated and sustained its escalation. Those changed conditions provide a new context so that processes which might contribute to conflict escalation are likely to result in de-escalation instead. Indeed, the changed conditions provide the context for whatever de-escalation policies are undertaken. In this section, we examine three sets of changing conditions: those within one of the adversaries in a struggle, those in the relationship between them, and those among parties not directly engaged in the struggle.

2.1 Internal Changes

Many kinds of changes within one or more of the adversary parties play critical roles in a struggle's de-escalation. Thus, a waning in the conviction among members of one of the adversary sides regarding the justness and morality of their cause greatly contributes to a de-escalation of a struggle. Such a weakening can be seen in the declining faith among Soviet citizens in Communist ideology and the Soviet system (Shlapentokh 1986).

The evident failure of past militant strategies are a powerful stimulus for partisans to consider turning to a more accomodationist approach. Adversaries generally seek to advance their own interests and to win as much as possible, and tend to rely on coercive, often violent, means. The transition to transformation often arises from a realization that those means were not achieving what was intended. Indeed, past policies may come to be seen as undermining the attainment of the ends sought.

Certain changes in the relative influence among the constituent parts of an adversary group are important precursors of a de-escalating transition. The emergence into prominence of groups interested in an accommodation with the adversary may lead to a shift in goals and means. The Palestinian uprising, the Intifada, which began in December 1987 provides a paradoxical example. It escalated the intensity of the struggle against the Israeli occupation, but also contributed to a moderating shift in the position of the PLO. The PLO leadership, seeking to represent all Palestinians, outside as well as inside the territories occupied by Israel, had long stressed the needs and desires of those Palestinians outside to return to their previous places of residence. The Intifada, however, increased the relative importance of the Palestinians in the occupied territories and their emerging local leadership. For those Palestinians, shaking off Israeli control of their lives was the primary objective. To represent the Palestinians in the occupied territories in their struggle, the PLO leadership, among other efforts, sought to open a dialogue with the US government as the recognized representative of the Palestinians. This required that they moderate their stated goals and the means to attain them.

Finally, some internal changes demand attention from an adversary's leaders, and divert them from external affairs, particularly antagonistic foreign relations. For example, beginning in the mid-1970s, the Soviet economy was clearly stagnating and living conditions were deteriorating. Life expectancy actually began to decline, unlike any other industrially developed country. Improving relations with the West offered the prospect of limiting the immense military defense expenditures and gaining access to Western technological developments and bettering everyday life (see *Economics of Disarmament: Certain Premises*). In 1985, Mikhail Gorbachev was chosen by the Communist Party to lead it and the then Soviet Union into a period of domestic reforms, and an accommodation with the West was regarded as necessary for that.

2.2 Changes in the Relationship

Changes in the relations between the adversaries which undermine the prospects of any of them unilaterally imposing a solution greatly contribute to a shift toward de-escalation. This frequently means that the adversaries are in a stalemate, and no party anticipates that the balance of forces will change to enable it to triumph. Furthermore, if the stalemate is highly unsatisfactory, so that the parties wish to escape from it, they are in what Touval and Zartman (1985) have called a "hurting stalemate." Such circumstances are often a prelude to a negotiated settlement of a conflict.

One other component is frequently critical for a transition away from escalation: the prospect of a better alternative than remaining in the stalemate. The alternative is a formula providing a mutually acceptable solution that appears to be attainable. A necessary element in any such formula is that the opponents do not threaten each other's most significant interests. Somehow, each side must convince the other that it accepts the other's survival or better, legitimacy.

For example, the American-Soviet nuclear weapons balance, by the end of the 1960s was a balance of terror. But at the same time, neither side had immediate goals which threatened vital interests of the other. Beginning with détente in the early 1970s, arms control agreements and many other measures appeared to demonstrate a mutual acceptance of each other as superpowers (see *Détente*). After years of negotiation in the Conference on Security and Cooperation in Europe (CSCE), the Helsinki Final Act was signed in 1975. This provided assurance to the then Soviet Union of the inviolability of the borders established in Europe after the end of the Second World War, including the western shift of Soviet borders and the division of Germany. With that assurance, the then Soviet Union and the East European countries it dominated reduced their barriers to Western influence (see *Security and Cooperation in Europe*).

2.3 Changes in Context

Shifts in the salience of various conflicts impact upon the possible de-escalation of each of the struggles. For example, the shift to détente in the early 1970s was fostered by changes in the salience of several other conflicts (Kriesberg 1992). Thus, the Soviet-Chinese antagonism had increased, indicated by the bloody border skirmishes in 1969; that provided an incentive for each of them to be less intransigent toward the United States. On the other side, the US engagement in the war in Vietnam was an overwhelming concern in 1969, when Richard M. Nixon was elected president. He and his advisors reasoned that an acceptable way out of Vietnam might be found by being more accommodating to the then Soviet Union and the People's Republic of China, playing one off against the other, and isolating North Vietnam. Furthermore, the newly elected Social Democratic government of then West Germany undertook a policy of accommodation with the then Soviet Union, East Germany, and other countries of Eastern Europe which eased and indeed fostered American-Soviet accommodation.

2.3.1 End of the Cold War

The end of the Cold War, marked by the fall of the Berlin Wall in 1989 and the dissolution of the then Soviet Union in 1993, impacted many conflicts throughout the world, including the struggles in Central America, Southern Africa, and in the Middle East. Policies pursued by many of the parties involved in each of those conflicts were based on the existence of the Cold War and these policies tended to perpetuate each conflict. The end of the Cold War required changes in those policies (see *Global Neighborhood: New Security Principles*).

The Cold War's demise for example, weakened support for both the Israelis and Palestinians. It lessened the value of Israel to the United States as an ally in the struggle against communism, and therefore threatened reduced support. On the other side, and more significantly, Soviet support for the PLO was lessened and Chairman Arafat was encouraged to find an accommodation with Israel. After the dissolution of the Soviet Union, Russia was even less likely to be antagonistic to the US policies in the region.

2.3.2 Other Regional Conflicts

The course of a struggle is often greatly affected by the outbreak or the ending of an intense armed combat in an adjacent region. For example, the outbreak of a fight may help forge new alliances or weaken support for one or more of the adversaries in the struggle.

The Iraqi attempt to incorporate Kuwait unleashed an intense war as the US and allied forces drove the Iraqi army out of Kuwait. The war divided the Arabs, particularly weakening the positions of the Palestinians, the PLO, and Jordan, who had not joined the anti-Iraqi government coalition. Furthermore, the threat Saddam Hussein was able to raise by appealing to popular anti-Israeli sentiments, was a powerful incentive for the US government to try to settle the Israeli-Arab conflict and help sustain the Arab governments with which it was allied in the war against Iraq. The war also appeared to leave the United States as the dominant regional as well as the dominant global power. The US government's incentive and ability to play a major intermediary role after the war were evident and led to the Middle East Peace Conference, in Madrid, according to a formula brokered by US Secretary of State James Baker (Quandt 1993).

2.3.3 Economic Changes

The increasingly integrated global economy also contributes to the de-escalation of international conflicts. For example, it contributed to the pressure felt by Soviet leaders to move toward an accommodation with the West in order to restructure their stagnating economy so as to function effectively within the global economy (see *World Economy, Social Change and Peace*). Also beginning in the early 1980s, economic conditions in many Arab countries deteriorated for most people. The great flow of income that the success of OPEC had generated for some Arab countries in the 1970s now slowed down. This contributed to the felt need to settle the Arab-Israeli conflict. In general, economic expansion which is a goal shared by many adversaries encourages cooperation and facilitates finding win/win outcomes.

In short, a combination of several changes is usually needed to bring about a transition into an enduring de-escalating movement, particularly for protracted conflicts. The changes occur within one or more adversary, in their relations, and in the social context. Quite different combinations of changed conditions can bring about the shift toward de-escalation. Thus, if a stalemate is very painful, then the formula to escape from it need not be as attractive as when the stalemate is more bearable.

The nature of the de-escalation and the resulting outcome is also likely to differ, depending upon the particular combination of conditions. There is little reason in theory or in experience to believe that the result of conflict de-escalation or termination will be equitable for all the adversaries.

The changing conditions create opportunities, but do not guarantee successful de-escalating efforts. No single kind of effort will work for every conflict in every circumstance. There must be a match between a particular set of policies and a particular set of conditions for de-escalation movement to occur.

3. De-escalation Policies

Undertaking an analysis of the prevailing conditions and trends relating to the struggle helps in selecting an effective policy to de-escalate a conflict (Keashley and Fisher 1995). It should be obvious that one tool does not fit all problems. To select the appropriate policy, the stage of escalation the conflict has already reached, how the conflict is like and unlike others, and the nature of de-escalation desired should be examined. That is, whether the circumstances are ripe for a particular de-escalating initiative must be considered (Kriesberg and Thorson 1991 and Zartman 1989). In addition, a wide range of alternative policies, and possible undertakers of the policies should be reviewed. Ideally, the sequencing of particular policies and the coordination of various actors and actions should be considered (Kriesberg 1996). All these tasks are rarely fully completed by persons engaged in a struggle or in trying to ameliorate it, but engaging in them tends to increase effectiveness.

3.1 Analytic Parameters

Alternative de-escalation policies are reviewed here in terms of the level of escalation a struggle has reached and the level of de-escalation the policies are targeted to achieve. This review will differentiate among four starting levels: little escalation, sharp escalation (or crises), protracted stalemate, and unilateral imposition, even though these levels tend to be mixed in actual struggles. Thus, a crisis may erupt in the context of a low level of contention or in the context of a protracted stalemate. Furthermore, various segments of a large-scale conflict may be in different stages simultaneously; for example, a struggle may be relatively stalemated in one area, but one side may be sharply escalating the fight in another arena.

3.1.1 Starting Levels

Before conflicts become protracted and destructive, they exhibit a relatively low level of overt struggle that is too often unnoticed or ignored (see *Conflict: Inherent and Contingent Theories*). One or more of the adversaries makes demands, probes for responses, threatens, or otherwise begins trying to gain its goals. Such actions, often precursors of much more severe conflicts in the near future, should serve as early warnings that a disastrous struggle may develop. Appropriate policies following such actions, by the partisans or by intermediaries, can often avert destructive escalation. Clearly, averting destructive escalation at an early stage is generally less costly, less risky, and more likely to be enduringly effective than it would be once the conflict has become protracted. Nevertheless, often adversaries think that others will prevent the conflict from escalating badly and meanwhile they must strive to reach their contested goal. Possible intermediaries generally do not act since they see high risks of failure and little potential gains, even if they succeed.

Efforts at de-escalation, particularly by intermediaries, often occur when a conflict has markedly escalated. Among the many forms of sharp escalation, one form is much examined in international relations: the crisis (Brecher 1993 and Snyder and Diesing 1977). In addition to crises, escalation surges occur when one of the parties greatly intensifies its means of struggle. In international conflicts this occurs when a threat is made, or an armed outburst erupts. The stage of intractable struggle is receiving increasing attention by scholars and policy makers (Kriesberg, Northrup and Thorson 1989 and Lederach 1995). In these long-standing struggles, neither side is able to impose a settlement on the other, nor is either willing to accept the terms insisted upon by the other in preference to continuing the struggle.

De-escalation policies can be distinguished in terms of four kinds of goals they are directed to

attain: preventing destructive escalation, stopping the ongoing violence, de-escalating the mutual antagonism, and using problem-solving means. The first two goals are relatively short-term, while the second two are relatively long-term.

3.2 From Low Level of Escalation

Everyone acknowledges that it is easier to stop a conflict from escalating destructively, if the struggle has not persisted for a long time and not yet escalated very far. This underlies the great interest among conflict resolution professionals in the potential of preventive diplomacy and in early warning. Despite the interest in early warning, the problem is not so much not knowing that a conflict is likely to escalate badly, but not knowing what might be done effectively, particularly because it is difficult to mobilize the necessary resources before the conflict has destructively escalated (Kriesberg 1997).

3.2.1 Short Term

This discussion is focused on tactical policies undertaken by partisans or by intermediaries that are directed at preventing struggles from escalating destructively.

The manner in which a challenging group pursues its goals and the other side responds, greatly affects the likelihood that a struggle will de-escalate constructively. For example, conflicts in which challenging groups use relatively non-provocative methods, such as conventional protest or nonviolent resistance, are less likely to escalate destructively than those in which challenging groups resort to violence. Similarly, conflicts in which the challenged parties respond in an equivalent way rather than by overreacting tend not to escalate destructively. Finally, destructive escalation is likely to be averted insofar as the partisans keep the issues in contention narrowly focused and isolated from other contentious issues.

Outside parties also may strive to prevent the conflict from spreading into neighboring countries or they may seek to stop or to limit the sale of weapons in the country where the struggle is underway. This is illustrated in the conduct of the United Nations and other international organizations and governments in limiting the scope of the wars in the former Yugoslavia (see *United Nations and NATO in Former Yugoslavia*). Thus, at the request of the President of the Yugoslav Republic of Macedonia, in December 1992, the UN Security Council authorized the deployment of troops under command of the United Nations Protection Force (UNPROFOR) along the Macedonian border with Albania and Yugoslavia (Serbia and Montenegro). The troops not only act as a deterrent to the spread of war, but also mediate border encounters and have succeeded in achieving the withdrawal of soldiers on both sides (Ackerman).

Within the international system, the UN and regional IGOs frequently exist which provide mediating, information gathering, facilitating, and consultative services to defuse nascent conflicts. In addition, nonofficial mediators or officials acting informally may also intervene to help settle community disputes, as is sometimes done by political and religious leaders. They often have bonds crossing religious and ethnic lines and use such connections to bring together leaders from disputing communal groups.

3.2.2 Long Term

Long-term de-escalation policies include the promotion of crosscutting ties, institutionalized procedures for resolving conflicts, improvement of the social, economic, and cultural way of life of the relatively disadvantaged in the social system, and the creation of shared identities and vested interests in advancing that shared identity, and fostering superordinate goals.

3.3 From Sharp Escalation

Great interest is exhibited by policy makers, analysts, and the public at large in the outbreak of crises and other sharp escalations, while there is relatively little attention to the avoidance of destructive escalation and the peaceful amelioration of conflicts. Nevertheless, insights about policies which have such results can be garnered from many sources.

3.3.1 Short Term

One of the essential qualities of a crisis is the sense of urgency engendered among the partisans. That urgency often hampers taking actions which would avoid a disastrous escalation. One of the ways to increase the likelihood of avoiding destructive escalation is for one or more adversaries to allow time for the other side to reflect on its course of action and not be pushed into a corner and face humiliation. This is exemplified in some degree by the US government's responses in the Cuban missile crisis of 1962.

3.3.2 Long Term

Among the many ways to stop sharp escalations from destructively increasing in scope and severity is to develop institutions and procedures that reduce the likelihood of such developments. This may take the form of improving the communication between the adversaries, making it swifter and better understood. For example, after the Cuban missile crisis, the US and Soviet governments established the "hotline," a direct

telephone line between the offices of the heads of the US and the Soviet governments.

Another long-term strategy is to develop groups, networks, or organizations including persons from opposing sides. These persons may sometimes be the primary representatives or advisors to them. Getting to know each other and their views reduces the likelihood of misunderstandings which may exacerbate conflicts. The cross-cutting networks also provide channels for quickly considering alternative paths out of a sharp escalation when that occurs. Such organizations have played a role in the transformation of the American-Soviet conflict. The Pugwash movement and the Dartmouth meetings are particularly noteworthy in this regard.

An additional policy developed in East-West relations in Europe contributed to reducing the likelihood of sharp escalations: the construction of Confidence Building Measures (CBMs). These measures included, for example, each side notifying the other in advance of large-scale military maneuvers and each side allowing representatives of the other to observe the maneuvers. Such measures provided reassurance and avoided misunderstandings and thus contributed to the end of the Cold War. This idea has been discussed and to some extent implemented between other sets of international and domestic adversaries (Feldman 1994). In the case of the East-West relations in Europe, they include measures reducing or excluding certain kinds of military activities which are deemed to be threatening, providing advanced notification of military exercises, and allowing for an exchange of observers of military exercises.

Finally, another way to prevent conflicts from escalating destructively is to avoid provocative acts. General agreements, even among unfriendly parties can implement methods to reduce or even stop particular kinds of actions. For example, politically-motivated airplane hijackings were widespread in the 1960s, but they were greatly reduced by improved security measures at airports and by international agreements to deny havens to hijackers.

3.4 From Protracted Struggle

Many large-scale conflicts persist for generation after generation, often destructively and appearing to be intractable. We discuss some of the many policies which enable adversaries to move to the resolution of such conflicts or into more constructive ways of conducting them.

3.4.1 Short Term

Even profound and long-term conflict transformations,

have small beginnings. Tactical policies, conducted by partisans and intermediaries are crucial in initiating and sustaining long-term change.

A fundamental difficulty in de-escalating destructive struggles is that one or more sides feels that its basic interests are threatened and it must fight on to sustain them. A crucial step in moving out of such a struggle is for all sides to undertake actions which counter those feelings. When such actions are made on a reciprocal basis, appear credible, and seem irreversible, protracted and intractable conflicts are in transformation. For example, the transformation in American-Soviet relations; which brought about the end of the Cold War occurred over a long time. There were periods of thaw in the Cold War and with them normalization of some aspects of American-Soviet relations; the actions of each side and the treaties signed by them indicated an acceptance of each other's continuing survival and even superpower status.

Policies to build support for de-escalation among members of one of the adversaries also contribute to the de-escalation of protracted conflicts, since these conflicts are especially dependent on the sentiments of the rank-and-file members of the opposing sides. A major set of such policies pertains to mobilizing popular support for the transformation, whether by the persons in leadership offices or by alternative groups. They are part of a long-term policy, or a short-term effort to rally support for a particular action. Mobilization may be attempted, for example, by social movement organizations arranging a demonstration or a campaign of protest against officials reluctant to change. Mobilization may also be sought by officials who hold major ceremonies which serve to make a public commitment to the transformation process. The officials may also hold a referendum to gain constituent support and campaign to get it.

Of course, significant internal opposition to ending a protracted conflict, on terms not unilaterally imposed, is very likely. Once the transition toward a joint solution has begun, opposition often intensifies, and how leaders handle that opposition to continuing with de-escalating moves is crucial. They may attempt to suppress it, placate it, or co-opt it, with varying success. Yet, having entered this path, the leaders of the opposing sides have a mutual interest in helping their negotiating partners stay in power and maintain support from their constituents. This poses a fundamental dilemma. The leaders must reassure their own followers that the course taken will yield them what they want and to reassure their former opponents they will not lose what they have sought.

Mediators and other intermediaries often play criti-cal roles in facilitating direct or indirect de-escalating negotiations, particularly in enduring struggles, when the adversaries are frozen in mistrust. Some of the various contributions mediators can provide are illustrated by the critical contributions the US government has made in de-escalating the Israeli-Arab/Palestinian conflict. This has included intensive mediation during high-level negotiations, as President Jimmy Carter and his associates did at Camp David in 1978, between Egyptian President Anwar al-Sadat and Prime Minister Menachem Begin and their associates. It has also included helping to construct a formula which would enable adversaries to begin negotiations, a particularly challenging task when the opposing parties do not recognize each other and do not officially meet. This was the case in 1991, when the US government, following the war against Iraq, sought to initiate comprehensive peace negotiations between the Israeli government and the neighboring Arab governments, and the Palestinians. After much shuttle diplomacy, a complex formula was constructed by Secretary of State Baker and his associates. It consisted of three arenas for negotiation: a general conference (preferred by Arab governments), bilateral meetings between Israel and each neighboring Arab government (long sought by the Israelis), and regional meetings on issues of common concern such as water, security, and refugees (to provide a wider mix of countries and matters of possible mutual benefit). The general conference was held briefly in Madrid in October 1991, bilateral negotiations followed, as did the regional meeting later. A breakthrough had been achieved, but progress then languished until the Israeli government changed in the election of June 1992, when the ruling Likud party was defeated by the Labor party (see *Arab-Israeli Conflict: Peace Plans and Proposals*).

3.4.2 Long Term

Moving out of intractable struggles usually takes a long time. Many small steps usually are needed before a major step can be taken. Furthermore, the effectiveness of the de-escalation efforts are likely to be enhanced if the actors consider the steps as a series and the actions of various actors are coordinated.

Two major strategic approaches partisans might take to change from a confrontational relationship to a more cooperative one have been presented in the literature. One is Graduated Reciprocation in Tension-reduction (GRIT), as set forth by Charles E. Osgood (1962), and the other is a tit-for-tat (TFT) strategy, as discussed in the work of Robert Axelrod (1984). According to the GRIT strategy, one of the parties in conflict unilaterally initiates a series of cooperative moves; these are announced and reciprocity is invited, but the conciliatory moves continue for an extended period, whether or not there is immediate reciprocity. GRIT was first prescribed in the early 1960s as a strategy for the United States to induce reciprocation from the then Soviet Union.

While GRIT strategy was inferred from social psychological theory and research, the TFT strategy was derived from game theory, particularly work on the prisoner's dilemma (PD) game. Experimental research and computer simulations of iterated games of PD indicate that cooperative relations often emerge, and the most successful strategy for developing cooperative relations and yielding the highest overall payoff is for one player to initiate the series of games by acting cooperatively and afterward simply reciprocating the other player's actions, whether a cooperative or a non-cooperative action.

Analysts have assessed these strategies by examining actual de-escalating interactions, particularly in the protracted US-Soviet conflict. For example, Etzioni (1967) has interpreted the de-escalation in American-Soviet antagonism in 1963 as an illustration of the GRIT strategy. He views it as beginning with President Kennedy's June 10th speech at American University announcing a unilateral halt to the atmospheric testing of nuclear weapons; the Soviets reciprocated and other cooperative moves were soon made, including the signing of the Limited Nuclear Test Ban in August 1963. The initial moves, however, were to some extent orchestrated by indirect communication between President Kennedy and Premier Khrushchev (Kriesberg 1981 and Cousins 1972).

A quantitative and case analysis of reciprocity in relations between the United States and the then Soviet Union, between the United States and the People's Republic of China (PRC), and between the Soviet Union and the PRC was conducted by Goldstein and Freeman (1990), for the period 1948-89.

It is ironic that GRIT was offered as a strategy to be undertaken by the US government to break out of the Cold War, but its most spectacular enactment was undertaken by a Soviet leader. Gorbachev announced a change in policy toward the United States and Western Europe and made many conciliatory moves. Goldstein and Freeman characterize it as super-GRIT. It led, they say, to normalized relations with China. It also transformed relations with the United States, although initially, as the Soviets offered concessions, US demands were raised.

Another long term policy is to strengthen shared identities and common institutions. For example,

Greece and Turkey's common membership in the North Atlantic Treaty Organization (NATO) has contributed to constraining the often threatening escalation of their embittered relationship. One of the ways that Gorbachev sought to end the Cold War was to embrace the rule of law, a shared commitment to human rights, and to stress that the then Soviet Union was part of a common European home (see *Glasnost and Perestroika*).

Policies pursued by non-governmental persons and organizations are also important in long-term de-escalating strategies. This includes efforts by segments of an adversary group to influence the leadership's relationship with their common opponent. For example, after President Sadat's visit to Jerusalem in November 1977, the Peace Now social movement arose within Israel to pressure the Likud-led Israeli government to be more forthcoming in its negotiations with the Egyptian government.

Finally, it should be noted that the failure to control and coordinate action sometimes undermines de-escalation too, once it has been undertaken. Insofar as the struggle has generated hostility and mistrust between the antagonists, de-escalating efforts must be clear and consistent to be effective. Subordinates carrying on routine activities or exhibiting extra zealousness may disrupt de-escalation progress. Some segments of the side undertaking to de-escalate a struggle sometimes so oppose the policy that they attempt to sabotage it. They may commit acts of violence against the adversary and so provoke responses which will escalate the conflict again. This has been the case many times in the Israeli-Palestinian peacemaking efforts.

Outside actors may also foster de-escalation over the long-run by imposing constraints on arms or by imposing sanctions. They may do this as interested parties, seeking to stop what they regard as abhorrent conditions and to bring about what they regard as a just outcome.

Intermediaries also often pursue long-term mediating strategies. These include actions to develop better mutual understandings and to foster recognition of possible mutual interests; the actions may be organizing dialogue groups and problem-solving workshops (Kelaman 1992). They may also entail large-scale assistance programs to help develop institutions for managing social conflicts or to help reduce economic problems.

Intermediaries have also played important roles in the transformation of American-Soviet relations. For example, the Conference on Security and Cooperation in Europe (CSCE) which formulated the Helsinki accords signed in 1975 by thirty-five countries, including the United States contributed immensely to the transformation of the Cold War (see *Helsinki Process*). The neutral and non-aligned countries represented at the CSCE meetings played important roles in negotiating an agreement (Leatherman, forthcoming).

4. Conclusions

In this contribution, we examined the processes, conditions, and policies which help explain how struggles can de-escalate without one party simply imposing its will on another. This review indicates that the choice of policies and their effectiveness depends on the existing circumstances and the goals sought.

The conditions underlying a large-scale conflict and the changes in these conditions do not wholly determine whether or not a conflict can be transformed nor whether that conflict is waged constructively. Nor can any person or group, no matter how powerful a role it plays, wholly determine how a conflict is waged. There is always a complex interaction between the prevailing conditions and the long and short term policies pursued by the protagonists, and by the intermediaries.

These interactions have two sets of implications. First, the underlying conditions set parameters within which de-escalating policies can be pursued. The conditions are more constraining for short-term policies than for long-term ones which may be directed at modifying the conditions themselves. Second, those persons and groups seeking to limit the destructiveness of a conflict or transform it into a constructively-waged one need to use an appropriate set of short-term and long-term policies.

In general, certain policies are likely to help prevent, limit, or transform destructive escalation. One useful policy is to minimize reliance on violence, particularly violence which threatens the opponent's existence or that is humiliating and provocative. This review also suggests the power of nonviolent inducements. These can be coercive, as when coalitions are built and allies are mobilized to support the goals being pursued in the struggle. Noncoercive inducements include persuasion and the promise of future benefits. Finally, consideration by each side of the concerns and fears of the other opens avenues for conducting a constructive de-escalation. That consideration must be conveyed convincingly, which is difficult but not impossible in the midst of an intense and protracted struggle.

There is no single path out of a seemingly intractable conflict. The various paths out lead in quite different directions, to greater integration in South Africa, to greater separation between Israelis and Palestinians, and to acceptance of the opponent's ideology, as happened in significant ways within the former Soviet Union. A critical component of successful new policies is a new vision of the nature of the relationship between the adversaries. This may be the result of new ways of thinking, perhaps arising from changes within one or more adversary, changes in the concrete broader situation, and changes in the relationship between the adversaries. After all, social conflicts are socially constructed, and they often can be restructured and reframed so they become a shared problem that requires a joint solution.

Such new visions are expressed in new ways of thinking about the relationship between the erstwhile enemies. They also are expressed in alterations in the set of parties primarily engaged in the conflict and its resolution, excluding intransigent parties or including accommodative new parties. For example, in settling the Cuban Missile Crisis in October 1992, the parties involved in the negotiations were essentially the Soviet and American leadership. Although the missile bases were established in Cuba and the Cuban government wanted them, it did not participate in the negotiations. The exclusion of the more intransigent party allowed an agreement to be reached. But the exclusion of a primary stakeholder sometimes can be viewed as appeasement and betrayal of an ally; this happened in 1938 when Czechoslovakia was not represented at the meeting in Munich when the representatives of England and France yielded to Hitler's demands for Germany to take over the Sudetenland areas of Czechoslovakia.

De-escalation generally proceeds in a step-by-step fashion. The ground must be prepared. What is also especially important is that the changes be done consistently and unequivocally, be in depth, and not be attempts to squeeze as much as possible from the adversary. Finally for leaders of each side, however, it is important to sustain a balance between relations with adversaries and with their constituents. It is important to sustain support from constituents, but that is best thought of in terms of their long range interests.

Transforming transitions tend to occur when a new way of thinking about their conflict becomes dominant in each of the primary adversaries. They each come to believe that the strategy they had been pursuing can not triumph or they can not gain more by continuing it, and an accommodative strategy promises to offer a better alternative. This is a more general statement than the suggestion that a negotiated settlement is reached when the adversaries are in a hurting stalemate and a formula for a settlement seems possible and acceptable. Intermediaries can play major roles in helping foster such reformulations.

The de-escalation of international conflicts is not the result of immutable, large-scale forces nor of the actions of a few brave and wise persons. Many circumstances need to converge and these must be interpreted in new ways in order for a seemingly intractable conflict to be transformed.

See also: *Crisis; Crisis Management; Theoretical Tradition of Peace and Conflict Studies; Evolutionary Movement Toward Peace*

Bibliography ————————————————————

Axelrod R 1984 *The Evolution of Cooperation*. Basic Books, New York

Borker S, Kriesberg L, Abdul-Quader A 1985 Conciliation, confrontation, and approval of the President. *Peace and Change* 11 (Spring)

Brecher M 1993 *Crises in World Politics*. Pergamon, Oxford

Breslauer G W, Tetlock P E (eds.) 1991 *Learning in US and Soviet Foreign Policy*. Westview Press, Boulder

Brockner J, Rubin J Z 1985 *Entrapment in Escalating Conflicts: A Social Psychological Analysis*. Springer Verlag, New York

Cousins N 1972 *The Impossible Triumvirate*. Norton, New York

Davis C, Feshback M 1980 *Rising Infant Mortality in the USSR in the 1970's*. US Department of Commerce, Bureau of the Census, US Printing Office, Washington, DC

DeBenedetti C (Charles Chatfield, Assisting Author) 1990 *An American Ordeal: The Antiwar Movement of the Vietnam Era*. Syracuse University Press, Syracuse

Etzioni A 1967 The Kennedy experiment. *The Western Political Q.* 20 (June)

Feldman S (ed.) 1994 *Confidence Building and Verification: Prospects in the Middle East*. JCSS Study No. 25, The Jerusalem Post, Jerusalem; Westview, Boulder

Fisher R 1964 Fractionating conflict. In: R Fisher (ed.) *International Conflict and Behavioral Science*. Basic Books, New York

Goldstein J S, Freeman J R 1990 *Three-Way Street*. The University of Chicago Press, Chicago and London

Goldstein A P, Michaels G Y 1985 *Empathy: Development, Training, and Consequences*. Lawrence Erlbaum Associates, Hillsdale, NJ

Holsti O R, Brody R A, North R C 1964 Measuring affect and action in international reaction models: Empirical materials from the 1962 Cuban crisis. *J. Peace Research* 3-4

Keashly L, Fisher R J 1995 Complementarity and coordination of conflict interventions: Taking a contingency perspective. In: J Bercovitch (ed.) *Resolving International Conflicts*. Lynne Riener, Boulder, London

Kelman H C 1992 Informal mediation by the scholar/practitioner. In: J Bercovitch, J Z Rubin (eds.) *Mediation in International Relations*. St. Martin's Press, New York

Kennedy R F 1971 *Thirteen Days: A Memoir of the Cuban Missile Crisis*. W.W. Norton, New York

Kriesberg L 1981 Noncoercive inducements in US-Soviet Conflicts: Ending the occupation of Austria and nuclear weapons tests. *J. Political and Military Sociology* 9 (Spring)

Kriesberg L 1992 *International Conflict Resolution: The US-USSR and Middle East Cases*. Yale University Press, New Haven

Kriesberg L (forthcoming) Preventive conflict resolution of communal conflicts. In: D Carment, P James (co-eds.) *The International Politics of Ethnic Conflict: Peacekeeping and Policy*. University of South Carolina Press

Kriesberg L 1995 Varieties of mediating activities and of mediators. In: J Bercovitch (ed.) *Resolving International Conflicts*. Lynne Riener, Boulder, Co

Kriesberg L, Northrop T A, Thorson S J (eds.) 1989 *Intractable Conflicts and Their Transformation*. Syracuse University Press, Syracuse, NY

Kriesberg L, Thorson S J (eds.) 1991 *Timing the De-Escalation of International Conflicts*. Syracuse University Press, Syracuse

Janie L (forthcoming) *Principles and Paradoxes of Peaceful Change*. Syracuse University Press, Syracuse

Lederach J P 1995 *Building Peace: Sustainable Reconciliation in Divided Societies*. The United Nations University, Tokyo

Mueller J E 1973 *War, Presidents and Public Opinion*. John Wiley, New York

Osgood C E 1962 *An Alternative to War or Surrender*. University of Illinois Press, Urbana

Quandt W B 1993 *Peace Process*. The Brookings Institution and Berkeley and Los Angeles, University of California Press, Washington, DC

Ramberg B 1978 *The Seabed Arms Control Negotiations*. Monograph series in World Affairs, Vol. 15. University of Denver, Denver

Schlesinger A M Jr. 1965 *A Thousand Days*. Houghton Mifflin, Boston

Snyder G H, Diesing P 1977 *Conflict among Nations*. Princeton University Press, Princeton

Touval S, Zartman I W (eds.) 1985. *International Mediation in Theory and Practice*. Westview Press, Boulder, Co

Zartman I W 1989 *Ripe for Resolution: Conflict and Intervention in Africa*. Oxford University Press (originally published in 1985), New York

LOUIS KRIESBERG

International Court of Justice

International judicial settlement (see *International Judicial Settlement*) is a refined form of international arbitration (see *Arbitration, International*) which reached its organized form with the establishment of the Permanent Court of International Justice after the establishment of the League of Nations (see *League of Nations*).

The jurisdiction of the Permanent Court was of a twofold character serving as a judicial tribunal for disputes between those states which were prepared to accept its jurisdiction, and also as an advisory body for the interpretation of those legal problems submitted to it by the League. By its Statute it was provided that in addition to the ad hoc jurisdiction which would arise whenever states in dispute decided to submit a specific issue for adjudication, the Court also possessed a compulsory jurisdiction at the option of those states wishing to declare their acceptance of the Court's role in advance of any dispute arising. By Article 36 of the Court's Statute, commonly known as the Optional Clause, it was open to states, members of the League, to announce in advance that they would accept the jurisdiction of the Court for any dispute affecting treaty interpretation or other issues of international law in relation to any other state accepting a similar commitment. This Declaration could be made conditionally and be subject to reservations, which made it of temporal character indicating that the jurisdiction was accepted only for issues arising thereafter, and of a substantive nature excluding particular types of issue, for example, as among members of the British Commonwealth, when it was considered that a more "friendly" form of settlement might be desirable (see *Peacebuilding and the Changing Role of International Law*). Again, it was recognized that specific treaties might provide for special tribunals, in which case the jurisdiction of the World Court would be excepted.

The judges of the Court were elected on their personal records, regardless of whether the countries of which they were nationals became parties to the Statute or not. Thus, although the United States declined to recognize the jurisdiction, American jurists played a major role in the practice of the Court, while a German jurist remained on the bench even after Germany withdrew from the League. The former Soviet Union never recognized the Court's jurisdiction and no then Soviet jurist ever joined the bench. In fact, the absence of the Soviet Union from the League enabled the Court to establish the principle that no advisory opinion could be delivered if the effect might touch upon the rights of a state not a party to the Statute or not acknowledging the jurisdiction.

The Treaty of Versailles, together with the other peace treaties terminating the First World War, included a number of provisions relating, for example, to the protection of minorities, international river navigation, internationalized territories, and the like, which were bound to give rise to dispute. The Court played a major role in developing the legal regimes which apply to such issues to this day. In addition, it dealt with problems relating to territorial limits, maritime criminal jurisdiction, and the servicing of international loans among others, again laying down broad principles which continue to be significant, although in many instances these rulings have now been affected by recent codification treaties (see *Treaties of the Modern Era*).

When the United Nations was established, the states participating in the San Francisco Conference were sufficiently conscious of the contribution made by the World Court to the development of international law that they embodied a revised Statute, largely based on that of the former Court, into the Charter as a separate chapter, expressly stating that the Court would constitute the judicial organ of the new world organization, with every member of the United Nations becoming ipso facto a party to the Court's Statute and amenable to its jurisdiction, if it should desire to make use of it. By virtue of the close relationship with the United Nations, the Court has played a major role in interpreting various issues of competence as well as delivering significant opinions on the status of the United Nations, the immunities and rights of its officials, the liabilities in so far as exceptional financial commitments are concerned, the obligations of members in exercising their discretion as to the qualifications of applicants for admission to membership, and perhaps most significantly a series of opinions on the obligations of South Africa as the mandatory for Southwest Africa, culminating in the legal determination of the status of Namibia and the right of the United Nations to terminate a mandate agreement, regardless of the views of the mandatory.

Despite the disappearance of the mandate and trusteeship systems, these opinions concerning the interpretation of agreements, the supreme competence of the United Nations and the nature of human rights are still of major significance. They remain of particular importance in view of the possible creation of new entities under some form of international supervision.

In order to ensure that there would be some jurisdictional basis for action from the moment of the new Court's creation—now to be known as the International Court of Justice—it was provided that any declarations under the Optional Clause of the former Permanent Court would remain valid, although it soon became clear that problems would arise in interpreting such documents. Compulsory jurisdiction on the basis of Article 36 of the Statute remained feasible, although its impact has been radically reduced by the introduction of what has come to be known as the Connolly Amendment by the United States. By this reservation the United States excluded from the jurisdiction of the Court any matter essentially within the domestic jurisdiction of the United States as determined by the United States. A number of other states, particularly among those newly created, made similar reservations. Although Article 36 provides that the Court alone will decide any dispute relating to its jurisdiction, it has upheld the validity of this particular reservation. Since states appear before that Court on a basis of absolute reciprocity, the reservation enables a state which has not added such a clause to its declaration under the Optional Clause to take advantage of it when sued by any state which has done so.

Article 38 of the Statute indicates the "sources" from which the Court will find its law. In the first instance, it is to have recourse to any treaty to which the states before it may be party. It is then to have recourse to principles of customary international law, and here problems arise since so many of the newer states refuse to acknowledge the validity of what has in the past been regarded as principles of customary law. In the third place, it is to have regard to the general principles of law recognized by civilized nations, although there is no indication of how a decision as to the standard of civilization is to be made, nor as to how a principle is to be recognized as general. In fact, the Court has never, in its majority opinions or judgments, made use of this "source," for any such principle would be treated as a rule of customary law. Moreover, it is now accepted that every independent sovereign state, especially if a member of the United Nations, is assumed to be "civilized" in the sense in which that term appears in Article 38. Finally, as a subsidiary means for the determination of rules of law, the Court is authorized to have recourse to its own jurisprudence and the writings of scholars. While a judgment is only authoritative for its own case and in respect of the parties thereto, the Court makes frequent use of earlier findings, and the judgments and opinions are given full respect by states and writers alike. However, the United States,

disagreeing with the Court's approach to jurisdiction in so far as its dispute with Nicaragua is concerned, has rejected the authority of the Court in this case and has denounced the Court as a political tool of anti-American interests. This decision has been made despite the use of the Court by the United States in its dispute with Iran concerning the seizure of the American embassy in Tehran, even though Iran refused to appear on that occasion. In this judgment the Court laid down some basic principles concerning the diplomatic function and the rights of diplomats (see *Ambassadors*). Further, despite the cancellation of its declaration under the Optional Clause, consequent upon the Nicaragua decision, the United States continues to recognize the Court's jurisdiction in connection with any treaty to which the United States is a party and which contains a jurisdictional clause in relation to the application of that treaty.

Unfortunately, the number of states prepared to accept the compulsory jurisdiction of the Court is still relatively small. However, a number of newly independent states have resorted to the Court for the settlement of boundary disputes, or for other issues arising from the legacy of colonial times. Nevertheless, it has made important contributions to the development of the law concerning the right of asylum, the limits of the continental shelf, state responsibility (see *State Responsibility*), the interpretation of the most favored nation clause, and the meaning of self-determination and human rights (see *Global Ethics, Human Rights Laws and Democratic Governance*). The Court's decision in the Nicaragua/United States case is of major significance as regards the meaning of self-defense, and its opinion on the legality of the use of nuclear weapons is extremely important in considering issues related to humanitarian law and the law of armed conflict. Its jurisdiction is final without any right of appeal. However, in the event of a state not carrying out a judgment, the successful party is able to refer the matter to the Security Council which *may* decide what action to take. In fact this means that a political organ has been given the right of supervision of a legal judgment.

The Court consists of fifteen judges elected by the Security Council and the General Assembly from among nominees put forward by states, bearing in mind the need for regional distribution and representation of the principal legal systems of the world. To date, the bench has always included a judge from the People's Republic of China, France, the former Soviet Union, the United Kingdom, and the United States, even though the People's Republic of China and the then Soviet Union have never had recourse thereto.

But Russia has announced its willingness to recognize the Court's jurisdiction in issues related to humanitarian treaties to which Russia is a party. If a case is presented and there is no judge of one of the parties on the bench, that party is entitled to nominate a judge ad hoc to preserve the appearance of reciprocity and equality, although in practice a judge ad hoc does not always possess the nationality of the state nominating him or her. A major departure in the personnel of the bench took place with the election of Judge Higgins from the United Kingdom. For the first time, a woman had been appointed a judge of the World Court. In recent years there has been a tendency for some states to question the independence of the Court and when making use of its services they have had recourse to a chamber made up of a smaller bench than the full Court. Unfortunately, they have tended not to accept the judges suggested by the President of the Court, but to insist that those appointed to such a chamber should be acceptable to, and even selected by, themselves. Such an attitude may be considered as directly contrary to the idea of the Court as a completely impartial tribunal, an impartiality which is preserved by granting the judges a reasonable tax-free salary, with full pension rights, and ensuring that they remain free of interference by any state in respect of their judicial activities.

It has often been asserted that the World Court can not decide "political" as distinct from "legal" issues. Against this it has been pointed out that the decision to go to Court and accept an impartial tribunal is a political decision, and that once made there is an acknowledgment that the issues in dispute will in fact be settled in accordance with the principles of international law. That the Court is prepared to consider the legal implications of any question, despite its political constituents, once the question has been referred to it was made clear in the Opinion on Nuclear Weapons. Unfortunately, more and more states are insisting that issues in dispute are political in character, affecting their national dignity, and of a kind that are not amenable to jurisdiction by a judicial tribunal. As a result the Court, in its present form, has not been employed as often as might otherwise have been the case, and it is not enough to suggest that part of this, when compared with the activities of its predecessor, may be put down to the absence of a peace treaty with Germany or of treaties concerning the welfare of minorities. On the other hand, it cannot be denied that the existence of such courts as the European Community, or the European and American Courts of Human Rights may well entail a diminution of activity, although the states resorting to these tribunals have never shown an excessive willingness to make use of the Court at The Hague.

See also: *Emerging Tool Chest of Peacebuilders; Pacific Settlement of International Disputes*

Bibliography ————————————

Gross L 1976 *The Future of the International Court.*

Hudson M O 1943 *The Permanent Court of International Justice, 1920-1942.* Longmans, London

Lowe V, Fitzmaurice M 1996 *Fifty Years of the International Court of Justice.* Cambridge University Press, Cambridge

Lauterpacht H 1958 *The Development of International Law by the International Court.* Stevens, London

Rosenne S 1997 *The Law and Practice of the International Court.* Leyden, Kluwer

Schwarzenberger G 1957 *International Law.* Stevens, London

LESLIE C. GREEN

International Criminal Law

International criminal law is understood as being that part of international law which defines offenses regarded as so heinous that any state would have the right to try the offender should he or she come within its jurisdiction. Normally, criminal jurisdiction depends upon the nationality of the offender, the nationality of the victim, or the location of the offense. In this case, however, none of these conditions is relevant, for it is international law which defines the offense.

One of the main difficulties in examining international criminal law is the absence of any international police force able to arrest the alleged offender or any international tribunal able to try him or her, although there is nothing to prevent any two or more states from establishing a special tribunal to try particular offenses or specific offenders, as was done in the case of the major German and Japanese war criminals at the end of the Second World War. In the absence of any permanent international criminal tribunal, the only way in which international criminal acts can be judged on an international level is by way of ad hoc tribunals specially established for that purpose, as has been done for the former Yugoslavia, with a tribunal sitting at The Hague, and for Rwanda, with a tribunal at Arusha. Otherwise, the decision to take proceedings against any offender rests with individual states, and the extent to which such states are prepared to give effect to the provisions of international criminal law depends upon national legislation. Some states are prepared to amend their legislation to give jurisdiction to national tribunals to try offenses which are defined as such by international law, particularly when the definition is to be found in a treaty to which the state in question is a party (see *State Responsibility*). It must be noted, however, that since the Middle Ages, all states, particularly those engaged in maritime commerce, have regarded piracy as an international crime, even though, prior to 1958, there was no treaty to this effect.

In feudal times the orders of chivalry recognized their own rules of conduct during conflict and tribunals made up of knights were established when necessary to try offenders against the accepted law. This was particularly true in the case of breach of parole or failure to pay a ransom or to observe the conditions attached to such ransom. This attitude to the law of chivalry may be seen in the modern approach to offenses against the laws and customs of war. While, for the main part, this law is embodied in the Hague Conventions of 1907 and the Geneva Conventions of 1949 as amended by the Protocols of 1977, it must be recognized that these conventions themselves to a very great extent are merely codifications of the customary behavior in time of conflict recognized as proper by the majority of national armed forces. This fact was emphasized during the Tokyo and Nuremberg proceedings (see *Nuremberg Principles*) when it was held that even the conventions had hardened into customary law. While the Hague Conventions prescribe the law to be observed, they make no provision for trial other than to recognize that states may be held liable for the activities of those under their command, nor is there any indication as to how that liability is to be enforced. Moreover, state practice indicates that criminal proceedings will be conducted by national military tribunals applying the law of armed conflict against the individuals personally liable for committing the war crimes in question, while the Geneva Conventions and Protocols expressly recognize personal liability for grave breaches. Although it has long been accepted that commanders may, depending on the circumstances, be responsible together with those under their command, it was not until the Nuremberg and Tokyo trials that any attempt was made to proceed against political leaders or members of a High Com-

mand who might have been responsible for the decision to go to war or for the overall policy once conflict was joined. Perhaps even more important was the introduction of the concept of crimes against humanity, intended for the protection of civilians and other non-combatants, including those rendered *hors de combat* originally directed to such matters as the Holocaust and other atrocities perpetrated by the Nazis in Europe, as well as by Japan in the Asian theatre during World War II. This concept has been greatly extended as a result of the growing international concern with the protection of human rights.

Traditionally, it was recognized at an early date that certain activities were so reprehensible that the perpetrators thereof might be considered as *hostes humani generis*, enemies of all humankind. The crime usually referred to in this connection is piracy on the high seas and every state is authorized to proceed against those accused of this offense, jurisdiction being based on the definition of the act regardless of any other consideration which might in normal circumstances be relevant in establishing jurisdiction. Moreover, this offense is based on the practice of maritime states and is intimately connected to the need to preserve the freedom of the seas and freedom of commerce. At various times and reflecting current moral standards, different activities have been regarded as amounting to international crimes carrying this universal right to exercise jurisdiction. Thus, during the nineteenth century with the growth of industrial activities, slave trading came to be treated as an international crime, although it has still been necessary in recent years to draft treaties condemning this activity, since not all states were prepared to concede that the trade in slaves was forbidden by customary international law. As a result of the evidence concerning the holocaust perpetrated in Nazi Germany between 1933 and 1945, genocide and other crimes against humanity received recognition as international crimes, although insofar as the former was concerned it was considered advisable to define it precisely by way of the Genocide Convention drawn up by the United Nations in 1948. In recent years, reflecting the rise in terrorism, the United Nations has adopted a number of treaties, covering such matters as hostage-taking, torture, traffic of narcotics and the like, which embody the principle of universal jurisdiction (see *Crime Trends and Crime Prevention Strategies*).

Among the oldest rules of international law have been those regarding the immunity and rights of foreign sovereigns and diplomatic representatives, and this principle is now confirmed in a United Nations convention which criminalizes attacks against diplomats or other internationally protected persons, such as representatives of the United Nations on official missions (see *Ambassadors*). However, the traditional immunity does not apply if the sovereign or diplomat is accused of ordering or committing an international criminal act. After the rise of anarchism in the nineteenth century, some states, particularly in Latin America, entered into agreements whereby they declared anarchists to be liable to the jurisdiction of any state capturing them and a similar liability was extended, even by some European states, to communists. The postulation of an international criminal law became more generally desirable after the assassinations of Alexander of Yugoslavia and the Foreign Minister of France in 1934, allegedly with the complicity of the Fascist government of Italy. As a result, the League of Nations (see *League of Nations*) drew up a convention condemning terrorism directed against political personalities in their political capacity, but this convention (1936) received only one ratification. At the same time some members of the League of Nations signed a concurrent convention establishing an international criminal tribunal with jurisdiction to try those committing offenses covered by the Terrorist Convention. However not a single state ratified this second convention, and neither has ever come into force. While the United Nations has been unable to agree upon a satisfactory definition of terrorism, it has adopted a number of resolutions condemning it (see *Contemporary International Terrorism, Nature of*). In addition, a number of conventions dealing with specific types of terrorism have been adopted, each of which affirms the right of universal jurisdiction. In addition, the International Law Commission has adopted a draft Statute for an International Criminal Court, which is now (May 1997) under consideration by the Geneva Assembly.

The drive to recognize the significance of international criminal law received a new impetus with the war crimes trials after 1945, and the General Assembly of the United Nations adopted a resolution recognizing aggression and crimes against peace as international crimes while reiterating the criminality of offenses against the laws of war and extending them to protect civilians by way of condemning crimes against humanity. The International Law Commission was instructed to draw up a draft convention on crimes against peace, but has not yet been successful in this task. As already indicated, a Genocide Convention was adopted in 1948, although not all members of the United Nations have become parties to it. Moreover, the convention recognizes that there is no international criminal tribunal and leaves it to the

courts of each country in which the genocide has been committed to proceed against those responsible. Since genocide is an offense that can only be committed with the connivance or consent of governmental authorities this convention is likely to remain a "paper tiger," even though some Western countries have amended their legislation to condemn genocide when committed by persons within their jurisdiction. Genocide is often regarded as the gravest offense against human rights, but it is the only such offense of the kind that is recognized as constituting an international crime. None of the other international instruments relating to human rights attempts to define any breach of its provisions as a criminal offense. However, in the light of the atrocities committed during conflicts in the former Yugoslavia and in Rwanda, the Security Council established ad hoc criminal tribunals, sifted with judges representing a variety of jurisdictions. These tribunals were empowered to try persons, regardless of position or rank, ordering or committing genocide, war crimes or crimes against humanity. Difficulties have, however, arisen in regard to securing the arrest of the most senior politicians or military commanders in the former Yugoslavia. In the absence of an international police force, the two tribunals are able to issue arrest warrants enforceable with the assistance of Interpol, and a number of countries have offered the necessary prison facilities for those convicted. These tribunals, however, only possess the limited jurisdiction indicated and have no competence in regard to offenses committed against the various antiterrorist conventions. Moreover, when they have completed their task regarding the former Yugoslavia and Rwanda they will cease to exist.

With the upsurge of aerial hijacking connected with the Arab/Israeli conflict in the Middle East, efforts were made to condemn acts of aerial terrorism. The General Assembly of the United Nations has adopted a series of resolutions condemning terrorism, but the effect of this condemnation has been mitigated somewhat by attaching thereto an exception on behalf of those waging wars of national liberation or otherwise seeking self-determination, insisting that eradicating the causes of terrorism is of equal importance as dealing with the acts of terrorism themselves (see *Psychological Causes of Oppositional Political Terrorism: A Model*). This reservation is rapidly becoming of less significance in view of the very reduced number of colonial territories still remaining and the increased status of the Palestine Authority, which has replaced the Palestine Liberation Organization as a national liberation movement (see *Arab-Israeli Conflict: Peace*

Plans and Proposals). In addition, regarding aerial hijacking a great deal of progress has been made under the auspices of the International Civil Aviation Organization under whose auspices the Tokyo, Hague, and Montreal Conventions of 1963, 1970, and 1971 were drawn up. The combined effect of these agreements is to ensure cooperation among the parties for punishing hijacking and other offenses against aircraft, with the obligation either to extradite—that is to say, for one state or authority to surrender an alleged criminal to another having jurisdiction to try the charge—or try those found within their territory against whom charges relating to such offenses might be lodged.

The United Nations has also been responsible for drawing up conventions relating to acts of terrorism against internationally protected persons, including diplomats (1973), and against the taking of hostages (1979). Both of these contain reservations in respect to acts done in the name of self-determination, but otherwise contain similar jurisdictional provisions to the antihijack treaties.

In the absence of treaties of the kind referred to above, the only way in which international cooperation for the punishment of criminal offenses is exercised is through the medium of extradition, but the obligation to extradite depends upon the existence of a bilateral treaty between the requesting and requested state, while the offense for which extradition is requested has to be listed in the treaty (see *Treaties of the Modern Era*). Moreover, most states have insisted that extradition would only be granted in respect to offenses enumerated in their own national extradition legislation. Furthermore, it has been generally recognized that extradition would not be granted in respect to political offenses, but the definition of a political offense has varied and has often reflected the political sympathies of the country of refuge. In recent years, reflecting the reaction against terrorism, even when politically inspired, there has been an increasing tendency to limit the scope of this defense. It is now frequent that if the offense has been committed with explosives or if persons, particularly non-governmental personnel, have been killed, the offense will not be considered political in character and the offender will be liable to extradition. At the same time, more and more extraditable treaties now abandon the specification of extraditable offenses providing for extradition if the alleged offense is subject to a jail sentence exceeding in many cases as little as twelve months or two years. Under the various antiterrorist conventions an attempt has been made to ensure that this defense cannot be used to evade extradition within the terms of the convention. How-

ever, a number of states sympathetic to terrorists have refused to become parties to these conventions, while many of the parties leave the decision as to the extraditability of an offense to be determined in accordance with their normal processes so that the treaty obligation is frequently evaded. In addition, the value of the limitation has been greatly reduced by the self-determination (see *Self-determination*) exception, and there are still many cases in which, despite current trends, individual judges have still protected alleged terrorists by way of the political offense defense. This has often been the case with members of the Irish Republican Army whose extradition Britain has sought from the United States.

The most serious crimes in modern international law are aggression (see *Aggression*), genocide, complicity in terrorism, and the like. Such crimes can, in most instances, only be committed with the connivance, complicity, or tolerance of state authorities, or may in fact be a matter of state policy. In former times it was possible for states to resort to war or occupation of territory in an effort to punish another state responsible for such activities. Today, particularly since every state has its friends and would probably be protected by a power possessing veto rights in the Security Council, such action is no longer considered possible. With the end of the Cold War, however, as well as the dissolution of the Soviet bloc, this situation is changing. Whereas in the past it was only possible to secure agreement to apply economic sanctions against such entities as the separatist administration in Rhodesia or the apartheid regime in South Africa, it is now possible to secure condemnation of and sanctions against countries supporting terrorism, traffic in narcotics and even to an extreme denial of human rights. Similarly, when Iraq invaded Kuwait, the Security Council agreed to authorize enforcement action (see *United Nations Peacekeeping Operations*), followed by severe sanctions against Iraq, including the establishment of nonfly zones with the threat of destruction of Iraqi aircrafts (see *Intervention*). The same willingness to take action has been seen in the case of the former Yugoslavia, which would have been most unlikely prior to the dissolution of the former Soviet Union (see *United Nations and* NATO *in Former Yugoslavia*). However, in view of the condemnation of the aggression and crimes against humanity which cannot be committed as a matter of individual enterprise, and in the light of the support and refuge given by a number of states to terrorists, as well as the condemnation by the United Nations of neocolonialism and those supporting it, the International Law Commission has devoted much of its energy to drafting an international code on state responsibility and has elaborated what might be regarded as an international criminal code. By Article 19 of the draft,

(a) An act of a State which constitutes a breach of an international obligation is an internationally wrongful act, regardless of the subject-matter of the obligation breached.

(b) An internationally wrongful act which results from the breach by a State of an international obligation so essential for the protection of fundamental interests of the international community that its breach is recognized as a crime by that community as a whole, constitutes an international crime.

(c) Subject to paragraph 2, and on the basis of the rules of international law in force, an international crime may result, *inter alia*, from:

(i) a serious breach of an international obligation of essential importance for the maintenance of international peace and security, such as that prohibiting aggression;

(ii) a serious breach of an international obligation for safeguarding the right of self-determination of peoples, such as that prohibiting the establishment or maintenance by force of colonial domination;

(iii) a serious breach on a widespread scale of an international obligation of essential importance for safeguarding the human being, such as those prohibiting slavery, genocide and *apartheid*;

(iv) a serious breach of an international obligation of essential importance for the safeguarding and preservation of the human environment, such as those prohibiting massive pollution of the atmosphere or of the seas.

This list of offenses is far from complete, but the offenses specified represent more the ideology of the Third World than the realities of international law. However, the International Law Commisson has followed this with a further draft Code of Offenses against the Peace and Security of Mankind which is somewhat less ideological in character, although still including such offenses as the traffic in narcotics which may be considered to be somewhat difficult to reconcile with the title of the Code. However, the jurisdiction of the International Criminal Court embodied in the Commission's draft statute is somewhat narrower than this. While there is a convention condemning apartheid as a crime against humanity (1973) this is far from being universally adopted.

Similarly, there is as yet no international law generally accepted relating to "the safeguarding and preservation of the human environment." And not all states are agreed as to what constitutes self-determination or colonial domination. It is also unlikely that there will ever be agreement as to what obligation is "so essential for the protection of fundamental interests of the international community that its breach is recognized as a crime by that community as a whole." Moreover, there is no indication in the draft of how any state resorting to any of these criminal activities is to be penalized or brought to justice, although it is provided that the liability of a state arises from the act of any state organ, regardless of the branch of government to which that organ pertains. This would imply that the only way in which a state can be penalized for its criminal behavior is by way of verbal condemnation or a decision of the Security Council to call for the application of some form of sanction, economic or military, against the offender. In the absence of this, the sole means of process would lie against an individual member of the government. And it is now clear that in many cases action in fact be taken against such persons either by way of an ad hoc tribunal established by the Security Council, or even by unilateral action by a state claiming to be seriously affected by the offender's conduct, as was the case when Israel seized Eichmann in Argentina, or as the United States has been doing increasingly with those alleged to be trafficking in narcotics.

While those parts of international criminal law which relate to aggression, genocide, and the like, if enforced, may contribute to the maintenance of peace and the upholding of the rule of law, there is little by way of true criminal law to be found in international law. International criminal law, therefore, may be defined as indicating those offenses which are regarded as such by the international community and the criminalization of which is postulated either by customary or treaty law. Until such time as there is an international criminal tribunal of a permanent character, the only reality for international criminal law lies in the extent to which individual states are prepared to legislate into their criminal statutes the proscription of the acts concerned. Enforcement of international criminal law depends on national legislation and national judicial processes, subject to the additional processes which might be created by specific treaties on an ad hoc basis. Even if an international criminal court is established, enforcement of its warrants of arrest as well as its judgements will depend, in the absence of an international police force and an acceptable place of detention, upon the willingness of states to give effective support to its activities. Further if such a court is to operate successfully and contribute to the proper establishment of a respected international rule of law, states will have to cooperate with the court, even if the accused is one of its own nationals, however regardless of the rank.

See also: *International Law; State Responsibility; Terrorism; Global Peace and Global Accountability; World Peace Order, Dimensions of a; New Morality for the Global Community*

Bibliography ———————————————

Bassiouni M C 1980 *International Criminal Law*. Sijthoff, Alphen aan den Rijn

Bassiouni M C, Nanda V P (eds.) 1973 *A Treatise on International Criminal Law*, 2 vols. Thomas, Springfield, Illinois

Green L C 1976 An international criminal code—NOW. *Dalhousie Law Journal* 3

Green L C 1981 New trends in international criminal law. *Israel Yearbook on Human Rights* 11

Lombois C 1971 Droit pénal international. Dalloz, Paris

Mueller G W, Wise E M (eds.) 1971 *International Criminal Law*. Sweet and Maxwell, London

Paust J J, Bassioni M C et al., 1996 *International Criminal Law*. Durham. NC, Carolina Academic Press

LESLIE C. GREEN

International Day of Peace and International Year of Peace

The International Day of Peace and the International Year of Peace (1986) were designed to promote and strengthen the ideals of peace both within and among all nations and peoples. The thirty-sixth session of the United Nations General Assembly unanimously adopted the International Day of Peace, every third Tuesday of September (the opening day of the United Nations in 1945) on November 30, 1981 in a Costa Rican resolution. The International Year of Peace in 1986 was unanimously adopted at the thirty-seventh session of the General Assembly on November 16, 1982, on the recommendation of the UN Economic and Social Council (ECOSOC).

The original proponent of the International Day and Year of Peace was Young Seek Choue, Founder-Chancellor of Kyung Hee University, Seoul, Republic of Korea, and then President of the International Association of University Presidents. The Costa Rican delegation headed by Ambassador Rodolfo Piza Escalante and Emilie C. de Barish, Alternate Permanent Representative of Costa Rica, proposed the resolution on the International Day of Peace at the thirty-sixth session of the UN General Assembly on behalf of Choue, a citizen of a nonmember state. The resolution was based on the Day of Peace resolution, inspired by Choue, adopted by the International Association of University Presidents (IAUP) on July 6, 1981, at its sixth triennial conference in Costa Rica. Among the many distinguished people who supported this resolution were Nasrolla S. Fatemi, Iranian Ambassador to the United Nations, Leland Miles, President of Bridgeport University, United States, and Rodrigo Carazo Odio, President of Costa Rica.

1. International Day of Peace

At its thirty-sixth session, in 1981, the UN General Assembly, recalling that the promotion of peace, both at the international and the national level, is among the main purposes of the UN, in conformity with its Charter, decided that it would be appropriate "to devote a specific time to concentrate the efforts of the United Nations and its Member States, as well as of the whole of mankind, to promoting the ideals of peace and to giving positive evidence of their commitment to peace in all viable ways." The Assembly therefore declared, in a resolution (A/36/L.29/Rev.1) adopted on November 30, 1981, that the third Tuesday in September, the opening day of its regular annual session, should be officially dedicated and observed as the International Day of Peace and should be devoted "to commemorating and strengthening the ideals of peace both within and among all nations and people." It invited all member states, organs and organizations, nongovernmental organizations, peoples, and individuals "to commemorate in an appropriate manner the International Day of Peace, especially through all means of education," and to cooperate with the UN in the observance of the Day.

The Assembly reaffirmed a belief set forth in the Charter of UNESCO that "since wars begin in the minds of men, it is in the minds of men that the defence of peace must be constructed," and that "peace must therefore be founded, if it is not to fail, upon the intellectual and moral solidarity of mankind."

The representatives of Costa Rica declared that the International Day of Peace "will serve as a reminder to all peoples that our Organization, with all its limitations, is a living instrument in the service of peace and should serve all of us here within the organization as a constantly pealing bell reminding us that our permanent commitment, above all interests of differences of any kind, is to peace. May this peace day indeed be a day of peace."

The first International Day of Peace was observed at UN Headquarters in New York on September 21, 1982, the opening day of the thirty-seventh session of the General Assembly. At the start of the session, delegates stood for one minute of silence in observance of the Day. Messages for the occasion were issued by Javier Perez De Cuellar, Secretary-General of the UN, Imre Hollai (Hungary) President of the General Assembly, and Masahiro Nisibori (Japan), President of the Security Council.

2. International Year of Peace

The resolution (A/36/l.29/Rev.1) on the International Day of Peace also invited the Economic and Social Council (ECOSOC) of the United Nations "to consider, at its first regular session of 1982, the possibility of declaring an International Year of Peace at the first practicable opportunity, taking into account the urgency and special nature of such an observance." In the meeting of May 4, 1982, ECOSOC unanimously recommended a Peace Year, resolving that 1986, the year of the UN's fortieth anniversary, be so designated. It is worth recalling, as did council members on this occasion, the preamble to the UN Charter: "To save succeeding generations from the scourge of war and for this end to practice tolerance and to live together in peace with one another as good neigh-

bors, and to unite their strength to maintain international peace and security."

On the first International Day of Peace, September 21, 1982, the General Assembly unanimously resolved to accept the ECOSOC recommendation and declared 1986 the International Year of Peace, to be proclaimed on October 24, 1985, the date beginning the observance of the UN's fortieth anniversary. The General Assembly requested the Secretary-General to prepare a draft program for the year in accordance with proposals by member states and in consultation with interested organizations and academic institutions, and to submit a report at its thirty-eighth session. The Secretary-General presented his report and his draft program in document A/38/413 and Add. 1 and 2. Arrangements regarding preparations for the International Year of Peace were presented in document A/C.5/38/60.

In resolution 38/56 of December 7, 1983, the General Assembly endorsed the principal objectives of the International Year of Peace. The Assembly invited "all states, all organizations within the United Nations system and interested non-governmental organizations to exert all possible efforts for the preparation and the observance of the International Year of Peace and to respond generously with contributions to attain the objectives of the years."

It is noteworthy that the resolutions on the International Day of Peace and the International Year of Peace were adopted without vote. This indicates a broad consensus among member states concerning the observance of this day and year of peace.

See also: *World Peace Day Association*

JONG-MIN HYUN

International Judicial Settlement

Of all the methods of settling interstate disputes the one that most resembles the processes within the state and demonstrates the realities of international law is judicial settlement. In this connection it must be pointed out that many issues that might result in interstate controversy, such as infringements by private individuals of the rights of diplomats (see *Ambassadors*), or failure by a state organ to meet its contractual obligations, most usually are settled in a national court. In the settlement of such issues the national tribunal is called upon to apply both national and international law (see *International Law*). It is only when a dispute arises between two states that there is any need to have recourse to an international

tribunal. Such a dispute may arise because one state alleges that its nationals have been denied justice by the judicial organs of the other, thus infringing the right of the first state to protect its own nationals. More usually, however, it arises from a breach of treaty or an allegation that one state has infringed upon the sovereign rights of another. Increasingly, however, with the achievement of independence by a number of former colonial territories, disputes have arisen concerning the continued validity of boundaries established by the former imperial powers. Similarly, with the adoption of law of the sea conventions a number of disputes have arisen concerning, in particular, the limits of the continental shelf, maritime frontiers and the regulation of fisheries.

It is a failing of international law that there is no permanent judicial tribunal enjoying compulsory jurisdiction with the power to compel any state to refer its disputes for determination, or to compel any state to appear before it as defendant, or to call upon any enforcement agency to give effect to any judgment that it may deliver (see *Pacific Settlement of International Disputes*). Superficially, therefore, to refer to international judicial settlement as a process to establish the law or rights under the law would appear to be an exercise in semantics. On the other hand, it cannot be denied that states have, since ancient times, sought to settle their differences without having recourse to armed force. Most usually this has been done by direct negotiation (see *Negotiations, Direct*), but on occasion they have referred their problem for impartial settlement to some neutral third party. As long ago as 600 BC arbitration was used by the Greek city-states, while in the Middle Ages it was by no means uncommon for interstate disputes to be referred to the Pope for ultimate settlement—a practice that has been revived only recently by Argentina and Chile in seeking a settlement of their dispute concerning sovereignty in the Beagle Channel. A more regular form of arbitration was introduced by the Jay Treaty (1794) whereby the United States and Great Britain agreed to settle a variety of differences stemming from the newly won independence of the United States. This was followed by the Treaty of Washington (1871) mainly concerned with determination of the dispute arising from the activities of the Confederate vessel *The Alabama* during the US Civil War, as well as with issues concerning US-Canadian relations. This arbitration clearly established that a state could not plead before an international tribunal that the deficiencies of its national law made it impossible for it to fulfill its international obligations. It also established the principle that an international tribunal should consist of an odd number of judges, with at least a president of neutral nationality (see *Neutrality*).

Arbitration became more popular and operated on a more extensive basis as a result of the First Hague Peace Conference, 1899, with the establishment of the Permanent Court of Arbitration. At the Second Hague Peace Conference, 1907, a Convention for the Pacific Settlement of International Disputes was adopted and this, for the first time, outlined a code of procedure for the Court to follow (see *Arbitration, International*). However, the Court was not a court in the normal sense of that word. While it had a permanent Registry at The Hague, there was no permanent court or tribunal. States wishing to make use of its services indicated from a list proposed by all parties to the Convention which persons were to hear their particular case, and the award was more in the form of a recommendation than a decision. However, once states had decided to refer a matter to independent arbitral settlement it could be assumed that they intended to accept the decision of that tribunal. Since the parties to the dispute are able to select the members of the tribunal, they will occasionally prefer this tribunal rather than the International Court of Justice where, unless the matter is to be heard by a chamber rather than the full bench, they have no control over the selection of judges (see *International Court of Justice*). Further, by resorting to the Permanent Court of Arbitration they and the tribunal are free of any restrictions that may flow from the Statute of the World Court of its Rules of Procedure.

The 1907 Conference also adopted the Convention of the Limitation of the Use of Force for the Recovery of Contract Debts. Here an attempt was made to use the judicial process rather than a resort to force. After Venezuela had defaulted on its debts, a number of creditor countries had in 1903 used force to ensure payment, and the Permanent Court of Arbitration held that the state resorting to force to ensure payment were to be treated as preferential creditors. By the Convention it was agreed that force to recover debts could be resorted to in the future only if the debtor refused to accept arbitration or if, after arbitration, it persisted in its refusal to meet its obligations disregarding the award.

International judicial settlement in the proper sense of the term began after the First World War. A variety of Mixed Arbitral Tribunals were established under the various Peace Treaties enabling the victorious powers to bring claims against the defeated Central Powers. Similar bilateral Mixed Claims Commissions were set up after the Mexican Revolution so that claims could be brought on behalf of non-Mexicans who had suffered injury during the revolutionary campaigns. Similarly, after the Second World War a number of Claims Commissions were established to deal with issues between some of the victors and Italy, particularly for claims put forward by "United Nations nationals" concerning expropriated property. While states continued to make use of bilateral ad hoc tribunals for specific cases as may be seen in such instances as the Claims Commission established by the United States and Iran to deal with issues consequent upon the overthrow of the Shah and the seizure of the United States embassy in Tehran, of far more importance from the point of view of international law was the establishment of the Permanent Court of International Justice in 1922, which continues today as the judicial organ of the United Nations with its name changed to the International Court of Justice. This was the first truly international judicial tribunal available to states seeking to make use of it, but denying to them any possibility of selecting their own nominees as judges. A bench of eminent jurists was elected whose instructions were to decide such issues as were referred to it in accordance with international law, subject to any special law that might be indicated by the parties by treaty or by other agreement. The personnel to hear any case are appointed by the President of the Court in the same way as is the case in national law. Moreover, the judges are elected for a fixed period and receive a predetermined salary, so that their remuneration no longer depends upon the parties to the dispute. In addition, to ensure their independence the judges are granted complete immunity in respect of their judicial activities. Interestingly enough, while the United States did not become a party to the Statute of the Court in the days of the League of Nations, eminent US jurists were elected to the bench. Today, the judges, fifteen in number, are elected by the Security Council and the General Assembly. They are supposed to represent the major legal systems of the world. In fact, geographic and political factors play a major role in the election and there are always judges from the People's Republic of China, France, the Soviet Union now Russia, the United Kingdom, and the United States. A major departure in the nature of international judicial settlement came in 1996 with the election of Judge Higgins, the first woman to serve on this capacity.

The Court has two distinct functions. In the first place, it is available to states in dispute for the settlement of that dispute. It also enjoys an advisory function which enabled the League of Nations (see *League of Nations*) to refer to the Court abstract issues on which guidance as to the law or the competence of the League might be given. Today this advisory jurisdiction has been widened and is open to the organs of the United Nations and the specialized agencies. However, since international law depends upon the consent and agreement of states, the Court lacks any compulsory jurisdiction. States resort to the Court by way of a special agreement for a particular dispute, or because there is a provision in a treaty to which they are parties prescribing reference to the Court, or because they have made a declaration in accordance with Article 36 of the Statute of the Court committing themselves to accepting jurisdiction for the

future on the basis of reciprocity. Although this obligation was widely accepted in the interwar period, the number of signatories, as a percentage of the members of international society, has declined since 1945 and neither the People's Republic of China nor Russia has expressed any intention of making such a declaration. Moreover, because of dissatisfaction with a decision, or unease over the political complexion of the bench, states have on occasion terminated their declarations of acceptance or, if time-limited, not renewed them.

Since there is no compulsion upon states to make any such declaration, Article 36 has become known as the "Optional Clause," but the jurisdiction thus created is known as compulsory jurisdiction, although it is only compulsory for the minority which have opted to accept it. Moreover, the Court, despite the provision in its Statute that it alone is competent to decide upon its jurisdiction, has held that states may reserve any class of issue from the purview of the declaration thus made. The Court has in fact held that this even goes so far as to accept as valid exceptions based on the Connally Amendment introduced by the United States, and copied by many others, reserving to the state itself all matters essentially within the domestic jurisdiction of the state as determined by the state (see *State Responsibility*). Such a reservation enables a state which has ostensibly accepted the jurisdiction to evade such an obligation by a simple assertion that the matter in dispute is within the domestic jurisdiction. Moreover, since parties appear before the Court on the basis of equality and reciprocity, it is open to a state which has not made such a reservation to claim its protection if the state seeking to take it to the Court has included such a clause in its declaration accepting the jurisdiction.

The fact that a state has accepted the jurisdiction of the Court does not guarantee that it will carry out an unfavorable decision. In such an event both the Statute of the Court and the Charter of the United Nations provide that a successful party may refer the matter to the Security Council, which may then decide either to take action which could involve military measures or to leave the defaulter in default (see *Status and Role of the United Nations*). This means that, while there is no method of judicial appeal in international law, there is nevertheless recourse to political appeal. Since the decision of the Security Council in such a matter is subject to the veto of the permanent members of the Council, it is open to the "protector" of a defeated state to frustrate the judgment of the Court, the judicial arm of the United Nations. To date, no attempt has been made to obtain

Security Council enforcement against a defaulting losing party. Whether, now that the Cold War is over, this will remain so in the future is yet to be seen. However, the fact that the parties have agreed to resort to judicial settlement implies a willingness to comply with the decision, however unfavorable this may be.

As with any national judicial process, proceedings before the International Court tend to be rather lengthy. In an attempt to preserve the peace and the status quo pending a decision, the Court has power to issue what may only be described as an interim injunction, and it may do this even prior to determining that it has jurisdiction to hear the merits of the dispute. This is what happened in regard to the United States' complaint against Iran in connection with the seizure of its embassy in Tehran, and also in regard to the Nicaraguan complaint of aggression against itself by the United States. In the later case the Court subsequently, with only the United States judge dissenting, upheld its jurisdiction only to find the United States refusing to appear for the hearing on the merits of the case, contending that the Court's interpretation of the law was wrong. Again, in an attempt to shorten the proceedings, it is open to parties to ask for a hearing before a small chamber rather than the full bench of fifteen judges. This occurred in relation to the dispute between the United States and Canada concerning their maritime boundary in the Gulf of Maine. In this case, however, the parties insisted on selection of the judges to constitute the chamber, a procedure completely contrary to the very concept of independent international judicial settlement. If states which do not like a judgment reject it or insist on selecting what they hope will be sympathetic judges, a blow will be delivered to international judicial settlement from which it will be unlikely to recover.

The International Court of Justice is not the only international judicial body now in existence. The members of the European Community (see *European Political Community*) have established a court of their own which has the unique characteristic that even individuals may appear before it and may bring allegations of noncompliance with the Treaty of Rome (the constitution of the Community), even as amended by the Treaty of Maastricht which replaced the European Community by the European Union (see *European Union*), even against their own government. The judgements of the European Court are binding upon all members of the Union, and they may even declare national legislation to be inconsistent with Union Law and so invalid. Perhaps even more significant are the European and American Courts of Human Rights, which have the competence to hear allegations of breaches of human rights conventions brought against those states which are parties to the European or American Human Rights Conventions, as the case may be. States which are parties to those Conventions and which have recognized the jurisdiction of the Court are bound by the judgements, even if this means amending national legislation.

Since states are free to exercise their sovereignty and thus to decline to appear before the International Court of Justice, it is open to them in any particular dispute to establish an ad hoc tribunal, which may or may not consist of a majority of neutral members and which may or may not be competent to deliver a binding judicial decision. Equally, there is nothing to prevent the members of any international organization from establishing a permanent tribunal to hear matters affecting the work or competence of that organization, issues affecting its members interests or in their relations with the organization itself. Thus, the United Nations has established an Administrative Tribunal to hear disputes between itself and its staff members, and the Tribunal is also available to the Staff of any specialized agency in dispute with such agency. In addition, a Law of the Sea tribunal has been established to deal with issues arising under the 1982 Law of the Sea Convention, and so has a tribunal for the World Trade Organization. It must be recognized, however, that for international judicial settlement to be successful and to make a positive contribution to peace the parties accepting the possibility of judicial settlement or resorting thereto must be willing to carry out the decisions of the tribunal, even when those decisions are contrary to their interests. Until recent years and the refusal of Albania to fulfill the decision in the Corfu Channel case, of Iran to carry out the decision in the embassy case, and of the United States to accept the jurisdiction in the case brought by Nicaragua, it was almost unknown for any state to reject an international judicial decision affecting itself. It can only be hoped that these incidents constitute aberrations of a passing character and will not serve as precedents to destroy the role of international judicial settlement as a major means of upholding the international rule of law as a vital factor in the campaign to preserve world peace. It might also help in establishing the rule of law if some nongovernmental agencies, such as the International Committee of the Red Cross (see Nobel Peace Prize Laureates: *International Red Cross*), as well as individual states were given the right to apply for advisory opinions.

See also : *World Peace Order, Dimensions of a; Emerging Tool Chest for Peacebuilders; Pacific Settlement of Internal Disputes*

Bibliography ————————————————

Carlston K S 1946 *The Process of International Arbitration*. Columbia University Press, New York

Hudson M O 1943 *The Permanent Court of International Justice, 1920-42: A Treatise*. MacMillan, New York

Hudson M O 1944 *International Tribunals*. Carnegie Endowment for International Peace, Brookings Institution, Washington, DC

Higgins R 1994 *Problems and Process*. Clarendon Press, ch. 11, Oxford

Lauterpacht H 1958 *The Development of International Law by the International Court*. Stevens, London

Lowe V, Fitzmaurice M 1996 *Fifty Years of the International Court of Justice*. Cambridge University Press, Cambridge

Ralston J H 1929 *International Arbitration from Athens to Locarno*. Stanford University Press, Stanford, California

Rosenne S 1997 *The Law and Practice of the International Court*. Leyden, Kluwer

LESLIE C. GREEN

International Law

For many people the cynical remark of one of the characters in *Exodus* by Leon Uris would sum up their view on international law: "The thing which the evil ignore and the righteous refuse to enforce." Such a view, however, ignores both the nature and the reality of international law.

Just as a person is not an island, so the modern state does not exist in isolation. Life demands an interplay with others based on mutual respect. Aristotle maintained that the essence of law was to treat equals equally and a similar concept underlies international law. As long ago as 1758 Vattel wrote in his *Le Droit des gens ou principes de la loi naturelle* that

> Nations, which are composed of men and may be regarded as so many free persons living together in a state of nature, are by nature equal and hold from nature the same obligations and the same rights. Strength or weakness, in this case, counts for nothing. A dwarf is as much a man as a giant is; a small Republic is no less a sovereign State than the most powerful Kingdom. From this equality it necessarily follows that what is lawful or unlawful for one Nation is equally lawful or unlawful for every other Nation.

The Charter of the United Nations (see *United Nations Charter*) confirms this in simpler language: "The Organization is based on the sovereign equality of all its Members." In order that this equality may be given reality and states may enjoy equal rights and be burdened by equal obligations, it is necessary for their relations, like those between individuals, to be controlled by a system that can give effect to that state of affairs. The system that seeks to do this is known as international law, a term first used by Jeremy Bentham (see *Bentham, Jeremy*), although states from time immemorial have recognized that their interrelationships must be regulated in an orderly fashion. In classical times this system was known as the *jus gentium*, which was often stated to be derived from natural law.

Our modern system of international law is generally dated from the seventeenth century, and the first major book on the subject is normally ascribed to Hugo Grotius, who published his *De Jure Belli ac Pacis* in 1625 (see *Grotius, Hugo*). Grotius, however, was not the first to write on international law, but the arguments put forward in his text proved most acceptable to the European states of his time, and they were frequently prepared to support their contentions by reference to his writings, for his comments were derived to a great extent from his experience as a diplomat.

In their relations, states often referred to events occurring in classical times, to general practice that had become popular and convenient, and to special agreements made between themselves with respect to specific issues. It was in this way that there developed the concept of the rights of merchants to travel and be protected when abroad, that safe-conducts gave way to the passport system, and that the freedom of the seas was recognized, and that a three-mile territorial sea developed from what was known as the cannon-shot rule conceding that a coastal state had the right to control its coastal waters up to the point of cannon-range. Even more important was recognition of the fact that if relations were to be conducted between states, the emissaries sent to conduct such relations were entitled to protection and immunities from local harassment. In early days they were considered to be under the protection of the gods, gradually this gave way to general acceptance based on state conduct, although today, with the appearance on the international scene of a large number of newly independent states, the law concerning diplomats has been codified in the Vienna Convention on Diplomatic Relations of 1961 (see *Ambassadors*). Despite the existence of the Convention, the International Court of Justice at The Hague has held, in the case arising from the seizure of the United States embassy in Tehran, that recognition of diplomatic privileges constitutes one of the most fundamental prerequisites for the conduct of international relations, having withstood the test of centuries. Traces are to be found as early as the Old Testament, while the term "diplomacy" finds its origins in the Greek *diploun*, or ward of office carried by the messenger sent by one city state to another.

Unlike the position within the state, there is no international legislature since the United Nations is not a parliament nor, in the words of the International Court, is it a state or a superstate. It is merely a standing diplomatic conference which, for the main part, discusses political issues and reaches its decisions in the light of the political views expressed by state delegates. Whether those decisions will be regarded as obligatory rests with the individual states. However, if the Security Council of the United Nations has made a decision under Chapter VII of the Charter concerning peace and security, that decision is binding upon all members of the organization. Just as there is no legislature, there is no international police force (although it could be claimed that various UN "peacekeeping forces" (*United Nations Peacekeeping Operations; Peacekeeping;* Nobel Peace Prize Laureates: *United Nations Peacekeeping Forces*) have performed a "policing" role and in recent years, such forces have come to take on a "peacemaking" or even "peace-enforcing" role). If the Security Council of the United Nations calls upon states to give effect to any decision reached by the Council, it remains the decision of those states whether they will give effect to that call or not. But if that "decision" relates to international peace and security, the members are bound, as happened in Korea and in regard to the invasion of Kuwait by Iraq. Lacking both a legislature and a police force, international law similarly has no automatic judicial authority which can give effect to or interpret any alleged legal rule or punish any breach. The International Court of Justice can only function if states in dispute decide by agreement to refer any dispute to the Court and it then rests with them whether to give effect to the decision that has been rendered (see *International Court of Justice*). Should a state contend that a decision in its favor has not been carried out, that state is entitled to refer the issue to the

Security Council which may decide to take steps to enforce the decision. The vote in the Security Council is, however, subject to veto so that enforcement depends upon political not legal rationalization. This explains why, during the Cold War, no successful party had recourse to this procedure. Now that the East-West confrontation has ended this may change. Although the usual law-making and law-enforcing processes are lacking on the international level, all states nevertheless do recognize that their interrelationships must be legally controlled and they maintain a legal service attached to their foreign ministries or have access to eminent legal scholars to advise whether their own conduct or that of any other nation conforms to international law.

Traditionally, international law has been derived from long-sustained practice of conformity which bas been regarded as obligatory, and breach of which has been considered as grounding a claim for reparation which may range from a mere apology through compensation to military action. Today, however, military action, unless taken in the name of self-defense and not condemned by the Security Council, would probably amount to a breach of the Charter of the United Nations, opening the door to retaliation against the user. Occasionally a victim of a breach of law has resorted to some illegal act of its own by way of reprisal. For such reprisal to be permitted it must be proportionate to the original act and intended to compel cessation of that earlier illegal act. So, as soon as the earlier act has ceased the reprisal must terminate. Rules of behavior based on general practice constitute customary law so long as they conform with *opinio juris*, that is to say, what the majority of states and writers on international law consider to be law.

Today, especially since the creation of a number of new states after the Second World War, states increasingly enter into multilateral treaties whereby they define what they consider their legal rights and obligations in a particular field to be (see *Multilateralism*). These international agreements, which may be known as treaties, or charters, covenants, agreements, understandings, or by any other name, may be compared with statutory law on the national level or, when entered into bilaterally, as if they were contracts. Since such agreements expressly indicate what the parties have agreed to, they must, if in any way ambiguous, be interpreted narrowly. Moreover, as statements of agreement, they will, as between the parties, override customary law to the contrary. However, in the Vienna Convention on the Law of Treaties (1969) it is provided that treaties are void if they conflict "with a peremptory norm of general international law . . . . A peremptory norm of general international law is a norm accepted and recognized by the international community of States as a whole as a norm from which no derogation is permitted and which can be modified only by a subsequent norm of general international law having the same character." Unfortunately, there is no indication in the Convention, nor is there general agreement among state, as to what norms may be considered peremptory in this sense. However, more and more agreements, especially when of a humanitarian character include a clause to this effect. Peremptory rules of this kind are known as *jus cogens*.

The need to ascertain what constitutes international law is not only one for states, it is also of importance if any judicial tribunal is called upon to determine whether particular activities constitute breaches of international law (see *International Judicial Settlement*). It is not only the International Court of Justice which needs to be aware of these sources of international law, for often national tribunals too are called upon to decide such issues. This may arise when a claim for immunity from jurisdiction has been put forward; in determining extradition issues; determining, in respect of countries which are parties to human rights agreements, whether national legislation conforms to international obligations, and the like. It is generally accepted that the most authoritative statement as to such sources is to be found in Article 38 of the Statute of the International Court and it is understood that the provisions of the Article are hierarchic in character, as follows:

(a) international conventions, whether general or particular, establishing rules expressly recognized by the contesting States;
(b) international custom, as evidence of a general practice accepted as law;
the general principles of law recognized by civilized nations;
(c) subject to the provisions of Article 59, judicial decisions and the teachings of the most highly qualified publicists of the various nations, as subsidiary means for the determination of rules of law.

The reference to "general principles of law" is not concerned with general principles of international law, but those general principles of "law" which are recognized by civilized nations. Unfortunately, it is not possible to determine what is meant by a civilized nation for, since the establishment of the League of Nations (see *League of Nations*), and even more so the United Nations (see *Status and Role of the United Nations*), it has been accepted that every rec-ognized state is civilized however abominable its policies or conduct might be from a moral point of view. Moreover, it is difficult to determine what principles are in fact generally recognized. In practice, courts tend to assume that any principle of law generally recognized by the majority of states in fact constitutes a rule of international customary law, which thus evades determining whether a particular nation is civilized or whether a specific principle is one which satisfies the provision.

Article 59 of the Statute, conforming to basic principles concerning sovereignty, provides that the decision in any dispute between states is authoritative for that case and those states alone and does not constitute a precedent in the usual sense of national jurisprudence. In practice, however, the International Court tends to follow its earlier reasoning in parallel issues and national courts and legal advisers frequently refer to such decisions as interpretative of international legal rules, and this practice is becoming increasingly common, particulary in regard to human rights, especially in countries which are parties to the European or American Conventions on Human Rights (see *Global Ethics, Human Rights Laws and Democratic Governance*). It is for this reason that the Article describes decisions merely as a subsidiary means for determining the rules of law. Similarly, as in the national sphere, doctrinal writings are not authoritative, only constituting suggestions as to what the law might be. It is only when a court accepts such an opinion that the statement acquires any status beyond that of an individual suggestion. It is only when states accept the views of a judicial body or a particular writer and behave accordingly, that it is possible to say that the judgment or writing is expressive of accepted international law.

In addition to the "sources" outlined in Article 59 it has become increasingly possible to find out what particular states consider international law to be. In recent years more and more states have been publishing their state papers, including the opinions of their legal advisers and their official reactions to specific incidents, such reactions being expressed in legal terms. Moreover, many national publications in international law now include sections devoted to the practice of their own state. As a result it is possible to ascertain the *opinio juris* of a fairly large number of states and to use such publications as evidence of what constitutes international law. In addition to the International Court of Justice, there are now a number of specialized international bodies established to deal with questions concerning the application or interpretation of particular treaties. Among these are the American and European Courts of Human Rights, The European Court overlooking the affairs of the European Union, as well as tribunals concerning the Law of the Sea Convention and the International Trade Agreement. There are also a number of bilateral tribunals, such as the Iranian-United States International Claims Commission, the tribunal set up under the United States-Canada Free trade Agreement, and that concerning the St. Lawrence waterway.

What has been said above is in line with the views of classical writers that international law is a law between states. With the establishment of the League of Nations and the International Labor Organization after 1919 it became clear that such an approach was unduly narrow, for both organizations operated on the international scene and in accordance with a constitution laid down in an international instrument. With the establishment of the United Nations and the proliferation of international organizations since 1945 it was obvious that the older definition of international law was completely inadequate. Moreover, since international law depends upon the consent of states, states may create any entity possessed of international legal status enjoying rights or being subject to obligations under international law. Even individuals may be given such rights as would appear to be the case in the field of human rights or for nationals of the members of the European Community who in certain circumstances enjoy the right of process before the European Court even against their own country.

A better definition of international law today, therefore, would appear to be that collection of rules and principles which states and others acting on the international scene regard as necessary for the maintenance of peace and good order in their relations among themselves, and which they recognize as binding in order to maintain that peace and good order.

The need to maintain international peace and good order extends into every facet of international life, and international law, therefore, has almost as many subdivisions as has national law. Traditionally one referred to the law of war and the law of peace—in fact the earliest writers so titled their books and paid more attention to the law of war than they did to the law of peace. Nowadays it is accepted that international law has a somewhat limited role to play in time of war, primarily concerned with the methods of waging war and the humanitarian principles necessary to reduce the horrors of war. This law is divided into the Hague Law derived from the Hague Conventions of 1907 and the Geneva Law based on the Con-

ventions of 1949 as extended by the Protocols of 1977. The tendency today is to describe both as constituting International Humanitarian Law (see *International Bill of Human Rights*), with breaches thereof rendering offenders liable to prosecution as war criminals (see *International Criminal Law*). Insofar as the law of peace is concerned, proper study of the law today frequently requires specialized knowledge and among the subdivisions we now have, among others, international constitutional law concerning international institutions, international business transactions, international pollution law, environmental law, river and water law, air and space law, human rights law, the law of the sea, and the like. Each of these subdivisions is directed to preserving good international relations and serving the needs of peace by maintaining the rule of law in international society.

See also: *World Peace Order, Dimensions of a; International Judicial Settlement; Treaties of the Modern Era; Pacific Settlement of International Disputes*

Bibliography ——————————————

Brierly J L 1963 *The Law of Nations*, 6th edn. Clarendon Press, Oxford

Brownlie I 1990 *Principles of Public International Law*, 4th edn. Oxford University Press, Oxford

De Visscher C 1957 *Theory and Reality in Public International Law*. Princeton University Press, Princeton, New Jersey

Green L C 1988 *International Law*. Carswell, Toronto

Jessup P C 1949 *A Modern Law of Nations: An Introduction*. Macmillan, New York

Kaplan M A, Katzenbach N de B 1961 *The Political Foundations of International Law*. Wiley, New York

McDougall M S, Feliciano F 1961 *Law and Minimum World Public Order: The Legal Regulation of International Coercion*. Yale University Press, New Haven, Connecticut

McDougall M S, Reisman W M 1981 *International Law in Contemporary Perspective*. Foundation Press, Mineola, New York

Oppenheim L F L 1996/1952 *International Law*, Vol. 1: *Peace*, 9th edn. Vol. 2: *Disputes, War and Neutrality*, 6th edn. Longmans, Green, London

R Higgins 1994 *Problems & Process: International Law and How We Use It*. Clarendon Press, Oxford

Schwarzenberger G, Brown E D 1976 *A Manual of Interanational Law*, 6th edn. Professional Books, Milton

Shaw M 1996 *International Law*. University Press, Cambridge

T M Franck 1995 *Fairness in International Law and Institutions*. Clarendon Press, Oxford

LESLIE C. GREEN

International Peace Research Association (IPRA)

The International Peace Research Association (IPRA) is a global association of researchers and educators whose work is devoted to the question of peace. It facilitates worldwide exchange and dissemination of peace research and promotes transnational cooperative research.

Founded in 1966, IPRA developed from a conference organized by the "Quaker International Conferences and Seminars" in Clarens, Switzerland, August 16-20, 1963. The participants decided to hold international Conferences on Research on International Peace and Security (COROIPAS), which would be organized by a Continuing Committee similar to the Pugwash Conferences (see *Pugwash Conferences on Sciences and World Affairs*). Under the leadership of John Burton, the Continuing Committee met in London, December 1-3, 1964. At that time they took steps to broaden the original concept of holding research conferences. The decision was made to form a professional association with the principal aim of increasing the quantity of research focused on world peace and ensuring its scientific quality. An Executive Committee including Bert V A. Röling, Secretary General (The Netherlands), John Burton (United Kingdom), Ljubivoje Acimovic (Yugoslavia), Jerzy Sawicki (Poland), and Johan Galtung (Norway) was appointed. This group was also designated as Nominating Committee for a 15-person Advisory Council to be elected at the first general conference of IPRA, to represent various regions, disciplines, and research interests in developing the work of the Association.

Since then IPRA has held seventeen biennial general conferences, the venues of which have been chosen with a view to reflecting the association's global scope: Groningen, Netherlands (1965); Tallberg, Sweden (1967); Karlovy Vary, Czechoslovakia (1969); Bled, Yugoslavia (1971); Varanasi, India (1974); Turku, Finland (1975); Oaxtepec, Mexico (1977); Königstein, FRG (1979); Orillia, Canada (1981); Gyor, Hungary (1983); Sussex, England (1986); Rio de Janeiro, Brazil (1988); Groningen, the Netherlands (1990); Kyoto, Japan (1992); Valetta, Malta (1994); Brisbane, Australia (1996); and Durban, South Africa (1998).

As a forum for the exchange of ideas about peace, IPRA offers a unique global perspective on the peace question. This is not only due to its global membership and scope, but also to the fact that IPRA has consistently been guided by a broad conception of "peace," conceived as including an absence not only of international war, but also of intra-state conflicts and "structural violence." (see *Structural Violence*

and the Definition of Conflict) "Positive peace" thus also includes a concern for human rights, economic and social development and ecological sustainability (see *Positive versus Negative Peace*).

In contrast to, for instance, the International Peace Science Society, IPRA is neither committed to any particular research methodology, nor restricted to any academic discipline. Its members come from as diverse disciplines as philosophy, theology, psychology, sociology, anthropology, political science, international relations, physics, medicine, geography, pedagogy and history. Finally, contrary to most academic associations, the thematic scope of IPRA also goes beyond pure research: Not only does it also include peace education (see *Peace Education*), but the association also encourages and facilitates a dialogue between researchers and peace activists.

The main purpose of IPRA, however, is to advance interdisciplinary research into the conditions of peace and the causes of war and other forms of violence. To this end IPRA aims to encourage worldwide cooperation designed to assist the advancement of peace research, and in particular: to promote national and international studies and teaching related to the pursuit of world peace; to facilitate contacts and cooperation between scholars and educators throughout the world; and to encourage the world-wide dissemination of results of peace research.

As a means to this end, IPRA publishes a quarterly *International Peace Research Newsletter*, devoted to disseminating information and analysis concerning current issues and activities involving peace researchers and educators. The current editor is Professor Mahendra Kumar (1715 Outram Lines, Kingsway Camp, Delhi 110 001, India).

Besides the newsletter, IPRA until the beginning of the 1990s published volumes of conference proceedings (1966-1988) as well as a variety of thematic anthologies. The *Journal of Peace Research* (PRIO, Oslo, since 1964) has, furthermore, been published under the auspices of IPRA, as has the *International Journal of Peace Studies* (since 1996). For a number of years, IPRA has further operated a listserv and a homepage, featuring basic information about the association, links to relevant peace research resources and a bulletin board on forthcoming events.

By June 1998, IPRA had a total of 1,060 individual members and 490 institutional and corporative members in 95 countries, 275 of whom were from Third World countries and 75 from former Communist states. Most members participate in one or several of

IPRA's commissions (until 1994 called "study groups"). These commissions are responsible for arranging workshops and panels at the biennial general conferences, in addition to which some operate newsletters and listservers for a continuing exchange of ideas. By 1998, there were eighteen such commissions with the following themes: Conflict Resolution and Peace Building, Culture and Communication, Eastern Europe, Ecological Security, Global Political Economy, Indigenous Peoples, Internal Conflicts, International Human Rights, Nonviolence, Peace Education, Peace History, Peace Movements, Peace Theories, Reconciliation, Religion and Peace, Refugees, Security and Disarmament, and Women and Peace.

IPRA further has five regional affiliates: the African Peace Research Association (AFPRA), the Asia Pacific Peace Research Association (APPRA), the Consejo Latinoamericano de Investigacion para la Paz (CLAIP), the European Peace Research Association (EUPRA) and the North America-based Consortium on Peace Research, Education and Development (COPRED).

IPRA holds consultative status with the United Nations Educational, Scientific, and Cultural Organization (UNESCO) and receives subventions for special projects from UNESCO via the International Social Science Council (ISSC). Other sources of income are dues from memberships and Newsletter subscriptions, as well as support from individuals and foundations.

In-between the general conferences, the highest authority within IPRA is the Council, consisting of at least fifteen members elected for a two year term, as well as ex-officio members. In all its elections, IPRA places great emphasis on gender and geographical diversity. In 1998, the IPRA Council comprised the following elected members: Ada Aharoni (Israel), Abdelwahab Biad (Algeria/France), Hendrik Bullens (Germany), Linda Groff (USA), Catherine Odora Hoppers (Uganda/Sweden), Mayoko Ishii (Japan), Mahendra Kumar (India), Kingsley Moghalu (Tanzania), Susan Nandutu (Uganda/Australia), Thania Paffenholz (Germany/Kenya), Sr. Mary-Soledad Perpinan (Philippines), Nielsen de Paula Pires (Brazil), Paul Rogers (UK), Maria Eugenia Villareal (Guatemala), and Howard Richards (USA).

Ex-officio members are the Secretary General as well as the holders of the new offices established in 1994 as president and vice-presidents. The first president was Kevin Clements (New Zealand/USA, 1994-98) as the successor to whom Ursula Oswald Spring (Mexico) was elected in 1998. Vice-presidents have included Judit Balasz (Hungary, 1996-98), Katsuya Kodama (Japan, since 1998), Regine Mehl (Germany, since 1998), Saana Osserian (France, 1994-96), Maria Elena Valenzuela (Chile, 1994-98) and Diyanama Ywassa (Togo, 1994-1998).

The association's headquarters are those of the home institution of the Secretary General. The Secretaries General of IPRA have been: Bert V. A. Röling (The Netherlands, 1964-1971), Asbjrn Eide (Norway, 1971-75); Raimo Väyrynen (Finland, 1975-79); Yoshikazu Sakamoto (Japan, 1979-83); Chadwick Alger (USA, 1983-1988); Elise Bouding (USA, 1988-91), Paul Smoker (USA, 1991-1994), Karlheinz Koppe (Germany, 1995-1997) and Bjørn Møller (Denmark, since 1997). The present headquarter (1997-2001) is thus at the Copenhagen Peace Research Institute (COPRI), Fredericiagade 18, DK-1310 Copenhagen K., Denmark (e-mail: bmoeller@copri.dk).

Bibliography:

International Peace Research Newsletter, Vols. 1-36 (since 1962)

IPRA Homepage. http://www.copri.dk/ipra/ipra.html

CHADWICK ALGER; BJØRN MØLLER

Internationalization

Internationalization is a basic process of the world economy which is deeply rooted in the nature of economic, technological, and political development, together with globalization (see *Globalization*) and transnationalization (see *Transnationalism*). Internationalization, globalization and transnationalization have become catchwords in the world of the outgoing 20th century. They are often used as identical categories in the vocabulary of political leaders and businessmen, academics and journalists, but first and foremost, the people, working in and managing the international organizations. The advance of internationalization, globalization and transnationalisation is based on the development of production, science and technology, transport, and telecommunications, and on the increased significance of the international division of labor. It presupposes a medium which is able to transmit effects between states. Depending on the intensity of relations, several effects may be resulting between the states: (a) isolated interactions; (b) intensive interactions; (c) mutual dependence/interdependence (see *Interdependence, International*); (d) complex interdependence; (e) economic integration (see *Economic Integration*); and (f) voluntary economic coalescence of states.

There is no universally accepted exact definition of the process of internationalization. Efforts, to give a single measure of its achieved level, are combinations of a number of indicators, the weighting of which is based on subjective judgements and not on any scientific theory. As in many other cases in the social sciences, the process can be characterized only by certain direct or indirect indicators. Internationalization, on the level of the world economy and of the national economies means on the one hand the increase of the importance of exports and imports of goods and services, information, knowledge, foreign investments migration in the system, and on the other hand the integration of state functions across jurisdictional boundaries. The most important quantitative indicators for characterizing the degree of internationalization of national economies are foreign trade volumes and, in proportions in gross output and consumption, external capital flows in investments, the share of technology imports in the applied new technologies and the migration of labor force in employment. The global aggregates of the same data reflect the degree of internationalization of the world economy (see *Global Integration*).

The beginnings of internationalization are connected with the modern industrial development of development and the birth of the world market. The process itself may be viewed as having various stages, with its nature at any particular time being determined by the socio-political framework of the given historical stage. The process of globalization is based on the internationalization and it is a higher stage of it. In a broader understanding it could be considered as the entirety of such universal processes as technological transformation, increasing interdependence of countries caused by mass communication, trade, and capital flows, the homogenization and standardization of production and consumption patterns, the predominance of world market orientation in trade, investments and other transactions (on the level of the firms), the spatial and institutional integration of the markets, the growing identity or similarity of economic regulations, institutions and policies across national boundaries, and the emergence of global problems, like environmental degradation and population growth. In a narrower, mainly economic understanding, globalization is a process, over which the national legislations have little or no control, and it is the strongest in capital and information flows. Transnationalization as a specific manifestation of internationalization is mainly a microeconomic

process, when the decisions on important areas of production, trade and capital flows, influencing many nations, are made by international firms outside of their territory, the transnational corporations. Internationalization in essence promotes economic progress. It increases the exchange of material and intellectual values and is beneficial to contacts among peoples. But the process takes place in a given economic and socio-political environment. The nature and value system of this environment may distort the process of internationalization, and may deprive certain groups of countries of its favorable effects. Colonialism, which imposed an international division of labor on large areas of the world, is a typical example of such distortive effects and of the associated unilateral gains to the metropole powers (see *Colonialism*).

There is a strong contradiction between the process of internationalization and the present political framework of our planet. Economic internationalization takes place in a world full of different sources of conflicts and tension, between the 200 or so "political units" coexisting in the world in the late twentieth century, but it is also creating common interest among them on a number of areas and issues. Many of the countries are multi-ethnic modern states. A great number of them are not "nation-states" in the European understanding of the word, where the definite ethnogenesis of the peoples living within specific territories, their accumulated social and historical experiences, the results of material production and intellectual work, the lessons gained from political struggle and from fighting against nature and foreign forces for the acquisition of the area, created specific ties. The common characteristic of the present states is that they are separate political and economic decision centers surrounded by boundaries, and maintain specific internal forces in motion which form the state institutional and organizational structure. Most probably, the states, with their specific internal economic and social structure of interests, will continue to remain basic factors in the modern world. Indeed, the role of the state framework and the significance of the state are still so great today that the probable economic and political shifts in the coming century will presumably, not influence its survival as a basic political-organizational unit of the world economy. However, the concept in which the state constituted a rather isolated unit with respect to sovereignty, community life, culture, language, defense, and economy can no longer be maintained, even theoretically (see *State, Theory of the*). Under normal circumstances, no modern state with any social system can exist without participating in international economic relations, and outside the accepted norms, rules and institutional structures of international cooperation, which not only sets certain limits to the states but serve as instruments for their policies and collective actions. Economic realities and necessities create—especially for smaller countries—*ab ovo* determined circumstances to which the state is bound to adjust itself (see *World Economy, Social Change and Peace*). The development of global organizations, intergovernmental cooperation regimes, transnational corporations, and the consequences of the policies and actions of these institutions are important factors in the collective management of the internationalization process.

Internationalization has always been developing with uneven spatial spread and sectoral intensity in technology, economics, finance, trade and culture. It is a source of a great number of relations between the different actors in a wide variety of fields. Some of these relations are integrative globally, others promote regional integration. Some of the consequences of internationalization can lead to disintegration and fragmentation. These processes are not necessarily developing as contradictory ones, which are crowding out each other. Parallel to the globalization process, and often as a reaction to it, the role of regionalism is growing. New regional organizations are emerging, mainly for economic cooperation, but also for security arrangements in certain cases, though not so strong as the European Union (see *European Union*) or the NATO (see *North Atlantic Treaty Organization (NATO)*). The process of fragmentation is influenced by and influencing the internationalization process. Larger political units are breaking down, without creating viable alternatives for the smaller countries. Many small states are increasingly marginalized and in fact excluded from the internationalization process and the globalizing framework.

The impact of internationalization is extremely complex and the changes in the welfare of the nations, the global division of incomes and wealth, and many issues of war and peace are very closely interrelated with the process of the degree and character of it. At present, close to 200 political units, among them 186 countries, (185 member states of the UN) are turning out what may be called the "world product." Never in the history of modern economic development have so many states existed at one time. Their simultaneous existence in itself has created a new and extremely complex situation from the point of view of the internationalization process, and not only because of the increased number of decision-making centers in political and economic affairs, or of the new political and economic frontiers (see *United Nations: Achievements and Agenda*). Indeed the new industries which

have unfolded on the basis of the new technologies require the construction of international frameworks. Scientific development underlying the technical changes is basically an international process. The output and consumption of many countries depend decisively or exclusively on whether they are able to provide for the import of vital raw materials and primary energy sources. Several countries are able to sustain modern economic growth only if they can import the necessary investment and consumer goods (and sometimes skills). Such international interaction calls for a high-level provision of financial flows and services, an international freight traffic network, transport, and communications—all to ensure a rapid and secure flow of goods and information between even the remotest points of the world. The effects of internationalization on countries may be of different natures: favorable or unfavorable, predetermined or spontaneous, and desirable or undesirable. Depending on the character of the areas concerned and on their mechanism, the effects may either work solely in economic life or go well beyond its limits. The contradictory requirements of the process of internationalization and the survival of the state framework are important sources of conflicts in the present world system. The forms of manifestation and the consequences of these conflicts, as well as the means and possibilities open to resolve them, are different in the various groups of countries defining the political units. The differences are basically rooted in the nature of the given systems and in the level of development of the countries concerned. In fact, there are great and varied differences among national economic structures existing and developing side by side. Countries with distorted or one-sided production structures and depending mostly on the international division of labor countries which are unable by themselves to carry out self-sustained economic growth, coexist with highly developed structures. But the highly developed, sophisticated economies are also differentiated, among other factors, by the size of their area (the size of the internal market), natural endowments, and so on. In spite of the structural and other differences which indicate the sources of external dependence, very few of the countries could maintain present (and expected) levels of national economic activity without increasing their economic relations with other countries and find solutions to the conflicting requirements of internationalization and political fragmentation. The answer to this requirements by the states in the internationalizing global economy is often the effort for regional economic integration.

Internationalization is also influenced by economic

power. The role of the change in international economic power relations in the progress of internationalization is rather complex. This is because the concept of economic power relations includes quantitative and qualitative, active and passive elements alike, and also can be interpreted in several dimensions. Owing to the fact that a few leading countries have control over a substantial part of production and consumption in the global economic relations, they have, even without resorting to political or economic pressure, much to say in deciding what should be the volume and pattern of international trade and capital flows. Their internal preferences and value judgments leave their mark on all major fields of internationalization.

Finally, it should be said that internationalization is not a linear and irreversible process. It may be reversed by major economic or political crises, which may lead to the disintegration of the world economy or to the collapse of existing institutional structures.

See also: *Integration, Regional; Interdependence, International; Global Economic Interdependence: Why Crisis?; Power; Imperialism; Functionalism*

Bibliography

Bergsten L F 1973 The Future of the International Economic Order: An Agenda for Research. *A Report to the Ford Foundation*. Heath, Lexington, Massachusetts
Brandt Commission 1983 *Common Crisis: The Brandt Commission Report*. Pan Books, London
Brown S 1974 *New Forces in World Politics*. Brookings Institution. Washington, DC
Camps M 1981 *Collective Management*. McGraw-Hill, New York
Cox R W, Jacobson H K 1973 *The Anatomy of Influence*. Yale University Press, New Haven, Connecticut
Hoffman S 1980 *Primacy or World Order*. McGraw-Hill, New York
Knorr K 1975 *The Power of Nations*. Basic Books, New York
Kuzmin E L 1975 *Mirovoe Gosudarstvo* [The Global State]. Mezhdunorodnie Otnoshenia, Moscow
Mandel E 1978 *Late Capitalism*. Gresham Press, London
Simai M 1981 Interdependence and Conflicts in the World Economy. Sijthoff and Noordhoff, Rockville, Maryland
Simai M 1994 *The Future of Global Governance: Managing Risks and Change in the International System*. USIP Press. Washington, DC
Simai M 1995 *The New Global Environment of the Development Process*. UNU Press. Tokyo
Simai M 1996 *International Business Policy*. IWE of the Hungarian Academy of Sciences, Budapest
United Nations 1996 *Globalization and Liberalisation: Effects of International Economic Relations on Poverty*. UNCTAD, Geneva, New York

MIHALY SIMAI

Internet: A New Vehicle for Global Peace Efforts

The Internet is an enormous and rapidly expanding global network of computers, users, resources and services. Often called a "network of networks," this global communication system was allowing as many as sixty million people, by July, 1997, to communicate with each other electronically and to have instant access to information and entertainment sources around the world. Most users access the Internet through regular telephone lines.

This revolutionary technological development has opened a new stage of possibilities for global peace efforts (see *Technology of Peace*). These possibilities can be understood by examining the Internet's history, its unique capacities, its effect on peace efforts, and its dangers and limitations.

1. The Internet Revolution

The Internet is a major step in the historical evolution of technology and global communications. It is a revolutionary event in the ability of human beings, worldwide, to communicate with each other as individuals and as groups. The Internet is transforming the ways people in the world community can relate to each other. It is creating new conditions and possibilities for peacemaking efforts.

The Internet is the third stage in the historical evolution of telecommunications. The first stage, the ability of *one-to-one* instantaneous communication over long distances, occurred with the invention of the telegraph (1844) and telephone (1875). This was a major event in the history of human communications. Accounts at the time marveled at this newfound ability. Expansive terms used at the time, such as "The Great Highway of Thought," are not unlike today's use of "The Information Super-highway" as a term for the Internet (Neuman 1996 p. 110). But as revolutionary as they were in permitting instantaneous long distance communication, the telegraph and telephone basically allowed only for one person to communicate with another.

The second major stage, again with revolutionary

effects on cultures, was the development of radio and television in the early twentieth century. These inventions permitted *one-to-many* communication (one person communicating with many people) instantaneously over long distances. These "second stage" devices became globally pervasive and have had a revolutionary effect on individuals and cultures worldwide.

As the third stage in the Telecommunications Revolution, the Internet's power results from its ability to allow for *many-to-many* communication. Essentially, anyone with a computer and telephone line, can communicate with anyone else on the globe. "Virtual groups" of people can electronically congregate and communicate among themselves, they can leave messages for others or the entire group, which can then be responded to at the receivers' convenience.

The instantaneous flow of information through international communications networks has transformed people's connectivity with the rest of the world. Millions of people everyday participate in global electronic conferences, electronically visit an astonishing variety of sites in "cuber-space," and receive highly specialized information from locations worldwide—all at little expense. These capabilities create a new world of possibilities for peacekeeping and international relations (see *Global Neighborhood: New Security Principles*).

2. The Age of the Internet

2.1 The Global Village

The Internet made the concept of the "Global Village" a reality. In 1962 Marshal McLuhan predicted that global media information networking would create a global village. Global villages and "virtual communities," featuring the unrestricted flow of information and discussion, represented a new stage in planetary communication. For the first time, on-going communities, created by global media information networking, could exist among members in geographic locations around the globe (see *Globalization*).

2.2 The Involvement of Government

These tremendous advances were a product of early government involvement. Governments have historically been closely involved with advances in communications, but their involvement has ranged from supportive to repressive. Even before Samuel Morse perfected the electric telegraph, France had banned the visual telegraph, or Chappe system, which was based on flag signals. The fear that workers might unite in an insurrection when they learned about each other's dissatisfactions, led the French, in 1837, to impose jail sentences and stiff fines on anyone transmitting unauthorized visual telegraph signals from one place to another (Neuman 1996).

With its potential for furthering peace efforts, it is ironic that the concept of the Internet had its origins in the Cold War following World War II. At that time, nuclear attack was a widespread fear. A highly de-centralized military command structure was established to avoid the destruction of the United States Government's ability to respond to nuclear threat. To avoid having any central computer that would be vulnerable to attack, the highly decentralized Internet-concept was developed.

Initially, the Internet was tightly controlled by the United States Department of Defense. The US National Science Foundation later extended the Internet to university supercomputer centers, then to the academic community at large, and finally to individuals. Today, both governmental and non-governmental institutions such as universities and corporations provide the funding for communication links. This interaction between the federal government, universities, and industry has fueled the American leadership in Internet technology. The Internet continues to function without a central authority. This decentralization continues partly from the original Cold War needs, and partly from the fiercely held anti-authoritarian ethic of the community of Internet users.

2.3 Global Usage

The Internet's growth outside the United States has become very rapid. Although the Internet has existed in its basic form for more than two decades, it has doubled in size every year since 1988 (Zerges 1996). By 1995, the biggest growth in Internet use was outside the United States in Asia, Europe and the Pacific (Frost 1996). By the summer of 1995, it already linked together more than 60,000 local, regional and national computer networks with some ninety-six countries having international Internet-connections. Three-fourths of the Global Internet Community in 1995 were in the United States with another 10 percent of users from Canada and Mexico. Ten percent were from Europe with less than two percent in Oceania and barely more than one percent in Asia and one percent in the rest of the world. In the year 2000, projections indicate that approximately one-hundred million people worldwide will have access (Swett 1995).

3. Opportunities and Dangers

3.1 The Internet's Special Capacities for Peace Efforts

The Internet has specific capabilities which create new possibilities for furthering peace efforts. The Internet's capacity to allow people all over the globe to interrelate and communicate with each other underlies many novel approaches. In this new stage of human communication the possibilities are only now beginning to be seen in areas of peace efforts such as conflict resolution projects, peace education, global collaborative projects and diplomatic-political activity. Many of the new possibilities stimulated by the Internet will be developed within the realms of universities, diplomacy, international business, and education.

These benefits derive from certain capabilities of the Internet such as its capacity (a) to create virtual communities, (b) to simplify global collaboration and teamwork, (c) to promote discussion of global issues, (d) to provide resources for conducting research, and (e) to make educational course work and training available worldwide.

3.1.1 Creating "Virtual Communities"

One of the most powerful capabilities of the Internet is its ability to make virtual communities possible. "Virtual communities" are electronic gathering places where people with common interests can communicate with each other. These virtual communities can make good use of certain of the Internet's capabilities. There are some ten thousand of these electronic conferences covering almost everything imaginable (Swett 1995).

3.1.2 Simplifying Global Collaboration and Teamwork

Global collaboration among a pair or team of geographically distant members becomes easy and inexpensive. International teams can work closely together to carry out complex international projects.

3.1.3 Promoting Global Discussion of Global Issues

It becomes easy and inexpensive for people, all over the globe, to be simultaneously engaged in a project or situation that may change hourly. Groups consisting of the most knowledgeable people worldwide can be easily formed to discuss global issues. This allows for the development of a "critical mass" of specialists who would not be available in a given institution, country, or continent or where circumstances did not exist to physically bring them together. A wider range of people who are not necessarily government representatives, can participate in discussions of global issues.

3.1.4 Providing Global Resources

It becomes possible to instantaneously locate and have access to peace related resources such as the electronic archives and press releases on the United Nations site. Worldwide resources ranging from inexpensive texts to multimedia resources and complex simulations are available in an unprecedented way. Electronic publications bring new research findings ever more quickly to their readers with the volume of scholarly information on the Internet doubling more than twice each year (Hopkins 1996). A wide range of professional organization and experts, freely sharing their expertise, has been an important part of Internet culture.

3.1.5 Providing Education and Learning

Educational course work and training resources are increasingly available to a world of potential students of all ages and backgrounds. Distance education through the Internet can be both informational and interactive. Collaborative learning, where students work together to accomplish academic tasks, is especially well suited for Internet usage (Ellsworth 1994 p. 391). The possibilities for learning are no longer confined by individuals time limitations and geographic proximity to educational institutions. Students, professors and researchers are finding a huge depository of updated documents which can be easily accessed through the Internet. The Internet is a bonanza for independent learners and scholars who can pursue studies on peace-related topics.

3.2 The Effect of the Internet's Capacities on Peace Efforts

3.2.1 New Opportunities

The new capacities offered by the Internet, create new opportunities for peace efforts within educational and research institutions as well as in government and corporate entities.

3.2.1.1 Education

Students and educational institutions are both major beneficiaries of the Internet's new capabilities. People's ability to learn is greatly enhanced as well as the academic and research institutions' ability to offer their expertise. Students using the Internet are able to learn other languages and cultures better because of their active communication in those languages and interaction with those cultures. These are valuable supplements to classroom instruction. Universities have begun to require their graduate students to post their master's theses and doctoral dissertations on the Internet, where scholars and the public around the world have free access to them. University libraries are being transformed to take advantage of this new world of instantaneously available resources. Long distance collaboration among individuals in academic and Government circles has continued as an on-going part of the Internet since the 1980s.

Simulations involving participants in different countries are easily conducted. Interactive courses on topics such as conflict resolution and international relations are now available with worldwide classes of students able to work closely together on course projects.

3.2.1.2 Government

The Internet increasingly plays a catalytic role in international affairs (Swett 1995). There are entirely new possibilities for grassroots peace efforts. The decentralized structure of the Internet gives people a more effective means to voice their concerns about society to a wide audience without being dependent on the traditional media and political establishment. Political activists are gaining powerful new abilities to involve large numbers of geographically distant people in their concerns and causes.

The Internet provides new ways for countries to carry out their foreign policy objectives. Internet advances are coinciding with other long term trends such as the end of the Cold War, the worldwide trend toward less centralized government, and the increasing importance of trade and economic, rather than political, relations. All of these developments are requiring major changes such as the way embassies function and diplomacy is conducted.

National governments will increasingly use the Internet as a diplomatic tool. The Internet will play an increasingly significant role in international conflict. When one country involved in a dispute with others begins to use the Internet as an additional tool in the political process, a catalytic effect occurs and other countries, involved in the conflict, enter officially into the electronic debate.

Ways to manage and resolve conflicts are important concerns to both governments and corporations, especially as their activities and involvements are increasingly global. The Internet could provide a forum and process for resolving conflicts among physically separated groups. Early attempts to work

with conflicts have been hampered by some of the limitations of the Internet such as its current confinement to text-based language.

History shows that governments have often been the first to react to, and restrict new ways for its people to communicate, or conspire. It is difficult for secretive, authoritarian governments to know how to respond to the Internet. "The Internet is the censor's biggest challenge and the tyrant's worst nightmare" (in Swett 1995 p. 9). There will be new competition for the established political parties and institutions. New political parties operating through the Internet will emerge. Politicians will invariably be drawn into the Internet before their competitors have the opportunity to dominate the political agenda or discussions.

The supra-national nature of the global communications network has already stretched the interpretation of laws and ethics and required new legislation to respond to issues such as intellectual property rights, commerce on the World Wide Web and governmental actions which could threaten the privacy of Internet users.

3.2.1.3 International Business

Peace efforts are often not associated with the world of international business. But, in fact, some of the most important findings about how international groups can best work together and resolve problems arising from cultural differences, are being learned in global corporations where global teamwork is an everyday necessity. Global corporations have large financial incentives for helping geographically distant work groups to function effectively with minimal friction.

In addition, global corporations have become major players on the world stage. A corporation's assets often exceed the assets of the countries in which they work. Corporations can have substantial effects on how countries will carry out their foreign policy objectives. The global communications system has allowed international businesses to maintain very close contact with employees scattered throughout the globe. Using increasingly sophisticated collaborative software and private intranet links, global corporations can synchronize the activities of geographically distant teams (see *Interdependence*).

3.2.2 Dangers and Hidden Impacts

The changes initiated by the Internet's new capacities can also present some dangers and produce unexpected effects. "Historically, changes in the means of communication—from speech to writing to the printing press—have transformed human development and society" (Harasim 1993 p. 16). Rather than merely "filling in" to preexisting social processes and ways people communicate, the Internet is actually transforming the nature of the processes themselves. The information age brings social cultural, psychological and legal changes to the way we live, interact and work. One unanticipated effect of the Internet, for example, is that large organizations tend to become less hierarchical and more cross-functional when employees can freely communicate with each other. The Internet could have a divisive affect by dividing the world's population into technological "haves" and "have nots" (see *Cultural Democracy*). Governments could threaten the privacy of Internet users.

The traditional mass media is being utterly transformed by the Internet. The long held monopoly of the traditional mass media will erode. The media, is losing its role as the gate keepers and filterers of information. (Swett 1995) Eventually, the audience may be able to ignore the "professional" journalists completely. At the first news of a crisis, Internet users can reach out to one another for information instead of being dependent on the traditional sources of news. (Neuman 1996) One difficulty this kind of usage creates, however, is that it may be difficult to know whether information is accurate or false and misleading. Governments and others can make offensive use of this difficulty by conducting dis-informational campaigns as part of their psychological operations (Sweet 1995). People and enterprises involved in peace efforts will want to redefine their work and how it is done in response to changes such as these.

3.2.2.1 Intercultural Communication

Global communication is also intercultural communication. Interacting with people from different cultural and national backgrounds has become a part of the lives of more people than ever before (see *Intercultural Relations and Peace Studies*). The Internet puts people from different cultures in sudden contact with people from other cultures, leaving no time to accomplish a crosscultural transition and to accommodate for crosscultural differences. Instantaneous contact can create intercultural misunderstandings particularly since it is still difficult on the Internet to convey the tone and nonverbal cues that make communication more accurate.

Virtual communities unrestricted by geography and national borders are easily created on the Internet. But as multi-cultural communities they face certain predictable dangers which can be exasperated by the absence of social cues. Facial expression, tone of voice, body language, race, nationality, gender, and age all convey much information that is lost when only text is used. Sensitivity to on-line cultural differences will be an important aspect of successful peace projects. New intercultural skills for good communication with people of other nationalities and cultures will be needed. Even though language translation software no longer unusual when using Internet mail, translated words can be misinterpreted. In these virtual communities, communication that is only text-based can easily lead to misunderstanding because communication is much more complex than text alone can easily convey (Aoki 1995). Fortunately, Internet text oriented e-mail will soon be replaced by multimedia messaging and video teleconferencing. These dangers will affect peace-related global projects as they are conducted increasingly through the Internet.

Particularly since the United States has been so instrumental in its development, the Internet strongly reflects American culture. An estimated ninety percent of the content on the World Wide Web, the more commercial and graphic portion of the Internet, is in English. There is a marked lack of diversity in language. Language continues to be a serious barrier for non-English speaking users, especially for those whose language is not written in the Roman alphabet. These factors can be felt as American cultural imperialism by less dominant, traditional cultures.

Americans, as a cultural group, may actually have some initial advantages in Internet usage. Americans are used to "low-context" communication in which the message is largely conveyed through words. People from East Asian cultures, however, usually rely more than Americans on face-to-face cues to accurately communicate. As a way to try to overcome this difficulty of making non-verbal expressions, symbols called "emoticons" have been developed as a way to convey non-verbal expressions. Since the American emoticons seemed inadequate to convey their emotions, the Japanese have developed their own set of emoticon symbols (Aoki 1995). For example the American emoticon for a smile (read sideways) is : -) while the Japanese emoticon for a smile is (^-^).

4. What the Internet Can Not Replace

The Internet has created a new world of possibilities for world peace efforts. But there are core aspects of international/intercultural relations that the Internet cannot replace. The Internet increases our range of human connectiveness and the number of ways people can make contact with each other, but it cannot replace other forms of developing international relationships.

Ultimately, successful global peace efforts are built upon people's ability to understand, interact effectively and collaborate with people from different cultural backgrounds. Global development, whether in the realm of international relations between governments, international education, or multi-national businesses is built on successful intercultural interactions (see *Social Progress and Human Survival*). Perhaps the greatest capacity of the Internet will turn out to be the capacity to enhance these human interrelationships.

See also: *Future of Humanity; Communication: Key to World Peace*

Bibliography ————————————————

Aoki K 1995 Virtual communities in Japan: Their cultures and infrastructure. *Asia-Pacific Exchange J.* 2(1) (March) Archived on http://naio.kcc. hawaii.edu. reports as file "kaoki.21"

Burgess G, Burgess H 1997 The World Wide Web: A Tool for Building Citizen Diplomacy Skills. *US Institutes of Peace Virtual Diplomacy Conference Paper*. Archived on http://www.usip.org, directory oc/confpapers.

Ellsworth J 1994 *Education on the Internet*. Indianapolis, Indiana USA

Frost R 1996 Web's heavy US accent grates on overseas ears. *Wall Street Journal* 26(September)

Harasim L (ed.) 1993 *Global Networks Computers and International Communication*. The Massachusetts Institute of Technology Press, Cambridge, Massachusetts

Hopkins J D 1996 New Technologies and the Future Dimension of the University. Opening Plenary Keynote Address.

Ortelius: The Database on Higher Education in Europe, Lauhcing Conference Palazzo degli Affari, Florence, Italy 17-19, May

Jauch D 1997 The Enterprise of Diplomacy in the Information Age. *US Institutes of Peace Virtual Diplomacy Conference Paper*. Archived on http://www.usip.org, directory oc/confpapers. Reports as file /infotech.html

Jones C 1997 Old hands give internet a helping hand. *Wired News Release*, September 5

McLuhan M 1962 *The Gutenberg Galaxy*. University of Toronto Press, Toronto

Neuman J 1996 The media's impact on international affairs, then and now. *SAIS Review,* The Johns Hopkins University Press

Noam E 1995 Electronics and the dim future of the university. *Science* 270

Rheingold H 1994 *The Virtual Community: Homesteading on the Electronic Frontier*. Harperperennial Library

Schmitz CA 1997 Changing the Way We Do Business in International Relations. *US Institutes of Peace Virtual Diplomacy Conference Paper*. Archived on http://www.usip.org, directory oc/confpapers, returns file schmits. html

Swett C 1995 *Strategic Assessment: The Internet*. Offices of the Assistant Secretary of Defense for Special Operations and Low-Intensity Conflict, The Pentagon, Washington, DC

Zerges K 1996 Using the Internet to Communicate with Future Students. Speech delivered at the conference "New Technologies for Information in Higher Education. Ortelius: An Example" University of Florence, Italy 17th and 18th of May 1996. Archived on http://www. eaie. nl directory ITHE, returns file zerges.html

ROBERT C. SMITH ; STEVI LISCHIN

Intervention

Nation-states experience a wide range of domestic conflicts, from peaceful protest demonstrations to civil wars. One principle of good conduct in international relations, well established in international law, is that a government should refrain from interfering in the domestic affairs of another country. But such interference takes place nonetheless, whether for humanitarian or military purposes.

An armed intervention is a particular type of interference by one government in another country, with four defining characteristics:

(a) The interference is overt, rather than covert.

(b) The interference is coercive, that is, armed forces from one country are assigned to combat in another country.

(c) There is an ongoing war between two rival internal groups, usually governmental forces and insurgents. The intervening force aids one side or the other rather than attacking just one or both of the domestic adversaries.

(d) The external forces fight as a separate party to the war rather than serving merely as volunteers or advisers to an internal force.

Although it is easy to confuse armed interventions with other uses of military force, attention to all four components can serve to avoid misclassifications. Covert military action in support of an antigovernmental insurgent is usually called subversion, as when the United States Central Intelligence Agency gave secret aid to the Contras, which were seeking to overthrow the Sandinista government of Nicaragua during the 1980s. Overt military action by one country across the borders of another is called invasion when it is unrelated to previously ongoing internal warfare. The Prussian attack on France in 1870 and subsequent occupation of Paris in 1871 is a classic example of an invasion. Interposition exists when an external armed force places itself between two warring armed forces in order to effect a cease-fire. The United Nations Emergency Force, for example, interposed itself between the armies of Egypt and Israel in 1956, thereby effecting a termination of the aggression of Israel and its allies, Britain and France, against Egypt. When an external force seeks to augment the warmaking capabilities of an internal warring faction, military aid is given. Governmental military aid for the Franco faction in the Spanish Civil War in 1936-1939 was provided by Germany and Italy, and the then Soviet Union aided the Republican Government of Spain. Nongovernmental aid came in the form of volunteers from Ireland to support Franco, while American, British, French, and other volunteers fought with the Spanish Republicans. The shipment of weapons and the extension of credits to foreign governments for the purchase of weapons are two of the most common examples of foreign military aid today.

Interventions take two forms—"pull" and "push" types of intervention (Little 1975 p. 3). Thucydides (1934) noted many instances in which a faction out of power in a Greek city-state called upon a foreign government to come to its aid; this is an example of a pull intervention, when a country invites ("pulls") an external power to solve a domestic problem. An example of a push intervention occurred after the success of the Bolshevik Revolution in Russia. In 1918, Russian dissident forces were joined by troops dispatched by the governments of Britain, France, Japan, and the United States in an effort to push out the new Soviet government; the unsuccessful intervention lasted until 1920.

Under international law, armed interventions can be justified in six situations:

(a) when the right to intervene is established specifically in a treaty;

(b) when a state unilaterally violates an agreement;

(c) when a state seeks to protect the safety of its own citizens in a civil conflict;

(d) when necessary for self-defense;

(e) when a state violates international law; and

(f) when intervention involves collective action by the international community, such as when the United Nations responds to threats to the peace or acts of aggression (Thomas and Thomas 1956, Vincent 1974 Chap. 8; see Falk 1964).

The particular circumstances of a situation preclude a more precise determination of what kinds of intervention are justifiable, so each intervening state may develop elaborate arguments to support actions that might be perceived elsewhere as unjustified. When the United Nations (UN) became involved in colonial and immediate postcolonial disputes that threatened to bring anarchy to a country, resolutions authorizing such intervention conspicuously avoided citing provisions in the UN Charter lest a firm precedent be established for later intervention (Miller 1967 p. 209). The ambiguity of the legal justification for humanitarian intervention is illustrated by the effort of Vietnam to drive the genocidal Khmer Rouge out of Cambodia through an armed intervention in 1978-79 and then to keep its troops in the country until 1989 because the Khmer Rouge, supplied by China, was poised at the Thai border to regain control of the country as soon as Vietnamese troops were withdrawn (Klintworth 1989).

During the Cold War, armed interventions in internal conflicts appeared to increase while interstate wars decreased. According to Little (1975 p. 4), there were three reasons:

(a) More nation-states had marginal defensive capabilities, as Grenada discovered when American troops arrived in 1983.

(b) The Cold War rivalry between the American and Soviet blocs gave almost every country's internal problems an international significance. A civil war in El Salvador, with allegations of aid to rebels from Soviet bloc countries formulated by Washington, was the occasion for military aid from the United States to the El Salvador government, starting in 1981.

(c) With the advent of nuclear weapons, direct superpower confrontation became too dangerous, so intervention and subversion were preferred methods in the competition between the superpowers for world dominance. Often the interventions became proxy wars, as in Cambodia after 1979, wherein China, the Soviet Union, and the United States backed three different groups seeking to control the country.

Not all armed interventions are successful in

achieving their aims. According to Chester Crocker (1996), effective intervention is a function of three general factors:

(a) the capabilities, leverage, and linkage of third parties to the conflict,

(b) the conflict's status, form, and rifeness, and

(c) the character of the parties to the conflict, their accessibility, and their decisionmaking systems.

Since the end of the Cold War, a greater consensus among the major powers has facilitated collective interventions with humanitarian aims, such as in Bosnia, Rwanda, and Somalia, where civil authority is in a state of collapse. The purpose of these efforts is generally to relieve human suffering while creating conditions conducive to the creation of a structure of civil authority acceptable to the people (Parekh 1997).

There have been some efforts to compile lists of interventions. Quincy Wright's (1965 pp. 641-46) listing of wars from 1480 to 1941 includes forty-four instances of civil wars with external intervention. Richard Little (1975 pp. 203-04) cites thirty-eight interventions from a larger compilation by Lewis Richardson (1960 pp. 40-111) for the years 1820-1945. J. David Singer and Melvin Small (1972 pp. 397-98) list thirty-four interventions from 1816 to 1965, which they call "internationalized civil wars," but in an expanded compilation for 1816-1980 they state that only twenty-one civil wars involved outside intervention (Small and Singer 1982 p. 278). Bruce Bueno de Mesquita (1981 pp. 205-07) enumerates one hundred and two conflict dyads from interventions from 1828 to 1968 involving major powers; his data source is Charles Gochman (1975). More recently, Herbert K. Tillema (1991) has provided a compendium of two hundred and sixty-nine interventions from 1945 to 1988.

See also: *Internal War*

Bibliography ─────────────────────

Bueno de Mesquita B 1981 *The War Trap*. Yale University Press, New Haven, Connecticut

Crocker C A 1996 The varieties of intervention. In: C A Crocker, F O Hampson, P Hall (eds.) *Managing Global Chaos: Sources of and Responses to International Conflict*. United States Institute of Peace, Washington, DC

Falk R A 1964 Janus tormented: The international law of internal war. In: Rosenau J N (ed.) *International Aspects of Civil Strife*. Princeton University Press, Princeton, New Jersey

Gochman C S 1975 Status, Conflict, and War: The Major Powers 1820-1970. Ph.D. dissertation, University of Michigan, Ann Arbor, Michigan

Klintworth G 1989 *Vietnam's Intervention in Cambodia in International Law*. Australian Government Publishing Service, Canberra

Little R 1975 *Intervention: External Involvement in Internal Wars*. Rowman and Littlefield, Totowa, New Jersey

Miller L B 1967 *World Order and Local Disorders: The United Nations and Internal Conflicts*. Princeton University Press, Princeton, New Jersey

Parekh B 1997 Rethinking humanitarian intervention. *Int'l Polit. Sci. Rev.* 18 (1)

Richardson L F 1960 *Statistics of Deadly Quarrels*. Quadrangle Books, Chicago, Illinois

Singer J D, Small M 1972 *The Wages of War, 1816-1965: A Statistical Handbook*. John Wiley and Sons, New York

Small M, Singer J D 1982 *Resort to Arms: International and Civil Wars 1816-1980*. Sage Publications, Beverly Hills, California

Thomas A Van W, Thomas A J 1956 *Non-intervention: The Law and its Impact in the Americas*. Southern Methodist University Press, Dallas, Texas

Thucydides 1934 *The Complete Writings of Thucydides*. Modern Library, New York

Tillema H K 1991 *International Armed Conflict Since 1945: A Bibliographic Handbook of Wars and Military Interventions*. Westview, Boulder, Colorado

Vincent R J 1974 *Nonintervention and International Order*. Princeton University Press, Princeton, New Jersey

Wright Q 1965 *A Study of War*. University of Chicago Press, Chicago, Illinois

MICHAEL HAAS

Islam

The concepts of war and peace in Islam originated in Arabia in the seventh century AD. Koranic instructions were revealed on particular occasions and addressed to specific communities. The Prophet's practice was influenced both by revelation and by the customs and practices of the time.

The most commonly used Arabic term denoting peace, or the absence of war, is *Salām*, meaning "harmony," "conciliation," "tranquility," and "peace." Other derivatives of the same root are *Musālim* (peaceful), *Tasālum* (peacemaking), *Istislām* (surrender), and *Muslim*. A Moslem (Muslim) is one who submits to God. He is, as Mohammed said, "the one of whom other Muslims should fear neither his hand nor his tongue."

Antonyms of *Salām* in Arabic are *Ḥarb* (war), *Qitāl* (fighting), and *Jihād*, which is "the exertion of one's power in God's path." *Jihād* can be achieved through dialogue, contribution to a just cause, or the fulfillment of a religious duty. A saying of the Prophet holds that the performance of the pilgrimage is the ultimate achievement of *Jihād*.

Salām is reflected in three interrelated areas of a Muslim's life: the religious, which concerns his relation with God; the social, which concerns his relations with others in the same community; and the political, which concerns intercommunal relations.

In a religious context *Salām* connotes the expected relationship between humankind and God in this world and in the hereafter. *Salām* emanates from God, although humankind is expected to strive to implement it on Earth by living in a state of peaceful coexistence in a world community whose members are all equal in the sight of God the Creator irrespective of their race, origin, nobility, or wealth.

These two themes are expressed in the terms *Taᶜāruf* (getting acquainted) and *Taqwā* (piety and God fearing). *Taqwā* is the key to the relationship between humankind and God through which individuals attains eternal bliss, *Salām*, in heaven. It also unites humankind in the faith and is hence the notion of the *Ummah*, a community or brotherhood that is united by the faith and accountable only to God.

The abode of God, Paradise, is known as *Dār* al-*Salām*, "the Abode of Peace and Eternal Bliss." Paradise is the reward of the believers for fulfilling their religious duties on Earth, and its peaceful life contrasts sharply with humankind's turbulent life on Earth. *Dār* al-*Salām* symbolizes man's desire for a more permanent and peaceful existence, which can be attained only in a metaphysical state.

At the communal level *Taᶜāruf*, *Taqwā*, and *Salām* can be implemented only within a social context. For Moslems, this social context was the *Ummah*, the Moslem community organized by Moḥammed, its earthly leader, with God as its head. Membership in the *Ummah* was based on religion rather than on kinship. The *Saḥīfah* (Charter of al-Madīnah), the first official document written by the Prophet (622 AD, defined the *Ummah* as a single community distinct from others and stated the obligations and expectations of all its members. The motto of the *Ummah* was "to command good and forbid evil." To ensure this, the Koran insists that Moslems practice justice and it emphasizes unity, cooperation, and sharing as prerequisites for communal peace.

To transform the *Ummah* from a pagan Arab community into a multiracial and multireligious one, both the Koran and the prophetic tradition prescribed an Islamic code of conduct in which *Salām* played an important role. At the social level the term *Salām* became a greeting with religious and moral implications, while at the political level it denoted a concept with religious, political, and international implications.

Although the Koran envisaged peace as the ultimate objective of Islam, it did not deny the need for a just war, or *Jihād*, under certain circumstances, provided it was of short duration, terminated in a peace agreement, and was carried out in accordance with Islamic law. Three types of just war were sanctioned in Islam by divine law: wars fought in defense of the faith and the Moslem community; wars fought to punish injustices inflicted upon the Moslem community; and wars fought against the idolaters, though only as a last resort in order to spread Islam. War was also allowed against any community that broke a treaty with the Moslems.

The interpretation of the concept of a just war in Islam differed according to the political conditions in the Islamic state at different times. During the Prophet's time the most dangerous enemies of the state were considered to be the idolaters, the polytheists of Arabia, and many Koranic verses were addressed to them. Early in the twelfth century, when the Moslem world was attacked for the first time by the Crusaders, the theory of *Jihād* focused on building Islamic morale and defined *Jihād* against the Crusaders from a position of weakness, especially in response to the First Crusade, as a purely defensive war.

In order to be just, a war had to be conducted according to a code of conduct prescribed in both the Koran and the prophetic tradition. The Prophet prohibited Moslems from committing acts of violence against their enemies, advising that if Moslems observed some evil activity they should try to change it through dialogue; if unsuccessful, they should pray for God's guidance for the offending person: and only if that did not work should they resort to force.

Like the theory of *Jihād*, the theory of peace crystallized in the Prophet's thought after his emigration to al-Madīnah in 622 AD. It was there that Mohammed developed a clearer concept of the Moslem community as well as of other religious communities in al-Madinah and its environs and, later on, in the whole of Arabia. This concept was first expressed in the *Saḥīfah* and thereafter in a number of letters pertaining to pacts and peace agreements with leaders of other communities.

Some early medieval jurists divided the world artificially into two zones: *Dār al-Islam* (the abode of Islam) and *Dār al-Ḥarb* (the abode of war). They defined the former as any territory whose inhabitants observed Islamic law and where Moslem authority prevailed, and the latter as any territory outside Islamic jurisdiction or hostile to Islam. Other medieval jurists added a third zone called *Dār al-Ṣulḥ* (the abode of peace). This third zone was the point of juncture between the two extremes, *Dār al-Islam* and *Dār al-Ḥarb*, and represented ideally a region where peace was expected to prevail in a theocratic state.

Although Islam prescribed a just war, the Koran also called for a just and lasting peace: "And if they hold aloof from you and wage not war against you and offer you peace, God allows you no way against them."

The basic rules regarding peaceful relations between the Islamic state and other communities or states were embodied in the concept of *Dhimmah*. *Dhimmah* in Islamic legal theory and practice meant both a guarantee of security or protection and a compact or obligation binding on Moslems and others. The term *Ahl al-Dhimma*h (protected religious minorities) was applied to the non-Moslem subjects of the Islamic state, such as the Christians, the Jews, the Zoroastrians, the Samaritans, and the Sabians. *Ahl al-Dhimmah*, also referred to as *Ahl al-Kitāb* (People of the Book), were allowed to live in an Islamic state provided they paid the *Jizyah* (poll tax). Their security, the freedom to practice their religion, and their defense were guaranteed by the state. However, the status of the *Dhimmis* fluctuated depending on time and place. Thus we find *Dhimmis* at times holding the highest offices in the Moslem state such as *Wazir*. At the same time we encounter in medieval Arabic chronicles accounts of incidents of mistreatment.

Dhimmah embodied three types of peace agreements between Moslems and others. The first, *Muᶜāhadah*, was an agreement between two communities or states regulating the nature of their relationship. Once a *Muᶜāhadah* had been signed or agreed upon orally between the Moslem community and another community, both parties were expected to adhere to it until the end of its term. Although the Prophet was strict about adhering to the terms of treaties, one early jurist suggested that a Moslem head of state could annul a peace treaty with a political enemy in certain circumstances, provided he did not attack before having sent its ruler an ultimatum.

The second, *Hudnah*, or *Muhādanah* or *Muwādaᶜah*—literally "tie" or "conjunction"—was a peace treaty of limited duration with specific stipulations that was signed between Moslems and non-Moslems. According to the terms of a *Hudnah*, whose maximum limit was usually ten years, neither side was allowed to attack or else the *Hudnah* was annulled. Captives taken by both sides were to be released and escorted to their respective territories, and the weaker opponent usually undertook to pay a fixed sum of money annually.

The third, *Aman*, was a pledge of security or safe conduct granted to non-Moslems who wanted to live in Islamic territory. The *Aman* was usually granted by the Moslem high official of state for a period not exceeding one year, in exchange for which the *Musta'min* (the person granted *Aman*) agreed to pay certain sums or commodities as security.

One can therefore say in conclusion that the main message of Islam is peace, a message that is perhaps best expressed in the following tradition: "O! People! Disseminate the word of peace [*Salām*]; feed the hungry; stay the night worshipping; and you will surely enter Paradise in peace [*bi-Salām*]."

It should be noted that at the present time Moslem states adhere to international law and abide by the provisions of the Charter of the United Nations.

See also: *Religion and Peace*

Bibliography

ᶜAbd Rabbihi A H 1975 *Falsafat al-Jihād fil-Islam* [The Philosophy of *Jihād* in Islam]. Al-Kitab al-Lubnani, Beirut

Armanāzī N 1930 *Al-Sharᶜ al-Duwalī fil-Islam* [International Law in Islam]. Ibn Zaydūn, Damascus

ᶜAzzām A 1964 *The Eternal Message of Muhammad*. Devin Adair, New York

Bosworth C E, Schact J (eds.) 1974 *The Legacy of Islam*. Clarendon, Oxford

Cahen C 1965 Dhimma. In: *Encyclopedia of Islam*, 2nd edn.

Coulson N J 1964 *A History of Islamic Law*. University of Edinburgh, Edinburgh

Fazlur Rahmān 1980 *Major Themes of the Qur'an*. Bibliotheca Islamica, Chicago, Illinois

Al-Ghunaimī M T 1968 *The Muslim Conception of International Law and the Western Approach*. Martinus Nijhoff, The Hague

Ibn Kathīr 1970 *Tafsī al-Qur'an al-ᶜAzīm* [Exegesis of the Great Qur'an]. Dar al-Fikr, Beirut

Ibn Manzūr 1956 *Lisān al-ᶜArab* [Lexicon of Arabic Language]. Dar Ṣādir, Beirut

Khaddūrī M 1955a *Law in the Middle East*. Middle East Institute, Washington, DC

Khaddūrī M 1955b *War and Peace in the Law of Islam*. Johns Hopkins University, Baltimore, Maryland

Khaddūrī M 1966 *The Islamic Law of Nations*. Johns Hopkins

University, Baltimore, Maryland

Maḥmasānī S 1972 *Al-Qānūn wal-ᶜAlāqāt al-Duwaliyyah fīl Islam* [Law and International Relations in Islam]. Dār al-ᶜIlm lil-Mālāyin, Beirut

Al-Qāsimī Z 1982 *Al-Jihād wal Ḥuqūq al-Duwaliyya al-ᶜAmmah fil-Islam* [*Jihād* and International rights in Islam]. Dār al-ᶜIlm lil-Malāyīn, Beirut

Al-Sarakhsī M 1958 *Sharḥ Kitāb al-Siyar al-Kabīr*. Miṣr, Cairo

Sival E *Interpretations of Islam: Past and Present*. Darwin Press, Princeton, New Jersey

Watt W M 1956 *Muhammad at Medina*. Clarendon, Oxford

HADIA DAJANI-SHAKEEL

Isolationism: United States

Diplomatic isolation can be said to mean an enforced exclusion of a nation from the world community, or the voluntary abstention from alliances by a country determined to pursue its own rights and interests in its own way. An instance of the former practice was the United States policy toward the People's Republic of China during the 1950s. But under Mao Zedong, the People's Republic of China itself pursued a policy largely designed to isolate itself from world affairs. In the 1970s, however, the People's Republic of China moved back to the position of the "open door," partly as a result of the strategy initiated by president Richard Nixon. Before the Anglo Japanese Alliance of 1902, Japan had existed without allies for over a thousand years. Between 1822 and 1902 British foreign policy reflected "splendid isolation," particularly in its approach to European affairs. Apart from the traditional alliance with Portugal, Britain entered only into *ad hoc* alliances to maintain what has been described as a "balance of power" on the European continent (see *Balance of Power*). During the last decades of the nineteenth century other European powers, such as Germany, tried to isolate their neighbors. This policy was effectively challenged by the Franco-Russian alliance of 1894, and in the decade leading up to the First World War no European power was isolated.

The word "isolationism," however, is usually taken to refer to the United States abstention from world politics. The original proponents of this idea could be said to have had a philosophy based on the premise of the moral superiority of the "New World" and the need to avoid entanglement in the machination of the power politics of the old order. It applied particularly to Europe, and the United States did not pursue the policy of non-involvement to the same extent in the pacific or the Far East. Implicit on the assumptions of this doctrine was the concept of an United States sphere of influence from which the European powers should be excluded. In the twentieth century "isolationism" came to be specifically identified with the policies initiated in congress during the interwar years, which were designed to prevent the United States from becoming involved in another world war in the same way in which it was perceived the United States had been drawn into the First World War.

1. Roots of United States Isolationism

The origins of "isolationism" can be traced to the period of the American Revolutionary Wars. In 1775 John Adams said that entire neutrality in all future European wars should be a first principle. Similarly, Thomas Jefferson argued that the United States, like the Turks, should have nothing to do with European affairs. Tom Paine, a recent immigrant from Britain, warned his American readers in 1776 that any submission to or dependence on Britain would involve their country in European wars and offend nations who would otherwise be friendly. In 1783 Congress resolved that the United States should be entangled as little as possible in "the politics and controversies of European nations."

The evolving doctrine was perhaps most fully expounded by George Washington in his Farewell Address of 1796:

> Europe has a set of primary interests which to us have none, or a very remote relation. Hence she must be engaged in frequent controversies the causes of which are essentially foreign to our concerns. Hence, therefore, it must be unwise in us to implicate ourselves, by artificial ties, in the ordinary vicissitudes of her politics, or the ordinary combinations and collisions of her friendships of enmities.

Washington acknowledged the need for temporary alliances but objected to ones that were of a permanent nature. Thomas Jefferson, in his inaugural address of 1801, elaborated this point: "peace, commerce, and honest friendship with all nations, entangling alliances with none."

These principles were enshrined by President James Monroe in his message to Congress of December 2, 1823. Mentioning the Old World and the New

World as separate spheres, he stated: "In the wars of the European powers, in matters relating to themselves, we have never taken part, nor does it comport with our policy so to do. *It is only when our rights are invaded, or seriously menaced* that we resent injuries, or make preparations for our defense." From 1852 this has been known as the Monroe Doctrine (see *Monroe Doctrine*).

2. Early Twentieth Century

Throughout the nineteenth and into the twentieth centuries the United States maintained, with modifications, an isolationist policy towards the European powers. This was largely possible because the politics of the European powers did not threaten United States interests. In the end United States security during this period rested on British supremacy, particularly on the seas. A belief grew in the United States, however, that this was more as a result of geographic isolation. Alongside this many saw a growth in the conviction of the moral supremacy of the New World, a view that was reinforced by the waves of immigration of those escaping the Old World and looking for a new life across the Atlantic. The Atlantic Ocean itself increasingly seemed a barrier to preserve the United States's isolationism. The Pacific and the East, however, were different. The United States acquired Hawaii, Guam, and the Philippines and pursued the policy of the "Open Door" in China, as well as expanding into Latin America and the Caribbean (see *Open Door Policy*). The foundations of twentieth century isolationism rested on a combination of these factors and reflected a strong Asia-first orientation. It was challenged by the rise of the German and Japanese armies and navies.

On the outbreak of the First World War, President Woodrow Wilson (see Nobel Peace Prize Laureates: *Woodrow Wilson*) asked the United States people to be neutral in thought, word, and deed. Germany finally challenged this: on January 31, 1917, it declared unrestricted submarine warfare in the Atlantic. But even when it entered the war, the United States did not make alliances with Germany's enemies, United States participation in the First World War seemed to convince many Americans that their boys should not again be sent to fight and die in alien countries for causes which did not concern them. As a result Wilson's ideas of a New World Order based on his Fourteen Points and the League of Nations were rejected by the United States Congress: the United States could not be involved in any commitments to maintain world stability.

During the 1920s the United States was a signatory to treaties concerned with the Far East, but it did not accept any real responsibilities in that area, and did not intervene in the Manchurian crisis of the early 1930s. In 1931 secretary of state Henry Stimson suggested a discretionary arms embargo which the president could apply in time of war against the side which had broken the peace. This resulted in debates about armaments manufacturers in the United States, and the extent to which they had benefited from the First World War. A Senate investigation, headed by Gerald P. Nye sat between 1934 and 1936, and with the assistance of a willing press sensationalized findings about the lobbying activities and profits of the munitions industry.

The growing isolationist lobby was also strengthened by the debates over the allies' refusal to repay war debts. Against the background of Mussolini's invasion of Abyssinian, Hitler's occupation of the Rhineland, and the Spanish Civil War, Congress passed successive neutrality acts. The 1935 act made it mandatory for the president to proclaim the outbreak of war between foreign states and to embargo the export of arms to such states. The 1937 legislation, however, while handicapping any belligerent obtaining war material or other supplies, aided Britain as it had command of the sea and the largest purse. The reason for this was the controversial "cash and carry" clause which was introduced for a trial period of two years.

3. Second World War

In July 1937, following the Marco Polo Bridge incident, it was evident that there was going to be a major clash between Japan and China in the Far East. The British Foreign Secretary, Anthony Eden (see *Eden, Anthony*), hoped to involve the United States alongside Britain in that area. He believed, together with some Foreign Office officials, that if this happened, the United States would automatically be involved with Britain in any war in Europe. But the United States refused joint action and would only take parallel action. Norman Davis, a presidential adviser, explained that his government was reluctant to "get mixed up with all Europe in the Far East." By October 1937, however, President F. D. Roosevelt was aware of the dangers of the international situation and of the need to educate public opinion. In his famous "quarantine speech" at Chicago he said: "It seems to be unfortunately true that the epidemic of world lawlessness is spreading. When an epidemic of physical disease starts to spread, the community approves and joins in a quarantine of the patients in order to protect the health of the community against the spread of the disease." Although British observers saw press comment as being favorable, the State Department viewed the response as hostile and determined United States foreign policy accordingly. Indeed isolationist sentiment in the United States was considered to be so strong that even when the Japanese attacked the USS *Panay* and HMS *Ladybird* in the Yangtse in December, the United States would not take joint action with Britain and was eager to accept the Japanese apology. Roosevelt, however, did arrange for Captain R. E. Ingersoll of the United States Navy to visit Britain, and these conversations, together with those of Commander T. C. Hampton of the Royal Navy in the United States in June 1939, laid the foundations of the Anglo-American military alliance.

In January 1938 Roosevelt proposed a peace plan to the British Prime Minister, Neville Chamberlain. The President was not offended by Chamberlain's hesitant response, and in any case against the background of isolationist sentiment in the United States the plan did not envisage the United States endangering its freedom from any commitment to involvement in world affairs. During the Munich crisis Roosevelt warned the British ambassador, sir Ronald Lindsay, that in indefinable circumstances the United States might again find itself involved in a European war, but so strong was isolationist opinion that even in such a case he thought it "almost inconceivable" that he would be able to send United States troops across the Atlantic. If Britain were invaded, however, it was possible that a wave of emotion would send the United States Army overseas.

Roosevelt was anxious to help Britain fight a war by blockade. He suggested this again in August 1939. The President wanted to help Britain, but was conscious, he said, that he could not move ahead of a difficult and very restive United States public opinion. Roosevelt, however, after Munich, through his friend, Colonel Arthur Murray, was able to let Chamberlain know that he hoped to provide Britain, if it were at war with the dictators, with basic materials—such as aluminum plates, steel casings for engines, and cylinder blocks—not covered by the neutrality acts, to enable the building of an extra 20,000 to 30,000 planes, to give superiority over Germany and Italy in the air. Roosevelt also urged that the King and Queen extend their planned tour of Canada in May 1939 to include the United States. He hoped to be able to present them with the repeal of the neutrality acts. But isolationist opinion in the United States was bolstered early in 1939 when a top secret United States aircraft

crashed killing a French official on board. Congress refused.

Public opinion in the United States, according to contemporary analysis, was inclined to blame Britain for not taking a strong enough stand against the dictators, rather than Hitler. On the refugee issue it felt that Britain should do everything: few Jewish refugees were admitted to the United States. On a diplomatic level, before the outbreak of the Second World War, a "special relationship" did exist between Britain and the United States: this was reflected in the full and frank exchange of information between the two governments. Roosevelt had a plan for aiding Britain. But he was hampered by domestic crises, and an isolationist Congress and public opinion. He said that he could go only as far as the public would allow him, though he tried to go further.

In his fireside chat on the outbreak of war, Roosevelt said that he could not ask the United States to be neutral in thought. By the end of 1939 he had managed to force "cash and carry" through Congress, arguing that it was a nonpartisan issue and wearing down reluctant isolationist senators through all-night sittings, opinion polls at the end of the year reflected stronger isolationist attitudes in the United States than at the outbreak of war. The isolationist lobby found focus with the American First Committee led by the aviator, Charles Lindbergh. But Hitler's invasion of Belgium aroused even the traditionally isolationist Middle West, and the Nazi invasion of Denmark and Norway, with the obvious implications for Greenland and Iceland, showed that a policy based on the continental America was not enough. Roosevelt bypassed Congress with his destroyer for bases deal in August 1940 and, reelected for a third term, secured the passing of Lend-Lease early in 1941. Critics argued that through passing Lend-Lease, with its implications of patrolling and convoying, Congress authorized Roosevelt to go to war. Indeed by November 1941, with incidents like the *Kearney* and the *Reuben James*, it could be argued that the United States was involved in a shooting war in the Atlantic.

It has been claimed that Roosevelt, unable to secure a declaration of war over the incidents in the Atlantic, concentrated on the Far East and tried to provoke Japan into firing the first shot. Extreme conspiracy theorists have even claimed that Roosevelt sacrificed the fleet at Pearl Harbor, and that the loss was deliberate rather than as a result of a series of blunders. A number of works published to mark the fortieth anniversary of Pearl Harbor have not resolved the issue; the answer probably lies in the British intelligence papers. Even after Pearl Harbor, isolationist sentiment in congress was so strong that had not Germany declared war on the United States, Congress would probably not have declared war on Germany.

4. Post-Second World War

After the end of the Second World War, the United States returned overnight to peacetime thinking: there was no guarantee that United States forces would even stay in Europe. This attitude was reflected in the Republican victories in the November 1946 congressional elections with the program of "return to normalcy." This threatened isolationism was only overcome through the adroit diplomacy of British officials, who managed to persuade the United States to see the world through British spectacles. It was the British Foreign Secretary, Ernest Bevin, who took the initiative and laid the foundations of the western security system based on the leadership of the United States. Starting with the assumption of responsibility for Greece and Turkey in February 1947, this developed into the United States' first peacetime entangling alliance through the formation of the North Atlantic Treaty Organization (NATO) (see *North Atlantic Treaty Organization (NATO)*) in April 1949. After the revolution in China, however, Britain had great difficulty in encouraging the United States to take the lead in Asia, but with the signing of National Security Council Paper NSC 48/2 at the end of 1949, which reflected British thinking, the United States was set to block communist expansion in Asia. It was only, however, with the stand at the beginning of the Korean war that London felt that the United States had finally withdrawn from isolationism and was standing up to its great new responsibility, perhaps as an "inexperienced colossus," and the Pax Britannica became the Pax Americana (see *Pax Americana*).

"Isolationism" is frequently viewed by those of liberal persuasion as having contributed to the outbreak of the second world war. In the 1960s, however, against the background of the Vietnam War, the "new left," implicitly supported the stance in their studies of the origins of the Cold War. During the presidencies of Ford and Carter there was a reappearance of isolationist sentiment in sections of the United States public. The Iranian hostage crisis of 1979 largely dispelled this, and president Ronald Reagan carried the American public with him in his reassertion of United States power and leadership in world affairs.

With the demise of the other superpower, the former Soviet Union, the United States remains as the only superpower capable of influencing global politics. Even with George Bush at the helm, the United States led the international community in taming a world menace, Iraq, which threatened world peace. Although seemingly suffering from fatigue and limitations of resources, the United States cannot free itself from the obligations of being the sole global leader. Its reluctance to get in deep involvement in ethnic or localized conflicts is justified by the limitation of its capacity to perform global leadership. But in the foreseeable future America will remain the world only superpower.

See also: *Self-Determination; Nonintervention and Noninterference*

Bibliography

Dallek R 1979 *Franklin D Roosevelt and American Foreign Policy, 1932-1945*. Oxford University Press, New York

De Conde A (ed.) 1957 *Isolationism and Security: Ideas and Interests in Twentieth century American Foreign Policy*. Duke University Press, Durham, North Carolina

Gaddis J L 1983 The emerging post-revisionist synthesis on the origins of the Cold War. *Diplomatic Hist.* 7(3)

Graebner N A 1956 *The New Isolationism: A Study in Politics and Foreign Policy since 1950*. Ronald Press, New York

Langer W L, Gleason E S 1952 *The Challenge to Isolation*. Harper, New York

Langer W L, Gleason E S 1953 *The Undeclared War*. Harper, New York

Morison S E, Commager H S, Leuchtenburg W E 1977 *A Concise History of the American Republic*. Oxford University Press, New York

Ovendale R 1975 *"Appeasement" and the English Speaking World: Britain, the United States, the Dominions, and the Policy of "Appeasement," 1937-1939*. University of Wales Press, Cardiff

Ovendale R 1985 *The English-speaking Alliance: Britain, the United States, the Dominions and the Cold War 1945-1951*. Allen and Unwin, London

Yahuda M 1983 *Towards the End of Isolationism: China's Foreign Policy after Mao*. Macmillan, London

RITCHIE OVENDALE; PEDRO B. BERNALDEZ

J

Jainism

Jainism is an old religion of India. It is a religion which is still very much alive. Several salient features of Indian culture, such as vegetarianism, nonviolence, tolerance, and nonaggression, may have been the results of Jaina influence. In the field of philosophy, Jainism has added a new dimension by propounding the doctrine of the multifaceted nature of truth (called *anekānta-vāda*). This is particularly relevant here for its significance lies in allowing peaceful coexistence of opposite viewpoints and opposing parties in this conflict-ridden world. It is a metaphysical thesis that goes directly against any form of extremism, dogmatism, and bigotry. It offers a metaphysical defense for negotiating with one's adversary, for forgiving one's enemy and for forbearing adverse misfortunes.

1. History

Around 600 BC in India the old Brahminical religion of ritual and sacrifice was challenged by a group of individual thinkers called *Śramaṇas*, who were wandering monks and free thinkers teaching their individual doctrines to the people who would follow them. Two major streams from the *Śramaṇa* thought survived. One was Buddhism, the other Jainism.

Jainism is as old as Buddhism, and it has been claimed that it is even older. The founder of Buddhism was the Buddha, but the Mahāvīra, also called Nirgrantha Jñātri-putra (or Nigantha Nātaputta in Pāli), a contemporary of the Buddha, was not the founder, but rather a *tīrthaṃkara* (a prophet), of Jainism. Jainism had at least one other historical *tīrthaṃkara*, Pārśva, who preceded Mahāvīra by more than two hundred years.

Mahāvīra was the son of Siddhārtha, a chief of the warrior class of the *Jñātrikas*. At the age of 30 he left his home in order to seek salvation. He wandered far and wide in the Ganges valley for 12 years before he found full enlightenment and became a *kevalin* (completed soul). He also became a *jina* (spiritual conqueror), from which the name Jainism was derived.

Having taught his doctrines for about 30 years and having founded a disciplined order of monks supported by many layfolk, he attained his *nirvātṇa* at the age of 72 at Pāvā, near Patna (468 BC).

The *Śramana* sect called the Ājīvakas, who preached a sort of fatalism and futility of human effort, was looked upon as the chief rival of both Buddhism and Jainism. Both Buddhism and Jainism were *Kriyāvādin* ("actionist") and preached that human effort is not futile for there is freedom of choice to work or not to work for final emancipation.

It is believed that Candragupta (c. 317-293 BC), the first Maurya Emperor, was a patron of Jainism and ultimately became a Jaina monk. Thus, like Buddhism, Jainism began to flourish during the Maurya period. The great schism of Jainism also took place at this time. Bhadrabāhu, the eleventh pontiff (called *gaṇadhara*) of the order, led the group of more orthodox, naked monks who called themselves the *Digambaras*, "the space-clad." Sthūlabhadra, another teacher, led the other group called the Śvetāmbaras, "the white-clad," who used to wear white robes. As in Buddhism, the sacred texts of Jainism were initially unwritten and were transmitted orally, being memorized by the monks. At that time Bhadrabāhu was the only monk who knew the entire sacred texts. Sthūlabhadra called a council of monks at Pātaliputra to conserve the sacred texts. Since Bhadrabāhu did not attend this council, the original canon was reconstructed as far as possible from the memory of Sthūlabhadra and other monks, and it was organized in the form of eleven limbs (*Aṅgas*). They were all authentic for the *Śvetāmbaras* only. The *Digambaras* disputed their authenticity.

Jainism spread both in the north and in the south. By 1000 AD many princes from the south gave their support. It spread to Gujarat and Rajasthan, where it still survives among layfolks as well as the monks. It is important to note that while Buddhism almost perished in India, but survived in countries outside India, Jainism never went beyond India's boundaries.

In the early eighteenth century a further schism

occurred when a group called *sthānakavāsins* broke away from the *Śvetāmbaras* in protest against their increasing iconolatry and temple worship. The new group became purist and held religious meetings in austere and unconsecrated buildings (*sthānaka*).

2. Literature

The Jaina canon as we have it today (45 texts of moderate size) represents for the most part a very old set of writings; the most important part of it goes back to the times of the Council of Pāṭaliputra. The language is chiefly the Ardhamāgadhī dialect of Prakrit. Hermann Jacobi furnished evidence and concluded that these texts belonged to the period roughly between 300 BC and 200 AD. This conclusion has never been seriously challenged.

The canon consists of eleven limbs (*Aṅgas*), twelve secondary limbs (*Upāṅga*), ten miscellaneous texts (*Prakīrṇaka*), six separate texts (*chedasūtra*), *Nandi* and *Anuyogadvāra* (two uncategorized texts), and four basic texts (*Mūlasūtra*). A huge mass of commentaries, represented by the successive stages of *niryukti, curṇī, tikā,* and *dīpikā,* came into existence afterwards. The non-canonical Jaina literature is also vast, and exists in various Prakrits, Apabhramsa, and Sanskrit.

One of the oldest independent Jaina philosophical treatises was Umāsvāti's *Tattvārthādhigamasūtra* in the first century AD, which has been the subject of many commentaries. The major writings in Jaina philosophy and logic were in Sanskrit, and such writings continued uninterrupted along with the development of Sanskrit literature. There are also many Jaina moral tales, poems in Sanskrit in the *Purāṇa* and *kāvya* styles, and scientific treatises.

3. Doctrines and Practices

According to the Jainas, the world is eternal and imperishable. No God created it. No Higher Being governs it. It is subject to its own laws. So far the Jaina view is consonant with modern scientists' view of the world, although it does not exactly coincide with the theory of evolution by natural selection. Jainism believes that the world remains unchanged in its essential parts although its components undergo constant change and modification.

The Jainas admit five imperishable elements, called "substances" (*dravya*): (a) *ākāśa* (space), (b) *dharma* (the medium for movement), (c) *adharma* (the medium for rest), (d) *pudgala* (matter), and (e) *jīva* (soul). Of these, the first three have spatial con-

notation. *Ākāśa* is coterminous with both this world and the nonworld (*aloka*), where all liberated souls rest or congregate, *dharma* is what allows motion, and *adharma* allows rest, but only in this world (*loka*) and not in the nonworld. *Padgalas* are actually minute indivisible atoms of matter; by combination they produce aggregates, which in turn produce the heterogeneous phenomena of the world we experience. *Jīvas* are innumerable and are distinguished from other elements by possession of consciousness and intelligence. A *jīva* is by nature omniscient, above joy or grief, possesses morality and unrestricted energy. But it just so happens that the soul is eternally affected by matter, in the form of *karman*, which is but a complex of very fine matter. *Karman* particles have been likened to those of a medical pill, which affects the whole body the way *karman* infects the soul. Thus infected, the soul's true qualities are blocked from being explicit. But, just as the soul is affected by the fine matter of *karman*, it can be rendered free from such obstacles. The technique is to stop the inflow of *karman* by religious and ethical practice and then to eliminate the already accumulated *karman*. When freed the soul develops its full potential and reaches the nonworld.

The central philosophy of Jainism is, however, *anekāntavada*, or "non-one-sidedness." It is a philosophy of nonradicalism and a unique contribution of Jainism to the philosophical tradition of India. It can also become a unique contribution in the global context. Literally the term *anekāntavāda* means "the theory of the many-sided nature of reality." Dasgupta has called it "relative pluralism." The later development of Jaina philosophy shows Jainism as a philosophy of synthesis, that is, a synthesized presentation of different metaphysical and epistemological theories of ancient and classical India. The seed of this "non-one-sidedness" doctrine lay in the canonical doctrine of *vibhajya-vāda*, the method of "analysis" or "breaking the knotty issue" (Matilal 1981). Both the Buddha and the *Mahāvīra* adopted the *vibhajya* doctrine—a doctrine of avoiding extremes. But while the Buddhist avoids extremes by an attitude of noncommitment and exclusion (the Middle Way), the Jaina avoids them by conditional acceptance of many extremes, thereby, neutralizing the conflict.

Combination of opposite viewpoints always presents some logical problems in philosophy. The Jainas were well-aware of such problems and developed a method to tackle them. This method consists of two doctrines: *nayavāda* (the doctrine of standpoints) and *syād-vāda* or *saptabhaṅgī* (the sevenfold truth predication to avoid absolute commitment to any thesis or position). A *naya* is defined as a particular standpoint—one that admits at the same time that there are different ones. A *naya* is therefore what captures a partial truth about an object or a thesis. The Jainas argue that different philosophers, when they construct different philosophical systems, emphasize different standpoints. As long as one develops a particular standpoint in full awareness of the fact that this is *only one* among many, equally viable, standpoints, one employs a *naya*, "a right philosophical behavior." But if one clings to one particular standpoint by excluding or rejecting all others as false, one employs a *durnaya*, "a censurable philosophical behavior." For example, when the Nyāya realists talk about the unchanging character of substances (or their atomic constituents) or of essences (universals), they adopt the "substance exists" standpoint (*dravyāstika-naya*). But the Buddhists in arguing in favor of the momentary and nonsubstantial nature of reality adopt the opposite standpoint, "modification exists" (*paryāyāstika-naya*). The Jainas say that both try to capture the truth but succeed only in getting it partially, and one can overcome this partiality and one-sidedness by integrating all standpoints into a totality, a vision that is possible only in the case of an omniscient being. Siddhasena, a well-known Jaina philosopher, observes:

All standpoints are right in their own respective sphere—but if they are taken to be refutations, each of the other, then they are wrong. But a man who knows the "non-one-sided" nature of reality never says that a particular view is absolutely wrong. (Matilal 1981 p. 31)

The above may also refer to the ambiguity of deciding conclusively what is an unmixed evil in man, and it may imply that "every cloud has a silver lining." This seems to be quite consistent with the doctrine of "nonviolence" (*ahimsa*) of Jainism.

Traditionally the Jainas came to talk about seven different standpoints, which can be subsumed under the two main ones already noted. These seven *nayas* have been variously named and differently interpreted in the literature. This article will follow Siddhasena in classifying them. According to him the "substance exists" standpoint bifurcates into two, the "general" (*samgraha*) and the "practical" (*vyavahāra*). The first is that adopted by the Vedānta school and Mahāyāna Buddhism, the second by the Vaiśeṣika and Sāmkhya schools. The "modification exists" standpoint has four subdivisions. The "straight-thread" (*rjusūtra*) is that adopted by the Sautrāntika Buddhists. The "verbal" (*śabda*) is the grammarians

preference. The "subtle" (*samabhirūḍha*) is the view that emphasizes etymologies of words to explain meanings or concepts. The "thus-happened" (*evambhūta*) is the way for the pragmatists, who believe, for example, that a cook is to be properly called a cook only when he or she is actually cooking. Akalanka, another Jaina philosopher, has described the standpoints as hidden intentions or presuppositions of the inquirers, different points of view or commitments of persons searching after the truth.

The *syād-vāda*, or the sevenfold truth predication, is the second doctrine of the Jaina logical methodology. The word *syāt* ordinarily means "perhaps" or "maybe," but there is another use of "*syāt*" to mean "possibility" (*sambhāvana*). The Jaina use of the *syāt* particle in attaching it to any sentence or thesis has a concessive force. It concedes the thesis only provisionally. But it concedes the opposing thesis not only to blunt the sharpness of the opponent's attack, but also to persuade the opponent to come to see another point of view. Thus, in Jainism, the particle has two forces—a disarming effect and (implicitly) a persuasive force.

The Jainas believe that the intrinsically pluralistic nature of reality cannot allow any proposition about it to be absolutely true or absolutely false. With a concessive *syāt* we can accept proposition p (=the pot exists) as being true from one point of view, and false from another. In addition, if we want to assert jointly truth and falsity of the same proposition in exactly the same sense, we will not succeed, given the nature of language and speech. In that case the said proposition would be ineffable, and we should say that we may assign a third value, ineffability, to p. These three fundamental values of truth predication, true (t), false (f), and ineffable (e), give rise to seven kinds of truth assigning to any proposition when they are taken one at a time, two at a time in combination, or all three: t, f, e, tf, te, fe, tfe.

The twin doctrines of *nayas* and *syāt* sustain the philosophical argument of the Jainas in favor of their *anekānta* theory. The truth is many faceted; pluralism is an essential part of realism. This is also very much consistent with the well-known ethical teaching of Jainism, *ahimsa* ("non-violence").

Nonviolence was the dominant trend in the whole *śramaṇa* movement. Abstention from killing (i.e., respect for life) was the first cardinal virtue to be practiced by everybody. The Jaina canonical texts emphasize that one should try to think of all living creatures as equal to one's own self and therefore should not try to harm anybody intentionally. Thus the *Acaranga sutra* notes:

All beings are fond of life, they like pleasure, hate pain, avoid decay, wish to live long. To all, life is dear . . . . All breathing, existing, living, sentient creatures should not be slain, nor treated with violence, nor abused, nor tormented, nor driven away. This is the pure, unchangeably eternal law, which the clever ones, who understand the world, have declared. (Jacobi 1968)

This need not mean that killing of any kind is sinful. Rather it dictates that we should live in this world in such a way as not to have to kill any living being. This is how a modern Jaina scholar, Malvania (1968), has put it. We should cultivate a feeling of kindness, compassion, and sympathy for all living creatures; killing or inflicting pain upon others may be allowed only when it is unavoidable. It is neither a Kantian ethic, nor utilitarian. It is a practical resolution without affecting the normative goal of nonviolence.

4. Relationship to Peace

The Mahāvīra carried the concept of nonviolence from the domain of ethics and practical behavior to the domain of intellectual and philosophical discussion. The Jaina principle of "respect for the life of others" gave rise, in the ontological domain, to the principle of respect for the views of others. This respect for the views, beliefs, and commitments of others, has been spelled out in the *anekānta* doctrine of "many-sidedness." Thus it has helped to cultivate the attitude of toleration towards the views, beliefs, and commitments of adversaries. It goes in fact further by persuading us to find out how and why our adversaries hold a different view or conviction. This creates the ground for reconciling seemingly contradictory positions into harmony. The centrality of this spirit of toleration, this attempt to reconcile and harmonize opposite parties, is unique to Jainism and is its most admirable trait. Seldom has such a sincere attempt been made to understand the adversary and to accept what is acceptable in the opposing position. In our present-day world, where peace, security, and even the survival of humankind is threatened by the nuclear menace and warmongering politicians, the Jaina spirit of toleration and reconciliation, its bold acceptance of a pluralistic universe, and its method of upholding noncommitment to any dogmatic position and any blind faith should be cultivated. To the maintenance of world peace and stability, Jainism can contribute a great deal.

See also: *Buddhism; Religion and Peace*

Bibliography

Bühler G 1903 *On the Indian Sect of the Jainas.* London
Dasgupta S 1963 *A History of Indian Philosophy*, Vol. I. Cambridge University Press, Cambridge
Glasenapp H von 1942 *The Doctrine of Karma in Jain Philosophy.* BVJP, Charity Fund, Bombay
Gopalan 1973 *Outlines of Jainism.* Wiley Eastern, New Delhi
Jacobi H 1968 *Jaina Sūtras.* Dover, New York
Jacobi H Jainism. *Encyclopedia of Religions and Ethics*, Vol. 7.
Jaini P S 1979 *The Jaina Path of Purification.* California University Press, Berkely, California
Malvania D 1968 Jaina theory and practice of nonviolence. *Sambodhi* 2(1)
Matilal B K 1981 *The Central Philosophy of Jainism (Anekāntavāda).* L.D. Institute, Ahmedabad

BIMAL KRISHNA MATILAL

Japan: Debates on Peace (1950s-1980s)

There are three main concepts necessary to analyze the postwar Japanese views on peace: idealism, realism, and globalism. There are movements associated with each of these concepts.

1. Idealism

After the Second World War in Japan those who have been called "idealists" came to the front, concerned whether they could remove totalitarianism and the Tenno system from Japan. In fact, in their situation they had nothing to do but idealize themselves and the difficult positions which they encountered as a result of the occupation of Japan by the United States. Consequently the idealists were isolated both intellectually and societally. They were concerned with the very nature of peace.

In the late 1940s the idealists, including pacifists, actively organized the Peace Study Group (Heiwa Mondai Danwakai) whose members were mostly scholars and leading scientists, including Goro Hani, Osamu Kuno, Hiroshi Minami, Yoshio Nakano, Shuichi Kato, and Masao Maruyana. Its purpose was more or less to make an impact on the policy-making process and peace movement for the future of Japan. It appealed for the future of world peace and made three key statements in the 1940s: the first, "A Statement by Scientists in Japan on the Problem of Peace

(1948);" the second, "A Statement by the Peace Study Group on the Problem of the Peace Settlement for Japan (1950);" and the third, "On Peace for the Third Time (1950)." In the first statement, they asserted that leading scientists needed to "cooperate" with people for the promotion of peace because, until 1945, scientists had not been able to cooperate to stop the Second World War. In the second, they emphasized that Japan faces two divided "worlds" the United States and the former Soviet Union. Japan should not support only one of them, nor should Japan conclude a peace treaty with only one of them. So the Peace Study Group concluded that Japan should be neutral toward both powers. In the third statement, they reconfirmed their attitudes towards peace and a peaceful world order. It was expressed symbolically that peace was a supreme value, while war was an absolute evil. These statements corresponded with the spirit of "no rearmament" in the new constitution.

The appeals and ideas of these above-mentioned statements were accepted by the communists and socialists and by most of the public as well as by later groups such as the Tokyo Peace Studies Group (Tokio Heiwa Kenkyu Group) and the Japan Peace Study Group (Nippon Heowa Kenkyu Konwakai). It was a significant event on postwar history that almost all Japanese explicitly or implicitly accepted these views. Consequently, the mainstream for peace movements took shape in the immediate postwar period in Japan. It continued to develop through the 1950s. In the 1960s, the peace movement separated into two groups, the communists and their supporters, and the socialists and their supporters. They began a controversy about "White" or "Red" nuclear weapons; weapons which the former could not classify but the latter could. Since this split the peace movement in Japan has been divided.

Above all, the idealists, including pacifists, idealized peace too abstractly with no relation to an unstable reality. While the optimistic idealists have still kept their standpoints, the pessimistic idealists have begun to look for a new view of peace, which will basically be committed to the globalist view.

2. Realism

After the Second World War up until the 1960s, the realists were not influential. As Japan achieved strong economic power in the 1960s, the realists—Masataka Kousaka, Younosuke Nagai, Seido Inoki, Makoto Momoi, and others—began to act. Their outlook on peace and national security began to emerge, and compete with, the idealist view. The realists

were increasingly in the vanguard of the new social situation. The realists questioned what the nature of a nation-state is in terms of their paradigm. The first realist answer to such a question appeared on two monthly magazines: "The Realists Talk for Peace" (Genjitsu-shugisha no Heiwaron) and "Is Japan a Bad Country?" (Nihon wa warui kunika), written by Masataka Kousaka. In the first article he discussed whether it was possible to realize the idealists' approach to peace. His answer was no. His second paper concluded that Japan was not and has not been bad. The second realist answer was described in a paper entitled "National Goals for Security and Dependence" (Kokka mokuhyo toshite no Anzen to Dokuritsu) by Yonosuke Nagai. After criticizing the idealists' approach to peace or peaceful order, he advanced a multiadaptive "Judo diplomacy" for a new Japanese method of diplomacy. He criticized the idealists because they had ignored the international political reality of the balance of power and its policies as a whole.

Above all, the realists—including the quasi-individualists, nationalists, the Rightists—thought of peace for Japan alone without considering its relationship to peace for other states. They failed to realize their goals or to express their ideals in terms which the world public might accept, although they did opportunely adapt their perspective to the specific peace order controlled by the two superpowers. While the optimistic realists still pursued their ideas of a nationcentric peace order and national security, the pessimistic realists developed a new view of peace embracing, in particular, the notion of collective security.

3. Globalism

From the 1970s, the globalist (Saburo Okita, Kinhide Mushakoji, Horoharu Seki, Shigeyuki Itow, etc.) discussed the future of Japan as well as about how to contribute to international society in order to protect Japan and achieve world peace in light of the fact that Japan has received much criticism from overseas countries. Saburo Okita proposed that Japan should contribute to world society by adopting a new diplomatic policy of being "defenseless on all sides." He emphasized that Japan needed to perform and support collective security in the long term. He criticized the realist-quasi-individualist view of peace and security—which proposed the strengthening of military power.

Collective security will be a useful idea in the next century. Shigeyuki Itow has asserted that Japan must create it, for Japan cannot now achieve the goal of maintaining peace by strengthening military power as the realists claimed or by reducing military power to zero as the idealists hoped. Kinhide Mushakoji and Hiroharu Seki also stressed changing a nationcentric approach into a global one to analyze present world affairs in the contest of international asymmetric structures. They talked about pursuing and achieving collective security as a new wisdom of humanity, able to protect us.

The globalists may be somewhat utopian without being scientific, and are thought of as idealizing realities instead of realizing ideals. They do not like to idealize peace too abstractly as the idealists did, nor do they like to realize it too concretely as the realists did, without ever considering relations to other states, other people, and the natural environment. The pessimistic globalist may change themselves into realists who pursue only their own nationcentric policy by pressuring members of the "nuclear club," while the optimistic globalist could take over their own creative points of view in helping to bridge the gap between ideals and reality, ends and means, and the national and the global levels.

4. Conclusion

The idealist approach to peace is nonstrategic, arm-chair, and slightly utopian but not militant; the realist approach is relatively powercentric, nationalistic, and militant; while the globalist approach is somewhat utopian but fundamentally creative, adaptive, informative, and cooperative.

Reviewing peace views and peace movements in their historical contexts up to 1986, we can summarize briefly that the idealists represented the mainstream in Japan in the 1950s, the realists in the 1960s, and the globalist in the 1970s. The question of how the 1980s will develop is unanswerable at present. All three movements are refusing to take the lead: each of the three continues to incite political agitation for or against various conceptions of peace, peace order, and security.

Bibliography

Hook G D 1981 Peace thought and ideas in postwar Japan. *Kokusaiseji* 69
Mushakoji K 1977 *Kokusai Seji O Miru Me* [Viewpoint for Seeing International Politics]. Iwanami Shoten, Tokyo
Seko H 1977 Heiwa no Seijigaku [Politics of Peace]. *Kodoron Lkouno Sejiigaku*. Iwanami, Shoten, Tokyo
Takahashi S, Nakamura K 1978 Sengo Nihon no heiwaron [Peace research in postwar Japan]. *Sekai* 6

SHIGEYUKI ITOW

Jingoism

Jingoism is a term describing an attitude of militaristic nationalism. Although it is similar in this sense to the word of French origin, chauvinism (see *Chauvinism*), it connotes greater emphasis on a warlike tendency. The origins of the two expressions are also suggestive of the nuances in implied meanings between them. Nicholas Chauvin, the eponym of chauvinism, was after all an ordinary French soldier who led a humble life, satisfied with his rewards, although he was devoted to the causes of patriotism and military glory in particular. The phrase "by jingo" itself can be traced to the rituals supposedly performed by magicians in medieval times, who used it as a part of their incantations. However, this has nothing to do with jingoism as the term came to be used.

The origin of jingoism was the war fever, basically a phenomenon of mass politics, that prevailed in Britain when a British squadron was despatched to Gallipoli to exert a restraining influence on Russia during the Russo-Turkish War in the late 1870s.

Those who advocated a strong policy against Russia was called "jingoes," which was derived from the phrase "by jingo" in the refrain of a song popular at that time:

> We don't want to fight, yet by jingo! if we do, we've got the ships, we've got the men, and got the money, too!

This kind of attitude did not pass away after the war but remained as a factor in British politics in the late nineteenth century, primarily in association with imperialistic wars. A typical case was the Boer War during which not only the policy of the government but also British society as a whole seemed to have fallen under its spell.

Bibliography

Black E C (ed.) 1969 *British Politics in the 19th Century*. New York
Judd D 1968 *Balfour and the British Empire*. London
Langer W L 1956 *The Diplomacy of Imperialism*. New York

Morris J 1968 *Pax Britannica*. Faber and Faber, London

Robinson R, Gallagher J, Denny A 1961 *Africa and the Victorians*. London

Taylor A J P 1954 *The Struggle for the Mastery in Europe*. Oxford University Press, Oxford

Thornton A P 1959 *The Imperial Idea and Its Enemies*. London

Thornton A P 1966 *The Habit of Authority*. Toronto

Winks R 1961 *British Imperialism: God, Gold, Glory*. New York

JONG-YIL RA

Judaism

The principal religious values of Judaism are justice and peace (*shalom*). A note on the range of meanings of the Hebrew word *shalom* will be followed by a brief introduction to the early rabbinic teachings on the nature of peace and the centrality of its place in Judaism. Particular emphasis will be placed on the tensions between *shalom* and other values and realities. The distinction between messianic peace and communal and individual peace will be traced in post-Talmudic Jewish sources. Prayers for peace and the use of *shalom* in the liturgy will then be considered. Reference will be made to the modern period, where two related issues dominate Jewish thinking on peace: peaceful Jewish existence in the nations of the world and, with especial urgency, peace between the State of Israel and her Arab neighbors. The last section will indicate elements of Jewish teaching that are of particular significance to the question of world peace and security.

1. Shalom

The Hebrew word *shalom* has a much wider range of usages than the English word "peace." The noun *shalom* is derived from the verbal root (*shalem*) "to be whole." The primary meaning of *shalom* is wholeness and completeness. This gives rise to a whole cluster of related concepts concerned with the state of being complete or whole, thus prosperity (e.g., Jeremiah 29:7, Job 15:21, Psalm 122:6), welfare (e.g., Jeremiah 15:15), health (Genesis 43:28), wellbeing (Genesis 29:6, 37:14), security (Leviticus 26:6), and safety (Genesis 33:18). It is also widely used to indicate a state of harmony: with reference to the individual, as peace of heart or mind, or tranquility (Isaiah 32:17, 48:22), or as a peaceful death (Genesis 15:15, 2 Kings 22:20); socially as friendship (Jeremiah 20:10, 38:22—"men of my peace"), allegiance (Judges 4:17), loyalty (Genesis 34:21, 1 Kings 8:6), communal harmony (Psalm 28:3, Jeremiah 9:8); nationally, politically and militarily, as peace as opposed to war (Ecclesiastes 3:8; Judges 4:17, 1 Samuel 7:14; 1 Kings 2:5, Psalm 120:7; Job 15:21; Obadiah 7); spiritually and morally, as peace (good)

in opposition to evil (Psalm 34:15, Job 25:2, Isaiah 52:7). At the core of biblical religion is God's covenantal relationship with his people Israel by means of an eternal covenant of peace (Isaiah 54:10, Ezekiel 34:25, 37:26). This covenant promises the correct relationship between God and his people, a relationship of peace. God is the author of peace (Isaiah 45:7) and peace ensures the presence of God (Numbers 6:26, 1 Chronicles 23:25). The words of the Lord are the words of peace (Psalm 85:8). Peace is the blessing to humankind, the gift from God (Psalm 29:11, Jeremiah 16:15), given particularly to the righteous (Isaiah 57:19, Psalm 37:37, 119:165). The covenant demands righteousness on the part of humankind (Zechariah 8:16, Psalm 34:14, 35:20) and the way of righteousness entails love of peace (Zechariah 8:19) and more concretely the pursuit of peace. The God of Israel is a God who detests war (Hosea 2:18; Psalm 49:6). The covenantal promise of peace led prophets, such as Isaiah and Micah, to a vision of an age of perfect peace to come, when peace would reign between people and between nations, a time when there will be no need of war:

> And they shall beat their swords into plowshares, And their spears into pruning hooks; Nation shall not lift up sword against nation, Neither shall they learn war any more. (Isaiah 2:4)

The people were blessed daily by the priests: "The Lord lift up His countenance upon you and give you peace" (Priestly Blessing, Numbers 6:24). The priests were responsible for the temple sacrifices including the central peace offering. These sacrifices were offered as thanksgiving, or for the fulfillment of a vow or as free-will offerings (Leviticus 3). The sacrificial cow or lamb was eaten by the offerer after the priests had shed the blood and taken their own portion. Enquiring after the peace of another (e.g., Genesis 43:27, 1 Kings 4:26) and the greeting "peace be with you" became in Hebrew the standard form of salutation. A world associated with *shalom*, the noun *menuhah*, derived from the verb "to rest," will be considered more fully in relation to the sabbath and liturgy below.

2. Rabbinic Teaching on Peace

There is a long history of Jewish groups retreating from general society in the attempt to live the life of peace. A first century account of one such movement, the Essenes, is given by Philo, the Alexandrian Jewish religious thinker, in one of his minor works (*Quod omnis probus liber sit*, 12-13). He describes a group who "avoid the cities," reject slavery, hold property in common, eat communally and "labor on the land and pursue such craft as cooperate with peace." Their commitment to peace is demonstrated by their stance on weapons:

> As for darts, Javelins, daggers, or the helmet, breastplate or shield, you could not find a single manufacturer of them, nor in general, any person making weapons or machinery or following industry concerned with war.

Peace was a central pillar of rabbinic thinking based on the vision of a world free of war and strife portrayed in the Torah (narrowly conceived as the *Five Books of Moses* and more broadly as the Written and Oral parts of the Torah). The rabbis held that there was a path to peace and that an end to all conflict and hostility could be achieved. This path was in the following of the ways of the Lord as given in the Hebrew Bible (Written Torah) and in its authoritative interpretation (Oral Torah).

Peace was incorporated by the rabbis into all aspects of Jewish life and thought. The principal sources for these rabbinic teachings was the Oral Law and its commentaries: primarily, the *Talmud* of Babylonia (redacted sixth century—the *Mishnah* together with the Babylonian *Gemara*, or commentary), the *Talmud* of Jerusalem (redacted fifth century—the Mishnah together with the Jerusalem *Gemara*), and the main *midrashic* (exegetical and homelitic interpretations of the Hebrew Bible) collections.

Peace and Torah are intimately related in rabbinic thought: "The whole of the Torah has for its purpose the promotion of peace" (Babylonian *Talmud* Gittin 59 B) and "The world is governed only with peace and all the Torah is peace" [*Midrash* (Rabbah), Numbers 21:1]. Only peace and Torah could possibly be compared, for it is true for both that "all its paths are peace" [Proverbs 3:17 see *Midrash* [Rabbah], Numbers 11:7]. The rabbis understood the fact that the civil laws (including those on peacemaking) come before Talmud, as being indicative of the priority of peace [*Midrash* (Mekilta), Mishpatim 1]. Peace is held to be not just a human aim and activity but as inherent to the order of creation itself: "The world endures because of three things, because of truth, because of justice and because of peace" (*Mishnah* Avot 1:18). Even the form of human origins is determined "in the interests of peace:"

> But a single man was created for the sake of peace among mankind, that none should say to his fellow, "My father was greater than your father." (*Mishnah*, Sanhedrin 4:5)

The rabbis cannot overestimate the importance of peace: "Great is peace for it is equal to everything" [*Midrash* (Rabbah), Numbers 17:7] and "Peace is one of the names of God" (compare Judges 6:24, Babylonian *Talmud* Shabbat 10B). At the heart of God's relationship with his people is peace. Peace is one of the ways in which God reaches out to people (see Babylonian *Talmud*, Berakot 16A-17A) and God's greatest gift to humankind is peace:

> When God sought to bless his people, He found no vessel which would contain all the blessings with which to bless them except peace, as it is said "The Lord blesses His people with peace" (Psalm 29:11). [*Midrash* (Rabbah), Deuteronomy 5:15. See also *Mishnah*, Uktzin 3:11-12, Babylonian *Talmud* Uktzin 83B]

In the same vein: "Great is peace, for all blessings are contained in it" [*Midrash* (Rabbah), Leviticus 9:9].

Peace and peacemaking have soteriological and eschatological implications. Making peace between human beings and their fellows is one of the activities which brings merits to people both in this world and in the world to come (*Mishnah*, Peah 1:1, Babylonian *Talmud* Kiddushin 39B). In relation to this world: "If a man exerts himself in maintaining peace in the family life of his friend and prevents its disruption he is promised that he himself will never suffer any grief in his own life" [*Midrash* (Mekilta) Jethro 1], and "No retribution will be visited upon one who makes peace between one man and another, between man and wife, between city and city, between nation and nation, between government and government and between family and family" [*Midrash* (Mekilta), Bahodesh, 11]. Peacemaking can be a protection against evil: "after he [Rabbi Meir] made peace between two men, they heard Satan cry out "Woe is me, Rabbi Meir has driven me from my house"(Babylonian *Talmud* Gittin 52A). The rabbis ask:

> Why then did Moses merit that his countenance should shine even in this world, with a light destined for the righteous in the next world? because ... he was ever-striving, yearning, watching to establish peace between Israel and their Father in Heaven. [*Midrash* (Tanna debe Eliyyahu) p. 17]

The messiah will bless humanity with peace: "The opening of his lips will be the blessing of peace" [*Midrash* (Pesikta de Rab Kahana) 149A] and the forerunner of the messiah, the prophet Elijah, will as a precondition of the coming of the messiah, make peace in the world (*Mishnah*, Edduyot, 8:7): " Before that time (The arising of the messiah) a prophet will arise, gathering in the exiles to guide and prepare Israel, his only desire will be to establish peace in the whole world" [*Midrash* (Pesikta Rabbati) 38].

The rabbis undertook a radical interpretation of the Hebrew Bible, in terms of their understanding of the importance of peace. For example, the warrior king David becomes, at the hands of the rabbis, a poet and a Torah-scholar (see e.g., Babylonian *Talmud*, Nedarim 32A on Genesis 14:14). The military heroes of the Bible become "heroes excellent in the combat of the Torah" [see Babylonian *Talmud*, Berakot 18B, Sanhedrin 44B, *Midrash* (Rabbah), Ruth 11:3]. The wars of the conquest of the land of Israel were also subject to similar interpretation (Neher 1966, Kimelman 1968).

Peace was achieved by the acceptance of the Torah and thus judges were particularly revered as peacemakers. The reward for penitence and righteousness was the blessing of peace [*Midrash* (Rabbah), Numbers 11:7]. But the most excellent way was by study: "Whoever so occupies himself with Torah for its own sake makes peace in the Heavenly Court and in the Earthly Court" (Babylonian *Talmud* Sanhedrin 99B). Scholars were held to increase peace in the world (Babylonian *Talmud* Berakot 64A).

According to rabbinic thought, people are endowed with two inclinations, a good inclination (*yetzer ha-tov*) and an evil inclination (*yetzer ha-ra*) (Stuart-Cohen 1984). They require both for life, for without the *yetzer ha-ra*, "No man would build a house, take a wife or beget children" [*Midrash* (Rabbah), Genesis 9:7], but without their *yetzer ha-tov* people would be reduced to the level of beasts. People must control, subdue, and direct their evil inclination by means of their good inclination. The most powerful antidote to the evil inclination is the study of the Torah. The control of the evil inclination ensures peace and one who controls these impulses is called "a true hero" (*Mishnah*, Avot 4:1) and the mightiest of heroes is "one who makes his enemy his friend" [*Midrash* (Avot de Rabbi Nathan), 23], thus making possible the achievement of peace.

The peacemaker par excellence was Aaron, the brother of Moses. Aaron promoted peace "between Israel and their Father in Heaven, between Israel and the learned, between the learned themselves, between a man and his fellow and especially between husband and wife" [*Midrash* (Avot de Rabbi Nathan) 48]. The Jew must not just revere and value peace—it is not enough to follow the commandment "You should not hate your brother in your heart" (Leviticus 19:17)—but like Aaron must actively "seek peace and pursue it" (Psalm 34:14). The rabbis understood this to mean:

> The law does not order you to run after or pursue the commandments, but only to fulfill them when the appropriate occasion arises .... But peace you must seek in your own place and run after it to another. [*Midrash* (Rabbah) Numbers 19:27].

Hillel said that one should: "Be of the disciples of Aaron, loving peace and pursuing peace, loving your fellow creatures, and drawing them near to Torah" (*Mishnah*, Avot 1:12). Some authorities hold that whilst the priesthood is limited to the "Sons of Aaron," "the disciples of Aaron" includes all Jewry: "Every Israelite must seek to promote peace in Israel, even as Aaron sought to promote peace." [*Midrash* (Avot de Rabbi Nathan) 26; see chap. 12 for the Legends of Aaron the peacemaker. Aaron was rewarded for his peacemaking by his sons and their sons blessing Israel with peace (Numbers 6:24).]

The pursuit of peace often stands in conflict with other values and realities. There are tensions between peace and idolatry, peace and truth, peace and law, peace and war and peace and justice. The rabbis placed such great store on peace that "Great is peace, for even if Israel commits idolatry but nevertheless lives in peace and brotherhood, judgment cannot touch them" [*Midrash* (Pesikta Rabbati) 199B, see also *Midrash* (Rabbah) Genesis 38:6, Numbers 11:7].

The talmud asserts "For the sake of peace truth may be sacrificed" (Babylonian, Yevamot 65B and Gittin 59B, compare 1 Samuel 16:2) and in connection with Genesis 50:16-17 it is held that "So great is peace, that scripture speaks fictitious words in order to make peace between Joseph and his brothers" [*Midrash* (Rabbah), Deuteronomy 5:15]. For the "sake of the ways of peace the wise say that we may flatter the wicked in this world" (Babylonian *Talmud* Sotah 41B). It is even permitted to blot out the holy name of God "to produce peace between man and wife" [*Midrash* (Rabbah) Leviticus 10:9 and based on Numbers 5:11-31, Jerusalem *Talmud* Sotah 1:4] and by extension "how much more for the sake of the peace of the whole world."

The law can be extended both within the community and without "for the sake of peace." Within the community the law is subject to extension and limitation in order to promote communal harmony (see for example, *Mishnah*, Gittin 5:4-9, Peah 3:1, Hullin 10:13). The relationship between Jew and gentile was based on the principle "for the sake of peace" so that charity and other laws (for example, visiting the sick, the burial of the dead, the comforting of mourners, and so on) were extended to those outside the community (Babylonian *Talmud*, Gittin 59B, 61A and Jerusalem *Talmud*, Demai 2:4). Likewise, Jews were to greet gentiles with "peace."

3. Peace and War

There is potential conflict between the values of peace and strict justice. This was often portrayed (for example Babylonian *Talmud* Sanhedrin 6A-7B) as a conflict between Moses (justice) and Aaron (peace), the most graphic illustration being the Golden Calf episode (see also Malachi 2:6).

The tensions between peace and war are the most significant in this regard and weapons were held to be disgraceful (Babylonian *Talmud* Shabbat 63A). It is not possible to be war loving and Jewish, for Judaism is based on the "Book" and "if the sword is there, there cannot be the Book, if the Book there cannot be the sword" (Babylonian *Talmud*, Avodah Zarah 17B). Peace is so preferable to war that:

> God told Moses to make war on Sihon (Deuteronomy 2:24) but they did not make war but instead they sent messengers of peace (verse 26). God said, "I ordered you to make war but you made overtures for peace, I shall disregard My word and endorse your action." [*Midrash* (Rabbah) Numbers 19:33]

Although war is held to be absolutely abhorrent and all steps should be taken to avert war, Judaism does not advocate an absolute pacifism. There is a great deal of rabbinic legislation and discussion on war but it is important to note that much of it presupposes the existence of a Jewish "state" in the land of Israel, which was not the case after the first century. Rabbinic thought does not allow for wars of vengeance and distinguishes between obligatory war [*milhemet hovah*, including the subclass of mandatory war (*milhemet mitzvah*)] and discretionary war (*milhemet reshut*) (Babylonian *Talmud* Sotah 44B). Obligatory wars are those commanded by God (for example the wars of conquest against the seven Canaanite nations) and defensive wars against already launched attacks. Discretionary wars are those launched for defensive strategic purposes (for example, according to the rabbis, the wars of King David). Such wars can only be sanctioned with the full support of the King and the Sanhedrin (*Mishnah* San-

hedrin 1:5). The rabbis do, in general, allow for pre-emptive strikes; "If a man comes to slay you, forestall by slaying him" (Babylonian *Talmud* Sanhedrin 72A) but this is only permitted to save one's own life. There are a great number of restrictions placed on discretionary wars; they must not be for conquest, plunder, or destruction, but only for the protection of Israel. Later authorities added even further restrictions. It is forbidden to wage war against a nation that has not attacked Israel. The rabbis, thus, restrict war to the defense and boundaries of Israel. There are further extreme limitations on the destruction, in war, of the property of an enemy (for example, trees must not be damaged, Deuteronomy 20:19) and many authorities hold that the prohibition against murder still stands in war. Selective conscientious objection is also permitted based on Deuteronomy 20:5-8 and 24:5. (For additional information on Judaism and war see Gendler 1978.)

Rabbinic Judaism does not envisage all mankind accepting Judaism as a precondition of a "share in the world to come" but insists that "the righteous of all nations have a share in the world to come" (Babylonian *Talmud* Baba Batra 10B). The genuine pluralistic prospective is vital as the foundation for understanding the above attitudes to defensive wars.

4. Peace in Prayer and Liturgy

Every aspect of Jewish life is imbued with the rabbinic teachings on peace and its pursuit. At the heart of Jewish prayer are the prayers for peace: "A man should pray for peace even to the last clod of earth (thrown on his grave)" (Babylonian *Talmud* Berakot 8A). The morning service commences with a version of the priestly blessing, "The Lord lift up his countenance upon you and give you peace," and the recitation of Peah 1:1. The core prayer of the liturgy, the *Amidah*, ends with a blessing for peace (Singer 1962 p. 55). To further emphasize the importance of ending with such a prayer there developed a tradition among a number of rabbinic sages of additional prayers for *shalom* after the completion of the *Amidah*. The reading from the scrolls of the Torah is followed by:

> And this is the law of Moses, set before the children of Israel, according to the commandment of the Lord by the hand of Moses. It is a tree of life to them that grasp it and of them that uphold it everyone is rendered happy. Its ways are ways of pleasantness and its paths are peace. (Singer 1962 p. 72)

Peace is also prayed for as the scrolls are returned to the Holy Ark. The major festivals and each new month entail particular prayers for peace and life. Each and every service must end with a prayer for peace [*Midrash* (Rabbah) Leviticus 9:9].

A central feature of Judaism is its emphasis upon home and family. Of primary concern is the concept of "home or family—*shalom*," this peace of the home and family is held to be especially significant and underlies other forms of peace: "He who makes peace in his house to him is as much merit as if he had made peace in Israel" [*Midrash* (Avot de Rabbi Nathan) 43A]. Each meal is followed by the Grace after Meals (Singer 1962 p. 254) which ends with a benediction for peace. Jewish family life begins at the wedding service with a blessing for peace (Singer 1962 p. 397; the couple's house is blessed with peace; circumcision and redemption of the firstborn (Singer 1962 pp. 405-6) all require prayers for peace. The burial service (p. 427) asks on behalf of the deceased "May (s)he come to his (her) place in peace" and the mourner's prayer (p. 80) recited on a daily basis for a year after death and thereafter on the anniversary of the death, calls for "abundant peace from Heaven and life for us and all Israel." The names of the deceased are always referred to with the plea "may they rest in peace."

Peace is held to be more than a pious hope for the messianic future and is incorporated into every week in the form of the sabbath. The sabbath is understood as a foretaste of the world to come and sabbath peace a foretaste of the final and complete peace. The sabbath day is referred to as a day of peace (*shalom*) and *menuhah* (rest) and correct sabbath observance, centered in the family, ensures peace. The synagogue service before the commencement of the sabbath calls for God to: "Spread over us the tabernacle of Your peace" (p. 152). At home the woman of the house's meditation which concludes ". . . grant that peace, light and joy always abide in our home" (Singer 1962 p. 141) and the lighting of the sabbath candles, which are said to make for peace in the home, begin the sabbath. Family members wish each other and others "a sabbath peace," the usual greeting for the sabbath day (*shabbat shalom*). The sabbath day is more than just a negative day of the cessation of labor, rather it is a positive day dedicated to harmony (*shalom*) in the home and family, with the natural world, and between people and their fellows. The rabbis interpret the injunction against kindling fire on the sabbath to include a prohibition on the kindling of the "fire of controversy and hear of anger on the sabbath day." Tradition holds that two angels of peace accompany all Jews on the way home from the synagogue on the sabbath, and bless their families "with peace." The sabbath ends with the words "Peace be upon Israel." In recent times the names of a number of synagogues contain the word shalom, for example, *Anshe Shalom* (People of Peace), *Rodefe Shalom* (Pursuers of Peace) or *Ohabe Shalom* (Lovers of Peace).

Medieval Jewry lived for the most part under Islam and Christianity and thus, doctrines and legislation dealing with war and peace between the nations was, of necessity, of theoretical import only. Jewish experience of the incessant wars between these religions and between factions within these religious traditions, led Jewish thinkers, most notably Saadia Gaon and Maimonides, to conceive of peace between the nations and religions as a possibility only in the messianic era. This limiting of the establishment of peace to the coming of the messiah resulted in medieval Jewish thinking on peace being focused on communal and individual peace. Bahya Ben Asher, a thirteenth century Jewish authority, understood individual peace to be the product of the observance of the Torah: "All the precepts of the Torah bring peace to the body (Exodus 15:26) and soul (Psalm 19:8)" (Chavel 1980 p. 620). He further understood unity to be "the essential cause of peace and dissension and change to be the roots of quarrel" (p. 450).

In Jewish mysticism the pursuit of peace has cosmic implications and peace on earth can bring about divine harmony. The hasidic tradition (beginning in the mid-eighteenth century) often offers a more "psychological" perspective, for example, the founder of hasidism, Rabbi Israel ben Eliezer, understood God's blessing of peace to be a blessing of inner strength. Other hasidic masters argued that peace could only be found in your own self, and that such peace, often conceived of as peace between body and spirit, must be prior to peace between people and their fellows. Rabbi Nahman saw the acceptance of prayer, the avoidance of terror, death and exile, and the rebuilding of Jerusalem, as being dependent upon peace (Band 1980). Rabbi Nahman further deemed individual peace and the overcoming of the experience that "there is no peace in my bones because of my sin" (Psalm 38:4) to be necessary in order to pray at all, and only this could lead to the messianic universal peace (Psalm 38:8) (see Greenbaum 1983).

5. The State of Israel

After more than a millennium and a half of the gentile persecution of the Jews in Europe, the rise of the nation-state gave to Jews the possibility of political emancipation, of living in peace on equal terms with their non-Jewish citizen-neighbors. The rejection of this Jewish political emancipation and the growth of political anti-Semitism culminating in the *Shoar* (Holocaust) raised the most profound doubts about that peaceful coexistence. Jewish security and welfare can never again be assumed or taken for granted. The "wholeness" of the Jewish people was broken and Jews can no longer feel so certain about their reliance on politically and legally granted freedoms. The eighteenth century Jew, Joel ben Abraham Shemariah, in his Will, advises his children, "To be at peace with all the world, with Jew and gentile must be your foremost aim in this terrestial life" (Abrahams 1926). He even advocated giving up his civil rights in the interest of peace. After the pogrom at Kishinev in 1903 Jewish intellectuals such as Bialik and Dubnov encouraged Russian Jews no longer to offer passive compliance with their own slaughter and to organize themselves into defensive groups (see Bialik's poem "City of Slaughter" in Klein 1948 Vol. I pp. 129-34). Jews responded to the Nazis with both physical and spiritual resistance. Jews are now actively engaged in seeking to protect Jewish communities whose *shalom* is threatened, such as in Syria, and in other places.

The State of Israel, established in 1948, is surrounded by nation-states who, apart from Egypt, steadfastly refuse to recognize her right to exist, and with whom Israel has found herself in a state of perpetual war, leading to actual armed conflict in 1948 (the War of Independence), 1956, (the Sinai Campaign), 1967 (the Six Day War), and 1973 (The Yom Kippur War). For the vast majority of Jews, in Israel, of course, and in the diaspora, the peace and security of Israel is the most urgent and pressing Jewish issue of our time. Most Jews in the diaspora recite a prayer for peace in Israel each sabbath (Singer 1962 p. 204). For a number of Jewish thinkers the obligatory war of self-defense has been revived in connection with the defense of Israel. The first Prime Minister of Israel, David ben Gurion, insisted that the Israel Defense Forces (armed services) follow strict guidelines in military activities so that such actions were solely defensive in nature (for details of this code— *tohar haneshek*, purity of arms—see Peil 1975). There has been a great deal of discussion in Israel concerning the moral and legal status of Israel's wars and military actions. The status of the conquered territories is an issue of much debate. There are those, such as the former Chief Rabbi of Israel, Yitzak Nissim, who insist that no territory, which is a gift from

God, can possibly be returned and must be defended according to God's will, and those such as Rabbi J.B. Soloveitchik, who consider that land should be returned without endangering security, as life is more precious than land.

Another issue of pressing concern is that of nuclear weapons. Drawing on traditional sources, there are Jewish thinkers who argue both for and against the holding of such weapons, although all support arms limitation (for two relevant studies see Jakobovits 1986 and Novak 1985).

6. Conclusion

The Jewish contribution to the understanding of peace is first, the vision of peace itself (extending to all creation), but more valuable than the vision is the insight that the value of life is dependent upon the possibility of the realization of that vision, the concrete possibility of peace. Further, for peace not to be just an abstraction it must be incorporated into all facets of daily life and thought and not just contemplated but actively pursued. Third, a recognition of a genuine pluralism, that is, that it is not necessary for all humanity to embrace Judaism, and lastly, not just that the vision of peace must never be lost sight of but that it remains the central concern of humankind: the end of all our work is peace.

> It is not your duty to complete the work, but neither are you free to desist from it. (Mishnah Avot 2:21, Rabbi Tarphon)

Bibliography

Abrahams I 1926 *Hebrew Ethical Wills.* Jewish Publication Society of America, Philadelphia, Pennsylvania

Altmann A, Lewy H, Heinemann I (trans.) 1979 *Three Jewish Philosophers*, Atheneum, New York

Band A (trans.) 1980 *The Tales (of Rabbi Nahman).* Paulist Press, New York

Baron S W, Wise G S (eds.) 1977 *Violence and Defence in the Jewish Tradition.* Jewish Publication Society of America, Philadelphia, Pennsylvania

Braude W (trans.) 1968 *Pesikta Rabbati.* Yale University Press, New Haven, Connecticut

Braude W (trans.) 1975 *Pesikta de Rab Kahana.* Jewish Publication Society of America, Philadelphia, Pennsylvania

Chavel B (trans.) 1980 *Encyclopedia of Torah Thoughts.* (Bahya ben Asher's *Kad Hakemah*). Shilo, New York

Cohn H H 1984 *Human Rights in Jewish Law.* Ktav, New York

Danby H (trans.) 1933 *The Mishnah.* Oxford University Press, Oxford

Epstein I (ed.) 1936 *The Talmud* (Babylonian), 35 Vols. Soncino, London

Fox M (ed.) 1975 *Modern Jewish Ethics*. Ohio State University Press, Columbus, Ohio

Freedman H, Simon M (eds.) 1939 *The Midrash*. (Rabbah), 10 Vols. Soncino, London

Friedlander G (trans.) 1965 *Pirkei de Rebbe Eliezer*. Sepher-Hermon, New York

Gendler E E 1978 War and the Jewish tradition. In: Kellner M M (ed.) 1978

Goldin J (trans.) 1955 *Avot de Rabbi Nathan*. Yale University Press, New Haven, Connecticut

Greenbaum A 1983 *Advice* (*Likutey Etzot*. Rabbi Nathan of Breslov on Rabbi Nahman). Breslov, New York

Hirsh R G 1974 *The Most Precious Gift: Peace in Jewish Tradition*. UAHC, New York

Jakobovits I 1986 The nuclear debate in the light of Jewish teachings. *Eylah* (Spring)

Kadushin M 1932 *The Theology of Seder Eliahu*. Bloch, New York

Kaplan M M 1970 *The Religion of Ethical Nationhood: Judaism's Contribution to World Peace*. Macmillan, London

Kapstein I, Braude W (trans.) 1981 *Tanna Debe Eliyyahu*. Jewish Publication Society of America, Philadelphia, Pennsylvania

Kellner M M (ed.) 1978 *Contemporary Jewish Ethics*. San-hedrin, New York

Kimelman R 1968 Non-violence in the Talmud. *Judaism*

Klein A M (trans.) 1948 *The Complete Works of Hayyim Nahman Bialik*. Bloch, New York

Kornfield J S 1935 *Judaism and International Peace*. The Tract Commission, Cincinnati, Ohio

Lew M S 1985 *The Humanity of Jewish Law*. Soncino, London

Neher A 1966 Rabbinic adumbrations of non-violence: Israel and Canaan: In: Loewe R (ed.) 1966 *Studies in Rationalism, Judaism and Universalism*. Routledge and Keegan Paul, London

Novak D 1985 The threat of nuclear war: Jewish perspectives. *Halakhah in a Theological Dimension*. Scholars Press, Chico, California

Peil M 1975 The dynamics of power: Morality in armed conflict after the Six Day War. In: Fox M (ed.) 1975

Shapiro D 1975 The Jewish attitude towards war and peace. *Studies in Jewish Thought*. Yeshivah University Press, New York

Singer S (trans.) 1962 *The Daily Prayer Book*. Eyre and Spottiswoode, London

Stuart-Cohen G H 1984 *The Struggle in Man Between Good and Evil*. Kok, Kampen

Wald M 1944 *Shalom: Jewish Teaching on Peace*. Bloch, New York

PAUL MORRIS

Jung, Carl Gustav

According to the analytical psychologist Carl Gustav Jung (1875-1961), people are inherently peaceful, as evidenced by his concept of the collective unconscious. This concept seriously challenges the notion of power rooted in conscious moral force. Jung's clarification of values through a better understanding of the collective unconscious allows for different methods of reconciliation and liberation.

To develop this interpretation more thoroughly, it might be helpful to describe the work of Jung on the collective unconscious. Initial support for his work began with the Jungian Psychological Club, financed in part by Edith Rockefeller McCormick. His work gained international recognition through the Jung Foundation and the Bollingen Foundation in Geneva chartered by, among others, Mary Conover Mellon and her friends.

Jung's work was most intensely concerned with the definition of "meaning," or the "experience of totality," synchronically linking conscious events to the collective unconscious. Jung proposed that the collective unconscious was first graphically encountered in the twentieth century by the *Blaue Reiter* school of expressionist painters in Munich, Germany—including Franz Marc, Wassily Kandinsky, and Paul Klee—in their kinesthetic, chthonic portrayals of the agonizing and bitter-sweet reality of war.

The collective unconscious in Jung's view has a "doppelgänger effect" as "a boundless realm that remains hidden because it is not (usually) connected with the ego-consciousness" (Jaffe 1971 p. 13, pp. 150-53). Jung took the example of Isaac Luria, a Jewish pacifist who explored the collective unconscious in terms of world order, as his prototype for defining the conscious import of the collective unconscious. Following years of painstaking analysis, Jung decided that the major threats to the collective unconscious are omnicidal weapons and the poverty of totalitarianism. These threats torture the collective unconscious, repressing the irregularities of reality (Jaffe 1971 pp. 122-27).

As Jung noted (1958), the search for peace is centered in one's personal reality and well-being, such that peace is:

... not based on differentiation and perfection, for

these only emphasize the differences or call forth the exact opposite; it is based, rather, on imperfection, on what is weak, helpless and in need of support—the very ground and motive of (inter)dependence.

From this interpretation of the collective unconscious, it appears that one should first reconcile consciously clashing ideologies and then revive the peaceable collective unconscious.

Put differently, Jung argued that our disregard for our collective unconscious has, in effect, starved the basic part of our self-image needed for mere survival—leading to the meaninglessness that is war. Starving the collective unconscious debases traditional techniques for solving domestic needs apart from nihilistic technologies, destroys abilities to dream or create alternative meaning, represses a personal understanding of one's own bisexuality in the collective unconscious, and most seriously of all, irreversibly negates reserve energies for comprehensive alternative future plans.

In denying the fundamental peaceableness of the collective unconscious, the consciousness of sovereignty undermines the global foundations for survival essential to both domestic and international legal structures as well. For example:

Ignorance in English law is no excuse for breaches of the law. In the collective unconscious, ignorance (or) unawareness is not only inexcusable, but the greatest offense with the most dire consequences. That is why in Greek myth, legend, and art, the villain is always the ignorance that serves as an image of unawareness; it is always the "not knowing," the nonrecognition of man's (human) inner eventfulness which is the real crime. (van der Post 1975)

Within the power of the collective unconscious lies the singular potential for world peace. "Instinctual" sovereignty has clouded our interpretation of the potential of the collective unconscious, obscuring basic questions of both solidarity and sovereignty within international relations.

Nevertheless, a great shift in our collective unconscious did occur during the Renaissance, with the recognition that we live in a heliocentric star system. This revelation caused conscious tension between individual, domestic, and international perceptions of security. The passage of European imperialism and colonialism from the political center of the world stage also threatened racial myths, sexual prejudices, and culturally imposed masks of militarism. In the future, awesome omnicidal weapons foreshadow another great subconscious shift in the foundations of our now global self-image.

See also: *Freud, Sigmund; Psychology of Peace*

Bibliography

Bernstein J S 1985 Jung, Jungians and the nuclear peril. *Psychological Perspectives* (Spring)
Jaffe A 1971 *The Myth of Meaning.* G. P. Putnam's Sons, New York
Jung C G 1958 *The Undiscovered Self.* Little, Brown, Boston, Massachusetts
Odajnyk V W 1976 *Jung and Politics: The Political and Social Ideas of C. G. Jung.* Harper and Row, New York
van der Post L 1975 *Jung and the Story of Our Time.* Pantheon Books, New York

ABDUL AZIZ SAID; PAUL HUBERS

Just War

The international law of war relies heavily on the doctrine of the just war, or as it was called in the Latin of the classical churchmen and lawyers, the *bellum justum*. This doctrine grew out of the shared culture and values—particularly a concern with justice—of early Greek and Roman civilization as expressed in writers such as Plato and Cicero (see *Cicero, Marcus Tullius*). It took root in Christian theology as developed by Augustine, Thomas Aquinas (see *St. Thomas Aquinas*), and the body of canon law. A secular branch of just war doctrine was also part of medieval customs and concepts of civilized behavior. De Vitoria, Suarez, Gentili, Grotius (see *Grotius, Hugo*), and later scholars were concerned with appropriate author-

ity to make war and to determine objectives, intent, and mode of conduct. Such concerns have taken modern form in various bilateral and multilateral treaties, acts of international courts and organizations, and academic works.

The doctrine of the just war has two major branches: justification for going to war, *jus ad bellum*; and justifiable acts in wartime, *jus in bello*.

1. Jus ad Bellum

The justification for going to war, *jus ad bellum*, depends on four principal elements (Johnson 1975 p. 26):

(a) Proper authority,

(b) Just cause,

(c) Right intent,

(d) Peaceful end.

1.1 Proper Authority

Classical writers insisted on the proper authority to engage war. Cicero, in Roman times, stated that "just war must be waged under the authority of the state" (Bainton 1978 p. 136). Subsequent scholars insisted that such authority must express itself through international due process. We find this element today in the importance that we give formal declarations of war and peace treaties to signal the beginning and ending of these contests.

The principle of proper authority also implies the validity of a decision not to wage war or join in a particular contest. Recognition of certain areas as war zones and certain states as belligerents implies that some areas may be peace zones and some states nonbelligerents.

Over the years, the legal status of neutrality has been safeguarded and developed to protect the rights of those who do not wish to become involved in wars. International law has paid special attention to freedom of the seas, particularly with regard to neutral commerce, and the inviolability of neutral territory. Larger powers have sometimes specifically contracted, through international treaties, to guarantee the territorial integrity of smaller neutral nations. Neutral states have elaborated different shades of neutrality to fit their needs (see *Neutrality*).

The concept of proper authority also inhibits intervention in the domestic conflicts of other states. Sovereigns alone have traditionally had proper authority on their own territory over their own subjects, a monopoly of violence within their own borders. Most states observe this norm most of the time. When they violate it, national leaders may claim that they are intervening on the side of proper authority, that there is no proper authority, or that the conflict is international rather than domestic. Examples of such intervention include foreign activities in the American, Russian, Spanish, Chinese, and Vietnamese revolutions as well as continuing foreign military participation in various contemporary struggles in Africa, Asia, and Latin America (see *Intervention*).

Proper authority withdraws the protection of international law, limited though it is, from actors who undertake unauthorized violence against duly constituted domestic governments. This principle tradition-

ally placed brigands and pirates outside the pale of law. Today, terrorists may fall in the same category, as do some activities of mercenary soldiers and multinational corporations.

1.2 Just Cause and Right Intent

In the modern world the principle of proper authority has come into conflict with, and lost ground to, other elements of just war such as just cause and right intent.

Insurrection against established government was once the most serious of crimes. Today it has become somewhat more acceptable, with the separation of church and state, the passing of absolute rule, and the prevalence of popular democratic and socialist standards of legitimacy.

Dissident subnational groups often find international support for violence in the name of basic political, social, economic, and cultural human rights. Examples range from the American Revolution, justified by the Declaration of Independence, down to contemporary Third World wars of national liberation and self-determination.

1.3 Peaceful End

The principles of just cause and right intent, in turn, have been weakened by the requirement that a just war be consistent with and supportive of peace. As war casualties have increased, the end of peace has become much more important. International values have gradually developed to restrict the use of violence.

Various international agreements have sought to maintain peace. Provisions in the Hague Conventions of 1899 and 1907, the Covenant of the League of Nations, the Kellogg-Briand Pact (Pact of Paris) of 1928, and the United Nations Charter laid down strong new regulations. In these agreements, nations promised to delay warlike activity until the processes of international law and organization had been given a chance to settle the dispute; not to engage in aggressive action against other states; and, in some instances, to abandon war altogether as a mode of national policy.

International law has implied penalties. Grotius believed that an unjust belligerent should pay reparations. In the twentieth century, this idea was reflected in provisions of the Fourth Hague Convention of 1907; in popular preoccupation with war guilt after both world wars; in the Treaty of Versailles assessments on Germany after the First World War; and in the Potsdam Agreement of 1945 that provided for German payments after the Second World War.

Some acts of war have been criminalized under

international law. The Charter of the International Military Tribunal that convened at Nuremberg specified the existence of a series of international crimes, including crimes against peace. Further, the Charter held individuals responsible for their actions.

In spite of such actions, crimes against peace remain rather ambiguous. Aggression, guilt, and responsibility have proved extremely difficult to define. The UN did not reach a consensual definition of aggressive war until 1974. The core of the definition is the priority principle, which establishes first action, including a first strike, as *prima facie* evidence of aggression. Nevertheless other relevant circumstances may mitigate the burden of priority. A state is not required quietly to wait for a first strike that may annihilate it; and initial violence may be justified in certain contexts of clear and present danger.

2. Jus in Bello

Once war has actually begun, international law helps define its limits. Despite claims of military necessity, the doctrine of *jus in bello* helps us say whether or not the war is being fought justly, whether the actions are legitimate, and the means are appropriate to the ends being sought.

We find early discussion of the limits on fighting in a number of places, for example, in Plato's *Republic*, which gave advice on the "usages of war," seeking to mitigate its more brutal aspects. The classic Islamic scholar Shaybānī formulated rules concerning the conduct of the army in enemy territory, the spoils of war, safe conduct, prisoners-of-war, peace treaties, and other related matters. The religious bonds that united Christian kings, and the secular, medieval codes of chivalry in Europe and Japan strictly prescribed appropriate and inappropriate battle conduct.

Contemporary limits on wartime violence, articulated through the doctrine of *jus in bello*, include two major elements: proportionality and discrimination (Johnson 1975 p. 26).

2.1 Proportionality

The principle of proportionality centers on the means of violence, which are supposed to be limited by the purpose at hand. For example, proportionality suggests that the battlefield use of particularly inhumane weapons should be restricted. Early international agreements limited the use of such "conventional" weapons as expanding bullets, or dumdums, named after a British arsenal in India in which such bullets had first been produced on a quantity basis (von

Glahn 1986). The Treaty of Versailles at the end of the First World War contained provisions against the use of poison gas.

Proportionality also implies that civilian injury or damage should not be disproportionate to the value of the main military target. Thus, contemporary treaties have attempted to restrict the worst modern weapons—atomic, biological, and chemical. A major argument for limiting their use is that the negative human effects of using such weapons are vastly disproportional to any military gains that a belligerent actor might hope to achieve by using them.

2.2 Discrimination

Discrimination is the second major principle of the *jus in bello*. The principle of discrimination centers on the objects of violence. It suggests that belligerents should discriminate between combatants and noncombatants and that noncombatants should be protected.

Noncombatants of a belligerent state have traditionally had a hard time of it. Invading armies historically ravaged and plundered; friendly armies lived off civilian food and shelter. Nevertheless, earlier wars were limited by available military techniques, and civilians were peripheral rather than central elements.

Modern war has made life much more difficult for noncombatants because it has tended to be total. Whole societies—rather than armies or navies—now go to war; and the distinction between soldiers and civilians has become blurred. Partly because of this blurring, the contemporary *jus in bello* includes new elements that seek to protect the innocent from indiscriminate slaughter.

The charter of the International Military Tribunal at Nuremberg specified two kinds of crimes in addition to crimes against peace. These were crimes against humanity and war crimes, both of which prohibited specified actions against noncombatants. The principles and judgments of Nuremberg were affirmed and incorporated into international law by a UN General Assembly resolution in December 1946, and the Genocide Convention of 1948 (see *Nuremberg Principles*).

International tribunals have assigned penalties for transgressions, and offenders have been prosecuted in a series of contemporary international proceedings. A trial at Leipzig in 1921 had preceded the Nuremberg proceedings of 1945-49. Additional trials took place in Manila, 1946; Tokyo, 1946-48; Jerusalem, 1961; Frankfurt, 1963-65; Stockholm and Roskilde, 1967. Many individuals have been found guilty and punished with imprisonment or death.

Red Cross conventions resulting from the Geneva Diplomatic Conference of 1949 reaffirmed and expanded the immunity of noncombatants. The four major conventions of the 1949 Geneva Conference attempted to provide safety to those who were once combatants, but who had ceased to be so—prisoners-of-war, the sick, wounded, and shipwrecked—as well as civilians.

Modern insurgency and counterinsurgency have shown the limits of the *just in bello*. The Vietnam war, for example, included various actions that might be classified as violating the principles of proportionality and discrimination. The United States used chemical defoliants with general negative, long-term effects on human, animal, and plant life. American leaders ordered massive bombing of North Vietnamese population centers. Both sides undertook attacks on civilians, including torture and assassination. There were violations of regulations concerning prisoners-of-war.

The best-known American attack on civilians occurred at the hamlet of My Lai, where the United States troops committed multiple war crimes. The final American action seems relatively mild, even laughable, given the nature of the offenses. The Army tried one person, Lieutenant William Calley, under the Uniform Code of Military Justice. The court found Lt. Calley guilty and sentenced him to life imprisonment. This sentence was later reduced, then overturned. Lt. Calley was released after serving two years in prison.

The trial of Lt. Calley, in spite of its slim results, symbolically reaffirmed the applicability of international law, not only to national leaders, but also to ordinary soldiers. It further undercut the defenses of military necessity or superior orders as blanket justifications for battlefield actions. Finally, it has led to a stronger emphasis on the provisions of international law in armed-service field manuals and basic training.

A four-year Diplomatic Conference on the Reaffirmation and Development of International Humanitarian Law in Armed Conflicts recently produced two additional protocols to the 1949 Geneva conventions. The Conference approved these in 1977, since when they have been open for national signatures.

These protocols extend the principles of proportionality and discrimination. They include revolutionaries and guerrilla fighters in certain civil wars. They grant immunity to prisoners-of-war and to the sick and wounded in armed conflicts in which colonialism, racism, and self-determination are central issues. They advance the protection of civilians.

The international law of war and the doctrine of the just war operate within severe restraints. There is no detailed international agreement on what is just and what is not. Rules are often badly defined, at cross-purposes, misapplied, or ignored. Yet, however primitive this body of law is, it does set some bounds to violence and hopefully stands as a foundation for future advances in international law and progress toward peace.

See also: *International Law*

Bibliography ───────────────────

Bainton R H 1978 *Christian Attitudes Toward War and Peace: A Historical Survey and Critical Revaluation*. Abingdon. Nashville, Tennesse

Johnson J T 1975 *Ideology, Reason and Limitation of War: Secular and Religious Concepts*. Princeton University Press, Princeton, New Jersey

Johnson J T 1981 *Just War Tradition and the Restraint of War: A Moral and Historical Inquiry*. Princeton University Press, Princeton, New Jersey

Johnson J T 1984 *Can Modern War Be Just?* Yale University Press, New Haven, Connecticut

Melzer Y 1975 *Concepts of Just War*. Sijthoff, Leyden

O'Brien W V 1981 *The Conduct of a Just and Limited War*. Praeger, New York

Phillips R L 1984 *War and Justice*. University of Oklahoma Press, Norman, Oklahoma

Ramsey P 1983 *The Just War: Force and Political Responsibility*. University Press of America, Lanham

Russell F H 1975 *The Just War in the Middle Ages*. Cambridge University Press, New York

Steinweg R 1980 *Der Gerechte Krieg: Christentum, Islam, Marxismus*. Suhrkamp, Frankfurt am Main

von Glahn G 1986 *Law Among Nations: An Introduction to International Law*, 5th edn. Macmillan, New York

Walzer M 1977 *Just and Unjust Wars: A Moral Argument With Historical Illustrations*. Basic Books, New York

FRANCIS A. BEER

Just War Theory

The Just War doctrine, stated philosophically by Plato and Aristotle, has been accepted by the Church since St. Ambrose and St. Augustine (see *St. Augustine*). This doctrine is generally accepted even now.

Psychosocial studies of Christians' attitudes to war confirm the widespread grass-roots support for this doctrine (see *Christianity*). The doctrine is invoked as a moral justification of nuclear deterrence. For example, the Catholic Archbishop of New York, Terence Cardinal Cooke, wrote that Catholic theology legitimises the development and maintenance of weapon systems in the nuclear age to deter other nations from war. He compared nuclear weapons to weapons carried by the police and he wrote:

> Millions of people may be alive in the world today precisely because government leaders in various nations know that if they attacked other nations, at least on a large scale, they themselves could suffer tremendous losses of human life or even be destroyed. It follows clearly that if a strategy of nuclear deterrence can be morally tolerated while a nation is sincerely trying to come up with a rational alternative, those who produce or are assigned to handle the weapons that make the strategy possible and workable can do so in good conscience.[1]

St. Augustine argued that he would never agree to attack anyone merely because they threatened him with an alternative set of beliefs. Nor would he kill in self defence, even if attacked by criminals and pagans. However, if the criminals were endangering the lives and well-being of helpless people, his commitment to the commands of Love would demand that he do his best to protect them. Violence is, thus, not used in doctrinal disputes but in social contexts and only when demanded by Justice. Unquestionably, such violence is evil, the hideous result of human frailty. But it is the lesser evil and, according to the ethical rule of double effect, is morally preferable to abandoning the innocent in their suffering. On such occasions one can only 'sin bravely.' John Courtney Murray S J affirms: There is no peace without justice, law and order. But 'law and order have need at times of the powerful arm of force' (Pope Pius XII). And the precept of peace itself requires that peace be defended against violation.[2]

Murray is fully aware of the 'tinderbox character of our world in which a spark may set off a conflagration,' but he sympathetically notes: "The Pope's reluctant realisation that . . . there are rulers who exempt themselves from the elementary laws of human society."[3]

Hence the Christian who loves justice and abhors the suffering of his neighbour must be prepared to engage in a just war against the evil doers.

In permitting such a war against these 'rulers who exempt themselves from the elementary laws,' the Just War theorists state various qualifications or limi-

tations. There are very stringent, if not impossible, qualifications stated in the Deuteronomic Law. These stipulate that all women, children, fruit trees, and springs of water should be spared. A way of escape should be kept open for the enemy. The newly wed, those engaged in new business enterprises, and those who are afraid should be exempted from military service. There would be few recruits today and of course it would be extremely difficult to fight even a very limited guerilla war under such conditions. I will argue that the qualifications listed by the modern Just War theorist almost as readily make a Just War impossible in an arena of conflict where nuclear weapons could be used.

These qualifications are both limitations on the right to wage war (*ius ad bellum*) and limitations on the conduct of the war (*ius in bello*). The war should not be 'total' where anything and everything is appropriate to ensure victory. The ethic of Christian love or humanitarianism is still important demanding some discriminations in the manner of conduct. St. Augustine wrote: "Even in war, cherish the spirit of the peacemaker" (Epistle 1886). This spirit is evident in the four following qualifications which are essential in traditional Just War theory.

1. Legal Authority

The first limiting factor is apparently innocuous: that is, the war must be declared by a lawfully constituted authority. Obviously, each state only needs to declare its own legality. So every state can declare war. However, considerable difficulty occurs when the individual decides that the war being conducted by the legal authority is unjust. It would seem that in a democratic state the onus should be on the citizen to evaluate each war contextually and to decide whether or not they can in good conscience participate (see *War*).

But, as we have seen through history, there are few, if any, societies which permit the individual to decide whether or not its particular war is just. The rulers of the state, who have the authority, determine whether or not there will be a war, and there is little or no place for an individual to decide. This was illustrated by the US Supreme Court Decision against Louis Negre in October 1970. Negre was a Christian but not a pacifist and therefore could not qualify as a conscientious objector (see *Conscientious Objection*). However, he believed that the Vietnam War was unjust and he did not want to participate in it. The court made it quite clear that his decision based on faith and morals was an 'incidental burden,' secondary to government interest. There could be no selective conscientious objection. Therefore, according to the theory, the individual should not expect the right to go against the governing authorities and decide whether or not a war was just.

2. Just Cause

As a second criterion within the Just War doctrine, it is alleged that there must be a 'just cause' with the 'right intention' to secure a good after-effect and to restore the order of justice violated by the offending state.[4]

In contemporary debate, this concern with 'after-effect' is crucial. Kant explained that war was the means to secure a preferred end. If such an end, e.g., a better society, could not be achieved, the war was pointless. However, the super-sophisticated thermonuclear weaponry we have at our disposal clearly proves that war itself is now our greatest enemy and that such war cannot be used 'to secure a good after-effect.' It is worrying to hear Alexander Haig say, 'There are things more valuable than peace.'

Since there is a theological ban against suicide, the Just War theorist, John Courtney Murray S J agrees that "annihilation is on every count morally intolerable: it is to be averted at all costs."[5]

However, Murray believes it is necessary to determine whether the war could be satisfactorily limited, and so he refers to what Pope Pius Xll calls "the solid possibility of success." Theodore Weber, in his commentary on Just War Theory, calls it the 'principle of proportionality.' Similar to the Marcusian 'historical calculus,' this moral cost-effect calculus weighs the 'human goods' involved, i.e., the end result, in terms of the 'immense sacrifices' demanded. If the end result is worthwhile, then so are the sacrifices. Weber explains that the probability of escalation (beyond the calculated estimate) is a risk not an intention,[6] and admits that the criteria for determining proportionality are very subjective and elusive.[7]

The view that nuclear war can secure a good after-effect, redress grievances and right injustice is tragically misguided. Indeed, in past conventional warfare, there never has been any guarantee that the 'morally just' would win. In 80 per cent of the wars between 1816 and 1935 the aggressors have been victorious. And since ethical terms such as 'morally just' and 'good' are so easily defined in terms of success, the victor is undoubtedly always in the right. Having been on the victorious side in the two World Wars, many of us, therefore, mistakenly believe that right can triumph through force of arms. This is often put into the religious framework: 'If God be for us who can be against us.'

Certainly, thermonuclear attack cannot be considered an instrument of justice. Its destruction is so widespread and indiscriminate that it is not possible to punish those specifically guilty of the evil. Innocent non-combatants are vaporised with the guilty combatants. More than ever G B Shaw's judgment is entirely appropriate: war does not establish who is right but only who is left. How theorists can value the 'principle of proportionality' in this situation defies the imagination. Also, I find it difficult to imagine how the 'probability of success' concept, the 'principle of proportionality,' and the intention to 'secure a good after effect' would differentiate a just war from a deliberate war of aggression. Every warmonger intends a limited war, a quick victory, and their good after-effect.

Furthermore, if war is permitted when there is 'just cause' to secure a good after-effect, why are there not more military sorties? There is widespread injustice and so perhaps it is morally obligatory for strong powers to use that pre-emptive first strike in the name of justice. Perhaps the cause of justice is so often ignored because it is recognised that war does not guarantee a good after-effect.

3. Humanising War

Thirdly, another criterion included in Just War theory, is the claim that the war should be humanised as far as possible. There must be just conduct among the belligerents and mercy must be shown to the defeated. Appropriate weaponry should be used so that the innocent would be immune from attack. Augustine allowed that it was permissible to kill the evil doers of another nation—but not the innocent. Paul Ramsey states that "the object of combat must always be counterforce, never counter people." Weber states that within the Just War there should be an implicit if not explicit bond of community among the belligerents.[8] In its idealistic terms he states:

> War must not intend vengeance towards nor dispossession of the enemy, and in particular it must not intend to destroy the enemy's society. War must be conducted in such a way as to point towards and permit the restoration of peaceful, political relationships.[9]

Two examples of attempts to legalise procedures for 'humanising' the 'game of war' are the Hague Convention of 1907 and the Geneva Convention of 1929. Ruled illegal are such activities as cruel treatment of prisoners of war, the use of poisoned weapons and the misuse of flags of truce.

Such criteria obviously rule out nuclear war. In no way could such requirements be met. As we all know, the slaughter would be wholesale and indiscriminate. Nuclear weapons are exceptionally destructive and make flags of truce and prisoners of war anachronistic. It has been said that if the USA attacked Russia with nuclear weaponry either China or Europe, depending on wind directions, would suffer from the lethal radioactive fallout. Indeed, as someone said, that with the long term almost eternal radioactive pollution, the living would envy the dead.

Actually, many of the Just War theorists recognise this problem of mass destruction. Weber says that:

All of these assumptions (of the Just War Theory) have been shaken if not altogether repudiated by the almost incredible destructive power of the newer weapons, the near impossibility of containing the destructive effects to spatially and temporally limited targets, the development of swift and long-range delivery vehicles, and the separation of man from weapons by technological control systems.[10]

Paul Ramsey, in particular, insists that non-combatants should not be directly and deliberately attacked. He condemns the destruction of Dresden, Hiroshima and Nagasaki and affirms that it is immoral and unjust to deliberately attack a city in a war even if it is to force the enemy to surrender. Also, he is critical of the nuclear deterrence theory where it has targeted cities for retaliation. However, Ramsey affirms that if a country makes the mistake of constructing military installations near population centres, then they have no recourse but to expect what are known in Pentagonese as 'collateral casualties.' The civilians, it is argued, will be 'indirectly' killed since it is the intention of the belligerent to destroy the installation and not the people. So if a Polaris submarine is berthed at the Auckland wharf, Auckland city is morally obliged to accept gracefully any collateral casualties resulting either from a direct hit or near miss or from the resulting fall-out.

Ethicists, such as Ramsey, who could not be happy with the policy of retaliation which aimed nuclear armed missiles at population centres and industrial sites, might well be pleased with recent developments in defence theory. With the new generation of missile systems being constructed, including the Trident (undersea long range missile system), the Pershing cruise missile and the new ICBMS, the Pentagon has admitted to a fundamental change in their nuclear policy. Instead of the defensive second strike, there is now this commitment to an allegedly counterforce

strategic policy. This, however entails the possibility of an offensive first-strike policy which Ramsey would not sanction (see *Nuclear Strategy*).

This policy change to counterforce is enabled because of the incredible accuracy of missiles. For example, the Trident submarine, which is described in the engineer's specifications as "an unanswerable first strike weapon" is a doomsday machine able to throw 408 nuclear weapons 6,000 miles with accuracy to 10 metres. In effect, it means that military strategists now believe that there may be some reasonable hope of a successful offensive strike which effectively disarms the weapon systems of the enemy. Recently, the US Secretary of Defense, Caspar Weinberger said "With them (Pershing II and C cruise missiles) we will be able to win a nuclear war."

However, the stipulation of accepting a Just War when it is restricted to counterforce is scarcely feasible in terms of these new dimensions of nuclear warfare. Ramsey's satisfaction derives from the fact that the tens of thousands who would be slaughtered as 'collateral casualties' of a limited counterforce strike were not 'directly' intended, but would be some sort of 'legitimate' side effect. Allegedly, this is far more preferable to the old counter city strategy where tens of millions would be destroyed. But this depends on a quixotic 'firebreak' between counterforce and counter-city strategic warfares. Certainly, there is a prima facie distinction, says Ramsey between: "The murderous policy of deliberately killing them (civilians) in totally devastating countercity warfare," as opposed to: "Tragically killing or sacrificing human beings as an indirect result of knocking out military targets (counterforce warfare)."[11]

But it is a quixotic, if not grotesque distinction, because of both the nature of a multi-megaton thermonuclear device with its long term, long range fall out, and because once a nuclear weapon is used (perhaps even a neutron bomb) it is difficult to imagine any stopping short of the final holocaust. Ramsey may say: "That counterforce nuclear war is the upper limit of rational, politically purposive military action."[12] But who really can believe the belligerents would be 'rational?' Herman Kahn, another defender of the nuclear arsenal, makes this same error. He argues: "Thermonuclear threats . . . must look and be both prudent and rational."[13]

Furthermore, there is a dangerous hidden agenda in this policy switch to counterforce. It implies that a nuclear power must strike first to survive. The old retaliatory theory left the possibility of both sides being destroyed. But with the counterforce first strike policy, it is contended that there is some possibility that the aggressor will partially survive and the opponent be destroyed or at least be effectively neutralised. Since in this game 'He who hesitates is lost' means that the button will be pressed to win. In a world so heavily armed and 'on the brink this policy is incredibly dangerous. And if the Warsaw Pact countries did have the advanced thermo-nuclear weaponry alleged by us Department of Defence strategists, then the success of the first strike must be seen as highly dubious (see *Nuclear Deterrence, Doctrine of*).

Also first strike is criminal in terms of the Nuremberg Judgment, which declared "to initiate a war of aggression is ... the supreme international crime," the United Nations Charter, and traditional Christian statements of the Just War theory.

The idea of humanising contemporary ABC warfare (atomic, bacterial and chemical) so that there could be, as Weber describes, a 'bond of community among the belligerents' seems to be another absurd pipe-dream of a cloistered academic. Certainly, gas was not used in World War II (except on several million Jews), the Red Cross was permitted some immunities and some prisoners were treated according to the Statutes of the Geneva Convention. But the expectation that there could be a community among the belligerents would involve an incredible trust in the moral calibre of the enemy, possibly a greater trust than was expected in times of peace. Undoubtedly, once declared, the modern nationalistic war would be fought for outright victory with no controls on the level of violence, if it serves the end of success. Clausewitz affirmed: "To introduce into the philosophy of war a principle of moderation would be absurd. War is an act of violence pursued to the uttermost." Winston Churchill declared in 1943 that there were "no lengths of violence to which we will not go." Hence the firebombing of Hamburg and Dresden, and hence, too, the annihilation of thousands of non-combatants at Hiroshima and Nagasaki which 'helped win the war.'

According to the Nuremberg Tribunal the leaders of the Third Reich rejected 'chivalrous warfare' and embraced the 'conception of total war' (see *Nuremberg Principles*).

> In this conception of 'total war' the moral ideas underlying the conventions which seek to make war more humane are no longer regarded as having force or validity. Everything is made subordinate to the overmastering dictates of war. Rules, regulations, assurances, and treaties, all alike, are of no moment; and so, freed from the restraining influence of international Law, the aggressive war is conducted by

the Nazi leaders in the most barbaric way. Accordingly, war crimes were committed wherever the Fuehrer and his close associates thought them to be advantageous.

And because the Nazi's repudiated the Just War limitations it became necessary that the allies do the same in that tragic fight to the end.

How on earth could Ramsey or anyone humanise a nuclear war? General Douglas MacArthur said: "Global war has become a Frankenstein to destroy both sides. If you lose you are annihilated. If you win, you stand only to lose. It contains only the germs of double suicide." President Eisenhower said: "In a nuclear war there can be no victors—only losers."

Incredibly, there are some who argue that just as the superpowers did not use gas in World War II, they would not use nuclear armaments in World War III. Professor Murphy, a war historian of Victoria University, New Zealand, affirms that the next war will be fought with conventional weapons. Paul Ramsey, similarly, insists that the Western nations "need increasingly to procure forces for sub-conventional and conventional warfare,"[14] to be able to defeat the 'Russian hordes.' Quite incredibly Ramsey argues that we are

> In mortal danger precisely because ... (our) unexamined reliance on deterrence of total war by threat of total war and mutual homicide policies are themselves of a piece with ... (our) unwillingness to prepare for any real trial of strength.[15]

This seems to be quite unrealistic. Rear Admiral La Rocque (USN) said that during the Formosan crisis in the 1950's the Admiral of a Pacific Fleet could not obey the order to prepare for a conventional war with China because of the overwhelming nuclear ordinance in the ships at his command. Also, we know that the Strategic Air Command bombers and nuclear powered warships are routinely carrying nuclear warheads—with the intention of using them, if need be. In a crisis, there would be only a few minutes available to a political leader and he would not want to make the wrong choice. From past experience, we can judge that the leader would rather err and be assured of victory rather than err and face the possibility of his own people's destruction: thus the leader would not hesitate to use the most effective killpower at his disposal.

4. Last Resort

A fourth and final limiting principle of the Just War

Doctrine is that war should only be participated in with a sense of tragic necessity, as a last resort when all other means have failed. But there is considerably more evidence for affirming that the Just War theorists are more concerned to justify war than to take seriously this qualifying criterion. To begin with, the concept 'last resort' is very subjective, and elusive, and could easily be compromised by eager or insecure combatants. If taken to its logical conclusion this phrase would seem to demand the adoption of a policy of unilateral disarmament and pacifism until the last moment.

Could it be said that all means have failed if there has been a refusal to try this approach? Of course, if it were tried the home side would be hopelessly outclassed and in no position to fight. Thus, the Just War theorist does not emphasise this qualification. The massive stockpiles of weaponry used for 'defense' and 'deterrence' prove the irrelevancy of this principle (see *Deterrence*). The efforts given to peacemaking pale into insignificance: the annual budget of the Peace Corps programme was the equivalent of 32 hours of the Vietnam War (see *Peace Corps*). There is far more honour in war exploits than in peacemaking, if media coverage of the Falkland Island crisis is any indication. There is so much fear mongering to win the votes of the electorate that anyone who would suggest a country should risk even a ten percent unilateral cut, as a means to begin the process of disarmament, is dismissed as irresponsible and 'unrealistic' according to Mr. Robert Muldoon, the former Prime Minister of New Zealand. Probably the most telling argument against the 'last resort' criterion is that to win a nuclear war in this era of first strike capability, it is necessary to incinerate the enemy before it has the opportunity to press the button. Initiating the holocaust can hardly be called a 'last resort.'

We should note again that the deterrence theory which has been used to legitimise the incredible escalations of nuclear weapons systems has appealed to the Just War theorists. Henry Kissinger explained: "We must maintain at all times an adequate retaliatory force and not shrink from using it if our survival is threatened." It is contended that this 'adequate retaliatory force' saves the world from destructive war. In this sense it is the lesser of two evils, an interim ethic using evil means in order to prevent the total evil of holocaust. This lesser evil in effect permits the theorist to assume the role of a peacemaker contributing to the avoidance of a wider, unlimited, total and ultimately evil war. The motto of the Strategic Air Command is 'Peace is our Profession.'

The logic of the deterrence argument is undoubtedly coherent. Ramsey calls it 'Pacifistic deterrence.'[16] But it is doubtful if it would work in practice.

The assumption that hideous and fearful weaponry deters is an inductive presumption that has little historical evidence to support it. According to calculations of the Norwegian Academy of Science, there have been 1656 major arms races since the 5th Century BC. Sixteen of these ended in economic collapse and all the rest ended in war. Building up an arsenal of weaponry seems to guarantee a conflagration. In fact, each side is doing its best to upset the balance of terror in its own favour. "We must have naval superiority," said Weinberger on March 4, 1981. And so it goes on in madness, to inevitable chaos. In terms of international attempts to secure peace and disarmament, the commitment to deterrence has been only detrimental and has itself spawned the spiralling nuclear arms race. Fear and mistrust increase with the manufacture and deployment of every new lethal weapon of megadeath. The enemy must believe such weapons will be used, otherwise they do not deter. The rhetoric of military and political advocates of deterrence must echo this willingness to use the weapons. So Pentagon officials declare: "We are taking the prospect of war seriously."[17] Such a belief forces the other side to gain superiority, so that it can use deterrence to its advantage. So the arsenals of Doomsday become like giant springs being wound up and up, until only the slightest provocation, error or malfunction causes it all to blow apart (see *Arms Race, Dynamics of*).

It may well be that the more horrendous, irrational and absurd the deterrent the less likely the more just power will use it. For example, Paul Ramsey who accepts the A bomb, is horrified by the H bomb. He says that in "its use, its possession, or the threat to use it, warfare has passed beyond all reasonable or justifiable limits." If the American leaders affirm deterrence like Ramsey then apparently they would be deterred from unleashing the thermo-nuclear holocaust upon their most detested enemy (see *Deterrence*). This, of course, would give the enemy a tremendous advantage. However, there seems to be little of this thinking in the Pentagon. Defense Secretaries and Presidents testify to their readiness to deploy nuclear weapons if it is "in our national interest" (President Ford). Speaking of Nixon, Kissinger said: "If the President had his way, we'd have a nuclear war every week." Towards the end of his Presidency, Nixon boasted: "I can go into my office and pick up the telephone and in 20 minutes 70 million people will be dead." The 'blackbox' was taken from Nixon a day or so before he resigned. Thus, from experience and the rhetoric we cannot suggest that the political-military leaders of the USA would be deterred from using what Ramsey found to be so objectionable. Similarly, in the USSR, Marshall Zhukov said in 1955: "The mere existence of nuclear weapons implies the possibility of their use." It seems tragically absurd to suggest that the threat of thermonuclear catastrophe should not be taken seriously.

In an ethical evaluation there is more at stake than mere political prudence. The basic structure of normative human values must be considered in light of the means used to achieve the so-called peace of the nuclear stalemate. How can those who profess the ethics of neighbourly love, reverence for life, and concern for future generations accept a theory or policy which prepares for the destruction of millions of people? As Ramsey admitted: "To press the button in counter-retaliation will . . . be the most unloving deed in the history of mankind . . . ." Reinhold Niebuhr another 'Just War' theorist agreed:

> We have come into the tragic position of developing a form of destruction which, if used by our enemies against us, would mean our physical annihilation, and if used by us against our enemies would mean our moral annihilation. What shall we do?

Such quotes from Just War theorists remind us of Buber, who said: "The use of unrighteousness as a means to righteousness makes the end itself unrighteous." And surely such quotes suggest that the Just War theory is anachronistic in the theatre of nuclear weapons. But can we imagine the leaders of the superpowers thinking like this? Unlike the Just War theorists, they have been tragically mesmerised by the cowboy logic which demands the biggest and best gun and, as in the old Wild West, demands the readiness to use it first. Hence in the spirit and according to the doctrine of the old Crusader, they are prepared to rush to the brink with nuclear-tipped missiles at the ready.

In fact, even war itself, like the Just War theory, is anachronistic in this new age. War is usually defined as the struggle to achieve victory through the force of arms. But with the push-button computerised, physicists' thermonuclear war there will only be the question of timing—probably not even who has the best weapons, but who can press the button first. It would be all over forever in just a few hours. As Ramsey said: "Megaton weapons are no longer weapons of war, and . . . their all-out use would not be war." It would be a holocaust from which no victor would emerge. Toynbee said that it is one thing to die for

your country and another to die with your country. Dr. Henry Cadbury wrote: "War itself is the enemy and the acquiescence of good men in it under the plea of a 'necessary evil' is their own honest yet tragic alliance with a greater and unnecessary evil." I believe therefore, that no one has the right to declare or even plan for a 'defensive' nuclear war. It would not only be murder but suicide for generations. The slogan 'Better dead than red' becomes blasphemous against creation. We should reply: "It is better to be dead than a mass murderer" (Heinrich Vogel). "The arms race is not only wicked in what it risks, but in terms of implicit intention" (Walter Stein).

Given modern ABC warfare the Just War doctrine is absurd. Our contemporary predicament with the horrendous stockpiles of thermo-nuclear weapons of superkill is absurd. The contemporary mentality which takes retaliatory strikes for granted and recommends pre-emptive 'surgical strikes' to destroy 500,000, as opposed to initiating the holocaust which would incinerate millions, is absurd. So practically speaking—in the light of this thoroughgoing madness, the appropriate action is to risk a policy of graduated unilateral disarmament. For non-nuclear States the risk must be non-alignment, being the outright refusal to participate in the most evil arms race known in human history. In effect, this and not the policy of Just War theory, is the lesser absurdity. Such a solution need not be a pragmatic desire to avoid megaton blasts, fire storms and radioactive clouds at all costs, but a positive affirmation that our international relationships can be different.

Once we are freed from our involvement in the Arms Race, our search for peace can take us past the Roman model of 'pax,' where there was merely an absence of conflict, in the direction of St. Augustine's *concordia* wherein the creative struggle for justice and reconciliation is possible. To achieve this we must not "learn to live with the bomb" (Professor Weizsacker). Rather we must embrace as 'co-survivalists' those whom the tricks and twists of history have caused us to declare enemies. Together we must find the new international community based on an accumulation of respect rather than on the weapons of holocaust. These weapons and their justifying theories, must be declared obsolete in this new age.

See also: *Global Wars; Just War*

Notes ————————————————————

1. *The Australian*, 17th December, 1981.
2. Murray, S. J., John Courtney. *Morality and Modern War.*

New York. The Council on Religion and International Affairs, 1959, p. 10.

3. *Ibid.*, p. 11.

4. Tucker, Robert W. "Bellum Justum and the Second Vatican Council: A Critique", in *Just War and the Vietnam Council*. Edited by Robert W. Tucker. New York: The Council on Religion and International Affairs, 1966, p. 8.

5. Murray, *op. cit.*, 1959, p. 17.

6. Weber, Theodore R. *Modern War and the Pursuit of Peace*, New York: The Council on Religion and International Affairs, 1968, p. 16.

7. *Ibid.*

8. *Ibid.*, p. 13.

9. *Ibid.*, p. 29.

10. *Ibid.*, p. 14.

11. Ramsey, Paul. *The Limits of Nuclear War*, New York: The Council on Religion and International Affairs, 1963, p. 9.

12. *Ibid.*, p. 10.

13. Kahn, Herman. *Thinking About the Unthinkable*, New York: Horizon Press 1962, p. 124.

14. *Op. cit.*, 1963, p. 31.

15. *Ibid.*

16. *Ibid.*, p. 11.

17. *Newsweek*, June 8th, 1981.

JOHN HINCHCLIFF

Justice and Peace

1. Introduction

Violence and war result out of unsettled conflicts. An ideal society living in harmony with its neighbours has no reason for warfare. A society living in harmony with itself will not experience civil war. Harmony as a sufficient condition of peace seems to be Utopian: Complete harmony is impossible in a world in which there was, is and always will be scarcity of goods. Scarcity of goods causes competition and conflict, i.e., disharmony. The political realist therefore might come to the conclusion that a world without internal and external conflicts including means of warfare is inconceivable. It was Plato who invented the idea that justice is a kind of harmony within the single person (within the psyche) and within society (polis) (see *Plato*). A good society is just insofar as every part of it knows its tasks and does not compete with each other. Externally it is independent from other societies' resources, autarky is the condition of external peace. A good society is therefore not expansionist. In Platonic terms, expansion, growth and change are indications for disharmony. The modern perspective cannot stick to this ancient ideal of autarky. But justice as the main precondition of peace prevails. Therefore we should delineate first what justice in general is, and proceed then to discuss the relations between justice and peace under modern conditions.

2. Personal and Political Justice

Justice is used as a moral criterion, in particular with regard to actions of individuals and social institutions. Personal justice is about a person's actions, how the person behaves towards other persons. Personal justice in this sense requires impartiality, it requires that I treat other persons equally. Equal treatment requires that I act without considering my personal preferences and advantages. Personal justice is a moral dimension which regards primarily those who are in power to decide matters concerning other persons' life. It is essential for parents that they treat their children in a just manner. Directors of firms should treat their employees justly. Personal justice is an ingredient of any hierarchical order. Without justice, every hierarchy would be reduced to mere power relations. But personal justice can be more than that, it can be a characteristic of the personality itself. One might call this usage of the term a Platonic one. The just person in this sense is in harmony with herself. She is able to balance different preferences and attitudes, she is able to judge impartially and discriminate between personal interests and moral requirements.

Instead, political justice is concerned with social institutions. Social institutions are just if they reveal impartiality or if they can be accepted from every point of view. A just society is not a society without conflicts. But just social institutions allow for settling these conflicts within an institutional frame which can be accepted by everybody. Political justice is a means to moderate conflicts in a way that violence and war do not evolve.

3. Subjective and Objective Justice

Sometimes a distinction is made between subjective justice (i.e., justice as a virtue) and objective justice (i.e., justice as a principle). The idea of subjective justice is often associated with the general idea that it is not simply one virtue among many, but rather the virtuousness of an individual as a whole—a supreme virtue, in which all other virtues are in some way subsumed. The broadest definition of justice is "congruitas ae proportionalitas quaedam"—that is some kind of congruence or proportion (Leibniz). This original meaning has been preserved to varying degrees in different languages of today. It has been largely lost, for example, in the German idiom, and the Italian word "guisto" can sometimes mean simply the factual correctness of something. This article is concerned primarily with justice as a relation between human beings or communities—that is, *homines ad hominen proportio* (Dante), and its impact on peace (see *Dante, Alighieri*).

4. Mythological Origins

Early conceptions of ethics conceived justice only in its general sense of conformity with a certain given order. Justice was primarily attributed—at least in monotheistic cultures—to the deity itself (significantly, other virtues such as courage, temperance, or self-constraint were generally not applied to the deity). In its application to human beings, justice was the epitome of flawless behaviour, in harmony with god-given norms. The prophets of the Old Testament, for example, condemn any disturbance of the social order as a breach of the law and the rights handed down by God (see Isaiah 1:16-23). In the New Testament, God redeems human sin through the life and death of Jesus Christ and, in His mercy, recognizes human righteousness: ". . . we conclude that a man is put right with God only through faith, and not by doing what the Law commands" (Romans 3:28). In the Old Testament, a person is righteous as long as she follows the will of God unconditionally and subjugates himself completely to the demands of justice, as imposed by God; the righteousness of God, of course, is of an entirely different nature. It is not the fulfillment of obligations; rather it is the equality of all men before God. This idea is also to be found in the Koran, being as inherent to Islam as it is to Christianity.

The expression δικαιοσύνη (justice/righteousness) does not appear in Greek mythology. Instead, there is the word "Themis" (divine justice). Themis gives counsel to Zeus and through her union with him, becomes the mother of Dike, the goddess of justice. Themis refers to the relation of mortals to the gods, and Dike refers to the relation among mortals.

5. Plato's General Theory of Justice

In the sixth century BC, the concept of *dikaiosyne* (justice) moved to the center of ethical thought. Theognis' pronouncement that justice is inclusive of all virtue even became a proverb. This concept of justice found its fullest expression in the works of Plato, who made it the fundamental principle for all individual and social relations. He rejected all conceptual systems that aimed at relegating the principle of justice to a subcategory of morality, claiming that justice is the execution of all that which is imposed upon a person or an institution (τα αὐτοῦ πράττειν). In this sense, justice becomes a virtue that rules, organizes, and delimits the actions of both the individual and the polis. A well-ordered community is analogous to a human soul in its perfection: just as reason, in a good human being, employs courage to moderate desire, in the ideal state it is the philosophers who enable the guardians(i.e., the executive forces) to keep the greed of the civilian population within bounds. In Plato's *Politeia* it is justice that brings the other three virtues—wisdom, courage, and temperance—into the proper relation. In *Nomoi* (Laws), his exposition of the "second-best state," codified law takes over the function of the guardians.

The hierarchical structure of Plato's model has been sharply criticized. Justified as this criticism may be, it has often obscured the real achievement of the Platonic theory of justice—namely, its incorporation of social theory into philosophical ethics and the theory of cognition and its recognition that people serve a variety of social functions. Subsequent thinkers on the subject of justice adhered to Plato's concept of it as an all-encompassing virtue but went on to formulate certain narrower definitions of justice parallel to this concept. Aristotle provides the clearest example of such a development.

6. The Classic Concept of Justice

Aristotle is known to have written a lengthy dialogue about justice, only a few passages of which, unfortunately, have survived until today. It could be that the dialogue, which was evidently intended as a counterpart to *Politeia*, was simply dwarfed by Plato's masterpiece, and thus for the most part ignored by posterity. There is a discussion of justice in Book V of Aristotle's *Nicomachean Ethics*, but it is confined to a relatively narrow juridical and social perspective, probably because the author did not want to repeat the more fundamental considerations he had already covered in the above-mentioned dialogue. While it is clear in Book IV of *Nicomachean Ethics* that Aristotle subscribes to the more general concept of justice, he detaches its definition from Plato's teachings about harmony within the soul and goes on to differentiate the concept of justice for application to several spheres. First, he draws a distinction between justice that is applied to human activities in general, and justice that guarantees equality as reason dictates (κατὰ μέροζ, or "according to one's part"). For the second type of justice he names two criteria to distinguish between moral judgements concerning relations among citizens and those concerning the apportioning of offices and goods. Medieval scholasticism took up Aristotle's differentiation and expanded on it, using the three concepts of *justitia legalis*, *justitia commutative* and *justitia distributiva*. For Aristotle, the first, "justitia legalis," has priority since human actions acquire their purpose from the ultimate realization of a good constitution of the community—that is, of conditions that promote the happiness of the community's citizens.

Distributive justice apportions goods and positions to each citizen in accordance with what he deserves. Distributive justice is thus the proper proportionality, and for this reason Aristotle characterizes it as a geometric proportion. Commutative justice regulates the relations of mutual exchange. Since the prerequisite for this is equality between the contract partners, Aristotle speaks of commutative justice in terms of an arithmetic proportion. Compensatory punitive justice is a subspecies of commutative justice. Here the punishment must conform to the damage done.

The various subspecies of justice in Aristotelian thought are not developed, however, in a logically stringent manner. This explains why even today interpreters of his philosophy disagree about whether it was Aristotle's intention to divide the concept of justice into two, three, or four subconcepts (see *Thomas Aquinas, Summa Theologica; Hirzel, Fechner, and Salomon*).

The Aristotelian definition of distributive justice nonetheless had a lasting impact on future generations. The Roman jurist Ulpian even declared it to be the foundation of justice itself, in his formulation: *justitia est constans et perpetua voluntas ius sumcuique trivuendi* (justice is the constant and perpetually continuing will to accord everyone the right to what he deserves).

The structure of the Roman legal system goes hand in hand with a detailed exposition of the substance of *ius suum cuique*. The formulation of the various rights, which were derived from the concept of justice in Greek philosophy, gave birth to a legal tradition that continues to have a normative impact to the present. For the Greeks, the connection between individual happiness and the general laws of the community was self-evident; but for the influential philosophical school of the Stoics and for the Christian theories of justice, the concept *suum cuique* (to each

his own) grew out of the natural order—or the God-given order of all things. It was only in the modern era that this framework was replaced in European thought with contract theories of justice.

7. Modern Theories of Justice

For Jean Bodin, in his *Six Livres de la republique* (1577), the state was still "the just government or administration, by a number of families, of that which is common to them," whereby the sovereignty of these few families is equated with the lasting and unrestricted power of the state. This sovereignty is expressed in the prerogative to enact legislation, which rests on the pure and unfettered will of the princes.

Hugo Grotius went a step further, with his theory of a just war (see *Grotius, Hugo*). In *De iure belli ac pacis* (1625), he bases this theory on the concept of natural right, which is discoverable by reason and which cannot be denied even if the existence of God is denied. It should be noted that the word "war" is used by Grotius to mean any encroachment on the natural power sphere of the individual or of a community, and thus war necessarily becomes the central object of any theory of justice. Grotius distinguishes between four different kinds of war: "war" between private individuals, which, in a civil context, must be limited to self-defense; "war" between an individual and the state, which is principally forbidden; "war" waged by the state against the individual, which is to be regulated through codes of criminal law derived from the principles of justice; and war between states, which falls under the jurisdiction of international law.

Machiavelli (1469-1527) rejected the central question of classical political philosophy: what makes a good citizen? His analysis focused on the way people behave in real life. Human actions cannot be subjugated to rigid principles because of concrete necessities which, if ignored, bring about one's own demise. For Machiavelli, justice is no external criterion for the quality of a community, but only acquires its definition within the context of a given society.

This realistic premise of Machiavelli's worldview served as the basis for Hobbes' "new founding" of political science. Hobbes, too, is concerned with man as he can be empirically observed—as a social being, which he is not by nature but by force of circumstance and for the sake of his own interests. For Hobbes, the objective is no longer the moral perfection of the individual in the polis (in order to promote the happiness of its citizens), but the creation of a ruling order that prevents the regression of man to his natural state (something that would endanger the life of every individual). Thus, justice has its origin in the will to survive, and the obligations of the citizen are derived from the inalienable right of every individual to self-preservation. The function of the state is limited to securing this right; its function is not to guarantee a just social order. According to Hobbes, there is no justice for man in his natural, aboriginal state, only the natural right of each individual to self-preservation by all means (see *Natural Rights*). Similarly, Hobbes' ethics recognizes no standards of justice for relations between sovereign states.

The liberalist doctrine of natural right has been of historical significance since the time of John Locke. In Locke's construct of natural, precivilian existence, the individual is the original and sole bearer of all rights. This liberty that was enjoyed by precivilian man is reflected in constitutional rights and liberties that protect the individual from the state. Liberalism draws a distinction between the state and society, and it postulates that social well-being would arise naturally in a stateless world. For the state, therefore, justice consists in providing the legal sanctions for social interaction which obeys its own laws, in this way securing the fundamental rights of its citizens. The classical concept of justice, which strives for the common good, is thus reduced to a "system of regulations governing competition" (Adam Smith).

Kant defines justice as the formal principle governing the possibility of law, whereby the word "law" is defined as "the content of those conditions under which the arbitrary will of one person and the arbitrary will of another can be brought together under a general law of liberty." Thus, it is quite correct to say that Kant did not develop a theory of substantive justice (see *Kant, Immanuel*).

Liberalism does not treat justice as a virtue in the classical sense. Very early on, however, this disintegration of the concept of justice met with strong resistance—in Rousseau's theory of social contract (1762) (see *Rousseau, Jean Jacques*). Rousseau does not accept the divorce of formal law from individual morality. For him the general will—and thus the law is necessarily just. This claim reinstates the classical identity of morality and the law. Rousseau goes even further, arguing that it is pointless to speculate whether a law can be unjust since nobody can be unjust to himself (Contrat Social I, 7). Rousseau himself shows this position to be immanently indefensible, however, by admitting elsewhere that it is quite possible for the will of all (volonté de tous) to diverge from the general will (volonté generale).

While the demand for justice has always been a central one for the socialist workers' movement, the movement's theoreticians have never developed their own theory of justice. In fact, the most influential current of thought in the labor movement, Marxism, considers any discussion of justice to be futile because the idea of justice belongs to the superstructure, whereas the goal of the workers' movement is the revolutionization of the economic base. For this reason, any thinking that focused on social justice is stigmatized as revisionist.

8. *Present-day Theories of Justice*

Present-day theories of justice reflect nearly all of the traditions of thought of the past. The most prominent example of this is the theory of John Rawls (1971), in which Aristotelian, Kantian, and liberal premises are brought to an interesting synthesis. Rawls takes up the tradition of contract theory and calls his concept of justice as fairness a Kantian one, but he also makes reference to viewing justice as a social virtue. His theory is meant to be an alternative to utilitarianism, the predominant theory—at least in the English-speaking world—of normative ethics today. Rawls views justice "objectively" as a fundamental obligation of political institutions, not "subjectively" as a personal attitude. He uses the methods of modern decision theory to reconstruct the basic idea of his contract theory. For Rawls, the principles of justice regulate the apportioning not of benefits but of "primary goods"— i.e., those that make a fulfilled life possible. These principles are applicable first and foremost to social institutions, not to the individual. Rawls' first principle of justice, that of "maximal equal liberties," has priority over the second one, the so-called "difference principle," which justifies social inequality only where this maximizes the welfare of the least advantaged members of society. In other words: maximal equal liberties for all may not be curtailed for the sake of an improvement of anyone's social welfare. With his theory, Rawls sparked a renaissance in thinking about justice, both in philosophical thought and in economic, political, and legal theory.

If one considers this theory as confined to the nation state, justice is the basis of internal peace. The central notion which makes the relation between justice and peace explicit, is that what Rawls calls "Sense of Justice." Persons behave according to a sense of justice if they act in conformity to those institutional arrangements which they take to be just. Those social groups which are worst-off in society, are most probable to assume that they live in an unjust society. According to the sense of justice, they would then act against the basic institutional structure of the respective social order. Rawls' theory answers this problem in the following way: Since the difference principle allows for unequal distributions only in case they are favourable for the situation of the worst-off persons in society. Therefore it is plausible to assume that a society, ordered according to Rawls' principle of justice, could secure peace, provided that there is a common sense of justice. This theory of justice can be expanded to the global system. In this case, world-wide justice according to the Rawlsian principles could secure peace, provided again that there is a common sense of justice in global society.

The entitlement theory of justice has emerged as the strongest antipode to Rawls' theory. This approach is formulated most poignantly by Robert Nozick in his book *Anarchy, State, and Utopia* (1976). The entitlement theory rejects all varieties of "timeslice theories of justice," its central thesis being that the justness of any apportionment depends on how a certain apportionment came about. In simplified terms, this means that a certain apportionment of goods or other commodities will always be just if it is the result of acceptable transfers from an originally just apportionment. This theory has, for the first time ever, brought a historical dimension to the definition of distributive justice. It holds that a moral evaluation of structures per se is not possible: what is more, it argues that simple adherence to a structure, even if the structure is perceived to be just, will inevitably conflict with individual liberties.

Libertarian theories like the entitlement conception of justice rely on the marketplace as the frame in which conflicts can be moderated efficiently. A precondition of the peace-securing role of the marketplace is that there are individual rights and liberties which are accepted by everybody. These individual rights and liberties can be extended to a liberal idea of human rights and state-rights. Libertarianism is minimalist concerning the moral requirements, but it is maximalist insofar as it expects conformity with these moral limits. Libertarianism disregards inequalities as a threat to peace.

9. Justice and Peace

The highest claim that is made on a political and social order is that it be just. This claim cannot be invalidated by other claims, nor can it be traded off against them. The idea of justice designates an unconditional moral obligation. No matter how well the laws and institutions of a political community may guarantee coordination, efficiency, or stability, if they are recognized to be unjust they must be eliminated or reformed. Even a just political social order can be found seriously deficient and in need of reform. If this is the case, however, the reform is a matter that concerns the whole community, not just a portion of it. In a just society, there will continue to be conflicts of interest, but the claims of one group or class against another will not be a justification for reform. This holds for every kind of political and social system, from the family to the world of sovereign states. Therefore, there is a logical connection between the moral justifiability of military conflicts and the principles of justice for international relations. The principles of justice governing the "coexistence" of states are ultimately the same as those governing relations between individuals or social groups (see *Peaceful Coexistence*).

According to both Kant and Rawls, a lawful or just social order is one that can combine the greatest possible freedom for the individual with the freedom of each other individual. Similarly, justice dictates that a maxim by which a state exercises its will in relation with other states be conceivable as a principle of a universal code of law (of a world state). Reason demands this, and reason ultimately proclaims the natural state, where each power is latently or openly at war against all others, to be immoral, and calls for the establishment of an international judicial order. Thus viewed, the idea of lasting peace is the product of practical reason, in the sense articulated by Kant (see *Perpetual Peace*). As long as an international judicial order (which would be guided by the postulates of substantive justice) has yet to be established, the morality of states' actions must be measured against the idea of such a judicial order. Indeed, certain impulses in this direction are already detectable today: policies of interstate relations based on the principle of maximizing the advantages for the individual state are being transformed into "world domestic policy" based on the principles of a just social order. Until now, these impulses have been confined for the most part to political speeches and publications, finding little expression in active foreign policy. World peace depends, to a certain extent, on how long it takes to put theory into practice.

10. Towards a Global Civil Society

The close relation between justice and peace results in the general outlook of a global civil society. For the time being there are institutional arrangements and citizen virtues which make sure that in many democratic societies in the world conflicts are settled peacefully. In the long run, there is only one chance to secure world peace, and this is to expand institutional settings and citizen virtues to the global frame. This does not necessarily lead to the establishment of a global state. There is no global government needed to make sure that there are stable institutional arrangements such that cooperation and conflict is possible without using means of war and violence. As individuals in a democratic society must learn to refrain from optimizing their personal interests in order to respect the interests of others, likewise states have to learn that they cannot optimize their respective interests to the detriment of the interests of other states. But there is a problem of underdetermination: Even if individuals understand that they have to respect other persons' values, cultural settings and interests, they need guidelines to know the limits. Institutional settings are designed to deliver these guidelines.

A global civil society can be built up only step by step. And indeed there are first steps in this direction if one takes, for example, transnational institutions like the European Community into consideration. Nowadays a war between members of the European Community is just unconceivable, notwithstanding a history of more than two thousand years of unending conflicts and wars until recently. The strength of transnational institutional arrangements depends on public legitimation. Justice is one of its main ingredients.

Bibliography

Aristoteles 330 BC *Nikomachean Ethics*. ca

Cassirer E 1941 *Logos, Dike, Kosmos in der Entwicklung der Griechischen Philosophie*. Göteborg

Chwaszcza C 1996 Ethik internationaler Beziehungen. In: Nida-Rümelin J (ed.) *Angewandte Ethik*. Kröner, Stuttgart

Faidherbe E 1934 *La justice distributive*. Paris

Galtung J 1994 *Menschenrechte—anders gesehen*. Suhrkamp, Frankfurt am Main

Hart H L A 1961 *The Concept of Law*. Clarendon, Oxford

Hayek F A 1982 *Law, Legislation and Liberty*. Routledge and Kegan Paul, London

Hobbes T 1651 *Leviathan*. London

Hobbes T 1647 *De Cive*. Paris

Jouvenel B de 1951 *The Ethics of Redistribution*. Cambridge University Press, Cambridge

Kaufmann A 1986 *Gerechtigkeit—Der vergessene Weg zum Frieden*. Pieper, München, Zürich

Locke J 1690 *Two Treatises of Government*. London

Machiavelli N 1531 *Discorsi Sopra la Prima Deca di Tito Livio*. Rom

Machiavelli N 1532 *Il Principe*. Rome

Nozick R 1974 *Anarchy, State and Utopia*. Blackwell, Oxford

O'Neill O 1991 Transnational justice. In: Held D (ed.) *Political Philosophy Today*. Stanford

Oppocher E 1977 *Analisi dell' idea della giustizia*. Milano

Pogge T 1994 An Egalitarian law of peoples. *Philosophy and Public Affairs* 23

Rawls J 1972 *A Theory of Justice*. Clarendon, Oxford

Rawls J 1993 The law of peoples. In: Hurley/Shute (eds.) *On Human Rights*. The Oxford Amnesty Lectures. New York

Rousseau J-J 1762 *Du contrat social*. Amsterdam

Rousseau J-J 1755 *Discours sur l'origine et les fondements de l'inégalité parmi les hommes*. Amsterdam

Sandel M J 1982 *Liberalism and the Limits of Justice*. Cambridge University Press, Cambridge

Sen A 1992 *Inequality Reexamined*. Clarendon, Oxford

Smith A 1759 *Theory of Moral Sentiments*. London

Sullivan W M 1982 *Reconstructing Public Philosophy*. University of California, Berkeley, California

Tawney R H 1964 *La giustizia*. Rome

Walzer M 1983 *Spheres of Justice: A Defense of Pluralism and Equality*. Basic Books, New York

Walzer M 1995 *Toward a Global Civil Society*. Oxford

JULIAN NIDA-RÜEMELIN

K

Kant, Immanuel

Immanuel Kant (1724-1804), German philosopher, lived en extraordinarily uneventful life, never wandering very far from Königsberg, a sedate university town in East Prussia. There Kant was born and educated, and there he quietly taught and wrote until the end of his days.

Kant's *Critique of Pure Reason* (1781) and *Critique of Practical Reason* (1788) established him as one of the towering figures of Western philosophy. In these and other works he sought to build on the rationalism of the Enlightenment, while attacking the Enlightenment's exclusive reliance on the environment as a means of apprehending reality. Kant argued that the human mind does not simply gather and reflect sensory impressions of the world, but imposes on those sensory perceptions "categories of understanding" which are innate in the mind itself. Perceptions of reality, then, are subjective rather than objective. They are the products of the mind's own faculties as well as of the impressions of the senses.

Kant believed that all of us possess an innate sense that we should do the right thing: a "categorical imperative" that tells us, essentially, not to do things to other people that we would not want them to do to us. This innate moral sensitivity was the basis for Kant's belief in God and the immortality of the soul.

Kant also believed in progress: both societal progress from barbarism to civilization and individual moral progress from slavery to impulse and passion to—ultimately—moral autonomy. In a state of moral autonomy, each individual will freely choose to obey the categorical imperative without external coercion.

Peace, Kant insisted, was a crucial prerequisite for humankind's ultimate societal and moral progress. War, he conceded, may once have played a constructive role in the development of civilization, but in his own day its waste and destructiveness made it the great enemy of further progress. Not only does each individual have a moral duty to work for peace under the categorical imperative, but states, which Kant saw as moral entities, also have a moral obligation to seek peace in their relationships with one another.

Kant regarded an end to war as something which was not only desirable, but which historical progress was making increasingly realizable. He thought that the major force in history was the tension between humankind's desire to satisfy its own wants, without regard to the well-being of others, and the realization that it is only through cooperation with others that it can have real chance for happiness. As a civilization develops, said Kant, people see increasingly clearly the truth that they must cooperate with one another, even if this means denial of their own passions and desires. Their relationships, therefore, become less violent as civilization develops. Their behavior is increasingly governed by law and morality rather than by brute force.

Kant was convinced that his own age was laying the groundwork for the extension of this increasing peacefulness to the relationships between states. He saw the growing tendency of political power to fall into the hands of representative institutions to be crucial to this development. Such institutions, he argued, put the power to decide whether or not to wage war into the hands of people who, actually suffered from its horrors. The representatives and their families and friends had to pay taxes to support wars; they had to risk being killed or maimed in battle; and they had to face the horrors of conquest and occupation in case of defeat. Inevitably, then, as civilization developed and progress was made, they would see more and more clearly that their true interests lay in peace rather than war. Kant pointed out that even in his own time wars over religious differences, which earlier had kept Europe in turmoil for over a century, had come to be seen as not worth waging. Surely in the future, he predicted, humankind would realize that other types of war were not worth the terrible price they exacted.

Kant confidently looked forward to a Europe of republics ruled by the representatives of free peoples. Their governments would increasingly avoid the evils of secret diplomacy and arms races; they would cease sowing hatred of one another among their citizens; they would bind themselves to one another in a network of friendly pacts. Perpetual peace, in short, would become the hallmark of the Western civilization of the future. Itself a product of that civilization's progress, it would in turn become the foundation for even greater progress.

Kant's ideas on peace, found most conveniently in his *Idea of a Universal History from a Cosmopolitan Point of View* (1784), *On the Common Saying* (1793), and *Perpetual Peace* (1795) have had a great deal of influence. By typing the idea of perpetual peace to a rational philosophy of history and theory of morals, Kant rescued it from being dismissed as just an idle dream of unrealistic naïfs. His work provided a powerful stimulus to much of the nineteenth century's thought and planning on how to limit and ultimately eliminate war on both sides of the Atlantic.

See also: *Perpetual Peace; Perpetual Peace: To Activate Peace in the 21st Century*

Bibliography

Friedrich C J 1969 *Inevitable Peace*. New York
Kant I 1963 *On History*. Indianapolis, Indiana
Kant I 1977 *Perpetual Peace: A Philosophic Essay*. Garland, New York
Williams H 1983 *Kant's Political Philosophy*. Oxford

GARRETT L. MCAINSH

Kekkonen, Urho

Since the Second World War Finland had succeeded in changing radically its relations with the former Soviet Union, ending an extensive period of animosity and wars and beginning a new experience of good neighborhood with a Superpower having a different social system and ideology. The long-term leader of this policy, President Urho Kekkonen, has often presented this success as an example for coexistence and cooperation between states of different national interests and beliefs (see *Peaceful Coexistence; Peaceful Societies*).

Urho Kaleva Kekkonen, born September 3, 1900 in Pielavesi, was elected, with a freshly gained degree of Doctor of Law, Member of Parliament as a candidate of the Agrarian Party in 1936. As Minister of the Interior (1937-39), he tried to suppress the Nazi-affiliated IKL Party. Having remained outside the war cabinets, he was called as Minister of Justice to the coalition government formed in November 1944 by J. K. Paasikivi and assisted him in creating a new foreign policy based on an understanding with the former Soviet Union. As a man in whom Paasikivi had confidence, Kekkonen played a key figure in the spring of 1948 in negotiating the Treaty of Friendship, Cooperation, and Mutual Assistance (FCMA) with the former Soviet Union.

Later, when five times Prime Minister in 1950-56, Kekkonen concluded the first long-term trade agreement with the former Soviet Union. This was the beginning of a multifarious economic cooperation between the two governments, unique in relations between socialist countries and countries practicing free enterprise.

Following Paasikivi as President of the Republic in March 1956, Kekkonen was reelected for three consecutive terms. In 1973 Parliament passed a special law extending his third term by four years but in 1977 he was elected again in the normal manner. Failing in health, he retired in November 1981.

Kekkonen dominated Finnish political life for more than 30 years. By his numerous visits abroad he was able to develop good personal relations, not only with Soviet leaders, but also with most heads of state and government in the West. Largely due to his top-level diplomacy the special position of Finland, still maintaining its FCMA treaty relations with the former Soviet Union but endeavoring to remain outside power conflicts, was finally recognized on the international scene.

Kekkonen was also a keen partisan of cooperation with Scandinavian countries and supported Finnish membership of the Nordic Council in 1955 (see *Nordic Council*). From 1956, when Finland was able to join the United Nations, Kekkonen encouraged Finnish activities in the organization, for example, in a large-scale participation in peace-safeguarding operations. In 1969 Kekkonen proposed a Finnish initiative for convening the first Conference on Security and Cooperation in Europe, the preparatory stage and the final phase of which were then held in Helsinki in 1972-73 and 1975 (see *Organization on Security and Cooperation in Europe (OSCE)*).

Anxious to remove the possibility that Finland would be implicated in tensions between the North Atlantic Treaty Organization and the Warsaw Pact, Kekkonen suggested in 1965 nonaggression treaty arrangements between Finland and Norway. Even better known is his proposal, made in 1963 and renewed in 1978, for the creation of a Nordic nuclear-free zone, extended both to Finland and Scandinavian countries. Despite increasing interest shown in the plan by public opinion and political parties throughout the countries concerned, no official steps have been taken, mainly because of overriding complications concerning both the Superpowers' strategies in Nordic space (see *Nuclear-Weapon-Free Zones: A History and Assessment*).

See also: *East-West Trade: Finland's Changing Role*

Bibliography ————————————————

Kekkonen U 1982 *A President's View*. Heinemann, London

JUKKA NEVAKIVI

Khan, Abdul Ghaffar

Khan Abdul Ghaffar Khan (born circa 1890), popularly called "Badshah Khan," is a Moslem Pathan leader from the Northwest Frontier Province (NWFP) of Pakistan whose nonviolent leadership during India's freedom struggle earned him the title "The Frontier Gandhi." After 80 years of active work (including 30 years in prison) in the cause of freedom and justice, Khan can legitimately be described as the greatest living exponent of nonviolence in the world.

In 1930 Khan formed the "Servants of God" (*Khudai Khidmatgars*), a self-styled nonviolent "army" of Moslem Pathans trained along military lines. During the 1930s and early 1940s, the "Red Shirts" (as they were popularly called) faced some of the most bitter repression of the Indian freedom struggle and provided an effective resistance to British rule. Gandhi pointed to the "Servants of God" as an example of the "nonviolence of the strong," when born fighters renounce their weapons to fight nonviolently. Khan's Red Shirts also challenged several prevailing myths about nonviolence: that it can be followed only by those who are gentle, that it cannot work against ruthless repression, and that nonviolence has no place in Islam (see *Nonviolence*).

Khan's nonviolent achievements were all the more significant because Pathans form one of the most violent societies in the world. Independent, austere, devoutly Moslem, Pathan society has long been steeped in intrigue and vendetta because the Pathan code of revenge, *badal*, requires the Pathan to avenge any insult. Pathans have long been feared on the Indian subcontinent for their military exploits. Most of the region's villages have fortified walls and "the rifle is an important symbol of manhood and independence" (Weekes 1964 p. 13). Whether a farmer, tradesperson, or artist, "every (Pathan) is a soldier" (Tendulkar 1964 p. 3).

To the British, the Pathans were less than civilized and commanded their attention only because the Pathan homelands included the strategic Khyber Pass, the "gateway to India." Long fearing Russian expansion through the Khyber into India, the British were determined to hold the area at any cost. During the latter half of the nineteenth century, the British sent scores of expeditions into the Pathans' hills, shelled their strongholds, burned (and later bombed) their villages, flogged and jailed Pathans by the thousands, deported many, and hung others—yet the Pathan homelands remained the only part of the British Empire never to be fully subjugated. To British soldiers throughout the Empire, the Northwest Frontier Province was known as "the Grim."

It was within this crucible of violence, despair, and political tyranny that Khan's work was achieved. He was born in 1890 near Peshawar, the provincial capital of the Northwest Frontier Province, and was the second son of a wealthy village chieftain, Behram Khan, widely respected in the area for his uprightness and—unique for a Pathan—his forgiveness. One of the first from his area to be educated (in a British mission school), Ghaffar Khan, at 19, turned down a prestigious commission in the elite Guides cavalry because of the patronizing attitude of the British officers toward Pathans. Not long after, he made what was to prove a pivotal decision when he yielded to his mother's wishes to remain home rather than go to England to study engineering. His elder brother, Khan Saheb, had preceded him there to study medicine, leaving Ghaffar the only son at home.

Given a village to oversee by his father, Khan married in 1912, and had a son. Moved by the poverty and ignorance of his people, Khan opened several Islamic schools in the area and helped to educate villagers in hygiene and agricultural methods. Khan came under the influence of a local social reformer, Haji Saheb, who awakened Khan's political consciousness and introduced him to the thinking of the fledgling, but potent, Moslem renaissance stirring in Northern India in the decade before the First World War.

Khan's increasing social and political activities brought him under suspicion from the British—who suspected his motives—as well as from the landed Khans and village priests who feared his reforms. Any sign of political or social awakening was seen as a threat to British security. Khan's teachers faced harassment and some of his schools were closed.

In 1919, Khan became active in Gandhi's first nationwide civil disobedience movement (see *Nonviolence: Philosophy and Politics of*) against the Rowlatt Acts and in the Khilafat movement. It was around this time that he became known as "Badshah Khan" (the chief Khan). He was arrested and served six months in prison. Freed when martial law was lifted, Khan resumed his reform work, was arrested again, and ordered to discontinue his reform work. He refused and received three years' imprisonment, much of it in solitary confinement and under harsh physical conditions in which he lost 50 pounds and developed scurvy.

In 1926 Khan visited the Islamic countries of the Middle East and was impressed by the rising nationalism he witnessed in countries like Egypt and Turkey. In 1928, Khan started the first Pathan journal, *Pakhtun*, to broaden his reach and to revive the Pathan language. Banned intermittently, the journal survived into the late 1940s when it was permanently discontinued by the Pakistani government.

1. The Servants of God

Khan attended the annual sessions of the Indian National Congress during the late 1920s, and gradually came increasingly under Gandhi's influence (see *Gandhi, Mohandas Karamchand*). In 1930, he formed the Khudai Khidmatgars, and placed them under the aegis of the Congress which was only three percent Moslem. Khudai Khidmatgars had to take an oath of nonviolence.

When Gandhi initiated the Salt *Satyagraha* in April 1930 (see *Satyagraha*), over 90,000 Indians went to jail. In the NWFP, there was intense repression, and the Khudai Khidmatgars grew to more than 50,000 strong. They faced machine-gun firings, attacks from armored cars, blockades, jailing, physical torture, and humiliation (Yunus 1947 pp. 118-120). But the Pathans held to their nonviolent discipline and there were innumerable stories of extraordinary nonviolent heroism and daring. In Peshawar, a troop of English soldiers began to fire without warning into an unarmed demonstration of men, women, and children. Gene Sharp (1960) records an account of what followed:

When those in front fell down wounded by the shots, those behind came forward with their breasts bared and exposed themselves to the fire, so much so that some people got as many as 21 bullet wounds in their bodies, and all the people stood their ground without getting into a panic. A young Sikh boy came and stood in front of a soldier and asked him to fire at him, which the soldier unhesitatingly did, killing him. The crowd kept standing at the spot facing the soldiers and were fired from time to time, until there were heaps of wounded and dying lying about. (Sharp 1960 p. 110)

One of the more extraordinary occurrences (which deeply alarmed the British with its echoes of the 1857 "mutiny") was the refusal of an entire platoon of the famous Garhwali rifles to fire upon the unarmed crowds. As a result of their refusal, "seventeen men were sentenced—one to transportation for life, another to fifteen years' imprisonment and the rest to terms of rigorous imprisonment, varying from three to ten years" (Tendulkar 1964 p. 70).

The nonviolence of these Pathans from the Northwest Province surprised Indians and British alike. But there was no doubt that in spite of their extreme suffering, the Pathans held to their nonviolence. The India League (of Great Britain) reported: "the severity of the repression has produced something like a war on the Frontier Province. That nonviolence still remains the rigidly observed rule of the nationalist movement in an area where arms are so readily obtainable is a tribute to the sincerity with which the creed has been embraced" (Tendulkar 1964 p. 53).

A direct consequence of Khan's movement was that the Northwest Frontier Province was granted the political reforms which had been advanced to the rest of India in 1919, but denied the Pathans at that time. Within three years, elections were held and the Red Shirts gained a majority of the legislative seats. Khan's brother, Dr. Khan Sahib, became prime minister.

In the meantime, Khan served another three years in prison then was banned from the province. He and his brother joined Gandhi at his ashram. Khan had become an all-India figure and was brought into the Congress leadership, but when offered the presidency of the Congress in 1934, he declined, saying, "I am only a soldier. I shall only render service." He has never sought elected office.

Khan is at heart a religious man, a reformer rather than a politician, shy, self-effacing, and childlike, who always preferred quiet village work to political life. Like Gandhi he preferred a simple life. His greatest love was living among the villagers, teaching and inspiring them.

In 1934, Khan was about to "bury himself" in village service when he was arrested again for speech-making. Although a general amnesty was in effect, he was nonetheless sentenced to two years in prison. Released in 1936, but still banned from his province, Khan again settled with Gandhi. In 1937 his brother, Dr. Khan Sahib, was elected prime minister of the NWFP and lifted the ban on his brother.

Gandhi visited the province twice in the late 1930s to observe at first hand Khan's experiment in turning Pathans into nonviolent soldiers—what Gandhi called the "nonviolence of the strong."

In 1942 Gandhi launched the Quit India movement and 60,000 Indians were arrested. Khan was jailed and had two ribs broken during his arrest. He served yet another three years until the general amnesty at the end of the war.

Negotiations for a free India began with the British in 1946. Dr. Khan Sahib was again elected prime minister of the NWFP. The Moslem League under Jinnah now demanded a separate Moslem state wherever Moslems were in the majority, as in the NWFP. In 1946 communal riots broke out between Hindus and Moslems and thousands were killed and left homeless. Gandhi, with Khan at his side, toured the worst areas and helped to pacify them.

2. Independence and Partition

In August 1947 the Congress agreed to partition in order to avoid civil war. The Hindu-Moslem tensions had so infected the NWFP that the Pathans, fearful of the "Hindu" Congress, voted to join the new Moslem state of Pakistan. The Moslem League, which had opposed Khan and the Khudai Khidmatgars, now took control of the NWFP.

Khan felt that the Congress had betrayed his movement and that the Khudai Khidmatgars had been "thrown to the wolves." Only Gandhi had opposed partition to the end. Khan felt that if the Congress had held out longer against partition, his province could have become part of India, or even an autonomous state.

Khan accepted Pakistan but asked for an autonomous Pathan province within a confederated union. He wanted the Pathans reunited as one family and called for "rule of the Pathans, by the Pathans, and for the Pathans." The Moslem League claimed he was anti-Pakistan, in league with Afghanistan and India (with whom Pakistan was at war over Kashmir), and arrested Khan. He was charged with sedition under the same Section 40 of the Frontier

Crimes Regulations by which he had been imprisoned 27 years earlier by the British. He refused to furnish security for "good behavior" and was sentenced to three years' rigorous imprisonment.

So began Khan's second ordeal in the cause of freedom and justice. His sentence was extended twice so that he served seven years before being released, only to be banned from his province, and then jailed again. During Pakistan's first 18 years of independence, Khan spent 15 in jail.

Shortly after Khan's first sentencing in June 1948, the Northwest Frontier Provincial government assumed extraordinary powers to "outlaw by ordinance all organizations 'objectionable to peace and security'." The Khudai Khidmatgars were banned and came under intense repression. More than 1,000 went to jail. In one village a mass firing killed hundreds of Khan's followers. The *Pakhtun*, often suspended under British rule, was finally silenced by the Pakistani government and the Khudai Khidmatgars' headquarters were razed.

When free, Khan continued to plead for a united Pathan province. But in 1954, the Pakistani government amalgamated all the provinces of West Pakistan into one unit. Khan asked for a referendum on the issue, but this was denied. Pakistan was governed by legislation passed during the colonial period and did not form a constitution until 1956. In 1957 Khan formed the coalition National Awami Party and campaigned against the "one-unit" rule. He gave 83 speeches in three months urging Pathans to resist the "one-unit" rule.

In 1958, Khan was again arrested, and shortly after General Ayub Khan assumed power in a military *coup d'état*, suspended the constitution, and declared martial law. Khan was released in 1959, then arrested again in April 1961 for "indulging in anti-state activities" (Tendulkar 1964 p. 517). Khan's six-month sentence was repeatedly extended until he was released in 1964 because his health had "deteriorated alarmingly."

In 1962 Khan was selected the "Prisoner of the Year" by Amnesty International which said in its statement: "Nonviolence has its martyrs. One of them, Abdul Ghaffar Khan, has been chosen by the Amnesty International as the 'Prisoner of the Year.' His example symbolizes the suffering of upwards of a million people all over the world who are in prison for their conscience. Despite appeals, the old man still lies in jail" Khan was 72.

In 1964 Khan sought medical treatment in England and then went into exile in Afghanistan, where he remained until the Pakistani Civil War in 1970.

His son, Wali Khan, led the opposition party during his absence. After a 15-year struggle, the "one-unit" rule was abolished, and the Northwest Frontier became a province again. Khan's party continued its demands for regional autonomy until it was outlawed in 1975, and both Khan and his son, Wali, were jailed for a year.

In 1983, popular demands for a return to democracy assumed the scale of a mass civil disobedience movement. Khan, at the age of 94, was drawn once again into nonviolent struggle for political freedom. He was arrested and placed in a "subjail" for several months until international pressure finally secured his release.

Despite almost continuous suffering and sacrifice in the struggle for freedom and justice, Khan remains unembittered. On the contrary, like his spiritual and political mentor, Gandhi, Khan appears to draw strength in suffering for the release of his oppressed and impoverished people.

Khan has several times in recent years been nominated for the Nobel Peace Prize as word of his work has begun to reach the West. In December 1985, Badshah Khan, nearing 100 years of age, was invited by India to address the centenary celebrations of the Congress Party.

See also: *Islam*

Bibliography ————————————————

Desai M 1935 *Two Servants of God.* Hindustan Times Press, Delhi

Khan A G 1969 *My Life and Struggle.* Hind Pocket Books, Delhi

Pyarelal N 1966 *Thrown to the Wolves.* Eastlight Book House, Calcutta

Sharp G 1960 *Gandhi Wields the Weapon of Moral Power.* Navajivan Publishing House, Ahmedabad

Spain J W 1962 *People of the Khyber: The Pathans of Pakistan.* Praeger, New York

Tendulkar D G 1964 *Abdul Ghaffar Khan: Faith is a Battle.* Gandhi Peace Foundation (Popular Prakashan), Bombay

Weekes R V 1964 *Pakistan: Birth and Growth of a Muslim Nation.* Van Nostrand, New York

Wolpert S 1982 *A New History of India.* Oxford University Press, London

Yunus M 1947 *Frontier Speaks.* Hind Kitabs, Bombay

EKNATH EASWARAN

Korean Armistice Agreement

The Korean Armistice Agreement is an agreement which was signed on July 27, 1953 between the hostile parties in the Korean War (1950-53). On June 25, 1950, North Korean forces initiated well-planned, massive attacks along a broad line across the 38th parallel, penetrating deep into the south. The Democratic People's Republic of Korea (North Korea) could not have initiated these attacks without help from the former Soviet Union. The United States quickly responded and went to the aid of the Republic of Korea (South Korea) despite its earlier position of placing Korea outside the United States defensive perimeter in Asia. The United States also successfully requested action by the United Nations Security Council against the North Korean aggression. United States military action in Korea then became a United Nations action. United Nations forces consisted primarily of United States forces, and were placed under American Command (see *United Nations Peacekeeping Operations*). When the tide of the war turned against North Korea, and United Nations forces pushed the war all the way to the North Korea-China border, Chinese forces intervened, forcing the United Nations forces to retreat south of the 38th parallel. Eventually, the war had to be stalemated as neither side wanted the conflict to extend beyond the Korean peninsula. The war was unable to alter the north-south division of the Korean peninsula.

On June 23, 1951, Jacob Malik, the Soviet representative to the United Nations Security Council, hinted at the possibility of a negotiated settlement to the Korean conflict. "The Soviet peoples," he stated, "believe that the most acute problem of the present day—the problem of the armed conflict in Korea—could . . . be settled." He also indicated that the communist side would accept the demands which had been made by the United Nations Command: (a) a ceasefire; (b) a demilitarized zone along the 38th parallel; and, (c) supervision of Korea during the armistice.

As the war had become bogged down to an impasse, the United States was intent on settling the conflict, despite strong opposition by President Syngman Rhee of South Korea, who still saw a golden opportunity to crush North Korea militarily and to unify the country by force. By this time, General MacArthur had been replaced by General Ridgway as Commander of United Nations Forces in

Korea, reflecting a fundamental change in policy towards the war by the United States.

On June 30, General Ridgway issued an invitation to the communist side for ceasefire talks. On the following day, Kim Il Sung, Supreme Commander of North Korean forces, and Peng Dehuai, Commander of the Chinese volunteers, agreed to such a meeting "in the area of Kaesong on the 38th parallel." On July 8, United Nations Command and communist liaison officers met at Kaesong to discuss preparation for the meetings. On July 10, the first in a series of meetings which lasted two years and seventeen days was held at Kaesong. Altogether, 575 regular meetings were held. Meanwhile, the meeting site was changed to Panmunjon, where a final agreement was signed.

The Korean Armistice represented only a *modus vivendi*, a temporary solution to the problem associated with the Korean division. It has been, since its inception, nothing more than a highly armed coexistence. The Armistice was not signed by South Korea, nor did it solve any of the problems that had caused the North Korean invasion of South Korea in the first place. The main provisions of the Armistice as finally agreed upon were: (a) a fixed military demarcation line and a demilitarized zone (4 kilometers wide), set up generally along the 38th parallel; (b) prohibition of any introduction into Korea of reinforcing military personnel and hardware; (c) the establishment of a Military Armistice Commission and a Neutral Nations Supervisory Commission to supervise the implementation of the Armistice agreement and to settle any violations of the Armistice provisions; and, (d) an arrangement for the release and repatriation of all prisoners of war in the custody of each side. It also recommended that, "within three months after the armistice agreement is signed and becomes effective, a political conference of a higher level of both sides be held by representatives appointed respectively to settle through negotiations the question of the withdrawal of all foreign forces from Korea and the peaceful settlement of the Korean question." As recommended, such a meeting was indeed held in Geneva in April-June 1954, but no solution for Korean unification ensued.

On the whole, the Armistice agreements have been more easily violated than truthfully honored. Both sides have made counterclaims for frequent violations, reducing the truce document to tatters. The Armistice halted the shooting conflict, but the North-South Korean situation remains unstable, threatening the peace and security of the area.

The Armistice agreement accomplished little more than a cessation of bloody hostilities, but such was the best that could have been expected at the time. The Armistice showed the futility of a victory on the battlefield, as long as there was a resolve by the larger powers to ensure a no-win scenario for the other side. Regardless of the political failures that followed the Korean Accord (1954 Geneva Conference on Korea), the concept of military takeover by either South or North, and the potential backing of such actions by their respective powerful allies, remains only the most remote of options. The fruitlessness of general warfare, particularly nuclear wars, especially where the Great Powers have staked a claim, was introduced to the modern era, through Korea. The accord that ended the conflict was symptomatic of the future relations between the Superpowers and their associates, a condition of neither peace nor war, characterized by belligerent coexistence.

The securing of the Armistice also points to the United Nations and its stabilizing and legitimizing role, at least with regard to South Korea. The fulfillment of its commitment to South Korea, although carried out mostly by the United States and at a time when the United Nations was dominated by the United States, nevertheless demonstrates the potential will of the United Nations to carry forward its decisions effectively with speed and force whenever it is pressed to do so. The resultant signing of the Armistice by UN participants lent a greater authority to the vast destruction, and the implications for a broader, more serious conflict. The accord was by no means an empty document. It did provide the initial step necessary for future resolution towards a more permanent peace.

The accord and the preceding war were, however, a testimonial to the potential will and resolve of both the United States and the United Nations. Both were perceived as too slow and too open to internal interference to respond quickly enough to counter the Soviet-backed North Korean invasion. To the demise of the Soviet and North Korean plans, the United States-led UN forces were giving credence to the notion of a "balance of power" within a few days of the initial North Korean advance.

Likewise, after the decision by Beijing to react to the northward movement of General MacArthur, the war and the subsequent accord was a testimonial to the major powers' willingness to opt for a belligerent coexistence rather than risk a new all-out conflict that might entail the use of nuclear weapons. The irony that the Soviet Ambassador to the United Nations, Malik, should be the initiator of the first ceasefire agreement in 1950 demonstrates the cognition of the no-win scenario by either side.

While by no means resolving the necessary issues to accomplish a rooted and stable peace (one which seemingly includes the resolution of the unification of Korea), the Armistice was a manifestation of some stabilizing realities by both the indigenous parties on the peninsula and the Superpowers. This recognition included the role that the People's Republic of China would play in the years to come, as an independent and powerful actor in Asia, and ensured the future role of the United Nations in attempts to resolve the deeper issues of the Korean peninsula. The added current dimension of China's emerging power and its place at the United Nations make the United Nations' involvement in the Armistice accords an all the more viable resource for the cause of peace and future resolution of the basic issues between North and South Korea.

Although the net result of the conflict itself was a modern pyrrhic victory, one where the original lines of demarcation agreed upon by the two great post-Second World War powers were reaffirmed, and one that saw Beijing begin to play a new assertive role on the global stage, the roots of the conflict, like those in Central Europe and a host of other divided areas, remain on standby, the situation unacceptable in the long run. Again, as in Central Europe, there has been a basic recognition that the military option had been tested and found wanting as a formula for achieving political goals.

See also: *Pacific Settlement of International Disputes*

Bibliography

Berger C 1964 *The Korean Knot: A Military-Political History.* University of Pennsylvania Press, Philadelphia, Pennsylvania

Cummings B 1981 *The Origins of the Korean War.* Princeton University Press, Princeton, New Jersey

Goodrich L M 1956 *Korea: A Study of US Policy in the United Nations.* Council on Foreign Relations, New York

Goulder J C 1982 *Korea: The Untold Story of the War.* Times Books, New York

Herms W G 1966 *Truce Tent and Fighting Front.* US Department of the Army, Washington, DC

Kim S J (ed.) 1976 *Korean Unification: Source Materials with an Introduction.* Research Center for Peace and Unification, Seoul

Oliver R T 1954 *Syngman Rhee: The Man Behind the Myth.* Dodd, Mead, New York

Vatcher W H 1958 *Panmunjom: The Story of the Korean Military Armistice Negotiations*, Praeger, New York

C. I. EUGENE KIM

Korean Reunification: Proposals

The end of World War II in 1945 brought liberation to the Korean people from Japanese colonial rule. Unfortunately, however, the Korean people then saw their country divided as a result of the dual occupation of the Korean peninsula by the United States and the Soviet Union and the ensuing Cold War structure.

In 1948, the Republic of Korea was established as the only legitimate government on the peninsula through free general elections conducted under the United Nation's supervision and on the basis of its resolution. But the North Korean communists rejected the UN-supervised free elections and established their own regime in the northern half of the peninsula—thus firming up the territorial division.

The state of the division of Korea constitutes the fundamental cause that has brought to the Korean people unspeakable sorrow and distress as well as the constant anxiety of another probable war. The Korean peninsula is the only place in the world where both the sheer separation and adversarial relations, characteristic of the Cold War period, still remain intact.

As the Korean people had lived in a unified country during the past thirteen centuries as a homogeneous race having a single language, culture and history, it is a historic imperative for them to achieve the reunification of their country as a peaceful and democratic nation. The task is enormously difficult because of ideological differences and mutual distrust between North and South Korea which resulted from a devastating, internecine war initiated by North Korea.

After the division, the Korean people suffered from the ravages of a bloody war as the North Korean communist regime launched a surprise and full-scale invasion of South Korea on June 25, 1950. The Korean War, which symbolized the East-West confrontation in the Cold War, resulted in enormous human casualties that reached 2 million as well as immense property damages. More importantly, it left a deep intra-national hostility between the two parts of the Korean peninsula.

As the 3-year Korean War finally ended, the 38th parallel—originally a demarcation line between the

North and South—was replaced by the truce line, and it has persisted until today under an extremely confrontational situation (see *Korean Armistice Agreement).*

Considering its geographical location and characteristics of the North-South competition, the Korean peninsula is sitting in the eye of a storm. If war breaks out again, it will bring about great catastrophe of immense destruction and numerous casualties that could result in the total extermination of the Korean nation. Moreover, it might be followed by the risk of destroying the peace in Northeast Asia.

1. Major Obstacles to Korean Reunification

While one of the major obstacles to peaceful unification is the ideological predisposition of the ruling class in North Korea, it can be said that more important is the difference in views of the North and South Koreans on the values of unification.

The people in the Republic of Korea, who enjoy the benefits of freedom and democracy, would not want to have unification without preserving these values, even though unification is their national aspiration. In fact, if South Koreans had wished to realize any form of unification at any cost, it could have been accomplished long ago. The anti-communism of South Koreans is not only due to anti-North Korea sentiment generated by the painful experience of the Korean War. Also added to this is their value orientation that unification under communist domination can not be allowed.

By contrast, the people in North Korea have been educated under the communist system for more than 52 years, through which they have formed the view that the capitalistic system in the Republic of Korea should be abolished and, as such, it is the main object of their struggle. At the present time, because North Koreans less than 52 years old have since their childhood only experienced the communist model, they are not able to compare different ideologies and systems, and neither are they competent in asserting critical ability.

Furthermore, because the ideological education rendered to North Koreans including its youths is based upon the historical view of class struggle that bolsters only ruthless efforts, while absolutely precluding the compromise with opposing classes, it is impossible under the present circumstances to solve the unification problems by transcending their view of class struggle and on the national stance. The obstacles to peaceful unification, which have been addressed so far, are all internal to Korea.

In addition to such internal obstacles, there are the impediments to peaceful unification arising from international circumstances. Since the interest relations of the surrounding superpowers are interwound in many respects including security, diplomatic and economic areas, it is infeasible to realize unification, which will be satisfactory to all of them. The superpowers surrounding the Korean peninsula tend to check each other to prevent a unified Korea from being under the influence of opposing powers. Such external factors make it more difficult to overcome the unification obstacles.

2. The Unification Proposals of the Republic of Korea

The unification formula of the South Korean government is well manifested in the so-called "Formula for National Reconciliation and Democratic Unification" and the "Korean National Community Unification Formula".

On January 22, 1982, the then President Chun Doo-Hwan of the Republic of Korea, in his New Year Policy Statement, announced "the Formula for National Reconciliation and Democratic Unification." In this formula, he proposed two fundamental approaches toward the accomplishment of unification. Like two wheels attached to one wagon, on the one hand, both Koreas work together for national harmony, and on the other hand, they foster the task of national unification so that their supreme goal, that is, unification, can be achieved. As a transitional measure to realize unification, the "Provisional Agreement on Basic Relations" was made so as to normalize mutual relations and then solve the obstacles to unification one by one with the opening of both societies through exchange and cooperation. Such a procedure is regarded as one of the important ways towards the promotion of national harmony. The contents of the "Provisional Agreement on Basic Relations" constitute the recognition of both sides, the peaceful settlement of disputes, the mutual non-interference in the internal affairs of the other side, the restriction of military competition to relax tension and prevent war, the opening of both societies, cooperative interchange, appreciation of international agreements and accords, and lastly the establishment of liaison representative offices in both Seoul and Pyongyang.

At the same time, the "Consultative Conference for National Reunification" consisting of the representatives of people from both Koreas will be organized, and a draft of the unified constitution made. The draft of unified constitution will be adopted by a national referendum to be held throughout Korea. Following this, the unified government will be established. This is the democratic unification procedure that the South Korean government has pursued.

While the concept of national harmony means an incorporation of the lesser conflicting elements, following the systematization of peaceful relation between two Koreas, the concept of democratic unification can be interpreted as a complete political incorporation.

On September 11, 1989, the then President Roh Tae-Woo of the Republic of Korea proposed a new policy for national unification under the name of "The Korean National Community Unification Formula." Asserting that the Korean commonwealth be organized as a transitory unification system, he based this unification proposal on three principles—independence, peace, and democracy. The establishment of a Unified Democratic Republic is proposed as an end-state unification system. In other words, national unification is to be pushed forward in an independent, peaceful, and democratic manner in which the self-determination of the people will be applied from the first to the last step, thereby excluding external intervention. The procedure to achieve national unification is through the formation of a commonwealth between North and South Korea to firstly establish a single national community and then a unified single nation-state. In the interim stage of national unification, the Korean Commonwealth is expected to perform such roles as promotion of mutual prosperity, homogenization of national community, and formation of national communal life zone. To accomplish this purpose, a Council of Presidents—an organization with the highest level of decision making power—a Council of Ministers composed of around ten members with ministerial posts, and a Council of Representatives of around 100 legislators, with equal numbers representing the two parts of Korea, are proposed. Five standing committees from the Council of Ministers would deal with issues such as the reunion of the separated families, the easing of political confrontation between North and South society, the promotion of multi-faceted exchanges and cooperation, the fostering of a national culture, formation of a common economic zone for mutual prosperity, the building of military confidence, arms control, and the replacement of the current Armistice Agreement with a peace agreement. A Council of Representatives would provide policy advice and recommendations to the Council of Ministers, draft the constitution of a unified Korea, and develop methods and procedures for fully unifying the country.

The procedure and vision for establishing a unified nation suggested by South Korea is as follows: In the first place, the Council of Representatives should discuss and agree on the political ideals, name and form of government for a unified Korea, its basic domestic and foreign policies, instruments, timing, and procedures for a general election to constitute its legislature. Both the South and the North would present their respective proposals for the constitution of a unified Korea to the Council of Representatives so that they can be combined into a single draft. The agreed draft of the constitution of a unified Korea should be finalized and promulgated through democratic methods and procedures. General elections would then be held under the promulgated constitution to form both a unified legislature and unified government. In the second place, a unified Korea should be at once a single nation-state and a democratic republic guaranteeing every citizen's freedom, human rights, and the right to seek happiness. Its legislature would be a bicameral parliament composed of an upper house based on regional representation and a lower house based on popular support.

A unified Korea should pursue the development of a democratic republic that would assure every citizen the right of participation as well as equal opportunity and freedom of expression, the promotion of welfare for all, firm preservation of national security and contribution to world peace, and the maintenance of good neighborly relations with all nations.

The "Korean National Community Unification Formula" is regarded as another comprehensive blueprint for unification, even though it is fundamentally not so different from the 1982 proposal entitled the "Formula for National Reconciliation and Democratic Unification." The new formula contains more advanced ideas as compared with its predecessor in terms of transitional institutional arrangement and the structure of parliament after unification. That is to say, the 1989 formula concretized and complemented the idea of the 1982 formula by devising the organization of commonwealth composed of equal number of delegates from North and South Korea, the creation of a Unification-Peace City, and a bicameral parliament system.

On the other hand, the 1989 formula and the 1982 formula have numerous similarities in their basic principles and approaches as follows:

First, the basic principles for unification of two formulas are virtually the same in spite of their different expressions. Among the three principles, the word "independence" used by the Roh Administration substantially has the same meaning as the term "national self-determination" employed by the Chun administration.

Second, the method of unification adopted by both administrations involves taking two main steps which are normalization of inter-Korean relations and realization of unification through general elections.

Third, the Council of Representatives of Korean Commonwealth is similar to the Consultative Conference for National Reunification proposed by the previous administration in its organization and function of drafting a unified constitution.

Fourth, the idea of adopting a Charter of the National Community is not so different from that of concluding a Provisional Agreement on Basic Relations between North and South Korea providing for a set of practical measures.

Fifth, the future policy of the new formula calling for the creation of a democratic state which guarantees liberty, human rights and the right to seek happiness is almost the same as the ideals of nationalism, democracy, liberty and welfare the 1982 formula pursued. Such is the case since the term "human rights" could be included in the ideology of democracy and liberty and the concept of the right to "seek happiness" is similar to the right to pursue "welfare." In addition, we can surmise that the ideal of nationalism in the 1982 formula is developed into the idea of building a national community.

Sixth, the proposal for the establishment of resident liaison missions to each other's capital is identical to both formulas.

Hence, it can be said that the new unification formula takes similar approach and framework in pursuing national unification as its 1982 predecessor. Fundamentally, the two formulas are based on the same principles and take a step-by-step approach which is known as the "functional or incremental approach to unification."

Nevertheless the new formula can be evaluated as being more developed and concretized one than the 1982 formula in the respect that it has delineated a detailed institutional framework for the intermediate stage to unification. If only North Korea accepts this proposal of transitional system, contacts, dialogue, and cooperation between North and South Korea, coexistence and co-prosperity for peaceful unification would be well regulated. Moreover, the 1989 formula has shown a more receptive posture toward North Korea by proposing all the interim institutions to be represented on a totally equal basis irrespective of population size of both sides. In this sense, the new formula is slightly more capacious than its 1982

predecessor even though it maintains the basic elements of earlier formula.

On July 6, 1993, president Kim Young-sam of the Republic of Korea put forward the unification policy of the new government in his opening address made at the Sixth Advisory Council on Democratic and Peaceful Unification.

In the formula, president Kim set forth a three-phased approach to unification—reconciliation and cooperation, the Korean Commonwealth and unified state—in conformity with the frame of the existing Korean National Community Unification Formula and in line with the spirit of the agreement on Reconciliation, Nonaggression and Exchanges and Cooperation between the South and the North.

As a base for the promotion of unification, the president called for a democratic national consensus, coexistence and co-prosperity and national well-being. Even though president Kim's unification policy is not fundamentally different from the "Korean National Community Formula for Unification" of the previous government, the position from which the policy is pursued is somewhat different in that democratic process is more strongly emphasized.

The approach to the issue of unification of Korea by president Kim Dae Jung of the new South Korean government which was launched in February 1998 can be summarized as follows: The Republic of Korea will never tolerate armed provocation of any kind; it has no intention to harm or absorb the North; and it will actively pursue reconciliation and cooperation between the South and North, beginning with those areas that can be most easily agreed upon.

President Kim has long maintained "three principles and three stages" for unification. The principles are peaceful coexistence, peaceful exchange and peaceful unification. The three stages are (a) a confederation of states, (b) then a federation "like the USA," and (c) complete unification.

3. The Unification Proposals of the Democratic People's Republic of Korea

North Korea, however, has shown negative reactions to the South Korean government's unification proposals, and insisted on the scheme for the establishment of so-called the "Korean Democratic Confederal Republic of Koryo." In the Party Central Committee report at the Sixth Congress of the Workers' Party on October 10, 1980, the late North Korean president Kim Il-sung put forward the idea saying as follows:

Our Party suggests that the fatherland be unified through the establishment of a confederal republic, in which the North and the South create a unified national government participated in equally by both sides, while recognizing and tolerating each other's ideology and system, with the two sides adhering to a regional autonomous system, respectively, with equal rights and obligations under the unified government.

It would be reasonable that in a unified country taking the form of confederation, a supreme national confederal conference could be organized among the same number of representatives from the North and the South and a proper number of our compatriots abroad which would then create a confederal standing committee with the task of guiding the regional governments in the North and the South and taking charge of overall policies of the confederate state.

The supreme national confederal conference and its standing body—the confederal standing committee—should, as the unified government of the confederal state, discuss and solve political issues, question of safeguarding the fatherland, external affairs and all other common problems linked to the overall interests of the country and the nation on a fair principle befitting the wishes for national unity, collaboration and unification; implement projects designed to ensure uniform development of the nation; and realize unity and collaboration between the North and the South in all fields. The unified government of the confederal state should respect the social systems and the views of the administrative organizations, political parties, factions and various strata and layers in the North and the South, while seeing to it that neither of the two sides ever attempts to impose its own opinion upon the other side.

Under the guidance of the confederal government, the regional governments of the North and the South should pursue their independent policies to the extent of meeting the basic interests and needs of the whole nation, and should strive to narrow the differences in all sectors of the North and the South, and to promote the uniform development of the country and the nation.

The name of the confederal state may well be "Democratic Confederal Republic of Koryo" after the name of our country's unified state widely known in the world and reflecting the common political ideals of the North and the South in pursuing democracy.

The "Democratic Confederal Republic of Koryo" should be a neutral state which does not affiliate itself with any political or military alliance or bloc. It is natural and most reasonable in reality that the Democratic Confederal Republic of Koryo would become a neutral country, on the condition that the regions of the North and the South with different ideologies and systems be unified into a single confederal state . . . .

Although North Korea's proposal for the establishment of the Confederated Republic of Koryo appears to be a peaceful unification plan, this proposal refuses to normalize South-North relations and to relax the tension between the two, before the actual institution of the Confederated Republic of Koryo. Furthermore, it even avoids to mention a democratic unification process.

North Korea's negative stance against democratic unification can be further proven by the fact that it boycotts the nation-wide election. North Korea presents the following claims:

"It has been our contention since the national liberation in 1945 that the unification be achieved through free nation-wide election . . . . Since then, as time has passed, the relations and conflicts between the North and South have become complicated and aggravated. The two have not only incompatible ideologies and systems, but also are in a militarily confrontational position along the truce line. Additionally, the political relation surrounding the Korean peninsula gets complex. Under such a circumstance, the fastest and the realistic way to accomplish unification is the formation of a confederated state, leaving the existing systems in both sides untouched (an editorial from the *Workers Newspaper* on February 20, 1982)."

The time when North Korea lastly advocated unification by way of holding nationwide elections under the precondition of the withdrawal of American military forces was in 1971 (the 8-Point Proposal for Peaceful Unification on April 12, 1971). And, the time when North Korea began to argue on unification through nationwide election as being unrealistic was after the 6th Workers' Party Congress in August, 1980, in which it proposed the plan for the establishment of the Confederated Republic of Koryo. Even after North Korea suggested the North-South confederation as a transitional stage toward the complete unification, it did not reject nationwide elections. As such, North Korea has changed its position on nationwide election because it wants to justify the North-South confederated system not as a transitional stage but as its unification plan. It was also because North Korea was not certain of achieving its preferred scenario of a communist unification without the presence of American military forces, resulting from the establishment of a unified government after nationwide election. It was also clearly related to the fact that North Korea could not but acknowledge its relative inferiority to South Korea in economic development as well as in the level of its people's quality of life.

North Korea has insisted time and again that the idea of a "confederation system" is the ideal unification formula under the present circumstances in North and South Korea. But, in spite of North Korea's propaganda campaign, there are several decisive defects in the system if taking note of the prerequisites attached to the realization of the confederation system and lack of democratic process.

First, North Korea's scheme includes preconditions unacceptable to South Korea. Second, it ignores democratic procedures for establishing a unified state. Third, it insists that the North and the South should continue to keep their conflicting ideologies and systems even after unification.

In particular, the three conditions demanded by North Korea—abolition of the National Security Law, the legalization of pro-communist activity, the withdrawal of the US military forces from South Korea—are in fact aimed at political disarmament and the weakening of defense capabilities of South Korea. These demands are actually intended for providing absolutely favorable conditions for North Korea's violent communist revolution or military conquest of South Korea.

4. Conclusion

For Koreans today, nothing is more difficult than the task of reunifying their divided motherland. The task involves highly complex and comprehensive issues, which will determine the future of the Korean peninsula and the fate of the entire Korean people.

Considering the fact that the two Koreas have been unable to normalize relations in more than half a century, it is all too obvious that the formulation and implementation of unification policies must be based not only on a justifiable, rational approach but also on a realistic approach if such policies are to be effective and workable.

Since the direction and form of unification will have a great bearing on the national fortunes and future destiny of the Korean people, unification must be pursued on the basis of justice and appropriateness. It can not, however, be expected to materialize unless it is pursued in a realistic, practicable manner.

In other words, while unification policy must be formulated in a reasonable, logical way, it must at the same time take existing realities fully into account. A unification policy must in no way be permitted to go against the pursuit of the national cause of the Korean people. A unification policy that is not workable and not practicable would only be a meaningless exercise in futility since there are so many obstacles that make unification perhaps the most difficult task facing the Korean people.

In order to overcome and resolve the sharp confrontation between North and South Korea, which have two different political systems and whose views of their interests are poles apart, it is essential for the two sides to explore and pursue an objective and elaborate unification approach that gives due consideration to each other's current situation and position.

See also: *Integration Theories, International Conflicts and Equilibria; Conflict Resolution, Process of*

Bibliography

Sohn J S 1991 *Peace and Unification of Korea.* Seoul Computer Press, Seoul

Han W S 1993 The Kim Young Sam government's unification policy: Basic structure and its three pillars. *Korea and World Affairs* 17(2)

Office of the South-North Dialogue, National Unification Board, 1993 *South-North Dialogue in Korea.* NUB, Seoul

National Unification Board 1982 *A White Paper on South-North Dialogue in Korea*

National Unification Board 1989 *To build a National Community through the Korean Commonwealth.* NUB, Seoul

The Seoul Forum for International Affairs 1998 *Managing Change on the Korean Peninsula.* Seoul

JAE-SHIK SOHN

L

Language and Peace

Peace is one of the fundamental principles and aspirations of humankind. The United Nations celebrated 1986 as the International Year of Peace (see *Year of Peace: Initiation, Promulgation and Commemoration*). Each year, the prestigious Nobel Peace Prize is awarded to recognize work for peace and humanitarian causes (see *Nobel Peace Prizes*). Peace conferences are regularly organized by national institutes or by supra- or international organizations that are devoted to the achievement of peace. The aim of the International Peace Research Association (IPRA), for example, is to advance disciplinary and interdisciplinary research into issues related to peace. Academic disciplines that focus on this research topic, notably peace studies, political science, history, international relations, study this issue, of course, from different perspectives, with different aims, and base their views on different methodological approaches (cf. Wenden 1995a).

The particular interest that linguists show in the largely political concept of peace is motivated by the fact that politics cannot be conducted without language, i.e., discourse. Politics is constituted to a large extent by text and talk. Aspects of particular interest for linguistics are found on all levels of linguistic research, and practically in all sub-disciplines of (applied) linguistics.

Etymology and *historical linguistics,* for example, study the origin of a word in a language and the history of its meaning. Attention is focused on how a word came into the language and with which other words it is related. For example, the English word 'peace' and the French word 'paix' are derived from the Latin 'pax'; the German word 'Frieden' derives from the old Anglo Saxon word 'freodo' and shares etymologically the same root as the modern English word 'freedom.' In addition to showing how the word forms developed, historical linguistics also studies how word meanings developed throughout history and in which contexts the word was used, e.g., looking at the meaning and use of the concept 'peace' from the Middle Ages through the time of Enlightenment up to the present day.

Lexical semantics is the linguistic discipline that is concerned with the meanings of words. Usually, a distinction is made between the denotation (as the context-independent, conventionally fixed meaning), and connotation (as additional components of word meaning which are related to emotional and other external circumstances). The word 'peace' is usually associated with positive values and emotions (see *Peace Theory: An Introduction*). Sometimes a comparative aspect is introduced into lexical semantics, that is, word meanings across languages and cultures are compared in order to find similarities and differences. Differences that are established in this process, reflect underlying philosophies and ideologies. With respect to the concept of 'peace,' differences in the meaning are due to the different traditions and strands of thought of Quakers, Christianity, Buddhism, Hinduism, Islam, Judaism, and others.

The results of such comparative studies find their practical application particularly in *lexicography* and in *translation theory and practice* (e.g., compilation of mono-, bi- or multilingual dictionaries, creation of terminological data banks, provision of lists with lexical equivalents). To compile monolingual dictionaries, lexicographers have to decide on criteria according to which they arrange the several meanings of a word (a lexical entry). For 'peace,' the *Concise Oxford Dictionary* lists three, albeit related, meanings:

(a) freedom from or cessation of war

(b) freedom from civil disorder

(c) quiet, tranquility, mental calm

The first two meanings are related to the area of politics, whereas the third one is related to intra-personal aspects, or to nature in a wider sense. These differences in the two main areas in which the word meanings apply also become obvious in collocations. 'Peace' can be interpreted (predominantly) as a political term in collocations such as 'peace negotiations, sign a peace treaty, fight for peace, a peacekeeping mission,' and as an everyday concept in collocations such as 'peace of mind, peaceful town, peaceful countryside.' Studying meanings beyond the level of the individual word, i.e., extending the analysis to the levels of collocations, phrases, sentences (and texts), is another task of the linguistic discipline of *semantics*.

In *lexical semantics*, political words offer a particular challenge. In the more traditional research such words have often been described as empty in meaning or as ideology-bound. Sometimes a standard meaning was distinguished from politically defined usage. In the case of 'peace,' semanticists and lexicographers have often found it easier to define it in terms of what it is not rather than what it is. As in the *Concise Oxford Dictionary*, 'peace' is mostly defined simply as 'absence of war.' Expanding the concept, Galtung (1964, 1969) contrasted this 'negative peace' with a 'positive peace' which describes the absence of any structural violence and introduces aspects of equality and harmony (see *Positive versus Negative Peace*).

These definitions that were developed in the discipline of peace studies can be linked to more recent approaches in linguistics. After decades of studying language as a system, in the late 1960s communicative and pragmatic aspects of language use gained more prominence. New sub-disciplines developed, such as *pragmatics, sociolinguistics, functional linguistics, communication studies, textlinguistics*. These frameworks made it possible to link linguistic forms to social, and hence also to political activities. In the 1970s, these developments were further enriched by a cognitive orientation within linguistics (e.g., *psycholinguistics, cognitive semantics*). All these developments resulted in new and/or deeper insights both into the structure and the functioning of language.

As mentioned above, politics is constituted to a great extent by text and talk. This holds equally true for the discourse on peace, on whatever political level or in whatever situation it is conducted, be it the United Nations debate on their *Agenda for Peace*, or when two states sign a peace treaty after a war had come to an end, or be it at home, in front of the TV set, when a family comments on TV reports about the prospects of a peace process in some area of the world. Whenever we open the newspaper, listen to the news on radio or TV, we frequently read or hear the word 'peace,' mostly, however, as a political concept. Taken at random from the special page 'Politics this week,' from two issues of the British weekly magazine *The Economist*, we find the following examples (my italics):

(a) India told Pakistan's new prime minister, Nawaz

Sharif, that it was willing to *resume peace talks* on a number of issues, including the dispute over Kashmir.

(b) Binyamin Netanyahu, back from Washington, denied reports that he had promised the Americans to freeze a plan to build 6,500 Jewish housing units on land seized in 1967 between Bethlehem and Jerusalem. "Illegal," said Yasser Arafat. Separately, 90 Bedouin were evicted from their West Bank homes to allow expansion of a Jewish settlement. "Racist," said an Israeli *peace group*. (*The Economist*, February 22, 1997 p. 6)

(c) Algeria held its first election since the army cancelled a vote the Islamists were about to win in 1992. Some 8,000 candidates from 39 parties competed for 380 seats in a relatively powerless National Assembly. The frontrunners were the president's National Democratic Rally and the moderate Islamist party, *Movement for a Peaceful Solution*. The main Islamist party remained banned. Bombs, blamed on Islamist militants, continued to explode.

(d) Nigerian warships bombarded targets in Sierra Leone, and American marines evacuated foreigners by helicopter. Fighting between rebellious soldiers and intervening Nigerian troops was halted while mediators sought a *peaceful solution*. (*The Economist*, June 7, 1997 p. 6)

In these short news items, different political actions are justified by reference to peace. Studies in *textlinguistics* and *Critical Discourse Analysis* (e.g., van Dijk 1980, 1988; Fairclough and Wodak 1997) have noted that words never come alone but they are embedded in concrete texts to fulfil a particular function. It is in the texts that words, and also political words, are repeatedly used, and it is, thus, in the texts that their meanings are stabilized, modified, or changed. Therefore, in the analysis of political discourse and political texts, the broader social and political framework in which such discourse is embedded has to be taken into consideration.

Applied to the examples above, the meaning of the word 'peace' in each of these short news items has to be interpreted against the specific context in which it is embedded. What these news items have in common is that they report about countries and/or areas of political problems or turmoil. In most of them, there are also additional lexical items that substantiate this claim, e.g., 'dispute' in example (1), 'evict' in (2), 'bombs' in (3), 'warships, fighting, soldiers, troops' in (4). In other words, the concepts of 'war' and 'peace' are often paired in the texts, either explicitly (as in 4), or the one is invoked by the other (as in 1-3). The words 'peace' or 'war' need not actually occur in the texts. Often, the concepts of war and peace are evoked by other words that belong to the associated conceptual scenario. For such conceptual structures, the terms frame, script, schema, scenario, etc., are used in cognitive linguistics. What they all have in common is an understanding that knowledge and experience is structured in the human mind. In other words, human beings experience the physical and social world in their given culture, and, based on this experience, they organize their knowledge about the world in their minds. This knowledge is organized in specific cognitive structures and it is used, or activated, in order to interpret (new) information. These organisational structures of knowledge provide the conceptual basis for lexical material, and vice versa, lexical structures encountered in a text evoke knowledge structures.

This cognitive orientation has led, amongst others, to the establishment of *frame semantics* as an approach to describe and explain word meanings. Applied to 'peace' and 'war,' it is noteworthy that the 'war frame' is much richer than a 'peace frame.' One form of representing frames is to start from a main predicate (an event, or an action, or a state) and, based on a textual analysis, to identify slots of the frame. For a war frame, the following slots can thus be identified:

(a) *agents* (the war-fighting parties, which exist at different levels, e.g., nations or states, groups/ alliances of nations, ethnic groups within a state, other political or ideological groups within a state);

(b) *patient* (the affected entity, the state, nation, or group against which some other state, nation, or groups is fighting a war);

(c) *instruments* (at a general level: weapons; or at a more specific level e.g., knives, swords, guns, canons, bombs, missiles—these instruments have changed in the course of history, and they may be culture specific);

(d) *reason/cause* (an actual or perceived threat by the other party or parties involved);

(e) *purpose/objective* (the ultimate aim of fighting the war, often identified as 'peace').

If the agent slot is taken by individuals, this points to 'war' in the non-political sense, i.e., inter-personal relations, but if the agent slot is taken by states, then we have 'war' as a political concept, in the context of international or inter state relations.

Other frame slots (semantic roles) could be added, e.g., *location* (where the war is being fought), and *time* (when it is being fought). Very often, more specific actions can be identified, e.g., attack, defend, bomb, fire. These actions can be characterized as sub-actions of the war frame, or even sub-frames with their own slots (e.g., an attack frame), with some of them being semantically linked to the *instruments* slot.

Textlinguistics and *frame semantics* have found that the (potential) slots of a frame are verbalized more or less frequently and extensively in the actual texts. For example, the *cause/reason* slot is often left implicit, or even empty, or specified differently in the mass media. This is evidence of the different political or ideological stance of the respective authors (e.g., mass media). Politicians and historians would speak of a hidden or a false reason (e.g., the beginning of the Second World War was presented by German Nazi propaganda as retaliation to an attack by Polish partisans on a German radio station). A similar phenomenon can be seen with respect to the purpose slot, which is often presented in a very general way (often as establishing peace), but always as a positive objective. In the texts, there are hardly ever explicit references to, so to speak, negative aims, e.g., occupying a territory, taking over power, destroying towns or states). What *frame semantics* contributes to the explanation of meanings is that it clearly shows that 'peace' and 'war' are semantically and conceptually related, i.e., that peace fills the *purpose* slot in a war frame.

Throughout human history, peace has very often been linked to war, as illustrated in the quotation by the Roman military writer Vegetius (379-395): 'Let him who desires peace, prepare for war' (*Oxford Dictionary of Political Quotations*, often quoted as 'If you want peace, prepare for war').

The fact that war is conceptualized as an action—in contrast to peace, which is conceptualized as a state—explains that the war frame is conceptually and semantically richer than the peace frame. But can we actually speak of a separate 'peace frame?' What would its slots be? When 'peace' takes the *purpose* slot in the war frame, it is negatively characterized as a state which the partners want to achieve by destroying each other. Galtung's positive peace would be defined as a state in which the partners want to guarantee the very existence of each other. Can such a concept (or frame) of 'peace' be established as a result of a text analysis? In which contexts could it be found?

Linguists and (critical) discourse analysts have conducted research on the basis of texts that were not devoted to actual wars or other violent conflicts. Thus, a substantial amount of analysis was done on the Cold War discourse (particularly in Europe and the United States of America), mainly in the 1970s up to the late 1980s, motivated in particular by NATO's 1979 decision to deploy more nuclear missiles on Western European territory to counter Russia's military build-up. This debate also led to an increased awareness of the social responsibility of scholars, also among linguists (e.g., Chilton, ed., 1985; Burkhardt, Hebel and Herberg, eds., 1989). In Germany, for example, a number of linguists started an initiative *Linguists for Peace* to stimulate research into the discourse on the nuclear debate, including studies on the meaning of the word 'peace' (e.g., Pasierbsky 1983).

Most of this research was based on mass media since they obviously play a significant role in the presentation of the world to their readership. For example, applying the textlinguistic methodology of the macrostructure analysis, Schäffner (e.g., 1986, 1995) identified the dominant macropropositions in the British weekly *The Economist* over the period 1979-84, and developing the analysis further, she identified the specific semantic profile of the major thematic words and thematic collocations (characterized as *textword-types*). For example, the specific word meaning (i.e., the textword-type) for 'peace' (1979-84) in *The Economist* was described as:

> (future) state between East and West in Europe in which a restored balance, i.e., a high number of nuclear missiles of NATO with a deterrence function, prevents the outbreak of war.

Alternatively, for the liberal British daily newspaper *The Guardian* the textword-type 'peace' (for 1979-86) was described as:

> state between east and west in Europe in which a negotiated low balance, i.e., few mainly non-nuclear missiles with a deterrence function, prevents the outbreak of war.

This example shows that political word meanings do not conform to a single norm, but rather to several norms. That is, depending on the textual embeddedness and the political stance of the text authors, these meanings (i.e., textword-types) may be valid for only one or a few political groups and only for a shorter or longer period of time.

The textlinguistic analyses also revealed systematic semantic and conceptual relations between 'peace,' 'balance,' and 'deterrence.' The link between 'deterrence' and 'peace,' for example, was presented as a conceptual relation of enablement, i.e., 'deterrence enables peace.' The typical instruments of deterrence at the time of the Cold War were nuclear missiles.

Missiles, the typical weapons of warfare, were reinterpreted in the Cold War discourse as instruments of peace. This is reflected in the following quotation:

> The invention of nuclear weapons has given man a historic opportunity to broaden the bounds of peace, as well as posing a fearful threat (*The Economist,* February 22, 1986) (headline: The long nuclear peace).

The collocation 'nuclear peace' may look like a contradiction in terms, and its semantic explanation would definitely pose problems for a semantic analysis that looks at words and collocations in isolation. A textlinguistic-discursive analysis, however, studies the intertextual sequence of occurrences and is, thus, able to explain the meanings of such collocations as being embedded in and determined by recurring macropropositions. Such an analysis, thus, revealed that 'nuclear peace' was presented as an instance of a positive peace in the Cold War discourse. This is illustrative of what Mehan and Skelley (1988: 43) called a "Pure War Culture" in which "the distinction between peace and war is blurred." *A Nuclear Dictionary* that was published in 1985 did not even include 'peace' as an entry.

Another important contribution by *cognitive semantics* to the study of word meanings and concepts is the research into *metaphors*. Metaphors are ways of conceptualizing (i.e., thinking about) the world. In texts relating to national security and inter-state relations, metaphors provide the basis and justification for the formulation and realization of government policy. Again, metaphors relating to war are much richer and more frequent than for peace (cf. Chilton and Lakoff 1995; Lakoff 1992).

Textual and cognitive approaches to the description and explanation of word meanings, a semantics of understanding (Fillmore 1985) has made it clear that word meaning cannot be treated as if it were an inherent property of verbal objects or a stable, fixed image. Words like 'peace' do not simply *have* meanings, but meanings are assigned to them by language users on the basis of cognitive processes in some concrete interaction and context.

What has also become clear is that the traditional definition of 'peace' as 'absence of war,' provided by lexical semantics, is not sufficient. From a discourse analytic perspective it is obvious that not every instance of non-war can be called 'peace' and that those instances which are called 'peace' do not necessarily share identical features.

The word 'peace' is used in discourse to express a state of no war between countries or between partners in international relations. This state holds true for a certain region and for a certain time. It is brought about or ensured by specific means, and it is precisely in respect of those means in which the various meanings of 'peace' can differ. The means are either (i) specific instruments (e.g., weapons with their specific purpose, as e.g., deterrence), or (ii) specific conditions (e.g., handing back captured territories), or (iii) themselves specific states, namely pre-condition states for the final state peace (e.g., security, justice—as described in the 1975 Helsinki Final Act of the Conference on Security and Co-operation in Europe).

The third case is mainly found in official texts published by supra- or international organizations, such as treaties or mission statements. The most frequent meaning of 'peace' that we encounter in text and discourse is the one in which the means are specified as some kind of weapons, although not necessarily nuclear weapons in the post-Cold War era. But weapons are still seen as being of decisive importance for ensuring peace. In other words, the line of argument is still linked to the concept of deterrence, as illustrated in the following examples:

> Alliance security policy aims to *preserve peace* in freedom by both political means and the maintenance of a military capability sufficient to prevent war and to provide for effective defense . . . . (A Comprehensive Concept of Arms Control and Disarmament, Brussels, May 29/30, 1989, NATO *Review*, vol. 37, no. 3, 1989, June)

> [Generals] argue that armour is increasingly relevant to peacekeeping: the lightly-armed UN mission to Bosnia proved ineffective, while the weightier NATO force which followed succeeded in intimidating all sides. (*The Economist*, February 1, 1997)

An example of 'peace' in which the instruments slot is filled by conditions is the following one, quoting an academic who comments on the Middle East:

> "Real peace will come to the area when Israel learns to live within the 1967 borders and when Palestinians accept it (Israel) in the area." (*Times Higher Education Supplement*, March 14, 1997)

The formulation 'real peace' points to some kind of ideal conception, to a cognitive model against which the actual situation is matched (Lakoff 1986, speaks of 'idealized cognitive models;' cf. also *prototype theory*, e.g., Rosch 1977). What would this ideal state 'peace' look like? Some indication of such an ideal state, albeit from the ideological position of Western democracies, is given in the following example:

> If we take 'world peace' to mean, and to require, mutual respect for self-government, national indepen-

dence, territorial integrity, self-determination and human rights—we are certainly not 'at peace' with the Soviet Union, because the Russians are engaged, and have been engaged for a very long time, in a conscious policy of international expansion . . . what exists between the Soviet Union and the West is not peace as it is normally understood in our societies. (Jeane Kirkpatrick in *Encounter*, November 1983)

These two examples show that a situation—although not (any more) being one of actual war—is still perceived as problematic and unstable. Collocations such as 'real peace' or quasi-definitions are used to modify the current state (e.g., not yet an end of occupation of specific territories, not yet full equality for all political and/or ethnic groups, no mutual trust). The aspect of latent instability is also referred to in the following quotation by Russia's President Boris Yeltsin at the summit meeting of the Conference on Security and Co-operation in Europe, December 1994: 'Europe is in danger of plunging into a cold peace.'

The United Nations' *Agenda for Peace* (1992) presents a programme on how the organization intends to work effectively in post-Cold War times. 'Peacemaking,' 'peace-keeping,' 'post-conflict peace-building,' and 'preventive diplomacy' are listed as the most important actions. A textlinguistic-discursive analysis of the *Agenda* reveals the following semantic and conceptual links: (latent) conflicts are the reasons for peacemaking, peacekeeping, post-conflict peace-building, and preventive diplomacy. The ultimate purpose of all these actions is to prevent the renewed upsurge of conflict and, thus, to achieve and/or preserve peace (see *Conflict Resolution, Process of*).

From a semantic and cognitive perspective, different conceptions and meanings of 'peace' underlie these actions, which are defined as follows in the *Agenda* (1992: 11):

(a) *Peacemaking* is action to bring hostile parties to agreement, essentially through such peaceful means as those foreseen in Chapter VI of the Charter of the United Nations.

(b) *Peacekeeping* is the deployment of a United Nations presence in the field, hitherto with the consent of all the parties concerned, normally involving United Nations military and/or police personnel and frequently civilians as well. Peacekeeping is a technique that expands the possibilities for both the prevention of conflict and the making of peace.

(c) *Post-conflict peace-building* [is] action to identify and support structures which will tend to strengthen and solidify peace in order to avoid a relapse into conflict.

These three actions can be seen as steps in the achievement of a state which deserves the name 'peace' and which is more than the absence of war or violent conflict. All these actions are aimed at stopping conflicts and/or preventing their recurrence, although 'peacemaking' and 'peacekeeping' are (still) conceived as involving military means. 'Preventive diplomacy,' too, is conceptually linked to perceived conflicts:

(d) *Preventive diplomacy* is action to prevent disputes from arising between parties, to prevent existing disputes from escalating into conflicts and to limit the spread of the latter when they occur.

Among the aims of the United Nations are:

(a) to seek to identify at the earliest possible stage situations that could produce conflict, and to try through diplomacy to remove the sources of danger before violence results; . . .

(b) to stand ready to assist in building bonds of peaceful mutual benefit among nations formerly at war,

(c) to address the deepest causes of conflict: economic despair, social injustice and political oppression (*Agenda* 1992: 7-8).

A linguistic analysis shows that in all these contexts, the understanding of 'peace' can be compared to what Galtung calls 'structural violence' (as opposed to 'direct violence,' i.e., war, at the international level, or physically hurting somebody, at the interpersonal level). Structural violence, i.e., exploitation, marginalization, oppression, inequality, injustice, etc., of specific groups or people, is the main reason why conflicts may (re)occur at any time (see *Structural Violence and the Definition of Conflict*).

Both direct and structural violence are related to, what Galtung calls 'negative peace', since the underlying conception is still that the parties involved have to be kept apart, to be stopped from fighting each other (see *Positive versus Negative Peace*). Forms of structural violence are determined by power relations, both within a country, i.e., power relations between social or political groups, and between countries and people, e.g., questions of dominance and hegemony on an international level. A question of interest for linguistic research is to find out how such forms of structural violence are reflected in discourse, either in certain genres or in individual texts. In this respect, the linguistic (sub)disciplines of *critical discourse analysis, conversational analysis, language policy*, and *contact linguistics* have made valuable contributions.

Being aware of the fact that linguistic differences sometimes cause inter-group conflict within nation states, *language policy,* for example, studies the role which individual languages play in a society. This discipline examines which languages are used (or allowed to be used) in which communicative situations, which provisions are made (e.g., by law) to ensure that all speakers are competent in their mother-tongue, which provisions are made for second and foreign language learning, etc. In other words, questions of *language planning* are an essential part of *language policy*, and there may even be situations in which language is a direct instrument of discrimination and oppression. *Contact linguistics*, in addition to studying the effects on linguistic systems (e.g., lexical borrowings), is particularly concerned with research on multilingualism in relation to the language users (the structuring of the social groups and their roles in a multicultural society, the status and the role of minority languages, the linguistic rights of minorities; cf. Nelde 1992).

Such studies are related to the general aspect of language and social discrimination, i.e., discriminatory social practices which adversely affect the relations between social groups in a state. Discriminatory practices may be based on race, social class, ethnicity, gender, or age. Linguistic research can provide insights into how language is used to communicate and consolidate ideologies (social beliefs, attitudes, values, stereotypes) that sustain social discrimination. For example, using the linguistic approaches of *conversational analysis or ethnomethodology* (which are, however, closely related to text and discourse analysis and to cognitive linguistics), it has been shown that lexical choices (e.g., 'Negroes' or 'Afro-Americans' or 'blacks'; or making gender linguistically visible by using double forms, such as 'he/she'), syntactic structures (e.g., active vs passive sentences), speech acts (e.g., orders, requests, promises), the selection or avoidance of arguments in particular discourses, the management or manipulation of turn-taking in interaction (e.g., in asymmetrical interaction, such as in interviews, or between teacher and student, or expert and layperson), etc., are all evidence of structural violence in a society (cf. the contributions in Schäffner and Wenden, eds, 1995). More recent developments in linguistics also study discourse on the environment and on the relationship between human beings and nature (*eco-linguistics*).

Linguistic research has demonstrated that language

directly or indirectly contributes to maintaining (and maybe even) justifying war and inegalitarian discursive practices. *Critical discourse analysis* (or *critical linguistics*) deals with power, dominance, hegemony, inequality, and the discursive processes of their enactment, concealment, legitimation and reproduction. Apart from uncovering (unequal) power relationships by investigating language behaviour in natural speech situations, amongst the aims of critical discourse analysis are included the need to draw up proposals for practical implementation (e.g., designing textbooks, conducting training seminars for teachers, lawyers, etc.).

In this respect, critical discourse analysis is closely linked with critical language education. Wenden (1995b) argues for an educational strategy which helps readers and listeners to acquire the knowledge and skills that are necessary in order to assess critically both text and talk. Moreover, the purpose of such a strategy is the empowerment of discourse participants to dissent, to raise for critical discussion, and, thus, change discursive practices which hinder the achievement of a comprehensive peace. With this practical orientation, critical discourse analysis has much in common with studies of peace education.

Critical discourse analysis aims to contribute, on the one hand, to the enhancement of the academic discipline, and, on the other hand, to the advancement of society. With this dual focus, it can provide useful contributions to interdisciplinary research into issues related to peace.

See also: *Communication: Key to World Peace*

Bibliography ——————————————————

Boutros-Ghali B 1992 *An Agenda for Peace: Preventive Diplomacy, Peacemaking and Peace-Keeping.* Report of the Secretary-General pursuant to the statement adopted by the Summit Meeting of the Security Council on 31 January 1992, United Nations, New York

Burkhardt A, Hebel F, Hoberg R (eds.) 1989 *Sprache zwischen Militär und Frieden: Aufrüstung der Begriffe?* Narr, Tübingen

Chilton P (ed.) 1985 *Language and the Nuclear Arms Debate: Nukespeak Today.* Pinter, London

Chilton P, Lakoff G 1995 Foreign policy by metaphor. In: Schäffner C, Wenden A (eds.) *Language and Peace.* Aldershot, Dartmouth

Fairclough N, Wodak R 1997 Critical discourse analysis. In: van Dijk T A (ed.) *Discourse as Social Interaction*, Vol. 2 of Discourse Studies: *A Multidisciplinary Introduction.* Sage, London

Fillmore C J 1985 Frames and the Semantics of Understanding.

Quaderni di Semantica vi(2)

Galtung J 1964 'Editorial'. *J. Peace Research* 1(1)

Galtung J 1969 Violence, peace, and peace research. *J. Peace Research* 6(3)

Jay A (ed.) 1996 The Oxford Dictionary of Political Quatitions. Oxford University Press, Oxford

Lakoff G 1986 *Cognitive Semantics.* Berkeley Cognitive Science Report 36, Berkeley

Lakoff G 1992 Metaphor and war. The metaphor system used to justify war in the Gulf. In: Pütz M (ed.) *Thirty Years of Linguistic Evolution. Studies in the Honour of René Dirven.* Benjamins, Philadelphia/ Amsterdam

Mehan H, Skelley J M 1988 Reykjavik: The breach and repair of the pure war script. In: Mehan H, Skelley J M (eds.) *Discourse of the Nuclear Arms Debate* (= *Multilingua*, Vol. 7, No. 1/2)

Nelde P 1992 Multilingualism and Contact Linguistics. In: Pütz Ma (ed.) *Thirty Years of Linguistic Evolution. Studies in the Honour of René Dirven.* Benjamins, Philadelphia/ Amsterdam

Pasierbsky F 1983 *Krieg und Frieden in der Sprache.* Fischer, Frankfurt/M

Rosch E 1977 Human categorization. In: Warren N (ed.) *Studies in Cross-Cultural Psychology,* Vol. 1. Academic Press, New York

Schäffner C 1986 Themawörter zum "NATO-Doppelbeschluß" im *Economist und Guardian.* In: Schäffner C, Neubert A (eds.) 1986 *Politischer Wortschatz in textueller Sicht, (= Linguistische Studien,* LS/ZISW/A, 146). Zentralinstitut für Sprachwissenschaft, Berlin

Schäffner C 1995 The balance metaphor in relation to peace. In: Schäffner C, Wenden A (eds.) *Language and Peace.* Aldershot, Dartmouth

Schäffner C, Wenden A (eds.) 1995 *Language and Peace.* Aldershot, Dartmouth

Stephenson M, Weal J (eds.) 1985 *Nuclear Dictionary.* Longman, Horlow

Sykes J B (ed.) 1976 *The Concise Oxford Dictionary of Current English*, 6th edn. Clarendon Press, Oxford

The Oxford Dictionary of Political Quotations 1996 edited by Jay A, Oxford University Press, Oxford

van Dijk T A 1980 *Macrostructures. An Interdisciplinary Study of Global Structures in Discourse, Interaction and Cognition.* Erlbaum, Hillsdale, NJ

van Dijk T A 1988 *News as Discourse.* Erlbaum, Hillsdale, NJ

Wenden A 1995a Defining peace: Perspectives from peace research. In: Schäffner C, Wenden A (eds.) *Language and Peace.* Aldershot, Dartmouth

Wenden A 1995b Critical language education. In: Schäffner C, Wenden A (eds.) *Language and Peace.* Aldershot, Dartmouth

CHRISTINA SCHÄFFNER

Lansbury, George

George Lansbury (1859-1940) was one of the leading figures of the British Labour Party in the first half of the twentieth century. Lansbury's political career, owing to his stubborn and uncompromising conscience, was extraordinarily turbulent. He began as a moderate in the Liberal Party, but by 1892 had converted to Marxism and joined the Social Democrats. By the end of the decade he had become disenchanted with Marxism and returned to a passionate belief in Christianity, which he maintained throughout his life.

Lansbury remained committed to socialism and became an active member of the new Labour Party. After holding various government offices in London, he was elected to parliament in 1910. Just two years later, though, discouraged by the Labour Party's general lack of militancy, particularly of the issue of women's suffrage which he strongly supported, Lansbury resigned his seat. In 1912 he ran, unsuccessfully, for election to parliament without party backing on a platform stressing votes for women.

When the First World War broke out, Lansbury again found himself at odds with most of the Labour Party because of his unswerving opposition to that conflict. Indeed, Lansbury was an uncompromising pacifist whose opposition to all war was mitigated only by the idea that a war against capitalism, which he considered to be the father of war and all other human miseries, might be worth fighting. Throughout the conflict he criticized Britain's participation from his position as editor of the radical weekly newspaper, *The Guardian.*

After the war, reconciled with the Labour Party, he was again elected to parliament in 1922, this time to serve until his death 18 years later. When the Labour Party came to power in 1929, Lansbury entered the cabinet as minister of works. His efforts to combat unemployment by sponsoring public works projects, while energetic, were overwhelmed by the Great Depression. In 1931 Lansbury led a revolt of militant Labourites against party leader Ramsay MacDonald's coalition with the Conservatives, and became the leader of what was left of the Labour Party in parliament. In 1935, however, when Fascist Italy invaded Ethiopia, the Labour Party voted to support whatever action the League of Nations took against Italy, even if this entailed war. As a pacifist, Lansbury campaigned strenuously against this position, and when he lost he resigned from the party leadership.

Lansbury spent the remainder of his life in a feverish campaign to try to halt the drift toward war. In addition to writing numerous pamphlets urging the adoption of pacifist principles, he counseled young conscientious objector (see *Conscientious Objection*) and traveled through Europe, imploring leaders everywhere to abandon their preparations for war. In parliament, he fought hard against British rearmament, which he felt increased the chances of war. His hopes were shattered by the Nazi invasion of Poland and Britain's declaration of war on Germany in September 1939. His health deteriorated rapidly after war broke out, and he died a few months later.

Bibliography

Lansbury G 1935 *Looking Backwards and Forwards.* London
Lansbury G 1938 *My Quest for Peace.* Michael Joseph, London
Lansbury G 1940 *This Way to Peace.* London
Naylor J F 1969 *Labour's International Policy.* Weidenfield and Nicolson, London
Postgate R 1951 *The Life of George Lansbury.* Longmans, London

GARRETT L. MCAINSH

Lao Tzu

Lao Tzu a Chinese philosopher of the sixth century BC, is known primarily as the author of a Taoist classic, the *Tao te Ching* (also known simply as the *Lao Tzu*).

Lao Tzu charged that poverty and starvation were caused by bad rulers, that greed and avarice resulted in wars and killing, and that the desire for wealth, power, and glory brought about the destruction of society. (His sage king "has no personal ideas. He regards the people's ideas as his own.") "The sage, in the government of his empire, has no subjective viewpoint. His mind forms a harmonious whole with that of his people."

Unlike Confucius, Lao Tzu emphasized the metaphysical principles of nature. Whereas Confucianism stressed the moral goodness of humankind as the key to happiness and peace, Taoism emphasized the harmony and simplicity of nature. To find peace and contentment, humankind must follow the Tao of the universe in which there is no strife, no competition, and no war. Unlike Confucius again, Lao Tzu considered that morality could not remove competition nor strife but that the great Tao is always without desire. Peace is accomplished not by action driven by desire, but by inaction inspired by the simplicity of the Tao. According to Lao Tzu,

> Tao invariably takes no action, and yet there is nothing left undone.
> If kings and barons can keep it, all things will transform spontaneously.
> If, after transformation, they should desire to be active.
> I would restrain them with simplicity, which has no name.
> Simplicity, which has no name, is free of desires.
> Being free of desires, it is tranquil.
> And the world will be at peace of its own accord.
> He who assists the ruler with Tao does not dominate the world with force.
> The use of force usually brings requital.
> Wherever armies are stationed, briers and thorns grow.
> Great wars are always followed by famines.
> A good [general] achieves his purpose and stops,
> But dares not seek to dominate the world.

Lao Tzu's advice to rulers is that they should govern as little as possible, keeping to the natural way, *laissez-faire*, letting people go their own way. He suggests that people are difficult to rule because the ruler does too many things. What the ruler should keep in mind is that "ruling a big country is like cooking a small fish." In cooking a small fish, one must take care not to handle it too roughly for too much handling will spoil it. In ruling a country, care must be taken not to push the people around, forcing them to rebel. When the people are satisfied there will be no rebellion or wars. Therefore, the less the government give to the people, the less war there will be. Thus, at the end of the *Tao te Ching*, Lao Tzu's utopia sounds like that of Jean-Jacques Rousseau's notions of insularity and solitude. Rousseau preferred *"un État très petit où le peuple soit facile à rassembler et où chaque citoyen puisse aisément connaître tous les autres."* For Rousseau, small was beautiful.

Like Rousseau, Lao Tzu preferred his community as small as possible.

> Let there be a small country with few people.
> Let there be ten times and a hundred times as many utensils.
> But let them not be used.
> Let the people value their lives highly and not migrate far.
> Even if there are ships and carriages, none will ride in them.
> *Even if there are armor and weapons, none will display them.*
> Let the people again knot cords and use them (in place of writing).
> Let them relish their food, beautify their clothing, be content with their homes, and delight in their customs.
> Though neighboring communities overlook one another and the crowing of cocks and barking of dogs can be heard,
> Yet the people there may grow old and die without ever visiting one another.

Lao Tzu's implicit naturalistic morality was based on condemnation of the assertive use of the will because this was the cause of all unnecessary suffering in the world. The content of the *Tao te Ching* consisted, first, in avoiding the consequences of such "willful action" as war, competition, exploitation of the common people, and alteration of the natural world, and second, in cultivating values such as simplicity and spontaneity that coincide with the ability "to act with no willful action."

See also: *Taoism*

Bibliography ───────────

Lao Tzu 1969 *Tao te Ching*. Penguin, Harmondsworth
Waley A D 1977 *The Way and its Power: The Tao te Ching and its Place in Chinese Thought*. Unwin, London

DAVID DAI

League of Arab States

This article provides the background as well as additional information about the Arab League. It also examines the role of the Arab League in general in addition to the conflict resolution in the region in

particular. In other words, it aims at understanding and reviewing the ability of the Arab League in creating a peaceful environment and coexisting among the Arab States (see *Peace and Regional Integration*).

This article deals with the establishment of the Arab League, the relation between the pact and role of the Arab League in achieving Arab unity, the role and the authority of the Secretary-General of the Arab League, and the Arab League and the conflict resolution in the region.

1. Historical Background: The Establishment of the Arab League

During the second world war, some Arab countries obtained their independence, and the "desire for greater unity and strength, was very popular among the Arabs" (Lenczowski 1956: 501). There was a widespread Arab hatred of the Western colonialists, who occupied most of the Arab countries, and especially Britain. Many revolutionary movements emerged against Britain which occupied many Arab countries. In this period and under these conditions, the British government decided to support some form of regional amalgamation in the Arab world[1].

There were some military and political considerations and interests which had been suggested as having influenced Britain's decision. Some of them were:

(a) To stop the widespread anti-British feeling, especially after Britain's decision to establish a national state for the Jews in Palestine.

(b) To earn the support of the Arab countries against the Axis states.

(c) An Arab Historian commented on the establishment of the Arab League and its Pact, saying that "Maybe Britain wanted the league as a device to prevent any Arab action serving Arab interest or threatening the British interests." (Mohafzah 1983 p. 52)

It has also been said "the league was born as a result of two main influences, Arab nationalism and British support" (Hassouna 1975 p. 3).

On September 25, 1944 a preparatory committee was formed from delegates of the only seven independent Arab States (Egypt, Lebanon, Iraq, Trans-Jordan, Saudi Arabia, Syria, and Yemen Arab Republic). They met in Alexandria (Egypt) to discuss proposals regarding Arab unity. The main issue discussed in the conference was the type of structural organization that would be established to help serve the Arab unity. Three political formations were discussed by the delegations:

First, "Full-union:" "It would have central authority over all Arab States" (Hassouna 1975 p. 6). This proposal was rejected by all but Syria.

Second, "Federated state:" "It would have an assembly representing the participating states and an executive committee responsible before the assembly and with full powers over federal issues" (Hassouna 1975 p. 6). This was also rejected.

Third, "Union without Executive Powers:" This was accepted by all states. Later on, it led to the formation of the Arab League.

It is worth noting that the consultations in the preparatory committee indicated that the Arab leaders were not serious about the idea of Arab unity. They also didn't intend to achieve such an Arab unity because they wanted to keep the regional divisions of the Arab world. Their purposes became apparent during the meeting. According to the president of the preparatory committee Mustapha al-Nahas Basha (the Prime Minister of Egypt) who made this case clear, " It has been unanimously decided not to form a central authority over all Arab countries; because it would be difficult to do that and it would cost the independence of each Arab country that wants to remain independent."[2]

The preparatory committee of the Alexandria conference ended its meeting on October 7, 1944, and signed an agreement which was called the "Alexandria protocol." The preparatory committee decided to form a political sub-committee to define the pact of the Arab league. It met in Cairo from February 14, to March 3, 1945, and it prepared the draft pact for the league. The preparatory committee held its second session to study and approve the draft pact on March 22, 1945, the seven Arab states approved this pact which was called the pact of the League of Arab States[3].

2. General Review of the League of Arab States

2.1 Aims of the League of Arab States

The aims of the Arab League were defined in the pact of the Arab League. These aims include the following:

(a) Strengthening the ralations between the member states, and encouraging political and economic cooperation as well as cooperation in Other Affairs (Article 2).

(b) Preserving the Arab States independence and their sovereignty (Article2).

(c) Dealing with the affairs and interests of the Arab States (Article 2).

(d) Maintaining peace and security in the Arab World (Article 5 and 6).

(e) Deciding upon ways of collaboration with other international organizations (Article 3).

2.2 Membership

The conditions of membership of the Arab league are defined by Article 1 of its pact:

(a) The member should be an Arab State.

(b) It should be an independent state.[4]

(c) It shall lodge a petition of adhesion to the league.

(d) The council of the Arab league will ratify this Arab state as a member in the Arab league.

2.3 Identity and Philosophy of the Arab League

The League of Arab States is a regional organization.[5] Its philosophy is based on Arab nationalism (see *Nationalism*).

In fact, the pact of the League of Arab states had not referred directly to the identity and philosophy of the Arab League[6], but we can deduce that from many aspects of the league. Firstly, the name of the League of Arab States indicates that the league belongs to Arab States.

Secondly, the most important factor regarding the conditions of membership in the League of Arab states is that all members should be Arab States, i.e., the league is Arab nationalist in identity.

Finally, the statements and declarations of some officials of the Arab League mentioned that the philosophy of the Arab League is based on Arab nationalism, for example: a previous Secretary-General of the Arab League[7] said on the League's fifteenth anniversary " the League is under obligation to Arab nationalism in all its activities."

2.4 Structure and Functions of the Arab League

The main bodies of the Arab League are:

The Council of the League of Arab States:

The council of the Arab states is the supreme power of the Arab League. It consists the representatives of member states. The level of representation is composed of the permanent representatives of the Arab League, or the Arab States foreign ministers, who are the main representatives, or the kings, presidents of Arab states. The council meets every year in two regular sessions, at the level of foreign ministers. The functions of the council are defined by the internal regulations of the council of the Arab League. Article 3 in the internal regulations of the council of the league defined the function as:

In order to fulfill the purposes of the League in accordance with the provisions of the pact, the council shall undertake the following:

(a) Formulating the general policy of the league and the work program of the council.

(b) Strengthening relations between member states, and coordinating their plans so as to achieve cooperation amongst them.

(c) Deciding on matters submitted to it by the Secretary-General or member states, and adopt the necessary resolutions thereon.

(d) Ensuring Implementation of its resolutions as well as of the agreements concluded by member states within the framework of the League.

(e) Examining the reports prepared by the specialized councils and organizations, and adopt the necessary resolutions thereon.

(f) Deciding on the means of cooperation with international organizations.

(g) Reviewing the administrative and financial affairs of the League.

The council may:

(a) Establish such consultative and technical committees as it deems necessary for the League to perform its functions, and select the members of these committees by secret ballot, from among candidates of member states specialized in the committee's respective field.

(b) Entrust to one or more of it members the study of a given subject and the presentation of a report thereon to be distributed among members at least one day prior to the meeting at which the subject is discussed.

Also, the pact of Arab League defined the functions of the council of the Arab League as:

(a) The resolution of disputes between the members of the Arab league by peaceful means. The council shall mediate in all differences which could threaten to lead to war between two member states or a member state and a third state, with a view to bringing about their reconciling (Article 5).

(b) Determining the measures necessary to repulse aggression or threat by one state (member of the league or non-member) against any member of the Arab League (Article 6).

(c) the council of the League appoints the Secretary-General, and it establishes an administrative regulation for the functions of the Secretariat-General, the permanent committee, and the council of the League (Articles 13 and 16-c).

(d) to approve the budget of the League, and fix the share of the expenses to be borne by each member of the Arab League (see Article 13 and 16-b).

The Permanent Committees

The pact of the Arab League mentions that special committees shall be formed in which the states participating in the League shall be represented. These committees shall be responsible for formulating the bases, extent and form of cooperation. Such bases shall be formulated as a draft agreement, to be presented to the council of the League.

There were also some committees formed by decision of the council of the League. The permanent committees are:

(a) Political Committee,

(b) Transport Committee,

(c) Legal Committee,

(d) Information Committee,

(e) Meteorological Observation Committee,

(f) Health Committee,

(g) Human Rights Committee,

(h) Financial and Administrative Committee,

(i) The Committee for the Communication of the Regional Offices for Israeli Boycott.

The Secretariat-General:

Article 12 in the pact of the Arab League mentioned the establishment of a Secretariat-General for the Arab League. The structure of the Secretariat-General is as seen in the diagram (for the role and authority of the secretary-general).

Joint Defense Council:

This council was established in 1950. It was formed by the Foreign and Defense Ministers of the Arab League members. Article 2, 3 and 4 of the Agreement of Joint Defense Council defined the main goals and tasks of this Council.

These goals and tasks can be summarized as follow:

(a) To support and defend, by all means including military means, any member of this council against any military aggression.

(b) To make efforts concerning common consultation and plans in case any threat against the security or independence of any member of the council.

(c) To improve cooperation between the members of the Arab League and reinforce the military capabilities of its members.

3. The Relation between the Pact and Role of Arab League in Achieving Arab Unity

The purpose here is not to analyze the details of the pact, but to review the ability and the extent to which the pact has been able to achieve Arab Unity, which is considered a strategic aim for and behind the Arab League, by mentioning some Articles of the Pact.

As it has been mentioned earlier, each Arab country in the preparatory committee of the Arab League was concerned with the protection of the principle which has led to the weakening of its role. It is reflected in the beginning of its pact namely in Article 2. This Article encourages cooperation among the members of the League, but without any surrender of their sovereignty to seek Arab unity. Thus, the principle of sovereignty of the Arab countries is opposed to the aim of Arab national unity.

Moreover, Article 1 of the Pact mentions the unanimity principle in voting. For example, votes and decisions of the league council are not binding for all the members. But only for those countries which accept its decisions. In other words the Arab League has no authority over any Arab State which refuses to accept the decisions of the Arab League, it can not oblige any state to agree on any step which leads to Arab unity.

Moreover, the Pact of the Arab League did not give (the league) effective instruments to oblige the members of the league to implement its decisions. Thus, some states may agree with the League's decisions but no body can force them to carry out these decisions.

In summary, it can be argued that the inclusion of these articles in the pact of the Arab League has not ensured the achievement of Arab unity.

4. The Role and the Authorities of Secretary-General

The Secretary-General is elected to a 5-year renewable term by the league's council. The Secretary-General has administrative, organizational as well as a political

Figure 1 The Structure of the Secretariat-General

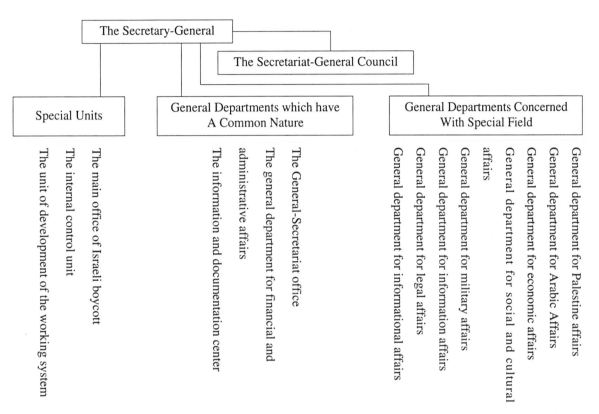

Source: This diagram is based on the data collected from: "the structural system of the Secretariat-General, the unit of development of the working system, and secretary of Arab League.

roles. The roles are defined in the pact of the Arab League, in the internal regulations of the secretariat, and through traditions and practices conducted by previous secretary generals. Most researchers state that the ineffectiveness of the legal framework (Macdonald 1965 pp. 240-243) and the absence of a judicial body to resolve disputes politically, led to and left room for the skills and personality of the Secretary-General as well as for his experience and relations to play an important role in making his political role more active particularly in resolving disputes peacefully.

The role and authorities of the Secretary-General can be summarized in the following points:

4.1 In the Administrative and Organizational Field

The Arab League through the Secretary-General usually invites the Arab States to participate in the emergency and the regular Arab League Summits.

In the regular summit, the League coordinates with the host country. In the emergency summits, it coordinates with the Arab States which call for the holding of the emergency summits.

The Secretariat-General which is headed by the Secretary-General prepares the drafts and the explanatory memoranda which relates to specific cases in the summits and the League Council. It organizes the secretariat works in co-operation with the host country. Articles 12-3, 4, 5 and 6 in the internal regulations of the council of the League mentions the main duties of the Secretariat/Secretary-General including:

(a) The Secretary-General shall undertake the organization of the secretariat of the council and its committees. He shall also supervise the drawing up of records of the deliberations which take place and the resolutions which are adopted. Verbatim records shall be prepared for all the meetings of the Council and its committees.

(b) The Secretariat-General shall receive and distribute the documents, reports and resolutions of the Council and its committees; shall prepare, print and circulate the records and the daily bulletins; shall file the documents, and shall undertake all the other functions required for the performance of the work of the council.

(c) The Secretary-General prepares the financial and administrative reports of the league which need the approval of the league council.

(d) The Secretary-General ensures the implementation of the decisions of the Arab Summit conferences or the league council.

(e) The Secretary-General executes the special functions that are assigned to the Arab League from the Arab Summit Conference or the league council.

4.2 In the Political Field

The Secretary-General usually attends the Meetings of the Arab summit conference, and he participates in the discussions of any case.

He encourages all the Arab states to participate in the summit conferences at the highest level.

He sometimes participates in the reconciliation of the differences between the Arab states during or after the ending of the Arab Summit meetings, by special meetings with the heads of state.

He presents the reports, studies and suggestions in political issues, which are submitted to the League from previous Arab Summits.

"The Secretary-General may draw the attention of the Council or the member states to any question which may prejudice the exiting relations among the Arab states or between them and other states" (Article 12-2 of internal regulation of the League Council).

Some Arab Summit conferences assigned the Secretary-General of the Arab League the task of making some political communications with some international political blocs.

He has also to ensure implementation of the political decisions of the Arab Summit Conferences.

The Secretary-General is given power by the internal regulation of the League Council. However, in reality, when meetings are held at the level of foreign ministers or Arab Leaders, it is the latter and not the Secretary-General who control the affairs of the meetings. The Secretary-General sometimes addresses a speech in the inaugural setting in the Arab Summit Conferences.

Sometimes he plays an important role in the coordination of the political positions and views of the Arab States in the international occasions and meetings with special attention given towards the Arab-Israeli conflict in particular.

In general, the political role of the Secretary-General is the settlement of the Arab disputes. His role depends on his personality and character, the political mission, the nature of the dispute, and disputing parties more than the legal or the political mechanism authorized to him by the League.

5. The Arab League and Conflict Resolution: Regional Disputes

5.1 The Arab League and the Arab Disputes

The pact of the Arab League defined, in Articles 5 and 6, the general framework for the roles and measures to be taken by the league to achieve a settlement of Arab disputes. The two articles mentioned:

Article 5: Any resort to force in order to resolve disputes arising between two or more member states of the League is prohibited. If there should arise among them a difference which does not concern a state's independence, sovereignty, or territorial integrity, and if the parties to the dispute have recourse to the council for the settlement of this deference, the decision of the council shall then be enforceable and obligatory.

In such a case, the states between whom the difference has arisen shall not participate in the deliberations and decisions of the council.

The council shall mediate in all differences which threaten to lead to war between two member states or a member state and a third state, with a view to bringing about their reconciliation.

Decisions of arbitration and mediation shall be taken by majority vote.

Article 6: In case of aggression or threat of aggression by one state against a member state, the state which has been attacked or threaten with aggression may demand the immediate convocation of the council.

The council shall by unanimous decision determine the measures necessary to repulse the aggression. If the aggressor is a member state, his vote shall not be counted in determining unanimity.

If, as a result of the attack, the government of the state attacked finds itself unable to communicate with the council, that state's representative in the council shall have the right to request the convocation of the council for the purpose indicated in the foregoing paragraph. In the event that this representative is unable to communicate with the council, any member state of the League shall have the right to request the convocation of the council.

Upon conducting a quantitative survey of the Arab League's role in the settlement of the Arab disputes from 1945 to 1981, the study found that the Arab League has not resolved but six out of sixty-seven Arab disputes that is only 8.95 percent of these disputes (Ahmed 1988 pp. 210-211). Moreover, the Arab League was not able to resolve a large number of the Arab disputes in the 1980s and 1990s. Some of which being: The Arab-Egyptian disputes (1979-89) , The Algerian, Moroccan, and Mauritania dispute (1979), The Iraqi-Syrian dispute (1979-96), The Jordanian-Syrian dispute (1980-85), The Jordanian-Palestinian dispute (1986-88), The Sudani, Yemeni, Iraqi-Kuwaiti dispute (1990-97),The Qatari-Bahrain dispute (1982-97), and the Saudi-Qatari dispute (1992).

The Arab League's role in the settlement of Arab disputes can be classified as follows:

(a) Disputes in which the Arab League did not interfere at all. For example, The Jordanian-PLO dispute in 1970 and the Saudi-Qatari dispute in 1992.

(b) Disputes which the Arab League made an attempt to resolve but failed to do so. For example, The Algerian, Moroccan, Morrotanian disputes (1979), The Iraqi-Kuwaiti dispute in 1990 (although the Arab league was not given a real opportunity to resolve this conflict due to regional, and international factors.

(c) Disputes in which the Arab League was able to play a key role in resolving, or at least in preventing such disputes from occurring. They include the Iraqi-Kuwaiti dispute in 1961, and the Libyan-Egyptian war 1977.

Article 5 of the pact of the Arab League stated that the two mechanisms to be used in resolving Arab disputes peacefully are mediation and arbitration.

Throughout its course, the Arab League has made use of two methods as complement mediation in resolving Arab disputes. They are the "fact finding" method and the "goodwill efforts." Moreover, the "buffer zone" method was used by sending joint-Arab troops under the leadership of the Arab League.

Another mechanism which was used by the Arab League to resolve Arab disputes is the Arab Summit conferences Diplomacy. The League participated in creating a positive atmosphere of diplomacy among the Arab leaders during the holding of the Arab Summit Conferences. This was done by encouraging the parties to discuss their disputes.

Although there has been a proposal for an Arab Court of Justice since its beginning in the 1950s, the Arab League still does not have a judicial body to resolve the Arab dispute in a peaceful manner. Most of the Arab states did not accept the proposal for an Arab court of justice for political reasons due to the nature of the Arab national regimes.

Usually, the party of the league which deal with Arab disputes is the League's Council in addition to Secretariat-General.

5.2 Arab League and the Arab-Israeli Conflict

The league has played an active role in the political, economical, and military aspects of the Arab-Israeli conflict since its beginning in the 1948.

5.2.1 In the Political Field

The League played an important role in unifying the Arab policies and stands towards Israel since its early stages. The League played a role in several issues: the Arab's opposition to the United Nations resolution regarding the partition of Palestine 1947, opposing the creation of an Israeli state in the Arab World in 1948, and in unifying the Arab stands toward opposing peace and negotiations with Israel until 1982. Nonetheless, the League accepted the Arab Israeli co-existence after that.

The Arab League also participated in gathering support to the Palestinians and the Palestinian issue at the Arab as well as international levels. It also passed a resolution calling for the forming of the PLO in 1964.

5.2.2 In the Economic Field

The Arab League participated in the coordination and unification of efforts toward imposing economical Arab sanctions against Israel. Nevertheless, the period of the 1990's has witnessed more flexibility on imposing these sanctions due to the Palestinian and Jordanian peace treaties with Israel.

The Arab League encouraged its members to lend economic support to the Palestinians and the Arab front-line states. During the Palestinian uprising, intifada, which started in December 1987, the Arab League specified a budget for the uprising through the Arab Summit Conference in 1988.

5.2.3 In the Military Field

The Arab League gathered Arab volunteers to support the Palestinians in the Arab-Israeli war in 1948. At the same time, it urged the Arab states to participate in the war against Israel. The League also gathered the Arab Armies in 1961 to prevent Israel from changing the flow of the Jordan River to its side.

The Joint Arab Defense Council of the Arab League sent armies as well as military equipment to the confrontation countries to strengthen their position against Israel during the Arab Israeli war in October 1973. Since then, the Arab League has not played a military role against Israel even during the Israeli invasion of Beirut in 1982.

6. Conclusion

The League of Arab States is under the control of the Arab regimes which have conflicting political views as well as policies. It cannot, therefore, challenge any Arab States whose policy may be against that of the Arab League or Arab unity. Also, it can not oblige any Arab State to follow the policy of Arab cooperation or unity. The practical position indicates that the Arab popular interaction with the Arab League is very limited. because it can not make marked achievements in the sphere of Arab Unity. It is also under the control of Arab regimes of which the majority lack popular support. Therefore, the Arab League is not a real decision-maker.

In summary, these points, while not forming a final or an overall evaluation of the Arab League, do indicate the inability of the league to achieve a serious Arab cooperation or unity, which is stated as one of its strategic aims without a serious Arab political will to improve and activate the political, military and economic role of the Arab League. However, this active role can be contradicted with the self-interest of most Arab regimes.

See also: *Pan-Arabism; Integration Regional; Integration Theories*

Notes

1. On 29 May 1941, Foreign Secretary Eden, declared "The Arab World has made greater strides since the settlement reached at the end of the last war, and many Arab thinkers desire for the Arab people a greater degree of unity than they now enjoy. In reaching out towards this unity they hope for support. No such appeal from our friends should go unanswered. It seems to me both natural and right that the cultural, and economic ties too, should be strengthened. His Majesty's Government for their part give their full support to any scheme that commands general approval. *The Times*, 30 May 1941, p. 5.

On 24 February 1943, he declared "As I have already made plain, the British Government would view with sympathy any movement among the Arab to promote economic, cultural or political unity, but clearly the initiative in any scheme would have to come from the Arab themselves. So far as I am aware, no such scheme which commands general approval has yet been worked out. *Parliamentary Debates*, House of Commons, Vol. 387, Col. 139, 24 February 1943.

2. The minutes of the preparatory committee, the fourth minutes which held in 2,10, 1944, p. 29, quoted in Shoun Arabia, no. 31, Sept. 1983, p. 31.

3. Later, all the Arab States signed this pact as members of the Arab League. They were: Libya 28/3/1953; Sudan 19/1/1956; Tunisia 1/10/1958; Morocco 1/10/1958; Kuwait 20/7/1961; Algeria 16/8/1962; People's Democratic Republic of Yemen 12/12/1967; Bahrain 11/9/1971; Qatar 11/9/1971; Oman 29/9/1971; United Arab Emirates 6/12/1971; Mauritania 26/11/1973; Somalia 14/ 2/1974; Palestine 9/9/1976; Djibouti 4/9/1977.

4. There was an exception for Palestine.

5. It has obtained recognition from the United Nations as a regional organization, and it has a permanent representative there.

6. The proposal of the pact amendment, which is waiting to be ratified by an Arab summit, mentioning directly that the league is an Arab nationalist organization.

7. He is Abdul Khalik Hassounah, who was the Secretary-General of the Arab league from 1952 to 1972.

8. Article 12/2.

Bibliography

Ahmed Y A 1988 *The Arab-Arab Conflicts: A Study of Survey 1945-1981*. Center for Arab Unity Studies, Beirut

Hassouna H 1975 *The League of Arab States and Regional Disputes: A Study of Middle East Conflicts*. Oceana Publications Inc

Internal Regulations of the Council of the League of Arab States

Internal Regulations of the Secretariat-General of the League of the Arab States

Lenczowoski G 1956 *The Middle East in World Affairs*, 2nd edn. Cornell University Press, New York

Macdonald R W 1965 *The League of Arab States: A Study in the Dynamic of Regional Organization*. Princeton Press, Princeton, NJ

Mater J et al. 1993 *The Arab League: The Historical Experience and the Development Projects*. Center for Political Research and Studies, Cairo University, Cairo

Mohafzah M et al. 1983 *The League of Arab States between the Current Situation and the Ambition*. Center for Arab Unity Studies, Beirut

The Agreement of Joint Defense and Economic Cooperation between the States of Arab League

The Pact of the League of Arab States

SAMI AL-KHAZENDAR

League of Nations

To dismiss the League of Nations simply as an organization that failed to prevent the Second World War is as facile and superficial as it is erroneous. As with the United Nations organization that succeeded it, the League can be seen as the flawed embodiment of human frailty in collective decision making; but it was also the first attempt at a framework to preserve the peace and pursue economic and technical unity in a global setting. To be aware of the true place of the League of Nations in history—to see it in the round, to balance its successes and failures, and to draw out its lessons—it has to be looked at in detail, with an awareness that all human institutions must be viewed in the mental and technical context of their time.

Both time and place were propitious for this first essay in world coordination. The idea of a "League of Nations" had been mooted in Europe for some time, but it fell to Woodrow Wilson, a constitutional lawyer and professor of political science who had become US President after that country had been dragged into the First World War in 1917 by the pressure of events, to push the idea at the Paris Peace Conference of 1919 in the last of his "Fourteen Points." Wilson chaired the Committee set up in January 1919 to draft the League of Nations Covenant, and in June of that year the Covenant was finally incorporated into the Treaty of Versailles. Meanwhile the League Secretariat had been set up in London under Sir Eric Drummond, its first Secretary-General, so that both the Treaty of Versailles and the League Covenant entered into force on January 10, 1920. In November 1920 the League moved its headquarters to the "Hotel National," later renamed the Palais Wilson and sited on the shore of Lake Geneva.

At the outset an uncertain political future for the League was foreshadowed in various ways, first of all by the uneasy accommodation that had to be reached between an uncomplicated but inexperienced world view as embodied in Wilson's Fourteen Points and the narrow nationalistic intriguing of hard-bitten Old World politicians, some of whom were intent, shortsightedly but perhaps not unnaturally, on squeezing the utmost in reparations out of a defeated warmongering antagonist.

Even the choice of Geneva as headquarters, against the rival claims of Brussels and Paris, was decided in part by extraneous personal advocacy, though the claims of Geneva in terms of location, humanitarian traditions, neutrality, and tolerance amid variety made it preeminent for the purpose (see *Geneva, Spirit of*).

But there were innate flaws in the League's conception. First, it was not truly a world body. By December 1920 its membership of 48 states did include over 70 percent of all nominally independent territories, while by 1937 this number had risen to 57, but there were some notable absentees and resignations. Despite Woodrow Wilson's original role, the US Senate eventually refused to accept League membership; Germany was excluded until 1926, and resigned, like Japan, in 1935; while the Soviet Union refused to join on ideological grounds until 1934. On the other hand, China was a member from 1920, as were a number of self-governing entities of the British Empire (Australia, Canada, and New Zealand) as well as India and South Africa. The ten states of Eastern Europe (excluding the Soviet Union) were all members by 1922, as was Switzerland, although the successful referendum required for that country to join was a close-run thing, except in Geneva itself.

Another flaw in the League's conception was the unanimity rule contained in Article 5 of the Covenant, which required that, with certain exceptions, decisions at the League's Assembly or Council should "require the agreement of all the Members . . . represented at the meeting"—at least insofar as decisions were binding on governments. As there was no quorum beyond a majority of members, while delegates abstaining were counted as absent, a distinction was made between decisions and majority recommendations. These and several other stratagems came to be used in practice to attain what looked like meaningful results. In Assembly Committees, decisions were commonly reached by simple majority. It was widely held that parties to disputes should not vote, but this rule, followed in five boundary cases between 1922 and 1927, was ignored in 1928 and 1931, when opposition, from Lithuania and Japan respectively, led to no decision being reached. Although less difficulty was experienced over the unanimity rule in the League's Council than in its Assembly, it was generally felt that the rule did considerably handicap the organization's ability to reach real decisions.

1. The League's Structure

Looking at the range of the League's activities one is struck first by the innovating "modernity" of the non-political side of the League's world view at a time when communications were rudimentary by today's standards and no precedents were on hand; and second, by how closely the League foreshadowed its successor, the United Nations, in certain respects.

The Covenant was the fundamental Charter that regulated acceptable peaceful behaviour by imposing acceptance of:

(a) An obligation not to resort to war and to safeguard peace,

(b) A perception of just and equitable relations between states,

(c) Undertakings of international law and maintenance of justice,

(d) Respect for all treaty obligations,

(e) Preservation of the territorial integrity and existing independence of all member states.

In Article 11 the Council was given the widest powers in exercising its task as the guardian of peace. Arbitration, or judicial settlement, was provided for in respect of any dispute involving a breach of an international obligation.

Article 16 provided for full sanctions by all members against any member resorting to war, in order to end hostilities. In addition and where necessary, the Council could recommend to governments concerned "what effective military, naval or air force the Members . . . shall severally contribute to the armed forces to be used to protect the covenants of the League." In 1929 the United Kingdom proposed to the tenth Assembly an amendment to the Covenant to prohibit all war except in self-protection or for approved police operations. After two years' work this was found impracticable and unpalatable to certain states so that the idea was eventually dropped.

To understand the League's wider field of action, an outline of its full structure is set out in Table 1.

The Assembly, comprising representatives of all member states, convened once a year in Geneva, normally at the beginning of September. Like its successor, the UN General Assembly, the Assembly was assisted by a number of committees dealing with special questions. At plenary sessions the public was admitted by card.

In the League's Covenant it was laid down that the Council, the other main political organ, should "consist of representatives of the Principal Allied and Associated Powers," together with those of four other members of the League selected by the Assembly "from time to time at its discretion." This meant that, like the UN Security Council, there were permanent members (initially intended to be the United Kingdom, France, Italy, Japan, and the United States) and nonpermanent elected members. Germany became a permanent member in 1926 and the then Soviet Union

in 1934. Nonpermanent members originally comprised Belgium, Brazil, Spain, and Greece, but the number was later increased to nine, with a wide range of states participating, including China. The Council met three or more times a year and, like the Assembly, was competent to deal with any question within the League's purview, or affecting world peace.

2. The League's Work

In the public mind the work of the League was overwhelmingly oriented to the maintenance of big-power peace and little else. This was, and is, in the case of the public's view of United Nations work today, encouraged by the fact that publicity media thrive on questions that offer confrontational headlines. It remains true, however, that any outline of the League's work must stress its very strong efforts to achieve global peace, hold down the arms trade, and resolve a widespread series of international disputes. This, as we know, was not a field in which the organization had any lasting success. Its real accomplishments lay in a range of far less dramatic but fundamental areas of international accord which can only be briefly mentioned.

The following are some foundations of international effort where serious work was pursued or begun:

(a) Abolition of war and quest for secure disarmament,

(b) Settlement of international disputes,

(c) Mandates system for dependent territories,

(d) Protection of national minorities,

(e) Economic and financial cooperation,

(f) Transport and communications cooperation,

(g) Health activity and disease control,

(h) Intellectual cooperation (in education, intellectual rights, films, and so on),

(i) Social and humanitarian work (welfare of women and children, detention, and so on),

(j) Campaign against drugs,

(k) Refugee relief work,

(l) Slavery,

(m) International law,

(n) Creation of common international statistics,

(o) Technical cooperation with states,

Figure 1
Structure of the League of Nations

LEAGUE OF NATIONS ASSEMBLY

COMMITTEES:
1. Legal and constitutional
2. Technical organizations
3. Reduction of armaments
4. Budgetary questions
5. Social and general questions
6. Political questions (mandates, slavery, and so on)

COUNCIL

SECRETARIAT

AUXILIARY ORGANIZATIONS:
1. Economic and Financial
2. Communications and Transit
3. Health
4. Intellectual Cooperation
5. Advisory Commission: Military, Naval, and Air
6. Mandates Commission
7. Commission of Enquiry for European Union
8. Advisory Commission for Protection and Welfare (children and so on)
9. A. Advisory Committee: Opium and Dangerous Drugs
   B. Central Opium Board
   C. Supervisory Body
10. Supervisory Commission
11. Committee on Allocation of Expenses
12. Advisory Committee of Experts on Slavery

HIGH COMMISSARIAT FOR THE FREE CITY OF DANZIG

INTERNATIONAL LABOUR ORGANIZATION

PERMANENT COURT OF INTERNATIONAL JUSTICE

SPECIAL INTERNATIONAL INSTITUTES:
1. Intellectual Cooperation (Paris)
2. Unification of Private Law (Rome)
3. Educational Cinematographic Institute (Rome)
4. Nansen Office for Refugees (Geneva)
5. Centre for Research on Leprosy (Rio de Janeiro)

Of many initiatives on peace and disarmament four major efforts should be mentioned. First, in 1924, Ramsay Macdonald and Edouard Herriot placed before the Assembly a resolution—the Protocol of Geneva—proposing general disarmament linked to compulsory arbitration and guarantees of security which, though not implemented, did inspire the League's subsequent work. Next, the Locarno Treaty of 1925, between the United Kingdom, France, Germany, Italy, and Belgium, served to achieve a temporary reconciliation between Germany and its Western partners which brought the former into League membership until 1933. In 1932 came a lengthy Conference on Disarmament and the Reduction of Armaments that had been planned since the League's early days. Despite wide public participation, however, this conference produced no tangible results. Just before this, in 1930, Aristide Briand of France had submitted a plan for a European Union inspired by the looming economic crisis of the 1930s and aimed also at an eventual political union of European states. Finally, we can mention the Argentine Anti-War Pact concluded at Rio de Janeiro in 1933, which was acceded to by 24 states, 18 in Latin America plus five European countries and the United States.

Although these major efforts produced relatively few lasting results, solutions were found to some of the many international disputes that received attention. This was true of some border problems, such as those between Greece and Bulgaria (1925) and between Colombia and Peru in 1933. But the organization proved unable to resolve a number of important conflicts such as those between China and Japan and between Italy and Ethiopia, as well as the key problem of German rearmament. These failures were to signal the declining influence and eventual collapse of the League.

The League's mandates system and other arrangements for the protection of minorities were prominent fields of activity of which the first has had some permanence. It originally covered 15 territories in Africa, the Middle East, and the Pacific, most of which had been under German control and for which mandates were exercised by the British Empire, France, and Belgium. Between 1919 and 1932, 15 states of Eastern Europe and the near East also assumed obligations to protect their nationals belonging to racial, religious, or linguistic minorities (see *Permanent Mandates Commission*).

Various economic and financial efforts formed a substantial part of the League's work. Though some may appear modest by today's standards, attempts were mounted to curb nationalism and protectionism with the convening of the London Economic and Monetary Conference of 1933, even though this did not realize its aims. There were agreements to abolish import and export restrictions, simplify customs formalities, regulate whale fishing, and deal with trade in wheat, among other things. Foundations were laid for international cooperation on transport, for example on inland waterways, road traffic signals and taxation, ports, and railway regimes. Even the cross-frontier transfer of electric energy and hydroelectric developments affecting more than one state received attention. All this work continues today in the Economic Commission for Europe and other UN regional commissions.

The nine other categories of League action distinguished above have equally been continued in the UN framework. Work on health and intellectual cooperation is now pursued globally through the World Health Organization and UNESCO, for example, but even so the ambitious if rudimentary schemes begun by the League must be seen as revolutionary in the context of knowledge, world-mindedness, and the state of communications in the 1920s and 1930s. One such activity was the organizing of epidemiological intelligence, standardized statistics, and public health assistance. The Eastern Bureau at Singapore prepared a weekly bulletin which was broadcast to countries of Africa, Asia, and Australasia where cholera, smallpox, and other diseases were prevalent, the data used being based on telegraphed reports on the public health position received from one hundred sixty three stations. Other areas were in touch with the Geneva Centre. In its entirety this health activity was planned to cover such matters as rural hygiene, housing, and biological standardization, as well as research on leprosy.

On intellectual cooperation the League's work sought to cover education as well as museums, art, university information, intellectual rights, films, and radio (see *Peace Museums*). Two examples may be cited: a convention on international circulation of educational films (1933), which obtained 24 ratifications, and another on the use of broadcasting in the cause of peace, concluded in 1936.

Much of what was called the League's social and humanitarian work, and which dealt with such questions as welfare of women and children, detention of prisoners, and so on, laid the foundations for what we know today as basic UN activities in such areas as human rights, refugee problems, narcotic drugs, and slavery. Some important international instruments concerned with human rights were instituted—for instance an international convention for suppression of traffic in women and children (1921) and the Slavery Convention of 1926. The convention of 1933 relating to the international status of refugees, an agreement covering a transit card for emigrants (1929), and numerous conventions on traffic in opium and dangerous drugs and on limitations on their manufacture and distribution—all recall today's continuing preoccupations. Similarly, the convention of 1927 establishing a separate International Relief Union, to deal with aid to populations suffering natural disasters, recalls today's action of UNDRO, the relatively new UN Disaster Relief Organization.

The Nansen International Office for Refugees (see Nobel Peace Prize Laureates: *Fridtjof Nansen and The Nansen Office*), later to become the Office of the High Commissioner for Refugees (see Nobel Peace Prize Laureates: *United Nations High Commissioner for Refugees (UNHCR)*), as well as all the League's auxiliary organizations listed in Table 1 and the International Labour Organization (see Nobel Peace Prize Laureates: *International Labour Organization (ILO)*), have continued to bear fruit today through UN activities; and the same is true of the last three categories of League effort—on the codifying of international law, technical assistance, and standardized statistics. Not only was the Permanent Court of International Justice and its Statutes a League creation of 1921 (see *International Court of Justice*), but a good deal of other work, including that on nationality laws and statelessness, were among types of activity now handled by the UN International Law Commission. Similarly, technical assistance, then only extended to a few states, has been enormously stepped up in today's developing world, so that whole organizations are now devoted to it.

3. *The League's Place in World Organization for Peace*

The League of Nations Council met for the last time on December 11, 1939, when it considered an appeal by Finland, but, despite the departure of its main staff and organizations, it continued to exist until the Assembly's final meeting in April 1946. Immediately afterwards the Palais des Nations became the European Office of the newly created United Nations.

The League was never a Parkinsonian expansionist body. While in 1920 its budget amounted to some 15 million Swiss francs, contributed in gold francs by member states, by 1938 this figure had only doubled to total 32 million francs, although both its work and its membership had greatly increased in the meantime.

In some respects the League was remarkably ambitious and modern, even by today's standards. At Prangins, near Geneva, Radio Nations, the League's radio station, was equipped with one long-wave telegraphic and two short-wave installations, for radio-telephony and broadcasting. Between 1932 and 1937 there were weekly broadcasts on the League's activities in English, French, and Spanish, but by 1937 the proceedings of the eighteenth Assembly came to be broadcast on a nightly basis.

Today's world organization has quietly built upon or adapted that of the 1920s and 1930s. In the measure of a slow, grudging but enforced acceptance of interdependence and a growing awareness of the linkages among all phenomena, the range, scale, and depth of internationalism have advanced as powers and expectations alike have been broadened by knowledge and innovative technique.

But circumstances change as well as powers, so that true development remains a slow interactive process. In two important respects there is a difference between the climate of the League's work and that surrounding the United Nations. On the negative side, the League's peace efforts were wrecked by political nationalism, a new fanaticism, and an impotent Europe—factors that persist today. But today's war climate—now inflamed to the point where world war equals world death—includes a new factor: a competitive, adversarial one-upmanship approach to peace and existence that did not hazard the 1920s

because the state that has overwhelmingly created it did not then belong to the organization.

Against all this, a new positive factor today is the rise of a vital and unifying bond of human rights thinking that did not exist at all in the days of the League. Perhaps the final lesson that emerges from these last 60 years of experience is that mere understanding and technical power to achieve peace are not enough—that the sources of war are at one with overwhelming economic fear and greed, against which an all-embracing code of rights and duties is the only option that remains.

See also: *United Nations Governance; United Nations Reform: Historical and Contemporary Perspectives*

Bibliography

League of Nations (Information Section) 1926 *The League of Nations: Its Constitution and Organization*. League of Nations, Geneva

League of Nations (Information Section) 1927 *The League of Nations: The Mandate System*. League of Nations, Geneva

League of Nations (Information Section) 1928a *The League of Nations: Political Activities*. League of Nations, Geneva

League of Nations (Information Section) 1928b *The League of Nations: Social and Humanitarian Work*, rev. edn. League of Nations, Geneva

League of Nations (Information Section) 1938 *The League of Nations: The Refugees*. League of Nations, Geneva

League of Nations (Information Section) 1939a *The League of Nations: Essential Facts About the League of Nations*. League of Nations, Geneva

League of Nations (Information Section) 1939b *The League of Nations: Towards a Better Economic World*. League of Nations, Geneva

League of Nations (Information Section) 1939c *The League of Nations: World Health and the League*. League of Nations, Geneva

Northedge F S 1986 *The League of Nations: Its Life and Times 1920-1946*. Leicester University Press, Leicester

Palthey G 1964 Geneva and the international organizations. In: Laederer B (ed.) 1964 *Geneva: Crossroad of the Nations*. Editions Generales, Geneva

Spinelli P P 1964 *Geneva and the International World*. CPII, Geneva

United Nations 1984 *Basic Facts About the United Nations*. United Nations, New York

Walters F P 1952 *A History of the League of Nations*, 2 vols. Oxford University Press, London

JAMES DILLOWAY

Lenin, Vladimir Ilyich

V. I. Lenin (1870-1924) was a great thinker and revolutionary, and founder of the first socialist state. He was the mainspring of the formulation of Soviet foreign policy. He laid its theoretical foundations, formed its major principles, and guided the practical international activity of the Soviet state. His ideas and behests serve as an unfailing impetus to creative work by his followers and successors on the problems of international relations, and as a pledge of the strength and efficiency of Soviet peace policy.

Having changed the very content of international relations, the October Revolution led to new, previously unknown, international political problems—those of relations between states with different social structures. The contradiction between socialism and capitalism became the basic and determining class contradiction of the time, and the chief contradiction in international relations. There arose the problem of peaceful coexistence—that is, the problem of relations between states with different socioeconomic systems. Lenin remarked that, since the victory of the Great October Socialist Revolution, international relations among "the whole world system of states are being determined by the struggle of a small group of imperialist nations against the Soviet movement and Soviet states, headed by Soviet Russia." The vast changes that have taken place in society over the last decades, the radical shifts in the alignment of forces in the international arena, the great changes in the system and structure of international relations have not removed this basic content of the relations between class-opposed systems. However, the trends of the present age make peaceful coexistence not only a more rational method of international intercourse but an absolute imperative, the main and only path to the survival of humankind.

As constant champions of peaceful coexistence, the then Soviet Union and the socialist countries felt deeply responsible for the fate of humankind. Socialism does not need to resort to violence for its confirmation and growth, since it draws on the invincible, objective laws of social progress. As far as the major question of today is concerned—that of war and peace—socialism sees that its class interests lie in close organic union with the interests of humankind rather than in isolation from them. It is only socialism that has the dual historic mission of revolutionary renewal in the world and of saving its peoples from war. The essence of the communist philosophy on peace is expressed in Lenin's words pronounced before the victory of the first socialist revolution: "The ending of war, peace between peoples, the stopping of pillage and violence, this is our ideal." These words carry a great ideological and moral-political potential.

When with the victory of the Great October Socialist Revolution, the relations between socialism and capitalism lay, for the first time at the foundation of all international life, there began to develop in the world arena opposition, antagonism, competition, and the difficulty of attaining peaceful coexistence between states with different social systems. Lenin's principles were enunciated in the historic Decree on Peace on the "freeing of mankind from the horrors of war and its consequences, combined with the resolution of the victorious proletariat to bring to a successful conclusion the question of peace and at the same time the liberation of the workers and exploited masses from all kinds of slavery and exploitation."

The scientific analysis of objective reality, the thorough consideration of the arrangement and alignment of forces in the world, formed the basis of Lenin's foreign policy program for the then Soviet Union. Calling on people "to look for new ways to solve our international problems," he himself resolved such problems at the highest level during the first years of the state's existence under the conditions of an embittered class struggle, civil war, foreign military intervention, blockade, and massive economic collapse.

Lenin's policy of peaceful coexistence was a direct refutation of slanderous statements about the "export of revolution" to which socialism is supposedly striving. The absolute rejection of war as a means of spreading revolution harmonizes, in Lenin's approach, with the logical defense of the right of oppressed peoples to engage in uprisings and revolutionary wars. Real peaceful coexistence presupposes opposition to the "export of counterrevolution" in whatever package it is presented, and offers a rebuff to imperialistic interference in the internal affairs of countries fighting for their independence.

A course toward peaceful coexistence of states with different social structures laid at the basis of Soviet policy with regard to the capitalist countries. It proceeded logically from the general tasks of socialist foreign policy, one task of which was the securing of the most favorable external conditions for the building of socialism, which can only mean conditions of peaceful coexistence with capitalist states.

An aggressive war is not only unnecessary to socialism for victory in competition with capitalism: it is generally foreign to its nature, to the nature of a system which has removed itself from the power of the bearers of militarism and aggression, the exploiting classes. The incompatibility of socialism and war, the indissolubility of socialism and peace, flows from the basic quality of peace as an essential condition for the strengthening of the new social order, the acceleration of its economic and social development, and the growth of its preeminence and its appeal. The most important task for socialist foreign policy has therefore become the struggle for peace.

From the very beginning Lenin's policy of peaceful coexistence was distinguished not only by its principled stand in defending the interests of socialism and of all revolutionary forces, but also in its realism when evaluating the conditions and possibilities for the practical realization of the tasks before it. In October 1917, when the first ever socialist state began the dogged struggle for peace, Lenin warned: "He who thought that peace is easy to achieve, that one only has to mention peace and the bourgeoisie will bring it to us on a plate, is an extremely naïve person." The rightness of this sober evaluation has been confirmed by history. Imperialism has not become reconciled with the new social order and has opposed its peace policy with blockades and intervention, aggression, and war.

When working out and implementing the policy of peaceful coexistence, it is of the greatest importance to consider carefully such objective factors of the development of international affairs as the alignment and disposition of forces on a global scale and within individual countries. Here, the Leninist understanding of "power" included not just the totality of economic, military, and other materials, but also moral-political factors, although by themselves they are, of course, extremely important in evaluating the balance of power. Seeing first of all in power its class content, Lenin examined from this standpoint not only circumstances as they formed but also the development of the relationship between the socialist powers and peace and between the imperialist powers and war. The analysis and prognosis of the alignment of class powers in the world arena in Lenin's methodology proceed from a general evaluation of the major natural laws of our time. Lenin's policy of peaceful coexistence is based on this only possible correct, scientific foundation. In this is the source of its vitality, its capacity not only to set specific tasks correctly and opportunely, but to indicate effective ways and means for resolving them, bearing in mind the great historical perspective.

The basic principles of Soviet foreign policy, the principles of proletarian internationalism and of peaceful coexistence of states with different social structures, found a basis and thorough practical testing in the activities of Lenin while he was governing the first ever socialist state, which was laying paths in economics and politics previously unknown. By thoroughly analyzing the specific historical situation, Lenin proved, first, the inevitability of the coexistence of states with different social structures during a whole historical period; second, the desirability and expediency in the interests of socialism of peaceful forms of this coexistence; third, the real possibility of peaceful coexistence of socialist and capitalist states, despite the difference in their socioeconomic systems and the aggressive aspirations of imperialism.

Leninism is the only correct and reliable compass in international affairs. It is only by firmly following its precepts that one can make out the extremely complex dynamics of the constantly interweaving and varying tendencies and processes of today, and interpret and note the chief prospects for peaceful development. It is in the area of international relations, where the interweaving of different objective and subjective factors has become especially complicated and where, since Lenin's lifetime, radical changes had taken place, that the full meaning of Lenin's ideas, of the entire Leninist legacy in the analysis of the international political realities of our time, and the great transforming power of Leninism manifested themselves with especial clarity.

International questions had always occupied the prime place in the theoretical and practical activity of the Communist Party of the Soviet Union (CPSU). This is bound up with the deeply international essence of the working class movement and its chief ideological weapon, Marxism-Leninism. At the present time the contribution of international relations and foreign policy to the process of the revolutionary transformation of the world is ever increasing. Lenin remarked that, with the victory of the Great October Socialist Revolution and the formation of the very first socialist state, the relations between the two systems—capitalism and socialism—had become the axis of all international life. Lenin's understanding of the struggle between the two social systems as the major content of the world revolutionary process relates to our time. The basic feature of this process, the contradiction between the socialist and capitalist systems, fully embraces all international relations.

The most characteristic feature of Leninist theory and practice in the area of international relations and foreign policy is the organic link, the oneness, of the analysis of international problems with that of problems related to the class struggle and the revolutionary movement. This characteristic shows up these days in the activity of those who continue Lenin's work.

Lenin's principles of socialist foreign policy formed the basis of the foreign policy activity of the former CPSU. The consistent creative application of these principles in conditions which firmly followed Lenin's course in international affairs constituted one of the most important foundations for the success of the Soviet state in the international arena. International political results invariably confirmed that this course was the only correct one, for it not only answered the interests of the Soviet peoples and of other socialist countries, but also reflected the aspirations and expectations of the overwhelming majority of the world population.

Leninist principles relating to the struggle for peace and socialism, against the forces of aggression and oppression of the world's peoples, determine this course of the Communist Party and the Soviet government. Faithfulness to Lenin's behests is the characteristic feature of the Party's policy and this found clear expression in the programs for peace worked out and accepted at the XXIV-XXVI Congress of the CPSU.

See also: *Militarism: Marxist-Leninist Critique; War: Marxist-Leninist Theory; Marxist-Leninist Concepts of Peace and Peaceful Coexistence; Peaceful Coexistence; Socialism, "Scientific"*

Bibliography ————————————————————

Lenin V I 1969-70 *Collected Works,* 45 vols. Lawrence and Wishart, London

OLEG N. BYKOV

Limited War

The concept of limited war has acquired increased significance in the nuclear age, because of the holocaust character of global nuclear war. It should not be confused with the intra-state wars of secession or succession that have become so frequent after the fall of the former Soviet Union and the end of the Cold War. Limited war refers to war between states; but intra-state wars can escalate into inter-state wars. Different types of limited war then have to be distinguished. Three main criteria can be used:

(a) geographic scope: global or world war versus limited or local war;

(b) ends or objectives: unconditional surrender or destruction of the opponent versus limited objectives, such as troop withdrawal or negotiated compromise;

(c) means: making restrained use of military capabilities such as limiting attacks to specific targets.

In most definitions of limited war the two last criteria are combined, as, for example, in the following definition by Robert Osgood (1957):

A war in which the parties restrict the purposes for which they fight to concrete, well-defined objectives that do not demand the utmost military effort of which the parties are capable and that can be accommodated in negotiated settlement.

If we first examine the difference in the geographic scope of wars we can again distinguish three categories: global or world war; limited wars fought by great versus small powers (military interventions); and limited (small, local) wars fought between small powers, such as the wars between Iran and Iraq or between Pakistan and India.

In the nuclear age a different distinction, though related to the means used in the war, has become very important, namely that between an all-out nuclear war or a limited and controlled nuclear war, either in the sense of limiting damage by agreeing on an early end of the war or by forcing one's opponent to submit by possessing escalation dominance. The latter concept means having a nuclear capability that would make it impossible for the opponent to move up the escalation ladder without suffering a far worse defeat or triggering mutual annihilation. There are thus many possible meaning to the concept of limited war.

The distinction between global and limited war in terms of geographical scope could arise in the twentieth century. Even though the war between 1914 and 1918 is commonly called the First World War, it started in Europe and still had Europe as its main theater of war. The Second World War was more global both in terms of the participating states and in terms of a much wider theater of war but was still primary European in its origin though Japan played a very important role. A global power balance and greatpower rivalry only came into being after 1945. The Cold War was the first truly global conflict. This global power rivalry has given war, limited in geographical scope, a new dimension since any war now affected the power balance between the two main rivals. Wars between the Great Powers fought out in a limited territory—such as the Crimean War of 1856—have not occurred since 1945. The main reason is of course that such direct military confrontations between the Great Powers might escalate into nuclear and global nuclear war.

Limited wars fought by one Great Power against or within a small state—in which other Great Power has sometimes supported the opposing side—have been much more frequent. These kinds of limited wars were often called military interventions.

Examples would be the interventions in Korea, Vietnam, Afghanistan, Hungary, or Czechoslovakia (see *Intervention*).

Wars between small powers have also been frequent. There the role of the Great Powers has often been to try to mitigate or end them. But the motive of trying to indirectly harm one's opponent has also played a role. That has, for example, been clear in the case of both the wars between India and Pakistan and the wars in the Middle East. In the war between Iran and Iraq, however, the Great Powers have abstained from any interference and have discussed ways to prevent escalation (see *Nonintervention and Noninterference*).

That makes it already clear that the nuclear balance between the Great Powers has had an impact upon their conflict conduct. It is necessary here to make a distinction between the doctrines of limited war upheld by the Great Powers and their actual behavior in situations of conflict.

The development of nuclear weapons has influenced the doctrines of limited war because of the recognition of the possibility of mutual destruction through nuclear war. In the past, wars were usually limited in their objectives. In balance-of-power doctrine (see *Balance of Power*), wars were not over fundamentals and were not supposed to lead to the destruction of the opponent. The ally of today could become the enemy of tomorrow, and vice versa. The East-West conflict (see *East-West Conflict*), however, was seen to be of a fundamental and irreconcilable nature. For that reason, restraint could only be possible because of the common danger and shared threat of mutual destruction. Limited War between the Great Powers therefore came to mean either a war in which the means were limited ("conventional" war) or one which would be controlled so as to limit damage and bring the conflict quickly to an end. The concept of limited war became quite popular in the

late 1950s. Since then, current theories of limited war found their inspiration in the works of Liddell Hart (1960). Its advocacy was for him not so much a response to the problem of nuclear weapons as to the conviction that wars should remain limited because of the horror and suffering implied in all modern war. His thinking resulted from the efforts starting in the late nineteenth century to maintain a clear distinction between combatants and civilians through prohibition of weapons of indiscriminate destruction and prohibitions of attacks on cities. According to Liddell Hart, war should be controlled and conducted with a minimum of disruption and without the barbarous excesses which were so clear during the Second World War.

To Liddell Hart nuclear weapons were essentially a continuation of the use of air power as a means of attrition of the enemy. But already soon after the first atomic bomb had felled on Hiroshima he wrote: when both sides possess atomic power, "total warfare" makes nonsense. Total warfare implies that the aim, the effort and the degree of violence are unlimited. Victory is pursued without regard to the consequences . . . and an unlimited war waged with atomic power would be worse than nonsense; it would be mutually suicidal."

Liddell Hart thus anticipated the argument that nuclear weapons would not make all warfare unthinkable. However: "Unless the political leaders are crazy, it is likely that any future war will be less unrestrained and more subject to mutually agreed rules. Within such limits it may develop new forms." Though that prediction has not come true, the concept of limited war has continued to play a very important role in thinking about military strategy and in arms-procurement policies, particularly when the United States proclaimed its nuclear strategy (see *Nuclear Strategy*) to be "massive retaliation." This concept meant that the United States threatened to respond to any attack which would affect its territory or that of its allies with a large-scale nuclear counterattack. Once the former Soviet Union also acquired the capacity to attack the territory of the United States, the strategy was criticized on the grounds that it left the American President in fact with no alternative but suicide or surrender. Liddell Hart already anticipated these arguments before the former Soviet Union had acquired that capacity. When the hydrogen bomb had been developed he wrote: "To the extent that the H-bomb precludes the likelihood of full-scale war, it increases the possibility of limited war pursued by widespread local aggression."

In the wake of Liddell Hart it was increasingly

argued in the 1950s that massive retaliation was not 'credible.'

The basic premise of the limited war theorists, of whom his book *Nuclear Weapons and Foreign Policy* (1957) made Henry Kissinger a prominent member, was that the means of deterrence (see *Deterrence*) should be proportionate to the objectives pursued. The theory of limited war thus left open two possibilities in the age of nuclear weapons: wars limited in geographic scope to be fought outside the main area of confrontation in Europe, that is to say primarily the Third World, and wars between the Great Powers that would be limited in their means, so as to be brought to a negotiated end before escalation into full-scale nuclear war.

These implications of nuclear war became clear at the time when the confrontation with the former Soviet Union was still conceived to be of a total and global nature. The limited war theorists therefore argued for moderation. Bernard Brodie for example wrote: "The one basic proposition which must be established in the minds of men if progress is to be made towards resolving our terrible military dilemma is this: limited war must mean also limited objectives." However, at the time Henry Kissinger, for example, still believed that a limited nuclear war fought in a rational manner and leaving the civilian population largely untouched, would be possible. His views were severely criticized as wishful thinking. The results of North Atlantic Treaty Organization (NATO) (see *North Atlantic Treaty Organization (NATO)*) exercises showed that limited "tactical" nuclear warfare in the then Federal Republic of Germany would result—even without the long-term effects of radiation—in more than five times the civilian casualties in Germany during the Second World War.

In Europe limited (nuclear) war would mean total destruction. Limited war theorizing, and particularly the criticism of massive retaliation and credibility, nevertheless had a very important influence on the nuclear strategy and arms-procurement policy of the Kennedy Administration. Kennedy's Secretary of Defense, McNamara, developed a new nuclear strategy, of which damage limitation and flexible response were the main catchwords. It was argued that the United States and NATO should have the means available for choosing different options to different kinds of probes or attacks by the opponent.

For that reason the new strategy emphasized limiting attacks to specific targets, that is to say shifting targeting policy from countercity to counterforce targets. This made a considerable increase in the number and types of nuclear weapons necessary. This move towards counterforce strategy, though abandoned again by McNamara himself in favor of the doctrine of mutually assured destruction (MAD) was taken up again in the 1970s by the Nixon Administration and defended by the need to have "limited nuclear options." President Reagan's Secretary of Defense Weinberger went still one step further in arguing that nuclear deterrence required having the capacity to wage protracted nuclear war. This was based on the idea of limiting war through possessing "escalation dominance," that is, military superiority on each level of the escalation ladder so as to prevent the opponent from taking such a next step. Limiting War in that conception logically leads to a continuing arms build-up. Soviet strategy was always based on war-fighting doctrines. The limited and limiting war doctrine of both Great Powers have been one of the most important driving forces of the arms race (see *Arms Race, Dynamics of*). Doctrines of limited war were an attempt to escape from the compelling realities of the nuclear age. In actual fact, limited war between the Great Powers has not occurred; there had not even been an exchange of gunshots between the military of the Great Powers.

The Great Powers in fact had behaved with great restraint towards each other, especially after the Cuban missile crisis of 1962. The primary reason for this was that neither of the Great powers could be certain that a military confrontation between them would not lead to the use of nuclear weapons nor whether once nuclear weapons had been used for a so-called "limited option" that would be the end of it. There is no complete certainty that the risk of escalation can be controlled. The crucial property of the nuclear age is therefore that the risk, no matter how small, that a nuclear war may come about, will always be infinitely more important than the possible gains of whatever use of military force. The relationship between risk and gain cannot be quantified anymore. A cost-benefit analysis becomes meaningless when faced with the possibilities of a nuclear holocaust. That grim reality can still not be avoided by the present or aspiring Great Powers. Forced restraint will have to characterize their conduct, as a future great war, comparable to the two world wars of this century, has become extremely unlikely.

The only still conceivable limited wars are conventional in nature though it is not impossible that chemical weapons may be used in the future. Limited nuclear war is only possible as the result of nuclear proliferation though at the moment the chances for such wars seem quite low. It is more advantageous and less risky for prospective nuclear states to demonstrate that they are able to produce nuclear weapons than, in fact, to produce them. New technology makes production of parts possible, that can easily be assembled in a short time period. Whether production of a nuclear weapon is likely to lead to (limited) nuclear wars, is still a matter of debate (Sagan and Waltz 1995). Limited nuclear war between the Great Powers is most unlikely, because of the many uncertainties involved and the ever-present possibility of escalation. There are as yet no indications that nuclear war can be controlled and kept limited. Though it may be argued from an ethical point of view that limited war would be better than all-out nuclear war (from the perspective of Great Powers at least; for the countries forming the battlefield it would still be a war of annihilation) the problem is that, if Great Powers plan for limited war and procure weapons for it, the chances of all-out nuclear war become greater. To prevent global nuclear war Great Powers should therefore stop preparing for limited (nuclear) war. If nuclear war cannot be controlled, the shared risk of nuclear war should remain, but be reduced as far as possible through arms control, crisis management, and confidence building (see *Arms Control, Evolution of; Confidence Building in International Diplomacy; Crisis Management*).

See also: *Deterrence; Global Wars; Local Wars Since 1945; Nuclear Deterrence, Doctrine of; War*

Bibliography ―――――――――――――

Ayoob M (ed.) 1980 *Conflict and Intervention in the Third World.* Croom Helm, London

Ball D 1981 Can nuclear war be controlled? *Adelphi Paper*, No. 169, London

Clark I 1982 *Limited Nuclear War.* Martin Robertson, Oxford

Freedman L 1981 *The Evolution of Nuclear Strategy.* Macmillan, London

Garnett J 1975 Limited War. In: Baylis J (ed.) 1975 *Contemporary Strategy.* Croom Helm, London

Holloway D 1983 *The Soviet Union and the Arms Race.* Yale University Press, New Haven, Connecticut

Kissinger H 1957 *Nuclear Weapons and Foreign Policy.* Westview, New York

Loddell Hart B H 1960 *Deterrence or Defense.* London

Osgood R E 1957 *Limited War: The Challenge to American Strategy.* University of Chicago Press, Chicago, Illinois

Sagan S D, Waltz K N 1995 *The Spread of Nuclear Weapons: A Debate.* Norton, New York/London

G. VAN BENTHEN VAN DEN BERGH

Local Wars Since 1945

The Second World War, despite being the most destructive armed conflict yet waged by humanity, has not brought an end to wars on Earth. The history of wars has continued to be written since 1945 (see *War*).

For the purposes of this article, wars are defined as armed conflicts in which all of the following occur:

(a) Activities of regular armed forces: military, police forces, and so on, at least on one side— that is, the presence and engagement of the armed forces of the government in power.

(b) A certain degree of organization and organized fighting on both sides, even if this extends to organized defense only.

(c) A certain continuity between the armed clashes, however sporadic. Centrally organized guerrilla forces are also regarded as making war, insofar as their activities extend over a considerable part of the country concerned.

Based on these criteria, there have been some 194 wars in the period 1945-92 (see Table 1), and according to some calculations 41 new wars started between 1982 and 1992. It is further calculated that in the 1945-82 period humanity experienced just 26 days without war. According to estimates, the casualties of these wars amounted to 25-30 million people, excluding the victims of the indirect consequences of armed conflict, such as famine and epidemics.

The wars waged between 1945 and 1992 took place on the territories of 90 countries. However, if the regular armies engaged on foreign lands are also taken into account, it can be concluded that approximately half of the countries on the globe have been engaged in armed conflicts in this period, while the number of countries in existence during that time has significantly grown.

Several features of present-day wars are different from those of the pre-Second World War period. While a more significant number of the wars before 1945 had Europe as their location, or at least were started by European states, almost all the armed conflicts of the postwar years have taken place outside Europe, in the developing countries or Third World —that is, parts of Asia, Africa, and Latin America.

Table 1
Local wars 1945-92

Theater of war	Year of beginning[a]	Theater of war	Year of beginning[a]	Theater of war	Year of beginning[a]
1. Greece	1944-	66. India-China	1962/	132. Ethiopia (Ogaden)	1977-
2. Algeria	1945/	67. Brunei	1962/	133. Zaire	1977/
3. Indonesia	1945-	68. Guinea-Bissau	1963-	134. South African	
4. Spain	1945-	69. Malaysia	1963-	Republic-neighbors	1977-
5. Indochina	1946-	70. Algeria-Morocco	1963/	135. Nicaragua	1977-
6. Greece	1946-	71. South Yemen	1963-	136. Guatemala	1977-
7. India	1946-	72. Dominican Republic	1963/	137. El Salvador	1978-
8. Philippines	1946-	73. Ethiopia-Somalia	1963-	138. Colombia	1978-
9. China	1946-	74. Zaire	1963-	139. Afghanistan	1978-
10. Iran	1946/	75. Rwanda	1963-	140. North Yemen-South Yemen	1978-
11. Paraguay	1947/	77. Kenya-Somalia	1963-	141. Zaire	1978/
12. Madagascar	1947-	78. Laos	1964-	142. Tanzania-Uganda	1978-
13. India (Hyderabad)	1947-	79. Israel-Palestine	1964-93	143. Spain (Basques)	1978-
14. India (Kashmir)	1947-	80. Columbia	1964-	144. Equatorial Guinea	1979/
15. Yemen	1948/	81. North Vietnam	1964-	145. North Yemen	1979-
16. Costa Rica	1948/	82. Mozambique	1964-	146. Cambodia	1979-
17. Burma	1948-	83. Iraq	1965-	147. Saudia Arabia (Mecca)	1979/
18. Colombia	1948-	84. India-Pakistan	1965/	148. Iran	1979-
19. Arab-Israeli conflicts	1948-	85. Dominican Republic	1965/	149. Syria	1979-
20. Malaysia	1948-	86. Peru	1965/	150. China-Vietnam	1979/
21. Bolivia	1949/	87. Oman (Dhofar)	1965-	151. Iraq-Iran	1980-
22. Korea	1950-	88. Sudan	1965-	152. Gambia	1981/
23. Egypt	1951-	89. Thailand	1965-	153. Uganda	1981-
24. Tunisia	1952-	90. India (Mizos)	1965-	154. Malvinas (Falkland Islands)	1982/
25. Bolivia	1952/	91. Bolivia	1967/	155. Bangladeshi	1982-
26. Kenya	1952-	92. Arab-Israeli conflicts	1967/	156. Syria	1982
27. Morocco	1952-	93. Zaire	1967/	157. Somalia	1982
28. Guatemala	1954/	94. Nigeria	1967-	158. Israel-Lebanon	1982
29. Colombia	1954-	95. Zimbabwe (Rhodesia)	1967-	159. Sudan	1982
30. Algeria	1954-	96. South Yemen	1968/	160. Nicaragua-Honduras	1982
31. China (islands)	1955/	97. Guatemala	1968-	161. Sri Lanka (Tamils)	1983
32. Costa Rica-Nicaragua	1955/	98. Chad	1968-	162. USA-Grenada	1983
33. Cyprus	1955-	99. El Salvador-Honduras	1969/	163. Sudan	1983-
34. Cameroon	1955-	100. South Yemen-Saudi Arabia	1969/	164. Sri Lanka	1983-
35. South Vietnam	1955-	101. United Kingdom (N. Ireland)	1969-	165. Turkey	1984-92
36. Oman	1955-	102. Kampuchea (Cambodia)	1970-	166. Mali-Burkina Fasso	1985
37. India (Nagas)	1956-	103. Sudan	1970/	167. South Yemen	1986
38. Hungary	1956/	104. Philippines	1970-	168. Surinam	1986
39. Egypt (Suez)	1956/	105. Jordan	1970/	169. Chad-Libya	1986-88
40. Cuba	1956-	106. Guinea	1970/	170. Philippines	1986-
41. Aden, Yemen	1956-	107. Pakistan (Bangladesh)	1971/	171. Peru	1986-
42. Indonesia	1957-	108. Sri Lanka	1971/	172. China-Vietnam	1987
43. Honduras-Nicaragua	1957/	109. Jordan	1971/	173. Honduras-Nicaragua	1988
44. Spanish Morocco	1957-	110. North Vietnam	1972-	174. Azerbaijan	1988-
45. Lebanon	1958/	111. Uganda-Tanzania	1972/	175. Brundi	1988-9?
46. Jordan	1958/	112. Burundi	1972/	176. Liberia	1989-
47. China (Quemoy, Matsu)	1958/	113. North Yemen-South Yemen	1972/	177. USA-Panama	1989
48. Nyasaland	1959/	114. Arab-Israeli conflicts	1973/	178. Papua New Guinea	1989
49. China (Tibet)	1959/	115. Iraq	1974-	179. India-Sri Lanka	1990
50. Laos	1959-	116. Ethiopia	1974-	180. Iraq-Kuwait (UN)	1990-9?
51. Dominican Republic	1959/	117. Cyprus	1974/	181. Rwanda	1990-
52. Paraguay	1959-	118. Lebanon	1975-	182. Croatia	1990
53. Zaire (Belgian Congo)	1960-	119. East Timor	1975-	183. Tajikistan	1991-
54. Angola	1961-	120. Angola	1975-	184. Somalia	1991-
55. Nepal	1961-	121. Namibia	1975-	185. Afghanistan	1991-9?
56. Cuba (Bay of Pigs)	1961/	122. West Sahara	1975-	186. Keyna	1991-9?
57. Tunisia (Biserta)	1961-	123. Argentina	1975-	187. Georgia	1992
58. Ethiopia	1961-	124. Indonesia	1975-	188. Moldova	1992
59. Iraq	1961-	125. Rhodesia-neighbors	1976-	189. S. Africa	1992
60. Venezuela	1961-	126. Mozambique	1975-	190. Bosnia Herzegovina	1992
61. India (Goa)	1961/	127. Iraq	1976-	191. Chad	1992-
62. Indonesia (West Iran)	1962/	128. Laos	1976-	192. India	1992-
63. Guatemala	1962-	129. Indonesia (West Irian)	1977-	193. Laos	1992-
64. Colombia	1962/	130. Kampuchea (Cambodia)	1977-	194. Myanmar	1992-
65. Yemen	1962-	131. North Yemen	1977/		

a – = and following year (s); / = ended same year

Source: 1945-76, Kende (1978) 1976-82, Kende et al. (1982)

Of the 194 wars waged between 1945 and 1992, 46 took place in the Middle East or African Arab countries, 45 in other parts of Asia, 35 in the rest of Africa, and 31 in Latin America.

Europe after 1945 has at the same time been the stage for hardly any wars and—with the exception of the civil wars in Greece immediately after the Second World War and the wars in former Yugoslavia in 1990s—those that were waged on its soil were of comparatively low intensity. The reasons for the absence of armed conflicts in Europe are not considered here; suffice it to say that this is a delicate peace based on the comparative balance of arms—and the most dangerous arms at that.

Important changes have also taken place in the character of war. While earlier the overwhelming majority of wars were waged between countries or groups of countries for territorial claims, over the borders of countries, wars of that type have constituted only a very small number of the total since 1945. At the same time, most of the wars in the latter period were waged inside countries very often colonies and not across frontiers: they were internal wars (see *Internal War*). The goal was usually to topple ruling governments: they were "anti-regime" wars. Up to about 1975-76 it was mainly colonial regimes which suffered revolt; thus the main type of war waged since the Second World War has been the independence struggle.

Another comparatively frequent type of war fought in this period arose out of internal conflicts within certain countries—fighting due to partial interests: nationalities, tribal groups, religious factions seeking partition or autonomy. In most cases there were no foreign troops involved.

The rarest type of war nowadays is that waged between states—that is, the type of war that used to be the most typical, fought between industrially advanced—mainly European—countries. It would, however, be false to conclude from this that industrially advanced countries were characterized by peace while the developing countries were characterized by war in this period. In a high proportion of wars since 1945 foreign troops have participated actively and the participating powers were mainly the industrially advanced countries. Between 1945 and 1960 the United Kingdom and France were the most active foreign participants; between 1960 and 1989 it was mainly the United States. It is the US Army that has been actively involved for the longest periods and in the most wars since 1945. However, other countries, such as Portugal have also been involved in wars in colonial territories.

Most post-1945 wars have been limited wars waged on a comparatively low level militarily (see *Limited War*). However, the period has also witnessed struggles, the intensity of which in many ways—such as the volume of explosives utilized—has surpassed that of the Second World War. In fact, during the Vietnam War the amount of explosive utilized was not just greater when specifically calculated—that is, in terms of the volume exploded on a territorial unit—but also when the *entire* volume is taken into consideration.

The history of wars after the Second World War has witnessed two periods during which the number and intensity of wars notably increased. Although the trend continued upward after 1945 up to the end of the 1960s, the increase was fastest between 1960 and 1967-68. One reason for this phenomenon is the significant change that has taken place in the policy of the United States. The new strategy of "flexible response" was called by some such as Henry Kissinger and R. E. Osgood, the strategy of "successful limited wars." It was in this period that the Vietnam War spread to North Vietnam, the Arab-Israeli Six Day War occurred, fighting continued and conflicts started in several countries of Africa (Zaire, Angola, Guinea-Bissau, Mozambique, Nigeria), the Bay of Pigs intervention attempt was made against Cuba, war in the Dominican Republic broke out, and guerrilla wars were waged in some Latin American countries.

The second period to witness a rapid increase in the number of armed conflicts started in 1975-76, and continues to the present day, with several new wars in Africa (new armed conflicts in Angola, West Sahara, Zaire, Ethiopia-Ogaden, Chad, and so on), in Asia (Cambodia, Afghanistan, the People's Republic of China-Vietnam, Iraq-Iran, and so on), and in Latin America (Nicaragua, El Salvador, Malvinas/Falkland Islands, and so on).

Between these two periods of intensified armed conflict there was a significant downward trend in the number of wars waged. Comparatively few new wars were launched, and in rapid succession several wars ended that had earlier been waged with high intensity and with significant influence on international politics. These included wars in Asia (Vietnam, Cambodia, Laos, and Afghanistan) and in Africa (Angola, Mozambique, Guinea-Bissau, and Somalia). It should be added, however, that some of these countries soon experienced the outbreak of new conflicts (Cambodia, Angola, Somalia).

As in the case of the first period of intensified warfare, these last two trends in the pattern of wars—

reduction from developments in international politics. The interim period of decreased warfare corresponds to a time of improved relations between the two main powers; détente was the catchword of this period (see *Détente*). When international conditions again deteriorated, in the second half of the 1970s, the second period of intensified warfare emerged.

Since the mid-1970s new developments have arisen in the history of wars. The reasons behind these are again related to a great extent to the changes occurring in general international conditions. The period of independence struggles has virtually ended. With a very few exceptions (the most significant of which is probably Namibia), the world is divided into legally independent countries; the dismemberment of the colonial empires has terminated. But the main type of war remains that fought "internally," within the boundaries of a given country. Wars of this type often concern national politics, with the national government on one side and an opposing party seeking to give the state a different political complexion on the other. Other wars of this type involve partial interests, as discussed above, where a group of the population, a tribe or a religious community rises against the government. Independence itself has added fresh fuel to such conflicts. The interests had existed for the most part during colonial times, but after the end of colonialism the problems which had been kept in check by the foreign power then destabilized the new national government. Whether related to the selection of the country's political-social trend, or to partial interests and secession attempts, many domestic conflicts have, after independence, immediately become problems of power. The conflicts then erupted into wars between social layers, groups of people who had once shared a common interest during colonial times—that of independence.

As noted previously, in the present period of intensified conflict, the theaters of wars have been changing, so affecting the international power balance. An unparalleled differentiation has lately taken place between the developing countries (for economic, political, and military reasons), leading to the dangerous possibility of the emergence of new regional power aspirations. This also involves the growing possibility for new wars between countries—the type of war which has in recent years become less frequent. This time, however, such wars are not between developed, industrially advanced countries, but between the so-called developing ones (e.g., the Iran-Iraq War).

The composition of states intervening with their troops in foreign wars is also changing. The deve-

loped market economy countries, which were previously the main intervention powers, now play lesser roles. The participation of the United Kingdom, France, and Portugal in modern wars was largely the consequence of their historical status as colonial powers; these positions were lost and the three countries were superseded by a more powerful intervention ally, the United States. This has made the presence of these countries less frequent in the wars since the 1960s, although French troops had intervened in some African countries (e.g., Chad) in this period. The United States, after leaving Indochina, refrained from taking part actively in military conflicts. The US invasion of Grenada (1983) and Panama (1989) is an exception. However, the United States has continued its involvement in warfare through supplying arms and "aid" to its "friends" in several conflicts. Indeed, according to the 1983-84 Strategic Survey by the London-based International Institute for Strategic Studies (IISS): "though still constrained by post-Vietnam domestic pressures, President Reagan had been considerably more willing to use military force in the pursuit of foreign-policy objectives than his two immediate predecessors. In 1983 alone, the US undertook a wide array of military actions."

Changes had also taken place in the military intervention of socialist countries in foreign territories. In earlier periods the troops of socialist countries were involved only in neighboring countries and in countries militarily allied to them (the People's Republic of China in the Korean War, the former Soviet Union in Hungary, Vietnam in Laos and Cambodia). More recently (after 1975), however, there had been new developments, including the participation of Cuban forces to assist the government of newly independent Luanda (formerly Angola) to repel the attacks of the army of the South African Republic, and the Cuban presence in Ethiopia. These constitute the first cases in which troops of a socialist country—with the arms and support of other socialist states—had participated militarily in wars waged outside its alliance (see *Alliance*) system and in a faraway continent. This in fact means that a recent earlier monopoly has ended: it is not only developed market economy countries that now have armies strong enough to provide military assistance, when needed, to their allies at localities far from their own territories.

Another new development in foreign participation in wars is that the armies of the developing countries have become more active on foreign soil. This includes the presence of the troops of Morocco, Libya, Tanzania, Gabon, Syria, and Honduras—among others—in wars in various developing countries. These involvements differ: some were legitimized by government request, whereas others contravened government request (and often led to a change of government under the foreign occupation). In fact, the latter case has become increasingly common in recent years; witness Cyprus (Turkish occupation), some Arab countries (Israeli), Angola and Mozambique (South African Republic). This is also partly the situation in East Timor and West Sahara. The presence of foreign troops naturally involves the permanent danger of the outbreak of conflicts.

The recent large and growing number of wars with increasing intensity on the territories of developing countries is related to the very rapid intensification of military preparation by these countries. In this respect, no changes have taken place since 1945, even during the time of temporary decrease in the number of armed conflicts. The period of détente, although having a limited effect on the actual wars waged, did not affect the increases in military budgets and imports of arms. The growth in military expenditures and importation of armaments in the developing countries continues at an ever-increasing rate. In addition, there has recently been an increase in the number of developing countries producing military equipment, arms, and war supplies, which are being exported in growing volumes. This phenomenon is made especially dangerous by the fact that a significant number of the developing countries not only store these weapons but also "consume" them.

The prevention of a third world war is in the interest of all humanity, and so, too, is the prevention of "local" wars. Not only are such wars being waged in larger number and with greater intensity these days—with thousands dying wounded, or made homeless—but they also carry the risk of escalation into larger conflicts. The danger is further increased by the fact that the strongest powers, through their policies becoming increasingly global, cannot necessarily remain neutral—moreover, as noted, in some cases they also take an active part in wars—and so the effect of these wars on the international balance of power may continue to grow. Finally, it must be remembered that local wars and the related arms race—together with the arms race developing independently from them—affect those territories most which are in greatest need of utilizing their resources for other goals: to use their energy, labor, and financial resources to change backward conditions, to improve the condition of the population and, in certain cases, to save their people from famine.

See also: *Aggression; Arms Race, Dynamics of; Cold War; Conflict: Inherent and Contingent Theories; Intervention; Limited War; Militarism and Militarization; War, Prediction of; Peace, Historical Views of*

Bibliography

Beer F A 1981 *Peace aganist War*. Freeman, San Francisco, California

Bertram C 1981 *Dritt-Welt-Konflikte und Internationale Sicherheit*. Osang, Bonn

Bouthoul G 1962 *Le Phénomene-Guerre*. Payot, Paris

Carver M 1980 *War since 1945*. Weidenfeld and Nicolson, London

Dupuy R E, Dupuy T N 1976 *The Encyclopedia of Military History from 3500 B.C. to the Present*. Jane's, London

Eide A, Thee M 1980 *Problems of Contemporary Militarism*. Croom Helm, London

Gantzel K J 1972 *System und Akteur*. Bertelsmann, Düsseldorf

Kende I 1971 Twenty-five years of local wars. *J. Peace Res.* 8(1)

Kende I 1978 Wars of ten years 1967-1976. *J. Peace Res.* 15(3)

Kende I 1979 *Local Wars in Asia, Africa and Latin America 1945-1969*. Center for Afro-Asian Research of the Hungarian Academy of Sciences, Budapest

Kende I 1982 *Kriege nach 1945*. Militärpolitik, Dokumentation Heft 27. Haag und Herchen, Frankfurt am Main

Kende I 1983 New features of the armed conflicts and armaments in developing countries. *Development and Peace* 4(1)

Kende I, Gantzel K J, Fabig K 1982 Die Kriege seit dem Zweiten Weltkrieg. *Weltpolitik*, Jahrbuch Nr. 2. Campus, Frankfurt

Khan K M, Matthies V 1981 *Regionalkonflikte in der Dritten Welt*. Weltforum, Munich

Kidron M, Smith D 1983 *The War Atlas*. Pan Books, London

Leitenberg M, Kalish R, Lombardi D 1977 *A Survey of Studies of Post World War II Wars, Conflicts and Military Coups*. Cornell University Press, Ithaca, New York

Matthies V 1982 *Kriege in der Dritten Welt*. Leske, Oplauen

Singer J D, Small M 1972 *The Wages of War: A Statistical Handbook*. Wiley, New York

Wallensteen P 1973 *Structure and War*. Rabén and Sjögren, Stockholm

Wood D 1968 *Conflict in the Twentieth Century*. Adelphi Papers No. 48. International Institute of Strategic Studies, London

Wright Q 1965 *A Study of War*. University of Chicago Press, Chicago, Illinois

ISTVÁN KENDE

M

MacArthur, Douglas

Douglas MacArthur (1880-1964) was one of the greatest commanders in the history of the United States. The son of a general, MacArthur spent his youth at various United States army bases and received his education at West Point, the United States' military academy. Upon graduation in 1903 he was commissioned as a lieutenant in the United States army, and embarked upon his long military career. He distinguished himself in the fighting in France, in the First World War, finishing the war as a general in command of a division. After the war he served as superintendent of West Point from 1919 to 1922, then in the Philippine Islands. Between 1930 and 1935 he was in Washington DC as Chief of Staff of the United States army, after which he went back to duty in the Philippines.

The Japanese invasion of the Philippines in December 1941 thrust MacArthur into the thick of the Second World War. He fought a brilliant delaying action against their attack, but his vastly outnumbered Filipino and United States troops were forced to surrender in the spring of 1942. By that time MacArthur, who had been appointed Supreme Commander of all allied forces in the southwest Pacific, had escaped to Australia. From there he orchestrated a series of attacks which succeeded in driving the Japanese from island to island over the next four years. MacArthur's strategy was not only successful, but is credited with achieving stunning victories with extraordinarily low losses to his own troops.

In September 1945, MacArthur accepted the formal surrender of the Japanese in Tokyo Bay and became, as Allied Supreme Commander in Japan, the effective ruler of that country. MacArthur's achievement in Japan was highly impressive. He presided over the destruction of Japanese militarism and the rebuilding of a shattered nation. More importantly, he instituted reforms in landholding, education, women's rights, the economic and social system, and politics which were the basis for the transformation of Japan into a stable, prosperous democracy.

When the Democratic People's Republic of Korea (North Korea) suddenly invaded the Republic of Korea (South Korea) in June 1950, MacArthur was given command of the United Nations forces when the world organization swiftly voted to come to the aid of South Korea. In a risky but highly successful move, he achieved the virtual destruction of the North Korean army by a massive landing far behind their lines, at Inchon, in September 1950. By late November United Nations forces occupied almost all of North Korea, but were then thrown back by a massive counterattack by communist Chinese soldiers. Not until the spring of 1951 was the front stabilized near the prewar boundary between North and South Korea (see *Korean Armistice Agreement*).

MacArthur, frustrated by this stalemate, began to demand that the United States government, which was leading the United Nations effort in Korea, give him the authority to attack the People's Republic of China directly. President Truman, however, did not wish to widen the war, and refused to accede. MacArthur's public criticism of Truman soon reached a level where it constituted an unacceptable challenge to the United States principle of civilian control over the military, and Truman dismissed MacArthur from his command in April 1951. MacArthur retired to private life, though he remained a vigorous spokesman for anticommunist causes until his death in 1964.

Though MacArthur is universally acknowledged as an outstanding general, he has never been without critics. His outspoken conservatism, combined with a towering ego and a rather aloof demeanor, alienated many. In particular, his insistence on attacking the People's Republic of China in 1951, despite that country's alliance with the former Soviet Union, impressed many observers as the act of an irresponsible militarist. He was widely accused of being so insensitive to the horrors of war that he would heedlessly risk a global nuclear conflict.

Whatever the wisdom of MacArthur's projected policies, it appears to be unjust to brand him as a man insensitive or indifferent to the tragedy of war. MacArthur was in fact a man who thought that war was a hopelessly foolish, outdated way to solve disputes, one which should be abolished. He went so far as to encourage the Japanese to renounce armed force and their right to wage war in their postwar constitution. However, MacArthur felt strongly that until war was abolished, decent people must be willing to wage war to defend themselves and their ideals. He was always hostile to those who preached pacifism and unilateral disarmament, saying at one point that to him, moral superiority rested with "a red-blooded and virile humanity which loves peace devotedly, but is willing to die in defense of the right."

Moreover, MacArthur rejected utterly the idea of fighting limited wars for limited political ends. He saw war not as an extension of politics, as had Clausewitz, but as a sign of the total failure of political means to achieve a rational solution to a problem.

Once war broke out, he said, the military must be given a completely free hand to win it. Victory, thus the restoration of peace, was to MacArthur the only legitimate goal of war. To him, for a political leader like Truman to try to reject military measures because of political considerations, once a war had broken out, was the height of immorality.

See also: *Militarism and Militarization; Truman Doctrine*

Bibliography

James D C 1970, 1975 *The Years of MacArthur*, 2 vols. Houghton Mifflin, Boston, Massachusetts

MacArthur D 1964 *Reminiscences*. McGraw Hill, New York

Manchester W 1978 *American Caesar: Douglas MacArthur, 1880-1964*. Little, Brown, Boston, Massachusetts

GARRETT L. MCAINSH

MacArthur Foundation Grants

On January 25, 1985, the John D. and Catherine T. MacArthur Foundation announced the award of US$ 25,000,000 over a three-year period (1985-88) to universities, independent nongovernmental institutions, and individuals to fund interdisciplinary and innovative peace studies, as well as to promote cooperation within the international community in matters relating to international security, conflict avoidance and nuclear arms control. The announced purpose of the grants was: (a) to encourage new approaches to the study of peace and security; (b) to encourage the application of theories and methods from diverse disciplines to issues of international peace and security; and (c) to support graduate training and dissertation research in international peace and security studies for students with training in the physical and biological sciences or the social and behavioral sciences, including foreign area studies.

By the end of the initial funding period, the Foundation's grants to institutions, public education and policy studies, international interactions, fellowships and exchanges, special initiatives, and research and writing grants to individuals reached over US$ 40,000,000 exceeding its original goal by US$ 15,000,000. From 1988-90 similar grants were made, totalling over US$ 78,900,000.

In 1991 the Foundation reexamined the program's direction and emphasis in the context of an emerging new world order. Four priority themes were identified for the Program on Peace and International Cooperation: (1) rethinking US foreign policy and national priorities in order to achieve a humane world order; (2) taking advantage of new opportunities for arms control, disarmament, and demobilization; (3) building sustainable democracy based on respect for human rights and equitable, environmentally sound economic participation; and, (4) strengthening mechanisms for cooperative international governance that are embedded in international civil society. In the area of sustainable democracy, special emphasis has been placed on supporting local or regional initiatives in Central America that promote government accountability, reduce the role of the military in society, and facilitate participation of new voices in the policy process. Reflecting the Foundation's new directions in its Program on Peace and Cooperation, US$ 84,900,000 was allocated in grants to individuals and institutions from 1991 to 1995. For the period 1985-95 peace grants of all types exceeded US$ 203,800,000.

The Foundation makes grants in areas other than peace and cooperation, such as health, population, world environment and resources, education, and the arts. From 1991 to 1995 the Foundation awarded US$ 730,100,000 in grants of all types. Its Program on Peace and International Cooperation accounted for 12 percent of the total. Foundation assets at the end of 1995 amounted to US$ 3.3 billion.

The Foundation gives grants to organizations,

institutions, and individuals. Grants to organizations and institutions fund public education projects, policy studies, and media productions for specialized and general audiences. Grants to individuals are made through three grantmaking competitions: *Research and Writing Grants for Individuals* foster promising approaches to the exploration of international peace and security. A brochure is available from the Foundation for individual, as well as for organization and institution grants. *The Social Science Research Council-MacArthur Foundation Fellowships* are awarded annually for innovative and multidisciplinary dissertation and postdoctoral projects that explore the security implications of worldwide cultural, military, social, economic environmental and political changes. Information and application materials are available from the Social Science Research Council, Program on International Peace and Security, 605 Third Avenue, New York, New York 10158 USA. *The Regional Program of Postgraduate Fellow-ships in the Social Sciences* is co-sponsored by the MacArthur and Ford Foundations. It is open only to citizens of Mexico and Central America. For information contact: Institute of International Education, Program de Becas Ford-MacArthur, Londres 16, 2° piso, Col. Juárez, México, D.F. 06600, México.

Information about the Foundation may be obtained by writing or calling: The John D. and Catherine T. MacArthur Foundation, Office of Grants Management, Research and Information, 140 South Dearborn Street, Chicago, Illinois 60603 USA.

See also: *Peace and Conflict Research Development*

Bibliography ————————————————

The John D and Catherine T MacArthur Foundation. *Annual Reports*. 1985-95. Chicago, Illinois

RICHARD B. GRAY

Machiavelli, Niccolò

Niccolò Machiavelli, statesman and political philosopher, was born in Florence on May 3, 1469, and entered public life at the age of 29 as Second Chancellor and secretary of the Council of the Ten in the republican period. He was from a Florentine family of landed property and noble ancestry which had been reduced to near poverty by the time of his birth. He was educated in classical and humanistic studies although he never learned Greek.

Machiavelli grew up in the midst of political turbulence dominated by such well-known personalities as Savonarola, Lorenzo il Magnifico, Charles VIII of France, and Pope Alexander VI. His family background as well as the political situation in which he grew up must have had enduring influences on his ideas on society and politics as easily discernible in his writings. Throughout his life he admired men with exceptional qualities and with great ambition, but thought little of the common people. He was fascinated by public activity, success, and struggle with Fortuna, the capricious goddess of fortune. For example, in a letter he wrote when he was 28 years old, Machiavelli described, with a display of power as a keen observer, his impressions of Savonarola, the religious and political reformer who dominated the Florentine republic in the 1490s. Machiavelli expressed a rather low opinion of his statesmanship, although characteristically he admired his persuasive ability.

In the course of his service as a public servant, Machiavelli was sent abroad on numerous diplomatic missions, including visits to France, Germany, and Switzerland. A number of his diplomatic despatches, containing his observations and evaluations of important personalities, including Cesare Borgia, survive today to indicate sources and directions of his insights which were later to be incorporated in his political writings.

After the fall of Machiavelli's close friend Soderini and the restoration of the Medici to power in Florence in 1512, Machiavelli was dismissed from his office and, on suspicion of involvement in a conspiracy against the Medici family, was imprisoned and tortured, the experiences of which he described in a poem beseeching help from Giuliano dei Medici. He was released from prison in 1513, but was banished from Florence. Debarred from active political life, he led an impoverished rural life for 13 years until he was recalled to government service. Nevertheless this period of retirement from politics proved to be the most fruitful for his literary talent. Living in Casciano, he wrote among other things his two major works, *The Prince* and *Discourses on the First Ten Books of Titus Livius*, while carrying on correspondence with his friends, notably Francesco Vettori, his patron and the Ambassador at the Holy See.

Machiavelli's political writings were not meant merely to be academic pursuits. They were written not only out of his active interest in contemporary public affairs, but at least partly with a view to regaining office, his perpetual hope. As he wrote to Vettori in a letter dated April 9, 1513:

> Fortune has determined that since I don't know how to talk about the silk business or the wool business, or about profits and losses, I have to talk about the government, and I must either make a vow of silence or discuss that.

At the end of another letter to Vettori, dated December 10, 1513, he wrote:

> In addition, there is my wish that our present Medici lords will make use of me, even if they begin by making me roll a stone; because then, if I could not gain their favour, I should complain of myself; and through this thing, if it [*The Prince*] were read they would see that for the fifteen years I have been studying the art of the state I have not slept or been playing; and well may anybody be glad to get the services of one who at the expense of others has become full of experience.

He was finally employed again by the Medici as secretary of a commission for the fortification of Flo-rence. But two years later the Medici were over-thrown and the Republic was reestablished. Machi-avelli hoped that he would be restored to his old position but he died suddenly of an abdominal sick-ness in 1527 before learning that someone else had been appointed to the position to which he had aspired.

See also: *Machiavellianism*

Bibliography

Burckhardt J 1929 *The Civilization of the Renaissance in Italy.* London
Butterfield H 1955 *The Statecraft of Machiavelli.* London
Morley J 1897 *Machiavelli* (The Romanes Lecture). London
Prezzolini G 1968 *Machiavelli.* London
Ridolfi R 1963 *The Life of Machiavelli.* London
Skinner Q 1981 *Machiavelli.* Oxford
Villari P 1898 *The Life and Times of Niccolò Machiavelli.* London
Whitfield J H 1965 *Machiavelli.* New York

JONG-YIL RA

Machiavellianism

Machiavellianism in common usage refers to the doctrine which holds that the end justifies the means, or that there is a different standard of ethics pertaining to the conduct of public affairs than that applied to private affairs. Norms of private ethics are seen as not only inapplicable but also positively harmful to the effective handling of public affairs. More specifically, the doctrine is associated with an idea concerning the modern nation-state: the idea that *raison d'état* is not and should not be bound by private ethics.

As on many of the cases on which a doctrine or a set of principles is attributed to the ideas of a single individual, Machiavellianism as it has been common-ly understood may not have much to do with the original intentions of Machiavelli himself (see *Machiavelli, Niccolò*). What Machiavellianism means exactly has been the object of various, and often misleading, interpretations and reinterpreta-tions. It is a controversial subject on which argu-ments are still in progress.

Against this background of general confusion pre-vailing over the "correct" understanding of Machiavel-lianism, it may be safely said that it is not a "vanishing type, but a constant and contemporary influence," as Lord Acton remarked, as the problems Machiavelli raised and the points he made pertain to some of the perennial factors of human society in general and its political life in particular. His longevity as a political theorist and the tenacity of Machiavellianism attest to this.

Trotsky noted a revival of Machiavellianism in his own times after an eclipse on the last century:

> This backward return to the most cruel Machiavel-lianism seems incomprehensible to those who only yesterday were cradled in the faith that human history moves according to a cultural and materialistic progress . . . . This is not true . . . . But in any case, no era of the past has ever been as cruel, without feeling, or as cynical as ours.

However, most important political thinkers in mod-ern times, liberals as well as Marxists, show traces of struggling with the teachings of Machiavelli in their theories, even if they were not in some cases actively conscious of the influence.

Machiavelli himself was not a scholar intent on care-fully constructing a system of theories. His political writings of which the most famous are *The Prince and Discourses on the First Ten Books of Titus Livius*—

were designed, at least in part, to win him support in his pursuit of office. In fact, some of his teachings are apparently contradictory and his concepts are loosely employed with different nuances according to the occasion, leaving it to posterity to argue over where his real message lies, what his true intention was, and in what his original achievement consisted.

Machiavelli enjoyed some reputation as a historian of Florence and as a playwright while he lived, but ironically his political writings received hardly any attention in his lifetime, even though he had hoped that they would be recognized by people of influence. In other words, Machiavellianism came into being only after Machiavelli himself had passed away.

For some time after his death, Machiavelli was chiefly to remain an object of intense hostility on religious or moralistic grounds. He was denounced as a counselor of tyrants, for having taught antireligious doctrines, and even for actually being responsible for certain political calamities, as he had allegedly had influence on their perpetrators. Thus Cardinal Reginald Pole wrote:

Reading it [*The Prince*], I found all the stratagems by means of which religion, justice and good will were invalidated and through which all human and divine virtues would become a prey of egoism, dissimulation and falsehood. It was written by a certain Machiavelli, native of Florence, entitled *The Prince*—and it is such a work that if Satan himself had had a son for a successor, I don't know what other maxims he could pass on to him.

It is understandable that in the time of the formation of nation-states in Europe, those who opposed this new order (for example, the Roman Catholic Church) being actively promoted by the state builders, the "princes" were bound to see in Machiavelli ideas dangerous to their status and their privileges, and above all to their moral foundations. At the same time the builders of the new order were not in a position openly to give him credit for his political perspicacity for obvious reasons, even if they knew of his works.

In any case, Machiavellianism had—and of course still has in part—a bad name, being identified with an open advocacy of the employment of evil means in politics such as treachery, deceit, and dissimulation. A paradox resulting from this is that we often find instances in which those who largely followed Machiavellian maxims in practice repudiated him vigorously in their words. Thus Edmund Spenser made ample use of Machiavellian ideas as expounded in *The Prince* when he gave counsel to Queen Elizabeth I on how to rule Ireland, while denouncing "Machiavellianism" as the art of atheism and deceit.

A better known example is the case of Frederick II of Prussia, who poured moralistic censure on Machiavelli in his famous *Anti-Machiavel*, while he himself was known as nothing but Machiavellian in his politics. Voltaire, who had closely cooperated with the king in the latter's work, later had this to say:

If Machiavelli had had a prince as a disciple, the first thing he would have done is to urge him to write against him.

Another case in point is the trial of Kamenev, an Old Bolshevik, during Stalin's purges in this century, on which Vyshinsky speaking as the prosecutor quoted, as evidence of Kamenev's political heresy, a paragraph from his essay on Machiavelli which mentioned him as a "master of political aphorism and a brilliant dialectician" (Abransky 1962).

In sharp contrast with the moralistic denunciation of Machiavellianism, some saw in Machiavelli a partisan of the republican cause, an ardent advocate of liberty who, feigning to give counsel to the tyrants, unravelled the realities of tyranny and warned the people against the ruses of tyrants, thus making it difficult for them to resort to their usual tricks. Spinola wrote:

Perhaps Machiavelli wanted to show that a free people should by no means entrust their own safety to one man, who unless he is conceited and thinks he can please everyone, must fear traps set for him at all times.

Rousseau remarked in a similar way: "He pretended to instruct kings, instead he taught the people a magnificent lesson. *The Prince* is a book for Republicans."

Some contemporary thinkers point out that Machiavelli contributed, though unintentionally, to liberal democracy by uncovering the basic dilemma inherent in the realities of the political world, which is beyond any hope of rational solution, namely the perennial conflict between different systems of values, and between ideals and the means to put them into practice. This conflict condemns people to a perpetual state of war with each other, thus pointing toward the direction of "pluralism, toleration, and compromise. In political life," people are left always to bring into question what the political authority is up to, regardless of the latter's claims of moral grounds for its actions, and to renounce the hope of finally solving all the problems of human society. Isaiah Berlin (1979) wrote:

Machiavelli's cardinal achievement . . . is his uncovering of an insoluble dilemma, the planting of a permanent question mark in the path of posterity.

Raymond Aron (1978), in comparing Machiavelli with Marx, remarked:

In a century during which so much blood has been spilled by those who hope for too much from politics and humanity, the Machiavellian sometimes appear as the defenders of freedom. Pessimism protects one from illusions and there is no prophet without illusion.

While Machiavelli was highly extolled by Mussolini as a scholar with penetrating insights into human nature and the nature of society, he was enlisted around the same time to the Marxist cause by the latter's political enemy, Gramsci, who saw *The Prince* as an anthropomorphical symbol which was to work on the disorganized people in order to arouse and organize their collective will—in other words, to create a political party based on the masses. Gramsci (1975) wrote:

The modern prince . . . cannot be a real person, a concrete individual it can only be an organism a complex element of society in which the cementing of a collective will, recognized and partially asserted, has already began.

In the course of nationalist movements, particularly in the countries where the process of the formation of nation-state were retarded, Machiavelli was seen as a champion of the nationalist cause, the founding theorist of the modern state. Thus, in the time of the Italian Risorgimento, he was hailed as a prophet of Italy's independence. He was also found and seized upon by German thinkers, mainly in the last century, as the teacher of the *raison d'état*—a term which Machiavelli himself never used.

Apart from moralistic judgments on him as either evil or good, and as either religious or antireligious Machiavelli has been widely acclaimed as one of the founders of the science of politics, who taught us how to distinguish values from facts' what we should do from what in fact we do. Francis Bacon was perhaps the first who gave Machiavelli credit for this:

We must be grateful to Machiavelli and to authors like him, who write about what men do and not about what they should do.

Others such as Ernst Cassirer (1946) and W. K. Hancock (1935-36) followed Bacon in acknowledging Machiavelli as a dispassionate scientist, morally neutral and politically uncommitted, who even anticipated Galileo in his inductive method.

Some, like Jakob Burckhardt (1929) and Charles Singleton (1953), viewed the political ideas of Machiavelli from "the perspective of art," considering that Machiavelli thought of politics as essentially an area of art, in which what matters primarily is the craftsmanship and the resulting products. Political action is removed in this sense from the realm of ethics, of "doing," into that of art, of "making."

As briefly reviewed above, Machiavellianism has been filled with various contents, as Machiavelli's work has always remained contemporary and as people have kept on going back to him in the light of their own experiences. His influences and relevance to the modern world have been so pervasive that it even appears sometimes that people have given up attempts strictly to adhere to his writings or his original intentions. As Giuseppe Prezzolini (1968) and Harvey Mansfield Jr. (1983) remarked respectively:

Machiavelli's reality consists not of what he left in writing, but of what readers of his works think of them.

Machiavellianism can advance without paying allegiance to Machiavelli.

The points Machiavelli bared concerning the basic realities of human society present unavoidable challenges to the contemporary world and to those who see no way out of the present crises on which the world finds itself except through the establishment of a lasting structure for peace on earth. They can ill afford to ignore Machiavelli.

His ideas on the wickedness of human nature, on the inevitability of constant turmoils and conflicts in human society, on the necessity of evil means such as violence and deceit on our political life, and on the need to seek perpetual expansion to preserve ourselves pose fundamental problems for any who seek and plan an ideal future for humankind—a Gordian knot, which, as Vanini and Leibniz are said to have remarked, can only be cut but never untied. However, Machiavelli also envisaged and indicated concrete ways of how to build a good society based on these basic realities by means of our own political actions.

Bibliography

Abransky C 1962 Kamenev's last essay. *New Left Rev.* 19

Aron R 1978 Machiavelli and Marz. *Politics and History.* New York

Berlin I 1979 The originality of Machiavelli. *Against the Current.* Penguin, Harmondsworth

Bondanella P, Musa M 1979 *The Portable Machiavelli.* Penguin. Harmondsworth

Burckhardt J 1972 *The Civilization of the Renaissance in Italy.*

London, 1929

Cassirer E 1946 *The Myth of the State*. London

Clark R C 1951 Machiavelli: Bibliographical spectrum. *Rev. Polit.* 13

Close A J 1969 Commonplace theories of art and nature in Classical Antiquity and in the Renaissance. *J. History of Ideas* 30

Ebenstein W 1957 Mussolini on Machiavelli. *Political Thought in Perspective*. New York

Fleisher M (ed.) 1972 *Machiavelli and the Nature of Political Thought*. London

Geerken J H 1982 Machiavelli studies since 1969. *History of Ideas* 14

Gilbert A H 1938 *Machiavelli's Forerunners*. Durham

Gilbert F 1954 The concept of nationalism in Machiavelli's *Princ. Studies in Renaissance* I

Gilbert F 1965 *Machiavelli's Forerunners*. Durham

Gramsci A 1975 *The Modern Prince and Other Writings*. New York

Hancock W K 1935-36 Machiavelli in modern dress. *History* 20

Hannaford I 1972 Machiavelli's concept of virtu in the Prince and the Discourses reconsidered. *Polit. Studies* 20

Harris P H 1941 Progress in Machiavelli studies. *Italica* 18

Ingersoll D E 1970 Machiaveli and Madison; Perspectives on political stability. *Polit. Sci. Q.* 85

Kraft J 1951 Truth and poetry in Machiavelli. *J. Modern History* 23

Lewis W 1951 *The Lion and the Fox*. London

McCoy C N R 1943 The place of Machivelli in the history of political thought. *Am. Polit. Sci. Rev.* August 1943

Mansfield H C Jr 1983 On the impersonality of the modern state: A comment of Machiavelli's use of stato. *Am. Polit. Sci. Rev.* 77

Mazzeo J A 1962 The poetry of power: Machiavelli's literary vision. *Rev. National Literature* 19

Meinecke F 1957 *Machiavellism*. London

Orwin C 1978 Machiavelli's unchristian charity. *Am. Polit. Sci. Rev.* 72

Peterman L 1982 Dante and the setting for Machiavellianism. *Am. Polit. Sci. Rev.* 76

Preus S 1979 Machiavelli''s functional analysis of religion: Context and object. *J. History of Ideas* 11

Prezzolini G 1968 *Machiavelli*. London

Prezzolini G 1970 The Christian roots of Machiavelli's moral pessimism. *Rev. National Literature* 1

Seren R 1957 A falsification by Machiavelli. *Renaissance News* 12

Singleton C S 1953 The perspective of art. *Kenyon Rev.* 15

Skinner Q 1981 *Machiavelli*. Oxford

Strauss L 1978 *Thoughts of Machiavelli*. Chicago, Illinois

Vogelin E 1951 Machiavelli's Prince: Background and formation. *Rev. Polti.* 13

Wood N 1967 Machiavelli's concept of virtu reconsidered. *Polit. Studies* 15

Wu J C H 1970 Machiavelli and legalists of Ancient China. *Rev. National Literature* 1

JONG-YIL RA

Madariaga, Salvador de

Salvador de Madariaga (1886-1978) was the person elected by the League of Nations to coordinate the League sessions on disarmament. In this position he became a focus of attention for the world's most powerful warring sovereign states. His experience in the 1936-39 Spanish Civil War had led him to ponder the realities of pacifism, collective security, solidarity, and sovereignty. He found no easy answers.

The principal legal instruments for use in international conflict resolution in the nineteenth century were the 1864 Law of Geneva for noncombatant casualties and the 1868 Law of the Hague for belligerents in war. Madariaga's early definitions of the nation-state consequently concerned standing armies and conscription. Political truth in this context was functional or instrumental, not related to goals for practical international disarmament.

Madariaga similarly defined "international relations" in his 1937 *Theory and Practice of International Relations* as the "mechanics of collective (consciously moral) forces" or the irrational mechanics of institutionalized power. These "collective forces" were subsequently defined as "all (conscious) manifestations of life endowed with power to influence collective events" (Bailey 1972; Madariaga 1935, 1937b). What this meant in reality was that "just" war principles were affirmed and thus a contemporary, Grenville Clark, for example, could draft the 1920 and 1940s United States conscription laws (Swomley 1964). The consciousness driving the world to war overwhelmed the League of Nations by the mid-1930s.

The central obstacle to implementing disarmament appeared to Madariaga to be the dilemma of sovereignty. He defined sovereignty as "a tendency, both primary and reactive, to consider or to assert the national will as the sole, or at least the final determinant of action" (Madariaga 1937b). Preeminent national sovereignty made international world peace almost impossible.

Madariaga saw the historical elements of sovereignty as fundamental to nationalism. Sovereignty started under Roman law and the laws of the Holy Roman Empire with the symbolic *fasces* of the Emperor, representing collective military might. Madariaga also viewed sovereignty as a more or less adolescent stage blocking the way to world solidarity, under the guise of various forms of expansionist imperialism or charismatic hero worship (Madariaga 1937a and 1937b). An analogy, however tenuous, might be that of sovereignty serving much like "apartheid," "gerrymandering," or "red lining," as understood, translated, and implemented on a world scale.

Sovereignty was the nemesis of solidarity for Madariaga. Solidarity, defined as the interdependence needed for existence between the parts and the sum total of international relations, undergirded world organization. Solidarity existed in either objective or subjective forms. Objective solidarity occurred in world power structures, while subjective solidarity occurred within countries. Objective solidarity included characteristics of territory, climate, habitat, food, resources, interdependence, race, world trade, and linguistic affinities.

Madariaga postulated that collective security resulted from military force. For this reason, he described Article X defining collective security enforced by common military intervention as the core Covenant article of the League of Nation Covenant. Implementation of Article X, through Article XI, was theoretically supposed to safeguard international peace between nations (Madariaga 1937b).

Practical implementations from the collective unconscious takes shape in the practice of world order. It was in the "hands-on" practice of world order that Madariaga began to critically question sovereignty, and opt instead for pragmatic conflict resolution. Madariaga found that actual implementation of world order required judicious transnationalism and solida-rity, instead of traditional collective security methods. His experience pointed to what actually worked, both in response to actual conditions and future trends.

Madariaga attempted to overcome the barrier of sovereignty in the practical operation of the League by the concept of solidarity. The term solidarity has apparently also been used within the United Nations in the sense of world order. Transnationalism and solidarity referred to a method reaching beyond the limits of national sovereignty or frontiers. At the same time, these terms relate to the behavior of nations and transnational corporate enterprise. The pragmatic shift of Madariaga on this point marked his recognition of heterogeneous methods for change and the implementation of power.

Madariaga noted that foreign affairs had literally ceased to exist in reality, since world affairs dominated any and all international relations. He recommended

that all foreign ministers be rechristened "ministers of world affairs." By 1938 he had begun to conceptualize solidarity in planning for world order, regarding tendencies and values incorporated through world trade and transportation. He predicted that world disarmament would only work on a planetary scale.

He redefined armaments as instruments of sovereignty, instead of as tools for world order. Recognizing that there would be no successful military deterrent to weapons of mass destruction, he perceived that the only other alternative was to create a world organism by world order. The fear of past war and economic autarky under the notion of sovereignty merely delayed healthy development of world institutions. He began to argue that sovereignty was functionally unnecessary.

He increased his call for non-national organizations as well, identifying these non-national or non-sovereign organizations in terms of world business and religion, thus transcending sovereign nationalism. He realized that the notion of sovereignty was very much alive, as illustrated by the Japanese inte-rests in East Asia reflecting the United States Monroe Doctrine in Latin America. He concluded in *Anarchy or Hierarchy* (1937) that the modern state should resume its local role in government, financially divest from international war trade, renounce international state sovereignty, and build institutions for peace (Carr and Madariaga 1941).

In effect, Madariaga called for world planning to avert the problems and consequences of war. His notion of international solidarity, in an international rather than socialist or capitalist sense, meant encouraging methods for transnationalism and discouraging national frontiers. He wanted to achieve world economic order and consciousness by overcoming world hunger, poverty, and the arms race.

World order would be reached when the notions of sovereignty and collective security became debatable or meaningless. Madariaga saw military confrontation as rooted in unorganized, anarchic answers to human necessities like housing, health, employment, and education. Internal well-being of the collective unconscious would advance when weapons of mass destruction and the poverty of totalitarianism became meaningless. He spent 39 years of his life in political exile from Spain, uncomfortable with espousing any particular nation, before dying in Switzerland in 1978.

Bibliography

Bailey S D 1972 *Prohibitions and Restraints in War*. Oxford University Press, New York

Carr E H, Madariaga S de 1941 *The Future of International Government*. Peace Aims Pamphlet No. 4. National Peace

Council, Oxford

Madariaga S de 1935 *The Price of Peace* (Richard Cobden Lecture). Cobden-Sanderson, London

Madariaga S de 1937a *Anarchy or Hierarchy*. Allen and Unwin, London

Madariaga S de 1937b *Theory and Practice in International Relations*. University of Pennsylvania Press, Philadelphia, Pennsylvania

Swomley J M Jr 1964 *The Military Establishment*. Beacon Press, Boston, Massachusetts

ABDUL AZIZ SAID; PAUL HUBERS

Magna Carta of Global Common Society

1. Retrospection on Human History and Civilization

There have been numerous hypotheses about the beginning of the universe. Among them, the most credible theory widely accepted by astrophysicists is that first formulated in 1965 by Nobel Laureate Robert Wilson of Bell Telephone Laboratory and astronomer Allen Sandage of Mt. Palour Observatory. By observing cosmic electromagnetic waves, they estimated that our galaxy was born about 13 billion years ago. Their claim has become currently an established theory largely because it substantiated the general theory of relativity by Albert Einstein.

Our solar system was by estimation created about 5 billion years ago around the arm of the Orion Constellation which is about 30,000 light years away from the center of our galaxy. The earth was born about 4.5-4.7 billion years ago. It rotates around the sun with the orbital distance of 150 million kilometers. With its radius extending about 6,380 kilometers, 1/108.7th of the sun's dimension, the earth looks like a half-boiled egg.

What then is the history of organisms on earth? The first evidence of life was the primitive virus, which could be either non-organic or organic depending on how one perceives it. It was discovered in Swaziland at the southern tip of Africa in the form of microfossil and was estimated to be about 2.8-3.4 billion years old.

Then about 2 billion years ago, the multi-cellular organisms came into being when oxygen was formed on earth. This means that there was no real life for 2.5-2.6 billion years after the earth came to existence.

Entering into the Paleozoic age, the real life forms were developed initially in the water. Algae in plant forms and trilobites and snails in animal forms began to appear on the scene. In the mid-Paleozoic age of 400-500 million years back, the vertebrate fish appeared.

About 50 million years after the plants spread to the land from the water, the amphibians with four legs emerged. They enjoyed maximum growth from the end of the Paleozoic to the Mesozoic era. Then appeared reptiles, the ancestor of birds and mammals. Such gigantic animals as Dinosaur showed up during this same period.

And approximately 100 million years later, which was about 60 million years before the present day, Dryopithecinae appeared on the land at last. However, we had to wait for another 56.8 million years for our ancestor Homo Habilis to be born, which was about 3.2 million years ago. This is evidenced by the discovery of a skull fossil at Kenya, Africa, by Louis Seymour Bozette Leaky.

Homo Erectus (Java Man and Peking Man) later succeeded the Homo Habilis. They came down from trees and laid the foundation of life on land, using verbal communications, fire, and instruments for hunting and collecting activities.

About 350,000 years ago, they evolved into Homo Sapiens (Neanderthal and Cro-Magnon) who were similar to modern man. They lived in caves and used wood, stone, and artifacts. They also wore animal skins and even enjoyed some cultural life such as painting on cave walls.

Scholars later came to discover and agree that Archaic Homo Sapiens of 100,000 years ago were even closer to us by the looks of their skull and body structures. They made elaborate abrasive stone instruments; moreover, they led a cooperative life and learned to bury the dead.

Then came the New Stone Age 40,000 years ago. The Archaic Homo Sapiens evolved into Modern Homo Sapiens, who settled in a habitat where they enjoyed productive lives by making pots with clay and raising livestock.

The real human-like life began only 10,000 years ago, and studies show that our cultural life started merely 5,000 to 6,000 years ago. Since then, man ushered in the historical epoch and developed four civilizations in different areas: the Mesopotamian civilization on the bank of the Tigris and Euphrates rivers, the Egyptian civilization at the Nile river bank, the Pamir high land civilization at an upper stream side of Indus and Ganges rivers, and the Great Yellow river civilization on a bank of the Great Yellow river of China.

From that time, progress included a division of labor through cooperation, differentiation of social status, creation of graphic symbols for writing, development of cities and markets and worship practices of primitive religions in accordance with ancient mythologies. Temple-building for gods inspired the development of architectural skills. In due course, humans gradually established theocratic political systems, which laid an incipient foundation for the modern civilized society of today. Indeed, human beings traveled a long way, crossing over the hills of the Ancient, Medieval, and Modern periods (see Young Seek Choue, *Oughtopia*, Oxford: Pergamon Press, 1979).

What should we reflect upon in this long course of human history? What are humans and what kind of life have they lived so far? Should we cheer over human victory when we consider the fact that only one percent or less of the original life forms have survived through the ages of 2.5-2.6 billion years and that only human beings have succeeded in developing civilization? Or, on the contrary, should we continue to engage in a life-and-death struggle with the strong-preying-on-the weak as we did in the past?

Distressingly enough, this is precisely the major predicament that humankind faces today. This is exactly the primary task for us to perform. Let us turn our eyes back a minute to the origin of things.

Nothing in this universe is immutable. The earth, the sun, the stars and even the galaxies are not free from evolutionary transformation. Accordingly, nothing in this world is truly permanent or unchanging. Everything develops in mutual interactions according to the ontological attributes of matter.

The life cycle of our galaxy is about 80 billion years and that of our sun and earth is about 10 billion years. Thus most of the stars are condensed from gas clouds and return to cosmic dust again after completing their life span. Therefore, our Galaxy will continue to expand for another 30 billion years, then fall into decay, and finally extinguish itself in 40 billion years. Our solar system also follows the same pattern. It has lived 5 out of 10 billion years of its total life span, and it is now enjoying the prime of its life.

In three billion years when the sun exhausts its hydrogen fuel at the core, it will expand by radiating a red glow and heating up. The expansion of the sun will destroy all life on earth, and the earth will eventually pulverize, terminating its life at the end of 5 billion years from now.

We cannot help but accept this reality which stems from the law of constant mutation and transformation. Such a dreadful realization of the facts and the fate of our life indeed haunts our sense of self-preservation.

This glaring truth suggests that mankind should have a correct view of the universe and look at the world realistically in order that people would understand life truthfully. This is the way human beings can abandon their futile rapacity, and live the rest of their life beautifully, valuably, and rewardingly.

In other words, we come to this world empty-handed, live briefly, and leave this world empty-handed again. But since we are already here, and have created cultural life, constantly seeking a life that is worth living, should not we continue cultivating a brighter cultural legacy for our neighbors, fellow countrymen, the entire humanity, and its posterity, so that they also could live a good peaceful life till death, while walking on the right, valuable and virtuous path?

I suggest, therefore, that we the humanity that is about to usher in the new century, contemplating on a new millennium take a new turn on our life, at this juncture of suffering the eschatological crises resulting from the decadence of the modern materialistic civilization, reflect on our past history, introspect on our own life, and thus formulate a desirable image of the future. That is to say that ultimately we should jointly construct a global cooperation society (GCS), which is a truly humanistic, civilized welfare, and universally democratic society.

2. Problems and the Future Prospect of Modern Society

What are the characteristics of modern human society? It is a society where people are spiritually poor in the midst of affluence achieved by materialistic civilization, where people are egoistic in spite of the necessity of becoming more social and compassionate. It is a society where man is neglected and alienated due to the predominance of machines and efficiency. It is a society where the materialistic pleasure-seeking and the self-proliferation of science and technology have become the goals.

Worried about the trend of modern society, Donald N. Michael said that we were running into a society that has had no preparation for the future; Alvin Toffler warned that we had no way of avoiding the shock of the future if the human society continues as it has; and Bertrand Russell asked if there was a hope in the future human society. As intellectuals in the world are worrying about the future of human society, what then are the problems facing us?

First, there is the climate of neglecting humanity due to the omnipotence of materialism. The belief in materialism in essence presupposes individualism, liberalism, egoism and exclusionism. It prefers pragmatic values such as profitability, efficiency, utility and pleasure to ethical and moral values like benevolence, righteousness, courteousness, decency, wisdom and faithfulness. Accordingly, these pragmatic values engender a cruel and heartless human society which lacks mutual trust and cooperation, making it impossible therefore to create a humanistic human society. In addition, commercialism leads to excessive consumption and the pursuit of decadent life.

Second, there are the abuses and aftereffects of the information-science society and the supremacy of science-technology. The development of science and technology has made human life convenient with material affluence. But if we are to indulge too much in science and technology for convenience and material affluence, we will be no longer the masters of science and technology.

Maximum production and maximum consumption will only make us worship science and technology and fall into the spiral of their self-proliferation. As a result, science and technology are today controlling man who is increasingly alienated and losing his humanity. Thus instead of serving man, science and technology are converting man into a cyborg living in a cyber space without humanity.

It is not hard to foresee that Internet will bring forth a total globalization and a world without borders, i.e., a society of virtual reality, and that DNA development and its mishandling will create a dehumanized society, giving rise to serious problems threatening the very existence of human society.

Third, there is the possibility of degeneration of democracy into an ignorant and mobocratic mass society. Democracy is the spirit of our world and our time and is the best political system up to date. But, a successful operation of the social instrument called democracy depends on how it is put to use.

Aristotle asserted at the early stage of its inception that democracy could be either the best system for a society of wise men or the worst system for that of the masses. After the bitter experiences following the end of World War II, the world has yet to register one single case among all the newly developing states which has succeeded in running a well-established democratic system after a simplistic importation of democracy without having the consciousness of democratic citizens.

Success of the democratic system depends on how able one is to handle it. The party system is good but it cannot escape from the partisan interests. The representative system is good, but it cannot flee from the personal relations of interests and advantages. The electoral system is good, but it is not immune to human favoritism. And the rule of law is good, but it is prone to the erratic inconsistency of "the morning enactment and evening amendments" at the discretion of policy makers.

If politics in democracy becomes politics of public opinion, it will be easily manipulated by the ruling elite. This is where again lies the major problem.

True, the public opinion and the majority rule must be upheld. But the essential question is whether it is the public opinion of informed people or that of particular self-interests, or worse yet, that of the popular opinion of the ignorant masses? That is the problem of the politics by public opinion. We must all heed that unconditional majority rule is synonymous to "tyrannical rule of the popular opinion," which easily falls prey to a mobocracy.

The 21st century will no doubt usher in a civil society ruled by public opinion. In this context, I welcome the emergence of a genuine civil society based on a participatory democracy. But in view of the worrisome trend of mass society today, we must guard against the possibility of democracy and the rule of law degenerating into a dictatorial society governed by public opinion.

Here is another grave problem. It is said that the law is sacred, for it is rooted in the eternal truth and therefore it is assumed that it must be obeyed by all. But natural law is variously interpreted according to the spirit of time and place. The positive law is changeable constantly depending on the interests and situations.

Moreover, in the enactment procedure, a law may pass or fail by one vote. Furthermore, positive laws are often enacted in the morning and amended in the evening. Whenever the law changes, good often becomes evil, and vice-versa. The change of law frequently overturns the judgement of history as well.

Now then, what is the standard for right and wrong or good and evil, and what is the criterion of its definition? Considering the importance of the questions, I shall address them in the next chapter when I deal with the civilizational view of history and the entailing values and norms.

Fourth, there are still the problems of exclusionism by nationalism, statism, class division and self-righteousness of religious and hegemonic forces. We cannot completely negate a partial rationale either to the nationalism of a people who has blood relations for thousands of years or to the class antagonism owing to ideological differences. But, how many conflicts and wars have we engaged in to burn, to destroy, and to kill each other and civilization itself precisely because of such exclusivism? There were no winners but all losers.

This is exactly the reason why we should take our lessons from the teachings of our past saints and sages on the reverence of human lives and the love of humanity. Today, all of humanity lives in the ethos of democratization, upholding the principles of liberty, equality, and cooperation of all the peoples of the world.

At this juncture, where the whole world is crying out for globalization, asserting co-existence and co-prosperity for all as a single human family, we may have to look back to the residual evils left by exclusive nationalism, imperialism, and class struggle to our civilization and to our humanity.

Self-righteousness is equally evil. Religions basically teach us to love even our enemies, forsake our greed and be merciful. Nonetheless, animosity, jealousy and hostility among different religions are constant throughout the ages, not to mention the endless factional contentions within the same denominations. In spite of these, religion is necessary and good.

Can we imagine a society without religion? No, it would be cold and bleak. It would be miserable and awful. Man is striving to be good and aspiring for self-perfection because there is religion. That is why we desire and pray for a true religion, rather than the religion of praying for "gift and fortune-blessing." With a truly religious mind, it may be possible for the entire humanity to become truly one single human family.

Self-righteous hegemonism is equally to blame. From Pax Romana of the ancient times down through the attempts of the world-empire construction by Genghis Khan, Hitler's Nazism, Mussolini's Fascism, Marx's class struggle, they are all for hegemonism. We must not loose sight of some nations which dream even today of world domination still imbued with the doomed fantasy of the past.

Clearly the spirit of our time has changed. It is no longer the era of monarchs or kings nor of exclusive nationalism and statism, it is the era of universal democracy founded on the principle of people's rule. That is why it is time for us to come together as a single human family under the banner of Pax UN and to construct what I call global common society (GCS) as we live in the era of humanization and globalization.

3. The Establishment of New Values and Norms Based on the Civilizational View of History

As a general rule, the natural world lives according to the law of nature, the world of animals according to their own instincts and conditioned reflex, and the human society according to reason and good sense founded upon humanness.

Regardless of the forms of government, our political society was founded on such human attributes and nature since the ancient times. First, the tribal chiefs ruled by primitive theocracy, followed by the absolute rule of kings by invoking divine right. Then with the advent of the modern age, political power was based on nationalism and statism in the name of nation, and then finally with the establishment of the theory of inalienable rights, democratic rule began to unfold in the republican form of government.

The legitimacy of such political systems was based on the divine right, the natural law, and the absolute authority of the people, state and classes, whereas the norms supporting such political systems were set forth by the absolute or reason-oriented view of history which are in fact derived from the natural norms. The problem with such norms is that they are simply based on the theory of force stemming from the belief in the supremacy of power.

We humans are controlled by the order imposed by the law of nature. But if we are to be detained meekly within that order like other creatures and animals, we cannot lead a human life. In other words, we cannot be human beings with cultural, social, and personality traits if we live under that condition. However, throughout the entire human history, men have lived unfortunately under the law of the jungle like animals with natural norms according to the naturalistic view of history.

How tragic the blood-stained human history was in retrospect! How absurd is our humanity with such superior wisdom and capacity, yet unable to elude the animal nature, and still living the life of the strong-preying-upon-the-weak and the winner-vanquishing-the-defeated!

At the threshold of the 21st century, if we are going to be cultured and civilized men, it is incumbent upon us to change our view of history into the civilizational view of history (a comprehensive view of history through a combination of spiritual culture and material civilization) so as to live a civilized life like genuine human beings with mutual respect and cooperation.

Let's meditate again for a moment with our eyes closed. We call ourselves human beings because we can think, live a cooperative life and possess culture and civilization. Only when we are rational and able to discern right from wrong and good from evil, live a cooperative life, construct a human community, and create cultural values, we would be true human beings.

Look around us a minute. Is there anything that is not civilized? Obviously our languages, letters, clothes, foods, housing, machines, customs, modes, institutions, installations, the necessities of life including tools and instruments, and living environment are all civilized. Could we call ourselves anything but civilized animals? We call people without civilization "primitive," with a low level of civilization "uncivilized," and with a higher level of civilization "civilized" and "intellectual."

Remember, we used to call the primitive people without civilization ape-men. Nevertheless, we humans still do not feel deeply the preciousness of the values of civilization. Civilization is certainly not a decoration or luxury. We must translate the history of mankind into the history of civilization.

It must be emphasized again that our view of history cannot be the naturalistic view of history nor can it be the rational view of history. It must be founded on the civilizational view of history so as to foster an environment of civilization and to build a house of civilization, i.e., the civilized society (see Young Seek Choue, *The Creation of Cultural World*, Taegu: Moonsungdang, 1951).

The civilizational view of history denies that nature and force are just or good. It upholds, instead, that man as the master of history and civilization is the center of society. It is founded on the idea of human-centrism, which conceives that all things in human society must be the factors and instruments to serve human life by creating human happiness and values (see Young Seek Choue, *Oughtopia*, Oxford: Pergamon Press, 1979). Humanity is so precious that it is even written in the New Testament, "What good would it be if a man gains the whole world, yet loses his life?"

Now then, what should be the standard criteria for judging the norms of civilization to serve as our social norms? As they must be established on the universal truth, I shall expound the question on the basis of the following five determinative criteria of right and wrong and good and evil.

First of all, since good is good of human society, anything that is truly humane, true and beneficial to human life is good. Anything that is neither humane nor beneficial to human life is evil.

Second, since man is a civilized being, anything that gives rise to civilization, preserves and develops it is good.

Third, because we live today in a democracy that is rooted in the principle of popular sovereignty, we should regard anything that is not for exclusivism but for universal democracy as good. In other words, all things that contribute to the securing of universal freedom, equality and co-prosperity and to the preserving of equal rights and co-existence of all states big or small alike are good. And anything that is against it is evil.

Fourth, man lives a collective social life. Since man has to cohabit in the domains of family, work place, and country, he is in fact incapable of surviving outside of society. Man's capability of creating and developing civilization and his enjoyment of a happy life is attributable only to his cooperative social life. So, anything that fosters cooperative social life is good, and anything that obstructs or destroys it is anti-peace and evil.

Fifth, it is my view that what is justice or injustice depends on whether it preserves and develops the above four criteria of good or not. I wish to make it clear that this is my standard of judging right and wrong and good and evil based on the norms of civilization derived from the civilizational view of history. However, changing the view of history is to change the optical angle to look at the world differently. It is, in fact, a work to change the understanding about history based on a changed view.

The theory of Greek astronomer Ptolemaios Klaudios in the 2nd century BC that the center of the universe was the earth and the sun rotated around it dominated the human civilization for a long time as a general belief. Only in 1543 did Nicolaus Copernicus come to proclaim the truth that the earth is not the center of the universe and rotated on its own axis and around the sun. And when in 1609 Galileo Galilei observed it for the first time in human history with a telescope and supported Copernicus' theory, he was condemned by the Inquisition.

This shows that we the contemporaries do not really know which view of history or which set of values and norms are correct and appropriate for our society. In this regard, my suggestion of changing the view of history should also be resorted to the judgement of history by the later generations.

4. The Reconstruction of Human Society and Its Future

Today human society is undergoing a total transformation. It is experiencing a metamorphic change. As the views of the universe, the world, and the state undergo drastic changes, so must the perspective of life.

As the revolutionary development of science and technology is compressing time and space, the walls of national boundaries have increasingly been lowered, turning the world into a global village. At the same time, the wide spread of democratic ideology has also accompanied the idea of human dignity and respect along with humanitarianism. As a result, yesterday's foreigners are becoming the members of the same human family today.

In other words, our world is transforming into a transnational society transcending national borders. And the revolutionary development in the field of transportation and communication has turned our world from "a space of the one-day-life" into "a space of simultaneous life."

The globalization of economy led by the development of the multinational corporations, the growth of trade volume, the opening of labor markets, and the increase of cultural exchange is making the world a truly cross-cultural society which will make all the people of the world global citizens with one single unified culture and sentiment. We can easily sense that a borderless world society, no longer requiring national boundaries, is changing the world into a place where there is no longer a need for arms race for hegemonic struggles.

Accordingly, we must break down the remnants of exclusionism statistic, hegemonic democracy, class socialism, and exclusionism, and establish the common goals, the common norms, and common tasks in order to rebuild the human society as a global common society where we can all co-exist and co-prosper (see Young Seek Choue, *Reconstruction of the Human Society*, Seoul: Ulyumunhwa Co., 1975).

In order to construct such a global common society, we must first establish a universal democratic society. In retrospect, the democratic systems we have had were either an exclusive nationalistic democracy or proletariat democracy (Communism).

Consequently, they did not go beyond the limits of attempting to secure the basic rights and well-being of their own people or classes in their own national communities. They believed and acted as if it were perfectly all right to persecute other people, to launch economic and armed aggression, or encroach on human rights as long as they did it for their own people or classes. Therefore, they were not true democratic systems for all.

I must reiterate that we must ensure freedom, equality and co-prosperity of all peoples as well as equal rights and co-existence of all nations, big or small, in accordance with the spirit of the United Nations Charter. That is why we must elevate our democracies of today to the universal democracy which I have advocated for a long time (see Young Seek Choue, *The Democratic Liberty*, Seoul: Hanil Publisher Co., 1948).

Second, we must build a human-centered society based on the principle of respect for humanity. We can no longer afford a dehumanized society like ours today where men are relegated to a level far less valued than materials, and where they are slighted and even despised by science and technology.

To transform our society into a society where humanity is respected, we should make materials, science and technology, all the social institutions, laws, systems, and organizations exist for and serve men as their instruments and means of achieving their humanistic goals. As one can see in the "Ordeal of Frankenstein," we must not create a society where machines and materials dominate men.

Third, we must establish ethical values and norms suitable to the new era. As it has been said already, the criteria for judging the standard of right and wrong and good and evil cannot be contingent on the naturalistic logic based on power expressed in "the victor is the king and the vanquished is the traitor." As long as such "law of jungle" or "the norms based on power" persists, our society can never escape from chaos. It makes the world to resemble the Pandemonium which is full of conflicts, distrust, manipulation, machination, struggles, and wars.

Man is a human being because he is in essence a spiritual-being with a body. Said in another way, because he has a highly developed spirit, he can cherish civilization, possess personality, and learn manners. Animals equally have both body and spirit but their spirits operate only instinctively and subject to conditioned reflex. That is what separates men from animals.

In the ever increasingly cruel society of today, one can easily see its dehumanizing process in the midst of the material affluence and convenience. We must realize that the pragmatic system of values, which encourages the calculation of advantages and disadvantages and gains and losses and the pursuance of utilitarian values, utility, and sensual pleasure, is producing all sorts of crimes, making our society a dreadful place.

Nevertheless, I am not discrediting all the contemporary values and urging to go back to the past to retain old ethical values. What I am proposing here is to blend the spiritual side of ethics, faithfulness, sense of propriety, morality, and conscience with the pragmatic values such as pleasure and calculation of gains and losses in order to create new ethical values and norms.

Fourth, we must build a global common society. Today we are all becoming citizens of the world community with the United Nations as its center. As the preamble of the United Nations Charter starts with "We the peoples of the United Nations," we are already professing ourselves subconsciously to be world citizens, democratic citizens, civilized citizens, and citizens of global welfare society. As our society is also becoming a society of science and technology as well as of information, we, the ordinary citizens in each nation, suddenly find ourselves becoming citizens of the world and of the universe.

But are we truly changing ourselves to fit to these realities? We claim that we are practicing democracy, yet we are holding on to the obsolete frame of exclusive national democracy. We are racing toward globalization, yet we do not hesitate to wage economic wars of preying on each other. While we are opening a space age, we offer prematurely a wide open cyber space over the national boundaries without counter-measures against abuses, and show even no scruples at manipulating DNA to clone human beings. An awful situation indeed!

That is not all. Even today, long since the downfall of the curtains of the Cold War, some nations are still developing high-tech weapons. There are also some countries which are not doing well economically but none the less racing to the development of nuclear weapons and missiles as delivery vehicles. Some of them are developing and producing missiles to earn hard currencies.

Man has aspired for peace ever since the opening of human society in the ancient times. Nonetheless, human history has constantly been stained with blood in the name of national interests and justice. And nations caught in the endless cycle of rise and fall have eventually ended up incurring only self-injury in the long run.

St. Augustine, who took pains in developing ideas of preventing wars, asserted that war was intolerable except those called "just wars." Hugo Grotius went so far as to suggest some concrete measures of preventing wars based on human reason. And Immanuel Kant offered a vision of permanent world peace which expounded that the only viable way of peace was to constitute a world republic through partial concession of sovereignty of each nation. Saint-Pierre argued that the only way of eliminating wars from the international community was through the formation of a league of nations.

Notwithstanding all these noble efforts including subsequent attempts by arms reduction measures, plans for checks and balances of power, or even the strategy of "star wars" like the Strategic Defense Initiative (SDI) were only partial schemes for peace, falling far short of eliminating wars on the face of the earth.

Then, how do we achieve our long desired permanent world peace and attain a civilized welfare society that will enable us to live a life that is worthy and rewarding? With this in mind, I dare offer here the following four ideas as the ways of improving our human society:

First, we must be conscious of the fact that we are no longer strangers to one another but global citizens sharing a common destiny. We must realize gravely that there will be neither winners nor losers in the future wars fought with chemical, biological, nuclear, and electronic weapons, for they will be the wars of Doomsday or Armageddon. They must be avoided under any and all circumstances, perceiving the mission as ordainment by God (see Young Seek Choue, *Proposal for Peace*, Seoul: Kyung Hee University Press, 1986).

Therefore, we should never allow any idea that under a certain circumstance war is inevitable and it must be fought. We must believe that peace—not war—is the dictate of history (see Young Seek Choue, *Proposal for*

Peace, Seoul: Kyung Hee University Press, 1986). Bearing that in mind, we must spread the peace-loving, peacekeeping and peace-making spirit and march together to construct a global cooperation society.

Second, in order to carry out successfully this historic mission for the human society, the major advanced powers which are well aware of the trend and tide of our times should take the lead in the vanguard of the movement.

To secure a world peace for all the nations based on a genuine democracy rather than under the domination of one nation like Pax Romana, we must achieve it under the United Nations if possible. And the initiative and leadership for peace must come from the leading major powers. I believe that in carrying out such a great task for the entire human society, the initiative and leadership of the leading powers are essential and would be more effective than those provided by ordinary nations.

This does not mean to exclude the general opinion of ordinary countries from the peace-making process but to emphasize that greater nations, not the strong nations, should exercise their leadership in addressing this historic task in broader perspectives.

Third, we first have to construct regional cooperation societies that are certainly not designed for the exclusive interests of nations but in perfect harmony for creating a universal democratic society. Ever since 1981, I have been developing the theory of regional cooperation society (RCS) and global cooperation society (GCS) to achieve world peace and submitted it to the United Nations, while working for its realization in collaboration with the International Association of University Presidents (IAUP).

The regional cooperation society is intended to bring together initially neighboring countries that are usually in the state of constant conflicts and wars so that they can begin a peace process through economic cooperation at the beginning and widen their cooperation to other fields including cultural and social fields. In the materialistic societies of today where material interests are considered most important, the successful promotion of mutual economic interests and benefits will be followed by the cooperation in other fields.

Such a regional integration can be compared with the hitting of two birds with one stone, for war can be avoided among the neighboring nations once they are intertwined by mutual economic interests (see Young Seek Choue, *World Peace in the Global Village*, Seoul: Kyung Hee University Press, 1987).

The European Union (EU) is a vivid example of such a case. Since the beginning of the Modern era, Europe was the site of war after war, including World War I and World War II. However, with the deepening of mutual economic relationship, the political picture of Europe has changed radically. The EU is the outcome of a successful economic cooperation among West European countries within the framework of the EEC and the EC. Eventually reorganized into the expanded EU, the solidarity of European states is stronger than ever before. The emerging of the EU is precisely an example of development of a regional cooperation society into the regional integrated society for which I have been advocating for a long time. Taking the EU as an example, we must develop the regional cooperation society into a regional integration society (RIS).

Once steps are taken to that direction, the existing national boundaries will eventually crumble down with further penetration of multinational corporations into each other, the opening of labor markets, and freedom of movement, employment and residence, while consolidating individual national security efforts into a single regional collective security system.

When the opening, cooperation, mutual benefits, solidarity, and security arrangement have reached such a stage, it will be hardly possible to wage a war among the members of the regional community. It is indeed a realistic and marvelous prospect we can aspire for.

However, contrary to my theory and purpose of regional cooperation society and global cooperation society, the process of regional integration today regretfully fails to overcome national blocism and to set their final goals on the establishment of lasting world peace and the construction of global common society. It is also regretful that today's regional organizations are being formed not within the framework of the United Nations. In other words, they are organizing themselves not within the framework of international democracy but within the framework of nationalistic democracy.

Fourth, the global cooperation society should then develop into a global integration society (GIS). With the spread of democratic ideas and with the revolutionary compression of time and space, we are already becoming world citizens looking forward to a global common society.

Accordingly, all the nations of the world in adhering to the spirit and the trend of our times have crossed their own borders to organize, first, regional cooperation organizations (i.e., regional cooperation societies) such as EC, OAS, OAU, ASEAN, NAFTA, MERCOSUL, and the Arab Community. They are now undertaking reorganization of the existing regional organizations into larger organizations. For example, the EC has already expanded into the EU; the NAFTA and the ASEAN are expanding into the APEC; and the EU and the ASEAN are cooperating

as the members of the ASEM.

I see this phenomenon not as a simple expansion of regions, but as a progressive integration of regional organizations (regional cooperation societies) into a global cooperation society and global integration society consciously or unconsciously, as the EEC has turned into the EC and finally into the EU in the name of globalization. In short, we are heading for the global cooperation society.

Since the global cooperation society is coming inevitably, what road are we to take then? We must endeavor to organize the regional cooperation societies and at the same time must drive for the global cooperation society. After these efforts successfully brought in the regional integration societies, we should then proceed to develop and consolidate the global integration society under the Pax United Nations.

At the initial stage of this scheme, the major nations of the EU, the APEC, the G-8, and China should assume leadership for the other countries in enlightening and encouraging the existing regional organizations to reshape themselves into genuine and viable regional cooperation societies. In doing so, it may be necessary for the major nations to provide various incentives to the existing regional organizations.

While undertaking this process, we must pay our attention seriously to the problems of arms control and collective security. We must reduce the stockpiles of chemical, biological, and nuclear weapons; forbid the development, transfer, and sale of new weapons and the related technologies; and develop a viable UN collective security system with a strong standing UN forces under the leadership of the major powers in order to deter and sanction aggression. These security measures should be transitional until the establishment of the global integration society under the Pax UN.

At the second stage, we must encourage and induce the newly organized regional cooperation societies not only to cooperate among them closely but also to reconstruct themselves into regional integration societies to the level of the EU today. At this stage, it will be most desirable and appropriate for the United Nations and the regional integration societies of the developed nations to provide the regional integration societies of the less developed nations various economic, social, cultural, and security considerations and benefits.

At the third and final stage, the regional organizations which have already transformed themselves successfully into the regional integration societies should then construct the global integration society under the banner of Pax UN and, while developing a Global Confederation of States, they should induce other RICs to join in. Analogically the United States of America is an excellent precedent for a global confederation of states. If the 50 states of various ethnic and cultural origins in the North American Continent could have been able to form a perfect union in federation, there would be a realistic chance that all the nations of the world can be united to form a global confederation of states in the 21st century. Today, we can see as a genuine example such integration process in the European Union (EU) which is rapidly shaping into "the United States of Europe."

After having successfully induced other regional integration societies to join the global confederation of states and complete it, we may be assured of the ending of the inhuman atrocities like mutual slaughtering and destruction. We may also be able to divert immense amounts of military expenditures to national development and welfare programs. I believe that only when we are able to reach this stage, we can achieve a lasting world peace for which mankind has been craving ever since the beginning of human history, and can construct a democratic, civilized, and welfare-oriented society which guarantees the co-existence and co-prosperity of all the people of the world. This briefly summarizes the essential points of my Oughtopian Peace Model which I developed in 1984 (see Young Seek Choue, *White Paper on World Peace*, Seoul: Kyung Hee University Press, 1991).

However, such achievements will not come automatically and easily. If we are not prepared for any unexpected incidents or situations that will obstruct the process of achieving the global integration society, we may encounter serious difficulties that may jeopardize this great historic task itself. So, all of humanity must earnestly exert their joint efforts toward that goal.

Let us ponder calmly on what we are really. Today, we are no longer ape-men. We are supposedly men with civilization and intellectuality. Nevertheless, we are still maintaining the animalistic norms and life of "preying and being preyed," and we have never seriously thought about it whether it is right or wrong. Also our exclusionism and egocentrism are destroying our history and staining it with blood all the while. But, we have never thought about a way of living peacefully together in harmony and cooperation.

We are at the point of leaving the 20th century and entering into the 21st century and a new millennium. It is still not too late to change the course of history. Instead of blindly and uncritically following the manners, customs, and institutions of the past, we must reform ourselves and rechart our human history by taking a lesson from the history of the universe as well as the entire process of human history.

For this task, we must become true human beings, possessing a correct view of the universe, a proper world outlook, an appropriate concept of the state, and a right attitude toward life. As true human beings, we must reconstruct the human society which will be spiritually beautiful, materially affluent, and humanly rewarding. This society is both desirable and feasible and I call it "Oughtopia."

I must say that if we ignore this historic call now, human history will remain forever unchanged as the history of animalistic world of "preying and being preyed" for thousands or millions or even billions of years to come.

There is a saying, "Where there is mind, there is action." If we are to be reborn and reconstruct our human society as a desirable one, we must reform our mind first. That was why, in 1995, the 50th anniversary year of the United Nations, I started to appeal to the whole world to join "the Second Renaissance Movement" at the threshold of a new millennium.

We know well that when the spiritual civilization of the West came to its utmost limit at the end of the Middle Ages, the intellectuals asserting "Let us return to nature" and "Let us restore humanity" initiated the Renaissance which led the Western world to the Reformation. The Renaissance and the Reformation were, in turn, responsible for bringing about democratic revolutions, an industrial revolution, and revolutions of science-technology and information, all of which in combination created today's brilliant materialistic civilization.

But, unfortunately, our materialistic civilization has also come to its limit, which is manifesting in the phenomena of disregard of humanity, alienation of man, and even the lack of humanity itself. Faced with this grim reality, it is a duty for all the intellectuals of the world to unite with all the non-governmental organizations (NGOs) and wave high the torch of the Second Renaissance Movement in order to overcome the eschatological crisis of today.

By reforming value concepts and to overcome this critical situation of today, we must launch a "Social Peace Movement" calling for the establishment of right morality and good conscience and for the restoration of humanity which are the basic ingredients of a solid foundation of peaceful and orderly social life.

We feel a solemn sense of mission when we realize that peace in mind, peace at home, peace at workplace, and peace among neighbors are the very foundation for peace in society. Without social peace, how can we expect co-existence and co-prosperity of all the peoples and all the nations of the world? Thus, social peace in individual societies and nations is the basic condition to peace and prosperity of the entire world.

All the participants to this memorable occasion, top leaders and intellectuals representing the world!

Let us all come hand-in-hand and join the Second Renaissance Movement in pursuit of this historical call! I am sure that it is the nobel mission of all human beings who are now closing the 20th century and facing the next millennium.

As *Noblesse Oblige* implies, the intellectual elite who recognize their special moral duty must take initiative. So must the developed great nations, largely responsible for shaping modern civilization, lead the way.

Only then may the later generations look back and say in profound gratitude and extolment that today's intellectuals and great nations marched out as a vanguard, led the salvation of the world and created the new desirable society, when the entire humanity was on the verge of Doomsday.

THE SEOUL DECLARATION
on a Global Common Society
for the New Millennium
—Magna Carta of Global Common Society—

Whereas human society is enjoying material affluence hitherto unknown in history, thanks to a large extent to the high degree of development of science, technology, information and telecommunication;

Whereas human beings have in the process tended to espouse the values of pragmatism, contributing to the corruption of our morals and of our conscience;

Whereas with our humanity belittled by the cultural process of self-proliferation of science and technology, we are transforming our society into a dehumanized community;

Whereas the development and deployment of arsenals of mass destruction including chemical, biological, radio-active and nuclear weapons on one side and the predominant trends of egoism and chauvinism on the other, as well as the discords between communities, religions, races and nations are seriously endangering peace and prosperity of humanity;

We, members of the world intellectual community and participants assembled in Seoul for the conference commemorating the 17th Anniversary of the UN International Day of Peace, September 24-26, 1998, stand at a historical crossroad to re-evaluate our experience with civilization at the closing of the century and the opening of the New Millennium, hereby Resolve to adopt the following Declaration:

First, we, the people who have experienced the excesses of an advanced state of materialism, science, and technology, should break away from the trends of a dehumanizing, alienating, and deprecating society, and construct a human-centered society where once again human beings become masters of their affairs and of history.

Second, we should establish righteous cultural norms based on a civilizational view of history in order to free ourselves from a social norm built on the rule of force and the law of the jungle with "the strong preying on the weak," and create a civilization where human beings live truly as human beings.

Third, we have come through exclusionary nationalism and class struggle ideologies and arrived today at the true era of a global village in a dynamic process of globalization and democratization. Therefore, we appeal to the world for the establishment of a Universal Democracy that guarantees the freedom, equality and prosperity of all humanity as well as equal rights and co-existence among the major and minor powers alike.

Fourth, at this historical juncture when we face a new age of globalization, democratization, humanization and welfarization, we, the people of the world, should overcome regional conflicts to create a Regional Cooperation Society and upgrade it to a Global Common Society under the rule of PAX UN to realize a permanent world peace and a culture-welfared society.

Fifth, we, the people assembled here, determined to achieve such objectives, propose hereby the promotion of a Social Peace Movement that would foster sincere mutual trust and the spirit of reconciliation and cooperation among all peoples, and we strongly urge the launching of a Second Renaissance Movement to construct a humanistic society, a culture-welfared society, and a universal democratic society.[1]

Note

1. The Seoul Declaration was initiated by Young Seek Choue and adopted at the International Peace Conference held in Seoul from September 24 to 26, 1998.

YOUNG SEEK CHOUE

Maldevelopment

If a development process is not and cannot mobilize the entire social force, and is such that the entire social force does not and cannot participate as well as contribute to the functions of production and distribution, decision making and implementation, consumption, and social exchange, one cannot conceive that it is a genuine and human-oriented development. If both the action and flow of a development is not "horizontal" and equitable toward all the components of society, it generates maldevelopment and malhealth. This sort of development can be termed as a development of imbalance or disequilibrium and characterized as "vertical growth."

Starting from the philosophical aspects, it can be stated that the world itself and human society proceeds through the stages of both the regular and irregular continuity of (a) proportionate balances and (b) disproportionalities or imbalances. In the case of proportionate balances, the process of continuity takes place more smoothly, though not in a linear way. In the case of disproportionalities and imbalances, there can be observed breaks, disruptions, disturbances, and dislocations. But the latter phenomena cannot be regarded as symptoms of discontinuity; rather they are rejections of outmoded and outdated elements, while some values continue to exist and contribute to the process of continuity. These values and determinants are, therefore, linkages between two opposites or contraries, the existing and the emerging, the present and the future processes.

In the process of continuity there cannot be any static moment or point of time or space. But certain moments or points of time and space may be considered as the basic moments or base points which can, scientifically, be termed as the moments and points of "dynamic stability" or stability in motion and conditional stability in continuity. This state is necessary in analyzing and understanding the all-round development of a nation or a geophysical territory. Therefor, this determinant is that of objective dynamism and judgment for understanding any process, system, culture, or civilization.

When a development process is based on imbalances, whether from the class and structural viewpoints; from the view of the factorial inputs, dimensions and determinants of social goals and means; from the aspects of production and distribution; or from the angles of mobilization and participation, it can definitely be classified as maldevelopment. Maldevelopment is, therefore, based on (a) wrong goals, means, and values, which generate (b) ill effects, in the sense of unhealthy, heterogeneous, unequal and inequitable social and human effects; and cause (c) malproduction from the standpoint of the society's satisfaction of fundamental social and human needs of goods and services; thus generating (d) malconsumption through oversufficiency of the

above needs or deprivation of basic needs; which causes (e) maldistribution of purchasing power, generally regarded as the indicator of the capacity to satisfy the need for goods and services.

Maldevelopment is a combination of overdevelopment, underdevelopment, and dependent development. The meanings of underdevelopment and dependent development are, perhaps, better understood than that of overdevelopment. The overdeveloped capitalist economies mistake vertical economic growth for development. They are still reluctant to accept the concept, determinants, and dimensions of overdevelopment, and regard economic factors and their components as the integral and basic parts of overall development. Therefore, their official concept is still econocentric. It is because of this fact that they still do not agree to confront conceptual as well as factual distinctions and differences between growth and development, between the verticality of the former and the horizontality of the latter. The state-capitalized socialist world is still very much in confusion. They base their plans and development on a growth-oriented model of a consumerist type, mistaking growth for social and human development, and their development goals include the concepts and elements of "desire," "comforts," and "luxuries" in relation to the basic human needs. Some of them have started arguing that the "above-basic" needs are "improved" needs which are the necessary conditions for improving social or human efficiency. Therefore, the dimensions of material growth and consequently, the determinants and factors contributing to such growth, have become the basic objectives of development in this world system too. Perhaps the failure to understand the distinction between needs and desires and the ambition to reach the overdeveloped living standards of the oversufficient capitalist economy is at the root of their confusing overdevelopment with development.

The economic concepts, considerations, and determinants of maldevelopment consist of elements, factors, and phenomena like:

(a) vertical or growth-oriented development policies, models, patterns, and tendencies, which have no regard for the needs, capacities, or potential of people or societies and their ability to absorb the results of these policies;

(b) the growth of population, without regard for a desired and balanced population growth policy, which does not keep pace with the economic development and development potential of the country and the society, and thus creates an imbalance in the relationship of people to the economy, between production and distribution, between the supply of produced commodities and services and people's consumption capacities;

(c) failure to adopt to changes in the patterns of social needs and social need-satisfying capabilities;

(d) incompetence in adjusting needs, demands, and needs-satisfying basic commodities, services, and supplies, at both the macro and micro levels of planning and achievement in every society;

(e) failure to correlate the appropriate technology to meet the needs of each society, both at the macro and micro levels, in order to keep the balance between human ecology and natural ecology, between human needs and capacities, and between natural capabilities and possibilities and so on.

The political concept of maldevelopment centers on the imbalance between the participatory and mobilizational functions of social beings, social and human rights and duties, equal and equitable rights to work and receive the benefits of work, freedom of expression and impression, and so on. In the West, in spite of vast economic progress, one can find between fifteen to twenty percent of the population living either at or below subsistence level or remaining illiterate, as well as being without the right to employment and hence without work or the possibility of earning purchasing power, without the basic human right to life and livelihood. The upper class and upper strata of society in capitalist political systems enjoy and over-enjoy both political and economic rights, while the lower class and the lower strata are subjected to the dominant class strata and the enforced dependence associated with this structure (see *Concept of Conflict and Peace: Class versus Structural School*). Alternatively, the state-capitalized socialist system has enforced compulsory political and human duties on the citizens of the countries belonging to it, with reduced political and human rights, in the name of sacrifice for the sake of building socialism for future generations. The imbalance of the relationship between political and human duties and political and human rights in the above society is a sign of genuine political maldevelopment and malpractice. Political education and education on scientific socialism and ideological convictions have now become relegated to the bookshelves. This is because of the uncoordinated relationship between political theory and daily practice in this system. That is why a black economy, an inclination to consumerism, and copying the Western mode of life

have become the outstanding features of the state-capitalized socialist system. The underdeveloped South cannot be put into any distinctive category. Here political rights can be purchased, are subject to bribery, can be suppressed, and can be negated.

The sociological concept of maldevelopment, which European sociologists and economists like to term as "unbalanced development," is manifested in the vertical form of both social and class formation, maintenance, and promotion with the strata of "more haves," "less haves," and "least haves" or with the classes of "more privileged," "less privileged," and "least privileged" or deprived. Liberal sociologists and economists describe this as "social mobility," while the Marxist terminology is "class formation." While social mobility is the result of less antagonistic social behavior, or the result of a passive social process under conditions of less social tension, class formation on the contrary, is the creation of antagonistic social behavior and processes (see *Social Conflicts and Peace*). The outcome of both the concepts and analysis is undoubtedly a socioeconomic imbalance and maldevelopment, and the main characteristic of maldevelopment is the polarization of abundance and privileges at one end and deprivation and poverty at the other end. Class theory presupposes that when the contrasts between different classes or, at least between two main groups or alliances of classes, become acute in a society or state there will follow class revolution in favor of the majority. But since the 1960s there has been no real revolution in any country. The reason behind this absence of any important and positive revolution is the continuous strengthening of the power, process, and mechanism of dominant structures. The structural concept and theory presumes that the world, or the national peripheries are governed and controlled by the international or national center, from the social, economic, political, cultural, and ecological points of view. Because of the modernization process through military, security, and functional control mechanisms, the structure of the center, though administered by the social minority, has become so strong and dominant that it can smash any revolutionary or popular action. That is why assumptions about the implications of class concept and class theory are less relevant in the present system, though in social class formation, class contrasts, class behavior and attitudes, class exploitation, modes and relations of production, and so on, their characteristics and validity remain relevant. Until and unless the relationship between social mobilization and social participation, or between social duties and social rights, or between social production and social distribution and consumption is horizontalized, there cannot and will not be any possibility of doing away with social maldevelopment and social malrelation. By social malrelation we mean the relationship between and among social beings, that is, human beings who interrelate in the day-to-day social process and management of production.

Cultural chauvinism and hegemony, dogmatism and conservatism, enforced dominance, and accepted dependence are some of the aspects of relational disequilibrium which can be found in all societies whether in the West or in the East, whether in the North or in the South. In any society or nation-state such unequal relationships can be found in the form of conscious or unconscious existence, desired or undesired application, active and passive behavioral aspects, and so on (see *Marxist-Leninist Concepts of Peace and Peaceful Coexistence*). The inclination to achieve and maintain power relationships is the essence of both class and structural concepts and the very existence of this inclination in the class, strata, group, or faction within the power, or dominant, position is at the root of the creation and maintenance as well as the promotion of social and cultural malrelation and maldevelopment. In capitalism, the accumulation of such power and dominance has continued for generations; in the feudal-capitalism of the South also, it has the same tendency of development. In the state-capitalized socialist world of the East this process can be characterized as a one-generation process, though in certain countries within this system one can observe the trend of a conversion from the one generation power base into a dynastical power base.

1. The First World or the Developed Free Market Economy

The overdeveloped and developed capitalist economies with high per capita gross national product (GNP) or gross national income, are categorized by the United Nations as the First World and are generally accepted as such by traditional social scientists all over the world. Therefore, countries with a high rate of economic growth and prosperity, high possession of capital and technology as well as consumer goods, high levels of production and consumption as well as per capita income or purchasing power, are considered as the First World. They are in this category by virtue of their possession of capital and technology, which are the results of past industrial revolution and present technological revolution, besides the enforced accumulation process and transfer of high surplus values

or optimum profits from their former colonies.

Class theory contends that the ever-increasing ownership pattern over the means and ends of production, based on *laissez-faire* principles of growth, combined with both an offensive and defensive military and armament structure, has enabled certain countries to become the dominant First World at the cost and deprivation of many others. However, in the First World not all are first class citizens from the point of view of privileges, opportunities, and development of aptitudes and talents. The privileged enjoy more possibilities and potential for betterment, a further section just manages them, while others struggle simply to survive. Polarization of wealth at one end and poverty at the other end are characteristic of this overdeveloped and developed capitalist world. Abundance and waste; affluence and deprivation; concentration of wealth and poverty; overconsumption and underconsumption; high levels of health amenities and treatment and the spread of new complicated, and expensive diseases; good housing conditions and increasing rates of slums—these are the two contrasting polarization trends which can be observed in the overdeveloped and developed capitalist economies of our time.

Structural theory and analysis suggest that both the growth and exploitation characteristic of the First World (consisting of the United States, Canada, Japan, Australia, New Zealand, South Africa, the United Arab Emirates, Saudi Arabia, the Federal Republic of Germany, France, the United Kingdom, and the other West European countries with the exception of Portugal and Turkey) are the results of the structural process and mechanism as well as structural violence. The administrative or functional, military, political, economic, and social power structure and their working mechanism are built up in such a way that the structure holds the power, and this structure is composed of the techno-bureaucracy, financial and commercial capitalism, multinational corporations, industrial oligarchy and cartels, and the share and commodity markets which promote, control, guide, and decide the present and future role of entire national and transnational systems (see *Neocolonialism*). Political parties with different ideological orientations and policies cannot strongly influence the course of policies decided and followed by the structure. The structural approach contends that the concept of class alliance is not really operative and effective in contemporary capitalism and so it is unrealistic to expect class revolution in contemporary modernized capitalism. With regard to the genesis of the First World the class analysis has its validity, while structural analysis is valid when it is related to the process, growth, and functional mechanism of the post-Second World War period.

There is a theory that the First World is proceeding towards an acute economic, political, and social crisis in the near future. This seems to be only partially true. There is a realistic prognosis that the First World will encounter difficulties in procuring nonrenewable raw materials, that is, minerals for their own industrial needs, since their own resources are either exhausted or are on the way to being exhausted, because of long-term irresponsible use. Both the state machinery and financial capital and technology will, of course, help the overdeveloped and developed capitalist economies to avoid crisis in producing internally and procuring from abroad renewable raw materials which are of agricultural origin. At the same time, because of the continued improvement in technology and large-scale use of innovations, capitalism has thus far avoided a crisis over the quality of products, which the Second World or socialist countries have encountered. In recent years, the First World has also been putting effort into avoiding wastage of materials in production, and applying the results of research for recycling waste in order to achieve optimum effects from materials used in production. The trend of overdevelopment, and its consequent effect—overconsumption—under the pretense of higher standards of living, is still dominant and is regarded as the inspiration for further economic growth by the multinational corporations and multinational capitalism. Besides these economic aspects, there can also be observed the political aspects of crisis. The democracy of the First World can no longer be regarded as popular democracy. It is, rather, a guided and structured democracy. A guided and structured democracy reduces the right of the citizens considerably and delegates a great deal of power to the executive machinery or mechanism. Thus the participatory function of the masses in decision making is heavily structured and the mobilizational function is greatly reduced.

At the social level, affluence has created frustration, particularly among the newer generation of citizens, because high levels of production and consumption cannot attract this generation much. This results in such phenomena as the ecological movements, increased drug abuse among a section of frustrated youth, and the involvement of many young people in mystical and naturalism-based religious activities. The theoretical and ideological works of the socialist countries, and the radicals as well as the New Leftists often attract the youth of the First World because these have not yet reached the stage of ideological bankruptcy. Monetary culture has gradually been infiltrating into the social life of the First World which seems to have become too impersonal, and the culture has started monetarizing family life also and generating alienation. Alienation, in its turn, may lead to sociopsychic problems and isolation for many of the people of these economies and societies, as is now feared by many social scientists.

However, accumulated experience will lead the First World to newer innovations in both civil and military technology, civil and armament production and exports of armaments as well as machinery, capital, and technology. The huge military research and development expenditure and armament production, which are socially unproductive and socially unusable, but whose burden is borne by society, do not contribute to the gross social product and are of no social use or benefit. Therefore, all military expenditure, under the pretext of defense, is nothing but a cause of inflation to the economy and the society. The average annual rate of such inflation is over eight percent in the First World, and over four percent in the Third World. Again, through export of arms the First World exports its inflation to the Third World, the buyer of armaments from this that very inflation being embodied in arms and munitions.

2. The Second World or the State-Capitalized Economy

The Second World or the State-Capitalized Socialism has disappeared with the collapse of the East European State-Capitalized Socialism, but as a concept and functional mechanism it will preserve its validity in history. Both the Mainland China (in a reformed way, as marked socialism) and Cuba (in its orthodox puritanian form) still try to hold the mantle of its validity.

The centrally planned economies, or countries having a socialized state capitalist mode and relation of production, which they themselves termed as socialist, had been categorized by the United Nations bureaucracy and socio-economic experts of the free market economic world as the Second World. In so determining that they had taken into consideration only the economic factors, determinants and dimensions, while neglecting those in the social, political, cultural, ecological and human aspects, besides the human rights, needs and duties. Attention was focused too narrowly on the economic indicator of the average or per capita gross national product of the economies belonging to this system.

Since the First, Second and the Third World had been the economic divisions of the global territories according to the average individual possession of economic wealth and poverty, the Second World was placed, as a self-reliant and self-sufficient system with a medium range of average gross national product, between the First World with high incomes and the poor Third World with low incomes.

The Second World was created after the Second World War. The economic blockade of Eastern Europe helped the region to attain economic self-reliance and self-sustenance based on its own sources and resources, though the region could not achieve a high degree of technological advancement like the First World or the developed free market economics. The Second World, on the economic front, had its own economic community known as the Council of Economic Mutual Assistance or COMECON which was parallel to the Western Europe's European Economic Community, now known as the European Union. Again, the Socialist World had its own military alliance in the past, but now defunct, known as the Warsaw Pact, which was parallel to the First World's North Atlantic Treaty Organization (NATO), which finds itself now at the stage of expansion and extension in the name of peace. On the military, ideological and political fronts the Second World did not compromise with the First World, but on the economic front it had had a certain type of convergence with the First World.

Countries belonging to the Second World had, with some variations, the following characteristics:

(a) basic social needs-based development,

(b) an almost egalitarian distribution system for the entire society,

(c) full employment though based on the over-employment policy and with less economic productivity,

(d) compulsory and free education,

(e) free child, maternity and health care system for the entire community,

(f) sufficient production and supply of the basic social needs-satisfying goods and services,

(g) insufficient development of goods and services of sophisticated nature entering into the categories of comforts and luxuries,

(h) less generation and guarantee of the non-basic and non-material human and social goods and services.

In the name of satisfying human needs which induce human duties, the Second World succeeded in bringing about enforced mobilization. But the attribution of both human and social rights to the inhabitants of each of these countries belonging to this system was much abandoned and neglected. Therefore, human rights in these countries lagged much behind human duties. That was the reason for the state-opposed movements for human rights, which were much encouraged both morally and materially by the politically and ideologically-motivated First World. Besides the goal-oriented positive points of the Second World, as mentioned above, some negative aspects of this system need be mentioned, which are as follows:

(a) oversupply of foodstuffs at state-subsidized cheaper prices, in the name of supplying more basic needs-satisfying goods,

(b) failure in product-improvement and sophistication, betterment of quality and lagging far behind the First World in respect of research and development in consumer goods and services as well as the improvement of the production process,

(c) failure of the static and dogmatic leadership to evaluate the dynamic aspirations of the people and introduce a dynamic outlook to the people whose ideological consciousness lacked far behind their material consciousness, etc.

The people of the Second World did enjoy less human rights, in the sense of expression, but they, on the other hand, were over-impressed by the window-display mode of life, manifested through consumerism.

The Second World intended to build a material socialism on the right premises but with wrong means. The big state enterprises and the huge state and collective farms were, very often, unmanageable, less efficient and less economically productive because of the bureaucratization and verticalization of the management and control and exaggerated centralization. Had the same been democratized and horizontalized on a local basis and structured on small and efficiently manageable scale, without making much ideological and systemic compromise, perhaps, the Second World model and mechanism of development and distribution could have been an ideal and acceptable model and mechanism for the entire world.

However, the Second and the First World did have some similarities on development approach, in the sense that they pursued the policy of economic growth rather than human and humanistic development. Both the models and approaches sought and seek to produce goods and services, irrespective of whether these are socially necessary, judged from the standpoint of fundamental social and human needs-satisfaction. They produce more for the people, put the same to the market where the edges of demand based on the possession of purchasing power and supply with profitability do determine the fate of the products and services, without thinking much of their social utility functions. The ultimate result of such an approach and function is an increase of the material consciousness of the people instead of human consciousness or consciousness about humanity.

Politically and from the point of view of the armaments build-up and armament-balance, the Second World functioned as an alternative and check-point between the First World and the Third World. The collapse of the Second World has enabled the First World to become monocentric and exercise greater control over the Third World. There are theories of historical analysis which try to prove that had the Second World not existed, the liberation of the Asian, African and Latin American former colonies would not have been possible. There exist also suspicions that the Third World could have been converted back into the political colonies of the First World, long ago. It is certainly true that the Third World countries of today are, more or less, economic and market colonies of the First World and the latter's military and security dependency on the First World is on the way of vertical increase.

The absence of the Second World in the world development arena has created a vacuum of alternatives to the neo-market economic mechanism, capitalization of the material and human resources, dehumanization aspects of development, etc. Closure of factories in the name of elimination of the unproductive units, huge unemployment, low level of pensions and lack of care of the older generation, closure of the state and privatised nurseries and kindergartens as well as lack of the children's health care, degradation of the quality of the health and specially, in the maternity sector, etc., are some of the malsymptoms of the present-day development process and measures in the now-defunct Second World systemic nations.

3. The Third World

The post-1950 colonies and semicolonies, which are economically underdeveloped and have been trying to be self-reliant in respect of satisfying the basic needs of their people and upgrading the average standard of living from the below-subsistence to the subsistence level, are defined and known as the Third World. Under the United Nations classification, based on gross national product and gross national income, the Third World countries are those having feudal, underdeveloped capitalist, neocolonized as well as semicolonized and vague social-ideological systems, with low average income. Though the Third World consists of the economically underdeveloped countries, now sophistically termed as "the developing countries," there are variations in the degree of development in these countries. Of course, from the social, moral, political, cultural, ecological, linguistic, and religious points of view, the Third World countries can be put into the categories of First and Second Worlds, in many cases. There is also a richer social stratum in the Third World which, in certain cases, live a more privileged and economically measured better life than many of the rich and privileged people in the First and the Second World.

A more rational and objective classification would be to categorize the world's people as well as the people of each nation-state into:

(a) over-sufficiency or social elite group or class of overpossession;

(b) sufficiency or middle class group or class of average possession; and

(c) under-sufficiency or below-subsistence group or class of poverty or underpossession.

It is the relation of ownership over the means of production as well as over the end of production, that is, distribution, which determines the economic strength, social position and prestige, political rights and privileges, and power to guide the development direction of culture. Therefore, the classification of the rich, self-sufficient, and poor countries is not, perhaps, the happiest one. It is class or class alliance and social-structural strata which either possess or control the means of production and natural resources of each country, and again there are classes who work with the means of production and natural resources, but receive less than is justified by their physical and intellectual labor input. The possessors are the privileged First World people while the possessed are the deprived Third World people.

Now, if we accept the geographical division of worlds from the standard of economic development, we find that a good number of the overdeveloped and developed capitalist countries have already utilized most of their nonrenewable natural resources and will, in the near future and automatically, be dependent on other countries, mainly those of the Third World, for the supply of a certain number of basic and strategic minerals, and since there is a limited chance of receiving these from the socialist régimes, the First World may either force the Third World to supply these nonrenewable raw materials or even wage war against some of them in order to procure what they wish, as is feared in certain quarters. Most of the resources or potential raw materials of both the nonrenewable and renewable types in the Third World have neither been prospected nor evaluated until recently. Their use, at both the macro and micro levels has also not been properly planned, because of the lack of the means and possibilities of production, and also because of the absence of planning or malplanning. This is because their ruling class or the structural mechanism either does not want a proper national planning policy on a coordinated basis of macro and micro planning with planned and proportionate use of the material and human resources of their countries in their own social interest, or because their metropolitan ideology-oriented planners stress the development and promotion of a socially parasitic and éilte desired production and distribution process . The Third World countries need to work out a development strategy which is based on the proper and horizontalized relationship of the utilization of human and material resources, in order to be self-reliant and self-sufficient, as far as possible, and to be able to meet fundamental material and nonmaterial social needs.

Since the processing of the work force does not take place in a planned way in most of the developing countries, there is an overproduction of the work force in white-collar jobs which cannot be absorbed by the national social economy, and this results in a brain drain from the less developed countries to the overdeveloped and developed capitalist countries, which avoid incurring any socioeconomic cost in processing such skilled labor. It is a huge social and economic loss for the Third World, while a considerable gain for the First World. Excepting a few processed products, the main exports of the Third World countries consist of primary and semiprocessed products, a good part of these coming back to them in the form of imported and expensive processed goods. This is because the Third World countries, with the exception of a few, have not been given opportunities by the First World through sufficient delivery of the means of production, and they themselves could not develop sufficient capacities for processing primary and semiprocessed products because of either a lack of proper financial resources or defective internal planning and

development strategies and mechanisms. Of course, the First World always prefers to import primary products in bulk instead of processed and semiprocessed materials from the less developed countries, in order to ensure the continuity of productivity of their own capital and assure employment of labor and the use of technology in their own countries. This sort of action can be characterized as neocolonialism or structural colonialism (see *Neocolonialism*).

Because of the defective goals of development and growth, most Third World countries are trying to catch up with the level of production and consumption and hence the standard of living of the First World. But these efforts of the Third World are based on a false hypothesis. They should understand that the First World economies are not static ones, their rate of growth is high and so highly dynamic and thus it is not rational to try to compete with them. Second, the Third World countries should not try to copy the mode and standard of consumerism of the First World; they should rather base their development strategies and goals on their own values, needs, possibilities and potentials, traditions and customs, and satisfaction of their own national and social needs. The Third World countries do have their own cultural entity, social identity, and political principles, of which they can be proud. But there do exist certain military and civil dictatorial régimes in certain underdeveloped countries where both human and civic rights are much suppressed, particularly among the national minorities and tribes, the casteless, and the ethnic groups.

The Third World countries are, by no means, the third class or the third category countries of the world, from the standpoint of political, cultural, and sociostructural identity. They constitute an effective alternative to both the First World and the entity of a third dimension which can function as an alternative to the extremes the First World.

If the Third World countries were grouped on a regional basis for cooperation and development for mutual horizontal interests and equity as well as equality they could, themselves, solve their own problems of development. However, political and ideological differences, religious and ethnic divergence, and mutual rivalries stand in the way of the realization of such regional cooperation.

4. The Fourth World

Many important considerations are not taken into account in categorizing the world on the basis of development. Overall development is always multidimensional. A country may be economically under-developed, but culturally, or socially, or politically may be better developed than some other countries put into the category of economically developed nations. Therefore, some of the economically developed and overdeveloped countries may find themselves in the categories of underdeveloped countries from the points of view of social, political, and ecological indicators. There are very rich and very poor people in both worlds. There are rich people in a Third World country like India, who, with feudocapitalist family management structures, live a more luxurious life than many millionaires in the United States or Japan. Again one can see about 20 percent of the people in the United States, the richest country of the world, living on the daily welfare coupons even in the 1980s. There are about 13 million people in the United Kingdom living at below-subsistence level. In the socialist world also about five percent of the people live below the subsistence level. In the great developed cities like New York, Paris, and London, the percentage of illiterates varies between 15 to 25 percent. If other than economic dimensions are applied, some economically poor countries may be found culturally rich and vice versa. Therefore, in terms of economic living standards, cultural heritage, child care, health and maternity benefits, distribution, social morality and crime, political and human rights and duties, educational facilities, housing and food supplies, employment opportunities, and so on, one can see the population group of the First World in the Third World and the population group of the Third World in the First World, and so on. This is due to both class structural violence in all the socioeconomic and political-cultural systems of the world. Neither class nor structural characteristics are sufficient to explain both the causes and effects of the above, but a combined analysis of both class and structural elements, causes, and phenomena is necessary in order to define and determine the characteristic of each of the First and Third World.

But what is the Fourth World? The Fourth World is composed of the neglected and oppressed people of the world who can be found in all the geographical territories, in all the socioeconomic, political-cultural, and ecological system. They are the aborigines, ethnic groups, minority tribes, and casteless communities. Because of both types of class and structural violence, power and technological violence, chauvinistic and hegemonic violence, dominance and imposed dependency types of violence, these people, who constitute the Fourth World, do not find themselves included in any of the existing human charters.

More than 90 million casteless Harijans and Girijans of India; the numerous tribes in the India-Bangladesh-Pakistan subcontinent; the ethnic Indian population groups in Northern, Central, and Southern Africa; the minority tribes in the African continent, the Beduins in the Arab world; the aborigines of Australia and New Zealand; certain sections of the Tibetans, Sinkiang-Uighurs, Mongolians, and the Central Asian people; the Gypsy communities all over the world—all who are the constituent parts of this Fourth World, are devoid of human rights and aspirations. They are like foreigners within their own geopolitical territories and socioeconomic structures. They have always been subjected to duties or forced work without being granted basic human rights. Their human needs are the same as the other people of the other three worlds, but these needs are never allowed to be fulfilled. Certain countries have introduced certain concessional measures on behalf of these people to be imposed from above. These concessions typically have the characteristic of mobilization and not the characteristic of participation, since the people belonging to the First, Second, and the Third Worlds consider themselves as the caretakers or patrons of the Fourth World, which is regarded as unfit to effect its own development, survival, and continuity. There is a systematic and continuous effort to technicalize and modernize these maintained half-human and half-slave people of the Fourth World, by charitable and missionary types of philanthropic measures from the other three socially, economically, and politically dominant groups. Every ethnic population group or nationally oppressed minority has its own outlook on different aspects and problems of social, political, and economic life; has its own specific mode of life and culture, religion, and traditions and, at the same time, its own values and value judgment. The modernization efforts by the first three Worlds have started the process of destroying the multilateral and multidimensional value of this Fourth World.

One of the specific characteristics of the Fourth World is that the relation between people and nature here is horizontal, that is, of interdependency and equality, and in most cases the religion of the people belonging to this World is animism and naturism whose essence lies in the horizontality of relation between people and nature, or, between human ecology and natural ecology. The religion of the first two Worlds is vertical in character, where the relationship between both God and humankind on the one hand, and between humankind and nature, on the other hand, is based on submission and obedience as well as dominance and dependence. One can not think of complementarity in this type of relationship.

The demand of the Fourth World is the right to self-determination, autocentric development of their own values and cultures, protection from infiltration and penetration from other dominant cultures, maintenance of their own traditions and all-round development based on their indigenous values instead of imposed values. In order to achieve such goals they have to become united, raise their voice, and start unified action. Though their problems are well-known on a global basis, very little has yet been done for their own rights and self-determination. They themselves are still loosely coordinated. In order to wage a long-term struggle they need to unite against both structural and class violence.

In order to undo both the maldevelopment and its mal-effects the human society of each global territory is to concentrate on the models and actions of relevant and sustainable development, to be based on their values, modes of life and culture, own sources and resources as much as possible. They are to use technology as far as national absorbable capacity, in each case, permits. The relationship between human resources and natural resources of each nation-state should be maintained at the equitable horizontal level in the development course and process. If one of the actors gains an edge over the other, there will be an imbalance which will generate maldevelopment. The end of the twentieth century has been witnessing a polarisation of development and richness in the First World and deprivance and poverty in the Fourth and Third World.

The development system and process of today generates inequities and it goes beyond human development, thus creating conflict between growth and equity. Unless the policies and measures of each nation-state are adjusted to undo the marginalization process of a section of its inhabitants these will unbalance people's lives, the worst consequence of maldevelopment. Therefore, the focus of development ought to be shifted from the greed to the need, from affluence to maintenance survival, from economic abundance to human ecology, etc.

See also: *Disarmament and Development; Human Rights and Peace; North-South Conflict; World Economy, Social Change, and Peace*

Bibliography

Dobozi E (ed.) 1980-85 *Development and Peace*, Vols. 1-6. Hungarian Peace Council, Budapest

Galtung J 1980 *The True Worlds*. Free Press, New York

Galtung J, Guha A et al., 1975 *Measuring World Development*, I, II, Vol. I. Nos. 3, 4, North-Holland Publishing, Amsterdam

Guha A 1983a Contemporary process of overdevelopment and dependent development: Some conceptual and analytical approaches. *Guru Nanak J. Sociol.* 4(1)

Guha A 1983b Concepts and misconcepts on alternative development and approaches. *Revue Roumaine d'Etudes Internationales* 15

Guha A 1983c Contemporary process and conceptual premises of maldevelopment. *Scand. J. Dev. Alternatives* 2(3)

Guha A 1985a *Conflict and Peace: Theory and Practice*. Institute for Alternative Development Research, Oslo

Guha A 1985b *Fourth World*. Institute for Alternative Development Research, Oslo

Guha A, Vivekananda F 1985 *Development Alternative*. Institute for Alternative Development Research, Oslo

Wien B J (ed.) 1984 *Peace and World Order Studies*. World Policy Institute, New York

AMALENDU GUHA

Malraux, André

André Malraux (1901-76), the French author, art critic, and soldier, had one of the most varied and adventurous lives of modern writers. He was born in Paris. Without finishing his *lycée* studies, he became interested in oriental art and started earning his living by dealing in secondhand books. He published some early texts in a surrealistic vein, just as original as those of many other authors of the early 1920s. He married a woman from the Jewish bourgeoisie (this marriage did not last) and, with her, left in 1923 for Indochina, then under French rule. His purpose was to discover valuable Cambodian sculptures to bring back for sale. At that time the French government had not officially declared all Cambodian ruins to be state property. Nevertheless, when, after a difficult trip into the jungle, he returned to Phnom Penh, he and his companions were arrested for theft.

Thanks partly to the efforts of his wife and several eminent French writers, he was sentenced to only three years' imprisonment, then retried but released, after payment of a fine. During the house arrest, interrogation, and trial, he experienced considerable humiliation—a theme which runs throughout his literary works and which has both political and metaphysical meaning. He briefly returned to France, then again left for Indochina. Having had dealings with the French authorities there, he had become strongly anticolonialist, and he founded a revolutionary movement, Young Annam, whose existence was brief, and helped run two anticolonialist newspapers. He particularly hated the colonial bureaucracy and the narrow-minded bourgeois who ran it. He visited Hong Kong and, because of the proximity of China, also became acquainted with Chinese revolutionaries who were arriving from Canton, but he did not participate in revolutionary activity on Chinese soil.

His experiences during these years in the Orient are reflected in his first three novels: *Les Conquérants* (1928), which concerns revolutionaries in Canton in 1925 and the historical character Pierre Garin; *La Voie royale* (1930), which recounts a chilling search for temple ruins in Cambodia; and *La Condition humaine* (1933), probably his finest work, which deals with the Shanghai uprisings in 1927 and the subsequent crushing of the Communists by Chiang Kai-Shek's Nationalist troops. Though it is not primarily a war novel, in this last text Malraux excels particularly in his descriptions of street fighting. It is a powerful testimony to the human willingness to die for a revolutionary cause and for fellow human beings. A fourth book on the Orient, *La Tentation de l'Occident* (1929), while not a novel in the true sense, presents fictionalized exchange of views on the culture of the East compared to that of the West.

Malraux had gone to Indochina as an art dealer and surrealist writer—essentially, an aesthetician—but he returned to France as a revolutionary, although the esthetic dimension of his interests remained powerful and his politics were always unorthodox and idiosyncratic. At all stages of his career he was concerned with what he called the absurd, whose origins were metaphysical at first, then cultural (what he called the "bankruptcy of the West"), and finally became political also. While never a member of the Communist Party, or a philosophic Marxist (that is, a subscriber to the dogmas of dialectical materialism), he was persuaded that only Marxist parties in Asia were truly revolutionary and capable of bringing about the political and social changes which seemed to him imperative in order to put an end to feudal enslavement; and he believed that communism was the only answer to political tyranny in the West. He favored violence as the only means of overthrowing colonial rule and capitalist exploitation, and wrote that he could not conceive of a young Annamite as being anything but a revolutionary.

Back in France, Malraux devoted himself to writing and to political activism. He recognized both the military and intellectual threats posed by Hitler, Mussolini, and Franco. He was elected president of the National Anti-Fascist Committee, and in 1934 visited Moscow, where he made a resounding but very unpopular speech against socialist realism at a rally intended to glorify Stalinist literature. With Gide (see *Gide, André*), he attempted to secure the release of the Bulgarian Communist leader Dimitroff, accused of setting fire to the Reichstag. Although Gide and Malraux were not given an audience with any top Nazi leader, they felt some degree of success when, later, Dimitroff was released, probably thanks in part to the publicity they had given his case. In 1935 Malraux published *Le Temps du mépris*, probably his weakest novel, but one which expresses clearly his horror of totalitarian governments and his belief in the revolutionary spirit. In 1934 he flew over Arabia in search of the ruins of the Queen of Sheba's palace.

When the Spanish Civil War erupted in 1936, Malraux was one of the very first Frenchmen to reach Spain. He immediately became head of an aviation squadron for the Republican side, and remained in Spain until the next year, flying (usually as a gunner) and seeing a great deal of action. During these months he composed his long novel on the war, *L'Espoir* (1937), which appeared before the war was over, and in 1938 made a film on the same subject. Both works stress how war is a collective experience, and, like *La Condition humaine*, they show the relationship of heroism, an individual achievement, to human brotherhood as a whole. Malraux also traveled to the United States in 1938 to collect funds for the Republican cause.

When the Second World War broke out, Malraux fought in an armored group. Captured and imprisoned (in the cathedral at Sens for much of the time), he escaped and made his way to the south. By 1943 he had joined a Resistance movement and was in command of a group in the Corrèze. In 1944 he was captured by Germans and, after prolonged interrogations and certainty that he would be tortured and put to death, he was rescued from prison in Toulouse as the city was freed. He then became head of the Brigade Alsace-Lorraine and fought on the Eastern Front in 1944-45.

Malraux's last work of fiction, *Les Noyers de l'Altenburg*, originally to have been called *La Lutte avec l'ange* and to be part of a longer work, was published in 1943 (During a search of his apartment in Paris the Germans destroyed much of the remaining manuscript). It tells of two generations, father and son, in two different conflicts, the First and Second World Wars, fighting on different sides because the elder, as an Alsatian, was a German citizen, and his son was French. It contains moving battle scenes which are related to the general themes of the book. In the First World War, as Russian soldiers are being gassed and the countryside is being devastated, German soldiers, including Vincent Berger, the hero, feel compelled to try to save some of their enemies, and Vincent manages to bring back an injured man before he himself dies. The scene is a powerful, if imaginary, account of widespread destruction through chemical warfare, and of the realization among some men that, when everything else is being destroyed, there is something in man that must continue to struggle, to affirm his humanity and reach out to others. In the Second World War, there is a splendid episode of a trapped tank, based on an incident from the author's own battle experiences. Another account tells of French soldiers imprisoned in Chartres Cathedral. Despite a strong intellectual element which makes *Les Noyers* a novel of ideas as much as a novel of action (and lends it an abstract quality which bothers some readers), it is a major statement on war in the twentieth century, partly because it shows the tragic distinction between the idea of "eternal man," as reflected in the description of the similar features of sculptures in the cathedral and ordinary French soldiers, and modern fratricidal man. Like the author's novels of the 1930s, it is a powerful plea for fraternity.

In 1945, Malraux met General de Gaulle. Although the Napoleonic phrase which the general is supposed to have pronounced, "At last I have met a man," is surely apocryphal, there is no doubt that these two men with strong personalities and brilliant minds had great respect for each other. In the Gaullist government of 1945-46 Malraux served as minister of information. Under the Fifth Republic he was minister of culture (until 1969). This change of political orientation, from sympathy for Marxism to support for the right-wing government of de Gaulle, requires some comment. Sartre, who did not like Malraux, thought he had simply sold out to the Right; this was the view held by many. Malraux, on the other hand, said that it was not he who had changed but the Marxists. He was referring, one may assume, to such events as the Nazi-Soviet Pact of 1939, the elimination of liberal democracy in Eastern European nations after 1945, the refusal of the French Communist Party to cooperate fully with the Forces Françaises de l'Int rieur during the war and to recognize the enormous contribution of Great Britain

to the victory. He came to realize that many of the communists in the Underground were not fighting for France but for Russia. Already the Spanish Civil War had shown him how difficult it was to reconcile purity of political intention with practical action. In 1936 he noted that there was a war mentality in Russia and that Soviet aid to Spain was prompted by calculating self-interest. Furthermore, the communists' secret-police tactics in Spain had disturbed him. He had no desire to see the Marxists take over postwar France, and between 1945 and 1950 lifted his voice frequently to warn that a communist coup was impending and that it would ruin France.

In short, Malraux reproached the communists for being willing to sacrifice any principle in order to achieve their end; this is one of the dilemmas discussed in *L'Espoir*. And, like many other fellow travelers of the 1930s, he had come to believe that Russian totalitarianism was not better than the Fascist kind—a rather late realization, since he had been aware earlier of the Moscow Trials and Soviet labor camps, but one which had been delayed by his desire to see the Soviets give essential support to the Spanish Republican forces to match the degree to which Fascist governments were supporting Franco. In truth, Malraux had always been a strong individualist, and even in his most communist-colored novels he seems to view the revolution as a means toward other ends, not an end in itself; his heroes are uninterested in doctrine and generally unwilling to sacrifice all their principles. Orthodox communist critics had already identified in his novels more than one streak of heresy. In fact, in *Les Conquérants and La Condition humaine*, revolution is to a considerable degree a school for heroism. Malraux's gradual recognition that Russian communism was only a means toward the erection of a powerful oppressive state put an end to his enthusiasm for the then Soviet Union.

After the war, Malraux devoted himself to his political activity, his speeches, and his writing, particularly his major texts on art such as the three volumes which make up *Le Musée imaginaire* (1947-49), *Saturne* (on Goya) (1950), and later *Les Voix du silence* (1951). While not held in uniformly high esteem by other critics, his art criticism includes major contributions to the understanding of what he calls "style"—the quality which makes it unique and transmissible—and to the concept of the "museum without walls," that is, art made available through photographic reproduction and related scholarship. As minister of culture he supported a wide variety of undertakings—the cleaning of Paris buildings, reorganization of the Louvre, renovation of museums and buildings, the redecoration of the Paris Opera by Chagall, and the founding of culture centers. Lest it be thought that his activity is not pertinent to the topics of war and peace, it must be stressed that for Malraux the questions of war were, from the beginning, closely connected to the question of culture (in the wide sense). To be sure, in *La Condition humaine* he portrays the Chinese coolies as chiefly the victims of economic exploitation (the immemorial enslavement of the peasants by the landowners, the new proletarian slavery by foreign capitalism), and shows that, until such systems are brought to an end, there can be no hope for millions; stomachs must be filled before minds. But the ultimate purpose of revolution goes beyond social reorganization. Like art, its aim is rebellion against the human condition. It is to allow the human spirit, or the "quality of man," that full development which alone can raise men from the condition of pitiable pawns of historic forces—"the vermin of the earth"—to the consciousness which is expressed in art and which will make them truly tragic figures. An agnostic, Malraux said nevertheless that he was "thirsty for transcendence." Art and culture express this spiritual dimension of the human race, and allow it to be understood and appropriated by others. As Malraux shows in *L'Espoir*, the eternal quality of human striving is the real hero of the Spanish Civil War. This is shown in several dramatic episodes, such as the execution of the soldiers, and the famous scene in which peasants bring down the aviators' bodies from the mountain. In *Les Noyers* he dramatizes his argument that history is not just a meaningless series of civilizations being born and dying; something endures and can pass from one culture to another. Wars and other struggles which seek to prevent the crushing of this spiritual dimension by totalitarianism are ultimately necessary wars.

Not surprisingly, anti-Gaullists who considered Malraux a traitor to the Leftist cause criticized most of what he wrote after 1945, including his statements on the conflict in Algeria. But it should be noted that in 1958, with Roger Martin du Gard, Francois Mauriac, and Sartre, he signed a petition protesting against the seizure of Henri Alleg's *La Question* (an exposé of the torture to which he had been subjected by the army in Algeria) and protesting against the use of torture denounced in the volume. And, like de Gaulle himself, Malraux did not ultimately oppose all negotiations with the Algerian rebels. Moreover, like many French, he was sympathetic to the People's Republic of China, which he visited in 1965. He was also interested in developing nations, and his travels embraced such countries as Egypt, Brazil, and India.

Malraux is considered by some to be overrated as a writer, an adventurer, an esthetician, and a politician. It would be foolish, however, to deny the very great literary qualities of *La Condition humaine* as well as its great human qualities which make it one of the outstanding novels of our century; to a lesser degree, his other books share in this excellence. He was a sensitive critic and a moving orator and stylist. His essays on such figures as T. E. Lawrence and D. H. Lawrence, while not scholarly in the standard sense, show a penetrating understanding of what makes their work significant; the same is true of his art criticism. With respect to his roles as soldier and adventurer, his participation in Spain was intense and important, as were his roles in the Resistance and the battles of 1944-45. His rather dominating personality did not preclude real sympathy for others. In short, his eminence is based on genuine achievement. His work is one of the outstanding literary testimonies in modern France to a powerful and searching human spirit which, while asking metaphysical questions, also must be concerned with political issues. Although he wrote more about waging war than maintaining peace, he did speak before many peace organizations in the 1930s, and, later, before UNESCO, where he gave a famous speech stating that the burning contemporary question was to know whether man was dead. His concern was always for enhancing human consciousness, and moving toward a world in which conflict could be reduced. When he spoke in *La Condition humaine* and later before UNESCO of the dignity of man ("the opposite of humiliation"), he proposed an ideal whose social and spiritual meaning can contribute to the promotion of peace.

Bibliography

Lacouture J 1973 *André Malraux, une vie dans le siècle*. Seuil, Paris

Langlois W A 1966 *André Malraux, the Indochina Adventure*. Praeger, New York

Malraux A 1928 *Les Conquérants*. Gallimard, Paris [1929 *The Conquerors*. Harcourt, Brace, New York]

Malraux A 1929 *La Tentation de l'Occident*. Gallimard, Paris [1961 *The Temptation of the West*. Vintage, New York]

Malraux A 1930 *La Voie Royale*. Gallimard, Paris [1935 *The Royal Way*. Random House, New York]

Malraux A 1933 *La Condition Humaine*. Gallimard, Paris [1934 *Man's Fate*. Random House, New York]

Malraux A 1935 *Le Temps du Mépris*. Gallimard, Paris [1936 *Days of Wrath*. Random House, New York]

Malraux A 1937 *L'Espoir*. Gallimard, Paris [1938 *Man's*

Hope. Random House, New York]

Malraux A 1945 *Les Noyers de l'Altenburg*. Skira, Geneva [1952 *The Walnut Trees of Altenburg*. Lehmann, London]

Malraux A 1947 *Le Musée Imaginaire*. Skira, Geneva [1949 *The Psychology of Art*, Vol. 1. Pantheon Books, New York; also 1967 *Museum Without Walls*. Doubleday, Garden City, New York]

Malraux A 1950 *Saturne: Essai sur Goya*. NRF, Paris [1957 *Saturn: An Essay on Goya*. Phaidon, New York]

Malraux A 1951 *Les Voix du Silence*. NRF, Paris [1953 *The Voices of Silence*. Doubleday, Garden City, New York]

Payne R A 1970 *A Portrait of André Malraux*. Prentice-Hall, Englewood Cliffs, New Jersey

CATHARINE SAVAGE BROSMAN

Malthusian Doctrine

The ideas of Thomas Robert Malthus on population growth and its consequences have played a major role in shaping Western social and economic thought in the nineteenth and twentieth-centuries. Born into an intellectually distinguished English family in 1766, Malthus graduated from Cambridge University in 1788. In 1805 he was named professor of history and political economy at the British East India Company's college at Haileybury, where he remained until his death in 1834.

In 1798 Malthus published, anonymously, a pamphlet entitled *An Essay on the Principle of Population as it Affects the Future Improvement of Society*. This burst onto an intellectual scene which, formed as it was by the optimism of the eighteenth century Enlightenment, tended to regard all human problems as the products of ignorance and traditions based on false ideas. Now that progress was sweeping away the clouds which had obscured the truth for so long, went the typical argument, human problems and human misery would soon be things of the past. Malthus vigorously opposed such optimism, by arguing that the pressure of inexorably growing populations would inevitably create problems for any society, even the most "enlightened." This sobering thought caught the popular imagination, and in 1801 Malthus issued a greatly expanded version of his pamphlet as a book. In all, he was to publish six revisions of his work on population during his lifetime.

The basic Malthusian doctrine of population growth is that, while a society's food supply will expand, at best, arithmetically, its population, unless checked somehow, will grow naturally at a geometric rate. Population, then, would inevitably tend to outstrip the food supply. Malthus then went on to discuss several factors which could counteract this normal geometric rate of population growth. First came the "positive checks" which cut population growth by raising the death rate: war, famine, and pestilence. These he characterized as "misery." Next came the "negative checks" which lowered the birth rate: abor-

tion, infanticide, and contraception. These he characterized pejoratively as "vice," seeing them all as immoral. Finally he admitted, somewhat reluctantly, that "moral restraint"—that is, marrying late to reduce the number of childbearing years, and remaining chaste before marriage—was another possibility. In theory, a society which practiced such restraint could balance its population growth with its food supply and even raise its material standard of living without the misery or vice. Malthus was most pessimistic about frail humanity actually ever having the foresight or willpower to behave so wisely, though.

The thrust of Malthus's argument, then, is that humankind is doomed to experience recurrent spasms of war, famine, and pestilence, horrors which could be made less frequent, in all probability, only by the basest immorality. Even though he could offer no conclusive evidence for his assertion that populations naturally expand at a geometric rate, the fact that his ideas appeared at a time of rapid population increase in Europe served to give them wide credence. In addition, since the Malthusian doctrine tended to lay the blame for the squalid living conditions of the poor on the backs of the poor themselves —if they could not support their children then obviously they were foolishly failing to practice "moral restraint"—the prosperous leaders of society found them very attractive.

Malthus's influence on Western thinking about peace and war is indirect, and difficult to measure. It would appear that his conclusions were one of the sources of the rather pessimistic intellectual atmosphere which replaced the boundless optimism of the eighteenth century Enlightenment. Rousseau (see *Rousseau, Jean-Jacques*), Bentham (see *Bentham, Jeremy*), and Kant (see *Kant, Immanuel; Perpetual Peace*) are just three of the major eighteenth century thinkers who had hoped that war might actually be eliminated from the world and who drew up plans for perpetual peace. This was an activity which had far less appeal for the major figures of nineteenth century thought. The ideas of Malthus, which made it easy to see war as something caused by sweeping historical forces rather than by human folly or evil, help to explain this shift.

In addition, Malthus's ideas imply that a struggle for existence, for access to ever more insufficient resources, is central to life. This idea was given even more explicit expression in the middle of the nineteenth century by Charles Darwin, who was influenced by Malthus. It was not a very great step to conclude that Malthus's ideas implied a future in which nations seeking more and more resources for their expanding populations would be led by harsh necessity to make war on one another. The bloodshed in such conflicts could even serve a vital purpose by "checking" the growth of population, in Malthusian terms. Malthusian thought, then, is one of the foundations of those nineteenth- and twentieth century philosophies, such as that of Heinrich von Treitschke, which see war as inevitable and even necessary for the well-being of the human race.

See also: *Malthusian Doctrine, Critiques of; Population Pressure, Women's Roles, and Peace; Human Security; Future of Humanity*

Bibliography —————————————————

McCleary G F 1953 *The Malthusian Population Theory*. Faber and Faber, London

Malthus T R 1960 *An Essay on the Principle of Population*. Modern Library, New York

Sauvy A 1961 *Fertility and Survival: Population Problems from Malthus to Mao Tse-tung*. Criterion Books, New York

Smith K 1978 *The Malthusian Controversy*. Octagon Books, New York

GARRETT L. MCAINSH

Malthusian Doctrine, Critiques of

The beginning of what the scientific and political world calls Malthusianism dates back to the edition of Malthus' first "Essay" in 1798, and its history is marked by an enduring battle between adherents and opponents. Malthus' ideas on the impending dangers to the mankind are simple to grasp and fundamental wisdom for the survival of man and because of that they are bound to provoke sharp debates on their empirical status and their applicability, under a political, economical, or ethical point of view.

1. Classical Points of Critique

The first "Essay" of 1798 is a harsh reaction to unlimited optimism of philosophers hailing the French Revolution and awaiting a bright future of mankind after having decided to implement the Revolution's plans. Some scholars assume, herein, a kind of a son's rebellion against the "progressive" ideas of his father who had corresponded with J. J. Rousseau (see *Rousseau, Jean Jacques*) and similar spirits of his time.

Actually, Malthus replied to those philosophers who believed in the endless perfectibility of humankind with a theory of persisting misery of man. The visible poverty of an industrializing England had led him to a lack of confidence in social progress. He was, on the contrary, convinced of the absolute impossibility from "the fixed laws of our nature, that the pressure of want can ever be completely removed from the lower classes . . . . The structure of society, in its great features, will probably always remain unchanged."

In spite of an elegant prose and an impressing kind to argue, Malthus proved out to be a shrewd pamphleteer. He gave a description of the mankind's life-wasting way through history and excluded any hope for a betterment of its brute destiny: because the alleged imbalance of population growth and nurture growth is fixed by laws of nature, i.e., sexually caused overpopulation exerts a constant pressure upon all means of subsistence.

In the Essay of 1798, the balance between rapid population growth and slowly growing means of subsistence is restored only by repressive "checks" (starvation, war, misery). Only in the subsequent editions, from 1803 onwards, figures additionally prevention (moral restraint, refrain from marriage) as a check which allows to escape the restoration of a man/subsistence-equilibrium by fatal events.

Malthus scandalized the public of his time for he looked pessimistically on man's lot, at a time when extreme optimism concerning man's and society's perfectibility filled the mainstream of thought. So he forced the advocates of political ideas who envisaged unbreakable progress in a revolutionary era, to take into account his disillusioning objections. But the fervent partisans of the French Revolution did not grow weary of blaming Malthus for clinging to theses which are misleading and stand against historical experience. The classical points of their critique read as follows:

1.1 Malthus presented the rhythms of growth of both the population and the life-supporting means as different. Increase in a geometrical ratio on the one side, and arithmetical ratio on the other, were due to an irrefutable natural law, leaving no room for any change through human reason and action. It became apparent very soon that these assumptions were stated beyond reality (see *Malthusian Doctrine*).

1.2 But also Malthus' fatal calculus pointing out a permanent shortage of means of life and a sentence to death by nature for many people came under attack.

1.3 As to the geometrical ratio of population growth, empirically minded scholars have argued that man's capacity to reproduce must not be confounded with the realistic mode of reproduction which is always much lower than man's physiological potential to procreate. Malthus was right in saying that fluctuations of climate and harvest would influence the family formation and the level of mortality. But he should have used his knowledge of the real world where nowhere an upsurge of population as indicated by a "geometric progression," over a longer period had ever been observed.

1.4 The apparent absence of misery in many countries has led Malthus to complement his theory on the drab situation of mankind with the human ability to prevention.

1.5 Population growth was overestimated.

1.6 Malthus' idea of a geometric progression of mankind stems from the untypical population growth in a closed precinct in the New World and cannot establish a general law of reproduction. The assumption of a doubling time of twenty-five years is unrealistic because it reflects an extreme demographic situation, i.e., a cleavage between a high level of births and a low level of mortality which only in the twentieth century emerged.

2. *Growth of Means of Subsistence—Underestimated*

In his first "Essay," Malthus stated a fixed and fateful relationship between population and its means to survive—always detrimental to the surplus population, i.e., to those for whom there is no blanket and no dishes on the table of nature for "the unhappy persons who, in the great lottery of life, have drawn a blank" (first Essay). This expression made him for a long time and in certain circles the representative of

an alleged brute and heartless economy. A further stumbling block was Malthus' insistence on the futility of battling against poverty with alms and charity because he believed the poor would convert them into additional offspring, and therefore, worsen their situation. The abolition of the English Poor Laws in 1834 was said to embody Malthusian arguments and this gave rise to criticism of the Malthusian doctrine as to be a set of reactionary ideas designed to petrify an unbearable class structure, and eager to abolish the poor instead of poverty as such.

On the whole, "means of subsistence" is more fruitful a concept than "food" or "nourishment" because it opens a wider view. It transgresses the narrow meaning of soil and harvest and points out to the variety of means which allow a population to exist at a particular level of living. But Malthus supposed a very slow upward creeping of the subsistence level in comparison with the growth potential of the population. He could not foresee the tremendous progress in all spheres of the society in nineteenth century Europe. Intensification of agriculture by chemical fertilizers multiplied the crop harvest and technological progress enabled a shift to industrial mass production of consumption goods. That raised the level of subsistence which came increasingly from the manufacturing sector.

3. *Summary of the Classical Points of Critique*

Populations grew much slower than envisaged, nurture grew much faster than imagined at the beginning of the nineteenth century. Scientific innovation in agriculture, expanded the narrow limits drawn by Malthus, cultural innovations in lifestyle and built-in safety valves in reproductive behavior to reduce population pressure spread throughout a new social stratification marked by an increasing middle class.

Technology and industrial organization expanded not only the "means of subsistence" but also extended the fields of production. Wages and earnings from industrial work became the dominant "means of subsistence" and overruled the ancient strangling law of the diminishing returns: after an optimal point, additional input of labor does not yield a corresponding additional output but a minor one. The rise of industrial fields of production made this agrarian law obsolete because an ever-growing number of people could be absorbed in new industrial sectors.

The nineteenth century saw developments which provoked a re-evaluation of some of the propositions of Malthus' rationale. What made the doctrine so questionable was not so much false inference which was Malthus' logic; it was much more the untamed economical, technological, and social progress which let the ancient fear that mankind will, sooner or later, run out of its means for living.

Malthus underestimated the outputs of the new industrial system, its capacity to improve the standards of living and the willingness to fight against death, once omnipresent in pre-industrial settings. New communication networks and modes of transportation helped to balance regions of affluence with those of poverty. For want of such knowledge, Malthus was led to place an undue emphasis on the impending shortage of arable and habitable land. Malthus could not foresee also the nineteenth century revolution in agricultural methods (chemical fertilizers, plant and animal breeding, improved livestock feed) which allowed European populations to grow fast by gaining a steadily improved condition of nutrition and health. In spite of the economic difficulties and the social ups and downs which displayed the new industrial system, the means of subsistence grew no less than the population did. Population more than doubled. Poverty became a problem of sectional deficiencies and a task for organized welfare policy but ceased to be mankind's lot.

4. The Malthusian Debate within the History of Social Sciences

Among the most prominent critics of Malthusianism we find liberal economists hailing the new technologies and resources. They considered Malthus' doctrine as an obsolete and drab outlook which had lost all its grounds.

The sharpest attacks on Malthusianism came from the Marxian thought. Notwithstanding the collapse of communism, this criticism is of interest because it deals with the "naturalism" and "animalism" as the base alleged of the Malthusian doctrine. Marxists, like Friedrich Engels, attacked it as a "vile and infamous doctrine," and as a "repulsive blasphemy against man and nature." According to Marx, no general law of population could be valid for all human societies, and invariable biological traits of nature exist only for plants and animals. Problems of overpopulation are the result of the prevailing economic and social order which a successful revolution or progress would resolve automatically. Marx asserted that poverty is the result of the unjust social institutions of capitalism rather than of population growth. The capitalistic machinery is eager to get rid of the wage earners who will build a surplus population—as a result of an economic calculation and not of a

"passion between the sexes" presupposed by Malthus. Karl Marx and Friedrich Engels strenuously fought against the Malthusian doctrine on population because it blamed poverty on the poor themselves rather than on the evils of social organization.

Industrial capitalism experienced ups and downs, business cycles and periods of stagnation which triggered off unemployment. That means also that an industrial labor market showed signs of surplus population, and it came to heavy disputes between Marxists and Liberals about the way out of the squeeze. It became clear, that this kind of deplorable surplus population was not engendered by mere sexuality and so Marx had called it an "industrial reserve army." This historical experience allowed a new sight on the mutual stimulation of demographic and economic growth fervently hailed by liberal economists. Crises in industrial capitalism, however, caused economic stagnation with employment problems which were replaced by phases of economic recovery. In the same manner, times of overpopulation will follow those of shortage of labor force. A realistic description of a "hot-cold-destiny" of population in highly industrialized capitalistic systems was found in a "theory of demographic alternation" (Ernst Wagemann).

Because of the rapid growth of the European population and the fact that better life gained ground foremost in the upper and middle classes, whereas the misery awaited the new-born in the lower social strata, the Malthus-Marx debate persisted throughout the nineteenth century. So this debate is due to the severe social inequality which early High Capitalism in the Western sphere had brought about.

5. "Welfare Theory" and "Demographic Transition Theory"—the Overthrow of the Malthusian Paradigm

In the first half of the twentieth century, further changes in the demographic and social sphere entailed also further criticism on the Malthusian doctrine considered as an inflexible body of knowledge unable to take into account the deep-rooted societal changes. About 1900, birth decline was registered in Western Europe and it cried out for an explanation where surplus population was meant to be the crucial factor in human history. Astonished by these facts, German economists put forward a "welfare theory of birth decline." It suggested that higher wages for people in the reproductive and the working age will not entail a greater number of children but a growing amount of consumption goods if being offered by advancing industrialized settings. That means that "alternatives" to the traditional family-centered lifestyle have come into being, and with them, a new form of coping with the necessities of one's life course. Communal tradition as guidance is fading while "competing options" of which personal choices are to be made begin to prevail. In this new situation, family and offspring will lose their central place in one's life and have to be put in accordance with other individual strivings, and chances. These findings challenged the logic of both Malthusianism and Marxism: Malthusianism because more familial resources will no longer mean an even greater number of children, but a minor one, and Marxism because the working class is no longer bound to impoverish and is not always willing to engage in collective action and revolution. Furthermore, it begins to look after better life chances and to display, seemingly to spite orthodox spirits, a mental *embourgeoisement.*

Birth decline was only an important part of a much greater movement which is considered, till these days and beyond Malthus and Marx, as the developmental solution for a growing population. It was embedded in a process in the West which had the appearance of a historical tendency called "industrialization" or "modernization." It has been well-documented in all regions and showed a wide range of phenomena and ways toward modernization. But an ideal picture can be given as follows: industrial development provides first an infrastructure which lowers mortality. Better living conditions, health services, and a transportation system which set back hunger and malnourishment were conducive to a decline of mortality in all age groups and to a steadily growing expectation of life. Ever more survivors caused a population growth whose end could not be seen. This explains why Malthusian warnings regained ground at the time, when demographic movements to make them obsolete had already begun to work. Only three generations later this process showed its contours and social scientists a new theoretical model: The initially perplexing birth decline could be seen as an adaptive movement to the declined mortality, allowed to complete a new overall-conception combining population growth, development and modernization under the title of a "theory of demographic transition."—Surplus population or "population explosion" turned out to be an intermediate "transitional" stage (low mortality, high birth rates) which relies a traditional demographic regime (high mortality and high birth rates) with a modern one showing a new balance at a low level of both deaths and births.

6. Early Neo-Malthusianism

At the end of the nineteenth century a *Neo-Malthusian*

movement came into being and declared a small family size among the poor to be the best way for reaching a better life. All over Europe the term "Neo-Malthusian" or even "Malthusian" meant the endeavor towards smaller families by contraception for making both ends meet better; and furthermore, the call for keeping nations and their life-supporting systems in balance: birth control and frugality in public and private will take the burden from man and nature and will bring about peace worldwide. Although Malthus as a clergyman would surely have disavowed birth control whose mass use of today's methods like infra-uterine device, "pill," and abortion he did not foresee. This "birth-control movement" (cf. Malthusian League) was the beginning of organized family counseling in Europe and Northern America. The on-going birth decline in Europe proved out to be an unexpected but long-lasting phenomenon and produced, in the early decades of the twentieth century, debates on the future of Western peoples. So Malthus' anxieties of an overpopulated world gave way to fears of the opposite, and even the suppression of birth control measures was taken into account. Malthus' writings seemed outmoded with the exception of those parts which dealt with the concept of "preventive checks" because it was clear that they were needed as a behavioral norm to bring about conscious parenthood, and after all, the demographic transition, i.e., the adaptation of the birth rate to an already lowered death rate in the course of modernization of a society.

7. Neo-Malthusianism after World War II—Population Problems in Developing Countries

After the Second World War the Malthusian doctrine regained an importance as an amazing population growth in the decolonized countries in Africa, Asia and Latin America (the "South" of the globe) emerged. This alarmed Europe and Northern America (the "North"). Because this growth was accompanied by the impoverishment of the "South;" it was, from then on, hard to deny that social and economic cleavages would divide the world. All modern societies have completed the demographic transition and the little and medium-sized Eastern Asian countries which run a successful economy are about to do so as well. But the overall situation, of less developed countries (LDCs) was apt to renew Malthusianism, in full awareness of the "laws" which the demographic transition model implies: at the beginning of the demographic transition, population harbors a "high growth potential" and will, after having entered the transitional stage, find themselves in a situation of developmental stress. If the growing population can not be absorbed by equally growing labor markets and nourished by an extended arable land, these countries will be caught in a so-called "Malthusian trap," which means that economic progress is annihilated by the costs of growing birth cohorts and lets a country creep at a low level of living.

So "development" can be defined as a successful avoidance of the Malthusian trap or as a planned and comprehensive endeavour to escape from it. On the best way to go onward the path of development, Malthusians and Anti-Malthusians made subject of hot debates. Malthusians pleaded for a manipulation of the demographic side, with the help of "birth control," "family planning," "containment of population growth," and so on. This would lessen the strain LDCs have to suffer. Anti-Malthusians of different kinds questioned this way from several points of view:

7.1 Marxist and "Third World" heroes proclaimed decolonization and social revolution for directing a LDC to development. As known today, the revolutionary hopes for many countries did not fulfill; on the contrary, demographic and economic problems seem, nowadays, to be severest in so-called centrally-planned systems constructed in accordance with the communist model.

7.2 The hard-core liberals were unfavorable to any intervention in a developmental stage. In their opinion, the factors of progress had to find themselves, because the solutions would come out of the problems. Therefore, their slogan read like this: "Doing nothing is the easiest way out."

7.3 "Developmentalists" who were also liberals on their own since they pleaded for a free market economy and democracy did not see how the Western-European way of modernization should come into being, somewhere else, automatically. In their opinion, a particular investment program had to propel economic and social progress and bring down a high birth level by even more alternatives to family life—such as proposed by the above-mentioned German "welfare theory." Their slogan was: "Development is the best pill." But also developmentalism had to cope with its own failures and misguidance of resources and so the Malthusians retorted ironically: "The best pill is the pill." "Family planning," however, needed preparatory work, trained staff and funded strategies. It turned out to be a conscious behavior which had to be harmonized between young couples and parents. Programs of that kind presupposed, for being success-

ful, the conviction of a lowered infant mortality, a greater chance of new-born that is required in the second stance, and a better economic outlook for parents with a reduced family size and for the children with an education and occupational formation.

The measures offered by authorities for the parent's planning of the number of children and the time space between the births must be in accordance with local culture. Otherwise, a family planning program is doomed when it is based on a mere propaganda and groundless promises. So the interconnection of demographic and economic factors during development became more and more clear and it got international confirmation at the UN World Population Conferences held once in a decade since the middle of the twentieth century.

A concluding paper of the World Population conference in Bucharest in 1974 stated, after days of passionate disputes, a "message" saying that only a wise combination of population policy and economic planning would be able to bring about progress and welfare in developing nations. This sounds like the triumph of the Malthusian doctrine and its critics alike whose incessant display of narrow-mindedness, deficiencies and misjudgments of Malthusian thought made it at last a renewed and useful body of knowledge. The next World Population Conference in 1984 in Mexico City was already held in this conciliatory spirit. The *World Bank's Development Report* published also in 1984 dealt exclusively with the population problem and delivered a masterpiece of an "enlightened Malthusianism" on whose grounds institutions could work. The UN-Conference on Population and Development held in 1994 in Cairo brought about the final breakthrough of family planning as a common good and practice under the extended title of "reproductive health and rights."

8. *"Carrying Capacity," Resources and Ecology*

The surge of ecological issues during the last decades of the twentieth century shows how ecology and environmentalism are indebted to Malthus and to his critics alike. The Malthusian theory and its corrections by virtue of empirical facts throw a light on the "state of the earth." The key concept to assess the "sustainability" of a population size over a long time is no longer "arable land" but "carrying capacity" of its living space. It refers to the long term capacity of the *natural* environment to shelter as well as the capacity of the *social* environment to provide a reasonable quality of life (D.F. Durham).

With the on-going process of civilization to higher forms of technology and social organization, the simple Malthusian contrasting of population against agriculture experienced an important widening, i.e., a shift toward the organizational skills of a population, even a stationary one, to produce the means for its constantly rising level of living. Shortage of land and efficient harvest as figuring in the classical model were transformed into an "ecological scarcity," the organizational level lagging behind its possibilities; it must be dynamically adapted for securing economic and social acquisitions such as a particular standard of living and an expectation of life.

The coping with ecological scarcity refers to an optimal (sustainable) use of resources within a given territory. To get, in this respect, a successful result, human capital and technological progress must work together to raise the carrying capacity and to improve the population-environment balance.

Neo-Malthusians of the most recent kind (*Paul* and *Anne Ehrlich, Lester Brown, Garnett Hardin, Virginia Abernethy*, and others) substituted the dichotomy population pressure—environmental decay by an impact-equation whose factors show how the relationship between population and environment is or should be kept in balance. According to the Ehrlichs the environmental impact (I) is equal to a population (P) at a particular level of prosperity of affluence (A) which is maintained by a technology (T) providing energy and resources. This $I = P \times A \times T$ formula looks rather mechanistic but widens the view on population and the shortage and gives chances to human action. It sends out signs of warning when a carrying capacity is endangered by deterioration. Pessimists will see in human action a danger to the earth's supportive capacity, but human reason can direct it to the opposite. Actions have raised the mankind's ability to transform formerly useless matter into resources and to extend the carrying capacity which had constrained a population by resource-based limiting factors. The same applies for technological progress as the most visible agent to loosen resource constraints. European history can be seen under ecological eyes: Malthus presupposed a filling of every empty corner of a carrying capacity with population. Some scholars speak of an *economy-pull hypothesis*. Surplus population (population in excess over carrying capacity), however, has not always brought death and misery but functioned as a stimulus for technological invention and change in production and its resource base. So some historians of agriculture like Ester Boserup formulated a *population-push hypothesis*. Population pressure and the response it triggers off are two forces of change reacting to each other. This dynamic view explains the European population growth and Europe's technico-economical progress as well.

The Anti-Malthusians consisting of liberal economists and sociologists criticize the overwhelming part which population plays in the balance of resource use. Since the 1970s, the resource-base of the world population and its outlook for the future became the battlefield for scholars on both sides. The sensational reports *"The Limits to Growth,"* (1972, Meadows et al.), and *Global 2000"* (1980), based on a neo-Malthusian thought, were attacked by sociologists and economists for underestimating the efforts which aimed at substituting raw materials whose price rises to an invaluable height: within a free market system the market prices will function as a measure of scarcity which human creativity is always eager to surmount. The motivation to advance and to be free from toil and trouble is the "ultimate resource" (J. Simon) which the mankind will never run out of. In a counter-attack, Malthusians insist upon the fact that the population of most LDCs is about to pass its transitional growth and will, presumably, arrive at 8 billions of people about the middle of the twenty-first century. This demographic growth will challenge all developmental forces to prevent mankind from a precarious situation with the necessaries of life, such as the so-called renewable resources of water, soil, air—if the non-renewable ones should have been replaced through technological invention.

This general feeling of coming shortages gives rise to positions which come closer to a Malthusian tradition than to others. But as the demographic transition model and the "message of Bucharest" tell, proper economic policies, education, and family planning must flow together into a general strategy. Population policy has to play a well integrated part and must not be the main thrust of development policy.

There are serious proposals to revert the European way to demographic transition for the ends of Third World's development. It must be completed much faster than in Europe because the incomparably high population growth rate of the South does not allow such a slow path to modernization. Mortality came down rather rapidly with the help from outside, and so foreign help will be needed for an equally faster going-down of the birth level. And furthermore, an idea begins to emerge that a foregoing stop to population growth would accelerate development. The European way, a reducing of fertility by raising the standard of living of the poor and by an influx of industrial mass consumption is impossible to be imitated in the Southern hemisphere. The focus has to be directed to fertility-reducing correlates such as an enhanced status and education of women, reducing infant mortality, and raising levels of health and family income. This would bring down population growth earlier and with fewer resources than by the European way, which would doubtlessly be detrimental to the present world's ecology.

9. Conclusion

Critique of Malthusianism did not extinguish the thought and the ideas bound up with it. Although Malthus' ground work seems to be simple, it is fundamental to many kinds of problem-solving: understood as a restoration of the population/carrying capacity-imbalances during the developmental stages of societies. The most important contribution of Malthus' critiques is the evidence that population *per se* is not nuisance or hope but a co-determining "accomplice" through the history of nations and mankind.

Malthusianism and its critique are not a matter of mutual exclusion, but how hesitatingly it developed an approximation of points of view on the way of construction of a body of knowledge and experience apt to overcome the crises impending in the twenty-first century.

See also: *Human Security; Future of Humanity; Social Progress and Human Survival*

Bibliography ——————————————————

Cole H S D, Fremann Che., Jahoda M, Pavitt K L R 1973 *Thinking about the Future—A Critique of the Limits to Growth*. Chatto & Windus, London

Coleman D, Schofield R (eds.) 1988 *The State of Population Theory*. Basil Blackwell Ltd., Oxford

Durham D F 1991 Notes on carrying capacity. In: *Population and Environment—A Journal of Interdisciplinary Studies* 13(2)

Mclaren D J, Skinner B J (eds.) 1987 *Resources and World Development*. John Wiley & Sons, New York

Neurath P 1994 *From Malthus to the Club of Rome and Back-Problems of Limits to Growth, Population Control, and Migrations*. M.E. Sharp, Inc., Armonk, NY

Simon J 1981 *The Ultimate Resource*. Princeton University Press, Princeton, NJ

Turner M (ed.) 1986 *Malthus and His Time*. Mcmillan, London

JOSEF SCHMID

Manifest Destiny

The term "Manifest Destiny," was a diplomatic slogan of common use in the United States during the 1840s and 1850s. It supported the belief of a supposed inevitability of the continental territorial expansion of the United States. The term was coined and first used by John L. O'Sullivan, a known expansionist who wrote in 1845, referring to the United States, that it was "our manifest destiny to overspread the continent allotted by Providence for the free development of our yearly multiplying millions."

Practically the slogan was a response to the phenomenal rate of growth of the country's population and the continuous expansion west and south of the 13 original colonies. By means of its application it was sought to obtain economic and commercial advantages and also to ratify the superiority of Anglo-Saxon talents and US political institutions over those of neighboring countries. Inasmuch as it was a response to the fear of foreign encroachment in the continent, it was a peculiar way of understanding and applying the principles of Monroe pronounced in 1823 and revived by President Polk in 1845 (see *Monroe Doctrine*).

Geopolitically Manifest Destiny was used as a justification for the annexation of Texas, for the demand for annexation of the territories won in the Mexican War of 1846-48 and for the policy followed in the controversy with the United Kingdom over the territory of Oregon. The political struggle that preceded the US Civil War also utilized the doctrine inasmuch as there was a will to annex new states to the Union in order to balance or unbalance the equilibrium among proslavery and antislavery states. Such an endeavor provided the rationale for expansionist overtures further away from "the continent alloted by Providence," as was the case for William Walker's incursions in Central America during the 1850s and the permanent desire of many to make Cuba a part of the Union. The principles of Manifest Destiny were also to be found in the argumentation behind the purchase of Alaska, the attempted annexation of Santo Domingo, and the later annexation of Hawaii and incorporation of the Caribbean and Pacific islands taken from Spain as a result of the war of 1898.

Bibliography ——————————————————

Weinberg A K 1935 *Manifest Destiny*. John Hopkins University Press, Baltimore, Maryland

RODRIGO ALBERTO CARAZO

Mao Zedong

Mao Zedong was one of the great charismatic leaders of the twentieth century but he is associated rather with wars and victories than with successful peace initiatives. The first impression is confirmed by his voluminous writings. While abundant in ideas on strategic and tactical problems—*On Tactics Against Japanese Imperialism* (1935), *Strategy in China's Revolutionary War* (1936), *Problems of Strategy in Guerrilla War Against Japan (1938), On Protracted War* (1938), *Problems of War and Strategy* (1938) to mention only some of the most important—they contain not a single major essay dealing exclusively with peace. This concentration on military issues does not mean, however, that reflections on peace are completely missing. The treaties *Strategy in China's Revolutionary War* for instance, written after the "Long March" and used by Mao for his lectures at the Red Army College in Northern Shensi, contains a small chapter that throws some light on his general attitude toward war and peace. "War, this monster of mutual slaughter among men, will be finally eliminated by the progress of human society, and in the not too distant future too. But there is only one way to eliminate it and that is to oppose war with war."

These introductory sentences underlie basic characteristics of Mao's personality—the messianic view of himself, his strong moral conviction, and his utopian optimism with apocalyptic undertones. Yet the following passages resound as well with a sense of reality that, in his thinking on war, expresses itself in the conviction that the phenomenon "war" does not vanish through rational communication and cooperation but only by means of war itself:

Mankind's era of wars will be brought to an end by our own efforts, and beyond doubt the war we wage is part of the final battle. But also beyond doubt the war we face will be part of the biggest and most ruthless of all wars. The biggest and most ruthless of unjust counter-revolutionary wars is hanging over us, and the vast majority of mankind will be ravaged unless we raise the banner of a just war. The banner of mankind's just war is the banner of mankind's salvation. The banner of China's just war is the banner of China's salvation. A war waged by the great majority of mankind and of the Chinese people is beyond doubt a just war, a most lofty and glorious undertaking for the salvation of mankind and China and a bridge to a new era in world history. (Mao 1965-77)

The imminent war against Japanese imperialism grew in Mao's perspective into a drama of world historic importance, in which Good and Evil confronted each other in a last showdown. Internationa.istic hopes and nationalistic ambitions amalgamated to an indissoluble entity; Karl Marx's vision of a classless society with Kang Yuwei's utopia of the "era of perpetual peace:" "When human society advances to the point where classes and states are eliminated, there will be no more wars, counter-revolutionary or revolutionary, unjust or just; that will be the era of perpetual peace (see *Perpetual Peace*) for mankind."

While Mao's chiliastic expectations of an imminent end of the old world and a dawning of a new one were soon replaced by the insight that the "era of perpetual peace" is still in the distant future and that even in this era the contradictions among men will last, Mao remained convinced up to his death that he was fighting for a better and a more peaceful world.

It was not a peaceful world into which Mao was born on December 26, 1893 in Shaoshan village of the province of Hunan as son of a small farmer. The scramble of the Western powers to partition the world among themselves was raging and the Chinese Empire was engaged in a desperate fight for survival. Beside the European powers and the United States, the emerging new Asian power, Japan, was fighting for its share of the booty. The Manchu Dynasty had succeeded up to this point in preserving its sovereignty, but the situation was far from encouraging. Many wars had been lost and each peace had to be bought dearly: with the opening of ports, the secession of rights and territories, and the retreat from neighboring states, which had lived for hundreds of years under Chinese suzerainty.

The attempts of the Chinese government to play the foreign powers off against each other had proved as unsuccessful as its half-hearted political and economic reforms. With its defeats the opposition grew, and while the dynasty managed to crush its opponents for a while, it finally had to abdicate. In 1912 China became a republic, though not a very fortunate one, for it was not Sun Yat-sen, the charismatic leader of the Republican movement who harvested the fruits of the victory but Yuan Shikai, the commander of China's most modern army, who had joined the revolution at the last minute. Since Yuan, however, was not interested in a republic, but intended to restore the monarchy and the old Confucian system, the war for a new China went on.

Mao was 14 years old when he first came in contact with the revolution. In October 1911, after the outbreak of the fighting, he joined a unit of Republican volunteers in Zhangsha, but left them after the victory to go back to school. Undecided what profession to choose he finally decided to become a teacher. He was mainly interested in political and social problems, read Adam Smith, J.S. Mill, Darwin, Spencer, Rousseau, and other Western authors, studied and admired the American War of Independence, and ardently hoped for a renewal of China. Under the influence of the avant-gardist journal *New Youth* (Xin Qingnian), edited by Chen Duxiu, Hu Shi, and other famous Chinese intellectuals, he came to the conclusion that such a renewal would be possible only on the basis of a comprehensive spiritual and cultural revolution. In 1917 he published his first article in the *New Youth*—entitled *A Study of Physical Culture*—in which he recommended physical exercise to his countrymen as a means of strengthening their bodies and hearts. "The principal aim of physical education," he stated explicitly, "is military heroism" (Schram 1963).

Mao's political activities increased: he founded societies and journals in which he propagated his ideas, and became, with the help of Li Dazhao, who was the main propagator of socialist ideas in China and later founder of the Communist Party, assistant librarian at Peking National University. Under the impression of the May Fourth Movement and the influence of Li Dazhao and Chen Duxiu, Mao turned more and more toward communist ideas. "By the summer of 1920," he later told Edgar Snow, "I had become, in theory and to some extent in action, a Marxist, and from this time on I considered myself a Marxist." In the summer of 1921 Mao participated as a delegate from Hunan at the foundation of the Communist Party and concentrated increasingly on the political education and organization of the Chinese industrial workers. In the meantime the Chinese communists had agreed under pressure from the Comintern to a coalition with the Kuomintang (KMT), the Nationalist Party of Sun Yat-sen. Mao entered the KMT and held high positions in it. However, in 1925 he became aware of the importance of the peasant problem and the peasant masses for the Chinese revolution. His *Report on an Investigation of the Peasant Movement in Honan* (March 1927) marked a decisive step in his revolutionary development. Not the then just-emerging urban proletariat, but the masses of poor peasants were in his view the main force in the Chinese revolution; their liberation was the precondition for the liberation of China. It was this discovery

that would establish decades later Mao's reputation as the founder of a new way toward socialism—a way not only relevant for China but for other developing countries as well. Later, in 1965, Lin Biao raised this insight of Mao's to the global level by stating that the world revolution depended more on wars in the rural areas of the world—that is, on the peoples in Asia, Africa, and Latin America—than on the urban proletariat of the West.

The bloody slaughter of the Chinese communists by Chiang Kai-shek(1927) and the conditions on the Jinggang Mountains, to which Mao had escaped with some followers, taught him however, that the mobilization of the peasants was not the only key to survival and victory. Some other "magic weapons" were needed. At least as important as the support of the peasant masses was the existence of armed forces, which were able to defend them and annihilate the armies of the KMT. And if political power comes out of the barrel of a gun, as experience taught, then it was indispensable to study the laws of war. The result was Mao's writings on strategy and tactics and his general reflections on war and peace, which provided these activities with an ideological and an existential legitimation.

Mao began his military studies in reaction against the efforts of Chiang Kai-shek to annihilate the communist areas. However, in the 1930s, the concentration on military problems became even more meaningful when the Japanese threat against China increased. In the fall of 1931, Japan occupied Manchuria; soon its preparations to invade other parts of China became immense. In the summer of 1937 the incident at the Marco Polo Bridge touched off the war. In the long run, the Japanese invasion proved to be fortunate for the communists: it not only saved them from the KMT troops, but put Mao in a position to win by an uncompromising anti-Japanese posture which engaged the sympathy of wide segments of the Chinese population and forced the KMT into a national united front against Japan (Xian incident). At the same time he made preparations, in the shadow of war, for the final battle with the nationalists, which started soon after the Japanese capitulation (September 1945) and ended in the summer of 1949 with the victory of the communists. Nearly three decades after founding the Communist Party and after more than two decades of war, Mao proclaimed on October 1, 1949 in Beijing the People's Republic of China. He was the unchallenged ideological and political leader, and held the most important positions in state and party. Mao had reached the zenith of his power.

Though the final victory of the communists

brought an era of bloody wars and civil wars to an end, it was only a first step in China's march toward a peaceful future. More, not less, difficult hindrances had to be overcome. There were two principal tasks which had to be carried out: the consolidation of communist power against its external enemies, and the creation of a society which met the ideals of socialism and the demands of the twentieth century. The tasks were equally difficult and in both fields the experience of Mao and the party was only limited. The solution of leaning on the then Soviet Union was therefore near at hand—internationally, in order to protect the People's Republic of China against the containment policy of Washington; internally, because only the Soviet leaders were in possession of concrete information concerning the establishment of a socialist economy. The Sino-Soviet Treaty on Mutual Assistance (February 1950) and the first Five Year Plan, with its stress on heavy industry and its neglect of agriculture, was completely oriented to the Soviet model. Soviet experiences dominated. Mao's call in 1938 for the "Sinification of Marxism" seemed forgotten and the development of a "Chinese Way" abandoned.

However, the developments following the death of Stalin proved this impression to be wrong. Mao was neither willing to subordinate China to the interests of Moscow's foreign policy, nor prepared to stick to the Soviet model when it did not work. The search for new ways started again and the Sino-Soviet monolith began to crumble. While Khrushchev's interest in the end of the Cold War and an arrangement with the West raised "peaceful coexistence" as the basic principle of the policy of the international communist movement, Mao insisted on the priority of "proletarian internationalism," renounced any compromise with the West, and propagated the offensive against imperialism. In his view, the world-historic weather conditions had changed: the east wind prevailed over the west wind—as he told Chinese students in November 1957 in Moscow. In the eyes of the world Mao had become the uncompromising protagonist of an offensive socialism; the People's Republic of China was the center of world revolution.

This impression was confirmed by the radicalization of internal events. Instead of approaching socialism by gradual collectivization and modernization, Mao decided on a "Great Leap Forward." The politics of the "Three Red Banners" (1958), based on the Yenan experiences and pushed by Mao despite misgivings in the party, broke with the Soviet model by putting the accent more on the creation of a highly motivated, unselfish "new man" and on new relations of production. Its center was the people's communes,

which were regarded as the "basic unit of the socialist society." They were not only expected to improve the effectiveness of the workers but also to lessen the differences between city and village, mental and manual labor, between workers and peasants, and to explore a faster route to communism. The challenge to Moscow was obvious.

However, the "run" was too short—the "Great Leap Forward" had disastrous consequences: the economy suffered heavy losses, the people were in uproar, but worst of all, the unity of the Communist Party was broken. A sequence of political and ideological struggles commenced that would last until Mao's death and shake the foundations of the People's Republic. The responsibility for the failure fell upon Mao, his reputation was damaged, and he retired to the "second line." Under the leadership of Liu Shaoqi and Deng Xiaoping, China returned to a pragmatic course, relying more heavily on material incentive and private initiative.

Mao's influence on Chinese politics declined. However, it was not only the loss of power that worried him—he was deeply troubled by the fatal consequences which the new politics had for his vision of a socialist society. He warned of "capitalistic tendencies" in the party and stressed the "continuation of class struggle" even under socialist conditions. Seeing his admonitions neglected, he finally proclaimed a "Great Cultural Revolution" in the summer of 1966. With the support of the "Red Guards" and parts of the Army he purged his opponents in the party and tried to realize again his ideas of an egalitarian society. The country sunk into chaos.

However, Mao failed to win back the initiative. In April 1969 under the threat of a dramatic deterioration in Sino-Soviet relations and under pressures from army leaders the Cultural Revolution was brought to an end. Law and order were restored, and with the help of Zhou Enlai many of the purged cadres were rehabilitated. Though handicapped by his ailing health, Mao was still able to keep his leading position and to balance hostile factions within the party. While sympathizing with Zhou's efforts to improve China's relations with the West in order to counter the Soviet threat, he remained highly suspicious of the politics of the "Four Modernizations" launched by the pragmatists.

In September 1976 Mao died. The fight between the opposed factions in the Party flared up again, but ended a short time later with the victory of the pragmatists. The leaders of the so-called "Maoist" faction, among them Mao's wife Jiang Jing, were purged and denounced as the "Gang of Four." Though influential forces in the party, mainly victims of the Cultural Revolution, pleaded for a de-Maoization, they failed. The majority were willing only to reduce the personality cult of Mao, which during the Cultural Revolution had assumed gigantic dimensions, and to subject Mao's politics to a thorough criticism. In the final analysis, they asserted, Mao's achievements for China by far exceeded his mistakes.

Bibliography

Ch'en J 1965 *Mao and the Chinese Revolution.* Oxford University Press, London

Chin S S K 1979 *The Thought of Mao Tse-tung. Form and Content.* University of Hong Kong, Hong Kong

Domes J 1972 *Die Ära Mao Tse-tung.* Stuttgart

MacFarquhar R 1974 *The Origins of the Cultural Revolution. I: Contradictions among the People 1956-1957.* Oxford University Press, London

Mao Tse-tung 1965-77 *Selected Works of Mao Tse-tung,* 5 vols. Foreign Languages Press, Beijing

Opitz P J 1972 *Maoismus.* Stuttgart

Schram S R 1963 *The Political Thought of Mao Tse-tung.* Praeger, New York

Schram S R 1967 *Mao Tse-tung.* Penguin, Harmondsworth

Schwartz B I 1951 *Chinese Communism and the Rise of Mao.* Harper Torchbook, Cambridge, Massachusetts

Snow E 1961 *Red Star over China.* Grove Press, New York

Starr J B 1979 *Continuing the Revolution: The Political Thought of Mao.* Princeton University Press, Princeton, New Jersey

Wakemann F 1973 *History and Will: Philosophical Perspectives of the Thought of Mao Tse-tung.* University of California Press, Berkeley, California

Womack B 1982 *The Foundations of Mao Zedong's Political Thought 1917-1935.* University Press of Hawaii, Honolulu, Hawaii

PETER J. OPITZ

Marxist-Leninist Concepts of Peace and Peaceful Coexistence

Marxism-Leninism analyzes peace from different angles: as a sociological category; as a state of international relations; as an end-station of social development; and as policy for a conscious avoidance of current wars and of elimination of war as a social phenomenon.

As absence of war, peace must be considered a concept of the same kind and order as war, that is, a sociopolitical category which reflects essential and universal properties and relationships of reality and cognition. Peace is a class and political phenomenon, an instrument of class policy. Its class and political content depend on the socioeconomic formation of the framework in which it exists and on the character of the policy whose instrument it is. It plays either a progressive or a reactionary role in history. It may be either just or unjust. Its character depends on the character of the policy which was waged in the war preceding it. Marxist-Leninists usually quote Lenin's saying that peace is the continuation of the policies of the preceding war. In the most general classification based on sociopolitical criteria, there are three types of peace:

(a) peace in an antagonistic society;

(b) peace in a nonantagonistic society; and

(c) peace under the conditions of the coexistence of two opposite systems on the interstate level—capitalism and socialism.

In the first type, a fierce competition is carried out without war; the second is characterized by a brotherly cooperation; and the third constitutes a combination of the former two with a mixture of warless economic competition and ideological struggle. This is the peace of today, which moreover is not complete, since it is also characterized by many local wars (see *Local Wars Since 1945*). The diversity of wars in our time means that, apart from the most general classification of the types of peace, a more detailed categorization could be made in which each kind of peace in a certain region and at a certain point of time could be characterized in connection with the character of the war which preceded it.

Marxist-Leninists frequently use the dichotomy of imperialist peace-democratic peace for the two basic divisions with which various kinds of contemporary peace might be classified. A second method of classification, based on sociohistorical and ethical criteria states two kinds of peace: (a) progressive and just peace, and (b) reactionary, and unjust peace.

In the past, peace was rarely just because of the aggressive and reactionary aims pursued by at least one side in the past war. A just peace was only achieved, in the Marxist-Leninist view, in victorious revolutionary or national liberation wars; other wars were settled in an unjust peace, which confirmed a changed balance of power and the then governing principles of domination and subordination. A truly just peace exists now only within the system of socialist states, and it is just and progressive in a dual sense: it epitomizes a new type of international relations between sovereign and equal states united by the bonds of mutual comradely help and all-round cooperation, and also it paves way to the future elimination of all wars, thus ensuring the prosperity and progress of all humanity.

Accordingly, like wars, peace may have different political contents. In a world consisting of states with different social systems, it may include some or all of the following components: political cooperation and strife, economic cooperation and competition, ideological struggle, and cultural and techno-scientific cooperation. The complex of these features makes a positive, or just, peace, so-called peaceful coexistence (see Sect. 2) (see *Peaceful Coexistence*). The existence of the imperialist part of the world generates, however, elements of negative peace (see *Positive versus Negative Peace*): inequality of nations, use of armed violence, neocolonialism, and militarism.

Peace may proceed through different phases and contain varying compositions of the above-mentioned components. Negative peace means simply absence of war and also absence of regular cooperation between states. Militarism dominates imperialist states, which prepare for war. Ideological struggle takes the form of psychological war. The Cold War of the 1950s exemplified this kind or phase of peace. During this phase peaceful forces struggle to overcome negative processes and move on to a higher phase of peace: positive, active peaceful coexistence. The latter also constitutes a process, in which peaceful forces aim at extending and strengthening all forms of cooperation and eliminating all forms of violence. The transition from political détente to military détente would make considerable progress toward establishing a stable, and perhaps eternal, peace.

1. Features of and Conditions for Stable Peace

Stable peace would be characterized by the following features and conditions.

(a) Stable peace is a democratic just peace. The principles for this condition in the international system are said to be formulated in the Constitution of the former Soviet Union: the principle of sovereignty and equality of all states; renunciation of the use of armed violence; inviolability of state boundaries; peaceful resolution of all conflicts; nonintervention in the internal affairs of other countries; respect for human rights and the right of nations to determine their internal order and ways of development; cooperation between states; and observation of international law. These are also the principles of peaceful coexistence (see Sect. 2).

(b) Stable peace is an indivisible peace. Real world peace is incompatible with regional (or local) wars, for several reasons. First, in human history local wars have caused more casualties and material destruction than world wars. Second, technological development has made the weapons used—or to be used—in local wars similar to nuclear weapons as regards their destructive power. Third, local wars can easily escalate to world wars. However, although world peace is inconceivable without peace in particular regions, it cannot be reduced to a simple sum of regional peaces. It depends on the peaceful solution of global conflicts, those between the global antagonistic camps.

(c) Stable peace assumes détente (see *Détente*), which means increased interstate economic, cultural, and techno-scientific cooperation. Political détente should be complemented, in the higher stage of positive peace, by military détente, which would mean stopping the arms race and beginning a gradual disarmament.

A really stable peace, however, can be achieved only by the worldwide victory of socialism (see *Socialism and Peace*); this is the final conclusion of Marxist-Leninists in their analysis of the political content of peace. Peaceful coexistence ought to pave the way to this final solution of the problem.

Stable peace does not include internal peace, that is, peace within the particular (capitalist) countries. This would be class peace, peace between the antagonistic classes and could mean the abandonment of the struggle for socialist revolution. The concept of positive peace includes the non-use of violence in relations between states but not between classes within states. However, positive peace creates favorable conditions for internal class struggle, since it deprives the oppressors of many ideological means which might serve to keep the popular masses in obedience, such as the necessity for national unity in the face of an alleged external threat. It is held that détente does not abolish the class contradictions, nor the laws of armed struggle. It does, however, create greater freedom of operation for these laws.

2. Toward Peaceful Coexistence

At the dawn of the communist movement, its founders and leaders regarded the struggle for peace as subordinated to the struggle for socialist revolution and did not consider peace as a separate and fundamental issue of theory and practice. They believed that socialism and communism would completely do away with the causes of war, rid mankind of the burden of militarism, arms races, and destructive armed conflicts, and ensure eternal peace. Durable peace under capitalism was unattainable, and under socialism was ensured, so the problem of peace in a world with coexisting capitalism and socialism was not discussed, since revolution was seen by them as winning simultaneously in all or almost all of the developed industrialized societies. Certainly, Marx and Engels criticized wars of their time, which they regarded as aggressive and reactionary; they supported the struggle against war preparations, and in the early 1890s Engels wrote that the social democratic parties could and should win by peaceful means. However, the position of the founders of Marxism was that the struggle for peace in general—not against concrete preparations for concrete wars in definite countries—is entirely devoid of meaning and content. The calls raised by the pacifists for removing the threat of war and liquidating arms "in general" within the framework of a somewhat improved capitalist society were regarded by Marx and Engels as futile; moreover, pacifism was seen by them as a form of bourgeois ideology which might divert the attention of the working masses away from the basic aim of the revolutionary movement—the socialist transformation of the world which would solve the problem of peace also. Lenin, who devoted all his attention and effort to the creation of a party for struggle, including armed struggle, and who during the First World War struggled for the transformation of international war into civil war, fiercely criticized pacifism and argued that only a socialist revolution of the proletariat would open the way to peace and disarmament. However, as the leader of the first socialist state he was confronted with the challenging task of ensuring the survival of it, and since no global revolution was in view, this aim could be achieved

only by the gradual and difficult realization of a policy of peaceful coexistence with the capitalist world, the "capitalist encirclement." This policy led to the formulation of the first ideas of the doctrine of peaceful coexistence which was to become the core of the Marxist-Leninist theory of peace.

Diplomatic practice was based on the assumption that many types of war were inevitable. Revolutions could not be accomplished without armed violence; colonies would fight for independence using military means; imperialist states would continue to compete and wage wars for a redivision of the world; and, last but not least, a series of armed collisions between the former Soviet Union and the capitalist countries was regarded as inevitable.

However, the former Soviet state badly needed peace. It had to defend its independence while being politically, economically, and militarily much weaker than the "capitalist encirclement." The bases of Marxist-Leninist ideology remained unchanged: The thesis that socialist revolution is the precondition for a stable peace, and the rejection of and combat against pacifism as an abstract but at the same time harmful ideology, in essence contrary to the policy of the revolutionary state and party. Certainly, peace was to be pursued, but as a separate goal, in concrete periods and concrete circumstances, that is, for ensuring a warless period for economic recovery, military build-up, and socialist construction for the former Soviet state.

Although Lenin believed stable peace and, even more, disarmament to be unattainable goals, several Soviet statements on peace and disarmament were issued in the first postrevolutionary years; for example the support by the former Soviet government of the principles of disarmament talks in 1922 and the Soviet proposal on "general disarmament" submitted in Geneva. In the same year, the Communist International stated that disarmament was infeasible as long as the bourgeoisie was in power, that is, before the victory of the proletarian revolution; communists had to seek in every way to unmask the false and backward essence of the disarmament slogans disseminated by the bourgeoisie and its agents, the social democrats. Thus, with the ideology unchanged, the immediate goal of Soviet public statements in favor of peace and disarmament was to create an image of a peaceful Soviet state, to attain propaganda successes, and to cause confusion in the adversary's camp. A change could be noted in 1935, when to meet the growing threat of Nazi war preparations it was decided to cooperate with antifascist forces in Europe and to create a common front against German fascism.

Fierce and uncompromising criticism of pacifist ideology was changed to a policy of linkage of the communist movement with pacifism for a common struggle against war. It was stressed especially in political propaganda that by untiring efforts the war that seemed imminent, as well as war between capitalist countries, could be prevented. The thesis that war between the first socialist state and capitalist countries was inevitable was set in a longterm perspective. At the same time, the idea that revolutionary wars were inevitable was seldom mentioned. With the signing of the pact between the former Soviet Union and Germany, this policy was, quite naturally, abandoned. The transitory character of the alliance with pacifism confirmed the supposition that Marxist-Leninists, both political leaders and theoreticians, still continued to cherish the doctrine of the inevitability of war, although the political use of it seemed to have varied with the political conjuncture.

In the early post Second World War period, however, the discrepancy between Marxist-Leninist theory and Soviet political practice resurged. Stalin started a large-scale political offensive for creating a worldwide anti-imperialist front, under the banner of the struggle for peace, against nuclear war. On the one hand, he wrote in 1952 (*The Economic Problems of Socialism in USSR*) that,

the inevitability of war among the capitalist states persists. They say that Lenin's thesis that imperialism necessarily produces wars should be considered obsolete as powerful popular forces have emerged demanding peace and opposing war. That is incorrect. The contemporary peace movement wants to rally the popular masses in the struggle for the preservation of peace and the prevention of another world war. That movement therefore is not struggling for the overthrow of capitalism and the establishment of socialism, but it limits itself to the democratic objectives of the struggle to safeguard peace . . . . That is not sufficient for, regardless of all the successes of the movement in defence of peace, imperialism still exists, hence the continued inevitability of wars. For the inevitability of wars to be removed, imperialism has to be destroyed.

The whole set of ideas concerning the inevitability of various types of war was restated as a central element of Marxist-Leninist ideology. The theory seemed to have reached its zenith at the climax of the Cold War (see *Cold War*). On the other hand, the above-mentioned peace offensive continued. The Soviet Communist Party and the state, in innumerable statements,

reiterated its peace-loving objectives and launched several initiatives on disarmament, nuclear in particular. Under the impact of this policy, most of the communist parties in the West supported both the world peace movement and peace initiatives in their countries. They remained skeptical, however, as regards the feasibility of a permanent peace, and even more, of disarmament, under contemporary conditions, especially in the face of the competition and struggle of the two antagonistic socioeconomic and political systems, and their continuous military build-up.

3. Theory of the Inevitability of Wars Renounced

As the policy of peaceful coexistence gradually began to replace the policy conducted during the Cold War, the theory of the inevitability of war was referred to less and less frequently, and at the Twentieth Party Congress held in 1956, it was officially renounced. In preparation for the Congress, Krushchev reexamined Marxist-Leninist doctrine to meet more adequately the conditions of the nuclear era and the problems of peaceful coexistence. Of the traditional view of the inevitability of war, all that remained was the orthodox assumption that the socioeconomic and political system of capitalism (in the stage of imperialism, as it was called) was the source of all wars. It was expressly declared, however, that all wars whatever their type could be avoided. There was no fatal inevitability about the occurrence of wars between the opposing social systems, or even of wars between capitalist states; the possibility of peaceful transition from capitalism to socialism in particular countries was declared; the inevitability of armed uprising as a means of national liberation was denied.

Moreover, a theoretical innovation was introduced: instead of referring separately to the avoidability of wars between the two antagonistic systems on the one hand, and between capitalist states on the other, the principle of the emerging doctrine of peaceful coexistence (wars could be avoided) was formulated so that it applied to all interstate wars in general. This radical change in the orthodox theory was immediately given an international scope. The Manifesto of Peace signed in Moscow in 1957 by the representatives of most communist parties read:

We, the representatives of communist and workers parties, declare that we are fully aware of our responsibility for the destiny of mankind: world war is not unavoidable, war can be prevented, peace can be secured and consolidated . . . . No-one can deny that the proposals submitted to the United Nations Organization as to how to stop the arms race—eliminate the threat of a nuclear war and establish peaceful coexistence among states—correspond to the vital interests of all nations .... We are calling on all of you to demand an end to the arms race which is daily increasing the danger of war which affects you, the working people, most.

Some of the contrasts between the new position and the traditional one were afterwards toned downed, however, by emphasizing the war-generating role of imperialism, by indicating the difficulties a peaceful seizure of power by the proletariat through parliamentary means would involve, and by stressing that the former Soviet Union and other socialist countries would support revolutionary civil wars and wars of national liberation whenever and wherever they may break out. Thus, as the theory of the inevitability of war was irrevocably abandoned and peaceful coexistence was said to be the order of the day, the continued existence of the danger of war was constantly repeated and the unchanging nature of imperialism as the source of all wars continued to be emphasized.

Insistence on the continuing danger of war—even if it did not seem probable at the time—can be explained by the conviction that a permanent struggle against war is a precondition for preventing it. Further, Soviet leaders might fear that in some indefinite future, under circumstances that cannot be defined, capitalist countries might be tempted to attack their socialist antagonists. Since the Soviet leaders regarded the military power of the former Soviet Union and its allies as the best guarantee against such an attack, their emphasis on the permanent threat from imperialism justified a continuous Soviet military build-up. Finally, the call for resolute struggle against the unchanged enemy might be an intentional exaggeration to demonstrate for the benefit of Soviet allies the necessity of maintaining the socialist military bloc under the leadership of the Soviet state, to motivate a call for unity in Soviet society, to help the struggle against foreign ideological penetration, and so on.

The abandonment of the theory of the inevitability of war may be explained by the changes that have occurred in international conditions and within particular countries. Marxism-Leninism regards as ineluctable the progressive development of society, that is, its evolution towards higher socioeconomic and political formations, of which communism is the highest. Those social phenomena and actions which are necessary to carry this process through are therefore inevitable. If progressive just wars were the only means of furthering progress, they would then be

absolutely inevitable; to the extent that they serve social development at less social cost than alternative means, they are relatively unavoidable. Thus Marxism-Leninism does not equate inevitability with automatism: social phenomena cannot occur without activity springing from social consciousness, but such activity will inevitably take place if it is required by social progress. Likewise reactionary and unjust wars directed against progressive forces are inevitable, but only so long as reactionary social forces are stronger than progressive ones. Certainly, wars may also be waged when one of the antagonistic social camps supposes that it is stronger and has reasonable chances for success.

The new Marxist-Leninist doctrine assumed that the conditions that had come to prevail by the mid-1950s were so radically different from those of any previous historical period that neither just nor unjust wars could be considered inevitable. The victories of the socialist system had had two effects: in the first place, it had become much more difficult for the reactionary forces to unleash unjust wars; second, possibilities had opened for the progressive forces to execute social transformations without resorting to armed violence. At the same time, the development of nuclear weapons had so greatly increased the potential social costs of war that even just wars were now more expensive than the nonmilitary methods that had become instrumental as a means of bringing about social revolutionary changes. To sum up, both kinds of war had ceased to be inevitable, even though they remained and will remain a theoretical possibility until capitalism is liquidated.

Thus, the changes in the theory of the inevitability of war were interrelated with the changes in the balance of power between the forces of progress and those fighting for the preservation of the status quo. The development of this proposition has led to the formulation of the theory of the correlation of world forces, which has become an important and integral part of Marxist-Leninist theory of both war and peace (see Sect. 8).

4. Peaceful Coexistence: Doctrine and Policy

In Marxist-Leninist theory, peaceful coexistence does not mean simply an ordinary principle—or set of principles—of international relations. It is presented as a state of the international system, as the inevitable simultaneous coexistence, for a more or less prolonged period of time, of states with different socioeconomic and political systems. Such a condition may cover a broad spectrum of international relations—at one extreme it is the most elementary state of peace (a simple absence of war), and at the other, extensive international cooperation.

Peaceful coexistence is said to be a phenomenon previously unknown in history, an inevitable—in the Marxist-Leninist terminology "lawful"—stage in social development. However, peaceful coexistence is more than this, it is a doctrine which underlies the policy of the socialist states, a set of principles which, in the Marxist-Leninist view, should govern international relations in our epoch and which require active policies pursuing definite political goals.

After the October Revolution, the inevitability of peaceful coexistence of the capitalist and socialist states was far from obvious, since the capitalist powers immediately intervened against the socialist state. However, in spite of the contemporary war, and the prospect that in the near or distant future the historical antagonism between capitalism and socialism had to be resolved by war, Lenin called for peaceful coexistence, Marxist-Leninists maintain. If only one of the links in the imperialist chain was broken, this meant, in Lenin's view, that the simultaneous existence of the first socialist state and capitalist countries was inevitable during the period of history covering the transition from capitalism to socialism on a worldwide scale. Lenin saw that the socialist state needed peace, and he expected that the interests of capitalist countries would in the near future demand the development, efficient organization, and expansion of commercial relations with the Soviet state. He asserted that there was a force more powerful than the wishes and the decisions of the government or classes hostile to the Soviets, and that force was to him world general economic relations; it would compel capitalist states to establish more or less normal relations with the Soviet republic. He also expected that peaceful coexistence would serve to curb and upset aggressive plans against the Soviets, gradually change the correlation of forces between socialism and capitalism in favor of the former, *inter alia* by promoting the consolidation of prosocialist forces throughout the world, and thereby creating preconditions for future new gains of socialism. In the interpretation which is given today to this doctrine and policy, and which requires at least a rough equality of power of the two competing social systems, it may be argued that in the interwar period peaceful coexistence was to the Soviet state a program for the future rather than actual contemporary policy. Some Marxist-Leninists assert that this was both the doctrine and the actual policy of the first socialist state from its very origin, whereas others say that peaceful coexis-

tence has become possible only relatively recently.

Not all kinds of peace, or to put it another way not all conceivable stages of peace, constitute peaceful coexistence, say Marxist-Leninists. "Negative peace" certainly does not. The build-up of peaceful coexistence begins with the renunciation of the use of armed violence by all states which is the *sine qua non* of the whole process of developing and strengthening peace. Formally this was achieved, for instance, by the signing of the Charter of United Nations (see *United Nations Charter*) by almost all states. In fact, however, the United States is said to repudiate such a renunciation and, in its politico-military strategy, it searches for fighting options that create capabilities for using military force below the level of total nuclear war. It does not seek to make peace more stable but it seeks the limit of militancy which would exclude only total nuclear carnage. Peaceful coexistence is therefore not an automatically emerging state of the international system but it must be pursued consciously, systematically, and continuously by active policy based on the following principles:

(a) *Inviolability of frontiers.* The present frontiers in Europe are to be finally recognized with all territorial claims by one country against another one completely excluded. Any attempt to change them, and particularly by an open or indirect use of violence, would break the peace in Europe.

(b) *Renunciation of the use of force or the threat of force.* All disputes are to be settled by peaceful means, through negotiations, in conformity with the basic principles of international law and in such a way that the legitimate interests, peace, and security of nations are not threatened.

(c) *Noninterference in internal affairs of other countries.* Recognition of the right of each nation to decide its own affairs. Nobody can impose a political system or a way of life on another nation. Peaceful coexistence means respect for the political, economic, and cultural foundations of other countries.

(d) *Strict respect for the sovereignty and equality of all nations.* Mutual understanding and trust between them; countries take into account each other's interests.

(e) *Expansion of economic, technological, and cultural cooperation.* On the basis of full equality and mutual advantage, broad and mutually advantageous all-round cooperation, also in such spheres as environmental protection and tourism. The development of comprehensive interstate relations will enhance the stability of the system of security and cooperation that is arising in Europe.

Peaceful coexistence in Europe is regarded by Marxist-Leninist theory of peace as the basis and part of a worldwide peace policy. This should include, for instance, the following measures:

(a) Elimination of the hotbeds of war in Southeast Asia, in the Middle East, in Central America, and everywhere in Africa. A political settlement should be promoted in all these areas on the basis of respect for legitimate rights of states and peoples subjected to aggression.

(b) More generally, renunciation of the use of armed violence in settling any international conflict.

(c) The invigoration of the struggle to stop the race in all types of weapons. The dismantling of foreign military bases. The reduction of armed forces and armaments in areas where military confrontation is especially dangerous.

(d) Putting a ban on nuclear, chemical, and bacteriological weapons. Putting an end to the testing of nuclear weapons. Stopping any attempt to militarize outer space.

(e) Abolition of all the remaining colonial regimes. Universal condemnation of racism and apartheid.

(f) Extension of all kinds of mutually advantageous economic, technological, and cultural relations between the states of various continents. Cooperation in settling such problems as the protection and conservation of the environment, development of power and other natural resources, development of transport and communication, prevention and eradication of the most dangerous and widespread diseases, and the exploration of outer space and the oceans.

5. Peace and Social Progress

Marxist-Leninist theory of peace calls for peaceful coexistence, not only because war causes terrible suffering and enormous destruction and loss of material and human resources, but also because, in the view of Marxist-Leninists, peace paves the way for the operation of the laws of social development to the advantage of socialism and communism (see *Socialism, "Scientific"*).

As regards socialist countries, peaceful coexistence makes it possible for social production to concentrate on the fulfillment of the society's economic and cultural requirements, and on the effective development of socialist democracy including civil rights and freedoms. Contrary to this, international tension and the threat of imperialist aggression, constant economic and political pressure, and various kinds of subversive activity from outside compel socialist governments to switch a large proportion of resources to defense and to take other measures to defend revolutionary gains. This has an adverse effect on economic development and on some aspects of social life and generates negative phenomena which slow down socialist construction.

Peace—and inversely tension—have a similar effect on the struggle for social progress (see *Social Progress and Human Survival*) within capitalist countries. International tension is used by imperialist countries as a justification for the militarization of the economy, and for suppressing any manifestation of class struggle against exploitation and oppression. By pointing to the alleged external communist threat, and by declaring themselves to be the only defenders of national interests, and thereby playing on the patriotic feelings of the popular masses, the governing strata can suppress any internal political opposition more easily. As Soviet theorists put it, peaceful coexistence locks the social and economic relations of capitalism in the narrow framework of its own natural laws where the contradictions flourish in full measure and the class struggle may be waged without being accused of being a conflict with alleged national interests.

Finally, as regards the newly independent postcolonial states, peaceful coexistence and, in particular, economic cooperation with the socialist countries considerably increases the ability of the new states to resist imperialist pressure and to establish fairer terms of trade and all other economic relations as well as to gain the possibility of acquiring modern technology and to take other measures to overcome the existing economic and cultural gap.

6. Peace and Global Problems of Humankind

Peace is said not only to favor the resolution of social contradictions and thereby to ensure social progress, but also to be a prerequisite for the solution of all vital issues faced by humanity, all the vital needs of humankind.

The first of these issues is to ensure material resources for supporting life of the growing population. If peace is preserved, and if international cooperation constantly increases, renewable sources of energy may be discovered through joint efforts. For instance, a controlled thermonuclear reaction may perhaps be used as an economical means of producing energy which will help to conserve the supplies of coal, oil, gas, and other raw materials now used for the production of power. The "green revolution" will spread, a rational approach to population growth will be taken, and famine, poverty, and mass epidemics will be eliminated, which *inter alia* will lead to the prolongation of life (see *Human Security*).

Another vital need of humankind is to bridge the gap between the economically developed countries and the underdeveloped or developing countries. This problem can be solved, if some conditions are fulfilled, say Marxist-Leninists. First, the resources of the developing nations must be concentrated on rapid and sound economic growth. This depends, however, on another condition, namely on radical social transformation, which will make possible the establishment of sound economic and social aims and plans for their accomplishment, the centralization of the management of material resources and the labor force creating a state sector which embraces the key branches of production, all this accompanied by structural changes on the basis of social justice. The third condition is the establishment of a just international economic order which would help to promote economic progress in the underdeveloped nations. This order would put an end to the system of unequal exchange and stop the neocolonial robbery of resources and the exploitation of the labor force of these countries (see *Maldevelopment*).

The third vital need is to protect the natural environment, to stop the pollution of it and to some realistic extent to reinstate the natural conditions of human activity. This is a global problem indeed, since in our planet, which is a single abode, environmental pollution in one portion of the globe will, sooner or later, affect the flora, fauna, and humans in its other parts (see *Global Environment and Peace*). Antipollution measures undertaken under the aegis of the United Nations and other international organizations, wholly supported by the socialist countries, can give considerable improvements; however, as Marxist-Leninist theory states, a fundamental change in the present situation necessitates a radical solution, namely the adoption of centralized, planned management of economic growth. This is possible, in this view, only in a socialist world, however. What can be done in the foreseeable future, is to replace the nonrenewable sources of energy by new ones: scien-

tific and technological progress can make it—and probably will make it—possible to develop renewable supplies of energy. Moreover, there are still huge reserves of some sources of energy, which have been erroneously regarded as giving cause for concern, such as coal, which could, with the atom, become the basis of future energy supplies.

All this reasoning is provided by Marxist-Leninist, scholars in order to demonstrate that:

(a) none of the humankind's urgent needs must lead to a catastrophe in the foreseeable future;

(b) none of them irresistibly pushes towards a world war;

(c) they can be partially and temporarily resolved if active international cooperation is developed; and

(d) all of the above needs can be completely satisfied only in a socialist and communist world.

Both the partial solutions and the final one require, however, stable peace. All of the vital needs of humankind may lead to war, and this danger alone points to the necessity for peace (see *Global Neighborhood: New Security Principles*).

7. Peaceful Coexistence is also Class Struggle

All the above-mentioned arguments for peace and peaceful coexistence concentrate on their impact on the cooperation between nations, on the solution by negotiation of all contradictions and conflicts. However, there is another side to the coin, and the Marxist-Leninist theory of peace does not lose any opportunity to underline it and to argue for it.

Class struggle manifests itself in political confrontation, economic competition and, primarily, ideological struggle. Soviet politicians and theoreticians stress that the imperialist camp also considers peaceful coexistence as a means of political class struggle. It aims at, on the one hand, defeating attempts to change the social status quo within the capitalist world and, on the other, to restore capitalist relations in the socialist countries. The basic means used is ideological struggle treated, however, in a particular way: not as a struggle of ideas or a discussion between the contrary ideologies, but as a combination of anticommunist propaganda, psychological warfare, and outright subversive activity within socialist countries which tries to direct the population against the government. This is accompanied by spreading war propaganda under the cover of "defense against the Communist threat." The Marxist-Leninist theory of peace devotes much attention to the condemnation of the class aims which "imperialism" is said to try to attain through peaceful coexistence. In this assessment, the difference between the character of the treatment of peaceful coexistence as a form of class struggle and the approach used by imperialism is that the former is in accord with the laws of social development and paves the way for progress while the latter is reactionary and unjust. Moreover, Marxist-Leninists stress that the class character of peaceful coexistence conducted by socialist countries has an international dimension: socialist countries do not export revolution and are also against the export of counterrevolution. They proceed from the sacred right of every nation to determine its fate independently, while imperialism tries to intervene in the internal affairs of other countries.

8. Peaceful Coexistence and the Correlation of World Forces

The key proposition of the Marxist-Leninist theory of peace is that peaceful coexistence has been possible and successful owing to the correlation of world forces which decisively changed in the favor of the forces of socialism and peace; further changes in the same direction—which are inevitable since they accord with the laws of social development—will ensure the further successes of peaceful coexistence. The main opposing sociopolitical forces in the contemporary world, as seen by the Marxist-Leninist theory of peace, are the two antagonistic systems: capitalism and socialism. A variant upon this opposition juxtaposes two worldwide classes: the world working class and the world bourgeoisie. Still another approach uses the concepts of "world socialism" and "world capitalism." World socialism includes the socialist countries, the socialist-oriented countries (in the Third World), the communist movement and all revolutionary forces which are united and interact with other social groups and political movements of an antiimperialist character. World capitalism includes the group of developed capitalist (also called imperialist) states, capitalist-oriented countries of the Third World, and various interacting conservative and reactionary political movements.

The approach most frequently applied sees the socialist side of the world equation of forces ("progressive" or "peace-loving" or "anti-imperialist") as consisting of the socialist states, the international workers movement, and the national liberation movement and states emerging from it. The respective parts of the other side of the equation are the

capitalist states, the international cooperation of monopolies, capitalist states and bourgeois parties, and the colonialist and neocolonialist powers. The three pairs of respective opponents give rise to three kinds of correlation of forces which constitute three components of the world correlation. The correlation of world forces underwent radical changes which may be described by four historical shifts.

The October Revolution in 1917 caused the first great shift in the correlation of world forces, according to the Marxist-Leninists. For the first time in history, the confrontation between the bourgeoisie and the proletariat, which previously had only a domestic character, acquired an interstate dimension. The second great shift took place after the Second World War: it was connected with the defeat of three major capitalist powers and the weakening of others, and with the emergence of a whole group (called a system) of socialist states. This became a political camp under the domination of the former Soviet Union. At the same time the rise of the United States to the status of a capitalist Superpower, beginning to play the chief role in the nonsocialist world, and the creation of the North Atlantic Treaty Organization (NATO) (see *North Atlantic Treaty Organization (NATO)*), contributed to the polarization of the international system into two camps. This consisted of two groups of states, including almost all the developed industrial countries, with their markedly different socioeconomic and political systems and antagonistic policies. The emergence of a large group of independent states in the 1950s and 1960s, which resulted from the explosion of the anticolonial (or, in the Marxist-Leninist terminology, the national liberation) movement, was viewed as the third basic shift in the correlation of world forces. This also marked the beginning of the third period in the so-called structural crisis of the world capitalist system. The new states were regarded as the natural allies of the socialist camp in its antiimperialist struggle. In the early 1970s, Marxist-Leninist politicians and writers began to point out a fourth basic shift in the correlation of world forces: the attainment by the former Soviet Union (and consequently by the entire socialist camp) of military strategic parity with the United States and the Western camp. It was the first time in history that a military development rather than a great sociopolitical change in the world structure was specified as constituting a basic shift in the correlation of world force.

The following influences of the correlation of world forces that are advantageous to the cause of peace and social progress are pointed out by the

Marxist-Leninist theory. First, it is held that the correlation of world forces has a positive impact on international conflicts. In general, it has limited the number and intensity of conflicts and particularly those between the two antagonistic camps. It has lowered the level, intensity, and scale of the use of military force in them. In many cases, such as the Israeli-Arab war of 1973 (see *Arab-Israeli Wars*), it has led to a localization and deescalation of war; in others it has influenced a transition from military operations to negotiations as in the Greece-Turkey conflict about Cyprus; it has led to a large decrease in the likelihood of conflicts in Europe, and in some cases to the elimination of conflicts (for instance, with regard to Berlin).

Second, the correlation hindered the outbreak of an intersystemic war; it would be a sheer suicide for the imperialist camp to start a nuclear war against the socialist camp; since a war between the particular countries of the opposing systems would cause the immediate outbreak of an intersystemic war, the former is also effectively prevented. As regards interstate local wars in the Third World, the correlation of world forces cannot eliminate their danger completely since they are rooted in the period of colonial domination, and break out for various national and social reasons, depending on the complex local politico-military situation. In the case of national liberation wars, either the progressive forces gave active military support to the insurgents, or paralyzed the attempts of a military counterintervention by the colonial powers, or else created such conditions that the oppressed peoples of the colonies achieved independence without armed struggle. The newly independent countries which strive for economic and social progress, and which face the danger of imperialist military intervention or indirect support of reactionary forces in their territories, can, owing to the prosocialist correlation of world forces, resist imperialist dictation. (On the other hand, their already substantial contribution to the common struggle for peace and the security of the peoples is likely to grow.) Finally, the correlation of world forces does not prevent internal revolutions of either national or social, or mixed, character, but it hinders armed intervention by the imperialist forces, it prevents escalation, and contributes to their termination.

However, while previously Marxist-Leninists had accepted that some wars—in spite of the suffering, destruction of material values and great cultural damage—ultimately had positive consequences in the social sense, that is, they created favorable conditions for revolutions, they now firmly state that wars can cause unprecedented destruction and endanger all the hitherto achieved gains of socialism. From now on socialism must try to advance along the path of internal development through new forms of nonviolent political struggle.

Third, the correlation of world forces positively affects the gradual restructuring of international relations. The world has changed from the balance of power (see *Balance of Power*) of a few great capitalist powers and their dominance over the world to the formal equality of more than 150 equal states and a world system based on two antagonistic camps. This process is leading the world away from international relations based on positions of strength and the dictates of Great Powers and toward relations in which the sovereignty of each state is respected and its interests taken into account. It is also leading away from confrontation to actual peaceful coexistence and cooperation.

This is the final and the most important impact of the correlation of world forces. Peaceful coexistence would be impossible without the correlation of world forces constantly improving in favor of the forces of socialism and peace. They not only prevent many wars, among them a catastrophic intersystemic total war, but also compel the imperialist camp to find a peaceful resolution to several conflicts and to arms control negotiations. In spite of the meager results hitherto achieved, these negotiations must and will continue since gradual disarmament is a condition of ensuring a stable peace.

9. The Chinese and the Yugoslav Variants

The above-characterized Marxist-Leninist theory of peace was the Soviet one. The Chinese and the Yugoslavian variants differed greatly in their assessment of the probability of wars in our epoch and the content and chances of peace. Unlike the Soviets, the Chinese assumed the inevitability of wars, although this contention with regard to the intersystemic war had seldom been mentioned in recent times, and when it had, it had seemed to refer to some indeterminate future. One new element in the Chinese position was the often-repeated statement that socialist countries would not be the first to start such a war. With regard to the interimperialist wars, the Chinese included here the conflict between the Superpowers. When the imperialist character of the former Soviet Union in relation to the countries of the Third World was pointed out, the Chinese emphasized the collaboration between the Superpowers, but when the relations between the latter were analyzed the long-run inevitability of an armed clash between them was mentioned. Both revolutionary wars and wars of national liberation were regarded as inevitable. Since capitalism wages a relentless struggle against the oppressed masses with the use of armed violence, civil revolutionary wars in an ever greater number of countries were to be expected. Apart from internal causes, each revolutionary war was, moreover, part of the international world revolution. Imperialists may be defeated by a series of revolutionary wars instead of one decisive world war. Thus, war between the antagonistic social systems became secondary in importance to revolutionary wars. In this approach, peaceful coexistence was both unrealistic and harmful. It was unrealistic because the national and social contradictions of the modern world lead inevitably to war; peaceful coexistence was nothing more than an unarmed truce unable to prevent local wars. Moreover, it was harmful because it amounted to a plot of the Superpowers to divide the world into spheres of influence without regard to the interests of the small and underdeveloped nations. and to suppress revolutionary movements and movements of national liberation.

The Yugoslav variant paralleled the Soviet one in the assumption that because the balance of power ceased to be favorable to imperialism (see *Imperialism*), and because of the policy of the socialist states on behalf of peace, wars of all types have ceased to be inevitable. The Yugoslavs stressed, however, much more than the Soviets do the national context of the struggle for both peace and revolution: internal conditions are always decisive for the choice of the right moment for the outbreak of revolution, and of the proper means for it, armed or peaceful, and any intervention from outside, even political, was undesirable. Accordingly, in the Yugoslav variant of peaceful coexistence, any armed intervention—even that launched to support some social or national revolution—was condemned. The second difference is that the Yugoslavs interpreted peaceful coexistence to mean coexistence between the states, not between blocs of states. They consider bloc building to increase hostility and to create conditions for future wars. True cooperation, which favors economic development, fosters national independence, and serves world peace, could only take place on a bilateral basis; being tied to a bloc only hinders a state from

such active peaceful coexistence. The alternative they propose was that the states followed independent policies, those of nonalignment. In this way bloc division would be overcome, international relations would be democratized, and since acute international problems could then be solved, peace would be preserved and strengthened.

10. Summary and Conclusion

The Marxist-Leninist theory of peace proceeds from the assumption that peace and war have ceased to be equally permissible historical alternatives as a means of attaining political goals. All types of international and internal wars are avoidable and should be avoided. Peaceful coexistence is the law of our times, says the theory; however, only an active policy for peace of states with different social systems can create an "operational freedom" for the action of this law. The correlation of world forces which in this view continuously changes to the advantage of the worldwide camp of peace, headed by the socialist countries, is an important factor acting on behalf of world peace.

See also: *Intercultural Relations and Peace Studies; Ethnic Conflict and International Relations; Emerging Tool Chest for Peace-builders*

Bibliography ⎯⎯⎯⎯⎯⎯⎯⎯⎯⎯⎯⎯⎯⎯

Inozemtsev N N 1978 *Leninskii kurs mezhdunarodnoi politiki* KPSS [The Leninist line of foreign policy of the CPSS], Izd.Mysl', Moscow
Inozemtsev N N (ed.) 1984 *Global Problems of Our Age*. Progress, Moscow
Kiessling G 1977 *Krieg und Frieden in Unserer Zeit*. Militärverlag der DDR, East Berlin
Korionov V 1975 *The Policy of Peaceful Coexistence in Action*. Progress, Moscow
Lider J 1979 *On the Nature of War*. Saxon House, Farnborough [1983 *Der Krieg, Deutungen und Doktrinen in Ost und West*. Campus, Frankfurt]
Problems of War and Peace. 1972 Progress, Moscow
Shakhnazarov G 1984 *The Coming World Order*. Progress, Moscow

JULIAN LIDER

Mediation

The term "mediation" comes from the Latin *medius*, "middle," and refers to ther process of stepping

between disputing parties in order to settle their differences. It is one of a family of techniques for pacific third-party intervention in conflict (*see Arbitration, International; Commission of Mediation, Conciliation, and Arbitration; Conflict Resolution, History of; Peacekeeping Forces; Problem Solving in Internationalised Conflicts*). Mediation has existed in various forms throughout history and in most parts of the world, but in recent years its importance has increased substantially. Its traditional areas of application included disputes within families and between employees and management. These have now been expanded to include community conflicts, ethnic group relations, confrontations between criminals and their victims, and many other areas. In international relations, mediation also has a long history, but it has been considerably less successful, and efforts are underway to improve its record. Traditionally, interstate mediation has been studied and practiced by political leaders, diplomats, and international lawyers; these have now been joined by peace researchers from a variety of disciplines. In the 1970s and 1980s, the surge of academic interest in both domestic and international mediation has produced a substantial body of scholarly literature, especially on the theoretical aspects of the subject. There appears to be a growing belief in the peace research community that the problems of war and injustice in the world could be significantly ameliorated if ways are found to match, at the interstate level, the achievements of intermediaries at the interpersonal and intergroup levels.

Strictly, mediation should be distinguished from the many other methods whereby a third party may facilitate the settlement or resolution of a conflict. There is no precise agreement about the meanings of the various terms for each of these, partly because they tend to overlap, and partly because third parties tend in practice to switch from one method to another when involved in a particular dispute. There is, however, general agreement that the various forms of pacific intervention may be arranged along a continuum, ranging from the weakest to the strongest methods of involvement. Mediation is in the center of the continuum, and is often described as a half-way house between conciliation and arbitration. But the term is sometimes used in a comprehensive sense, to describe the entire range of techniques of pacific intervention. In this usage, the "mediator" becomes a person or organization employing all relevant methods in an effort to resolve a conflict in a peaceable fashion.

The weakest form of pacific intervention consists of steps to restore and improve communication between parties whose conflict has caused the breakdown of their relationship. At the interpersonal and intergroup levels, there may be bitterness, estrangement, and hostility. At the higher levels of political relationships, normal communication channels may have been cut completely, so that the only contact between the parties may consist of actions designed to injure or destroy each other. In either situation, initial assistance can take the form of carrying messages back and forth—an activity typical of the "quiet diplomacy" practiced by private groups such as the Quakers (see *Quakerism*), or undertaken in highly publicized fashion when a "special envoy" is dispatched to a region of conflict by the government of a state. Once indirect contact is achieved, the parties or their representatives can be helped to negotiate face-to-face. The extension of "good offices " to those in dispute can provide them with a neutral and safe location at which to meet and talk.

With the parties restored to direct contact, the task of the third party may be completed; negotiation may then enable the disputants to manage their own conflict without further assistance (see *Negotiations, Direct*). But if the malign characteristics of conflict dynamics are present, including polarization, stereotyping, rigidity, and the escalation of acts of violence, then negotiation alone may be unsuccessful (see *Conflict: Inherent and Contingent Theories; War*). It may therefore be necessary and possible for the third party to move to the next stage of pacific intervention: conciliation.

Conciliation requires the third party to become involved in the substance of the dispute, although only to a limited degree. Conciliation is an eclectic process, consisting of whatever steps seem to be appropriate to enable the parties to reach a mutually acceptable settlement of their dispute by themselves. The conciliator therefore always stops short of making substantive proposals, while at the same time assisting the negotiations between the parties in every possible way. The strategies of conciliation are to elucidate the nature of the conflict, which the parties may have difficulty in seeing clearly if they are angry and aggrieved; to clarify the attitudes of the parties to each other, ideally in each other's presence; and to explore with the parties the possible range of options open to each of them.

The procedures of conciliation, therefore, are supportive, nondirective, and facilitative. The most important part of the task consists of listening to the parties' own accounts of their shared problem. But some more active tactics may also be employed. If the dispute is between individuals or small groups, conciliation may include personal and psychological counseling, as in marriage guidance and probation work. If the dispute is between occupational groups, organizations, or political groups, conciliation may extend to fact finding or "inquiry," together with authoritative interpretation and advice about legal arrangements which may apply to the matters under dispute. However, these more active steps continue, under conciliation, to serve the purpose of assisting the parties rather than directing them. The highest achievement of the technique is "reconciliation," whereby the conflict between the parties is completely resolved and their relationship is restored to normality.

If conciliation is insufficient, then the third party's next step is mediation. A mediator employs all the basic techniques of conflict management, up to and including conciliation. But in addition, the mediator goes beyond supportive activities into the formulation of constructive proposals to lay before the parties. Whereas a conciliator's work is restricted to clarifying the views of the parties and providing technical advice on attitudes or on the implications of a particular option, the mediator takes the further step of suggesting various ways around the obstacles in the path toward a settlement. As in all pacific third-party activities, the mediator seeks to maintain absolute neutrality in this delicate process, because the rule of impartiality is easily violated when proposals about the outcome of a conflict are being laid on the table. To be acceptable to the parties, the mediator's role must be perceived not only as disinterested but also as legitimate and expert. For this reason there is now much emphasis in the United States, where the study and practice of mediation is most advanced, on the development of training schemes and codes of conduct. This has led in turn to the emergence of an independent profession of mediators, basing their work on the discovery that mediation "is ideally suited to polycentric disputes and conflicts between those with a continuing relationship, since it minimizes intrusion, emphasizes cooperation, involves self-determined criteria of resolution, and provides a model of interaction for future disputes" (Folberg and Taylor 1984 p. 13).

However, both conciliation and mediation may fail. In that case, it may be possible for the conflict management process to move, via mediation, to the strongest end of the spectrum of available methods: legal settlement. This requires the parties to submit their dispute to the decision of an impartial authority, such as an arbitrator, a panel of judges, or an independent commission. At this end of the continuum, conflict management techniques merge into the executive process of government. Government consists of the authoritative allocation of values which are in dispute between individuals or groups, and is made possible by a mixture of coercion, tradition, and the general consent of the governed. Both the political process (whereby issues are identified and personnel selected for government) and the governmental process (making policies and laws, enforcing them, and adjudicating them) involve continual conflict management. On the political or input side of government, the usual techniques are conciliation and mediation, as when a political party leader persuades an assortment of conflicting groups to form a consensus and merge into a broad coalition. On the executive or output side of government, the usual techniques are coercive, carried out by agencies which are backed by the power to enforce compliance.

Arbitration and judicial settlement, therefore, closely resemble government. The parties decide, perhaps with the assistance of a mediator, to grant their consent in advance to a judgment to be made by an outside body. The process falls short of government in that the consent granted by the parties is limited to the matter under dispute, and also because compliance cannot be guaranteed in the absence of a coercive authority. It follows that legal settlement is most likely to be effective when the parties are easily identified, and when the issues are clear-cut or concern the interpretation of an agreement. It is widely practiced in disputes over property, in conflicts over pay or conditions of work, and generally where problems arise within a well-defined hierarchy. It works least effectively in situations where the parties are dispersed or poorly led, where issues of principle arise, where attitudes are inflamed, and where the stakes have been raised by acts of violence.

In many sectors of domestic society, legal settlement has been successfully institutionalized. More generally, conflict management using all the forms of pacific intervention is widely practiced in many countries of the world. In consequence, academic interest has in the past generation shifted away from its traditional concern with the laws and forms of government as a means of managing the simpler types of disputes, and toward the most intractable kinds of conflicts—those for which conciliation and mediation are the most appropriate methods (Kolb 1983, Folberg and Taylor 1984, Marshall 1984).

In the world society as a whole, the picture is very different. Extensive machinery for most forms of pacific intervention in conflict does exist in international relations, notably direct negotiation through diplomacy, along with a considerable array of procedures and institutions for legal settlement (see Merrills 1984, for a comprehensive account). However, it is traditional in both the theory and practice of international relations to lay the greatest weight on the procedures available at the extreme ends of the spectrum: negotiation (bilateral or multilateral) on the one hand; and legal settlement on the other. The assumption, traditionally, has been that where good offices and negotiations fail, arbitration and other quasi-governmental processes are the next significant step. The success rate of legal settlement, however, is extremely poor, as Merrills notes (pp. 184-87); if negotiations cannot solve a problem, then it is common practice in world affairs either for the problem to remain unsolved, or to be dealt with by force. It is of course the case that the intermediate stages of peaceful conflict management, conciliation, and mediation, are provided for in the institutions and practices of international relations. But they are infrequently used by comparison with their rate of employment in domestic society; they have been little studied until recently; and they have rarely been successful. As Burton (in Azar and Burton 1986 pp. 40-55) and other scholars have pointed out, this gap in international relations theory and practice contrasts sharply with domestic theory and practice where conciliation and mediation are now the main focus of attention. Filling the gap in international relations provides a major opportunity for peace research activity, and may be the basis for the most significant reform that is possible in international relations.

There has been extensive discussion, among scholars and practitioners, of the reasons for the almost routine failure of the mechanisms for the legal settlement of international problems. Three distinct views have emerged. First, the traditional analysis, advanced by diplomats, international lawyers, and some political scientists of a "realist" persuasion, has identified the international "anarchy" (that is, the absence of world government) as the major obstacle. In the absence of coercive authority, it is argued, many of the worst disputes in international relations are inherently resistant to conciliation or mediation, still less to arbitration and judicial settlement. International disputes are often said to be "nonjusticiable" (that is, political rather than legal in character). It is noticeable that states lack both the willingness to yield control of their most serious disputes to an external authority, and to accept (or impose) sanctions which could enforce compliance with its decisions. The conclusion of the traditional analysis is that no progress is possible.

A second group of scholars, however, note that a great deal of mediation is actually conducted, although it takes place within the diplomatic framework, rather than the legal one. They suggest that the study and practical development of this activity could bring many of the benefits of legal settlement techniques to world affairs. The international system does possess some characteristics of order and stability which are quasi-governmental in character; they are created by the vast discrepancies in power and resources between the strongest states and the weakest states. Leaders of major states often regard themselves as holding responsibility for the management of conflicts within and between weaker states, and can draw upon the whole range of foreign policy instruments, including military means, to do so (see *Intervention*). In this context, the use by diplomatic officials of good offices, negotiation, and mediation is relatively commonplace, and the settlements that they bring about sometimes have the binding character of international law.

As Touval and Zartman report, this "mediation as power politics" (1985 p. 11) has a significant record of success. Prominent cases include the Camp David Accords of 1978 (see *Camp David Accords*), the Zimbabwe Settlement of 1979, and the ending of the United States Hostage Crisis in Iran in 1980. The success is based largely upon the superior resources or bargaining position of the mediating state, which can provide "leverage" enabling it to offer inducements and threaten penalties in order to impose a settlement. Mediation of this type should be regarded as a branch of foreign policy, rather than as an autonomous technique of pacific third-party intervention, because there is no question of the mediator being impartial. The mediator's political interest in the dispute is well-understood by all parties, and the diplomat who intervenes becomes in effect a participating party in relation to the issues under dispute.

A third group of scholars has emerged in recent years, arguing that neither the means of legal settlement as studied by the lawyers, nor the negotiation activities of the diplomats, are adequate approaches to the problems of world politics under contemporary conditions. They justify their position by reference both to the dismal record of conflict management in world affairs (with particular reference to the prospect of nuclear war and the high incidence of terrorism, local war, and guerrilla warfare), and also to the underdeveloped condition of the techniques of conciliation and mediation at the international level. They stress that the conflicts which are charateristic of world society as a whole cannot be treated only as static disputes between states, but must instead be seen as dynamic social processes. International conflicts, in this view, have roots which run much deeper than clashes of interest between governments. These roots include ideology, clashes between ethnic groups, rigidities and misperceptions in decision making, the spillover of domestic difficulties into foreign policy, and profound structural problems caused by economic and political injustice. Before conflicts of this extremely complex type can be resolved or even settled by a compromise agreement, they must be fully understood by those involved in them. Once analysis has been carried out and understanding achieved, the knowledge gained enables the parties to make adjustments which can mitigate the worst aspects of their relationship. A highly analytic form of conciliation and mediation, therefore, is seen as the appropriate means for dealing with international disputes.

The terminology employed to describe this new approach has been evolving rapidly in recent years. Early work by Burton, Doob, Kelman, and others during the 1960s and 1970s described the technique as "controlled communication," the "casework method," or "the therapeutic workshop," all of which reflected its origin in the methods of mediation developed in the handling of domestic disputes. Later publications have referred to "prenegotiation," to "problem-solving workshops" (Light in Banks 1984), and to "third-party consultancy" (Mitchell 1981). It seems likely that "the problem-solving approach" will become the standard term (see *Problem Solving in International Relations*). All the scholars working in this area lay heavy stress on the importance of nondirective techniques, so that the method is much closer to conciliation than to mediation. Where the third party makes suggestions, it is argued, they should never include matters of substance in relation to the dispute, but instead focus on "academic" points drawn from conflict theory and the procedures of communication. Of the scholars working in this

area, de Bono (1985) comes closest to advocating a strongly directive role for the mediator.

See also: *Alternative Dispute Resolution; Arbitration, International; Confidence Building in International Diplomacy; International Judicial Settlement*

Bibliography

Advisory Conciliation and Arbitration Service (ACAS) 1984 *The ACAS Role in Conciliation, Arbitration and Mediation.* ACAS, London

Azar E E, Burton J W (eds.) 1986 *International Conflict Resolution: Theory and Practice.* Wheatsheaf, Brighton

Banks M (ed.) 1984 *Conflict in World Society: A New Perspective on International Relations.* Wheatsheaf, Brighton

Berman M R, Johnson J E (eds.) 1977 *Unofficial Diplomats.* Columbia University Press, New York

Bercovitch J 1984 *Social Conflicts and Third Parties: Strategies of Conflict Resolution.* Westview, Boulder, Colorado

de Bono E 1985 *Conflicts: A Better Way to Resolve Them.* Harrap, London

Folberg J, Taylor A 1984 *Mediation: A Comprehensive Guide to Resolving Conflicts Without Litigation.* Jossey-Bass, San Francisco, California

Kolb D M 1983 *The Mediators.* MIT Press, Cambridge, Massachusetts

Marshall T F 1984 *Reparation, Conciliation and Mediation.* Home Office Research and Planning Unit Paper 27. Home Office, London

Merrills J G 1984 *International Dispute Settlement.* Sweet and Maxwell, London

Mitchell C R 1981 *Peacekeeping and the Consultant's Role.* Gower, Farnborough

Touval S, Zartman I W (eds.) 1985 *International Mediation in Theory and Practice.* Westview, Boulder, Colorado

MICHAEL BANKS

Mediation: A Tool for Peace Oriented Transformation

1. Definition

Mediation may be defined as the attempt to bring together two or more conflicting parties for serious discussions about how they can escape the trap of reciprocal violence. Seriousness is emphasised because there are instances of people agreeing to talk only because they think they can thereby gain some political or tactical advantage. But no, there must be at least some desire to end the conflict, to make some

sort of compromise, to abandon some principle, to make some slight sacrifice.

We shall not be discussing the type of mediation which is fuelled by the use (or the capability to use) military, political or economic force to gain ends desired by the mediator. We shall concentrate on 'pure' mediation that relies on the power of good will, common sense and experience to discover a way out of the trap of violence that is acceptable to all parties involved.

However, although mediation, is an ideal method of peacemaking, the best means of transforming a violent into a truly peaceful relationship, it is one which may not always be possible to apply.

2. Grounds for Accepting or Rejecting Mediation

The most usual reasons why one or more conflicting parties may reject mediation is that they think they can get a better deal by continued violence; or that they feel certain of outright victory and see no reason why they should consider the negotiation and bargaining that mediation may lead to; or fear that mediation might weaken their position with their friends or help their opposition; or that the situation is so complex and anarchic that no one individual or faction can either accept or initiate any diplomatic move.

By contrast mediation may be accepted also for a variety of motives. There may be an apparently unbreakable stalemate in the field or in negotiation; all parties may feel too damaged and depleted to continue the struggle; they may feel that their cause is suffering disproportionately from the continued conflict; or their yearning for peace may transcend the motives that led to the struggle.

Or, for some other reason, there may be a change of perception by the protagonists—of the conflict, of their opponent, of themselves.

There are, of course, an infinite number of struggles to which mediation could be appropriate. These range from the interpersonal—a married couple, for example—by way of communal, ethnic, religious, political and comparable feuds right up to the large scale violence of intra—or international war. It could be argued that mediation at the domestic level would have nothing in common with what would go by the same word, but which might involve huge armies.

Most of the writer's experience has been in large scale violent conflict. The people he has dealt with have been decision makers—heads of state, ministers and other high officials, and/or warlords and guerrilla leaders. But he has also been involved in community disputes in the inner city of London where he lives. The underlying principles at both macro and micro levels are very similar; it is easy to understand that a common thread runs through the various ways in which conflicts are expressed. After all, the presidents and the guerrilla generals all share the humanity of their humbler fellow citizen, and their responses to threat are much the same.

But if the parties agree to accept mediation, it is the best of all peacemaking procedures. The use of threats and promises, which characterises most great-power mediation, may force governments to a cease-fire, but no amount of arm twisting will make people like or be eager to cooperate with each other; when pressure is removed, hostilities may recommence. But mediation, which lacks conventional power, aims to *change peoples perceptions*—of each other, of the conflict, and of themselves.

3. The Psychology of Mediation

This means that mediators have a largely psychological role. They must never say so, of course; that would be seen as an insult. Paradoxically their discussions with the key decision makers will be largely about political, military and economic matters. But their relationship with these people must be based on a deep sense of shared humanity, and empathy for the stress, desperation and guilt which—in this writer's experience at least—they feel for the suffering they are causing.

In this sense, the role of mediators is to befriend. Leaders are often lonely, they are afraid of assassination or a coup, they don't know whom they can trust. But they may be able to relax best with outsiders who have no political or economic axes to grind. Instead of having to maintain their face, both to their ministers and more importantly, to themselves, they can let go; talk frankly, and listen freely without the filters which block out any denial or speculation.

In this way, they may at least temporarily forget the mirror image. This is one of the great obstacles to peace. General X has the terrible responsibility of sending young men into battle to kill other young men. He is under the pressure of guilt, fear, resentment, vanity, and other demands of his ego. He copes with these uncomfortable feelings by projecting them onto his opposite number. *He* is the one responsible for all this intolerable situation. X builds up his threatened self-esteem by transferring his doubt and guilt onto his enemy, Colonel Y. X is a peace lover, he is only at war to defend his people from the intolerable aggression of Y, who is nothing but a war criminal (see *Psychology of Peace*).

The mediator next hears much the same story from Y—it is X who is the war criminal, Y himself wants nothing but to live in harmony with his neighbours. He is outraged to hear what X says about him. There is, of course, some exaggeration, but the two are being seventy-five percent sincere. They really believe what they are saying.

And these sincere beliefs must be changed if the two men are to meet and discuss the peace they both really want.

But how can this be achieved?

It need hardly be said that patience and tact are essential. To bully people into peace may work in the short run but not in the long. Never push for results, because this is really pushing for one's own ego, which is an irrelevant intruder; and if any peacemaking is motivated by the personal need to succeed—it will certainly fail.

4. Problems of the Mediator

I also need not say that it is essential to be well-informed. A would-be peace-maker who obviously lacks a clear understanding of the situation will not be treated seriously. Equally dangerous is for mediators to express personal opinions on the situation, except to deplore the suffering caused by the conflict to all parties. Anything beyond this will always be condemned by one side or the other as showing partiality. Above all, any attempt by mediators to offer solutions to the conflict will not only be seen as partiality but also—and rightly—as presumptuous. Mediators cannot know what is best for people of another culture or historical background. They must never think that they know best, nor that those they are dealing with know worst.

This, of course, is a negative list of "don't." But they are things which interfere with the mediators real quest; to bring the conflicting groups into meaningful negotiation *aimed at solving their own problems by their own efforts.* It is a delicate tight-rope. One particular difficulty is that mediators must reach a good, even close, relationship with decision makers on all sides of the quarrel. But both General X and Colonel Y are of course aware that the mediators whom they have come to trust, are also friendly with their hated opposite numbers. How can this be? Most of the time they appear to accept the fact with a certain puzzled reluctance. But if something goes wrong; if the mediators deviate minutely from the principles we have mentioned, there will be trouble.

5. The Mediator's Approach

For mediators to be at all effective they must display—and also in fact *feel* consistent good will. Their concern must never falter. They must never yield to irritation at the seeming lack of reason that frustrates most peace initiatives; they can only remind themselves that war *is* basically unreasonable.

We have seen that embattled leaders need friends. They lack the support of people in whom they have faith, whom they know to be of undemanding good will, who have no personal interests in the present situation, and so with whom it is impossible to unburden their own hopes and fears. But within the safety of their relationship with a mediator who is both well-wishing and impersonal, they may be released from the psychological tyrannies that destroy a clear-headed perception of things. But the mediator, like a lover, must expect no return for his care and concern.

From these moments of objectivity may come the wise and humane decisions that bring the conflict to an end. But of course there will be no true peace unless the culture of violence is weakened; for example, the imposed 'peace' in Bosnia did little to do this and consequently the violence persisted long after the cease fire was declared (see *United Nations and NATO in Former Yugoslavia*). By the same token, there will be no adequate reduction in this culture unless the actual hostilities have come to an end. Thus the peacemaking tasks of the mediator may persist long after the official end of hostilities.

6. Failures of Mediation

Although mediation is a peerless means of transforming violence into peace, it is by no means always successful. The disorder and negative feelings that evoke violence often fail to yield completely to non-coercive approaches. Nevertheless, the very fact that mediation is sincerely agreed to by the participants in a struggle ensures that it will have some effect, if not always as comprehensive as had been expected and hoped for.

There may be some softening of the conflict—a cease fire to facilitate the evacuation of civilians, an exchange of wounded prisoners, a peace settlement less harsh than expected. At the end of one partially successful mediation, the mediators were told that the negotiated settlement had been made easier because they had constantly kept the idea of peace before the minds of the combatants.

See also: *Arbitration, International; Nonintervention and Noninterference; Conflict Resolution, Process of; Conflict Resolution, History of*

ADAM CURLE

Mencius

There is no doubt that Mencius (Meng-zi) exercised the greatest influence upon the development of Confucian thought second only to Confucius because for over a thousand years the *Mencius* was read side by side with the *Analects* by every schoolboy in China. Mencius not only developed some of the ideas of Confucius but also discussed problems untouched by him.

Little is known about Mencius other than what we can glean from the book named after him. True, there is a biography of him in the *Shin Ji* (*Records of the Grand Historian*), written at the beginning of the first century BC by Si-ma Qian yet it contains hardly any facts not to be found in the *Mencius*. We do not even know the date of his birth and death. It is rather generally accepted that he lived from about 372 to about 289 BC.

It is said that Mencius was born in a small state adjacent to the native state of Confucius in northeast China and his ancestors belonged to the Meng family of the State of Lu which had been one of the "three families" that dominated Lu in the days of Confucius. He studied the teachings of Confucius with the disciples of the grandson of Confucius, Zi Si, and dedicated himself to the development of the Confucian School. Like Confucius, he travelled from one feudal state to another seeking a hearing for his ideas on government. He was granted hearings (which are described in the *Mencius*) but none of the rulers seemed to have seriously considered putting his ideas into practice. He then retired and gave exposition of the Shu Jing (the *Odes*) and the Shu Jing (the *History*) and developed the ideas of Confucius.

Mencius lived in the Warring States Period (403-221 BC). Avarice, deceit, and ruthlessness characterized the political life of the age. In spite of this, he insisted that men are basically good by nature. They commit evils only as a result of distortion of their original goodness. In a world where economic and military power seemed to be the sole deciding factors in the struggle for political survival, he nevertheless counseled rulers to pursue virtuous and benevolent government, assuring them that "the benevolent man has no match" (*Mencius* I A.5).

Mencius asserted that every human is moral creature and Heaven has planted a moral heart in humankind. If the "original heart" can be preserved untainted then it is possible for the individual to contemplate upon moral duty, priorities, the purpose and destiny of humankind, and the role of the individual in the universe.

According to Mencius, there are four incipient tendencies in the heart. These he called "the heart of compassion," "the heart of shame," "the heart of courtesy and modesty," and "the heart of right and wrong." He further pointed out that "the heart of compassion is the germ of benevolence; the heart of shame, the germ of dutifulness; the heart of courtesy and modesty, the germ of observance of the rites; the heart of right and wrong, the germ of wisdom" (*Mencius* II A.6).

The political philosophy of Mencius was not only consistent with his moral philosophy but was derived from it. He looked upon politics as a branch of morals, that is, the relationship between the ruler and the subject was looked upon as a special case of the moral relationship which holds between individuals. He maintained that the ruler is set up for the benefit of the people. Hence whether a ruler deserves to remain a ruler depends on whether he carries out his duty or not. If he does not, he should be removed and in this circumstance the people have the right to rebel. Mencius stated:

> The people are of supreme importance; the altars to the gods of earth and grain [symbol of the independence of the state] come next; last comes the ruler (*Mencius* VII. B. 14).

Thus we can see the full significance of the supremacy of the people.

For Mencius, an individual who does not act with benevolence and rightness is an outcast. This principle applies even if that individual is an emperor; indeed, it makes the situation worse. Mencius stated:

> Only the benevolent man is fit to be in high position. For a cruel man to be in high position is for him to disseminate his wickedness among the people. (*Mencius* IV. A. I)

And there is no higher position than that of the emperor. So long as the ruler is motivated by benevolence, he is granted the Mandate of Heaven (*Tion Ming*) and the people will understand and accept whatever measure he finds it necessary to take. "If the services of the people were used with a view to sparing them hardship, they would not complain even when hard driven. If people were put to death in pursuance of a policy to keep them alive, they would die bearing no ill-will toward the man who put them to death" (*Mencius* VII. A. 12).

The attitude of Mencius toward war followed on logically from his belief in the supremacy of the people. War brings great suffering to the people as they are the ones who get killed and it is their land that is laid waste. So war must be condemned. However, according to Mencius, war may be justified if two conditions are fulfilled. First, war may be used to remove wicked rulers who cannot be removed by any other means. Second, even when directed towards this end, war should only be initiated by someone who has the authority. When these two conditions are fulfilled, the result is what Mencius would call a punitive war. To a ruler—and so to a state—war is what punishment is to the criminal. So Mencius declared that those who delight in their skill in strategy are, in fact, great criminals.

To sum up, Mencius believed that all men are good, and equally good by nature and everyone has a "taintless heart" planted by Heaven which contains embryonic moral tendencies. If we all keep our "hearts" untainted, no-one will become evil. Mencius

al.. advocated a benevolent government and insisted th.. ne ruler must work for the good of the people oth.. .vise he has to be removed. He was strongly op|..·d to war but he gave no objection to righteous wai ...-Iis philosophy, though established over two thou.. .id years ago, is still applicable to society toda..

See a.. *'onfucianism and Neo-Confucianism; Con-fuciu·*

Biblio.. ·

Dobson W. A H 1963 *Mencius*. Oxford University Press, London
Lan D C 1970 *Mencius*. Penguin, Harmondsworth

KENNETH P. H. HO

Mercosul

1. Introduction

Created by the Treaty of Asunción of March 26, 1991 between Argentina, Brazil, Paraguay and Uruguay, the free trade zone of Mercosul has had a consistent history of success since its inception and became a model for initiatives of its kind. Aimed at creating a common market for the region, Mercosul had the initial objectives of achieving, by January 1, 1995, a) the free movement of people, goods, capital and services; b) the creation of a common external trade tariff and the establishment of a common external trade policy; and c) the coordination of macro-economic policies. On July 25, 1996 MERCOSUL signed a free trade agreement with Chile and, on December 17, 1996 with Bolivia.

In strict trade terms, Mercosul has been enormously successful. Internal trade went from US$ 4 billion in 1990 in a constantly ascending curve to US$ 14 billion in 1995, US$18 billion in 1996 and an estimated US$ 22 billion in 1997. This was accompanied by a movement towards trade liberalisation with third parties as well. In the case of Brazil, the average tariff went from 58 percent in 1989 to 12.6 percent as a consequence of the implementation of the CET. Accordingly, the growth of regional trade was not achieved at the expense of extraregional imports, which leapt from US$ 25 billion in 1990 to US$ 55 billion in 1995. These figures amply confirm Mercosul's objectives of practising an open regionalism in tune with the goals of commercial liberalisation and increasing participation in the world trade of goods and services (see *Integration, Regional*).

This favourable trade picture, taken with an economic scenario of stabilised currencies, has been well received by the international community as a whole, and enhanced the attractiveness of Mercosul member states with respect to foreign direct investment, which rose in a continuously ascending curve from US$ 2 billion in 1991 to approximately US$14 billion in 1996. Major investments from extraregional sources have been made in the recent past in the motor and the pharmaceutical sectors. In addition, regional investments have also increased, many related to agri-business. The regional agricultural sector, which is largely complementary, has greatly benefited from a substantial market free from the distortions created by the grotesque practice of subsidies—unfortunately still in vogue in much of the world.

2. Administration

Clause 9 of the Treaty of Asunción establishes that the administration and resolutions adopted by Mercosul will be carried by the Common Market Council and the Common Market Group. The Council, which is composed of the Minister of Foreign Affairs and the Minister of Economy of each of the signatory countries, is the highest decision-making body. It is responsible for the political guidance of the Common Market and for assuring that the purposes and terms established for the implementation of Mercosul are met.

The Common Market Group is the executive body. It is coordinated by the Ministry of Foreign Affairs of each country and is composed of four members and four substitute members per country. These members are representatives of the Ministry of Foreign Affairs, the Ministry of Economy and the head of the Central Bank of the respective member States.

According to Article 17 of the Internal Rules of the Common Market Group, the group is allowed to create subgroups of work, when necessary to accomplish the obligations of the Common Market Group. Each subgroup of work will have a national coordinator, indicated by each signatory country, and while its commission may have the participation of private sector members, private sector members are not allowed to participate in the decision making.

Resolution 8/93 of the Common Market Group mandates that the Administrative Secretary is to carry out a quarterly review of the practice and application of the Decisions of the Common Market Council and the Common Market Group.

The Administrative Secretary of Mercosul was created by the Protocol of Ouro Preto (Article 40) with the main purpose to maintain the files of all Mercosul Documents, to facilitate the organization's publicity, and to facilitate the direct contact of the authorities of the Common Market Group. The Administrative Secretary which is based in Montevideo, Uruguay, also functions as a center of communication and exchange of information related to Mercosul and guarantees the legal effect in each signatory country of the decisions of the organs of Mercosul.

3. Regulation Procedures

As per Article 2 of the Protocol of Ouro Preto, the decisions of Mercosul may operate as follows:

(i)   Once a rule is approved, the signatory countries will adopt the necessary measures to incorporate that rule in their national legislation and communicate its incorporation to the Administrative Secretary of Mercosul;

(ii) When all the signatory countries have communicated the incorporation mentioned in item (i) above, the Administrative Secretary of Mercosul will communicate such act to the other signatory countries; and,

(iii) The approved rule will simultaneously come into force in the signatory countries 30 days after the communication described in item (ii) above.

For the purpose of implementing and following such rules the Common Market Group in its XII Meeting held in Montevideo on January 13 and 14, 1994, determined that the subgroups of work would report quarterly on the degree of implementation of the decisions and resolutions adopted by Mercosul in each signatory country.

4. Dispute Resolution

The Protocol of Dispute Settlement, signed by the signatory countries of Mercosul in Brasília on December 17, 1991 and promulgated in Brazil by Decree 922 of September 10, 1993, recognizes the importance of the Treaty of Asunción and is an effective mechanism to guarantee the accomplishment of the treaty.

5. The Common External Tariff (CET)

The Common External Tariff (CET), which has been in force since 1995, is set at 11 different levels from zero to 20 percent, with an average of approximately 12 percent. Each member country was allowed an exception quota of 300 items from the CET (Paraguay with 399), with a linear and automatic convergence set to be achieved for most items by the year 2001. Products in the areas of information technology and telecommunications will converge only by 2006.

Trade within Mercosul is mostly tariff-free, but there are some relevant albeit temporary exceptions such as cars in the industrial sector and sugar and related products in the agricultural sector. In addition, there are groups of products considered sensitive trade by the member states that are subject to internal tariffs to be eliminated by 1999 for Argentina and Brazil and by 2000 for the others. Those exceptions amounted to 29 items for Brazil, 221 for Argentina, 427 for Paraguay and 950 for Uruguay. In December 1994, during the Ouro Preto meeting, a special supranational body was created, the Mercosul Trade Commission, with the objective of overseeing the dismantling of the non-tariff barriers and the homogenisation of phyto-sanitary, technical and safety rules. At the same time, a common customs code was adopted for the member states incorporating customs procedures, import valuation norms and rules of origin.

6. Rules of Origin

Another important issue for Mercosul concerns rules of origin, which define the proportion of domestic components (originating in Mercosul) which products must contain. To this end, a program has been established to achieve the convergence of individual country rules, to be implemented on a uniform and gradual basis, to reach the general norm (60/40) by 2001.

Mercosul's rules of origin, which were established by the Agreement of Economic Complementation no. 18, was replaced by the Eighth Additional Protocol of the Agreement of Economic Complementation (ACE/18) signed by the signatory countries of Mercosul on December 30, 1994.

7. Services

In spite of the importance of the services sector for both the Argentine and the Brazilian economies, where it accounts for, approximately, 55 percent of the GDP, the area has yet to be formally regulated by Mercosul. By means of the Protocol of Ouro Preto, signed by the heads of state of the four member countries on December 17, 1994, an "ad-hoc" group on trade in services was created with a view to preparing a framework agreement for the liberalisation of services within Mercosul.

The "ad-hoc" group has been quite active in the formation of this agreement. Taking into consideration the regional specificities in accordance with the guidelines of the General Agreement on Trade in Services (GATS) within such negotiations, it was deemed apposite by the representatives of the member states to prepare additional agreements in three areas of services which were not concluded during the Uruguay Round of the GATT, namely (a) financial services including banking, insurance and reinsurance; (b) telecommunications; and (c) air transportation (see *General Agreements on Tariffs and Trade*). Such agreements have been drafted with the view of liberalising the internal rendering of services, rather than creating barriers to third countries.

Concomitantly with the negotiations for the framework agreement on services, some initiatives have already been taken by the Mercosul member states in connection with some very specific areas in the financial sector. For instance, Resolution 10/93 of Mercosul adopted the minimum capital and equity requirements established by the Basel Committee. Similarly, Decision 8/93 of Mercosul established the minimum regulation of the capital markets to be in force in the member states, as well as a common terminology. In addition, the same Decision revoked the existing limitations on intraregional capital movements by citizens of Mercosul. At this point, it must

be emphasised that, at present, of all Mercosul countries, Brazil is the only one with exchange controls.

On the other hand, Decision 12/94 established basic principles of consolidated banking supervision as well as defined accepted practices and criteria, with a view towards the preservation of the solvency and liquidity of the financial sector within Mercosul. The Colonia Protocol for the Promotion and Regional Protection of Investments within Mercosul was signed on January 17, 1994 and established most favoured nation privileges, in addition to regulating in detail monetary transfers. Such must be effected in convertible currencies, in accordance with the regulations adopted by the recipient country of the respective investment. The Colonia Protocol further assures convertible currency cover for remittances of repatriation of capital; profits; interest; repayment of loans; royalties and fees; indemnification and other limited purposes.

Investments by Brazilian citizens abroad in Mercosul's stock exchanges are limited to operations liquidated at sight and in Mercosul's futures and option markets are limited to hedging operations for trade transactions.

In addition to such internal initiatives, Mercosul countries have been liberalising their financial markets before third countries. This tendency started sooner in Argentina, which eliminated the state reinsurance monopoly and opened its banking sector to foreign capital, to such an extent that today, out of the five largest private banks in that country, four are controlled by foreign banks. Nowadays, insurance companies in Argentina tend to belong to banking groups, whereas in the past they were largely independent, many of which controlled by trade unions.

The same situation can be verified in Brazil. On August 25, 1995, the Brazilian Official Gazette published an administrative act by which the President eliminated the restrictions imposed by the 1988 Constitution by formally recognising the country's interest in the increased participation of foreign financial institutions in the local banking market. Less than two years later, there are approximately seventy banks controlled by foreign capital in Brazil, including the country's 4th largest bank, in addition to some seventy representative offices of foreign banks. Similarly, Constitutional Amendment number 13 of August 21, 1996 lifted the reinsurance monopoly which existed in favour of the National Institute of Reinsurance, soon to be privatised.

Uruguay has long had an international banking center which is quite liberalised and relies extensively on off-shore activities. Paraguay's banking sector is at present the least developed of the four member states of Mercosul and faces at the moment the challenges of a major restructuring effort on the part of the country's government. With the recent liquidation of the two largest national capital banks, now the five largest banks in operation in Paraguay are controlled by foreign capital.

It remains indisputable that the single most important obstacle to the full consolidation of Mercosul, as well as to the liberalisation of its services markets, is the anachronic existence of exchange controls in Brazil. One of the pillars of the Brazilian economic stabilisation programme successfully created three years ago by the then Finance Minister, Mr. Fernando Henrique Cardoso, who is today the country's president, was to have an overvalued local currency (the "Real").

This was done with a view to check inflation via relatively cheap imports, whilst the structural reforms introduced before Congress were not approved and the major privatizations had not taken place. The other pillar of the economic stabilisation plan is of course the policy of very high interest rates, which prevents the economy from overheating.

This situation is seen both in Brazil as well as within Mercosul in general with mixed feelings. On the upperside, there are, of course, the enormous benefits of a stabilised economy. On the downside, however for the Brazilian private sector, such policies have been considerably detrimental to its trade competitiveness in local as well as in the international markets. For Brazil's Mercosul partners, the existence of exchange controls is seen as an obstacle for further integration and for market access. Accordingly, Mercosul's Decision 8/93 not only recognises that restrictions on capital transfers impose serious tension on the financial markets, but also establishes an annual review of the objective of free movement of capital.

8. Environment

As the world attends to environmental protection, which measures can affect the comparative advantages of some countries, thus creating barriers to the access of some markets and altering their competitiveness by an increase in production costs, Mercosul signatories (SubGroup of Work no. 6), through the Ministries of the Environment of each signatory country will:

(a) analyze the restrictions and non-tariff measures which relate to the environment;

(b) elaborate a proposal of harmonization and elimi-

nation of exclusive measures;

(c) promote studies that analyze the environmental costs to the productive process, which has to be concluded by December 1997;

(d) follow the process of elaboration, discussion, definition and implementation of ISO 14,000—Environmental administration—and analyze the impact of its application as a differential agent to the competitiveness of the products originating from Mercosul in the international market;

(e) harmonize its environmental legislation;

(f) develop and make operative a system of environmental information; and

(g) create a green label that represents the guarantee that a product was produced in accordance with the industrial guidelines not harmful to the environment.

9. Agriculture

In order to facilitate the free circulation of combined agriculture and stock raising, as well as agroindustrial products, Subgroup No. 8 of Mercosul will harmonize the Health and Sanitation Agreement of Mercosul with the rules of the WTO. In order to determine the basis of coordination at regional levels, the actions and instruments for the agriculture areas, Mercosul will analyze the agricultural policies of each signatory country.

10. Labour

Mercosul will also continue to follow the rules established by the International Labor Organization. Subgroup of Work No. 10 will analyze the reports prepared by the BIRD (Inter-American Development Bank) on labor costs and labor migration and make proposals related to these matters. It is also the intention of Mercosul to sign multilateral agreements on Social Security and to implement a system of technical cooperation in the area of professional education.

11. Future Plans

As the main scope of Mercosul until year 2000 will be integration through the consolidation of the Customs Union, the Common Market Council, on August 4, 1995 asked the Common Market Group to prepare a programme of action for Mercosul until year 2000, which was approved by the Common

Market Council by decision 9/95.

The delegations of the signatory countries will exchange ideas and the content of the document "Mercosul 2000", which was presented to the Common Market Group during the recent meeting of the Mercosul held in Punta del Este, Uruguay, on December, 1995.

Mercosul 2000 reflects the political intention of the governments of the signatory countries and develops the actions that finalize integration. It specifies the following goals to be reached by 2000, divided into the following topics:

(a) Consolidation of the improvement of the Customs Union. According to the document Mercosul 2000 such consolidation and improvement will be reached by (i) the consolidation of free commerce through the free access of products, elimination of non-tariff restrictions, elimination of commercial obstacles and the use of technical regulations. The document also points out the necessity of guaranteeing equal conditions of access to free trade by the conclusion of a Protocol of Consumer Protection and also guarantees for consumers rights by establishing the Common Rule of Consumer Protection; (ii) improvement of common commercial policies; (iii) implementation of the agreements already signed; (iv) adoption of new common instruments of commercial policies such as the Common Rules against unfair trade, Rules of Safeguards, both in accordance with the rules of the WTO and also, the adoption of sectoral commercial policies for the Automotive Industry to be in force in the year 2000 based on the total liberalization of the trade of the signatory countries, the application of the CET and exclusion of national incentives, and for the sugar industry, for which the definition of a regime of adequation must be concluded by December 1997 and will be effective from January 2001. Also, by Resolution 124/94 a technical committee will study the necessity of the creation of a sectoral commercial policy pertaining to the textile sector;

(b) improving the productivity of agriculture, restructuring the competitiveness of the industry, cooperation and exchange of technology to promote the development of regional mining; adequate use and conservation of energy, and promoting joint actions concerning telecommunications, among others; and

(c) the rules of Mercosul are to be consistent with the rules of GATT and the agreements resulting from the Uruguay Round. Additionally, agreements signed with ALADI members are to be renegotiated, the agreement signed with the EU is to be implemented, and the understandings with members of NAFTA are to be continued.

Mercosul 2000 also foresees the diffusion of regional arts, improvement of health, improvement of the quality of education, strengthening of science and technology, elaboration of agreements on intellectual property and special treatment for matters related to immigration.

12. Competition and Dumping

Through Decision No. 21/94 of the Common Market Council, the basic guidelines on competition have been approved in order to make a coordinated effort of the signatory countries to stop practices affecting free competition.

Such Decision forbids agreements and concentrated practices between economic entities, as well as the decisions of associations of companies which have the intention of stopping, restricting or distorting competition and the free access to the market in the production, processing, distribution and selling of goods and services, in full or in part, that can affect commerce between the signatory countries. The Decision forbids limitations or control of production, of distribution, of technological development or investments, the division of the goods and services market or sources of supply of raw materials, and any agreements or acts that affect or can affect competition in bids or public auctions, among other areas.

It is also forbidden for one or more economic entities to abuse a dominant position, in all or in a substantial part of Mercosul, such as to impose directly or indirectly, the prices of sales and purchases, denying, unjustifiably, the selling of goods or services. The Decision also determines that every time that an operation of any nature between companies that results in an economic concentration amounting to a participation of 20 percent or more of the market will be submitted for consideration.

Decision No. 18/96 of the Common Market Council introduced the Protocol of Competition of Mercosul, which, by promoting free competition, contributes to the goal of free trade established by the Treaty of Asuncion. Through this Decision, the investigation on dumping (introduction in another country of a good with prices less than fair value of the same good in the exporting country) related to the imports from another signatory country will have to be made in accordance with national legislation until December 31, 2000, when the dumping rules of Mercosul will come into force.

13. Safeguards

The safeguards measures were created by Annex IV of the Treaty of Asunción with the main purpose of allowing any of the signatory countries to stop complying, temporarily, with an obligation assumed in Mercosul when the country faces a new situation that may cause harm to its economy. At the Meeting of Fortaleza, held in the second semester of 1996, the rules related to the application of measures of safeguards to the imports from non-signatory countries were approved by Decision No. 17/96 of the Common Market Council.

The approval of such Decision affords protection to the industries in Mercosul countries against unfair imports from non-signatory countries. Decision 17/96 also creates the Committee of Commercial Protection and Safeguards, establishing December, 1998 as the month in which it will come into force. Until this date, any signatory country may adopt its own national legislation regarding the subject.

14. Conclusion

In December 1995, the member states of Mercosul agreed on a five-year plan with a view to evolving in the direction set by the Treaty of Asuncion, perfecting the free trade area and customs union and resolving the pending agenda. Among the points still outstanding is the question of the free movement of people, which remains unresolved. For Mercosul, this question does not have the importance it had for the European Union, because of the relatively liberal rules in place before the creation of the free trade area, but nevertheless retains considerable relevance because a common market cannot be achieved with-

out it. Another important question to be addressed involves the harmonisation of the economic policies of the member states. Of course, since 1991, the degree of harmonisation of policies within Mercosul has been unprecedented, but closer cooperation is required for the future, and that should include the effects of exchange controls in Brazil, which prevent the free flow of capital within the free trade area.

Coordination of external trade policies has been so effective that, at present, the negotiations on the creation a Free Trade Area of the Americas (FTAA) are being conducted by Mercosul as a bloc. In addition to the free trade agreements signed between Mercosul and Chile, and Mercosul and Bolivia, similar negotiations are going on with other Latin American countries such as Venezuela, Peru, Ecuador and Colombia. A point still subject to some degree of controversy pertains to the structure of supranational institutions. The Argentines seem to favour the creation of a structure similar to that in place in the European Union, whereas the Brazilians wish to maintain as small a bureaucracy as possible. Some believe part of the success of Mercosul is due to this minimalist approach, valid in a part of the world historically plagued by red tape. In any case, a new system for the resolution of disputes, at present very inefficient, will have to be examined.

As with any regional trade agreement, there is still much to be done within Mercosul. There are also many political and economic risks facing this initiative. However, for its member states, Mercosul has represented the greatest strategic programme carried out this century and one that could very well leverage their respective societies and economies to the developed world.

See also: *Peace and Regional Integration; Economic Integration; Integration, Regional; Integration Theories*

DURVAL DE NORONHA GOYOS JR.

Middle East Crisis: Origin and Solution

It is quite ironic that the Middle East region, which is considered to be the most sacred in the world, has been torn asunder with struggles and conflicts for so many years. The source of the Middle East crisis is so complex that numerous books could be written about it over the next several decades. In order to comprehend the source of this problem as to provide a practical solution, we need to view the entire Mid-

dle East crisis from as many angles as possible, at least from the viewpoint of Iraq itself, the United Nations, and the United States.

1. Iraqi Views of the Situation

When a nation is ruled by the military, like in the case of Iraq, it is obvious that a final solution to every problem encountered rests with the military. In spite of the fact that we have learned from history the futility of military solutions on a lasting basis, we keep on resorting unwisely to such a means.

For quite a few years, Iraq and Iran were at war with each other which brought the massacre of tens of thousands of civilians on both sides and which destroyed most of the rich cultural heritage of this global area. The moment they said war was over, both Iraq and Iran began to rearm once more for an eventual future replica of war. What is surprising is the fact that both Iraq and Iran were guided by dictatorial regimes which proclaimed to be strongly Islamic. Supposedly, both were guided by the Koran and both shared belief in the same God, commonly known as Allah. But these two Islamic nations did not use the Koran as their guide, nor did they use Allah as their refuge and source of strength. Instead, they sought for guidance from the military and for the source of strength from horrendous weapons of destruction.

When during the Gulf War Iraq used chemical weapons, the whole world became alerted. The United Nations became seriously concerned and a resolution was passed to set an embargo on Iraq as to isolate it from the rest of the world.

In spite of the fact that Iraqi people suffered from lack of adequate nourishment and from lack of medicine, they would not abandon the only means they felt was their protector from the enemy, the chemical weapons. Due to increased tensions in the Middle East, steps were taken by the United Nations to send a team for purpose of verifying the destruction of Iraq's brutal weaponry system. Iraq's hesitance to let the UN team have access to every single area of the country, raised suspicion among some nations. It was believed that Iraq was not sincere in its promise of cooperation. At the same time, Iraq showed readiness to bargain militarily in exchange of the upliftment of the embargo.

2. United Nations' Resolution

Although there has been disagreement among UN members relative to the means that could be used to make Iraq comply with the UN Resolution, there has been a unanimous consensus relative to the need for the implementation of the UN Resolution itself. Some nations, like the United States and the United Kingdom, have advocated the use of force. In fact, the United States was not hesitant in sending a military force in the Gulf and in seeking moral support for its intended military action from Iraq's neighboring countries. At the same time, the United Kingdom pledged that it would support the United States fully in the event that a war breaks out against Iraq.

On the other hand, Russia, China and France voiced their opposition to military intervention in solving the Iraqi problem. Apparently, these three nations must have learned from history that a military solution would never work in the long range. Although the majority of the world body of nations expressed interest in seeing all chemical weapons destroyed from the Iraqi territory, almost no one favored a military solution. As far as the Middle East crisis is concerned, the United Nations is faced with a great challenge. As a matter of fact, the UN Secretary-General has a key role to play in proving to the world the eventual importance for the United Nations' presence and the consequent justification for its continued existence.

In visiting Iraq recently, UN Secretary-General Kofi Annan took a gigantic step in the right direction. He found that a solution to the crisis was not only possible but also feasible. Apparently, Iraq was not against the UN inspection of its military facilities but against the US involvement in it. Iraq seems to view the United States as the policeman of the world with no legitimate mandate to pursue this objective. Also, Iraq sees the United States' determination to furnish weapons of destruction to any country which is willing to pay the right price, as revealed in the Iran/Contra affair, as a threat to international stability.

Needless to say, Iraq feels somewhat nervous in seeing its surrounding nations being equipped with weapons of destruction mostly furnished by the United States. This is felt to be a threat to the security of the Iraqi nation. Also, this means that the United Nations must realize that if Iraq is to eliminate its chemical weapons and other sanctioned military equipment, at least Iraq's surrounding nations must do likewise. Of course, that would include Israel and Turkey as well.

3. United States' Political Role

As the only world super-power, the United States feels the obligation to protect the world from any foreseeable catastrophe. To this end, it wants to furnish military weapons to all nations conceivable. Just over the past 24 months alone, the United States sold weapons of destruction to 144 nations across every continent. US embassies all over the world are urged to advertise American industry which specifically includes military weapons.

Instead of embarking upon a program of demilitarization of nations, the United States has embarked on a program of continued military armament on the assumption that war is imminent. Sooner or later there is bound to be either a Third World War or several regional wars fought in various global areas. The reaction to this assumption is now very well known. Keep on improving the weaponry system and have as many nations as possible prepared for war. Instead of forming and strengthening a European alliance based on economic and educational development as well as based on a good health care system, the United States is concentrating on the continued strengthening of the weapons industrial complex through a military alliance commonly known as NATO—the North Atlantic Treaty Organization (see *North Atlantic Treaty Organization (NATO)*).

The presence of NATO is not only a threat to the economic development of member-countries, but it constitutes a hindrance to the development of good educational programs and a sound health care system. The European Economic Community grew and flourished not because of the military program it had to offer, but because it developed an atmosphere of fraternal peaceful relations that led to the elimination of passport and to the right of every citizen within the European community to work and settle anywhere one wants within the said community itself (see *European Union*). Like Retired Rear Admiral Gene La Rocque and other top US military and former Pentagon officials stated on more than one occasion, the United States sells weapons everywhere not for the defense of the nation but merely for profit. Once more, the Iran/Contra affair is a vivid example of this.

Based on the tangible experience the world has of the United States relative to the manufacture and sales of weapons, let us assume that all the dangerous weapons Iraq has are found by the UN inspection team and are then destroyed. If at some future date Iraq wants to purchase such weapons from the US weapons industry, Iraq will have everything it would want as long as it pays the right price. In this regard, Iraq could get some advise from its neighbor Iran as how to go about to secure from the United States all weapons of destruction conceivable including landmines.

4. Capitalism and the World's Future

We need to keep in mind that the United States, as a capitalist nation, is primarily concerned with money which comes through profit-making. This explains why the United States has equipped notorious military rulers in Nigeria, Indonesia, the former Zaire, Guatemala and several others with all the military equipment they wanted to the detriment of the civilian population itself. Profit was being made, besides

the fact that American industrialists were given the green light to exploit the resources of these respective nations.

When the United States encounters a country which prohibits the foreigner from going there to exploit its resources, then the United States raises its eyebrows. It would soon label such countries as socialists or communists like it did with the case of Nicaragua under Ortega, Chile under Allende, Iran under Mossadeq, and Cuba under Castro, among others. Several years ago, Pope John Paul II said in Mexico that two of the greatest evils of this century were communism and capitalism because they both achieve their objectives through the exploitation of people. The difference, the Pope said, lies only in the method of approach. Shortly after the Pope made such a statement, communism collapsed and it was predicted that the years of capitalism were numbered.

At this stage of history, it is very obvious that social democracy is all the world needs where people will hopefully stop experiencing any longer the ravage of exploitation. Social democracy is capable of promoting a genuine world peace through the abolition of war which comes through disarmament and development. Is is also capable of procuring people everywhere with free education from the cradle to the grave where the human talent is given the opportunity to search for the solution to such maladies as cancer, AIDS, malnutrition, multiple sclerosis, epilepsy, heart disease, juvenile delinquency, organized crime, and drug abuse which includes nicotine addiction, among others. This form of government is also capable of providing people with a good health care system which is free from birth to death.

In view of what has been stated, we may conclude that at this stage of history the weapons industry has become a malignant tumor of our earthly community and it needs to be surgically removed, the sooner the better. The continued presence of the military in our world today has become a cancerous tissue whose presence is never to preserve peace but always to promote war.

5. Availability of Practical Solutions

From Iraq's policy of using the military to get what it wants, we should learn to avoid this very old mistake. As we already know, first Iraq got engaged into war with Iran and then it used its military to march into Kuwait and annex it as one of its provinces, same way as Hitler did with Austria prior to World War II. Kuwait was afterwards liberated from Iraq by allied forces at the cost of thousands of innocent people who lost their lives, not to mention the many buildings and bridges which were destroyed.

Besides, the air and water were polluted badly with toxic wastes which probably has caused cancer to numerous people. If Egypt tried to use the military to regain the Sinai peninsula, countless thousands of lives would have been lost in vain and the Sinai peninsula, in all probability, would have still been today under Israeli control. Iraq needs to follow the footsteps of Costa Rica by taking immediately a bold step in abolishing the military. Like Costa Rica, Iraq would become an Island of Peace in the Middle East Region. Its civilian economy would grow by leaps and bounds and the entire nation may eventually develop into an earthly paradise.

The United Nations needs to learn that there is no wisdom at all for the larger nations to compete with each other in military terms. Such competition reveals how backward nations may still prove themselves to be at a time when the entire planet has become so vitally and indispensably interdependent. The abolition of nuclear weapons and landmines by the year 2,000 AD should become a top priority in the UN agenda. "Disarmament and Development" needs to become the new motto of the United Nations.

The United States needs to persuade itself that its military presence in the world is not appreciated at all. If the crisis in the Middle East is solved to the satisfaction of everyone involved it will not be because of but "in spite of" the US military presence. Above all, the United States should stop its policy of furnishing weapons of destruction to virtually every single country on earth, friends and enemies alike. Instead, it should initiate a program of world demilitarization where the military becomes merely history.

See also: Arab-Israeli Conflict; Nonintervention and Noninterference

CHARLES MERCIECA

Militarism and Militarization

A main sociopolitical feature of modern times is the growing role of the army and the military profession in national and international affairs. There is widespread use of organized violence for the purpose of coercion—internally and externally. International relations are essentially power relations determined by the military factor. The arms race has become a global phenomenon, encompassing big powers and small nations alike (see *Arms Race, Dynamics of*). Military rivalry is at the core of major power relations, while military strength plays an important role in structuring the dominance-dependence relationship between North and South. Global military expenditures have grown unabated since the Second World War, reaching in the 1980s the equivalent of the gross national income of the poorer half of the world's population (see *Economics of Disarmament and Conversion*). At the same time, weapons have not been lying idle. Since the Second World War approximately 130 large-scale armed conflicts have taken place. These have been fought largely on the grounds of the Third World, and with weapons mainly supplied by major powers, as in Korea, Vietnam, Afghanistan, the Persian Gulf and Bosnia. The result has been tens of millions of casualties, military and civilian.

1. The Notions of Militarism and Militarization

The above developments and the systemic features involved are variously termed "militarism" and "militarization." But although they are widely used, there is no unanimity about the real meaning of these terms. Too often they are misused for political ends, each side pointing with an accusing finger at the adversary. Generally militarism is defined differently by the Left on the one hand, and by the western liberal school on the other hand. While the Left emphasizes expansion, aggression, and the class structure of society as the main features of militarism, the western liberal school rather pays greater attention to the prevalence of the military over civilian affairs, to excesses in the use of military force, and to the cult of power within society (see *Theoretical Traditions of Peace and Conflict Studies*).

There are also historical and situational dimensions to the use of the notions of militarism and militarization. The term "militarism" emerged in the nineteenth century following the imposition of universal military conscription and the rise of large national armies headed by a well-knit professional officer corps. The prime examples of militarism, most often cited, are the Prusso-German and Japanese military build-ups and expansion before and after the First World War. Today's militarism and militarization differ from these paradigmatic examples in many respects, however, in line with the changed nature of the nation-state and the transformation of international relations after the Second World War. Not only have nuclear weapons changed military horizons, and not only have the major powers wielded key political influence on the international scene, but also the colonial system has been dismantled, with about half of the developing Third World countries having come under military rule. Given these new military and sociopolitical circumstances, the notions of militarism and militarization have also acquired new meaning. Militarism and militarization exhibit today diverse features according to the size, traditions, class structure, culture, economic strength, and military power of the societies and states in question. These two terms should therefore be considered not as static but as dynamic, circumstantial, and historic phenomena.

2. Differences Between Militarism and Militarization

A distinction should be made between militarism and militarization. The latter represents a process leading in the direction of militarism, during which military interests and values acquire increasing influence in state and society, in a direct or indirect way. Militarization may proceed on the national, regional, or global level. On the national level, militarization is reflected in the extent of armaments and the ascending leverage of military influence. It finds expression in the political, military, economic, social, and cultural domains. Politically, it actuates the concentration of power, the weakening of democratic governance, the infringement of human rights, and the institution of authoritarian rule. Militarily, it prompts armaments: the development, acquisition, and deployment of new weapons and weapon systems. Economically, it tends to give preference to military expenditures, thus impairing efforts for development. Socially, it leads towards a less equitable distribution of national income, and the restriction of human autonomy (see *Military Research and Development, Role of*). Culturally, it tends to corrupt human values, predicating the preponderance of means over ends, and sapping the spiritual, ethical, and moral fabric of society. On the regional level, militarization serves to stimulate the arms race and military-political polarization. On the global level, its most detrimental impact lies in the militarization of international relations. Intense armaments do not buy security, the arms race has made the world more insecure than ever. At the same time, high armament levels maintain and petrify the global hierarchy of power and the social inequalities between nations.

Militarism should be seen as the systemic apex of the process of militarization. As a rule, militarism embodies three ingredients: a value system, a sociopolitical structure, and a specific function. These component elements can be defined as follows:

(a) a system of beliefs and values that views organized violence and the use of force as indispensible tools of orderly governance, social order, and international ascendance;

(b) a system of government that relies structurally on a more or less institutionalized alliance or fusion of the military establishment, the state bureaucracy, and the dominant economic interest groups;

(c) a system whose executive function consists internally of the repressive exercise of power in the interests of the existing social order and ruling elites, and externally in the use of force as an instrument of nationalistic and expansionistic policy and diplomacy.

The systemic dynamics of militarism builds on the legitimate role of the military in society. Constitutionally, military organizations are allotted the task of the application of organized violence in the defense of state and nation against foreign encroachment. Militarization and militarism take off by abusing this legitimate function and extending their influence into civilian domains, internally and externally. One way of doing this is by stirring up nationalistic and fundamentalist sentiments, and then following this up by enhancing the image of the military as the guardian of national independence and security. After seizing power, the military usually tends to discipline society into submission gravitating to dictatorial rule.

3. Sociopolitical Indicators

A number of indicators may be helpful in detecting militaristic tendencies at an early stage.

Elements of ideology:

(a) nationalism, chauvinism, ethnocentrism, xenophobia;

(b) expansionism, aggressiveness, bellicosity;

(c) glorification of power, of the army, and of the military establishment;

(d) stress on hierarchy, discipline, regimentation, and redistributive authority; and

(e) ideological dogmatism—political, religious, or tribal-traditional.

Systemic features:

(a) position of the military in state and government: ruling force, decisive influence, co-partnership, or high authority under civilian supremacy; and

(b) deviation from democratic rule: dictatorship, authoritarian government, denial of democratic freedoms, repressive measures. In special cases, governments are established in the wake of a *coup d'état*.

Policy orientation and execution:

(a) high military expenditures and preferential treatment of the armed forces;

(b) military build-up and application of military strength as an instrument of diplomacy;

(c) participation in military alliances;

(d) imperial and neocolonial postures;

(e) special care for police forces and participation of the army in internal security operations;

(f) military interference in shaping socioeconomic goals and policy; and

(g) arbitrary decision-making processes.

Not all of these indicators need coexist together or be characteristic of a particular variant of militarism. The existence of but some of them may be sufficient to cause concern.

4. Variants of Militarism

Two basic manifestations of contemporary militarism and militarization can be distinguished: the great power and small nation variants. Militarization of the leading major powers is mainly outward oriented: it strives to maintain and enlarge their spheres of domination and influence and to impose some type of neocolonial control on countries within the reach of their power. Military rule in smaller countries, while claiming to act in the interests of national security, is mainly inner directed. It aims at the domination of all aspects of national life and the suppression of any protest against undemocratic forms of government.

In both cases, the establishments reveal a propensity to act on the impulse of the military imperative. That is, they will respond to security dilemmas and conflict situations not by the search for political and social solutions but by the use of force. This leads not to lasting conflict resolution but to conflict domi-

nation or suppression fraught with a continuation of tension and discord. Elements of conflict are thus perpetuated with no real solutions in sight. This propensity to opt for military rather than political solutions is a basic source of internal dissension, regional conflicts and international strain (see *Conflict Formation, Elements in*).

Some theorists have maintained that in the young, newly independent Third World countries, military rule is in fact beneficial: it introduces needed discipline, promotes modernization, and serves the process of nation building. This theory of the "modernizing soldier" is based on the assumption that the military commands organizational skill, has an understanding of the modern technology required by the army, and is a bearer of patriotism and national cohesion. According to this theory, the military in the Third World is eminently suited to serve as a vehicle for social change, economic advancement, and progressive political transformation.

Those who repudiate this theory of the "modernizing soldier" point to the waste of productive resources by the military regimes due to high spending for armaments and the needs of the army; to the distortion of economic priorities by the emphasis on weapon acquisition and the maintenance of sizeable armies; to the stifling of the people's creative initiative, indispensable for national development efforts; and to the stimulation of corruption through uncontrolled authority (see *Economics of Disarmament and Conversion*). It is questionable, critics of the "modernizing soldier" theory maintain, whether the military, with its rigid outlook, has the ability to show flexibility and apply modern social and economic theory to problems of development. Technical solutions, these critics say, cannot substitute for fundamental sociopolitical reform and structural change.

5. Militarism Dynamics and Armaments Dynamics

Militarism dynamics and armaments dynamics are closely interrelated. The common denominator is to be found in what President Eisenhower termed in his 1961 farewell address "the military-industrial complex" (see *Military-Industrial Complex*). President Eisenhower stated, among other things:

> This conjunction of an immense military establishment and a large arms industry is new in the American experience. The total influence—economic, political, even spiritual—is felt in every city, every state house, every office of the federal government. Yet we must not fail to comprehend its grave implica-

tions. Our toil, resources, and livelihood are all involved: so is the very structure of our society.

In the councils of government, we must guard against the acquisition of unwarranted influence, whether sought or unsought, by the military-industrial complex. The potential for the disastrous rise of misplaced power exists and will persist.

We must never let the weight of this combination endanger our liberties or democratic processes.

This statement clearly identifies three pressure groups with vested interests in armaments: the military establishment, the arms industry, and the state political bureaucracy "in the councils of government." In conjunction with imperial rivalries and the momentum inherent in the race in military technology, the push by these three interest groups serves to impel the arms race.

The military-industrial complex existed and acted also in the former Soviet Union, though under different systemic conditions. The above three component elements of this complex formed also in Russia exhibited a symbiotic relationship: the political bureaucracy, as in the United States, was very interested in using modern arms as an instrument of policy and diplomacy; the military craves more and better arms, and the arms industry was vitally interested in a continuous flow of orders for new weapons. Nor was the profit motive absent in Russia. It was reflected in the rank, status, privilege, and income differentials accorded to the elites in the military-industrial complex.

Obviously, the armaments drive of the major powers is an innate and organic part of the process of militarization.

It may seem difficult to speak of a fully fledged military-industrial complex in the Third World countries, especially in those in which an arms industry is only in its infancy or does not exist at all. Yet the military establishment and the state bureaucracy too often form an alliance, the impact of which is reminiscent of the workings of the military-industrial complex. The armaments dynamics in developing countries is reinforced by arms supplies from abroad. Thus, while in the case of the major powers, armaments dynamics are mainly inner directed—the technological momentum in addition to the thrust of the military-industrial complex playing a crucial role—in the case of the Third World countries, armaments dynamics are only partly inner directed. To a large extent, they are also externally impelled, stimulated by the global arms race. Since developing countries are also bound to the major powers in many other domains of their economic life, such clientship on military supplies, spare parts, and repair and military training makes the militarization process in these countries a dependent phenomenon. The world horizons and structure of both armaments and militarization are shaped mainly by the major powers.

6. The World Military Order

There is structure and hierarchy in the global military order—the web of interests animating armaments and militarization. This is most clearly reflected in the global investment in armaments and the flow of arms around the world. Approximately two-thirds of all global military expenditures were spent in the 1980s by the two military alliances, the North Atlantic Treaty Organization (NATO) (see *North Atlantic Treaty Organization (NATO)*) and the Warsaw Pact, with the United States and the former Soviet Union alone underwriting 50 percent of global spendings (see *Cold War*). The two alliances combined accounted at that time for around 90 percent of worldwide weapons traffic. In the post-Cold War era a new arms trade pattern emerged, primarily because of the collapse of the Soviet Union. While in the period between 1987-90 the United States accounted for 21 percent and the USSR for 48 percent of weapon deliveries to the Third World, in the years 1991-94 the proportions changed dramatically: total weapon transfers to the Third World by the United States amounted to 48 percent, while the share of USSR/Russia came down to 13 percent. At the same time armaments expenditures of Third World countries showed signs of a growth rate exceeding that of the industrial countries. This gives grounds for concern, as the waste on armaments in developing countries has a more adverse impact than in the wealthier countries of the North. In addition, weapon purchases by the Third World countries aggravate the acute debt problem. Not only do expenditures spent on arms by the Third World countries weaken their economies; these expenses makes them also more dependent on the major powers (see *Economics of Disarmament: Certain Premises*).

The arms trade contributes to the establishment of a patron-client relationship, as weapon imports involve not only a kind of political collaboration but also long-term technological dependence. At the same time, the arms trade in advanced weapons boosts the horizontal-geographical and the vertical-technological proliferation of armaments. The arms trade becomes an important element in the global militarization process. It serves to buttress the position of the military-industrial complex in the exporting countries, and of military influences in the recipient countries. The arms trade is part of a system reproduction built around military-technological cooperation.

The pattern of armaments expenditures and the structure of arms trade have a basic bearing on the global conflict configuration. They mirror a world hierarchy of power and a military order which sustains the North-South dominance-dependence relationship. Developing countries may, of course, rebel against this dependence relationship, and they often do. However, the choice is rather limited; in fact, military-technological dependence on the major powers remains a constant feature.

Arms supplies to the Third World have a pernicious effect on the internal and external relations of many developing countries. Internal militarization tends to incite indigenous friction, and this in turn leads to external interference and intervention by the weapons suppliers. The world hierarchy of power and the world military order acquire a dynamic permanence.

Militarism and militarization exert a profound influence on contemporary international relations. No stable peace can be established unless these issues can be addressed seriously and ways can be found to cure the world of the disease of militarism. A primary precondition for success here is progress in efforts for disarmament.

See also: *Emerging Tool Chest for Peacebuilders*

Bibliography ⎯⎯⎯⎯⎯⎯⎯⎯⎯⎯⎯⎯⎯⎯

Andrzejewski S 1954 *Military Organization and Society*. Humanities Press, New York

Berghahn V R 1981 *Militarism: The History of an International Debate 1861-1979*. Berg, Leamington Spa

Charisius A, Engelhardt K, Fiedler H (eds.) 1979 *Militarismus heute. Wesen und Erscheinungsformen des Militarismus der Gegenwart*. Militärverlag der DDR, Berlin

Eide A, Thee M (eds.) 1980 *Problems of Contemporary Militarism*. Croom Helm, London

Finer S E 1962 *The Man on Horseback: The Role of the Military in Politics*. Praeger, New York

Huntington S P 1957 *The Soldier and the State: The Theory and Politics of Civil-Military Relations*. Harvard University Press, Cambridge, Massachusetts

Janowitz M 1964 *The Military in the Political Development of New Nations*. Chicago University Press, Chicago, Illinois

Klare M T 1996 The arms trade in the 1990s: Changing patterns, rising dangers. *Third World Q.* 17(5)

Perlmutter A 1977 *The Military and Politics in Modern Times*. Yale University Press, New Haven. Connecticut

Vagts A 1967 *A History of Militarism*. Free Press, New York

MAREK THEE

Militarism: Marxist-Leninist Critique

Marxism-Leninism sees militarism as a product and as an inherent feature of developed capitalist society. The various aspects of this concept include:

(a) the types of relations in the political superstructure of society;

(b) the corresponding types of state policy;

(c) characteristics of the internal and external functions of the capitalist state; and

(d) the ideology which justifies militarism and which is at the same time its instrument.

All these aspects, or components, of militarism are said to be deeply anchored in the respective elements of the socioeconomic basis of capitalist society.

1. Militaristic State Apparatus

Militarism as a structure can be conceived in three forms. First, it is an authoritarian rule based largely on military power as a means of keeping the population obedient. Second, it is a close association of civilian and military elites which requires the military establishment to play a significant role in foreign and domestic policies. Finally, it may take the form of coercive intervention by the military in the process of government, with or without an open military takeover, but in clear violation of legally institutionalized procedures. In all three cases, the military largely or entirely control the government or at least possess an undue and excessive influence on its policy; however, in all three cases the military cannot be regarded as a separate social force but as a representative of the interests of the bourgeoisie as a whole, and in the highly developed countries of the top stratum of it, monopoly capital. These interests consist, in the Marxist-Leninist view, in protecting the system based on the private ownership of the means of production and in ensuring privileges and big profits outside the country. Both of these basic interests require military power, preferably without its open use, that is, without recourse to interstate war or internal use of armed violence against social opposition, but if this is impossible, then by means of open armed violence. The use of militarism by rulers to consolidate and expand their domination, to preserve the existing system, and to generate big profits within and outside the country was born with the division of society into classes and with the appearance of the exploiting class, according to Marxist-Leninists. Inheriting militarism from other antagonistic class societies, the bourgeoisie took over the most reactionary elements in it and adapted them to the contemporary conditions, and to its interests and needs. In the monopolist stage of capitalism, militarism has reached a size and intensity unprecedented in history.

2. Militaristic Policy

The militaristic structure involves a corresponding policy. Militarism is thus also defined as a system of economic, political, ideological, and directly military measures for the purpose of suppressing any internal opposition and for preparing and conducting interstate wars or for exerting military pressure on other states. The complex of both internal and external measures includes: the militarization of the economy, science, and education; the arms race; the build-up of military blocs; the growth of the armed forces; the acceleration of preparations for wars; the repression of workers' movements and the national liberation struggle; the spreading of militaristic propaganda; and so on.

In the Marxist-Leninist view, the militaristic policy of the great capitalist powers is expanding and intensifying. The necessity for increasing militarization, perceived by the ruling elites of the great capitalist powers, is said to be rooted in the general crisis of capitalism. The imperialist bourgeoisie is said to have exhausted the economic means provided by the capitalist economic system for the exploitation of domestic labor; the unhindered exploitation of the colonies and dependent countries as sources of raw material and markets has also come to an end (see *Imperialism*). Thus noneconomic measures of compulsion, both internal and external, have been considered more necessary than ever before. This has led to two world wars and it is now creating the danger of a most destructive war encompassing the whole world.

3. Functions of Militarism

The functions of militarism are said to derive from the main functions of the capitalist state, which is quite

natural, and are similar to those of the armed forces. The internal function is that of preserving and strengthening the existing system, of keeping the working masses in subjection and repressing their struggle for liberation. The external function consists in promoting and defending the interests of the ruling elite abroad. These functions are interrelated, and both aim at defending and increasing the power of the rulers and securing their profits. Contemporary militarism is a variant of this traditional phenomenon linked to the period of aggravation of all class contradictions, both internal and international, in the imperialist world. It is assigned the task of not simply defending the interests of the rulers, but of preserving their threatened rule. For this purpose, it must employ not only armed forces, but the whole apparatus of the state (including the police) and the whole of its administrative, economic, and ideological power.

It is not surprising that, in this interpretation, both functions expand and grow more intense. The internal one becomes more severe and resorts more and more to terrorist methods. The armed forces are extensively used to put down strikes, antiracist and antiwar demonstrations, student rebellions, and protest action of peasants. These functions are then formalized by corresponding legislative enactments. Ideological indoctrination plays an important role in complementing violent action by diverting the attention of the working masses from internal political and economic crises. It includes and uses nationalistic, chauvinistic, and racialist ideas.

As the external function expands it acquires new features. First, at the beginning of the twentieth century, this function was exercised in interimperialist rivalries. The monopolies of individual countries aspired toward increasing monopolization of the sources of raw materials and of markets which could be achieved only by physical seizure and national domination of them as well as by domination over competing monopoly groups. The struggle for world domination inevitably led to world wars; the victory in them could be secured only when all the resources of the beligerent nations were utilized, which necessitated the militarization of the whole society. Militarism and preparations for war greatly accelerated the process of intensive merging of monopolies with the state, the development of state monopoly economy. This was a two-sided process: monopolies strove toward militarism, while militarism rested on the monopolies as its economic base.

Following the October Revolution of 1917, and particularly since the emergence of the socialist camp, the external function of the great capitalist powers has been tinged with antisocialist militarism, with emphasis on the destruction of the socialist system, suppression of the international labor and national liberation movements, and the reestablishment of capitalism throughout the world.

The third feature is that militarism now encompasses all imperialist countries, and according to Marxist-Leninists, ties them into a common knot, which enables the United States to impose its will on its allies who are also, however, its competitors.

Fourth, war and the threat of war have now become the main instruments of the militarist external policy. Initially, Marxist-Leninists tended to exaggerate the conscious and deliberate character of the war preparations of the great capitalist powers and the influential militarist forces within them, but recently they have emphasized more the uncontrollable arms race which is constantly escalating and preparing the material prerequisites for war, even if the deliberate policy of unleashing war has significantly weakened. The arms race serves on the one hand as a basic means of increasing the hold of the militarists over all aspects of capitalist society and, on the other, as an instrument of influencing international relations. It has a clear antisocialist character, not only because it prepares the material means of an antisocialist war, but also because the intention of Western militarists is to place an extra burden on the economy of the former Soviet Union and other socialist states, to force them to increase their military expenditure, and to make it more difficult for them to put their large social programs into operation, thus weakening the attraction of socialism. Finally the arms race which is presented by militarists as not constituting a potential cause of war per se is in the Marxist-Leninist view extremely dangerous for two reasons. First, it generates the danger of "self-conflagration" which could occur in the following circumstances: when an accidental strike is delivered by one side and when it is interpreted by the other side as a preemptive strike. Second, it is not so much that the arms race may start a war, as that a war started for any other reason would become a war that destroys all life on earth. In addition, not only accidents but a variety of evil intentions must also be taken into account as well as the possibility of irrational behavior of the leaders in an acute crisis which might escalate with lightning speed.

4. Bases of Militarist Ideology

Militarism is said to include—but is not to be reduced to—ideological justification and indoctrination. It must be justified in order to infect the population and to gain their acceptance and support for the military build-up and policy.

Two basic propositions are said to underlie militarism. The first is that military force is a determining factor in social development. Military force is said to ensure sovereignty, to provide the motive force of progress, and the indispensable means of resolving all political disputes. In other words, it is both necessary and inevitable—in the internal development of individual countries and in international relations.

The other, and interconnected, proposition is that the use of violence is a law of history. Violence is considered a primary force rooted in human nature, and the use of it the main means of the struggle for people's rights and interests. It is also the main method applied by states, when they attempt to impose their will on other states. In this perspective, the search for power becomes the basic idea of the strategy of using internal and international violence, since to possess power means to be able to apply violence. Concomitantly, the proposition on the exclusive role of violence in history sees the roots of violence in the nature of individuals, society, or the state. One corollary is that the very origin of states is rooted in wars, that is, armed violence. Violence was used in primitive societies and led to the establishment of special groups for the purpose of warfare: these became the embryo of the state apparatus and its armed forces. This assertion illustrates the equation of violence with armed violence: when the proponents of this view of violence quote historical examples of the use of violence, these usually concern only wars or armed uprisings.

Moreover, several ideas concerning the role of war and armed forces constitute direct corollaries of this propositions, such as:

(a) the proposition that armed violence is the only method of resolving international conflicts and that armed forces as an instrument of such violence are, therefore, the main factor in international relations;

(b) the assumption about the inevitability of war, which would be a direct consequence of treating the use of violence as a law and a universal phenomenon; and

(c) the assertion that the socialist system of states can be destroyed by means of armed violence, as well as the similar assertion that the revolutionary and national liberation movements can be suppressed in the same way.

The two propositions about the exclusive role of

violence and armed forces in history are said to be underpinned, confirmed, and strengthened by the whole range of reactionary bourgeois theories of the roots and causes of war. These include, for instance, biological theories based on the assumptions that (a) all forms of life, from plants to humans, are engaged in a constant struggle in which only the fittest survive, and war is one of the forms of this struggle, and (b) humans are driven by instinct to struggle and make war; psychological and sociopsychological theories which emphasize the influence of the social or group psyche on the outbreak and course of war; anthropological theories which see war as a product of cultural development and experience, and especially those which assert that wars were the vehicle of progress, since they perfected the human race and culture and stimulated the development of nations and nation-states and the means of production; ecological theories which consider war to be a manifestation of the struggle for better environmental conditions and/or an instrument in this struggle; geopolitical theories which postulate that war is a manifestation or a form of the struggle for a larger space and more secure frontiers; and ethical theories which approach war as an instrument in a moral system, that is, a moral or moral-religious imperative, or as a means of perfecting humans, society, or the state. As an example of the way in which such theories are deployed to justify militarism, it is pointed out that militarism is presented as a way of thinking—and accordingly acting—about policy and society in terms of military virtues and values (see *Theoretical Traditions of Peace and Conflict Studies*).

The Marxist-Leninist critique of militarism pays special attention to what is regarded as a modern approach which justifies militarism, namely the technoindustrial approach to wars. This is said to assume that wars today are generated by industrial, scientific, and technological progress which creates both fierce interstate competition and the means of struggle which seem to favor its resolution by military forces. The constant underlying philosophy is political realism which regards the search for power and resort to war as a normal and necessary means of maintaining international relations. War and the threat of war, the arms race, and the demonstration of force are presented by modern militarism not only as inevitable but also as the engines of technological and scientific—and consequently social—progress.

The exclusive role of armed violence and its carrier—military force—in history, which in the Marxist-Leninist view underlies the Western ideology of militarism, is sharply criticized by the former. Violence, and even more so, armed violence, cannot be considered a primary force in human and social life, since it is a product of social (and ultimately economic) forces. Its use cannot be presented as a law of history, and a historical necessity, since it only constitutes a social instrument, which the reactionary forces, and, correspondingly, also the progressive force, may or may not use in the class struggle. This depends on the historical circumstances, that is, on whether the use of violence meets or does not meet any social requirements. The same can be said of the armed forces, the carrier of armed violence. The decision to form a state and its armed forces constitutes the final result of a process and of social development: it is necessitated by the needs of the emergent class system. Social institutions are created and social activities appear when they are needed to meet social demands. Armed violence—war—and armed forces appeared when the exploiting classes began to need them for the defense, strengthening, and extension of their rule.

A corollary of these errors is the neglect of the distinction to be made between revolutionary and counterrevolutionary violence and armed forces. Such a distinction is of primary importance not only for understanding the genesis and essence of particular wars, but also for assessing and predicting their consequences and their role in history. The outcome of wars, and their progressive or reactionary consequences, depend greatly on the character of social forces which cause them and, correspondingly, on the just or unjust, progressive or reactionary, character of violence itself. Militarism, the armed forces on which it is based, and wars, which it prepares or which it threatens, are necessarily unjust, since they are the instrument of imperialism, the basic reactionary force of our times and the root of all wars. In international relations, Marxist-Leninists assert the necessity of eliminating any kind of armed violence: this is said to be useless for resolving the antagonistic contradiction of our time. Only internal violence, in the form of social revolution, may result in the continual creation of new societies and its cumulative effects may bring about a radical transformation of the international system. Internal violence need not necessarily take an armed form. Owing to the correlation of world forces, advantageous to socialism, revolutions may be accomplished without war. Moreover, internal wars may easily escalate to international ones, and these must be avoided.

5. Apologia for the Militarization of Economy

The apologia for the militarization of economy occupies a special place in the ideological arsenal of militarism, according to Marxist-Leninists. It is justified and praised for the following alleged social and economic merits:

(a) militarization of economy increases the global national product;

(b) it reduces unemployment;

(c) it reduces production costs and increases consumption;

(d) it improves the distribution of the national product; and

(e) it results in the growth of the role of state and a consequent decline in the extent of private ownership of the means of production, and thus in the reduction of social inequalities and conflicts.

The above list of merits is also related to the apologia for the militarization of science. Western theorists are accused of attempting to justify the militarization of science by citing the requirements of present-day warfare and the natural interaction of economic, scientific, and military affairs. They contend that the growth of the size and intensity of wars requires the development of the branches of science and technology that are connected with warfare and an increase of the use of them for military purposes. The requirements of war have stimulated the development of many sectors of science and the creation of many technical devices, such as those in the fields of ballistics, probabilistic theory, radar, automated systems, aerodynamics, missiles, and so on. The enormous requirements of the military machine thus have required the diversion of many scientific inventions and discoveries and enormous material resources towards military purposes and the creation of an enormous military-industrial apparatus with its own relatively independent economic basis.

Concerning these alleged advantages of militarizing the economy, and also the explanation that it is required by modern war, three main objections have been raised. First, militarization is always carried out at the cost of the working classes, and it worsens their material conditions. Second, militarization is not only unproductive but also counter-productive: it draws material resources and human talents from fields that are crucial to economic and social development and diverts them to fields of little use to the national economy. Finally, the entire process of inter-

action between science, technology, and military affairs, involving the militarization of science and technology, has a social causation, the essence and the consequences of which are contrary to those asserted by the apologists for it. The use of scientific and technological achievements in military affairs is determined primarily by the narrow class of monopolist capitalists who need them for making extraordinarily high profits, preparing aggressive wars, and countering the acute class struggle. The militarization of science and technology provides temporary additional sources and incentives for economic development, but aggravates the rottenness and parasitism of capitalism. The increase in production is used not in the interest of society as a whole but against it. Social inequality increases, not decreases as the proponents of the militarization of science, technology, and economy allege. The production of weapons of mass destruction swallows an enormous part of the national income; the growing production enriches only a handful of monopolists, while the number of unemployed workers, intellectuals, and peasants grows. The extreme aggravation of the internal social contradictions makes the economic and political development of particular countries even more uneven. The adverse psychological consequences of militarization and of constant preparedness for war and fear of war are enormous and difficult to estimate.

6. Marxist-Leninist Criticisms

The intrinsic feature of the ideological arsenal of militarism, which in the Marxist-Leninist view underlies all the apologies for it, is the presentation of it as of a non-class phenomenon. Militarism is said to be treated by its defenders as either an eternal phenomenon and defined in a way that conceals its class nature, or else it is presented as a new phenomenon generated by modern conditions, atypical of the classical capitalist system. In using the former method, scholars present militarism as a regime based on military force or emphasize armed violence, accepting such a regime and a policy, without giving any indication as to the identity of the makers of this policy. In the second approach, militarism is presented as the outcome of the modern military technological revolution and specific modern conditions.

Criticism by Marxist-Leninists of this proposition concerning the exclusive role of armed violence and military force in history as the theoretical bases of militarism may be here supplemented by criticism of views concerning the alleged nonclass character of militarism.

It is said that militarism and militaristic preparations for war are new phenomena which are not linked to the character of the socioeconomic and political system. However, they have characterized all class societies, and especially the capitalist system, from its very beginnings. The process of the militarization of the economy, followed by the militarization of the whole life of society, accelerated in the second half of the nineteenth century, with the transition to monopoly capitalism, with the concentration and centralization of production, and the search for mass markets for the goods of monopoly production. Militarism pushed toward unleashing wars, and wars favored the further growth of militarism. The series of imperialist wars initiated by the United States in 1898, and participation in the First World War and in the military campaign against the young Soviet republic stimulated the development of American militarism. Since the Second World War the growth of militarism in the United States and other capitalist countries has been occurring at an enormous rate. This process testifies to the fact that the development of militarism is in full accord with the development of capitalist society, a quite logical and natural process which accompanies the development of capitalism in its monopolist stage with the increased interventionism of its state apparatus.

Thus scientific and technological progress cannot be regarded as the main cause of militarism and the increased bellicosity of the ruling elites in modern times. These achievements do not give impulses to war per se; they may as well be placed in the service of peace. The same may be said of the possession of armed forces. Almost all states have them, but not all are militaristic. It is only when the governing and exploiting class, or its elite, consciously increases state armaments, the armed forces, and preparations for predatory wars, as well as its internal oppression, that one can speak of militarism. Naturally, this phenomenon is characteristic of antagonistic class societies only.

7. The Military-Industrial Complex

The growth of present-day militarism cannot be properly understood without the analysis of the so-called military-industrial complex, which has become the driving force of militaristic ideology and policy. It reflects both the new conditions under which the ruling class is acting vis-á-vis other classes and other states, and the shifts in the alignment of forces within monopoly capital itself.

The social basis of militarism has always been made up of the ruling-class groups directly interested in the privileged role of the military establishment within a given country, and their safeguarding role with regard to the governing socioeconomic and political system, as well as their direct interest in foreign policy and aggressive wars. Thus these groups always included, apart from the military proper, also those who capitalized on the acquisition of foreign territories and on exploitation of other peoples.

At the dawn of capitalism and at the time of its premonopoly maturity, arms manufacturers occupied a modest place in the structure of militarism. The first large arms companies emerged at the turn of this century, and they played a considerable role in the preparations for both world wars. The German and Japanese arms concerns were active not only in the preparations for the Second World War, according to Marxist-Leninists, but they participated in the mass annihilation of civilians and in the exploitation of slave labor in the seized territories. The military monopolies and the Nazi and militarist elites were so closely intertwined that the delimitation between them was disappearing, but the non-German "merchants of death" also gave financial support to the emerging Nazi rule and contributed to their preparations for war.

In the United States, and other Western states during the Second World War, several comparatively small military companies grew into big corporations with a turnover of hundreds of millions of dollars; among them were, for instance, the American Lockheed, Boeing, and United Aircraft companies, and the submarine-building Electric Boat Company which later formed the nucleus of the multibranch General Dynamics. However, in the Marxist-Leninist view, it was only after the setting up of the North Atlantic Treaty Organization (NATO) (see *North Atlantic Treaty Organization (NATO)*) in 1949, when the spending of many billions of dollars on armaments became a constant element of reproduction in peacetime, that the corporations dealing with the production of armaments began to flourish and to gain a constantly increasing influence on the state machinery of the United States and, to a somewhat lower degree, of its allies. This process has led to the emergence of the military-industrial complex, which in the Marxist-Leninist definition has been defined as the alliance between the imperialist monopolies, the reactionary military, and a part of the state apparatus. The top echelon of state bureaucracy joins the monopoly groups and the military hierarchy, and the whole gigantic military machine serves as its basis. Affiliated to them are science, technology, and many other spheres which, in one way or another, serve the military conveyor or live off it. The military-industrial complex exerts great influence on the entire policy-making process, on the militarization of the economy, and on techno-scientific research. Two consequences are emphasized by Marxist-Leninists: one is the growth of the danger of war, and the other is the further concentration of capital and the increase in social inequality.

As regards the former, although the interests of the military-industrial complex are inseparable from the interests of monopoly capital as a whole in the struggle against socialism and the national liberation movements and in its defense of its positions in the interimperialist rivalry, the military-industrial complex has also its own particular interests: it profits from the preparation for war and the conduct of war. Thus its interests are directly oriented toward war. The arms race which it unleashes and carries out creates two basic dangers: first, war may break out from self-conflagration of the arms race, and second, a war caused for any reason can, thanks to the arms race, become totally nuclear.

The development of the American military-industrial complex in the last decades had been the focus of the Marxist-Leninist, basically Soviet, criticism. In the 1950s and 1960s the ties of the corporations which deal with the production of armaments with the military establishment and with the state apparatus grew stronger. Among the thousands of Pentagon's contractors, the dozen biggest monopolies accounted for about two-thirds of the entire arms market. A considerable number of Pentagon officials and top commanders in the army, navy, and air force have links with the military business. They push contracts for the arms dealers and are rewarded with lavish subsidies, and upon retirement from military service receive well-paid posts in the corporations. Both in Congress and in practically all the other parts of the political system there is a permanent clan of people who are supported by the military corporations and who in turn constitute a powerful lobby that promotes the interests of the military business. Another development pointed out by the critics is that although on the whole the major military corporations have had to rely, financially, on provincial groupings, such as the Bank of America group in California, the growing profitability of military business has gradually attracted increasingly more of the financial oligarchy.

The forced end of the Vietnamese war, détente, and the Strategic Arms Limitation Talks (SALT) treaties endangered a sharp reduction in the growth of profits, and in the 1970s a relative lull set in for the military business. This was only transitory, however. The Reagan Administration set in motion major armaments programs and declared that they were designed for many years ahead. This was to ensure a long-term steady growth of the armaments industry. The Administration's main idea has become to sustain a practically uninterrupted military build-up, consisting in providing new systems along the whole spectrum of armaments, and modernization in it, both enabling the military industry to operate to full capacity, thus eliminating intervals when generations of weapons succeed one another. To back up the arms race, appropriate military doctrines, said to create conditions for waging limited wars and winning them as well as to create favorable conditions for the negotiations on arms control and disarmament have been elaborated. These ideas and programs were crowned by the transfer of the arms race to outer space, where antisatellite weapons were expected to be deployed and a large-scale antiballistic missile (ABM) system to be set up. The new doctrines and the military build-up has been wholeheartedly supported by the military-industrial complex, in which, among others, the key positions have been occupied by the Californian financial group, which includes the military-industrial corporations Lockheed, Boeing, and Rockwell International. These top echelons of economic, military, and political power also take part in transnational business; one of the main directions of their foreign expansion is the developing countries. The military-industrial complex seeks allies from the monopoly capital not associated with the armaments production. It tries to arrange cooperation with them for three aims: to wage a common policy with regard to the developing countries; to exert economic and financial pressure on the monopolies in Western Europe and Japan in order to weaken their competitive power; and to contribute to the political campaign which demands state measures to limit the working people's rights in both national politics and the socioeconomic base.

Characteristic of the late 1970s and 1980s, in the Marxist-Leninist view, is the internationalization of the military-industrial complex which makes militarism an even more international structure and policy than ever before. In recent years there has been a considerable growth of arms production and the strengthening of military corporation in Western Europe and Japan. The NATO decision to increase military spending annually by three percent in real terms contributed to this growth, which has been especially fast in the Germany, France, and the United Kingdom. Japan formally observes the principle of using no more than 1 percent of its gross national product (GNP) for military purposes but the actual military expenditures greatly outstrip the GNP growth. The concentration and militarization of industrial production is constantly growing: 60-80 percent of the output of the aircraft industry, nearly 30 percent of electronics, and up to 20 percent of ships produced in the United Kingdom, Germany and France are used for military purposes. Germany the 30 biggest firms account for 59 percent of the military industry turnover. The critics point out that ever-greater intertwining of West European and Japanese concerns with the United States military-industrial complex. United States aircraft and missile giants have a large portion of the shares of the Dutch, French, Italian, and other West European corporations, and components for American weapons systems are often produced in Europe. Around 320 joint Japanese-American programs of military technical cooperation are being carried out, including the manufacture of armaments from US licenses. Thus the military-industrial complexes of European NATO members and Japan have a stake in the continued arms race led by the American complex, and in promoting the militaristic course in international relations. They greatly contributed to the increased threat of war, which can be judged from the following signs. First, there is the enormous number of weapons which have accumulated in the world. The nuclear potential of the United States is 12 times greater than required for the destruction of the population of the whole earth. Second, there is the constant growth in military expenditure, which in the mid-1980s reached more than 500 billion dollars; US military expenditure accounts for almost a half of this. Third, the number of zones saturated with arms constantly increases. Fourth, nuclear weapons are spreading in spite of the Non-Proliferation Treaty. Finally, a gigantic intellectual potential is concentrated on inventing new types of weapons of mass destruction. Weapons are being developed which will be able to use radiation energy beams for defense, and electric power to launch supersonic missiles. The development of highly effective chemical lasers and various kinds of chemical weapons is underway. The solution of vital problems which face mankind is hampered by the designation of the gigantic financial and human resources for the accelerating arms race—the product of militaristic policy in which military-industrial complex plays the crucial role.

While in the capitalist world the military-industrial complex constantly grows and becomes internationalized, socialist countries know no such phenomena according to Marxist-Leninists. First, a socialist state concentrates its resources on a multifaceted and wide-scale constructive program in the economic, cultural, technological, and scientific fields, which is the basis of socialist construction. Left to itself, no socialist country would form armed forces and spend considerable funds on defense. It is the urgent need to defend themselves which forces the countries of the socialist world to maintain armed forces. These not only serve the cause of defense but also exercise a peace-safeguarding function by preventing future major wars. Second, within the structure of the socialist society, there is no social stratum which would be consciously oriented toward war. Finally, and likewise, under socialism there is no social stratum which could derive particular advantage from the military build-up or from militarization of the entire social life. Such a stratum is not composed of the personnel employed in the military industry or in the armed forces for the simple reason that they could find employment anywhere outside the military sphere. Nor is there a danger that a rapid reduction of the armed forces and the military production would cause any difficulties in the spheres of the economy and employment. On the contrary, in a socialist country, where there is absence of unemployment and a constant demand for workers and material resources to fulfill the creative tasks of socialist construction, personnel and resources can be switched in a relatively short time from the military sector to the goals of peaceful development.

8. Criticisms of Chinese Militarism

In the past three decades, the term militarism has also been used in Marxist-Leninist literature to denote a socioeconomic and political system different from the United States and its allies.

The People's Republic of China has been assessed in a good deal of Marxist-Leninist studies, as militaristic. The governing ideology and policy have been said to be directed towards converting the People's Republic of China into a powerful militaristic state and establishing its world hegemony. The situation in the People's Republic of China is said fully to correspond to the main tenets of the concept of militarism as the subordination of economic, political, and social life to the aims of preparing predatory wars and as the transposition of the forms and methods of military organization into the field of civilian relationships. Since, in Marxist-Leninist theory, militarism as a structure and a policy is combined with certain special functions of the state and its military machinery as well as justified by a set of ideological assumptions, let us see how these characteristics of Chinese society are described.

According to these Marxist-Leninists, the Chinese state has ceased to be a proletarian dictatorship and has turned into the dictatorship of a military-bureaucratic elite. Since the character of a state depends on its socioeconomic system, the Chinese elite has to correspond to some specific kind of such system. This is, however, unclear: the Chinese socioeconomic structure does not represent any variant of the capitalist system, and it has not been stated *expressis verbis* that it is not a socialist one. The assessment of the Chinese social structure as a kind of militarism may invalidate the proposition that in our times militarism characterized imperialism only.

The focus has therefore shifted to the description of Chinese ideology as well as domestic and foreign policies and the dominant role of the armed forces in their conduct. The ideology of Chinese militarism is said to be rooted in both the whole history of the nation and in the specific character of the Chinese Revolution; both have resulted in the present set of militaristic ideas and goals.

The ideology which is said to underlie the policy of Chinese militarism includes several ideas presented by the critics as characteristic of the entire Chinese history: nationalism (in its most extreme chauvinistic form—the great Han tradition) (see *Chauvinism*); the apologia for the absolute power of the ruler and the unconditional obedience of the masses; the view of war as a justified and legitimate means of maintaining absolute rule, and as the universal means of resolving all internal and international conflicts; and the related idea of a privileged position for the armed forces in society.

At the same time the underlying ideology is said to be based on the specific features of the Chinese Revolution which was pushed through mainly by the petty bourgeoisie—primarily the peasants—and which was therefore characterized by anarchism, social utopianism, "populism," voluntarism, and ignorance of the laws of history. The complex of these attitudes and ideas which accompanied the Chinese Revolution was mixed with the above-mentioned traditional ideology of nationalism and the apologia for war and the armed forces. Marxist-Leninist analysts contend that the nationalism of Chinese "petty-bourgeois pseudo-revolutionaries" who speculated on the real needs of China as an underdeveloped country gave rise to an ideology which praised the policy of expansion of the Chinese nation and Sinocentric conceptions. It culminated in the idea of China's

supremacy "on the five continents."

This idea was not presented directly, however, say the critics, but it was an inherent part of the more general theory of world development in our times. Initially, the struggle for national liberation, rather than the policy of the socialist states and the working-class revolutionary movement, were presented as the main front of war against imperialism and the basic contradiction was that between the underdeveloped oppressed nations and the developed capitalist countries of North America and Western Europe. In a revised version, presented by Mao Zedong (see *Mao Zedong*) in the 1970s, the world was seen as consisting of three camps called "worlds." The two Superpowers constituted the First World, Japan, Europe, and Canada the Second World, and Asia (with the exception of Japan) including the People's Republic of China, Africa, and Latin America the Third World. The two Superpowers exploited and oppressed the nations of the Third World and also competed to subjugate them. In the Chinese view, the former Soviet Union which wanted to expand, but was inferior to the United States in economic strength, must rely chiefly on its military power. Because of the unprecedented centralization of the economy in the former Soviet Union and the creation of a state-monopoly capitalist economy and a fascist dictatorship regime it was easier for this state than for the United States to put the entire economy on a military footing and militarize the whole apparatus of the state. The Second World oppressed and exploited the Third World but was at the same time controlled and bullied by the Superpowers. Thus the developing countries played the leading role in the fight against imperialism.

As regards the second main conceptual problem of militarism, the functions of the armed forces, both the internal and the external functions are said to have undergone basic transformations in the People's Republic of China in the 1960s and 1970s. The internal function which in a normal socialist society tends to wither away, in the People's Republic of China has become the main one, and even more: the army began to dominate society, to exercise not only military, but also economic, political, and cultural functions. The whole society, critics maintained, was structured like a military institution, and military methods were being introduced in all fields of social activity. Not only in the first post-revolution decade but also afterwards, millions of officers and soldiers were assigned to all levels of the state, party, and social apparatus. During the "Great Leap Forward" in the late 1950s a militarized "people's commune" was declared "the first unit of the future communist society." The expansion of the repressive apparatus, the growing influence of the army in the Party's central organs and in the country's highest legislative organ as well as the occupation by the military of leading positions at all levels of political, economic, and ideological guidance of society testify to the internal role of the armed forces as the main support of the military bureaucratic dictatorship.

As regards the external function, the normal task of preparing a defense against imperialist aggression has been toned down. The relation to the countries of the Third World has also changed: instead of supporting their trend toward full political and economic independence, the Chinese army often fights against them, as it did in India in 1962. This change of the functions of the Chinese armed forces, which were recognized as the main force of the anti-imperialist revolution, like the change in the character of the state, was not explained in Soviet writings by corresponding changes in the socioeconomic base. The only explanation provided was that the "Cultural Revolution" was, in fact, a counter-revolutionary *coup d'état*, and the takeover of the armed forces by the military bureaucratic elite was the decisive action in this counterrevolution. The transformation of the social character of the army and its functions was performed by means of political indoctrination and "purging" the army of anti-Maoist elements. This is a quite unorthodox argument in Marxist-Leninist terms, as basic changes in the social role of the army are said always to correspond to changes in the character of the socioeconomic structure.

Mao's death and the great changes subsequently made in the fields of the economy and administration have not changed the basic tenets of the theory underlying Chinese militarism and its practice. The Chinese rapprochement with the United States has confirmed and reinforced the political implications of militarism. More than before militaristic policy aimed at splitting the socialist camp and undermining the unity of action of anti-imperialist forces as a whole. The People's Republic of China has become an ally of the imperialist bloc in the fight against socialism and it cooperates with reactionary nationalistic states in the Third World. It accepts the inevitability of a world war and directly supports the forces moving towards war.

To sum up, the inclusion of the Chinese system, policy, and in particular the armed forces in the concept of militarism has made the Soviet theory of militarism inconsistent: the whole argument connected with the social causation of militarism, and inter alia with the attribution of contemporary militarism to the imperialist socioeconomic basis must—seemingly—be revised, to encompass both the main "variants" of it.

9. Some Differences in Approaches

There are basic differences between Marxist-Leninist and the non-Marxist approaches to the concept and practice of militarism. The main point of disagreement resides in its very concept. In the West the term is interpreted so variously by different schools and scholars, and so many aspects of a structural, attitudinal, and political nature have been subsumed under this concept that almost any political or economic policy, or any theory of war and armed forces may be termed militaristic. In the Marxist-Leninist approach, all the connotations of militarism may be reduced to a common one: militarism is a conscious activity on the part of the monopolist bourgeoisie, which aims at increasing its own power and intensifying its reactionary internal and external policy. It uses the growing role of the military forces and armed violence as an instrument of such a policy. Thus the following differences in approaches may be pointed out.

(a) While in the non-Marxist attitudes the point of departure is the increasing role of the military and their tendency to become relatively autonomous, without, however, any indication of their role as the defender and instrument of the exploiting classes, in Marxist-Leninist theory the emphasis is not on the military regarded solely as the instrument, but on the class or stratum which uses it, that is, the bourgeois monopolists.

(b) Thus, while in non-Marxist approaches militarism usually means the abuse by military personnel of their legitimate function and the usurpation of roles and prerogatives which normally are not theirs, in Marxist-Leninist studies it is the rulers who use the military to increase their own power.

(c) In this connection also, the Marxist-Leninists, unlike the non-Marxists, place militarism in the framework of the class struggle between the two antagonistic classes—the exploiters and the exploited masses—and emphasize the internal function of militarism as aiming at increasing this exploitation and making it more effective by using noneconomic means.

(d) As a corollary, the non-Marxists present the external function of militarism mainly as a consequence of the primordial status of the military, and partly as a justification and a rationalization of their privileged position. In the Marxist-Leninist approach, both the internal and the international functions are closely linked together in the service of the same class and the same class interests. Which of them comes to the fore depends on the period and the situation: at present the external function of militarism and its aggressive tendencies are the more dangerous.

(e) In the West, the growth in the role of the military is seen as the usual determining characteristic of militarism, or of the process of militarization. The large role of the military in the former Soviet Union and the policy of large-scale armaments lead non-Marxists to term the Soviet system and policy militaristic, and to point to the role which the Soviet military-industrial complex played in this policy. Soviet scholars sharply criticized such a standpoint as anti-Soviet propaganda.

(f) In the West the military-industrial complex is criticized by many as related to militarism, as spreading warlike influences, and plundering natural and human resources for the sake of superfluous military measures, and also as corrupting the state apparatus and making excessive profits. Marxist-Leninists agree with these charges but take issue with the assumption, usual in the West, that it is an abnormal phenomenon which can be liquidated by improving the existing capitalist system. This is not a disease which can be cured by reforms, they say, but, like militarism itself, it is a natural and inevitable product of the imperialist system, which has to be liquidated together with the system itself.

(g) In the West, the ideology of militarism is often regarded as a deviation from democracy, and even a departure from it. However, Marxist-Leninists point out that it does not mean anything new, since bourgeois democracy, which never was real democracy, in its imperialist variant has always been militaristic—with its concept of an absolute role of force in history, in contemporary international relations, and in domestic affairs. Such ideas underlie the traditional theory of the balance of power, according to which violence and war are the supreme arbiters and normal instruments of policy, justified by the interests of nations. Militarism means that this apologia for war and its perpetuation has only become more open and explicit.

(h) Marxist-Leninists also take issue with the attempts to present militarism as a kind of ideology, or subculture, or a set of values dominating in society. No ideology can be separated from its socioeconomic roots and from the interests of the class which tries to impose it on society. Such a presentation ignores the fact that militarism owes its existence to the class nature of society and this means an artificial separation of the spiritual sphere of society from its dominating economic basis and the policy of the ruling classes in it.

(i) Finally, a special point of disagreement seems to be the assessment of militarism in the countries of the Third World. While in the non-Marxist literature Third World militarism is sometimes considered one of the two main variants of militarism, Marxist-Leninists seem to view it quite differently. The emphasis in the developing countries on strengthening the armed forces, they say, is rooted in the weakness of the political life and economy rather than in the deliberate intention of the governing classes to suppress, exploit, and increase profits. It can, with time, become an instrument of imperialistic militarism, and its ally and servant but it cannot be termed a variant of the same order.

10. Conclusion

The Marxist-Leninist criticism of the political nature of militarism and its aims is a part of the criticism of the whole of the so-called imperialist policy. The assessment of the ideological apologia for militarism is similar to that of the so-called bourgeois theories of the genesis and nature of war, and of theories of violence as the determining force in history. Militarism is simply equated with modern capitalism. This assessment stands and falls together with Marxist-Leninist theory as a whole. Marxist-Leninist criticism of militarism constitutes simultaneously an argument for peace *sui generis*. It supplements the political campaign for peaceful coexistence in the Soviet version.

See also: *Marxist-Leninist Concepts of Peace and Peaceful Coexistence; Militarism and Militarization; Military-Industrial Complex*

Bibliography

Apalin G, Mityayev I 1980 *Militarism in Peking Policies.* Progress, Moscow

Denisov V V 1975 *Sotsiologya Nasiliya* [Sociology of Violence]. Izd. Politicheskoi Literatury, Moscow

Faramazyan R A 1970 *SShA: Militarizm i Ekonomika* [USA: Militarism and Economy]. Izd. Mysl, Moscow

Lider J 1981 *Military Force: An Analysis of Marxist-Leninist Concepts.* Gower, Farnborough

Faramazyan R A (ed.) 1983 *Militarism: Tsifry i Fakty* [Militarism: Numbers and Facts]. Izd. Politicheskoi Literatury, Moscow

Sheinin Yu M 1963 *Nauka i Militarizm v SShA* [Science and

Militarism in the USA]. Izd. Akademii Nauk SSSR, Moscow

Sheinin Yu M 1972 *Voennaya Sila i Mezhdunarodnye Otnosheniya* [Military Force and International Relations]. Izd. Mezhdunarodnye Otnosheniya, Moscow

Sheinin Yu M 1974 *Voina, Istoriya, Ideologiya* [War, History and Ideology]. Izd. Politicheskoi Literatury, Moscow

JULIAN LIDER

Military Research and Development, Role of

For better or worse, science and technology exert a powerful and pervasive influence on society—economic, political, social, cultural and spiritual. The huge benefits for humankind are unquestionable. But alongside these, concern is growing about the dubious and adverse by-products of science and technology. Most of all, anxiety is increasing about the effects of the race in science-based military technology. In the nuclear age, the consequences of this race are indeed unpredictable.

In the post-Cold War circumstances, weapon modernisation and the maintenance of elaborate military R&D laboratories acquired particular importance. Taking account of a volatile international situation punctured by violence, in conditions of shifting power relations, development of new generations of sophisticated weapon systems with a foresight far into the future became crucial. New weapon systems on the drawing table became of greater interest than available, often outmoded, weapon systems. A shift in military thinking has taken place from the emphasis on deployed to rapidly producible and deployable new, more effective, weapon systems. Armaments tend thus to concentrate rather on the development of new designs and test models, postponing their production until moments of acute crisis, when these weapons would actually be needed. Contingency future oriented military planning became closely linked to the work of weapon laboratories and military R&D.

1. Impact on the Arms Race

One of the first to draw attention to the effects of military research and development was President Eisenhower. In his widely quoted 1961 farewell address he pointed to the "sweeping changes in our industrial-military posture" caused by "the technological revolution during recent decades." Eisenhower stressed:

In this revolution, research has become central; it also becomes more formalized, complex and costly. A steadily increasing share is conducted for, by, or at the direction of, the federal government. Today, the solitary inventor, tinkering in his shop, has been overshadowed by task forces of scientists in laboratories and testing fields. In the same fashion, the free university, historically the fountainhead of free ideas and scientific discovery, has experienced a revolution in the conduct of research. Partly because of huge costs involved, a government contract becomes virtually a substitute for intellectual curiosity. For every old blackboard there are now hundreds of new electronic computers.

The prospect of domination of the nation's scholars by federal employment, project allocations, and the power of money is ever present—and is gravely to be regarded.

Yet, in holding scientific research and discovery in respect, as we should, we must also be alert to the equal and opposite danger that public policy could itself become the captive of a scientific-technological elite. (*Reproduced in Air Force Magazine* October 1983)

Military research and development (R&D) commands enormous human and material resources. Reliable estimates suggest that military R&D of the major powers—which accounts for about 80-90 percent of global R&D—consumes 10-15 percent of their military expenditure. Though there was a decline in military R&D in the post-Cold War period, particularly in Russia because of economic reversion, world military R&D expenditures, according to *SIPRI Yearbook 1996*, amounted to US dollars 55-60 billion, of which dol. 39 billion was accounted for the United States, and dol. 50 billion for NATO. Among major investors in military R&D were also China, India, Japan and South Korea.

Military R&D also uses enormous human resources. According to the *UNESCO Statistical Yearbook 1988*, in 1980, on a global scale, 3,756,100 scientists and engineers were employed in scientific laboratories.

Assuming, following general assessments, that a quarter of this labor force was working for the military sector, we arrive at a figure of about one million highly qualified scientists and engineers that at the end of the Cold War were employed by military R&D. This in itself must have a dramatic effect on the arms race.

But sheer numbers, even if determinative, may not tell the whole story. More important are the structural features, the goal resoluteness, and the laws of operation of military R&D.

Military R&D is a close-knit undertaking, science-based and mission-oriented, which aims to maximize the race in military technology. Though a giant empire, it is ingeniously structured to enhance the pursuit of the highest achievements in modern military technology.

A most important feature of military R&D is the long lead times required for the invention, conceptualization, recurrent model and prototype production, feasibility studies, repeated testing, development, improvement, and production of new weapon systems. The average gestation period is 10-15 years, with increment innovation and modernization extending this even further. Such long lead times infuse constancy and continuity into the arms race. Military R&D serves to project the arms race far into the future. It is a futuristic enterprise in the sense that existing weapon systems are assumed to be obsolete, and exotic future weapons are perceived as the ultimate reality. Weapons on the drawing table of military R&D today, will predetermine military capabilities and shape military-political horizons for years to come.

Compounding the effects of long R&D cycles is the operational routine in military R&D: to follow up any achievements in weapon development with further quests for weapon improvement and refinement—the so-called "follow-on imperative." This relates especially to the interaction between offense and defense. Military R&D proceeds as a matter of compulsion to complement any new offensive device with counter-devices in defense, and vice versa, on the assumption that the adversary has had similar achievements or may even be ahead. This sets into motion a spiral of R&D efforts in offense and defense. Weapon improvement and modernization, as well as the pursuit for new generations of weapon systems, are ceaseless endeavors. In combination with the long R&D lead times, the follow-on imperative adds permanency to the armaments effort. The arms race acquires stability and buoyancy.

Moreover, a sacrosanct rule in military R&D is worst-case analysis and planning. Lacking precise information on the achievements of the adversary, military R&D presumes the worst, as a matter of conservative prudence. It values the assets, capabilities, and performance of the opponent much higher than an unprejudiced examination of evidence would suggest, at the same time undervaluing its own accomplishments. Worst-case analysis is subjective and arbitrary in nature. It is fueled both by excessive secrecy surrounding military R&D and by vague intelligence data which are not trusted. Eventually, judgments are made, not on the basis of available information about the achievements of the adversary, but on the basis of one's own accomplishments which are also credited to the opponent. These then serve to impel the competition. Military R&D ends up racing against its own achievements.

Worst-case analysis has a critical attitudinal aspect: it instills the mind of military planners to excess. In conditions of complex military technology and diverse force structures of the opposed military camps, worst-case postures create a cognitive asymmetry, distorting the very perception of the relation of forces. It then acts to confound strategic calculations. Facts and myths on capabilities and intentions of the adversary are mixed up and become difficult to disentangle. The outcome is an intensification of the arms race (see *Arms Race, Dynamics of*).

All the above features and operational imperatives of military R&D intertwine, reinforcing each other. They combine to produce a forceful inner thrust to the armaments drive.

2. Impact on Development

The impact of military R&D on society is not limited to its effects on the arms race. Other, less visible but no less important effects can be found, especially in the field of development, in the corruption and perversion of science, in the distortion of cultural-ethical values, and in the general malfunction of society.

Today's global R&D budget, military and civilian, is largely dominated by investments in military research. Military R&D spendings alone exceed the global financial resources devoted to R&D on health, energy, agriculture, and pollution control. Military R&D is the most massive and concentrated scientific-engineering endeavor within the entire global R&D framework.

Military R&D is not confined to one specific domain. It has expanded into almost all fields of scientific inquiry, both natural and social sciences, from nuclear energy, electronics, aerodynamics, chemistry, information technology, and automation, to behavioral and medical sciences. The aim is to master warfare in all environments and all possible spheres of human engagement. As a corollary, military R&D acquired a commanding position in the structure and operation of all R&D, including civilian domains. In the process, the general R&D effort is becoming corrupted by the pervasive impact of military R&D. On the one hand, civilian R&D is being crippled by the maldistribution of human and material resources (see *Economics of Disarmament and Conversion*). On the other hand, it is exposed to constant pressures from military R&D. Military R&D is inherently antithetic to purposes of development. It is a distinctly mission-oriented branch of science and technology, striving for the most effective application of scientific and engineering achievements to advance the art of organized violence and destruction. True, some spinoff has been noted in civilian domains, especially in dual use technologies such as computer sciences, semi-conductor devices and electronics (and this is often used to justify investments in military R&D). But military R&D also draws heavily on exploits of the civilian economy, variedly called spin-on or spin-in features. Yet spin-offs from military R&D are as a rule in no proportion to the magnitude of investments.

All the above aspects affect both developed and developing societies. But those who are already most deprived suffer most. First, the maldistribution of resources in global R&D has extreme proportions in relation to developing countries. According to the *UNESCO Statistical Yearbook 1988*, only 11 percent of world scientist and engineers engaged in R&D were to be found in developing countries.

Second, military R&D is inherently geared to the requirements of rich industrial countries, reaching out as it does for the highest technology. It is attuned to technological, capital-intensive, and labor-saving production. Thus, military R&D is alien and adverse to intermediate and appropriate technology most felt lacking in developing countries. It does not respond to the true needs of the populations in developing countries, their level of education, cultural habits, or socioeconomic conditions.

Third, when introduced in developing countries, military R&D diverts precious intellectual and material resources from real science and technology needs. Instead, it sets skewed priorities which distort and hamper genuine developmental efforts. Strategically emplaced in the core of R&D, military R&D saps society of its developmental vitality. This is also perceptible in industrial societies where emphasis on military R&D has a determined effect on general productivity and growth.

Fourth, interposed in developing countries, military R&D acts to reinforce relations of dependence on industrial metropolises and major powers. It becomes part and parcel of the dominance-dependence structure in international relations. Developing countries can hardly compete with the pace of military technological advances of the major powers. Even if they acquire an initial foothold in autonomous arms production, their dependence on the flow of increasingly sophisticated military technology tends to accrue.

Cumulatively, military R&D has a pernicious impact on development. Its properties are geared to militarization of society and submission to political-military pressures from the international environment. All the phenomena related to the impact of military R&D attest to a malaise in science and society of wide consequences. No single sphere of human activity seems today untouched by this malaise: the interlocking effects in so many domains of our daily life, present and future, serve to sap the developmental vitality of society.

See also: *Military-industrial Complex, Disarmament and Development; Militarism and Militarization*

Bibliography

Acland-Hood M 1984 Statistics on military research and development expenditure. *World Armaments and Disarmament, SIPRI Yearbook 1984*. Taylor and Francis, London

Arnett E 1966 Military Research and Development. *SIPRI Yearbook 1996*

Brooks H I 975 The military innovation system and the qualitative arms race. *Daedalus* 104(3)

Brown R 1982 R&D for a sustainable society. *Am. Sci.* 70(1)

Feld B et al., (eds.) 1971 *Impact of New Technologies on the Arms Race: A Pugwash Monograph*. MIT Press, Cambridge, Massachusetts

Forsberg R 1972 *Resources Devoted to Military Research and Development*. Stockholm International Peace Research Institute (SIPRI), Stockholm

Long F A, Reppy J (eds.) 1980 *The Genesis of New Weapons: Decision Making for Military R&D*. Pergamon, New York

Melman 5 1975 Twelve propositions on productivity and the war economy. *Armed Forces and Society* 1(4)

Norman C 1981 *The God That Limps: Science and Technology in the Eighties*. Norton, New York

Rotblat J (ed.) 1982 *Scientists, the Arms Race and Disarmament: A UNESCO/Pugwash Symposium*. Taylor and Francis, London

Thee M (ed.) 1978 Military research and development: The driving force behind armaments. *Bulletin of Peace Proposals* 9(1)

Thee M 1990 Science and Technology: Between Civilian and Military Research and Development. United Nations

Institute for Development Research, Geneva

Thee M 1991 *Whatever happened to the Peace Dividend? The Post-Cold War Armaments Momentum.* Spokesman for European Labour Forum, Nottingham

Thee M 1992 The post-cold war technological armaments Spiral. *Peace Research* 24(1)

United Nations 1982 *Study on the Relationship between Disarmament and Development. Report of the Secretary-General.* United Nations, New York

MAREK THEE

Military Restructuring and Conversion

The armed forces are being restructured almost everywhere, albeit neither along the same dimension nor in the same direction, and partly for different reasons.

(a) In Western Europe and the United States, the end of the Cold War and the disappearance of the enemy has left the military establishments effectively without a *raison d'être*. Their main mission is no longer national defence, but various forms of peace support operations.

(b) In the former Eastern Europe, the armed forces are being reorganized for national defence and prepared for integration with NATO.

(c) In the former Soviet Union, the previously perceived need for a defence against the West has largely been replaced with a need to hold the country together, i.e., to defeat secessionist attempts in Russia's 'near abroad.' The other states of the former Soviet Union have similar problems, in addition to that of fielding a national defence against Russia as well.

(d) In the Middle East, the general level of militarization remains high, but has fallen slightly *inter alia* because of the ongoing peace process (see *Militarism and Militarization*).

(e) In the Persian Gulf region, changes have been dramatic. Iran is still rebuilding its society and armed forces after the Iran-Iraq War, but remains ostracized, hence, is purchasing weapons from odd sources. Iraq is under the United Nations 'administration' but with a large part of its military strength intact after its defeat in the 1991 Gulf War. The members of the GCC (Gulf Cooperation Council) are engaged in a massive arms build-up that may alter the regional balance of power.

(f) In Southeast Asia and Indochina, the guerrilla struggles that previously determined military needs have largely come to an end, leading to a restructuring of the armed forces to conventional military defence against external threats, yet without identifying the possible sources of such threats. As a result, most countries are engaged in an arms build-up, yet without any clear strategic orientation.

(g) China may be aiming for an enhanced power projection capability that could underpin a role as a regional hegemon in East Asia. Even though it has numerically reduced its armed forces over the last decade, their quality is improving significantly because of technological modernization.

(h) In Africa, South Africa is reorganizing its armed forces from being instruments of the apartheid regime, directed against the black majority as well as neighbouring states, toward a defence of the nation as a whole. Most of the rest of Southern Africa is only slowly recovering from decades-long civil wars, with armed forces that are in a very poor shape.

1. Disarmament

The general trend in world military expenditures has been downwards since 1987, yet seems to have reached a plateau since around 1992. It should also be kept in mind that the previous level was exceptionally high, hence, a certain build-down was almost inevitable. Global military expenditures are thus far from low, only somewhat lower than a decade ago: 840 billion constant 1994 USD in 1994 compared with the all-time peak of 1.3 trillion in 1987 (ACDA 1995). There are several reasons for the build-down:

Above all, the threat has disappeared that provided the rationale for the very high military spending in the North throughout the Cold War.

Furthermore, the previous deadlock in arms control negotiations was broken in the late 1980s, and the last ten years have seen a number of agreements which differ from their predecessors in several respects: They are no longer merely proscribing what neither side intended to do anyhow, but banning or regulating military activities that have actually been planned for, sometimes even implemented. Furthermore, arms control is no longer merely placing ceilings on deployments but entails reductions of weapons and armed forces, sometimes even major ones (see *Disarmament and Development*).

Even though global military expenditures have declined, there are exceptions to this trend: both Southeast Asia and the Persian Gulf region have seen rising defence expenditures through the 1990s, as has China. On the other hand, because of the collapse of the former Warsaw Pact and Soviet Union, the West's total share of global military spending has risen: the US share is thus 34 percent, and that of NATO as a whole is 56 percent (ACDA 1995).

In addition to such quantitative changes, there have also been rather dramatic qualitative changes in the world's military order, stemming from several sources: Technological developments, the appearance of new military missions, the adoption of new strategic doctrines, and the adaptation to changing social and demographic patterns.

2. New Forms of War and New Military Missions

Some authors have argued that major international war has become obsolete, either as a result of a learning process, or because of the global spread of democracy and the market economy that make states less war-prone (Mueller 1989; Brown & et al. 1996).

First of all, however, this assessment needs to be qualified: While international war may be obsolete in the 'zone of peace' (North America, Western Europe, Japan, Oceania), it remains an option taken seriously beyond its confines, i.e., in the 'zone of turmoil.' War between states at least remains a possibility in the Middle East, the Persian Gulf region, South Asia, East Asia (e.g., the Korean Peninsula), and on the periphery of Europe: (e.g., between Greece and Turkey and between the various successor states to former Yugoslavia and the former Soviet Union) (Singer & Wildawsky 1993).

Secondly, the receding frequency of international war is not tantamount to the disappearance of war as a social phenomenon. The predominant form of armed struggle may simply have become intra-state war, for instance, stemming from ethnic tensions. Such conflicts may either assume the form of 'traditional civil' wars or revert to 'chaos,' featuring struggling clans, gangs and other groupings (Van Creveld 1991; Snow 1996) (see *Civil Wars: Dynamics and Consequences of*).

While national defence thus remains a relevant mission for the armed forces in parts of the 'zone of tur-

moil,' it has largely become redundant in the zone of peace. Neither the states in North America nor Western Europe face major threats to their sovereignty or territorial integrity that require a national defence. In its place has come a wide and diverse panoply of military missions, among which the following stand out: Collective security missions, humanitarian intervention and various 'Operations Other Than War.'

3. Collective Security and Humanitarian Intervention

Collective security implies that the rest of the world's states commit themselves to come to the assistance of whichever state is being attacked. This was envisioned under Chapter VII in the United Nations Charter (see *United Nations Charter*), where Article 42 mentions the need to 'take such action by air, sea, or land forces as may be necessary to maintain or restore international peace and security.' During the Cold War the UN was prevented from functioning as envisioned by the bipolar division of the world, which was reflected in the composition of the UN Security Council that alone had the power to decide on 'Article 42 operations.' Whatever operations might have been called for were blocked by either a Soviet or an American veto, with one partial exception: the Korean War (1950-53), where US and other forces fought on behalf of the United Nations.

The end of the Cold War removed this constraint, and it was immediately followed by an almost classical instance of collective security: Iraq's conquest of Kuwait, to which the United Nations responded by, first, imposing sanctions on the aggressor (as envisioned in Article 41 of the Charter) and secondly, by asking member states (the US and others) to evict the aggressor by force, as happened through Operation Desert Storm in 1991. This achievement spurred a renewed academic and political interest in collective security and its requirements (Weiss 1993; Downs 1994) (see *Collective Security and Collective Self-defense*). However, as there has been no new international war since the defeat of Iraq, it is impossible to tell whether collective security would have worked or not.

The war against Iraq was also followed by an instance of what has been called 'humanitarian intervention,' when the allies established 'safe havens' in northern and southern Iraq for Kurdish and Shi'ite insurgents that were being bombarded by Iraqi forces. Subsequent humanitarian interventions have been undertaken in Somalia (to end the clan war) and Haiti (to restore democracy). Some observers believe that these are indications of a trend towards increasingly frequent humanitarian interventions, i.e., military interventions in defence of human rights, yet in infringement of the principle of state sovereignty and non-interference in other states' internal affairs. Others disagree, pointing to the fact that, significantly, none of the interventions mentioned were labelled 'humanitarian,' but all were legitimized with reference to 'international security,' probably because of the continuing strength of the non-interference norm (Rodley 1992) (see *Nonintervention and Noninterference*).

Both collective security and humanitarian intervention require that the UN has at its disposal certain military capabilities, either in the form of UN troops or national forces that are assigned to UN operations, either on an *ad hoc* basis or in the form of 'earmarking.' Such forces should possess sufficient (sometimes quite substantial) fighting power, as they would be assigned to actual combat duties (see *Intervention*). Furthermore, because both types of operations may, in principle at least, be called for anywhere in the world, long-range power projection capabilities are required, both with regard to weapons, logistics (sea or airlift) and command, control, communications and intelligence systems. At present, only the great powers (and above all the United States) possess such capabilities.

4. Peace Support Operations

Other military missions conducted under the UN's auspices are less demanding in these respects, such as those that fall under Chapter VI of the Charter, even though they are not explicitly mentioned there.

During the Cold War, the UN launched several peacekeeping missions, typically in the form of an interposition of UN troops ('blue helmets') between two former warring parties after (and as a means of monitoring) a cease fire. After the Cold War, both the number and the typical scale of peacekeeping operations have risen steeply. Not only are they now sometimes initiated before a ceasefire, i.e., as 'peace enforcement' operations, or before a war actually breaks out, i.e., in the form of preventive deployment (sometimes with the consent of only one side). In most cases they are also employed to bring an end to intra-state rather than international armed conflicts, which is often very demanding (Ratner 1995).

Such 'peace operations' (peacekeeping and peace enforcement) are not particularly demanding in terms of equipment, where the need is mostly surveillance aircraft, infantry weapons and transport systems (see *Peacekeeping Forces*). However, they are very demanding in terms of military personnel, where special qualities are called for: not so much soldierly (i.e., combat) skills as non-military skills in mediation, conflict prevention and resolution. Blue helmets are not supposed to take sides but to remain impartial, which may be extremely difficult, especially when they are deployed before a ceasefire. While the great powers tend to be best suited for collective security and humanitarian intervention, small states are often better at the tasks involved with peace operations, in which they also tend to have a longer experience.

5. Military Doctrines and Strategies

Partly as a reflection of the emergence of such new missions and the receding saliency of old ones, military doctrines and strategies are also being amended around the world. Changes point in many different directions, however, generalizations are impossible.

(a) Some states have replaced offensive with more defensive military doctrines, albeit for different reasons. For instance, South Africa has done so as a way of making a 'clean break' with its apartheid past and of building peaceful relations with its neighbours; and Taiwan has done so in belated recognition of the infeasibility of a forceful conquest of mainland China and a reorientation towards a gradual and peaceful reunification strategy.

(b) Other states seem to be moving in a more offensive direction. The United States has thus adopted a doctrine calling for the ability to wage and prevail in two 'major regional conflicts' nearly simultaneously, and in an offensive mode (Davis 1994); Russia has abandoned its former no-first-use doctrine for nuclear weapons and proclaimed vital interests in its 'near abroads;' China has amended its former 'people's war, doctrine in favour of an 'active defence' (or 'people's war' under modern conditions) and may be heading in the direction of enhanced power projection capabilities in support of territorial claims in East Asia and a possible hegemonic role; and Japan may be gradually shedding its post-war constraints on military activities, etc.

Besides the divergence of views on the relative merits of offensive and defensive military doctrines, there is also a divergence of views about how to prioritize the different arms of service (army, navy, air force, special forces), and about the trade-offs between quality and quantity: Are large, but primitively equipped forces preferable to smaller but better armed forces, or vice versa?

6. Defence Reforms

The new missions described above have obvious implications for military requirements, both in terms of manpower and equipment.

The number of soldiers worldwide is coming down. Compared to 28.7 million in 1988, the number for 1994 was a 'mere' 23.4 million (ACDA 1995). However, this downward trend is almost completely confined to the developed countries, i.e., the 'zone of peace.' The emerging picture is thus one of much smaller, but increasingly well-equipped soldiers from the developed world, as opposed to very numerous, but poorly and primitively equipped soldiers from the developing world.

As a reflection of the aforementioned trend towards intra-state wars, the armed forces in large parts of the developing world (especially in Africa) increasingly consist of irregulars: militias, child soldiers, mercenaries and sheer bandits. Because of the declining requirement for mass armies, conscription is on its way out in the developed world, where it is either being completely abolished or partially replaced by other personnel structures. An additional reason for this trend is that it makes less sense to conscript a nation's youth for military missions that have little if anything to do with national security (Burk 1994).

The typical equipment of soldiers in the developing world is only changing little: the AK-47 assault rifle remains the typical weapon of the insurgent as well as of other combatants in intra-state wars. Nations with more 'conventional' defence requirements tend to purchase the same type of armaments as developed states (tanks, artillery, armoured personnel carriers, combat aircraft, warships, etc.)—only with a slightly lower degree of sophistication and usually in smaller numbers. Because of larger stretches of water many Third World countries need to patrol as a result of the Law of the Sea, many states have also felt the need to move from 'brown' to 'green water' navies with a longer reach and staying power. However, it is still only the very great powers in the developed world (the United States and Britain) that can afford genuine 'blue water' navies.

The trend towards nuclear proliferation seems to have been stopped, or even reversed. Several countries have abandoned their nuclear weapons development programmes (Argentina, Brazil and, less voluntarily, Iraq and North Korea), while South Africa has destroyed the nuclear weapons it had clandestinely built during the apartheid regime. The only serious proliferation risks thus appear to stem from Israel (that almost certainly has nuclear weapons), and India and Pakistan, which may also have them (see *Nuclear Strategy*). However, many countries in the Third World continue to field, or have acquired other alternative weapons of mass destruction (WMD), such as chemical or biological weapons. Furthermore, several have acquired medium-to-long range ballistic missiles that would be suitable means of delivery for such WMD.

In the developed world, the typical military equipment is changing quite radically, for several reasons:

(a) Nuclear weapons are being built down quite drastically, both because of arms control agreements and because of their diminished utility (as a result of the disappearence of the bloc division);

(b) major conventional weaponry in Europe has been drastically reduced as a result of the 1990 CFE (Conventional Armed Forces in Europe) Treaty;

(c) the new missions (peace support operations, for instance) generally require lighter equipment, but in many cases more demanding logistical structures for long-range power projection;

(d) military missions are increasingly multinational and entail actual combat (as opposed to the more passive deterrence functions during the Cold War), hence the need for standardization and interoperability;

(e) the opinion is gaining ground that something dramatic has happened in the field of military technology.

7. Revolution in Military Affairs?

The US has drawn the lesson from the victorious Gulf War (Cordesman & Wagner 1996) that its Air Land Battle doctrine was vindicated, and that its military technology stood the test of combat. Many observers have drawn the conclusion from this experience that the world is witnessing a fully-fledged 'Revolution in Military Affairs' (RMA), also labelled the Military-Technological Revolution (MTR). These theories are based on the following beliefs, which are probably myths, even though they certainly contain a grain of truth:

(a) that air power can be decisive, in the sense that

future wars may be fought almost entirely from the air;

(b) that information dominance may be decisive;

(c) that technological supremacy is decisive, hence 'the best weapons win;'

(d) that surgical precision is achievable, especially with air strikes, so that collateral damage can be minimized and wars waged in full conformity with just war criteria;

(e) that determined offensives, initiated by air strikes, can break through all defences.

To the extent that they believe in these presumed 'lessons', states will feel the need for a comprehensive replacement of old (presumably obsolete) equipments with new and state-of-the art ones.

8. Implications for the Arms Industries

The aforementioned general downward trend in the world's military expenditures obviously implies a shrinking global demand for weaponry, even though the restructuring of the armed forces and military establishments worldwide entails requirements for new types of weapons. The emerging new demand, however, is insufficient to make up for overall decline. The shrinking demand must, sooner or later, be reflected in a reduction of the global supply of armaments, i.e., in a contraction of the arms industries. This will have negative consequences for employment as well as, in many cases, for national balances of payment.

Faced with a receding domestic demand for their products, however, arms industries tend to defer a build-down of their production capacity by a search for other customers, i.e., they seek growing arms exports as a means of making up for declining domestic demand. Even though this is bound to be a futile quest in the long run (because of the, probably irreversable, declining global demand), it may be economically rational in the short or medium term, where it may be possible to acquire a larger share of the global arms market. It is thus only natural that the above changes in military missions and requirement have also affected the pattern of global arms transfers.

9. Arms Exports

Global arms transfers have changed in several

respects, both with regard to total volume and geographical distribution. First of all, the total volume has declined dramatically, from 83 billion constant (1994) USD in 1984 to a 'mere' 22 billion in 1994 (ACDA 1995).

Secondly, there has been a realignment among the suppliers, as one of the former main exporting countries has practically disappeared from the market, namely the then Soviet Union. Even though Russia in 1994-95 managed to recapture a significant share of the market (six percent), this was due almost entirely to its selling equipment held in stock that was either obsolete or which had to be disposed of as a result of arms control agreements. The United States has thus established itself as the unchallenged number one arms supplier, with a share of 56 percent. West European countries (the UK, Germany, France and others) count for another 26 percent, making the total western share of arms exports as high as 84 percent (ACDA 1995). This has been due, in no small measure, to the spreading belief in the above-mentioned 'Gulf war lessons,' which have also served to prevent Russia from reestablishing itself on the market, as the presumed implication is that Russian (Soviet) weapons perform poorly compared with American ones. Other arms exporting countries include countries such as China and North Korea, but they mainly provide weaponry to countries that are, for whatever reason, subjected to embargoes from the main suppliers.

Thirdly, there has been a significant change in the pattern of imports: Western Europe remains a major recipient of arms, partly because of the above-mentioned restructuring for new missions and partly because of an arms build-up in Greece and Turkey. While arms purchases in the Middle East have been declining slowly, those of the Persian Gulf Region have risen steeply. Finally, Southeast Asia has established itself as a booming market, both because of the high economic growth rates (that facilitate rising military expenditures) and because of a restructuring from anti-guerilla to conventional military missions.

10. Conversion

Aggressive marketing of arms for exports will, at best, postpone a contraction of one nation's arms industry at the expence of those of other countries. In the long run, the global arms industry will have to adjust to the falling demand, either by plant closures or by reorganization (Møller & Voronkov 1996; Renner 1992).

Some analysts recommend a *laissez faire* approach to the problem, similar to what is common for other sectors of the economy: Governments should simply reduce their military expenditures, using the savings to reduce national debt and/or lower taxes. While this will inevitably result in some unemployment in arms factories (and other military establishments), the beneficial effects of the savings will presumably stimulate the economy sufficiently to create plentiful new jobs—albeit perhaps in other sectors of the economy and/or other parts of the country in question. Others have recommended a conversion of the economy in general, and the arms industries in particular, with a view to minimize the negative effects of the adjustment. A useful distinction is that between macro and micro conversion (see *Economics of Disarmament and Conversion; Economics of Disarmament: Certain Premises*).

'Micro conversion' refers to the local or plant level, where the problem is finding alternative employment for both soldiers and other military employees and/or finding alternative production lines (and markets) for the arms industry, thereby salvaging employment for the workers. Generally, however, micro conversion is not only made all the more desirable, but also hampered by the high concentration of both military facilities and the arms industry which tend to cluster in localities with little alternative employment and, consequently, a high dependency on the military. A further obstacle to plant-level conversion of the arms industry is that it has often been kept isolated from the rest of the economy. Even in large corporations with a wide range of civilian production lines, arms production has usually been kept separate from the rest. In some cases, however, a diversification of production is possible, i.e., the introduction of civilian alongside the military production.

'Micro conversion' refers to a conversion of the arms industry or the entire economy (Brauer & Gissy 1997; Klein & al. 1995). The term may even refer to society as a whole that should change from a 'war footing' to a 'peace footing.' Viewed from this angle, 'conversion' may rather be a question of national policies to create new jobs (rather than preserving existing ones) and of preventing a major economic recession, rather than of salvaging particular industries or firms.

Seen from a macro perspective, it may also be of political security importance to maintain the ability to arm the nation's military, hence of preserving a national arms production base (Davis 1994). Even though an attack may be regarded as highly unlikely in the short or medium term, it may still be held to be conceivable in the longer term, hence there may be a perceived need to be prepared for such an eventuali-

ty. This is, in fact, one of the most common arguments against a conversion, hence for the maintenance of the arms industry, with all the implications thereof, in terms of demands for new arms acquisitions and/or for furthering arms exports.

To the extent that one takes the notion of unpredictability seriously, it becomes important to be able to combine declining military expenditures and actual arms purchases with a maintenance of a production base that would permit a remobilization of the nation for war. Seen from this perspective, 'conversion' would tend to be synonymous with diversification, i.e., arms factories should increasingly produce civilian commodities, while preserving the ability to shift back to military production; research and development (perhaps including the production of prototypes) should be upgraded over actual production; and conversion should, as a matter of principle, be reversible i.e., allow for a 'conversion' back to military production.

See also: *Civil Wars: Dynamics and Consequences*

Bibliography

ACDA (Arms Control and Disarmament Agency) *World Military Expenditures and Arms Transfers.* Government Printing Office, annually, Washington, DC

Brauer J, Gissy W G (eds.) 1997 *Economics of Conflict and Peace.* Aldershot, Avebury

Brown M E, Lynn-Jones S, Miller S E (eds.) 1996 *Debating the Democratic Peace.* The MIT Press, Cambridge, MA

Burk J (ed.) 1994 *The Military in New Times. Adapting Armed Forces to a Turbulent World.* Westview Press, Boulder, CO

Cordesman A, Wagner A R 1996 *The Lessons of Modern War,* Vol. 4: *The Gulf War.* Westview, Boulder

Creveld M V 1991 *The Transformation of War.* The Free Press, New York

Davis P (ed.) 1994 *New Challenges for Defense Planning. Rethinking How Much is Enough.* RAND, Santa Monica

Downs G W (ed.) 1994 *Collective Security beyond the Cold War.* University of Michigan Press, Ann Arbor, Michigan

Klein L R, Lo F-C, McKibbin W J (eds.) 1995 *Arms Reduction. Economic Implications in the Post-Cold War Era.* United Nations University Press, Tokyo

Møller B, Voronkov L (eds.) 1996 *Defence Doctrines and Conversion.* Dartmouth, Aldershot

Mueller J 1989 *Retreat from Doomsday: The Obsolescence of Major War.* Basic Books, New York

Ratner S R 1995 *The New UN Peacekeeping. Building Peace in Lands of Conflict after the Cold War.* St. Martin's Press and Council of Foreign Relations, New York

Renner M 1992 *Economic Adjustments after the Cold War. Strategies for Conversion.* Dartmouth, Aldershot

Rodley N (ed.) 1992 *To Loose the Bands of Wickedness. International Intervention in Defence of Human Rights.* Brassey's Defence Publishers, London

Singer M, Wildawsky A 1993 *The Real World Order. Zones of Peace / Zones of Turmoil.* Chatham House Publishers, Chatham, NJ

SIPRI Yearbooks, Stockholm International Peace Research Institute, Stockholm, Oxford University Press, Oxford, annually

Snow D M 1996 *UnCivil Wars: International Security and the New Pattern of Internal War.* Lynne Rienner Publishers, Boulder, CO

Weiss T G (ed.) 1993 *Collective Security in a Changing World.* Lynne Rienner Publishers, Boulder & London

BJØRN MØLLER

Military-Industrial Complex

The phrase "military-industrial complex," coined by one of President Eisenhower's speech-writers, was first used by the President in his Farewell Address in January 1961. The speech attracted widespread attention at the time, and has subsequently led to extensive controversy and research.

"Military-industrial complex" refers to the collusive relationship which is alleged to exist between those industrialists involved in the production of military technology, and leading members of the military establishment. Together, this group is seen as having a vested interest in high levels of spending on defense, a degree of international tension, and a militarized approach to the problems of foreign policy. If left unchecked, the policy-making power of this special interest group would grow to the detriment of civilian authority, international security, and economic progress. Originally, the concept of the military-industrial complex was applied to the United States, but subsequently it has been used in relation to all the major military powers in the industrialized world.

Theories about the "military-industrial complex" have been closely associated with the patterns of arms production and procurement which characterized the period after the Second World War. In the 1980s and 1990s, however, a number of political changes, and economic and technological developments, have challenged the Cold War model of military-industrial activity. These developments pose new questions for theorists of the military-industrial complex and underline the extent to which it is necessary to locate such theories in historical context.

1. Eisenhower's Warning

In his Farewell Address, Eisenhower noted that until the Second World War there had been no permanent armaments industry in the United States; but reliance on "emergency improvization" was seen as too risky in the Cold War circumstances in which the United States had found itself. As a result, the President added: "We have been compelled to create a permanent armaments industry of vast proportions;" on top of this, there were three and a half million men and women directly engaged in the armed services. Then followed the most famous passage in the outgoing President's speech:

> Now this conjunction of an immense military establishment and a large arms industry is new in the American experience. The total influence—economic, political, even spiritual—is felt in every city, every State House, every office of the Federal Government . . . . Our toil, our resources and livelihood are all involved; so is the very structure of our society. In the councils of Government, we must guard against the acquisition of unwarranted influence, whether sought or unsought, by the military-industrial complex. The potential for the disastrous rise of misplaced power exists and will persist.

Later, in a press conference, Eisenhower said that he was not thinking so much of a willful abuse of power by military and industrial interests, but of "an almost insidious penetration of our own minds that the only thing this country is engaged in is weaponry and missiles—and I'll tell you we can't afford that." Eisenhower's warning reverberated through the nation, coming as it did from a famous old soldier who had close associates among the country's industrialists and who in the past had praised the contribution of industry to US security.

Eisenhower's warning had both historical and intellectual antecedents. Woodrow Wilson (see Nobel Peace Prize Laureates: *Woodrow Wilson*) was but one of the civilian leaders who, over the centuries, had raised the alarm against the possibility of undue military influence on government. Conceptually, the idea of the "military-industrial complex" was related to Harold Lasswell's "garrison state hypothesis," first published in 1941, and C. Wright Mills's *Power Elite*, first published in 1956. Lasswell had warned of the way in which the "specialists in violence," under the pressure of modern technical imperatives and international tension, were coming to dominate key points in national decision-making structures, while Mills conceived a homogenous and firmly entrenched "power elite"—comprising the leaders of the major national institutions—which was characterized by rising military influence and policies resulting in an escalating arms race.

Earlier, various liberal and socialist analyses of the causes of war had ascribed great significance to the insidious role of special interest groups, and particularly those involved in financing and producing the equipment for war. These old radical scapegoats were the infamous "arms traffikers," "merchants of death," and "war profiteers" who were said to have perverted national interests for their own ends. According to this "devil theory" the naturally peace-loving peoples of the world have been pushed into conflict and poverty by governments under the influence of evil and conspiratorial special interests. The modern concept of the military-industrial complex is an extension of these ideas, and so it was not surprising that it was readily embraced by radical critics of US external behavior.

While exaggerated emphasis has been given to the idea both by those who favor it as a "devil theory" explanation of international politics, and those of a Marxist persuasion who see the phenomenon as systemic in capitalist society, the concept is not without significance. A sufficient body of empirical research has now built up both to verify the concept as a term of analysis and to expose it as a cause for political concern.

2. Military-Industrial Activity after the Second World War

The great turning point in the relationship between government, industry, and the military establishment in the United States, as Eisenhower pointed out, was the Second World War. The generally uneasy relationship which had existed between these bodies became transformed into what has been seen as a symbiotic one. Those involved—scientists and engineers, managers and financiers, politicians and the armed forces—recognized that modern military power demanded the maintenance of very close relations. The traditional images which these groups had of each other changed, as the "arsenal of democracy" became a "permanent war economy."

But along with the growth of the military-industrial might to meet the problems of the Cold War (see *Cold War*) situation, there also occurred the growth

of vested interests, challenges to civilian authority, and threats to rational defense decision-making. And researchers on the military-industrial complex soon noted that the problem was wider than the alleged collusion between the military establishment and the defense industrialists whose power and status, and in the latter case profits, were all threatened by the prospect of peace breaking out. The influence of the military-industrial complex was also seen in the outlook, interests, and behavior of certain politicians, universities, high-level researchers, labor unions, and industries and services in local communities. In one way or another, all these groups developed stakes in the military-industrial complex; directly or indirectly they all received benefits from the vast amounts of money being disgorged by the Department of Defense. Some companies came to depend heavily or even exclusively on defense contracts; retired officers were employed to solicit contracts and advise on weapon development; governments became dependent on certain key defense contractors, the electorates of some districts came to be comprised of large numbers of people involved in military-related industries; the economics of some regions became significantly dependent on the continuation of armaments manufacture; and much academic research, both in the social and natural sciences, was diverted down profitable military channels.

In the Cold War years defense was good business. Big profits were to be made and vested interests were pursued. The widespread involvement in defense-related activities undoubtedly made it easy for US politicians to generate support for huge military programs to counter the "communist threat." Other consequences occurred in the economic and technical fields. Here it has been argued that while huge military programs did provide employment, profits, and growth in the aftermath of the Second World War, the long-term results have been deleterious for the US economy. Complaints against the big defense industries have included their cost-overruns, the delays in the production of weapons, the encouragement of technical stagnation and unemployment in other sectors of the economy, the stimulus given to inflation by the expansion of jobs in the military sector, and the increasing tendency to produce unreliable and overcomplex weapons systems.

While recognizing the danger of simply transposing a concept derived from one political system onto that of another, critics have charged that the defense sector in the former Soviet Union was also characterized by congeries of interests committed to heavy defense outlays and with a stake in a degree of international tension. Furthermore, both the defense industries and the military establishment in the former Soviet Union were gigantic and powerful, and the contacts between them regular and close. But did this add up to a military-industrial complex? Soviet propaganda denied it, and there was little or no evidence to prove that successive Soviet leaders were the creatures of the defense industry-military establishment nexus. Historically, the Soviet Ministry of Defense was notably underrepresented in the Politburo, and the military were periodically on the losing end of struggles with a totalitarian party anxious to subordinate all professional bodies. In the former Soviet Union ultimate decision-making power was located in the supreme party body, the Politburo. Ever since 1917 there was a fear within the Communist Party of "Bonapartism," the rise of undue military influence.

Such arguments as those just advanced must be seen, however, in relation to the widespread view that the former Soviet Union, as a whole, was a "militarized" society. From the outset the state was invariably committed to overinsurance in the military field, and Party-military consultation was usually close and regular at the highest levels of decision-making. On crucial issues such as arms control, the strategic build-up, and European security, Soviet leaders sought regular military advice; and by the 1960s, this tendency was encouraged by the fact that policy-making in the former Soviet Union was more bureaucratic and consultative than under Stalin. Informal relationships also developed between the Party and military hierarchies. Of primary importance was the role of the military as one of that trinity of organizations, together with the Party apparatus and the Committee of State Security (KGB), which every new Soviet leader sought to win over.

During the Soviet era, the Party was preoccupied with security and the need to have military backing for its policies; this relationship was seen as crucial because of the high military content of key areas of foreign policy. To a degree, therefore, the Party was both reliant on and susceptible to military advice. And both required the products of the defense industries. There was, therefore, a vital area of interdependence between the political, military, and heavy industrial leaders, and research has shown that a discrete military-industrial special interest group took consistent positions on particular issues, and especially those concerning resource allocation. In practice, the satisfying of military requirements was not something which Soviet leaders found difficult, for the Soviet "civilian" leadership was probably the most security conscious in the industrialized world.

Thus the "civilian/military" distinction was so ambiguous in the former Soviet Union that it is unprofitable to dwell too long on trying to determine the precise extent of "military" influence. Equally, the boundary between the military-industrial complex and the rest of Soviet society was not a sharp one. Indeed, just as Soviet civilian leaders held militarized attitudes, so in some senses the Soviet state as a whole could be regarded as a military-industrial complex.

3. Recent Trends in Military-Industrial Activity

In the 1980s and 1990s, a number of new developments have challenged the ways in which analysts conceptualize and investigate the defense sector. In particular, the increasing economic and technological pressures affecting the defense industries, and the decline in demand for armaments which followed the end of the Cold War, have challenged the distinctive status and familiar national frameworks which formerly characterized military-industrial activity. These developments may in turn have important implications for theories about the military-industrial complex. Most importantly, recent trends suggest a shift away from the character of the defense economies of the US and the former Soviet Union during the Cold War period and thus lend support to the view that it is necessary to locate theories about the "military-industrial complex" in historical context.

In the industrialized world, in the period since 1945, the defense sector came to constitute a key economic asset due to its role as a "technology driver" for the economy as a whole. Thus for economic, as well as security reasons, the defense sector acquired a "special status" protected from the commercial practices which characterized the civil sector and excluded from international trade agreements. Significantly, it is this protected "special status" enjoyed by the defense sector which has served as the basis for theories of the "military-industrial complex."

Since the 1980s, however, a number of commentators have noted that the defense sector has been undergoing a process of "normalization" or "secularization" whereby the practices of defense industries move closer to those of the civil economy. Firstly, arms production has become subject to a process of internationalization where the trend towards participation in transnational joint ventures has modified the "national champion" status of arms producing firms. Secondly, a number of governments have sought to liberalize defense markets by attempting to introduce market principles and commercial practices to the defense sector. Finally, the traditional relationship between defense and civil technologies has been undergoing significant change in response to new developments in civil technology. These trends have all served to reduce the distinctiveness of the defense sector and moved its practices closer to those of the civil economy.

Moreover, in the 1990s, the decline in demand for armaments which accompanied the end of the Cold War has impacted upon military-industrial interests in both the US and the former Soviet Union. Defense cuts in the US have led to mergers and acquisitions among leading arms producers and substantial cuts in production capacity and employment. Because these developments have been driven by supply-side initiatives and have not led to reduced profits, the restructuring process has not generated much opposition from vested interests. Not surprisingly, this transition process has been smoother in the US than in the former Soviet Union.

Key questions regarding the role of military-industrial activity have yet to be resolved in the "new Russia," as is the case in other states traditionally dependent on heavy arms sales. For example, for maximizing employment prospects and export potential. The main change has involved a reduction in military-industrial capacity. Data presented by Sköns and Gill, for example, suggest that between 1991 and 1995 military output fell to one-sixth of its level in 1991. In addition to this, procurement reforms have sought to replace the former principles of central planning in the defense sector with privatization.

It could be argued that the level of opposition to these policies, and their limited results, suggests support for theorists' claims about the entrenched interests of the military-industrial complex. The influence of military-industrial interests remains an important factor in post-Soviet politics. In addition, the impact of institutional reform has been constrained by the continuing influence of former Soviet officials. Although powerful agencies such as the Military-Industrial Commission and Gosplan have been replaced by new departments under the Russian Ministry of Industry, the new bodies continue to be staffed by officials from the old regime.

Moreover, Izyumov records coalitions of resistance to the reforms which are reminiscent of early theories about the military-industrial complex. For example, in 1991, a coalition of defense industry leaders, bureaucrats, members of the military, and sympathetic politicians aligned themselves in opposition to the "treason" of the government's conversion program. It was among these conservative elements

that support was found for the attempted *coup d'état* against Yeltsin in August 1991. According to Izyumov, "four out of the eight members of the short-lived junta were representatives of the military-industrial complex."

It is significant that other elements in the military-industrial complex have not resisted the reforms. Izyumov argues that the "more liberal, better educated and more insightful members of military industrial management" were less hostile to the reform program. More importantly, opposition to the conversion program can be explained by looking at defects in the policy itself. Izyumov suggests that the reforms neglected to address the effects of conversion on professionals in the defense industry who had been accustomed during previous years to being lauded as contributors to their country's welfare. Opposition to policy change is thus not necessarily evidence of a "military-industrial complex."

4. The Significance of the MIC

During the Cold War, the concept of the military-industrial complex attracted attention from academic researchers, radical critics of the global military order, peace movements, and from those searching for scapegoats for the ills of the Cold War international situation. To its advocates, the military-industrial complex offered a convenient monocausal explanation for the superpower arms race, international tension, and big defense outlays. But the extreme formulation of the concept needs to be set in a wider perspective. It can explain some of the pressures which exacerbate arms races and international tension, but it is far from being the whole story.

As an explanation of the traditionally mistrustful state of international politics, the extreme conspiratorial interpretation of the military-industrial complex overplays the vested interests which some groups might have in international tension. Several alternative considerations and pieces of evidence need to be advanced. First, theories of the "military-industrial complex" are not in themselves an explanation for either the bipolar situation which characterized the Cold War or international conflict more generally. Given the historical legacy of Soviet-American relations before the Second World War, it was not a radical surprise that hostile imaging, competitive arms building, action-reaction behavior, and confrontation in all arenas came to the fore once the common cause of defeating Hitler had been achieved. The aberration in US-Soviet relations was the wartime alliance, not the Cold War. Thus even those on both sides without a stake in big defense recognized that an "objective" threat existed, which had to be countered. Second, during the Cold War, the dynamics of the US-Soviet arms race reflected the problem of continuous technological innovation in the weapons field. The imperatives of highly technical military confrontations place heavy demands on readiness, the continuous modernization of equipment, and the possession of "state of the art" technology; as weapons readily become obsolete there is a fear of significant military breakthroughs by an adversary. There is therefore a rational strategic-technical dynamic to the arms race (see *Arms Race, Dynamics of*). Third, it is easy to exaggerate the extent to which the military-industrial complex, or particular components of it, may become "out of control." The rate of increase in defense spending has not constantly risen, the procurement of some weapons has been checked, the practices of defense industries have been scrutinized, arms races have sometimes moderated as well as escalated, and détente has sometimes broken out.

In addition, there is little evidence that those who profit from war or international tension have either successfully instigated such outcomes or have had the ability to direct a state's foreign policy in such directions. Finally, the record shows that military establishments are not always as "hawkish" as their image when it comes to involvement in foreign conflicts or the advocacy of adventuristic foreign policies. It should be apparent that not all decisions in the field of defense policy are determined by a combination of the profit motive on the part of armaments manufacturers and the desire of military establishments for power and status. Arms races, superpower rivalry, economic stagnation, and international tension therefore have more complex causes than the alleged influence over policy of a complex of interests who profit, in one way or another, from big defense. Unless one simply believes in the concept of the military-industrial complex as an article of faith, it can be seen that the degree to which it is systemic, conspiratorial, the product of impersonal forces, or technologically determined, can be exaggerated. This is also true of the extent to which it is alleged to be out of control.

However, all this is not to say that the military-industrial complex has no role in shaping policies and attitudes. The phenomenon has been established empirically. There is a symbiotic relationship between defense industries and the military, a military-industrial complex did acquire momentum during the Cold War period, lobbying does go on, vested interests are pursued, the pace of weapons innovation is increased by the heavy dependence some firms have on defense contracts, and political influence is sought by special interest groups. To the extent the military-industrial complex exists, and represents illegitimate power, it is in the interests of rational civilian control of policy that it be curbed. It is in the interests of international peace and security, as well as domestic development that this be done; peace cannot be expected to flourish if, by a process of "insidious penetration," our thinking about foreign policy remains dominated by militarized notions, which give undue weight in policy-making to the details of the military inventories of nations, which emphasize threats but ignore reassurance in international relationships, and which are driven by the idea that there is an inevitable correlation between national military strength and national security. Military build-ups which add to one's own destructive power can increase the sense of insecurity in the minds of one's adversaries, and so do not necessarily enhance one's security in the long run.

Bibliography

Hislop D, Law A 1996 *Restructuring the Defense Industry After the Cold War*. University of Edinburgh Working Papers in Sociology No. 8, Edinburgh

Journal of International Affairs 26(1) 1972 (Issue devoted to The Military-Industrial Complex: USSR/USA)

Izyumov A 1993 The Soviet Union: Arms Control and Conversion-plan and Reality. In: Wulf H 1993 *Arms Industry Ltd*. Oxford University Press, Oxford

Lasswell H D 1941 The garrison state and the specialists on violence. *American Journal of Sociology* 47

Lens S 1970 *The Military-Industrial Complex*. Pilgrim Press, Philadelphia, Pennsylvania

Melman S 1974 *The Permanent War Economy*. Simon and Schuster, New York

Mills C W 1956 *The Power Elite*. Oxford University Press, London

Pilisuk M, Hayden T 1965 Is there a military-industrial complex which prevents peace? *J. Social Issues* 21 (3)

Rosen S 1973 *Testing the Theory of the Military-Industrial Complex*. Lexington Books, Lexington, Massachusetts

Sarkesian S C (ed.) 1972 *The Military-Industrial Complex: A Reassessment*. Sage, Beverly Hills, California

Sköns E, Gill B 1996 Arms Production. In: *SIPRI Yearbook 1996: Armaments, Disarmament and International Security*. SIPRI, Stockholm

KEN BOOTH; PAULINE EWAN

Monnet, Jean

Jean Monnet (1888-1979), French economist and statesman, was one of the leading figures in the movement for European integration which followed the Second World War. The son of a wealthy brandy distiller, Monnet received an excellent education and rose rapidly in the service of the French government. He developed an early interest in international affairs, representing his country in several international forums during and after the First World War. From 1919 to 1923 he served as deputy secretary general and as financial adviser to the League of Nations, the international organization which grew out of the longing for peace after the First World War. He soon became disillusioned by the League's ineffectiveness and left, spending the years until 1939 pursuing an international business career with great success.

Monnet returned to the French government in 1939, shortly before the outbreak of the Second World War. His work in the early years of war centered on strengthening the ability of France and Britain, two hard-pressed allies, to coordinate their political and economic efforts intelligently. He is credited with having been the driving force behind Winston Churchill's bold but abortive all for common Anglo-French citizenship in the dark days of the spring of 1940.

Monnet spent most of the war after the fall of France in the United States, as a member of the British Supply Council. There he strongly urged the Americans to enter the war against Hitler, and played an important role in convincing the American government to consider what would be necessary, economically, if America did in fact enter the war. America's relatively advanced level of economic planning for war at the time when the Japanese attack on Pearl Harbor suddenly thrust it into the conflict owed much to Monnet's efforts.

Though Monnet did not get along well with Free French leader Charles de Gaulle, who was suspicious of his broad international outlook, Monnet's expertise won him a position as minister of commerce in the provisional government which de Gaulle formed as France was liberated from the Nazis in 1944. Monnet remained in government service after the end of the war, going on to play a leading role in France's dramatic postwar economic recovery. A skilled and enthusiastic advocate of economic development following a rational plan, Monnet is regarded as the father of France's highly successful planning efforts in the late 1940s and 1950s. He held the post of commissioner general for planning in the French government from 1947 to 1955.

Having experienced two hideously destructive European wars, Monnet was determined to do whatever he could try to prevent a third such calamity. He was no visionary who believed that high ideals and principles alone would lead to a more peaceful world. Nor, after the dismal failure of the League of Nations (see *League of Nations*), did he feel that international organizations such as the Federation of Europe or the United Nations could ever completely defuse the violence inherent in clashing national ambitions. Instead, he wished to create new political and economic patterns which would ultimately smother the national rivalries and distrust which had so often led to war in the past. It was his opinion that the national hatreds and rivalries which had fed those conflicts could be defused if the democracies of Europe were integrated into a unified bloc. If the nations of Europe could abandon their traditional economic protectionism and begin to cooperate with one another economically and politically, a loyalty to Europe could be developed which would overcome the narrow national loyalties which had proved so destructive in the past. He hoped that a more integrated Europe could build political institutions which would provide a forum where the differences between nations could be settled peacefully, in the same way that disputes between groups and individuals within nations are settled. He expressed his distrust of traditional national sovereignty in 1968 as follows: "Within national frontiers, men long ago found and developed civilized ways of dealing with conflicts of interest; they no longer need to defend themselves .... But across their frontiers, nations still behave as individuals would if there were no laws and no institutions. Each ... clings to national sovereignty ... each reserves the right to be judge in its own cause."

Few individuals have done more than Monnet to break down such concepts of national sovereignty in Europe. After the Second World War he was consumed with the idea that unless some alternative to a Europe divided into hostile, sullen, and suspicious nation-states was found, another war was absolutely inevitable. This feeling was the driving force behind his boldly advanced, innovative plans for achieving European unity. As he himself put it in the now-famous 1950 memo in which he described his new approach to the problem of European unity, his proposal was meant to "lay the first concrete foundations of the European Federation which is indispensable to the maintenance of peace." Reflecting on this phrase later, in his memoirs, he emphasized that "the last word was the most important: peace."

The result of Monnet's memo was the establishment, in 1951, of the European Coal and Steel Community (ECSC). In this organization, six European nations—France, Italy, the then Federal Republic of Germany, Belgium, the Netherlands, and Luxembourg—in effect surrendered control over their own iron, coal, and steel industries to an international authority. This was the first significant voluntary abrogation of national sovereignty in Western Europe, particularly meaningful because these heavy industries have so much military significance. In effect, these nations were surrendering the right to prepare for or to wage war without their neighbor's consent (see *Peace and Regional Integration*).

Monnet became the ECSC's first president, serving until 1955. As such he helped to lay the basis for its broadening into a general union of all aspects of the economic life of the members in 1957. Monnet is thus one of the most influential figures behind the birth of the European Economic Community (also known as the Common Market) and the European Atomic Energy Community (Euratom).

In 1955 Monnet organized the Action Committee for the United States of Europe, and became its president in 1956, serving until 1975. This organization, under his leadership, lobbied for steps that would increase the political, as well as the economic, unifi-

cation of Europe. Though Monnet was always impatient at the slow pace of political integration, and at the tenacious strength of nationalism even within the European Community (EC), by the time of his death in 1979 he had done much to lay the groundwork for a more unified and peaceful Europe. His service in this cause was given recognition in 1966, when the University of Bonn made him the first recipient of its prestigious Robert Schumann Prize. This award, named after another of the fathers of postwar European integration, was established to honor those who have distinguished themselves in the cause of European unity.

See also: *Transnationalism: The European Case; European Political Community; Integration, Regional*

Bibliography

Bromberger M, Bromberger S 1968 *Les Coulisses de l'Europe.* Presses de la Cité, Paris [1969 *Jean Monnet and the United States of Europe.* Coward-McCann, New York]

Lister L 1960 *Europe's Coal and Steel Community.* Twentieth Century Fund, New York

Mayne R 1973 *The Recovery of Europe, 1945-1973.* Anchor Press, Garden City, New York

Monnet J 1976 *Mémoires.* Fayard, Paris [1978 *Memoirs.* Collins, London]

GARRETT L. MCAINSH

Monroe Doctrine

The Monroe Doctrine encompasses principles of foreign policy that have guided, with several interpretations through time, the relations of the United States with various other nations in the Western Hemisphere. The Doctrine basically excludes the possibility of intervention in the affairs of North and Latin America on the part of any external Europe or other political system.

The principles that were to form the Doctrine were originally expressed in the Annual Message of President James Monroe to the US Congress on December 2, 1823. Several weeks of preparation and discussions in Monroe's Cabinet preceded its formulation and delivery. However, the roots of the principles contained in the Message must be searched for in the first years of existence of new North American Republic.

In effect, and notwithstanding the fact that the rev-

olutionary government of the United States had signed a treaty with France in February 1778 by means of which both countries had agreed to "make war and peace together" and aid one another in their endeavors, once the Revolution had consolidated independence, the United States decided to follow a distinct and then unique foreign policy. In 1793, Washington enunciated the "Neutrality Proclamation," later followed by principles set out in his Farewell Address of 1796, which were highlighted by a general principle of action under which the United States would not be part of any permanent alliance, nor would be involved in foreign wars; it was the principle of "nonentanglement."

Such principles permitted the rising nation to avoid involvement in the Napoleonic Wars and the subsequent events directed to restore order in Europe. In 1819 the United States was invited by Russia to be part of the Holy Alliance, an opportunity that was seized by Monroe's Secretary of State, John Quincy Adams, to declare that the two systems (that of Europe, monarchical, and that of the United States, republican) "should be kept as separate and distinct as possible."

Meanwhile, in other latitudes of the Western Hemisphere, the invasion of Spain by Napoleon in 1810 had ignited an independence movement among Spain's colonies in Latin America. By the end of the decade the tide was clearly against Spain, and some of the European powers had thought of interposing themselves in the affairs of the Spanish colonies, filling the vacuum left by Spain by means of an intervention in the mother country (notably the Congress of Aix-La-Chapelle of 1818 and the Congress of Verona of 1822 discussed this matter). Great Britain, opposed to such intervention and interposition, had begun to drift apart from the Continental powers. By 1821 several of the former Spanish colonies had already declared and consolidated their independence and the United States had moved to recognize the countries thus formed.

1. The Preparation

Two events triggered the formulation of a set of foreign policy principles in the State of the Union message of President Monroe:

(a) The Russian Czar had granted to the Russian American Company exclusive trading rights in the northwestern coast of North America, down to the 55° parallel.

(b) The United Kingdom, guided by George Canning, had begun a quest for political understanding with the United States regarding Latin America, by means of which London and Washington would manifest their pledge of nonintervention in the internal affairs of the Latin American countries. At the same time they intended to indicate that any recovery attempt by Spain was hopeless and that no transfer of any portion of territory from Spain to any other power would be accepted.

The relevant passages of the Message were the product of the ideas of President Monroe as well as of John Quincy Adams, who by then was a leading contender for the Presidential elections to be held at the end of 1823. The fact that other main contenders were also in Monroe's Cabinet has prompted some authors to argue that heavy domestic policy determi-

nants were involved and conditioned the formulation of this piece of foreign policy.

It was decided that the foreign policy pronouncement should be made by means of a Presidential declaration, intended to be known not only by the Congress and people of the United States but also by the concerned foreign powers.

2. The Document

The document itself comprised two distinct parts. The first was related to Russia's intentions on the northwest coast of the continent. In view of "the rights and interests of the United States," it was asserted that "the American continents . . . are henceforth not to be considered as subjects for future colonization by any European power." This policy has come to be known as the "principle of noncolonization," and was in fact a repetition of a previous statement by Secretary of State Adams.

The second section referred to the situation in Latin America. The document reaffirmed the principle of nonentanglement and the neutrality proclamation, and declared the superiority of the US policy system over that practiced by the European powers. The principle set out in this second part of the Message was that the United States "should consider any attempt on their [the European powers'] part to extend their system to any portion of this hemisphere as dangerous to our peace and safety." The United States, it said, has respected, and will continue to do so, Europe's existing colonies in the hemisphere, but would not be indifferent to any attempt at interposition by other powers tending to subdue the new Latin American governments.

3. The Immediate Effects

The declaration was forceful. Monroe sincerely believed that there was a threat posed by the Holy Alliance powers and decided to confront it. Historians now generally agree that such a threat was non-existent or unsustainable, but anyhow Monroe's admonition was at the time both courageous and menacing, even though the might of the United States was not then comparable to that of the powers addressed.

The declaration itself was a skillful piece of open diplomacy: it was preemptive with respect to Great Britain's intentions as well as in its insistence that an alliance was not desired by the United States government or by the people; and it served to cement relations with the emerging nations in South America.

In Europe the Presidential declaration was received

as an unpleasant surprise. Metternich, among others, harshly commented on the Message as "a new act of revolt, unprovoked, audacious, dangerous, intending not only to set power against power but also altar against altar." In the United States, however, the President's Message aroused the enthusiasm of the people. It was viewed as a declaration in which the President spoke not only for his people but for his age—the Age of Enlightenment. The inclusion of the US political system and the consecration of the principle of the two spheres are the notions that have given continuity in time, for the Old and the New World, to the Monroe Doctrine.

4. Application: The Nineteenth Century

Monroe's pronouncement was to play a most important role, not only in the diplomatic history of the United States, through diverse applications down the years, but also in the fields of international relations and diplomacy. But for more than two decades the message was ignored by all policy makers. Subsequent administrations did not establish closer relations with the Latin American countries. Great Britain filled—commercially—the vacuum left by Spain, establishing economic domination of the new Latin American countries.

It was not until 1845 when President James K. Polk, confronted by Britain's and France's opposition to the US annexation of Texas, as well as by disputes with Britain over the territory of Oregon and California, that Monroe's message was revived, stressing that the country would not tolerate any armed or diplomatic intervention by any European power. A few years later, when Yucatan rebelled against Mexico, President Polk once more invoked Monroe's principles and clearly expressed that neither Great Britain nor Spain should intervene in Yucatan and that, if the situation so required, it was the United States that should move in to control the problem.

The events of the late 1840s and the 1850s permitted Monroe's principles to be converted into a national dogma and take the form of a doctrine. The United States had begun to be involved commercially with its nearby countries in the Caribbean Basin. The United States' interests soon clashed in Nicaragua with those of the British, and this led to the Clayton-Bulwer Treaty of 1850 between the two powers; while restraining further British colonization in Central America, this treaty did not take into consideration the principles of the Doctrine inasmuch as it provided that both countries would share control over Nicaragua's transoceanic route.

The US Civil War caused a significant lapse in the application and development of the Doctrine. The United States, involved in its internal conflagration, did not react in response to three European involvements in Latin America: (a) the British occupied the Malvinas (Falkland) Islands; (b) Spain reasserted sovereignty over the Dominican Republic; and (c) Louis Napoleon instigated a French invasion of Mexico that resulted in the placing in power of the Austrian Archduke Maximilian. Once the Civil War was over, the Spanish left the Dominican Republic, the British were entrenched in the Malvinas—unperturbed until the 1980s—and the us government only exercised the dictums of the Doctrine in regard to Mexico's occupation, applying pressure on France to withdraw. France did withdraw, although the main drive for this came not from the us government but from the Mexican patriots themselves led by Benito Juárez.

The late-1870s and early-1880s witnessed an intense effort by the United States to exclude any other power from participating in the projects for building an interoceanic canal. The Clayton-Bulwer Treaty was repealed and the United States obtained exclusive rights to Nicaragua's interoceanic route. Intense us involvement developed in the isthmus of Panama, then under Colombian rule, and the United States saw to it that the Lesseps enterprise to build a Panama canal did not succeed. If a canal was to be built, it was argued, it should be under exclusive guarantee of the United States.

A dispute over the boundary demarcation in the Esequibo area developed between Venezuela and Great Britain, and in 1895 President Grover Cleveland compelled the British to arbitration over the dispute. In the name of the Monroe Doctrine, it was stated, the United States should be involved in the conflict as a "paternal overlord" with regard to the Latin American nations. Again, in 1902 Venezuela, greatly in debt to European powers, suffered a blockade led by Great Britain, Germany, and Italy, who were attempting to collect their credits. The action aroused acute irritation in the United States. President Theodore Roosevelt originally acquiesced to the blockade but later claimed that he had pushed for the settlement that rapidly ended the dispute—a fact that has not been historically confirmed.

As has been mentioned, the United States had been intensively involved in the projects relating to the construction of an interoceanic canal. It developed very close ties with Colombia while negotiating a canal agreement, helping at the same time to ensure tranquility in the province of Panama. However, when the Colombians demanded additional concessions on the draft treaty, the United States turned its back on them, impeding the Colombian armed forces access to suppress a revolt in Panama and readily signing, with the new independent government, the Panama Canal Treaty of 1903, only 15 days after the country had declared independence.

5. The Roosevelt Corollary

At the beginning of the twentieth century the countries of the Caribbean Basin were plagued by international debts, internal strife, and complete bankruptcy. Fear of intervention by European powers in any or some of the countries in the area assailed the United States and led President Theodore Roosevelt to proclaim in 1904 the "Roosevelt Corollary of the Monroe Doctrine," an extension of the Doctrine by means of which the United States asserted its right to intervene in any Latin American nation to prevent involvement by any European power.

The status of the region, now of special interest to the United States because of the Panama Canal, began to be seen as one of specific security concern for the country, which was also willing to consolidate economic hegemony in the area. Any foreign intervention would hamper or block such intentions and therefore had to be prevented. The Corollary, which was applied to secure intervention in independent states in order to control customs revenues, was carried further and came to be used as a vindication for direct military occupation by the United States of the territories of independent nations: Haiti, Cuba, the Dominican Republic, Honduras, Nicaragua, and Panama were among those to which this policy was applied, for decades at a time in some cases.

The Corollary became a most offensive piece of "diplomatic" action. It embodied the "Big Stick Policy" and consecrated the United States as the police force of the area. In Latin America such actions raised suspicion and dislike. Through experience, countries in the area became more afraid of intervention from the United States than from Europe, and, suffering intermittent US occupation and meddling in their internal affairs, developed intense resentment toward their Northern neighbor, resentments which in many cases survive to the present day. For its own part the United States under President Wilson declared that it was a task of the country to aid the people of the Caribbean in the establishment and maintenance of honest and responsible governments to such extent as might be necessary in each particular case.

6. The Internationalization of the Doctrine

The First World War produced for the first time the reluctant participation of the United States in global political affairs. The United States exited the war as a very powerful nation, and President Wilson himself led the victors in delineating the new world order through the Treaty of Versailles and the Covenant of the League of Nations. The Pact was seen by Wilson as being an extension to the macro-international level of the principles of 1823, inasmuch as it provided the possibility of resorting to collective action against an aggressor. However, the United States did not ultimately join the League of Nations despite Wilson's wishes.

When ratifying the treaty establishing the World Court, the United States made a specific reservation covering the principles of the Doctrine, and also introduced with the same purpose a gloss in the Kellog-Briand Pact to outlaw war in 1929.

7. The "Good Neighbor" Policy

The "Memorandum on the Monroe Doctrine," or "Clark Memorandum" (named after its author, J. Reuben Clark) repudiated officially in 1929 the Roosevelt Corollary. The experience of the United States through three decades of open military intervention and the effects and costs of the Great Depression made it necessary for the country to retreat once more into isolation from world politics, including its immediate area of influence. The Monroe Doctrine then came to be interpreted and based on the principle of self-defense. In the 1930s the task of the United States, self-imposed and also affected by the stance taken by the Latin American nations in the various Inter-American Conferences held, was one of cooperation and assistance rather than that of direct domination, albeit preserving "the rights of the United States (in regard to intervention) under international law" (Protocol of Montevideo 1933). Later on, in Buenos Aires in 1936, the reservations were done away with.

With the advent of the Second World War new situations came to test the application of the Doctrine. The fall of France and Holland into German occupation brought forth the issue of several dependencies of those countries being taken over by the Axis power. The United States made it clear once again that it would not accept any transfer of sovereignty from any European power in the hemisphere's area to any other power, and reiterated that it had the right to step in and "act in the manner which its own defense or that of the Continent" required. At Havana in 1940 the Pan-American Conference declared that an attack against any American states was to be considered as an attack on all. During the war, the provisions of the Doctrine were understood to cover Canada and Greenland, as parts of the hemisphere.

8. The Post-Second World War Period

After the war the focus of attention and preoccupation of the United States came to be the possible subversion of governments promoted by international communism. In 1945, in Chapultepec, the principle of collective action in the case of external attack was restated. In 1947 the Inter-American Treaty of Reciprocal Assistance was signed in Rio de Janeiro; by this treaty the Latin American countries and the United States agreed on an alliance under which aggression against one country would be met with sanctions against the aggressor imposed by all. In 1948, the Organization of American States was formally established, having among its principles of action that of ruling out intervention by one state in the affairs of others (see *Organization of American States (OAS)*).

The containment of communism has been the major factor in the postwar hemispheric relations of the United States. In 1954 a meeting of the Pan-American Conference in Caracas, analyzing the situation of Guatemala, concluded that "the domination or control of the political institutions of any American state by the international communist movement, extending to this hemisphere the political system of an extracontinental power, would constitute a threat to the sovereignty and political independence of the American states, endangering the peace of America...."

The Guatemalan problem was soon dealt with through indirect participation of the United States. A more direct application of the Monroe Doctrine and its extensions was that of the US invasion of Grenada in 1983. In the intervening years and beyond to the present the condition of Cuba (since 1959) and of Nicaragua (since 1979) have provoked a situation in which the United States has come to accept—or fight—the inclination toward and adoption by hemispheric nations of doctrines and systems alien to the United States' perception of how such nations should be run.

The last test for the application of the Doctrine came in 1982 on the occasion of the Malvinas (Falkland) Islands dispute. The United States found itself linked by formal alliances with the two belligerents and, after attempting unsuccessfully to mediate in the dispute, announced that it would give full support and assistance to the United Kingdom, accusing Argentina of being the aggressor.

9. Concluding Remarks

The principles of the Monroe Doctrine have developed over time and have been subject to modifications, extensions, and divergent interpretations. Nevertheless, they have had significance for more than 160 years as a great influence and undeniable force on the behavior of the various us administrations vis-à-vis their southern neighbors.

See also: *Caribbean Basin Initiative (CBI); Intervention; Pan-Americanism; Nonintervention and Noninterference*

Bibliography

Alvarez A 1924 *The Monroe Doctrine: Its Importance in the International Life of the States of the New World.* Oxford University Press, New York
May E R 1976 *The Making of the Monroe Doctrine.* Harvard University Press, Cambridge, Massachusetts
Perkins D 1955 *A History of the Monroe Doctrine.* Little, Brown, Boston, Massachusetts

RODRIGO ALBERTO CARAZO

Montaigne

Michel Eyquem, born in 1533 in the castle of Montaigne in Perigord, France, was the son of a wealthy Bordeaux merchant who had been made a noble in 1519. As a young man Montaigne received training in Latin, then went on to study philosophy in Bordeaux and law in Toulouse.

From 1554-70 Montaigne pursued a career as a magistrate, entering the Parliament of Bordeaux in 1557. However his political ambitions were not realized and this period of Montaigne's public life yielded him little satisfaction. In 1571 Montaigne retired to devote himself to study and meditation, and shortly afterwards began working on his *Essays* while reading Seneca and Plutarch. However Montaigne was unable to remain isolated from public affairs and in 1574, during the Wars of Religion, he assumed command of a section of the Royal Army.

In 1580-81 Montaigne, who suffered from kidney stones, undertook a European voyage in search of a cure, and in order to add to this store of experience.

While still on this journey Montaigne was elected mayor of Bordeaux which afforded him the opportunity of acting as a diplomatic link between the many factions dividing France at the time.

In 1588 a new and expanded edition of the *Essays* appeared. Montaigne spent his final years revising, correcting, and adding to his works, until his death in 1592.

The *Essays* are a journal of Montaigne's search for wisdom, by using his natural faculties. Setting a new precedent in French literature, the author speaks about himself candidly and without restraint. The evolution of Montaigne's thought is demonstrated by the transition from the early works, which lean heavily on classic authors, to the later works which present his own independent point of view. Montaigne tells us that he himself is the subject of his essays—his disposition, feelings, ideas, experiences. However, unlike the romantic *Confessions* of Rousseau, the aim of the sober and lucid Essays is not self-exaltation but the acquisition of wisdom. Since each person represents the entire human condition the individual case has value as an example.

Renaissance humanism and the Reformation have a common origin in the return to the text. While the German monk Martin Luther was protesting against the abuses of the Church, the reformation in France started with the Evangelical movement, that is, the return to sacred Scriptures as the only authentic source of Christian beliefs. Thus, most of the humanists, who were in conflict with the established Catholic view that Scripture must be accompanied by the traditional commentaries of the Church Fathers, had to choose between orthodoxy and the new faith. Calvinism, with is austere moral doctrine, eventually became the guiding force of the French Reformation.

The unity of French Christianity having been disrupted, the religious conflict eventually led to civil war. Attempts were made to suppress the Reformation by means of violence. The political ramifications of the Reformation stem from the democratic tendencies of Calvinism and the religious alienation of a sovereign and his people. Adding to the social upheaval was the degradation of royal authority. While François I and Henri II had been powerful and respected monarchs, various influences weakened the authority of later Renaissance rulers.

From 1562-93 eight separate wars ravaged France with fragile truces marking a pause in the battles and massacres. In 1593 Henri IV reconquered the capital, Paris, and by the Edict of Nantes (1598) peace was finally brought to the country (see *Henri IV*).

French literature was profoundly influenced by the Reformation and Wars of Religion, when tracts and discourses treated theological questions in a sometimes violent tone. In contrast to this violent literature, Montaigne is a voice of moderation amidst the intolerance and fanaticism surrounding him.

In one of his essays, Montaigne tells us that justice in only a pretext for wars of religion which are caused by human passions. People use religion for their own purposes, instead of serving the cause of religion. Montaigne decried the religious factionalism of his day in which the parties were equally guilty of injustice, violence, and worldly ambitions. Few of those fighting were motivated by religious zeal, or even the desire to protect their country and serve their king. Montaigne held that the underlying cause of the social turmoil was the haphazard way in which public affairs were conducted.

See also: *Religion and Peace*

Bibliography ⸻

Burke P 1981 *Montaigne*. Oxford University Press, Oxford

Joukovsky F 1972 *Montaigne et le probleme du temps*. Nizet, Paris

Moreau P 1939 *Montaigne*. Hatier, Paris

Micha A 1964 *Le Singulier Montaigne*. Nizet, Paris

Supple J J 1985 *Arms versus Letters: The Military and Literary Ideals in the 'Essais' of Montaigne*. Oxford University Press, Oxford

THERESA M. HYUN

Moral Development and Peace

To many philosophers, historians, and religious thinkers (e.g., Kant, Toynbee, Jesus) the equation of peace with a higher moral development and sensitivity, and of war with a deficient or arrested moral development, has long seemed obvious. Because science has traditionally been reluctant to involve itself with "value judgments," this has been an assumption for which empirical data have been, until recently, generally lacking.

A study in 1984 by the Institute for Futures Forecasting in California was designed to fill this need for research into the possible connection between moral sensitivity and peace in two regards: directly through correlations with the results of a new test of moral sensitivity developed and recently validated by Loye, and indirectly through supportive inference from correlations with group perceptions of the probabilities for nuclear war in the 1980s and 1990s.

The original study, which provided an extensive database of potentially relevant personal information, was of nearly 1,500 people in a variety of groups from 33 states throughout the United States. From this original study, six groups were selected for a follow-up study in the fall of 1984. The three primary groups were 35 people belonging to defense-oriented groups, including defense (for example, nuclear missile) system management trainees and Southern police officers (identified in Tables 1 and 2 as DF); 22 people belonging to peace-oriented groups, such as Freeze Voter, Creative and Planetary Initiatives (PE); and 52 individuals of diverse backgrounds, selected to provide a comparison group of approximately equal numbers of women and men and of conservatives and liberals—or, in the terminology of this study, norm maintainers and norm changers (designated IN, for Individuals). Additionally, there were three other comparison groups: a group of 24 nurses in California and Utah (NU); 35 women and men from throughout the United States with business occupations (BO); and 62 readers of a "New Age" publication (NA).

1. Moral Sensitivity Testing

Among tests administered to members of these groups was a new test of moral sensitivity, developed by Loye, of the following nature. As is well-known among many social scientists now actively studying moral development, the key established work in this area is that of Lawrence Kohlberg at Harvard.

Kohlberg's scale, however, standardized on all-male samples, was shown to be sexually biased in the standards it establishes for morality. Harvard professor Carol Gilligan found that while stressing a male-oriented, cognitive dimension of "justice," Kohlberg's work (and his widely used morality interview measure and developmental scale), not only slighted, but in effect also largely ignored, an equally important female-oriented, affective, or emotional dimension of "caring."

Seeing a potential connection between the two Kohlberg-Gilligan dimensions, earlier two-factor views of morality by Kant and Rawls, and the findings of social psychologist Milton Rokeach establishing "freedom" and "equality" as the dominant values in systems governance, Loye used this perception to guide the development of a new measure of moral sensitivity. This measure is nonsexually biased and in tests with a variety of groups seems to assess with some accuracy how individuals relate to the needs and rights of others (the valuing of equality) or to the needs and rights of ourselves (the valuing of freedom).

Table 1 shows a rank ordering for all six groups earlier defined on the following scales: MSE, measuring the valuing of equality; MSF, measuring the valuing of freedom; MSC, equality and freedom combined; MSB, moral sensitivity as measured by self-reported behavior; and MSN for moral "neutrality," or a relative insensitivity to moral issues. As can be seen in Table 1, the peace group is high on MSE, MSC, and MSB, and lowest on MSN. The defense group is lowest on MSE, MSC, and MSB, and also on the high side for MSN. The exception is the MSF or freedom dimension.

Here the defense group is higher than the peace group, but only by a quite insignificant margin (means of 2.5 vs. 2.4. where significantly wider margins are observable on all the other scales).

This difference on the freedom scale is of interest

Table 1
Moral sensitivity

MSE	MSF	MSC	MSB	MSN
PE 2.8	BO 2.7	PE 10.9	PE 2.1	BO 8.4
NA 2.6	NU 2.6	NA 10.2	NA 1.8	NA 8.4
NU 2.4	DF 2.5	NU 10.1	NU 1.7	DF 8.3
IN 2.4	IN 2.5	IN 9.9	IN 1.6	IN 8.2
BO 2.1	PE 2.4	BO 8.8	BO 1.4	NU 7.8
DF 1.9	NA 2.4	DF 8.2	DF 1.4	PE 7.5

A rank ordering of six groups (PE, DF, IN, plus NA, NU, and BO) according to differences of means on the following dimensions: MSE=moral sensitivity to value of equality; MSF=moral sensitivity to value of freedom; MSC=equality and freedom combined rating; MSB=moral sensitivity registered by behavior; MSN=moral "neutrality"

Table 2
Predictions of nuclear war

Groups	1980s	Percentage	1990s	Percentage
Peace	90% probability	22.7	90% probability	36.4
(PE)	50-50	54.6	50-50	45.4
	90% improbability	22.7	90% improbability	18.2
Defense	90% probability	0.0	90% probability	2.9
(DF)	50-50	8.6	50-50	22.9
	90% improbability	91.4	90% improbability	74.2
Individuals	90% probability	1.9	90% probability	3.9
(IN)	50-50	13.5	50-50	34.6
	90% improbability	84.6	90% improbability	61.5
New Age	90% probability	3.3	90% probability	15.0
(NA)	50-50	23.3	50-50	33.3
	90% improbability	73.3	90% improbability	51.7
Nurses	90% probability	0.0	90% probability	20.8
(NU)	50-50	37.5	50-50	54.2
	90% improbability	62.5	90% improbability	25.0
Business	90% probability	2.8	90% probability	19.4
(BO)	50-50	30.6	50-50	22.2
	90% improbability	66.6	90% improbability	58.4

for two reasons. First, the finding fits not only the occupational thrust but also the basic systems protective function for the defense group. That is, in this world of predominantly violence-, conflict-, and warfare-oriented social controls, if a social system is to maintain its freedom or survive, its leaders feel they must heavily invest in military and police protection.

The great dilemma of our time, which peace groups are responsive to, is that because of the nuclear arms build-up, this defensive investment actually increasingly threatens rather than enhances our chance for survival. Secondly, within the context of other research with this new moral sensitivity profile, it is evident that by itself, a high reading on sensitivity to freedom seems to represent little more than ethnocentricity. In other words, without the counterbalancing effect of also having a high sensitivity to equality, high MSF seems to represent primarily sensitivity to the needs of oneself and one's extremely limited own particular group—a characteristic of most conservative or norm-maintaining individuals. It is instructive that, by contrast, the norm-changing peace group is comparatively high on both scales.

It is also instructive that a greater sensitivity to others—as measured by a low score on moral neutrality or MSN—should be more characteristic of the peace group, for in groups animated by a peace-oriented drive both toward systems survival and a human developmental ideal, we would expect to find people generally registering highest in moral sensitivity and lowest in moral neutrality or insensitivity.

Likewise, we would expect to find those responsible for military and authoritarian systems maintenance—which heavily depends on the capacity of humans to be insensitive to the needs and rights of others—to be generally lowest in moral sensitivity and highest in moral neutrality or insensitivity. And in both instances this is what Table 1 shows.

2. Predictions of the Probability of Nuclear War

Shedding possible further light on this matter of the relation between moral sensitivity development and peace are data from the responses to a question asked of those who filled out the moral sensitivity profile. Participants were asked to predict the likelihood of nuclear war in the next two decades.

Despite the fact that historically new weapons have always been eventually used in warfare, that nuclear weapons have in fact already been used by the United States in the Second World War, and that significant nuclear arsenals and the threat of nuclear terrorism still remains with us, the members of the predominantly norm-maintaining defense group overwhelmingly responded that in their estimation there is a very low risk of nuclear war.

As shown in Table 2, of the three primary groups, by far the highest percentage predicting a 90 percent improbability of nuclear war in the 1980s and 1990s was the defense group (predictions of a 91.4 percent improbability for the 1980s and 74.2 percent for the 1990s). One explanation for this finding could be that because of the desensitizing to violence that is part of prevailing world cultural socialization processes (for example, the distancing of one's emotions from the real human implications of war "games" and our barrage of violent "entertainment"), norm-maintainers would tend to block out that there is any reality to fears of nuclear war. By contrast, of the three primary groups, by far the highest percentage predicting a 90 percent probability of nuclear war in the 1980s and 1990s was the predominantly norm-changing peace group (22.7 percent for 1980, 36.4 percent for 1990, Table 2).

To summarize, confirming the observations of Kant, Toynbee, Jesus, and many other moral philosophers, historians, and religious thinkers, the picture this empirically gathered data reveals is that groups for peace score high in moral sensitivity, and are highly concerned about the dangers of nuclear war, and groups involved in the formal defense of our social systems score low in moral sensitivity, and are relatively insensitive to the risks of nuclear war.

See also: *Psychology of Peace; Peace Education; Peace and Peace Education: A Holistic View; From Morality to Ethic: Toward an Ideal Community*

Bibliography

Beck L W 1949 *Kant's Critique of Practical Reason and Other Writings in Moral Philosophy*. University of Chicago Press, Chicago, Illinois

Eisler R 1987 *The Chalice and the Blade: Our History, Our Future*. Harper and Row, San Francisco, California

Gilligan C 1982 *In a Different Voice*. Harvard University Press, Cambridge, Massachusetts

Kohlberg L 1981 *The Philosophy of Moral Development*. Harper and Row, San Francisco, California

Loye D 1971 *The Healing of a Nation*. Norton, New York

Loye D 1983 *The Sphinx and the Rainbow: Brain, Mind, and Future Vision*. New Science Library, Boulder, Colorado

Loye D (in press) *The Glacier and the Flame: The Rediscovery of Goodness*

Rawls J 1971 *A Theory of Justice*. Harvard University Press, Cambridge, Massachusetts

Rokeach M 1973 *The Nature of Human Values*. Free Press, New York

DAVID LOYE

More, Thomas

Sir Thomas More (1477-1535), English humanist and statesman, has won lasting fame in two very different contexts. Firstly, his *Utopia* remains one of the best-read books of the European Renaissance; secondly, his beheading at the hands of Henry VIII was among the most dramatic events of the Reformation. More was educated as a lawyer, and entered royal service in England in 1517. He undertook numerous diplomatic missions for Henry VIII, was made speaker of the House of Commons when parliament met in 1523, and became Lord Chancellor of England in 1529. By then, however, Henry had decided to divorce his wife, Catherine of Aragon, a step which led inexorably to England breaking away from the Roman Catholic Church.

Almost alone among Henry's thoroughly intimidated subjects, More refused to compromise his conscience. He felt that the divorce, carried out in defiance of papal orders, was totally invalid. More had always been an extremely devout Catholic. Throughout his adult life he devoted a great deal of time and energy to religious devotions, regularly fasting and wearing a hair shirt to subordinate his flesh to his spirit. When the Reformation began in Germany, More put his learning and wit at the service of his faith by writing a number of tracts against the Protestants. Thus when Henry VIII demanded in 1534 that More swear an oath which implied approval of Henry's break with the Roman Catholic Church, More refused to do so. He bravely maintained this uncompromising stand even as it became increasingly apparent that it would end in his own death. He was executed by Henry VIII in 1535; 400 years later, in 1935, his church recognized him as one of its saints.

More is also remembered as an eminent humanist scholar. He and his circle of like-minded friends felt that the application of common sense and reason to the problems facing their society could eliminate much of the misery and despair which blighted so many lives. They realized that an end to war, with its incalculable human suffering and its prodigious waste of resources, was central to any such improvement in the human condition. This conviction is given eloquent voice in More's delightfully satiric *Utopia*, which was published in 1516. In the "Dialogue of Counsel," or first part of *Utopia*, war is prominent among the features of his world which More subjects to withering criticism. War is characterized as a base and brutalizing endeavor, the root cause of which is greed—the ruthless, insatiable quest for more and more on the part of a priviliged few whom he regarded as having too much wealth and power already. "The majority of princes," one character in the dialogue points out, "have more delight in warlike matters . . . than in good feats of peace; and spend much more study on how by right or by wrong to enlarge their dominions than on how well and peaceably to rule and govern what they have already." The misery war causes, More continued, does not end with the return of peace. At war's end the soldiers, with no skills save those of violence, are thrown back into society to live through rapine and theft.

The second part of *Utopia* purports to be a traveler's description of the happy, until then undiscovered, island of Utopia (in Greek, literally, "no place"), which had largely avoided the ills then bedeviling Europe. The key to the Utopians' success, said More, was their renunciation of private property. The Utopians held their goods in common, are in communal messes, and shared happily in whatever work needed to be done. They lived frugally and rationally, rejoicing in labor and in such simple pastimes as reading and gardening. They shunned utterly the ostentatious displays of wealth and power which consumed so many of More's fellow Europeans. Thus greed, which More considered to be the root cause of war and of nearly all the other ills of his own place and time, had never been allowed to take root among the wise and gentle Utopians.

More emphasized that the Utopians "abhor war or battle as a thing very beastly." They regarded the shedding of blood as contrary to the natural goodness of human nature, and did not even hunt or butcher animals. These pursuits were shunned lest they weaken the Utopians' natural distaste for violence and cruelty, and led them to regard the slaughter of their fellow humans with less than their usual horror.

Averse as they were to war, though, the presence of aggressive states nearby forced even the Utopians to keep themselves ready to fight. Indeed, with the exception of what would now be called conscientious objectors, every Utopian citizen—women and children as well as men—was a well-trained, well-armed soldier. More presents them as being willing to fight to repel invasion, and in other cases where war was necessary to protect or to extend their own rational, superior way of life. Such cases included avenging the murder of one of their citizens by foreigners, gaining unused land needed by their own expanding population, and rescuing neighboring peoples from tyranny and injustice. More apparently felt that the human benefits of such wars, particularly the preserving and spreading of Utopian rationality, would outweigh their human costs. It seems likely that he hoped to emphasize a contrast between the Utopians' refusal to fight for anything except rational goals and the frivolous and selfish cause of the wars then racking Europe.

The manner in which More had the Utopians fight was also a tremendous contrast to the way in which the Europeans waged their wars. Where the latter saw war as an opportunity to win honor and fame, the Utopians disdained chivalric concepts of military glory. Once a war began, their only object was to bring it to a victorious conclusion as quickly and as bloodlessly as possible. This included such inglorious tactics as hiring foreign mercenaries to do as much of the fighting as possible, moving beacons to mislead and destroy enemy fleets, and encouraging assassins to murder the leaders of their foes. By glorifying such practices More sought to discredit the traditional chivalrous view of war as a glamorous and ennobling adventure. To More and his Utopians, war was a horrible evil to be ended as soon as possible, by whatever means would accomplish this goal. Glory and honor could never play a role in such a bestial enterprise.

See also: *Utopia; Utopianism*

Bibliography

Adams R P 1962 *The Better Part of Valor: More, Erasmus, Colet, and Vives on Humanism, War, and Peace, 1496-1535.* University of Washington Press, Seattle, Washington

Caspari F 1946 Sir Thomas More and *Justum Bellum. Ethics* LVI

Hexter J 1952 *More's Utopia.* Princeton University Press, Princeton, New Jersey

Marius R 1984 *Thomas More.* Knopf, New York

More T 1516 *Utopia.* Penguin. Harmondsworth

Wolfers A, Martin L W (eds.) 1956 *The Anglo-American Tradition in Foreign Affairs: Readings from Thomas More to Woodrow Wilson.* London

GARRETT L. MCAINSH

Movement for Reunion of Separated Families in Korea

The term "separated families" refers to involuntarily divided family members. The family unit can become fractured by both natural and artificial means. Earthquakes, flooding and other natural disasters are examples of the former factor, while war, domestic turbulence and social instability are of the latter.

The tragedy of the separated family has afflicted the world throughout history. Korea, too, has had several hundreds of thousands of families separated throughout her history, owing mostly to incessant warfare. In the Chosun Dynasty, for instance, large numbers of families were unwillingly separated due to the Imjin-Japanese Invasion and the Bungja-Chinese Invasion. In world history, the problem of separated families reached its zenith when the Portuguese infringed upon the human rights of Africans, through slavery, an institution that still is in place in some parts of the modern world. Owing to the separation of families resulting from two World Wars and the world-wide outbreak of Wars of National Liberation, the twentieth century has been labeled by many as the "Century of the Uprooted."

In Korea, the two million separated families that had migrated to Russia and China during the Japanese occupation were freed to visit each other following World War II thanks to normalization of diplomatic relations with those countries. As a result of the Korean War, however, and the 1953 demarcation of the peninsula which it produced, the Korean people suffered once more, this time by having over ten million of their families separated.

There were three major reasons for the huge number of forced family separations following Japanese colonization. First, ideological conflict between the former USSR and the US and their "divide and rule" policy of the Korean peninsula after the Second World War, induced about 3.5 million men and women to leave their families to pursue one of these two contending doctrines. Second, the Korean War (1950-53) led many to take refuge from North Korea. In addition to those that passed through the demarcation line to go north, North Korean troops kidnapped a large number of retreating civilians. Although some came down with the South Korean troops to meet their earlier departed family members, in the end, as a result of the Korean War more families were separated than were reunited. Third, a considerable number of Korean Japanese, although fewer than the two prior cases, were enticed to move to "the Worker's Paradise" of North Korea.

The reunion of these separated families should be advocated on the grounds of both human rights and dignity. This idea was first upheld at the December 10, 1948 United Nations General Assembly conference in the form of the "Universal Declaration of Human Rights" which recognized family reunion as a right under the basis of the following articles:

All human beings are born free and equal in dignity and rights. They are endowed with reason and conscience and should act towards one another in a spirit of brotherhood (Article 1).

Everyone has the right to recognition everywhere as a person before the law (Article 6).

All are equal before the law and are entitled without any discrimination to equal protection of the law (Article 7).

The family is the natural and fundamental group unit of society and is entitled to protection by society and the state (Article 16, III).

Men and women of full age, without any limitation due to race, nationality or religion, have the right to marry and to found a family. They are entitled to equal rights as to marriages, during marriage and at its dissolution (Article 16, I).

No one shall be subjected to arbitrary interference with his privacy, family, home or correspondence, nor to attacks upon his honor and reputation. Everyone has the right to the protection of the law against such interference or attacks (Article 12).

Everyone has the right to leave any country, including his own, and to return to his country (Article 13, II) and everyone has the right to seek and enjoy in other countries asylum from persecution (Article 14, I).

When family reunion is recognized as a right, it creates an obligation to be upheld by nations, organizations and individuals. The right of returning home should not be blocked or infringed upon since it is a basic human right. This right was recognized in the Universal Declaration of Human Rights (see *Declaration of the Rights of Man*), which articulated the importance of the right to return home by manifesting its supremacy, independent of the freedom of residence (Article 13, I). Again, at the Geneva April 1976 International Humanity Agreement, it was declared that the right to return home was more basic a human right than the simple need of family members to be able to communicate with each other and lead a happy life together. The basic point of these Declarations was that the reunion of separated families is a humanitarian issue, which outweighs political, ideological and institutional interests.

The reunion of the separated families in the Korean peninsula also serves as a promising way to decrease tensions between the North and South, in addition to easing the nostalgic pain of divided families. It also represents the next certain step toward reunification. In other words, since the reunion of the separated families symbolizes trust building between the two Koreas and addresses a core human rights issue, this issue should be treated as an important precondition to every effort by the South to communicate with North Korea.

It is nothing more than a self-contradiction to speak of trust building and peaceful reunification on the Korean peninsula without first taking into consideration the separated families reunion issue, which provides the fundamental basis for promoting relations between the two Koreas. In the cases of other formerly divided countries such as Germany, Vietnam and Yemen, communication between separated families was followed by a gradual extension of relations in other fields, for instance, politics, economics and sports.

The other presently divided country, Taiwan, is also able to maintain a desirable relationship with its other half: Mainland China. The two countries permit visitation by relatives and human exchange for the purpose of mutual promotion of tourism and business. In addition to allowing correspondence, both sides also established extensive telephone communications. Korean citizens, however, have not yet been permitted to exchange even letters with their families on the other side, and are unable to answer even the most basic question of whether their relatives are still alive.

Let us review some of the recent history of the relations between the South and the North concerning the separated family issue. Efforts were initiated by the South, when on August 12, 1971, the president of the Korean Red Cross issued a special statement calling for the earliest solution of problems of a purely humanitarian nature. In the statement he asked his counterpart to come to the negotiation table, and proposed a "Search Campaign for Separated Families" to determine the dimensions of the problem. He also identified the barrier between two Koreas as the origin of the tragedy and proclaimed that the separated family issue was one symbolic of grief in the twentieth century. Two days later the North side replied positively to his proposal for meetings.

After twenty five preliminary meetings beginning in August 20, 1971 and the 7.4 Joint Statement which invigorated the inactive negotiations, the first main talk was held in Pyongyang on August 30, 1972. The first talk addressed five topics; (a) ascertaining the living status and location of the separated families, (b) bringing about free visitation and meetings between the two sides' relatives and families, (c) allowing free correspondence among separated families and relatives, (d) reuniting separated families on the basis of their free will, and (e) other humanitarian issues. The first talk drew world-wide interest, but produced no actual results, and the second talk was held the same year in Seoul, on September 13. At the second talk, the South Korean Red Cross suggested three basic principles for the meeting; (a) advocating the free will of separated families and relatives, (b) carrying out the program in accordance with the Red Cross' spiritual principles, and, (c) the prompt and precise execution of the program in conformance to the common ways of the international Red Cross Society. The North, however, broke off all further discourse. The only fruit of the second talk was the agreement for earnest dialogue on the topics to be discussed in the third talk.

The third talk, which dealt with the same topics, was held on October 24, 1972, in Pyongyang. The South Red Cross once again, offered principles for the talk: (a) the program should be solely controlled by the Red Cross Society and in accordance with its principles of humanitarianism and neutrality, (b) the separated families, the subject of the talk, should be able to take part based on their own free will and should not be manipulated by either side, (c) the pure purpose of restoring family relations should not be contaminated by any procedural misbehavior, and (d) topics should be discussed one at a time, with any agreement that was reached put into operation immediately.

At the onset of the third talk, the South suggested filling out the current status of separated families on a special report form as a practical preparatory step. In response, though, the North side steadfastly stuck to its usual political rhetoric, and as a result, the talks reached a stalemate. At the fourth talk held in Seoul on November 22, 1976, both sides agreed to establish a South-North Joint Committee of the Red Cross and a joint office for common administration. Despite this apparent success, however, both sides stubbornly maintained their positions, and no further agreements were produced. The two sides met three more times without any progress, until the negotiations finally concluded at the seventh talk in Pyongyang, July 12, 1973. When the North announced the suspension of the South-North discourse on August 28, 1973, the South-North Coordination Committee established by the Joint Communiqué of July 4, 1972 was also disbanded. For the next ten years, the South and North maintained a stand-off on the issue, lacking even intermittent gestures.

In the 1980s, the separated family issue was raised again for discussion, this time on May 27, 1985 at the Eighth South-North Red Cross Conference. At the talks, both sides reached agreement on two proposals: the exchange of "Home Visit Teams and Artist Groups." According to the agreement, each side would form a group consisting of home visit teams and artist groups (amounting to 151 people in total, including 50 home visitors) that would be invited by the other side. As a result of this agreement, thirty five South Korean visitors met their separated families in Pyongyang and thirty North Korean visitors met their lost brothers and sisters in Seoul. Meanwhile, the artist groups of both sides performed twice in each other's capital city on September 21 and 22.

Although this initial achievement of exchanging select teams was limited in size and scope, it had a few definitely positive features. First and foremost, it established the precedent of separated families reuniting despite ideological barriers. It also marked the first time that separated families had been able to visit each other's side since the Military Armistice Committee had made a few abortive attempts to reunite separated families. The "Home Visit Teams" were the first visible fruit of a fourteen-year long "Ten Million Separated Families Search Campaign," and demonstrated that the South-North Red Cross Conference could serve to provide solutions to the problem. After the first exchange of "Home Visit Teams and Artist Groups" however, it was quite some time before the Korean Red Cross made further progress.

The next step forward came when the offices of the North and South Korean Red Cross reached agreement on another exchange program for separated families. The agreement to hold discussions was affirmed by the North at a press conference of the Seventh South-North high level talks, held in Seoul in May 1992, when they declared that the "separated families issue should be handled without any preconditions." Although the proposed number of each side's home visit team was to be limited to only one hundred, the South was in no position to pass over the first opportunity for progress since the first exchange of home visit teams in 1985. The South expected that talks would provide momentum for further exchange and agreed to a four day/three night visitation schedule from August 25 to 28. Unfortunately, though, the North placed three preconditions on the exchange of teams that the South deemed unacceptable, and the agreement was scrapped.

Previously in 1989, after seven working-level meetings between the South and North, the North had also annulled an earlier agreement on the same subject, the exchange of home visit teams. The North had postponed the agreed exchange of 501 member home visit delegations (comprised of 300 home visitors, 100 artists, 100 attendants and a leader), demanding that the revolutionary opera "Flower-selling Lady" be performed as a precondition.

The North was entirely responsible for breaking both agreements by attaching additional conditions onto completed deals in order to ruin what had already been signed. The North Korean government might have been worried that the legitimacy of its system of one-man rule would be threatened as a consequence of increased contact with the South Korean delegation and its culture. After all, the North Korean government has consistently sought to evade international pressure to open up through delaying tactics or deceptive strategies.

As private organizations, the "People from the Five Northern Provinces," and the "Korean Assembly for Reunion of Ten Million Separated Families" have made significant contributions to the separated families reunion campaign. The former organization was established to provide services to homeless Northern immigrants, and publishes the bulletin '*Minbo*,' which carries the regular section 'Find' in order to help people search for their lost families. The "People of Five Northern Provinces" also issues a bulletin, '*Yibuk-Kongbo*,' which contains a section titled 'Separated Families' which serves the same purpose as '*Minbo*.'

Mass media efforts to unify separated families have been channeled through the "Separated Families Search Campaign" led by Korean Broadcasting Services (KBS), *Hankuk-ilbo*, *Chosun-ilbo* and *Seoul-Sinmun*. The KBS live broadcast of the "Separated Families Search Campaign" was especially successful in focusing world-wide attention upon the separated families issue on the Korean peninsula and facilitating the reunion of many separated families within South Korea.

One of the private organizations most active in the search for lost family members has been the "Korean Assembly for Reunion of Ten Million Separated Families" set up on December 20, 1982 by separated families who sought to pressure the North, after the North's sabotage of the failed South-North Red Cross conference. After electing Young Seek Choue, Chancellor of Kyung Hee University, as Chairman on December 20, 1982 at their main office, the "People From the Five Northern Provinces," was officially inaugurated on February 9, 1983 at the Sejong Hall, in Seoul with 6,000 representatives in attendance.

That the separated families participated in organizing activities in their common interest signified that they had abandoned passively lamenting their situation and instead had begun to embrace a more active approach.

The Committee attempted to actively increase awareness in the separated family issue both at home and abroad through year round activities such as hosting academic conferences, researching on the current status of separated families, and appealing for cooperation from international organizations. The Committee also decided to commemorate August 12, 1971, the day when the Chairman of the South Korean Red Cross first proposed "South-North Red Cross Talks" for the reunion of separated families, as the 'Day of Separated Families' (after the first home visitation was achieved the commemoration day was changed to every year on September 20). When KBS TV telecast the live program, "Separated Families Search Campaign" the Committee, led by Young Seek Choue, provided services and facilities in concert with Korean Red Cross. Even after the campaign, the Committee jointly operated a 'Reunion Plaza' with the same partner to provide continuous service.

From August 26 to September 7, 1990, twelve members of the "Overseas Delegation for Facilitation of Separated Families Reunion" led by Young Seek Choue visited the United Nations, the International Red Cross, the International Human Rights Association, UNESCO, and other related institutions and presented the tragic picture of separated families in the Korean peninsula, appealing for the reunion of separated families, the free exchange of letters, and unimpeded visitation rights.

In addition, Young Seek Choue, chairman of "Korean Assembly for Reunion of Ten Million Separated Families" put forward an 'International Day of Peace' and an 'International Year of Peace' to the United Nations General Assembly via a third country, Costa Rica. Young Seek Choue, who holds lifetime honorary chairmanships of both the International Association of University Presidents and the International Club for Brighter Society has made an immense contribution to the Korean separated families reunion campaign.

His committee signed up 21,202,192 people in support of the reunion of separated families during the "Worldwide Signature Drive for Urging Reunion of Separated Families" held from June 1, 1993 to August 15, 1994. The signature campaign, in which 153 nations participated, was acknowledged by the International Guinness Committee as the world record for the largest signature campaign with the greatest number of countries participating. It was no wonder that, as a result of the signature campaign, the heart-breaking struggle of separated families yearning for reunion became inscribed in the hearts of an incalculable number of people. Through the worldwide signature campaign, Young Seek Choue attempted to bring an undesirable historical event back out of oblivion and pointed out the injustice of the forced partition of the Korean peninsula so that citizens of the world would cooperate to ease the suffering of the separated families.

Since the first generation of Korea's separated families is decreasing due to attrition, their reunion should be treated by the government with the utmost urgency. Finally, the new South Korean government led by Dae-Jung Kim has put forward a flexible new approach to South-North relations that places exceptional interest in and emphasis upon the separated family issue. Even though the North Korean government has yet to demonstrate any tangible signs of turnaround in policy, the fact that the North has also abandoned its antagonistic attitude toward the South is sufficient to provide the separated families with new expectations and hopes for reunification.

Bibliography

Korean Assembly for Reunion of Ten Million Separated Families 1983a *Korean Separated Families and its Reunion*

Korean Assembly for Reunion of Ten Million Separated Families 1983b *When will the Tragedy End?*

Korean Assembly for Reunion of Ten Million Separated Families 1985 *International Cooperation for the Reunion of Separated Families*

Korean Assembly for Reunion of Ten Million Separated Families 1986 *The Reunion of Separated Families and Korean Reunification Policy*

Korean Assembly for Reunion of Ten Million Separated Families 1996 *Beyond the Wall of Separation. Cases of Correspondence and Meeting of Separated Family Members*

National Unification Board, Republic of Korea 1997a *A White Paper on Reunification*

National Unification Board, Republic of Korea 1997b *Guidelines for Cooperative Exchange of South-North Separated Families*

South Korean Red Cross 1976 *A White Paper on Separated Families I*

South Korean Red Cross 1986 *A White Paper on Separated Families II*

DONG-YOUNG CHOUE; JONG-HOI KIM

Moving the Substantive Agenda Forward: CONGO's NGO Committees

The NGO Committee on Disarmament, Inc. at UN headquarters in New York and the NGO Special Committee on Disarmament at the UN in Geneva cooperate on a wide range of international disarmament issues. Each takes the leadership on matters in their respective locations. The effectiveness of our activity was praised in the closing remarks of Chairman Jayantha Dhanapala at the 1995 Non-Proliferation Review and Extension Conference with, "Over the past twenty-five years non-governmental organizations have performed valuable services for the Non-Proliferation Treaty (NPT)—in encouragement, ideas, public support and advocacy of further progress toward the goals of the treaty. I should like to pay them a sincere tribute for their dedication."

A major example of this cooperation is our focus on the NPT PrepComs in Geneva in 1998 and in New York in 1997 (in NY again in 1999). Early on we informed NGOs of the opportunities we sought for full input from NGO experts during the governmental PrepComs. The success of these efforts was a result of both our advance contacts with diplomats and help from the UN Centre (which became the current Department) for Disarmament Affairs. Before describing our achievements in the NPT process and other specific results of our work, as well as the difficulties we encounter, we will describe our objectives and activities more generally.

Both Disarmament Committees network with national and international peace and disarmament NGOs around the world, which are accredited to the UN:

(a) providing them with resources;

(b) soliciting their views;

(c) supporting their campaigns, such as the International Campaign to Ban Landmines;

(d) encouraging their activity with the UN;

(e) informing them of UN and international progress on disarmament issues through publications and conferences;

(f) supporting coalitions which form around topics, such as Abolition 2000, a global network for the elimination of nuclear weapons through a UN Nuclear Weapons Convention.

The New York Committee also publishes six regular issues of *Disarmament Times* each year and special issues when events merit. Its publication schedule relates to scheduled intergovernmental meetings on disarmament. This is the only independent professionally produced newspaper devoted exclusively to accurate, objective reporting on arms control and disarmament activities in the UN context. In addition to the UN community, the paper reaches a world-wide readership of policymakers, researchers, students, organizations and concerned individuals. Readers can follow an initiative as it develops into a draft agreements or even a treaty.

During Special Sessions on Disarmament and other major UN disarmament conferences, the Disarmament Committees serve as liaison between the UN and NGOs. During such events we facilitate NGO participation in sessions, sponsor an information center and arrange forums, briefings, meetings with delegates and with the UN press corps. We also encourage NGOs to present their concerns in a clear and compelling fashion to their own, and other, governments on a regular basis.

A primary objective of our Conferences and Fora is to bring NGO expertise into the mix of ideas being considered by governments and at the UN. Until greater access is obtained, this is often the only way to introduce such ideas. The Forums provide an opportunity for outside experts to present their proposals at the UN. Sometimes held in cooperation with UN secretariats of Disarmament Affairs and Public Information, forums bring together ambassadors, negotiators, technical experts, UN officials, scholars, journalists and members of the public for close examination of disarmament issues. In New York during Disarmament Week in October 1998 our panels are grouped under the title "The World at a Critical Turning Point." Other recent titles are "Emerging Disarmament Issues," "The Future of Disarmament" and "New Realities: Disarmament, Peace-building and Global Security." Forum topics considered during the past decade have included reductions of nuclear weapons, prevention of an arms race in outer space, disarmament and development, chemical and biological weapons treaties, alternate security systems, a comprehensive test ban, problems in verification, nuclear non-proliferation, nuclear-free zones, 'transparency" in the arms trade and the convention to ban landmines. UN cooperation has enabled us to publish more than ten edited transcripts of these forums.

Both Committees offer internship for students interested in disarmament issues. They have the opportunity to deepen their knowledge of international relations, attend UN and NGO meetings, study UN documents and assist with the work of the Committees.

Returning to specific achievements, the pattern which we developed from experiences in the 1995 NPT Conference and then the 1997 NPT PrepCom is one which served us well in 1998. It is our model for the 1999 NPT PrepCom and useful for future disarmament conferences. Well in advance we requested all interested NGOs to submit topics for our presentations during the PrepCom. These topics were grouped and the NGOs concerned with each group developed a joint statement and selected a presenter. We asked the Conference Chairperson for a scheduled time to make these 13 presentations. After consultation with his Bureau, there was agreement that on the second day NGOs would have a half-day session for this purpose, after which delegates could ask questions. We also compiled our statements in a booklet for each delegate. The session was well attended. Both this process and the NGO contributions were commended by the Chairperson and several delegations. Earlier the Abolition 2,000 Network gave the Chairperson an appeal for the elimination of nuclear weapons signed by 13 million people. Regretfully, after the initial period of exchange of views, NGOs were not allowed to attend meetings except for the formal closing. This is a barrier we are still trying to overcome, for NPT, First Committee of the UN General Assembly (GA), and other disarmament fora. However, press conferences and a series of NGO meetings paralleling those of the States parties were valuable for exchanging NGO views and for networking.

The contributions of NGOs in the field of disarmament have been less than in the economic and social fields, and regards both policy making and implementation, but they have nevertheless played an important role. In the 1950s and 1960s individual scientists, experts, research institutions and various NGOs were very active in campaigns to stop radioactive fallout from nuclear testing and to prevent nuclear proliferation. By disseminating accurate information and warnings about the dangers of nuclear testing and the spread of nuclear weapons they stimulated public interest and pressures. This helped generate political will for governments to ban testing in the atmosphere in 1963, and to agree on the Nuclear Non-Proliferation Treaty in 1968.

In more recent times NGOs helped to initiate and promote the efforts to amend the 1963 Partial Test Ban Treaty and to convene the Test Ban Amendment Conference in 1991. These revived the efforts for a comprehensive test ban and restored that item to a top place on the international agenda. They also played an active role in promoting the achievement of the Chemical Weapons Convention and its verifi-

cation systems. Similarly, it was a group of NGOs that initiated and promoted the "World Court Project" that led to the advisory opinion of the International Court of Justice on the legality of the threat or use of nuclear weapons in July 1996.

Two NGOs with consultative status with ECOSOC were awarded the Nobel Peace Prize for their efforts to promote a world free of nuclear weapons—the International Physicians for the Prevention of Nuclear War in 1985 and the Pugwash Conferences on Science and World Affairs in 1995. Then in 1997 the Prize was awarded to the International Campaign to Ban Landmines, a coalition including many accredited NGOs. Now in mid-September, 1998, the required 40th country ratified the Convention on the Prohibition of the Use, Stockpiling, Production and Transfer of Anti-Personnel Mines and on their Destruction, so it will go into effect in March, 1999. Universality is the goal and countries which have signed continue to ratify. A book, *To Walk Without Fear*, has just been published on this unique NGO and governmental cooperation which produced the Convention, spurs mine clearance and provides humanitarian aid. UN Secretary General Kofi Annan described this partnership as a "remarkable expression of the *new diplomacy*." By their very nature, NGOs tend to reflect the views of civil society at the grassroots, and in turn, by providing accurate and timely information to their members, help to shape those views and generate support for the UN and its work.

We have been active in the efforts to get fuller access for all NGOs in the UN, but obviously our experience is in the disarmament area. We seek to follow disarmament in the UN as closely as we can, but our actual participation is very limited. In the First Committee of the GA and the Disarmament Commission, we are allowed to attend public sessions, but not informal or closed sessions or meetings of sub-committees or working groups. We are allowed access to the floor of the meeting room and to delegations only before or after the actual meetings. We cannot make oral or written presentations but are permitted to leave printed material on tables outside the meeting rooms.

At the Conference on Disarmament in Geneva, NGOs may attend meetings where they sit in the public section. They may send communications to the Conference which are listed in a document that is circulated periodically to the Committee and made available to delegations upon request, a very rare occurrence. At special conferences and meetings, such as the international Conference on Disarmament and Development in 1987 and Special Session of Disarmament (SSOD) III in 1988, one day was set aside by the main committee of the whole for some selected NGOs to make oral presentations. These necessarily had to be very short.

It has also become established practice for individual NGOs to work in private with individual UN delegations to promote consideration and action on specific disarmament issues. It was close contact and relations of this nature that made it possible for NGOs to make the contributions described above and many others.

There is now a growing feeling among delegations, the UN Secretariat and the NGOs that the contributions of NGOs could be greatly increased and be more effective, including participation of NGOs from developing countries, if current practices were placed on an official, formal, open basis similar to current ECOSOC practice. In particular, we have requested that NGO participation be expanded in the following ways:

1. That in the First Committee we be given:

(a) some official status that would allow us to attend all open and closed meetings of the First Committee and of any sub-committees and working groups established by it;

(b) the right to submit written proposals that would be circulated as documents of the First Committee;

(c) the right for a selected number of NGOs to make oral presentations on appropriate occasions to the Committee and to its subsidiary bodies;

(d) the right to receive all documents of the First Committee when they are issued.

2. That the same privileges should be provided to NGOs with respect to other Committees of the GA and to international conferences and special sessions that deal with disarmament affairs. It is hoped that the granting of these privileges would also be carried over to the Conference on Disarmament and the review conferences and other conferences held pursuant to any international treaty and preparatory committees therefor.

We believe these are constructive suggestions. It is clear from the accomplishments of 50 years that NGO contributions have been substantial and are growing. No group has a monopoly on wisdom. But NGOs bring to the table both an idealistic and practical perspective, certainly not a narrow political one. We often speak for those otherwise unable to make their voices heard. We intend to be full partners with governments in service to humanity through the United Nations.

VERNON C. NICHOLS

Multilateralism

In public debate, multilateralism is normally contrasted with unilateralism. In this context, the multilateral approach is to try to change or constrain the policies of two or more States through international negotiations and treaties, rather than by independent (i.e., unilateral) actions. The negotiations could relate to military, political, economic, and any other issues with an international dimension. However, although most of the discussion that follows would be relevant to any of these issues, this article will draw upon experience in the area of arms control and disarmament. The next section outlines some of the potential advantages and disadvantages of seeking arms control or disarmament through multilateral agreements rather than unilateral actions,

There is another dimension to the debate about multilateralism—people often disagree about how many nations multilateral negotiations should include. Several of the most important arms control agreements, such as the Anti-Ballistic Missile (ABM) Treaty and the Strategic Arms Limitations Talks (SALT) I and II agreements between the United States

and the then Soviet Union, are really "bilateral" rather than multilateral. The question of how many countries should participate in negotiations, and which countries these should be, raises important technical, strategic, and political issues. These are discussed in the second part of this article, followed by a brief historical summary of how some important multilateral negotiations and treaties were approached.

1. Formal Negotiations and Treaties

International negotiations are time consuming and fallible. There is little point in engaging in them if the desired objectives can be satisfactorily achieved by unilateral action. Military preparations to enhance deterrence or precautions against accidental war are normally carried out without prior negotiations with adversaries, though allies might be consulted. Similarly, if international stability can be increased by removing sources of conflict through independent political initiatives, or by reducing tension through unilateral changes on military policy, then there is a good case for going ahead immediately.

Even in this situation, however, there are some potential advantages to the multilateral approach. Sometimes the process of negotiating can be important in itself. It can symbolize a commitment to take other countries' interests into account and provide a public platform on which the issues can be highlighted. Furthermore, international procedures and institutions may be established which may prove valuable in the future even if they are unnecessary at the time of negotiation. Against this, unilateral actions can also have a powerful symbolic effect if they are clear and well-explained. Procedures and international institutions may equally well be established after the initiative has been taken, with less danger of distracting side-issues being raised during negotiations. The negotiating format can be used as a delaying tactic by domestic groups that are opposed to the change. For example, many analysts believe that the United States Administration agreed to East-West talks on troop reductions in Central Europe in 1973 in order to forestall moves in Congress to reduce US troops unilaterally rather than agree to mutual reductions with the Warsaw Pact.

In situations where the desired objectives can be achieved only through the actions of more than one state, the case for formal talks is obviously stronger. Even where there is little competition between the states involved, measures might be carried through much more efficiently if the action of each state was coordinated through prior negotiations and agreements. For example the North Atlantic Treaty Organization (NATO) (see *North Atlantic Treaty Organization (NATO)*) allies have regularly engaged in negotiations to establish a consensus on arms programs or changes in strategy.

To resolve problems or achieve cooperative measures between competitors or adversaries may require hard bargaining, strong pressures, and mutual guarantees. Even within military alliances there are elements of competition, as each state seeks to promote its own economic and political interests and its own preferences for alliance strategy. Yet these concern are minor compared to the rivalry and suspicion between potential military adversaries such as the United States and the former Soviet Union. Even while they are pursuing measures in areas of mutual advantage, such adversaries are likely to maneuver to try to score propaganda points and secure relative advantages. At the least they may suspect the others of trying to do so.

In this context, formal negotiations and treaties have clear attractions. On some issues, each state

may be unwilling to limit or change its policy until its adversaries have explicitly agreed to simultaneous and similar constraints on their own policies, with the important details and verification procedures already hammered out and guaranteed by international treaty. Even where a government judges that it could afford the risk of taking unilateral action without guaranteed reciprocation, there are still attractions to the multilateral approach. Reciprocation may be more likely, and include concessions in the areas that cause most concern in a particular government, if the proposed measures are used to strengthen that government's bargaining position rather than conceded in advance.

Formal negotiations are not essential for hard bargaining, but detailed and direct discussions of draft treaties may allow details and procedures to be better specified and technical issues to be resolved. Furthermore, a formal bargaining process would encourage governments to properly engage with their adversaries' concern. Differences in historical, social, and economic structure, geostrategic position, and asymmetries in force structures inevitably lead to differences in countries' priorities and concerns. Such asymmetries mean that trade-offs are likely to be necessary for an equitable agreement. Trade-offs can become very complex, and a clear negotiating structure may be necessary to bring the bargaining process to a successful conclusion.

Negotiations can also help to create institutions with an interest in securing an agreement—partially counterbalancing the influence of groups opposed to the implementation of the measures concerned. In the SALT process, for example, large negotiating teams and their various supporting institutions developed which had direct access to decision makers and a professional commitment to the success of the talks. In the former Soviet Union this provided the Politburo with an additional source of information outside of their military establishments. In the United States it even led to concern amongst opponents of SALT that these institutions were so strong that the United States was pursuing agreement for agreement's sake.

There are also advantages on basing an agreement on a legally drafted treaty, specifying obligations and procedures for verification or settling disputes. Less detailed agreements would leave more room for future differences in interpretation which might undermine the agreement. And although international law is not enforced by a higher supranational authority, a formal and ratified treaty does strengthen the pressures for compliance.

These advantages can be very strong, as is testified by the fact that states have devoted so much time and energy to the multilateral approach. Nevertheless the experience of strategic arms negotiations, in particular, has emphasized a number of potential disadvantages. A key problem is that the negotiating process encourages inflexibility, and even the development of weapons as "bargaining chips." This problem is intrinsic to the bargaining process, but it can be argued that formal negotiations exacerbate the difficulties. Their very formality and the visibility of the resulting agreement may discourage the floating of compromises and make each side more determined to ensure that the final deal clearly requires concessions from adversaries which are at least equivalent to its own. This can distort a government's view of its interests and objectives and invest asymmetries (for example in numbers or types of weapons) with an importance they do not deserve. In order to preserve their reputation as tough bargainers, states might even reject deals that would actually be to their overall advantage just because other states seem to gain even more.

These inflexibilities, combined with the intrinsic complexity of the issues and of preparing a legal treaty, all tend to make negotiations last a long time. Yet, during the course of negotiations, political, economic, military, and technological developments continue and may have undermined the basis or value of the negotiations before they are completed. For example, during the seven years it took to negotiate the SALT II treaty relations between the United States and the then Soviet Union moved from détente to a "new Cold War." Meanwhile, the emergence of the US Pershing II and ground-launched Cruise missiles and the Soviet SS20 missiles and Backfire bombers reopened disputes about what constituted a strategic weapon. Similarly, the development of Multiple Independent Reentry Vehicle (MIRV) technology during the SALT I negotiations greatly reduced the value of the agreed limits on the numbers of strategic missiles, since the number of deliverable strategic warheads could continue to increase.

Finally, attempts to secure a fully ratified treaty can cause more problems than they are worth. Although a joint declaration may be less precise than a treaty and lack the status of international law, the sanctions against abrogation can be almost as severe and no treaty can be drawn up so tightly that all signatories are bound to honor the spirit as well as the letter of the agreement.

So there are both potential advantages and potential disadvantages to the multilateral approach. In practice, however, multilateral negotiations can be combined with more informal or unilateral processes.

For example the negotiations between the United States, the erstwhile Soviet Union, and the United Kingdom for a ban on nuclear weapon tests in the 1950s and early 1960s was stimulated by a three-year unilateral moratorium on warhead tests by all sides. The political atmosphere after the Cuban Missile Crisis was improved by a series of unilateral tension-reduction measures, which contributed to the agreement on the partial Test Ban Treaty. Similarly the formal treaty may simply consolidate measures achieved through other means. The 1967 Outer Space Treaty banning nuclear weapons being placed in orbit was only signed after several years of tacit restraint on the part of both Superpowers.

2. How Multilateral Should Negotiations Be?

On the face of it, decisions about which states should participate in multilateral negotiations or treaties should be straightforward. If a state has a direct interest in the issues under discussion and/or is likely to have a direct role in implementing or maintaining any agreement that emerges, then it ought to be included. However, in practice the decision can often be difficult or controversial.

If the above criterion is interpreted liberally, the negotiations may become unmanageably large. To take an extreme example, it could be argued that every state has a direct interest in constraints on the nuclear arms face. But the problems of negotiating the bilateral SALT and Strategic Arms Reduction Talks (START) were bad enough with only two states involved. Expanding them to include over 150 states would probably remove any chance of success. In general, each additional negotiating partner with a direct interest in the issues involved will have its own priorities and constraints and will complicate the task of arriving at a mutually acceptable agreement. Even if the substantive issues were put to one side, the negotiating process is likely to be more drawn out, complex, and prone to disruption. There is therefore an incentive to keep the number of states involved to a minimum.

However, there are also problems if the criterion for participation is interpreted too strictly. Excluding an influential state whose interests could be affected by the agreement can create more problems than it solves, even if the treaty does not directly place it under any obligations. Furthermore, states without a major role in the problem under discussion may be able to mediate between the opposing sides and propose compromises, increasing flexibility and facilitating agreement. Non-nuclear neutral and nonaligned countries such as Sweden and Mexico have, for example, made valuable contributions in this role during arms control and disarmament negotiations.

Decisions about participation can have important political implications, and therefore can be fiercely contested. These decisions can imply a certain interpretation of the problem and may greatly influence the character of the agreement likely to emerge. Each state will argue for participation and procedures that will promote its own perspectives and objectives. Thus, there have been major disputes about the participation of the Palestine Liberation Organization (PLO) in negotiations to resolve conflicts on the Middle East, and on whether to tackle the problems through a series of bilateral negotiations of a single regional conference (see *Arab-Israeli Conflict: Peace Plans and Proposals*).

Participation in negotiations can be used by a state to assert the status and legitimacy of its interests in the issues under discussion. Thus they can be used to assert Great Power or Superpower status—part of the definition of a Superpower is wide acceptance that it has an important role or interests throughout the world, particularly on security issues. In the context of the Middle East, for example, the former Soviet Union had promoted the idea of a regional conference, in which it would naturally participate. The United States was keen to deny that the former Soviet Union had a useful role to play, particularly after Kissinger successfully reduced Soviet influence in the Middle East in the early 1970s. This is part of the reason why the United States prefers bilateral negotiations between the Middle Eastern countries themselves: confident of its own influence in the region, the United States can afford to play a background role.

Similarly, as the Superpowers increasingly abandoned multilateral talks in favor of bilateral negotiations in the 1960s, many neutral and nonaligned states tried to resist this trend and retain the US-Soviet talks within a United Nations framework. In part this was an assertion of their own interests in nuclear arms control and disarmament.

The allies of the United States and former Soviet Union have a clear security interest in the arms policies of their respective Superpower. On nuclear issues they had generally been satisfied with bilateral negotiations, and had sought to protect their interests through representations to their Superpower ally. This has made the actual process of negotiating more manageable, but at the cost of sometimes complicating the decision-making process between negotiating sessions. For example, suspicions on the part of the former Federal Republic of Germany and the United Kingdom that the Carter Administration might sacrifice some West European military options in order to secure the SALT II agreement slowed down the whole SALT process just at the time that the whole process was coming under intense, and ultimately fatal, criticisms from within the United States itself.

To add to the problems of obtaining the optimum participation in multilateral negotiations, key states may be unwilling to join the talks. This could be because they do not regard the agreement that may emerge as being in their national interests. It could also be because they disagree with any definition of the problem which implies that their participation is necessary. For example, the United Kingdom and France refused any involvement in the Strategic Arms Limitation or Intermediate Range Nuclear Forces talks, partly because they did not want any constraints to be imposed on their nuclear forces and partly because they denied that their forces were relevant until the Superpowers had radically reduced their own arsenals. For its part, the United States was pleased to omit them because it wanted to obtain equal constraints with the former Soviet Union, while the former Soviet Union was arguing for a NATO-Warsaw Pact balance. The People's Republic of China and France refused to participate in negotiations for a Comprehensive Test Ban Treaty (CTBT) or to sign the Non-Proliferation Treaty (NPT) (see *Non-Proliferation Treaty (NPT)*) for similar reasons: they rejected legal constraints on countries' nuclear weapon programs while the Superpowers maintained their own enormous nuclear arsenals.

3. Historical Summary of the Role of Multilateralism in Arms Control and Disarmament Negotiations

These brief comments do not, and cannot, aim at a comprehensive survey of multilateral negotiations. They seek only to illustrate the historical experience of arms control and disarmament negotiations, and to indicate how the problems of scope and participation have been handled and how multilateral fora have related to bilateral talks. In this section, multilateralism is used in contrast to bilateralism (or trilateralism).

If one neglects some early arms control and disarmament treaties such as the prohibition on war elephants by the Rome-Carthage Treaty of 201 BC, the history of the multilateral approach to international security begins at the end of the nineteenth century. In previous centuries governments had negotiated over treaties to end wars, but the Hague Conferences of 1899 and 1907 were the first international conferences between governments which were convened to discuss how to preserve peace.

Czar Nicholas convened the Hague Conferences to promote international disarmament, stimulated by the strains military preparations imposed on Russian finances. In the event, government in countries such as Germany and Britain regarded such aims as utopian and the conferences concentrated on more limited objectives. They established the Permanent Court of Arbitrator at the Hague, clarified the status of neutral countries, and codified certain rules of war, at least as far as declared wars between "civilized" nations were concerned—colonial wars were treated as internal conflicts.

In the interwar years, the Geneva Protocols of 1924 effectively banned the first use of chemical or biological weapons. The 1928 Kellogg-Briand Pact condemned the use of force to resolve international disputes and was signed by 65 states. This Pact provided impetus for the League of Nations to convene the 1932 World Disarmament Conference in Geneva, which discussed a universal reduction and limitation of all types of armaments. More than 60 governments sent representatives, making it the largest international gathering until that date. Subcommittees were set up on a wide range of issues but, after long negotiations and many notable proposals, the conference was dissolved in deadlock. Although nations agreed in principle to a collective security system and to international limitations on arms, they could not agree on effective ways of operating the security system or on the way in which the relative strengths of each country's armed forces should be fixed.

Rearmament, not disarmament, became the rule after 1933. After Hitler came to power, Germany withdrew from the World Disarmament Conference and from the League of Nations. In 1934 Japan gave notice that it would withdraw from naval arms control treaties with Britain and the United States (see *Naval Limitation Treaties between the World Wars*).

After the bombing of Hiroshima and Nagasaki, the restriction or abolition of nuclear weapons went straight to the top of the political agenda. In January 1946, the United Nations General Assembly unanimously approved the creation of an Atomic Energy Commission (AEC) within which negotiations were to be conducted "for the elimination from national armaments of atomic weapons." In 1947 the UN Security Council established the Commission for Conventional Armaments to negotiate a general reduction in armaments and armed forces and satisfactory procedures for verification and sanctions.

In the context of increasing rivalry and suspicion between the former Soviet Union and the West, these negotiations achieved nothing. In an attempt to break the impasse the two negotiating bodies were consolidated into a single Disarmament Commission composed of the eleven members of the Security Council plus Canada. This new commission had the objective of negotiating a plan for general and complete disarmament (GCD) acceptable to both the Eastern and Western blocs. This plan would then be presented to the General Assembly. The ultimate aim was to reduce all armed forces and military facilities of all nations to the minimum level necessary for maintaining internal security within each country.

In the face of a continuing lack of progress within the negotiations themselves, the UN juggled with the multilateral fora. The Disarmament Commission was the primary disarmament body for five years. Then it was expanded in 1957 and 1958 to include every member of the UN, with the effect that it became uselessly large and held only two further sessions in 1960 and 1965. Meanwhile a subcommittee was created in 1954 consisting of Canada, France, the United Kingdom, the United States, and the former Soviet Union which was expanded five years later to become the Ten Nation Committee on Disarmament and which then took over as the main negotiating forum. East and West were equally represented with five members each. If nothing else, these exercises illustrated vividly that the obstacles to agreement could not be overcome by adjusting procedures and participation alone.

Many people had actually hoped that comprehensive GCD proposals would actually be more likely to succeed than more limited proposals. They recognized that nuclear strategy, particularly in NATO, was linked to the fear of conventional attack, and also that the former Soviet Union, the United States, and their allies were unlikely to abolish their conventional forces while other states retained theirs. GCD supporters hoped that fully comprehensive negotiations would be able to take all these linkages into account and thus overcome obstacles that would block more partial talks. Potential regional instabilities could be avoided while disarmament was implemented, problems of definition would be avoided because all weapons would be included, and circumvention would be easier to detect because all military forces would be monitored.

Thus the GCD approach—multilateralism par excellence—had great internal coherence. The problem was that its very comprehensiveness would have made it extraordinarily hard to negotiate. Even if an agreement had been achieved, the process of implementation would have been so unwieldy and prone to disruption that it would have been difficult to carry through in the face of the inevitable suspicions and opposing vested interests.

In the event the negotiations did not pass the first hurdle of securing an agreement between the former Soviet Union and the United States. Eight definitions and principles were agreed in September 1961 (known as the McCloy-Zorin Principles after the representatives who negotiated them). The principles included commitment to the common objective of GCD supervised by the UN, which would be provided with its own international peace forces. Disarmament would be carried out in an agreed sequence of stages until complete, and at no stage would any state gain even temporary advantage.

These principles remain official policy, and have been endorsed by most nations of the world. However, they have manifestly not led to a disarmament agreement. During the last serious negotiations on the issue which ended in 1964, the United States continued to insist upon substantial conventional disarmament and veto-free international inspection before it would abandon nuclear weapons, whereas the former Soviet Union insisted upon nuclear disarmament at an early stage with inspection and major conventional disarmament deferred to later stages. Since then, attention has focused on more limited, and hopefully more achievable, arms control and disarmament measures.

By 1962 the growing number of nonaligned nations in the United Nations had become very frustrated with the negotiating performance of the nuclear alliances, and eight of their group joined the Ten Nation committee, creating the Eighteen Nation Disarmament Committee (ENDC). This was further expanded to include 26 nations in 1969, 31 nations in 1975, and as of 1986 it consisted of 40 states and was known as the Conference on Disarmament (CD). On June 17, 1996, the Conference admitted 23 more states as its members. In the words of the UN, it remains "the single multilateral disarmament negotiating forum of the international community." However, after it expanded to include neutral and nonaligned states in 1962, the former Soviet Union and the United States increasingly went outside the ENDC and its successors to negotiate bilaterally. Nevertheless, as illustrated below, the UN multilateral negotiating fora have played a useful and creative role.

Since the original proposal by Prime Minister Nehru of India, a comprehensive ban on nuclear tests has been a long term priority of the UN. Direct negotiations between the United States, the United Kingdom, and the former Soviet Union began in 1958 after unilateral moratoria on testing had been announced and reciprocated. When the trilateral talks broke down in January 1962, the ENDC established a subcommittee on the issue. An initiative by the eight nonaligned or neutral members of the committee resulted in the three nuclear weapon states resuming negotiations in April 1962 within the framework of the ENDC. In June 1963 these states decided to go outside the ENDC to finalize the Partial Test Ban Treaty, which was duly signed on August 5, 1963, and by 1986 had 111 signatories.

After 1963 various neutral and nonaligned countries, particularly Sweden, carried out studies and made proposals through the ENDC in order to promote negotiations on a comprehensive test ban treaty (CTBT). In 1976 the (expanded) UN committee established an Ad Hoc Group of Scientific Experts on seismic verification techniques, and promoted the trilateral talks that resumed in June 1977.

This interaction between bilateral (and trilateral) negotiations and multilateral talks existed also for other arms control issues. The process leading to the Non-proliferation Treaty (NPT) began in 1959 with an Irish proposal to the Ten Nation Disarmament Committee, which was then raised in subsequent years by other countries. In 1965 the NPT dominated ENDC business. The United States and the then Soviet Union submitted draft treaties for discussion and in the autumn of 1966 began private negotiations on the issue. They returned one year later to present identical draft treaties to the ENDC. After revisions by neutral and nonaligned countries the NPT was opened for signature on July 1968, and came into force in 1970. Since then there have been five-yearly review conferences. There are now only five states worldwide outside the NPT regime (Brazil, Cuba, India, Israel, and Pakistan). In June 1997, Brazil announced its intention to join the Treaty (see *Non-Proliferation Treaty (NPT)*).

In a similar way, the UN negotiating machinery contributed to the following treaties, amongst others: the Outer Space Treaty (1967), the Treaty of Tlateloco (1967) (establishing the Latin American nuclear weapon free zone), the Sea Bed Treaty (1971), the Biological Warfare Convention (1972), and the Environmental Modification (Enmod) Convention (1977), the South Pacific Nuclear Weapons Free Zone Treaty (1985), Chemical Weapons Convention (1993), African Nuclear Weapons Free Zone Treaty (1996), and Ottawa Treaty (1997). It has also played a key role on discussions on nuclear weapon free zones (see *Nuclear-Weapon-Free Zones: A History and Assessment*), a ban on chemical weapons, and proposals to establish the Indian Ocean as a so-called Zone of Peace (see *Indian Ocean: The Duality of Zone of Peace Concept and Politics of Security Revisited*).

However, some multilateral arms control negotiations have taken place almost entirely outside UN structures. For example, following Chancellor Willy Brandt's Ostpolitik policy in the late 1960s and early 1970s (see *Ostpolitik*), the Conference on Security and Cooperation in Europe (CSCE) began in 1973. It was a complicated set of negotiations in which 35 States (United States, Canada, and every European state except Albania) sought to reach consensus agreements in three areas: military confidence-building measures; economic, scientific, and technical cooperation; cultural and educational exchanges and the freer movement of people and dissemination of information.

In spite of the complexities, an agreement was signed in all three areas in 1975—the so-called Helsinki Final Act. In the course of the negotiations the NATO, Warsaw Pact, and neutral and nonaligned states tended to form three groups with common negotiating positions, simplifying the negotiating process. However countries sometimes broke ranks with their group: Romania, for example, went much further than the rest of the Warsaw Pact in promoting military confidence-building measures. The CSCE was seen as an ongoing process after 1975, with regular Review Conferences (see *Organization on Security and Cooperation in Europe (OSCE); Helsinki Process)*).

The Mutual Balanced Force Reduction (MBFR) talks began in October 1973, shortly after the CSCE negotiations were launched. They covered only the Central European area, and only Warsaw Pact and NATO states participated. States with armed forces deployed in Central Europe were included as "direct participants," while the other members of the two military alliances were given secondary status as "indirect participants." Each alliance has adopted a common negotiating position and the issues have remained fairly simple—focusing on small reductions in troop numbers. However, the absence of a strong political will on either side to reach an agreement, and the lack of mediators, has led to the talks being deadlocked over issues that should easily be resolved. Since 1976 the main obstacle was a disagreement over the number of Warsaw Pact troops in Central Europe.

The Conference on Disarmament in Europe (CDE), begun in Stockholm in January 1984 to strengthen the confidence-building measures established in the 1975 Helsinki Final Act, seemed to be more promising: it has the same participants and negotiating practice as the CSCE process. Despite the different negotiating positions between the NATO and Warsaw Pact, the CDE was ended in November 1986. The Stockholm CDE Conference contributed to the development of the CSCE arms control regime from the first generation of CBMs to the second generation of CSBMs: among other things, (a) the CDE extended the application zone of confidence building measures; (b) it lowered the notification threshold; (c) it introduced on-site inspection provisions; and (d) it contained constraining measures.

4. Conclusions

Multilateralism has established itself as a key approach to resolving international problems that endanger world peace and security. Several important agreements have been established through it. The idea of tackling regional or global problems through a multilateral process rather than by each state pursuing its own individual interests is now widely accepted. However, analysis and historical experience shows that multilateralism in the narrower sense of pursuing international change through formal negotiations between a number of states should generally be regarded as a valuable element in a broader strategy for change which also involves informal, bilateral, and unilateral processes.

See also: *Arms Control, Evolution of; Collective Security and Collective Self-defense; Confidence Building in International Diplomacy; Negotiations, Direct; Problem-solving in Internationalised Conflicts; Treaties of the Modern Era; Unilateralism*

Bibliography ———————————————

Bechhoefer B 1961 *Post-War Negotiations for Arms Control.* Brookings Institutoon, Washington, DC
Goldblat J 1982 *Arms Control Agreements: A Handbook.* SIPRI/ Taylor and Francis, London
Lall A S (ed.) 1985 *Multilateral Negotiation and Mediation Instruments and Methods.* Pergamon, Oxford
Myrdal A 1980 *The Game of Disarmament: How the United States and Russia Run the Arms Race.* Spokesman Books, Nottingham
National Academy of Sciences 1985 *Nuclear Arms Control Background and Issues.* National Academy Press. Washington, DC
Noel-Baker P 1958 *The Arms Race: A Programme for World*

Disarmament. Atlantic Books, London

Sizoo J, Jurrjens R Th 1984 CSCE *Decision Making: The Madrid Experience*. Martinus Nijhoff, The Hague

United Nations Department for Disarmament Affairs 1985 *The*

United Nations and Disarmament: 1945-1985. United Nations, New York

OWEN GREENE; KI-JOON HONG

Multinational Corporation and Peace

The globalization of economic exchange and production has become a reality, and nowhere is this reality more evident than in the proliferation of multinational corporations (MNCs). MNCs are enterprises with headquarters in one country that are active in other countries. Many MNCs originate in developed countries and, like the governments of those countries, advocate a free market, and many have a "global reach," with economic interests in almost every corner of the world.[1]

By engaging in cross-border production and distribution, these corporations have produced unprecedented interdependence among societies (see *Interdependence, International*). Whether they are a force for peace or war is a subject for debate. In the eyes of some observers, MNCs are engines of modernity and harbingers of global peace, homogenizing, enriching, and integrating diverse societies, the multinational corporations (MNCs) is either a force for peace and modernity (see *Global Integration*). The influence of MNCs is welcomed in advanced Western societies and Japan where they are regarded as benign, and are seen as global engines of free enterprise and modernization whose effects include providing prosperity, homogenizing attitudes and producing "modern" attitudes, linking people in numerous societies, and placing economic issues at the top of the global agenda.

For critics, MNCs are the agents of global capitalism, fostering economic and political inequality among states and perpetuating a global class system based on the exploitation of the many in the developing world by the few in advanced capitalist countries. Observers with this ideological slant, then, regard the MNC as a creature of advanced capitalism that perpetuates Third World poverty and provokes class warfare on a global scale.

1. The Emergence of the Multinational Corporation

MNCs are not a recent phenomenon; indeed, trading groups such as the Hudson Bay Company, the Portuguese Mozambique Company, and the English and Dutch East India companies were imperial entrepreneurs that "were not only authorized to use violence but were endowed with nearly all the powers of sovereignty."[2] In some cases, they were immensely profitable. Writing of the English East India Company, John Strachey declared: "Seldom in human history has a small chance-picked body of men had so much actual cash to gain and to lose."[3]

Although the autonomy of these companies varied, most were able to operate with little government interference. By the charter given to the Dutch East India Company in 1602, the company could make war and peace, establish colonies, seize foreign ships, and even coin money. For its part, the Dutch state was given a share of the corporation's profits. In all, they played a key role in extending European influence by establishing regular contacts between Europe and China, Japan, India, and elsewhere.

The modern MNC dates from early in the twentieth century, especially the oil industry. After the 1909 breakup of the Standard Oil Trust in the United States, Standard Oil of New Jersey expanded rapidly overseas, especially in the Middle East and Venezuela, in search of new sources of oil. Other European and American oil companies followed suit, and by the late 1920s seven companies—the "seven sisters" (Standard Oil Company of New Jersey, Royal Dutch/Shell, British Petroleum, Gulf Oil, Texaco, Standard Oil of California, and Mobil)—controlled production, refining, and distribution of oil globally. After World War II manufacturing industries followed the example of the oil companies, investing heavily overseas.

The role of MNCs has grown dramatically in recent decades, and are today leviathans in their own right. Of the fifty wealthiest economic entities in the world as measured by gross domestic product and total corporate revenue,[4] almost one-third are MNCs.[5] These include industrial, service, and resource-extraction enterprises from a variety of home states, though especially Japan and the United States: Mitsubishi, Mitsui, Itochu, Sumitomo, General Motors, Marubeni, Ford, Exxon, Nisso Iwai, Royal Dutch, Toyota, Wal-Mart, Hitachi, and Nippon Life Insurance.

Although many MNCs originate in developed countries, some of the fastest growing are from newly industrializing countries (NICs), such as Samsung and Hyundai in Korea and Pemex in Mexico.[6] Whatever their national origins, MNCs pursue their own inter-ests—the most important of which include increased market share, cost reduction, sales growth, and risk reduction—rather than those of any country. MNCs now span the globe and operate in all sectors in both developed and developing countries.

Today, there are about 37,000 MNCs, with more than 200,000 foreign affiliates,[7] and as much as a quarter of world trade involves the movement of goods and service among MNCs subsidiaries in differ-ent countries. MNCs span the globe, control immense economic resources, and their names are household words. They are centrally organized but have no home, and the loyalty of their executives are to their corporations first and foremost. Thus a Japanese girl arriving in Los Angeles said to her mother: "Look mom, they have McDonald's here too."[8]

2. MNC Objectives

Corporations have a variety of motives for expanding overseas. Although profits are principal motivation for corporate behavior, many corporate decisions reflect a willingness to accept losses in order to assure market share and, therefore, profits in the long term.

First, they seek access to new markets, sometime markets that offer only slim prospects for profit in the near future. Thus, some years ago one observer expressed bewilderment at the willingness of US automobile manufacturers to compete for shares of Brazil's market, a market that at the time was barely able to support a single producer. "For some reason other than profits," he declared, Ford, Chrysler, and GM stay in Brazil, expand, and hope for the *mañana* that never seems to come.[9]

By establishing subsidiaries in a region or by join-ing with local corporations in joint ventures, MNCs can get around import barriers and tax obligations. Along with franchising and licensing arrangements, this relatively recent approach to foreign investment allows the local enterprise to raise capital, "while the foreign owned firm (FOF) supplies capital only (or mainly) in the invisible form of the costs sunk in developing new technologies and/or management expertise, and in developing and publicising a brand name or a corporate reputation."[10] Using these sophis-ticated tools, US and Asian enterprises expanded dra-matically into Europe after the European Community proposed the Single Market Act of 1985 to create an area in "which persons, goods, and capital shall move freely under conditions identical to those obtaining within a Member State."[11] Similarly, Euro-

pean and Japanese firms have invested heavily in Mexico to get inside NAFTA. And Japanese invest-ment in the United States, for example for construct-ing plants for automobile assembly, has been an effective way to get around nontariff barriers that limit the import of automobiles and other manufac-tures into the United States.

Corporations also expand overseas to obtain access to local capital markets, raw materials, or to reduce the costs of labor. Japanese and American corporations have established facilities in countries like Mexico and Thailand to keep down the cost of labor and maintain a competitive edge. In recent decades, US firms have established a great number of *maquiladoras* (mills) just across the border in Mexico, which employs seve-ral hundred-thousand Mexicans at wages about two-fifths as high as those in the United States. Japanese firms have expanded significantly "offshore" into Southeast Asia in recent years, especially because of the strength of the yen but also to reduce trade surplus-es Japan enjoys with countries like the United States. Indeed, the dramatic reduction in the imbalance between Japanese exports and imports is largely accounted for by "imports" of Japanese products pro-duced outside the country.

Whatever, the motivation of MNCs, escalating for-eign investment has globalized production. Today, products like automobiles often include parts made in several countries, and MNCs are producing goods and services that, though altered in some respects to appeal to local taste, is much the same no matter where it is sold.[12] As a result, many corporations have progressively fewer ties to their home country. When America's Big Three automobile manufactur-ers—General Motors, Ford, and Chrysler—invoke patriotism in urging Americans to forsake Japanese cars and "come home," they do not publicize the fact that "American" cars are assembled in many coun-tries and are made from parts produced all over the world. In some respects, "domestic" corporations as Chrysler are no more American than Nissan, Toyota, Honda, or Hyundai which have subsidiaries in the United States and employ large numbers of Ameri-can workers and managers.

3. MNCs and the Sovereign State

Corporations become multinational in varying degrees. Some remain ethnocentric, reflecting the values and interests of their home country. Such enterprises are organized to maximize control by managers at home. Although they have worldwide operations, they remain national in spirit. Other cor-

porations—akin to holding companies—are organized more loosely, giving local affiliates latitude to
make decisions and allowing local managers to enjoy
authority. Subsidiaries are managed locally but
receive assistance from the center. Like franchise
operations, such corporations benefit by marketing
products of local firms. Such arrangements help corporations mobilize local support and evade national
restrictions.

As corporations extend across borders and diversi-
fy production, it becomes more and more difficult for
individual states to control them or for states to
remain masters of their own economic destinies.
With expansion and the mixing of human and material resources from a variety of national sources, their
identities become more ambiguous in terms of
nationality. As corporations acquire a multinational
perspective, they no longer distinguish between
"domestic" and "foreign" business and begin to plan
globally.

Multinationals seek to invest wherever there is a
potential for return, often even if such investment
vitiates the foreign policy of "home" states. They
view national impediments to trade and investment
as providing advantages to competitors (which are
not subject to such limitations) and do not want
"politics" to interrupt the smooth transaction of business. It was in this spirit that MNCs fiercely opposed
the United States policy in 1974, linking Soviet emigration policy to granting that country most-favored
nation trade status. MNCs also opposed President
Jimmy Carter's imposing sanctions on the USSR after
the 1979 Afghanistan invasion, and President Ronald
Reagan's efforts to limit Western high-technology
exports to the then Soviet Union after martial law
was declared in Poland in 1981. Although the US
government had its way in the first two cases, it
incurred political costs in doing so, and was forced to
reverse its policy in the third.

Tension between governments and MNCs is perhaps
inevitable because of their differing objectives and
perspectives. This was evident when the Clinton
administration forced Conoco to cancel a deal to
develop an oil field in Iran in 1995.[13] Conoco was
quickly replaced by Royal Dutch Shell and the
French-based Total.[14] The efforts of US multinationals to persuade Washington to ignore human rights
and make strategic considerations take a back seat in
relations with China reflect the same perspective
articulated by a corporate executive to the US under-
secretary of state fifty years earlier:

His argument was direct and simple. His corporation,

he said, was not in politics of any kind. If the United
States wished to have a quarrel with the Nazi government of Germany, that was the government's privilege; but his corporation with its foreign operations
could not be involved, and did not feel bound to
accommodate itself to American policy expressed in
a "moral embargo."[15]

Whether MNCs can, in Raymond Vernon's colorful
phrase, keep "sovereignty at bay,"[16] there is little
question that they have acquired a "global reach."[17]
With proliferating links among national economies
and revolutions in communication, transportation,
and computer technologies, MNCs have become global actors. In one sense, most governments enjoy ultimate control over their own territory, but many corporations make important decisions over which governments have limited control. States have resources
they can use against MNCs, among them taxation, regulation, and nationalization; but, because states need
investments and corporations need a warm business
climate, they may find themselves dependent on each
other; when they collide, both may be losers.

Those who claim that sovereign states remain the
chief actors in global politics point to the fact that
states retain control over the means of coercion.
However, coercion avails little when capital takes
flight, currencies fluctuate, or habitual trade deficits
produce unemployment. In any event, the flexibility
of MNCs allows them to take advantage of the global
market and helps them to play off states against each
other and to overcome local labor unrest or an
unfriendly local political climate. Flexibility helps
MNCs compensate for their lack of coercive power.
Writes one commentator:

While multinational companies can invest or disin-
vest, merge with others or go it alone, rise from nothing or disappear in bankruptcy, the state seems
stodgy and stuck in comparison. The state is glued
more or less to one piece of territory, fighting off
entropy and budget crises, the national community
usually assessing the latest foreign attacks upon a
condition of declining competitiveness and the vulnerability in its domestic markets.[18]

In recent decades, MNCs have become even more
important participants in global politics owing to the
growing importance of market shares as a critical
element of national power and the greater role of
capital costs in comparison to land and even labor,
especially but not solely in high-technology sectors
of the economy. Thus, Susan Strange argues that
states seek "allies among foreign-owned firms."

"These firms may be persuaded, in exchange for access to the national market, to raise the finance, apply their technology, provide the management and the access to export markets—in short, to take all the steps necessary to locate production of goods or services within the territory of the host state."[19]

Direct investment—investment eagerly sought by countries for economic development and modernization—provides a significant source of MNC political influence. Between 1985 and 1990, foreign direct investment grew on an average of 34 percent a year, and, as Susan Strange observes, "sometime around the mid-1980s, . . . the total of international production—output of the affiliates of TNCs[20] outside their home base—overtook the volume of world exports of manufactures."[21] The expansion of American and Japanese enterprises has been especially important in this regard. In 1991, after five years in which Japan's direct overseas investment outstripped US investment, the Americans regained the lead. In 1993, US direct foreign investment jumped to US$ 69 billion or three times the next biggest investor, and in the first nine months of 1995 the annual rate was up to US$ 74 billion, more than double the 1992 figure.[22] Americans again accounted for the lion's share of total overseas investment much of which went to Asia, especially China.[23]

Over two decades ago, it had become apparent to Peter Drucker that something had changed dramatically. "For the first time in 400 years—since the end of the sixteenth century when the word 'sovereignty' was coined—the territorial political unit and the economic unit are no longer congruent."[24] For Susan Strange, this change "is not so much the emergence of the 'multinationals'" as it is "the change from production mostly designed and destined for one local or national market, to production mostly designed and destined for a world market."[25] The result is "increased power and influence of the multinationals"[26] and reduced autonomy for states.

4. *MNCs and the Developing World*

It is in the developing world that the presence of MNCs has generated the most heated debate. A desperate need for capital, technology, skilled management, and employment opportunities may dissuade governments from limiting corporate freedom of operation. Corporations are sometimes able to enlist political aid from home countries. American intervention in support of MNCs, whether in aiding the overthrow of Chile's Salvador Allende or Guatemala's Jacobo Arbenz, is well remembered in Latin America. Thus, in 1931 US Marine

General Smedley D. Butler boasted:

> I helped make Mexico safe for American oil interests in 1914. I helped make Haiti and Cuba a decent place for the National City Bank boys to collect revenues in. I helped purify Nicaragua for the international banking house of Brown Brothers . . . . I helped make Honduras "right" for American fruit companies. Looking back on it, I might have given Al Capone a few hints.[27]

MNC influence is that the developing world is further increased by control over technology and global marketing and distribution networks.

During the 1960s and 1970s, many developing countries were highly suspicious of MNCs, and it was in this climate that the concept of "dépendencia" flourished in Latin America. In the version articulated by Raúl Prebisch, then Executive Secretary of UNCTAD, Latin America, like other developing regions, was relegated to exporting primary commodities in the global economy, while importing finished goods from the industrialized countries. Foreign-owned extractive industries and agriculture, according to Prebisch, were monopoly enclaves within host countries. These enclaves, he believed, provided little of value to local economies, but the exports they produced were critical to the position of host countries in world trade (see *Imperialism*).

Foreign enterprises, argued dependency theorists, often simply expropriated a local resource and exported it for the company's benefit. Or, these corporations made products for export rather than products that would be useful to local populations consisting of poor peasants and residents of teeming urban slums. Far from providing capital for local growth, the corporations competed for local capital, driving up rates for local enterprises. In doing so, the companies earned exorbitant "excess" profits which were repatriated to home countries, creating a serious drain on the balance of payments of host countries. In the process, poor countries lost control over their own assets. The economic welfare of Latin America was not only dependent upon decisions made by foreign firms but, in a more general sense, upon the vicissitudes of the world commodities markets. Prebisch argued that the terms of trade between developed and developing countries were gradually worsening; the price of primary commodities was steadily declining while the costs of finished goods were rising.

Dependency theorists viewed penetration by MNCs as part of a broader process of marginalization with both international and domestic dimensions. From an international perspective, this meant that MNCs contributed to widening the gap between "center" or "core" (developed) countries and "periphery" (developing) countries (see *Maldevelopment*). The domestic side was a pattern of what dependency theorists called "internal colonialism" between modern cities and traditional countryside with "zones of misery" (urban slums) constituting an intermediate zone. Capital-intensive MNCS, they argued, created little employment in host countries, overcharged for imported and often obsolete technology, and created and sustained a domestic elite with little incentive to support policies that would widen local markets or redistribute income.

Under the influence of these and similar ideas, many developing countries pursued "import substitution" policies, emphasizing industrialization at home to produce for local consumption those goods that had previously been imported. In fact, far from lessening dependence, these policies increased it because much of the resulting industrialization required additional foreign investment and led to high debt levels.

In an effort to curb alleged corporate abuses, the United Nations proposed a code of conduct early in the 1970s, and two centers were established in the mid-1970s to render MNC activity more "transparent." The Center on Transnational Corporations collects and disseminates information about MNCs to familiarize the global community with their range of activities,[28] and the Commission on Transnational Corporations checks on complaints against MNCs and manages the Center.[29] Some regional groups established their own codes of conduct for eliminating improper corporate behavior. Among the first was the Andean Group (see *Integration, Regional*), founded in 1969 by Bolivia, Colombia, Ecuador, Peru, and Venezuela, which limited repatriation of MNCs profits, set standards for transferring corporate technology to host countries, and required that, eventually, foreign ownership of local affiliates be surrendered.[30] In other cases, hosts required majority local control before permitting MNC investment. Some countries simply prohibited foreign investment in specified industries, believing that it would infringe upon their sovereignty and increase their economic dependency.

Finally, a few countries nationalized MNC property in the late 1960s and early 1970s, Peru, Libya, and Venezuela, among others, nationalized foreign petroleum industries in their countries, and Bolivia and Chile nationalized the tin and copper industries.[31] Nationalization is a dangerous path, however, because it spurs conflict with rich states and brings an end to investment and foreign aid.

In the 1980s and 1990s, hostility toward MNCs in the developing world diminished. Many of the old dependency arguments had become obsolete as the essential nature of MNCs changed, most importantly from extraction and agriculture to processing and services, a change that was translated into higher paying local jobs. "As a result," declares Strange, "nothing is more striking in recent world economic history than the U-turns of at least thirty Asian, Latin American and even African governments on the matter of policies toward foreign investment and toward state vs. private ownership of enterprises."[32]

The end of the Cold War left developing countries with less bargaining leverage with the West where support for foreign assistance declined. To attract foreign investment, it was increasingly necessary for developing state to follow neoliberal economic policies, including privatization of local enterprises and creating a warmer atmosphere for foreign firms. Moreover, as the number of MNCs increased, developing states could be more selective about which they would permit to operate and could exploit competition among MNCs to get better contracts and investments. Larger numbers of MNCs also reduced the prospect that corporations would pull up stakes because others could replace them. The most important developments, however, were the growing pursuit of free-market policies in the developing world, accompanied by rising MNC investment in countries like China, Brazil, Indonesia, Malaysia, and India. As the climate for investment improved, MNC investment in the Third World climbed, reaching US\$ 80 billion in 1993.[33] In the last few years, the bargaining strength of developing states was weakened by a shift in corporate investment patterns away from the Third World to the former Soviet-bloc countries and to the more secure environment of the developed countries.[34]

5. Conclusion

The jury is still out as regards the role that MNCs play in fostering peace or war. Probably the answer is a little of both. As sources of enormous amounts of capital and high technology, MNCs are critical elements in providing the wherewithal for economic growth and development and, therefore, economic prosperity. As purveyors of modernity, they produce unprecedented cultural homogeneity, at least among urban elites, around the world. In these respects, MNCs reduce barriers among countries and create webs of interdependence that provide prosperity that can only be sustained under conditions of peace.

On the other hand, MNCs accelerate processes that

foster instability and conflict both within and among different societies. On the one hand, they foster economic inequality within countries, providing prosperity for urban elites that, like feudal elites in past centuries, have more in common with similar elites in other countries than with the poor in their own societies. In addition, their preference for political stability conditions them to ignore human rights violations and authoritarian solutions. On the other hand, their desire for profit and security leads them to invest heavily in relatively few countries, thereby exacerbating economic gaps among countries especially in the Third World.

What is clear is that, as one observer puts it, the "globalization of business and finance will permit these organizations to remain outside the effective control of any single national government."[35] Since MNCS are independent players in global politics that control significant resources, national leaders have to take account of their interests and preferences. To the degree that war is inimical to those interests, the world will be a safer place. Finally, MNCS reflect, perhaps more clearly than any other phenomenon, the declining significance of territory as a source of prosperity or security. Conquest of neighboring countries is far less profitable than becoming a recipient of direct corporate investment.

See also: *Globalization; Global Economic Interdependence: Why Crisis?; Imperialism; Human Security; Global Peace and Global Accountability; Global Neighbourhood: New Security Principles*

Notes

1. See Richard J. Barnet and Ronald E. Muller, *Global Reach* (New York: Simon and Schuster, 1974).

2. These trading companies "were not only authorized to use violence but were endowed with nearly all the powers of sovereignty." Janice E. Thomson, *Mercenaries, Pirates, and Sovereigns* (Princeton: Princeton University Press, 1994), p. 32. Founded in 1600, the English East India Company at its height administered large areas of India.

3. John Strachey, *The End of Empire* (New York: Praeger, 1964), p. 23.

4. *World Development Report 1995* (New York: Oxford University Press, 1995), pp. 166-167, and *Fortune* August 7, 1995 p. F-1

5. This measure inflates states' relative ranking because GDP includes corporate sales.

6. Until the 1970s, MNCS were regarded largely as extensions of American power, and in consequence they produced unease in Europe as well as the developing world. See, for example, J. J. Servan-Schreiber, *The American Challenge* (New York: Atheneum, 1968).

7. "Globe-totting," *The Economist*, September 3-9, 1994, p. 62.

8. Cited in Thomas L. Friedman, *New York Times,* December 11, 1996, p. A21. There are some 2,000 McDonald's restaurants in Japan.

9. J. Wilner Sundelson, "U.S. Automotive Investments Abroad," in Charles P. Kindleberger, ed., *The International Corporation* (Cambridge, MA: MIT Press, 1970), p. 246.

10. Susan Strange, *The Retreat of the State: The Diffusion of Power in the World Economy* (Cambridge, UK: Cambridge University Press, 1996), p. 47. Strange observes that growth in 'new, invisible and largely uncounted (and probably uncountable) investments in licensing, joint ventures, franchising, and so forth" makes it likely that statistics in recent years undercount the explosion in foreign investment.

11. Cited in Derek Unwin, *The Community of Europe* (London: Longman, 1991), p. 231.

12. See, for example, Richard W. Stevenson, "Ford Sets Its Sights on a 'World Car'," *The New York Times,* September 2, 1993, pp. C1, C4.

13. Robert S. Greenberger and Allanna Sullivan, "Clinton Bars Conoco's Plan For Iran Project," *The Wall Street Journal,* March 15, 1995, p. A3.

14. Youssef M. Ibrahim, "Teheran Finds Other Buyers for Its Oil After U.S. Sales Are Ended," *The New York Times,* June 21, 1995, p. A6.

15. Adolf A. Berle, *The Twentieth Century Capitalist* Revolution (New York: Harcourt, Brace, Jovanovich, 1954), p. 133.

16. Raymond Vernon, *Sovereignty at Bay* (New York: Basic Books, 1971).

17. See Richard J. Barnet and Ronald E. Muller, *Global Reach* (New York: Simon and Schuster, 1974).

18. Robert A. Isaak, *Managing World Economic Change,* 2nd ed. (Englewood Cliffs, NJ: Prentice-Hall, 1995), p. 264.

19. Strange, *The Retreat of the State,* p. 9.

20. Strange uses "TNC" (transnational corporations) instead of "MNCS" (multinational corporations).

21. Strange, *The Retreat of the State,* p. 47.

22. G. Pascal Zaschery, "U.S. Companies Again Hold Wide Lead Over Rivals in Direct Investing Abroad," *The Wall Street Journal,* December 6, 1995, p. A2; Allen R. Myerson, "American Money Makes the Whole World Sing," *The New York Times,* December 17, 1995, Section 4, pp. 1, 14.

23. Fred R. Bleakley, "Foreign Investment in U.S. Surged in 1994," *The Wall Street Journal,* March 15, 1995, p. A2.

24. Peter F. Drucker, "Multinational and Developing Countries: Myths and Realities," *Foreign Affairs* 53:1 (October 1974), p. 133.

25. Strange, *The Retreat of the State,* p. 44.

26. Ibid., p. 43.

27. Cited in Carlos F. Dia Alejandro, "Direct Investment in Latin America," in Kindleberger, ed., *The International Corporation,* p. 320.

28. See United Nations Centre on Transnational Corporations, *Transnational Corporations in World Development* (New York: United Nations, 1988).

29. Joan E. Spero and Jeffrey A. Hart, *The Politics of International Economic Relations,* 5th ed. (New York: St. Martin's, 1997), pp. 140.

30. Robert S. Walters and David H. Blake, *The Politics of Global Economic Relations,* 4th ed. (Englewood Cliffs, NJ: Prentice-Hall, 1992), p. 148.

31. Barnet and Muller, *Global Reach,* p. 188. Some of these industries were later returned to their corporate owners.

32. Strange, *The Retreat of the State,* p. 49.

33. James Brooke, "U. S. Businesses Flocking to Brazilian

Ventures," *The New York Times,* May 9, 1994, pp. C1, C4; Fred R. Bleakley, "Foreign Investment by Multinationals Rebounds, Benefiting China, U.N. Says," *The Wall Street Journal,* August 31, 1994, pp. A2, A5.

34. Growth in the number of TNCs looking for worldwide opportunities has provided compensatory bargaining leverage for some countries.

35. Joseph LaPalombara, "International Firms and National Governments: Some dilemmas," in Brad Roberts, ed., *New Forces in the World Economy* (Cambridge, MA: MIT Press, 1994), p. 434.

RICHARD W. MANSBACH

Muste, Abraham Johannes

Few pacifists have contributed as substantially as Abraham Johannes Muste to our understanding of war and peace in the modern world. He left this mark because he brought to the subject a rare blend of social activism and theoretical analysis, and because his "Christian pacifism" was imbued with a relentless realism not usually expected from one who renounces war in favor of universal love.

Abraham Johannes Muste was born on January 8, 1885 in the Netherlands. Six years later, he moved with his family to the United States. Raised in an environment of little means and of devout Dutch Reformism, he became a minister of the Reformed Church of America, but he would not spend much of his life in the pulpit. His conversion to pacifism during the First World War started A. J. Muste on a long, influential career of radical activism, which was by no means limited to the issue of war. By the late 1920s, he had become so deeply involved in the still young and struggling American labor movement that he temporarily traded his pacifism for a thorough-going Marxism-Leninism. In 1936, disillusioned with the violent methods of his fellow Trotskyites, he returned to pacifism and redoubled his efforts to achieve radical change through nonviolent means.

Through such organizations as the Fellowship of Reconciliation—which he served as Executive Secretary (1940-53) and Secretary Emeritus—the American Friends Service Committee, SANE, the War Resisters League, the Committee for Nonviolent Action, and many others, Muste distinguished himself as a tireless agitator for social justice, racial equality, nuclear disarmament, and the repudiation of military force as a tool of national policy. When he died in 1967, this staunch opponent of the First World War was lending his experience and insight to the movement to end the war in Vietnam. For more than five decades of political commitment and struggle, he had addressed his need "to *experience* ideas . . . to learn what they mean in practice . . . to act them out" (Hentoff 1970 p. 136). Not surprisingly, then, Muste's reputation at the time of his death was,

first and foremost, that of an activist.

In the long run, however, Muste's impact will most likely be measured by the ideas, theories, and analyses found in his published writings. It is here that the greatest benefit of his activism emerges: the lessons of his practical experience in the political arena enrich, sharpen, and modify the details of his Christian pacifist vision.

That vision is spelled out primarily in three volumes: *Non-violence in an Aggressive World* (1940), *Not By Might* (1947), and *The Essays of A. J. Muste* (1970), edited by Nat Hentoff. In the first, Muste focused on democracy and organized religion, both of which are characterized as being in the throes of a profound crisis. Setting down the major tenets of his pacifism, he argued that only a commitment to the nonviolent way of life can ensure the interdependent survival of these institutions. The second book reiterated and expanded upon earlier themes, but the experience of another world war had provided a new, updated focus—atomic weaponry. The volume of essays included most of Muste's contributions to journals and pamphlets, as well as the first installments of an unfinished autobiography. Organized chronologically from 1905 to 1966, this collection of articles conveys the evolution and durability of Muste's pacifism.

The pacifism explained in these books and essays is firmly rooted in Muste's deep Christian faith. While his commitment to nonviolence was tested, rejected, reconfirmed, and developed in the crucible of practical political activity and analysis, it would always be informed by scriptural interpretation and theological propositions. In his view, the Christian justification for nonviolence was so persuasive that the term "Christian pacifism" was actually redundant. For Muste, Christianity is pacifism, and pacifism is Christianity (see *Christianity*). "Christian pacifism arises out of and is bound up with the very essence of the Christian world-view, the most precious and distinctive doctrines of our faith" (Muste 1940 p. 11).

According to this world-view, the universe (and

everything in it) is the creation of God. The essence of god is love. Thus, "at its central core, the universe is love" (Muste 1947 p. 86). History has a definite purpose, or goal: the achievement of the Kingdom of God on earth, that is, God's reign of peace, brotherhood, and justice. The means to the fulfillment of this goal, which amounts to salvation for the individual and for humankind, is the love of God as revealed in Jesus Christ. The cross provides an applicable standard of moral judgment for the behavior of individual persons, who must become active agents in the march toward the ultimate goal (see *Pax Christi International*).

In other words, the realm of human activity is governed by the same law that defines the purpose of the universe. "To love and to be loved . . . is of the essence of man's nature" (Muste 1940 p. 104).

Muste's theological explanations were inevitably laced with words and concepts that might suggest a romanticist, even unrealistic view of the world. Aside from the fact that many Christians reject his brand of Christianity, anyone concerned about the complex problem of war might find recurring concepts such as "love," "faith," "redemption," "salvation," and "Jesus" too amorphous to offer meaningful hope. But Muste was much too sophisticated to believe that war and other forms of violence can be eradicated simply by advocating "love" and "faith."

The Christian source of his pacifism gave him the courage of his convictions about nonviolence and established a personal system of values that stressed the integrity and dignity of the individual. It did not prevent him from seeing the complexities, contradictions, and ambiguities of any effort to eliminate war, especially one using nonviolent means (see *Nonviolence*).

Muste's conviction that the problem of war can only be solved through nonviolent means was based on much more than his spiritual faith. He maintained that an objective analysis of war led to the same conclusion. If his appeal to Christian doctrine tempts us to underestimate him as too idealistic and simplistic, his treatment of the nature and causes of war reveals a realist whose definition of the problem is anything but simplistic and naive. In fact, he suggested that the problem of war is even more complicated, far reaching, and stubborn than many self-proclaimed "realists" dare to admit.

Put simply, Muste insists that war is not just the effect of certain causes, but rather part of a complex vicious circle characterized mainly by violence (see *War*). It is part of a total system, a pervasive way of life which breeds war and which is further sustained by war.

In the area of international relations, several conditions contribute to the outbreak of specific wars and to the long-run perpetuation of the war system. Nation-states are in constant competition with each other, seeking advantage and security. Fueled by the mass emotions of nationalism and racism, the competition is fiercest in the areas of economics and arms.

According to Muste, economic inequality is a primary cause of war. The maldistribution of wealth and resources among nations makes war an acceptable policy tool for the weak and the strong alike. Meanwhile, the search for military superiority or just "security" generates arms races which inevitably produce less security and often lead directly to war (see *Arms Race, Dynamics of*). At the very least, they nourish an atmosphere of distrust, conflict, and hatred among nations.

The international system, ruled by competition and power politics, lacks a sense of community and the formal machinery for implementing fundamental principles of justice and equity. War persists in part because there is no world government. Thus, Muste concluded, the elimination of war requires not only a radical economic readjustment among nations and comprehensive disarmament, but also the creation of a federalized world government (see *Federalism, World*).

The problem of war is greatly complicated by the internal structure and domestic conditions of the nation-states that do battle in the international arena. Muste was especially critical of capitalist states, agreeing with Marx, Lenin, and Hobson that they display an inherent tendency toward militaristic imperialism. Capitalism favors and generates policies leading directly to war, but it also contributes indirectly to the problem by producing within states a general climate of unfettered competition, self-aggrandizement, and exploitation, all of which do nothing to discourage aggression and violence in individuals.

But capitalism is merely the most extreme example of a more general phenomenon. The real culprit, Muste maintained, is "the modern sovereign power state whose function is war" (Muste 1947 p. 152). Whatever the ideological hue of any modern power state, its political, economic, social, cultural, and psychological forces are geared toward massive military planning. The centralization and regimentation needed to maintain such a posture create societies that are increasingly pyramidal, authoritarian, and structured around the threat of internal, governmental violence.

To the extent that the domestic features of modern power states increase the perils of international anarchy, the internal structure of states can be identified as a cause of war. On the other hand, since the centralization and regimentation are rationalized and accepted as necessary to maintain the society's security against external foes, war and the threat of war constitute a cause of those domestic conditions. This is a clear example of the vicious circle effect described by Muste, of how war can be considered a cause of war.

Muste proposed that the modern power state be dismantled. By emphasizing the need to attack economic exploitation, social injustice, and authoritarian institutions, all of which are endemic to the modern power state, Muste challenged what he called "bourgeois pacifism," the belief that war can be abolished without "profound changes in the economic order and in the structure of society" (Hentoff 1963 p. 230). But he took the argument further. Just as a "pacifist" must be concerned with economic change, those who struggle primarily for economic change and social justice must realize that their goal is impeded by the continuation of war and other forms of violence. For Muste, the two struggles are inseparable. If economic injustice is a major "taproot" of war, war is "the greatest single obstacle to social change" (Muste 1940 p. 98).

This led Muste to identify another major source of the problem: the nature of human beings as individuals. War is caused in no small way by certain psychological dispositions and human beliefs (see *Aggression*). The "thoroughly bad mental state" that sparks particular wars and sustains the war system, is itself partly a product of the forces, conditions, and influences found in the structure of states and in the anarchy of international relations. However, Muste also attributed it to people's inherent capacity for sin (see *Human Nature Theories of War*). Noting that pacifists are often criticized for adhering to "a superficial, optimistic, 19th century liberal view of the nature of man, which minimizes sin and its power in the hearts of men and in history," he contended that the situation is actually "much worse than we ordinarily think it is" (Muste 1947 p. 109).

As powerful and destructive as the human capacity for sin might be, it is equalled by the potential for grace, and this is where Muste turns for hope. Despite the complexity of the war system and the multiplicity of interacting causes, the vicious circle can only be broken by human decision and action. Muste wrote of "an act of will," "a moral and political decision," "a new pattern of action." Individuals can and must make a commitment to seek peace and justice in the nonviolent way of Christ's teachings, not just for the sake of pursuing a kind of ethical

purity, but because those teachings express a psychological and political realism about violence. "Violence," wrote Muste, "begets violence and not something else" (Muste 1947 p. 104). Having believed, during his Trotskyite interlude, that the route to democracy, brotherhood, and peace was through dictatorship, hate, repression, and violence, he was "brought up hard against the realization that by that very pragmatic test which I had chosen, the method did not produce the desired results" (Hentoff 1970 p. 209).

This emphasis on appropriate means was at the heart of Muste's pacifism and general political philosophy. If war is part of a total way of life, and if that way of life is known principally by its violence, then we must approach human affairs in a manner that repudiates and defeats this central feature. We must proceed on the basis of a belief, or faith, in the ultimate unity of humankind, in the infinite worth and dignity of each and every human being. Although Muste traced *his* faith in this approach to specifically Christian doctrine, it is essentially an approach that humanist philosophers (e.g., Karl Popper) have termed a "rationalist" attitude, or an attitude of reasonableness. Whatever it is called, this approach is central to the theory and practice of democracy and to the scientific method.

Muste left no doubt about the connection between his "Christian pacifism" and democracy and science. He asserted that democracy and violence are incompatible; that the goal of treating persons as ends in themselves requires democratic institutions and procedures; that resorting to compulsion or violence is an abandonment of democratic process; that war is less likely if societies are built on justice, fellowship, and broad participation in a decentralized, antiauthoritarian setting. With the scientist, Muste shared the belief that all humans are potential bearers, or sources, of truth and that a "scientific" approach calls for experimentation, flexibility, and open-mindedness.

What sets Muste apart from the typical champion of democracy and from most practicing scientists is his absolute commitment to this rationalist attitude, his unqualified refusal to abandon it for compulsion or violence, his insistence that unless we apply this principle in all aspects of our human affairs, our most noble goals will be frustrated by the vicious circle that so prominently includes war.

These notions also set Muste apart from many others: those who would attempt to abolish war by focusing only on the reform of international relations; "radicals" who seek profound change in societies without challenging the use of war and violence as political tools; "pacifists" who refuse to participate in war without actively engaging themselves in efforts to modify the conditions making for war. Few of these have done more than A. J. Muste to explain the complexity of war and the enormity of the task, or to convince us that "peace is indivisible . . . the way of peace is really a seamless garment that must cover the whole of life and must be applied in all its relationships" (Hentoff 1970 p. 200).

One who comes to Muste's writings believing that pacifism is simplistic, native, and unrealistic would be surprised to discover that Muste was not prepared to guarantee that his pacifist approach would bring an end to war and usher in a reign of peace, brotherhood, and justice. He only insisted that we learn from past experience, which tells us that these ends will definitely not be achieved through violent means.

See also: *Pacifism*

Bibliography ─────────────────────────

Hentoff N 1963 *Peace Agitator: The Story of A. Muste.* Macmillan, New York
Hentoff N (ed.) 1970 *The Essays of A. J. Muste.* Simon and Schuster, New York
Muste A J 1940 *Non-violence in an Aggressive World.* Harper and Brothers, New York
Muste A J 1947 *Not By Might.* Harper and Brothers, New York

ALBERT DALMOLEN

Myrdal, Gunnar

Gunnar Myrdal was an economist, important mainly for his contributions on development issues and methodological questions. Born December 6, 1898 in Solvarbo, Sweden; he died May 17, 1987 in Stockholm, Sweden. Myrdal won the Nobel Prize for economics in 1974; in 1970 he and his wife Alva were awarded the major peace prize of the then Federal Republic of Germany, and in 1981 both received the Nehru award for international understanding. Myrdal's wife (married in 1924, three children) was a pioneering emancipator of women and both author and activist in peace research and policy (see Nobel Peace Prize Laureates: *Alva Myrdal*); she was active in Swedish politics and on the international and United Nations level as well.

1. Scientist and Politician

Myrdal himself attributed his faith in the Puritan work ethic and his egalitarianism to his sturdy farming background. Although initially interested in natural sciences, he started to read law at Stockholm University to learn about how society functioned, but soon changed to economics. He did his doctoral dissertation on price formation and economic change in 1927. In 1933 he succeeded his main teacher G. Cassel to the chair in political economy and financial sciences at Stockholm University. At first a pure theorist, his year in the United States as a Rockefeller fellow in 1929-30 turned his interest to political issues. On his return from the United States he became active in politics; this experience turned him from a "theoretical" economist into a political economist and what he himself described as an "institutionalist."

When the Labor Party came to power in Sweden in 1932, he was involved in the work of several royal commissions and public committees, and in 1935 became a member of parliament. In 1938 he was selected to carry out a major investigation of the black problem in the United States (see Myrdal 1962). In Sweden, he headed the committee that drafted the Social Democratic postwar program. Having returned to parliament, he became one of the directors of the Swedish Bank, chairman of the Swedish planning commission, and Minister for Trade and Commerce (1945-47). In 1947 he became executive secretary of the United Nations Economic Commission for Europe in Geneva. Ten years later, he embarked on a 10-year study of development in Asia resulting in the monumental *Asian Drama* (1968). He was also a member of the governing council of the United Nations Research Institute for Social Development. The UN accepted his approach to development policy in 1969 as the integrated or unified strategy of development.

2. Main Theoretical Positions

In his early theoretical work, Myrdal systematically introduced expectations into the analysis of prices, profits, and changes in capital values. The main contribution of his microeconomic work (Mydal 1939) was the formulation of the distinction between anticipations and results. The concepts *ex ante* and *ex post* greatly clarified the discussion of savings, investment, and income, and their effects on prices. Myrdal made a major contribution to liberalizing economics from a static theory, in which the future is like the past (i.e., things always remain the same) and to paving the way for dynamics, in which time, uncertainty, and expectations enter in an essential way.

Methodological questions have always occupied Myrdal's thought, and he was well-equipped to criticize the economic establishment. In particular, he is best known for his critique of conventional economic theory applied uncritically to underdeveloped countries. He called for urgent reconstruction of such theory. The main elements of his criticism were the following:

(a) *The limitation of economic thinking by Eurocentricity.* Many basic concepts, models, theories, and paradigms are "Western" because they fit the reality of advanced industrialized countries; they are therefore mostly inadequate to describe or interpret the reality of underdeveloped societies. Myrdal's critique is not primarily directed to abstraction or selection, but stresses that the abstractions follow the wrong lines, and that irrelevant features are selected. He subjects commonly used concepts to close scrutiny and finds that most dissolve when applied to underdeveloped societies. For example, "employment" should be replaced by the richer and more realistic concept of "labor utilization."

(b) *The narrow definition of development as economic growth.* Myrdal replaces it by the concept of modernization ideals while emphasizing the actual needs and values of real people instead of created intellectual abstractions.

(c) *The narrow definitions and limits of scientific disciplines.* The essence of Myrdal's institutional approach is to bring all relevant knowledge and techniques to bear on the analysis of social problems, which must always be studied not in isolation but in their mutual relationships.

(d) *False objectivity.* Under the pretense of scientific analysis, false objectivity conceals political valuations and interests; this pseudoscience should be replaced by explicit valuations as far as possible.

(e) *Bias.* Myrdal criticized bias arising from twisted terminology.

While always emphasizing realistic and relevant research and stressing the need to purge economic thinking of systematic bias, Myrdal often attacked his colleagues, especially for their tendency to isolate themselves from other social sciences and to ignore conflicts and real contradictions by excluding considerations of noneconomic factors. Contrary to the regular run of economists, Myrdal himself stressed clearly the importance of social and political institutions, particularly for economic development. For example, one of his main theorems states that policy measures leading to greater equality by institutional reforms could lead to more rapid growth, while mainstream economists normally assume that there is a trade-off between equality and growth, and therefore equality, which impedes growth by reason of lower productivity, has to be sacrificed or postponed.

Myrdal's views on this and on similar questions are methodologically based on his well-known theory of circular or cumulative causation. His conclusions on "vicious" or "virtuous circles" were first developed fully in *An American Dilemma* and then applied to general development theory. Traditional theory explains inequality—for instance between the economic development course of different countries—as the result of differential resource endowments. But Myrdal looks upon resources as being the result, not the cause of income and wealth; capital, for example, is much more the result than the cause of economic growth. The principle of cumulative causation postulates increasing returns through specialization and economics of scale, and shows how small advantages are magnified; this can be used to show movements away from an equilibrium position as a result of the interaction of several variables. For creating instability, however, the numerical values of the coefficients of interdependence have to be above a critical minimum size. In *Economic Theory and Underdeveloped Regions* (1957) Myrdal showed how the advantages of growth poles can become cumulative, while the backward regions may become relatively or even absolutely impoverished. He also applied his ideas successfully to the interaction between economic and sociological variables. In the analysis of development, he elaborated the relationships between nutrition, health, education, and productivity, and showed the possibility of both positive and negative "circles" of cumulative effects to which conventional economic analysis was blind. Myrdal's conception also guards against unicausal explanations and universal remedies. Furthermore, cumulative causation is based not only on interaction in a social system but also on interaction in time; therefore memory and expectations are of high importance. Further important methodical instruments of Mydal's analysis of development are the concepts of "backwash" and "spread" effects, explaining the movement of regions or countries at different stages of development and the effects of unification. Altogether, the significance of Myrdal's methodological contributions has been in providing a more realistic and productive alternative to the conventional stable equilibrium analysis which neglected the aspects both of dynamics in time and of social structure.

3. Significance for Development Policy

Myrdal's political analysis of development problems stresses mainly the importance of institutional factors and the urgent need for reforms. In particular, the need of land reform, he stated again and again, is extremely urgent because the great majority of humankind depends on agriculture for its livelihood. Having been an early critic of the euphoria of the "Green Revolution" he always demanded real structural change in rural areas as an indispensable condition for national economic development by balanced growth. Other important fields of needed action and necessary reform are population policy, education, and health.

Myrdal has never been as optimistic as the conventional development technocrats in science and policy because of his recognition of the role of the state and the elites in most developing countries. He judges the phenomenon he calls the "soft state" as a grave obstacle to development: "softness" does not concern the degree of coercion and violence exercised by many states, but refers to their unwillingness and inefficiency to coerce in order to implement declared policy goals of social and economic development; this is not mere weakness, but it reflects the power structure and a gap between professed and real intentions. Complementary to the various forms of lack of social discipline resulting in deficiencies in legislation and law observation and enforcement, corruption is an important feature of the soft state and an overall constraint to development measures.

Later Myrdal explained this situation by the existence of an "elitist conspiracy" and by the "neocolonial mechanism." In spite of significant historical and socioeconomic differences, one unifying trait for nearly all developing countries is political domination by a small upper and middle class leading to the establishment of an elite class structure. Owing to the influence of diversified but powerful elite groups there has been little progress in land reform and none at all in stamping out corruption. Although the needed reforms are in line with Western ideals and have been more or less carried out in the developed countries, little or no influence is exercised by the latter to secure such socioeconomic change in developing countries. However, according to the traditions of colonialism (see *Colonialism; Neocolonialism*), met-

ropolitan powers are likely to ally themselves with the privileged ruling groups or even create new such groups. This is because all transactions with underdeveloped countries have to be conducted with the upper class elites, and in the developed countries little attention is paid to the prevailing inegalitarian power structure, impeding not only greater equality but also economic development.

Advancing in years, Myrdal became even more politically radical. Formerly an active supporter of the Western policy of development aid, and even designing a good deal of Swedish and also of United Nations aid conceptions, in the 1980s he has become increasingly critical of the present form of aid. He states that the most important reason for his changed attitude is the knowledge of the utter destitution and want among the people in less developed countries. He now demands relief instead of development aid (Myrdal 1981): besides poverty and catastrophe relief the only acceptable form of aid is to prevent predictable situations of want, but aid for industrial development must be discontinued. Myrdal stresses as further reasons for his radical change the dominance of exploitative regimes in nearly all developing countries and growing corruption, both of which hinder all urgently needed institutional reforms. So, the present way of development will bring about only more poverty and misery, and therefore only direct and controlled help for the poor is reasonable. Even the demand for a New International Economic Order (see *New International Economic Order*) by developing countries will be deceptive as long as hardly any of their elite's representatives will stress or even mention the need for a new economic order at home. To change this, pressure from below is necessary, but because such pressure is either missing or ineffective in most cases development aid should strengthen the hand of those who are fighting for reforms in those countries. Myrdal also recommended the provision of support to firmly established and popular liberation movements, and to countries like Nicaragua or Tanzania which he looked upon as genuinely willing to realize structural change (see *World Economy, Social Change and Peace*).

4. Myrdal's Third Way

"Myrdal had never been easy to typecast. On many issues, he fired at both sides of the conventional barricade and liked to emphasize the false shared premises of the combatants" (Streeten 1972). In spite of his recent position on development aid and his sharp criticism of established economics and conventional economic policy throughout his life work, Myrdal never had been a radical in order to change the Western capitalistic system essentially. He did not draw revolutionary conclusions but relies on the admittedly difficult possibility of self-reform. His approach to economic policy was neither strict central planning by force of the state nor capitalistic *laissez-faire*, but that of using prices for planning purposes and of attacking attitudes and institutions directly to make them instruments of reform. With regard to development policy, however, this did not work as he himself finally had to recognize: any reform and development measure within a given power structure may yet strengthen that very structure.

Gunnar Myrdal, the great critic of methodical biases, had some bias of his own, too. His modernization ideals, even though not as uncritically applied as in the older modernization theories, obviously derive from his work in the United States which was an important personal experience for him: US aspirations and ideals, and the "American creed," were kindred to his own beliefs, as he admitted himself. Another source of his political thinking was his experience of the Swedish welfare state which doubtless provided criteria for Myrdal's criticism of the state in developing countries. However, besides his and his wife's personal political work in favor of development and peace, his most important lasting significance will be his methodological criticism. This work was an urgently needed antidote to deceptive scientific self-confidence, even when it failed to provide productive alternatives.

See also: *Human Security; Future of Humanity; Maldevelopment; World Economy, Social Change and Peace; Equitable Equality: Gandhian Concept*

Bibliography

Angresano J 1997 *The Political Economy of Gunnar Myrdal: An Institutional Basis for the Transformation Problem.* Cheltenham

Assarsson-Rizzi K 1984 *Gunnar Myrdal: A Bibliography, 1919-1981.* New York

Dostaler G 1994 *Gunnar Myrdal and His Works.* Montreal

Myrdal G 1939 *Monetary Equilibrium.* London

Myrdal G 1953 *The Political Element in the Development of Economic Theory.* London

Myrdal G 1957 *Economic Theory and Underdeveloped Regions.* New York

Myrdal G 1962 *An American Dilemma: The Negro Problem and Modern Democracy.* New York

Myrdal G 1963 *Beyond the Welfare State: Economic Planning in the Welfare States and Its International Implications.* New Haven

Myrdal G 1968 *Asian Drama: An Inquiry Into the Poverty of Nations,* 3 vols. New York

Myrdal G 1968 *Value in Social Theory: A Selection of Essays on Methodology.* London

Myrdal G 1969 *Objectivity in Social Research.* New York

Myrdal G 1970 *The Challenge of World Poverty: A World Anti-poverty Program in Outline.* New York

Myrdal G 1973 *Against the Stream: Critical Essays on Economics.* New York

Myrdal G 1979 Underdevelopment and the evolutionary imperative. *Third World Q.* 1(2)

Myrdal G 1981 Relief instead of development aid. *Inter-economics* (March/April)

Streeten P 1972 Gunnar Myrdal. In: Sills D C (ed.) 1972 *International Encyclopaedia of Social Sciences,* Vol. 18. London

REINHARD WESEL

Myth, Identity, and the Politics of Conviction: Participation in the Struggle for a Just World Order*

The fact that one is a citizen of a particular state does not detract in any way from his membership in the human family as a whole, nor from his citizenship in the world community.
  – Pope John XXIII. *Pacen in Terris,* April 10, 1963

A riot is the voice of the unheard.
  – Martin Luther King, Jr.

My propositions serve as elucidations in the following way; anyone who understands me eventually recognizes them as nonsensical, when he has used them—as steps—to climb beyond them. (He must, so to speak, throw away the ladder after he has climbed up it.)
  – Ludwig Wittgenstein. *Tractatus Logico-Philosophicus.* London 1981 p. 189

1. Introduction: Mythmaking as Political Practice

Myths and mythmaking are important to peoples' lives. Myths articulate a people's history, they bridge past, present, future: they bring together reason and desire, thought, feeling and action: they hold together time and space. All cultures and societies have mythmakers—storytellers—who spin their plots and narratives to capture the texture of their peoples' lives: their hopes, fears, and joys; their rituals, traditions, and institutions. Myths and mythmaking carry the spirituality and history of its peoples. In short, "myth . . . [is] a story usually of historical events that unfolds a worldview of a people: the origin, destiny, practices, and beliefs of a people."

As stories and worldviews of a people, that is, as historical constructions of identities and practices, myths and mythmaking have always been a significant, and indeed, difficult and complex—if not contested—part of the economic, political, and cultural terrain; and it has often been said that whoever masters the commanding myth of a society controls its politics.

Of the many constructed myths that are part of the human legacy, one is of particular interest to us. Part of this myth underscores the idea that since the neolithic period—when hunting and foraging human bands settled around the great river basins and created agriculture some 7,000 to 10,000 years ago—humans have lived with, and by, the myth of a territorially fixed identity. Not surprisingly, it was also during this period that war, slavery, patriarchy, and the state emerged. And while belief, religious system, and blood lines have always transcended territory, and while human identities will continue to be shaped by gender, status, class, occupation, and the like, this myth of a territorially fixed identity has been the commanding myth of human polity.

However, according to other interpreters of this myth, our planet is at an "axial moment," a "great transition" comparable to the period noted above, when human societies moved from an essentially nomadic-hunting existence to this essentially territorial-agricultural way of life. In fact, this transition, precisely because it is a transition, is characterized both by the breaking down and resurgence of statist myths and values in the light of profound political, economic, and cultural transformations that shape human life, leading not only through a crisis of identity, but toward the emergence of a truly planetary civilization. Human history—and the many histories that comprise it—is undergoing a process of change that puts into question not only the structures and processes of the present world system, but also the underlying myths and values that inform these structures and processes.

Moreover, at the heart of this myth is the idea that in the context of the transformations in political, economic, and cultural life in this century, we are witnessing the creation, articulation, and the implementation of a new myth of human identity. It is a myth

of "a planetary people," namely, the human race that is transcending the territorially fixed identity noted above. By this we mean the capacity in each of us to identify, empathize, and act—to imagine to use the apt terminology of Benedict Anderson—with and on behalf of the human species, and in the end, for the planet we inhabit.

It is not our intention to suggest that this myth—the myth of specie identity (or global citizenship)—was the overarching political motif of the last twenty years let alone of the next two decades. Nor are we suggesting that this myth replace all other myths of identity that have been constructed and that continue to shape human life on this planet. Rather, we want to explore different dimensions of this myth; and see how such a myth can play an important role in the creation of political practices that are adequate to the emerging global polity of our time. And while myth and mythmaking are not the usual stuff for policy consideration, we want to suggest that participating in the transformation of the structures and processes of our time may require the articulation and construction of such a myth, not so much as a mawkish, sentimental, pietistic claim for the brotherhood or sisterhood of humanity, but rather as a challenge to develop cooperative solutions for a common political life for all the peoples of the planet. In short, we want to explore the ways in which myth and mythmaking (of the kind noted above)—as *historical and contingent constructions of human identity, interest, and practice*—can be dimensions of a transformative political practice for our time.

2. From Philosophies of the Subject to the Practices of the Subject

The connections between philosophy and politics have a long, not to mention contested, history. In fact, one could claim without much difficulty that many of the critical political issues of our day, including the meaning and significance of transformative political practice, are being worked out in the philosophical debates of our time. For example, the recent edited work entitled, *Who Comes after the Subject?* by Eduardo Cadava, Peter Connor, and Jean-Luc Nancy, asks rather provocatively the *philosophical* question that concerns us *politically* in this essay. Seeking to come to terms with the challenge posed by both structuralists and poststructuralists concerning the (philosophical and political) status of the Subject (including questions about subjectivity), contributors to this volume may be read as suggesting that despite—perhaps because of—the profound difficulties of identifying *who* the Subject is and *what* subjectivity is, it is nonetheless important both for philosophy and politics to come to some provisional understanding, if not resolution, of the problems arising around these issues.

To be sure, the philosophical question of the Subject—which has a long contested history—is of great significance, and will continue to haunt us in years to come. Without pretending to have overcome the philosophical *aporias* of the Subject identified by thinkers like Jacques Derrida, Michel Foucault, and Jean-Francois Lyotard and the poststructuralists, we want to pose the question of the Subject, less as a philosophical and more as a *political* problem, recognizing that in the end, philosophy and politics are inseparable, but believing that moving through these intractable philosophical problems may very well be achieved through the constructions of political practices. What is especially interesting to us, particularly in the context of our concern for myth and mythmaking, is the suggestion, underscored by much of the literature on "critical social movements," "civil society," and "democracy and democratization," that, perhaps, the impetus for social change, if not its bearers, will be those critical social movements, what the participants of the Global Civilization Project of the World Order Models Project (WOMP) have called "global civil society." And more important, that the practices of these critical social movements are articulations, however provisional, of this myth of specie identity, or of the global citizen.

In short, while we are sympathetic with the concerns raised by the poststructuralists noted above, in this paper we want to explore a slightly divergent trajectory, namely, from questions of "Who and what the Subject and subjectivity are?" to the question of "What is entailed in being a Subject?" Put in its political/convictional and institutional form, the question is: "How is it possible to increase the number of human beings who realize that a just world order is possible?"

3. Different Narratives of the Current Situation

In order to answer the question, it seems sensible to review the ways in which our contemporary global society is presently operating. Consider, in this regard, the statement of former President George Bush at the UN Conference on Environment and Development (UNCED) after he declined to sign the Biodiversity Convention and watered down the Convention on Global Climate Change: "I am the President of the United States, not the President of the world, and I will do what is best to defend US interests." Even more instructive is the statement of James Woolsey, at one time the Clinton administration's nominee for Director of the Central Intelligence Agency, during his confirmation hearings:

> Yes we have slain a large dragon, but we live now in a jungle filled with a bewildering variety of poisonous snakes. And in many ways, the dragon was easier to keep track of.

Of course, as Richard Falk observed, the dragon referred to by Woolsey is the former Soviet Union and the snakes referred to are all the myriad problems we confront today: former Yugoslavia, Somalia, proliferation of weapons, terrorism, to name only a few. The fact is, having left the rhetoric of the new world order, as indeed Bush himself did, the Clinton administration still sees the world, if the statement by Woolsey is any indication, primarily as a jungle of competing and dangerous self-interests.

A second narrative, in contrast to the statements of Woolsey, is what is reflected in the work of former UN Secretary-General Boutros Boutros-Ghali, in particular, his 1992 "Report on the Work of the Organization" and the "Agenda for Peace"—two major documents that no doubt will shape the future of the normative order. In both instances not only is there a recognition that the "healthy globalization of contemporary life" is critical to the preservation of local or national identities, but, more significantly, that there is a sober acknowledgment that the "time of absolute and exclusive sovereignty has passed; its theory was never matched by reality."

To be sure (written) words do not always lead to appropriate action. At the same time anyone who has had to fight the battle of words in international organizations and bureaucracies is very much aware that the words stem from embodiment in the real world. They arise from interest, values, and social forces, and they may be used to promote significant political change far beyond the original expectations of the authors. The "Declaration of Human Rights" (see *Declaration of the Rights of Man*) and "Helsinki Accords" are two notable examples of documents that have had this impact. So, too, are the Boutros-Ghali documents noted above.

There is another point well worth mentioning. The statement of Boutros-Ghali, in contrast to those of Bush and Woolsey, affirms the promise rather than the threat that the present offers, and the sense that the old order of narrowly defined national interests could be passing away and a new, truly global order, is emerging. In fact, it may be argued that there are, at least, two narratives of the world that are today vying for dominance. And while they are not necessarily in contradiction with one another, they certainly provide very different emphases and perspectives and imply different trajectories, on our world. They embody, in a manner of speaking, contesting images—myths, if you will—of the global polity. One affirms the possibility of a truly global polity, the other retreats into a world of national polities.

A third narrative, even of greater contrast to the first two might be called a "popular internationalism," which is deeply critical of the present world system, while at the same time, cognizant not only of the limits of "enlightened self-interest" within a statist and capitalist-driven global polity, but also of the possibilities of creating an "effective front" built on the universalist values of the Enlightenment and of the socialist movement. And while this perspective places the emphasis on the role of what we call "global civil society" in creating a genuinely global polity, it accepts, as the other narratives do, the necessity of states, as we know them, for any future global polity. As Samir Amin writes:

> A humane and progressive response to the problems of the contemporary world implies the construction of a popular internationalism that can engender a genuinely universalist value system, completing the unfinished projects of the Enlightenment and the socialist movement. This is the only way to build an effective front against the internationalism of capital and the false universalism of its value system.

4. An Alternative Narrative of the Present Situation

It is possible to understand the first two narratives, as simply attempts by self-interested states or international institutions to gain better access to the world's political, economic, and cultural resources. It is even possible to read these events as the triumph of pragmatic realpolitik. We refuse this somewhat jaded view. For despite the differences in these readings, a number of profound underlying themes, best captured in the third narrative, seem to present themselves, not only as lessons of history, but as constructions of an alternative human identity, the articulation of transformative practices reflecting, if not an emerging global subject, then surely, of a multiplicity of subjects (and subject positions) that are locally situated and globally oriented. These may be stated thus: the growth of an alternative normative order; the presence of a strong transnational peace and justice movement; and the preference for, and efficacy of, nonviolent activism.

First, the balance of power system (see *Balance of Power*) based on national interest, national security states, shifting alliances, and ultimately, the willingness to use military systems, had its own normative framework. This century, however, has witnessed the growth of an alternative normative order in which the validity—in both a pragmatic and ethical sense—of the use of large-scale organized violence has been scrutinized and found wanting not only by policy officials, but by wide sectors of the world's population. The Hague Conference at the turn of the twentieth century with its regulations on the rules of warfare is followed by the Geneva Conventions, the League of Nations, the Pact of Paris, the United Nations Charter, Article 2 (4), the codification of the Nuremberg Judgment, and the many declarations, resolutions and instruments, and, the special sessions on disarmament. Worthy of note, as well, are some twenty-five NGO fora—the global citizens' initiatives: Stockholm (1972), Nairobi (1975), Rio de Janeiro (1992), and, Beijing (1995), to name only four. These are all part of that normative movement. Again, as noted above, the practice does not always follow words; but words hammered out in negotiations, dialogue, and confrontations do have impact on behavior.

Second, there has been a strong transnational peace and justice movement in this century. It has drawn upon religious and traditional belief systems throughout the planet going back two or three millennia. While there are a number of movements that have focused on coherent alternatives, both short- and long-term, for resolving disputes and curtailing violence, for the most part, most movements have waxed and waned around particular wars. But their dialogue and practices have questioned the validity of large-scale organized violence and are attracting more adherents.

Third, nonviolent activism as a preferred method of achieving radical social change is another strand in this emergent myth of the Subject. Mahatma Gandhi (see *Gandhi, Mohandas Karamchand*), Martin Luther King, Jr. (see *Conscientious Objection*), early Solidarity in Poland, and other formations of "civil society" in what used to be Eastern Europe, the Filipino people's deposing of Marcos, the Chinese students at Tiananmen Square, among many others, all attest to the growing realization of both the limits and possibilities of nonviolent activism. Not only are they another strand in the process of delegitimatizing violence, but they also contribute to an ethos where the question of how to eliminate war and other forms of violence becomes a more credible political project for those concerned with the transformation of our planet in this "axial moment" of planetary history.

5. The Legacy and Promise of Historical Transformation: Democratic Global Constitutionalism, Global Civil Society, and Human Identity/Interest

Perhaps, most important of all, to read the current situation in this way is to suggest, at a minimum, that the war system, militarism, as well as other forms of violence need not be forever with us; they are not inevitable. Indeed, the historical achievements of the past—the delegitimization of the divine right of kings, of slavery and colonialism, and of apartheid—all attest to the fact that, as Margaret Mead once declared, war is a human invention and can be eliminated. The "Servile Declaration on Violence" puts it even more forcefully that while aggression is part of the human condition (or what might be called "human nature"), organized warfare (and, we might add, all forms of violence) is not (see *Human Nature Theories of War; Aggression*). That the legacy of historical transformation includes the possibility of social change will need to be part of the story, the narrative, the making of myths, in order to convince others of the desirability and possibility of constructing a world that is peaceful and just.

Within the context of competing alternative interpretations of the contemporary scene, the various strands of delegitimatizing war, militarism, and violence, as well as the rich historical traditions of dismantling oppressive structures, we would like to suggest three additional propositions that could be part of the global transformative practices for our time. These propositions not only inform and motivate our practice, they are part of the historical construction of our identities. They are: (i) "a riot is the voice of the unheard;" (ii) "*Ubi Societ as Ibi Lex*" (wherever there is society there is law); and, (iii) "to think, feel and act as a global citizen is essential for analyzing, prescribing, and implementing struggles for a just world order."

The first of these propositions has its origin in the lives and voices of the oppressed, and, in fact, is initiated by the voices of the unheard. It was Martin Luther King, Jr., who observed that "a riot is the voice of the unheard." We have the responsibility to identify where the unheard are located; what their grievances, needs, and claims are; what personal, political, and institutional opportunities they have to be heard, not to mention satisfying their aspirations; and yes, we also need to honor their sensibilities and feelings with our own evaluation of the validity of these aspirations. Surely one of the major matters we will need to attend to in all of this is the riot, and the use of violence. Since we are profoundly aware of

structural violence, as well as direct violence that is visited upon the oppressed, our understanding and even empathy for self-defense or counter conflict is appreciable. At the same time we need to be aware that in legitimatizing this latter kind of violence, we may legitimatize violence itself. We need to weave these perplexing and vexing dilemmas into our narratives, practices, and identities.

6. Democratic Global Constitutionalism

It was Machiavelli who noted in *The Prince* that "there are two methods of fighting, the one by law, the other by force. The first method is that of men [sic], the second of beasts. But, as the first method is often insufficient, one must have recourse to the second." We take it that the task is to assist in the great effort to eliminate recourse to the second. And what we wish here to note is the role that law, the constitutive order, and democratic global constitutionalism play in the construction of our narratives, practices, and identities.

The twentieth century has been witness to two contradictory trends. On the one hand, it ranks as one of the bloodiest, war-ridden, and violent periods of human history. World War I, Manchuria, Ethiopia, Hitler's conquest of Europe, World War II, the Holocaust, the use of atomic weapons in Hiroshima and Nagasaki, the bloody partitioning of India and Pakistan, the Arab-Israeli Wars, Korea, Vietnam, the Gulf War, Yugoslavia, Somalia, Rwanda, and more, are testimony enough to horrify any human being. Simultaneously, as we tried to suggest earlier, this century has produced a normative history unique in human society, including, among other things, the attempt to control and discourage by law large-scale organized violence. In short, the international community has embarked on a normative journey to outlaw war and crimes against humanity; to make recourse to aggressive war illegal and even criminal, and barbarous treatment of citizens by state officials; indeed, to outlaw and delegitimatize all forms of violence against both human beings and nature.

Under these conditions of divergence between practices of violence and the normative claims for peace and justice, the ideas of democratic constitutionalism as the formal and contextual political/legal foundation for global polity grows increasingly attractive. Here the developments around the League of Nations and the United Nations become more interesting. For as bilateral, regional, functional, and transnational treaties and organizational arrangements expand, such developments, almost of necessity, will refashion the state system, revealing its rigid tendencies and yet suggesting alternative political arrangements within and beyond the state. No doubt this is already happening as the activities around the Declaration of Human Rights, the two Covenants, and the Rights of the Child have clearly illustrated.

Between 1930 and the year 2000 the world's population will have tripled from two billion to more than six billion. These six billion people will be more mutually aware of one another than every prior generation of earthly inhabitants (see *Future of Humanity*). Furthermore, the process of interdependence, integration, and intermingling are producing transnational forms and structures of economic, social, cultural, and political relations that place great pressure on the old systems and suggest the urgent need for new forms of governance and polity (see *Transnationalism*). The year 1995 was the fiftieth anniversary of the United Nations. Citizen organizations throughout the world are beginning to focus on how to democratize the UN and how to make it more responsive and accountable to the citizens of the globe (see *Future of Humanity*). It is becoming increasingly clear that a profound concern for new forms of democratic governance and polity at the global level is emergent.

And so let us be very clear that what is being called for here is *democratic* global constitutionalism. We noted above the maxim in Western jurisprudence, *Ubi Societas Ibi Lex*, where there is society there is law. We strongly believe, perhaps it is even demonstrable, that global society has emerged. We dare suggest, moreover, that some form of global law is emerging. Thus, the question that remains is: What kind of law? Administered by whom? And, for what purposes and values?

7. Global Civil Society

The emergence of a global civil society is also important to emphasize. Large-scale transformations always bring forth new political actors and new forms of political action. Social movements, as one of the important components of civil society, are particularly significant in this respect. Indeed, it is fair to argue that these movements that are transnational in scope are the critical mass from which global civil society is emerging and being molded. These transnational movements have, it should be pointed out, dealt with individual states, i.e., the antiapartheid movement against South Africa; clusters of states, i.e., the European peace movement against NATO; multinational businesses, i.e., the campaign against Nestle's baby formula program;

and international organizations, i.e., alternative conferences on environment, development, women, human rights, and the like. Greenpeace, Amnesty International, and other groupings have made themselves part of this transnational civil network; and it is fair to say that many states and organizations that are targeted by these groups recognize their influence (see *Non-governmental Organizations (NGOs)*).

At the same time, our efforts need to be directed toward exploring and explaining not only the emergence of global society and law, but of community; and how, in the final analysis, we should participate—and enable others to participate—in shaping it. We start with the idea, both empirically demonstrated and philosophically desired, that community is local in origin, but global in reach. We are concerned to know how many beings—whatever their differences and diversities that we, no doubt, are willing and sometimes eager to affirm—can and should be seen also as members of one "global" community. The lessons of human history do suggest that there is a "human condition," and that it is a valid, if not desirable, starting point especially if it is sundered from some of modernity's ontological or epistemological pretensions noted above. In this context, it will be necessary to modify our maxim *Ubi Societas Ibi Lex* to read *Ubi Communitas Ibi Justa Lex*: where there is community there is just law.

8. Human Identity/Interest

Finally, to think of society, community, and law, and especially at this moment of history with its emphasis on participation and democracy of people is to point directly to the notion of civil society and to the role of the citizen in it. This is where the third proposition finds its place, namely, to think, feel, and act as a global citizen is essential in the construction of human identity and interest (see *Education for Global Citizenship*).

It is extremely difficult to conceptualize, let alone construct, the idea and practice of human identity or interest. The historical, ideological, and epistemological weight of statist construals of identity and interest seem to inveigh against such a goal. One need only survey the literatures and practices under the sign of the realist consensus to realize that identity and interest are often tied to territorially, ethnically, and linguistically bounded communities. Often, these communities understand themselves as being in perpetual conflict and competition with other communities—a trace, to borrow a Derridean notion, of a Hobbesian "state of nature." Indeed, one might point to the present conflicts in the former Yugoslavia, the former Soviet Union—to name only the most prominent—as confirmation of the resilience, if not permanence, of conflicting and irreconcilable national identities and interests. Our third proposition, some may opine, is nothing more than utopian.

To be sure, not unlike the other two, this proposition that is essential to constructing the idea and practice of global citizenship calls for much broader, deeper, and wider discussion. The problems noted above have no easy solution; and it will not do to impose yet another identity, let alone an identity that aspires toward globally oriented norms and claims, on our multilayered, multistranded lives. Yet, it is precisely because such identities often tend to overlook some of the wider (some might argue, "ecological") dimensions of human experience that we make this almost nonsensical, if not arrogant, claim. Our politics is nourished by the conviction that the notion of citizenship will have to be extended beyond its present statist-, ethnic-, and gender-based limitations. We want to suggest further that any reconstruction of the idea and practice of citizenship must be accompanied by a corresponding deconstruction and reconstruction of the ideas of identity and interest, particularly as they are construed within the discourses of the so-called realist consensus.

Such a task is not to be taken lightly. But neither are we traveling the pathways of a *creatio ex nihilo*. Indeed, this idea of global citizenship that is sustained by the idea of a human identity (as opposed to ethnic, national identity) and interest, but especially of dignity, is being constructed by individuals and groups throughout the planet.

9. Political Practice as Mythmaking: From a Politics of Conviction to the Practices of Struggle for a Just World Order

Participants in WOMP and the Global Civilization Project have consistently maintained that convictions about political action proceed from moral imperatives as well as practical necessities. Such a perspective arises not only from profound reservations about the adequacy of the dominant myths and values under the sign of the realist consensus to interpret human history, and to provide both the moral ground and the political will for transformative practice in the present and the future; but, also from the deep realization of the limits of human reason and passion to comprehend what might be called the *Zeitgeist* and practices of our time.

If one reviews the literatures of "future studies,"

international relations, and political science, particularly in the last decade, it becomes fairly clear that scholars, public policy experts, and activists failed to comprehend what turned out to be profound and extraordinary transformations in human history that coalesced between 1989 and 1992. This is not simply the result of what is believed to be an imperfect, though perfectible, social-scientific method, but rather a reminder of the real limits of the human capacity to understand and interpret the world in which human beings find themselves. Rather than seeking refuge in the Cartesian pretensions of discovering that "Archimedean point," or modernity's illusion of the quest for certainty; and, indeed, rather than capitulating to the deception that lack of knowledge must be accompanied by lack of action, we prefer to argue for a "politics of conviction" that is rooted in *practices of struggle* for a just world order.

This politics of conviction is more than belief; and while it is always personal, it cannot be individual. It is a common practice that includes the articulation of preferred objectives for an *imagined community* that is global in reach, the identification of concrete social forces and agents of transformation, and, the creation and nurture of fundamentally new and better relationships, already in existence and still to be constructed, and the institutionalization of structures and processes that will bring about the transformation—without denying the major difficulties, hostile actors, and deep structures that need to be overcome. This politics of conviction is articulated as historical and contingent practice of transformation, which include, in the language of an earlier essay, articulating a "transition strategy," or better still, transition strategies, that takes seriously those struggles for a just world order as a "defining moment" within a larger quest for human identity and interest.

We noted above that the first proposition in our alternative narrative is "a riot is the voice of the unheard." This political idea has a methodological correlate within the context of a politics of conviction. Not only is political resistance critical, indeed, integral, to the process of transformation, but the sensibility of resistance (of what Hegel may have meant by the notion of "negativity"—or its embodiment in radical critique) dislocates these logics, particularly the logics of domination. It not only underscores the contingent and precarious character of what we seek to challenge, thereby opening it to transformation, but also reminds us of our own historicity, thus creating a climate where limits are affirmed as conditions of possibility rather than signs of failure; where empathy and shared vulnerabilities shape common aspirations even as they illumine the limits and possibilities of human action.

It is in this sense that our politics of conviction, which moves beyond an uncritical Weberian voluntarism, oriented around a structurally based "ethicotheoretical decision," is nourished by a commitment and call to individuals, groups, organizations, and leadership of progressive governments throughout the planet to join in a common effort and engage in practices of struggle for a just world order. It bears repeating that we are very much aware that war, imperialism, authoritarianism, poverty, social injustice, ecological instability, and alienation are problems faced by human beings throughout the planet; that the interaction of these problems produces and reproduces a global system in which militarism is deeply rooted and where the logics of the state system often go unchallenged. It is against this background that we commit ourselves to a set of interrelated aspirations: peace, social justice, economic well-being, ecological balance, and positive identity. These aspirations are not only normative, however. They form the basis of our analytical method in comprehending our world.

We also know and take heart in the fact that there are a growing number of people throughout the entire planet who are concerned and ready to act, even to resist, to change these structures and processes. Indeed, it is worth reiterating that we are at an "axial moment" in human history, a time when the old myths of identity are giving way to new ones. There are literally hundreds, indeed thousands, of struggles attempting to create local communities as well as a global society that are inspired by the imperative to provide acceptable conditions for material living, appropriate social and political participation, an ecologically sound environment, and a polity free from militarism. We recognize that the nation-state in the Third World has been a progressive institution and does provide some protection and some security against forms of domination by stronger states and institutions. Yet we also acknowledge that this very system of states as it is presently constituted is incapable of dealing with global crises.

10. Principles, Images, Norms

With a global system that is at once fragmenting and integrating, and a situation that is profoundly contested, conflictual, and uneven perceptually and empirically, we are the first to acknowledge the profound difficulties in offering principles, strategies, and tactics to overcome the problems we face. This is especially problematic where claims are being made, par-

ticularly by those perceived to be in positions of privilege, about the global applicability, not to mention desirability, of these recommendations. At the same time, not only does our politics of convictions refuse to yield to the luxury of inaction; more importantly, we are emboldened by the reality that our recommendations spring forth from the very practices of participants in an emerging global civil society—which we are here seeking to articulate. "The Iowa Declaration," the full text of which is included as an appendix is one such articulation that we offer as an example of these practices. One critical point also needs to be underscored. That is, the following principles, images, and norms are not in the first instance policy recommendations, but are articulations, indeed, constructions, of particular practices—and for this reason, are to be understood as part of the process of creating and nurturing a myth of global citizenship. They are, to return to Wittgenstein, "steps . . . to climb beyond them."

In this context, we emphasize three principles that are emerging in these practices, namely, accountability, participation, and transnationalization/globalization. These three mean, for example, that it is critical

(a) to the maximum extent possible, to form decentralized units of production, consumption, and community participation; units informed by globally oriented as well as locally constructed values and practices—with some right of appeal to some unit outside this formation;

(b) to develop unique and creative forms of transnational cooperation to promote global values and practices; but to engage only in those political, social and cultural projects that benefit humanity. If that criterion proves to be too difficult, select only those projects that directly benefit the lowest 40 percent of humanity in terms of material well-being and meaningful participation in decision making, and, select projects that have the capacity to mobilize between five percent and 20 percent of the polity in which the project will take place;

(c) to increase accountability, wide participation in the creation and management of global institutions and global problems. Here, the use of violence should be avoided, if at all possible. If used, it should be used only against targets that are themselves the direct source of oppression. Further, the decision to use violence should be subjected not only to "local" people but wherever possible to a transnational group of like-minded individuals.

11. Conclusion: The Myth of the Global Citizen

We are "Citizens of the World." We demand that our borders be opened. We want commercial and cultural exchange, and the right to export our labor force abroad. We want freedom to leave China in order to study on a semistudy, semiwork basis. We demand to be able to travel freely, and to take care of our pre-requisites.

The Alliance appeals for support from the Chinese masses, and from human rights organizations throughout the world.

• *Manifesto of the Alliance for Human Rights in China*, January 1, 1979 (Founding members: Ren Wanding, Zhao Xing, Xing Guang, Li Guangli, Quan Wei, Song Yi, Li Wei, and two other comrades)

This essay began with a statement by that good human being Pope John XXIII, introducing the notion of citizenship in the world community. That notion coming from Pope John XXIII—even given his extraordinary moral, intellectual, and political leadership—undoubtedly elicits the response that it is the statement of an idealist—it is at best, some would argue, aspirational, and at its worst, pietistic.

The quote above deploys similar language. However, it clearly comes from a much different context. Here we have a group in struggle, facing repression and oppression, and using the terminology of citizens of the world to express their grievances and claims. This is not a mawkish, sentimental declaration of "globalists" from Western society. Rather these are individuals who are confronting one of the most authoritarian governments in the world. Beyond that, what makes their statement so revealing in terms of the emergence of the myth of global citizenship is precisely the fact that it is occurring in China. According to traditional Chinese myth, China is the center of the universe; other cultures and civilizations are expected to live accordingly, as symbolized in the ceremony of the kowtow. In utilizing, therefore, universal terminologies, these dissidents may be interpreted as revealing the extent to which the idea of a global civilization of the kind we have been exploring resides even at the center of the universe in terms of the psychopolitical visions and feelings located precisely within the center.

The statement seems so arresting that we have attempted to discover who these individuals were. While we are unable to state definitively who they were, our research indicates that none of them were "cosmopolitan" in the sense of having traveled abroad. They seem to have been relatively well educated, so

their internalization of the notion of citizen of the world is one that is quite significant and instructive.

There are other illustrations of the emergence of the myth of global citizenship that need recounting. Three, in particular, may be useful. First, Jimmy Carter, on the occasion of his inauguration as US President, issued a one-page statement to the world with the following introductory paragraph:

I have chosen the occasion of my inauguration as President to speak not only to my own countrymen—which is traditional—but also to you, citizens of the world who did not participate in our election, but who will nevertheless be affected by my decisions.

That this modest, very bright person, upon assuming what could very well be the most powerful office on the planet should feel the necessity of speaking to "citizens of the world" is still another indication of the emergence of the myth of global citizenship.

Second, we should also point to the statement made by Chancellor Helmut Kohl in November 1992 in eulogizing Willie Brandt. Chancellor Helmut Kohl described Mr. Brandt as a "citizen of the world," and saluted him for having built "bridges over walls and barbed wires, bridges to our eastern neighbors, bridges between North and South." That Chancellor Kohl, perhaps the most nationalist leader in Germany since Konrad Adenauer, would characterize Willie Brandt in his eulogy as a citizen of the world in affirming, positive terms is thus all the more significant.

And finally, as we noted earlier in this paper, the emergence of a global civil society, perhaps best exemplified by those citizens' initiatives that are often local in origin but global in vision, for example, the Nairobi world conference of women and the counter-conference to UNCED at Rio, all attest to the existence of the myth of the global citizen.

It is our conviction, borne of our experience in an emerging global, indeed, planetary consciousness and practice, that the myth of the Subject, is today being articulated in the practices of an emerging global citizen: one who thinks, feels, and acts, as if he or she *belongs* to the planet earth, and who imagines that she or he is *responsible* for the planet earth. This is myth and mythmaking at its best: the creation of a narrative rooted in a practice that is already coming into being as both promise and fulfillment.

12. The Iowa Declaration

This Declaration, which is part of an ongoing process initiated by Saul Mendlovitz and formalized in 1992, has been discussed and revised in a number of workshops and conferences throughout the globe. The program outlined below for what we call here the Movement(s) for a Just World Order is based on the view that there are five major interactive problems facing human society. They are: militarism and war; poverty and maldevelopment; ecological imbalance; social injustice; and alienation. The Movement(s) attempts to address these problems by optimizing the values of peace, economic well-being, ecological balance, social justice, and positive identity through organized political, social, economic, and cultural activities. This value framework is used as an analytical frame for understanding the global social system and thus is seen as a supplement to or perhaps even substitute for a traditional power analysis.

In addition, the Movement(s) considers this period of history to be axial—that is to say, a fundamental change is taking place in the value system(s) of human society that has enormous impact on organization, norms, and concerns. Specifically, the nation-state system, state sovereignty, and practices and notions of governance as we have experienced and understood them for the past 300 to 500 years are undergoing profound transformation.

In selecting the particular program and projects, we have attempted to take into account the vast variety and disparity in income, power, and influence among the many groupings of human beings throughout the globe.

The Iowa Declaration

WE, PEOPLES OF THE UNITED NATIONS AND CITIZENS OF THE WORLD,

HAVING MET AT IOWA CITY, IOWA, FROM 12 TO 14 APRIL 1995 AND AT OTHER TIMES PRECEDING TO CELEBRATE THE FUTURE OF THE UNITED NATIONS ON THE OCCASION OF ITS FIFTIETH ANNIVERSARY,

DETERMINED

1. to save the world from the scourge of war, which often in our lifetimes has brought untold sorrow to humankind, and

2. to reaffirm faith in fundamental human rights, in the dignity and worth of the human person, in the equal rights of men and women and of nations large and small, and

3. to promote social progress and better standards of life in larger freedom, and

4. to protect and preserve the integrity and sustainability of our earth-space environment, and

5. to establish conditions under which justice and respect for the obligations arising from treaties and other sources of international law can be maintained,

DO HEREBY DECLARE OUR COMMITMENT TO PARTICIPATE IN MOVEMENTS FOR HUMANE GOVERNANCE THROUGHOUT THE GLOBE AND, IN FURTHERANCE OF THIS COMMITMENT, TO DEDICATE OURSELVES TO THE FOLLOWING CONCRETE GOALS WHICH, SEPARATELY AND TOGETHER, CONSTITUTE OUR COVENANT WITH THE WORLD BY THE YEARS 2010-2020:

1. a democratic constitutional framework for global institutions on global matters, supported by a global tax regime and including a global court system with compulsory jurisdiction (*democratic global governance*);

2. general and complete disarmament with a comprehensive global security structure in place under civilian control (*demilitarization/peace*);

3. global and regional human rights regimes with compulsory law-making and law-enforcing jurisdiction (*human rights/social justice*);

4. a basic-needs regime and the eradication of base poverty and maldevelopment for all humankind (*economic well-being/development*);

5. global and regional environmental regimes with compulsory decision-making authority and control (*sustainable ecological balance*);

AND TO THESE ENDS, CONVINCED THAT WE ARE AT AN OPEN MOMENT IN HISTORY WHEREIN REALITY— NEVER FIXED—CAN BE SIGNIFICANTLY TRANSFORMED, AND RESOLVED TO COMBINE OUR LOCAL, NATIONAL, AND TRANSNATIONAL EFFORTS TO ACCOMPLISH THESE AIMS, WE CALL UPON THE UNITED NATIONS, MEMBER STATES, AND INDIVIDUALS AND GROUPS EVERYWHERE TO TAKE JOINT AND SEPARATE ACTION IN RESPECT OF THE FOLLOWING SHORT-TERM (1995-2000) AND INTERMEDIATE-TERM (2000-2010) TRANSITIONAL OBJECTIVES AND STRATEGIES:

A. Short-Term Transitional Objectives/Strategies (1995-2000) Facilitating Political Processes

1. Establish and actively participate in coalitions, cadres, and cells of concerned citizens resolved to fulfill globally oriented peace and justice agendas for local and national governments, including: (a) active and informed citizen participation in political processes; (b) fair, equitable, and restorative criminal justice systems; (c) the

elimination of racism, sexism, and religious and other forms of social intolerance; (d) enlarged provision for quality education, adequate housing, expert health care, and income sufficient to ensure every person's potential; and (e) effective laws and policies to ensure an ecologically sound and healthy natural environment.

2. Support individuals for office, both electoral and appointive, who commit to the values of a just world order within a globally oriented policy framework for the governance of their local and national societies.

3. Initiate a continuing summit of the world's religious leaders, moral philosophers, and other qualified persons who are committed to global governance to develop and recommend solutions to the principal problems dividing humanity, especially the problems of war, civil and political injusitce, poverty and maldevelopment, ecological degradation, and sociopolitical alienation.

Democratic Global Governance

4. Work to ensure strong financial and political support of a reformed and revitalized United Nations system that takes seriously (a) an equitable sharing of power within the UN Security Council and General Assembly; (b) faithful adherence to principles of gender equality; and (c) increased participation by, and/or representation of, citizen action organizations (CAOs, also known as NGOs), indigenous peoples, and other underrepresented groups.

5. Publicize and promote the United Nations Decade of International Law, including submission to the compulsory jurisdiction of the International Court of Justice in respect of all treaties entered into after 1994, and otherwise work to expand and strengthen the world rule of law.

6. Support the movement for an international criminal code and court to deal with individuals and groups who engage in crimes against humanity, terrorism, torture, and other heinous behaviors that fall below standards of basic human decency.

Demilitarization/Peace

7. Campaign for a five-year, 50 percent reduction of national defense budgets (redesignated "national security budgets") that will (a) significantly reduce spending on offensive weapons systems; (b) provide for peacekeeping and peacemaking

training and planning as part of the military mission; (c) encourage and adequately fund economic conversion programs for defense-related industries; and (d) allocate the resulting savings to meeting basic needs both domestically and globally and to United Nations peacekeeping and other multilateral peace operations.

8. Facilitate the successful resolution of an advisory opinion of the International Court of Justice on the illegality of the threat and use of nuclear weapons.

9. Work to establish a continuing United Nations Conference on World Security and Cooperation (analogous to the Conference on Security and Cooperation in Europe) and equivalent regional forums to define and develop mechanisms and institutions for the reduction of nuclear, "conventional," biological, and chemical arms, the clearing of land mines, the regulation of the arms trade, and the peaceful resolution of national and international disputes.

10. Promote the creation of a small but permanent and reliably financed United Nations peacekeeping force both for humanitarian intervention in civil wars and instances of genocide and for monitoring and moderating violent conflicts between States.

11. Advocate and help to inculcate a culture of nonviolence at all levels of social organization and, to this end, develop popular and institutional support for both public and private conflict mitigation and dispute resolution initiatives, including an expanded right of individual and group petition to United Nations and regional bodies, peace teams, environmental negotiations, and reconciliation projects involving interpersonal and intergroup conciliation, mediation arbitration, and other means of peaceful settlement.

Human Rights/Social Justice

12. Assist in the investigation and exposure of human rights violations everywhere, especially where egregious State behavior is involved, and, to these ends, help especially to enforce the 1948 Convention on the Prevention and Punishment of the Crime of Genocide and to secure worldwide ratification and enforcement of the 1966 International Covenant on Economic, Social and Cultural Rights, the 1966 International Covenant on Civil and Political Rights, the 1966 Convention on the Elimination of All Forms of Racial Discrimina-

tion, the 1979 Convention on the Elimination of All Forms of Discrimination Against Women, and the 1989 Convention on the Rights of the Child.

13. Work to (a) promote the work of the UN High Commissioner for Human Rights; (b) ensure that the United Nations and regional organizations receive and act on early warning of interethnic conflicts; (c) establish regional human rights courts where they do not now exist; (d) further the World Decade for Human Rights Education launched by UNESCO in December 1994; and (e) encourage all nations to develop action plans stating how they will promote and protect internationally recognized human rights.

14. Help to implement "The Nairobi Forward-Looking Strategies for the Advancement of Women to the Year 2000" of the 1985 United Nations World Conference to Review and Approve the Achievements of the United Nations Decade for Women, participate in the 1995 Beijing Fourth World Conference on Women, and support its adopted "Platform of Action" promoting equality, development, and peace.

15. Promote the work of the United Nations High Commissioner for Refugees, and, to this end, (a) facilitate strong institutional and financial support to meet at least the basic needs of the more than 50 million refugees and other displaced persons presently existing; (b) expose and help to remove the conditions of militarism and maldevelopment, among others, that produce refugees and other displaced persons; and (c) otherwise help to cause refugee and displaced person status to be only a temporary evil of human existence.

16. Endeavor to inaugurate and strengthen economic and political democracy in all societies throughout the world.

Economic Well-Development

17. Help to bring about an effective worldwide basic needs regime, supported by an equitable global tax scheme capable of maintaining it and by an appropriate monitoring and regulation of transnational enterprises, each governed by principles of decentralization of production and consumption and by maximum community participation in decision making, involving especially representatives of labor in local and national communities.

18. Strive to eradicate economic misery and maldevelopment among the world's poor by (a)

encouraging radical national and international debt-reduction programs, including the equivalent of bankruptcy proceedings, for heavily indebted developing countries; (b) supporting efforts to cause all wealthy countries to commit at least 0.7 percent of GDP for genuine and appropriate economic and technological assistance; (c) working to empower the Economic and Social Council (ECOSOC) or a substitute Economic Security Council to integrate issues of Socioeconomic development and security; and (d) helping to facilitate among all global and regional developmental agencies and institutions, especially the World Bank (IBRD), the International Monetary Fund (IMF), and the International Development Association (IDA), more democratic decision-making processes and enhanced communication, coordination, and accountability.

19. Promote economic security and equal opportunity for working men and women everywhere by (a) supporting the work of the International Labour Organization to achieve full employment, the raising of living standards, and improvements in the conditions of work; and (b) encouraging greater access to labor-intensive services in the services regime of the newly formed GATT World Trade Organization (WTO).

Sustainable Ecological Balance

20. Prioritize and act upon Agenda 21 of the 1992 United Nations Conference on Environment and Development (UNCED) and, to these ends, work to secure universal ratification of, among other agreements, the 1982 United Nations Convention on the Law of the Sea and its progeny, the 1992 United Nations Framework Convention on Climate Change, and the 1992 Convention on Biological Diversity.

21. Initiate and promote a multilateral convention against ecocide that would make it a crime, in time of peace or war, intentionally to disrupt or destroy a human ecosystem in whole or in part.

B. Intermediate-Term Traditional Objectives/Strategies (2000-2010) Facilitating Political Processes

1. Continue to establish and actively participate in coalitions, cadres, and cells of concerned citizens resolved to fulfill globally oriented peace and justice agendas for local and national governments (as recommended in Short-Term Transitional Objective/Strategy 1, above).

2. Continue to support individuals for office who commit to the values of a just world order within a globally-oriented policy framework for the governance of their local and national societies (as recommended in Short-Term Transitional Objective/Strategy 2, above).

3. Continue to sponsor and promote summits of the world's religious leaders, moral philosophers, and other qualified persons who are committed to global governance to develop and recommend solutions to the principal problems on the human agenda (as recommended in Short-Term Transitional Objective/Strategy 3, above).

Democratic Global Governance

4. Further ensure strong financial and political support to a reformed and revitalized United Nations system (as recommended in Short-Term Transitional Objective/Strategy 4, above) by, among other things, charging interest on unpaid United Nations dues and assessments and taxing international arms sales, international currency trading, and the transnational pollution of the "global commons."

5. Continue to promote the world rule of law and help to strengthen the international criminal code and court recommended in Short-Term Transitional Objective/Strategy 6 (above) and established in 1995-2000.

Demilitarization/Peace

6. Continue to support the United Nations Conference on World Security and equivalent regional forums established in 1995-2000 to facilitate arms reduction, the clearing of land mines, the regulation of the arms trade, and the peaceful resolution of national and international disputes.

7. Work to provide effective United Nations and regional monitoring, inspection, evaluation, and reporting of the worldwide arms trade and all arms transfers.

8. Strive to eliminate all nuclear weapons and all nuclear power projects that could contribute to weapons production, and work to prohibit unconditionally the development, manufacture, and testing of all nuclear, biological, and chemical weapons on a worldwide basis.

9. Help to establish "nonprovocative defense" national security systems and continue to advocate a culture of nonviolence and peaceful settlement of disputes (as recommended in Short-Term Transitional Objective/Strategy 11, above).

Human Rights/Social Justice

10. Continue to investigate and expose human rights violations, especially where egregious State behavior is involved and, to this end, continue to enforce the 1948 Convention on the Prevention and Punishment of the Crime of Genocide and all other fundamental human rights agreements and conventions.

11. Endeavor to require all nations to develop action plans stating how they win promote and protect internationally recognized human rights and redouble support for (a) the World Decade for Human Rights Education launched by the United Nations in December 1994, (b) the work of the UN High Commissioner for Human Rights, (c) United Nations and regional efforts to receive and act on early warning of interethnic conflicts, and (d) the use of established regional human rights courts whenever possible.

12. Help to ensure that women are guaranteed equity in all policy-and decision-making offices in the United Nations and in all legislative and executive offices in government, business, and professional organizations throughout the world.

13. Redouble support of the work of the United Nations High Commissioner for Refugees (as recommended in Short-Term Transitional Objective/Strategy 16, above).

Economic Well-Being/Development

14. Strive to ensure adequate nutrition for all people through the world and, to this end, make adequate nutrition a first call on resources and secure the establishment of a global food agency to implement the right to food that would consolidate and give focus to the diverse food programs currently in existence.

15. Work to empower the World Health Organization (WHO) to provide basic health services for all human beings, including effective, medically safe, and noncoercive family planning on a universally available basis.

16. Further support and work for a serious and effecitve worldwide basic needs regime (as recommended in Transitional Objective/Strategy 17, above), and to this end promote the formal establishment of, among other things, a new System of

National Accounts and broader Quality of Life indicators to provide a framework and criteria for development projects funded by United Nations agencies and other international institutions.

17. Continue to work toward the eradication of economic misery and maldevelopment among the world's poor (as recommended in Short-Term Transitional Objective/Strategy 18, above).

18. Further help to achieve economic security and equal opportunity for working men and women everywhere (as recommended in short-Term Transitional Objective/Strategy 19, above).

19. Endeavor to secure the widespread adoption of a Global Code of Conduct for transnational corporations and State trading associations that would be accountable to the values of a just world order as well as the test of profitability.

Sustainable Ecological Balance

20. Continue to act upon Agenda 21 of the 1992 United Nations Conference on Environment and Development (UNCED), paying particular attention to safeguarding the genetic and biological diversity of flora and fauna throughout the world.

21. Work to secure the universal ratification and enforcement of a multilateral convention against ecocide that would make it a crime, in time of peace or war, intentionally to disrupt or destroy a human ecosystem in whole or in part.

FINALLY, WE BELIEVE THAT, ON THE OCCASION OF THE FIFTIETH ANNIVERSARY OF THE UNITED NATIONS, THE TIME IS LONG OVERDUE WHEN OUR ENTIRE PLANET MUST BE VIEWED AS THE BEGINNING AND END OF HUMAN IDENTITY AND LOYALTY. TO THIS END, WE COMMIT OURSELVES TO A NEW GEOPOLITICAL ETHOS OF PLANETARY STEWARDSHIP OR CITIZENSHIP. TO THINK AND FEEL AND ACT AS A GLOBAL CITIZEN IS, WE BELIEVE, ESSENTIAL TO THE REALIZATION OF A REVITALIZED UNITED NATIONS AND HUMANE GLOBAL GOVERNANCE GENERALLY. WE CALL UPON EVERYONE EVERYWHERE AND AT ALL LEVELS OF SOCIAL ORGANIZATION TO JOIN WITH US IN THIS STRUGGLE.

The Iowa Declaration was adopted at a symposium of 240 concerned citizens held April 12-14, 1995 at The University of Iowa in Iowa City, Iowa, USA to commemorate the fiftieth anniversary of the founding of the United Nations. The symposium, entitled, "UN50: Preferred Futures for the United Nations," was cosponsored by the Iowa Division of the United Nations Association-USA, the International and Comparative Legal Studies Program of The University of Iowa, the World Order Models Project (New York City), and The Stanley Foundation (Muscatine, Iowa) in cooperation with the American Society of International Law (Washington, DC), the Center for Global and Regional Environment Research of the University of Iowa, The United Nations Association-USA (New York City), and the United States Institute of Peace (Washington, DC). The Declaration originated among the organizers of the symposium and in six preparatory community forums held in Iowa and in Illinois, Jamaica, and Nigeria during 1994-95, cosponsored by the Iowa Division of the United Nations Association-USA, the Iowa Humanities Board (a State Program of the National Endowment for the Humanities), The Stanley Foundation, and the World Federation of United Nations Associations (WFUNA). For additional copies of the Declaration, contact: Iowa Division of the United Nations Association-USA, 20 East Market Street, Iowa City. IA, 52245-1728 (Phone/ Fax: 319-337-7290; E-Mail: unaiowa@igc.apc.org).

SAUL H. MENDLOVITZ; LESTER EDWIN J. RUIZ

N

National Interest

The concept of national interest has replaced the older one of the interest of a state as an extension of its monarch. The interest of the dynastic state was formally expressed as "the dignity, honor, and interests of the Crown." A distinction between the public interest and the private interest of the king did not emerge before the seventeenth and eighteenth centuries. In the dynastic age foreign affairs were still to a large extent personalized as the relations entertained by a king with his fellow monarchs. However, once sovereignty and legitimate authority no longer rested with the person of the king but with the nation seen as a sovereign people, the concept of national interest could come into being. The French Revolution was an important watershed in this development.

The concept of national interest provides for a demarcation in two directions: to the interior and to the exterior. In the first place it puts the interest of nation and state as a whole above that of the private interests of specific individuals or groups within the state. It is thus in clear opposition to a slogan such as "what is good for General Motors is good for the United States." It can thus also implicitly refer to a hierarchy of public interests, as we will come to see. Secondly, the concept of national interest provides a demarcation toward the outside world in placing the interest of the state above the interest of humankind or humanity. It implicitly sees humankind as being naturally divided into sovereign states, each with their own specific character, role, and interests, symbolized the idea of the nation. The term national interest presupposes the desirability of the continuous existence of a particular nation-state and thus ultimately will be identical with the survival as an independent entity of what is usually seen as organized as a state. The national interest is then seen as identical with survival of the state and its 'national' security. It may imply that this interest is unitary and unequivocal. It can also be taken to mean that other interests have to be subordinated to the national interest. So, for example, national security in the United States has long been supposed to demand a so-called bipartisan foreign policy, an agreement of the two main political parties not to disagree about the main lines of foreign policy. The term national interest can therefore easily be used for propaganda or rather for special pleading under the guise of something held to be beyond doubt or any different interpretation. The terms "national interest" and "national security" are usually invoked by those who claim that the political leaders pay insufficient attention to the external threats facing them and to the build-up of military strength it requires. They are symbols which are often invoked against those who would rely more on international cooperation or detente. However, as soon as one tries to define the national interest in more than the minimum sense of physical survival it becomes ambiguous. If that is done, reference is usually made to values or objectives, so as for example in the following definitions of national security: ". . . a nation is secure to the extent to which it is not in danger of having to sacrifice core values if it wishes to avoid war, and is able, if challenged, to maintain them by victory in such a war" (Walter Lippmann), or "security, in an objective sense, measures the absence of threats to acquired values, in a subjective sense, the absence of fear that such values will be attacked" (Wolfers 1962).

But "core" or acquired values are subject to interpretation and cannot be objectively defined. Such notions "tend towards an absolute view of security, a great power orientation and the notion that national security has some firm and readily identifiable meaning" (Buzan 1983). If that is already the case with the narrow interpretation of survival as the national interest, it will be even more true of a broader conception. The national interest taken in a wider sense than survival or national security becomes increasingly ambiguous and open to interpretation. It cannot serve as a guide to the making of foreign policy but can only defend a particular policy as claimed to be in the national interest. There can always be debate however not only about the content of the national interest or of national security but also about the means to achieve it. A good example may be the national interest of Germany. As it was seen to be the German nation as a combination of the Federal Republic and the Democratic Republic, its unification had to be in the national interest. But in both German states that conception of the national interest was up to 1989 subordinated to the preservation of their own political identity and separate survival.

Different conceptions of national interest also underlie the debates about the maintenance of peace: should one rely primarily on one's own military power or on security cooperation in the UN including strengthening shared interests in arms control and nuclear disarmament? Should one orient oneself to national rather than to international security? The peace movements that have become so numerous in the recent past defend such alternative conceptions of the national interest to that of the political and military establishments. The national interest, again, is open to interpretation .

But that different interpretations of the national interest are unavoidable does not make the concept devoid of meaning. It can simply refer to the interests as pursued by a particular nation-state vis-à-vis other states. The question then becomes how states perceive their interests.

As with all interests defended and pursued in politics, a distinction can then be made between short-term and long-term interests and between narrow or wide conceptions of interest. The defense of narrowly conceived interests can come into conflict with the broader long-term interest of a nation. The pursuit of a specific short-term interest may jeopardize the development of a common market arrangement or of long-term arms control agreements. To then evoke the national interest in order to defend a particular solution for foreign policy dilemmas is no more than propaganda.

Nevertheless, the basic meaning of the concept of national interest or national security still stands, no matter how ambiguous and open to different interpretations it may be. Independent rivaling states are forced, because of the absence of an international monopoly of violence, to rely upon their own resources or on alliances with other states to protect themselves and defend their interests. The most important duty of every government must therefore be to protect and further the interests of its own people against the competing interests of other people. As Martin Wight (1979) has written: "A foreign minister is chosen and paid to look after the interests of his country, and not to be a delegate for the human race." The question again is:

what are the interests of a particular country? Every country considers certain things as essential for its continued survival and independence. Every country thus has certain vital interests. The question then becomes: are there particular vital interests which provide for continuity in the foreign policy of a particular state? The question can be turned around: if there is continuity in foreign policy it can only be based on a durable conception of its vital interests. Such vital interests derive primarily from the position which a state occupies in a particular network of rival states. In his *In Defense of the National Interest* (1951), Hans Morgenthau argues that for the national interest of the United States two things are vital: its position as a predominant power without rival in the Western hemisphere and the maintenance of the balance of power both in Europe and in Asia. It can thus be seen that the vital interests of Great Powers in a sense determine, or at least presuppose each other. Preservation of the balance of power (see *Balance of Power*) in Europe implies the maintenance and defense of the North Atlantic Alliance even after 1991. For the then Soviet Union the same goal meant the maintenance of its control over Eastern Europe in the context of the Warsaw Pact. Russia as its successor—partly at least—has difficulty in accepting a limited role in Europe.

Vital interests mean something quite different to great and to small powers, both in terms of content and in terms of geographic scope. For small powers it can mean either seeking protection from one of the Great Powers or a guaranteed neutrality. Vital interests can change with the transformation of the structure of international power relations.

In the context of the British Empire it had always been a vital interest for Britain to keep control over the Suez Canal. But when put to the test in 1956 that interest proved no longer vital, because Great Britain was no longer either an imperial or a global power. Similar reassessments become needed after the end of the Cold War.

The idea of the national interest can be seen in the same way as the former concept of the reason of state (*raison d état*). That conception implies that one should further only the interests of one's own state, if necessary by force, without regard either to the demands of morality or the interests of other states. Such a narrow conception of national interest was superseded for the first time by the policies prescribed by Europe's classical balance of power. As Lord Brougham wrote in the eighteenth century:

"All particular interests, prejudices, or partialities have to be sacrificed to the higher interest . . . of uniting against oppression or against the measures which appear to place the security of all in jeopardy. No previous quarrel with any given state, no existing condition even of actual hostility must be suffered to interfere with the general security."

Balance of power policies presuppose the recognition that the national interest of all states is served by its subordination to the higher interest of preserving the balance of power. Prince Metternich already wrote:

". . . we must always view the society of states as the essential condition of the modern world . . . . The great axioms of political science proceed from the knowledge of the true political interests of all states; it is upon these general interests that rests the guarantee of their existence . . . . In the ancient world isolation and the practice of the most absolute selfishness without any other restraint than that of prudence was the sum of politics . . . . Modern society on the other hand exhibits the principle of solidarity and of the balance of power between states."

Balance of power policies as practiced by dynastic states and continuing in the Concert of Europe of the nineteenth century can thus be said to have been a first attempt to see the relations between states as a structure with regularities and dynamics of its own and to act upon such a shared perspective rather than on a narrow view of the immediate interest of one's own state. But when the power balance changes to the advantage of a particular aspiring great power such a perception of a common interest in preserving the balance of power may fade away.

In the nuclear age, however, the narrow conception of the national interest is no longer possible. The shared danger of nuclear war forces the nuclear great powers to cooperate, if in a limited sense. Their rivalry can no longer be allowed to lead to a direct military confrontation, because that could escalate into nuclear war. International security therefore becomes a necessary aspect of national security. This can be illustrated by the concept of deterrence (see *Deterrence*). As still commonly perceived, deterrence is a policy of power A against power B. The military posture of power A should be capable of deterring power B from any kind of attack. But in the nuclear age both powers are rather being deterred from risky conduct by the common danger of nuclear war, intended or unintended.

Deterrence is no longer unilateral, it has become shared. In the nuclear age Great Powers the United States, China, Russia and to some extent France and the United Kingdom thus have to respect each other's security needs and interests. They also have to pay attention to the security problems of smaller states, so as not to get embroiled in a political crisis that could lead to a military confrontation with their opponent. There is therefore an even stronger tension between the narrow and short-term conception of the national interest and the broad or holistic conception of interest and security that the nuclear age demands. In the nuclear age too much emphasis on the national interest is inimical to the preservation of peace. It can also form an obstacle to the international cooperation globalizing processes demand. The same goes for regional cooperation (see *Integration, Regional*), as even the development of the European Union (see *European Union*) shows.

See also: *Balance of Power; Nuclear Deterrence, Doctrine of*

Bibliography

Buzan B 1983 *People, States and Fear: The National Security Problem in International Relations*. Wheatsheaf Books, Brighton

Howard M 1983 *The Causes of War*. M.T. Smith, London

Kratochwill F 1982 On the notion of "interest" in international relations. *Int'l Organization* 36(1)

Morgenthau H 1951 *In Defense of the National Interest*. University Press of America, New York

Rochester J M 1978 The paradigm debate in international relations and its implications for foreign policy-making: Towards a redefinition of the national interest. *Western Political Q.* 31(1)

Wight M 1979 *Power Politics*. Penguin, Harmondsworth

Wolfers A 1962 The goals of foreign policy: National security as an ambiguous symbol. *Discord and Collaboration: Essays on International Politics*. Baltimore, Maryland

G. VAN BENTHEM VAN DEN BERGH

National Socialism

National Socialism, commonly referred to as Nazism, was the political creed proclaimed by the National Socialist German Workers party (*Nationalsozialistische deutsche Arbeiterpartei*, NSDAP). The party, which evolved in 1920 from the Munich-based German Workers Party (DAP), was initially only one of several factions of the radical right whose rivalries and in-fighting characterized the troubled politics of post-First World War Bavaria. But under the direction of Adolf Hitler, who joined the DAP in September 1919, and who usurped the leadership of the NSDAP in July 1921, it became within 12 years the most successful populist party in Weimar Germany, with more seats in the *Reichstag* than any other group. A paramilitary section, the *Sturmabteilung* (SA) was formed in 1921, and following the failure of Hitler to effect a successful Putsch against the Bavarian state government in November 1923 and his subsequent imprisonment, the NSDAP was reorganized as a mass party with parliamentary aspirations. Its growing membership and its successes in provincial and national elections in the years 1929-32 provided Hitler with a power base which was to be a vital element in bringing about his appointment as German Chancellor in January 1933, and the establishment of his dictatorship. The emergence of sibling National Socialist movements in Austria and amongst the German-speaking communities of Danzig and Czechoslovakia also helped to determine the course of Germany's territorial aggrandizement in the 1930s. It would indeed be impossible to understand either the politics or the policies of the Third Reich without some appreciation of the appeal and nature of National Socialism

In theory, at least, the NSDAP represented a reconciliation between nationalism and socialism. Hitler himself offered an explanation of what this implied. "I am a German nationalist," he wrote in 1928. "This means that I proclaim my nationalism. My whole thought and action belongs to it. I am a socialist. I see no class and social estate before me, but that community of blood, united by a language, and subject to the same general fate." He thus equated his socialism, not with the common ownership of the means of production and distribution, but with the subordination of class and corporate interests to those of the ethnic community, or *Volksgemeinschaft.* True, the party's "official program" called for the abolition of unearned income, the elimination of middlemen, the nationalization of trusts and holding companies, support for individual businessmen, and the closure of chain and departmental stores. There were also those amongst the party's leadership, like Gregor Strasser, the NSDAP organizer in north Germany, who evidently took seriously such anticapitalist slogans. It is, however, questionable whether Hitler and his closest associates regarded these as anything more than propaganda. Hitler was in any case far less concerned with expropriating big business than with extolling the virtues of racial consciousness and purity. The National Socialist revolution which he foresaw was

not one of class, but one of race.

Much of what passes for Nazi ideology, and which found expression in the writings of Walther Darré, Dietrich Eckart, Gottfried Feder and Alfred Rosenberg, as well as those of Hitler, was inconsistent, irrational, and intellectually arid. At its core was the notion of the primacy of the *Volk*—the racial group perceived as the nation. This was combined with a Social Darwinian vision of the world in which races, like species, were engaged in a struggle for survival, a belief in the innate superiority of Nordic man, a rabid anti-Semitism, and a rejection of Marxism and parliamentary democracy, both of which were regarded as stifling personal ability and talent. Some cohesion was given to these ideas by Hitler in *Mein Kampf,* the two volumes of which were published in 1925 and 1928. In this curious concoction of autobiography and political analysis Hitler expounded his essentially Manichean conception of history in which the creative forces, represented by the Aryans, were locked in conflict with the Jewish destroyers of culture. He maintained that although the Germans, the *Volk* with whom he was most concerned, were not a pure racial group, pockets of pure Aryan stock could be found amongst them, and that it was the task of the *Völkisch* state to foster and preserve their racial strength. Germany's rejuvenation therefore required the adoption of an authoritarian order, which Hitler conceived of in terms of the leadership principle (that is, "authority of every leader downward and responsibility upward"), and government by those who understood the processes of history and who had the will to act ruthlessly in accordance with the laws of nature. "A state," he predicted (1926), "which in this age of racial poisoning dedicates itself to the care of its best racial elements must some day be lord of the earth."

It was in the context of this pseudoscientific theorizing that Hitler also explained his views on German foreign policy. These he refined and reaffirmed in a second manuscript, which he completed in 1928, but which remained unpublished until 1961, when it appeared in English as *Hitler's Secret Book.* They reflected his basic assumption that Germany's future depended upon it attaining the status of a world power, his desire to ensure that its rapidly expanding population should be kept within the bounds of a single state, to which should be added his native Austria, and his romantic attachment to the idea of a peasantry amply provided with soil for its sustenance. Thus, after having rejected birth control, internal colonization, and industrial and commercial policies as solutions to Germany's demographic problems, on the grounds that they would have a deleterious effect upon the quality of the *Volk*, he urged the need for military conquest and territorial aggrandizement. Living space, or *Lebensraum*, for the German people could, he insisted (1926), best be found in "*Russia* and her vassal border states," lands which were already subject to, or threatened by, what he viewed as the latest Jewish attempt at world domination in the guise of Russian Bolshevism. At the same time, he denounced the obsession of Weimar politicians with regaining the territories lost by Germany in 1919, and he recommended that Germany should seek alliances with the United Kingdom and Italy as a means in the first instance of coping with its "grimmest enemy," France.

Mein Kampf clearly cannot be divorced from the decade in which it was written: a period in which Germans were having to face the consequences of military defeat and revolution, and in which the French still seemed determined to enforce the Treaty of Versailles. Yet the roots of National Socialism, like those of Italian Fascism, stretch far back into the nineteenth century. The growth of the secular state and the industrialization of Europe had nurtured new and more virulent forms of nationalism which were eventually translated into radical imperialisms. This process was accompanied by attempts, such as those made by Alfred de Gobineau and Houston Stewart Chamberlain, to apply biological principles to the explanation of social and political phenomena. Anti-Semitism also became more widespread in the last quarter of the century, manifesting itself in France during the Dreyfus affair and in the Vienna of von Schönerer and Karl Lueger. The German-speaking peoples seemed particularly susceptible to such tendencies. In the absence until 1871 of a single united German state, there had emerged amongst them an organic nationalism which emphasized their common culture, language, and descent, rather than loyalty to a specific political entity (see *Pan-Germanism*). Moreover, Slavonic nationalism and the progress of urbanization menaced the identity and status of Germans living in Austria-Hungary and in scattered enclaves in the western borderlands of the Russian empire (see *Pan-Slavism*). It was no accident that the first National Socialist party, the German National Socialist Workers Party, was formed in Bohemia a few months before the collapse of the Hapsburg monarchy. Nor was it odd that several of the leading figures within the movement in Germany, including both Hitler and Rosenberg, were born and educated outside the frontiers of the Prusso-German state. Their National Socialism was in some respects the response of a beleagured minority to the competing claims of other ethnic groups, and the challenges posed by the advance of modern capitalism and the

Bolshevik revolution.

The obsolete political structure of the Wilhelmine Reich had in the meanwhile hardly been conducive to the growth of democratic attitudes and institutions in Germany. Despite the industrialization of the country's economy, the German aristocracy succeeded in maintaining its political preeminence, and historians of the Fritz Fischer school have argued that the efforts of Germany's traditional rulers to overcome dissension at home led to the pursuit of a peculiarly aggressive foreign policy. The draconian terms which the German military leadership imposed on Bolshevik Russia at Brest Litovsk (1918) have thus been seen both as evidence of the acquisitive ambitions of the Kaiser's Germany, and as a model for the expansionist designs of Hitler. The inclination of the German middle class to identify its interests with those of the Wilhelmine state, and its failure to develop a political consciousness commensurate with its economic role, also served to weaken the Weimar Republic. Shocked by Germany's collapse in 1918, frightened by the prospect of revolution, and angered by the inability of republican governments to protect them against the catastrophic effects of inflation and economic depression, the lower middle class voters of Protestant Germany deserted the conservative and liberal parties of the right and center-right. At the end of the 1920s they, along with the recently politicized peasantry, turned towards the NSDAP, the party which promised the restoration of Germany's political health, and action against communists, monopoly capitalists, and Jewish profiteers. This shift in electoral loyalties was in large part responsible for providing the Nazis with 107 seats in the *Reichstag* and 18.3 percent of the vote in September 1930, and 230 seats and 37.6 percent of the vote in July 1932. But Hitler's appointment as the head of a coalition government in January 1933 was in the end the result of pressures brought to bear upon the aged President Hindenburg by representatives of the traditional right, including industrialists and aristocrats, who mistakenly believed that they could contain Nazi radicalism and use it to maintain their own authority in Germany.

Once in office, Hitler and his cohorts made use of terror tactics and the law in order to consolidate their power. Hermann Goering, the new Prussian minister of the interior, began the Nazification of the German police, and the *Reichstag* fire of February 27, 1933, which the Nazis blamed upon the communists, was followed by a presidential decree which suspended political rights guaranteed by the constitution. Then, after fresh elections, in which they were still unable to win a majority in the *Reichstag*, the National

Socialists, in alliance with the nationalists, and with the acquiescence of other parties of the right and center, secured the passage of an enabling act which left the government free to legislate without parliamentary sanction. During the next 18 months the Nazis established a one-party state, the SA was purged of its troublesome and unruly leadership, and after Hindenburg's death in August 1934, Hitler combined the presidency with the chancellorship. Opponents of the regime were rooted out, locked up, and otherwise disposed of, and the NSDAP continued to extend its control over the country through a process of administrative and political coordination (*Gleichschaltung*), and the creation of a variety of party organizations which paralleled existing state institutions. Nevertheless, both the relevance of National Socialist ideology to the government of the Third Reich and the relationship between the movement and the state remain matters of academic controversy.

Few modern historians would dismiss National Socialism as simply an instrument fashioned by a power-hungry politician in order to fullfill his Machiavellian designs. Hitler was certainly a master in the art of public persuasion, and the party rallies, in which elaborate ceremonies were enacted against dramatic and inspiring settings, doubtless served to emphasize the authority of the state. But National Socialism also represented an attempt to transform German society and values. The evocation of ancient Germanic myths and denunciation of non-Aryan culture were facets of a doctrine which aimed at converting the German people to the belief that their common ethnic relationship was the most important thing in their lives. It would, in any event, be very difficult to explain the anti-Semitic legislation of the 1930s and the extermination of some six million Jews without reference to the ideological foundations of the Nazi state. Even the armed forces and the business world, which had initially appeared to effect a compromise with Hitler, were in time to find themselves subject to the dictates of National Socialism. Goering, who from 1936 was in charge of the four-year plan, was thus able to replace the conservative domination of military and economic affairs with his own administrative machine. This radicalization of the Third Reich has been linked to the polyocratic structure of the regime (Broszat, 1981). Far from being a monolithic dictatorship, National Socialist Germany resembled an authoritarian anarchy in which individuals and state and party agencies vied for influence, with Hitler acting as a sort of final arbiter. Nazi leaders, such as Heinrich Himmler, the *Reichsfürer* of the paramilitary *Schutzstaffel* (SS), and Goering, were to devote much

of their time and energy to constructing bureaucratic empires in which older departments of state were eventually submerged.

Germany's foreign policy in these years has likewise been portrayed as a function, rather than an objective, of the National Socialist system. Hitler's first foreign minister, Constantin von Neurath, had constantly to reckon with the efforts of leading party members, including his successor, Joachim von Ribbentrop, to have a say in policy making. Vital decisions, as for instance in matters relating to the handling of Austria and Czechoslovakia, had sometimes to be taken in response to the initiatives of Nazis at home and abroad. And even if Hitler may still be regarded as having been primarily responsible for determining the broad lines of foreign policy, there remains the question of what his intentions were. The prevailing view amongst scholars in the aftermath of the Second World War was that from 1933 until 1941 Hitler had relentlessly pursued the long-term goal of *Lebensraum* in accordance with the course projected in *Mein Kampf*. This assumption was, however, challenged by A. J. P. Taylor, who in his celebrated study of the origins of the Second World War (1961) depicted Hitler as essentially an opportunist. Other historians in the 1960s pointed to the inconsistencies between Hitler's early writings and Nazi foreign policy. Since then there has been an inclination, especially in Germany, to see Hitler's foreign policy as having been rooted in the racialist ideology of National Socialism. Hillgruber(1974) has thus suggested that although Hitler's tactics may have been flexible his foreign policy strategy amounted to a phased program (*Stufenplan*), by which, after first consolidating Germany's position in central Europe, he intended to expand towards the east and to achieve continental hegemony as a prelude to a war for world domination. Some support has been lent to this interpretation by Overy (1982), who has recently concluded that from the mid-1930s onwards the German economy and military machine was being prepared for a long and total war which Hitler anticipated would take place in the following decade. Germany's premature involvement in a major European war in September 1939 was due to Hitler's miscalculation of the likely reactions of the United Kingdom and France, and his failure to repeat against Poland the sort of coup that had previously enabled him to annex Austria and eliminate Czechoslovakia.

Further evidence of the key role played by ideology in the conduct of Nazi Germany is to be found in Hitler's invasion of the then Soviet Union in 1941. The application of racial dogma in the administration of occupied eastern Europe obstructed the economic exploitation of the region, alienated potential allies, and hampered the German war effort. Quiet apart, however, from the tragic consequences of the holocaust, the message of National Socialism was a profoundly pessimistic one. There was no socialist utopia in Hitler's *Weltanschauung*. The racial conflict, he perceived, would only be brought to an end when one people, presumably the Germans, strengthened and purified by its participation in the struggle, achieved world domination. All of this is, nevertheless, primarily of historical interest. National Socialist Germany was defeated in 1945, and although neo-Nazi organizations have occasionally reemerged in the Federal Republic and in other parts of Europe, they have not obtained any substantial electoral support. Nationalism, racism, and authoritarian systems of government are likely to remain features of the modern world. So too is an inclination in some developed and developing countries to revert to the norms and values of preindustrial society. But history rarely repeats itself, and the particular set of circumstances which led to the triumph of National Socialism in one of the most powerful countries in the world is unlikely to recur.

See also: *Fascism; Hegemony; Imperialism; Nationalism*

Bibliography ————————————————

Bracher K D 1971 *The German Dictatorship: The Origins, Structure and Effects of National Socialism*. Weidenfeld and Nicolson, London
Broszat M 1981 *The Hitler State: The Foundation and Development of the Internal Structure of the Third Reich*. Longman, Harlow
Hiden J, Farquharson J 1983 *Explaining Hitler's Germany: Historians and the Third Reich*. Batsford, London
Hildebrand K 1973 *The Foreign Policy of the Third Reich*. Batsford, London
Hillgruber A 1974 England's place in Hitler's plans for world dominion. *J. Contemporary History* 9(1)
Lane B, Rupp L 1978 *Nazi Ideology Before 1933: A Documentation*. University of Texas, Austin, Texas
Overy R J 1982 Hitler's war and the German economy: A Reinterpretation. *Econ. History Rev.* 35
Taylor A J P 1961 *The Origins of the Second World War*. Hamish Hamilton, London

KEITH HAMILTON

Nationalism

Nationalism as an empirical fact refers to a particular form of "consciousness of kind," "identification," or "loyalty," as distinct from narrower attachments such as tribalism and parochialism and broader ones such as humanitarianism. Such descriptive usage is sometimes called "national consciousness," perhaps in order to distinguish the consciousness itself from its social and political consequences or to give nationalism a base in human nature.

When a distinction is made between "nationalism" and "national consciousness," the term nationalism is clearly reserved for some normative view about the way one's loyalties "ought" to be ordered, as in the following definition: "Nationalism may be defined as a state of mind in which the individual feels that everyone owes his supreme secular loyalty to the nation-state" (Kohn 1974 p. 851). This definition is empirically valid only if we assume that a tacit "ought" is present. It is obviously not true that nationalists believe everyone to be a nationalist: what nationalists feel (according to the quoted article) is that everyone ought to owe his supreme secular loyalty to the nation-state. If one makes the "ought" explicit, however, it is by no means certain that

nationalism entails the view that loyalty to the nation-state must be one's supreme secular loyalty. Such a view accords with a definition of National Socialism rather than nationalism.

Another difficulty in representing nationalism as normative is that we already have a term—patriotism—which shows loyalty to one's nation or country as a good. If, as many say, nationalism is (a) as good and (b) as recent as the nation-state, what shall we say about *"Dulce et decorum est pro patria mori?"* Should we call it "patriotism" because it preceded the concept of a nation-state and thus imply that one can be patriotic without being nationalistic, and nationalistic without being patriotic?

A solution to this problem may be found in defining nationalism as a "political creed." If nationalism is a creed, something believed rather than felt, it exists only when the concept of nation-state exists, although it can exist even where an actual nation-state does not exist, as with the French-Canadian, Kurdish, and Basque nationalisms. The problem with this solution can be seen in George Orwell's extension of the concept of nationalism to cover "such movements and tendencies as Communism, political

Catholicism, Zionism, anti-Semitism, Trotskyism and Pacifism" (Orwell 1945). All these can certainly be called "political creeds" or at least "creeds having political consequences," but so can virtually any belief. If we start along this path, "nationalism" becomes too vague and general a concept to serve any function.

Hans Kohn evades the whole problem by restricting nationalism to the kind of political creed "that underlies the cohesion of modern societies and legitimizes their claim to authority" (Kohn 1968 p. 63). The difficulty with this limitation, however, is that nationalism today promotes neither cohesion nor legitimacy but has the opposite effect. Thus the Basque, French-Canadian, Kurdish, and Scottish nationalists deny that present state jurisdictions are legitimate. Kohn's approach really describes nineteenth century nationalism. What we need is a definition which covers both the unifying, legitimizing effects of nationalism and the fragmentation of states which is characteristic of present-day nationalistic movements. In each case, nationalism is the operative concept. What is this concept?

The word "nation," from which nationalism is derived, has long been used with reference to a "people" as opposed to "humankind." Here, a "nation" is that division of humankind which regards itself as capable of forming a social unit that is not biologically based—that is, is not a "race" or "tribe" —and is not necessarily an actual political unit (this last case is exemplified by the "people" of Israel before their state was created). Since the rise of the nation state, the concept of "nation" has been distinctly politicized: a "nation" is now the people believing themselves capable of forming a viable political unit and as such legitimately entitled "self-determination" (see *Self-determination*) to resist claims to sovereignty made by any state not so based.

The following definition of nationalism may now be suggested: nationalism is the ideological view that the sociological or psychological concept of "nation" defines *de jure* sovereignty. Hence it defines *de facto* sovereignty that is not in accord with its principles as illegitimate, even if the *de facto* sovereign is arrived at "democratically." Under nationalism, democracy is not itself legitimate—it is not "true" democracy— unless the state is a nation.

The concept of "nation" can precede and lead to the formation of states, as it did in much of Europe during the nineteenth century under the influence of the Romantic concept of a "folk." But it can also follow the formation of a state, as seems to have been the case with Switzerland and the United States.

When the concept follows the formation of a state, the concept of "freedom" replaces that of a "folk" as the unifying element. An alliance formed to resist a common threat creates a "nation," not just a state, when the members consider that they have "freedom" as a common value rather than simply as a common interest that will disappear with the disappearance of the threat (see *Alliance*).

1. Development of the Idea

If we think of nationalism as an expression of one of the many loyalties or emotional attachments, its rise can be "explained" by referring to the decline of other loyalties: "the rise of nationalism is closely linked with . . . the lessening of the older religious, tribal, clannish and feudal loyalties" (Kohn 1968 p. 64). But such an explanation has no more than tautological validity: logically the rise of nationalism must mean that other loyalties declined. What we need is an explanation of the change.

The peculiarity of loyalty to a nation and the reason nationalism developed late in human history is that unlike other loyalties it is allegiance to a concept and is better understood in terms of ideology than what we usually call "loyalty." If we ignore history, we are likely to become conceptually confused about the origin and hence the nature of nationalism. Historically, a shift parallel to one from personal to conceptual or ideological loyalty preceded nationalism: the shift from the fealty of feudalism to sovereignty. However, whether the concept of sovereignty is a necessary antecedent of nationalism is not clear. In Machiavelli the two are intermingled, whereas in Hobbes' conception of sovereignty nationalism is ignored.

What is certain, however, is that when recognition of sovereignty is felt to be a condition for the existence of norms, nationalism is one of the concepts marking the distinction between *de jure* and *de facto* sovereignty. Jurists such as Lord Acton saw a danger in the development, but then the use of nationalism as a means of making the distinction was a fact that political theorists had to accept and could not resist merely on the ground that it conflicted with juristic conceptions of legitimacy. Even as Acton objected, nationalism was transforming the map of Europe in a way which showed the weakness of certain juristic formulations. Whatever else nationalism did in the nineteenth century, it established that the concept of sovereignty is not merely a theoretical construct peculiar to jurists and political theorists but an actual force in human behavior.

What deserves attention is the connection between

the concepts of nationalism and democracy. By postulating "people" as "nation" (a conceptual abstract above all else), nationalism served to exclude anarchistic aspects from the concept of democracy. Nineteenth century democracy was thus thought of as government "of" and "for" the people (nationalism) and not "by" the people (anarchism). Democracy so conceived raised no problem with regard to sovereignty, although it played havoc with the juristic idea of "legitimacy," for it promoted the fragmentation of empires and the unification of historically independent states. Such "democracy" (actually nationalism) could be and was supported by those of a marked aristocratic tendency.

This merging of nationalism and democracy has had important effects on political theory. It has blocked all attempts to base democracy on anything other than the "nation" (e.g., on interest groups). So long as the social unit underlying the state is thought to be the "nation," any other basis is dismissed as "undemocratic."

1.1 The "Folk"

In the late eighteenth and early nineteenth centuries the Romantics in England and Continental Europe (especially Germany) consciously countered the view that the cosmos can only be understood analytically. Between ego and Homo sapiens—giving identity to the individual among the mass of humankind and also requiring as part of one's fundamental nature that one be more than egoistic—was the concept of "folk." It accorded with biblical views about race and tribe and with conditions in Europe, in which there seemed to be one "race." The idea of "folk" required a return to an original condition which agreed with nature, intuition, and revelation. Expressed politically, the result was "nationalism," for which the groundwork had been laid by Rousseau (1702-72), a characteristic that was promoted by the brothers Grimm (Jakob, 1785-1863 and Wilhelm, 1786-1859), who sought scientific support for the "folk" in language and myth, and by Johann Gottfried von Herder (1774-1803), who developed the theory of the folk-soul later to be adapted by Carl Jung into the concept of the "collective unconscious."

Few people question the psychoanalytical adaptation of the Romantics' concept of "folk" for it has no obvious social or political consequences; however, when linked with biology, as by Joseph de Gobineau (1816-82) and H.S. Chamberlain (1885-1927), it has come under very strong attack. So long as it remained "Romantic"—vague and unscientific—it

could be treated as a poetic fancy, but when given any kind of scientific support it is called racism (see *Race and Racial Prejudice*) and is attacked as "unscientific." Science is presumably opposed to any divisions whatsoever in the concept homo sapiens.

1.2 Hegel

Apart from the hostility of science to the Romantic conception of the "folk" as the natural basis for community and state, the Swiss and Americans—among others—had established that it is not a necessary basis. The Romantics could ignore such discrepancies, but a philosopher like Hegel (1770-1830) could not, even though he was strongly influenced by the Romantic concept (see *Hegel, Georg Wilhelm Friedrich*). Hegel presented the state as a sort of superpersonality; he retained the Romantics' view that we must begin with the person rather than the machine and must end with individuals rather than interchangeable cogs—as mechanistic-oriented science was arguing.

Since we have decided that democracy requires us to adopt the mechanistic view that the ideal condition—the meaning of equality—is the interchangeability of human cogs, Hegel's views on nationalism have been rejected as undemocratic and unscientific. They are indeed such if mechanism is the assumed foundation for science and democracy. But they are certainly not unphilosophic. We are still confronted by the fact that science and democracy demand that we pay no attention to our sense of being individuals who have affinities with others, where the affinities are not based on congeniality or prudential considerations but expressive of fundamental values defining us as individuals. If we explain this "sense" biologically, we shall talk of "race," but if we recognize the inadequacies of such a view, we are left with something resembling the Hegelian concept of the role of the nation-state with regard to individuality and human values. Nationalism today, however, as encountered for instance in Africa, often uses the Romantics' conception of "folk" to justify or rationalize a tribalism and racism that is incompatible with the original concept. It is also the "hurrah" word for those Western liberals who use it to justify "racist" views which they would not countenance anywhere else. In the end, they are not likely to give Hegel any credit for having made a contribution to the concept. But the evidence is that he did so and that we need to rethink the relativism that science and democracy have been promoting.

The application of essentially European notions of

nationalism (in particular those, as was said earlier, which identify nationalism and democracy) to Africa leads to serious difficulties. Those who think of themselves as a "people"—a tribe—are often not numerous enough to form a viable nation-state. The states that exist are based on territorial divisions established by European states in their colonialist days. Thus it has hardly been possible to create "democratic" states on the basis of nationalism. A solution to this problem has been to substitute socialism—government "for" the people—for nationalism's government "of" the people. This very policy has in fact been called nationalism. But such "nationalism" seems to be no more than a technique of government to retain jurisdiction over a certain territory, as well as over the people therein, by a sort of "bread and circuses" generosity.

The fusion of the Romantic conception of a "folk" with Hegelianism encouraged the type of imperialism characteristic of German late nineteenth century (and subsequent) policies inspired by Heinrich von Treitschke (1834-96), who advocated "unbridled" nationalism (John Bowle's expression, 1964). (Note, for instance, Treitschke's defense of the annexation of Alsace and Lorraine: "These provinces are ours by the right of the sword and we will rule them by virtue of a higher right . . . the right of the German nation to prevent the permanent estrangement from the German Empire of her lost children. We desire, even against their will, to restore them to themselves.")

Because most contemporary philosophers and historians are relativists who reject both the concept of a "folk" and that of "civilization" as a superior culture, we dismiss Treitschke's statement as a rationalization of aggression (see *Aggression*) and search elsewhere for the real motives of imperialism (see *Imperialism*). It does not follow, however, that an unsound or unjust motive cannot be a motive. It is evident that the notions of "civilization" (and "duty") once represented actual convictions which motivated not only governments but the citizens themselves and that—even without the concept of "folk"—the concept of "civilization" was sufficient to motivate the expansionist nationalism of a citizenry (Jingoism) (see *Jingoism*). Thus the westward expansion of the United States and the acquisition of Texas and California were little more than a ratification by the US government of the policy initiated by citizens inspired by the view that they were enlarging the area of civilization. This view accorded with the Hegelian idea of the state, but derived more from Hegel's assumptions about the nature of civilization than from a knowledge of his reasoning.

1.3 The Modern View

The modern tendency is to encourage a relativistic attitude to the nation-state and define the "nation" as the state within its present territorial boundaries (also to equate "state" and "nation"—a common American practice), and to represent any other view as warmongering if not downright fascist. Certainly, to deny that the culture of a state epitomizes "civilization"—that is a superior form of culture—is conducive to peace so long as all states adopt this view, but it also removes an essential element in patriotism necessary to defense. If it really does not matter under what political system one lives or what one's nationality is, then all states must encourage a relativist attitude to their culture (and nonrelativists to be regarded as warmongers).

The Romantic concept of a "folk" untainted by the concept of civilization—and repudiating the latter as excessively rational—set limits of justifiable aggression: war was seen as the response of a tyrannical state to the efforts of a "folk" to attain independence or freedom from the consequences of earlier aggression by imperialists. To Giuseppe Mazzini (1805-72), the "folk" and its desire to form an independent political unit represented a step towards an eventual brotherhood of mankind. He saw all nationalist movements based on a "folk" as having a common goal.

Such a conception of "folk" transcending family and tribal loyalties can still serve a function in emerging nations in Africa. An alternative is to use ideology as evidence of civilization. Thus a Marxist-oriented government is likely to see itself as a "civilizing" force which is justified in pursuing an expansionist policy. A democratic government, on the other hand, has no real way of opposing tribalism and promoting liberal nationalism, especially now that democracy is essentially relativistic. Indeed, ideology, operating as Hegel saw "civilization" functioning, seems at present to be the basis of aggressive nationalism. (This, incidentally, testifies to the long-acknowledged duality of Hegelian vision: containing a sinister, illiberal component in addition to its philosophic, liberalizing part, accounted for earlier.)

Even if we regard the idea of a "folk" as a Romantic myth and the Hegelian philosophy of the state as a rationalization, nationalism reflects the psychological need of the individual—of the human self—to have a continuity in time, a history more extensive than the limits set by his or her own birth and death. The decline of the belief in an afterlife required looking back to a hypothetic earlier unity—being a member of a "folk"—whose characteristics explained one's self and defined the state of which one was a member either as an imperialist entity or as a fragment of a larger unity. Consequently, there has been in modern times a series of wars that rearranged the political map of Europe until an accommodation was reached between nation as "folk" and nation as state or viable politico-economic unit. Since the accommodation is but a *modus vivendi*, idealists—such as Scottish or Flemish nationalists—have sought further adjustments; their efforts, however, represent more of a domestic nuisance than a threat to peace. Governments can afford to be tolerant, for most people are pragmatists who, despite their sympathies, are ultimately concerned with the question of whether the ideal represents a viable state.

In some countries where there was previously no hypothetic history of a "folk," as in the New World, an actual history has now existed long enough for members of a state to think of themselves as part of a continuity—a nation—with set limits: the established territorial boundaries of the state. Consequently, war between (say) the Unites States and Canada is inconceivable.

In some other parts of the world a continuity in time in the form of a history of the state does not yet exist. Thus in Africa "nationalism" reflects the ambitions of particular individuals who, as heads of state, have the power to set policy. Such leaders are imperialists in the tradition of Napoleon or the Zulu King Shaka rather than nationalists: they can operate because there is no nationalist spirit to oppose them or be exploited by them.

2. The Nature and Consequences of Modern Nationalism

Like many "isms," over the years nationalism has changed its meaning. Being a compound of specific beliefs and values, it can—when only slight shifts in emphasis occur—give rise to markedly different views. Nineteenth century advocates of the idea would wonder why we describe as nationalism any behavior performed in the name of the state. Is terrorism nationalism? Surely not.

Yet there is a continuity in past and present nationalism. If nationalism in the Third World today is premised on the state itself rather than on its members—the "folk" of traditional nationalism—it is because such a continuity exists. Nineteenth-century nationalism gave rise to the modern nation-state, to the concept of self-determination, and to sepa-

ratism—characteristics of nationalism in the twentieth century *outside* the Third World.

2.1 Self-Determination of Nations

The idea of self-determination (which found a noted advocate in Woodrow Wilson) (see Nobel Peace Prize Laureates: *Woodrow Wilson*) implies a principle of international law, a norm that can be defined as the majority rule operating within the concept of nationalism. Having originated as a democratic principle, it raises the important question of the limits of tolerance. Wilson's emphasis on self-determination linked ideology (exclusively democratic, in his terms) with nationalism (equated with the "people," not the state), so that self-determination no longer refers exclusively to membership in a "folk" but to adherence to an ideology determining whether a given body of people is a nation.

Self-determination being a norm of international law, what matters is its effect on the attitudes of national states to the international situation. It shifts one from questions of personal feeling and background to the normative interest in what is happening to people who are not like oneself. In terms of traditional Christian ethics, self-determination politicizes Jesus Christ's parable of the Good Samaritan (see *Peace According to the New Testament*).

2.2 Separatism

Characteristically modern nationalism in Europe and North America has been separatist: it identifies itself as nationalism by separatism. (Thus one can refer to Scottish nationalists as separatists and Quebec separatists as nationalists, for separatists and nationalists are interchangeable terms).

This should not be taken to mean that Scottish nationalism and Quebec nationalism are of the same nature. Scottish nationalism is like pride of family—the pride of Mrs. Sparsit in Dickens's *Hard Times*. Her relatives were both Scottish and English [including the families of Powlers and Scadgers]; her stance implied that there is no perceptible cultural differences between the English and the Scots; also that the Scots have a proud history, as in Burns's 'Pean to National Pride.' It is Pride in their history, family pride, as it were, that sustains Scottish nationalism.

French-Canadian nationalism, however, is a matter of preserving self-identity. The cultural pressures from English Canada and the USA are such that only a degree of political autonomy capable of enforcing French Canadian culture is likely to allow Quebecers of the twenty-first century to recognize one another.

Given the psychological distinction between 'national pride' and 'personal identity' nationalism, we can return to the political question of the link between nationalism and separatism.

The reason for the link can be found in international law, although it is not clear whether there is an explicit principle in international law that all territory has to be under the jurisdiction of some sovereign body (state or international). All territory now falls under some jurisdiction—a situation very different from the nineteenth century when large parts of the globe, especially in what we now call the Third World, were not so administered.

The concept of national sovereignty is now being used in international law to solve the very problem once conceived as inherent in "nationalism" and "sovereignty"—namely that of war. All territory—except when assigned to a new "nation" by a separatist movement—is now considered inalienable; hence, any infringement on territory is defined as aggression.

2.3 Ethnic Nationalism

Politically, the rise of ethnic nationalism is the assertion of one's sense of self as a matter of group right—an identity shared in the face of a society that insists that only the majority really counts and that consequently all conceptions of the good are necessarily relativistic.

(An increasing assertion of ethnic nationalism in our time can be in part traced to the shift from ideological democracy—liberty, equality and fraternity as fundamental social values—to majoritarian views: a shift that apparently took place under the influence of latter-day utilitarianism.)

It is the relativistic view that explains the readiness of those not themselves asserting some type of ethnic nationalism—the liberally inclined—to accept such nationalism as a matter of elementary justice. Ethnically speaking, twentieth century ethnic nationalism is the way relativism manifests itself politically.

So long as relativist demands stop short of a demand for actual political independence—of forming a state recognized in international law (see *International Law*)—they can be enormously advantageous to those making them. Thus native Indian tribes in Canada, calling themselves 'nations' (and referring to their demands as 'treaty negotiations'), have been guaranteed large economic concessions amounting to millions of dollars for each member of the tribe. But they can enjoy such wealth only so long as they do not form a nation-state. Should they become inde-

pendent, their state(s) would not be economically viable. At present most members of such tribes are almost entirely dependent on provincial and federal welfare payments. Hunting-gathering cultures are by nature subsistence societies: no political change can alter this fact.

Current tribal nationalism—as one might call this form of ethnic nationalism—has no relation to nineteenth century nationalism that had a basis in an ideology. On the other hand, twentieth century tribal nationalism is often a political ploy used by those with no desire to become an active nation, but well aware of the potential economic advantage when arguing from the premises of relativism against their 'opponents' who are liberals, and therefore ready to accept their argument.

Unlike genuine ethnic nationalists who want political autonomy and are separatists (who, like Patrick Henry are prepared to say "Give me liberty or give me death!"), tribal nationalists in North America usually do not mount the barricades but rather hire lawyers, whose fees are paid by the state they pretend to oppose. "Compensation" for historical 'exploitation' constitutes their basic demands.

2.4 Third World Nationalism

The above developments have affected the nature of nationalism in the Third World, for they have given political geography a status in international law, a status it never had before the present century. Because a state's boundaries are now thought of as circumscribing a "nation," no matter what the ethnic of tribal features are, what is done by nationals in that state—whenever the action is not self-directed—is liable to be labeled "nationalism."

Little of what is called nationalism in the Third World resembles what is called by this name elsewhere. What exists is often tantamount to racism, which may be a legacy of colonialism (see *Colonialism*)—resentment against another race's arrogance and domination—or merely a misunderstanding of "nationalism."

Racism differs from nationalism for it says nothing about ethnicism—cultural resemblances and differences—the principal focus of nationalism. Racism is based on mythical biology which reputedly explains irreconcilable hostility: black against white; Arab against European. In its extremist form it is akin to the mythology of the National Socialist era in Germany (1933-45) when racism was entrenched as the ideology of the Third Reich. (Either expulsion of a "race" from the territory or Hitler's "final solution" is the racist's solution to social and political problems.)

The direct consequence of the substitution of racism for nationalism is terrorism used as a political tool (see *Structural Causes of Oppositional Political Terrorism: Towards a Causal Model*). A racist by definition abandons the concept of innocence with regard to relations with the outgroup: it is as nonsensical to the terrorist to speak of killing innocent people by a bomb as to speak of innocent bacteria being killed by a germicide.

Tribalism, which may at some remote period in European history have provided the conditions that in the nineteenth century supplied the ethnic basis for nationalism, is unlikely to function this way in the developing countries. As units, tribes are usually too small to form viable nation-states or to give a basis to "national sovereignty."

The consequence of nationhood in the developing countries is not so much separatism as tribal struggle for political power (see *Problems of Ethnicity and Religion in the Philippines*). Leaders who wish to become heads of state are faced with the formidable task of having to shift allegiance from tribe to nation, as defined by the political boundaries of the nation—state rather than a concept of "folk," which would have been the natural form of development from tribalism to nationalism.

Does this kind of "nationalism" entail a threat to peace? Characteristically, in some Third World states the demand for majority rule can be seen as a demand for nationalism. But the adaptation of the majority rule principle to nationalist purposes distorts its traditional function as a democratic device. What those states seek is an appearance of unanimity which would imply unity—or a common national spirit—which is achieved by manipulation of the voting process. It seems that when the issue is nationalism it does not matter that the vote fraud is undemocratic.

Many of the Third World states have grotesquely corrupt governments which are often a threat to peace. Terrorism is in a sense an alternative to corruption: it seeks to achieve unity by making a common enemy of foreign states. It has been argued that it is for the sake of international peace that Western democracies have shown a willingness to support obviously corrupt regimes.

Nationalism has been incorporated into international law for the sake of international order: peace without appeasement. Thus, under the Charter of Human Rights, human beings have a "right" to self-determination; in international law national boundaries—as they now exist—are nearly always deemed inviolable. Nationalism is used to hinder imperialism

and expansionism, to defeat arguments for *Lebensraum*, and so forth.

In effect, nationalism functions as an ethical limitation on the expansion of sovereignty as well as an ethical claim by subject people seeking redress from the world community. Perhaps it is the only concept in international law that is basically ethical rather than concerned with mutual accommodation. Thus respect for nationalism reflects a nation's commitment to international law. In this regard, the West comes out very well. This cannot be said about communist states.

2.5 The Third World: Tribalism and Kinship

A most intractable problem facing Third World States (few of whom can be called 'nations' or 'nation-states') is 'tribalism,' which, unlike nationalism, makes kinship—genetic and affinal relations—the basis of all social relations. As a result, those who are not kin are by definition 'strangers:' xenophobia characterizes all tribal societies.

Some argue that on the basis of their perception of what history and social evolution had established, tribal and clan-based societies can evolve into nation-states in the way Europe supposedly had. Or, if we accept Tacitus's *Germania* as a description of tribalism in what is now Europe, some can argue that the Third World countries can also 'evolve' their way out of tribalism into modern nation-states; perhaps with the example of Europe before them they can do it even faster.

However, insights derived from the tradition of political theory lead elsewhere. Social contract theory in all its varieties provides the argument that the coercive state is based on the prudential considerations of its members, not on their sense of kinship. Thus both the Swiss and Americans, despite the diversity of their component cultures, are quite nationalistic.

Under present conditions, there is little likelihood that African tribal societies could come to resemble European states. For one thing, they are hostile to European culture. More importantly, their present governments represent tribal loyalties, not contractual considerations. The sad fact is that African societies were better off under European imperialism than they are under pseudo-democratic tribalism. Imperialism imposed on prevailing cultural diversity a type of social contract; it also held out the potential for national development. Government by dominant tribes ensures only corruption and squalor, or—as Hobbes, the contractualist, put it when arguing from, primitive, pre-contractual conditions—a life that is 'nasty, brutish and short.'

2.5.1 Africa

In Africa, nationalism is not an indigenous phenomenon except, perhaps, for Egypt and Ethiopia. Everywhere else, the boundaries of states were determined by European colonizers so that even under independence citizens of particular states tend to refer to themselves in tribal terms and to use references to their nationality merely to locate their homeland and kindred geographically. (Thus a Kenyan will seldom describe himself as Kenyan but rather will say 'I am *from* Kenya.') Typically, an African does not recognize 'nationalism' as a feeling capable of leading to a specific action, as it does for a European. What certainly exists in Africa is a desire for independence in the sense of an urge to control resources and power, but not nationalism.

Will genuine nationalism ever emerge there? Tribalism—a sense of kinship—is not likely to 'evolve' into 'nationalism'—a political conception transcending kinship. Nationalism—an ideological concept—in recent years has been deliberately and quite cynically conflated with kinship for ideological reasons: politically correct Westerners want to pretend that 'native people' (tribes) are 'nations' and as such have a right under international law to proclaim independence from a state. Hence the evidence that African 'nationalism' has been promulgated by non-Africans; it appeals to greed for property and power rather than to what is understood as nationalism.

2.5.2 Asia

Nationalism in Asia is different. Throughout history virtually every present Asian state has been at least nominally part of some empire: remarkably, the relationship has not necessarily been conceived of as exploitative, but as part of the glorious past. It was, for instance, legends about the Khmers that led to the discovery of the ruins of Anghor Wat.

The ancient nature of civilization in Asia has helped limit European influence to a minimum—in most cases to market place matters and technology. (The important exceptions being India and Hong Kong.) In some old Asian societies Europe and Europeans have been looked upon as 'barbarians.' If Americans had realized this, they would not have made the appalling miscalculations in Vietnam: they believed that so long as they controlled the cities—their notion of the 'civilized' parts of the country—

they had a hold on the country as a whole. This was not so. The countryside with its villages was the heart of the country and the center of nationalism. The cities—the product of European influence—were a kind of 'hinterland.'

Only those reasoning from the importance of centralized power to national unity—the importance of Rome to the Roman Empire, of Washington to the unity of the United States and of Paris to France—could make such a naive mistake. If they had recognized that nationalism in Asia is not the result of European influence, it is unlikely that they would have acted in this way.

2.6 Nationalism and Communism

Originally, Marx claimed that "the struggle for the proletariat with the bourgeoisie is at first a national struggle," but he misunderstood the strength of nationalism. Marx and Engels left an ambiguous legacy with regard to nationalist movements. Thus they supported the struggle of certain peoples (like the Poles and Hungarians) for national liberation, while branding Pan-Slavism (see *Pan-Slavism*) as reactionary. To the Marxists, nationalism, as a factor undermining imperialism (of the Russian or Austrian variety), had its limited uses; these uses, however, were always subordinated to the doctrinal requirements of the class struggle (see *Socialist International*). Marx wanted nationalism to disappear eventually and be replaced by "proletarian internationalism."

Expediency can explain the instrumental value that Moscow policy makers attached to nationalism in certain parts of the world. They fostered wars of "national liberation" in the Third World with the aim of modernizing undeveloped countries through industrialization—a process in which nationalism emerges as a politico-economic movement (running parallel to the historical dialectical process whose end is "freedom").

2.6.1 After the Demise of the Soviet Empire

Like the Holy Roman Empire—neither 'holy' nor an 'Empire,' the former Union of Soviet Socialist Republics was never a 'Union,' never administered by 'soviets,'—never 'socialist' and never made up of 'republics.' But it beats the Holy Roman Empire by one more deception: the former USSR was an empire in the classical, Alexandrian sense of being a conglomerate of states, nations, tribes and administrative units held together by the Fuhrer Principle of fascism—the 'cult of personality' that post-Stalinist Communists denounced after it became impracticable.

Because the USSR was a classical empire and a conglomerate of disparate units, the collapse of the central authority in 1991, calls in the minds of political analysts for a number of leading questions, such as: Which of the administrative units became nations? Which members of an artificial unity—'union'—show evidence of 'nationalism' by attempting to form nations? Which—while showing a sense of nationality—attempt to revert to earlier boundaries? And which behave as if it did not matter that the central authority is no longer the 'sovereign' power (in the Hobbesian sense)? Answers to such questions—which are beyond the scope of this article—could supply empirical evidence about the relative roles of sovereignty and nationalism.

In East Central Europe the situation of the satellites began to change even before the Soviet empire crumbled. Following the example of Poland—which was the first to shed the yoke of the Communist Party as early as in the summer of 1989—they one by one reclaimed their sovereignty in the months that followed. Their tradition of national identity helped to sever formal ties with the wider ideological unit—the USSR (before the Empire's demise)—and make possible escape from Soviet domination. It is the same national/cultural tradition (not to speak of rejection of totalitarianism) that made these countries opt for the West and press for joining Western Europe (see *Eastern Europe, Transformation of*). It was hoped that this goal could be achieved in two stages; first, by trying for membership in NATO (see *North Atlantic Treaty Organization (NATO)*) and ultimately in the European Union (see *European Union*) (scheduled for extension around 2003)—the very policy to which Russian leaders have shown a varying degree of opposition and hostility.

There is ample evidence that it is extremely difficult to shake off the legacy of Communist regimes: in several states ex-Communists were back in power within a few years: in Poland, Hungary, Lithuania, the Czech Republic. A society's ideological past cannot evidently be entirely renounced, the ostensible espousal of a democratic system of Government and a measure of nationalist tradition notwithstanding. But what is worse, is the general post-Communist paranoia that enhances greed, inter-personal hostility, extreme egoism, scorn and smallness—all contributing to a general moral chaos. (This was specifically said of Poland in the Spring of 1997 but a similar situation is reflected throughout that part of Europe). In the Polish Parliament the group in power in 1997 is the 'post Communist majority' which in fact amounts

to minority-rule, with the President being of the same ex-Communist persuasion. The consequences of all this are potentially serious. The ideological ties that some leading politicians now have with their pre-1989 past may not only bias their government's future policies towards Russia (with whose nationals they maintain old-established links) but also obscure and befuddle the issues relating to the very purposes of their national goals and the way these goals are pursued.

Within Russia itself there is the question of boundary adjustment in accord with nationalism: the 'republics' of the former USSR were the product of the fiats of central power in the way that African 'nations' are the consequence of colonialism. In the Western parts of the former USSR very definite perceptions of nationalism have been violated by political divisions. Armenians, for instance, are convinced that the Armenian Soviet Socialist Republic was not the whole of 'Armenia.' What are the international consequences of a situation in which several states occupy—as they do now—parts of 'Armenia?'

Then there are the Central Asian Republics: Kazakh, Kirgiz, Tadzhik, Turkmen and Uzbek. They seem to be administrative units based on tribal consideration. In some ways they are like American states and Canadian provinces: political units that were created by a central power. In other ways they are like African tribal units—neither 'nations' nor 'states,' and nobody has any real notion of what they 'should' be (least of all the members of these 'republics'). At present they may not be showing any strong sense of nationalism, but there is no telling what the future holds.

2.6.2 Russian Imperialism

It was fascism and pre-fascists (such as certain national movements in nineteenth century Italy) that invented the irredentist justification for imperialism and enabled Hitler to take over the Sudetenland (and get away with the *Anschluss*), but it is Russia that is now likely to benefit from irredentism. Under Communism, massive shifts of population were enforced in the USSR in order to both populate the Northern regions—such as Siberia—and to weaken nationalist movements by making the populations less homogenous than before the resettlements. Thus throughout Asia, where historically there were few or no Russians, there are now extensive enclaves of ethnic Russians who, under irredentism, offer a potential justification for future Russian imperialism. In addition, the considerable Russian ethnic influx into the

Baltic states since 1945 has created strong Russian minorities there (Latvia, Estonia) —a source of conflict with authochton nations and a potential tool of imperialism.

Yet, if imperialism is to be anything more than verbal posturing and appeal to past glories, two things are needed: a stable central power and a disciplined army. So long as neither of these exist, there is no reason why Russian enclaves scattered across Asia and Eastern Europe would effectively help to revive imperialism.

However, what many former Soviet republics and *all* former satellites fear, is the restoration of the concept of 'satellite'—the USSR version of 'hegemony.'

In international law, 'hegemony' has only quasi-legal status (see *Hegemony*); that is, the Monroe Doctrine—a declaration by the US that it has 'hegemony' over the New World—has effect only in so far as the US can enforce it. It had no effect, for instance, as long as Canada was part of the British Empire—until after 1867. Then it came to matter, as one might guess from the curious configurations of the Alaskan Panhandle, which looks so much like 'gerry mandering' (also an American politico-territorial conception).

'Hegemony' poses a threat to nations contiguous with Russia because in international law it allows for a degree of control over a nation, a control that is *not* subject to international law. 'Imperialism'—the incorporation of territory into an imperium—is now disallowed by international law. In theory, the 'international community' is expected to act, exercising control similar to that of confederation within a 'balance of power' (see *Balance of Power*). But hegemony—the status as satellite—is not subject to this control. Thus, without any effective opposition by international powers, the former USSR could in theory reassert the satellite status of its former satellites. Under 'hegemony,' an independent state has only nominal independence—the kind that led to the Hungarian uprising and the Prague Spring, and of course, their suppression. This, of course, happened under the Communist USSR. But even now, in the waning years of the twentieth century, Russia is no democracy. There are also serious signs that the Russian Orthodox Church—the traditional tool of Tsarist imperialism—has again begun to bolster nationalism. It is this situation that causes apprehension in Central Europe.

2.7 Nationalism and Religion

Back in the 1920s, G.B. Shaw recognized in *St Joan* that religion can come to express and epitomize nationalism when the prevailing ideology denies the significance of a 'people' or 'nation' as a significant social unit. The passing of Communism as an ideology 'transcending' nationalism has revived the issue put forward in *St Joan*. Once more, religion—Islam in North Africa and the Middle East, Christians and Muslims in the former Yugoslavia, Catholicism and the IRA in Ireland—has come to the fore (see *Ethnic-Religions Conflict: Nationalism and Tolerance*). As well, utterly factitious unions of entirely imaginary 'religions' and imaginary 'races,' have come to haunt a society which failed to deal honestly with the issues of race and nationalism: the politically ambitious recognize an opportunity when they see it.

One tends to forget that 'religion'—as virtually everyone outside the Third World thinks of it—represents a 'catholicized' or universalized version of what had formerly been an early expression of 'nationalism'—the 'chosen' people or 'true (and only) humans' idea. Thus Christianity is catholicized Judaism, the parable of the 'good Samaritan' marking the break with nationalism; Buddhism is catholicized Hinduism, in which race and caste are no longer relevant; so, too, Islam sees itself as 'truly' universal by being purely ritualistic: it does not matter who you are or what you believe so long as you observe certain rituals.

There is one further step in this ideological development which one disciple of any religion takes, for it makes the function of religion as supplying significance to consciousness irrelevant—the step of relativism, the conviction that belief does not matter for all beliefs are 'equal.'

The evidence is that Western society as a whole has taken this step and cannot understand why entire cultures are acting the way St Joan and all other martyrs did. For these cultures the pragmatic effect of self-sacrifice is irrelevant. It is nonsense—they retort—to say that sacrifice is in vain: 'you others are denying my existence and my significance; I assert both by scorning you; you cannot defeat me by threats or persecution.'

Now, to concentrate on three particular areas relevant to the issue of nationalism and religion—Ireland, the Balkans, and the Middle East and Islam:

2.7.1 Ireland

Historically, it was Henry VIII—designated by the Pope himself as 'Defender of the Faith' when Henry was 'Catholic'—who established the opposition of religion and nationalism in Ireland. When Henry became a heretic, his political ambitions in Ireland became a question of religious affiliation: 'legitimate' descendants of Henry—William of Orange et al.—came to epitomize the religious and political divisions that Henry had established.

In Ireland, nationalism manifests itself in terms of religious opposition—Catholic versus Protestant—because there is no other way to talk about 'nationalism;' apart from religious affiliation there is no problem with regard to nationalism in Ireland: attempts to assert that there is one—as by pretending that Protestants are English and not Irish—are manifest fabrication. The issues of religion and nationalism in Ireland come down to the degree to which Irish state policy can be secularized. This is the question which should be addressed. It is fatuous to argue that Protestants should get out of Ireland because they are really English and historically do not belong there. It is much too late to argue about the policy of Henry VIII as if it were still politically relevant.

2.7.2 The Balkans

In the Balkans, where geographic conditions are such that cultural fragmentation—hence nationalism—is inevitable, the resulting political units are incompatible with the economic realities of modern nation-states. Montenegrans, Albanians, Macedonians, Serbians and others are without question genuine nationalities, but they do not form viable independent political units without consigning themselves to the permanent status of Third World nations—'Hewers of wood and drawers of water.'

It is a bit of historical speculation to ask what the current situation in the Balkans would be if it were not for the overthrow of the symbol of unity, the monarchy. Yugoslavia—an artificial unity designed to solve the problem of disunity—was a political entity under King Peter, but it was not a nation. It was fictive; it was *de jure*, not *de facto*. By an act of the international community (as distinct from the citizens of Yugoslavia), the Balkans were converted into a Third World nation.

The Balkans, unlike Ireland (and the Middle East) do not want to be unified religiously or nationally, whereas those outside the area feel that 'world peace' would be promoted if the nationalist and religious differences in the Balkans did not exist. The problem is a difference between those who have no real respect for religious and national differences on one hand, and on the other those who feel that these are the fundamental existentialist questions.

History and geography have made the Balkans 'the powder keg of Europe.' National relations are so intertwined that a single incident—like the assassination of the reigning family by an anarchist in 1914—could bring on a world war. However now in the late 1990s the consequences of the existing tensions for world peace are not likely to be so disastrous. Yet the very complexity of the divisions of nation and religion makes the situation explosive. In the Balkans we find in actual physical conjunction: the great schism in Christianity of 1054 between Eastern and Western Christianity, the division between Christianity (see *Christianity*) and Islam (see *Islam*) of 622, as well as the divisions between nationalities consequent on geography. These divisions are exacerbated because for a variety of reasons—historical, genetical and cultural—everybody in the area is related. What is even more important, politically, no one can look on the other as historical 'oppressor' in the way the Irish can look at the English. Since these ethnic groups have long lived in separate communities, they could, theoretically, join together in a common purpose for mutual benefit as in the Hobbesian conception of the social contract.

2.7.3 Caveat: Ethnic Cleansing

Although what in the 1990s came to be known as 'ethnic cleansing' and the older term 'balkanization' originated as references to the situation in the Balkans, few people recognize the relationships between them. Ethnic cleansing conceived of (by the perpetrators) as a 'good,' creates the situation we condemn as 'balkanization' and ensures that people who are closely related ethnically will remain at odds politically: it also guarantees that they will be unable to form the kind of federation that would be to their common advantage.

There is no question that ethnic homogeneity is beneficial: it allows a government to arrive at a conception of 'national interest' (see *National Interest*) that under multiculturalism is not even discernible. (Indeed, democratic governments faced with multiculturalism are necessarily preoccupied with attaining and retaining political power rather than with 'governing.')

However, attempting to arrive at cultural homogeneity by means of ethnic cleansing results in one thing only—the conversion of a domestic problem into one of international relations. Since no one has jurisdiction over the international sphere, a problem that might have been solved when it was internal, is made intractable because it is converted into a threat by foreign interests that are motivated by a desire for revenge and restitution.

2.7.4 Islam

Benjamin Franklin's dictum 'We must all hang together or we will hang separately' is a good rule of thumb explanation of 'solidarity' movements such as Islamic fundamentalism in the Middle East. If we recognize that the collapse of Communism entailed the world political hegemony of the USA, we can understand why the American democratic and secular tradition has not triumphed but rather has evoked fanatic resistance in the Middle East.

Before Islam came to express a collective opposition to Westernization—a resistance that Kipling thought impossible: 'East is East and West is West and never the twain shall meet'—panarabism was tried, the simple fact being that a good many political leaders in the East (like many in the West) are only nominally religious. But panarabism could not succeed even though a natural state—the United Arab Republic—did exist for a brief time (see *Pan-Arabism*). Actual national feelings prevented so artificial a union: Iranian, Afghans, Syrians, Irakians and so forth are just not 'Arabs,' whereas they are definitely Muslims and feel this to be important. The crucial fact is that 'Western' views and Western culture derive from Christianity. Opposition to Westernization, then, is best expressed religiously—by emphasizing Islamic fundamentalism.

In the US curiously enough, political fanaticism can be manifested under the guise of religious fanaticism. Thus it is no coincidence that an entirely imaginary 'religion,' called 'Black Muslims,' should arise as an expression of civil problems. Perhaps it is not surprising that Islamic 'fundamentalism' should evince hostility to the US rather than mere doctrinalism. (A note is in order about the doctrinal 'tolerance' attributed to Islam. Although presumably the Koran 'counsels' tolerance, there is no sign of it in the international behavior inspired by Muslim fundamentalism. Note the terrorist policy (see *Terrorism*) that originated with the Rushdie affair and the persistent blackmailing to which foreign states—and their publishers—were subjected by Iran.)

There are some specific reasons why in the twentieth century 'Islam' should revive as counterweight to the American hegemony. For domestic political reasons, the Department of State has been promoting Israel, a state based on religion. Muslims are under no illusion who is responsible for the situation, as bombings in America's 'client' state, Saudi Arabia, have clearly established. Nor have people in the Middle East any doubt as to why the US does not choose to ignore the Middle East in the way it had ignored the Balkans for a long time. Middle East oil is essential to the American economy as well as defense. Thus the Department of State is trapped between the needs of American politicians to support Israel and the needs to ensure oil supplies. In view of the American divisions, fundamentalism is the basis for Islam's solidarity.

2.7.5 Muslim Terrorism

Since only one major normative system in modern times, Christianity, has consistently represented organized violence—war and militance—as morally wrong, one should not be surprised that the decline in its influence should be marked by a rise in the use of organized violence to achieve personal and political ends. Nor should one be surprised that those defining themselves as non-Christian (and even anti-Christian) should be the most militant. Until the collapse of its organizational center in the USSR in 1991, Communism was the main source of organized violence in the twentieth century. Islam has now inherited the role.

The revived militance of Islam (after a 'pause' lasting three centuries) seems to be related to the non-Islamic acceptance of the behaviorist view that violence reflects frustration. According to Western frustration-aggression theory, violence reflects a justified personal grievance ('frustration') rather than an anti-social attitude, and is therefore best resolved by concessions—relief of the 'frustrations.' Hence the peculiar readiness of Western society to make concessions to demands that used to be considered criminal blackmail and were resisted for this very reason. The demands, of course, increase in direct proportion to the granting of concessions, since another behaviorist position (proved experimentally and historically) is that behavior, if rewarded, is 'reinforced' by having attained its object. If terrorism works—i.e., if concessions are made—blackmailing will persist out of self-interest, not out of faith in Islam.

See also: *Revolution; Self-determination; State, Theory of the; Supranationalism; Transnationalism; Socialist International; Tolerance in an Age of Conflict*

Bibliography

Berlin I 1981 Nationalism: Past neglect and present power. In: *Against the Current*. Oxford University Press, Oxford

Berlin I 1991 *On the rise of nationalism*. In: *The Crooked Timber of Humanity*. Alfred A. Knopf, New York

Bowle J 1964 *Politics and Opinion in the Nineteenth Century*. Oxford University Press. Oxford

Breuilly J 1982 *Nationalism and the State*. Manchester University Press, Manchester

Caplan R, Feffer J (eds.) 1996 *Europe's New Nationalism: States and Minorities in Conflict*. Oxford University Press, New York

Cobban A 1945 *National Self-Determination*. Oxford University Press, Oxford

Cobban A 1969 *The Nation-State and National Self-Determination*. Collins/Fontana, London

Emerson R 1960 *From Empire to Nation. The Rise to Self-Assertion of Asian and African Peoples*. Harvard University Press. Cambridge, Massachusetts

Gellner E 1983 *Nations and Nationalism*. Basil Blackwell, Oxford

Hayse C J H 1931 *The Historical Evolution of Modern Nationalism*. Richard R Smith, New York

Himmelfarb G 1995 The dark and bloody crossroads: Where nationalism and religion meet. In: *Looking into the Abyss*. Vintage Books, Random House, New York

Kamenka E (ed.) 1976 *Nationalism: The Nature and Evolution of an Idea*. Edward Arnold, London

Keating M 1996 *Nations Against the State: The New Politics of Nationalism in Quebec, Catatonia and Scotland*. Macmillan Press, London

Kedourie E 1960 *Nationalism*. Hutchinson, London

Kedourie E (ed.) 1971 *Nationalism in Asia and Africa*. Weidenfeld and Nicolson, London

Kiss E 1993 Five theses on nationalism. In: *NOMOS XXXVIII, Political Order*. New York University Press, New York

Kohn H 1944 *The Idea of Nationalism: A Study of Its Origins and Background*. MacMillan, New York

Kohn H 1955 *Nationalism: Its Meaning and History*. Van Nostrand, New York

Kohn H 1962 *The Age of Nationalism*. Harper, New York

Kohn H 1968 Nationalism. In: *International Encyclopedia of the Social Sciences*, Vol. XI. New York

Kohn H 1974 Nationalism. In: *Encyclopaedia Britannica*, Vol. 12. Encyclopaedia Britannica, Chicago, Illinois

Minogue K R 1967 *Nationalism*. Batsford, London

O'Brien C C 1988 *God Land: Reflections on Religion and Nationalism*. Harvard University Press, Cambridge, Massachusets

Orwell G 1945 Notes on Nationalism. *Polemic* (October). (Repr. 1965) In: *Decline of the English Murder and Other Essays*. Penguin, Harmondsworth

Seton-Watson H 1977 *Nations and States*. Methuen, London

Shafer B C 1955 *Nationalism: Myth and Reality*. Harcourt Brace and World, New York

Shafer B C 1972 *Faces of Nationalism: New Realities and Old Myths*. Harcourt Brace, New York

Silvert K H 1963 *Expectant Peoples: Nationalism and Development*. Random House, New York

Smith A D 1971 *Theories of Nationalism*. Duckworth, London

Smith A D 1981 *The Ethnic Revival*. Cambridge University Press, Cambridge

Smith A D 1995 *Nations and Nationalism in a Global Era*. Polity Press, Cambridge, UK

Snyder L L 1976 *Varieties of Nationalism: A Comparative Study*. Dryden Press, Hinsdale

Snyder L L 1990 *Encyclopedia of Nationalism*. Paragon House, New York

Sugar P F (ed.) 1995 *Eastern European Nationalism in the Twentieth Century*. The American University Press, Washington, DC

Symmons-Symonolewicz K 1968 *Modern Nationalism*. Polish Institute of Arts and Sciences in America. New York

Tilly C (ed.) 1975 *The Formation of National States in Western Europe*. Princeton University Press, Princeton, New Jersey

Tivey L (ed.) 1981 *The Nation-State: The Formation of Modern Politics*. Martin Robertson, Oxford

Unger J, Barné G R et al., (eds.) 1996 *Chinese Nationalism*. M.E. Sharpe, Armonk, New York

Whitaker U G Jr (ed.) 1961 *Nationalism and International Progress*. Chandler, San Francisco, California

Worsley P 1964 *The Third World*. Weidenfeld and Nicolson, London

The Exit from Communism. In: *Daedalus*, (Spring) 1992. Cambridge, Massachusetts

W. J. STANKIEWICZ

Natural Rights

Natural rights are those rights which belong to human beings by nature, resting not on custom or convention, but on self-evident principles or fundamental laws of reason. The foundation of natural rights is the doctrine of natural law.

The concept of natural rights is based on Western political philosophy. Traditionally, it has included life, liberty, and property. These rights are inalienable, imprescriptible, and appear as a manifestation of individualism, considering the nature of the person independently of any political allegiance. The concept of natural rights, recast in the rhetoric of "human rights," is a crucial tenet of modern liberalism.

The dignity of each person is supposed to take precedence over any social order. Hence, the authority of government must be limited. The United States Declaration of Independence (1776) and the French Declaration of the Rights of Man and Citizen (1789), for example, argued that citizens must be protected against abuses by the sovereign power. In the modern era, the notion of natural rights has been extended to the social or cultural domain due, at least in part, to pressures from Third World nations.

The Universal Declaration of Human Rights (December 10, 1948) is a United Nations document which sets forth a variety of rights, including the following: right to life, liberty, and security of person; equal rights of men and women; equal protection of the law; freedom from arbitrary arrest, detention, or exile; fair and public hearing by an independent and impartial tribunal: freedom of movement and residence within borders of each state; right to leave any country, including one's own, and to return to one's own country; asylum from persecution; right to a nationality and the right to change one's nationality; right to own property; freedom of thought, conscience, and religion; freedom of peaceful assembly and association; universal and equal suffrage; right to work; equal pay for equal work; right to rest and leisure; and right to education.

The concept of natural right, therefore, has expanded from a Western emphasis on life, liberty, and property to an international standard of political, cultural, and social rights.

See also: *Human Rights and Peace; International Bill of Human Rights; Human Security; Declaration of the Rights of Man*

Bibliography —————————

Charmont J 1927 *La Renaissance du droit naturel*, 2nd edn. Duchemin, Paris
Hobbes T 1651 *Leviathan*. Anderw Crooke, London
Locke J 1690 *Two Treatises of Government*. Churchill, London
United Nations 1948 *Universal Declaration of Human Rights*, UN General Assembly Resolution 217 A (III). United Nations, New York.
Wechsler H 1961 *Principle, Politics, and Fundamental Law: Selected Essays*. Harvard University Press, Cambridge, Massachusetts

ROBERT H. PUCKETT

Naval Limitation Treaties between the World Wars

The First World War precipitated a determined search for policies and instruments to prevent the recurrence of such a catastrophe. Prominent among the causes which were held responsible for the outbreak of war in 1914 were the arms races between the powers, with the naval race between Britain and Germany arousing particular attention in the English speaking world. Until the mid-1930s, disarmament and arms limitation proposals of all kinds continued to excite interest and raise hopes for the future. Politicians and diplomats devoted a great deal of time and energy to these many-sided questions. Yet the only significant (and then only temporary) progress to be achieved was in the area of naval limitation. Success here was not without its critics at the time, while the Second World War persuaded many in Britain and the United States that the naval treaties had been worse than a failure. The treaties, it was argued, had weakened the forces of those powers which might otherwise have been able to deter the aggressors, and had worsened the setbacks which the Allies experienced in the early stages of the conflict. Thus a cloud hung over the one major experiment in arms control up to that time (the Anglo-American agreements concerning the Canadian frontier in the previous century had been on a much smaller scale),

and which was to retain its unique position until the era of détente between the United States and the former Soviet Union in the early 1970s. Given that so little tangible progress has been made in arms control at any time, treaties which embraced the three leading naval powers (and to a lesser extent others as well), and which were in operation from 1922 until the later 1930s, deserve careful study.

A number of questions are worth considering. What circumstances and policies made them possible? What were their deficiencies at the time? What more could have been done to rectify or lessen their defects? Why did they break down? Did they contribute anything to the cause of peace? Or must the balance, in the end, be tilted against them, and their overall effect upon international relations be described as damaging rather than constructive? Space will not permit an investigation of the question why interwar progress in naval limitation was not repeated with armies and air forces.

1. The Background to the Washington Conference

Surprising though it might seem, the First World War was immediately followed by an incipient naval race between the United States, Japan, and Great Britain.

Until 1914, the United States had been content to accept Britain's claim that, given her position as the world's leading shipping, trading, and colonial power, she was entitled to the world's largest navy. The United States was already building up its navy against Germany and Japan, while the experience of war persuaded many that the United States needed a navy "second to none" if its interests were to enjoy due respect and protection in the future. British interference with United States shipping as long as it remained neutral during the war was much resented. At the same time the Japanese seized the opportunity, while the other powers were preoccupied by the war in Europe, to extend their influence in the Far East to a degree and by methods which were seen as damaging to the United States. Some Americans, indeed, began to argue by 1919 that their country needed a navy equal to those of Britain and Japan combined. Fear, pride, and professional ambition were all at work. Rival American and Japanese warship construction thus continued after the war, and by 1921 the British, although financially impoverished by the war and anxious for time in which to assess the implications of air and submarine warfare before embarking on extensive surface ship construction, felt obliged to respond. At least on paper a naval race as serious as that between Britain and Germany before 1914 was in the offing. This was the background to the Washington Conference which sat between November 21, 1921 and February 6, 1922.

British readiness to come to terms with the United States can be traced back to 1919 when even the Admiralty recognized that the strength of the latter was such that naval parity of some sort would have to be conceded. If financial considerations were paramount, one need not entirely discount other motives in this readiness to discuss naval limitation. The Japanese, too, by 1921, were beginning to feel the strain of empire building and inflated arms expenditure, with some of their service chiefs acknowledging that in any prolonged naval race the United States was bound to win. Simultaneously, any hopes in United States governing circles that they could achieve a significant naval advantage for bargaining purposes over Britain and Japan were being dispelled by the refusal of the Senate to vote the necessary funds. Popular protests against naval expansion were of real consequence in the United States. An international conference was thus possible and productive, because in all three key capitals moderates and supporters of economy were in control. The other major participants, France and Italy, were too weak to exert much influence as long as the most expensive naval units were under discussion,

although the French refusal to agree to the abolition or strict limitation of the submarine contributed, with the serious Anglo-American differences over their respective needs in cruisers and destroyers, to the failure to reach any quantitative agreements about such warships. The submarine, the French insisted, was "the defensive weapon of lesser navies." Nor was it even possible to secure a satisfactory resolution of the question as to what rules should govern the use of submarines against merchant shipping in the event of war. The shadow of unrestricted warfare as practiced by Germany in 1915-18 was not lifted.

2. The Washington Treaties

Such naval limitation as was achieved at Washington was also dependent upon a number of other agreements. To reassure the United States, the British and Japanese agreed to end the alliance which had bound them since 1902. Its renewal would have strengthened the "big navy" enthusiasts in the United States. Various agreements were concluded to try to restrain Great Power rivalry in China, and in particular to cut back the influence which Japan had attained in East Asia aided by world events since 1914. Japan, for its part, was compensated for its acceptance of a smaller battle fleet than that of either Britain or the United States by the promise of the Anglo-Saxon powers to fortify no bases nearer to Japan than in Hawaii and Singapore. At Washington no less than nine treaties and twelve resolutions were negotiated, clear evidence of the dependence of naval limitation on the settlement of other questions, political and economic.

Under the treaty for the limitation of naval armaments of February 6, 1922 some 1.7 million tons of old and partially built battleships and battle cruisers were scrapped by Britain, the United States, and Japan. This was about 300,000 tons more than they retained. The reality was less impressive. Much of the discarded tonnage was obsolete or at a very early stage of construction. Some exceptions were allowed in the 10-year "holiday" in capital ship construction, though limits were imposed on the size of the new ships and the caliber of their largest guns. These were fixed at 35,000 tons and 16 inches respectively. Ratios were roughly established between the battle fleets of the five main powers (Britain 10, the United States 10, Japan 6, France 3.5 and Italy 3.5). No aircraft carrier was to exceed 27,000 tons, with Britain and the United States each being allocated 135,000 tons, Japan 81,000 tons, and France and Italy 60,000 tons apiece. With respect to cruisers, for reasons already mentioned, only qualitative restrictions proved possible. Cruisers were not to exceed 10,000 tons or carry larger than 8-inch guns. Unfortunately these figures represented a new type of cruiser, and helped to trigger off something of a mini naval race in the construction of such ships. Indeed, the British had agreed to these specifications without looking deeply into the relevance of this type of ship to their strategic needs. The Washington negotiations also demonstrated that even when the powers were interested in arms limitation, the differences in the needs and composition of their fleets made fair comparison difficult if not impossible. Many supposedly comparable ships in the British navy, for instance, were smaller and older than their United States counterparts. Finally the French were reluctant to discuss arms limitation in isolation from the question of military guarantees from Britain and the United States.

Any conclusions concerning the Washington Conference must obviously be mixed. Certainly tension was reduced between the United States and Japan. Naval expenditure was cut back, though the cruiser agreement was in time to generate serious dissension between Britain and the United States. To no small degree, naval competition in general was transferred from the largest classes of warships to smaller ones. The future prospects of naval limitation were clearly dependent on the character of the environment in East Asia and probably in Europe as well. The question has sometimes been asked why more was not achieved at Washington, if not in the limitation clauses themselves with all their technical complications then at least at the political level, to try to reinforce what had already been achieved and to provide momentum for the future. Some critics complained that the treaties lacked teeth. They were dependent on the good faith and self-restraint of each power. Guarantees, enforcement, or penalty clauses were absent. But here one must stress the overriding obstacles presented by each power's concern for its national sovereignty. This was made most apparent in the deliberations on the treaties in the United States. When President Harding submitted the results of the conference to the Senate for approval, he insisted that the most significant political instrument, the Four Power Treaty of December 13, 1921 between the three leading naval powers and France, entailed no commitment to armed force. There was no alliance, only "covenants for peace." As it was, the Senate ratified the treaties only after it had added a reservation of its own against formal commitments of any kind.

One must not be too critical of the United States on this point. One generation, however hard it may try,

cannot bind another. Circumstances and attitudes change. Obligations are continually reviewed in the light of currently perceived interests. Furthermore, down to 1931, the degree to which the foundations of Washington were being undermined was by no means evident.

3. The Geneva Conference and After

The question of naval limitation was far from forgotten, and in 1927 resulted in a second conference which met in Geneva. Here an extraordinary (and in the longer term a largely irrelevant) controversy arose between the British and American delegations. This helped to obscure further the real threats to Washington. Failure resulted largely from the inability of Britain and the United States to agree on a definition of parity when the attempt was made to extend it to other classes of warship, especially cruisers.

The Geneva Conference, although a disappointment, warrants some study if only to demonstrate how, even when war between two powers seems improbable, arms limitation can still give rise to major problems. As at Washington there was a strong desire to save money. Winston Churchill, the British Chancellor of the Exchequer, was to be found in the unfamiliar role of a forceful advocate of naval economies (see *Churchill, Winston*). The United States, on whose initiative the conference had been called, was mainly concerned to achieve parity in cruisers with the British and at the least expense to themselves. The British, in return, were also anxious for an agreement, but one which would check the building of the large expensive cruisers (the type favored by the United States, given their needs in the Pacific) and allow the Royal Navy to equip itself with sufficient smaller ships to protect the vulnerable sea lanes of the empire. Hence the British proposal that they should receive an allocation of 70 cruisers as against 47 for the United States and only 21 for Japan. Had this been conceded the British would have dramatically enhanced their security by way of naval limitation: The United States, however, were outraged alike by the proposed disparity, and the size of the building programs envisaged by Britain. Although many ingenious solutions were put forward, it proved impossible to bridge the differences. Basically the United States wished to build a certain number of 8 inch gun cruisers and confine the British cruiser fleet, however constituted, to broadly the same overall tonnage as themselves. The British were equally determined to restrict the number of 8-inch gun cruisers and retain a much larger overall tonnage of cruisers than the United States was willing to accept. The stalemate persisted although each government was anxious for agreement, and each was aware that a new treaty would be popular at home (except among the more nationalistic and navalist groups). As for the Japanese, the British delegation commended their efforts to promote a settlement.

The Geneva Conference failed in part because of inadequate preparation. Diplomats and politicians too readily assumed that further progress on the lines of Washington would not be difficult to achieve. Unfortunately, too, among the United States delegation the admirals achieved a dominant influence, so that narrow technical and professional considerations were allowed to prevail. These certainly restricted the opportunities for maneuver. On the other hand, one American historian, Gerald E. Wheeler (1963), has interestingly argued that the American navy chiefs were, as early as 1927, mainly guided in their thinking by the possibility of a war with Japan, but they dared not make this public. Strict parity with Britain was a more acceptable breaking-point. Certainly in view of what was to happen, the United States and Britain could happily have accepted each other's demands, though such an outcome would not have been pleasing to the Japanese. As it happened, this conference, followed by the abortive Anglo-French disarmament proposals of July 1928, reduced Anglo-American relations to their lowest point between the wars. In the end, however, reason and good sense began to prevail, and evoked reassuring words from President Coolidge: "What we need in these discussions is men who, taking the broader and more statesmanlike view, will start from the point of view that war between us shall not take place." The atmosphere was also improved by the concurrent negotiation and signature of the Kellogg-Briand Peace Pact (August 27, 1928). In the same year, the assumption in British defense planning that there would be no war for 10 years was confirmed and even strengthened.

At the end of the 1920s the possibility of war between Japan and the Anglo-Saxon powers still seemed remote. Since Washington, however, the Japanese had built more warships than Britain and the United States combined. Eight of their new cruisers exceeded the tonnage permitted by the limitation treaty. But in general the British seemed to have more immediate cause for worry in Europe than the Far East. The German navy, which had been drastically cut back by the Treaty of Versailles, was beginning to display new vigor. At the end of the decade, the Germans were developing the so-called "pocket battleship," a ship which was nominally within the

10,000 ton limit imposed by the peace treaty, but which, given its range and formidable armament, appeared to possess great potential as a commerce raider. The British were also worried by the naval ambitions of the French and the Italians. The French continued to build submarines in disturbing numbers, and to resist all Italian claims to naval parity. Thus naval building in Europe could, in time, begin to threaten such agreements as had been concluded between the three main naval powers with their eyes mainly on the Pacific, and impede any further efforts to make such agreements more comprehensive.

4. The First London Conference

In 1929 both Britain and the United States acquired leaders who were deeply interested in peace and disarmament. President Hoover, with his Quaker background, had had direct experience of organizing relief for a war-devastated Europe. The new Labour prime minister, Ramsay MacDonald, though not a pacifist, had been a critic of British policy in 1914-18. Together they encouraged efforts to find a "yardstick" whereby Britain's insistence on a large number of small cruisers could be reconciled with the United States requirement for heavy cruisers, and at the same time prevent a situation whereby Japan's ratio of heavy cruisers against the United States would not threaten British security in the Far East. Preparations for another naval conference were also complicated by the fact that some groups in Japan were increasingly anxious to obtain a more favorable ratio with the Anglo-Saxon powers, and there were other knock-on effects from the Franco-Italian naval rivalry in the Mediterranean. Nevertheless in 1929 both the British and United States governments began to slow up their building programs, and in the preparations for the London conference politicians and diplomats provided much more direction and control than at the ill-fated meetings in Geneva. In the winter of 1929 the British cabinet took a most important step when it decided that British interests could be met with only 50 cruisers and not the 70 on which the Admiralty had always insisted. Its case was strengthened by the fact that 50 approximated to the current cruiser fleet, and any increase in the foreseeable future seemed unlikely. The United States, too, was showing more flexibility, with one influential admiral insisting that aircraft carriers would be more useful in any war in the Pacific than heavy cruisers. The London Conference therefore opened on January 21, 1930 with the ground reasonably well-prepared for a compromise.

The negotiations, nevertheless, were complicated and difficult. In March the conference was near to failure because the demands of the French threatened to undermine the crucial compromises which had been agreed by the British and the United States. The French argued that they had to take account of Italian and German intentions, especially as long as the Anglo-Saxons showed no interest in a treaty to guarantee French security. The British remained unsympathetic, and tended to find the representatives of fascist Italy more reasonable and moderate than those of republican France. Of course the Italians, as the weaker party, were only too happy to agree to many of the proposed limitations, provided the French conceded parity.

An Anglo-American compromise was also contingent upon a satisfactory settlement of the naval ratios with Japan, and there the conference was helped by the electoral success of the moderates in February 1930. In the short run this facilitated agreement, although the terms ominously inflamed and strengthened those elements in Japan (especially in the Japanese navy) which were dissatisfied with the existing ratios, and which argued that Japan could be secure only if the Americans were allowed a much narrower (if any) margin of superiority. As it was, elaborate formulas were required to settle the cruiser issue. In the end, by the Treaty of London of April 22, 1930, the percentages allowed to the Japanese in the various classes of surface warships ranged from 60-70, with parity in submarines. The three powers also agreed to postpone new battleship construction for five years. It proved impossible to bridge the differences between France and Italy, so they were not included in the main limitation agreements. The British continued to look for ways to bring these two powers within a comprehensive settlement, but without success. This enhanced the significance of Article 21 of the Treaty of London, by which each of the three main signatories was permitted in certain circumstances to increase its naval tonnage in response to excessive building by powers which were not party to the treaty. Contrary to expectations, however, the main challenge to the treaty soon began to develop not in Europe but in the Far East.

5. Japanese Naval Expansion

In 1931 the moderate politicians in Japan who favored understandings with Britain and the United States began to lose influence, and to be threatened by militant elements in the army and navy. The latter believed that the political, economic, and military policies pursued since 1922 were failing to safeguard and advance Japan's interests. These were, it was said, damaging to Japan's prestige and influence on the Asiatic mainland. The militants could point to the growing self-confidence of the Chinese. It was too soon to talk of a united China, and an immediate threat to Japan. But Chinese nationalism was strong enough to pose problems for Japanese interests in southern Manchuria. In the longer term, too, the former Soviet Union could be expected to exert more influence in the Far East. At home, the militants were assisted by the growing discontent, even suffering, of vast numbers of Japanese as the Great Depression devastated the country's economy. In such conditions it was easy to win support for the argument that it was no longer appropriate for Japan to allow itself to be confined to the role of a junior partner by the Anglo-Saxons.

Treaty supporters among the admirals began to lose ground to the so-called "fleet faction" led by Admiral Kato Kanji, a man steeped in the samurai tradition. This faction argued that the treaties allowed Japan too few warships of all kinds. They wanted equality in many classes. When their opponents warned that such aims would precipitate a new naval race, the "fleet faction" replied that despite its superior resources the United States would probably lack the will to compete effectively, and, even if it did, so large a growth in relative United States power would alienate world opinion to the benefit of Japan. It might even lead to an Anglo-Japanese rapprochement. In the early 1930s the "fleet faction" came to control the Japanese navy, while in 1931-32 the whole political balance in the country began to move in favor of the expansionists following the army's successful takeover in Manchuria at the expense of the Chinese and Russians. Parliamentary government in Japan had been little better than a facade in the 1920s, and it speedily crumbled in the face of such challenges. In 1933 Japan withdrew from the League of Nations (see *League of Nations*), and continued to make territorial gains at the expense of the Chinese. The whole Far Eastern environment was being rapidly transformed, with Japan relying increasingly on force and control of territory rather than diplomacy, international treaties, and economic influence to promote its interests. Indeed, a growing number of Japanese now believed that the country must acquire a formal and informal empire which would make it economically self-sufficient and militarily invulnerable. The liberal, internationalist policies of the 1920s, however modest, were outdated.

Both services consequently set out to diminish,

control, and even eliminate Western influence in China. Soon the European empires in Southern Asia were included in this projected sphere of influence. Such aims were not to the taste of all ministers, some of whom hoped to preserve the limitation treaties in some form in return for at least tacit United States acceptance of Japan's enlarged role in East Asia. By 1934, however, it was evident that this policy would not succeed. The United States refused to recognize Japanese claims, and were beginning to expand their fleet, although only in those classes of warship where the United States had not built right up to the treaty limits. The Japanese admirals, in their turn, were confident that they could wage a successful campaign of attrition against any American attempt at an offensive across the Pacific. Basically they thought this could be done by ensuring that the Japanese navy, and its supporting aircraft, could compensate for any deficiency in numbers by superior quality. Great faith was placed in a new design of superbattleship, and to a lesser degree in submarines. The potential of the aircraft carrier was underestimated. By 1934-35, therefore, the Japanese navy was not really interested in naval limitation except essentially as a propaganda weapon at home and abroad. Certainly nothing was to be conceded at any future conference which would threaten the navy's capacity to win the envisaged defensive battle of attrition. To the unwary the Japanese navy's case might have appeared to be primarily a plea for equality and security. In practice it was designed to isolate China, and facilitate that country's subordination to Japan.

6. The Second London Conference

By 1935 the Japanese had made good progress in the planning and development of their new fleet. They already possessed ships which infringed the limitation treaties. An end to treaty limitation would free the country to build precisely the types of warship best suited to its needs—especially superbattleships and submarines. It was claimed that with no excessive increase in cost, Japan could be made secure whatever the United States response. The expense of widening and deepening the Panama Canal, for instance, was expected to deter the United States from trying to compete with the superbattleship. Stress was also laid on the United States' economic problems—the recovery there from the Depression was less rapid than in Japan. In general the United States appeared unsure and deeply introverted. The Japanese were further encouraged by the military revival of Germany. This diminished what little

chance there was of war with Britain. The navy leaders pressed their views on the government in the preparations for the second London Naval Conference, and for good measure hinted darkly that a military coup was possible if the Japanese delegation failed to follow the navy's wishes.

The mood in the United States, meanwhile, was totally different. The Depression, popular hostility to further United States involvement in foreign wars, and suspicion of the role of United States bankers and arms manufacturers in the First World War all made it essential for the government to speak up for disarmament. The Roosevelt Administration, in any case, believed that peace and prosperity were interdependent—that an arms race and fear of war would impede an economic recovery in the United States and the world as a whole. Through a revival of prosperity it was also hoped that the aggressive elements in Europe and Japan would lose their appeal and influence. But the administration was also determined not to leave Japan a free hand in the Far East, even if it could do no more than express moral disapproval. Naval limitation therefore remained a major matter for the United States, with the president himself expressing the hope that real reductions might yet be secured.

The British approached the 1935 conference in a much less optimistic mood. They were unsure of United States support in a crisis in the Far East, and were being obliged to take more account of developments in Europe than at any time since the Washington Conference. Italian naval construction was beginning to cause concern as well as that of other powers. The British rather desperately, and—as it proved—vainly, tried to argue the case for smaller and cheaper battleships. In general, Britain's global military commitments were well in excess of her resources, so that it is not surprising that the British clutched at any straw—the possibility of further naval limitation, an understanding of some sort with Japan, the appeasement of Germany, and the elimination of outstanding Anglo-American naval differences—to improve their security.

These considerations help to explain what must otherwise be regarded as the highly injudicious British decision to conclude a unilateral naval limitation agreement with Germany on June 18, 1935. The Germans, who had recently repudiated the Treaty of Versailles armament restrictions, were eager to reassure the British in what was one of their sensitive concerns, the Royal Navy. By such an agreement they could also hope to drive a wedge between Britain and France. The German offer to limit their surface fleet to 35 percent of that of the British (they demand-ed more in submarines) for six years cost them noth-ing. They did not possess the resources or inclination to build more in the mid-1930s, while, given Hitler's approach to international treaties, the agreement could be repudiated once it became inconvenient (as happened in April 1939). Promises that they would not resort to indiscriminate submarine warfare were thrown in for good measure. "The British were not wholly credulous, but the German offer seemed too good to refuse. Here was a promise of limitation at a time when so much else seemed in a state of flux. In the longer run, if the Germans were sincere, it might even contribute to the whole process of appeasing Germany's grievances and turning her into a peaceful and cooperative member of the community of Europe and the League of Nations.

Little need be said of the work of the second Lon-don Naval Conference which met between December 10, 1935 and March 21, 1936. The Japanese, obdu-rate on the question of naval equality, withdrew in the middle of January. The French vetoed a British suggestion that Germany and Russia be invited to participate in the final stage of the conference. In practice it proved possible for Britain, the United States and France among the leading naval powers, and later Britain and the former Soviet Union (August 1936) to reach agreement on certain qualitative restrictions (such as the size and armament of battle-ships and cruisers), while by the end of 1936 all the main powers, including Italy, Germany, and Japan, had ratified a special protocol prohibiting the unre-stricted use of submarines against merchant ships. Many lesser states also signed. The British naval his-torian, Stephen Roskill (1976), comments: "The value of these signatures may be regarded as justifi-cation for cynicism about attempts to 'humanize' war." Yet he also argues that, despite the short-lived utility of such limited results as were achieved at London, the conference should not be dismissed as a colossal waste of time. It was right to continue or preserve the work of the 1922 and 1930 conferences. Contemporaries could not be sure that failure was inevitable. The negotiations before and during the conference did much to improve Anglo-American relations which, in view of what was to happen, can be accounted a gain for those who had to fight the crucial naval battles in the war against Germany, Italy, and Japan. The second London treaty included escape clauses, so that thereafter British and United States rearmament, whatever the effects of earlier treaties, were slowed only by internal political, finan-cial, and industrial constraints.

7. Conclusions

Any conclusions concerning this experiment in naval limitation between 1922 and 1936 must be tentative and complicated. Nor can the origins and effects of the treaties be easily distinguished from the general course of events in the same period. The overall international environment of the 1920s was very dif-ferent from that of the ensuing decade. Economic problems interacted with revulsion against war to facilitate restraints. The United States in 1921 pro-vides the clearest evidence of idealistic popular pres-sures, though their influence cannot be discounted on other occasions. But in general in the 1920s govern-ments believed that national prosperity was not assist-ed by large armament programs. Lower taxation was expected to stimulate the civilian economy, and prove electorally popular. Obviously governments weighed all naval limitation agreements against the needs of national security, but given the confidence between Britain, the United States, and Japan, for instance, that their competition for influence and economic advantage in China would be conducted according to well-understood rules and conventions, it seemed pos-sible to reconcile the needs of financial restraint and national security. If war is the continuation of politics by other means, then naval limitation was the quest for security by more economical methods.

Once the international environment began to change in the 1930s, with the continuing effects of the Depression, and the dramatic political changes in Ger-many and Japan, all that had been painfully construct-ed between 1921 and 1930 began to crumble. Had moderate regimes survived in Germany and Japan, had both countries been discreetly handled by the rest, had China remained too disunited to disturb the Japan-ese, had the former Soviet Union remained paralyzed by its internal problems, one might tentatively suggest that the first London Naval Conference need not have proved the climax to the era of naval limitation. But on the other hand it does not seem possible to argue that, had naval limitation made even greater progress in the 1920s, this, by itself, could have done anything to check the swing to extremism in the ensuing decade. Only offers of a free hand in Central Europe and the Far East might have kept tolerably responsible regimes in power in Berlin and Tokyo.

Arms limitation, therefore, may help to consolidate and improve a benign environment. Constructive negotiations, pursued with sufficient determination and skill on the part of all the participants, may also, as illustrated at Washington, divert the powers from a potentially dangerous course. On the other hand it can be argued that the failure of the United States, for most of the 1930s, to demonstrate its readiness to respond to Japan's naval challenge strengthened the claims of the Japanese extremists that their expansionist policies could be followed at tolerable cost to the Japanese economy, that Japan had little or no cause to fear the United States, and that with a moderate increase to the Japanese fleet the country could be permanently safeguarded from United States attack. Too late the Japanese discovered that the United States was preparing to fight, and given time would be able to amass strength far in excess of their earlier calculations. Thus American restraint in the early 1930s may well have been one of the contributory causes of Pearl Harbor.

See also: *Treaties of the Modern Era; Arms Race, Dynamics of; Arms Control, Evolution of*

Bibliography ————————————

Buckley T H 1970 *The United States and the Washington Conference, 1920-1922*. University of Tennessee Press, Knoxville, Tennessee

Mckercher R J C 1984 *The Second Baldwin Government and the United States, 1924-1929*. University Press, Cambridge

O'Connor R G 1962 *Perilous Equilibrium. The US and the London Naval Conference of 1930*. Kansas University Press, Lawrence, Kansas

Pelz S E 1974 *Race to Pearl Harbor*. Harvard University Press, Cambridge, Massachusetts

Roskill S 1968 *Naval Policy between the Wars, 1919-29*. Collins, London

Roskill S 1976 *Naval Policy between the Wars, 1930-1939*. Collins, London

Wheeler G E 1963 *Prelude to Pearl Harbor: The United States Navy and the Far East, 1921-1931*. University of Missouri Press, Columbia, Missouri

CHRISTOPHER J. BARTLETT

Negotiations, Direct

International interactions are so diverse that the actions of one state can affect another state in a variety of ways. When conflicts occur, several ways of managing or reducing the seriousness of the conflicts are available. One of the most important methods for coping with conflict situations is to have the relevant parties establish some sort of contact. If states seek to collaborate more fully, they use direct discussions in order to establish the basis for such increased joint activities.

Direct negotiations, therefore, occur when two or more nations hold discussions with a view to harmonizing their relations, moving either from more conflictual interactions to less conflictual relations or from a state of occasional friendship to a condition of more regular and productive contact.

Direct negotiations are to be contrasted with indirect negotiations. In the latter case, two governments do not communicate verbally, but one country seeks to modify the foreign policy behaviors of the other through actions, such as troop mobilizations or unilateral troop reductions, that tacitly call for the other side to reciprocate. Deterrence is one major example of indirect negotiations (Schelling 1936) (*see Deterrence*). The yearly Lunar New Year Truce in the Vietnamese War of 1965-73 was arranged through indirect (tacit) bargaining.

Deescalation (see *Internationalized Conflicts, Deescalation of*) by means of reciprocated initiatives for tension reduction, as advocated by Charles Osgood

(1962), was pursued by President John Kennedy (1963) after his "Toward a strategy of peace" speech. The result of Kennedy's efforts was a thaw in Soviet-United States relations that led to a detente in the 1960s (Etzioni 1967) and 1970s (Wolfe 1979). The Strategic Arms Limitations Agreements of 1972 and 1980 as well as increased trade between the two Superpowers were direct results.

Direct negotiations may take place at many levels. If heads of government do the negotiating, their efforts are called summit diplomacy. Johan Galtung (1964) has identified 147 such meetings between 1941 and 1961; based on their results over the two decades, he urges that summit conferences should be regularized. Usually, however, negotiations between states are delegated by the heads of governments to subordinate officials, leaving governmental leaders with the ceremonial role of signing a document that has been negotiated by their agents in accordance with strict instructions.

Direct negotiations may touch upon three types of subjects. Perhaps the most familiar subject is the termination of ongoing violence (treaties of peace, treaties of surrender, and armistices); a second is the drawing up of new agreements unrelated to violence (treaties in peacetime); a third is the revision of former treaties and agreements (peaceful change) (see *Treaties of the Modern Era*).

The treaty of peace is the most common form of

direct negotiation to terminate war. Quincy Wright (see *Wright, Quincy*) (1965) finds that 178 wars were concluded by treaties of peace between 1550 and 1941; some wars, of course, stopped without a treaty. Treaties are more common in modern times than they were in earlier periods; they are less likely when wars are fought outside Europe; and a treaty is more likely to conclude a war with many participants than a war between just two belligerents.

A treaty of surrender, such as the Treaty of Brest-Litovsk in which Bolshevik Russia capitulated to Germany in 1917, is concluded largely by unilateral dictation on one side and self-abnegation on the other. One of the reasons why the People's Republic of China insisted on the return of Hong Kong was that the treaty signed with Britain that assigned perpetual rights to the latter over Hong Kong was a treaty of surrender and thus an "unequal treaty" that was considered by Beijing to be unenforceable under international law.

An armistice, finally, is a temporary cessation in hostilities. An armistice may be negotiated via unilateral capitulation (the surrender of the Confederate States of America to the United States of America in 1865), through third-party intervention (the Peace of God in Medieval Europe), or may be the result of direct negotiations (the Paris Accord of 1973 that ended American participation in the war in Vietnam). Many armistices are merely preparatory steps toward the conclusion of peace treaties (November 11, 1918); some are broken and fighting continues thereafter (Arab-Israeli armistices); still others in effect become peace settlements due to the absence of a formal treaty of peace (Korea after 1953) (see *Korean Armistice Agreement*).

Considerable research has been conducted into so-called normal negotiations, that is, agreements in peacetime. Many researchers focus on how a negotiator can gain a relative advantage (Lockhart 1979); others study factors that account for cooperative behavior, that is, which enhance the probability of making concessions to ensure a compromise settlement or to develop strategies for evoking altruistic behavior from previously selfish opponents (Sawyer and Guetzkow 1965). In both cases the strategies of negotiation applied to more normal negotiating situations can be applied to other subjects.

The revision of former agreements is usually called peaceful change. Drafters of the Treaty of Versailles of 1919 thought that no treaty should freeze a status quo but instead should be subject to revision through legal means. The establishment of the League of Nations was seen as an institutional expression of the concept of peaceful change (see *League of Nations*).

See also: *Arbitration, International*

Bibliography ──────────────────────────

Etzioni A 1967 The Kennedy experiment. *Western Political Q.* 20

Galtung J 1964 Summit meetings and international relations. *J. Peace Research* 1(1)

Kennedy J F 1963 Toward a strategy of peace. *Department of State Bulletin* 44

Lockhart C 1979 *Bargaining in International Conflicts.* Columbia University Press, New York

Osgood C E 1962 *An Alternative to War or Surrender.* University of Illinois Press, Urbana, Illinois

Sawyer J, Guetzkow H 1965 Bargaining and negotiation in international relations. In: Kelman H C (ed.) 1965 *International Behavior.* Holt, Rinehart and Winston, New York

Schelling T C 1963 *The Strategy of Conflict.* Galaxy, New York

Wolfe T W 1979 *The SALT Experience.* Ballinger, Cambridge, Massachussetts

Wright Q 1965 *A Study of War.* University of Chicago Press, Chicago, Illinois

MICHAEL HAAS

Nehru, Jawaharlal

Jawaharlal Nehru was born on November 14, 1889. During 1905-12 he received his school and university education in England. In 1920 he joined the Non-cooperation Movement and was elected President of the Indian National Congress in 1929, 1936, and 1937. He was the first Prime Minister and Minister of External Affairs of Independent India from August 15, 1947 until his death on May 27, 1964.

1. Nehru and Gandhi

Peace was conceived by Jawaharlal Nehru as follows: "Peace can only come when nations are free and also when human beings everywhere have freedom and security and opportunity. Peace and freedom, therefore, have to be considered both in their political and economic aspects."

If one compares this definition with Mahatma Gandhi's perception, the most distinctive feature is their differing approaches. For Gandhi, peace was based on a particular anthropological concept of social order, the prime impetus being people's quest for peace within themselves and in their relations with their fellows (see *Gandhi, Mohandas Karamchand*). Nehru, on the other hand, focused on the nation-states, on the realm of institutionalized political power. The foremost task of national governments was a twofold one: in the domestic sphere to push forward the process of nation building and economic progress through the process of "modernization" and the inculcation of a "scientific temper" among people; in the international sphere he wanted efforts to be made to establish a world order which could secure peace.

To realize this distinction is important for assessing the relationship between Gandhi and Nehru, who was chosen by the former as the Prime Minister of India. It also explained their different roles in India's struggle for freedom. Gandhi, the "Father of the Nation," provided the vision of a free Indian people, but felt increasingly alienated by the political strategy adopted by the Indian National Congress during and after the 1930s. It was Nehru who became the real architect of "modern India," who started to establish the country as a progressing nation and as a fully fledged member of the international community.

Both of them were guided by a strong idealistic inclination which harmonized with reality only under great difficulties. Gandhi had to realize this with regard to his religiously inspired perception of universal peace (see *World Order: Gandhi's Concepts and Contributions*). Nehru suffered a similar disenchantment concerning his concept of a peaceful world community. He experienced the gravest deviation from his ideal when India was defeated by the Chinese in 1962.

2. "One World"

Being an agnostic and a liberal humanist, Nehru visualized peace among humankind by way of a global community: "We have arrived at a stage in human affairs when the ideal of One World and some kind of World Federation seems to be essential, though there are many dangers and obstacles in the way."

The idea of "One World," of a world government, was not Nehru's own creation, but was widely discussed among various ideological groupings in the first half of this century (see *World Government*). It was stimulated by the disastrous experiences of the

First World War and later the Second World War, by the lessons drawn from the League of Nations' failure, and finally by the high hopes pinned on the newly created United Nations Organization. Keeping in mind Nehru's own cosmopolitan upbringing and his international outlook, it seemed quite natural for him to feel attracted by this idea. Yet he did not advocate the idea unconditionally and modified it in the course of his growing experience as Prime Minister of the Indian nation-state.

For that reason, it is noticeable that his idea of securing world peace underwent a change, if not a certain degree of disillusionment. He started off by defining independence not in "the old type of narrow, exclusive independence," but in a context where "separate warring national States should be ended." The United Nations (see *United Nations Reform: Historical and Contemporary Perspective*), in spite of its shortcomings, seemed to him an appropriate body through which to implement the conception of One World. He outlined his way of achieving this in his speech in the United Nations General Assembly in 1956: "I hope that, gradually, each representative here, while obviously not forgetting the interests of his country, will begin to think that he is something more than the representative of his country, that he represents, in a smaller measure perhaps, the world community."

Even more appropriate to his intentions of linking internationalism and nationalism was the idea of a "world commonwealth." This concept had the advantage of taking political constraints into account more realistically. Instead of a superstate ruled by one central government, a world commonwealth would enable the various nation-states to maintain their identity, their sovereignty, and to establish their international relations on equal terms (see *World Government*).

This approach took into consideration not only Nehru's personal ambitions, but also the desire of the Indian nation to emerge as a great nation on the international scene. He perceived India's greatness not in terms of military power potential, but in terms of cultural heritage; geographical size and location which destined India to be a meeting point for Eastern and Western thought; vast economic potential which called for immediate development; the peaceful way by which India had won independence and set an example for other freedom movements; and finally moral prestige which Mahatma Gandhi had achieved for his people.

In a psychological respect, this perception explained the very motive of Nehru's political ambitions. Being gifted with a clear, scientific mind, provided with an exceptional education at the most prestigious institutions in England, tutored into domestic politics by an outstanding father, adopted and respected by Mahatma Gandhi as his favorite disciple, Nehru longed to pay back all these efforts by raising India to the position of an esteemed member of the global community. To participate in global politics as India's prime representative, at the same time corresponded with his own international outlook.

Against this background Nehru, as Prime Minister of India, clearly stated his priorities. While earnestly advocating international goodwill, peace, and freedom, he identified the prime task of every government as serving the immediate needs of its own country: "Therefore, we propose to look after India's interest in the context of world cooperation and world peace, in so far as world peace can be preserved." If India's national interests could not be satisfactorily pursued in the frame of a world federation, then the country should participate in changing this conflict-prone world order or seek for alternative options to safeguard her security needs.

3. Panch Sheel

Various components shaped Nehru's perception of how to secure global and national peace. Inspired by his vision of "One World," he considered the Five Principles of Peaceful Coexistence (*Panch Sheel*) to be India's contribution to world peace. His strategy of nonalignment (see *Nonalignment*) provided the operational frame in which India's security interests could be ensured. At the same time, nonalignment would place the Indian government in a position to choose the most appropriate assistance for developing the economy, which according to Nehru's conviction could only be achieved by a socialist economic policy.

Panch Sheel comprised the following five principles: (a) mutual respect for each other's territorial integrity and sovereignty; (b) nonaggression; (c) mutual noninterference; (d) equality and mutual benefit; and (e) peaceful coexistence. For the first time, *Panch Sheel* was mentioned in the Preamble of the Indo-Chinese Treaty of 1954 concerning trade and intercourse between Tibet and India. In 1955, the principles were adopted as the doctrine of the nonaligned countries at the Bandung Conference (see *Bandung Conference*).

Nehru described the principles of *Panch Sheel* as the basis of India's relations with other nations, as the normative force of India's foreign policy, and as

the revival of ancient Indian traditions reaching back to the great Buddhist emperor Ashoka in 250 BC. He conceded that they were not new ideas. This is true, for he merely revived principles repeatedly referred to whenever the peaceful intentions of a government or organization were to be emphasized. For example, peaceful conduct between sovereign nations was proclaimed as a basic principle in the United Nations Charter (see *United Nations Charter*).

The remarkable aspect of introducing *Panch Sheel* into diplomatic parlance has, however, to be seen in the particular context in which Nehru applied them for the first time, namely, in the framework of a treaty between India and her rival, the People's Republic of China. They were obviously supposed to safeguard India's security vis-à-vis China's territorial claims and growing ambitions in the international arena.

How could the Five Principles fulfill their protective function for India's national interests? Nehru saw in them the "message of tolerance." India could claim "the credit for spreading this conception of a peaceful settlement, and above all, of noninterference," because India had already gained "a measure of respect and attention." Propagating peaceful coexistence basically meant to acknowledge that "there are different ways of progress, possibly different outlooks, but ultimate objectives may be the same."

Panch Sheel was the nearest way in which Nehru could adopt Gandhi's precepts of nonviolence to a pattern of international relations. The pragmatic doctrine, "do not interfere in my affairs, then I will not interfere in yours" combined with the moral stance, "take my practice of tolerance as an example" aimed at a twofold objective: to secure peace for India and to achieve international recognition of India's views (see *Peaceful Coexistence*).

4. Nonalignment

Though the Five Principles of Peaceful Coexistence were set forth only after the strategy of nonalignment had already been put into practice, they embodied its very essence. They supplemented each other insofar as *Panch Sheel* highlighted the moral aspect, and nonalignment the operational one. None of them involved a grand design, but gained their attraction from the particular circumstances under which they were proclaimed and—in this respect one has to concur with Nehru's perception—from the fact that the Indian nation did indeed become prominent in the early postwar period.

Nehru rightly admitted that the strategy of nonalignment gained its international importance because it was put forward by a large country like India, while it would soon have been done away with by the Superpowers if propagated by a small nation. Again, the twin function becomes obvious. By acting as advocate of smaller, politically less influential nations, India could revalue her position vis-à-vis the Great Powers and simultaneously ensure the support of the newly independent countries. Basically, Nehru applied the same tactic in international politics as Mahatma Gandhi had done in the domestic field.

Nonalignment essentially meant keeping aloof from the two big power blocs which had emerged soon after the Second World War. Still maintaining close links with the former colonial ruler, India was naturally expected to join the Western bloc after her formal independence. But Nehru had realized at an early stage that the growing political and economic strength of the United States would encourage her imperialistic ambitions. Therefore, immediately after he became Vice-President and Member-in-charge of External Affairs of the Interim Government in September 1946, Nehru announced the Indian intention not to join any of the power groups. In December 1947, now Prime Minister of the first independent government, he confirmed his earlier stance. It took only two more years, during which the Indian nation reached a considerable domestic stability and consolidated her international position, for nonalignment to become an accepted policy of the Indian government.

The most significant feature of the Indian perception of nonalignment was described by Nehru in the following way: "But I should like to make it clear that the policy India has sought to pursue is not a negative and neutral policy. It is positive and a vital policy that flows from our struggle for freedom and from the teachings of Mahatma Gandhi." As in the case of nonviolent resistance (see *Nonviolence*), the decision to participate in solving a conflict was taken out of a position of strength. Only if the Indian government anticipated some effect, should it bring to bear its reputation.

Reflecting the newly restored self-esteem of the Indian people as well as the conviction that the peace and prosperity of a nation could be achieved in different, though equally valid ways, Nehru stressed the point: "Every nation should be free to choose the path it considers best" (see *Self-Determination*).

5. Implications for India's Economic Policy

That leads to the other motivation which justified nonalignment as the only appropriate framework for India's foreign policy. As described above, Nehru

comprehended peace and freedom as comprising both political sovereignty of the nation and economic progress of the people (see *Peace with Freedom*). Foreign policy was basically determined by the economic policy a government decided to pursue for the sake of developing the national economy.

In the late 1940s, the Indian leadership had not yet formulated a coherent economic policy, although Nehru had been involved in the work of the Congress Planning Commission for nearly 20 years. The Indian economy was closely linked with the British, structured according to the capitalist system, and increasingly exposed to United States influence. The Indian government could not afford to reject Western, especially United States development assistance. On the other hand, it wanted to keep its options open.

The nonaligned strategy was considered to overcome this dilemma. If the government demonstrated its political self-determination, it hoped to achieve a fourfold aim: (a) to attract development assistance from both sides; (b) with its increased bargaining power to reduce as far as possible political strings attached to economic aid; (c) to be placed in a position wherein Nehru himself could determine the right mix of capitalist and socialist elements in its development policy; and (d) to maintain only a small defense budget because the rival Superpowers would prevent any interference by the respective opponent.

This tactic started to pay off in the 1950s, when the former Soviet Union, under Khrushchev, remunerated India's role as protagonist against colonialism and imperialism in the Third World. It also coincided with the introduction of a "mixed economy" in India.

Nehru's personal *credo* was a socialist development strategy combined with the use of modern technology: "I am convinced that the only solution of the World's problems and of India's problems lies in Socialism, and when I use this word I do so not in a vague humanitarian way but in the scientific economic sense." Yet, his pragmatism softened his radical conviction. The influential Indian private capitalists could only be won by a compromise. The private sector elements of the "mixed economy" could ensure their support as well as United States development aid, while the public sector elements could secure the government's planning priorities and attract Soviet assistance.

6. Evaluation of Nonalignment

To conclude, the strategy of nonalignment was perceived by Nehru not as a principle per se but as a pragmatic framework for India's foreign policy. In a conflict-prone global setting dominated by two rival

Superpowers, it should enable the Indian government to decide for itself on the most appropriate option in a particular situation. What India needed most, after having gained formal independence, was a period of peace and consolidation in order to develop economic resources. For that purpose, the government had to avoid being dragged into the power struggle of the industrialized countries. The more India could prevent any interference in her own affairs as well as in the affairs of befriended decolonized nations, the higher the guarantee would be for peace. This strategy necessitated a direct link between national and global peace. Therefore, Nehru's India advocated a policy which postulated mutual respect between sovereign opponents, sought to lessen international tensions by negotiation, and attempted to prevent future conflicts by an increased global cooperation.

The main strength as well as weakness of this policy has to be seen in its nondoctrinal approach. Nehru had defined the active element as being that the Indian government would decide, on the merit of each case, whether to participate or even mediate in a conflict. As a result of this selective approach, a comprehensive analysis of the nonaligned policy has to concentrate on the empirical side, how the policy was operationalized on various occasions and if it functioned in the long run according to its initial intentions. The latter are outlined in this article and assessed in the context of Nehru's personal perceptions as well as India's national ambitions. An empirical investigation would, however, reveal the contradictions which Nehru, as its prime protagonist, had to face, and the compromises to which he was forced to agree.

Bibliography

Dutt V 1979 *Gandhi, Nehru and the Challenge*. New Delhi

Maxwell N 1974 Jawaharlal Nehru: Of pride and principle. *Foreign Affairs* 52(3)

Nanda B R (ed.) 1976 *Indian Foreign Policy: The Nehru Years*. University Press of Hawaii, Hawaii

Nasenko Y 1977 *Jawaharlal Nehru and India's Foreign Policy*. Verry, New Delhi

Nehru J 1961 *India's Foreign Policy. Selected Speeches: September 1946-April 1961*. New Delhi

Nehru J 1981 *An Anthology*. Oxford University Press, Delhi

Rajan M S (ed.) 1976 *India's Foreign Relations during the Nehru Era*. Asia Publishing, Bombay

Rana A P 1976 *Imperatives of Non-Alignment: A Conceptual Study of India's Foreign Policy Strategy in the Nehru Period*. South Asia Books, Delhi

Range W 1961 *Jawaharlal Nehru's World View: A Theory of International Relations*. University of Georgia Press, Athens, Georgia

CITHA D. MAASS

Neocolonialism

Colonialism in its literal form means the transplanting of emigrants from the mother country to form a new community at a distant location. The more sophisticated and widely used sense of the term is, however, to connote a superior-inferior relationship between the mother country and the dependent area. It implies the subjugation of a less developed and technologically inferior people by a more developed and powerful state. The term also pertains to a historical development when the West, enjoying its military prowess, conquered much of the non-West and engaged in a subsequent exploitation of captive peoples and resources. Colonialism is basically antithetical to peace because by definition peace is based on a just and harmonious relationship. Although almost all former colonies became independent following the Second World War, a similar colonial superior-inferior relationship still exists between ex-colonial powers and the newly created independent states. This superior-inferior relationship between the advanced, industrialized nations and the former colonies has been identified as neocolonialism.

Many of the newly independent countries were not prepared for independence and lacked adequate resources for independent statehood. Earlier, as colonies, they served the interests of imperial metropolitan powers as markets for manufactured goods, sources of raw materials, investment opportunities for the rich, strategic locations and sources of personnel for national defense, and as the symbols of prestige associated with Great Power status. Some modern features were introduced under the general scheme of exploitation, enough to wet the appetite toward a nationalistic agitation for independence and to disrupt the traditional status quo. The colonial powers receded first from Latin America. Following the Second World War the remaining colonial powers were forced to readjust their power relationships with dependent states due in part to their inability to hold on to the expensive remnants of their past glories. Since the Second World War almost all remaining colonies have become independent through either force or peaceful negotiation, or some combination of the two.

Given the unprepared state of newly independent countries, however, a dependency relationship has continued between industrialized, developed nations (mostly former colonial powers) and the newly independent countries. Not being able to meet their developmental needs, the newly independent countries have been forced to rely on the industrial and administrative know-how and financial wealth of the developed nations. Furthermore, by not being able to meet their security needs the newly independent countries have been forced to invite protection from the more militarily powerful developed nations. Such dependency, however, has meant obligation, whether it is the payment on a large external debt or through the fulfillment of some security alliance responsibility. When these obligations are not met external political intervention often ensues.

Neocolonialism encompasses many areas of the world and manifests itself in diverse fields. The Wars of Independence in Latin America in the early nineteenth century succeeded in the removal of Spanish authority in the Americas, but they were followed by a massive influx of British, German, and US capital. As a result, by 1900 foreigners owned all or most of the transportation facilities, communication systems, mines and mineral deposits, plantations and ranches, manufacturing and processing plants, and banks and trading companies in the region. These foreign interests were not concerned with the internal redistribution of their wealth. Their enterprises were profit motivated and they often allied themselves with the conservative forces in the host countries to preserve the lucrative *status quo*. The results of such neocolonial practice have been the uneven development of dependent areas and the widening of the gap between rich and poor, that is, between the developed, Western sector and the underdeveloped, underprivileged traditional sector (see *Maldevelopment*). Latin America is today a society divided. Latin American revolutionary political movements have advocated economic nationalism and expropriation of foreign-owned enterprises. They have also rejected foreign interventionism.

The above course of development in Latin America closely approximated the neocolonial relationship between the First and Second World developed nations and the Third World developing countries in Asia and Africa in the post Second World War era. During the colonial period, Third World countries of Asia and Africa were a focus of primary product production, which, besides petroleum, included the prin-

cipal products of sugar, cocoa, copper, oil seeds and nuts, coffee, and ores of various types. The basic market for such primary products was as an export to the dominant colonial power. The removal of the overt domination by the colonial powers after the Second World War, however, did not turn back the clock and undo the type of developmental damage incurred previously. Consequently, dependence on the Western (homeland) market and the reliance on from one to four commodities for the majority of export earnings remained and continues to be one of the principal features of the Third World economy. This market relationship in and of itself does not contribute to "less peaceful development," but the nature of the commodity market dependency relationship does critically impact on development.

In Ghana, for instance, the cocoa price in constant value widely fluctuated from 21.5 cents per pound in 1949 to 25.8 cents in 1971, and reached the unprecedented height of 231 cents in 1977. The Zambian copper worker, the Brazilian coffee worker, and the producers of sisal in Tanzania know that these wildly fluctuating prices are not an isolated circumstance. They do in fact typify the disharmony and instability in pricing arrangements between rich and poor nations. It is this market relationship that makes planning, debt responsibilities, and inflation potentially volatile political-economic problems at practically a moment's notice, leaving the poor developing countries in a position of virtual powerlessness.

While the discussion of commodities reveals the content of colonialism that remains with a new face, it is the vehicle of neocolonialism and the "modernization" they offer that draw greater attention. It is the enticing relationship with the multinational corporations (MNCs) (see *Multinational Corporations and Peace*) that may unleash so much of the destabilizing activity described in Barnett and Muller's *Global Reach* (1974). And yet, the MNCs remain as an attractive option. Commonly observed advantages to MNC associations are openings for a quick influx of capital, assistance with balance of payments (which also may be short lived), the hope of producing domestically what was previously imported, and likewise the creation of new export markets, a rapid growth in the industrial sector, and finally some relief from local employment problems. The MNCs also offer technical and managerial expertise along with access to both capital and markets that developing countries can rarely match. But these advantages are outweighed by many negative factors. The capital-technological intensive style of development offered by most MNCs very often contributes to a skewed developmental pattern involving the enrichment of a local elite, the employment and relative comfort of a few more, and the entanglements associated with foreign finance and debt. Multinational corporations rarely train or employ indigenous people in their highest ranks, relying on local populations to supply only the skilled and semiskilled labor and junior management roles. Those at the very top remain foreign. Also, for the same reasons that make them so attractive, the MNCs can come quickly to dominate local firms. In Brazil, in 1970, 70 percent of the profits in the fastest growing portions of the economy were accounted for by MNCs. The intent, as it was from the beginning in any such relationship, is not to contribute to the well-being of a particular country, but to maximize profits for mostly foreign investors and foreign owners. While the MNC may appear to be a net employer, its preference for capital-intensive techniques may mean greater imports, as well as jobs, lost through more labor-intensive styles of development. While realizing the potential complexities and diversity of relationships between developing countries and MNCs, one must constantly remember that the basis for the presence of the MNC is to make money and ship it home. This reflects the historical patterning of the neocolonial relationship: the dominator still takes more out than it puts in.

Another leading aspect of neocolonialism is the concept of cultural imperialism. Interdependent with all the notions associated with neocolonialism, cultural imperialism is perhaps the most intangible. It is a much more difficult aspect to pin down than the concrete notions of cocoa prices or reported profit levels of MNCs. There are, however, some revealing statistics that illustrate physically what is in depth a very abstract occurrence. Statistically, for example, the largest advertising companies in Indonesia, Pakistan, Thailand, Malaysia, Nigeria, Ghana, Kenya, Colombia, and Peru are all from the United States. In India, Mexico, and Argentina, three of the top five are all from the United States. While US and British TV, for example, average 2 and 13 percent respectively in foreign content programming, contrasting figures for some developing countries are Zambia, 65 percent; Chile, 50 percent; Egypt, 41 percent; and Guatemala, 84 percent. These figures, of course, do not show the personal side to cultural imperialism. They do, however, portray the substantive argument.

Cultural imperialism is both the contrived and unintentional destruction of local culture and values. It is the inculcation of simple transient Western consumer values brought to bear by the most sophisticated uses of the marketplace and the media. This imperialism fosters role models, consumer tastes, and images of the future that are unattainable for most Third World persons. This imperialism is made all the more complex because it is so often a self-inflicted wound—made, to be sure, with the cooperation of outsiders, but brought on by the presentation and reaction to a reality-fantasy world that is both confusing and attractive to unsophisticated consumers.

See also: *Colonialism; Imperialism*

Bibliography

Barnett R J, Muller R E 1974 *Global Reach*. Simon and Schuster, New York

Brwon M B 1974 *The Economics of Imperialism*. Penguin, New York

Fannon F 1967 *The Wretched of the Earth*. Penguin, New York

Frank A G 1969 *Capitalism and Underdevelopment in Latin America*. Monthly Review Press, New York

Harrison P 1981 *Inside the Third World*. Penguin, New York

Myrdal G 1968 *Asian Drama*. Penguin, New York

Snyder L C (ed.) 1962 *The Imperialism Reader*. Van Nostrand, New York

United Nations, Commission on Transnational Corporations 1978 *Transnational Corporations in World Development : A Re-examination*. United Nations, New York

Ziring L, Kim C I E 1985 *The Asian Political Dictionary*. ABC-CLIO, Santa Barbara, California

C. I. EUGENE KIM

Neutrality

The term "neutrality" originates in the Latin word *neuter* which means "neither of them." It always refers to a conflict and implies being neither on one nor on the other side in an armed conflict. Defined in this broad sense, neutrality can be said to have existed in all regional and universal state systems known in history.

Viewed from today's perspective and conceptualizing neutrality in a more restricted sense, the institution of neutrality emerged at the beginning of the modern state system. In the Middle Ages neutrality was deemed unacceptable because men thought the universe to be governed by universally valid laws based on absolute justice. Hence, conflicts arising between states were to be seen as conflicts between right and wrong or good and bad. It was regarded as immoral to remain indifferent with regard to good and bad. Wars were either just or unjust wars (see *War*). However, once the universalistic claims of divine or natural law and just-war thinking began to wither away, there was a place for neutrality.

The institution of neutrality became firmly established only when the principle of sovereignty emerged as the key concept guiding international relations. It is indicative that the first authors writing about neutrality, Hugo Grotius (1583-1645) (see *Grotius, Hugo*) and Emerich de Vattel (1714-69), also wrote extensively about sovereignty, independence, and noninterference. Both philosophically and historically these concepts belong together. It is important to recall the close interrelationship existing between the principle of neutrality and the principle of sovereignty. Whenever sovereignty has been generally recognized in the international system, there was also ample form for neutrality. On the other hand, whenever sovereignty was made relative by absolute claims of religion or ideology, neutrality was jeopardized, rejected for being logically impossible, and even despised for its alleged immorality.

The contemporary international system, in this respect, offers no safe environment for neutrality. To the extent that world policy is determined by ideological motives, neutrality is clearly not given a proper place. According to the Marxist-Leninist worldview, for instance, the world is perceived as the arena of a permanent class struggle; any state is either on the side of the "exploiters" or the "exploited" (see *Marxist-Leninist Concepts of Peace and Peaceful Coexistence*). And on such a polarized context, no third stance such as neutrality is perceived to be feasible. It seems that any ideological claims make neutrality relative at best, and impossible at worst.

1. The Legal Basis of Neutrality

Any policy of neutrality directly or indirectly refers to specific legal norms pertaining to neutrality. Neutrality, as a legal term, did not exist until 1907; that definition still remains valid today despite the significant changes which the international system has undergone in the meantime. No effort undertaken to adapt the classical definition of neutrality to the modern world since the Second World War has been successful. Therefore the 1907 definition still represents the only universally acknowledged legal basis of neutrality.

The law of neutrality, as agreed upon in 1907, is written down in the *Vth Convention Concerning the Rights and Duties of Neutral Powers and Persons in Case of War on Land*, signed in the context of the Hague Peace Conference, on October 18, 1907. This convention stipulates a number of rights of the neutral state to be observed by belligerent states, and duties to be observed by the neutral state. Belligerents are obliged to respect the territory of neutral powers, since this territory is inviolable. They are also forbidden to move troops or convoys of either munitions of war of supplies across the territory of a neutral power. Finally, the fact of a neutral power resisting, even by force, attempts to violate its neutrality cannot be regarded as a hostile act by the belligerent.

On the other hand, the government of the neutral state must not allow military activities to take place on its neutral territory. In addition, every measure of restriction or prohibition taken by a neutral government with regard to commercial and other transactions must be impartially applied by it to both belligerent.

The Hague Convention, in Articles 6 and 7, explicitly limits the duties to be observed by neutral powers: these duties refer to official governmental acts only, and they do not oblige private persons or firms; in particular, the government of a neutral power is not called upon to prevent the export or transport, on behalf of one or other of the belligerent, of arms, munitions of war, or in general of anything which can be of use to an army or a fleet.

The legal obligations addressed by international law to neutral powers can be said to represent a minimum set of duties only. Neutral countries have a strong interest in keeping their obligations limited, as suggested by the Vth Hague Convention. They have good reasons for rejecting additional obligations which the belligerent would like to impose on the neutral. In particular, neutral countries have no reason whatsoever to restrict their press freedom in order to guarantee "neutrality" of public opinion. In international law there is no such thing as "ideological neutrality" or "political neutrality." Neutral governments and citizens of neutral countries are free to express their views about any conflict and the conflicting adversaries. Nor are neutral governments obliged to control or direct their external trade in order to achieve symmetry in their trade with the conflicting parties. It is also important to note that neutrality, strictly speaking, always refers to an armed conflict. International law does not give any precise indications about how neutral states have to behave in peacetime.

2. The Political Basis of Neutrality

Many countries have chosen a policy line which is oriented to nonparticipation in any future war between other states. In other words, they have adopted the stance of permanent neutrality. In political terms, by contrast to legal terms, the concept of neutrality refers to a foreign-policy orientation which is shaped in order to be able to apply the law of neutrality in the event of any future war. The foreign policy of a permanently neutral country hence requires certain steps to be taken in peacetime. Chief among them is the decision of not joining any alliance or, more generally, avoiding any commitment or entanglement that might jeopardize the country's neutral stance in case of war between other states. Such measures constitute what is called the "policy of neutrality." They are essentially voluntary and are taken at the discretion of the neutral country concerned.

While all neutral countries share in common the legal basis of their neutrality as defined by the Vth Hague Convention, they do differ with respect to their policy of neutrality. The actual shaping of this policy of course depends on the geopolitical and strategic context in which the country concerned is situated. However, it is correct to generalize that in all cases of permanent neutrality this policy has been adopted and is conducted for the sake of defending the respective country's national independence and integrity.

3. The Practice of Permanent Neutrality in the Contemporary International System

3.1 Switzerland and Austria

Free from commitments to military alliances, neutral Switzerland with neutral Austria constitute a kind of "looking device" across the center of Europe. Situated between the North Atlantic Treaty Organization (NATO) (see *North Atlantic Treaty Organization (NATO)*) and the former Warsaw Pact, this "looking device" was important in the context of the tension between the two power blocs. The freedom of Austria and Switzerland from alliances was, for NATO, an obstacle in the direct link between NATO forces in Central and Northern Europe (former Federal Republic of Germany, Benelux countries, Denmark, and Norway) and its forces in Southern Europe (Italy and other Mediterranean countries). On the other hand, the Swiss-Austrian "looking device" could be useful to the Warsaw Pact countries by securing their flank in

operations in Germany or Yugoslavia/Northern Italy, or by using it as a corridor for a "Blitz" push to the West. In the event of tension or open conflict, both alliances would be tempted to invade Swiss or Austrian territory, either by NATO forces, moving in a north-south direction, or by Warsaw Pact troops, moving in an east-west direction. Their interests were thus seen to cancel each other out. Consequently, the neutral "looking device" could be eliminated as a factor in the tension between the two power blocs in Europe. Both Austria and Switzerland have undertaken considerable efforts for military defense. Although their forces, of course, do not match the mighty forces of a potential aggressor, they do constitute an unmistakable reminder to a potential aggressor that a military invasion of these countries would involve the aggressor in heavy losses in men and material; that the aggressor should expect much destruction and a lengthy campaign, thus being obliged to pay a high "admissions price." This strategy of "dissuasion" is, in effect, the equivalent available to a small country of the strategy of deterrence available to Great Powers (see *Deterrence*). Austria and Switzerland are also able to exploit their mountain area as a natural tank barrier, and both the Austrian and the Swiss armies are trained to fight a highly mobile war of in-depth defensive action that would oblige a potential aggressor to deploy a disproportionately high number of troops for the occupation and control of their territory.

3.2 Sweden and Finland

Both the Swedish policy of nonalignment and Finnish neutrality have to be seen in the context of the so-called "Nordic balance" system. On the western flank of this system, Denmark and Norway have been members of NATO, having agreed, however, to a partial commitment only; in peacetime they do not allow the stationing of American troops or nuclear weapons on their soil. On the eastern flank, Finland had been in practice committed to the former Soviet Union; the Finnish-Soviet Treaty for Friendship, Cooperation, and Mutual Assistance stipulated mandatory consultations in case of a threat to the security of the signatories. Sweden, which had no engagements of any kind to any side, is situated in the center of the Nordic balance system. Finland's independence as well as Sweden's nonalignment are ensured by the potential abandoning of the partial commitment status by Denmark and Norway and their fully joining the ranks of NATO—and vice versa: any Norwegian or Danish steps toward granting United States troops permission to establish military bases and nuclear weapons stocks on their soil would inevitably have triggered Soviet pressure on Finland and possibly also Sweden. Hence there existed a delicately balanced equilibrium between the former Soviet Union and NATO with regard to the Nordic countries. As in the case of Switzerland and Austria, Sweden and Finland tried to reinforce their neutrality by considerable defense efforts. In addition, as the stability of the Nordic balance depended on the degree of tensions existing between East and West, both countries have had a very strong interest in preventing tensions and in promoting East-West détente (see *Détente*).

3.3 Ireland

The singular stance of Ireland is largely determined by Ireland's relation to the United Kingdom. Both historical traditions and the continuing dispute about Northern Ireland led the Republic of Ireland to abstain from joining NATO, and hence to stay neutral. In other words, Irish neutrality, to a large extent, is a function of Anglo-Irish relations. By contrast to the Central European and Nordic neutral, Ireland did not hesitate to join the European Economic community (EEC) as a full member, while the other neutral abstained from such a step for reasons of their neutrality.

3.4 Costa Rica

The Central American state of Costa Rica is the most recent example of a country having adopted a policy of permanent neutrality. It did so by a constitutional reform made in November 1983, proclaiming the "permanent, active, and unarmed neutrality" of the country. Costa Rican neutrality is unarmed because the Costa Rican army had already been abolished. Still, Costa Rica has a police force of 7,000. Costa Rica's adoption of a policy of permanent unarmed neutrality has to be seen in the context of the rising level of tensions affecting the Central American region. In addition, a territorial dispute with Nicaragua regarding some border areas may play a role. Costa Rica assumes that by declaring its neutrality it may be less vulnerable to potential Nicaragua aggression because any aggressor would hesitate to attack an innocent neutral and thus raise protests from world public opinion (see *Costa Rica: Neutrality*).

4. Neutrality and Nonalignment

The policy of nonalignment is far more prominent in the contemporary international system than the policy of neutrality (see *Nonalignment*). Today more than 90 countries, most of them Third World countries, practice a policy of nonalignment. Although there is no formal secretariat or any other institutional infrastructure of the nonaligned movement, the members of this movement, to a certain extent, do coordinate their policies, and they hold regular meetings of ministers for foreign affairs as well as heads of state and government.

Comparing neutral countries with nonaligned countries leads to identifying both divergences and contrasts. First of all, the aims of neutrality differ from those of nonalignment. The fundamental purposes of the nonaligned movement, since its very beginning in the early 1960s, comprise a reform of the international system, the strengthening of national independence, accelerated economic and social development, and many additional goals which are not included in the policy of neutrality properly speaking.

Also the frames of reference differ considerably. Whereas neutrality is oriented towards a specific relationship between belligerent and nonbelligerent states, clearly defined by classical international law, nonalignment does not refer to any legal criteria. There is a policy of nonalignment, but there is no such thing as a law of nonalignment, nonalignment being defined primarily in political terms.

It should also be borne in mind that the nonaligned movement mainly consists of new emerging nations striving for economic development which in turn implies a high degree of variety of individual forms of nonalignment to be discerned inside the movement. Originally, nonalignment meant abstention from, or indifference with regard to, the conflict between the two major powers. However, in its present form, the nonaligned movement offers a great variety of attitudes even with respect to this conflict; this can be seen in the fact that the movement comprises members such as Cuba, on the one hand, and the Ivory Coast, on the other hand. Finally it should also be borne in mind that some nonaligned countries are deeply involved in local and regional conflicts and even bloody and protracted wars among themselves, as in the case of the war between Iraq and Iran.

5. Neutrality and Neutralization

Neutrality must not be confused with neutralization. While neutrality constitutes a freely chosen policy of a country to refrain from participation in any conflict among other belligerent states, neutralization originates in decisions taken by the conflicting parties themselves, irrespective of the interest of the neutralized state or area. Viewed in this perspective, neutralization virtually amounts to disengagement. If two opposing parties realize that their forces are mutually deadlocked in a stalemate or if they prefer to continue their conflict without further direct armed confrontation, they may decide to withdraw their forces, on a mutual basis, and thus to establish a kind of a buffer zone.

Related to this are mutual arrangements regarding the so-called "thinning out" of certain zones, that is, the prohibition not to station certain types of weapons or the limitation of the number of troops allowed in a certain zone on each side of the line of demarcation. Sometimes such disengagement measures comprise areas of rather limited extension, such as border zones or single cities, islands, rivers, gulfs, etc. Sometimes, however, they may concern entire countries such as Persia, Afghanistan, and Burma in the framework of the competition among colonialist countries at the beginning of the twentieth century. Today, similar agreements, based on a mutual albeit tacit understanding, seem to have been implemented in many African regions south of the Sahara, at least as far as the direct interference of the two major powers is concerned.

Disengagement schemes and neutralized zones or states are always prone to collapse. Each side is suspiciously watching whether or not the opponent is inclined to interfere in the neutralized zone despite the arrangement. The slightest doubt about the opponent's compliance with the arrangement leads to a preventive reoccupation of the neutralized zone. As either side suspects the other side of the same mischievous intention, each will be willing to push forward as quickly as possible to preempt any action from the other side. Neutralized zones are the more susceptible to collapse the more important their economic and strategic value to the two opponents. That is why any neutralization scheme involving states with a considerable economic, demographic, and geostrategic potential is hardly feasible and, if nevertheless agreement is reached, will not be stable for a very long time. For instance, a reunification and simultaneous neutralization of divided Germany would therefore be quite unthinkable because a reunified Germany would represent too high a stake for East and West as to let it shift or be absorbed by the other side.

The idea of neutralization clearly offers no panacea for the solution of international disputes. It seems that only the "miniature version" of neutralization, that is, disengagement from, or demilitarization of, restricted border areas and buffer zones does make sense, provided a minimum of stability in the relationship between the two conflicting parties is ascertained.

6. Neutrality and Peace: The Passive Component

The contribution of neutrality to peace has both a passive and an active component. Passively neutral states strengthen peace by not engaging themselves in conflict. By keeping themselves outside of hostilities, they help to limit conflict.

In addition, any policy of neutrality clearly implies a purely defensive attitude. This is also reflected in the strategic posture of all neutral states. No neutral state has the kind of troops and equipment required for attacking its neighbor or intervening far abroad. Most neutral armies are structured and trained in the tradition of territorial defense, putting the emphasis on defensive weapons, interdiction of airspace, border fortifications, and an infrastructure highly suitable for mobilizing national resources against any invader, yet refraining from acquiring offensive weapons such as long-range bombers or intercontinental missiles armed with nuclear warheads. Such a defensive posture is highly conducive to generating trust. No neighbors, let alone far away countries, have any reasons to be afraid of the neutral states. In this way, neutral states are perceived as islands of relaxation in a tense environment characterized by hostility, crises, and unrest. They can be said to be factors of stability in the international system.

In the first instance, however, neutrality as a principle of foreign policy is adopted by a country not with the intention in mind to make peace but rather in order to be left in peace. Yet in this connection the question arises on which factors the security of neutral countries depends. The following eight factors deserve to be taken into consideration:

(a) Denying the conflicting parties the use of the neutral territory. Seen from the vantage point of an army commander or head of government involved in a bloody war, it is not neutrality which counts but the value of that neutrality as an element in a cost-benefit analysis in strategic decision-making. To a belligerent, the neutrality of a third country may be of some value for the simple reason that it prevents the enemy from profiting from the neutral territory. In other words, the first and foremost motive for respecting neutrality is denial of the neutral asset to the other side. Provided both adversaries are interested in not letting the neutral territory shift into enemy control, the situation of the neutral country remains relatively safe and stable. However, once a belligerent con-

cludes that its own advantage from occupying the neutral territory exceeds the advantage of denying the same advantage to the adversary, it will not hesitate to violate the neutrality concerned.

Hence neutrality can survive if, and only if, there is a symmetry or an equilibrium of interests (or disinterest), on the part of all potential adversaries in keeping the respective territory neutral. Of course symmetry or asymmetry of interests exists outside the control of the neutral country itself. The neutral cannot change the objective reality of geopolitics and geostrategy. It cannot choose its neighbors. It cannot rearrange the international equilibrium.

(b) Mutual perceptions by the belligerent. Yet even if there is a situation of rough equilibrium prevailing in the vicinity of a neutral country, the situation is still prone to destabilization. Either belligerent will watch suspiciously the other side's intentions with regard to the neutral territory. Each side will be ready to preempt the action of the other by incorporating the neutral territory. (In game theory, this situation is known as the so-called "Prisoner's Dilemma.") Each side will suspect the adversary of planning to encroach upon the neutral territory, and if one side thinks that the adversary's move is imminent, it will not hesitate to attack the neutral first—and so does the other side. Hence, more often than not, neutral countries are virtually crushed between the two belligerent as soon as tension mounts. Their situation can be stable only if each side perceives the respective adversary to be not ready or not interested in violating the neutrality of the neutral country (see *Game Theory*).

(c) Dissuading potential aggressors. A purely passive neutrality is clearly less viable than an active neutrality. The neutral country must try to influence the cost-benefit calculations made by the belligerent. In particular, it must try to create disincentives to invasion, in other words influencing the perceptions of costs. For this reason, all European neutrals have adopted a doctrine of armed neutrality. By their military preparedness, they dissuade a potential invader from invading the country. They offer clues as to the costs the potential invader would have to pay by meeting armed resistance and thus exact a kind of "entry fee" that would hardly be worth the benefit of swallowing the neutral country. Apart from military defense, a potential aggressor may also be dissuaded by the prospect of a population which, for love of its independence, will harass the invader by employing all kinds of civilian resistance. From what has been said before, it is clear that the neutral state's defense

preparations are the more important the less there is an equilibrium of interests, on the part of the belligerent, in respecting the inviolability of the neutral territory. The neutral, in other words, must try to cover the net difference that might arise between the two belligerents' interests. (One might be tempted to use the formula: $N > A - B$.)

(d) Signaling to each side that its respective adversary is also unwelcome. Fourthly, by demonstrating to each side that the other side will meet resistance when trying to invade the neutral country, each side becomes convinced that, to the other side, it will hardly make sense to attack the neutral—hence each side's trust in the neutral is reinforced. Each side will ask itself: "why should I attack the neutral if my enemy cannot do it, or do it at relatively high cost only?" There is a subtle dialectic in the existence of a neutral country situated between two hostile camps. The government of a neutral country has to be well-aware of the implications this particular dialectic has on the shaping of mutual expectations and perceptions held by the adversaries.

The neutral state can influence perceptions by constantly signaling its impartiality in strategic terms to all sides. Of course this does not require ideological and political impartiality. But it does mean that the neutral country, by a strict implementation of the rights and duties of a neutral power, demonstrates to each side that it will not grant any privileges or advantages to the other side. In more practical terms, this implies that the neutral adopts an attitude of watchful circumspection, rejecting any infringement on neutrality (such as small incursions in the border zone or violation of air space), even symbolic and insignificant ones. If it has no sufficient means available to repulse such incursions, the neutral government should at least loudly protest against it. It is only by such a strict impartiality and constant vigilance that the neutral can build confidence in the perceptions held by the conflicting parties. Confidence in the reliability of the neutral government and the credibility of its strict observance of neutrality are the only means for mitigating the suspicions inherent to any belligerent's view of the neutral.

(e) Enhancing credibility as a neutral by public support for neutrality. The credibility of neutrality as perceived by potential violators of neutrality can also be enhanced by expressions of political will, more precisely by public declarations and demonstrations of the neutral's firm determination to adhere to neutrality and to defend it if necessary. Confidence in

neutrality can be greatly promoted if the outside world realizes that there is full unanimity among the people as well as between the people and its government. Potential conflicting parties and, even more so, belligerent, are extremely sensitive and jealous in this regard. Once they doubt the reliability of the neutral country to remain neutral in all contingencies, they may quickly be led to believe that it might be better to secure the neutral territory before the adversary can do so. The present-day neutral countries in Europe are characterized by a full and unlimited support for neutrality on the part of the overwhelming majority of the population and by all significant parties and groups. As they are free, democratic countries with an open society, foreign powers are convinced that their willingness to adhere to neutrality is genuine and sincere. So there are good reasons to assume that a democratic nation is in a much better position than any other nation to signal a credible neutrality. A policy of permanent neutrality, freely adopted by a free people, is much more credible than a neutrality decided upon by an authoritarian government in disregard of what the people feels and thinks.

(f) Enhancing credibility as a neutral by tradition. It can be concluded from the forgoing analysis that the longer the duration of neutrality, the better the credibility. The permanence of permanent neutrality constitutes a definitive advantage because the perceptions held by the conflicting parties are shaped by it. A country relying on permanent neutrality as one of the foundations of its security may be well-advised to refrain from modifying it. It goes without saying that once neutrality is abandoned, the state's credibility would be compromised in the event that it subsequently reaffirmed its neutrality. Anything that tends to stabilize the views held by the conflicting parties contributes to the strengthening of confidence on neutrality, and vice versa, anything that tends to shift the image of the neutral concerned may be detrimental to this confidence.

(g) Protection by the nimbus of neutral innocence? It cannot be denied that the violation of the integrity and sovereignty of a neutral country, once it occurs, constitutes an act that will not enhance the prestige of an aggressor. On the other hand, neutral countries, by their inherent peace-mindedness, enjoy the prestige of innocence. A breach of neutrality therefore may provoke worldwide indignation against the aggressor. Yet, it is one thing protesting against and condemning the aggressor but quite another to deter it from committing such an act. Potential violators of

neutrality may take the reaction of world public opinion into account; however, this element is in general not considered as important as the purely strategic considerations which may recommend attacking the neutral. In no case of aggression against a neutral country (Belgium 1914, Norway/Denmark 1940, Cambodia 1968, etc.) were the aggressors deterred or surprised by the outcry of world public opinion—they had already taken this reaction into account in their calculations.

(h) Neutrality as a trigger of collective security mechanisms? Related to the above is the assumption that the violation of neutrality will very probably trigger action by collective security mechanisms and/or friends and allies (see *Collective Security and Collective Self-defense*). For instance, the United Kingdom would perhaps have refrained from participating in the First World War had Imperial Germany respected and guaranteed the neutrality of Belgium. However, premature conclusions must be avoided because this, and other cases, should be analyzed in a much broader context. If third parties, alliances, and collective security organs take sanctions against an aggressor, the question arises whether they do so because they are enraged by the aggressor's breach of international law or simply in response to assessments of their own vital security interests. The record of both the history of alliances and collective security arrangements (League of Nations (see *League of Nations*), United Nations (UN) (see *Status and Role of the United Nations*), Organization of American States (OAS) (see *Organization of American States (OAS)*), Organization of African Unity (OAU) (see *Organization of African Unity (OAU)*), etc.) rather point at the latter. Hence, the additional protective effect of neutrality through the triggering of sanctions (and, of course, thus deterring aggression) is delimited by the equilibrium of interests held by the conflicting parties in denying the use of the neutral territory to the other side. The matter rests solely with the structure and intensity of those interests.

7. Neutrality and Peace: The Active Component

The relevance of neutrality for peace has also an active component. Neutrality is an ideal prerequisite for good offices and mediation. All neutral countries have a long-standing record of useful service for the sake of peace and understanding. The neutral territory is often the sole place where enemies can meet and discuss terms of an armistice. Neutral states often accept mandates for good offices once diplomatic relations between two hostile powers have been broken. Their territory also serves as a platform for all kinds of international institutions, such as regional offices of the United Nations, the international Red Cross, refugee organizations, and international conferences. In many circumstances, neutral governments have also acted as intermediaries, launching peace initiatives and offering suggestions and proposals for a peaceful resolution of conflicts.

The potential of neutral states as mediators must, however, not be overestimated. More often than not, peace initiatives undertaken by representatives of neutral governments have been abortive, being all too welcome to one side while unacceptable to the other side. The role of a neutral mediator is a delicate one. Unfortunately, peaceful and good intentions and the commitment to helping adversaries to resolve their conflict are not sufficient for successful mediation—finding the proper moment, soberly diagnosing the situation, and obtaining the agreement in principle by both parties have proved much more crucial. That is why neutral governments sometimes hesitate to intervene in conflicts and to offer their good offices and mediation unless the basic conditions for success seem to be available. In more operational terms this means that neutral diplomats, as a rule, do not become active before their mandate is accepted, in principle, by all sides concerned.

However, even if neutral governments prefer not to launch spectacular and highly risky diplomatic initiatives, they may play an important role at the level of discreet diplomacy going on behind the scene, in the lobbies of international organizations, especially the United Nations General Assembly. Here, in the multilateral context, neutral countries often and successfully play the role of honest broker and catalyst for achieving consensus. In addition, the multilateral context offers a variety of opportunities for offering good offices. In this connection it is interesting to note that UN peacekeeping forces ("Blue Helmets") are preferably recruited in neutral countries (see *Peacekeeping Forces*). Similar functions fulfilled by neutral countries can be observed in regional contexts: for instance, neutral and nonaligned countries participating in the Organization for Security and Cooperation in Europe (OSCE) (see *Organization of Security and Cooperation in Europe (OSCE)*) joined together in the so-called "N+N Group" which often worked out compromises to overcome deadlocks and evolved a number of initiatives for promoting peace, particularly in the field of confidence-building measures.

In the post-Cold War era, where the former superpower confrontation no longer divide nations geopoli-

tically as existed in the East-West conflict, the notion and policy of neutrality has somewhat derived a new meaning. Neutrality is no longer associated with a nation's non-alignment with any bloc nor any superpower. Neutrality is also more abstract than before. The notion of neutrality is a status of a possible non-relationship between a particular country and the rest of the world. It does not imply a rejection by a country of any relationship between itself and a potential aggressor but *any* aggressor in the world arena.

On the other hand, with the growth and concomitant increase of regionalism and "regional states," it is possible in the long run that the concept of neutrality will acquire new meaning. It is highly expected that neutrality will acquire nuances which will be brought about by the possibility of occurrence of so-called "clash of civilization." In this sense neutrality of a certain country may go beyond more political security considerations but will include elements of cultural affinities.

Therefore, it is highly likely that present neutral countries will be presented by choices which will call for reconsideration of their policy of neutrality. The changing characteristics of conflict and peace will bring with them new policy inputs to the doctrine of neutrality.

See also: *Neutrality, Permanent*

Bibliography

Andren N 1967 *Power Balance and Non-Alignment: A Perspective on Swedish Foreign Policy*. Almqvist and Wiksell, Stockholm

Baumann G 1982 *Die Blockfreien-Bewegung*. Knoth, Melle

Birnbaum K E, Neuhold H P (eds.) 1981 *Neutrality and Non-Alignment in Europe*. Braumüller, Vienna

Black C E et al., 1968 *Neutralization and World Politics*. Princeton University Press, Princeton, New Jersey

Blix H 1970 *Sovereignty, Aggression and Neutrality*. Uppsala

Burton J W (ed.) 1966 *Nonalignment*. Deutsch, London

Driscoll D 1982 Is Ireland really 'neutral'? *Irish Stud. Internat. Affairs* 1(3)

Frei D 1967 *Neutralität Ideal oder Kalkül?* Frauenfeld

Frei D 1969 *Dimensionen neutraler Politik*. Geneva

Frei D 1971 Neutrality and nonalignment. *Korea and World Affairs* 3(3)

Frei D 1981 Kriegsverhütung durch Neutralität? *Beiträge zur Konflikforschung* 11(4)

Ginther K 1975 *Neutralität und Neutralitätspolitik*. Springer, Vienna

Hakovirta H 1983a Effects of non-alignment on neutrality in

Europe. *Cooperation and Conflict* 18

Hakovirta H 1983b The Soviet Union and the varieties of neutrality in Europe. *World Politics* 35(4)

Holst J J (ed.) 1973 *Five Roads to Nordic Security.* Universitetsforlaget, Oslo

Jakobson M 1968 *Finnish Neutrality.* London

Keatinge P 1984 *A Singular Stance: Irish Neutrality in the 1980s.* Dublin

Khan R 1981 *Perspectives on Non-Alignment.* Kalamkar Prakashan, New Delhi

Köpfer J 1975 *Die Neutralität im Wandel der Erscheinungsformen Militärischer Auseinandersetzungen.* Munich

Lutz D S, Jütte-Grosse A (eds.) 1982 *Neutralität: Eine Alternative?* Nomos, Baden-Baden

Lyon P 1963 *Neutralism.* Leicester University Press, Leiceter

Martin L W 1963 *Neutralism and Nonalignment.* Praeger, New York

Neuhold H P 1979 Permanent neutrality and nonalignment: Similarities and contrasts. *Oesterreichische Zeitschrift für Aussenpolitik* 19(2)

Neuhold H P 1982 Permanent neutrality in contemporary international relations. *Irish Stud. Internat. Affairs* 1(3)

Ogley R 1970 *The Theory and Practice of Neutrality in the Twentieth Century.* Routledge and Kegan Paul, London

Rotter M 1981 *Die Dauernde Neutralität.* Duncker und Humblot, Berlin

Schindler D 1975 Dauernde Neutralität. In: *Handbuch der schweizerischen Aussenpolitik.* Bern

Schindler D 1980 Die Lehre von den Vorwrkungen der Neutralität. In: *Festschrift für R. Bindschedler.* Bern

Singham A W 1977 *The Non-Aligned Movement in World Politics.* Westpoint

Tuzmukhamedov R 1976 *Soviet Union and Non-Aligned Nations.* Bombay

Vigor P H 1975 *The Soviet View of War, Peace and Neutrality.* Routledge and Kegan Paul, London

Vukadinovic R 1979 *Non-Aligned Countries and Denente.* Jugos-lovenska Stvarnost, Belgrade

Willetts P 1978 *The Non-Aligned Movement.* Frances Pointer, London

Zemanek K 1977 'Zeitgemässe' Neutralität? In: Frei D (ed.) 1977 *Die Schweiz in einer sich wandelnden Welt.* Zurich

DANIEL FREI; PEDRO B. BERNALDEZ

Neutrality, Permanent

Permanent neutrality is an international legal term. A state which has the legal status of permanent neutrality must pursue a domestic and foreign policy which does not make the maintenance of neutrality impossible in any future war, and must fulfill its subsequent obligations. Particularly, it cannot join any military alliance, it cannot set up such an alliance jointly with other neutral states, and must not sign any other kind of treaty on collective defense or security. It cannot permit the setting up of foreign military bases on its territory, or the transit of foreign military units for any purpose, including flight over its territory or navigation in its territorial waters. At the same time, it has the right—according to some opinions it is obliged—to maintain armed forces in order to defend its country from external attack or to protect its neutral status from violation. For this purpose, it can enter into cooperation with other states in the sphere of pure military technology, and it is not out of the question for it to train its military personnel in other countries. It can produce and export weapons.

A permanently neutral state has to adopt a special attitude in its foreign economic policy, for example, it cannot join any economic and monetary union, where the close economic intermingling with its members would make the preservation of its neutrality difficult in the case of an armed conflict. It can announce opinions on foreign political issues, and it is not compelled to maintain ideological neutrality in the struggle between the two world systems. At the same time, for a neutral state, overviolent foreign political actions endanger credibility, and it is advisable for it to adopt a moderate attitude in criticizing the policy of other states.

1. Establishing Permanent Neutrality

Permanent neutrality can be attained with a multilateral international agreement or with concordant and correlating declarations, which include the undertaking of explicitly international legal obligations. The professional literature includes the view that the unilateral undertaking of obligations has the same effect, but in such a case, other states would not be obliged to respect the neutral status of another state. In fact, the essence of permanent neutrality is that the obligation by nature is always multilateral; the states maintaining relations with the neutral states, and undertaking related obligations, may not do anything which would violate the special status of the neutral states. It is not necessary that the concerned parties—primarily the major powers—should also guarantee neutrality. Some authors actually regard this as explicitly dangerous for neutrality, because, under this pretext, the guarantor state may acquire too much influence in its relationship to the neutral state. The international legal status of permanent neutrality should be distinguished from the status of a state merely carrying out a neutral policy (e.g., Sweden). The latter is legally not obliged to remain neutral in a future conflict, thus it can change its policy at any time.

It is a particular feature of the status of permanent neutrality that the above stated sphere of international obligations were not laid down in any agreement, consequently the regulations developed as customary law in practice.

2. Switzerland, Belgium and Luxembourg

The first state to gain the status of permanent neutrality was Switzerland, which according to the intentions of the powers concluding the Napoleonic Wars, should have become a buffer state on the border of France. Articles 84 and 92 of the Act of the 1815 Vienna Congress (see *Congress of Vienna*) and the Declaration signed on November 20, 1815 in Paris by Austria, France, Great Britain, Prussia, and Russia recognized that "The neutrality and integrity [of Switzerland] and her independence from alien influence stands in the interest of all Europe." Therefore, solemnly and explicitly these powers recognized the neutrality of Switzerland and guaranteed the inviolability of her territory defined by the Vienna Congress.

Later, Belgium received the same status, and was declared a neutral state by the London Agreement concluded on November 15, 1831. Luxembourg acquired neutral status through the Agreement of May 11, 1867. The signatory states also guaranteed their territories and independence. However, at the beginning of the First World War, Germany—although, as a consequence of state succession of Prussia, it was among the guarantor states—attacked Belgium and Luxembourg, and invaded their territories. Consequently, these states drew the conclusion that the status of neutrality did not exempt them from the obligation to participate in the war, and declared that they did not wish further to maintain their status. The Peace Treaty in Versailles revoked their neutral status. At the same time, the fact that Switzerland could preserve her neutrality, both in the First and in the Second World War, undoubtedly confirmed the legal institution of neutrality.

3. Austria

Switzerland's international legal status served as an example in the settlement of the Austrian question after the Second World War. The Austrian state annexed by Germany in the *Anschluss* before the war, was occupied by the Allies at its end. Initially, its destiny was linked to that of Germany, even after 1949, when the latter was split. At the 1954 Berlin Conference, the Declaration of Neutrality and reunification of the two Germanies emerged; however, the major powers could not reach agreement. Shortly afterwards the former Soviet Union seemed to be ready to separate Austria's status from that of Germany. The Soviet Union recognized the strategic significance of the separation of the North Atlantic Treaty Organization (NATO) (see *North Atlantic Treaty Organization (NATO)*) forces stationed in the former Federal Republic of Germany from those stationed in Italy by a neutral zone consisting of Switzerland and Austria. At the same time, the NATO powers were interested in the withdrawal of Soviet troops from the territory of Austria and the maintenance of a Western political system in that country.

The Austrian-Soviet negotiations held in Moscow in April 1955, reached a formal agreement on the status of Austria. The Moscow Memorandum published after the negotiations contained the conditions, the fulfillment of which would enable the restoration of the country's sovereignty. One of these conditions was the obligation undertaken by Austria that, "Austria will undertake a neutral attitude for good, similarly to Switzerland." After the conclusion of the Austrian State Treaty and the withdrawal of the last occupying soldiers from the country, on October 26, 1955 the Austrian Parliament "with unaminous free decision and in order to ensure its independence, protect its territorial integrity and maintain internal law and order, declared eternal neutrality." The constitution was amended accordingly, and the signatories of the treaty (the four major powers) confirmed this modification on December 6 of the same year, and recognize the permanent neutrality of Austria. Later, several other states made similar declarations with which in fact the mutually binding legal obligation of the concerned parties came into being. However, on this occasion the guarantee of neutral status was not included.

4. Laos

Attempts were made to settle the increasingly complex Laotian question in the Indochinese situation with the help of the institution of permanent neutrality. As the result of the 1961-62 Geneva Conference, the Laotian Kingdom made a neutrality declaration on July 9, 1962. It promised to protect and respect its own sovereignty, independence, neutrality, and integrity, not to participate in any military alliance or in any other agreement incompatible with its neutrality, and to forbid any other state to use its territory for military purposes or for intervention in the domestic jurisdiction of other states. The other participant states—including the United States—promised to recognize the permanent neutrality of Laos and to refrain from all actions which would directly of indirectly affect the sovereignty, neutrality, and integrity of Laos. These were the first written documents which endeavored to determine and interpret the content of permanent neutrality. However, because of further developments in Indochina the provisions were not enforced in practice.

5. United Nations Membership

Certain differences can be discovered in the foreign political practice of the two presently actually existing neutral countries. The most important concerns United Nations membership. Because of the stipulations of the UN concerning collective security (namely, that the Security Council can theoretically compel any state to engage in military action against an eventual aggressor state) Switzerland did not join the world organization at that time, and although the idea of joining has occasionally emerged since then, it has not yet been accomplished.

Austria did not follow this example; after acquiring her full independence, Austria maintained its former application to be admitted to the UN, which was approved without any countervote. The Austrian government considered that the Security Council individually decides on the employment of force, and the four major powers would be in contravention of their obligation undertaken in 1955 if they compelled Austria to participate in such an act. In addition, according to Article 43 of the Charter UN members, for the purpose of force employment, undertake to make available armed forces, assistance, and facilities, including rights of passage, only in accordance with a special agreement between the Security Council and individual member states. Thus if the Security Council does not enter into such an agreement with Austria, the danger of violating neutrality does not exist.

In practice, UN membership has not caused any problem for Austria; moreover, in 1973-74 the Austrian state became a member of the Security Council and participated in the economic sanctions brought against Rhodesia in 1966 and 1968. As this only involved a civil war, it was not regarded as taking a stand in the war of two states. With regard to Switzerland, neutral status was not an obstacle in providing a

venue for the UN European Headquarters, and Switzerland also participated in the sanctions against Rhodesia. Both states sent armed forces to participate in the UN peacekeeping operations.

6. Economic Neutrality

In the 1960s, the problem of economic neutrality emerged in the case of both countries. The European Economic Community (see *European Union*) started to exercise a considerable attraction to the countries outside it, and joining or association with the organization was mentioned, both in regard to Switzerland and Austria. However, the question of membership was immediately dropped from the agenda, as the decision-making norms of the Community allow the passing of binding majority decisions, namely, the voting down of a member country in certain defined cases. And this would obviously be incompatible with the neutrality status of both countries. A lengthy debate then ensued about the problem of association. The former Soviet Union—which at that time adopted an opposing standpoint against the European Economic Community—protested sharply against Austria's association. However, ultimately the negotiations ended unsuccessfully, because of the resistance of France and Italy, among other reasons. Negotiations about Switzerland's association were interrupted even earlier. However, in 1972 both neutral countries entered into a commercial agreement with the Community, according to which a free trade zone was set up between them—that is, they lifted the customs duties on industrial products in their trade turnover. As both countries are part of the European Free Trade Association (EFTA), they practically became members of a comprehensive West European zone. No reservations against this were declared by the major powers concerned.

7. The Contribution of Switzerland and Austria

Both Switzerland and Austria have played a positive role in international relations. This has been made particularly possible since, as a result of détente (see *Détente*), opportunities for the participation of small countries in world affairs increased. They had equally the trust of the two groups of countries of opposite social systems, and in this way, had provided a bridge between East and West in several cases, both in the physical sense (by providing a venue for bilateral and multilateral meetings) and in the political sense (particularly in the case of Austria) by the endeavor to contribute to the easing of international tension. In this respect, they entered into successful cooperation with other neutral and nonaligned states. Their cooperation was particularly useful at the Madrid follow-up conference of the Helsinki process.

See also: *Costa Rica: Neutrality; Nonalignment*

Bibliography ———————————————

Birnbaum K, Neuhold H (ed.) 1982 *Neutrality and Non-Alignment in Europe: The Laxenburg Papers*. Austrian Institute for International Affairs, (AHA) Vienna

Bonjour E 1978 *Geschichte der schweizerischen Neutralität, Helbing und Lichtenhahn*. Basel

Ginther K 1975 *Neutralität und Neutralitätspolitik*. Springer, Vienna

Kunz J L 1956 Austria's permanent neutrality. *Am. J. of Int. Law* 50

Lalive J-F 1974 International organization and neutrality. *Br. Yearb. of Int. Law* 24

Verdross A 1977 *Die immerwahrende Neutralität Österreichs*. Verlag für Geschichte und Politik, Vienna

Verosta S 1967 *Die dauernde Neutralität: Ein Grundriss*. Manzsche Verlags-und Universitäts buchhandlung, Vienna

LÁSZLÓ VALKI

New Ethics in the Industrialized and Informationalized Society

1. Introductory Remarks

Today's world is at a crossroads and in a transitional dilemma, with the signs of optimism and pessimism equally viable and equally potent. On one hand, a dawn of new age, qualitatively different from the previous ones, is opening grandiosely before our eyes with space exploration, genetic engineering, and computopia and a myriad of other technological breakthroughs that promise a bright future. On the other hand, our world is, however, being torn apart by racial, religious, ethnical and social conflicts as never before. The doomsday signs abound.

What then is the primary force behind these complex, paradoxical and antinomic signs?

The major causal factors that bring forth these paradoxical and antinomic phenomena stem from the dual forces of industrialization and gone so far and so fast that the advanced societies are, according to Daniel Bell, moving into the stage of the "post-industrial era." Kenneth Boulding sees of the emergent "post-industrial age." Alvin Tofler also echoes Bell and Boulding by saying that the smoke-stack industries are giving ways to more smooth and sophisticated "third-wave industries."

What then is the force bringing forth the post-industrial and post-civilization third wave changes? It is none other than the rapid process of informationization. Just as capital has been the backbone of industries in the past, information is fast supplanting capital as the primary engine of the "post-industrial society." As Marshall MacLuhan's adage goes, we live in a "global village" created by the "information superhighway." In *Racing Toward 2001*, Russell Chandeler enumerates the following "possible scenarios" of the future information age:

(a) "Our available information base will increase dramatically"—With the capability to reproduce the equivalent of 1,000 books on just one 3.5-inch compact disk, a personal library of 10,000 volumes will be within reach of anyone with a personal computer.

(b) "Low-cost memories will enable us to store unlimited information"—Continuous newscasts and other information will be delivered through local fiber optic networks to our homes.

(c) "Multiple video channels provided by both long-distance and local networks offer the potential for people at widely separate location to participate simultaneously in business meetings"—Inter-active video conferences have already been used very successfully, but worldwide networks will connect people globally.

(d) "Technology, through robots and artificial intelligence, will revolutionarize workplace and speed up the way many tasks are performed"—Robots and artificial intelligence will be used by manufacturers to custom-design and produce goods and control inventories as well as construct the machines.

In *The Road Ahead*, Bill Gates of Microsoft writes: "There will be a day, not far distant, when you will be able to conduct business, study, explore the world and its cultures, call up any great entertainment, make friends, attend neighborhood markets, and show pictures to distant relatives—without leaving your desk or armchair. Instead of the "information superhighway," he talks about "Information At Your Fingertips," for information has become easily accessible to anyone eager to learn. Through the Internet (see *Internet: A New Vehicle for Global Peace Efforts*), one can gain access to every kind of information at his finger tip.

2. Antinomic Phenomena in the Information Age

However, we should not lose sight of the other side of the coin. While we consider these technological wonders at the threshold of the third millennium, we should at the same time grasp the limitations and potential harms inherent in information technology.

Information is caught on the horns of dilemma plagued with counter-productive results.

The first is the problem of "information indigestion." The explosive amount of information is such that nobody, however intelligent, could hope to keep up to date with it, even in a quite narrow field of specialty. If a man tries to absorb every information available to him, he is bound to suffer from digestive disorder. Furthermore, we must note that the vast bulk of "information" is rubbish, the intellectual equivalent of junk mail.

The second is the problem of "the Gresham's law." The "principle that bad money will drive good money out of circulation" is also operating here. When two or more kinds of information of seemingly equal importance but unequal intrinsic values are in circulation at the same time, the one of less value will drive away the one of greater value. In the Internet, pornography—writings and pictures intended to arouse sexual desires—can be readily accessible to teenagers. Recently, it was reported in the press that some people use the computer networks for gambling.

The third is the problem of "individual privacy." The power and versatility of digital technology has raised a new concern about individual privacy. Since any amount of data can be stored in the computer, the government tends to put all sorts of information on individual citizens. Such an action must be condemned as an illegal invasion into the privacy, but most of the government agencies seem to disregard such a protest. The information society should serve all of its citizens, but it tends to serve the technically sophisticated and economically privileged people. Also, it should be noted that "national security" is being endangered. If an enemy agent breaks into the secret code of a government, he may gain access to all sorts of information about the nation.

The last, but certainly not the least, is the problem of "illicit use of information." As a saying goes, "Information misused is worse than sheer ignorance." Today, rotten politicians are making use of the sophisticated information networks to manipulate and deceive their opponents as we saw in the Watergate case. Business firms are doing the same in their efforts to crush their competitive companies. Of course, it is not the politicians nor the businessmen who are using scientific information as the tool of evildoing. In Japan, the yakuza groups, the organized gangsters, have control over activities such a gambling, prostitution, labor racketeering, and loan-sharking within each territory through the use of their well-lubricated information networks. In the United States, the Mafias import their narcotics from Colombia and the "golden triangle" of Thailand and Myanmar by using airplanes and ships through the use of sophisticated electronics communication.

We see clear antinomic signs—the signs of historical retrogression. In the *Beginning of the End*, Tim Lahaye writes, "Today, man's inhumanity to his fellow man is one of three most conspicuous elements of history. At no time in world history has there been so much worldwide grief, effecting so many people, as has existed in the recent decades. More wars, revolutions, insurrections, and plagues have beset mankind than in any comparable period in history. More people are fearful, uptight, and filled with heartache than ever before."

3. The Principal Cause of Today's Crisis

We realize that the real source of economic ruin, social disarray, political marginalization, and ecological catastrophe is in the main caused by ethical anarchy. The crisis is not so much sociopolitical as it is moral and spiritual. The real culprit is within ourselves.

The modern man in this information age has become, in the words of Herbert Marcuse, "one dimensional." Money has become his sole yardstick of success. Covetous for material possessions, proud and extremely egocentric, he thinks about nothing but his own selfish desires. Sexual perversion is rampant in today's advanced societies. Homosexuality is prevalent. In San Francisco, homosexuals have been granted marriage licenses. As a result, AIDS has become a most deadly disease in many countries.

In most advanced societies, the greatest single problem is the nationwide breakdown of the home and soaring divorce rate. The US Census Bureau gave, for instance, the following figures: In 1920, 1 divorce for every 7 marriages; in 1960, 1 divorce for every 4 marriages; in 1972, 1 divorce for every 3 marriages, and today, it is the ratio of 1 to 2. In *Against the Night*, Chuck Coleson maintains that we are coming into a new dark age, an age of moral and ethical nightfall.

Let us now take the violent student demonstration on the campus of Yonsei University—the worst of its kind in recent decades in Korea. Why? Why? Why? Most, if not all, of us were tormented by this tantalizing question for days with eyes glued to TV wondering what would be the outcome of this unusually violent student demonstration that lasted for 9 days. Why were these students so militant in their pitched battle against the riot police, causing so many casualties on the both sides, including one death? The scenes of the demonstration appearing on TV looked like frontline military combats.

Do those students really believe in the *Juche* ideology of North Korea? Are they really determined to give their lives for the sake of the national unification in line with the North Korean propaganda? To me, however, Ms. Mary B. Kim's analysis that appeared on the *Korea Herald* seems to have touched the core of the answer. She wrote, "Undermotivated in their scholarly pursuits in an increasingly materialistic society, they are left with a spiritual vacuum." Amid material affluence, we see a spiritual vacuum.

How can we then rectify the situation?

4. The Renaissance of the Changeless Ethical Principles

Viewed from this deep socio-psychological perspective, Ms. Mary Kim's diagnosis of the crisis of our college students becomes obvious. In the past, our ideological education always told them that Communism is wrong and Liberal Democracy is right. With the downfall of the Soviet system, Communism has been proven wrong. But what then is the state of Liberal Democracy in our country? To our dismay, liberty in our society has degenerated into licentiousness and democracy into a mobocracy. Capitalism no longer has the Protestant ethics that Max Weber so vehemently claimed. On the contrary, it is run by the Law of the Jungle.

By placing material values at the apex of his hierarchy of values, our society has been too busy to make money. During the past few decades, the goal of the government has been invariably set in terms of the growth of GNP. Personal happiness has been equated with how much personal income one makes per annum. In a certain sense, mammonism has taken over the role of Liberal Democracy. Take, for instance, the case of the America-educated professor who murdered his father to inherit his money. As Ms. Kim laments, the young people are "left with a spiritual vacuum."

Without justifying the reckless actions of those radical students, I feel that responsibility of the violent demonstration that we witnessed should be borne by the older generation, namely my generation. We have not given our youth any spiritual cause to fight for. As the Bible says, "man shall not live by bread alone." A spiritual being, man by nature wants struggle for a higher cause than his own selfish desire. "Give me liberty or give me death" was not the cry of only one person, Patrick Henry. Kim Koo, the greatest patriot of our times, cried out, "Our national reunification is my heart's desire even in my dream."

Entrapped by mammonism, the older generation has lost their most precious innate ability—the ability of loving others. Most of us are being controlled by their sensual and carnal desires alone. Extremely self-centered, modern man is devoid of the sense of social responsibility. Extremely egoistic, his ego erects its center in itself as the axis of all the universal whole.

What then is the most effective remedial measure available? It is always so much easier to talk about "what" and "why" of the ethical anarchy than to find out "how" to resolve the crisis.

To rectify the agonizing situation, what is needed is not a mere new ideological education but what President Vaclav Havel of the Republic of Czechs calls "the revolution in the realm of human consciousness." The basis for spiritual revolution is found in the teachings of the ancient saints—the "golden rule" in human relations: We must treat others as we wish others to treat us. We must make a commitment to respect life, dignity, individuality and freedom of other people, so that every person is treated humanely.

How can we then transform a person from his innate egoism to altruism? In religion, this process is called "conversion." But in secular universities, we cannot apply the same method of religious organizations.

However, we, educators, can teach our students what psychologists call "enlightened self-interest." This is a real workable paradigm shift. There is a universal moral law that has worked in human history ever since man appeared on the earth. The essence of this moral law is rather simple. Everyone, educated or illiterate, can enrich his life by practicing this law: In order to gain, you should serve others. "Give, and it will be given to you. A good measure, pressed down, shaken together and running over, will be poured into your lap," said the Master.

This golden rule can be applied in international relations as well. In history, those nations which were willing to assist other weak nations prospered. When the United States was the number one donor nation, it was at the apex of prosperity. Korea used to be a receiving nation in the past, but now it has become a giving nation. For two years in the past, I served as chairman of the Rice of Love of the Korean Church. We have given rice to 14 countries in need. The rich psychological compensation we receive as the result of our giving cannot be measured by any monetary yardstick.

In this sense, I strongly endorse Young Seek Choue's "The Second Renaissance Movement" (see *Second Renaissance*). The renaissance in Italy during the 14-15th century was not the mere restoration of the Greco-Roman classics. It was not a movement to return to the past. Rather, it was a forward-looking movement by regaining the wisdom of the past. What is needed today urgently and imperatively is to regain humanity in our minds by reviving the changeless ethical principles based on the moral law operation in human history. By the renaissance of the ancient tradition of the "golden rule" through the paradigm shift of "enlightened self-interest," we can, I believe, resolve the current crisis of the world. Who should take the major burden of this movement? It will be none other than the educators who mold the characters of their students, the leaders of the 21st century.

WON SUL LEE

New International Economic Order (NIEO)

The demand for a new international economic order (NIEO) was raised formally in 1974 by the states of the developing nations and carried by a majority vote in the sixth special session of the United Nations General Assembly. It should be noted that the demand for a remodeling of the world economic system and some of the central single demands of the NIEO were, since the beginning of the UN Conference on Trade and Development (UNCTAD) in 1964, repeatedly the subject of negotiations between industrialized and developing countries. That the presentation of a conceptional, compact, and politically solid demand by the developing nations for a reorganization of the world economy only came about in 1974 cohered with a series of both agricultural and political factors, the most essential points of which are outlined briefly below.

(a) The growing bitterness of developing countries over unfulfilled demands made to industrialized countries in a series of international conferences.

(b) The crisis of development altogether, as seen in the increase of underdevelopment and poverty in the developing countries.

(c) The crisis of politics toward developing countries, which became evident in the failure of conventional aid to developing countries, for example, in the failure of the concept of "aid through trade."

(d) The leading role played by the nonaligned movement which within a few years had raised the question of the developing countries to a political issue of the first order (see *Nonalignment*). For example, it was stated in an "explanation of nonalignment and economic progress" of the heads of state and government of nonaligned countries in Lusaka in September 1970 that: "The continuation of a persisting unjust economic system in today's neocolonialism inherited from the colonial past is an impediment to the deliverance from poverty and from the fetters of economic dependence. The quickly deepening rift between rich and poor is a threat to international peace and international security." Here for the first time the United Nations Organization (see *Status and Role of the United Nations*) was summoned to use the apparatus at its disposal for a swift remodeling of the world economic system in the areas of commerce, finance, and technology in order to allow economic cooperation to replace predominance.

(e) The constantly intensifying cooperation of the nonaligned movement with the pressure group of the states of the Third World, namely the Group of 77, not lastly conditional on the membership of many states of the Third World in both organizations.

(f) The widespread opinion that the "old" world economic order had proved itself incapable of doing justice to the specific interests of the growing number of states obtaining political sovereignty as a result of decolonialization.

(g) The "Energy Crisis" 1973-74 and the success of the Organization of Petroleum-Exporting Countries (OPEC) in employing oil as a political instrument in obtaining economic power.

(h) And finally the crisis of international relations and organizations characterized by a shifting of weight from the questions of the East-West conflicts to those of the North-South "problematique," in the course of decolonialization of further parts of Asia and Africa in the 1960s more and more young states of the Third World joined the United Nations and made this increasingly a political forum at which they discussed and further dealt with their specific interests and wishes. According to the principle of "one state, one vote" the UN General Assembly in particular could in time be dominated by Third World states.

While the factors outlined above changed the world's political climate in favor of the developing countries, it is indisputable that the "oil crisis" of 1973 was the key factor in stimulating the demand for a New International Economic Order. The officiating president of the nonaligned movement, the Algerian head of state Boumediene, called a special conference of the UN General Assembly as a countermove to an energy conference of the industrialized countries called for February 1974 in Washington DC by the United States. This Sixth Special Session of the UN General Assembly took place from April 9-May 2, 1974 in New York. On May 1 the Declaration and Programme of Action for the Establishment of a New International Economic Order was passed (UN Doc. A/Res 3201 and 3202 (S-NA)).

Although the contents of the declaration had yet to be realized and still existed at most as a "programmatic outline" or "a subject of dispute and negotiation" between industrialized and developing countries, the demand for an NIEO represented for the industrialized countries a weighty political and economic challenge. It aimed, in essence, for a fundamental change in the relations between North and South in favor of the interests of the developing countries and therefore called into question the time-honored privileges of the industrialized countries. The Declaration and the Programme of Action were the subject of negotiations in all UNCTAD as well as UNIDO conferences. Some of the most crucial statements under discussion were:

Full permanent sovereignty of every State over its national resources and all economic activities including the right to nationalization or transfer of ownership to its nationals. (Declaration; 4e)

Just and equitable relationship between the prices of:

... goods exported by developing countries and the prices of goods imported by them with the aim of bringing about sustained improvement in their unsatisfactory terms of trade and the expansion of the world economy. (Declaration; 4j)

... to work for a link between the prices of exports of developing countries and the prices of their imports from developed countries. (Programme of Action; 1, 1d)

Improving the competitiveness of natural materials facing competition from synthetic substitutes. (Declaration; 4m)

Preferential and non-reciprocal treatment for developing countries wherever feasible, in all fields of international economic co-operation. (Declaration; 4n)

Facilitating the role which producers' associations may play within the framework of international co-operation . . . . (Declaration; 4t)

To take measures to promote the processing of raw materials in the producer developing countries. (Programme of Action; 1, 1g)

... each developed country should facilitate the expansion of imports from developing countries. (Programme of Action 1, 3a(v))

... receipts from customs duties, taxes and other protective measure should be reimbursed in full to the exporting, developing countries or devoted to providing additional resources to meet their development needs. (Programme of Action; 1, 3(vi))

Implementation, improvement and enlargement of the Generalized System of Preferences for exports of agricultural primary commodities, manufactures and semi-manufactures from developing countries . . . (Programme of Action; 1, 3a (x))

To promote an increasing and equitable participation of developing countries in the world shipping tonnage (Programme of Action; 1, 4(i))

Measures to eliminate the instability of the international monetary system . . . (Programme of Action; 11, 1b)

The developed countries should encourage investors to finance industrial production projects, particularly export-oriented production, in developing countries, in agreement with the latter and within the context of their laws and regulations. (Programme of Action; II, 16)

To give access on improved terms to modern technology and the adaptation of that technology, as appropriate to specific economic, social and ecological conditions and varying stages of development in developing countries. (Programme of Action; IV)

... an international code of conduct for transnational corporations in order to ... prevent interference in the internal affairs ... regulate the repatriation of the profits accruing from their operations taking into account the legitimate interests of all parties concerned-promote reinvestment of their profits in developing countries. (Programme of Action; V)

The Charter of Economic Rights and Duties of States represents the most important document for the NIEO, which at the twenty-ninth UN General Assembly on December 12, 1974 was passed as a "quasi-legal act" by 120 states. The United States and the European Community states of the then Federal Republic of Germany, the United Kingdom, Belgium, Luxembourg, and Denmark voted against the Charter because on 3 of the 34 article agreement could not be reached. The first area of disagreement concerned the question of the expropriation and indemnity of foreign investments (Art. 2), because in cases of dispute this allowed for the possibility of nationalization according to the internal laws of the nationalizing state; the second concerned the right of states to form producer cartels in the area of raw materials (Art. 5) in order to develop their national economies and therefore achieve a stable financing of their development: and the third concerned the statesí endeavors to work toward the adjustment of developing countreisé export prices to their import prices (known as "prices indexing") which gave rise to the fear of a controlled world economy amongst industrialized countries.

However, closer analysis showed that the Declaration and the Charter were in no way aimed toward the creation of a basic new order but, rather, in principle adhered to the conventional mechanism of the international division of labor and were essentially trade oriented on nature. For example, Article 14 of the Charter-obliged every state to help on furthering a constant and increasing expansion and liberalization of world trade and an improvement of the well-being and standard of living of all nations. It also called upon all states to work together for the management of world trade through the gradual removal of trade impediments and the improvement of the international framework. Nevertheless, proposals regarding the politics of raw materials did contain aspects which could give the producing countries a "bigger slice of the cake." They can be summarized as follows:

(a) Increase in the profits gained by exporting raw materials;

(b) Increased control over the production, marketing, and processing of raw materials by transnational corporations;

(c) Increased involvement in the marketing and processing of raw materials.

These and other demands were however basically nothing more than a corrective mechanism of the "character" of free international competition which always tended to concede advantages of the weak in favor of the strong. In brief they were to serve, as they do internally in many an industrialized country with a social market economy, to protect the weak through special flanking measures.

Misgivings and objections to the specific elements of the proposal for a New International Economic Order were not confined to governments alone. The political debate was mirrored in discussions in academic circles. Three stances were identified:

(a) Those who welcomed the demands of the Third World states for an NIEO without criticism and presumed that a quick solution to the problems of the developing countries will flow from its establishment.

(b) Those who saw and feared in the demands a tendency towards "controlled economy" although they were in favor of an improved integration of developing countries within the international division of labor.

(c) Those who saw, on the one hand, the demands for an NIEO as the expression of the self-interest of Third World elites and, on the other hand, an important prerequisite for the success of every economical and political reform in "dissociation" from Third World economics.

Since the mid-seventies representatives of the developing countries were increasingly embittered over the persisting resistance of the industrialized countries against structural reforms and reinforced transfer of resources. As a consequence, their demands grew even more radical which in turn was met with criticism and rejection by the public of the West, an attitude progressively taken on by the World Organization itself. The developing countries had not only noticeably lost respect but, as a result, the industrialized countries withdrew from a number of special organizations, such as the United States from the UNESCO in 1984, after the developing countries had too rigorously carried through their position with them.

Neither the UNCTAD conferences nor 30 additional international conferences, negotiating the demands of the developing countries, brought about any visible results. Thus the countries of the South increasingly realized that global demands connected with the creation of a New Economic World Order did not lead any further. In view of drastic political changes in the entire world after the fall of the Soviet imperium and the end of the East-West conflict as such, utilized to their advantage by the states of the Third World to carry through their demands, even within the UN, a remodeling of international economic relations was initiated in the early nineties. Evidence for this change is demonstrated by the Res. S-18/3 of May 1, 1990 on the "Economic Cooperation of States," accepted by common consent. It emphasizes both the responsibility of each individual state for its own development and the special possibilities of influence of the industrialized nations on the world economy and the consequences that will evolve. With this new orientation the debate on the creation of a New International Economic Order which would have satisfied the conceptions and needs of the states of the South will probably have come to an end.

See also: *Disarmament and Development; North-South Conflict; United Nations Charter; World Peace Order, Dimensions of a*

Bibliography ———————————

Alting von Geusau F M A (ed.) 1977 *The Lome Convention and New International Economic Order.* Leyden

Bhagwati J N (ed.) 1977 *The New International Economic Order: The North-South Debate.* MIT Press, Cambridge, Massachusetts

Commission of the European Communities 1982 *Memorandum on the Community's Development Politics.* Brussels

Eisold H, Hasenpflug R (eds.) 1984 Time for reorientation in Lome III ? *Intereconomics* 19(2)

Ferdowsi M A (ed.) 1983 *Die Verträge von Lome zwischen Modell und Mythos: Zur Entwicklungspolitik der EG in der Dritten Welt.* Minerva-Publication, Munich

Frey-Wouters A E 1980 *The European Community and the Third World: The Lome-Convention and its Impact.* New York

Galtung J 1978a Some reflections on the "new international economic order"—the old, the new, and the future. In: Galtung J (ed.) 1978 *Toward Self-Reliance and Global Interdependence: Reflections on a New International Order and North South Cooperation.* Canadian International Development Agency, Ottawa, Ontario

Galtung J 1978b Poor countries vs rich: Poor people vs rich—whom will the NIEO benefit? In: Galtung J (ed.) *Toward Self-reliance and Global Interdependence: Reflection on a New International Order and North-South Cooperation.* Canadian International Development Agency, Ottawa, Ontario

Pisani E 1983 Les Enjeux de la Convention de Lome. Aout

Sauvant K P, Hasenpflug H (eds.) 1978 *The New International Economic Order: Confrontation or Cooperation between North and South?* Westview Press, Boulder, Co

MIR A. FERDOWSI

New Morality for the Global Community

1. Introduction

Sitting comfortably in a Glasgow flat far away from the sweltering heat of the Seoul summer, I nonetheless have been feverishly infatuated with the disturbing world news. They are not in small numbers, from the capricious fates of the Bosnian war to the swaggering Gaullist stubborn resistance to the hybrid antinuclear protests. We have nourished the illusion that the world is nearer the new order of international understanding and cooperation. It is now clear that we got it wrong. National and international behavior still seems to be primarily on a struggle for power, interests and gains. Seeing such global problems, I ask myself the conventional question: should there be no discussions on the moral constitution of the global world?

'Globalization' (see *Globalization*) has become an increasingly important theme in the social sciences since the begining of the 90's and generated the debates about various problems concerning its processes, and so it is fair to expect that the very moral nature of globalization has been looked into; and yet it is surprising that it has been largely left out and remained unexplored. The inheritance of social sciences is in a fundamental way deeper than that of value-free science. They were cast within the terms of moral reconstruction, as their founders, despite crucial differences, equally illustrated. Since social science began to be conceived in narrow 'scientific terms,' morality has been reduced to a personal decision to make within the private sphere. The apple has fallen a very long way from the tree. The globalization theorists have helpfully illuminated the ways the global world is being constructed through political, economic, and cultural interdependence. But they have so far failed to recover and sustain a moral voice within their own disciplines.

This paper intends to look at the globalization of the environmental concerns by heightening the connections between social analysis and morality.

2. The Images of Globality

Social sciences have long been interested in social change on the global scale, proposing various vocabularies such as diffusion, modernization, development/underdevelopment, world-system, internationalization, lately globalization. All of these refer to the processes by which the populace of the world is becoming more incorporated into a single world, through a technological, economic, political, and cultural synchronization or hybridization. It is not difficult to find this trend in the major classical sociological versions. In the words of Marx, it was already prognosticated that "National differences and antagonism between peoples are daily more and more vanishing, owing to the development of the bourgeoisie, to freedom of commerce, to the world market, to uniformity in the mode of production and in the conditions of life corresponding thereto" (Marx 1988 p. 73). Marx's theory is most explicitly committed to the globalization of capitalist development. In parallel, Weber made a profound contribution to the conceptualization of rationalization as the globalizing process. Although one can hardly disagree with the unmatched brilliance of Weber's comparative-historical scholarship, one may well be tempted to challenge his famous thesis of the 'Protestant Ethic' that the emergence of bourgeois capitalism is 'unique to the West,' and, hence, extend significantly his argument about the iron cage of bureaucratic rationalization (Weber 1930). A similar comment may be made on Durkheim's theories of differentiation as a global social change (Durkheim 1964).

Some measure of world-wide expansion or globalization existed for centuries, even before the rise of modern nation-states (Waters 1995). However, as more recent decades testify, it has unconceivably exploded in terms of intensities, rates, levels, velocities. The global flow of goods, capital, services, personnel, ideas sees no closed boundaries. The recent focus on globalization is the kind of intellectual exercise that captures something already out there ready to be captured, a widely perceived but not yet fully articulated reality that has long begged for analytic attention. Even though the word 'global' is over 400 years old, it was not recognized as a significant concept in social sciences until the early or the mid-1980's, when R. Robertson and others began to include the word in the titles of their published works. The term 'globalization' as a social process is still not widely used, but is gaining its currency in social sciences (Waters 1995 pp. 2-3).

Globalization has various themes, but it can be defined as a process "in which the constraints of geography on social and cultural arrangements recede and in which people become increasingly aware that they are receding" (Waters 1995 p. 3). Production,

consumption, and exchanges are no longer rooted in localized or nationalized factories, shops, and markets. Territorial boundaries that are coterminous with nation-states tend to have different spatial meanings. Furthermore, in contemporary society the rapid circulation of information on the global scale has come about through electronic communication, with computers as its most potent carrier (see *Internet: A New Vehicle for Global Peace Efforts*). Extensive media technology turns the world more and more into a 'global village.' Many from different disciplines have rushed to the globalization paradigm. In economics, the focus is on the global economy generated by the expansion of capitalist market relations and the internationalization of production and finance. Globalization in political science refers to global politics where the density of interstate relations is ever increasing. In anthropology and sociology, the focus is on the spread of science and technology, global communication, standardization, cultural interpenetration and interaction. Globalization embraces virtually every aspect of contemporary life and represents all sorts of world images.

Certain intrinsic conflicts are therefore understandable as an inherent tendency of globalization (Park 1994a). One of the most central seems to be between the structurally boundless possibilities of resource accumulation and appropriation and the cognitively bounded pursuit of interests. The structural constraints are shattered, but the deep cognitive moulds are hardly opened up. Even after decades of explosive growth in globalization, nation-states hold fast to their centuries old dream of imperializing empires. Examine the many new nations which, emancipated from the Western powers, follow and behave just like the classical imperialist examples of their former masters such as England and France. Globalization is no guarantee of world peace and stability. It generates new possibilities for conflicts, as it opens up new structural time-spaces. This calls for critical self-understanding and reflection. Before we come to this discussion, let us briefly look into the global condition where conflicts arise.

3. The Rise of Global Conflicts

The manner in which global conflicts arise is manifold and perceived at various levels, but there is one which becomes particularly salient. For good or ill, nation-states are thrown in a global conceptualization of their historical and political projects, which in turn challenges their traditional notion of sovereignty. There must be a readjustment, a conscious balancing between 'the national' and 'the global,' and a gradual sliding into the global space. The processes of globalization are not exhaustively understood only at the institutional levels; their embodiments are brought about by historical agents, transforming actors, and carriers of new values. It is, however, not to be construed that agency does not originate from the institutional loci, and vice versa. Conflicts of a global nature emerge from the collision of institutional arrangements with agents.

Cross-cutting these two levels (institutional and agency), we arrive at a fourfold typology as shown below:

Table 1. The Types of Global Conflicts

		level of agency	
		national	global
level of institution	national	1	3
	global	2	4

We may illustrate these types with reference to the environmental problems.

3.1 This may be called 'the Tobacco type.' Consider the movement against the tabacco import in Korea in the late 80's. The YMCA initiated a campaign to halt imports of tobacco from the United States. For them, it is just like imports of hazardous waste from an industrialized country that pose a threat to health and the environment. This type of conflict is characterized by disagreement between two sides divided by national boundaries. The powerful nation-states advance the interests of their corporations with little concern about human health in other countries. The national businesses often tend to identify more with core business interest in the West rather than with people of their own peripheral region (see *Imperialism*). Institutional behavior and agency are primarily based on core-periphery interest, yet to be incorporated into the global processes. Conflicts arise principally between two national boundaries.

3.2 This may be conceived of as 'the Muruora type.' An action by state collides with the global action groups. In light of the new global circumstances, no nation-state can exercise its sovereignty as a legal right of state without modifying it. The global condition makes it possible for the environmental groups to connect the local with the global by asserting that states are obliged to limit sovereignty for inhabitants of the earth as a common home. The world public is beginning to share the causes of common environ-

mental problems such as global pollution. Conflicts arose when the state and the carriers of global environmental causes clash against each other. This cannot be better illustrated by the French operation to seize the Greenpeace ship Rainbow Warrior II near the Muruora nuclear test site in French Polynesia. It took place ironically, in July 1995, exactly a decade after the sinking of the first Rainbow Warrior by the French secret service in Auckland Harbour. The second Greenpeace vessel breached the exclusion zone around the test site to protest Jacques Chirac's decision to carry out underground nuclear tests. The French commandos stormed the vessel, smashing windows and tear-gasing the cabin. The protesters aboard shut themselves in the radio room and broadcast the situation to the world. Most of the 22 crew, three passengers and six journalist on board were detained on shore (*The Independent*, July 11, 1995). The drama goes on, as the French government has announced to postpone the test only to this September.

3.3 This may be represented as 'the China type.' The issues such as air pollution, global warming, and ozone depletion are addressed at the national and international levels. Of these, ozone depletion problem is the area in which there has been much progress in consensus building. United Nations Environment Programme began to examine the problem in 1978 and held a global convention in Vienna in 1985. This culminated into the Montreal Protocol which entered into force in 1992. China, along with many of the so-called Third World states has not ratified it. There is no need to mention that China is a conspicuous case, since it has the largest population and rapidly growing industrial sector. This type points to the locus of conflict between the nation-states and the international protocols to regulate and safeguard the earth's stability.

3.4 This may be termed as 'the Convention type.' Ever since public concern was heightened by a series of environmental disasters in the 60's and the 70's, there has been a rapid growth of environmental interest groups called NGOs (see *Non-governmental Organizations (NGOs)*). They come into conflict with the transnational corporations, which have been able to create a global network of alliances and have an interest in maximizing profits by means of the low-cost production and disposal which is possible in the non-Western countries. In the international conferences, environmental NGOs press for more drastic measure such as a ban on exports of hazardous wastes and products, and thus they come to align with developing countries. Sometimes, they criticize the industrialized countries for their refusal to commit to specific steps to reduce their own industrial pollution and push for significant reduction of global inequities. The locus of conflict is among/between environmental interest groups and the international bodies of nation-states.

Given that globalization is a virtually unavoidable pattern of social change, it becomes difficult to keep the national/indigenous completely divorced from the global/transnational; and so conflicts tend to shift to the global level. As seen in type 1, the problem of imports/exports of hazardous product or waste is likely to transform into type 2 or type 3, and eventually type 4. The idea of the fragmentation of the human problem as an isolated unit is clearly obsolete and practically untenable in a globalized world. Any problem has global implications. It is particularly so in the area of the environment, because the public has most readily become aware of the earth as a single environmental space. In the past, issues such as waste disposal, resource shortages, and air quality were considered as national problems and, consequently, as something for each country to tackle. During the past few decades, much of this situation has changed. As the new scientific findings have shown more about the specific causes of the environmental damages, they have found their way into the global media, by which the public has come to have a heightened sense of crisis about life on earth. There is a growing awareness that damage in one part of the world, caused by one state or one corporation, can have a direct effect on the rest of the world. It is precisely at this point that the existing claims of sovereignty come into question, as the new perception of the 'global community' looms large in the minds of the people of the world.

4. For a New Moral Basis

If it is right that the space of life has expanded to such an extent that it is beginning to be perceived as the global community, it has to be asked: could we expect to achieve a true community while continuing to employ the existing approaches to global problems? We have to examine the basis on which various agents and institutions carry on their respective projects. This will be discussed within the context of critical self-understanding. Durkheim was probably the first in the history of sociological thought who linked the process of social change to the morality of society (see *Social Progress and Human Survival*).

He believed that society moves in the direction of growing division of labor and functional differentiation, and proposed a dichotomous typology of societies as a chronological scheme. The isolated, self-sufficient, uniform 'mechanical solidarity' turns into highly differentiated, mutually dependent, diversified 'organic solidarity.' This change brings about a breakdown or weakening of the moral order of the former and demands for a new moral order relevant to the latter (Durkheim 1964). Following him, it may be stated that when demographic density is low, familistic morality served well as the basis of social bonds, as exemplified in the case of the kinship society. With a high demographic density, society can no longer be characterized as intimate and close-knitted, and thus need more open, more inclusive moral values. What Durkheim really meant was, then, a renewal of the moral community.

Regarding the global condition, we are faced with the problem of that version of morality that can be developed to have a decisive impact on human interactions, give a guide to forming and sustaining global solidarity, and help resolve global conflicts. This task involves a critical assessment of the underlying assumptions about the patterns of institutional behavior and of human action. In order to accomplish this task, we must discuss at least two kinds of orientation which seem to be responsible for the pathological situation of global life, destroying the environment and threatening the survival of humanity. The first is economism which is closely tied to the practical understanding of everyday life in modern society, and the second is statism which is to maintain and defend the actions of the nation-states with old claims of sovereignty.

4.1 Economism has to do with the modern project that humanity would be able to master the physical world through the development of scientific-technical knowledge. Ironically both market capitalism and socialist command economy have identified development with the advance of technology and the domination of the natural world. Modernization was conceived as a transformation of pre-industrial society into an industrial society that had technical capabilities for sustained economic development and concomitant social reorganization, as characterized in the 'economically' prosperous Western societies. Economism is a world view that defines the interests and values on the basis of calculating costs and gains, fosters a sheer competition with each other for profits that often dispenses with a sense of human dignity, and results in the failure to develop and transmit a sense of solidarity among societal members. All tenets seem to have surrendered to economic growth and development. Transnational corporations have an inherent tendency to go into areas that best serve their own profits and struggle for more gains, and thus cause environmental degradation, both directly and indirectly. The priority of economistic interests and values has been established, on a world-wide scale, as the taken-for-granted world view of modern life, that governs not only corporation behavior, but also everyday interactions and interpersonal relations.

An adequate global vision must challenge the hegemony of the current 'economistic' logic. It needs to propose a new framework that lays ground for a global morality within which the interests and values can be redefined beyond the utilitarian calculus and the scope of human concern can be expanded beyond the confines of technical-instrumental civilization. This does not demand a return to some romantic golden age, but advocates engaging critically with the control and domination of the physical world as the basis of development and the notion of infinite appropriation as the source of well-being. To construct a sustainable globe, the globalization of economic exploitation must be checked. For these purposes, the creative religious and cultural resources of many different traditions must be mobilized to provide alternative moral visions of how we can better collectively live within our global space with an acute sense of collective responsibility for the consequences of our actions on a global scale. The potential alternative moral visions are often compromised and blocked by being subordinated to the advance of economistic instrumentalism. For example, the success story of the so-called 'Four Tigers' of the newly developing countries in Asia is related to the Confucian ethos, and yet its other side is a case of the uncritical adherence of Confucian tradition to economism (Park 1994b, 1995) (see *Confucianism and Neo-confucianism*). It is therefore required that the alternative visions of life be tested in practice.

4.2 Statism has to do with the traditional state-centric realism that states are primarily perceived as institutions and actors to play the role by self-interest, inevitably to engage in a struggle for power and domination. The process of state-building originally began from European feudalism and subsequently expanded through both concentralization and colonialization, creating opportunity for further interests. Capitalist or not, state power has been used to promote the interests of the states. Third World revolu-

tions since World War II, too, have broken the formal relations of colonial dependency and created sovereignty, and followed their former masters' steps to further their own interests. The global field that is created by the rapid development of a multinational structure provides opportunities for interests of which states take advantage. Global conflicts emerge as nation-states as both institutions and agents seek to increase control over global resources through a range of political and military measures. The powerful nations tend to perpetuate its power and domination in such a way that the old relations of colonial dependency is virtually recreated. In this sense, a powerful modern state is practically a 'monarchy' in the modern guise. States should not be viewed simply as instruments of dominant class interests nor should their policies be determined by economic conditions (Skocpol 1994). Nonetheless, states seek to use the global field to promote 'state egoism,' not to develop a new sense of responsibility capable of acting as moral institutions. They identify with the utilitarian interests and values, and act on the basis of calculation of costs and benefits, treating the physical world as a resource to be exploited for the ends of states (see *Conflict and Peace: Class versus Structural School*).

A new vision of the states is required to go beyond such statism which justifies national and international behavior primarily based on power, domination, and self-interests. This statism thus creates a framework of conflicting relationships between and among nation-states, in which resources are appropriated and controlled. But in the global condition, where states both as sole agents and real institutions are irrelevant, if not withering away, a more appropriate notion of the nation-states is needed, not restricted to economistic and militaristic dominance but capable of enhancing the moral capability of the world and fostering collective responsibility for global problems. Since global problems transcend national boundaries, nation-states should free themselves from the old notions and strategies used to expand power and control resources. Often statism has been effectively checked by transgovernmental institutions and organizations that are created to address the global issues in a cooperative manner. As seen in power dynamics between industrialized and industrializing countries, however, collective efforts, without means of legal enforcement, are frequently hampered by the dominance of states' actions based on the criteria of political and economic self-interests. Hence the key to developing a solution to the prevalence of statism is not merely to set up intergovernmental, transgovernmental, and transnational organizations. Rather, the key, more fundamentally, is to generate a moral practice that is capable of effectively questioning the criteria on which nation-states make decisions, and develop a capacity for moral reasoning on the basis of the criteria of human dignity and solidarity.

If we are capable of conceiving the global life space as a community, then the prevailing criteria of decision-makings—i.e., utilitarian calculations and state egoism—must change. If the global space is to be a global community, it has to be based on a new set of shared meanings and experiences in which we can relate to each other. In other words, we, as inhabitants of the planet as a common home, have to share a sense of collective destiny. Otherwise, we live in this physical world not as authentic members of the global community but as individual actors hopelessly dissociated from each other. The question is whether we are prepared to appreciate that community project and search our common energy in the pursuit of the global goods (see *Global Peace and Global Accountability*).

5. Global Practice: Thinking and Acting Morally

There seems to be no window of hope for an optimistic future. The people as well as their nation-states are keen to take advantage of the globalization of economic processes and bring an immediate commercial gain. Whenever this becomes a factor, they simply retreat from engagement with any affairs of a global dimension, and turn away from all meaningful actions. The dramatic example is our attitude toward the war in the former Yugoslavia. We are well aware that it is caused by the deep-seated ethnic hatred and nationalistic aspirations remaining fresh in the consciousness of the people of the territory. Irredentist claims and nationally 'pure' states seem to have been their goal, that has joined the state and the people together. The people of the region, politicians and peasants, do not seek to live with 'mixed' parties of different religions and opposing factions. These complexities may have succeeded in building a massive defense wall of the 'cautious realist camp' against arguments for active engagement from a globalist camp. This has, however, hidden the entrenched forms of life and relationships that are characterized by the utilitarian criteria for decision-making both by the governments and the people of the world.

In a Seoul conference on the issues of globalization, a journalist participant deplored the narrow scopes of the Korean media by stating that newspapers and television channels had continued to reduce the coverage of the world affairs, as managers, editors, and the media consumers were combined to form an enclave of provincialism in contemporary Korean society. They are all respectively infiltrated by individual self-interests, instrumental values, and continue to allocate more energies for incredibly rich street gossip on outside of their immediate surroundings. Yet such narcicistic and inward looking insularism is not confined to this side of the world. In a recent article, one British commentator's opinion criticizing the insularity of British people, quoted a survey which showed that documentaries on international topics on the four main television channels in Britain had fallen by 40 per cent over five years. ITV, for instance, produced 173 hours in 1989-90; by 1993-94 it dwindled to 39 hours (O'Shaughnessy 1995 p. 20). The authors of the famed book *Habits of the Hearts* (Bellah et al.), which began the discussion of the issues about the American social and cultural ecology, also identified one of the problems as 'radical individualism' that "emphasizes strategic action to maximize self-interest, action that rather sharply distinguishes between means and ends" (Bellah 1988 p. 271).

In the culture of atomistic individualism, there seems to be little space for a strong sense of obligations to a larger globe beyond the private world. Is it possible that we could become committed to the global problems? Do we have any source of possibility for enhancing the global community? I think we have or at least we should have. The environmental problems are useful topics for questioning the dominant conceptions of the world as involving the control and appropriation of nature. As far as the environmental movements are concerned, there seems to be a possibility for an optimistic future, although the same can not be easily said concerning other dimensions of globalization (see *Green Security*).

First, in the midst of this cultural milieu, however, globalization contains within its processes a certain kind of openness, structurally an obstacle to protect the enclave of life unchallenged. Those who are withdrawing from all meaningful involvement with the global issues cannot completely close their eyes to news footage of global disasters, such as the Chernobel explosion. Many forces underlying the globalizing processes are impersonal and beyond the intentions of 'localized' individuals. The dimension of the spatial compression of globalization makes it difficult to define itself as the opposite of localization, as the term 'globalization' is often used to describe this situation (Robertson 1995). No doubt today's individualists, unlike those of the past, are more likely to be shaped by the global condition.

Second, there are already individual carriers and collective actors of a morality for global social action. Environmental NGOs, including 'Greenpeace' and various organizations, have not only challenged the commercial concept of the global world but affected environmental behavior and policy by taking legal proceedings against states they considered to be out of compliance with environmental law (Miller 1995). The rise of the environment movements is at once freeing us from the enclave of self-interest and encouraging our global impulse. What we are seeing and hearing is a moral practice, keeping alive the possibility of solidarity within the global community, regardless of national citizenship and beyond the fetters of traditional communal and national bonds. Indeed, we are of late witnessing the hitherto unthinkable, unprecedented threats of 'minuscule' Greenpeace to the national power of 'mighty' France, almost signaling the coming of "the new politics," as a columnist aptly coined, "or, at least, the shift in powers from national government to the global markets" such as boycotting throughout the world (Marr 1995 p. 1).

Third, a moral discourse for the global community can take the advantage of making use of the large amount of human and social scientific debates along the line of the communitarian critique of liberalism (Mulhall and Swift 1992). What is perceived to be a major achievement in these studies is the notion of obligations to future generations, for which no justifications can be provided by the utilitarian, contractarian, and rights-based liberal theories. These obligations arise from a 'non-contractual' element (Durkheim 1964), "a sense of community that stretches and extends over generations and into future"(de-Shalit 1995 p. 14). Community is not only concerned with its members of 'here and now,' but also with its descendants. The current discussions of globalization has largely neglected the concern with, and obligations to, future generations as important, tilting toward spatial dimensions. This moral perspective defines clearly the global environmental problems such as nuclear effects that would result not only in all areas of the world but also the descendants of the whole population.

Thus, the reaffirmation of our global community is, at least, not an impossible task. Collective efforts to reconstruct the life space at the global level can and do generate both new forms of action and new concepts of power. Global movements are no longer based on the old forms of social movements and movement organizations, but on the ability to produce new fields.

6. Conclusion

Much of contemporary social sciences is indebted to the ideas of the Enlightenment. Both the bourgeois liberals and Marxist thinkers are its offsprings. It is those intellectuals who created 'the economistic' and 'realist' vision of the world, from which they now find it unable to release themselves. The laissez-faire economics was merely an extreme case. Their theories were born with little knowledge about how limited the global natural resources were, much less about the transgenerational genetic damages at the global scale caused by radiation. Even if J.S. Mill conceived the possibility that the natural resources such as 'air' would have 'commodity value' (Mill 1900 p. 7; de-Shalit 1995 p. 134), economists have not ventured to exercise critical arguments about the notion that clean air is not a part of wealth but always cheap. Today no country, not even the most powerful, can be thought of outside the context of the global condition. The realist idea of states was also conceived without the vision of globality. In this global age, we have to advance a new conception of reality that is capable of legitimating a moral commitment to a community of global connections and relations. What is needed in this new global situation is for us to acquire a new moral vision, namely a global morality.

Only when and if we are able to (re)affirm a global community, and if we secure our identity both within the community and through obligations to it, we would truly be able to remedy the global pathologies of today, and resolve the conflicts that arise from global confrontations and foster a genuine global community.

See also: *Global Environment and Peace; Emergence of Global Community and the Establishment of New Global Ethics*

Bibliography —————————————

Bellah R N, R Madsen, W M Sullivan, A Swidler, S M Tipton 1988 *Habits of the Hearts: Individualism and Commitment in American Life*. University of California Press, Berkeley

Bellah R 1988 The idea of practices in habits: A response. In: C H Reynolds, R V Norman (ed.) *Community in America: The Challenge of Habits of the Hearts*. University of California Press, Berkeley

Durkheim E 1964 *The Division of Labour in Society*. Free Press, New York

Marr A 1995 Green Power in the World's Saloon Bar. *The Independent* 11(July)

Marx K 1988 *The Communist Manifesto* (A Norton Critical Edition). W. W. Norton, New York

Miller M A L 1995 *The Third World in Global Environmental Politics*. Open University Press, Buckingham

Mulhall S, Swift A 1992 *Liberals & Communitarians*. Blackwee, Oxford

Park Y S 1994a Pomsegyehwa-wa kanung sege. [The Possible World of Globalization]. *Hyonsang-gwa Inshik* [The Quarterly Journal of Humanities and Social Sciences] 18(1)

Park Y S 1994b The socio-cultural dynamic of a newly industrializing country: The experience of Korea. In: R H Brown (ed.) *Culture, Politics, and Economic Growth: Experiences in East Asia*. Studies in Third World Societies, Pub. No. 52

Park Y S 1995 *Uri-sahoe-ui Songchaljok Inshik* [A Reflective Understanding of Korean Society]. Hyonsang-gwa Inshik, Seoul

O'Shaughnessy H 1995 Pull the courtains tight. The light hurts our eyes and we are tired. *The Independent on Sunday* 13 (August)

Robertson R 1995 Globalization: Time-Space and Homogeneity. In: M Featherstone, S Lash, R Robertson (eds.) *Global Modernities*. Sage, London

de Shalit A 1995 *Why Posterity Matters: Environmental Policies and Future Generations*. Routledge, London

Skocpol T 1994 *Social Revolutions in the Modern World*. Cambridge University Press, Cambridge

Waters M 1995 *Globalization*. Routledge, London

Weber M 1930 *The Protestant Ethic and the Spirit of Capitalism*. Charles Scribner's, New York

YONG SHIN PARK

New World Order and New State-Nations

1. The New World Order or "The New World Order"

It is too early to discuss the new world order as fully conceptualised and particularly as a materialised concept for one simple reason: lack of clear and final proliferation of the contents of such a concept despite the clear hints of objectives and methods of establishing "the new world order." Whether it will really lead to, in history already so many times flamboyantly announced, circumstances of the establishment of the new world order and even more, whether such an establishment be carried out in the form which at present seems to be inevitable to great many people is to be found out. Future being an offspring of history and presence mainly looks like its ancestors and always mostly appears to be something new, what it really is, its own self as presence.

Therefore we cannot presently discuss the establishment of "the new world order" but only endeavours made in order to establish it as well as the results of those endeavours. For that reason it is quite rational to add quotation marks in front of this term thereby not diminishing its importance as the subject of research.

It is important for this topic that the establishment of the new world order appears only at first glance as the establishment of global domination of one centre of collective power, one state, one ideology. As a matter of fact, there are clearly expressed continental and regional domination of the emerging world powers with the tendency to increase all its resources of power ever more not subordinated to the formal centre of the global domination (see *World Peace Order, Dimensions of a*).

The ratio in the economic power as a base of the total power of three already existing economic and technological world centres (USA, EEC with Germany on the top and Japan as moderator of the economic trends and power of the Far East) will decide whether USA will retain in not so long future the top position of the highest position of the global power or it will have to share it with somebody else and maybe even leave it. Their present and probably future domineering position in the sphere of the military power will not be worth much without keeping economic power as the benchmark of general supremacy just as the expressed military power pays much nowadays neither to the CIS nor China.

It can be expected that the powers like Germany and Japan will not strive in the future, despite increase in their military power, to achieve their interests by using military power on the international plan, especially by using their own powers, but to do so by channels of economic and technological and financial influence in particular with comprehensive use of multilateral institutions. This explains persistence in the attempts of Germany and Japan, as well as some regional powers to enter the UN Security Council as soon as possible so that in the capacity of permanent members they could get as much of the cake of the political power as possible in decision-making and global influence as a strong resistance to that expressed by USA, but also France and England as third-rate powers gaining their political power mostly owing to possession of such a positional advantage against Germany and Japan. In any way, USA itself has for the time being "higher cooptative power than the others" due to its domineering position in the majority of the international organisations and institutions (OUN, IMF, GATT, OECD, NATO) (see *Emerging Tool Chest for Peacebuilders*). Yet, although this position of USA has been historically achieved and determined, it is not, in the contrast to the positions of Great Britain and France in which their political powers primarily lie in historical position on which they have been found such as permanent membership in UN Security Council, primarily contained in certain historical right to power but it is also, to the contrary, a very clear expression at the same time of present overall and enormous political, economic and military power of USA.

If political, economic and especially financial power are such kinds of power to which an increasing importance has been attached for winning over dominant position in global relations, the military power is and will remain in the future such a form of power which is to be decisive factor of domination in the regional frameworks. Neither Turkey nor Brazil, India nor Nigeria are likely to become soon political, economic and the least financial powers, but they certainly are and will long remain regional powers thanks to their military powers.

The commitment to intermediating in global scales from the positions of power as new and possible general way of cooperation with others, especially those disobedient nations and countries has been particularly expressed in relation to the sovereignty of other states.

According to all this, "the new world order" also implies transformation of understanding right to self-determination since it has been up to now construed by its architects as the right of the nation to national, but not political and particularly not economic self-determination.

2. The Modern State-Nations

Being not only one of the consequences of establishing "the new world order" but also the condition of its appearance and duration is disappearance and recognition of the new state-nations as modern countries. Dissolution of the multinational federation and establishment of new state-nations offers possibilities for proving domination not only of the great over the small but also of "the mature" on the territory of "the delayed" nations, the territory of which is conducive for that. The disintegration of former territory of the USSR as a multinational empire as well as once stable

multiethnic countries like the Federal Republic of Yugoslavia into larger and smaller, mutually belligerent countries only at first glance enables easier supervision over them and easier implementation of foreign military, political and economic interest in the regions in which the newly established state-nations elated by their national "awakening" and supported more by the past than the vision of the future inexorably enter into mutual conflicts and thus other forms of dependence upon other countries, primarily great powers.

Since modern national state represents "actual part of the historical process which connects past with future" (Czempiel 1987 p. 361) we can talk about at least two types of modern state-nations—about the state-nations found in modern times and about newly established, and/or emerging states nation (Rejai & Enloe p. 37).

State-nations found in the modern times have behind them the time of greatest hardships including totalitarianism and the fact they have been included among the modern state-nations they mostly owe to their traditional approach to the questions of the state-hood and the nation. They have been reviewed as a notion and mentioned in this text more in the function of their explanation as a political phenomenon.

Unlike them, the newly established or emerging state-nations respectively are a true challenge to researchers of social and political phenomena. The mysteries of their rapid and mass appearance like phoenix of the reiteration of the archaic concept of the state national (which have since long ago been considered from East to West as historically lived up and outdated) and it is conditioned only by an attempt of clarifying not only the cause or conditions and circumstances but also themselves as apparently by many specific political phenomena whose appearance and existence significantly influenced featuring not so much of "the end of history" as general nature and characteristics of the end of 20th century.

There is no doubt that the phenomena of newly established state-nations is closely connected to the process of establishing "the new world order" and/or that it has been caused to great extent by disappearance of the block equilibrium due to the dissolution of the Eastern Block upon permission of USSR, disintegration of USSR itself and historical failure of socialism as a system.

The break of a historic game which resulted in withdrawing of the socialist ideology from the scene of the societies in which there was the state ideology rendered it possible that the national conscience and long suppressed and formally eliminated national passions and religious disputes appear on the surface breaking out to the front position of the social events not only in the countries—regions of former socialist, especially federate and multiethnic countries in which until recently there was "brotherhood and unity" but in those regions first with the expressed tendency of expansion also to other multiethnic and multireligious communities and regions, primarily underdeveloped countries like the Indian subcontinent and Africa, but also in Europe and other economically more developed and potentially conflictuous hotbeds of ethnic composition. At this moment seventy-five such hotbeds worldwide have been identified by OUN with the possibility of drastical increase of this figure having in mind the fact that there were until recently twenty-two federations in the world in which as much as 40 percent of the world population lived.

The characteristic features of these processes are very important for this topic which appeared during the dissolution of "the socialist empire" and the Socialist Federal Republic of Yugoslavia as a sort of a rarity incarnated in the fact that much higher efficiency was shown in such a dissolution by internal factors than external factors (some internal factors which have been "unpredicted" because their involvement was, among other things, less expected according to the Western analysts, whereas the Eastern analysts did not dare doubt those factors), in any case more than the internal factors which were generally regarded as the possible forces of the destruction of the socialist systems. It is primarily the matter of the role of red-tape party and state elite which used to be a national and then turned into more nationally than internationally committed groups as they started to discover in the weaknesses of the system the possibility of their own profitability—establishment of the state-nations like their personal empires, at any rate and regardless of the fact that those empires often remained within the confines of caricature territory dimensions and irrespectable military, political and economic significance. The resistance of these structures to the new conditions as a proof of their vitality has been proved by the fact that nowadays they ate the ones that rule mainly in the states which were not dependent in a rather degrading way on Moscow. Old and new "emperors" have shown that they recognize political trends and fashion—priest's garment was soon replaced by the national coloured vestment. However, in the fashion world it is not unusual that designers wear their own designs thereby exercising their influence from the position of the first and exclusive model to the public by the power

of their importance and the importance of the social position they have.

Yet, despite the undeniable role of the advocates of the materialization of the idea about "the new world order" in these events, their trends have taken to the influences of the other, sometimes unidentifiable or hardly definable, factors.

The fact that these leaderships did not only flee in front of danger but made endeavors to instrumentalise it by adapting themselves to the new conditions does not illustrate their character or moral as personal qualities but rather will for power as rationality which is, like irrationality, the quality of mankind. It is these just mentioned transformation processes of the totalitarian system of the socialist countries that prove that the irrationalism is inherent to man and politics. One irrational or, at least more irrational than rational, political system has been dismantled by means of nationalism which is completely characterized by irrationality, which does not mean it was only by means of that, since the irrational most frequently appears in human, and especially in political behavior only as subsidiary derive of the rational comprehension of the rationally determined goals.

The impossibility of rational control of the party and state elite encouraged their conflicts and later their attempts to get support in the public which they previously had not sought. Mass mobilization with a view to proving correctness of the political attitudes of the elite and firmness of the position of power could have been most easily and quickly achieved by means of intensifying national and religious feelings as so far unused reservoir of irrationality in the society.

3. The Characteristics of New State-Nations in Eastern Europe—Particularly in the Territory of Former Yugoslavia

The key characteristics of the majority of new state-nations in Eastern Europe, and particularly in the territory of former Yugoslavia, are violence and the perception of the nation as something sacred (see *Eastern Europe, Transformation of*). Therein lie the roots of their current problems.

This can be explained in the following way. In already existing state-nations legal tradition is in the main the decisive criteria for the treatment of the state as a state-nation. In contrast the second type of contemporary state-nation, this is the emerging state-nation, on the whole considers even the category of state as something sacred, as a national holy thing. And the very method of the creation of the state nation of this type leads to its being considered a holy thing, to the general perception of the state as something sacred. This is because any excessive enthusiasm for an action (and this includes enthusiasm that is provoked both intentionally and unintentionally, and also formally excessive national enthusiasm) contributes to the overestimation and idolization of that action and its consequences, and the transformation of secular matters into sacred matters.

The historical basis for the emergence of this type of state-nation also lies in the aspiration of the so-called qualitatively belated (which does not always mean quantitatively small) nations to "achieve maturity" by becoming state constructive. The ultimate or sufficient maturity of a nation is confirmed, according to the conviction of its leadership, by statehood, or mainly by statehood. This is why the creation of its own state-nation represents the highest goal absolutely for the definitive international identification of the nation; there is no legitimacy of the civilization maturity, nor is there absolute proof of the adulthood of the nation.

When thus defined, the contemporary state-nation of this type has had to be perceived as something sacred in the social and habitual conditions in which it arose. As everything that is sacred seeks sacrifice as the confirmation of its value and importance, leading therefore to holy violence, this accounts for the quantity of violence whether large or small that, in various forms, has accompanied the emergence of this type of contemporary state-nation.

Since such state-nations come about on the territory of former multinational state communities, violence therefore starts as institutional destruction—as a kind of structural violence against the previous state. The strength of political and general social and national agitation, primarily in Eastern Europe, modified the slogan "the preservation of the state is the most important task" into the slogan "the creation of the state-nation is the most important task" (of a nation and socialist republic). And the secret of the non-freedom of the multi-national community has given way to the secret of the non-freedom of the orgiastically proven particularity of the nation and its state in the contemporary age.

Whether direct physical violence will come about, and if so to that extent, depends on several factors. Firstly, it depends on the conduct of national movements (and these are usually inter-nationally conflicting and territorially competitive), and this ultimately means that it depends on the conduct of their leaderships in the capacity of national elite. These leaderships, aspiring to seize their own states in several senses of the word, can or must behave on different levels of conflict depending on a series of factors—from the degree of their knowledge (or lack of knowledge) and skill, to factors such as the pronounced interest commitment of powerful international state and legal subjects in the form of complete approbation and support or disapprobation. At all events, the national leadership that are building up new states in Eastern Europe, and particularly on the territory of former Yugoslavia, never completely renounce force, particularly force conceived as counter-force and as the last option available for achieving their goal—the state-nation as the fulfillment of the national political dream.

It is an ancient rule that states that wish to be recognized must be able to wage war. Newly emerging state-nations transform this archaic possibility into a necessity for their contemporary action inside or outside their borders.

The main source of these conflicts is the defining of national territory as state territory (Rokkan and Urwin 1982 pp. 1-11, 424-436). Namely, each of the newly emerging state-nation sets itself the task of achieving borders on the basis of its historical vision (see *National Interest*). But this is not on the basis of some kind of general or average historical vision, but is always the vision from the period of (where applicable), previous statehood, or territorial occupation by the nation when the "national" elite of that time had, or claimed the right to, the largest territory as national territory (Rokkan, Urwin, Aarebrot, Malaba, Sande 1987 pp. 17-25). Since neighboring state-nations aggrandize totally different periods of their histories, it is no wonder that borders thus conceived and desired overlap, and quickly become a reason for intolerance and war. The reason for war is all the greater if it is possible to "liberate" members of ones own nation in another state-nation. That is why there are so many wars on territories of former ethnic federations, and particularly on the territory of former Yugoslavia, since in that region it is virtually impossible to avoid a situation where members of some "new" nations are also living in large numbers beyond the borders of their state-nation (see *Ethnic Conflict and International Relations*). It is therefore far more natural not to expect the newly emerging state-nations to honor any kind of borders, but rather to expect their expansion, or the demand for expansion (even beyond all reasonable limits), as reflected in the words: "our land extends to wherever even the smallest part of our nation lives," which can, ultimately, be interpreted as being where one individual lives.

The absence of restraint where violence is concerned is also due to the fact that the orgiastic, barbarian characteristic that is contained in the genetic code of every nation is not finally eliminated with the emergence of the state-nation, as is claimed in the euphoria and manifestos of the newly-founded state-nations, but, it is rather, depending on the political interest, merely assuaged or even stimulated further with the goal of jeopardizing and destroying other nations and, in general, the enemies of the given nation (see *Nationalism*). The interpretive function of nationalistic ideology is here revealed in endeavors to justify such an approach to violence, and even to genocide, as a proof of the power, strength and vitality of the nation.

Furthermore, an exceptionally important factor in the presence of violence at the moment of the emergence of new state-nations is the existence or non-existence of the culture of death, and it is broader than the culture of politics and encompasses the approach to the dying of both man and the state.

The essential anachronism lies in the fact that the state is not considered in a new-democratic, process-dynamic way, but rather in an old-democratic, static way as a structure—the materialization of mystic national power. The anachronic-ritual treatment of the state as a holy structure requires that the custom be honored of building some blood sacrifice into the foundations of the structure in order that the structure might become more precious and more stable, and for it to assume "great suggestive power over the will of men, over world public opinion, and over the perceptions and feelings of the state with the rule of law" (Schmitt C. 1934 pp. 7-14).

Generally speaking, in Eastern Europe, and especially in former Yugoslavia, that is in the areas of the emergence of new state-nations, both the official and the unofficial emphasis on the greater value of the newly-established state has its roots in this very thing—the quantity of blood shed and the magnitude, that is the "size" of the sacrifice.

If, habitually, the native territories, of the newly emerging state-nations value every sacrifice highly, and particularly mass sacrifice and the sacrifice of the innocent, then, through normative and civilizational influences, violence becomes extremely easy—not only a habitual but also a state ritual. Thereby there is also a selection of interests. The selection of habitual norms is carried out according to the criterion of usefulness for day to day nationalistic policy.

As a rule, whenever they are unable, for various specific reasons, to be satisfied with the traditional approach concerning the general requirement of state-nations "that the individuality of consciousness

must be offered in sacrifice" (Hegel G. W. F. 1987 p. 270) in the name of the national, that is the collective interest, the new state nations, particularly on the territory of former Yugoslavia, demand and offer a blood sacrifice. Then the "negative form of emergence as a real power of the community and the strength of its self-preservation" (Hegel G. W. F. 1987 p. 320) is manifested, and the freed collective energy and the will to risk having a bloodstained statehood that combines individuals into a nation of state or a state-constructive nation become fully prominent.

There is also the clear commitment on the part of all newly emerging state-nations to define and declare themselves as states with rule of law, although they do not always act as such. Generally speaking, the rule of law is encountered far more frequently as a term in technical use than it is felt in the political life of the newly-formed state-nations. This is, among other things, certainly also due to the fact that the new system is not being built on a new foundation, but on the foundations of the previous system. For this reason, the excessive use of the term "rule of law" has not only become superfluous as a result of the real achievement of the legality of the state and the new system, but has become absolutely essential as a mask of legality and the generally good, democratic regulation of society. Alongside the over-frequent disregard of human rights and the freedoms of the citizens who do not belong to the state-constructive nation, the principle of dominant and even absolute leadership is over-emphasized in the political life of the newly formed state-nations. Such leadership is incompatible with the principle of the rule of law, and brings the newly-formed state-nation nearer to the model of patriarchal democracy as a frequently closer form of social system from a historical and civilisational point of view. Another specific feature of newly emerging state-nations is that they imitate the principle of absolute leadership. They do not implement it as a principle of personal leadership, but as the leadership of a national movement that is usually so predominant that, even when it encompasses several parties, there are no substantial differences among them in the perception of national interest and sovereignty. This makes possible the existence of the thesis on a new form of political monism. That is to say, although all the newly-formed state-nations on the territory of former Yugoslavia extol their political pluralism, what is actually involved here is the manifestation of the rule of one single, markedly national movement.

The problem also lies in the fact that the newly-formed state-nations in Eastern Europe and former Yugoslavia endeavors to be at the same time both a state with a marked rule of law and a totally state-nation, and this is not incompatible in certain segments of the political system, but it is evidently not possible as a lasting basis for predominantly conflict-free political life in such a state. From a normative point of view, the newly-formed state-nations are states with the rule of law since they possess the actual legal order that provides norms for the form of political life. However, the concept of state nation loses all sense in the equation of the state and law, or that of the principle of leadership and statehood. A state-nation may only be conceived as a state with the rule of law if it is accepted that the nation, the state and the law represent relatively independent elements of one social system.

Since the contemporary state-nation expresses the nationalistic conception of the state and its national values as primary values with the aim of ensuring the national regulation of life, in every state-nation there exists the objective subordination of the individual as a social subject to the nation as the highest value. The predominance of the collective over the individual is the lasting principle of the functioning of state-nation. This does not, of course, mean the state nation is not and cannot at present be a state with the rule of law in its form, for this political principle is nothing other than the principle of domination, that is the principle through which every state with rule of law is in fact formed. Newly-formed state-nations, with both the image of being and the potential to be states with the rule of law, are differentiated only by the form in which variants of individual or collective domination are expressed.

The greatest problem evidently lies in the fact that the best conceived program of collective happiness and welfare for even leading nations, not only legally but also politically, easily becomes transformed into the forced happiness of individuals and the basis for imperium paternal, which is the "greatest possible despotism" (Kant I. 1964 p. 145) . The sacrifice of the autonomous social subjectivity of the individual on the altar of national unity and in the interest of the fulfillment of "higher national goals" only accelerates the transformation of the nation into a global community of the totalitarian type that aspires to absorb into itself the totality of the human personality, whereby room for the democratic freedom of the individual and social groups and for the autonomy of civil society is drastically reduced.

4. The Perspectives

Mass emerging of the new state-nations is the most important in the series of increasing hints that present, although in many ways not legitimate and guaranteed enough, still relatively stable relation of placing of the nations and other ethnic groups within the states and their present boundaries will not take long and that the situation of moderate satisfaction of the ethnicity for the reasons of ethnic position, increasingly turn into the state of ethnic dissatisfaction and possible nationalist explosion of planetary scopes.

Having national-status rights, not even when they are equal, is not any longer enough. The state or the autonomy close to the statehood status is obviously the future target of ethnic hydra which is more than ready to throw down the gauntlet to up to now state organization of the world. The discrepancy between the number of 3,600 ever more "awaken" ethnic groups (with permanent tendency of launching "the new") and their settling into "only" 179 states world over, the wish of the ethnic groups, unaffirmed as states, is expressed ever more to cease existing as "possible nations" any longer but due to the civilization conditions created for that (such as respecting the fact that numerous borders of the developing countries, particularly in Africa, Near East and Middle East were drawn by "colonial ruler" (see *Colonialism*) without taking a special care about ethnic, or more precisely tribe divisions and relations or due to the increasing international-subjective tolerance of interpreting and thus confirming recognition of the right to ethnic individuality as the right to turning into a nation), turns into danger and reality of the new trend which will most likely notably mark the profile of the end of 20th century and the early 21st century—mass formation and even more massive attempts to establish new state nation by separations peacefully or by means of violence as well as intensifying international backing up or preventing those endeavors.

Although it is beyond dispute that the global economy offers the chance for the small nations to gain momentum and for development of regional economies and that way for civilization maturing of the lagging nations, they must in their striving to get their own state bear in mind present unwritten rule of the architect of "the new world order," whose resolution legalization by OUN is expected, and which says that there can be no separation without relying of the separatists onto the greatest powers of "the new world order" and accepting complete dependence upon them when it comes to the future of their newly established state nations (see *World Economy, Social Change and Peace*). So, the interest of the great is expressed here, too as a criterion for helping small and lagging nations no matter how justified their wishes may be.

According to all this, the survival or disappearance of ethnically complex states by hook or by crook will probably depend a great deal as presently on the consent or distinction of the interests respectively, as well as on the balance of powers rather international agents and particularly on the reconciliation of the interests of those states with the interests of the masters of "the new world order."

For the time being the development of such processes has been slowed down by some attempts which, to tell the truth, do not show much in the political solutions not only of the architects of the "new world order" but in the solutions of other states, too. Among these endeavors which are mainly funded in the respect of interests, from the theoretic point of view it is worth to draw attention to those which advocate maintaining and formation of ethnic con-societies in which coexistence of different ethnic groups on the principle of equal footing would be viable; the closer to equality, the more viable attempts would be. This nice theoretic assumption in practice has so far encountered this unresolved problem that whoever has surplus of rights and power does not want to waive them otherwise but formally and that ethnic federalism does not work unless it has been established upon anybody's rule, even if it is the rule of the majority.

If the predictions of Mr. Boutros Ghali do become true, expressed in the form of fear in mid-1992, the thesis of Carl Friedrich about nationalism being the strongest power of the planet will become a final truth. In the analysis of the beginnings of that process which may or may not be stopped, but the process which has definitely started, will become increasingly clear that no ghost of nationalism of the world scales was given up out of the bottle but that it is a matter of the nonmistical process of interest transformation of the human mankind into not only those new forms imposed by the new post-industrial organization of life in the society but also into those forms characterized by neglect of the interests and needs of the ethnicity in the name of speed and profit

which inevitably results in convulsions of their spontaneous self-development and interventionism in the function of their statehood as currently fastest and politically most profitable solution by which the problems of those ethnicities are not actually solved but only conceived. Therefore, unless this process has been stopped, the major problem of "the new world order" will be one day the question of the organization of the world as "a broken mirror" which as a task, at least at this moment, entirely exceeds the possibilities of any power which does not mean only informatively, military, technologically and economically most industrialized countries but of their international economic, political and military organizations and alliances, too.

See also: *Neocolonialism; Role of Europe in the Management of Global Problems; World Order; World Order: Gandhi's Concepts and Contributions; Globalization; Global Integration*

Bibliography

Stein R, Derek U W 1982 *The Politics of Territorial Identity.* Sage Publ., London, Beverly Hills, New Delhi

Stein R, Derek U W, Frank A H, Pamela M, Terje S 1987 *Centre-Periphery Structures in Europe.* Campus Verlag, Frankfurt, New York

Schmitt C 1934 *Nationalsozialismus und Rechtstaat: Juristisce Wochenschrift.* H 12/13, Berlin/Leipzig

Hegel G W F 1987 *Phanomenologie des Geistes.* Reclam Nr. 8460(6), Stuttgart

Kant I 1964 *Ueber den Gemeinspruch: Das mag in der Theorie richtig sein, taugt aber nicht für die Praxis.* Werke, hrsh. v.W.Weischhedel, band VI, Darmstadt

Fleck L 1983 *Erfahrung und Tatsachen.* Bonn

Czempiel E-O 1987 Die Zukunft des Nationalstaates. In: Beyme K von, Czempiel E, Kielmansegg P Graf: Politik 2, Frankfurt am Main

Mostafa R, Cynthia H E 1981 Nation-states and State-nations. In: Perspectives on World Politics (A Reader Edited by M. Smith, R. Little and M. Shackleton at the Open University), London/Sydney/Wolfeboro/New Hampshire (rep. 1986)

DRAGAN SIMEUNOVIC

New Zealand's Contribution to Nuclear Disarmament

Although antipodean isolation saved it from the territorial ravages of war throughout the twentieth century, New Zealand lost a disproportionately large number of its people on active service during the two World Wars. Perhaps because of this personal experience of loss, together with an awareness of world events, citizens of this country gradually developed a determined and active opposition to nuclear armaments policing the global village.

In the 1980s its anti-nuclear stance had become a matter of national pride, perhaps even a defining characteristic for a significant majority of New Zealanders. By the end of the 1990s it has become a political non-issue being a *fait accompli*—a cornerstone of New Zealand's sense of nationhood.

But it has not been without political cost. The USA, France and the UK sought to counter the anti-nuclear punch of this determinedly "clean and green" country. A brief outline of some of the history demonstrates that it was a sustained and successful people's protest over many years.

1945: A few days after the Hiroshima and Nagasaki catastrophes in August perhaps the world's first anti-nuclear meeting occurred at Canterbury University College in Christchurch—the *alma mater* of Lord Ernest Rutherford who first split the atom and who asserted the technology could never be used for destructive purposes. The speaker was a Viennese refugee, the as yet unrecognised philosopher, Karl Popper, who declared in a packed auditorium: "When the first atomic bomb exploded the world as we have known it came, I believe, to an end." His concluding comment is still pertinent: "The fundamental struggle in life is the moral struggle to limit the power men wield over their fellow man."

August 1947: The first Hiroshima Day march occurred in Christchurch organized by the Peace Union.

1950: 20,000 New Zealanders signed a world-wide anti-nuclear petition drafted by the Peace Committee in Stockholm.

1951: 250 delegates attended the New Zealand Committee Peace Congress.

New Zealand, Australia and the USA signed the ANZUS agreement a year after New Zealand entered the Korean War.

1956: A petition was organized by the Quakers, National Council of Churches, National Council of Women, the Federation of Labour and others against British nuclear testing.

1957: 1600 people crowded into the Auckland Town Hall seeking to ban the H-bomb which the British were testing at Christmas Island. The Labour Party formed a government promising to "oppose all further tests of nuclear weapons!"

1958: The Campaign for Nuclear Disarmament (CND) established in New Zealand and has since then organized many annual marches and petitions.

1959: Walter Nash's Labour Government sought a

test ban treaty and helped develop a Nuclear Weapon Free Zone in Antarctica (see *Nuclear-Weapon-Free Zones: A History and Assessment*).

Nobel prize winner, Dr Linus Pauling, was invited to New Zealand by the Peace Council to explain the dangerous effects of nuclear testing.

1960: New Zealand voted in favour of the United Nations' resolution urging France to stop nuclear testing. Australia abstained. The US and UK voted with France against the resolution. The nuclear armed and nuclear powered United States submarine Halibut docked in Auckland.

1962: The National Government under Keith Holyoake criticised as "surprising and regrettable" the US decision to conduct atmospheric tests in the Pacific. The US detonated ninety nuclear devices in Micronesia.

The British ended a series of twenty nuclear tests above Christmas Island and the Australian desert.

1963: CND organized a petition signed by 80,000 proposing a Southern Hemisphere nuclear weapon free zone. "No bombs south of the Line" the petitioners proclaimed.

The Labour Party campaigned for a Nuclear Weapon Free Zone in the Southern Hemisphere.

A Nuclear Test Ban Treaty opposing atmospheric tests was signed by UK, USA and USSR with New Zealand the first country to ratify it after the three original signatories (see *CTBT Negotiations: Analysis and Assessment*).

The Government appealed to the French not to commence nuclear testing in the Pacific.

1964: France was determined to continue atmospheric testing and moved its base to Moruroa in the South Pacific. Four hundred New Zealand organisations protested.

1966: France exploded its first of many nuclear devices in French Polynesia disdainful of the Test Ban Treaty and outrage expressed by people in the Pacific since 1962.

1968: A campaign successfully opposed the USA establishing an Omega navigation system ground station which uses low-frequency radio waves to assist the US nuclear missiles carried by the new Polaris submarines. It was re-sited in Victoria, Australia.

Strong public criticism focused on the French for exploding their first H-bomb in the South Pacific.

1971: The Government was asked by a CND petition to establish a nuclear weapon-free Southern Hemisphere.

1972: 100,000 signed a petition launched by Radio Hauraki against French nuclear tests. Greenpeace organized a yacht to sail into the testing zone. The

Peace Research Media Project organized three more vessels to join the Greenpeace vessel.

1973: The newly elected Labour Government, under Norman Kirk, included in its manifesto the nuclear weapon free proposal. The Government sent the frigate *Otago*, with Cabinet Minister Fraser Colman, and later the frigate *Canterbury* into the testing zone. The Peace Research Media's ship *Fri* was arrested.

1974: New Zealand joined Australia in asking the International Court of Justice at the Hague to stop French testing. The Court declared the tests were in breach of international law. The French soon after agreed to stop atmospheric tests but planned to go underground on the fragile atolls of Moruroa and Faungataufa.

1975: Co-sponsored by New Zealand and Fiji and supported by the South Pacific Forum nations a resolution was successfully steered through the United Nations for a nuclear free zone in the South Pacific. The vote was 110 in favour, none against, and 20 abstentions.

The US Government sought permission under the ANZUS agreement to have a nuclear powered ship berth in New Zealand.

The Peace Squadron was formed by the Rev Dr George Armstrong to engage in active non-violence and prevent the US ship from entering the Auckland Harbour.

Labour was heavily defeated by the National Party. One of the Prime Minister Muldoon's first actions was to close the Nuclear Weapons Free Zone desk in the Ministry responsible for Foreign Affairs, and, although supporting a ban on nuclear testing and land-based nuclear weapons, announced a welcome to USA nuclear ships and reaffirmed the commitment to ANZUS.

1976: Visits to Wellington by the guided missile frigate *Truxtun* and to Auckland by the guided missile cruiser *Long Beach* were confronted by the Peace Squadron's flotilla comprising yachts, launches, kayaks and surfboards. Eighty craft filled the Auckland Harbour in a spectacular, internationally covered act of defiance. There would be eight such visits.

1977: At the International Convention for Peace Action in Wellington, 30 international speakers, including US Congressman and presidential candidate in 1972 Paul McCloskey, Nobel Peace prize winner Mairead Corrigan from Northern Ireland, the scientist Sir Marc Oliphant and Australian Senator Gordon MacIntosh meet with several hundred New Zealanders from many cooperating peace movements to debate eighty action proposals to stop the nuclear arms race.

1978: The National Government won another election but with the three main opposition parties all vigorously anti-nuclear.

1979: The US nuclear submarine *Haddo* met a huge flotilla of small craft in the Auckland harbour. New Zealand's Air Force helicopters stirred the water in an attempt to disrupt the protesters. But the determined protesters managed to stop the submarine briefly, pelt it with paint filled balloons and one protester leapt from his surf boat onto the deck of this sophisticated weapon of mass destruction.

1981: The Christchurch based Nuclear Free Zone Committee asked local government to declare their towns and cities nuclear free zones. So successful was this initiative that by 1986 there were 104 local bodies involved, covering seventy-two percent of New Zealand's population.

1983: The Australian, Dr Helen Caldicott, returned to address large crowds. As a consequence, WAND (Women Asking for Nuclear Disarmament) formed and organized in Auckland the largest anti-nuclear march of 25,000 women.

1984: The Labour Government led by David Lange was elected with the promise both to ban nuclear powered and nuclear armed vessels and to renegotiate the ANZUS Treaty. The Social Credit and the New Zealand Party vowed to withdraw from ANZUS while the defeated National Party expressed its commitment to ANZUS.

1985: About forty years after Hiroshima, in January, the Labour Government announced that nuclear powered, nuclear armed, and nuclear capable ships would be refused entry. Seeking to test this announcement, the USA requested permission for the ageing and conventionally powered USS *Buchanan* to visit on their terms, i.e., "to neither confirm nor deny" the presence of nuclear weapons on board, allegedly a requirement for "strategic reasons." The Lange Government refused, affirming the principle, "If in doubt, keep it out."

It is worth noting that for a brief time Lange himself was diffident after being attacked by US military and intelligence agencies, and after discussions with the Australian Labour Prime Minister, Bob Hawke. However, deluged by letters and confronted by enormous public concern which demanded he "tow the party line," Lange, probably being true to his own feelings, could say to Schultz, "We would like to help but we'd be voted out if we did." Lange became the articulate David of anti-nuclear sentiment standing against the powerful, pro-nuclear Goliath.

This stance differed from the Danish policy which said in effect "no nuclear weapons in our ports but we trust our nuclear allies to honour this policy." Certainly, it differed from the Australian Labour Government which permitted nuclear powered or nuclear armed vessels providing they were in transit. Tiny Vanuatu, like New Zealand, refused to accept the "neither confirm nor deny" requirement of the US Navy. Interestingly, Rear Admiral da Roque, former Commander of the US Pacific fleet, in congressional testimony, admitted the US had violated treaty arrangements with Japan by carrying nuclear warheads into their harbours. He affirmed: "US Navy vessels capable of carrying nuclear weapons are carrying them all the time and do not off-load them when entering foreign ports."

On Hiroshima Day, August 6, New Zealand supported the Rarotonga Forum's resolution to establish the South Pacific Nuclear Free Zone Treaty banning testing, nuclear bases and the dumping of nuclear wastes (see *Nuclear-Weapon-Free Zones: A History and Assessment*). Vanuatu initially opposed the Treaty because it lacked substance, arguing in effect that it was like a group of non-smokers deciding to put up a smoke-free zone. But when the strongest smoker appears, none can police it. But New Zealand viewed it symbolically as a useful step. It lacked substance because the USA had persuaded Australia to draft protocols favouring their strategic interests. To be effective, it required ratification by the nuclear powers. China and the USSR signed some of the protocols but the US, UK and France opposed it (until 1996).

As a consequence of New Zealand's actions, an angry and acrimonious US Government downgraded New Zealand from being an "ally" to a "friend" for military sales, refused to engage with New Zealand officials and politicians for a decade (a more severe restriction than imposed upon China, Zaire or Iraq), ended the ANZUS security guarantee, halted the sharing of intelligence analyses, ended joint military activities, and denied preferential access to military materials. There were hints that a trade embargo might occur. Lange later affirmed that the Government's advisors "told me our trade in Europe depended on our surrender to the doctrines of nuclear preparedness" (Speech to Annual Conference of Labour Party in 1988). But anti-nuclear Americans began a campaign to promote the purchase of nuclear free New Zealand products. And New Zealand-USA trade expanded during the four years of the Labour Government.

A US official in Washington, DC warned that New Zealand threatened the Western alliance in its struggle against communism. A US naval authority suggested that the martyrdom of David Lange might be the price that had to be paid for stopping the "New Zealand disease." Ralph McGhee, a CIA field director, explained that his government would have to educate New Zealanders that actions opposing the USA's strategic interests were the work of leftist communist dupes. The Labour Party was merely "playing politics" with "nuclear phobia" and would be a "free rider" hiding under the protective skirts of the US, UK and France. A Heritage Foundation Defence Analyst blamed New Zealand's opposition on "leftist trade unions, self-proclaimed peace groups and a few Church organisations."

But the more the Americans threatened and vilified New Zealand the stronger became the resistance. A most unusual pro-Government demonstration was held in front of Parliament to condemn the bullying tactics of the USA and to affirm the Government's resistance.

August 1985: The notorious act of the sinking, in the Auckland Harbour, of the Greenpeace vessel preparing to protest against French testing, shattered New Zealanders. The violent end of the *Rainbow Warrior*, with the loss of a crew member, brought the issue home. Despite their subterfuge, responsibility was traced to the highest reaches of French Government. The act served to stiffen the New Zealand persistence especially when there was no condemnation from the British or Americans. The delayed and grudging apology from the French did little to appease the outrage.

1986: A Defence Review attracted submissions from many New Zealanders seeking a nuclear free defense system.

1987: The Labour Government was losing public support because of its radical economic reforms. Also, the US and British governments were vigorously opposing the Government's determination to write their opposition into legislation. On July 4, the very popular New Zealand Nuclear Free Zone and Arms Control and Disarmament Act was passed into law. Thus, legally, New Zealand followed Iceland, Vanuatu, Solomons and Fiji. Labour won the election with a reduced majority. The National Party experienced public antagonism because of their perceived pro-nuclear positioning.

1990: The National Government, characteristically more conservative and traditionally supportive of ANZUS and military strength, was elected primarily because of dissatisfaction with Labour's economic policies. However, to be elected, National had to promise the electorate they would not compromise the nuclear free stance.

1991: A Heylen Opinion Poll confirmed that 73

percent of New Zealanders wanted to retain the Nuclear Free Legislation precisely as it was written.

1993: All parties went into the election affirming the nuclear free Act.

1995: The Bolger Government strongly opposed the continued French nuclear testing on Moruroa and Faungataufa in several ways. They supported the flotilla of craft sailing into the testing zone. They initiated a request to examine the legal implications of the judgment made by the Court of International Justice in 1974, and nominated Sir Geoffrey Palmer, former Labour Prime Minister, as an ad hoc judge, and they publicly endorsed the ATOM (Against Testing on Moruroa) team's protests in France. An illustration of the international exposure to New Zealand's opposition to French testing was the decline in Japanese students enrolling in New Zealand because they feared radiation poisoning.

President Clinton acknowledged New Zealand's determination to support the Comprehensive Test Ban Treaty and announced US support. On the same day New Zealand Prime Minister Jim Bolger received an invitation to visit the White House.

1997: The US Army's Pacific command in Hawaii provided a folio to journalists describing how nations were permitted to relate with the USA's military. See below, a Herald Graphic representation (*NZ Herald* November 28, 1997 p. A17).

As can be seen New Zealand ranks with Vietnam and is not regarded as well as countries like India, Cambodia, Russia and Indonesia. Not that New Zealanders would worry!

The anti-nuclear stand taken by New Zealand still annoys. A senior Defence Department official described their reaction: "Pound for pound no country punches above its weight better than New Zealand. In the Gulf, in Bosnia, everywhere that there has been a need for assistance, New Zealand has been there." But "New Zealand has not shown the political will" to repair the anti-nuclear caused fracture with the USA. (Quote cited by John Roughan *NZ Herald* November 28, 1977 p. A17).

Key international events sharpened the development of our national conscience over the years. The list included the British testing of nuclear devices in Australia; the Americans testing on Bikini Atoll, especially the tragic aftermath of an American test suffered by the people of Rongalap Island; the threats to use nuclear weapons during the Cold War, e.g., Cuban missile crisis, and the various nuclear accidents including Browns Ferry, Three-Mile Island and Chernobyl.

Seminars, conferences, speeches and articles galore, films such as *The War Game*, protests and marches told various messages such as the following.

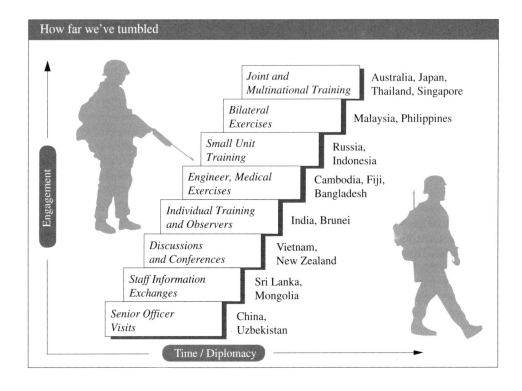

How far we've tumbled

It is impossible to wage a Just War or defend ourselves with nuclear weapons. Nuclear deterrence is an invitation to nuclear catastrophe.

The "red-scare" rhetoric, e.g., "Better dead than red," and the wild west logic of "Might makes right" threatened perhaps a "nuclear winter" and the end of civilisation.

The presence of nuclear weapons whether stored or in transit creates a target.

The list of "broken arrows", or near disastrous accidents, involving nuclear weapons, e.g., the dropping of a 24 megaton bomb by accident near Goldsboro, North Carolina, with 5 of the 6 safety locks not holding, demonstrated in a frightening way the risk of catastrophe. The threat of nuclear terrorism is a possibility especially with the lack of control over fissionable materials within the former Soviet Union.

The horrendous costs of the arms race while people starve, suffer from curable illness and are homeless, appals our conscience.

Again and again, campaigners emphasised that the protests were not anti-American nor anti-British, nor anti-French: just anti their nuclear policies. The writings of many Americans, who could not be dismissed as "naïve trendy lefties," assisted the peace activities including Einstein, Eisenhower in his farewell speech, Nimmitz in his retirement speech, the politically powerful Herbert York who wrote *Race to Oblivion*, Rear Admiral La Roque, the Pugwash scientists, and Robert Aldridge, Head of the design team for the Marv missile for the Trident submarine.

The nuclear disarmament movement in New Zealand achieved success because, fundamentally, it was a people's movement. In the 1970s, and 1980s as many as 300 active peace organisations supported by hundreds of concerned citizens encouraged the politicians to realise nuclear disarmament was civilisation's only alternative. The politicians were forced to heed an alert, well educated, widely travelled, and "security literate" populace.

Peace organisations may have had different emphases in their goals and objectives but demonstrated an unusual degree of cooperation. The Campaign for Nuclear Disarmament, the Foundation for Peace Studies, the World Peace Council, Greenpeace Scientists Against Nuclear Arms, Peace Movement Aotearoa, Just Defense, LIMIT, Pacific People's Anti-Nuclear Action Committee, Nuclear Free Peacemaking Association, Coalition Against Nuclear Warships, Peace Squadron, and various professional groups including physicians, clergy and engineers, etc., involved hundreds of dedicated people and hours of their time. The Churches, Unions, Maori groups, educational institutions and women's groups could always be relied on for support. But it also came from people such as Judge Harold Evans and Sir Robert Jones, a wealthy property developer and boxing aficionado.

New Zealand has welcomed and thrived on the support given by people around the world who oppose the "mad momentum" of the arms race which could blow apart civilisation in a crazy game of thermonuclear roulette. It has has not sought to impose its sense of disease on other countries.

However, in the concluding words of *Nuclear Free —the New Zealand Way*, David Lange affirmed: "New Zealand will always be an affront to the advocates of deterrence and always be a comfort to the supporters of disarmament." Legislators in the Philippines, who voted for a nuclear free constitution, thus ending US activities in the Subic Bay, claimed inspiration from New Zealand's actions. Sweden acknowledges New Zealand's example in strengthening its nuclear free policy by demanding to know whether visiting warships carry nuclear weapons. Similarly, it is alleged that anti-nuclear movements in Japan, Australia, and Norway have found encouragement in New Zealand's stance.

Thus, by strengthening the cause of disarmament, New Zealand's actions have constituted a significant threat to the Western Alliance. Thus, the USA, UK and France have sought to oppose and change our political will. They will not succeed. Hopefully, we have helped to change theirs.

See also: *Nuclear Weapons Abolition; Campaign for Nuclear Disarmament (CND); Disarmament and Development*

JOHN HINCHCLIFF

Nicolai, Georg Friedrich

Georg Friedrich Nicolai (born Berlin 1874, died Santiago, Chile 1964), physician, biologist, social philosopher, educator, and humanist, was famous during and after the First World War as the most daring opponent of German militarism. Long neglected by historians, he has been restored to his place as a pacifist thinker and activist of the first rank, thanks to the discovery of his literary estate ("Nicolai Archive," now at the Institut für Zeitgeschichte in Munich) and the studies published recently by modern scholars. Nicolai's magnum opus, *Die Biologie des Krieges* [*The Biology of War*], a milestone of pacifist thought of enduring interest even in the nuclear age, first published in 1917, was reissued in 1983 (Verlag Darmstädter Blätter, 3rd edition) and again, with valuable supplemental material, in 1985 (4th edition).

This work, written in a Prussian fortress in 1915 against a tide of patriotic fanaticism, was the protest of a far-seeing scientist and humanist against the destruction of European civilization by "the barbarians on both sides." Seeking to place pacifism on an objective scientific basis, Nicolai combined biological data and population statistics with historical and cultural arguments to support his thesis that war in the technological age had become an anachronism, analogous to cannibalism and slavery as an obsolete, inefficient, and morally unacceptable means of resolving conflicts of interest between nations. Dismissing the warlike passions of his contemporaries as atavistic remnants of a primitive stage in human history, and refuting at the same time the popular pseudo-Darwinian notion that war ("the bath of steel") assured the survival of the fittest, he called the fratricidal slaughter a biological and moral catastrophe and an obstacle to the evolution of a higher (that is, more intelligent) type of human being. "Reason never can, nor ever will justify war, and modern attempts to do so in the face of contrary evidence have failed miserably. The morality of the future must be compatible with evolutionary interests of the species."

Coming from a man who in peacetime had been a renowned professor at the University of Berlin and who was already suspected of harboring "antinational" (that is, pacifist) views, this was a dangerous heresy. The authorities regarded *The Biology of War* as a threat to the war morale of the public and confiscated the plates. But Nicolai, who meanwhile had been forcibly drafted into the army and served as a lowly orderly in the medical corps, had taken the precaution of smuggling copies of the manuscript across the Swiss border. After a delay of almost two years, the book appeared in Zurich, ostensibly without the author's knowledge. Nicolai was court-martialed for violating the Articles of War. Though his "crime" called for a jail sentence, the military judges, afraid of creating a martyr, let him off with a modest fine. But the book created an international sensation and overnight placed Nicolai in a position of moral and intellectual leadership among pacifists everywhere. Suppressed and boycotted in Germany even after the war, the book quickly appeared in English, Danish,

Swedish, Finnish, and, ultimately, Romanian, Russian, Japanese, and Spanish translations, carrying Nicolai's ideas to every corner of the war-weary globe. Romain Rolland in his voluntary exile on Lake Geneva called him "Le Grand Européen" and asked Albert Einstein, who happened to be in Switzerland just then, to convey his admiration to "this great, free and serene spirit." He then wrote a two-part essay on Nicolai, which he later incorporated in his book *Les Précurseurs*, and in 1918, with the war still going on, he wrote the preface to the next edition of Nicolai's work. In 1919, Nicolai in turn translated Rolland's great postwar manifesto calling for the reconciliation of Europe's intellectuals and asked his countrymen to support it. The two men, by ignoring the hatred of their peoples for each other, set the most striking example for overcoming it.

The Biology of War contained a wealth of ideas that have since become commonplace but were novel and daring at a time when war was still looked upon as legitimate and even desirable. The Germans especially, proud of their military tradition and blinded by the government's propaganda, glorified the war of 1914-18 as an heroic struggle against numerically superior but morally inferior enemies. Nicolai tried to open their eyes to its destructiveness not only in the physical sphere—the loss of lives, the mutilization of young, able-bodied men, the famines and epidemics afflicting the civilian populations, the devastation of the landscape—but in the moral sphere, through the brutalization of the national psyche that resulted from the mass killings. He foresaw the downfall of the Hohenzollerns, the horrors of the Third Reich, genocide, the waning of European influence in world affairs, and the breakdown of an international order that granted sovereignty—and with it the right to make war—to political entities organized as national states.

The personal courage it took to utter such ideas while the war was still in progress and while Nicolai himself was still in the German military gave his book its unique moral weight. Most of his academic brethren were ardent supporters of the war. Nicolai had opposed it from the start. With the publication of *The Biology of War* he had crossed his Rubicon: he had become the only German academic publicly to condemn the war and to speak of the chauvinism of his colleagues as "the bankruptcy of the German intellect." From this point on he was a pariah, regarded as a traitor not only to his country but to his class, the professorial caste.

Nicolai had not been an active pacifist before 1914, nor did he join any pacifist group during the war, preferring to fight his battles alone. He was in fact an unlikely candidate for the role of a martyr for the cause of peace. Professor of Physiology and Medicine at Berlin; senior physician at the *Charité* Germany's most prestigious teaching hospital; world-renowned as an expert in electrocardiography; one-time co-worker of Ivan Pavlov in St. Petersburg and of equally distinguished scientists in Holland and Italy; socially prominent in Wilhelmine Germany; married to an heiress whose father was an industrialist and confidant of the Kaiser; consulted by the aristocracy and even the Imperial family; he might have been expected to conform to the patriotic spirit that pervaded all levels of German society in the August days of 1914. But hidden underneath the glamorous Wilhelmine personage was the incorruptible intellect of a rational thinker. He came from a family of dissidents to whom the very name of Bismarck was anathema. His father, an old-line democrat who had fought on the barricades in 1848, gave up a prized position as assistant to the great chemist Bunsen in order to join the battle for a democratic constitution as a political journalist. His mother, an emancipated woman, leaned toward socialism and surrounded herself with "radical" friends. Nicolai himself, brilliant, precocious, and rebellious, was expelled from several schools but acquired a vast fund of knowledge from extracurricular readings—Aristotle, Thomas More, Kant, Goethe, Schopenhauer, and Nietzsche, but also Karl, Marx, J. S. Mill, and Henry George, and above all Darwin. Later he studied medicine, attracted no doubt by its scientific aspects. He spent a semester in Paris where he was exposed to Gallic mores but also to French utopian socialism, and from where he returned with a lifelong admiration for all things French. After graduating from Heidelberg University he did his doctoral thesis in Leipzig under the great physiologist Ewald Hering. Before accepting a position he traveled for a year in the Far East, observing the various oriental cultures. After returning to Germany (1902) he advanced rapidly, thanks to a phenomenal memory and an almost superhuman capacity for work. He was an enthusiastic participant in international scientific congresses, corresponded with foreign colleagues, and attracted graduate students from abroad, especially from Russia.

For such a man a European war was madness, but he kept quiet until he felt challenged by the publication of the notorious "Manifesto of the 93," in which the flower of German *Kultur*, scientists, artists, and writers, defended the rape of Belgium and proclaimed its solidarity with German militarism. For Nicolai, who saw himself as a citizen of a Republic of Letters that knew no national boundaries, this was intellectual treason. He could not blame the military, whose business it was to fight wars, nor the uneducated masses who were easily seduced by propaganda, but he believed the educated elite had a duty to restrain these elements. In collaboration with Albert Einstein and the astronomer Wilhelm Förster, he promptly (October 1914) drafted a countermanifesto, "Appeal to the Europeans." The "Appeal" deplored the disruption of cultural and economic ties at the very time when advances in technology and communications called for unity. It attributed the war to the "faulty organization" of Europe, comparable to that which led to the decline of the Greek city-states. It predicted that the war, regardless of its outcome, would produce no winners, only losers, and it called upon "the educated men of all nations" to use their influence "so that the terms of the peace do not become the source of future wars."

Only one person, a close friend of Nicolai, was willing to sign the "Appeal." It remained unpublished until 1917, when it appeared in *The Biology of War*. Nicolai meanwhile expressed his views in a lecture series on cultural-biological interactions in human evolution, a topic in which he had long been interested, but which the war had now rendered acute. Rejecting unofficial warnings as threats to academic freedom, he continued his lectures until he was ordered under an administrative pretext to leave Berlin and report for duty at a hospital for contagious diseases in the West Prussian fortress of Graudenz. Here, in the summer of 1915, he expanded his lecture notes into the book that was to be known as *The Biology of War*. He made no secret of his pacifist feelings and was denounced by a colleague for declaring the sinking of the Lusitania, the use of poison gas, and the invasion of Belgium to be reprehensible as well as stupid. Following an investigation for possible treason, and a punitive transfer to a camp for Russian prisoners of war, Nicolai returned to Berlin and resumed his lectures. He was then (April 1916) assigned to the base hospital of the fortress in Danzig. There the commanding officer informed him that he was to refrain from all political utterances, verbal or written. He protested that as a civilian he was not subject to military orders, whereupon he was told to take the oath to the colors. He refused, stating that as a 40-year-old married physician he was not liable to the draft. Within 24 hours he was inducted—illegally, as he maintained—into the army as a private and assigned to laboratory duty as an orderly.

The degradation of a professor was a serious matter in class-conscious Wilhelmine Germany, and the

"Nicolai Case" was brought up in the Reichstag by socialist and progressive deputies and reported in the press, but to no avail. After 18 months in the medical corps—during which he provoked his superiors into court-martialing him again, this time for disciplinary offenses—Nicolai was transferred to the musketeers and sent to a small garrison near Leipzig. Ordered to carry side arms, he refused on the grounds that his rights as a physician and conscientious objector under the Geneva Convention were being violated. Threatened with imprisonment, he went into hiding, reasoning that with the publication of *The Biology of War* the year before he had achieved his purpose and that he had nothing to gain from losing his freedom. Soon afterwards (June 1918) he made a dramatic escape by airplane to Denmark, causing a new international sensation. Having refused to take the oath, he did not consider himself a deserter. The embarrassed German government declared him insane in absentia.

With the eyes of the world focused on him, Nicolai worked hard to bring about a compromise peace. He lectured in many cities throughout Scandinavia and established contact with leading citizens. He founded an international pacifist magazine, *Das werdende Europa* (roughly, "The Europe of the Future"), on whose editorial board such prominent figures as the writer Georg Brandes, the polar explorer Fridtjof Nansen (see Nobel Peace Prize Laureates: *Fridtjof Nansen and The Nansen Office*), the educator Ellen Key, and the Secretary of the prewar Interparliamentary Union, Christian Lange (see Nobel Peace Prize Laureates: *Christian Lange*) agreed to serve. But the war was drawing to a close, and only one issue of Nicolai's magazine appeared before the Armistice.

Meanwhile he was offered Soviet citizenship by Lev Kamenev, Lenin's associate. He refused; he condemned the Bolsheviks for their violence, and in any case he was a bourgeois and considered himself a true German patriot.

In late November 1918 he returned to Germany, where by now the monarchy and the military regime had been toppled. Skeptical but hopeful, Nicolai took a leading part in the efforts to strengthen the fragile democracy of the young Republic and to reestablish contact with the former enemies. He joined the Bund Neues Vaterland, as association of like-minded spirits that included Albert Einstein (see *Einstein, Albert*), Carl von Ossietzky (see Nobel Peace Prize Laureates: *Carl von Ossietzky*), Harry Count Kessler, E. J. Gumbel, the former army officer H. G. von Beerfelde, and the well-known feminist Helene Stöcker. He drafted some of the Bund's manifestos, he

wrote articles for liberal and socialist newspapers and magazines, and spoke at rallies in many cities. He was one of the leaders of the delegation sent to Bern to represent Germany at the conference charged with planning the League of Nations in March 1919, and in 1922 he and two fellow Bund members went to Paris to establish rapport with the peace-minded Ligue des Droits de l'Homme. No one was more dedicated, energetic, and imaginative in trying to restore postwar Germany to a place in the family of Western nations.

But his enemies, the academics whom he had offended with his scathing criticisms during the war, were preparing their revenge. The right-wing press mounted a campaign of hate and slander against the "deserter-professor." In January 1920, when Nicolai tried to resume his medical lectures at the University, he found himself confronted by a mob of rioting nationalist students. He appealed to the academic authorities, but their sympathies lay with the rioters. The Rector, the famous historian Eduard Mayer, a fanatic nationalist, arranged for hearings ostensibly intended to clarify the situation but actually designed to provide a pretext for removing Nicolai from the faculty. The Academic Senate, composed of such distinguished scholars as the theologian Adolf von Harnack, pronounced Nicolai unfit to be a teacher of German academic youth, because his conduct during the war had been harmful to the Reich. It was not a judicial process but the excommunication of a heretic. Abroad Nicolai's expulsion was called "a German Dreyfus affair."

Nicolai fought back. He appealed to the Minister of Education, to the courts, the press, and the public at large, but except for Albert Einstein he found not a single defender among academics. The universities like the courts, were firmly in the hands of the reactionary Old Guard. After a long and bitter struggle, Nicolai gave up and accepted an offer from the Argentine University of Córdoba, then controlled by revolutionary (*reformista*) students. Except for three brief visits he never returned to Germany.

The second half of his long and active life cannot be dealt with in this space. He became an intellectual force in Argentina, later in Chile, and finally throughout Latin America, revered as a teacher and thinker by two generations of students, intellectuals, and progressive politicians, among them Victor Raúl Haya de la Torre, Alfredo Palacios, José Ingenieros, Anibal Ponce, Luis Alberto Sanchez, Gabriela Mistral, and Pablo Neruda. The many books and essays Nicolai wrote between 1925 and 1954, dealing no longer with the specific topic of pacifism but with ethics in general and their relation to science, with epistemology, relativity, dialectics, the psychoanalytic method, and socioeconomic problems, all carefully researched, constitute a rich and still largely unexplored legacy. Thus far none have been translated from the Spanish in which they were written.

Nicolai's central theme in these later works was the relationship between morality and science. Humans must conform to their biological destiny as thinking animals. The history of the species is the history of "cerebralization," he wrote in *El mundo fisico y moral*. The moral sense, he asserted, is not a rational system of thought but a poorly developed instinct inherited from human ancestors. It is compatible with immoral acts. The great "subjective moralists" like Jesus and Socrates failed because they relied on the free will of the individual. "To entrust the moral law to the free will is to remove it from rational examination. It is a fundamental error to consider science and ethics as separate spheres." The future of humans is determined by biological history. "He who understands what it means to be human is ipso facto objectively moral."

Bibliography
Nicolai G F 1917 *Die Biologie des Kriges, Betrachtungen eines Deutschen Naturforschers*. Orell Füssli, Zurich [Grande C, Grande J (transl.) 1919 *The Biology of War*. Dent, London]

Nicolai G F 1923 *Aufruf an die Europäer, gesammelte Aufsätze zum Wiederaufbau Europas*. Wiener Graphischen Werk stätte, Leipzig

Nicolai G F 1931 *El mundo fisico y moral en su concepción cientifica, un ensayo biológico-moral*. Talleres Graficos Argentinos, Buenos Aires

Relgis E 1949 *Georg Fr. Nicolai, un sabio y un hombre del porvenir*. Ediciones Reconstruir, Buenos Aires

Rolland R 1923 Un grand Européen. *Les Précurseurs*. Albin Michel, Paris

Sanchez L A 1938 Georg Frederic Nicolai, "El Gran Europeo," "Ciudadano del Mundo." *Hoy* 1 (June)

Urrutia G 1966 Jorge Nicolai, Un sabio contradictorio. *Hombres y Pueblos*. Editora Austral, Santiago

Vom Brocke B 1985 Wissenschaft und Militarismus. Der "Aufruf an die Kulturwelt der 93" und der Zusammenbruch der internationalen Gelehrtenrepublik. In: Calder W M III, Flascher H, Lindken T (eds.) 1985 *Wilamowitz nach 50 Jahren*. Wissenschaftliche Buchgesellschaft, Darmstadt

Vom Brocke B 1985 Wissenschaft versus Militarismus: Nicolai, Einstein und die "Biologie des Krieges." Mit einer "Dokumentation" von Rektor und Senat der Universität Berlin und einem Ausblick auf die Theologie Karl Barths ("Wissenschaft und Militarismus" II). *Annali dell'Instituto storico italo-germanico* X

Winter I 1960 G. F. Nicolai. *Forschen und Wirken*. Festschrift zur 150-Jahr-Feier der Humboldt Universität

Zuelzer W 1974 Deutscher Geist und der Krieg, II. Im Kampf mit der Macht, Georg Friedrich Nicolai. *Merkur* 28(12)

Zuelzer W 1982 *The Nicolai Case, A Biography*. Wayne State University Press, Detroit, Michigan [1981 *Der Fall Nicolai*, Frankfurter Societäts, Frankfurt]

WOLF ZUELZER

Niemöller, Martin

Martin Niemöller (1892-1984) was a Protestant parson, the President of the Church of Hessen-Nassau, and Chairman of the German Peace Society (Section of the International of Conscientious Objectors). Ecclesiastical resistance to Nazism and Christian opposition to European nuclear armament are inseparably linked with his name. Niemöller's activities were a symbol for conscience-motivated intervention in politics and had considerable influence upon Christian participation in the peace movement of the then Federal Republic of Germany.

Niemöller was brought up in a protestant parsonage in Westphalia. He initially decided upon a career as an imperial naval officer—a choice consistent with the German Protestant tradition of the alliance between "throne and altar" and with the contemporary adage "A good Christian is a good soldier." During the First World War he was a commanding officer of a submarine stationed in the Mediterranean. But after the disbandment of the imperial navy following the war he became a parson and by 1931 was a well-known pastor in the German capital, Berlin.

As a result of his belief in the direct example of Jesus for all Christians, Niemöller came into conflict with the ruling regime when the Nazis came to power and attempted to bring the Protestant church into line in 1933. From his parish, he organized the "Pfarrernotbund," the core of an anti-Nazi group within the Protestant church known as the "Bekennende Kirche." Support spread rapidly throughout Germany. Although resistance was confined strictly to spiritual and ecclesiastical questions, Niemöller was arrested and put in a concentration camp (KZ) as a "personal prisoner of Hitler" until the Allied forces liberated Germany.

After the Second World War Niemöller was appointed Vice Chairman of the Protestant Church in Germany (EKD) and leader of the EKD Foreign Bureau. In 1947 he was elected President of the Evangelical Church in Hessen-Nassau where he remained until 1964; he declined to hold the title of bishop.

In an extensive series of lectures and sermons which were widely reported in the press, Niemöller attracted considerable publicity for his sharp criticism of postwar society. This criticism sprang from his religious beliefs and, in particular, his interpretation of the New Testament. As a result of his stand, many young Christians adopted an increasingly political interpretation of Christianity. Niemöller was opposed to German rearmament for two reasons: he interpreted the fall of the Third Reich as a judgment, asserting that "God has destroyed our weapons," he also felt that rearmament would result in the permanent division of the German people. Although he stressed repeatedly that he did not wish to involve himself in party politics, he did take part in several initiatives against the remilitarization and division of Germany. In 1954, after a discussion with a nuclear physicist, Otto Hahn, Niemöller formed a more radical opinion, reaching the conclusion that the use of force is irreconcilable with a life in the Imitation of Christ. Thereafter, he was a radical opponent of military service. He also rejected the doctrine of deterrence in many inter-ecclesiastical debates. After his retirement in 1964 he increasingly voiced his criticism of the nuclear deterrent in public: "It is my opinion that the existence of nuclear extermination capacity is a blasphemy of the living God" (Schmidt 1982 p. 42). In Niemöller's view, the doctrine of deterrence as an instrument of international policy exhibited a profound distrust of Jesus Christ. He referred back to the Barmer Theological Declaration (dating from the time of the ecclesiastical resistance to Nazism) which stated: "Jesus Christ constitutes God's powerful claim to our whole life." There are no realms "in which we belong not to Jesus Christ but to other masters" ["*Jesus Christus . . . ist . . . Gottes Kräftiger Anspruch auf unser ganzes Leben.*" *Es gebe keine Bereiche, "in denen wir nicht Jesus Christus, sondern anderen Herren Zu eigen wären.*" (Huber 1983 pp. 19-20)].

For Niemöller the split between thinking and acting in the private sphere on the one hand and the public sphere on the other did not accord with the message of the Bible. He called upon Christians to live and act in the Imitation of Christ in both their private and their public lives. This point of view was sharply criticized by both the press and the public and he was once again accused of being a troublemaker. But the religious values and the unimpeachable anti-Nazi background of Niemöller spoke for themselves and they stood in sharp contrast to the political class of the Federal Republic of the time.

Bibliography

Huber W 1983 *Folgen christlicher Freiheit: Ethik und Theorie der Kirche im Horizont der Barmer Theologischen Erklärung*
Niemöller M 1934 *Vom U-Boot zur Kanzel*
Niemöller M 1935 *Predigtsammlungen*
Niemöller M 1957 *Reden*, 4 vols
Niemöller M 1977 *Reden, Predigten, Denkanstösse 1964-76*
Schmidt D 1959 *Martin Niemöller*
Schmidt D 1982 Der unruhige Lebensweg des Pastors Martin Niemöller. In: Kloppenburg H et al., (eds.) *Martin Niemöller: Festschrift zum 90. Geburtstag*

HANS KARL RUPP

Nobel Peace Prizes

The Nobel Peace Prize[1] is considered the most prestigious recognition of work for peace and humanitarian causes. Alfred Nobel (1833-96), the Swedish inventor of dynamite, left the bulk of his large fortune for the establishment of annual prizes for "those who during the preceding year shall have conferred the greatest benefit on mankind." Prizes in physics, chemistry, medicine, and literature were to be granted by Swedish institutions; the fifth prize was to be given to the person "who shall have done the most or the best for fraternity between nations, for the abolition or reduction of standing armies and for the holding and promotion of peace congresses." It was to be awarded by a committee of five persons to be elected by the Storting, the parliament of Norway, then united with Sweden under a common monarch.

Nobel had first become interested in peace in his youthful reading of Shelley. While his fortune came mostly from the production of explosives, these were mainly used in mining and the building of railroad tunnels and canals. He knew that his inventions increased the effectiveness of the engines of war, but he thought that this process would ultimately make war so terrible that it would be brought to an end. Through his Austrian friend, Baroness Bertha von Suttner (see Nobel Peace Prize Laureates: *Bertha van Suttner*), Nobel learned about the peace movement, which was organizing internationally in the early 1890s, with the Baroness as one of its chief leaders (see *Peace Movement in the Nineteenth Century*). He made generous contributions to support her activities by writing and playing a major role in international peace congresses. He told her that one day he would do something really important for the peace movement, and this is what he had in mind when he wrote his will.

Since Nobel did not like lawyers, he wrote the will himself. It was loosely drawn, and the executors had a difficult time getting it probated. At stake was an estate amounting to over 33 million Swedish kronor, and the tax authorities and Nobel's relatives had to be settled with. The executors also had to secure the agreement of the institutions that were to award the prizes and the approval of the King of Sweden. Finally the Nobel Foundation was set up to administer the funds and oversee the prize procedures. Its directors have done a remarkable job of handling the finances, especially in recent years. In 1996 the amount of each prize was 7.4 million Swedish kronor (about US$ 1.2 million). The 1997 prize was supposed to be 7.5 million Swedish kronor.

The Foundation's statutes govern the awards. Nominations are to be submitted by February 1 to the respective juries in order to be considered for the year's prize and should be accompanied by supporting documentation. Nobel's directive to reward work of "the previous year" is to be interpreted to include earlier achievements when their value has recently become recognized. Prizes may be divided, but not into more than three parts. A prize body may postpone a decision for the following year and then decide to withhold the prize altogether but in every five-year period, beginning with the first awards, at least one prize must be granted. Information about the decision making is not to be divulged. All the prizes are to be awarded in ceremonies in Stockholm and Oslo on December 10, the anniversary of Nobel's death. At that time or within six months every laureate is expected to give a lecture in the city of the award. In Oslo the lecture is now usually presented as part of the award ceremony.

Within these general statutes each prize-awarding body is free to develop its own policies and procedures. For example, the regulations for the Peace Prize explicitly provide that awards may be made to institutions as well as individuals, in contrast to the other four. These regulations call for six-year terms for members of the Norwegian Storting's committee, arranged so that three terms end at one time and two at another. Originally high government officials, including premiers and foreign ministers, were members, but in 1937 the regulations were amended to exclude all sitting cabinet members, so that the independence of the committee from the government of Norway would be made clear. Today, active Storting deputies are no longer elected to the committee, although its membership generally reflects the political strengths of the parties in the parliament. A further effort to highlight the committee's independence was the change of name in 1977 from the Nobel Committee of the Norwegian Storting to the Norwegian Nobel Committee.

According to the regulations, those eligible to submit nominations for the Peace Prize are restricted to the following categories:

(a) active and former members and advisors of the committee;

(b) members of national governments and legislatures and of the Inter-Parliamentary Union;

(c) members of the International Court of Arbitration at The Hague;

(d) members of the Commission of the Permanent International Peace Bureau;

(e) members of the Institute of International Law;

(f) university professors of political science, jurisprudence, history, and philosophy;

(g) previous recipients of the Peace Prize.

In the fall of each year the secretary of the committee sends out several thousand announcements soliciting nominations. From the several hundred communications received, a list of those properly nominated is drawn up. For the 1997 prize there were 129, of which twenty-six were organizations. The secretary is the only nonmember of the committee who attends its meetings. He is also Director of the Norwegian Nobel Institute, the scientific institution which each prize body is authorized to establish to assist it in its work.

In its first meeting the committee decides on a short list of nominees, on each one of which the secretary or one of the other three advisors prepares a report. These reports are circulated to the members of the committee who seek to arrive at a decision in the first part of October. No minutes are taken at the meetings, and over the years the commitment to confidentiality has been exceptionally well-maintained. The announcement of the Prize winner is usually made by the chairperson shortly before the middle of October, with a short communication which has been approved by the committee, giving the reasons for the decision. This is the only public document about this rationale from the committee as a whole. At the award ceremony on December 10, the chair or another member of the committee gives a fuller statement in the speech of presentation, but while he or she might refer to the thinking of the committee, there is no committee approval beforehand. The ceremony, which was for many years held in the large auditorium of the University of Oslo, has since 1990 taken place in the more capacious assembly space at Oslo's city hall.

Nobel may have expected that his Peace Prizes would mainly go to activists like Bertha von Suttner, but his will was phrased in very general terms, and in seeing such a testament through probate the executors made much of the point that in his working relationships Nobel would often express an idea and then leave it to be carried out by those in whom he had confidence. In just this way the Norwegian Nobel committees have tried to remain faithful to Nobel's larger purpose as they have understood it, while going about this in their own fashion. Of the three types of peace endeavor that Nobel did specify in his will, the committees have made awards for arms control efforts and promotion of peace congresses, but they have given an ever-broader interpretation to Nobel's phrase about working for "fraternity between nations," eventually coming to consider any distinguished achievement for human solidarity as qualified for the award.

In the years before the First World War the committee did honor many leaders of the organized peace movement and also practitioners of international law who were trying to extend the area of relations between states that would be subject to the rule of law. In its very first award, however, the committee struck out on its own by sharing the 1901 prize between Frédéric Passy of France, doyen of the international organized peace movement, and Henry Dunant, founder of the Red Cross. Baroness von Suttner and her co-workers complained that the latter organization, however worthy its relief of suffering caused by war, did nothing to prevent it. To the first Nobel Peace Prize committee, however, the work of the Red Cross was a demonstration of human fraternity even in the midst of fratricidal conflict, and later committees honored Red Cross organizations on three separate occasions.

The Dunant award was the first of many for humanitarian effort. The list includes the Norwegian explorer, Fridtjof Nansen (1922), called "the patron saint of the refugees" for his work for the homeless and uprooted under the League of Nations (see *League of Nations*); the organizations of the League of Nations and the United Nations (see *Status and Role of the United Nations*) that continued his work; and those inspired by their religious convictions to help the victims of war, poverty, and disease, such as the Quakers (1947), Albert Schweitzer (1952), and Mother Teresa (1979). Jane Addams of Hull House (1931) was honored as both a great humanitarian and the leading spirit of the Women's International League for Peace and Freedom (WILPF). The committees have also recognized efforts to provide food for the world's hungry, with awards to Lord Boyd Orr (1949), the British physician who headed the Food and Agriculture Organization (FAO) and then was president of the World Union of Peace Organizations, and to Norman Borlaug (1970), the American scientist whose research led to increased agricultural production.

In the period before the First World War, almost half of all the prizes went to veterans of the organized peace movement. In the period between the two World Wars, prizes went to Christian Lange of Norway (1921), for many years the soul of the Inter-Parliamentary Union; to the German and French peace leaders Ludwig Quidde and Ferdinand Buisson (1927), in recognition of the Franco-German reconciliation after the war; and to Lord Cecil (1937), who had qualified as the British cofounder of the League of Nations and then for his help in shaping its institutions as a government delegate in Geneva. He received the prize much later, after he had left government service to organize a powerful movement of opinion in support of the League. Since World War II the peace activists who received the prize have included Emily Greene Balch (1946), who succeeded Jane Addams as leader of the WILPF; Philip J. Noel-Baker (1959), the British crusader for disarmament, to Linus Pauling (1962), who led an international campaign among scientists that helped produce an atomic test ban treaty, Betty Williams and Mairead Corrigan (now Maguire), co-workers for peace between Catholics and Protestants in Northern Ireland (1976); International Physicians for the Prevention of Nuclear War (1985); and the physicist Joseph Rotblat, a longtime opponent of nuclear weapons, who shared the 1995 prize with the Pugwash Conferences on Science and World Affairs (see *Pugwash Conferences on Science and World Affairs*), the organization he headed.

As the awards to peace activists declined, those for statesmen increased, and the majority of the total number of awards have gone to them. The first was in 1906, when the committee honored President Theodore Roosevelt for his role as mediator in ending the Russo-Japanese War. Between the World Wars there were ten awards to statesmen, and even more after the Second World War. It was these awards that first made the Peace Prize newsworthy, but some of them have been the most controversial. Critics have argued that statesmen should be *hors de combat*, since their achievements are made possible by the office they hold, and they are not to be compared with men and women who devote their lives to peacemaking. But a persuasive case can be made for judging political contributions in a much longer perspective. The awards to Roosevelt, Foreign Minister Gustav Stresemann of Germany (1926), and Secretary of State Frank B. Kellogg (1929) , for example, have not stood up very well in the light of historical research. There is always the possibility that a statesman may make a significant contribution to peace and then become a warrior, like Menachem Begin (1978). In the case of Henry Kissinger (1973), whose award produced widespread protests because of United States policy in Indochina, the ceasefire agreement for which he and Le Duc Tho of North Vietnam were named for the Prize, did not hold up. Le Duc Tho refused to accept the Prize, and Kissinger tried unsuccessfully to return it later. The committee takes the position that it makes an award for a particular effort for peace, whether this turns out to be successful or not.

There have, indeed, been statesman awards that have enhanced the reputation of the committee; Woodrow Wilson (1919), for the League of Nations; Arthur Henderson (1934), the dedicated British chairman of the League Disarmament Conference; Secretary of State Cordell Hull (1945) for his "Good Neighbor" policy toward Latin America and his role in the establishment of the United Nations; Ralph Bunche (1950), the UN mediator who ended the Arab-Israeli hostilities over Palestine in 1949, who was the first Black to receive the prize; UN Secretary-General Dag Hammarskjöld of Sweden (1961), the only posthumous award (now permitted only if the laureate dies after the prize has been first announced); the German Chancellor Willy Brandt (1971), for his reconciling *Ostpolitik* (see *Ostpolitik*). None of these awards, of course, was without its critics.

In more recent statesman awards, the committee has been explicit in declaring that the prize was intended not just to reward past efforts, but to encourage and facilitate peacemaking already under way. Such was the case with the prize for President Oscar Arias Sanchez of Costa Rica (1987), whose initiatives to end civil wars in Central America began a process that ended successfully only ten years later. After the award to Mikhail Gorbachev (1990) for his contribution toward ending the Cold War, the committee again played a peacemaking role itself, using the prize to help promote ongoing efforts to end a conflict. In 1993 the committee divided the award between President F.W. de Klerk of South Africa and the leader of the opposition to apartheid, Nelson Mandela, President of the African National Congress. The following year, in accordance for the first time with the Nobel Foundation statutes permitting the prize to be shared between three parties, the committee awarded it jointly to Yasser Arafat, President of the Palestinian National Authority and head of the Palestinian Liberation Organization, and two Israeli leaders, Yitzhak Rabin, Prime Minister, and Shimon Peres, Foreign Minister.

In explaining these awards, Committee Chairman Egil Arvik declared in 1983, "Nobel's will does not state this, but the will was made in another time. Today we realize that peace cannot be established without a full respect for freedom." The precedent for such prizes was the courageous award for the Nazi concentration camp prisoner Carl von Ossietzky (1935). He was an antimilitarist journalist, on behalf of whose candidacy an international campaign was organized that enlisted the support of some of the most prominent intellectuals and politicians of the time.

The line of more recent human rights laureates began with Albert Lutuli (1960), the Zulu chieftain who led the first important movement for Blacks in South Africa. Just as Lutuli resisted the policies of the South African government, later human rights awardees have similarly braved the wrath of their governments for holding to their principles. Andrei Sakharov (1975), the Soviet nuclear scientist, was sent into internal exile for his courageous stand for human rights, disarmament, and international cooperation; Adolfo Pérez Esquivel (1980), Argentinian leader of the major international association for human rights is Latin America, was in prison when he was nominated for the prize; Lech Walesa (1983) was detained by the Polish government because of his struggle for the rights of workers to organize; Aung San Suu Kyi (1971) was for years held under house arrest by the military dictatorship of Myanmar (Burma); Rigoberta Menchú Tum (1992), the Mayan Indian whose parents were murdered by the Guatemalan military, spent most of her time in Mexico beyond their reach. The staunch opposition to apartheid of Bishop Tutu (1984) was tolerated by the South African government because of his religious identity, as was also the case with Bishop Belo of East Timor (1996), whose protests against the violation of human rights by the Indonesian occupying troops vastly displeased the authorities in Jakarta. It has never been safe for his fellow-laureate, José Ramos-Horta, to return to East Timor since the Indonesian invasion in 1975. In his years of exile, Ramos-Horta has defended the human rights of the East Timorese people, just as the Dalai Lama of Tibet (1989), also self-exiled, has been doing for his own people. In all these awards the committee has made the point that the laureates were working for their objectives by nonviolent means.

Other awards for human rights have gone to Martin Luther King, Jr. (1964) for his role in the civil rights movement in the United States; to the author of the United Nations Declaration of Human Rights (see *Declaration of the Rights of Man*), René Cassin of France (1968); to Amnesty International (1977), the organization that defends prisoners of conscience all over the world; to Sean MacBride (1974), who was prominent in the work of Amnesty International and has labored for peace and human rights on many fronts; and to Elie Wiesel (1986), the Holocaust survivor and interpreter, who has become a witness for truth and justice and human unity.

Peace researchers have criticized the committee for its failure to develop a basic theory of peace. Its earlier approach has been as one of its chairmen declared long ago, to be on the watch for *all* development which may have future potentialities for peace. With more justice the committee has been criticized for its earlier pro-Western orientation, which has naturally been a reflection of the international outlook of most Norwegians. The country with the greatest number of awards is the United States with eighteen, followed by the United Kingdom with eleven, France with seven, and Sweden with five. Not until 1960 did the committee begin to think globally, with the prize for Lutuli. The first Asian to be chosen was Le Duc Tho in 1973, who declined. In the very next year the committee named former Premier Sato of Japan, and it has continued since then to give more recognitions to regions of the non-West. Of the thirteen individual laureates from 1986 to 1996, only one was from the United States and one from the United Kingdom, while 4 were from Eastern Asia, three were from the Middle East, two from South Africa, and two from Central America.

On other counts as well, recent awards have met earlier criticisms. Nobel had hoped his Prizes would endow younger laureates with the resources to go on to higher achievement. In all five fields, however, the prizes have most frequently gone to older laureates, whose greatest achievements were behind them. This was especially true for the peace prize in its earliest years, when the committee wanted to honor the older veterans of the organized peace movement. In the last twenty years the average age of the twenty-two individual prize winners is about fifty-six, with only two octogenarians on the list and a number of laureates in their thirties and forties with many years left for peacemaking.

Nobel would have been surprised that Baroness von Suttner was not honored until the fifth year of the award. In the first seventy-five years, in fact, there were only two other women laureates, Addams (1931) and Balch (1946). Between 1977 and 1982, however, four more were added, Williams and Corrigan (1976), Mother Teresa (1979) and Alva Myrdal (1982), who worked for arms control at the United Nations and later became a peace activist. Then in 1991 and 1992, Aung San Suu Kyi and Menchú Tum were named, for a total of only nine awards to women. Ever since 1949 there has been a woman member of the committee, however, and for more than a decade a woman was chair.

Nobel had expected that his prizes would be given only to individuals. Of the 101 peace prizes, however, seventeen have been granted to institutions. He had intended that the prizes would be given every year, but in the seventy-three peacetime years the committees withheld the prize on ten occasions, either failing to agree or agreeing that there was no qualified candidate. In the twelve years when world wars were raging, the committees made only two awards, both to the Red Cross. Twenty-one prizes have been divided, but only once into three parts. Since 1972, when no prize was awarded, the committee has not missed a year, although the award for 1976 was postponed until the next year, when Corrigan and Williams received it.

While certain of Nobel's intentions might have been disregarded or modified in many of the Peace awards, the Norwegian Nobel Committees have actually made of the prize something far greater than Nobel could ever have dreamed. It has been no easy task to identify the worthiest peacemakers in a century of violence. Committee members have had to grow accustomed to criticism and controversy. Theirs has also been a service for peace. Once every year, in the midst of wars and rumors of wars, the world's attention is turned to the search for peace and human solidarity. With the best of their awards, the Peace Prize committees have inspired what Martin Luther King called in his Oslo address "an audacious faith in mankind."

Notes

1. Articles on each individual Nobel Laureate in Peace may be found in Volume III.

Bibliography

Abrams I 1962 Bertha von Suttner and the Nobel Peace Prize. *J. Central European Affairs* 22

Abrams I (ed.) 1997 *Nobel Lectures, Peace, 1972-1990*, 2 vols. World Scientific, Singapore & River Edge, NJ

Abrams I 1988 *The Nobel Peace Prize and the Laureates. An Illustrated Biographical History, 1901-1987*. Hall, Boston, MA. Revision in process.

Abrams I (ed.) 1995 *The Words of Peace. Selections from the Speeches of the Winners of the Nobel Peace Prize*, rev. edn. Newmarket, New York

Falnes O J 1938 *Norway and the Nobel Peace Prize*. Columbia University Press, New York

Fant K 1993 *Alfred Nobel. A Biography*. tr. from Swedish. Arcade, New York

Gray T 1976 *Champions of Peace*. Paddington Press, London

Haberman F W (ed.) 1972 *Nobel Lectures. Peace, 1901-1970*. 3 vols. Elsevier, New York

Heillberg T, L M Jansson 1986 *Alfred Nobel*. tr. from Swedish. rev. edn. Lagerblads, Karlshamm, Sweden

Holl K, A C Kjelling (eds.) 1994 *The Nobel Peace Prize and the Laureates . . . . The Meaning and Acceptance of the Nobel Peace Prize in the Prize Winnersd' Countries*. Lang, Frankfurt am Main

Nobel Foundation 1901-*Les Prix Nobel*. (published annually) Almqvist Wiksell International, Stockholm

Nobel Foundation 1972 *Nobel, The Man and His Prizes*, 3rd rev. edn. Elsevier, New York

The Nobel Prize Annual 1988 1989-(published annually) IMG Publishing, New York

Sohlman R 1983 *The Legacy of Alfred Nobel*. tr. from Swedish. Bodley Head, London

Sverdrup J 1984 Norway and the Peace Prize. *Peace and Change: A Journal of Peace Research* 10

IRWIN ABRAMS

Nonalignment

Of the many momentous changes brought about by the Second World War (1939-45), the emergence of the US of America and the former Soviet Union as the two major contending powers, each convinced of the superiority of their respective ideologies and social systems, was perhaps the most important in shaping the postwar world. The second most important development was the dissolution of the European and the Japanese empires and the birth of colonial territories as independent nations. Both these developments in their own way contributed to the emergence of nonalignment as an instrument of foreign policy. The first gave rise to the "Cold War" (see *Cold War*), and it was the desire of the newly emerging countries not to become involved with the Cold War which gave birth to the idea of nonalignment. In doing so, the developing countries were, possibly not consciously, following in the footsteps of the US of America in her early stages of development. As early as April 1793 President George Washington issued a proclamation of neutrality (see *Neutrality; Neutrality, Permanent*) advocating "a conduct friendly and impartial toward the belligerent powers" (Perkins 1995 p. 67). In his Farewell Address, the president had stated: "With me, a predominant motive has been to endeavor to

gain time to our country to settle and mature its yet recent institutions and to progress without interruption to the degree of strength and constancy *which is necessary to give it command of its own fortunes*" (italics mine) (ibid., p. 67). To have the command of one's own fortunes has been the very basic motivation of nonalignment in the post-Second World War.

Both economically and militarily, the US had come out of the Second World War stronger than ever before. Between 1939 and 1945 the US gross national product in constant dollars (1939) had risen from $88.6 billion to $135 billion. During the four years between 1940 and 1944 the industrial production increased at an annual unprecedented rate of fifteen per cent per annum. Much of this consisted of war production but the manufactures for civilian uses had increased significantly. By the end of the war, nearly half of world's total manufactures and a third of total output of goods of all types was being produced within the US (Kennedy 1988 p. 358). The problem, of course, was that such a level of production could not be maintained for the lack of purchasing power in the war devastated countries in Europe and in Asia. The reconstruction of the war devastated Europe and Asia required vast infusion of the US economic assistance. Yet, the public opinion within the US considered international problems less important than domestic ones and the Truman Administration was apprehensive that any major request for funding foreign assistance may be turned down by the Congress unless the President presented the issues to the American public in terms of a crusade against communism "to scare the hell out of the country" as Senator Vandenberg had suggested to the president (Freehand 1985 p. 89). It was in this context that in his address to the joint session of the Congress on March 12, 1947, President Truman (see *Truman Doctrine*) stated:

> At the present moment in world history nearly every nation must choose between alternative ways of life. The choice is often not a free one. One way of life is based upon the will of the majority, and is distinguished by free institutions, representative government, free elections, guaranteeing of individual liberty, freedom of speech and religion, and freedom from political oppression. The second way of life is based upon the will of a minority forcibly imposed upon the majority. It relies upon terror and oppression, a controlled press and radio, fixed elections, and suppression of personal freedom.
>
> I believe that it must be the policy of the US to support free peoples who are resisting attempted subjugation by armed minorities or by outside pressures .... I believe that our help should be primarily through economic and financial aid which is essential to economic stability and orderly political process ....
> (Freehand 1985 pp. 85-86)

It was an enunciation of a foreign policy so wide-ranging in implication that it virtually denied the right of armed revolution to an independence movement in a colony or against a tyrannical government, for it could be claimed by those under threat that they were fighting a communist insurgency or a nationalist leader could be branded as a communist. Some of these elements of the Doctrine came to be challenged even within the US. Walter Lippmann, the veteran journalist, "attacked Truman for by-passing the United Nations and for the open-ended nature of his pledge of assistance. Lippmann also questioned the wisdom of helping the [then] reactionary Greek government" (Ambrose 1985 pp. 86-7). US Secretary of State George Marshall, at that time in Paris en route to Moscow, was "somewhat startled to see the extent to which the anti-communist element of the speech was stressed" (Freehand 1985 p. 100). George Kennan also had serious reservations regarding the universal nature of the policy statement and he wondered whether the US had the ability to meet such a

wide-ranging commitment. From then on the US policy began to be presented in more and more emotional terms. For instance, President Eisenhower called the US-Soviet struggle as "Forces of good and evil are massed and armed and opposed as rarely before in history. Freedom is pitted against slavery, lightness against dark" (Kennedy 1988 p. 372) (see *Peace with Freedom*).

No doubt, much of this political rhetoric was for domestic consumption yet it must have infuriated the Soviet leadership. The former Soviet Union had felt cheated when it was excluded from any major gains in Japan. General MacArthur was a Supreme Allied Commander responsible to all the governments at war with Japan but he ignored governments other than the American (Ambrose 1985 p. 53). Another major bone of contention was the status of the Eastern European countries. These countries were liberated by the the Red Army and were under the Soviet control. The American leadership, while acknowledging that the Russian security required friendly governments in the Eastern European countries insisted on these countries having democracy, freedom of religion and speech and free enterprise. Given the history of Eastern Europe, a free election would rarely elect a government friendly to the Soviet Union (ibid., p. 56). The American arguments in favor of democracy and related human freedoms were, to say the least, disingenuous. It was well-known that from the early days of American expansionism in the Western Hemisphere "the US maintained a near hegemony over Central and South America (through military dictatorships in most cases). It was true that free elections in East Europe would result in anti-Soviet governments, but it was equally true that free elections in Latin America probably would bring power to anti-American governments" (ibid., p. 63). Between 1898 and 1934 the US had launched more than thirty military interventions in Latin America partly to protect their economic interests and partly to assert their geopolitical hegemony. Some of these interventions were short-lived, yet in others military occupations lasted several years. "In Nicaragua, American forces occupied the country almost constantly from 1909 to 1934; in Haiti, US troops lingered from 1915 to 1934; in Dominican Republic, they established military rule from 1916 to 1924. The basic goal of US policy, as commentators repeatedly said at the time, was to convert the Caribbean into an 'American lake' (Smith 1996 pp. 52-3) (see *Pax Americana*). It is difficult to say whether, in determining its East European policies, the Soviet leadership was taking its clue from the long history of US hegemony in Latin America; it is doubtful whether they would be totally oblivious to it. Nevertheless, in the development of the concept and the practice of nonalignment, the newly emerging countries had to learn much from the Latin American experience.

Confident of its economic and military might, the US Administration gave snub after snub to the former Soviet Union. When Truman met the Soviet Foreign Minister, V. M. Molotov, in April 1945, he not only vigorously chided him but also warned him that no reconstruction aid would be forthcoming unless the then Soviet Union was prepared to accept the US's interpretation of the Yalta accords. The former Soviet Union was exposed to various other provocations by the US and its allies. Only three days after Victory in Europe (V.E.) Day, Lend-Lease aid to the former Soviet Union and other allies was abruptly cut. The decision to stop shipment to the former Soviet Union was implemented with such zeal that the US officials "turned back ships already at sea" (Paterson 1973 p. 44). Later, Truman reversed his previous executive order and the supplies were resumed (Ambrose 1985 p. 66). A subsequent request for loans by the former Soviet Union for postwar reconstruction was repeatedly deferred for political reasons while generous loans were given to the United Kingdom, France and Italy. In spite of the fact that the Yalta Conference had promised to restore the former rights—the rights discontinued after the Japanese take-over of Manchuria—of the former Soviet Union in Manchuria, Chiang Kai-Shek refused Soviet requests to establish joint companies in Manchuria. Similarly, Soviet oil concessions in Iran were refused. In 1948 export controls were introduced to reduce trade with communist countries and to halt the flow of defense equipment to the then Soviet Union. All this gave the then Soviet Union a feeling that the US was creating an anti-Soviet bloc.

In response to the Truman Administration's hard line, the former Soviet Union began to consolidate and to assert its influence in the Eastern European countries through bilateral treaties, reparation collections, and joint ownership of industries. The former Soviet Union signed trade treaties with Bulgaria, Rumania, and Hungary in 1945 giving the former Soviet Union considerable influence in their economies. By mid-1946, barter deals between Bulgaria, Rumania, Hungary, Poland, and Czechoslovakia on the one hand and the former Soviet Union on the other enabled the latter to receive regular supplies of coal from Poland, and oil from Rumania. A number of joint ventures with 50 percent Soviet equity participation were also established in Rumania and Hungary. All this togeth-

er with the Soviet refusal to allow free elections to be held in these countries was considered by the US to be an "exclusive penetration" of these countries by the former Soviet Union and a hostile act toward the US as was the spate of nationalization of industries in the Eastern European countries. When the US government announced the Marshall Plan which was to be administered bilaterally under US supervision, the former Soviet Union countered this by signing trade treaties with the Eastern European countries and tying them together in the Molotov Plan (Paterson 1973 p. 29). In February 1948 a Soviet-inspired *coup d'état* brought communism to Czechoslovakia. The Danubian Conference held in February 1948 clearly showed that the former Soviet Union was not prepared to compromise where its security was potentially at risk. It was in March 1948 that the US imposed a full-scale export control on products destined for the former Soviet Union and the Eastern European countries. Thus, by the Spring of 1948 the scene for future Soviet-American confrontation was set and the two superpowers were already in control of their spheres of influence. The former Soviet Union did not yet have the atomic bomb, but it did not take long to produce one. A nuclear device was exploded by the former Soviet Union in September 1949 and it had the bomb early the next year. It was in this atmosphere of growing East-West tension (see *East-West Conflict*) that many newly emerging countries were born as independent nations.

1. Nature of Nonalignment as Principle of Foreign Policy

Majority of the newly independent countries under colonial rule, had the experience of being dragged without choice into big power rivalries and wars. They were also acquainted with the fate of the Latin American and the Eastern European countries who in spite of their political independence had little freedom of action. After having won their freedom after long struggles, the newly independent countries intended to guard their freedom jealously and avoid being subservient once again to foreign powers. Therefore, it was natural for them to distance themselves from the superpowers.

The advocates of nonalignment as principle of foreign policy have been clear about the distinction between "neutrality" and "nonalignment." "Neutrality" to them has been a passive act of nonparticipation in a conflict between two or more warring nations (see *Neutrality*). "Nonalignment," as they see it, is an active creed to promote a world where weaker nations can live unmolested by powerful nations, choosing their own ideologies and developing political and economic systems in accordance with their own traditions, needs, and potentialities, an ambition not very different to those expressed by President George Washington quoted above.

In this sense nonalignment becomes the cornerstone of developing countries' foreign policy and its constituent elements such as support for liberation movements, opposition to racism and to the arms race, the regulation and control of multinational corporations, or the call for a New International Economic Order (see *New International Economic Order (NIEO)*), have been the natural outcome of their colonial past and the subsequent search for dignity and for the command of their own fortunes. Nonalignment as a principle of foreign policy has been deeply rooted in the belief that poverty, colonization, racism, the domination of the world by major world powers, and the arms race are not isolated events but interrelated phenomena aimed at the perpetuation, in one form or another, of control and influence by the economically and militarily powerful countries. It is the inequitable distribution of wealth and power both within a country and between countries which gives rise to internal as well as international conflicts. In order to sustain their world supremacy the richer countries, particularly at the height of the superpower rivalry, developed more and more sophisticated weapons and built up their nuclear arsenals. Mutual suspicion coupled with the desire to attain superiority of one over the other, further fueled the arms race endangering the very existence of humankind (see *Arms Race, Dynamics of*). The piling up of the increasingly sophisticated weapons of assured mutual destruction made it unthinkable for the superpowers to contemplate direct confrontation. At the same time, promoting military-strategic interests led the superpowers to coopt allies and satellite nations by economic and more so military ties fueling disastrous regional proxy wars with untold human misery. Proxy wars, supported with weapon exports rather than dispatch of troops, are far cheaper, and less troublesome politically. "A US soldier in Egypt for example, would cost $150,000 a year, while an Egyptian soldier costs $2,100 a year" (SIPRI 1982 p. 180). Such export of arms and related military training to satellite states run by ruthless dictators also provided them with the means for internal repression of democratic and reformist forces. At the height of the Cold War, the extension of hegemonic interests of the two superpowers tended to widen the zones of conflict. In such an atmosphere, in principle, nonalignment of a

nation tended to narrow this zone of conflict. Taken to its logical conclusion, nonalignment of nations could isolate the two superpowers. Thus isolated, the superpowers, finding that a direct confrontation might inevitably bring about their mutual annihilation, would try to find ways and means to avoid such a catastrophe. In this sense nonalignment as principle of foreign policy can be an instrument of peace.

2. Economic and Cultural Emancipation as Key to Political Sovereignty

The newly emerging countries, on their independence, invariably found that their political sovereignty did not have real meaning unless they had economic freedom as well. As a result of their colonial past, they continued to be the producers of primary commodities, their fate being directly linked with the economic and international trade policies of the richer countries. The shipping, processing, and marketing of such products were still largely controlled by the transnational corporations (TNCs) (see *Multinational Corporation and Peace*). In many cases the banking, insurance, and financial institutions of developing countries together with the key manufacturing industries were also dominated by the TNCs. It has not been uncommon that through patronage and bribing of local elites (Ball 1976 p. 295), the TNCs have not only extracted economic and financial concessions but also undermined domestic economic and social policies, particularly labor legislation. Attempts at nationalizing foreign interests by a developing country has incurred the wrath of the countries to which transnational corporations belong. The overthrow of popularly elected governments of Mohammed Mossadegh in Iran in 1953 (Ambrose 1985 p. 155), Arbenz Guzman in Guatemala in 1954 (Smith 1985 pp. 135-37) and of Salvador Allende in Chile in 1973 (Smith 1996 pp. 175-76) were in direct response of their taking over transnational property. In all these cases, the overthrow was organized and overseen by foreign intelligence services. The fear of foreign intervention has been one of the main reasons behind developing countries' reluctance to allow transnationals to operate in their countries. In much the same way, in the early stages of modernization during the Meiji Japan, "the policy in regard to receiving foreign capital was based not so much on purely economic considerations as on worries about international political risks" (Beers 1967 p. 169; Okita and Miki 1967 pp. 139-67).

Blatant interventions in defense of transnational's interests have given way to more subtle ways of promoting private enterprise through the International

Financial Institutions (IFIS), such as the World Bank and the International Monetary Fund (IMF). From their very inception, these agencies have been used by the US as a tool of its foreign policy and a means of economic penetration of developing countries by its transnationals. The dominance of the citizens of the US and other capitalist nations in key positions in these agencies has ensured the imposition of market-oriented development strategy on developing countries. Their most ambitious program of "economic reform" to transform developing countries into "market economies," many elements of which even Adam Smith would have found unacceptable, was set out to help the debt-ridden developing countries of the 1980s (Sinha 1995 pp. 557-75). The economic reform consists of two sets of policies: stabilization, the responsibility of the IMF, and the structural adjustment, the responsibility of the World Bank. "While stabilization aims at controlling inflation and improving balance of payments in order to maintain a reasonable flow of debt servicing, structural adjustment stresses the opening of a country to foreign trade by reducing trade barriers (particularly non-tariff barriers), changing the sectoral balance in the country's development strategy from heavy capital goods to textiles and other consumer goods industries and toward agriculture and from import-substituting industrialization (ISI) to export promoting ones, and enlarging the domain of the private sector (including those of foreign enterprises)" (ibid., p. 558). Some of the other policy measures such as reduction in direct taxes and the increase in indirect ones, the cut-back in public provision of social security, health and higher education and the privatization of social services and public enterprises are aimed at altering the property relations, and hence the distribution of wealth and political power toward the greater empowerment of the rich and big business (both domestic and the foreign), and the renters at the cost of the poor. Most studies suggest that with a few exceptions, structural adjustment has worsened the hard-core poverty even in countries implementing structural adjustment successfully (Toye 1991 p. 169).

Apart from the increasing pressures from the IFIs, developing countries were undergoing some changes from within. There was a genuine concern about the inefficiencies of public enterprises and the ever-expanding size of the bureaucracy had come under criticism. A rapid growth of the Chinese economy after the return of sanity from the chaos of the Cultural Revolution and economic reform introduced by Deng Xiao Ping in 1978 in contrast with the growing economic malaise of the former Soviet Union and the

Eastern European countries was undermining the very *raison d'être* of a planned economic system. The success of other East Asian economies also was, somewhat erroneously, being seen not only as the outcome of private enterprise but also of foreign capital. This was inspite of the fact that the two most successful East Asian countries, Japan and the Republic of Korea had allowed foreign technology but not much of foreign capital in their early stages of development. This distinction between foreign technology and foreign capital has either been glossed over or not sufficiently appreciated. It is also not recognized that except for Hong Kong and Singapore inflow of foreign direct investment (FDI) was not very significant before 1985; it gathered momentum only after the phenomenal appreciation of the yen in 1985. Even then, other than Singapore, FDI as a percentage of gross domestic investment (GDI), between 1986 and 1991 was only eleven per cent in the case of Hong Kong and ten per cent in the case of Malaysia. In Taiwan it was less than four per cent and in the Korean Republic only one per cent (UNCTAD 1994 Tab.1 p. 73). According to the UNCTAD study Malaysia was successful in targeting and attracting electronic assembly which was much more capital- and skill-intensive than the labor-intensive industries attracted by neighboring countries. It had also succeeded in imposing equity-sharing and other conditions on investors. Yet, the study suggested, "however, Malaysia's technological base is small and underdeveloped, TNCs have low local content . . . . The pattern of industrial development has been skewed towards electronics and electrical industries—still assembly operations (though now fairly capital- rather than labor-intensive) with low levels of linkages with local firms, little local design-and-development activity and no independent marketing capability" (ibid., p. 74). Latin America too had begun to attract FDI, until 1990, mainly under the debt-equity swap, an arrangement by which a developing country could reduce its debt while increasing the access to transnationals to its domestic industries and subsequently, by privatization. Much of the FDI into the Latin American countries went into services (telecommunications, tourism, financial and professional services) and natural-resource sectors, petroleum and gas, and gold and copper mining. Overall, with the exception of Mexico and to a certain extent Argentina, manufacturing has failed to attract much FDI (ibid., pp. 84-6). The inflow of FDI into Africa has been rather small and nearly three quarters of the total inflow is limited to oil-exporting countries. (ibid., p. 94). A predominance of natural resources and fuel as the main recipients of FDI runs the risk of the reemergence of a colonial pattern of development both in Africa and Latin America.

Nevertheless, the pro-market and pro-transnational corporation views have become more acceptable in most developing countries because of the large number of returnee students who had gone through the "neoclassical orthodoxy" of the American universities and business schools. The period also saw the emergence of a new class of *nouveau riche* who disliked living an austere life because of trade protectionism and the limited range and the low quality of domestically produced luxuries. They have, like in most Latin American countries, emerged as a new socio-political force favoring market opening and a red-carpet treatment to transnationals for producing a wide range of luxuries while the majority of populations continue living on the margin of subsistence.

Transnationals, particularly, those with defense-industrial capacity, are also the beneficiaries of arms trade, currently (1991-95) averaging nearly thirty billion dollars per year. Ninety per cent of the deliveries come from only four countries, the US, the UK, France and Russia; the US alone accounting for nearly half of the total deliveries. Sustaining the national defense industry and allowing for the upgrading of the advance weapons system have been the avowed aim of both the UK and France for nearly four decades; Russia adopted a similar policy in 1992 and the US in 1995 (IISS 1995-96 pp. 280-81). The advantage of arms trade goes much beyond the defense sectors. In an electronic age the distinction between defense and civilian production is getting ever narrower and the arms-exporting countries have heavily subsidized industries, such as aerospace, electronics and super-computers, having considerable commercial spin-off (Porter 1990 p. 305).

3. Other Forms of Subversion

There have been other forms of interventions with the freedom of the poorer nations to determine their own economic destiny. In order to convert the elite of the developing countries to their own way of thinking, the developed countries offer training, fellowship, and other forms of cultural exchange. News media—the newspapers, radio, and television—supplement these efforts. Such activities, though a form of ideological and cultural subversion, are perfectly legitimate so long as there is an open choice and the developing country governments and elites know who is offering what. In reality, more pernicious attempts at ideological and cultural subversion are

quite common. As Indira Gandhi said in her inaugural address to the Meeting of the Coordinating Bureau of the Non-Aligned Movement held in Algiers in 1976:

> In spite of political sovereignty, most of us who have emerged from a colonial or semi-colonial past continue to have a rather unequal cultural and economic relationship with our respective former overlords. They often remain the main source of equipment and technological guidance. The European language we speak itself becomes a conditioning element. Inadequacy of indigenous educational materials makes us dependent on the books of these dominant countries, especially at the university stage. We imbibe their prejudices. Even our image of ourselves, not to speak of the view of other countries, tends to conform to theirs. The self-deprecation and inferiority complex of some people of former colonies make them easy prey to infiltration through forms of academic colonialism . . . .
> The media of powerful countries want to depict the governments of their erstwhile colonies as inept and corrupt and their people as yearning for the good old days. This cannot be attributed entirely to the common human failing of nostalgia. To a large extent there is a deliberate purpose. Leaders who uphold their national interests and resist the blandishments of multinational corporations and agencies are denigrated and their image falsified in every conceivable way. (Van Dinh 1977 pp. 78-79)

When Indira Gandhi spoke these words, the memories of the US subversion of the legitimate government of Chile were fresh in her mind. Reportedly, the US Central Intelligence Agency (CIA) had spent US $1.5 million in support of *El Mercurio*, the largest Chilean newspaper which became the most important channel for anti-Allende propaganda. The CIA "funded a wide range of propaganda activities. It produced several magazines with national circulations and a large number of books and special studies. It developed material for placement in the *El Mercurio* chain (amounting to a total daily circulation of over 300,000); opposition party newspapers; two weekly newspapers; all radio stations controlled by opposition parties; and on several regular television shows on three channels" (Schiller 1977 p. 37). Such activities are not the monopoly of the CIA; other intelligence agencies from both the West and East attempt to infiltrate the news media of developing countries. It is in this context that the call for a New World Information and Communication Order (NWICO) was made. The idea that the developing countries pool their resources and coordinate their efforts in collecting and disseminating information about each other to improve their self-image should in no way have threatened the Western news media; there was no suggestion of reduced access of the Western media to developing countries' news or advertising. Nor was there any suggestion for state control of the press beyond what was currently the case. Yet there was a considerable opposition to the idea in the West. One of the reasons for the US and the British withdrawal from UNESCO was the organization's support for the NWICO. Earlier the US State Department under Dean Acheson had "unsuccessfully tried to persuade Latin America to abolish the Economic Commission for Latin America, a UN agency. The commission irritated US officials by issuing reports demonstrating that the prices of raw materials and food exports were declining relative to the prices of imported manufactures, and by suggesting that the solution to these declining terms of trade was to attract development capital, presumably from the US government, for industrialization and economic diversification" (Rabe 1988 p. 19). For similar reasons the UN Conference on Trade and Development (UNCTAD) did not find much favor with US administrations.

In an ultimate sense, nonalignment as a principle of foreign policy originated from the belief that all peoples and nations have an inalienable right to determine the forms of governments and methods of economic, social, and cultural development of their own choice unhindered by the richer and militarily more powerful nations. In its rejection of a hegemonical and hierarchical world, nonalignment as a principle of foreign policy has been a major breakthrough in the history of political thought and international relations. It is ironic that the very same country, which deserves some credit for the development of the concept of nonalignment (then termed as neutrality) in its embryonic form, came to see nonalignment as a threat to its hegemony. It violated international law repeatedly by destabilizing foreign governments by covert actions and at times, organizing assassinations of foreign heads of state, an act prohibited also by the US laws. Time and again, it unilaterally intervened (see *Intervention*) in the internal affairs of the Latin American countries in spite of its treaty obligations not to do so. It is not surprising that:

In terms of its contribution to the US relations with the Third World, paramilitary actions has had minimal positive results. The US committed itself to long-term assistance in Iran, Guatemala, and Chile that eventually dwarfed the dollar costs of the original CIA projects. The numerous failures contributed nothing. Moreover, it can be argued that the effort as a whole helped to fuel the rise of the "nonaligned" movement, neutralism in the world affairs, the success of which

comes at the expense of cold war strategies. (Prados 1986 p. 468)

4. Nonalignment as Movement

Nonalignment as a movement simply developed out of the cooperation between those newly emerging countries which had adopted nonalignment as the basis of their foreign policy. The idea of the Asian and African countries coming closer together was initially raised in 1945 by the delegates of the two continents attending the constituent conference of the US in San Francisco (Jaisingh 1983 p. 7). The idea was translated into action by convening the Asian Relations Conference in New Delhi in March-April 1947, which was attended by 28 countries. Some republics of the former Soviet Union had also attended. Among the international organizations the US and the Arab League (see *League of Arab States*) had sent their observers. In his address to the Conference Jawaharlal Nehru, the Indian Prime Minister, expressed the hope that the newly independent nations would follow an independent foreign policy. Burma and Ceylon (now Sri Lanka) supported the idea while Pakistan did not. However, the term nonalignment was not used during the conference. The first collective action by the Asian countries came in 1949 in response to the Dutch intervention in Indonesia. The Asians saw the action as an attempt to reimpose colonial rule on the Asian countries. At the request of Burma a summit of the Asian nations held in New Delhi demanded the withdrawal of the Dutch from Indonesia. The same year another conference held in New Delhi gave birth to the idea of a formal Afro-Asian group within the UN.

The late 1940s and early 1950s saw a further intensification of the Cold War. In June 1948 came the Berlin blockade. The North Atlantic Treaty Organization (NATO) (see *North Atlantic Treaty Organization (NATO)*) was set up in 1949. The North Korean invasion of the South brought in the US and the Chinese military involvement in Korea in 1950. The war lasted for three years, the armistice being signed in July 1953. Until the international settlement negotiated in Geneva in 1954, France continued its military efforts to reimpose colonial rule on Indochina. These efforts were fully endorsed by the US. By 1954 the US government was paying about 80 percent of the cost of the French military efforts in Indochina (Myrdal 1968 p. 173). The increasing involvement of the US in the war in Vietnam began immediately after the Geneva Settlement of the French colonial war in Indochina (Myrdal 1968 p. 227). Geneva Settlement of 1954 stressed that the military demarcation line at the 17th parallel was only provisional. It had also provided for an impartial election within two years and had prohibited the introduction of further troops, Vietnamese involvement in military alliances, as well as the establishment of foreign military bases. The US government did not respect these conditions and backed the secessionist government of Ngo Dinh Diem in the South with economic and military support. Between 1960 and 1964 the deployment of US military personnel increased from 800 in 1960 to 21,000 in 1964. At the beginning of 1966 more than 180,000 US soldiers were participating in war operations in Vietnam (Myrdal 1968 p. 407). When the American ground troops were withdrawn in January 1972, their number totalled 410,000 (Sultzberger 1987 p. 122). Another 58,000 American soldiers had been killed (Lind 1996 p. 149n). The total bombs dropped from 1966 to 1968 amounted to 2.87 million tons and from 1969 to July 1973, 4.53 million tons (Ball 1976 p. 335 note 6). Apart from the devastation caused by massive bombing, destruction of trees and vegetation by chemical defoliants resulted in flooding and soil erosion. Paddy fields were flooded by salt water because of destruction of dikes making resumption of farming difficult (Chomsky 1982 pp. 25-6). As many as 223,748 South Vietnamese soldiers died in action; the numbers of North Vietnamese and Viet Cong soldiers is estimated at one million and civilian deaths at nearly 4 million (Storey and Robinson 1995 p. 27).

Vietnam attended the nonaligned summit in Colombo in August 1976 and wished to follow a truly nonaligned foreign policy. Ideally they wanted to have a "quadripartite" aid for postwar reconstruction, half being provided by the Soviet bloc and China and the other half provided by the Western industrialized countries, Western Europe, the US, Canada and Japan. The Vietnamese effort to have an equidistant relationship both with China and the former Soviet Union could not materialize. The Chinese did not agree to make any long-term commitment; the former Soviet Union provided soft loans for Vietnam's five year plan (1976-80) but it expected Vietnam supporting the Soviet line in world affairs, which the Vietnamese were not keen to do. Nor were they inclined to take sides in the Sino-Soviet dispute. They made every effort to avoid China or Soviet Union meddling in South Vietnam and invited France, Norway, India and Japan to undertake project in the South, while not allowing both then Soviet Union and China to open consulates in Ho Chi Minh City (Chanda 1986 pp. 180-81). Hanoi annoyed the

Soviet Union also by joining the IMF in September 1976 while at the same time refusing to join the Soviet-led Council for Mutual Economic Assistance (CMEA) (ibid., pp. 182-83). Gradually, the Soviet aid began to drop and Vietnam was looking more eagerly to normalizing its relations with the US and to obtaining economic assistance from the West. The US decided, however, to give priority to the normalization of relations with China before doing so with Vietnam. Soon after Vietnam signed a friendship treaty with the former Soviet Union. The treaty with the former Soviet Union, Vietnam's invasion of Cambodia and a massive exodus of the "boat people," those who were escaping from Vietnam by boat, made the diplomatic ties with the US increasingly impossible (ibid., p. 291). Thus, the brave efforts of Vietnam to adopt a nonaligned policy became a victim of the Soviet-China rivalry, and the US seemingly siding with China.

The Afro-Asian group within the UN was actively involved in the pursuit of peace right through the Korean and the Indochinese dispute. It played a part in bringing peace to Korea and in the Geneva Settlement of 1954 which brought a temporary peace in Indochina. A major boost to the idea of nonalignment as a movement came in 1955 at the Bandung Conference (see *Bandung Conference*) which was attended by 29 Afro-Asian countries. The conference adopted a Declaration on World Peace and Cooperation confirming its faith in the aims and principles of the UN Charter, and the inalienable right of sovereign nations to live without foreign interference and advocated the settlement of all international disputes by peaceful means. The Bandung signatories were in essence attempting to present a combined moral and political presence in the world which might make it difficult for the richer countries, particularly, the superpowers, to indulge in indiscriminate actions against poorer and weaker countries. Beyond applying moral pressure, there was nothing much they could do. The rampage against the poorer countries by the major powers continued after Bandung. Almost within a year of the Bandung Conference came the invasion of Egypt by the combined forces of the UK, France, and Israel in retaliation for the Egyptian nationalization of the Suez Canal. The Cold War was further intensified at the beginning of the 1960s. In 1960 an American reconnaissance plane which was flying over Soviet territory was shot down and this led to the failure of the Paris Great Power Summit. In 1961 came the Bay of Pigs. This was a blatant attempt by the US government to engineer the overthrow of Fidel Castro in Cuba. Only two years earlier, John Foster Dulles (see *Dulles, John Foster*) had said that Castro was not a communist agent and Dean Acheson believed that Castro was a democrat and a social reformer. Even after Castro had legalized the communist party, threw out the moderates from his government and appointed himself the Premier of Cuba and organized a public trial and execution of 550 supporters of Fulgencio Batista, the deposed dictator of Cuba, Allen Dulles, the Director of the CIA, compared the Cuban to the French Revolution. What enraged the US government was Castro's Agrarian Reform Law which expropriated farmlands of the sugar barons, many of them American, the nationalization of the sugar industry and his advocacy of nonalignment as a proper foreign policy stance for developing countries in the Cold War (Rabe 1988 pp. 122-25).

It was in this context of growing world crisis that the first formal Conference of the Heads of State of Nonaligned Countries was convened in Belgrade in 1961. The conference was attended by twenty countries as full members and three as observers. The conference was largely concerned with political issues such as decolonization, particularly, the granting of independence to Algeria and Angola; the withdrawal of French troops from Tunisia; cessation of foreign military intervention in the Congo; ending of apartheid in South Africa; and granting the legitimate rights of the Arabs in Palestine. In its search for peace the conference appealed both to President Kennedy and Premier Khruschev "to renew their negotiations, so as to remove the danger of war in the world and enable mankind to embark upon the road to peace" (Government of India 1981 pp. 7-8).

Since the Belgrade summit several other summits have followed; the seventh was held in New Delhi in 1983. Following the Conference on the Problems of Economic Development held in Cairo in 1962 the movement turned its attention to economic and social issues. Particular mention must be made of the Lusaka Summit in 1970 and the Algiers Summit in 1973 where economic issues came to the fore. It was at Algiers that the Summit documents presented for the first time comprehensive and inter-related political and economic objectives, which have since inspired the policies of the nonaligned and developing countries. The fifth Summit held at Colombo in 1976 called for a new international order in the fields of information and mass communications. More recently, the Jakarta Summit (September 1992), meeting in the wake of the disintegration of the then Soviet Union, condemned ethnic strife, religious intolerance and narrowly conceived nationalism and reiterated its

resolve to continue working for a peaceful resolution of international disputes. The latest summit at Cartagena, the emphasis was more on the issues of poverty reduction and the promotion of equity. Other issues discussed included terrorism, nuclear weapons and the reform of the UN system.

Currently, the movement operates through three decision-making institutional devices other than the triennial summit meetings of the nonaligned heads of states: (a) The Conference of Foreign Ministers of Nonaligned Countries; (b) The Coordinating Bureau; and (c) The Group Meeting of Representatives of Nonaligned Countries at the UN, New York.

The Conference of Foreign Ministers meets roughly midway between two summit conferences. It is responsible both for reviewing prevailing trends in the international situation and for making recommendations for the forthcoming summit. It is also responsible for assessing the pace of implementation of decisions and resolutions of the previous summit.

The Coordinating Bureau is charged with the responsibility of maintaining contact between nonaligned countries between summits, for preparation of agenda for ministerial meetings, and for coordinating nonaligned activities. The Coordinating Bureau meets periodically at three levels: (a) ambassadorial; (b) ministerial; and (c) permanent representation of nonaligned countries at the UN in New York. The Bureau has thirty-six members; seventeen come from Africa, twelve from Asia, five from Latin America, one from Europe, and the remaining one seat is shared alternately between Europe and Africa.

The Group Meetings of Representatives of Nonaligned Countries at the UN are held at the level of permanent representatives to the UN at regular intervals, at least one in two months or more frequently if needed. So far the idea of a permanent secretariat is not favored by the movement. However, a Nonaligned Documentation Center has been established in Colombo.

5. Post-Cold War Years

Arguably, with the disintegration of the former Soviet Union and the presumed victory of the West, the rationale for the continuation of the nonaligned movement is seemingly undermined. Nevertheless, even a cursory picture of the present world might suggest that the crucial issue—the rights of the developing countries to live with peace and dignity and with freedom of choice to decide their economic and political destiny—that gave birth to the Nonaligned Movement, still eludes their grasp. In fact, with Russia, increasingly depending upon the Western largesse for saving it from economic collapse, the US, the only superpower, finds itself with much less restraints to its power to act unilaterally against the developing countries. Of late, the UN, particularly, the Security Council has been converted as never before into "a dangerous and uncontrolled arm of the American government, with no countervailing power to balance it. In 1991, it launched the Gulf War; in 1992, it organized sanctions against Libya; in 1993, it permitted the bombing of Mogadishu. All was done in the name of the UN" (Gott 1993 p. 24). This reflects, probably a change in style—reflected in the indecent haste with which the Clinton Administration had publicly let it be known that the reelection of Boutros-Ghali was no more acceptable to the US government—and not of content. Contrary to the belief in the Western world that the Soviet veto and the hostility of the Third World had made the UN ineffective, it was the US which used vetos most. From 1970 through 1989, the US vetoed forty-five Security Council resolutions alone, eleven others with the UK, four with the UK and France; Britain came next with twenty-six vetoes (eleven with the US and four with US and France); and France used vetoes eleven times (seven times alone). As against this former Soviet Union had used vetoes only eight times (one with China) (Chomsky 1991 p. 213 note 40). Conscious of this imbalance of power within the UN, the non-aligned movement has repeatedly called for UN reforms in order to give a fairer share of power to developing countries. The US, with a view to further entrench the hold of the richer countries in the UN, is only interested in the inclusion of Germany and Japan as permanent members in the Security Council. However, more recently, it has shown some willingness to accept three more permanent members to represent each of the three regions, Africa, Asia and Latin America. Whether the US Congress would approve of such a change is not yet certain; after all it is the Congress which, in defiance of the world public opinion, has often stood in the way of the US government paying its long-standing dues to the UN.

In any case, the US has rarely cared about world opinion or international law when it takes unilateral action in pursuance of its perceived interests. For instance, Senator Moynihan commenting on the Grenada invasion by the Reagan Administration on October 25, 1983 called it "an elemental violation of the Charter." He further added that "a 'realist' school had developed which looked upon international law as a delusion of the well-intentioned but inexperienced" (Moynihan 1990 pp. 130-31). In 1989, in the

seventy-fifth anniversary issue of the *New Republic*, Charles Krauthammer wrote "the law—international law—is an ass. It has nothing to offer. Foreign policy is best made without it" (ibid., p. 131). Similarly, the mining of the harbors in Nicaragua, in the opinions of both Senators Patrick Moynihan and Barry Goldwater, was "an act violating international law" and "an act of war" but Jeane Kirkpatrick asserted that "unilateral compliance with the [UN] Charter's (see *United Nations Charter*) principles of non-intervention and non-use of force may make sense in some specific, isolated instances, but hardly a sound basis for either US policy or for international peace and stability" (ibid., p. 133). When Nicaragua went to International Court of Justice (see *International Court of Justice*), the Reagan Administration gave notice, effective immediately, that the US did not consider the Court's jurisdictions compulsory. This was counter to the commitment made by the US in 1946 that it would give at least six months notice before renouncing the compulsory jurisdiction of the Court (ibid., pp. 143-44). The Invasion of Panama in December 20, 1989 came after George Kennan had suggested that "the era of containment was finally over" (ibid., p. 150). Although the invasion was an infringement of international law, President Bush claimed that the deployment of the US forces was "an exercise of the right of self-defense recognized in Article 51 of the UN Charter . . . ." In Senator Moynihan's view it was doubtful if "the drafters of the UN Charter would have judged the right of self-defense to extend to the invasion of Panama" (ibid., pp. 171-72). It was also against the Organization of American States (OAS) (see *Organization of American States (OAS)*) Charter as well as the Panama Canal treaty. OAS condemned the invasion of Panama by a vote of 17-1, with a few abstentions. The only opposition came, obviously from the US (Chomsky 1991 pp. 147-48). However, when Iraq invaded Kuwait, the US Administration was invoking international law which it had repeatedly violated in the cases of Nicaragua and Panama. Iraq had built up its military machine with the help of economic assistance from the US and its Western allies. By 1987, forty per cent of Iraq's food was imported from the US and much of the Iraqi oil went to the US. Even in the face of the Iraqi invasion of Iran, and Saddam Hussein's use of poison gas against the Iranian troops and its own Kurdish citizens or the forced relocation of half a million Kurds and Syrians, prominent American businessmen and diplomats praised Saddam Hussein for his moderation and his progress towards democracy (ibid., pp. 194-95). The Bush Administration went ahead with military escalation when the majority of the UN wished to give some more time to economic sanctions and negotiations. The US allies were critical. Germany refused to support the US military expenses in Saudi Arabia on grounds that the action was not authorized by the UN. The EU, while providing some financial support, found the US military action autonomously taken. The UK was the only enthusiastic supporter (ibid., p. 203). The Third World watched with dismay and disbelief that the US had once again opted for a military solution. There was a growing belief among many that after the destruction of the Iranian military power in the Iran-Iraqi War, in which the US had supported Iraq, the US wished to destroy the military power of Iraq lest it did threaten Israel and the other US allies in the Gulf. In doing so, President Bush had no reason to worry because Russia, in the need of Western money, was on his side. The invasion of Panama and the military solution in Iraq set the pattern that the developing countries might expect if they were to threaten US interests abroad. This was very clearly laid down in the National Security Strategy report in early 1990 (ibid., p. 29).

The growing concern with proliferation of nuclear weapons in the wake of the disintegration of the former Soviet Union and ready access of the ex-Soviet states to nuclear weapons led to the nuclear states hastening the progress toward a Comprehensive Test Ban Treaty (CTBT). Such a treaty was first proposed by Jawaharlal Nehru. In the last four decades every time it was taken up, the nuclear powers thwarted the efforts towards a treaty. When the treaty was near completion in 1996, India refused to sign on grounds that the nuclear powers had not earnestly endeavored to take steps to abolishing all nuclear weapons (see *CTBT in Indian Perception*). To make matters worse France followed by China resumed a limited number of tests and the US is likely to do the same. It has given India the excuse that the nuclear powers were using CTBT as a device for "freezing inequality." More recently, in the Helsinki Summit in March 1997, the US and Russia have reached an agreement regarding a new arms-control treaty, known as Start III. Under the treaty each side will reduce by 2007, its nuclear warheads to anything between 2,000 to 2,500. However, Start II remains unratified by Russia and without its ratification Start III cannot be implemented (*Guardian Weekly* March 30, 1997 p. 15). The proposed cuts bring the level of the nuclear weapons to one fifth of what they were five years before but what the developing countries have to fear are not nuclear weapons but the high-tech weapons and the stealth planes used in the Gulf War. The US is

reportedly developing nuclear devices that could go deep down to destroy any structure which may be housing nuclear or chemical weapon development programs. It is feared that in the future, the US government will use pre-emptive strikes for destroying such projects in developing countries (see *CTBT Negotiations: Analysis and Assessment*).

Trade and economic sanctions will also continue to be used against some of the developing countries, not considered "unsavory" by the US government. The US allies have increasingly come to question the use of continuing sanctions against Cuba. An editorial of the *Guardian Weekly* wrote a few years ago, "the sight of the world's greatest power waging a vendetta over more than three decades against the little neighbor which chose a different way of life (and the wrong friends) has never been a happy one." It further added, "the debate over whether the US should seek to normalize relations with Cuba must be one of the most one-sided, in terms of common-sense logic, in international affairs today. Ranged against the affirmative case is little more than historical prejudice, the sort of spite which ostracized Vietnam (with disastrous knock-on effects for Cambodia) for over a decade and political nervousness over alienating the Florida electorate. The argument in favor is soundly grounded in US self-interest, let alone the interest of the Cuban people, which should actually be the first consideration" (Comment *Guardian Weekly* August 28, 1994 p. 12). Questions regarding the direction of the Cuba policy have also been raised within the US. Writing in the *Washington Post*, Bernard Aronson, the former Assistant Secretary of State for Inter-American Affairs, argues in favor of "a bipartisan initiative for peaceful democratization" of Cuba, and suggests "for its part the US should be prepared to place on the table: (a) withdrawal from the US naval base at Guatanamo Bay and relinquishing of the US base rights; (b) confidence-building measures to reassure the Cuban military that the US would not take advantage of a democratic opening to intervene; and (c) a step-by-step relaxation of the provisions of the embargo in exchange for concrete steps by the Cuban government to move irreversibly toward democracy" (Aronson 1994 p. 17). The latest in the series of Cuba-bashing is the Helms-Burton Act, which emphasizes the extra-territorial power of US law, and proposes that foreign companies trading with Cuba in defiance of the US embargo would be liable in American courts. The provisions of Helms-Burton Act have also been extended to cover trade with Iran (Walker 1997 p. 6). This has infuriated the US allies, particularly, the European Union (see *Euro-*

pean Union). The Russians have also refused to comply and continue to sell arms and nuclear technology to Iran. Turkey, another US ally, has also been developing closer economic ties with Iran. Yet, the American government refuses to change its policy towards world issues. In the words of William Taylor, the director of political military studies of the Centre for Strategic and International Studies: "We are supposed to be the leader of the free world, so the rest of the world had better fall into step here . . ." (ibid., p. 6). Clearly, such an attitude does not augur well for the Third World.

On the economic front too, developing countries may be pressurized to continue market-opening measures even though such policies have been creating wide income differentials. The US economic model, as against the European and the Japanese, is being promoted as the only relevant model for the developing countries. Unfortunately, the US economic policies in recent years have polarized the society ever more. Under Reagan and Bush administrations "only the rich got significantly richer" (Lind 1996 p. 191). As Lind highlights, "between 1929 and 1969, the inequality in the US declined. Since 1969, inequality has dramatically risen" (ibid., p. 195). As against this "income inequality in Germany, Japan and other industrial democracies has remained much lower than in the US in the post-1969 period" (ibid., p. 195). To Lind, the lower level of income inequality in Germany and Japan is the result of generous government policies and the stronger labor movements. On the other hand, in Britain, Australia, New Zealand and Canada, *laissez-faire* reforms have resulted in rising inequality, falling wages and growing underclass (ibid., p. 195n). Galbraith also expresses similar views on the emergence of an underclass in America consisting of "members of minority groups, blacks or people of Hispanic origin" (Galbraith 1992 p. 31). He also highlights the growing differentials between the earnings of average workers and executives of large corporations. "In 1980, the chief executive officers of the three hundred largest American companies had incomes twenty-nine times that of the average manufacturing worker. Ten years later the incomes of the top executives were ninety-three times greater. The income of the average employed American declined slightly in those years" (ibid., pp. 55-6). Lind calls this polarization of the American society into a small rich and white oligarchy and the growing underclass the "Braziliazation" of America. Increasing polarization has meant that "the cities of the US resemble those of the Third World, with swarms of homeless vagrants, often insane or addict-

ed to drugs. And thanks to its lack of effective gun control laws, the US has by far the highest rates of homicide and imprisonment, not only among English-speaking democracies but all democratic countries. America is not significantly freer or more democratic than other industrial democracies today. It does, however, lead Europe and Japan in beggars, murders and prisons per capita" (Lind 1996 p. 233).

Clearly, with a much higher degree of poverty and inequality of income and wealth, developing countries have to be careful in opting for a Western capitalist model because there is more than one. If a planned economy—not many developing countries other than the communist ones were really planned economies—failed to solve the problem of poverty and inequality in developing countries, it is highly unlikely that a purely "market-oriented" policy would be able to do so. An indiscriminate race toward market-opening may intensify the polarization of society already divided by privilege, wealth and political power and thereby aggravate the problems of political instability facing many developing countries. Thus, the appropriate choice of their economic destiny will be a challenge facing most developing countries, even for those which have achieved impressive rates of economic growth (see *World Economy, Social Change and Peace*).

6. Conclusion

In so far as the movement is concerned with creating a sense of awareness among the member countries of the need for collective action against the arbitrary actions of the superpowers, the aim has been achieved to a considerable extent. Developing countries—not all of them are members of the nonaligned movement—are increasingly coordinating their actions within and outside the UN system.

On economic issues, the achievements of the movement have been few. Except for a short period during the early 1970s when the Organization of the Petroleum Exporting Countries (OPEC) was ascendant, the richer countries have not shown any willingness to make meaningful concessions. It was during this period that the UNCTAD was successful in negotiating the Generalized Systems of Preferences (GSP) under which the richer countries agreed to provide concessionary market access to poorer countries.

Colonialism (see *Colonialism*) and racism (see *Race and Racial Prejudice*), have by now become much less respectable than they used to be before or immediately after the Second World War. The movement must receive some credit for this change. Apartheid is a thing of the past in South Africa which has emerged as a democratic country with Nelson Mandela (see Nobel Peace Prize Laureates: *Nelson Mandela*) as the first president of the country. Some credit for the majority rule in South Africa must go to the movement. However, the change was largely brought about by the growing internal opposition of the blacks, particularly black young school children, and in an atmosphere of increasing spate of violence and counterviolence, world opinion turned against apartheid regime. A world-wide disinvestment campaign forced the foreign companies to sell-off their interests in South Africa, damaging greatly the already weakened economy and a politically unstable society. A UN embargo on export of arms, actively advocated by the movement, also helped. Some halting progress has also been made in meeting the legitimate aspirations of the Palestinian people. Much of this was achieved by the unarmed revolt of the Palestinian youths, *intifada*, as well as by the pressures brought about by the peace movements within Israel (see *Arab-Israel Conflict: Peace Plans and Proposals*). How far the ultimate solution would be fairer to the Palestinians is difficult to tell, but the realism both in Israel and among the Arab countries is a hopeful sign. Occasional nudging from the US has also helped but the domestic sensitivities stand in the way of the US taking a decisive action.

In the field of world politics, the movement scored an unparalleled victory in October 1971 in admitting the People's Republic of China to the UN by a two third's majority defeating the US veto against the Chinese entry. Britain voted against the US (Mercer 1988 p. 1037). However, with respect to disarmament and peace, the direct contribution of the movement, for obvious reasons, is rather limited. In some cases such as the Iran hostage crisis, nonalignment provided the basis for Algerian success in defusing the crisis. However, the movement has been plagued by the continuing tendency among member countries to take to arms to solve their territorial disputes with other member countries. This has certainly undermined the credibility of the movement.

The movement has also been criticized for lacking cohesiveness in terms of ideology as well as organizational structure. Critics have underlined the heterogeneity of the membership and have argued that such a large unwieldy body cannot take any practical decision. This may well be true but on the other hand it can be argued that diversity, looseness, and flexibility is the strength of the movement. After all, the member countries "belong to different continents and cultures, their nature and level of socio-economic

development is not the same, their geo-political compulsions vary considerably, their historical experience is distinctive and above all, the international political perspectives of their ruling elites, though broadly similar, are far from identical. In other words, there is a great deal of variety and diversity which calls for a fair degree of flexibility and dynamism" (Misra 1982 p. 63). Nonalignment, if it is to survive as an effective international movement encompassing more than two-thirds of the countries of the world, should prescribe only broad and generalized ideology, leaving the specifics and the details to each country to fill according to its national needs and requirements.

Another criticism of the movement refers to the lack of evenhandedness of its opposition to the superpowers. The movement has, in the past, taken a less critical view of the Eastern bloc than of the West. Typical examples of this would be a more vocal criticism by India of the Anglo-French action on Suez than of the Soviet action on Hungary or Czechoslovakia. The less vociferous criticism of the Soviet involvement in Afghanistan compared to the US action in Vietnam may be another example. This lack of evenhandedness can be explained largely in terms of the dominance of the world economy and the trading system as well as of the international organizations by the West, particularly by the US. As a result of this dominance the chances of conflict between the US and the West on the one hand and the developing countries on the other have been much greater than with the Eastern bloc countries and the former Soviet Union. The American attitude of seeing all world problems with the prism of East-West confrontation is another reason for the disenchantment of the developing countries with the US. On the other hand, in Afghanistan the former Soviet Union did not behave much differently than what the US had done in Vietnam. However, with the disintegration of the former Soviet Union, the threat from the former Soviet Union has receded; while at the same time, the chances of unilateral action by the US has increased. It is therefore important for the nonaligned movement to take such threats seriously and raise its collective voice against them if it hopes to retain its credibility.

The movement, concerned as it is with the political, economic, social, and cultural emancipation of humankind, must also show a readiness to censure its member nations for denying similar rights to their own people. This would certainly be a divisive issue and might undermine the solidarity of the movement, but on the other hand by continuing its silence on the violations of human rights and other injustices perpetrated by member nations on their own people, the very *raison d'être* of the movement will be lost.

See also: *New International Economic Order (NIEO); New World Order and New State-Nations*

Bibliography

Aronson B 1974 Consensus Needed on Cuba. *The Washington Post*, reproduced in *Guardian Weekly*, August 28, 1994
Ball G W 1976 *Diplomacy for a Crowded World: An American Foreign Policy*. The Bodley Head, London
Bandyopadyaya J 1977 The non-aligned movement and international relations. *India Q.* 33
Beers J S 1967 Comments on the paper by Dr. Okita and Dr. Miki. In: Adler J H 1967 *Capital Movements: Proceedings of a Conference held by the International Economic Association*. Macmillan, London
Chanda N 1986 *Brother Enemy: The War after the War*. Harcourt Brace Jovanovich Publishers, San Diego
Chomsky N 1982 *Towards a New Cold War: Essays on the Current Crisis and How We Got There*. Pantheon Books, New York
Chomsky N 1991 *Deterring Democracy*. Verso, London
Freeland R M 1985 *The Truman Doctrine and the Origins of McArthyism: Foreign Policy, Domestic Politics, and Internal Security, 1946-1948*. New York University Press, New York
Galbraith J K 1992 *The Culture of Contentment*. Houghton Miffin Company, Boston
Gott R 1993 Nations Divided by a Lost Vision. *Guardian Weekly*, September 12
Government of India 1981 *Documents of Gatherings of Non-aligned Countries*. Ministry of Foreign Affairs, New Delhi
Graham J A 1980 The Non-aligned Movement after the Havana Summit. *Journal of International Affairs* 34(1)
Grobe-Jutte A M 1981 From Hierarchical to Egalitarian International Decision Structures: Non-aligned Policies in the UN system. In: Jutte R (ed.) 1981 *Future Prospects of International Organization*. Frances Pinter, London
Institute of International Strategic Studies (IISS) 1995-96. *International Arms Trade*. London
Jaisingh H 1983 *India and the Non-aligned World: Search for a New Order*. Vikas, New Delhi
Jankowitsch O, Sauvant K P (eds.) 1978 *The Third World without Superpowers: The Collected Documents of the Non-aligned Countries*. Oceana, New York
Jankowitsch O, Sauvant K P 1981 The Initiating Role of the Non-aligned Countries. In: Sauvant K P (ed.) *Changing Priorities on the International Agenda: The New International Economic Order*. Pergamon, Elmsford, New York

Kennedy P 1988 *The Rise and Fall of the Great Powers: Economic Change and Military Conflict from 1500 to 2000*. Unwin Hymen, London
Kodikara S V 1982 Non-aligned Institutional Forms and Democratization of International Relations. In: Kochler H (ed.) 1982 *The Principles of Non-alignment*. Third World Press, London
Krishnan N 1982 Non-alignment-Movement or Organization? Criteria of Membership. In: Mishra K P, Narayanan K R (eds.) *Nonglignment in Contemporary International Relations*. Vikas, New Delhi
Lind M 1996 *The Next American Nation: The New Nationalism & the Forth American Revolution*. Free Press Paperbacks, New York
Mercer D (ed.) 1988 *Chronicle of the 20th Century*. Chronicle, London
Misara K P 1982 Ideological Bases of Non-alignment. In: Kochler H (ed.) *The Principles of Non-alignment*. Third World Press, London
Mortimer R A 1980 *The Third World Coalition in International Politics*. New York
Moynihan D P 1990 *On the Law of Nations*. Harvard University Press, Cambridge, Mass
Myrdal G 1968 *Asian Drama: An Inquiry into the Poverty of Nations*. Penguin, Harmondsworth
Okita S, Miki T 1967 Treatment of Foreign Capital—A Case Study for Japan. In: Adler J H *Capital Movements: Proceedings of a Conference held by the International Economic Association*. Macmillan, London
Paterson T G 1973 *Soviet-American Confrontation: Post War Reconstruction and the Origins of the Cold War*. Johns Hopkins University Press, Baltimore, Maryland
Perkins B 1995 *The Cambridge History of American Foreign Relations* (Paperback). Cambridge University Press, New York
Porter M E 1990 *The Competitive Edge of Nations*. The Free Press, New York
Prados J 1986 *Presidents' Secret Wars: CIA and Pentagon Covert Operations from World War II through Iranscam*. Quill William Morrow, New York
Rabe S G 1988 *Eisenhower & Latin America: The Foreign Policy of Anti-Communism*. The University of North Carolina Press, Chapel Hill
Schiller H I 1977 Mechanisms of Cultural Imperialism. In: Singham A W (ed.) *The Nonaligned Movement in World Politics*. Lawrence Hill, Westport, Connecticut
Singham A W (ed.) 1977 *The Non-Aligned Movement in World Politics*. Lawrence Hill, Westport Connecticut
Sinha R 1995 Economic Reform in Developing Countries: Some Conceptual Issues. *World Development* 23(4)
SIPRI 1982 *Yearbook of World Armament and Disarmament, 1982*. Taylor and Francis, London
Smith P H 1996 *Talons of the Eagle: Dynamics of U.S.-Latin*

American Relations. Oxford University Press, New York

Storey R, Daniel R 1995 *Vietnam*, 3rd edn. Lonely Planet Publications, Hawthorn

Sulzberger C L 1987 *The World and Richard Nixon*. Prentice Hall Press, New York

Toye J 1991 Ghana. In: Mosley Paul, Harrington Jane, Toye John *Aid and Power: The World Bank & Policy-based Lending (2)*. Routledge, London

Walker M 1997 Clinton Stumbles over Foreign Affairs. *Guardian Weekly*, June 23

RADHA SINHA

Non-governmental Organizations (NGOs)

Non-governmental organizations (NGOs) comprise a vast universe of non-state groups and associations operating at the local, regional, national, and global level. All NGOs exist in order to facilitate the shared interests of their members, and in many cases this involves attempts to influence public policy by bringing pressure to bear, directly or indirectly, on authoritative bodies and by stimulating public opinion. The principal types of NGOs are: sectoral groups (usually representing economic sectors such as agriculture or employers), professional associations, religious groups, and social movement organizations (representing broad, long-term interests such as human rights, the environment and peace). There is also a small but growing category of NGOs that provide services, aid or support. Examples include the International Red Cross, Medicins sans Frontieres, and the Internet Assigned Numbers Authority. NGOs are increasingly involved in reporting and monitoring of international agreements, and are emerging in some cases as partners of governments and international agencies in the implementation of certain policies and programs. The Union of International Associations estimates the number of international NGOs to be as high as 38,000.

Non-governmental transnational movements have existed as long as states have, representing religions, economic sectors and professions. A good example of an early international movement that spawned what today would be called like-minded NGOs in different countries was the movement to abolish slavery, which lasted roughly 100 years from the late 1780s. The International Red Cross was founded in 1863. Not surprisingly, many NGOs arose in the first decades after the First and Second World Wars, primarily in response to the foundation of the League of Nations and the United Nations respectively. Over 1,000 NGOs attended the UN Founding Conference and managed to attain, through lobbying the attending delegates, an official status in the new organization. Article 71 of the UN Charter states that "The Economic and Social Council (ECOSOC) may make suitable arrangements for consultation with non-governmental organizations concerned with matters within its competence." This was crystallized in a resolution of the Economic and Social Council (ECOSOC) of the UN in 1968 (resolution 1296). In a 1996 resolution, ECOSOC urged all UN agencies to review their consultative mechanisms and participation of NGOs in their deliberations. More than 1500 Non-Governmental Organizations (NGOs) have consultative status with ECOSOC, classified into three categories: category I organizations are concerned with most of the Council's activities; category II organizations have special competence in specific areas; and organizations on the Roster are those that make only occasional contributions to the Council's work.

NGOs are now routinely consulted by most other Specialized Agencies in the UN. These consultative relationships which vary widely are complex, but they do provide NGOs with considerable opportunities to exercise influence. For example, bodies such as the International Labour Organization (ILO), the Food and Agriculture Organization (FAO), the Human Rights Commission, and the World Intellectual Property Organization (WIPO) are forums in which specialized NGOs can bring their expertise to bear with some effect. The International Confederation of Free Trade Unions not only has consultative status with the ILO, but also sends delegates to its meetings. Such organizations as the International Federation of Agricultural Producers (IFAP) are counted on for their expertise by the FAO, as is the World Medical Association by the World Health Organization.

In some cases, sustained pressure by NGOs has contributed to the establishment of Specialized Agencies, such as the Office of the High Commissioner for Refugees, the UN Commission on Human Rights, the UN Commission on the Status of Women, and the High Commissioner for Human Rights. Conversely, the advent of such agencies has often prompted the establishment of international NGOs. For example, the ILO gave rise to the IOIE. International NGOs can influence policy as well through the definition of standards and considerations in international agreements. In the case of human rights, for example, strong lobbying efforts at the UN have changed the terms of debate around women's rights and acceptable standards for social services. The same is true of NGO contributions to the standards whereby global warming is measured, or technical standards for the telecommunications industry. Because NGOs are primarily lobbyists within the UN system (though in highly technical, scientific areas, the influence of sectoral or professional associations is very strong), their influence is seen primarily through institution building and changed terms of debates. These influences then cascade (though often very slowly) down to the national level.

NGOs with consultative status can sometimes, but not always, be involved in preparing the agenda and documentation for UN sponsored conferences on special topics. A sign of the growing maturity of the international NGO system, however, is seen in the development of parallel "NGO Forums" to the official UN conference. This began with the Stockholm Conference on the Human Environment in 1972, and continued with subsequent world conferences—the Rio Summit on the Environment (1992), the Vienna Conference on Human Rights (1993), the Cairo Conference on the Family (1994), the Beijing Conference on Women's Rights (1995) and the Istanbul Conference on Settlements (1996). NGO Forums for world conferences now routinely attract over 1000 NGOs from around the world. Beyond the numbers of NGOs is the increasing capacity they have to coordinate and communicate globally. This has been helped significantly by the Internet (see *Internet: A New Vehicle for Global Peace Efforts*). The Association for Progressive Communications, an NGO with UN consultative status, now provides electronic communication services to NGOs at UN conferences. In addition to having a parallel forum, NGOs have fought for and won the right (though this varies by conference) to make presentations and directly monitor discussions. The practice of having "five year after" reviews (this happened with the Rio, Vienna and Cairo Declarations) also gives the international NGO community a chance to publicize failures and accomplishments, and pressure governments to do more.

The international influence of NGOs is not limited to the UN. As globalization advances, there are more and more opportunities as well as challenges for international NGOs (see *Globalization*). The development of supra-national organizations like the European Union (EU) (see *European Union*), is a good example. As EU institutions have developed, and as power has shifted from national capitals to Brussels, sectoral organizations have had to develop EU-wide

constituencies and mandates. Good examples are the Union of Industries and Employers' Confederations of Europe and European Trade Union Confederation. The Economic and Social Committee of the EU (established in 1957) has 222 members drawn from social and economic interests of Europe. Another example comes from the increasing importance of international agreements that establish important governance regimes in specific policy fields. Trade agreements, such as the North American Free Trade Agreement and the Mercosur, are prime examples, as was the attempt to develop a Multilateral Agreement on Investment. NGOs concerned with human rights, environmental and cultural issues have had to organize international coalitions and lobbying efforts to deal with these increasingly common initiatives.

Changes to the global peace and security environment have also changed, and possibly enhanced, the role of NGOs. For most of the post-war period, until the collapse of the former Soviet Union in the late 1980s, peace and security were defined in traditionally military terms and revolved around an axis of superpower rivalry. NGOs combined in a variety of peace and anti-nuclear movements, most notably the Campaign for Nuclear Disarmament (see *Campaign for Nuclear Disarmament (CND)*). But these movements were classic "outsiders," engaging in street protests, marches and sit-ins, and were largely ignored by the military and security agencies of national governments or by military alliances such as the North Atlantic Treaty Organization (NATO) (see *North Atlantic Treaty Organization (NATO)*). This has changed significantly with the end of the Cold War. Security and peace issues are no longer defined primarily in bipolar military terms, but with respect to both broad and localized threats to global social, political, economic and ecological stability. This includes everything from global warming to underdevelopment and internecine ethnic strife. As the security agenda has expanded, so has the recognition of the potential contribution of NGOs. In 1994, for example, NATO launched its Partnership for Peace Program, which envisages both greater cooperation of military forces and better civil society-military understanding in efforts towards peace-building.

One of the most dramatic recent examples of the new configuration of influence between NGOs and governments was the International Campaign to Ban Landmines (ICBL) (see Nobel Peace Prize Laureates: *International Campaign to Ban Landmines*). Eventually consisting of over 1,000 organizations around the world, the ICBL was, in the beginning, almost exclusively driven by a small group of NGOs. Within a few years the issue had taken on an international profile. With modern communications technologies, the ICBL was able to rapidly develop a well-coordinated global coalition of NGOs that cut across a variety of traditionally distinct NGO sectors (e.g., peace, human rights, women and development). Even as wide a coalition as this, however, would not likely have succeeded in achieving a convention against landmines. Canada, along with several like-minded states, met with NGOs in 1996 and issued a challenged to the world community to meet again in Ottawa in late 1997 to ratify a convention. What followed was a hybrid strategy of traditional state diplomacy and NGO public advocacy and pressure to persuade reluctant governments. In December 1997, at a meeting of 150 state representatives and hundreds of NGOs, 122 governments signed the "Convention on the Prohibition of the Use, Stockpiling, Production and Transfer of Anti-Personnel Mines and on their Destruction." The 1997 Nobel Peace Prize was awarded to the ICBL and its co-ordinator, Jody Williams (see Nobel Peace Prize Laureates: *Jody Williams*). By June 1998, 20 countries had ratified the Convention. Most remarkably, the United States did not support the ban, and the success of the ICBL and its partner governments perhaps signalled the emergence of a post-Cold War, international grassroots type of diplomatic campaign (see *Peacebuilding from Below*). A global partnership of NGOs and middle- and small-power states achieved significant success in first focusing and then shaping world public opinion.

The contribution of NGOs to peace and security is not always positive. Religious fundamentalist groups, American militias, terrorists, and world-wide networks of Nazi sympathizers are also NGOs in the broad sense of the term. There is circumstantial evidence that the number of organized groups dedicated to the destabilization of existing regimes is increasing. However, if we consider NGOs as groups dedicated to non-violent political change through negotiation and influence over public opinion—and these groups appear to be growing in number as well—then the vast majority of NGOs are oriented to peaceful action.

A key question is the influence that NGOs wield over policy formation at both the national and international levels. As noted earlier, there appears to be a trend among governments to rely increasingly on NGOs for the delivery of certain services in partnership with government agencies. At the national level this embraces social service delivery, or the privatization or commercialization of certain government services such as airports, food inspection, or parks maintenance. The best example from the international arena is the delivery of overseas aid, for

which most countries rely on varying degrees of partnership with domestic and internationally based aid agencies. Another example is monitoring and publicizing of government abuses—Amnesty International and Friends of the Earth are examples of organizations working in the human rights and environmental fields that provide information that would otherwise be operationally or politically difficult for international agencies to generate themselves. Humanitarian agencies provide invaluable services in delivering emergency aid to strife-torn areas of the world.

The story is more complicated in terms of policy formation—the influence that NGOs have over formal positions, conventions and agreements. The derailing of talks in 1998 on the MAI was hailed by many as a victory for anti-MAI NGOs, many of whom were part of traditional coalitions of human rights and global social movement groups worried about the increasing role of business and free markets. The Landmines Convention is another recent example of what appears to be surprising NGO influence over policy formation. Various examples of successful "peoples' movements"—supported by global NGO coalitions—include the collapse of communism in the former East European bloc, and of apartheid in South Africa. There are several factors at play here. First, the capacity of global movements to organize and develop coalitions on a very broad scale is greatly enhanced by modern communications technologies. Groups can also, if they use the media astutely, get their messages out to global audiences much more quickly and efficiently. In this sense, global agenda-setting is more powerfully influenced by NGOs today than previously. Second, the permeability of international organizations to NGO influence has increased over the years. The UN now routinely hears from NGOs in most of its specialized agencies; NGOs now run parallel conferences at most major international fora; other international organizations such as the EU, the Organization for Economic Co-operation and Development, and the World Trade Organization have developed mechanisms for the consideration of NGO views and opinions. Third, the globalization of production and consumption has made some corporations more vulnerable to international boycotts—particularly corporations whose products (such as soft drinks or clothing) are aimed at consumer markets in the west. Counterbalancing these trends, however, are several other forces. The international NGO community in any given policy area is often fractious, divided, and competitive—a good example is the global environmental movement. There is strong NGO consensus on many key issues, but by their nature these groups tend to be issue-specific and therefore difficult to organize into broadly focused coalitions. Another problem is the burgeoning number of NGOs. Communications technologies make it possible for ever larger numbers of ever more narrowly focused groups to gain a platform and some attention. This compounds the problem of presenting consensus positions to international policy-makers.

The number, visibility and influence of NGOs continues to grow. In 1945 they were interlopers on the diplomatic stage; by the end of the millennium they are important actors in their own right. NGOs and the movements they represent are often messy and fractious, but they will continue to have long-term impact.

Bibliography

Castells M 1996 *The Rise of the Network Society*. Blackwell, Oxford

Keck M E, Kathryn S 1998 *Activists Beyond Borders: Advocacy Networks in International Politics*. Cornell University Press, New York

Pross A P 1986 *Group Politics and Public Policy*. Oxford University Press, Toronto

Smith J, Charles C, Ron P (eds.) 1997 *Transnational Social Movements and Global Politics: Solidarity Beyond the State*. Syracuse Studies on Peace and Conflict Resolution, Syracuse University Press, New York

Tarrow S G 1998 *Power in Movement: Social Movements and Contentious Politics*. Cambridge Studies in Comparative Politics, Cambridge University Press, Cambridge

LESLIE A. PAL

Nonintervention and Noninterference

In a formal sense, nonintervention is a principle that is generally accepted in customary international law. In a broader and less formal sense, especially in its form of noninterference in domestic affairs, it is generally endorsed by the community of nations. But in international law there are a number of generally sanctioned exceptions to the observance of this principle, and in general international practice the principle is frequently violated. Indeed, one might observe that intervention (see *Intervention*), rather than nonintervention, whether on generally accepted legal grounds or in violation of such grounds, seems to be a pervasive feature of contemporary international relations.

There is a large body of international law that deals with intervention and its converse, nonintervention. Two representative definitional statements by recognized authorities on international law will bring out both the more general and the more formal ways in which the term "intervention" is used in international law. Briefly (1963) states that "intervention is a word which is often used quite generally to denote almost any act of interference by one state in the affairs of another; but in a more special sense it means dictatorial interference in the domestic or foreign affairs of another state which impairs that state's independence." Bishop (1953) points out that "the term 'intervention' is at times used in the sense of presenting an international claim against another state; but it is more usually employed to indicate forcible action of some type taken in the interference with the affairs of a state by another state, by several states, or by a collectivity of states."

In general, therefore, intervention must be regarded as action that is a violation of international law and international obligations; but international law has also recognized several forms of intervention and interference in domestic affairs that are accepted as valid. Brierly explains the two faces of the legal approach to intervention in these words: "Intervention, being a violation of another state's independence, was recognized to be in principle contrary to international law, so that any act of intervention had to be justified as a legitimate case of reprisal, protection of nationals abroad or self-defense or, alternatively, as authorized under a treaty with the state concerned." Moore (1906) lists the grounds for legally acceptable intervention as including "self-preservation," "intervention in restraint of wrong doing," "intervention by invitation to [by] a party to a civil war," "intervention under the authority of the body of states," and "intervention to preserve the rights to succession to thrones." These legally accepted forms of intervention are so broad, and are subject to such varying interpretations by interested parties ("self-defense," for example, is a common rationalization or alleged justification for acts of aggression and other acts that threaten the peace), that they seem to raise the basic question of the real and precise status of intervention in international law and international practice.

The dilemmas posed in international law and international practice over the major issues of intervention and nonintervention are further illustrated by the United Nations Charter (see *United Nations Charter*), and by the rather sorry record of the UN as an agency to promote peace by discouraging and, if need be, organizing collective action against acts of intervention (see *Collective Security and Collective Self-defense*). The ambiguity, and even impotence, of the United Nations regarding such acts is brought out in Article 2(7) of the Charter, the article that lays down the basic principles of the organization. This article reads as follows: "Nothing contained in the present Charter shall authorize the United Nations to intervene in matters which are essentially within the domestic jurisdiction of any state or shall require the Members to submit such matters to settlement under the present Charter; but this principle shall not prejudice the application of enforcement measures under Chapter VII." According to this article the United Nations is not authorized "to intervene in matters which are essentially within the domestic jurisdiction of any state," but no reference is made to a similar obligation on the part of members of the organization. Moreover, the "enforcement measures" referred to in Chapter VII—the chapter entitled "Action with respect to threats to the peace, breaches of the peace, and acts of aggression"—include a wide range of actions that certainly would constitute intervention, sometimes in rather extreme forms, however much they may be sanctioned in the Charter and in international law and however much they may be justified as necessary actions to deal with major threats to peace. Article 41 of Chapter VII refers to "measures not involving the use of armed force" that may be employed by members of the United Nations to give effect to Security Council decisions, with specific mention of "complete or partial interruption of economic relations and of rail, sea, air, postal, telegraphic, radio, and other means of communication, and the severance of diplomatic relations;" and the following article authorizes the Security Council to "take such action by air, sea, of land forces as may be necessary to maintain or restore international peace and security," if the Council concludes that the "measurers provided for in Article 41 would be inadequate or have proved to be inadequate." "Such action," the article states, "may include demonstrations, blockade, and other operations by air, sea, or land forces of Members of the United Nations." (see *Economic Blockade*) The fact that Chapter VII of the Charter has seldom been invoked, has never been fully implemented, and has in fact been largely a "dead letter" does not qualify the general point about intervention that is being made here—namely, that the United Nations Charter both endorses the general principle of nonintervention and at the same time envisions the possible necessity of sponsoring various actions that, however

justifiable, would constitute a varied pattern of interventionary measures.

In December 1965 the United Nations General Assembly, which has passed a number of resolutions and declarations in support of the principle of nonintervention and noninterference in domestic affairs, adopted a comprehensive "Declarations of the Inadmissibility of Intervention in the Domestic Affairs of States and the Protection of Their Independence and Sovereignty."

Some international documents have contained a more unqualified affirmation of the principle of nonintervention and noninterference in domestic affairs. Article 8 of the Convention on the Rights and Duties of States, signed in Montevideo by representatives of the American Republics in 1933, flatly stated that "No state has the right to intervene in the internal or external affairs of another." In 1937 both the Council and the Assembly of the League of Nations approved a resolution stating that "every State is under an obligation to refrain from intervening in the internal affairs of another State." Article 15 of the Charter of the Organization of American States (see *Organization of American States (OAS)*) asserted the same principle in an even more unqualified and comprehensive way: "No State or group of States has the right to intervene, directly or indirectly, for any reason whatever, in the internal or external affairs of any other State. The foregoing principle prohibits not only armed force but also any other form of interference or attempted threat against the personality of the State or against its political, economic and cultural elements."

For understandable reasons, weaker and less developed nations have been particularly supportive of efforts to strengthen the international prohibition of intervention and interference; and they have been particularly critical of Great Powers for frequently resorting to such acts. They have sponsored, and otherwise promoted, innumerable declarations and resolutions, at international conferences, in international organizations, in joint communiqués, and so on, opposing intervention and interference in domestic affairs, and they have repeatedly made formal protests to stronger nations against alleged acts of interference and intervention. But many of them have occasionally justified and/or cooperated in taking interventionary measures, such as intervention to help to end colonialism, or to counter intervention, especially by major powers. They have also acquiesced in, and often have even sought, a variety of forms of assistance by other states which they regarded as essential for their security and/or development but which could certainly be regarded as highly intrusive and interventionary measures. These include economic and military assistance, and various patterns of political, economic, social, and cultural relations and interactions.

Throughout history, Great Powers, in particular, have resorted to various forms of intervention and interference in other states or areas. This was a marked feature of the policies of the major European powers in the nineteenth century, and it is a marked feature of the behavior of the major powers today. In a sense it could be argued that a Superpower—perhaps even a Great Power—can not be other than an interventionary force. Certainly the present great powers are so regarded, and with considerable justification. Each follows patterns of action and behavior which it regards as essential for the promotion of its national interests, and which in any event may be unavoidable because of its global reach and power, and which can only be described as interventionary, in essence and in effect. Each also justifies certain forms of intervention for ideological or other reasons. The former Soviet Union, for example, had repeatedly proclaimed that it would support "wars of national liberation," and the United States insists that it would take whatever measures may be necessary to resist and contain Communist expansion.

As has been indicated, intervention and interferences in domestic affairs may take many forms, and may indeed be an inescapable feature of contemporary international life. Various patterns of political, economic, military, social, cultural, and psychological actions and relations could be characterized as forms of intervention and interference, whatever their more positive aspects may be. Other classifications of forms of intervention and interference are often suggested—for example, subversive intervention, preventive intervention, preemptive intervention, even humanitarian intervention and counter-intervention.

For governments and peoples that are concerned with human welfare and human rights throughout the world (see *Human Rights and Peace*), humanitarian intervention is a justifiable exception to the general prohibition on nonintervention and noninterference in domestic affairs. The argument is that where these goals are being violated, outside intervention—whether by collective or bilateral action, by official or unofficial groups—is not only justifiable, but imperative, to ensure the observance of minimal standards of individual and national behavior. Sohn (1982) has found out that "(g)ross violations of human rights are now considered to be matters of international rather than domestic concern, and to represent possible threats to

the peace." Akehurst (1993) asserts that "because furthering human rights is a purpose of the United Nations and collective action for that purpose is pledged by its members, and, further, because the United Nations institutional efforts at moral suasion in this regard often have been intellectual, efforts beyond the statutory limitations of the United Nations might reasonably be acceptable for such a high purpose." This was the effect of the UN coalition that was formed to contain and punish Iraq's actions in Kuwait in 1991, as well as the multinational intervention in Somalia, and the protracted intervention in the Balkan region to stop the slaughter of thousands of civilians in the name of "ethnic cleansing."

In pursuit of preserving the peace and security of a community of citizens against intentional actions to commit genocide, humanitarian intervention by the international community by any means deem necessary is considered justified. Another arena of appropriate intervention would be where the semblance of responsible government has disappeared and large populations are killed, or are threatened with death from at least two sources: indiscriminate warfare between two belligerents and consequent life-threatening devastation of food and water distribution systems.

As Falk (1968), one of the authorities on international law who believes that humanitarian intervention is often legally warranted, acknowledges, "the relation between domestic suppression of human rights and the use of international intervention as a technique of liberation is . . . a matter that lies along the frontier of a developing world law system."

Nonintervention in the sense of noninterference in internal affairs becomes particularly difficult in the case of civil conflict or internal war in a state or states that creates special spillover problems for neighboring states or for the international community. Unfortunately there are numerous contemporary examples of domestic conflict with spillover effects which have had adverse internal and external repercussions and which have led to external involvement and intervention. It has often been pointed out that the United Nations Charter says nothing explicit about external intervention in internal struggles. These struggles, now all too common, are among the most disturbing features of the contemporary international scene, for they not only threaten the stability or even the survival of the nation or nations immediately concerned, but they often have spillover effects that lead to external intervention and interference that might escalate into major threats to world peace.

Generally speaking, it may be argued that nonintervention and noninterference in domestic affairs help to create conditions of peace, and that intervention and interference pose threats to peace. But even this seemingly logical generalization is not always valid, especially when the wide gamut of international behavior subsumed in the terms "intervention" and "interference," and the linkages between national and international conduct and developments, are given careful consideration.

See also: *Intervention*

Bibliography ———————————————

Akehurst M 1993 Human intervention. In: Gillespie T R Unwanted responsibility: Humanitarian military intervention to advance human rights. *Peace and Change* 18(3)
Bishop W W 1953 *International Law: Cases and Materials.* Little, Brown, Boston, Massachusetts
Briefly J L 1963 *The Law of Nations,* 6th edn. Oxford, New York
Falk R A 1968 *Legal Order in a Violent World.* Princeton University Press, Princeton, New Jersey
Franck T M, Weisband E 1972 *World Politics: Verbal Strategy among the Superpowers.* Oxford, New York
Henkin L 1968 *How Nations Behave: Law and Foreign Policy,* 2nd edn. Praeger, New York
Kane W E 1972 *Civil Strife in Latin America.* Johns Hopkins University Press, Baltimore, Maryland
Little R 1975 *Intervention: External Involvement in Internal Wars.* Rowman and Littlefield, Totowa, New Jersey
Moore J B 1906 *A Digest of International Law.* US Government Printing Office, Washington, DC
Morgenthau H J 1967 To intervene or not to intervene. *Foreign Affairs* 45(3)
Rosenau J N (ed.) 1964 *International Aspects of Civil Strife.* Princeton University Press, Princeton, New Jersey
Rosenau J N 1969 Intervention as a scientific concept. *J. Conflict Resolution* 13
Rosenau J N 1980 *The Scientific Study of Foreign Policy,* rev. edn. Nichols, New York
Sohn L B 1982 The new international law: Protection of the rights of individuals rather than states. *American University Law Review*
Thomas A V W, Thomas A J Jr 1956 *Non-intervention: The Law and Its Import in the Americas.* Southern Methodist University Press, Dallas, Texas
Vincent R J 1974 *Nonintervention and International Order.* Princeton University Press, Princeton, New Jersey

NORMAN D. PALMER; PEDRO B. BERNALDEZ

Non-offensive Defence

Non-offensive defence (NOD) is a form of defence possessing as little offensive capabilities as possible. There are several terms for this concept, each of which highlights a specific aspect:

(a) 'Non-offensive defense' (NOD), emphasizing that it possesses little or no offensive (i.e., attack) capabilities;

(b) 'Structural inability to attack' (SIA), which underlines that this non-offensiveness is a function of the structure of the armed forces;

(c) 'Defensive defense' (DD) which focuses on the defensive capabilities;

(d) 'Defensive restructuring' emphasizes the gradual nature of the envisaged build-down of offensive and simultaneous strengthening of defensive capabilities.

(e) 'Non-provocative defense' (NPD), which highlights the fact that the absence of offensive capabilities means avoiding unnecessary provocation of adversaries;

(f) 'Confidence-building defense' (CBD), which stresses that this contributes to building trust among states.

1. The Rationale

While they may disagree on the means to achieve them, almost all NOD proponents agree on the ends, most important among which are the following:

(a) Disarmament, which is favoured both as a contribution to the ends below and as a means to free resources for civilian consumption (see *Economics of Disarmament and Conversion*). Generally, NOD advocates have little faith in arms control by negotiation and tend to prefer a combination of unilateralism and gradualism. Regardless of the method, however, what matters most is to reduce the element of mutual threat in arms acquisitions so as to escape the action-reaction pattern. The latter is a reflection of the 'security dilemma,' implying that what a state does for its own security tends to damage the security of its adversaries. As the latter respond in a similar fashion, the security of both sides deteriorates (if 'balance' is maintained), while both spend (i.e., waste) more and more resources. To the extent that armaments are strictly defensive, however, they will pose no threat to a state's enemies, who are thus under no pressure to respond. Not only does an escape thus become possible from the arms race, it may also be possible to reverse the dynamics: To the extent that a state's adversaries are driven by merely a quest for national security, they may emulate a defensive restructuring of the armed forces, whence may ensue a 'restructuring and disarmament race.'

(b) War Prevention, as NOD will make certain wars well-nigh inconceivable without increasing the risk of other forms of war. If states possess merely such forces as cannot be used for attack, their respective adversaries will have no incentive to start preventive wars or launch pre-emptive attacks. They will stand a better chance of prevailing if they wait for the respective other side to attack. Against premeditated attack, on the other hand, an NOD-type defence should possess undiminished strength as a form of 'deterrence by denial:' the country should be difficult to invade and even harder to occupy (see *Deterrence*). A state with an NOD-type defense would, however, benefit from the clarity provided by the defensive nature of its forces: They could be mobilized and readied for combat upon early warning without risk of thereby provoking an otherwise avoidable war.

(c) Defensive Strength is required for war prevention. Some NOD advocates believe that a civilian-based defense would be adequate for dissuasion of an aggressor, as it would make occupation costly and unrewarding. Most disagree and believe that military forces are required, but that they may do without offensive capabilities.

(d) Damage Limitation is to be achieved by deemphasizing nuclear weapons (or removing them altogether), thereby escaping the dilemma that some forms of defense would destroy what they were supposed to protect.

(e) Détente and Confidence-building would benefit from a defensive restructuring of the armed forces. NOD can help dismantle enemy images by removing their foundations, as well as by enhancing transparency; and it may serve as a confidence-building measure in its own right (see *Détente*). NOD is simply the military application of the principle of Common Security, promulgated by the Palme Commission in 1982: Security cannot be attained at the expence of one's adversary (who would merely respond, thereby damaging one's own security) but presupposes that both sides of an adversarial dyad are secure.

2. Premises

The claim that NOD would be a means to the ends listed above rests on two basic assumptions: that 'offensive' and 'defensive' are distinguishable, and that defense is superior to offence.

2.1. Offence/Defence Distinction

The offence/defense distinction does not apply to individual weapons or weapons systems, as all can be used for both defense and attack. It is a matter of intentions, activities, plans, options and capabilities:

(a) Intentions: To seek territorial expansion or the establishment of control over other states is offensive, while to seek to preserve one's national sovereignty and territorial integrity is defensive.

(b) Actions: Attack is offensive, but counterattack need not be—in fact tactical counterattack is a precondition for successful defence. However, large-scale border-crossing ('strategic') counter-offensives (e.g., intended to occupy the aggressor's homeland) are generally to be counted as offensive.

(c) Plans: Strategies that envision border-crossing attacks and/or large-scale counter-offensives are offensive, while such as merely envisage fighting on home ground to repulse an attacker are defensive. Offensive tactics that envision attacking an invader's forces on one's own ground are entirely compatible with a defensive orientation.

(d) Options: To be in a position to launch attacks or large-scale counter-offensives is offensive (albeit sometimes unavoidable), whereas to eschew such options is defensive. This may be a matter of political constraints (e.g., constitutional prohibitions against aggression), political structures and civil-military relations (firm democratic civilian control of the armed forces, for instance); and/or of military capabilities.

(e) Capabilities: Some combinations of personnel, weapons, logistics, and deployment patterns (i.e., military postures) are well-suited for the execution of offensive strategies, hence offensive, while other postures are inadequate for such actions, hence defensive.

What is offensive or defensive further depends on

context, both historically and geographically: One military posture may have been offensive in the past, but have ceased to be so; and one military posture may be offensive in one geographical setting, but not in another. Island states, for instance, can neither attack nor be attacked by means of armies alone. Finally, 'offensive' and 'defensive' are relative and relational terms: A posture may be more or less offensive, but is rarely entirely one or the other; and it may be offensive vis-á-vis one opponent, but not against another.

That there is thus no such thing as an offensive or defensive posture of universal validity does not imply that distinctions cannot be made. In a specific context, informed observers will have little difficulty with determining whether one posture is more offensive than another, or what might make a predominantly offensive posture less so.

2.2. Defensive Superiority

Preferably two adversaries should be so strong on the defensive and weak on the offensive that the situation would be one of mutual defensive superiority: Neither side should be capable of winning a war of aggression, whilst both would be sure to prevail in a defensive war against the other as aggressor. Such a situation is captured in the formula (where D and O stand for defensive and offensive strength, and A and B are two states):

$$D_A > O_B \ \& \ D_B > O_A$$

Such a stance can be achieved both by a strengthening of defensive and a build-down of offensive capabilities, or both simultaneously.

As argued by Clausewitz, the defensive is inherently the stronger form of combat, as the defender enjoys several advantages: He is able to fight on his home ground, which can be prepared for defense; he can exercise more realistically; he benefits from interior lines of communication; he has easier access to civilian infrastructure and other resources; and there are certain capabilities that he does not need (long-range mobility, for instance), hence he can specialize on those needed for defence. To what extent it is possible to make the defender actually stronger depends, however, on what form of NOD-type defence is chosen.

3. NOD Models

The main NOD models are the following (see Alternative Defence Commission 1983; Möller 1991; Møller 1995):

(a) Area-covering territorial defence as in the seminal proposal of Horst Afheldt, or the 'spider-and-web' concept of the SAS (Study Group Alternative Security Policy). The latter envisages a combination of an area-covering defence web with mobile forces ('spiders'), including tanks and other armoured vehicles. Even though the latter are *per se* suitable

NOD COMPARED WITH TRADITIONAL MILITARY POSTURES		
None	Fewer	More
GROUND FORCES		
Theatre nuclear weapons Short-range nuclear weapons	Main battle tanks Infantry Fighting Behicles	Trucks, Motorcycles Anti-tank weapons (guns, recoilless rifles, mortars, grenade launchers, etc.)
Battlefield nuclear weapons Chemical weapons	Combat helicopters Large-calibre, self-propelled artillery	Air defence weapons (guns, portable SAMs) Obstacle-creating means (anti-tank mines etc.)
AIR FORCES		
Strategic bombers Long-range ballistic missiles	Fighter-bombers CAS-aircraft Air superiority fighters Helicopters	Surface-to-Air missiles Interceptor aircraft
MARITIME FORCES		
Tactical naval nuclear weapons Aircraft carriers	Land attack weapons Submarines Large surface ships Amphibious forces	Minelayers Land-based naval aviation Small surface ships Coastal artillery

for offensive operations, they are made dependent on the web, hence very mobile within, but virtually not beyond it, i.e., on enemy ground.

(b) Stronghold defence (also known as 'selective area defence' or 'bastion-type defence'), as suggested by members of the SAS group for the Middle East and other regions with low force-to-space ratios and/or long borders. This implies concentrating the defence on certain areas that are politically important and/or which allow for a cohesive defence.

(c) Forward defence, for instance by means of 'fire barriers' and/or fortifications and fixed obstacles along the border. Without mobile ground forces that are capable of taking and holding ground, such a defence may be entirely non-offensive even if long-range striking power (aircraft, missiles) is included.

(d) The 'inverted synergy' (or 'missing link') approach, according to which an otherwise offensive force posture may become strictly defensive by the absence of one or several components, for instance long-range and/or mobile air defence capability, mobile anti-tank defence, or river-crossing equipment.

(e) Disengagement, implying the withdrawal of certain forces (usually the most offensive-capable ones) from the border area to rearward locations, combined with a forward defence by strictly defensive means: typically tantamount to a tank-free zone in the border region, to be defended by infantry armed with anti-tank weaponry, or otherwise.

(f) 'Stepping down,' implying that the general level of readiness should be reduced: forces should be cadred (e.g., through a shift to a reserve army system) or otherwise prevented from launching surprise attacks, say by a separation of munitions from weapons.

Which model is preferable depends on the context: Countries with little strategic depth (e.g., Israel or Singapore) cannot rely on territorial defence; nor can countries with too much territory such as Russia; while countries with very long borders cannot defend them all in a forward mode; and disengagement only makes sense in some cases, etc. That not every NOD model is suitable for every context, however, does not imply that NOD as such is inapplicable.

In the table above, a typical NOD military posture is compared with a traditional one. However, it is merely intended to illustrate the shifts of emphasis implied by the adoption of NOD as the guideline for defence planning.

4. History of the NOD Debate

Interest in NOD-like conceptions goes back for several decades. Even before that we find precursors of modern NOD theory, i.e., writers who have developed some of the elements of what has become modern NOD models.

4.1 Precursors

The ancient Chinese strategic writer Sun Tzu has inspired NOD proponents with his emphasis on asymmetry: There is no need to 'meet like with like,' but tanks may, for instance, be countered with anti-tank weapons, nuclear weapons with dispersal, etc.

As mentioned above, the German strategist Carl Von Clausewitz held the defensive to be the stronger form of combat. He further emphasized that it had the effect of creating pauses in fighting, as a result of which the political ends might come to take precedence over the military objectives. He also described how a defensive 'people's war' (i.e., guerrilla war) would work in this direction.

The Polish banker Ivan Bloch in 1889 wrote about the strengthening of the defensive as a result of technological innovations such as barbed wire, machine-guns and railways. He thus predicted that future wars of aggression would develop into protracted and extremely costly war of attrition—as happened in World War I.

4.2 1918-40

The debate about (what today is called) NOD in the inter-war years was spurred above all by the desire to avoid a repetition of the unprecedented disaster of the First World War. There was a rather widespread recognition that this disaster had been brought about by a combination of factors:

(a) an erroneous belief in the strength of the offensive, manifested, *inter alia*, in the German 'Schlieffen Plan' and its French counterpart, the 'Plan 17;'

(b) an arms race resulting in extraordinarily high level of armaments;

(c) a last-minute mobilization race which acquired an unstoppable momentum, since no state dared be caught off-guard by an attacker.

From this recognition sprang, on the one hand, a quest for viable supranational or international institutions, i.e., for a form of collective security (personified in the League of Nations); secondly disarmament negotiations in the 1920s and 1930s, especially the 1932 World Disarmament Conference. While the focus was placed on reducing or abolishing 'offensive weapons,' it proved impossible to find any definition of such weapons which was acceptable to all participating states, and the negotiations were exploited for launching allegations against adversaries. One of the few partly successful set of disarmament negotiations was that on naval armaments, especially the 1922 Washington Naval Conference, which managed to slow down the (offensive) naval arms race, whereas the 1930 and 1932-36 conferences in London were largely unsuccessful.

There was also a debate in certain countries on the prevailing trends in weapons technology and their effects on the offence/defence balance, as well as concrete suggestions for strengthening the defensive. In the UK, the belief in the supremacy of the defence (advocated above all by Liddell Hart) supported the policy of continental disengagement and 'appeasement' associated with the Chamberlain government which, in their turn, facilitated Hitler's expansionist drive (see *Appeasement Policy*). In France, similar beliefs led to the construction of the Maginot Line, a comprehensive system of fortifications along the north-eastern border of France. Whereas this defensive line was probably quite effective, successive French governments failed to complement it with mobile reserves capable of dealing with breakthroughs and circumventions. The (in hindsight partly erroneous) belief in the supremacy of the defensive left the European democracies vulnerable to German attacks which exploited the recently discovered offensive potentials of tanks and aircraft, working in combination, for *blitzkrieg* strategies.

In China, the communist guerillas in the last half of the 1930s fought quite a successful resistance struggle against the Japanese invaders. In this connection they applied a defensive guerila strategy of battle avoidance and protracted war, formulated by Mao Zedong. Later NOD strategists have drawn heavily on the experience from this war, as well as from subsequent guerila wars, especially as far as tactical concepts are concerned.

4.3 The 1950s

In the 1950s, after the development of the bipolar system in Europe, German rearmament was debated against a background of a large-scale introduction of tactical and theatre nuclear weapons all over Europe. This was seen as dangerous developments that would both heighten the risk of war and spoil the last chances of German reunification. Hence a number of proposals were put forward for various forms of disengagement pertaining to Germany—both by Germans (Bogislav Von Bonin, the SPD, the FDP, and others) and by foreigners (George Kennal, Hugh Gaitskill, and others).

The disengagement proposals were accompanied by some thinking on alternative means of defence. Some of the aforementioned disengagement advocates accompanied their proposals with sketchy suggestions for other ways of defending Germany and Europe. Whereas von Bonin proposed a genuine military NOD-type defence, Kennan came close to an advocacy of non-violent defence. Others arrived at similar conclusions and recommended a shift to non-violent defence (Steven King-Hall among others).

4.4 The Second Cold War

The renewed debate about NOD in the late 1970s and early 1980s reflected similar fears of war. Nuclear strategy appeared to many observers to be heading in a dangerous direction which was made to look even more frightening because the arsenals on both sides had by now reached the 'over-kill' level. Arms control negotiations appeared to have ended in a *cul de sac*. This spurred both more 'hawkish' attitudes towards arms control and détente (particularly in the USA) and a number of critical theoretical analysis of the logic of arms control, with Robert Jervis standing out for his proposals for distinguishing between offensive and defensive weapons. In Europe Horst Afheldt and others in 1976 put forward the first detailed proposal for an alternative and strictly defensive military defence of Central Europe.

The gradual spread of anti-nuclear sentiments in the late 1970s was accompanied by a growing interest in all sorts of alternatives to NATO's 'nuclear-infected' flexible response strategy. It was realized that nuclear weapons were there for a purpose, hence, they had to be rendered superfluous before their abolition would become a realistic goal. Concrete proposals were made for a restructuring of the armed forces, intended to ensure that NATO would possess a conventional posture which would be adequate for deterring a Soviet attack, thus rendering nuclear deterrence redundant.

4.5 The Second Détente

NOD proposals were not taken seriously by most governments in NATO before the late 1980s, but were either ignored or rejected as incompatible with NATO strategy and *ipso facto* unacceptable. In the latter half of the 1980s this situation changed when, quite unexpectedly, the former Soviet Union endorsed the idea of NOD. Until then, nearly all NOD proposals had been addressed to NATO, both because their proponents were westerners, and because it was regarded as inconceivable that the East might be persuaded to change its strategy. At best, western NOD proponents had hoped for inducing a change indirectly: by persuading NATO to reform its strategy first, thereby hopefully motivating the USSR to change course as well.

The Soviet sea-change thus came as a complete surprise, *inter alia* because the strategy and operational and tactical conceptions of the Red Army had hitherto been highly offensive. In the course of a couple of years, however, the Soviet (communist) leadership had committed itself politically to a complete shift to NOD, accompanied by an equally wholesale commitment on the part of the Warsaw Pact. This was not only reflected in a certain (albeit rather slow and, from a Western point of view, unsatisfactory) unilateral restructuring and build-down of the armed forces, but also in numerous concrete proposals for negotiations concerning both nuclear and conventional forces.

One result thereof was the start of a new set of negotiations on conventional armed forces in Europe, to replace the unsuccessful MBFR (Mutual and Balanced Force Reductions) negotiations. The mandate of the new CFE (Conventional Armed Forces in Europe) talks was initially likewise limited to conventional ground forces in Europe. It was, however, somewhat broader, both geographically (by covering the entire area from the Atlantic to the Urals) and thematically: by dealing with equipment, i.e., major army weapons systems as well as combat aircraft and helicopters. The mandate was also more focused and relevant, since the proclaimed intention was to reduce offensive capabilities in general, and those of surprise attacks in particular.

The talks were, in one sense, remarkably successful, and a treaty was signed as in 1990. In another sense, however, they had clearly been overtaken by events: the division of the participating states into two alliances had been rendered obsolete by the effective collapse (and subsequent formal dissolution) of the Warsaw Pact; one participating state (the GDR, i.e., East Germany) had shifted sides and subsequently ceased to be through a 'merger' with West Germany; and, finally, the pace and magnitude of the unilateral reductions exceeded those stipulated in the CFE treaty.

By the early 1990s, many NOD conceptions had been incorporated into the 'establishment' strategic discourse, and many of the goals set by NOD proponents had at least been partly achieved. On the other hand, as the threat of large-scale and nuclear war had receded, interest in NOD also declined in Europe where the main problems were no longer military ones such as those which NOD might help solving.

5. Relevance of NOD in the Post-Cold War Era?

While NOD is thus less relevant as a hedge against large-scale war in Europe than it was during the Cold War, it remains relevant for the following areas, where these is also a significant interest in the topic:

(a) In the former Soviet Union, NOD is a relevant guideline for restructuring of the armed forces of both Russia and the other successor states. For Russia it is important not to be perceived as a threat, while what matters most for the others is to achieve a cost-effective defence that will allow for a transfer of resources from military to civilian purposes. In both instances, NOD-type forces would be preferable to offensive-capable ones. It will, however, be difficult for Russia to cover its entire territory without a long-range mobility that may be tantamount to offensive capability.

(b) In East-Central Europe, it is important to find ways of making NATO membership more acceptable to Russia. NOD-type armed forces combined with constraints on the deployment of foreign troops and weapons would ensure Russia that the accession to NATO by Poland, Hungary, the Czech and the Slovak Republics would not represent a threat.

(c) In South and South-East Europe, a defensive structure of the armed forces in the states created on the territory of the former Yugoslavia (including the two entities in the former Bosnia) would be important for ensuring that the new states constitute no threat to each other. This is a necessary, albeit far from sufficient, precondition for a lasting peace. Defensive restructuring of the armed forces of Turkey and Greece would also constitute a hedge against a war between these two states, that might erupt over Cyprus or the division of territorial waters in the Aegean Sea.

(d) In South Asia, it is important that India is not seen by Pakistan as a military threat, which might make a preventive war or pre-emptive attack seem both necessary and promising (as a lesser evil). It is similarly important for Pakistan not to give India any pretext for an attack. It is especially important to maintain peace between these two states because both may have nuclear weapons.

(e) In the Middle East, NOD would be a valuable component of an Israeli-Syrian peace treaty. Israel would need assurances that the Golan Heights would not be used for a surprise attack by Syria, and vice versa. NOD would also seem to be the only conceivable form that armed forces of a future Palestinian state could take, as it would be unacceptable to Israel to have offensive-capable hostile forces stationed on the West Bank and/or Gaza.

(f) In the Persian Gulf area, the international community has already acknowledged the need to limit and contain the offensive capabilities of Iraq in order to prevent a new aggression against neighbouring states. However, it is also important that the small but rich states belonging to the Gulf Cooperation Council are not perceived as a threat by either Iraq or Iran, especially as they are counted as US allies. Hence, defensive restructuring would seem to be a precondition for a stable peace in the region.

(g) In East Asia, the situation is potentially even more unstable. North and South Korea have frequently been on the brink of war, as each perceives the other as a mortal threat. Both sides have formidable offensive capabilities, and North Korea has apparently sought to build a nuclear potential. Defensive restructuring would mitigate these risks and might pave the way for a general relaxation of tension that would be a precondition for reunification. Upon reunification, it will also be important for regional stability that the combined armed forces are as defensive as possible, otherwise they might trigger a regional arms race. Such an arms race might also be set in motion via Chinese arms build-up, if this is seen as providing China with offensive capabilities. In that case, Japan might abandon its NOD-type military constraints, a step which the rest of Asia (*inter alia* because of history) would see as a serious threat to their security.

(h) In Southern Africa, NOD-type restructuring is an important means for post-apartheid South Africa to assert its leading regional role without being perceived as a threat. The defence review process in 1996 and the resultant *White Paper* clearly acknowledged this.

6. NOD, Alliances and Collective Security

While NOD would make states less of a threat to their neighbours, it cannot solve all defence problems, *inter alia* because of differences of size. Very large states (like Russia or China) need forces with a long range merely to defend their own territory. These ranges almost inevitably provides them with the ability to invade smaller neighbours. Hence the need of these small states for additional safeguards, either in the form of allies or collective security arrangements.

Both alliances and collective security, however, require armed forces with a long range and offensive shock power (for the liberation of conquered territory). A possible solution to this dilemma may be a division of labour: States could eliminate their offensive capabilities on the national scale by not having a full panoply of long-range forces, but only elements thereof (e.g., some long-range aircraft, but no mobile ground forces). Offensive capability would only materialize upon the bringing together of such force elements in multinational joint task forces, which would (in most cases) be regarded as much less threatening.

See also: *Collective Security and Collective Self-defense*

Bibliography

Alternative Defence Commission 1983 *Defence without the Bomb*. Taylor & Francis, New York

Booth K, Baylis J 1988 *Britain, NATO and Nuclear Weapons. Alternative Defence versus Alliance Reform*. Macmillan London

Borg M, Smit W (eds.) 1989 *Non-provocative Defence as a Principle of Arms Control and its Implications for Assessing Defence Technologies*. Free University Press, Amsterdam

Boserup A, Neild R (eds.) 1990 *The Foundations of Defensive Defence*. Macmillan, London

Cawthra G, Møller B (eds.) 1997 *Defensive Restructuring of the Armed Forces in Southern Africa*. Dartmoth, Aldershot

Dean J 1987 *Watershed in Europe. Dismantling the East-West Military Confrontation*. Lexington Books, Lexington

Gates D 1991 *Non-Offensive Defence. An Alternative Strategy for NATO?* Macmillan, London

Möller B 1991 *Resolving the Security Dilemma in Europe. The German Debate on Non-Offensive Defence*. Brassey's Defence Publishers, London

Möller B 1992 *Common Security and Nonoffensive Defense. A Neorealist Perspective*. UCL Press, Boulder; Lynne Rienner, London

Möller B 1995 *Dictionary of Alternative Defence*. Adamantine Press, Boulder; Lynne Rienner, London

Möller B, Wiberg H (eds.) 1994 *Non-Offensive Defence for the Twenty-First Century*. Westview, Boulder & London

Neild R 1990 *An Essay on Strategy as it Affects the Achievement of Peace in a Nuclear Setting*. Macmillan, London

Singh J, Vatroslav V (eds.) 1989 *Non-Provocative Defence.*

The Search for Equal Security. Lancer, New Delhi

UNIDIR (ed.) 1990 *Nonoffensive Defense. A Global Perspective*. Taylor & Francis, New York

BJØRN MØLLER

Non-Proliferation Treaty (NPT)

The history of postwar efforts to prevent nuclear proliferation began in January 1946, when the very first United Nations General Assembly resolution envisaged the elimination of nuclear weapons from national arsenals. A few months later, the United States government proposed the Baruch Plan (see *Baruch Plan*) in the United Nations. This would have involved the establishment of an international authority to control atomic energy activities dangerous to world security, but the initiative failed. Shortly after this the then Soviet Union (1949), the United Kingdom (1952), France (1960), and the People's Republic of China (1964) became nuclear powers.

During this period nuclear technology for the production of electric power advanced with great speed, and the links between peaceful and military uses of nuclear power became stronger. In fact, the first nuclear reactors were built to produce plutonium for weapons, not to generate electricity; to this day it is impossible to generate electricity in a reactor without using or producing materials that could be used for nuclear weapons. Thus, "horizontal proliferation"—the increase in nuclear weapon states—has been regarded by many as an inescapable risk of the widespread use of nuclear energy for peaceful purposes and the dissemination of nuclear technology.

Negotiations to achieve the Non-Proliferation Treaty (NPT) ended on June 12, 1968, and the Treaty entered into force on March 5, 1970. It was the outcome of a decade of diplomatic effort.

1. The Terms of the NPT

The primary purpose of the NPT is to prevent "horizontal proliferation" and in particular, at the time it was negotiated, to prevent the former Federal Republic of Germany and other Western states from gaining a nuclear weapon capability. The Treaty consists of a preamble and 11 articles. The preamble deals with the dangers of nuclear warfare, recognizing the necessity of full cooperation in the application and the improvement of the International Atomic Energy Agency (IAEA) safeguards system. It also reaffirms the principle that the benefits of peaceful applications of nuclear technology should be available (for peaceful purposes) to all parties in the Treaty, and recalls the importance of exchange of scientific information about peaceful applications of atomic energy. It expresses the intention of all parties, "to achieve at the earliest possible date the cessation of the nuclear arms race and to undertake effective measures in the direction of nuclear disarmament." Finally, the preamble affirms again the determination expressed by the parties in the 1963 Treaty banning nuclear weapons tests above ground, "to achieve the discontinuance of all test explosions of nuclear weapons for all times." The Comprehensive Test Ban Treaty was opened for signature in 1996.

The essence of NPT is contained in its first two articles. Article 1 obliges the nuclear weapon states (NWSs) not to transfer nuclear weapons to any recipient whatsoever. Article 2 pledges the non-nuclear weapon states (NNWSs) not to receive, acquire, or develop nuclear weapons. Article 3 obliges the NNWSs to accept the International Atomic Energy Agency (IAEA) safeguards on their nuclear activities to prevent diversion of nuclear material for weapon purposes. Article 4 affirms that all states party to the treaty have the right to undertake research, production, and exploitation of nuclear energy for peaceful purposes. Article 5 obliges NWSs to assist NNWSs in the development of nuclear energy for peaceful purposes. Article 6 stipulates that all parties to the treaty undertake to pursue negotiations in good faith on effective measures for nuclear disarmament and general and complete disarmament. Article 7 states that nothing in the treaty affects the rights of nations to agree on nuclear-free zones. Articles 8-11 are largely procedural: Article 8 states that any party may propose an amendment to the Treaty and says also that a conference to review the operation of the Treaty shall be held five years after its entry into force; Article 9 defines a NWS as one which has manufactured and exploded a nuclear weapon prior to January 1, 1967. Article 10 gives each party the right to withdraw from the Treaty if its "supreme interests are jeopardized by extraordinary events" and also gives the treaty an initial duration of 25 years.

In 1995, after 25 years, the NPT was extended indefinitely. In the early 1990s, the NPT had became nearly universal, with several states that had previously refused to join signing or acceding. By 1998, only five countries with significant nuclear activities remained outside the Treaty: Brazil (which is a State Party to the Latin American Nuclear Weapon Free Zone), Cuba, India, Israel and Pakistan. Of these, India, Israel and Pakistan achieved the capability to produce nuclear weapons since 1970 but are not eligible to sign the NPT as NWSs since they did not test before 1968.

2. The Major Problems

To most observers, the NPT is a vital part of the world order, preventing the spread of nuclear weapons and preserving global security. To critics, the Treaty is flawed. What are the main problems?

(a) The NPT was intended to serve two main purposes: to stop the spread of nuclear weapons capability (horizontal proliferation) while regulating commerce in peaceful nuclear technology; to stop and reverse the nuclear arms race (vertical proliferation). Although the efforts to prevent horizontal proliferation have been largely successful and holdings of nuclear weapons have decreased in all of the NWSs party to the Treaty since the end of the Cold War, it has become apparent that complete nuclear disarmament will not happen for several decades at least.

(b) Horizontal proliferation remains a real threat because, despite improvements in the inspection system of the IAEA since Iraq was caught cheating in 1991, States Parties can still withdraw from the Treaty with nuclear material in their possession, as North Korea did in 1994. While these two are the only States Parties ever found to be in clear violation with the Treaty (North Korea violated its safeguards agreement before withdrawing), suspicions of non-compliance remain among other States Parties. Some of Japan's neighbors suspect it of creating a nuclear weapon option, for example, and the United States has claimed that Iran is in violation, though it has not formally made this charge to the IAEA.

(c) Nuclear energy has not provided the benefits expected in the 1960s, when the optimistic belief that nuclear energy would solve energy problems was prevalent. For most NNWSs the cost, with the additional safety and environmental risks, is now prohibitive. Furthermore, in some cases nonparties have received better assistance (for instance, Brazil is buying a complete nuclear fuel cycle from the then Federal Republic of Germany, and Argentina received equipment for the production of heavy water from Switzerland before signing).

3. Criticisms of the NPT

The NPT has been criticized by India on the grounds that it establishes a "nuclear club" with unequal benefits and obligations for NWSs and NNWSs. While this argument was popular ten years ago, India has lost the support of once supportive states, even before trying to block the CTBT in 1996 and resuming nuclear testing in 1998. NNWSs party to the Treaty still express concern about the pace of progress on Article 6, but it is much less common to accept that this is a fundamental flaw in the Treaty.

Indeed, a more common criticism is that the Treaty is still not universal. NNWSs in the Middle East in particular raise the universality issue, which has prevented progress in the Arms Control and Regional Security track of the Arab-Israeli Peace process. Safe energy and environmental groups criticize the NPT because it promotes nuclear power and disturbs the introduction of safer and cheaper energy alternatives. In their opinion, nuclear power is an expensive, risky way of producing energy. Moreover, antinuclear groups consider the distinction between peaceful and military nuclear technology to be absolutely artificial. The nuclear proliferation problem, as posed, is, according these groups, insoluble: it is simply impossible to promote nuclear energy for peaceful purposes and, at the same time, prevent the spread of nuclear weapons. As the Indian and Pakistani nuclear tests in 1998 reminded the international community, nuclear proliferation remains one of the great problems facing humanity. The NPT has had a central role in preventing the emergence of more nuclear weapons states, while offering a forum in which non-nuclear weapon states can encourage nuclear disarmament.

See also: *Arms Control, Evolution of; Nuclear-Weapon-Free Zones: A History and Assessment*

Bibliography

Arnett E 1996 *Nuclear Weapons after the Comprehensive Test Ban: Implications for Modernization and Proliferation.* Oxford University Press, Oxford

Arnett E 1997 *The Comprehensive Nuclear Test-Ban Treaty,"* SIPRI *Yearbook 1997: Armaments, Disarmament and*

International Security. Oxford University Press, Oxford

Cowen Karp R 1992 *Security Without Nuclear Weapons? Different Perspective on Non-Nuclear Security.* Oxford University Press, Oxford

Kokoski R 1995 *Technology and the Proliferation of Nuclear Weapons.* Oxford University Press, Oxford

Simpson J 1996 *The Nuclear Non-Proliferation Regime after the NPT Review and Extension Conference, SIPRI Yearbook 1996: Armaments, Disarmament and International Security.* Oxford University Press, Oxford

RAFAEL GRASA; ERIC ARNETT

Nonviolence

Peace research today has reached a consensus that the opposite of peace is not war, but violence (Schneider 1973 p. 149). It would follow that the opposite of violence, namely nonviolence, is in some way identical to peace. Often regarded as a subtopic of peace, especially in academic circles, nonviolence may prove to be the key to peace.

It is therefore doubly unfortunate that the systematic study of nonviolence and its conscious use as a social force are so recent that the word is used (and the phenomenon understood) in different, not infrequently contradictory senses. On a descriptive level, the distinction between nonviolence and violence is unproblematic—and unilluminating: nonviolence is the absence of violence (see *Positive versus Negative Peace*). However, just as with the concept of "negative peace," that is, the absence of war, problems arise in the first place because not all violence is physical. Most (but not all) theorists today would consider an abusive word or gesture not to be nonviolence, even if that word or gesture is not accompanied by blows; on the other hand, actual blows, if they are delivered to a bully not out of hatred or fear but to protect someone might well be considered nonviolence.

1. Definitions

The term "nonviolence" in general use today seems to inherit the meanings of earlier terms like (Christian) nonresistance as understood by writers such as Adin Ballou, under the influence of Sanskrit *ahimsā*, "nonviolence, noninjury" made current by Gandhi (Ballou 1972; nonresistance is listed in the Oxford English Dictionary as meaning only passive obedience). Most speakers, however, do not use the word "nonviolence" with anything like the full meaning of *ahimsa* as Gandhi understood it. Like many a-privative compounds in Sanskrit, *ahimsa* connotes not merely the absence of the thing negated but the positive quality which is its opposite (compare *abhāya*, literally "nonfear," meaning "courage").

Second, *ahimsa* is what linguists call a desiderative formed on the root $\sqrt{han}$ "strike," "slay," "injure"

(Bondurant 1965 p. 23). Thus the word denotes an intensely positive state of affect towards other beings in which even the desire to harm cannot arise, a state which Gandhi, Martin Luther King Jr., and others identified with *agape*, or spiritual love (see *Sustainable Peace*). This force Gandhi regarded as latent in all human beings, becoming manifest to the degree that negative emotions such as anger (for example, the perfectly natural anger arising from a perception of injustice) were converted into their positive—and some would say original—forms: anger to compassion, greed into generosity, and so forth. In its full sense, then, nonviolence is that force or principle which comes increasingly to motivate a person who transforms the desire to injure others into its positive counterpart. It is anything but negative.

The terms in use in other European languages show the same negative bent; for example French *nonviolence* and German *gewaltlosigkeit*, which can literally mean "absence of power or authority." With the introduction of nonviolent principles and methods into the central political arena by the Green parties, particularly in Germany, a new and more accurate connotation has become somewhat current, e.g., through the word *gewaltfreiheit* or "freedom from violence." This is what we might call a 'Shalom' definition of nonviolence (see Zampaglione 1973 pp. 185-187).

Just as in common parlance "peace" nearly always means the mere absence of war, so the term "nonviolence" usually and just as erroneously suggests the mere absence of injurious force (see *Words of Peace and War*). What is more, since we have come to equate injurious force with force purely and simply, people shun 'nonviolence' as *gewaltlosigkeit*, the absence of any force what so ever. Just as the profound peace of which Augustine spoke so eloquently in Book XIX of the *City of God* has only been enjoyed by a few rare individuals, and not become the social order, so what Gandhi called the "nonviolence of the brave" has rarely been met within human history (see *Gandhi, Mohandas, Karamchand*). Nonetheless it is, he believed, discretely present as the active force behind innumerable partial forms of nonviolence that one does encounter in individuals, movements, and societies.

In this article, "nonviolence" will be used for that positive and (at first nonphysically) active force; for convenience the older punctuation "non-violence" will be reserved, following David Dellinger, for all lesser forms, that is, the mere absence of violence, as in common parlance, or presence of some partial commitment to nonviolence. Fully realized nonviolence is usually called today "committed" nonviolence as opposed to merely "strategic" nonviolence, but a variety of other qualifications are also current. We may begin by considering some of these more common and observable forms and their relations to the less tangible force or principle which empowers them (see Sharp 1973 for a comprehensive analysis along somewhat different lines of division).

2. Forms and Gradations

The Druze of Palestine who nonviolently resisted Israeli attempts to absorb their cultural and political identity, but who served in the Israeli Defense Force would seem to be using non-violence for a particular purpose without being committed to it as a universal principle of ethics. The Druze may have felt that nonviolent resistance only applies to struggles *within* the state—an honest mistake which Gandhi himself only gradually outgrew (Brock 1981). Or they may have felt that as long as they were living under Israeli protection they were bound to accept military service in it—a position Gandhi might have approved to the end, for anyone who did not yet feel the call to principled "nonviolence of the brave." But they may also have abjured violence against the Israeli occupation—and accepted it in Israeli military service—out of fear. Gandhi and all who follow him would regard this as the precise opposite of nonviolence, and a serious tactical error in the long run.

To further complicate matters, not only may individual Palestinian Druze have adopted the same policy from different motives but within each one of them different motives, as in any individual, may have been mixed and contending. This is the human condition: it is rarely a yes or no matter whether or what kind of nonviolence is at work in a given situation.

A test would be, what would they do if their non (-) violence were answered by violent repression? A wave of non-violent resistance to Apartheid ended after the Sharpeville massacre of 1960, and turned into sullen submission punctuated by violent outbursts

(which can be considered as two sides of the same coin from the nonviolence viewpoint). To try "nonviolence" conditionally, thinking that "if the other side picks up the gun we will be forced to do likewise," is really worse than nothing: it would be better, Gandhi constantly maintained, to use the gun until you no longer believe in it.

These are examples of partial or provisional commitments to non-violence, and they are commonly met with. Their exact relationship to nonviolence resists simple analysis; nonetheless, some attempts to analyze such situations are important—not to pass judgment on any participant but to understand a critical but very little understood practical dynamism (and Gandhi, like Kant, did not accept that morality was impractical; contrast Galtung 1965 p. 249). From any of these commitments to non-violence an individual or group can move closer to nonviolence, and thus gain power and long-term effectiveness. This is perhaps least true from the position of cowardice, but even there one can become more nonviolent by, paradoxically, first becoming overtly violent. One must be *capable* of violence in order to renounce it.

The difference, then, between non-violence and nonviolence may be not so much one of philosophical principle as one of developmental levels within a process through which humankind has to pass individually and socially. Historically, nonviolence can generate what might be called a "weak force" in the social field. It is much less likely to produce counterproductive side-effects or compromise the long-term development of a relationship than violence, but it is nothing like as predictable or efficacious as the deployment of full "dehyphenated" nonviolence, which, as in Gandhi's case, not only rectified a major situational injustice but changed world history. This is the "strong force," or in Gandhi's terms "the greatest power mankind has been endowed with."

No harm attaches to a limited or provisional use of nonviolent strategies by those who are incapable of violence or afraid to use it, by those yet unconvinced that nonviolence is in fact either a universal ethical or effective principle—except the harm that comes when you or onlookers think you have tested "nonviolence" and found that it doesn't work. As Theodore Roszak often says: "People try nonviolence for a week, and when it doesn't 'work' they go back to violence, which hasn't worked for centuries."

If the resisters in Sharpeville or Prague (see below) had realized that their limited successes came from a mere fraction of the power available to them, they might have found ways to consolidate their gains and go forward.

3. Misconceptions

The prevalent misconceptions about nonviolence all seem latent in the misleading negative term for it. As Bishop Tutu has said of the former practice of calling Black South Africans "non-whites" or "non-Europeans," it is very difficult to appreciate fully something we constantly refer to as the absence of something else.

Gandhi himself responded to this difficulty by rejecting the term "passive resistance" for his experiments with nonviolent principles in the struggles of indentured laborers of South Africa in 1906, substituting *Satyagraha*, "holding to truth," or "truth force," a new coinage he partly arrived at by a contest (see *Satyagraha*). Satyagraha was to remain his word for nonviolence in action, especially in the social field, throughout his subsequent campaigns in India. However helpful, neither this nor his tireless activities have as yet set the misunderstanding to rest.

Two common myths arise directly from the inability to conceptualize nonviolence as an active force in its own right:

(a) nonviolence is passive; it is offered best by the meek,

(b) it is only effective against weak opposition: "It would never have worked against the Nazis."

Both these myths were exploded by Khan Abdul Ghaffar Khan and his work in the Northwest Frontier province of India during the 1930s and early 1940s (Easwaran 1984) (see *Khan, Abdul Ghaffar*). Khan, known as the "Frontier Gandhi," raised a non-violent "army" of fierce Pathans who renounced a centuries-old tradition of retaliation and turned their phenomenal courage instead to the patient bearing up under savage oppression from British military authorities—an oppression fully equal to Nazi determination and savagery. For that matter, limited, uncultivated nonviolence worked very well against the Nazis themselves (see now Stolzfuss 1996) and against the Soviet invasion of Czechoslovakia in 1968 (Sharp 1985).

A related if not as mischievous myth is that for the nonviolent person physical violence is absolutely ruled out under any circumstances. Nonviolence is not really, unlike pacifism, a moral norm, but as Gandhi always insisted, a principle, or a force. In an emergency (Gandhi used the example of a madman with a naked sword) even lethal physical violence can be allowable, indeed demanded—that is, for the protection of others.

Yet in such an emergency three things which lie mainly outside the domain of physical behavior would be required of a positively nonviolent person: (a) to accept any consequences of his or her physically violent action; (b) to ask why the situation arose in the first place and what he or she—or society in general—could do to prevent such things (in technical terms: is "structural violence" lurking in the social situation, for example in mass media programs which criminalize viewers); and (c) not to entertain the slightest ill-will toward the assailant, even if physical violence must be applied against him or her. These situations rarely arise, but in a theoretical sense it is useful to know that even injurious force is not inherently violent: violence is, as the Sanskrit word implies, "*intention* to harm."

4. The Nonviolent Paradigm

The fact that nonviolence draws its power from unseen, pre-behavioral sources has made its political and scientific development difficult in the present material age. We seem to have reached the era in human history which most urgently needs nonviolence and which in terms of the cognitive development of human consciousness has a new opportunity to conceptualize it. The awareness of violence *per se* as a distinct phenomenon (and conversely of nonviolence as a unique social resource capable of intentional development) has taken on a new clarity, as well as urgency, as Jacques Ellul says: "This is not so much the age of violence as the dawning of our *awareness (conscience)* of violence." It is also, sadly, an age of marked physical or external orientation. As Emerson said prophetically: "Things are in the saddle and rule mankind." Nonviolence is entirely a matter not of things but of consciousness; as Galtung and others have pointed out, it concerns our interior life (Galtung 1965 p. 251f). It would be well, then, to explain some elements of the nonviolent belief system, or paradigm.

Nonviolence rests on a belief in (and non-violence on a presentiment of) the fundamental unity of all life: "I subscribe to the belief or philosophy that all life in its essence is one and that the humans are working consciously or unconsciously toward the realization of that identity" (Tendulkar 1953 p. 219). From this flow numerous practical consequences.

As a Danish proverb has it: "In every man there is a king. Speak to him; he will come forth." The faith of the nonviolent actor stands on the assumption—or perception—that ways can be found to speak to the better side of all human nature. As the Quakers say: "There is *that of God* in everyone." Therefore every human individual must be respected, and so no individual can fail to respond, on some level, to genuine respect and kindness (see *Quakerism*).

We are not speaking here of a sentimental kindness, but a genuine concern for the true well-being of the "opponent," compatible with one's own genuine needs for fulfillment. In fact a second article of faith is that all conflict-producing difficulties rest ultimately in perception; no true benefits to oneself are detrimental to others; likewise, in the economic sphere, Gandhi's pregnant aphorism that "there is enough in the world for every man's need; there is not enough for every man's greed." Third, Gandhi and others believed that all history is moving toward a realization of perfect harmony (Boulding 1978 pp. 80-122), and this adds an unseen force to every correctly aligned thought, word, or deed (see World Order: *Gandhi's Concepts and Contributions*). The ontological basis of these beliefs has been perhaps best expressed as follows (Gandhi 1928 p. 433):

"The world rests upon the bedrock of *satya* or truth. *Asatya* meaning untruth also means non-existence, and satya or truth means that which is. If untruth does not so much as exist, its victory is out of the question. And truth being that which is can never be destroyed. This is the doctrine of *Satyagraha* in a nutshell."

5. Logic and Values

Contrary to the tendency of most people to regard successes in the slowly gathering history of nonviolence as "lucky," its advocates hold nonviolence to be a science with absolutely predictable results.

Given the frame of reference we have just briefly described, it is clear that nonviolent logic offers a complete alternative to what game theorists call the zero-sum distributive model of interaction by which in order for one "player" to win the other has to lose. In fact the categories "win" and "lose," "us versus them" lose their hypnotic significance: conflict becomes a stage on a scale of interaction modes in which all participants can gain, not the least by achieving a closer integration with one another, which is part of the overall purpose of life. The paradigm of zero-sum distribution is replaced by that of positive-sum integration (see *Game Theory; Peace, Systems View of*).

In this way the introduction of a nonviolent actor changes the field of interaction, like a magnet in a whorl of metal filings; while conflicts are of course resolved by nonviolence (and sometimes non-violence), whether or not they are resolved, the conflict

relationship is restructured (Flinders in Easwaran 1978 pp. 157-66, Juergensmeyer 1984 pp. 3-66). Thus, advocates of positive nonviolence, like those of positive peace, do not shun conflict, regarding most cases of conflict as an opportunity for psychic and social growth.

The apparent moral contradictions of nonviolence are often susceptible of logical explanation within its own frame of reference; for example, while accepting physical violence for the protection of others (and possibly of oneself) in an emergency, Gandhi came to oppose preparations and organization for violence, which precludes war. The reason is not only one of scale. He undoubtedly would have argued that if one has the time to organize and prepare for violence one also has the time to organize and prepare for nonviolence, as one does not in the isolated (and in practice very rare) emergency. There is much more to what René Girard has called "*la logique de la nonviolence*" (Girard 1978 p. 236), but this may serve as a practical introduction to this fledgling science.

6. Nonviolent Action: Strategies and Principles

There seem to be three general principles underlying successful nonviolent action, or *Satyagraha*:

(a) *Respect for persons*. The nonviolent actor constantly distinguishes the opponent's person from the deed or attitude deemed objectionable, for example, by offering the person constructive alternatives consistent with his or her dignity even while firmly refusing to cooperate with indignities toward oneself.

(b) *Persuasion rather than coercion*. This is practised wherever possible, that is, in all but the most extreme emergencies. The attempt is always to educate the opponent (or co-educate him or her along with oneself: in this respect the enterprise really has no opponent), to draw rather than push. To compel another's action without educating his or her will is at best an emergency measure, never part of a truly nonviolent strategy.

(c) *Means and ends*. The nonviolent actor cannot use means incongruent with the desired nonviolent ends. An entire theory of action lies behind this principle which space forbids entering here (Gandhi 1955 pp. 48-72; Duncan 1971 pp. 33-39).

From these principles have sprung an infinite variety of tactics which in the most successful long-term efforts have been deployed in two complementary modes. These are (to use the terms from Gandhi's major campaigns) constructive program and civil disobedience.

(a) *Constructive program*. It is very important to begin constructively. The major emphasis of a nonviolent campaign should fall always and wherever possible on ongoing, constructive, nonconfrontational efforts to improve one's own situation rather than trying to force changes in the opponent. Gandhi's spinning campaign (*charkha*) is a classic example, along with the other ongoing programs of cultural, moral, and economic self-uplift that made up "Constructive Program" (Gandhi 1941).

Ignorance of this constructive principle is probably the most serious shortcoming of almost all non-violent actions today. It is not that no work is being done on decentralized economies, regionalism and politics based on human values, but activists are so often (for understandable emotional reasons) caught up in positions which are antiwar or anti some other particular form of violence that they forget to reach for a clear, positive alternative.

(b) *Obstructive program*. When constructive uplift of one's own community is bogged down and efforts to educate ones opponent are falling on deaf ears (in the Indian case, such crises seem to have developed roughly every ten years) it becomes necessary to non-cooperate or offer civil disobedience. Here again, there is a well-worked-out set of guidelines for true civil disobedience, the most important being that the civil resister must not operate secretly or attempt to avoid legal penalties: one's resistance is to a law, not to the principle of Law. Thoreau and Gandhi discovered these principles independently (contrary to popular opinion, Gandhi read Thoreau only after Satyagraha had been worked out in South Africa).

As a form of communication, which they are, nonviolent actions often have a symbolic value. By undertaking to suffer in a just cause, one bears witness to the truth. Yet this should not be taken to mean that bearing witness is sufficient by itself. Gandhi's efforts were never aimed only at media or other forms of symbolic attention, they were always primarily substantive: the spinning wheel was a real tool for producing badly needed cloth, his march to the sea (1930) was first a way to get to a source of salt, and a dramatic gesture only secondarily.

It is important to realize that a lot of peace efforts today, for example, protest marches and demonstrations, have no constructive component, and are very often only symbolic. This is not to say such acts are either useless or wrong, but they cannot be expected to teach us much about the full potential of nonviolence. If such undertakings fail, it does not mean that nonviolence has failed. It may also be that the reactive and symbolic nature of much peace activities accounts in large part for their limited effectiveness.

7. Assessing Nonviolent Effectiveness

As we have already seen, there is an invisible dimension to nonviolent energy. Whether or to what degree nonviolence was at work in a given act, word, or thought is hard for an outsider to judge (or for many insiders), since for one thing so much depends on intentions in such matters (Naess 1974 p. 115). Furthermore, as Gandhi pointed out in his classic pamphlet, *Hind Swaraj*, (Gandhi 1909 ch. XVII), "history" has come to mean the record of violent interruptions in the real process of the world, and we are so conditioned by that view of history that we decide "nonviolence doesn't work" if there is a single setback, while the effectiveness of violence is not questioned even in the face of massive defeats and repercussions.

Similarly, nonviolent actors try to view their efforts as part of a long-term process. While military strategists look to the Cuban Missile Crisis as an exemplary success of threat and coercion, advocates of nonviolence would look before the event to ask what dynamics had brought the United States and former Soviet Union to that pass, and after it to point out that the Soviets' defeat stiffened their resistance and increased their determination never to be humiliated again by American power.

Finally it must always be borne in mind that the success or failure of an event has a personal, psychological dimension. Martin Luther King, Jr. wanted never to allow his opponent to bring him so low as to make him hate that person, just as St. Augustine (see *St. Augustine*) had pointed out the folly of thinking our *enemy* could hurt us more than our *enmity*. If an individual is injured or even killed during an apparently unsuccessful attempt to offer nonviolent resistance, he or she may nonetheless have avoided the psychic injury of hating—and the opponent may have been touched more than superficially appears, may have been made readier to be persuaded at a subsequent interaction.

8. Nonviolence and Peace

From his South Africa days, Gandhi often referred to his volunteers as "soldiers." In addition to correcting the fundamental misconception that nonviolence is a "nonsomething," this way of speaking serves to remind us that nonviolence requires if anything more discipline, training, and preparation than soldiering, and that we must expect it to require at least as much sacrifice, though of a different kind.

Alongside obvious differences between militancy and nonviolence, one that is less obvious seems fundamental: militarism's de-emphasis of the individual human being. It would seem inevitable within military psychology to regard human beings as means to an end; a tendency which reached extreme proportions during the need to euphemize the levels of destruction of nuclear weapons but which has remained with us through the media presentation of the Gulf War.

The nonviolent person will try never under any circumstances to forget the humanity of the other. For him or her, countries are never strategic pawns and persons never to be obscured by labels like "foreigner" or "criminal." In the familiar Quaker adage, "there is that of God in every man," nonviolence obeys Kant's law that the human being should never be treated as a means but as an end in him—or herself. Even during large-scale conflict.

While there is no *a priori* reason nonviolence would not apply to conflicts between states (Galtung 1965 p. 237), this remains the least tested and perhaps most urgently needed arena for nonviolence. In the present (twentieth) century, that is beginning to change. A certain body of historical experience has accumulated, theory has begun to develop and bibliography accumulated around two types of action can be distinguished which could in time put an end to war by the employment of nonviolence principles.

The first to become to any degree noted by scholars and the public grew up in response to fears of a massive Soviet land invasion during the Cold War stalemate (Sharp 1985): this is generally known as Civilian-Based Defense (not to be confused with civil defense) or social defense (*soziale verteidigung*). It is basically a form of nonviolent noncooperation by ordinary citizens who resolutely refuse to cooperate with the invasion plans of the attacker, while actively fraternizing with the attackers as human beings. Tentative, spontaneous and undeveloped examples of this form of defense, which Gandhi proposed to his countrymen in the event of a Japanese invasion (Walker 1981 pp. 68-70; Tendulkar 1953 Vol. 6), have been the German resistance to the Franco-Belgian occupation of the Ruhr in 1923 and the often-cited "Prague Spring" (1968) in which a spontaneous noncooperation by the Czech (see *Conscientious Objection*) people frustrated a Soviet invasion force of 800,000 troops for eight months (Sharp 1973 Vol. 1 p. 17, 46). The successes of even these limited forms, and the soundness of the theory explaining them, has now attracted serious attention in the security establishments of Western European and other states and given rise to several research institutions and programs.

The other, and more recently recognized possibility is nonviolent intervention. Interventionary or interpositionary action by an unarmed and usually nongovernmental third party has become an attractive possibility in the post Cold War world of intense local warfare (and the infamous "low-intensity" warfare practised on Central American peoples) (see *Intervention*). By their mere presence and/or a variety of support activities and mediation, groups of volunteers have been intervening successfully to protect individuals whose lives are at risk in oppressive regimes (e.g., Guatemala and Columbia) (see *Mediation*), prevent groups of citizens or non-violent demonstrators from being attacked by police (Hebron, Sri Lanka, Haiti) and also to prevent the raiding of villages, especially in Contra-ridden Nicaragua (see *Peace Brigades, Peace Teams*).

Both social defense and peace brigades were foreseen and in part instituted by Gandhi, the latter as the *Shanti Sena* or "Peace Army" which had an uneven history in India after his assassination (Weber 1996); since his time dramatic but largely unknown efforts have been made to send large unarmed expeditionary "forces" into areas of desperate conflict like former Yugoslavia (Moser-Puangsuwan and Weber). The greatest successes, understandably, have been with those small-scale "micro-interventions" known as protective accompaniment, like those carried out by Peace Brigades International in Central America and elsewhere. Here the logistical problems and cultural misunderstandings are not out of scale for the modest resources of the volunteer, under-funded and largely non-governmental organizations involved (see *Mediation: A Tool for Peace Oriented Transformation*). Here also volunteers can be selected with a bent for nonviolence and get a modest amount of training for the strange new role they are called upon to play as the pioneers of peace for the third millennium after Christ.

Since war ultimately arises from conflicts at the intrasocial, interpersonal, or even intrapersonal levels, or some combinations of these, and since nonviolence acts to resolve conflicts creatively at all those levels, it seems probable that quite apart from the question of alternative defense, which enters the picture only after conflict has mushroomed, nonviolence is the most powerful and least developed resource in the world today for security and peace (see *Conflict Formations, Elements in*).

See also: *Alternative Defense; Civilian-based Defense; Nonviolence, Philosophy and Politics of*

Bibliography —————————————

Ballou A 1972 *Christian Non-Resistance in All its Important Bearings Illustrated and Defended.* Ozer, New York (original edition 1846)

Bondurant J 1965 *Conquest of Violence.* University of California, Berkeley, California

Boulding K E 1978 *Stable Peace.* University of Texas, Austin, Texas

Brock P 1981 Gandhi's Nonviolence and His War Service. *Peace and Change* 7

Duncan R 1971 *Gandhi. Selected Writings.* Harper Colophon, New York

Easwaran E 1978 *Gandhi the Man.* Nilgiri Press, Petaluma, California

Easwaran E 1984 *A Man to Match His Mountains: Badshah Khan Nonviolent Soldier of Islam.* Nilgiri Press, Petaluma, California

Galtung J 1965 On the Meaning of Nonviolence. *J. Peace Res.* 3

Gandhi M K 1928 *Satyagraha in South Africa.* Triplicane, Madras

Gandhi M K 1941 *Constructive Programme: Its Meaning and Place.* Navajivan, Ahmedabad

Gandhi M K 1955 *My Religion.* Navajivan, Ahmedabad

Girard R 1978 *Des Choses Cachées Depuis la Fondation du monde.* Grasset, Paris

Juergensmeyer M 1984 *Fighting with Gandhi.* Harper and Row, New York

Naess A 1974 *Gandhi and Group Conflict.* Universitetsforlaget, Oslo

Schneider H 1973 *Friedensverständniß in Vergangenheit und Gegenwart.* In: Weiler R, Zsifkovits v (eds.) *Unterwegs zum Frieden.* Herder, Vienna

Sharp G 1973 *The Politics of Nonviolent Action.* Porter Sargent, Boston, Massachusetts

Sharp G 1985 *National Security through Civilian Based Defense.* Association for Transarmament Studies, Omaha, Nebraska

Stolzfus N 1996 *Resistance of the Heart: Intermarriage and the Rosenstrasse Protest in Nazi Germany.* Norton, New York

Tendulkar D G 1953 *Mahatma: Life of Mohandas Karamchand Gandhi.* Government of India, New Delhi

Walker C C 1981 *A World Peace Guard: An Unarmed Agency for Peacekeeping.* Academy of Gandhian Studies, Hyderabad

Zampaglione G 1973 *The Idea of Peace in Antiquity.* Dunn R (trans.), University of Notre Dame

MICHAEL N. NAGLER

Nonviolence, Philosophy and Politics of

Nonviolence is not easy to define. Is it only a new term which includes very old-established positions and practices? Is being a nonviolent person the same as to be nonviolent? Does nonviolence consist of a force, a different way of achieving power, as some people consider, or is it weakness, a tame acceptance of the established order? What is the limit, if there is one, in giving up the use of physical force? What are the methods of nonviolence? Are they effective? Is it possible to be nonviolent when supporting nonconfessional, agnostic attitudes, for example? As these questions show, it is not easy to speak generically about the philosophy of nonviolence and related subjects, such as civil disobedience, pacifism, nonviolent direct action, nonviolent popular defense, and so on.

1. Positive and Negative Aspects of Nonviolence

Though the practice and theory that one should not return evil for evil is old, it was not always named nonviolent behavior. Tolstoy was maybe the first to use the phrase when he spoke of "nonviolent resistance to evil" (see *Tolstoy, Leo*). Gandhi, influenced by Tolstoy, used "nonviolence" to translate the Sanskrit term *ahimsa*; it soon became customary to write *nonviolence* as one word in English. The translation of *ahimsa* is not perfect however; *ahimsa* means in fact "no harm." The terminological explanation allows us to avoid a common error: nonviolence does not aim to stop the use of physical force, or any form of moral coercion or aggression. If so, nonviolent direct action would be incomprehensible. Believers in nonviolence try at any price not to damage their adversaries. They consider that the absolute limit of their action is their respect for life.

We have seen the negative aspect of nonviolence: the nonreturn of evil for evil. We can find precedents for this attitude in Confucius, in Buddha ("If a man hurts me, I'll return him my affection and good will; the more he hurts me, the kinder I must be; the perfume of goodness reaches me, and the sad air of evil blows towards him"), in the Laotian tradition, and even in Socratic-Platonic thought, when Plato says through Socrates' words in *Critó*: "It is never licit to commit an injustice nor to return injustice for injustice, nor to take revenge on someone who suffers, returning him evil for evil."

The Christian tradition includes this element, too, as some of the new Testament writing, especially those of John, James, and Paul, abundantly show (see *Peace According to the New Testament*). This moral norm spread slowly, mainly because of the progressive implantation of Christianity in the West (see *Christianity*), to such an extent that it enjoys wide theoretical acceptance (though it is far from being followed by the majority as a common way of behaving), and a lay formulation in the categorical imperative in Kant's formal ethics.

2. Positive Resistance

Nonviolence has a positive aspect, frequently emphasized with adjectives such as "active nonviolence," "nonviolent direct action," or "nonviolent resistance." In plain words, nonviolence has always implied a struggle, admittedly in the field of conscience or will, but a struggle nevertheless. Nonviolence presupposes action and initiative, which implies the use of "weapons," tactics, and strategies based on the principle of overcoming evil through good (see *Nonviolence*). Without any obligation, nonviolence would not exist. Gandhi was explicit in the matter: "*Ahimsa* is not the way of the timid or the cowardly. It is the way of the brave ready to face death. He who perished sword in hand is no doubt brave, but he who faces death without raising his little finger and without flinching is braver. But he who surrenders his rice bags for fear of being beaten is a coward and no votary of *ahimsa*." It is a question of turning nonviolence into a rule of life, of getting involved in it totally. It is not possible to act nonviolently, according to this theory, in one activity and violently in others; if so, we would convert nonviolence into a policy and not a way of life. The obligation must be total.

What happens when the nonviolent person faces a conflict in which agreements or obligations are not possible, a situation which must be solved by means of struggle? Those who do not trust nonviolence as a method for solving conflicts efficiently usually think that this kind of conflict can only be settled by choosing between surrender or passive submission and violence, and since victory requires violence, they consider there is no other remedy left but to direct oneself towards a threat and the use of violence, whatever its forms are. The truth is that violence is not the only efficient action in such conflicts. Throughout history, various people and groups, in several places all over the world and under a variety of political regimes, have supported nonviolent resistance. Martin Luther King and the buses boycott in Montgomery (see *Nobel Peace Prize Laureates: Martin Luther King, Jr.*), Gandhi and the Salt March (see *Gandhi, Mohandas Karamchand*), César Chaves and the fight on behalf of the "chicanos" are well-known examples, There are, however, many other examples: the Hungarian resistance against Austria from 1850-67, the Chinese boycotts of Japanese goods in the early twentieth century, the fights in the Russian Empire in 1905-06, the action launched in support of the legitimate government of the Weimar Republic of Germany and against the rightish Kapp *Putsch*, the German resistance (in 1923) to the French and Belgian occupation of the Ruhr, the struggles against the Nazis in Norway, Denmark, and the Netherlands, using nonviolent methods.

The examples above show that nonviolent strategy is a strategy of resistance, of nonsubmission to the enemy's will. Those who decide on this strategy refuse to accept passively the sufferings their adversaries impose on them. They defy their authority and oppose their power until they defeat them. This strategy is based mainly on the analysis of the psychological mechanism which sets off nonviolence. This mechanism has been studied by Richard Gregg. His view is that when people attack with physical violence they expect one of two responses: fear, which will lead to submission or escape; or a violent response. Attackers gain some moral security if they face the response they expect, it allows them to take the initiative and reaffirms that they did well when deciding on that kind of behavior. What happens when the response breaks the scheme and there is neither fear nor counterviolence? The aggressor is met with calm, firmness, serenity, a lack of resistance in the physical sense. All resistance is centered in the moral attitude, in the insistence on persisting with this attitude, not remaining silent. The aggressor may think the attacked one is silly or a coward, but this attitude will have to change if the latter keeps firm. Therefore it is fundamental that nonviolent people show perseverance, and continue to work hard at their calm and pacific attitude, so that their aggressors may lose their own moral balance.

Nonviolence is, in Gregg's words, a "moral jiujitsu." As the nonviolent person does not resist as the aggressor expects, the force of the aggression confronts a gap and the aggressor's moral balance is lost.

This puzzles the attacker, who is not prepared to assume the kindness of the attacked one; moreover, if there are spectators, the aggressor's insecurity will be even more serious. In any case, the moral "jiu-jitsu" would be impossible without an attitude of veracity, without an attitude of total truth in the attacked one. To quote Gandhi:

> Truth should be the very breath of our life. When once this stage in the pilgrim's progress is reached, all other rules of correct living will come without effort, and obedience to them will be instinctive. But without Truth it would be impossible to observe any principles or rules in life.
>
> Generally speaking, observing the law of Truth is merely understood to mean that we must speak the truth. But we in the Ashram understand the word *Satya* or Truth in a much wider sense. There should be Truth in thought, Truth in speech, Truth in action.

Moral resolution, attachment to the truth, leads the nonviolent person to the report (legal or illegal), to negative coercion (noncooperation, strike, boycott, civil disobedience) or even to positive coercion (meetings, sit-downs, occupation of public centers or places of work, obstruction of roads, sabotage, and any other means which do not imply compulsory transition to bloody violence).

3. Nonviolence and Political Power

These diverse levels of nonviolent resistance have a philosophical support: political power is not intrinsic to the power holder. The roots of political power reach beyond and below the formal structure of the state, into society itself. According to Gene Sharp (1973), the main sources of political power are: authority, human resources ("the number of persons who obey him, cooperate with him, or provide him with special assistance"), the skills and knowledge of such persons, intangible factors (habits and attitudes toward obedience and submission, presence or absence of a common faith, and so on), and the degree to which rulers control material resources (financial, natural, means of communication and transportation, and so on), and the extent and the type of sanctions at their disposal. But all these sources depend on obedience.

It was probably Étienne de la Boétie (1976), speaking about the power of a tyrant, who best described (in the sixteenth century) the importance of obedience, of people's complicity, in the exercise of power. He maintained that all the means a tyrant uses to conquer a nation come from the nation itself; they supply the tyrant with the instruments that are used to

conquer them. La Boétie also stated the principle of noncollaboration. "You will manage to be free, even if you don't try it, it is enough wanting it. Be prepared to stop serving and you will be free." (Boétie 1976 p. 174). If everybody agrees in disobeying then there is no tyranny possible, a thought which Henry Thoreau took up when speaking about "resistance to Civil Government" (civil disobedience in our vocabulary). Civil disobedience—a deliberate peaceful violation of particular laws, decrees, regulations, ordinances, military or police orders, and the like—is based on the consideration that there are inherently immoral, unjust, or tyrannical laws; in such cases, it is correct to prefer moral conscience to prevailing legality, it is fair to disobey. The acts of civil disobedience seek to call public attention to the view that a principle of moral importance is held to be violated by a law or a policy sanctioned by public authorities. It is therefore a good means of political education for citizens, a good means of avoiding consent, since disobedience is essentially voluntary.

Nonviolence also presupposes a new approach to political control. According to Gene Sharp (1973), the approach based on the withdrawal of support and noncooperation in its various forms, from official obstruction to disguised obedience or judicial noncooperation, should be added to the traditional methods (rulers' self-limitation, institutional agreements and dispositions, use of violent means—rioting, assassination, violent revolution, guerrilla warfare, civil and international war, *coup d'état*, and the like). In accordance with it, one of the main advantages of nonviolence rests on its wide range of fighting and resistance tactics. Sharp catalogs 198 ways in his *The Politics of Nonviolent Action*, classified under the following sections: protest and persuasion; social noncooperation; economic noncooperation/boycotts; economic noncooperation/strikes; political noncooperation; and nonviolent intervention.

4. Success in Nonviolence

The most widespread criticism of nonviolent philosophy (in its field of individual action as well as when it prepares defense alternatives) is that it has hardly any success, that is to say, it is ineffective and utopian. Nonviolent people usually counterargue by falling back on historical examples and, much more importantly, pointing out that there are several ways of exercising nonviolent strategy with possibilities of success. The first is conversion: the opponent, as the result of the action of a nonviolent person or group, comes around to a new point of view which embraces the ends of the nonviolent actor. Conversion is based on Gandhi's idea of not humiliating the opponent, of avoiding hostility towards people. We fight, practice noncooperation, against systems or methods and not against people; with the result that through actions we look for the heart, for feelings, not only for repression (which is not often searched or wished for). But conversion runs into many difficulties: the barrier of social distance between the confronted groups, the structure of the opponent's personality, the role of a third party in disagreement, and so on. Gandhi, however, enumerated a series of requirements or controls which nonviolent people should apply themselves to favor conversion: (a) abstain from violence and hostility; (b) gain the confidence of the adversary, telling the truth, mentioning one's own plans, behaving with a degree of fair play (postpone an action in the face of a natural catastrophe, for example); (c) avoid the adversaries' humiliation; (d) make the sacrifices for one's cause visible; (e) carry out constructive tasks; (f) keep up a personal contact with the opponent; (g) show one's confidence in the opponent, (h) develop an attitude of good will and patience towards the antagonist.

Another less radical strategy with possibilities of success is accommodation: "In the mechanism of accommodation the opponent resolves to grant the demands of the nonviolent actionists without having changed his mind fundamentally about the issues involved" (Sharp 1973 p. 733). There is no conversion or repression; nonviolent people see themselves more as a "nuisance" than a "threat" and it generates some "tolerance."

The third strategy, nonviolent coercion, is used when opponents do not cooperate with the demands of those who practice the nonviolent action. These demands are achieved against the opponents' will; that is to say, they may be nonviolently coerced. As Sharp points out, "this type of nonviolent change has often been neglected in favor of the other two mechanisms, . . . because it has left the field clear for advocates of violence" (Sharp 1973 p. 741). Thus nonviolent coercion consists of pressing by nonphysical means, including moral force, which repressive power is unable to control, or rather preventing the development of the political, social, and economic system by means of noncooperation and rivalry.

How is nonviolent direct action organized? According to a text written by the Fellowship of Reconciliation, at the request of Martin Luther King, one must start with four basic principles: (a) define your objectives, your short-range objective and your long-range goal; (b) be honest and listen well, because a crucial part of nonviolent direct action is the understanding that no one knows the complete truth about the issues at hand; (c) love your enemies; (d) give your opponents a way out. The action is carried out in six strategic stages: (a) investigate, get the facts; (b) negotiate, meet with opponents and put the case to them; (c) educate, keep campaign participants and supporters well-informed of the issues; (d) demonstrate, (picketing, vigiling, mass rallies); (e) resist: this may mean a boycott, a fast, a strike, task resistance, or other forms of civil disobedience; (f) be patient, meaningful change cannot be accomplished overnight. As Thomas Merton said, "concentrate not on the results, but on the value, the rightness, the truth of the work itself."

5. Conclusion

Nonviolence is not a mere philosophy, it has a strong political dimension, of theory for action and social change. For nonviolence the causes of social problems are both personal and systemic. To end injustices, both people and institutions must evolve new values and behavior; furthermore, social changes are more likely to persist if they are made by people voluntarily.

To sum up, nonviolence is much more than a philosophy, in spite of its vast history in philosophical or religious thought; it is also a method of action, a way of life, and a political theory which dares even to discuss radical social change. Its peculiarity rests on emphasizing that aims and means must coincide: for the adherents of nonviolence a just and egalitarian society is impossible if we use violent means to bring it about. The changing of the structures is not enough, people have to change, too. We must learn to act and think differently, we must dare to disobey, to deny our consent to those who misuse it. As Gandhi said, "the law of the majority has nothing to say where conscience is in turn to speak." It is not the law which should suggest what justice is, but justice should dictate the law. That is the force of nonviolence, the moral force of the example and of truth. On the other hand, nonviolence has created a great many tactics and fighting methods, of nonviolent direct action, which, alone, constitute an excellent and relevant instrument to achieve peace, as their growing use proves. Indeed, they are used even by those who do not wholly share the philosophical and moral principles of nonviolence.

See also: *Gandhi, Mohandas Karamchand*

Bibliography ————————————————

Bedau H A 1968 *Civil Disobedience: Theory and Practice.* New American Library, New York

Boétie E de la 1976 *Discours de la servitude volontaire.* Payot, Paris

Duncan R (ed.) 1971 *The Writings of Gandhi.* Fontana, London

Fischer L (ed.) 1963 *The Essential Gandhi.* Allen and Unwin, London

Gregg B 1960 *The Power of Nonviolence.* James and Clarke, London

Müller J M 1981 *Straté gie de l'action non-violente.* Du seuil, Paris

Sharp G 1973 *The Politics of Nonviolent Action.* Porter Sargent, Boston, Massachusetts

Sibley M Q 1963 *The Quiet Battle: Writings on the Theory and Practice of Non-violent Resistance.* Doubleday, New York

Thoreau H 1980 *On the Duty of Civil Disobedience.* Housmans, London

Tolstoy L 1963 *Letter to a Hindu.* Peace News, London

RAFAEL GRASA

Nordic Council

The Nordic countries are internationally recognized as small, peace-loving states with firmly established democratic systems of government, sound and effective economies, only slight class differences, and highly developed social security systems. One important feature of Nordic life, however, has only to a limited degree attracted the attention of the outside world. That is the extensive cooperation which the peoples of Scandinavia have established among themselves in almost every walk of life.

Nordic cooperation started 150 years ago as a cultural movement. At government level the breakthrough came after the Second World War under the impression of war and occupation. The main single event was the establishment of the Nordic Council, whose first session was held in February 1953. Denmark, Iceland, Norway, and Sweden were all represented from the start. Finland, for reasons of foreign policy, did not become a member until December 1955.

The decision of Great Britain in 1961 to seek membership of the European Economic Community (EEC) created fears of a serious threat to the main aspects or Nordic cooperation, since the Nordic countries predictably would not have identical attitudes towards the EEC. In an effort to prevent a potential menace to their concord the Nordic Council in 1962 recommended, and the national legislatures adopted, the Nordic Convention of Cooperation—the so-called Helsinki Agreement. This convention for the first time codified the results and the aims of political Nordic cooperation in an international treaty. Hitherto the practical results of Nordic agreement on individual problems had been enacted as national laws in the individual countries.

A significant extension of the scope of the Helsinki Agreement of 1962 was brought about in 1971. The statutes of the Nordic Council were raised from individual national legislation to be included in the revised international treaty, which in this way became the supreme Nordic document, codifying the general provisions for cooperation. The revised treaty also created a Nordic Council of Ministers responsible for coordinating all forms of cooperation at government level. To the Convention on Cooperation were added a Cultural Treaty in 1971, a Transportation Treaty in 1972, and an Environmental Protection Convention in 1974.

In 1970 the Faroe Islands in the North Atlantic and Aaland in the Baltic Sea, which enjoy a considerable degree of self-government under the sovereignty of Denmark and Finland, respectively, were allowed representation in the Nordic Council. The Faroes were permitted to send two members as part of the Danish delegation and Aaland was allowed to send one member as part of the Finnish delegation. By a new amendment to the Nordic Convention in 1983 the Faroes and Aaland—as well as Greenland, which has now acquired autonomy within the Kingdom of Denmark—each elect two members to the Nordic Council.

The Nordic Council has two kinds of members: 87 elected by the legislative assemblies among their own members, and a number of cabinet ministers appointed by the governments of the five states and the three autonomous regions.

The Icelandic Althing elects seven members, the Stoating of Norway and the Riksdag of Sweden 20 each, the Folketing of Denmark 16, who together with the two chosen by the Lagting of the Faroes and the two by the Landsting of Greenland form the delegation of 20 of the Kingdom of Denmark. Likewise the two members elected by the Landsting of Aaland join the 18 members chosen by the Finnish Eduskunta to form the delegation of the Republic of Finland.

As the Council has only advisory competence, it is possible to give the individual countries the number of members mentioned, irrespective of the size of their populations, in order that most parties can be reasonably well-represented. The elected members constitute the core of the Council. They alone have the right to vote; they alone express the Council's will or opinion through their recommendations and "statements." The Committees and the Presidium are also composed solely of elected members.

In addition to the members chosen by the parliaments and the other legislative assemblies, the Council includes ministers appointed by the governments before each session, the number of which the governments themselves decide. The ministers have seats in the Council's Plenary Assembly and take part in the discussions on an equal footing with the elected members. But they have no vote. Under the Statute they also have access to the Committees of the Council, but once again without the right to vote. The governments have always been well-represented at the Council sessions; on average about 50 ministers take part in each session.

Experience has shown that, during council activities, valuable direct contact is formed between government representatives and parliamentarians, particularly in the committees. The ministers are drawn into the consideration of matters at an early stage, allowing a constructive exchange of viewpoints between the two groups and thereby the drafting of realistic recommendations.

Since the Council's parliamentary members generally speaking are chosen on a proportional system, almost every party in the legislative assemblies is represented by one or more members. During the last few years they have organized themselves into four groups: Social Democrats, Conservatives, Communists and other left-wingers, and a Center group uniting the representatives of the Liberal, the Social-Liberal and the Christian-Social members. This establishment of party groups has contributed to strengthening the influence of the Council.

The Nordic Council normally assembles once a year by turns in one of the five Nordic capitals. The central factor in its activities are the five permanent committees which meet several times a year: committees on economic matters, cultural affairs, legal problems, communications and technology questions, and on social and environmental issues. The common financial grants for the manifold activities of Nordic cooperation are scrutinized by the Council's Budgetary Committee. However, the final decision on the budget rests with the national parliaments.

The Nordic Council of Ministers, which—as mentioned above—was established in 1971 as the official joint organ for cooperation among the Nordic governments, is composed of one member from the government of each state and self-governing territory. Which ministers take a seat in the Ministerial Council depends upon the issues to be considered. The Council is therefore a group of changing members.

One of the departmental ministers from each country is entitled the Minister for Nordic Cooperation. Upon this small group of ministers rests the responsibility of coordinating those common activities and problems at government level which do not belong under any special departmental minister. Each Minister for Nordic Cooperation is assisted by a high-ranking civil servant. Together these officials form the Committee of Deputies. In a similar manner Committees of Senior Officials have been established for each of the departmental areas, 17 in all.

In their Nordic activities the governments were assisted by two Ministerial Council Secretariats, one in Copenhagen for cultural matters and one in Oslo for all other questions. In 1985 it was decided to combine them into one, to be located in Copenhagen from 1986.

The Nordic Council is a forum for cooperation between the parliaments and governments of the Nordic countries and its purpose is to promote and initiate cooperation between the member-states. In sum, significant accomplishments of the Council include the abolition of passport regulations for Nordic citizens travelling within the region, policies for an open labor market and social security policies.

The Nordic Council of Ministers is tasked to safeguard and develop Nordic cooperation and to consult each other on matters of mutual interest in collaboration with Europe and other international organizations. The Council deals with issues concerning legal, cultural, social and economic fields and also the environment and communications. Very recently, the Council decided to include matters of foreign policy and security. For this purpose the Ministers of Foreign Affairs meet regularly.

See also: *Nordic Political Cooperation*

Bibliography ———————————————

Anderson S V 1967 *The Nordic Council.* University of Washington Press, Seattle, Washington
Bukdahl J et al., (eds.) 1959 *Scandinavia Past and Present, 3* vols. Arnkrone, Odense
Engellau P, Henning U (eds.) 1984 *Nordic Views and Values.* Nordic Council, Stockholm
Friis H (ed.) 1950 *Scandinavia: Between East and West.* Cornell University Press, Ithaca, New York

Heldal H 1965 *Nordic Cooperation in the Social and Labour Field*. Ministry of Social Affairs, Oslo

Herlitz N 1969 *Elements of Nordic Public Law*. Norstedt, Stockholm

Lyche I 1974 *Nordic Cultural Cooperation*. Universitetsforlaget, Oslo

Scott F D 1975 *Scandinavia*. Harvard University Press, Cambridge, Massachusetts

Strath B 1978 *Nordic Industry and Nordic Economic Cooperation*. Almqvist and Wicksell, Stockholm

Sundelius B 1978 *Managing Transnationalism in Northern Europe*. Westview Press, Boulder, Colorado

Turner B 1982 *The Other European Community: Integration and Cooperation in Nordic Europe*. St Martin's Press, New York

The Nordic Countries: The Nordic Council. http://www.randburg.com/nordic/overview-6.html

Wendt F 1981 *Cooperation in the Nordic Countries: Achievements and Obstacles*. Almqvist and Wicksell, Stockholm

FRANTZ W. WENDT; PEDRO B. BERNALDEZ

Nordic Political Cooperation

The results of Nordic political cooperation are very comprehensive, although some important attempts did not succeed. Negotiations in 1948-49 for a defensive alliance failed. Later, more than 10 years of preparations for creating a common market were overtaken by the establishment of the European Free Trade Association (EFTA) in 1960. Denmark, Iceland, Norway, and Sweden joined the EFTA, while Finland signed a separate agreement with the Association. However, through membership of the EFTA the Nordic countries achieved many of the goals they had aimed at when planning their common market. In 1966-67, all duties on industrial products were abolished. Consequently, their mutual trade rose from 12.1 percent in 1955 to 23.3 percent in 1973.

However, the idea of creating a closer economic association had not been abandoned. After surmounting a great number of practical difficulties due to the different economic interests of the countries, the governments and the Nordic Council in February 1970 reached agreement on a proposal for the so-called NORDEK treaty, the aim of which was to establish a comprehensive economic union (see *Nordic Council*). However this most important single project ever contemplated through Nordic cooperation never became a reality. Although one of the declared purposes of the negotiations had been to facilitate the participation or collaboration of the countries or some of them in an expanded European Economic Community (EEC) (see *European Union*), the government of Finland in March 1970 decided not to sign the draft treaty it had approved the month before. The reason given was that Denmark, Norway, and Sweden intended to explore their possible membership of the EEC, which in December 1969 had given its approval to British application.

This failure of the NORDEK project was a setback to Nordic cooperation. Furthermore, when Denmark alone became a member of the EEC in January 1973, some further concern was felt about the future of Nordic cooperation. However, such anxiety has proved groundless. The trade treaties which the four other countries entered into with the EEC preserved the Nordic free trade area that had been created within the EFTA. It has therefore been possible to continue the high level of exchange of goods and the growing industrial cooperation that had been the result of EFTA membership. In spite of Danish membership of the EEC, almost every kind of Nordic cooperation has continued and been further developed. Moreover, Denmark's membership also benefits the other Nordic countries, Denmark acting as an effective Nordic spokesperson in the various organs of the European communities.

1. Concrete Economic Measures

Although the more ambitious schemes had failed, Nordic economic cooperation continued by the "step-by-step" method that had been practiced ever since 1945 and had given so many positive results. The strengthening of the constitutional instruments of Nordic cooperation through the 1971 revision of the Helsinki Treaty contributed to an increase in the efficiency of the efforts. In the 1980s great interest has been centered on proposals to make the Nordic countries into a "common home market." This endeavor is greatly facilitated by their geographical proximity, the similarities of their peoples in tastes and business customs, their community of language, and the extensive harmonization of legislation and standards.

In order to remove "invisible trade restrictions" a great number of steps have been taken to facilitate coordination of economic activities. Such measures include mutual approval of material testing, identical standards in many fields, control of electrical materials, as well as harmonization of building materials and building regulations.

Common enterprises to strengthen the economy of the individual countries include cooperation in the study of atomic energy, initiatives in the exploitation of oil and natural gas, research in energy saving, cooperation in production and transmission of electric power, a fund for technical and industrial development statistical studies and information, export credit arrangements, and collaboration of the central banks, as well as a Nordic investment bank to procure capital for large joint enterprises and for financing exports of interest to two or more of the countries.

2. Legal Cooperation

An important reason for the considerable results of Nordic cooperation is the close cultural community of the Nordic nations. This is especially true within the field of the law, due to the fact that they share a common view of justice and therefore trust the legal systems of each other. Consequently, it was a natural objective for the Scandinavian movement, when it started in the middle of the nineteenth century, to bring about greater uniformity in the legal systems. As a general rule, however, this uniformity was not brought about by adopting joint laws or treaties, but by negotiating uniform solutions on the basis of which the individual countries enacted their own national laws. In fact, that is the method still employed in most fields of Nordic cooperation. Treaties and conventions are used only to a limited extent.

These efforts have continued to the present day. New fields of legislation are constantly included, according to the needs of the community, and existing laws are taken up for revision.

Legal cooperation today covers a great variety of subjects: marriage, divorce, and the financial aspects of both; citizenship; naturalization; purchase and sale of goods; trademarks; trade registers; cheques, bills of exchange, and instruments of debt; commercial agents; maritime law; air traffic; insurance; contracts; patents and copyrights; consumer protection; installment purchases; and several other fields of activity.

Of particular interest are the uniform laws of citizenship, which not only make it possible for citizens of one Nordic country to be naturalized in another Nordic country of residence after a shorter stay than non-Scandinavians, but also give them the automatic right to become citizens after a continuous residence of seven years in their new country.

Nordic legal cooperation also covers important fields of the administration of justice. The courts pos-

sess the authority to try crimes committed in any Nordic country. Likewise, all the countries have introduced legislation for the execution of sentences pronounced in the other countries. The Swedish Minister of Justice, Herman Kling, once characterized this legislation as "an extremely advanced form of cooperation which is without parallel elsewhere in the world; indeed. the cooperation ... between the Nordic countries in this field is more intimate than is the case between the states of a federation."

3. Cooperation in Social Matters

While the earliest agreement in the legal field was obtained as far back as 1880's cooperation in social matters did not start until the 1920s and first gained real impetus after the Second World War. Since then, such significant results have been obtained that a Scandinavian who resides in a Nordic country other than that of which he of she is a citizen, enjoys, on the whole, the same social benefits as the citizens of his or her country of residence. Therefore one may actually speak of a Nordic social citizenship.

Behind this is the fact that all the Nordic countries make up a common labor market for many trades and professions, in which no special license or authorization is required. But even for several other professions there exist special agreements, in consequence of which similar common and open labor markets have been created. This is the case for primary-school teachers as well as for physicians, dentists, nurses, pharmacists, veterinarians, and 13 other groups within the health sector.

To make life safer for the several hundred thousand Scandinavians who avail themselves of the common labor market, a citizen of one of the countries who lives in another country is entitled to the same social benefits in his or her new country of residence as those enjoyed by its own citizens. These agreements are primarily concerned with old age pensions and other pensions, as well as social insurance covering illness, accidents, and unemployment.

4. Cooperation within the Health Sector

As far as health services are concerned, cooperation has gone further than the common labor market for the medical professions mentioned above. A common pharmacopoeia has been established. The national health services work closely together. A Nordic School of Health in Gothenburg, Sweden, offers advanced courses for physicians, nurses, hospital administrators, and other groups within the health sector. The authorities cooperate closely in the fields of job environment, industrial medicine, and hygiene, as well as labor protection in general. Prescriptions issued in one country are valid in all of them. The governments join forces in combating trade in illicit drugs and in conducting research related to alcohol and drug abuse. A Nordic institute tests odontological materials. The so-called Scandia-transplant organizes the search for kidneys of recently deceased persons for transplantation purposes. In the area of consumer protection, a comprehensive body of rules has grown up regarding labeling as well as food inspection and research.

5. Cooperation Regarding the Environment

The Nordic countries have been pioneers in the efforts to improve the environment. The Convention on the Environment of 1974 states that the damage inflicted by an industrial enterprise in another country is to be placed on the same footing as damage inflicted in the home land, and the perpetrator may be prosecuted in a similar way. The Nordic countries also cooperate in a very concrete manner in combating pollution of the seas that surround them, chiefly the vulnerable waters of the Baltic, the Gulf of Bothnia, and the Sound. In international organizations they have been active in combating air pollution.

6. Facilitating Communications

In the view of Scandinavians as well as foreigners the most conspicuous practical manifestation of Nordic cooperation is the Nordic Passport Union. It is not necessary for Scandinavians to show a passport when entering another Nordic country. Non-Scandinavians must undergo passport control only when entering or leaving the Nordic area, but not when crossing inter-Nordic frontiers. Customs inspection of luggage and automobiles has been greatly simplified. Where it takes place at all, it is often carried out by the customs officers of one country on behalf of both countries involved.

Prominent in the field of communications are the Nordic Postal Union and the Nordic Telecommunications Union (NORDTEL). The managements of the national railroads work closely together. The Nordic telecommunications authorities rent a joint telephone and telexnet in the transatlantic cables. The Nordic Telecommunications Satellite Committee has established a joint station north of Gothenburg, Sweden; through this station, and via a satellite in the INTELSAT system, is sent much of the telephone and telex

traffic between the Nordic countries and the United States.

The Nordic Tourist Traffic Committee coordinates the activities of the national tourist organizations in a number of cities abroad. Scandinavian Airlines System (SAS), combining the Danish, Norwegian, and Swedish national airlines, is one of the largest enterprises in the world of aviation, a striking example of the effectiveness of Nordic cooperation. As a logical consequence of the establishment of the SAS, the three governments have established close contact among their national aviation authorities. The three SAS countries act together at international meetings and at diplomatic level to defend their interests in the air.

7. Cultural Cooperation

Inter-Scandinavian cooperation in the cultural field took place on a wide scale before 1940, having gradually developed since the start of the Scandinavian movement in the middle of the nineteenth century. For almost 100 years, however, cultural cooperation was almost exclusively the result of private efforts in many walks of life. Not until after 1945 did national governments become involved in the systematic development of cultural relations.

Many joint Nordic institutions in various fields of higher education and research have been established to coordinate advanced scientific research and instruction among the individual countries. This is important, as in many cases each of these small nations has only a limited number of scholars, scientists, and funds in each field of study. That is why it has been found useful—often indispensable—to concentrate both professors and students in joint institutions, to set up Councils to organize cooperation between research groups, and to establish a division of labor between research centers in different countries.

By these various kinds of cooperation it is possible to provide an adequate basis for qualified research and training in subjects where the number of scholars and students is very limited, to avoid duplication, achieve a more effective of cheaper use of investments in equipment, laboratories, libraries, and so on, and to provide a broader professional environment and greater inspiration between research workers.

The fields of scholarship represented by the various common institutes are very diverse. They include nuclear physics, folklore, social planning, volcanology, African, Asian, and Latin American studies, and East European research, as well as advanced courses in journalism. Other subjects are research in traffic safety and in the abuse of alcohol and drugs, acceleration physics, marine biology, oceanography, ecology, Arctic medicine, international politics and peace research, agricultural and forest research, as well as research into mass media.

A number of joint Nordic courses provide high-level instruction in such fields as the literature, languages, history, archeology, and ethnology of the Nordic nations. Cooperation between research libraries and an extensive documentation and information service in many fields of study makes possible a common utilization of the library resources of the individual countries. The publication of joint Scandinavian scholarly and scientific journals plays an important role, since through them the results of Nordic research are presented to readers both abroad and at home.

As a result of the ability of the majority of Scandinavians to understand each other, closely related languages (the Finns are the main exception), radio and above all television are important tools for strengthening cultural bonds. Many people are able to receive television broadcasts directly from a neighboring country. There is furthermore a close cooperation among the state broadcasting corporations. A joint agency, *Nordvision*, organizes a systematic exchange of TV programs and arranges coproductions.

The Nordic Council and the Nordic governments have for 20 years discussed the subject of television cooperation. After 1975 the interest centered on a common satellite, called NORDSAT. It has, however, proved very difficult to agree upon a solution. A project—called *Telex*—based upon Swedish technology has in 1985 finally succeeded in gaining support for a three-year trial period from Sweden, Finland, Norway, and Iceland. Attempts have been made to obtain the participation of Denmark.

The Nordic Council and the governments take an interest in disseminating each other's national literature. For that purpose the Nordic Council Literary Prize was established on 1962. The 75,000 tax-free Danish crowns are awarded every year. Grants are also available for translations, which are of special interest to those who read only Finnish and to the inhabitants of the Faroes, Iceland, and Greenland, as well as to the Samis (Lapps) in the northern region of the Scandinavian peninsula,

Knowledge of arts other than literature is likewise promoted through common efforts. The Nordic countries share a common pavilion at the famous Biennial in Venice. A Nordic center for pictorial art has been established in the old fortress of Sveaborg in Helsinki harbor. Arts exhibitions, guest performances of theater and opera companies, and the exchange of orchestras, soloists, conductors, and critics are subsidized. The Nordic Council Music Prize, awarded every second year, amounts, like the Literary Prize, to 75,000 tax-free Danish crowns.

A valuable cultural initiative is represented by the Nordic House in Reykjavik, Iceland. The purpose of this institution is to strengthen Nordic interests among the Icelanders by means of exhibitions, concerts, film shows, and theatrical performances, as well as by means of a well-equipped library. The House in the Icelandic capital has become the model for the Nordic House in Tórshavn, capital of the Faroes, as well as for the Nordic Institute in Aaland.

The many problems facing the small numbers of Samis (Lapps), spread across the northern reaches of Norway, Sweden, and Finland, have been of great concern to the Nordic Council. One of its initiatives has been the establishment in the Norwegian town of Kautokeino far above the Arctic Circle, of a Nordic Sami Institute to strengthen the culture of the Lapps and the basis for their way of life.

Besides the regular grants on the Nordic budget for the many scientific and cultural activities, a special Nordic Cultural Fund finances a wide assortment of one-off projects, such as exhibitions, courses, congresses, study trips, publications, and so on.

8. Cultural and Political Bonds

The five countries maintain mutuality in their agreements on trade and commerce, the employment market, communications and related areas. There is therefore a growing tendency, both within the Nordic countries and outside them, to consider the region as a single market area. Social matters such as environmental issues, sexual equality, education and social welfare receive equal attention and priority within the Nordic countries.

Internationally, it can be said that the Nordic countries often stand together and are thus able to wield more influence on political and cultural matters than they could ever have individually. This sort of a united front has been a result of long-standing cooperation both at inter-governmental and unofficial levels.

Company executives often meet to discuss business strategies. Likewise, in the cultural sector, artists in all fields have been meeting and working with their colleagues.

Cultural and political cooperation have had many benefits for all countries. Sharing knowledge and opinions has helped in forming common policies for implementation at home and in an international context. Naturally, projects which are too large for one country to handle can be deal with on a concerted basis. Such is the importance of the cultural and political bonds that have existed among Nordic countries since centuries ago till now.

9. Institutional Aspects of Nordic Cooperation

An important feature of inter-Nordic cooperation is the close contact among organizations and institutions of all kinds in the Scandinavian countries. The movement started in the second half of the nineteenth century and has continuously covered new fields ever since. Today it will therefore be difficult to find any organization without some kind of relationship with its counterparts in the other Nordic countries.

A special kind of organization is the NORDEN Association, which with its national branches in all the countries and with their numerous local bodies, has for its sole purpose to promote mutual understanding and cooperation.

When the first attempts at organized Nordic cooperation at government level were made in the last decades of the nineteenth century, they were prepared by ad hoc groups of experts. During the First World War the governments started meetings to discuss urgent matters of common interest, especially neutrality policy and mutual economic assistance. In the 1920s and 1930s meetings of ministers in other fields, too, became more frequent, though still intermittent.

The experiences of the Second World War gave a very strong impetus to Nordic cooperation at government level, and during the following four decades it has been growing steadily. At present almost all cabinet ministers hold regular meetings. A great number of permanent groups of high-ranking civil servants and numerous expert groups and many kinds of institutes of cooperation have been established.

In 1952 a parliamentary organ of cooperation, the Nordic Council, was constituted and held its first session in 1953. Its founding members were Denmark, Iceland, Norway, and Sweden. In 1955 Finland was able to join. In 1970 the self-governing territories of the Faroes and the Aaland Islands were allowed to choose their own representatives, who joined respectively the Danish and the Finnish delegation. In 1984, Greenland attained the same right. Its representatives became members of the Danish delegation.

Since 1984 the Nordic Council has been made up of 87 members elected by the respective legislative assemblies among their own members, and a number of cabinet members appointed by the governments and the executive organs of the self-governing territories in numbers they themselves decide. Normally about 60 cabinet ministers take part in the yearly Council session which is held alternately in the five state capitals.

The Danish Folketing elects 16 members, the Faroeish Lagting two members and the Greenland Landsting two members, who together form the delegation of the Kingdom of Denmark. The Finnish Rikesdag elects 18 members, who, together with the two elected by Aaland's Landsting, constitute the Finnish delegation. Iceland's Althing elects seven members, Norway's Storting 20, and Sweden's Riksdag 20 members.

The elected members and the Cabinet members are all members of the Council, but only the elected members have the right to vote.

In 1962 the general objects of Nordic cooperation were formulated in the so-called Helsinki Treaty of Nordic Cooperation. By a revision in 1971, a Nordic Council of Ministers was established, to be served by a cultural secretariat in Copenhagen and a secretariat for all other matters in Oslo. From 1986 the two secretariats were to be merged into a single ministerial secretariat in Copenhagen. A special Cultural Treaty was adopted in 1971 and a Transport Agreement in 1972.

Although the Nordic Council has only advisory power, its influence is considerable and growing, due to the fact that the parties usually elect influential members to join the Council. Its importance has also been augmented by the fact that the elected members of the various delegations have organized themselves across national frontiers according to their political affiliations. There are four such groups in the Council: the Conservatives, the middle parties (moderate Liberals, and Social Liberals, Center parties, Christian People's parties), Social Democrats, and finally Left-wing Socialists and Communists.

10. Meetings of Foreign Ministers

The cooperation between the Nordic states is not limited to their internal problems. Although the countries differ in their foreign associations and their security policies (see *Nordic Security Problems*), their foreign ministers meet regularly, at least twice yearly. At these meetings they inform each other of their views concerning international issues directly involving their countries or otherwise of interest to them. The divergent attitudes of the Nordic countries to security policy problems give their diplomatic services access to information which is consequently broader in scope than the diplomats of any single one of the countries could obtain. Furthermore, the mutual trust which usually exists between the participants of the meetings allows them to exchange views and information in full openness and confidence. In spite of the completely informal and uncommitted nature of the meetings they are an important element in Nordic cooperation.

11. The Nordic Countries in the United Nations

At one of the biannual meetings of the foreign ministers, matters on the agenda of the autumn General Assembly of the United Nations are always discussed. The Nordic countries participate in UN activities on the basis of their common cultural and social ideals. As small and peaceloving nations they are agreed about the need to strengthen the UN as a worldwide, peace-establishing organization which also has a duty to promote economic and social improvement for the peoples of the world. The similarity of their views and ideals has made it natural for the Nordic countries to reach similar attitudes to the concrete issues in the world organization. Contact between their representatives is very close in all spheres of UN activities, and they try wherever possible to coordinate their views. In matters not relating to security policy nor too strongly affected by the clash of interests between the Great powers, the representative of one of the countries often speaks on behalf of all of them.

The Nordic cooperation taking place in the General Assembly and its committees thrives no less in the UN specialized agencies including ECOSOC and its subsidiary organ the Economic Commission for Europe (ECE).

At the request of the UN, the Nordic countries have provided military contingents to some of the peace-keeping forces organized by the UN (see *Peacekeeping Forces*). This has been the case several times after the wars between Israel and its neighbors as well as in the Congo 1960-64 and in Cyprus since 1964.

At the suggestion of the Secretary-General of the UN, Denmark, Finland, Norway, and Sweden (Iceland has no military) in 1974 established the Nordic Standby Force in UN service. Under certain conditions a contingent of about 5,000 men in all should be made available to the UN. The units are organized separately in each country, but in a way that will allow them to function as a joint Nordic unit, if required.

The ministers of defense meet half-yearly to discuss problems related to the force. Their meetings are prepared by the Joint Nordic committee for Military UN Matters.

12. Cooperation in Other International Organizations

In the international economic organizations and institutions established after the Second World War, and at the many trade and monetary conferences, it is natural for Nordic representatives to maintain very close contact and, when possible, support joint policies. This is particularly the case on the organization for Economic Cooperation and Development (OECD) and the General Agreement on Trade and Tariffs (GATT), in the International Monetary Fund (IMF) and in the International Bank for Reconstruction and Development (IBRD). The close relationship between the Nordic countries is accepted as a fact by the international organizations and institutions. The Nordic countries are therefore considered as a single geographic region which must always be represented in the various committees and working groups.

13. The Nordic Treaties and International Common Action

The Nordic concord of attitudes and actions in international institutions and organizations originated spontaneously, but has since been expressly formulated in the various inter-Nordic treaties of cooperation. The Helsinki Agreement of 1962 contains an article stating that "the Contracting Parties should, whenever possible and appropriate, consult one another regarding questions of mutual interest which are dealt with by international organizations and at international conferences." The Cultural Treaty of 1971 contains a provision that "the Contracting Parties shall aim at joint action in international connections within those areas covered by this Treaty." They are likewise required to cooperate concerning the spreading of information abroad on the cultural life of the Nordic countries and the achieving of a common or coordinated attitude in international cultural cooperation. The 1972 agreement on cooperation in the field of transport and communications stresses that it is important that a Nordic country, participating in international cooperation in transport and communications, "when not all the countries are represented, bears in mind the interests of the other countries." The agreement also contains a requirement "to work towards a common Nordic approach internationally ... when this is appropriate in view of the coincidence of the countries' interests, or in other respects."

In accordance with the treaties, the Nordic representatives keep close contact in the Council of Europe's cultural organ, the CCC (Council for Cultural Cooperation), while the Nordic Postal Union is a firm foundation for joint action in the Universal Postal Union. The organs for telecommunications cooperate in the International Telecommunications Union (ITU), as do the broadcasting companies in the European Broadcasting Union (EBU).

14. Assistance to Developing Countries

In relation to their own resources, the Nordic countries have always been among the largest contributors to the programs of assistance started soon after the Second World War to help the developing countries. About a half of this Nordic assistance is provided through the multilateral arrangements under the UN and the specialized agencies. However, quite large sums are also provided for bilateral agreements between the individual Nordic countries and a number of developing countries.

The Helsinki Agreement added a new aspect. One of its articles states that "the Contracting Parties should, whenever it is possible and expedient, coordinate their activities for aid to and cooperation with the developing countries." Nevertheless, the major part of the contributions continued to be channeled via the United Nations and its organs. It was agreed that where investments or other economic matters were concerned, even Nordic cooperation could do little in the way of development assistance. Instead the Nordic countries could make an effective joint contribution in education and in various aspects of technical assistance. Another consideration advanced was that the Nordic countries could serve as a model for the new African states by showing that sovereign states are able to cooperate in joint projects without having to base their cooperation upon common defense and foreign policy.

The costs of the individual projects are shared by the Nordic states, but one of the governments is in charge of the administration of each project. The Nordic activities have been concentrated in Tanzania (mostly educational institutions), Kenya (cooperative schools), and Mozambique (agricultural development).

15. The Nordic Countries and Europe

The Nordic countries recognize the need for active participation in giving shape to a united Europe. Sweden and Finland became members of the EU in 1995; prior to that Denmark had been a long-time member. Cooperation with Europe is considered a part of Nordic collaboration. It is not being seen as an alternative.

See also: Nordic Council; Nordic Security Problems; Peace and Regional Integration; Integration, Regional

Bibliography ————————————————————

Anderson S V 1967 *The Nordic Council: A Study of Scandinavian Regionalism.* University of Washington Press, Seattle, Washington, DC

Andrén N 1967 Nordic integration—Aspects and problems. *Cooperation and Conflict*

Andrén N 1984 Nordic integration and cooperation—Illusion and reality. *Cooperation and Conflict*

Bukdahl J et al. (eds.) 1959 *Scandinavia Past and Present I-III.* Arnkrone, Odense

Etzioni A 1965 *Political Unification.* Columbia Institute of War and Peace, New York

Friis H (ed.) 1950 *Scandinavia: Between East and West.* Cornell University Press, Ithaca, New York

Haskel B G 1976 *The Scandinavian Option.* Universitetsforlaget, Oslo

Heldal H (ed.) 1965 *Nordic Cooperation in the Social and Labour Field.* Ministry of Social Affairs, Oslo

Herlitz N 1969 *Elements of Nordic Public Law.* Institute for Legal Research, Stockholm

Lyche I 1974 *Nordic Cultural Cooperation.* Universitetsforlaget, Oslo

Nordic Countries: Cultural and Political Bonds. http://www.randburg.com/Nordic/overview 5. html

Scott F D 1975 *Scandinavia.* Harvard University Press, Cambridge, Massachusetts

Solem E 1977 *The Nordic Council and Scandinavian Integration.* Praeger, New York

Sundelius B 1976 *Nordic Cooperation: A Dynamic Integration Process.* University of Denver, Denver, Co

Sundelius B 1978 *Managing Transnationalism in Northern Europe.* Westview Press. Boulder, Co

Sundelius B (ed.) 1982 *Foreign Policies of Northern Europe.* Westview Press, Boulder, Co

Wendt F 1959 *The Nordic Council and Co-operation in Scandinavia.* Munksgaard, Copenhagen

Wendt F 1981 *Cooperation in the Nordic Countries—Achievements and Obstacles.* Almqvist and Wiksell, Stockholm

Wisti F (ed.) 1981 *Nordic Democracy, Ideas, Issues, and Institutions in Politics, Economy, Education, Social and Cultural Affairs of Denmark, Finland, Iceland, Norway, and Sweden.* Det Danske Selskab and Munksgaard, Copenhagen

FRANTZ WENDT; PEDRO B. BERNALDEZ

Nordic Security Problems

For decades, even during the First World War, Denmark, Iceland, Norway, and Sweden had been able to stay neutral. In 1935 Finland's parliament and government expressly declared their country's accession to the Scandinavian policy of neutrality (see *Neutrality*). As a natural consequence of their countries' attitude, the Nordic foreign ministers, assembled in Oslo, Norway, on August 31,1939, and declared that their governments, in case of the war that seemed imminent, intended to maintain strict neutrality toward the contending parties.

This policy, however, did not prevent Finland from being invaded by the former Soviet Union three months later, while, on April 9, 1940, Germany attacked Norway and invaded Denmark. Some weeks later the United Kingdom, as a countermove to the German actions, occupied the Faroes and Iceland. Only Sweden was able—apart from minor concessions to Germany—to maintain a heavily armed neutrality throughout the war.

When the hostilities ceased in 1945, Denmark and Norway rejoined Sweden in their traditional neutral position, which was now limited by the obligations they had taken upon themselves as members of the United Nations. However, the collective security system of this newly founded international organization raised hopes of a safer world for weak countries.

Finland was in a situation quite different from the other Nordic nations. To recover the land it had lost in the winter war of 1939-40 it had in June 1941 joined Germany in its attack on the former Soviet Union, but was forced to sign an armistice in September 1944. Obviously, its freedom of action was strictly limited, and it was greatly dependent on its all-powerful Eastern neighbor.

1. The Fear of Soviet Expansion

Very soon after the cessation of hostilities in Europe, the international situation became dominated by the growing tension between the former Soviet Union and its former Western allies. The first victim of the aggravated state of affairs was the collective security system of the United Nations (see *Collective Security and Collective Self-defense*). As decisions of its Security Council presupposed unanimity of its Great Power members, the antagonism of the former allies deprived small nations of the protection the international organization might have offered them.

The Nordic countries quickly registered this change of climate. The increasing domination of the former

Soviet Union in the countries of Eastern Europe and in its German occupation zone, as well as its enhanced naval presence on the Baltic, created resentment among the Western powers as well as great worry in the Scandinavian countries.

Two events, especially, made a strong impression in the Nordic capitals. The communist coup d'état in Prague on February 23,1948 overthrew the democratic regime in Czechoslovakia and added to the fear of a Soviet push forward in Europe. This anxiety was heightened, when on February 27, the Soviet government summoned Finland to sign a pact of friendship, cooperation, and mutual assistance. Did this indicate that Finland was going to suffer the fate of the other neighboring countries of the former Soviet Union? And would the other small Nordic countries be able to resist the overwhelming military and political pressure of the communist Superpower? What were in fact the intentions of Moscow toward the small Nordic countries that formed a barrier between the Baltic and the North Sea and the Atlantic Ocean?

2. Failure of Nordic Defense Union Plans

Influenced by the above considerations, the prime ministers of Denmark, Norway, and Sweden, soon after the Finnish pact was signed, started secret deliberations which resulted in a decision by their foreign ministers in September 1948 to let an expert committee examine the possibilities and conditions for a jointly binding defense alliance within the framework of Articles 52-54 of the UN Charter.

On the basis of the proposals of the experts the three governments accepted in principle the idea of a regional military agreement. Its purpose was to establish solidarity concerning the defense of the territories of the three states, with the express exclusion of Greenland and the Faroes which are under the sovereignty of Denmark, and Svalbard and Jan Mayen under that of Norway. The cooperation was to comprise the coordination of national defense plans, the armed forces, and the military productions of the three states.

However, although the three governments agreed in principle upon the contents of the plan, they differed as to its wider international implications. While the Swedes insisted that the Nordic defensive union must be without any kind of military ties with other states or groups of countries, the Norwegians, with no less determination, claimed the right to discuss with the Western democracies what assistance these countries might furnish in case of future conflicts, as well as delivery of much-needed arms in the event of such conflict.

On this basic difference of opinion the grand scheme of a Nordic Defense Union was wrecked in January 1949. A Danish suggestion of a Dano-Swedish defense union was rejected by Sweden as it regarded the risks involved to outweigh the advantages.

3. Denmark and Norway Join NATO

In the same months of 1948-49 as the Nordic governments examined the possibility of a defensive alliance, the Western powers were preparing what was to become the North Atlantic Treaty Organization (NATO) (see *North Atlantic Treaty Organization (NATO)*). Around New Year 1949 Denmark and Norway had secretly been contacted and asked whether they might wish to join such a pact as founding members. Both countries had asked to postpone their answers until they had studied the report of the expert committee. When there was no longer any doubt about the outcome of the Nordic defense deliberations, first Norway and then Denmark accepted the offer by the United States to join NATO. They—as well as Iceland— were among the signatories on April 4, 1949.

The failure of the attempt to form a defense union did not create bad feeling among the Scandinavians. In fact, the Swedish Prime Minister, Tage Erlander, privately let his Danish opposite number know that it would create no great surprise in Sweden, if Denmark felt obliged to follow Norway in joining NATO.

But to prevent the wider consequences of their countries following divergent roads in these most important fields of foreign policy and national security, Denmark, Norway, Sweden, and Iceland three years after the failure of the defense union project decided to establish the Nordic Council (see *Nordic Council*). Although the problems of foreign policy and defense were not excluded from the agenda of the Council, it was generally agreed that they were not to be the subject of resolutions by the assembly. This attitude was strengthened after Finland joined the Council in 1955.

4. Denmark's Strategic Position

The United States and the United Kingdom had been eager to have Denmark, Norway, and Iceland join NATO, as these countries formed an advanced bastion against a potential attack by the former Soviet Union. The three Nordic countries shared an even greater interest in the protection their Western allies might

lend them, as in their case it might be a question of being safeguarded from becoming satellites of the communist Superpower. With their location in the line of possible Soviet forward thrusts against the Western powers, the two groups of NATO members had a common interest in each other's fate.

Of the three countries, Denmark in the 1950s and 1960s was regarded to be in the most directly exposed position. Small, split up into many parts, without any natural internal obstacles, it lies across the three straits connecting the Baltic and the North Sea. To ensure free passage for the oceangoing warships of its Baltic fleet would obviously be of great importance to the former Soviet Union. That could be obtained by occupying Denmark. Such a step would have the further advantage for the aggressor of opening the way for attacks on Norway from the south and on the former Federal Republic of Germany between Lübeck and Hamburg from the north. Furthermore Denmark would provide excellent bases for air attacks on the United Kingdom and on shipping between the UK and Western Europe.

All these benefits to the former Soviet Union of a conquest of Denmark were therefore considered to be serious threats to the NATO powers, who consequently were interested in barring enemy exits from the Baltic and in preventing the former Soviet Union from using Danish air fields. As Denmark is far too weak to resist an invasion of some size by means of its own small military force, arrangements were made with the NATO leadership to bring assistance, especially in the shape of American and British airplanes, and troops chiefly from the United Kingdom. These reinforcements may, however, only be sent at the request of the Danish government. Necessary supplies for assisting foreign airplanes have been stockpiled on Danish territory.

The NATO reinforcements in case of attack are obviously essential to the defense of Denmark. At the same time the Danes attach great importance to being defensive in their attitude in order not to provoke the former Soviet Union unnecessarily. They therefore declared in 1957 that "in the present circumstances" they wished to receive neither nuclear arms nor foreign troops on their territory. It is the Danish authorities alone who decide in these matters.

5. The Importance of the Kola Peninsula

Although the Warsaw Pact naval forces in the western part of the Baltic are strong, and their vessels regularly patrol the seas surrounding the island of Zealand and other Danish strategic waters, there is no doubt that the center of gravity of the former Soviet Union's military efforts during the last 25 years has been transferred from the Baltic and the Danish straits to the Kola Peninsula and the North Atlantic and adjoining seas. This development greatly increases the strategic importance of the Northern flank of Scandinavia and thereby the latent threat to Norway. In fact, Norway has been termed the strategic key position of Northern Europe.

Ever since the end of the Second World War the former Soviet Union had been developing an increasingly strong military presence on the Kola Peninsula in Northern Russia and on the Barents Sea. Here was concentrated a large and constantly growing force of strategic submarines, many carrying long-range nuclear missiles, as well as a considerable number of surface warships and airplanes.

The strategic situation in the North Atlantic, where the United States and the United Kingdom hitherto had exercised an unchallenged supremacy, has therefore changed. The Soviet naval forces based on the Kola Peninsula had the dual role in case of war of directly threatening the United States with nuclear missile attacks from the submarines and of attacking the vital transport of supplies across the Atlantic from the United States to Western Europe. As the strength of the Soviet Kola forces increased they steadily moved their maneuvers farther south towards Iceland and the Faroes. An important purpose of this strategy was to keep the American naval and air forces as far away as possible from the Barents Sea and the Kola base. The reason for this was the change in American strategy since the 1970s from a more defensive attitude in the North Atlantic and the Norwegian Sea to a sustained forward thrust to the North in order to get at the Soviet submarines before they leave the rather shallow Barents Sea and to be close enough to strike direct blows against the Kola base by means of the low-flying Cruise missiles.

6. Northern Norway's Exposed Position

The Soviet presence, which constituted a latent menace to Northern Norway—especially since the two countries had a common frontier gained by Finland's cession of Petsamo to the former Soviet Union—was the main motive behind Norway's eagerness to obtain the protection of the NATO shield. The intensified rivalry between the Soviet and NATO navies in the seas bordering Norway increased Norwegian fears of Soviet attacks. The former Soviet Union might want to take possession of parts of Norway as advanced positions in the defense of the Kola Penin-

sula installations or as forward bases for naval and air attacks on the North Atlantic sea lanes between America and Europe.

The Norwegian underlying concerns were greatly increased by the prospects of the strengthened Soviet naval presence in the Norwegian Sea preventing the allied forces guaranteed to Norway as a member of NATO from arriving in time to repel the Soviet attack. Detailed plans had been made, stipulating that American, British, and Canadian forces were to come to the assistance of Norway. Now further allied reinforcements in the form of aircraft, and troops to be brought by air, were agreed upon, as well as stockpiling in Norway of guns, trucks, munitions, fuel, and spare parts.

It was a matter of vital importance to the Norwegian authorities to be able to count on the assistance of allied forces in defending the country. But, as in the case of Denmark, they sought to avoid measures which the former Soviet Union might regard as provocative; therefore the government declared in 1957 and 1960 that nuclear arms would not be stockpiled or deployed on Norwegian territory. Nor would foreign troops be allowed there (except for training maneuvers and stockpiling of material) as long as the country was not attacked or subject to threat of attack. These renunciations were purely one-sided declarations by Norway which alone could decide to cancel them.

Likewise allied troops were not allowed to hold maneuvers in the North of Norway, closer than 800 kilometers by road from the frontier to the former Soviet Union. The presence of allied aircraft and warships was not permitted in Norwegian air and sea territory across the 24th Eastern Meridian.

Under the NATO strategy it was the task of Denmark and the former Federal Republic of Germany to defend the access to Southern Norway. The Norwegians were therefore able to concentrate most of their defense in the northern parts of the country. To demonstrate Norway's peaceful intentions only a very small force was located close to the Russian frontier.

7. The Importance of Iceland

The rising confrontation of the superpowers in the North Atlantic and the Norwegian Sea since 1960 had increased the importance of Iceland in the Nordic security system. During the Second World War the country was invaded by the United Kingdom on May 10, 1940. By a treaty between Iceland and the United States of July 7, 1941 the British troops were replaced by Americans. The main purpose of the United States presence was to secure the transport routes across the Atlantic between the United States and Europe. After the cessation of hostilities in 1945 the American forces left the country, but the United States were granted permission to use Keflavik Airport as long as they had responsibilities in Germany.

When Iceland in 1949 was invited to become a founding member of NATO it accepted, having no defense of its own and being aware of its increasingly exposed position should the antagonism between the United States and the former Soviet Union develop into hostilities. In 1951, under the impression of the increased tension between East and West in the wake of the Korean War, Iceland concluded an agreement with the United States within the framework of NATO to defend Iceland and "to preserve peace and security in the North Atlantic Area."

From then on Iceland became the center of an intense American activity to supervise—and in case of war to prevent—the passage of Soviet nuclear-armed submarines and other warships through the Greenland-Iceland-United Kingdom gap. Airplanes, early warning aircraft, submarines, aircraft carriers and other vessels, mines, radar, and sound surveillance systems are the instruments the Americans use to control the gap. The United States presence in Iceland was concentrated in the airbase at Keflavik on the coast south-west of Reykjavik.

8. The Faroes and Greenland

To the east, between Iceland and the west coast of Norway, a radar and Loran (Long Range Navigation System) stationed in the self-governing Danish territory of the Faroes formed part of the North Atlantic warning system.

According to a treaty of 1951 between Denmark and the United States within the framework of NATO the defense of Greenland was a joint responsibility of the two countries. This fact was expressed through the provision that the national flags of both countries should fly over the defense areas. In practice, however, it was naturally the Americans who carried the chief load of the burden. The installations were mostly early warning systems against Soviet missiles directed against the United States and Canada.

9. Nonaligned Sweden

While Denmark, Norway and Iceland were members of NATO, and Finland had a special relationship with the former Soviet Union, Sweden was the only one of the Nordic states without any kind of military treaty or arrangement with a group of states or a single power. The fact that for more than a century and a half the country has avoided being involved in war explains its determined resolution to keep aloof of Great Power rivalries and alliances. This policy, which was defined as "nonalignment in peace aiming at neutrality in war" had a necessary prerequisite in a rather strong defense.

No parts of Sweden were strategically as sensitive as the Danish Straits and the northern parts of Norway. However, the Swedes felt obliged to take into consideration that a power attacking either of these important targets might feel tempted to invade Swedish territory in order more easily to gain its objectives. Under the influence of the menace to Norwegian territory caused by the confrontation of NATO and the former Soviet Union in the North Atlantic and the Norwegian Sea, Sweden has strengthened its defense in its northern region. The frequent presence of more or less unidentified submarines in Swedish territorial waters has likewise led to increased supervision by the navy.

10. Finland's Special Relationship

Finland's geographical position between the former Soviet Union and neutral Sweden makes its position strategically important. It was a priority to the Soviet government in Moscow to prevent attack through Finland against Leningrad and the Murmansk railroad to the naval base on the Kola Peninsula, or against the base itself. On the other hand, it is not in the Soviet interest to conquer Finland or make it into a satellite state like the Warsaw Pact countries, because such an action would in all likelihood force Sweden to give up its neutrality and join Denmark and Norway in NATO. These decisions to keep Finland and Sweden as buffer states explain the former Soviet Union's aim in obtaining the Treaty of Friendship, Cooperation, and Mutual Assistance with Finland (FCMA).

Finland, on the other hand, had most skillfully turned the situation to its best advantage by being able to maintain her special relationship with the former Soviet Union and at the same time making the Western powers (the United States, the United Kingdom, France) acknowledge Finland as a neutral country. By this policy it had made an important contribution to removing an element of tension in this part of Europe.

The FCMA Treaty (concluded in 1948) provided that in the eventuality of Finland, or the former Soviet Union through Finnish territory, becoming the object of armed attack by Germany or any state allied with Germany, Finland would fight to repel the attack with all its available forces within its frontiers, and, if necessary, with the assistance of the former Soviet Union.

It is expressly laid down that Finland had to request the help, and that the countries should confer with each other, if it is established that the threat of an armed attack is present. Finnish military cooperation was not automatic and is expressly restricted to Finnish territory. Both parties had the right to propose consultations, if they both agreed that the threat of an armed attack exists.

There was general agreement that Finland would not be exposed to attack except by an aggressor who wants to pass Finnish territory in order to invade the Soviet Union. At the time of the signing of the FCMA Treaty the zone of military tension—seen from the Finnish point of view—was in the northern part of the Baltic and in the Gulf of Finland, close to the south coast of Finland. However, in the following decade it moved away from Finland to the western part of the Baltic, close to the Danish Straits. At the same time the headquarters of the Soviet Baltic fleet was moved from Kronstadt to Kaliningrad (formerly Königsberg).

From the 1960s onwards the confrontation between NATO and the former Soviet Union in the North Atlantic and the Norwegian Sea, as well as the prospect of Northern Norway becoming a battleground, turned the attention of Finland's government towards Lapland. As this northernmost part of the country is located between the Norwegian Finmarken and the former Soviet Union, the Finnish authorities decided to reinforce troops and send fighter aircraft up there to vindicate the nation's neutrality.

11. The Nordic Balance

The former Federal Republic of Germany was admitted to NATO in 1955. In 1961 negotiations were conducted about the establishment of a NATO unity of command, covering Denmark, Schleswig-Holstein, and Hamburg. This close cooperation between German and Danish military forces as well as NATO naval exercises in the western part of the Baltic and the visit to Norway of the Minister of Defense of the former Federal Republic of Germany provoked sharp Soviet reaction. Among other steps the Soviet government invoking the FCMA Treaty, demanded military consultations with Finland and insisted upon deliberations between the military staffs of the two countries.

The Finnish President, Urho Kekkonen, flew to see First Secretary Nikita Khrushchev in Novosibirsk and warned him against military consultations that might create "war psychosis" and military counter-measures in the other Nordic countries. Khrushchev accepted Kekkonen's advice and abandoned the idea.

The Finnish President had evaluated the situation correctly. Foreign Minister Halvard Lange of Norway expressed the hope that the existing balance in the Nordic region might be preserved. The Minister of Defense, Gudmund Harlem, was more outspoken. Attempts to put pressure on Norway, he declared, might make the country move into closer relations with NATO. He referred specifically to Norway's decision concerning nuclear arms in Norwegian territory.

By employing the term "Nordic Balance" the Norwegian Foreign Minister had coined an expression which since then has been used to characterize the particular strategic relationship of the Nordic countries among themselves and to the respective Superpowers. The prerequisite of this "Balance" is the fact that their different attitudes in high politics should not create bad feeling among them. On the contrary, there is general agreement that each country by choosing that solution which serves its own interests best has in fact contributed to keeping the tension in the Nordic region at a reasonably low level.

This is particularly true of the decision by Denmark and Norway not to install nuclear arms or station foreign troops or establish NATO bases on their territory, but to remain willing to receive reinforcements from outside, if they are threatened or attacked—a fact which may make an outside power less eager to disturb the peace of the region. Sweden, firmly determined to defend her neutrality, is thus able to discourage any Great Power from attempting to cross her territory in a push against either Finland or Norway. Finland's pact with the former Soviet Union expressly recognized the country's right to stay neutral, except when it was exposed to an attack from Germany and her allies.

12. A Nordic Nuclear Free Zone

In the peace treaty of 1947 Finland agreed not to possess or procure nuclear arms. The arrangement of 1951 between the United States and Iceland concerning the airport at Keflavik contained the provision that nuclear weapons were not to be brought into the country without the consent of the Reykjavik government. Denmark and Norway on 1957 declared that they did not want nuclear arms in times of peace. Sweden, which was the only of the Nordic countries that seriously considered producing her own nuclear arms, abandoned the idea in 1958.

Thus, the whole Nordic area was in fact a nuclear free zone.

Referring to this state of affairs the Soviet Prime Minister, Bulganin, in 1958 proposed to the Danish and Norwegian governments to turn what he termed "Northern Europe" into a zone without atomic and hydrogen weapons.

In 1963 President Kekkonen of Finland (see *Kekkonen, Urho*) called on the Nordic Countries to confirm the de facto nuclear free zone by the signing of mutual declarations, In the 1960s and 1970s communist and other left-wing party members of the Nordic Council on several occasions presented motions of similar content.

For more than 20 years these various initiatives were fruitless. Neither the Danes nor the Norwegians, whose national security in the last resort depended upon the nuclear arms of their great NATO allies, were willing to sign away their protective shield.

A Norwegian government report which was critical of the proposal stressed that the establishment of a nuclear free zone would in no way whatever change the strategic importance of Norwegian territory. Whether or not a state could stay outside a European conflict would depend upon the importance the belligerents attach to its territory and not upon its being nuclear free or not. If Norway were declared nuclear-free in war and peace, it could not guarantee that allied forces would be sent to assist it, if they were not able to use nuclear arms to defend themselves. Participation in an isolated nuclear free zone would not be compatible with participation in NATO's reciprocal collective defense.

A negative guarantee—for instance from the former Soviet Union—would, according to the report, not provide Norway with the same security as NATO's positive guarantee to assist it against all kinds of attack. A nuclear power may at any time retract its negative guarantee. A negative guarantee might also create a formal basis for Soviet inspection of Norwegian defense without giving Norway similar rights in the former Soviet Union.

An important consequence of Norway's abandonment of the allied common defense would, according to the report, be a distinct change in the balance of power in the former Soviet Union's favor in the northern region. The NATO countries would in all probability try to re-establish the balance by an increased military presence in the seas to the north and west of Norway, which are so important to their security. The result would be disruption of the present low tension in the northern region.

13. The Nuclear Free Zone Becomes a Popular Issue

For almost two decades the idea of a Nordic nuclear free zone had been a problem of more or less theoretical discussion and had been met with great skepticism, as the Norwegian report shows. However, from about 1980 it suddenly became the object of interest in ever-widening groups within the Nordic nations. The main reason behind this development was the intense discussion which arose in most West European countries about NATO's decision in December 1979 to station Pershing II and Cruise missiles in some of the member countries—though not in Denmark and Norway. This coincided with increasing tension between the Superpowers and resulted in an intensified dread of an atomic war.

The Nordic countries were not to receive any of the new nuclear arms, but the wave of reaction against them from abroad took shape in the form of a hitherto unknown popular support of the idea of a Nordic nuclear free zone. At the political level the governments of Sweden and Finland—the two countries which had already renounced the use of the atomic bomb and did not seek the protection of the nuclear shield of NATO—raised the question with the other Nordic governments. From September 1981 the problems became a standing item on the agenda of the twice-yearly meetings of the Nordic foreign ministers.

At the parliamentary level the Social Democratic Parties in Denmark and Norway took the lead in advocating the establishment of the nuclear free zone. In Norway—whose military position is the most exposed—the parties reached an agreement to study the whole problem in a parliamentary committee. In Denmark, Parliament, on the initiative of the Social Democratic opposition, charged the government to work actively in all relevant international organizations to ensure Denmark's remaining free of nuclear arms in peace, crisis, and war. The party, however, stressed that it did not want any unilateral Danish steps. It very much prefers to make Denmark free of nuclear arms by means of the Nordic nuclear free zone. The Danish Social Democrats also emphasize that there is no reason to doubt the party's positive attitude to NATO.

The Conservative Prime Minister in a government of nonsocialist parties declared that it will continuously review the matter with the other Nordic countries and Denmark's NATO partners.

The Swedish government, which is the most active protagonist of the Nordic nuclear free zone, wants the atomic powers to commit themselves not to use or threaten to use nuclear arms against the territories of the Nordic countries. But in the opinion of the government the establishment of the Nordic nuclear free zone must also mean the absence of nuclear arms from the Baltic as well as the removal from the neighborhood of the zone of nuclear arms directed or capable of being directed against the zone.

On November 29-30, 1985, representatives of the governments and political parties of all the Nordic countries met on Copenhagen for the first conference of its kind on the subject of the Nordic countries as a nuclear free zone. As before, the Social Democrat and the Socialist Parties presented a rather optimistic view of the usefulness of such a zone, while the representatives of the Conservative parties as before expressed doubt as to whether such an arrangement would enhance the security of the Nordic countries.

After the collapse of the former Soviet Union, security matters concerning the Nordic countries largely changed. There are those who see Russia as not giving up its expansion aims or irredentism. Taking cognizance of Russian action in Chetchenia or hot disputes between Russia and Ukraine over the Black Sea flotilla, renewed security concerns address Russian "threats" to Northern Europe—Nordic security thus includes also the Baltic area.

Feelings of security among Nordic countries can be related to their membership in alliances. Being members of the European Union seems to give Finland and Sweden some feeling of security. This may also be true of Denmark, Iceland and Norway who are members of NATO.

On the whole, the role of West European Union (WEU) will be increasing. NATO is going to rely for its military resources on all European states who are members in it. The Nordic countries are well-equipped and have well-skilled military forces. Security cooperation needs further strengthening.

See also: *Nordic Political Cooperation; Nuclear-Weapon-Free Zones: A Historical and Assessment*

Bibliography

Andrén N 1977 *The Future of the Nordic Balance*. Ministry of Defense, Stockholm

Brundtland A O 1982 The Nordic balance and its possible relevance for Europe. In: Frei D (ed.) 1982 *Sicherheit durch Gleichgewicht*. Schulthess Polygraphischer Verlag, Zürich

Cooperation and Conflict Vol. 17(14) 1982 (Issue devoted to Nordic Security Today)

Holst J J 1973 *Five Roads to Nordic Security*. Universitets forlaget, Oslo

Holst J J 1981 Norway's search for a Nordpolitikk. *Foreign Affairs 60*

Jakobson M 1980 Finland: Substance and appearance. *Foreign Affairs 58*

Korhonen K 1975 *Urho Kekkonen: A Statesman for Peace*. Otava, Helsinki

Maude G 1976 *The Finnish Dilemma*. Oxford University Press, Oxford

Petersen N 1980 *Britain, the United States and Scandinavian Defence 1945-49*. Institute of Political Science, Aarhus

Security Problems in the Nordic Countries. http://rubiin.physic.ut.ee/~toomasr/security.html

Sundelius B (ed.) 1982 *Foreign Policies of Northern Europe*. Westview Press, Boulder, Colorado

Wallin L B (ed.) 1982 *The Northern Flank in a Central European War*. Swedish National Defense Research Institute, Stockholm

FRANTZ WENDT; PEDRO B. BERNALDEZ